Comparing Nations and Cultures

Comparing Nations and Cultures

Readings in a Cross-Disciplinary Perspective

Edited by

Alex Inkeles
Stanford University

Masamichi Sasaki
Hyogo Kyoiku University

Prentice Hall
Englewood Cliffs • New Jersey 07632

Library of Congress Cataloguing-in-Publication Data

Comparing nations and cultures: readings in a cross-disciplinary
   perspective / edited by Alex Inkeles and Masamichi Sasaki.
     p. cm.
   Includes bibliographical references (p.).
   ISBN 0-13-297029-5
   1. Sociology—Research—Methodology.   2. Cross-cultural studies.
   I. Inkeles, Alex. II. Sasaki, Masamichi S.
   HM48.C645 1996
   300—dc20   94-47519
                                       CIP

Acquisitions Editor: Nancy Roberts
Editorial/production supervision: John Svatek
Cover design: Bruce Kenselaar
Buyer: Mary Ann Gloriande

Printed in the United States of America
10 9 8 7 6 5 4 3 2 1

ISBN 0-13-297029-5

Prentice-Hall International (UK) Limited, *London*
Prentice-Hall of Australia Pty. Limited, *Sydney*
Prentice-Hall Canada Inc., *Toronto*
Prentice-Hall Hispanoamericana, S.A., *Mexico*
Prentice-Hall of India Private Limited, *New Delhi*
Prentice-Hall of Japan, Inc., *Tokyo*
Simon & Schuster Asia Pte. Ltd., *Singapore*
Editora Prentice-Hall do Brasil, Ltda., *Rio de Janeiro*

Contents

Preface

Comparing Societies and Cultures

Virtually without exception the precursors and founders of modern social science were comparativists. This was true of the most conservative such as Machiavelli, and the most radical such as Marx. They also consistently were generalists, that is, they studied societies, cultures, and groups within them not mainly to describe their unique or distinctive properties but rather to extract from a set of different social arrangements that which was, if not universal, at least generally true of a large number of cases. This pattern is perhaps best exemplified in the work of Durkheim and his search for the general law that would explain variation in suicide rates across nations, religions, occupations, and other status groups. But even when one of these early great scholars took as his problem the understanding of a single nation in its uniqueness, as de Tocqueville did in his enduring masterpiece *Democracy in America,* he sought to achieve his objective mainly by comparing and contrasting the United States with other countries, and especially with those in Europe.

Although modern social science got its start in Europe, its further development in the last two-thirds of the twentieth century was largely concentrated in the United States. The process had started in the 1930s but was accelerated after World War II as the United States

emerged as the overwhelmingly dominant force worldwide in matters political, economic, and intellectual. But a strange transformation overcame much of social science as it migrated across the seas. In America it became much more local, even provincial. The process is perhaps best exemplified by what happened to sociology. In that field the University of Chicago came to dominate, but its sociologists relied heavily on the city of Chicago as their laboratory to study processes of urban development, stratification, delinquency, crime, and divorce. And they either slighted comparisons with these processes as they operated in other national settings or, more serious, seemed to assume that what applied to Chicago was some sort of general law of social development that would apply everywhere else. On a larger scale, the domination of the world scene by the United States after World War II encouraged a careless tendency to assume that developments in the United States must somehow mirror or anticipate developments in other nations, other societies, and other social groups.

The last two decades have seen some correction in this situation. This has come about partly through the revival of the social sciences in Europe, associated with the general recovery from the devastation of World War II. New and different voices, some entirely without any trace of American accent, demanded to be heard. From among the European leaders we have found a place in this collection for Stein Rokkan, Erwin Scheuch, and Meinolf Dierkes.

An additional stimulus for the internationalization of the social sciences was the development of regional centers of social research in other parts of the world, notably in Latin America and Asia, which stimulated and interacted with groups in the United States who were highly critical of the sociological establishment there. They vigorously rejected the mainstream models of national development, such as modernization theory, and championed new models such as "'dependency' theory" and "world systems" analysis. These are represented in our collection by Theotonio dos Santos, Immanuel Wallerstein, and Eric Wright.

Probably the most important corrective for parochialism in American social science, however, came from within the American establishment itself as some of the brightest and most energetic scholars such as Almond and Verba, Deutsch, and Huntington in political science, and Lipset, Kohn, and Smelser in sociology, made the case for the comparative perspective and exemplified the productivity of that approach in their research. All are represented in this volume.

Although an awareness of the virtues, even of the necessity, for more widely adopting a comparative approach to social research has been growing rapidly in the social science community, very few systematic guides are available for those who would like to pursue this approach, and suitable teaching materials are especially rare. This perception motivated us to assemble the collection of papers presented in this book of readings. It has two main elements. First, it offers, although in necessarily brief compass, an introduction to the comparative approach which explains and justifies its relevance for social theory and practice, and explicates some of the methodological requirements and challenges the approach presents. Second, and this element fills some five-sixths of the volume, it presents a wide-ranging array

of more than thirty examples of the application of the comparative method to the analysis of many dozens of social institutions, social problems, and social actions. Yet, however wide-ranging we sought to be, we were constrained by limits of space and assessments of the limits on students' time and interest, and so we had to adopt some principles for selection from among the plethora of choices we might have made. This requires that we explain, at least briefly, the considerations that guided us in putting together this collection.

Our Guiding Principles

Initially we scanned bibliographic databases, and the bibliographies of major books, encyclopedias, and the like to develop a comprehensive list of titles which suggested that the question presented a comparative analysis of societies, cultures, institutions, and social behavior. In this we went all the way back to 1950 but gave most attention to the scholarly output of the last two decades. From the thousands of titles we found, we selected those which seemed on the basis of title, topic, or author to be most relevant to our purpose of presenting a broad and representative survey, and if a preliminary quick scanning supported that assessment we placed the article in our candidate pool. We ended up with some four hundred articles that seemed to merit further attention, each of which we read and briefly annotated. To make our final selections, which meant accepting something like one in ten, we were guided by a series of considerations, which might also be thought of as selection criteria. Not every criterion was distinct from the others, and no criterion alone was sufficient to determine final selection. Rather, we tried the intellectual exercise of keeping all the criteria in mind at once. We knew this was an impossible feat but decided nevertheless to attempt it by considering each of the following:

Scope   There are separate and relatively well-established and defined fields of comparative politics and comparative economics. We felt it impractical to attempt a reader that would properly represent those fields and still also do justice to sociology, in which we have our main professional interest, or to anthropology and social psychology, to which we had a lesser but not negligible commitment. Moreover, restricting ourselves to the analysis of societies, cultures, nations, major institutions, and social movements and actions seemed to provide a broad enough scope. But even within the sociological tradition alone we had the choice of covering only a few topics in greater depth or trying to better reflect the range of work in the field by dealing with as many topics as feasible while still having some depth in each. We elected to cover ten or more topical areas with the hope we could have about three articles in each area. There are, of course, more than ten or twelve generally recognized major topical or substantive divisions in the field of sociology, and we had to leave out some that some audiences would have insisted on including. In such matters one can never please everyone, or even almost everyone. We are satisfied, however, that the topics we chose to cover are all important and are of interest to substantial constituencies.

Depth and Balance   The issue of scope also arises when one confronts the problem of how to represent work in a single area such as "deviance." One strategy calls for trying for as much depth as possible, for example, by using the three slots available in each section to go at least a bit into depth on a single topic such as suicide or homicide. A different goal is to strive for more balance or representativeness, to illustrate as many different facets of a problem as possible, approached in as many ways as the available space permits. That is the approach we favored, so that under deviance, for example, we have articles not only on suicide but also on homicide and on juvenile delinquency.

Variety of Research Styles   Increasingly sociology journals are full of articles using the most advanced and complex methods of multivariate data analysis. These advances in method are very important to the general development of sociology, and we do not mean to fault them. But such methods are not the only ones used by researchers who are nevertheless systematic comparativists. Neither are those who use the most advanced methods those who necessarily provide us with the most knowledge or insight. Someone with a great new idea pursued with the most simple of statistical methods may help us to learn a great deal more than another who can practice the most demanding statistical exercise but has no good ideas to guide his or her methodological gymnastics. Therefore, to represent the varieties of research styles actually extant in the field, and because they often add considerably to knowledge and understanding, we have supplemented the articles using complex multivariate statistical analysis with others following a different research style. These include multicountry studies of a single institution, such as the social security system, treated in nonstatistical terms as a problem in organizations; comparisons of as few as two countries, using only descriptive statistics; and, among still others, comparisons of a single institution or form of social action, tracing development over time in a set of nations operating under different historical and objective conditions.

Readability and Accessibility   We certainly did not think of this book as a technical manual. It is meant more for the intermediate undergraduate and graduate student, and for faculty members who would like a chance to sample what comparativists are doing in the behavioral sciences so that they might better assess the achievements and the promise of this approach. We therefore set as a criterion that to be selected an article had to be *readable by and accessible to* a person not a specialist in the topic nor adept in the method utilized. Many articles without any statistical apparatus at all proved neither readable nor readily comprehensible. And a number of articles using very advanced statistics not only were written in a very readable way, but even the results of their statistical tables, while not interpretable as such by all readers, had the results presented in the text in a way that made the findings accessible to the less specialized reader.

Interest   Given that our book is meant as an introduction to comparative sociology, and as a broad-ranging sampler for readers who may not yet be committed to the comparative approach, or even to sociology itself, we felt we had to stress as much as possible the intrinsic interest of the subject of an article and its treatment. If this is sugarcoating a pill, we do not mind so long as the medicine proves intellectually beneficial. Looking over the array of articles we finally settled on, we do not think we can be accused of being simple popularizers who selected materials only because they would pander to the lowest common denominator of common taste. But our criterion did mean that occasionally an article that was reputed to be important in the development of the field but was very dull was bypassed for one that might have a lesser reputation but promised more to engage the interest of most readers.

Currency   In the natural sciences, unless one is doing the history of a science, one insists rigorously on the very latest work that has been done on a topic. In those disciplines research ages very quickly as a field moves rapidly ahead to new ground, and the latest work incorporates and reflects what is firmly known and widely accepted from past work. This is much less true for the social sciences. They are much given to what Pitirim Sorokin called "fads and foibles," so that important and productive lines of work are neglected, or may be totally abandoned, even though the knowledge they generated continues to have validity and the promise of future gains is considerable. While we recognized the importance of presenting the latest research, we did not feel it would be honest to pretend that all or most of what was recently

published in the fields we were concerned with was necessarily more correct or more informative than work published some time earlier. In any event, we had many other considerations, as described here, to keep in mind in making our selections. We therefore felt under no compulsion to have all or most of our selections come from publications appearing in the last two or three years. Rather, we selected articles on other grounds, even if they were published as much as a decade ago, so long as we judged them of the highest quality and had reason to believe that subsequent work had not proved their conclusions wrong, at least as applied to the period and data under considerations. Not to be current is not the same as being wrong, just as to be most current is no guarantee of being right, to say nothing of being relevant.

Influence   Some individuals and some particular articles have had so wide an influence that no effort to reflect the field at large could be considered complete without including them. On the other hand, if we limited ourselves to famous authors and much-cited articles we would have produced an array without form or structure, one lacking focus and coherence. Of course we made a special effort to represent major figures in the field. We also felt that we should include at least some articles that had achieved the status of "classic" because they were so often and so widely referred to. So, the apparent influence of an article was made an important factor in selecting from among candidates that on other grounds might seem equally worthy to be included. Indeed, we consulted the citation index to locate articles cited so often by other workers in the field that they became serious candidates by this criterion alone. We also checked the index to assess the impact of articles we had selected on other grounds. Frequency of citation was, however, never in itself *the single criterion* for either the selection or the exclusion of an article. And inevitably, many whose contribution and reputation would warrant their appearance are not represented because we found none of their work to quite fit our outline and our other selection criteria.

Frankness The comparative method has its share of difficulties and ambiguities, and those who believe in the uniqueness of each society and culture may challenge the whole enterprise. We determined not to put a gloss on the theoretical challenges and the methodological critiques that frequently confront comparative studies. Rather, we tried to represent the most common and profound criticisms, not pointedly seeking them out but allowing their voice to be heard as such issues were routinely raised in the relevant scholarly literature.

Brevity Although we mention this criterion last, it certainly was not least. We were keenly aware that to keep the cost of our book reasonable, we had to keep its size within strict limits. And we were not insensitive to the often-heard complaint of students that their reading assignments are too long. Yet many papers of otherwise good quality, and sometimes important in their impact on the field, were closer in length to a monograph than to the limits of the typical journal article. We thought twenty

printed pages was room enough to say quite a lot, and favored examples that stayed within those limits.

Authenticity In a very few cases an article we very much wanted to present was far too long or technical, and we secured the permission of the author to omit some material. In general, however, respect for the author and an interest in preserving the historical record led us to reproduce the articles as they originally appeared. Where it seemed unmistakable that a typesetting error had created confusion, however, we did sometimes change a word to clarify what seemed the obvious intent of the author. And to give the text a more uniform quality we made minor adjustments in the form in which numbers were presented, in the location of quotation marks, and in other editorial routines.

Balancing all these considerations, we settled on some forty articles organized in thirteen topical sections. We tried to give each section breadth and variety, and to make the whole ensemble readable, representative, and authoritative. We hope the result does justice to the field and serves our readers well.

Comparing Nations and Cultures

The Case for a Comparative Approach

To launch our book of readings, we present four papers that make the case for approaching social institutions and social issues from a comparative perspective. We also get introduced to the scholarly work of individuals who have been pioneers in the development and application of cross-national research, and who did much to demonstrate its potential for deepening our knowledge about and understanding of social and political institutions and human behavior more generally.

Karl Deutsch traces the beginnings of comparative social analysis back more than two thousand years to the Greek historian Herodotus, and then carries the story forward in time to Karl Marx and on to such contemporaries as the Nobel Prize winner Herbert Simon. Clearly this approach has been found useful by a wide range of great thinkers. Indeed, Deutsch, himself a political scientist and sociologist, considered the method to be intrinsically cross-disciplinary. More important, he felt it to be indispensable for progress in the social sciences.

Antal, Dierkes, and Weiler carry Deutsch's argument further in the course of a review of comparative studies as they relate to understanding and shaping public policy. They stress the challenges—theoretical, methodological, and organizational—that confront the effort to do comparative research that has relevance for the policymaker. And they certainly are not dogmatic about the outcome, feeling it to be an open question as to whether or not comparative cross-national research can really lead to con-clusions that in turn can be the basis for sound social policy. Students reading the articles we have brought together in this collection should regularly raise the question as to whether a given research has potential policy implications, and should practice formulating those implications.

Coming next to Stein Rokkan, we once again meet one of the founding fathers of modern comparative analysis. Rokkan's perspective is very broad, encompassing not only cross-national studies but also cross-societal and cross-cultural research. He calls attention to the tension between those who insist on the distinctiveness, even the uniqueness, of the societies and cultures they study as against those who make the "universalist assumption" that all societies, past, present, or future, are appropriate units for potential comparison. Of course, the comparative method can be used to prove either the universal or the unique. Rokkan also distinguishes two different styles of making macrolevel comparisons. In one the societies compared are broadly alike in certain respects, say size and importance, but represent different cultural areas. He illustrates this approach by reference to Reinhard Bendix's classic study of citizenship and nation building in countries as diverse as Germany, Russia, India, and Japan. In the other style an effort is made to select all the nations examined from the same historical period and the same cultural set, for example, to study all the nations of Europe in the period of the Industrial Revolution.

Melvin Kohn, in an article representing more recent developments, nevertheless echoes many of the arguments for the comparative approach and makes similar distinctions to those introduced by Deutsh and Rokkan. He too considers cross-national research as being "indispensable" for establishing the validity of the generalizations that are derived initially from studying something in only one country. And he too stresses the utility of cross-national research for seeking out not only the similarities but also the differences in the way things work in different national settings. For example, if you studied only the United States you would reach the seemingly obvious conclusion that being higher on the socioeconomic scale generally means you are subject to less distress in daily life. But it turns out that in Japan there is no connection between the two, while in "Socialist" Poland the situation was reversed—with the well placed and economically advantaged experiencing not less but rather more distress.

CHAPTER ONE

Prologue: Achievements and Challenges in 2000 Years of Comparative Research*

Karl W. Deutsch

A large part of human learning has always occurred through comparison. The first four steps in the learning process of science entail *curiosity, recognition of patterns, counting* cases of recognition, and perception of *similarities* and hence general classes. The words "state," "king," and "money," for example, each refer to a class of observations that have something in common. "Fruit" may refer to apples or oranges which, despite their differences, may sometimes be treated as a single category for purposes of diet or as perishable goods for freight or storage. After the recognition of classes comes the recognition of *differences,* followed by the recognition of unique cases and then the processes among and across different units, classes, or unique events. Most often general classes and concepts precede the study of specific differences. The recognition that two events belong to some sort of class renders them comparable. But the study of differences within a class or in many classes is indispensable if social science is to progress and theory to avoid sterility.

States, kingdoms, and principalities have been compared for approximately 2,500 years. In the history of the social sciences, comparisons among nations as a focus of research arose late, as nations arose late. Modern nations began in the sixteenth and seventeenth centuries in England, in the eighteenth in America and France, in the nineteenth in much of Western and parts of Central Europe, in the twentieth even more strongly in Eastern Europe and in Asia, and in the second half of the twentieth century in Africa south of the Sahara.

By now the nation-state has become widespread, even though the word "nation" applied to Nigeria does not have exactly the same meaning as when applied to France. Even so, the number of modern states has risen and the field of comparative politics has expanded vastly.

Comparison has followed a zigzag path. The early observation of cases was practiced by the Greek historian Herodotus. Conceptual analysis is found, for example, in the works of Plato, where such general concepts as monarchy, aristocracy, timocracy (the rule of the rich), democracy, and tyranny are developed and then applied to the events in many Greek states. To this is coupled the prediction that this sequence is also observed in reality, but that after the inevitable collapse of tyrannies, the cycle closes again and then returns either to aristocracy or to one of the other earlier stages. These are basic types and they have remained in the vocabulary of political science to this day. A Greek historian, Thucydides, compared Athens and Sparta, and within Athens he compared Athenian aspirations as enunciated by Pericles in his funeral oration with Athenian cynical practices, as shown in the dialogue of the Athenian Ambassador with the people of the Island of Melos, or else in the disastrous Athenian popular decision to send an expedition to Sicily. Thucydides used comparisons with such devastating effect that we could call him one of the great satirical writers of his age, as well as one of the great historians.

Aristotle combined the Platonic methods of abstraction with the study of concrete cases.

He sent his assistants around the Mediterranean to collect the constitutions of 128 city-states. The result was Aristotle's *Politics,* a valuable piece of theory which has endured over the centuries. Plutarch compared the lives of outstanding persons, matching them in pairs, and showing what could be made out of comparative biography. Medieval political thought, as in Thomas Aquinas, again seeks abstractions and general principles, somewhat in the Platonic method, such as justice, the just ruler, the just war, the common good, and Aquinas went far enough to seek abstractions from the differences between Christians and non-Christians, and in the *Summa against the Gentiles* he sought to define a common good for Christians and non-Christians.

Machiavelli once again revels in specific cases. What his Prince did at this or that place or occasion, what cruelties he committed, which throats he cut, how he did it more or less judicially is described with relish in *The Prince.* But he used these cases and these anecdotes to look for a general abstraction, for the principles of the politics of power. So did his successors Thomas Hobbes and Alexander Hamilton, and down to the days of Hans Morgenthau thinkers of this bent have tried to find general rules for the politics of power. Other thinkers have tried on a broader basis to find out what could be a general pattern in history. Philosophers such as Immanuel Kant, Hegel, Marx, Lenin, or the Italian Ignacio Silone—who tried to write a general theory of fascism—all tried to study cases in order to arrive at theories. The Aristotelian tradition of mingling a concern for differences with the search for general principles was carried on by Montesquieu in the eighteenth century, and by Arnold Toynbee in the twentieth century. In the meantime, new factors have been introduced to the discussion of the course of history. Vilfredo Pareto introduced irrationality and the use of symbols; Max Weber reminded us of the importance of culture, which may produce quite different reactions to similar economic situations.

Throughout the centuries, comparative studies in the grand manner have been conducted—broad comparative surveys leading to broad generalizations. *Most of these cross-state comparisons are also cross-disciplinary.* The ancients used philosophy and history together with political analysis. Some of the nineteenth- and twentieth-century thinkers included the new discipline of economics and to some extent cultural anthropology, psychology, and sociology. But the success of the grand theories was at best limited. They illuminated aspects of historical occurrences but failed to account for the totality of development.

In the meantime nationalism was expressed by national prophets; and gradually, in the course of social mobilization, it was reaching the *masses,* at first intermittently but later with a steady hold. This development had started in England in the seventeenth century, in the American colonies and France in the eighteenth, in much of Western Europe and in Latin America in the nineteenth, in Eastern Europe and in much of Asia in the first half of the twentieth century, and in black Africa mainly after 1945. The result is a multiplication of modern states, from less than 30 in 1880 to more than 150 in 1980, and with each such state now having to perform a much wider range of tasks of defense and domination. Public sectors in modern states grew between 1900 and 1980 on the average from 10 percent or less of GNP to 30 percent or more. In other words, there was a threefold expansion of politics within the states and a fivefold increase in the number of states. The public sectors of world events—those not *directly* determined by either tradition or market processes—have grown by factor of about 15 from about 2 or 3 percent of the total of the gross product of the world to about 30–45 percent that now pass through the public sectors of the world's nations. Compared to this secular change since 1900, the attempts of some national governments in the early 1980s to reduce once again the public sectors seem unlikely to win major long-term successes.

In addition, at least two social orders have arisen among the more highly industrialized states, communism and capitalism, and by now also among states in developing countries, such as China, Cuba, or Vietnam on the one hand, and the many market-oriented developing countries on the other. All these developments offered greatly increased opportunities for comparative research but they multiplied its difficulties by vastly increased complexity.

For the last sixty years, comprehensive theory—what is sometimes called *grand theory*—has been a victim of this development. Since 1920, few if any such theories have been proposed, let alone accepted. Josef Schumpeter and Colin Clark in economics, Pitirim Sorokim and Talcott Parsons in sociology, Erik Erikson in psychology, Claude Lévi-Strauss in anthropology, Arnold Toynbee in history, and Quincy Wright in political science made perhaps the most impressive efforts toward grand theory, but they rarely reached the scope and stature of their predecessors before 1920 and most of their professional colleagues kept their distance from their generalizations. Only Toynbee's work was a conspicuous exception. It is a Grand Theory in the classic sense, but here, too, most historians kept their distance from it.

The dominant forms of comparative research in the last sixty years have focused on improving empirical methods and data and the host of what have been called "middle-range theories," after a term made popular by the sociologist Karl Mannheim after 1935, and later by the sociologist Robert Merton.

There is no room for a complete inventory of these developments, but [the following are] some examples of the new empirical methods.

Aggregate Data Analysis

This is a much more serious set of data collected by governments and other agencies for their own purposes. Such data have biases and errors in them, so that a general problem of communication arises here—namely how to separate a signal from noise—and one tries to find out how much noise or how much inaccuracy in the data can be tolerated in relation to each particular social science question that has to be studied. Another problem in each case is whether it is enough to stick to the average or central tendency of each statistical series and to what extent the *variances* have to be taken into account. Examples of substantial work are the surveys and analyses by Arthur Banks and Robert Textor, by Bruce Russett and his collaborators, by Charles Taylor and Michael Hudson, and more recently by Charles Taylor at the Wissenschaftszentrum Berlin für Sozialforschung.

The New Survey Research

The works by Paul F. Lazarfeld, Herbert Hyman, Seymour M. Lipset, Angus Campbell, Philip Converse, and Warren Miller have been examples. Alex Inkeles, whose six-country study (1974) on the psychological and sociological effects of work in factories and other organizations was based on survey research, has led to the operational qualification of the concepts of modernization and modernity. In Germany, the work of Rudolf Wildenmann, Max Kaase, Elisabeth Noelle-Neumann, Erwin Scheuch, and others has won international respect.

Content Analysis

This is a powerful tool of analysis, pioneered before World War I by a German literary scholar, Konrad Burdach on a book from the year 1400, *Der Ackermann aus Böhmen*. In the 1930s and 1940s, this method was brought to political science by Harold Lasswell and it was developed further by R. R. Anderson at the State University of Michigan, by Ithiel de Sola Pool, Dan Lerner, and Alexander George, and then by Philip Stone for the use of the computer. This computer-assisted method was then applied by Zwi Namenwirth and again by Harold Lasswell, and by Hans-Dieter Klingemann. The result is a series of content analysis enterprises with data we never had before.

Game Theory and
Game Experiments

Anatol Rapoport has probably done more than anyone in the mathematical and experimental analysis of two-party conflicts. Other important work has been done by Thomas C. Schelling, Philip Nash, and Robert Axelrod.

National Character Studies

This is another development, derived from cultural anthropology and social psychology by Ruth Benedict, Margaret Mead, Abraham Kardiner, Nathan Leites and the important survey of the field by Alex Inkeles and Daniel Levinson. Today we do not like to speak of national character, because the term has been misused, and we prefer to speak of "culture" or "modal personality structure," but the phenomenon referred to has remained much the same.

Computer-Assisted World Models

These began with the Forrester-Meadows model at MIT, supported by the Club of Rome, and went on to the models by Iran Mesatovic and Eduard Pestel, the model by the Bariloche-Group of Carlos Mallmann, Hugo Scolnik, and others, the British model SARUM, the Japanese world model FUJI, the more limited FAO-model MOIRA, as well as others, and now the political GLOBUS-model at the Wissenschaftszentrum Berlin für Sozialforschung. All these models consume data but they also produce them.

Very often empirical data that are available are not used for testing. Views that have become popular appear plausible, even if they are erroneous. Empirical data on human behavior are not confronted with the assumptions of theoretical economics textbooks. The late psychologist George Katona made an important contribution to economics by starting to *ask* prospective consumers themselves about their economic attitudes and expectations.

Similarly, empirical data rarely have been brought to bear on the assumptions of theories

of deterrence. All too often, deterrence theory involves a piece of cognitive regression. As one knows, "regression" means that one falls back from the adult way of thinking and feeling back to the level of childhood. Consider what one can read in the popular press and in the pronouncements of statesmen in many countries about other countries. The other country, it is often said "understands nothing but force," or at best, a combination of bribes and threats. Only in this way, it is suggested, could the other nation or its government be more controlled, like an obstreperous donkey, with "a carrot and a stick." The method rarely works for long and not only because the economic carrot usually is too small and the thermonuclear stick is far too big. Carrot-and-stick methods have failed in outside efforts to control small countries like Afghanistan, Algeria, and Cuba. They have no chance of controlling the behavior of large countries like the United States, China, India, or the Soviet Union.

Some United States officers studying at Harvard made studies of military writings on deterrence, asking in particular how much of the findings of professional psychological research were used in them. It turned out none whatever.

Another set of empirical data which are underutilized are *time data*. There is one comparative survey in which Alexander Szalai of Hungary, Philip Converse of the United States, and others took part which compared the use of time by people in seven countries. We know far too little about the use of time, and much of the theory of communication and control requires time data. A large field of comparative research remains wide open.

A considerable number of middle-range theories have been developed concurrently. In a certain sense, the theory of money and employment by John M. Keynes is such a middle-range theory. There is the work of Joan Robinson and E. H. Chamberlin on the theory of monopolistic competition. Karl Mannheim's theory of the "fundamental democratization" of the world, and Joseph Schumpeter's contribution on the fundamental importance of innovation in the economic process are other cases in point. Fritz Machlup developed the theory on the transition from the industrial society to the information society. Robert Merton explicitly defended the use of middle-range theories and did excellent work on the interactions of science in societal development. Thomas Kuhn has contributed to our understanding of the interplay of scientific and social conditions leading to changes in the predominant images and patterns of concepts that he called "paradigms" in different fields of science. In my own work, I have studied nationalism and supranational integration; the results were middle-range theories and not comprehensive ones. Recently Mancur Olson has attempted to generate a middle-range theory of why states decline. A closer look shows that Olson's theory and theories of monopolistic competition have much in common, even though Olson may have come to his ideas quite independently.

In the meantime, comparative research has begun to compare many systems on a smaller scale — subsystems within larger ones. Of course, not only political science and political psychology have begun to compare such subsystems; the anthropologist John Whiting and his collaborators did this for families and child-rearing patterns in many black African societies. Comparative cultural anthropology has produced huge collections of cultural surveys and other data, some of which have been assembled in the Human Relations Area Files (HRAF) at Yale and other universities.

Political scientists have compared constitutions ever since Aristotle. More recently they have compared voting behavior. Large comparative studies of party structure and party behavior and pioneering comparative studies of elites have been conducted. There are comparisons of economic institutions, such as comparisons of labor-management relations in different countries. Comparisons have also been conducted of administrative behavior, for example by Herbert Simon, and for the Third World by Gunnar Myrdal, who proposed the

notions of a "soft state," the state where the government's commands are often not carried out, and a "hard state," similar to the modern Western state, where the government operates on cybernetic characteristics, such as information intake, information storage, information processing, feedback, and information output characteristics.

We also need comparative studies of error frequencies. Any computer manufacturer would like to know at least for internal purposes how often his computers break down. The armed forces, in constructing sophisticated missile systems, speak of "circular error probability" (CEP) around a target, the distance from the target within which half the missiles fired at it will fail. But what is the CEP of government officials or policies that are supposed to produce some particular results? Shouldn't we know? Shouldn't we know how often miscarriages of justice occur in particular systems of law or how often in certain safety procedures, for example, fire inspection experts fail to identify the causes of a fire? How often can we find out in foreign policy decisions whether the expected results were actually achieved after the policy had been set in motion? Concerns about the likelihood of failures and of error are basic in engineering, and this is one of the reasons why most engineering work is reliable. Work in politics is more difficult to assess, but is this a reason for knowing nothing about errors? It is not assumed that policy is perfect, but we need to know approximately how frequent and how large its expectable errors may be.

In sum, we now have a multitude of data with many middle-range theories, but they are sectoral, and some sectors are missing entirely. Moreover, the entire information is out of context. We have no common ground for most of the middle-range theories and no comon context for much of the data. Neither mainstream nor Marxist theory since 1920 has been able to offer such a possible context. Only a few world models offer at least a challenge and an opportunity in this respect. They must be interdisciplinary and long-range; they must be both state-centered and also world-centered. Perhaps in the future they could be extended to cultural factors on the one side and to technological factors on the other. They would have to integrate many of the confirmed middle-range theories that are now available. This is impossible if one stays at a level of middle-range theories, but it is a challenge to integrate them.

In the end, the world models may succeed. How long this will take and how hard it will be, no one can tell for certain. But integrating knowledge accumulated from comparative research into such a model presents one of the most important challenges to social scientists and one of the best uses to be made of the rich body of theories and data generated by comparative research. It is with these goals in mind that we have contributed to this book.

Note

* From *Comparative Policy Research: Learning from Experience,* edited by Meinolf Dierkes, Hans N. Weiler, and Ariane B. Antal (New York: St. Martin's Press, 1978). By permission of St. Martin's Press, Incorporated. Copyright 1978 by M. Dierkes, H. N. Weiler, and A. B. Antal.

Cross-National Policy Research: Traditions, Achievements, and Challenges*

Ariane Berthoin Antal, Meinolf Dierkes, and Hans N. Weiler

Even though cross-national or international comparative research[1] has long been a part of the social science agenda, there has clearly been a major leap forward since the Second World War. This expansion is attributable to developments in both the sociopolitical environment and the scientific community. The increase in comparative research can be seen as a response to "the accelerated interdependence of the world arena, an interdependence that was shockingly dramatized by World War II, by the biopolarized tensions between the communist and the noncommunist worlds, and by the anti-colonialist emergence of new nation states in Africa and Asia" (Lasswell 1968: 3). At the same time, other trends in scientific thought and in our societies have produced conditions which favored the development of comparative research:

Among the principal intellectual influences which fed into it [comparative social research] are: 1. the growing body of data on non-Western political systems; 2. the introduction into foreign political studies of concepts and methods that had emerged in research on American political processes; 3. anthropological, psychological, and psychoanalytical theories of culture and personality; 4. the concepts and insights of historical sociology and sociological theory. (Almond 1968: 333)

The purposes of cross-national research are numerous and the expectations regarding its contributions have been high. Comparisons of a more implicit and figurative kind have been part of social and political analyses as far back as the Greek theorists and have played an im-

portant role—as Karl Deutsch has described in chapter 1—in many of the classics of social thought: Marx, Weber, Tocqueville, Durkheim, Schumpeter, to name but some of the most prominent examples. However, systematic comparative approaches in sociology, economics, and political science did not emerge until the second half of this century. This development is due in large measure to the enhanced analytical self-consciousness of the social science community, notably in North America and Europe, and to the resulting appreciation of the analytical potential of more systematic comparisons across different social and political systems (Rokkan 1968; Przeworski and Teune 1970; Niessen and Peschar 1982). Its general justification and rationale are widely shared: "Cross-national research is needed and conducted because it is the closest approximation to the controlled laboratory experiment of the natural scientists which is available to social scientists" (Lisle 1978: 475).

A first central goal of comparative research is "to develop concepts and generalizations at a level between what is true of all societies and what is true of one society at one point in time and space" (Bendix 1973: 532). Comparison— be it intertemporal, interregional, or intersectoral—permits the stepwise and controlled falsification of hypotheses generated within a specific sectoral, regional, or national context. It defines the limits of generalization by specifying the conditions under which hypotheses are valid. This task has been approached from two angles: testing macrohypotheses concerning the interrelations of structural elements of total systems, and conducting microreplications in other national and cultural settings to test a proposition already validated in one setting (Rokkan 1966: 19–20).

A second central purpose of comparative research is to contribute to the development of a relevant knowledge base for both domestic and foreign policy. Comparative research can fill important gaps in knowledge about how other countries deal with similar situations, about the background and effects of alternative strategies for solving common problems (or avoiding their emergence in the first place). Structured comparison provides a framework for determining those aspects of a situation which are due to unique circumstances, and those which are more generally applicable — and therefore possibly appropriate to consider transferring to other contexts. Focused cross-national studies can help to locate those variables amenable to planned change by policy-making agencies (Berting et al., 1979: 161), as well as those which are beyond the control of the policymaker. Comparative research can aid in the specification of the conditions under which one country can learn from another. In short, comparison can put our judgments about policy processes and outcomes into a broader and more refined perspective. Identifying the differences among various national approaches to a given policy problem can assist in the specification of the structural, institutional, and cultural constraints of the public policy. An awareness of alternatives challenges the political and cultural assumptions on which a nation's policies are based. It brings to light underlying, often unquestioned premises. Researchers conducting comparative investigations often find that they learn as much, if not more, about their own political system by studying others. Not only do they find new policy options in other countries, but they also discover latent policy constraints and opportunities within their own system.

Another related reason for conducting comparative research stems from the increasing interdependence which characterizes the world today. Problems, policies, and issues cross borders and the policies of one country may strongly affect other countries. In this situation we need to know how other countries deal with problems, not only to learn how we might be able to deal with them ourselves, but also in order to estimate what kind of impact their problem-solving strategies might have on our own situation. The economic, environmental, cultural, and political interdependence of nations, the fact that the problems faced by one nation also influence others, and the realization that the difficulties in one country may be caused by another country's domestic policy together are leading to efforts to harmonize national policies on certain issues. Herein lies a major reason behind much of today's comparative research. The attempts by international and transnational organizations — such as the European Community — to establish common standards in different policy areas has motivated research on the various experiences countries have had in addressing common problems.

Can comparative research satisfy these great and varied expectations? Can it fulfill both the scientific and policy goals set for it? In one of the early efforts to evaluate the state of the art, with a special focus on the field of comparative politics, Roy Macridis arrived at a rather devastating conclusion. He found this field to be "essentially noncomparative . . . essentially descriptive . . . essentially parochial . . . essentially static . . . [and] essentially monographic" (Macridis 1955: 7, 12). In order to assess the progress made in comparative research since Macridis wrote this harsh critique it is first necessary to understand some of the key elements in the heritage of cross-national policy research, for the foci and approaches of the different research strands that have fed into this field of research have significant implications for the course the development of the field has taken and for the strengths and weaknesses characteristic of the state of the art today.

Cross-national policy research can be seen as a hybrid between academic inquiry and policy-making information. While a central message of this book is that the needs of policy making are best served by conducting solid scholarly research and that therefore the distinction between the two kinds of information needs can be misleading, it is instructive to review the distinct roots of this kind of research and examine how and to what extent a fusion has occurred.

A significant characteristic of the scholarly side of comparative research is the fact that it has been largely unidisciplinary in nature. The interaction between the various disciplines has been rather limited. Comparative politics is an interesting example because its systemic approach has had a major impact on the development of the field. As Almond (1966: 877) pointed out,

It is not accidental that it fell to comparative politics to be particularly active in reestablishing the relationship between the analysis of individual political systems and their classes and varieties with general political theory, and that it dramatized the necessity of reforging the links between historical political theory, empirical political theory, and normative political theory.

In the development of theory about political systems and processes, comparative political analysis has made its most significant contributions by either testing macrohypotheses on the interrelations of structural characteristics of political systems (for example, between social structures and party systems) or by replicating in other cultural and national settings propositions (for example, about determinants of voting behavior) already validated in one system (Rokkan 1968). The scope of comparative inquiry along these lines has been considerable, and has ranged from studies on the role and functions of particular types of political institutions such as legislatures (Loewenberg and Patterson 1979) or political parties (Dahl 1966; Lipset and Rokkan 1967; Rokkan 1970; Sartori 1976) and the analysis of key issues in political development such as the breakdown of democratic regimes (Linz and Stepan 1978), regime stability (Huntington 1968), to the complex interaction between the cultural and structural properties of political systems (Almond and Verba 1963; 1980) and more recently the development of the welfare state (Flora and Heidenheimer 1981). The overall significance of the new departure that came to be known as "comparative politics" has perhaps been captured best by Verba (1967: 11):

The revolution in comparative politics started with a number of brave principles: look beyond description to more theoretically relevant problems; look beyond the single case to the comparison of many cases; look beyond the formal institutions of government to political processes and political functions; and look beyond the countries of Western Europe to the new nations of Asia, Africa, and Latin America. The new comparative politics aimed at the creation and testing of generalizations and theories about politics and, especially, about macro-political systems. The macro-political perspective was perhaps forced on the practitioners of comparative politics by the nature of their subject matter. It creates the strength of the work being done in the field as well as many of its special problems.

Beyond this task of consolidating political theory and its validity across different political systems, comparative political analysis has also substantially expanded the scope of descriptive knowledge about political phenomena in quite a variety of political settings. The association between comparative politics and the emergence of area studies (notably for non-Western areas) greatly facilitated this expansion by opening up and systematically cultivating a vast amount of information about a wide range of political systems and processes. While the analytical penetration and theoretical utilization of this database has varied greatly, substantial progress in the development, modification, and validation of theoretical propositions about the nature of political processes has been made through the expansion of comparative political analysis beyond the realm of North America and Western Europe (e.g., Almond and Coleman 1960; Pye and Verba 1965; Michelena 1971; Cockroft et al. 1972; Verba 1978; Eisenstadt 1978).

Policy, seen as an element in the "performance" of political systems, and its determinants became and remained an important part on the conceptual agenda of much comparative political analysis (Almond and Powell 1978: part IV). But the explanatory interest of comparative politics research was not primarily directed at a better understanding of the making and implementation of public policy and of its effects. The information needs of policymakers was not met directly by this line of research. Not surprisingly, therefore, a different line of comparative inquiry—parallel to this growing scholarly concern with the comparative and cross-national study of political and social phenomena—began to take shape in the 1960s that was more specifically and explicitly directed at the study of public policy.

This new field of comparative policy research has its more immediate ancestry in policy analysis (Nagel 1975; Dye 1976) and it reflects the influence of such fields as public administration, history, social psychology, political sociology, and—perhaps most importantly—economics. It is located, as Heidenheimer et al. (1983: 8) put it, "at a busy crossroads in the social sciences" and "provides a setting where political scientists, sociologists, historians, and economists are learning from one another." The primary characteristics which distinguish it from the type of scholarly research described above include its problem orientation and its multidisciplinarity. While the emphasis of comparative politics, for example, was on scholarship, the focus of public administration research was on applicability. As Nagel (1984: 1) explains:

Policy studies relates closely to both public administration and political science. It shares with public administration a concern for the effects of public policies; in contrast, political science stresses their formation. With political science it shares a concern for establishing cause-and-effect relations on a level more general than that characteristic of public administration. Policy studies thus usefully links the more pragmatic aspects of public administration

with the more theoretical aspects of political science.

In the most concise definition available, the field of comparative public policy is described as "the study of how, why, and to what effect different governments pursue a particular course of action or inaction" (Heidenheimer et al. 1983: 2–3). While this definition covers a wide range of different concerns and analytical approaches, it captures some of the more important items of the agenda of most comparative analyses of policy, notably the emphasis on explanation and the importance of the effects (intended as well as unintended) which government policies have on the lives and welfare of their citizens. This explicit concern with the human and social consequences of policy distinguishes comparative policy analysis as a field from some of its related comparative enterprises such as comparative government or comparative political behavior. Put slightly differently and even more pointedly, "the primary purpose of comparative policy research . . . is not to establish the universality of relationships, . . . [but] to enhance the credibility of specific predictions about specific cases" and thus to "get useful rather than general knowledge in the short run" (Teune 1978: 54).

Cross-national policy research is unique in its search to brook the disjuncture in the research community between "pure research" and "pure policy advice." Two major consequences for the development of cross-national policy research stem from the public administration root. On the one hand, bridging the gap between theory and practice has not always been easy, while the lack of theory and a more general framework has hindered the cumulation of research results. And, on the other hand, the comparative approach is not central to the tradition of public administration research. Such research tends by nature to be ethnocentric and parochial in its problem-solving orientation. Consequently, the methods and concepts developed specifically for the study of issues in the American context have sometimes been transferred to comparative policy research. Their application in different social, political, and cultural contexts has often proved problematic.

The problems arising from transferring analytical models and concepts from one national context directly to another represent only one set of complications confronting comparative research derived from implicit assumptions underlying specific projects. While concepts and analytical constructs may be culturally bound or limited, other implicit assumptions may affect the cross-national applicability of research approaches as well as findings. Considering, for example, the close proximity between the comparative analysis of policy and the stark reality of the common and individual good, it is not surprising that the issue of normative elements in comparative policy research has become an important theme in recent investigations. Since, for Anderson, a policy "is a conscious contrivance, reflecting human purposiveness, and . . . in some sense a moral act," there is inevitably "a normative element at the very heart of any effort to develop a systematic, comparative study of public policy" (Anderson 1978: 20). Just how to deal with this normative element in comparative policy is a matter of considerable debate. There seems to be substantial agreement, however, on the need for treating the normative assumptions underlying policy decisions as a key variable in the comparative analysis of policy in an attempt to "unravel the subtle interactions between political culture and public policy predispositions" (Heidenheimer et al. 1983: 5). This becomes particularly important as the question of choice assumes increasingly greater significance in the comparative policy field. Among the themes are choice between different policy objectives and different policy instruments, choice between maintaining the status quo and innovation or reform, choice between public and private responsibilities, and choice between different patterns and ben-

eficiaries for the distribution of public resources. Indeed, it is difficult to conceive of policy without invoking the notion of choice, and it is difficult to deal with the theme of choice without coming to terms with the issue of norms and values (Heidenheimer et al. 1983: 12–13 and passim; Apter 1971; Rae and Eismeier 1979).

Another critical dilemma in the development of comparative policy research is also related to issues of implicit versus explicit assumptions underlying approaches and influencing findings: the use of inductive versus deductive reasoning in research design. Heidenheimer and his colleagues, for example, while leaning toward a more inductive approach in their own work, recognize and document the attractiveness of proceeding into a comparative analysis of policy from the basis of a given set of assumptions about how the state, social classes, bureaucratic organizations, or other participants in the policy process tend to behave, and show that such a preference is by no means limited to premises that are derived from Marxist traditions (Heidenheimer et al. 1983: 3–4). The increasing predominance of rational choice approaches and formal modeling in American political science are certain to have an impact on future public policy analysis, both in domestic and in cross-national contexts. . . .

There are, then, a number of tensions inherent in the challenge of cross-national policy research whose impact is particularly important for the development of knowledge over time. The combination of the diverse disciplinary heritage of the field and the pressures for immediate policy relevance have called into question the ability of the field to claim theoretical unity (Feldman 1978). In a recent review of the literature, Hancock (1983: 298–9) found that the problem lies less in the lack of theories, for "theories abound within the subdiscipline and have profitably helped focus research and analysis within each of the designated approaches." Rather, he concludes, the tension lies in the fact that "the very existence of sharply divergent conceptualizations and research foci has severely inhibited cumulative scholarship within the subdiscipline as a whole" (Hancock 1983: 293). The fragmentation of the field can also result from the sectoral approach to the definition and treatment of policy problems. While bridging disciplinary boundaries with a certain degree of success, researchers are only now beginning to integrate their knowledge derived from diverse policy sectors into a more comprehensive understanding of the way the public policy system as a whole functions.

This rather fragmented state of affairs in comparative policy analysis is natural enough, considering the origins and history of the field and its varied audiences. This fragmentation, however, together with the enormous proliferation of work in the comparative policy field, has also made it increasingly difficult to identify common themes and theoretical propositions, convergent or contradictory trends in findings, methodological similarities or complementarities, consistent patterns in the utilization of findings, discernible types of organizational arrangements, or clear directions for future research. The process of learning from what has been discovered so far, synthesizing knowledge and benefiting from the rich background of experience that has accumulated over the years in comparative policy research appeared to require a conscious focused effort. This was a motivating factor behind the organizing of a major review of cross-national research in several policy areas. There was a strong sense that an updated, broader, and more penetrating analysis of experience in comparative research was needed in order to assess the state of the art and to reevaluate both the possibilities and limitations of comparative research vis-à-vis the expectations of the research and decision-making communities. Four quite different policy sectors were chosen, each having their own research approaches and traditions, methodologies, and target groups in national (and sometimes international) policy-making

communities. The review strategy involved an examination of a number of individual projects within each of the fields in order to develop a sounder empirical basis for discussing these questions.

In the light of the problems identified in previous assessments of cross-national research in general, and comparative policy research in particular, four central types of issue were crystallized for analysis in the policy fields selected for review. While in practice these issues are closely intertwined, for analytical purposes they are best first treated individually before their interaction can be properly understood.

1. *Theoretical issues.* As discussed above, two of the main criticisms leveled at cross-national policy research are, on the one hand, that the search for policy relevance has been at the expense of theoretical rigor, and, on the other hand, that the multitude of theoretical backgrounds have impeded overall cumulation. Based on the observation that research projects often contain implicit theories and assumptions, it is important to discover the specific theoretical and epistemological underpinnings in individual cases to examine the extent to which they have influenced the results of the research. In other words, to what extent are research findings really contradictory, and where can more general conclusions be drawn across research projects when cloudy theoretical assumptions are clarified?

2. *Methodological issues.* The discussion about the existence of a special methodology for comparative research seems to have subsided in the conclusion that in general the issues are the same as those faced in noncomparative research but are made more complex by the different contexts in which the research is conducted (Przeworski and Teune 1970). But the focus of most studies on methodological problems has been on the cross-national and cross-cultural validity of specific measures, particularly in survey research. The problems that emerge in cross-national *policy* research have received far less attention.

3. *Organizational issues.* The importance given to organizational issues in conducting cross-national research is evidenced in the efforts sponsored by the International Social Science Council, the Vienna Centre, for example, and it was an important item on the agenda of the

emerging comparative politics community (Merritt and Rokkan 1966: part IV; Rokkan 1966). Of particular interest, for example, are Rokkan's reflections on the possibilities for "linking up" projects in different countries in such a way as to optimize the comparisons of designs, methodologies, and findings (Rokkan 1979: 5–6). In spite of such efforts, however, the organization of research projects is often handled pragmatically, with little regard for the theoretical implications and little knowledge of previous experiences. This is probably largely attributable to the fact that research reports usually focus on the substantive side of the project rather than discussing the difficulties faced and mistakes made in organizing the research. Little systematic and comprehensive research has been done to evaluate the strengths and drawbacks of different organizational strategies and their appropriateness for specific types of research tasks. By examining the experiences of a broad range of individual projects, the intention of this review was to learn from the past and to establish more clearly how the tendency to reinvent the wheel can be counteracted in the future.

4. *Issues relating to policy relevance.* The question of the transferability of research results is essential in comparative policy research. One school of thought holds that, since each cultural context is unique, lessons learned in other contexts cannot be applied elsewhere. A related argument is that only when a very high level of abstraction is reached can the differences between settings be bridged, so that the resulting conclusions must necessarily be equally abstract and therefore unsuited to policy practice. Thus, one central question requiring empirical examination is the extent to which past research can be considered to have been policy-relevant and which conditions seem to have favored this.

In the light of the background which this chapter has attempted to trace, there was clearly much more to this task than a mere inventory, ambitious as that alone would have been. Instead, the review was designed in such a way as to identify and make transparent patterns, trends, and directions in this vast array of comparative policy research. It was the hope of the authors, reviewers, and editors that, in the process, an answer might emerge to the question which a number of critics have raised,

namely whether there really was any significant cumulative quality about the field of comparative policy research. Berting, in his conclusions following a UNESCO-sponsored symposium in the Netherlands in 1979, was one of the more outspoken skeptics with regard to the prospect of ever overcoming the many difficulties which tend to prevent the effective cumulation of comparative research findings (Berting et al. 1979). This project set out to examine his pessimism and the concerns of others against the background of a major body of comparative research in four major policy areas, and this volume presents the results of this effort. The reader will have to judge how, in the burgeoning field of comparative policy research, the forces of cumulation and the forces of dispersion measure up against each other.

Notes

*   From *Comparative Policy Research: Learning from Experience,* edited by Meinolf Dierkes, Hans N. Weiler, and Ariane B. Antal (New York: St. Martin's Press, 1978), 13–25, by permission of St. Martin's Press, Incorporated. Copyright 1978 by M. Dierkes, H. N. Weiler, and A. B. Antal.

1. The terms "international" and "cross-national comparative" research are used interchangeably throughout the volume to describe research efforts that systematically study similar phenomena (such as institutions, groups, individuals, attitudes, goals, behaviors, social processes) in different socioeconomic, political, and cultural settings.

References

Almond, Gabriel A. 1966. "Political Theory and Political Science," *American Political Science Review,* vol. 60, no. 4 (December), pp. 869–79.

Almond, Gabriel A. 1968. "Comparative Politics," *International Encyclopedia of the Social Sciences,* vol. 12, New York: Macmillan and Free Press, pp. 331–6.

Almond, Gabriel A. and James S. Coleman, eds. 1960. *The Politics of the Developing Areas.* Princeton: Princeton University Press.

Almond, Gabriel A. and G. Bingham Powell, Jr. 1978. *Comparative Politics: System, Process, and Policy,* 2nd edn. Boston: Little, Brown.

Almond, Gabriel A. and Sidney Verba. 1963. *The Civic Culture: Political Attitudes and Democracy in Five Nations.* Princeton: Princeton University Press.

Almond, Gabriel A. and Sidney Verba, eds. 1980. *The Civic Culture Revisited.* Boston: Little, Brown.

Anderson, Charles W. 1978. "The Logic of Public Problems: Evaluation in Comparative Policy Research" in Douglas E. Ashford, ed., *Comparing Public Policies: New Concepts and Methods.* Beverly Hills: Sage, pp. 19–41.

Apter, David E. 1971. *Choice and the Politics of Allocation.* New Haven: Yale University Press.

Ashford, Douglas E., ed. 1978. *Comparing Public Policies: New Concepts and Methods.* Beverly Hills: Sage.

Bendix, Reinhard. 1973. *State and Society: A Reader in Comparative Political Sociology.* Berkeley: University of California Press.

Berting, Jan, Felix Geyer, and Ray Jurkovich, eds. 1979. *Problems in International Comparative Research in the Social Sciences.* Oxford: Pergamon.

Carnoy, Martin. 1984. *The State and Political Theory.* Princeton: Princeton University Press.

Cockroft, James D., et al. 1972. *Dependence and Underdevelopment: Latin America's Political Economy.* Garden City, NJ: Doubleday.

Dahl, Robert A. 1966. *Political Oppositions in Western Democracies.* New Haven: Yale University Press.

Dye, Thomas R. 1976. *Policy Analysis: What Governments Do, Why They Do It, and What Difference It Makes.* University, AL: The University of Alabama Press.

Eisenstadt, S. N. 1978. *Revolution and the Transformation of Societies: A Comparative Study of Civilizations.* New York: Free Press.

Feldman, Elliot J. 1978. "Comparative Public Policy: Field or Method?" *Comparative Politics,* vol. 10, pp. 287–305.

Flora, Peter and Arnold J. Heidenheimer, eds. 1981. *The Development of the Welfare State in Europe and America.* New Brunswick, NJ: Transaction.

Hancock, Donald M. 1983. "Comparative Public Policy: An Assessment" in Ada W. Finifter, ed., *Political Science. The State of the Discipline.* Washington DC: American Political Science Association, pp. 283–308.

Hanson, Charles, Sheila Jackson and Douglas Miller. 1981. *The Closed Shop: A Comparative Study in Public Policy and Trade Union Security in Britain, the USA, and West Germany.* New York: St. Martin's Press.

Heidenheimer, Arnold J. 1974. "The Politics of Educational Reform: Explaining Different Outcomes of School Comprehensivization Attempts in Sweden and West Germany," *Comparative Education Review,* vol. 18, no. 3 (October), pp. 388–410.

Heidenheimer, Arnold J., Hugh Heclo, and Carolyn Teich Adams. 1983. *Comparative Public Policy: The Politics of Social Choice in Europe and America.* 2nd edn. New York: St. Martin's Press.

Hirschman, Albert O. 1970. *Exit, Voice, and Loyalty: Responses to Decline in Firms, Organizations, and States.* Cambridge, MA: Harvard University Press.

Holt, Robert T. and John E. Turner. 1970. *The Methodology of Comparative Research.* New York: Free Press.

Huntington, Samuel. 1968. *Political Order in Changing Societies.* New Haven: Yale University Press.

Kelman, Steven. 1980. *Regulating America, Regulating Sweden: A Comparative Study of Occupational Safety and Health Policy.* Cambridge, MA: MIT Press.

Lasswell, Harold. 1968. "The Future of the Comparative Method," *Comparative Politics,* vol. 1, no. 1 (October), pp. 3–18.

Lijphart, Arend. 1975. "The Comparable-Cases Strategy in Comparative Research," *Comparative Political Studies,* vol. 58, no. 2 (July), pp. 158–77.

Linz, Juan J. and Alfred Stepan. 1978. *The Breakdown of Democratic Regimes: Europe.* Baltimore: Johns Hopkins University Press.

Lipset, Seymour Martin and Stein Rokkan, eds. 1967. *Party Systems and Voter Alignments.* New York: Free Press.

Lisle, A. 1978. Chapter 14, in Meinholf Dierkes, Hans N. Weiler, and Ariane B. Antal, eds., *Comparative Policy Research: Learning from Experience.* New York: St. Martin's Press.

Loewenberg, Gerhard and Samuel C. Patterson. 1979. *Comparing Legislatures.* Boston: Little, Brown.

Lowi, Theodore J. 1975. "What Political Scientists Don't Need to Ask About Policy Analysis" in Stuart S. Nagel, ed., *Policy Studies and the So-*

cial Sciences. Lexington, MA: Lexington Books, pp. 267–73.

Macridis, Roy C. 1955. *The Study of Comparative Government.* Garden City, NY: Doubleday.

Merritt, Richard L. and Stein Rokkan, eds. 1966. *Comparing Nations: The Use of Quantitative Data in Cross-National Research.* New Haven: Yale University Press.

Michelena, Jose A. Silva. 1971. *The Illusion of Democracy in Dependent Nations.* Cambridge, MA: MIT Press.

Nagel, Stuart S., ed. 1975. *Policy Studies and the Social Sciences.* Lexington, MA: Lexington Books.

Nagel, Stuart. 1984. *Contemporary Public Policy Analysis.* University, AL: of Alabama Press.

Niessen, Manfred and Jules Peschar, eds. 1982. *International Comparative Research: Problems of Theory, Methodology and Organisation in Eastern and Western Europe.* Oxford: Pergamon Press.

Pateman, Carole. 1980. "The Civic Culture: A Philosophic Critique" in Gabriel A. Almond and Sidney Verba, eds., *The Civic Culture Revisited.* Boston: Little, Brown, pp. 57–102.

Przeworski, Adam and Henry Teune. 1970. *The Logic of Comparative Social Inquiry.* New York: Wiley-Interscience.

Pye, Lucian W. and Sidney Verba, eds. 1965. *Political Culture and Political Development.* Princeton: Princeton University Press.

Rae, Douglas and Theodore J. Eismeier, eds. 1979. *Public Policy and Public Choice.* Beverly Hills: Sage.

Roberts, Geoffrey K. 1972. *What Is Comparative Politics?* New York: Macmillan.

Rokkan, Stein, ed. 1966. *Data Archives for the Social Sciences.* Paris: Mouton.

Rokkan, Stein, ed. 1968. *Comparative Research Across Cultures and Nations.* Paris: Mouton.

Rokkan, Stein. 1970. *Citizens, Elections, Parties.* New York: McKay.

Rokkan, Stein. 1979. *A Quarter Century of International Social Science: Papers and Reports on Developments, 1952–1977.* New Delhi: Concept Publishing Co.

Rokkan, Stein, Jean Viet, Sidney Verba, and Elina Almasy, eds. 1969. *Comparative Survey Analysis.* The Hague: Mouton.

Rose, Richard, ed. 1976. *The Dynamics of Public Policy: A Comparative Analysis.* London and Beverly Hills: Sage.

Sartori, Giovanni. 1976. *Parties and Party Systems.* Cambridge: Cambridge University Press, 1976.

Scase, Richard, ed. 1980. *The State in Western Europe.* New York: St. Martin's Press.

Skocpol, Theda. 1979. *States and Social Revolution: A Comparative Analysis of France, Russia, and China.* Cambridge: Cambridge University Press.

Spiro, Shimon E. and Ephraim Yuchtman-Yaar, eds. 1983. *Evaluating the Welfare State: Social and Political Perspectives.* New York: Academic Press.

Stepan, Alfred C. 1978. *The State and Society: Peru in Comparative Perspective.* Princeton: Princeton University Press.

Teune, Henry. 1978. "A Logic of Comparative Policy Analysis" in Douglas E. Ashford, ed., *Comparing Public Policies: New Concepts and Methods.* Beverly Hills: Sage, pp. 43–55.

Verba, Sidney. 1967. "Some Dilemmas in Comparative Research," *World Politics,* vol. 20, no. 1 (October), pp. 111–27.

Verba, Sidney, Norman H. Nie, and Jae-on Kim. 1978. *Participation and Political Equality: A Seven-Nation Comparison.* Cambridge: Cambridge University Press.

Weiler, Hans N. 1983. "Legalization, Expertise, and Participation: Strategies of Compensatory Legitimation in Educational Policy," *Comparative Education Review,* vol. 27, no. 2 (June), pp. 259–77.

CHAPTER THREE

Cross-Cultural, Cross-Societal, and Cross-National Research[*]

Stein Rokkan

We propose to direct our attention to one single, central set of issues in the development of a worldwide science of Man and Society: the possibilities of translating "grand theory" into empirically workable *typologies of "macrosettings"* for variations in human behavior, and the consequences of such typologies for decisions on the cultural and the geographical range of comparisons at the level of communities, households, and individuals.

These issues cut across all the disciplines of the human and the social sciences: they are of central importance in the disciplines devoted to the study of structures of interaction among human beings. Much of the literature on comparative anthropology focuses on the merits of alternative typologies and on the possibilities of establishing regional ranges for cross-societal comparisons.[1] The argument opposing anthropologists and economists over the analysis and interpretation of data on production, manpower, and barter in preliterate societies bears on similar issues: how far is it meaningful to "stretch" models developed at one end of the continuum to cover the twilight zones of part-monetized, part-mobilized communities in developing countries? Similar controversies have arisen in the wake of the eager attempts of sociologists and political scientists to introduce their techniques and styles of analysis into the new nations of the "Third World": anthropologists and other area specialists have strenuously opposed such efforts to establish a data basis for comparisons across societies differing so fundamentally in structure and in ethos. The attacks against the universalist assumptions

underlying Murdock's statistical correlations for samples of the world's societies have their counterpart in the criticisms leveled by anthropologists and historians against such attempts at worldwide data archiving as Karl Deutsch's, and at such universal models of socio-cultural-political development as those sketched by Talcott Parsons among sociologists and by Gabriel Almond, Lucian Pye, and their partners in the comparative politics movement.

The extremes in this controversy are easily stated: at the one pole of opposition, all societies, past, present, or future, constitute units of potential comparison and ought eventually to be subjected to tests against unified models of universal hypothetico-deductive explanation; at the other pole, all societies are culturally and historically unique and defy understanding through comparisons with others.

The Murdock school comes closest to the universalist extreme: they want to make sure that all known variants get a chance to be represented in the sample and see few if any direct barriers to meaningful comparisons across the major regions of the world. To this school, the diffusion of cultural characteristics and the sharing of historical experiences constitute so many disturbing elements in the design of the sample of societies, and do not constitute criteria for the limitation of comparisons. The protracted controversy over what has come to be known as "Galton's problem" tells us a great deal about the ways in which differences in intellectual styles affect the organization of comparative research. The English anthropologist Edward Tylor presented the first "cross-cultural" table of associated characteristics for a sample of societies in a famous lecture in 1889, and was attacked by the statistician Galton for failing to consider possibilities of cultural diffusion. Tylor had set up a two-by-two table to test the association between the traits "in-law avoidance" and "patrilocal residence," but had included in his count of cases a number of societies which were geographically and culturally closely related and might have derived the given combination of traits from a common source.[2] Tylor's followers have heeded this warning and have tried their best to weed out of their samples societies likely to be interpreted as so many "duplicate copies of the same original," to use Galton's phrase.[3] But this is hardly a lasting strategy in a world constantly shrinking through the diffusion of technologies and ideas and through the accelerated sharing of historical experiences. The Murdock strategy would be eminently applicable in a world of isolated societies and local religions, but runs into a variety of technical, logical, and statistical difficulties in a world of proselytizing religions and ideologies, of constantly expanding networks of communication, exchange, and organization.

Comparative sociologists such as Shmuel Eisenstadt, Reinhard Bendix, Seymour Martin Lipset, Barrington Moore, and Talcott Parsons, and comparative political analysts such as Gabriel Almond, Karl Deutsch, Samuel Huntington, Robert Holt, and John Turner have deliberately opted for the alternative solution: to build the communication–diffusion–innovation variables directly into their models and to focus their comparative analyses on units developed through the merger of smaller societies of the type studied by anthropologists. Jack Goody and Ian Watt have epigrammatically identified anthropology as the science of man as a talking animal and sociology as the science of man as a writing animal:[4] this is the crux of the division between the comparisons of isolated societies in the Tylor-Murdock style and comparisons of empires and nation-states by the followers of Montesquieu, Tocqueville,

and Weber. The introduction of written communication extends the possibilities of control over space and time and alters the character of the social structure. Talcott Parsons has stressed this "cybernetic" interpretation in his recent statement on the comparative history of societies. His wide-ranging account runs from the socially-culturally-politically least differentiated preliterate societies, over the "ideographically" literate early empires and the alphabetized "seedbed" societies of Israel and Greece, to the advanced nation-states of the modern age.[5] Such sweeping interpretive statements may at times take on the character of exercises in the philosophy of history but do point to important tasks of detailed comparison.

The best-documented historical comparisons have focused on limited ranges of cases or on shorter spans of time: on the conditions for the formation of centralized bureaucracies and differentiated national polities and on the stages and sequences of integration and consolidation, stagnation and decline.

These studies differ markedly in their strategies. We may conveniently distinguish three styles:

- Analyses focused on the identification of *one type of polity* and on the construction of a paradigm for the comparison of all historical cases close to this type, wherever they may have occurred in time or space;
- Comparisons of pairs or multiples of *leading or innovating polities* across all world regions over roughly the same span of time;
- Comparisons of all polities within *one culturally-historically homogeneous region* of the world.

Shmuel Eisenstadt's gigantic work on the emergence and decline of bureaucratic empires[6] offers an excellent example of comparisons of the first type. Nothing of similar scope and analytical depth has as yet been attempted for the other major type of cross-community organization for resource mobilization and territorial control: the nation-state.

Karl Deutsch has given us a suggestive cybernetic model of nation-building processes but has applied it to only a few empirical cases. His pioneering work on *Nationalism and Social Communication* limited its quantitative comparisons to four countries,[7] and the data bank built up by him for analyses of variations among nation-states does not cover sufficiently long spans of time to allow the testing of developmental models.[8] Perhaps his greatest contribution lies in his effort to codify procedures for the establishment of indicators of variation in the rates of mobilization within the actual or potential territories of nation-states:[9] this work has inspired a variety of attempts at empirical testing and has acted as a springboard for further theorizing.[10]

The Deutsch models fired the imagination of a number of scholars, but they were limited to only one of the many sets of processes inherent in the formation of national political communities: they focused on variables explaining the rates of incorporation of underlying local populations at different physical and/or cultural distances from the national center, and gave much less attention to variations over time in the political or administrative measures of national standardization and consolidation taken at the territorial centers, or to the dimensions of elite conflicts over such policies. In Deutsch's work with Weilenmann on the formation of the Swiss polity,[11] there are intriguing pointers toward the construction of a model of variations in the processes of alliance formation at the national center, but the implications of this style of analysis remain to be worked out for other cases of multicultural nation building such as the Dutch, Belgian, Canadian, and Lebanese.

The paradigm developed in successive steps within the Almond-Pye Committee on Comparative Politics[12] offers a better balance between "state formation" variables describing processes at the center of each system, and "nation-building" variables accounting for processes of change in the underlying territorial populations. The Almond-Pye scheme posits six crises of development. These define sets of challenges, decision points, or policy tasks in the path of any central elite or counterelite endeavoring to consolidate a national territorial community. This amounts to a proposal to study all historically given nation-states within one conceptual grid, whether old-established or newly constituted, whether in Europe, European settler areas overseas, in Asia or in Africa. The aim is worldwide comparative analysis: the paradigm is a tool in the ordering of data on the sequences of decisions and reactions leading to the formation of nation-states at different levels of cultural consolidation, political mobilization, and organizational capacity.

Three of the six crises arise out of conflicts in the extension and differentiation of the administrative apparatus of the nation-state:

- The *penetration* crisis—the crucial initial challenge of the establishment of a coordinated network of territorial administrative agents independent of local power resources and responsive to directives from the central decision-making organs;
- The *integration* crisis—clashes over the establishment of allocation rules for the equalization of the shares of administrative offices, benefits, and resources among all the culturally-territorially-politically-distinct segments and sectors of the national community;
- The *distribution* crisis—conflicts over the expansion of the administrative apparatus of the nation-state through the organization of services and the imposition of control measures for the equalization of economic conditions between the different strata of the population and between localities differing in their resources and levels of production.

The other three crises arise out of conflicts between elites and counterelites in the definition and differentiation of the territorial population:

- The *identity* crisis—the crucial initial challenge in the establishment and extension of a common culture and the development of media and agencies for the socialization of future citizens into this community of shared codes, values, memories, and symbols;

- The *legitimacy* crisis—clashes over the establishment of central structures of political communication, consultation, and representation commanding the loyalty and confidence of significant sections of the national population and ensuring regular conformity to rules and regulations issued by the agencies authorized by the system;
- The *participation* crisis—the conflict over the extension of rights of consultation and representation to all strata of the territorial population and over the protection of rights of association, demonstration, and opposition.

The paradigm does not posit any fixed sequence in the solution of the six crises; on the contrary, the purpose of the scheme is to pinpoint variations in the sequences of challenges, policy conflicts and full-scale crises among historically given polities and to generate hypotheses concerning the conditions for the emergence of such variations in processes of nation building. Unfortunately, little concrete work has been done on the operationalization of this set of general concepts or on the classification of historical sequences of conflicts and decisions within this framework. Characteristically, most of the examples used in the presentation and discussion of the scheme have been taken from the brief histories of the nation-states emerging from colonial status following World War II.

Indeed, the decisive intellectual motivation for the development of the scheme was the urge for some ordering and codification of the insights accumulated in the initial study of these new states. There was no similar attempt to bring order into the wealth of historical information at hand on the already functioning nation-states in Europe and the European settler areas. There is little doubt that the scheme can prove useful in the comparative study of these older nation-states, but the concrete experience of operationalization, classification, and interpretation has not yet been made.[13]

Whatever the results of such concrete tests, it is clear that this paradigm of crises does not in itself constitute a model for the explanation of variations in the outcomes of nation-building processes. The paradigm helps to order the information about each bundle of processes but has not been built into a body of propositions concerning the consequences of varying sequences of crises and of varying alignments of elites and underlying populations in the solution of the crises.

This has been a field of great intellectual excitement during recent years. A number of sociologists and political scientists have tried to develop models for the explanation of variations in the choice of elite strategies in the building of national communities and have sought to derive propositions concerning the consequences of different alliance strategies for the further development of each system.

We may conveniently distinguish two styles of macrocomparisons along these lines:

- *Large-nation comparisons* across *contrasting* cultural areas;
- Comparisons of *all units*, smaller as well as larger, within *one* cultural area.

Reinhard Bendix focuses his work on *Nation-Building and Citizenship* on the growth of territorial systems of public authority in four contrasting national communities: Germany and Russia, India and Japan. Samuel Huntington seeks to define the "fusion of functions" and "division of powers" characteristic of the United States through an analysis of the contrasting developments in England and France.[14] In both cases the explanatory variables are sought in the processes of interaction, alliance, and conflict among the elites controlling the principal resources of social, economic, and/or cultural power in each population; the dependent variables are characteristics of the resultant structures of administrative and political institutions. In another set of "leader-nation" comparisons, by the political scientists Robert Holt and John Turner,[15] these administrative-political variables in their turn offer a basis for the explanation of contrasts in the timing of the takeoff to economic growth: the early industrializers in each cultural context, England and Japan, are systematically compared and contrasted with the two later industrializers, France and China, in an effort to test propositions concerning the consequences of political centralization for the initiation and spread of economic innovations.

This theme, the interlinkages between processes of economic growth and processes of political-constitutional change, is equally central in Barrington Moore's pioneering analysis of the conditions for the rise of democratic opposition politics versus monolithic dictatorships in the leading states of the modern world.[16]

Moore distinguishes three "paths to the modern age": the *democratic and capitalist,* the *fascist* and the *communist,* and seeks to compare the histories of the leading nations which followed each of these paths in Europe, America, and Asia. He compares the three highly divergent cases of capitalist democracy in the West, England, France, and the United States of America, with the one nation which may still follow this path in Asia: India. He then compares two nations which, at least for a period in their history, chose the fascist route to modernization: Germany in Europe and Japan in Asia. Finally, he compares the two giant leaders of the communist nations: Russia and China. These comparisons are linked through a unifying model of alliances and oppositions among four sets of actors: the central bureaucracy, the commercial and the industrial bourgeoisie, the larger landowners, and the underlying peasant population. The logic of this analysis is very simple but its implications far-reaching: once an alliance or an opposition has established itself through a revolution or through a slower process of interaction, the total political system tends to assume a definite style which will limit options for future decision makers. This emphasis on irreversibilities in the "typing" of nation-states through early alliances and oppositions has significant con-

sequences for comparative cross-national research: we shall spell this out further below in our discussion of the Lipset-Rokkan model for the explanation of variations among party systems. The great strength of Moore's analysis lies in its discussion of the consequences of alternative alliances and oppositions among the controllers of different types of power resources: the alliance of the landed aristocracy and the urban bourgeoisie *against* the monarchy in England, *through* the monarchy in France, the alliance of Northern capitalists and Western farmers against Southern plantation owners in the United States, the alliance of landowners and royal administrators in Prussia and in Japan, the weaknesses of all alliances between economic power holders and "agrarian bureaucracies" in Russia and China. The emphasis throughout is on strategies for the acquiring of maximum power resources and for the organization of countervailing checks. At least in the core model of explanation, there is very little concern for cultural variables influencing strategies and outcomes: no discussion of the role of linguistic loyalties as a factor in decisions on alliance or opposition, no mention of churches and sects as possible resources for the mobilization of support or protest. This may well be justified in a parsimonious model of explanation for just those eight countries, but surely limits the scope of the analysis too rigidly. Moore argues that his model does not require testing beyond these leading countries: the crucial political innovations occurred in these larger units and any further comparison of developments in the smaller countries would help to account for processes of diffusion and adaptation only:

This study concentrates on certain important stages in a prolonged social process which has worked itself out in several countries. As part of this process new social arrangements have grown up by violence or in other ways which have made certain countries political leaders at different points in time during the first half of the twentieth century. The focus of interest is on innovation that has led to political power, not on the spread and reception of institutions that have been hammered out elsewhere, except where they have led to significant power in world politics. The fact that smaller countries depend economically and politically on big and powerful ones means that the decisive causes of their politics lie outside their own boundaries. It also means that their political problems are not really comparable to those of larger countries. Therefore a general statement about the historical preconditions of democracy or authoritarianism covering small countries as well as large would very likely be so broad as to be abstractly platitudinous.[17]

These arguments for the concentration of analytical efforts on leader nations, on systems wielding "significant power in world politics," raise intriguing issues of research strategy. First of all, what intellectual reasons are there for restricting the endeavors of comparativists to the analysis of conflict and innovation in the major power centers? It would not seem difficult to make as good a case for concerted research on processes of diffusion and reception: after all, most of the units open to comparative study are "follower" nations rather than leaders. Secondly, political innovation surely cannot be treated as a function of size alone. Two small polities, Greece and Israel, generated the greatest innovations of the ancient world. In the modern world, small polities such as Iceland, Switzerland, the Netherlands, and Sweden have fostered institutional innovations without any direct counterpart in the larger leader units. Talcott Parsons, in his theoretical statement on differentiations among modern societies, has gone so far as to assert that innovations have been more likely to occur in isolated units at the peripheries of major power systems: the Italian city-states, the Dutch provinces, and the English monarchy of the seventeenth and eighteenth centuries offered "sanctuaries in which new developments could mature before having to encounter the more severe tests of broader institutionalization."[18]

Whatever the merits of this argument, the smaller nations constitute worthy objects of comparative study: they have managed to survive a world dominated by larger and stronger units; they have developed their own distinctive institutions; there are enough of them to allow detailed studies of variations along several different dimensions. Whether it will prove fruitful to apply the models used for the larger nations and world powers to all these smaller units remains doubtful, even if we disregard the "microstates" currently studied by the United Nations Institute for Training and Research.[19] In our comparative analysis of the development of party systems, Seymour Martin Lipset and I have fitted sixteen European systems, eleven smaller and five larger ones, into the same core model of explanation,[20] but this does not necessarily succeed for other dependent variables.

In fact, we have become convinced that a good case can be made for Moore's rejection of small-polity comparisons *if they cut across major cultural areas of the world:* "leader" nations can be meaningfully compared independently of the larger cultural contexts, but smaller units tend to be so heavily dependent on their surroundings that it will be more fruitful to compare them area by area rather than indiscriminately across continents. This certainly goes for comparisons of political and religious institutions, organizations, and behaviors, but would also seem to be true for other elements of social structure: ecological configurations, social and economic stratification, educational institutions and achievements. Our comparisons of democratization processes and party-political development in Western Europe suggest that the smaller units are more likely to become structured along cultural dimensions than the larger ones: linguistic/ethnic boundaries cut across Belgium, Switzerland, and Finland and have deeply affected the internal politics of Ireland, Denmark, and Norway; conflicts over religious identities have found distinctive institutional expressions in the Low Countries, in Switzerland, and in Austria. Similar lines of cleavage can of course be traced within the larger countries as well, but they have not so heavily influenced the structuring of institutions and organizations within the national community. One of the hypotheses we hope to substantiate in our current study of the Smaller European Democracies[21] is that the larger nations have commanded greater resources for coping with such forces of cultural divisiveness: the weight of the centralizing standardization machineries has tended to be heavier and the willingness to accept and to institutionalize cultural distinctiveness has been less pronounced than in the smaller units.

This would argue strongly for limiting comparisons of the inner structure of smaller units to clusters of national communities grown out of the same historical experiences of cultural conflict and integration: the polities which emerged out of the Western Roman Empire and the clashes between secular rulers and the Roman Catholic Church, the polities which emerged from the Eastern Roman Empire and the Orthodox Church, the polities of the Muslim world, the polities which grew out of the partition of the Spanish and the Portuguese Empires in the Americas, and so on. This would be tantamount to acceptance of Galton's point in his critique of Tylor: the smaller units should not enter the statistical tables indiscriminately but be grouped by areas of cultural communality. This is the third of the strategies distinguished at the beginning of this section: the comparative analysis of dimensions of variation among polities within one culturally-historically homogeneous region. We shall conclude our review of styles of macro-comparison by a brief account of one such attempt at within-region analysis.

The Lipset-Rokkan model of variations in party systems[22] is strictly limited to the set of polities that grew out of the cultural clashes of the Renaissance and Reformation and established their structural characteristics under the joint impact of the Democratic Revolution in France and the Industrial Revolution in England. The task set for the model is also strictly limited. Its purpose is to specify, with a maximum of parsimony, the variables needed to account for the observed variations in full-suffrage party systems among the countries initially delimited.

The purpose is *not* to explain the emergence of one or the other national party system, but to identify the crucial dimensions of cross-polity variation that account for the presence or absence of different party-political alternatives during the elections following the introduction of universal manhood suffrage.

This is done in three steps:

- First a set of fundamental dimensions of nation building are identified and the corresponding sequences of elite options are spelled out;
- Secondly, a set of propositions is generated concerning the consequences of the decisions at each option point for the formation of lasting electoral party fronts;
- Thirdly, these propositions are tested against the historically given party alternatives and each deviant case is discussed in some detail.

The model posits four initial dimensions of nation building and four corresponding "critical option poinfts" for the national elites:

Cultural dimensions:	Corresponding option points:
I. Center–periphery	One standardized national language or several?
II. State–Church	Establishment of national Church vs. alliance with a supranational Church vs. establishment of competing secular agencies

Economic dimensions:	Corresponding option points:
III. Urban–rural	Protection of urban vs. rural products against foreign competition: the tariff issue
IV. Owner–worker	Protection of rights of property vs. equalization of economic conditions through union and/or state action

This listing of dimensions and options could of course be used in studies of *any* nation-state, whether European, American, Asian, or African, but this would not of itself make for theoretically fruitful comparisons: just as in the case of the Almond-Pye paradigm the initially posited dimensions of variability must be linked up with each other and with an explicitly stated set of dependent variables in a series of potentially testable propositions. Thus far we have been able to formulate such a set of propositions for one set of dependent variables for sixteen countries of Western Europe. Other scholars are at work on similar exercises in model building for Latin America, but this work has not yet advanced far enough to yield definite results.[23] One very good reason is that the range of dependent variables in the model is much broader and the variables themselves are not as easy to operationalize.

These attempts at codification and empirical testing not only promise further advances in the comparative study of nation-building processes, but are bound to have an impact on further work with data at the microlevel of each political system. In fact, we were directly motivated to develop our model for the explanation of the European party systems by the difficulties encountered in attempts to interpret cross-national data on mass reactions to politics in different countries of the West. Seymour Martin Lipset and his colleague Juan Linz had made a major effort in the midfifties to collate data from many countries on the political preferences of a variety of occupations and professions, but found it extremely difficult to compare information at this level because of the variations in the political alternatives offered the voters in the different countries.[24] The Lipset-Rokkan model represented a response to the challenge of this earlier effort: it served to specify the dimensions of the dependent variables in comparative studies of voting behavior, and made it possible to group countries by the extent of similarity of alternatives and to order parties by their degree of national dis-

tinctiveness. What makes this operation so intriguing is that it has opened up a new perspective on the interaction of micro- and macrovariations in political systems. By focusing with such determination on the macrolevel, the *Party Systems* volume has in fact helped to bring about a reversal in the strategies of comparison. Instead of proceeding as though sociocultural distinctions determined political behavior through some process of direct translation, the new emphasis is on the parties as agencies of mass mobilization and on the sociocultural divisions within the electorates as so many openings for or barriers against efforts of mobilization. In this model the null hypothesis would be that each party succeeds equally well in all divisions of the electorate: the structure of departures from these average mobilization successes would then define the given party system. This implies a fundamental change in the direction of analysis. Instead of seeking to establish more and more multivariate regularities in the determination of microbehaviors, we resolutely start out with the parties and use the microdata to characterize the macroalternatives in each system. This strategy was elucidated in some detail at a recent conference organized by the Committee on Political Sociology of the International Sociological Association. Richard Rose and Derek Urwin presented a plan for the use of data from sample surveys from twelve to fifteen countries in a comparative analysis of the cohesion and distinctiveness of party electorates:[25] they did not want to use microdata to test propositions at the level of individual voters, but to generate typologies of macroalternatives as a step in the formulation and testing of higher-order hypotheses.

Such shuttling between different levels of comparative analysis is likely to become common in most fields of social science inquiry. It is of course no accident that the examples of such procedures so far given have come from comparative politics. Anyone concerned with nations as units of analysis must of necessity consider dimensions of political decision making—not only because nations define areas of homogeneous practices in data gathering and data evaluation, but also because so much of what happens and is registered within a nation reflects conflicts and compromises among political elites and within the populations they have been able to mobilize. In this sense, all cross-national comparisons confront the social scientist with tasks of political analysis: no body of social science data, even purely demographic or linguistic, can be compared without some consideration of the political contexts in which they were generated.

Notes

* From *Main Trends of Research in the Human and the Social Sciences* by UNESCO, with preface by René Meheu (Paris: Mouton, 1970), 667–76, and 684–89, by permission of UNESCO. Copyright 1976 by UNESCO.

1. See O. Lewis, "Comparisons in Cultural Anthropology," in: W. L. Thomas, Jr. (ed.), *Current Anthropology,* Chicago, University of Chicago Press, 1956.

2. E. B. Tylor, "On a Method of Investigating the Development of Institutions," *Journal of the Royal Anthropological Institute* 28, 1889, pp. 245–280.

3. See R. Naroll, "Two Solutions to Galton's Problem," in: F. W. Moore (ed.), *Readings in Cross-Cultural Methodology,* New Haven, HRAF Press, 1961, and *Data Quality Control: A New Research Technique,* Glencoe, Free Press, 1962.

4. J. Goody and I. Watt, "The Consequences of Literacy," *Comparative Studies in Society and History* 5, 1963, pp. 304–345.

5. T. Parsons, *Societies: Comparative and Evolutionary Perspectives,* Englewood Cliffs, Prentice-Hall, 1967, and *The System of Modern Societies,* Englewood Cliffs, Prentice-Hall, 1970.

6. S. N. Eisenstadt, *The Political Systems of Empires,* New York, Free Press, 1963.

7. K. W. Deutsch, *Nationalism and Social Communication,* Cambridge, MIT Press, 1953, rev. ed. 1966.

8. The revised edition of the Russett et al., *World Handbook* [should] however include several 20–30 year time series for the advanced countries. . . .

9. K. W. Deutsch, "Social Mobilization and Political Development," *American Political Science Review* 65 (3), Sept. 1961, pp. 493–514.

10. See S. Rokkan and H. Valen, "The Mobilization of the Periphery," in: S. Rokkan (ed.), *Approaches to the Study of Political Participation,* Bergen, Michelsen Institute, 1962; S. Rokkan, "Electoral Mobilization, Party Competition, and National Integration," in: J. La Palombara and M. Weiner (eds.), *Political Parties and Political Development,* Princeton, Princeton University Press, 1966; P. Nettl, *Political Mobilization,* London, Faber, 1967; and S. M. Lipset and S. Rokkan (eds.), *Party Systems and Voter Alignments,* New York, Free Press, 1967.

11. See K. W. Deutsch and H. Weilenmann, "The Swiss City Canton: A Political Invention," *Comparative Studies in Society and History* 7 (4), 1965, pp. 393–408, and the forthcoming volume by the same authors, *United for Diversity: The Political Integration of Switzerland.*

12. The initial formulations appeared in G. Almond and J. Coleman (eds.), *The Politics of the Developing Areas,* Princeton, Princeton University Press, 1960. For subsequent stages in the elaboration see the six volumes of the series *Studies in Political Development,* Princeton, Princeton University Press, 1963–1966, and the following theoretical presentations: G. Almond, "A Developmental Approach to Political Systems," *World Politics* 17, 1965, pp. 183–214; L. W. Pye, "The Concept of Political Development," *Annals of the American Academy of Political and Social Science* 358, 1965, pp. 1–114; G. Almond and L. B. Powell, *Comparative Politics: A Developmental Approach,* Boston, Little Brown, 1966; and L. W. Pye, "Political Systems and Political Development," in: S. Rokkan (ed.), *Comparative Research across Cultures and Nations,* Paris, Mouton, 1968. Manuscripts of five draft chapters toward the forthcoming collective volume on *Crises of Political Development* were in circulation in 1966; the volume is due to be published in 1970.

13. For an initial discussion of a scheme of operationalization see S. Rokkan, "Models and

Methods in the Comparative Study of Nation-Building," *Acta Sociologica* 12 (2), 1969, pp. 53–73.

14. S. Huntington, "Political Modernization: America vs. Europe," *World Politics* 18 (3), 1966, pp. 378–414.

15. R. Holt and J. Turner, *The Political Basis of Economic Development,* Princeton, Van Nostrand, 1966.

16. B. Moore, *The Social Origins of Dictatorship and Democracy,* Boston, Beacon Press, 1966.

17. B. Moore, *op cit.,* pp. XII–XIII.

18. T. Parsons, *The System of Modern Societies,* Englewood Cliffs, NJ, Prentice-Hall, 1970.

19. UNITAR, *The Status and Problems of Very Small States and Territories,* New York, UNITAR, 1967, mimeo.

20. S. M. Lipset and S. Rokkan, "Cleavage Structures, Party Systems and Voter Alignments: An Introduction," in: S. M. Lipset and S. Rokkan (eds.), *Party System and Voter Alignments,* New York, Free Press, 1967. For further amplification see S. Rokkan, "The Structuring of Mass Politics in the Smaller European Democracies," *Comparative Studies in Society and History* 10 (2), 1968, pp. 173–210, and *Citizens, Elections, Parties,* New York, D. McKay, 1970.

21. On this project, see V. R. Lorwin, "Historians and Other Social Scientists: The Comparative Analysis of Nation-Building in Western Societies," in: S. Rokkan (ed.), *Comparative Research across Cultures and Nations, op cit.* The "SED" project covers the five Nordic countries, the three Benelux countries, Ireland, Switzerland and Austria. Most of the analyses undertaken compare these countries among each other, but on occasion attempts are made to compare the "smaller" ones (of which two are "micro" states, Iceland and Luxembourg, while two are medium sized by European standards: Belgium and the Netherlands) with the four larger democracies, Great Britain, France, Germany and Italy, and sometimes even with "polycephalic" Spain.

22. S. M. Lipset and S. Rokkan, "Cleavage Structures, Party Systems, and Voter Alignments: An Introduction," in: S. M. Lipset and S. Rokkan (eds.), *Party System and Voter Alignments,* New York, Free Press, 1967.

23. O. Cornblit et al., "A Model for Political Change in Latin America," *Social Science Information* 7 (2), 1968, pp. 13–48.

24. S. M. Lipset and J. J. Linz, *The Social Bases of Political Diversity,* Stanford, Center for Advanced Study, 1956, mimeo. Only a small part of the information gathered in this collection was later presented in Lipset's work *Political Man,* Garden City, NJ, Doubleday, 1960.

25. R. Rose and D. Urwin, "The Cohesion of Political Parties: A Comparative Analysis," Paper, International Voting Conference, Loch Lomond, July 1968, later published as "Social Cohesion, Political Parties and Strains in Regimes," *Comparative Political Studies* 2 (1) April 1969, pp. 7–67.

Cross-National Research as an Analytic Strategy: American Sociological Association, 1987 Presidential Address[*]

Melvin L. Kohn[†]

In this essay, I discuss some of the uses and dilemmas of cross-national research. I argue that cross-national research is valuable, even indispensable, for establishing the generality of findings and the validity of interpretations derived from single-nation studies. In no other way can we be certain that what we believe to be social-structural regularities are not merely particularities, the product of some limited set of historical or cultural or political circumstances. I also argue that cross-national research is equally valuable, perhaps even more valuable, for forcing us to revise our interpretations to take account of cross-national differences and inconsistencies that could never be uncovered in single-nation research.

My thesis is that cross-national research provides an especially useful method for generating, testing, and further developing sociological theory. As with any research strategy, cross-national research comes at a price. It is costly in time and money, it is difficult to do, and it often seems to raise more interpretive problems than it solves. Yet it is potentially invaluable and, in my judgment, grossly underutilized. This is hardly a radically new thesis. As Stein Rokkan (1964) long ago pointed out, to do cross-national research is to return to the preferred analytic strategy of the forefathers of sociology, a strategy that was nearly abandoned in sociology's quest for methodological rigor but now can be pursued anew with the much more powerful methodological tools available today.[1]

A sensible discussion of the uses and dilemmas of cross-national research requires that I first define the domain and delineate the principal types of cross-national research. Then I illustrate some of these uses and dilemmas by scrutinizing the body of cross-national research I know best, namely my own, my rationale being William Form's (1979) cogent observation that "probably no field has generated more methodological advice on a smaller data base with fewer results than has [cross-national] comparative sociology." Using my research as a source of illustration makes it possible to discuss the issues concretely. I review this research in sufficient detail to highlight its accomplishments and its failures, my concern being only in part with the substance of the research for its own sake; I also want to extrapolate from this concrete example, to make some more general observations. Finally, I discuss some fundamental issues about the conduct of cross-national research. In so doing, I bring in studies dealing with quite different substantive problems from those that I have addressed in my own research, and using quite different methods, to see whether my conclusions apply as well to a much broader range of studies.

The broadest possible definition of cross-national research is any research that transcends national boundaries. This definition is somewhat ambiguous, though, because many studies of single societies are implicitly cross-national, in that the investigators interpret their findings by contrasting what they learn about the country they actually study with what is known or is believed to be true about some other country or countries. I prefer to restrict the term, cross-national, to studies that utilize systematically comparable data from two or more nations.

In restricting the term to explicitly comparative studies, I do not mean to belittle the importance of studies that are only implicitly comparative. Such studies contribute importantly to our understanding; witness, for example, the distinguished series of studies of American society by foreign observers, beginning with Alexis de Tocqueville's *Democracy in America.* Consider, too, studies in which the selection of some one country is particularly appropriate for testing a general proposition—as in Kelley and Klein's (1981) use of the Bolivian revolution of 1952 to test their theory that "radical revolutions" inevitably lead to an increase in inequality, or Chirot and Ragin's (1975) use of the Romanian peasant rebellions of 1907 to test competing interpretations of the intensity of peasant rebellions. And consider, finally, those pivotal studies—Stephen Bunker's (1985) *Underdeveloping the Amazon* is a particularly good example—where some country or region of a country is selected for study precisely because it exemplifies a more general social phenomenon. I leave such research out of my purview not because it is unimportant, but because to include it would make the bounds of "cross-national" so large and ambiguous that it would be difficult to say what, other than research focused single-mindedly on a particular country, is *not* cross-national.

Within the large genre of research that is explicitly comparative, I would further distinguish four types of cross-national research of somewhat differing intent. The four types are those in which nation is *object* of study; those in which nation is *context* of study; those in which nation is *unit of analysis;* and those that are *transnational* in character.[2] Although these four types of research shade into one another,

their purposes are distinguishable and their theoretical implications somewhat different. My analysis will apply mainly to the second of the four types, in which nation is context of study.

In the first type of cross-national research, where nations are the *object* of study, the investigator's interest is primarily in the particular countries studied: how Germany compares to the United States, France to the Soviet Union, or India to Pakistan. Alternatively, the investigator may be interested in comparing particular institutions in these countries: the social security systems of the United States and Australia; the educational systems of the German Democratic Republic and the Federal Republic of Germany. At their best, as in the systematic comparisons of Finland and Poland by Erik Allardt, Wlodzimierz Wesolowski, and their collaborators (1978), such studies can lead to well-informed interpretations that apply far beyond the particular countries studied. What distinguishes such research, though, is its primary interest in understanding the particular countries. In this research, one wants to know about Finland and Poland for their own sakes; the investigator does not select them for study just because they happen to be useful settings for pursuing some general hypothesis.

By contrast, I wish to focus on cross-national studies in which, to borrow from Erwin Scheuch's (1967) apt phrase, nation is *context.* In such research, one is primarily interested in testing the generality of findings and interpretations about how certain social institutions operate or about how certain aspects of social structure impinge on personality. In Burawoy and Lukacs's (1987) comparison of a U.S. machine shop with a Hungarian machine shop, for example, their primary interest is not in the United States and Hungary for their own sakes, nor certainly in the particular machine shops, but in these machine shops as exemplifying the relative efficiency of capitalist and socialist industrial enterprises. Admittedly, it may be difficult to differentiate research in which nation is object from research in which nation is context. When Robin Williams (1985) studies the use of threats in U.S./U.S.S.R. relations, he clearly is interested in the United States and the U.S.S.R. both for their own sakes and as exemplifying superpowers in a nuclear age; there is no way of separating the two purposes. It is nevertheless generally useful to distinguish between research whose primary purpose is to tell us more about the particular countries studied and research whose primary purpose is to use these countries as the vehicle for investigating the contexts in which social institutions operate. My examination of cross-national research as an analytic strategy will be addressed mainly to research where nation is context.

This domain includes such diverse studies as Theda Skocpol's (1979) comparative analysis of revolution, and also, from quite a different theoretical perspective, Michael Burton and John Higley's (1987) analysis of the conditions under which competing elites settle their differences in grand political compromises; Donald Treiman's (1977) analysis of the stratification systems of the industrialized world; William Form's (1976) study of the complexity of industrial technology, workers' skill levels, and the quality of workers' social interactions; Janet Chafetz and Anthony Dworkin's (1986) analysis of the determinants of the size and range of ideologies of women's movements throughout the world; and my colleagues' and my comparative research on social stratification and psychological functioning in Poland, Japan, and the United States (Slomczynski, Miller, and Kohn 1981; Naoi and Schooler 1985).

It is useful to differentiate research where nation is context from two other types of cross-national research that are not central to my discussion here. In the first, where nation is the *unit* of analysis, investigators seek to establish relationships among characteristics of nations qua nations. In such research, one no longer speaks of countries by name, but instead classifies countries along one or more dimensions — their gross national product, or average level of

educational attainment, or position along some scale of income inequality. A prototypic example is Bornschier and Chase-Dunn's (1985) analysis of the relationship between the penetration of national economies by transnational corporations and the hypothesized long-run stagnation of those economies. Other pertinent examples are Blumberg and Winch's (1972) analysis of the relationship between societal complexity and familial complexity; and Ellis, Lee, and Petersen's (1978) test of the hypothesis that there is a positive relationship between how closely adults are supervised in a society and the degree to which parents in that society value obedience for children.

What distinguishes research that treats nation as the unit of analysis is its primary concern with understanding how social institutions and processes are systematically related to variations in national characteristics. Such analyses need not treat each nation as a homogeneous entity, but may study intranation institutions and processes, as Meyer, Hannan, and their colleagues (1979) have done in their analyses of national development. Nor need research that treats nation as unit of analysis assume that each nation exists in an international vacuum. As Bornschier and Chase-Dunn (1985, p. 65) put it, ". . . we do not contend that nation-states are closed systems. A unit of analysis does not need to be a closed system. When we compare individuals or schools we know that these units interact with one another and are parts of a larger social context. The unit of analysis in comparative research is any unit in which the process of interest is known to operate."

In distinguishing research that treats nation as the unit of analysis from research that treats nation as the context for analysis, we are again dealing with gradations, not sharp differences. As will become evident later, attempts to understand cross-national differences sooner or later require one to search for the pertinent dimensions that differentiate the nations qua nations. One can, in fact, argue that research in which nation is treated as context is simply a way station to more general analyses in which the pivotal distinguishing characteristics of nations become variables in the analysis. In principle, as Rokkan (1964), Przeworski and Teune (1970), Hopkins and Wallerstein (1967), and Chase-Dunn (1982) all argue, one can and should convert descriptive differences between countries into analytic variables. I have no quarrel with this objective, only a belief that in many fields of sociological inquiry there is much to learn from research in which nation is treated as context before we are ready to translate "nations" into "variables."

Research that treats nations as the unit of analysis requires that one be able to discern which of the many differences between countries are the pertinent analytic variables; that one be able to formulate meaningful hypotheses at the appropriate level of abstraction; and—if one is ever to test such interpretations—that one have at hand or have the potential to collect data from a sizable sample of countries. It also requires much better data than are generally available in multination data sources. I hope that an essay on cross-national research written ten or twenty years from now will be able to focus much more on such research than I believe is warranted today.

And then, finally, there are studies that treat nations as components of larger international systems. Borrowing a term from economists and political scientists who have studied corporations (and I hope not distorting their usage of the term), I call this *transnational* research. Immanuel Wallerstein's (1974, 1980) analysis of the capitalist world system and Fernando Cardoso and Enzo Faletto's (1979) analysis of dependency and development in Latin America are prominent examples. We are at a rather early stage in the development of appropriate methodologies for transnational research (Meyer and Hannan 1979; Chase-Dunn 1979; Chase-Dunn, Pallas, and Kentor 1982). Even now, though, transnational research has proved its importance by demonstrating that the nations we compare in *all* types of cross-national research are not isolated entities but are systematically interrelated.

I see all four types of cross-national inquiry as useful, each for particular substantive problems. I focus on research that uses nation as context, not because I consider this type of cross-national research inherently more valuable than the others, but because I think that for many sociological problems—particularly, I must admit, for those in which I have the greatest substantive interest—this type of research has especially great utility in the present state of knowledge. In particular, such research affords the opportunity to study each of the countries with sufficient thoroughness for intensive comparison.

Establishing the Generality of Relationships and the Limits of Generality

Many discussions of cross-national research (Ragin and Zaret [1983] is a thoughtful example) contrast two research *strategies*—one that looks for statistical regularities, another that searches for cultural or historical differences. I prefer to pose the distinction, not in terms of research strategies, nor of methodological preferences, nor even of theoretical proclivities toward "transhistorical" generalizations or "historically contextualized knowledge," but in terms of interpreting the two basic types of research *findings*—similarities and differences. Granted, investigators' theoretical and methodological preferences make it more or less likely that they will discover cross-national similarities; granted, too, what can be treated as a similarity at one level of analysis can be thought of as a myriad of differences at more detailed levels of analysis. Still, the critical issue is how to interpret similarities, and how to interpret differences, when you find them.

Finding cross-national similarities greatly extends the scope of sociological knowledge. Moreover, cross-national similarities lend themselves readily to sociological interpretation; cross-national differences are much more difficult to interpret. As Kazimierz Slomczynski, Joanne Miller, and I argued (albeit a little too categorically) in our first comparative analysis of the United States and Poland:

Insofar as cross-national analyses of social structure and personality yield similar findings in the countries studied, our interpretation can ignore whatever differences there may be in the cultures, political and economic systems, and historical circumstances of the particular countries, to deal instead with social-structural universals. But when the relationships between social structure and personality differ from country to country, then we must look to what is idiosyncratic about the particular countries for our interpretations. (1981, p. 740)

The first half of this formulation asserts that when the relationship between social structure and personality is the *same* in two or more countries, then the unique historical experiences of each country, their distinctive cultures, and their particular political systems are not of focal importance for interpreting the relationship. The formulation does *not* assert that history, culture, and political context have been irrelevant in shaping social structures, but that the resultant social structures have a cross-nationally consistent impact on people. The explanation of this impact should be sought in terms of how people experience the resultant social structures, rather than in the historical or cultural processes that shaped those structures. Admittedly, this may not always be the best interpretive strategy. Apparent similarities can mask profound differences; what seems to call for a unitary interpretation may actually require entirely different explanations. Nevertheless, I believe that where we find cross-national similarities, the most efficient strategy in searching for an explanation is to focus on what is structurally similar in the countries being compared, not on the often divergent historical processes that produced these social-structural similarities. The basic and very simple point is that social-structural similarities may have been brought about by very different historical processes and yet have es-

sentially similar social and psychological consequences.

The second half of the formulation directs us to interpret cross-national *differences* in terms of historical, cultural, political, or economic idiosyncrasies. Przeworski and Teune (1970) argued that what appear to be cross-national differences may really be instances of lawful regularities, if thought of in terms of some larger, more encompassing interpretation. I agree, but I also believe that developing such interpretations is an immensely difficult task. A necessary first step is to try to discover which of the many differences in history, culture, and political or economic systems that distinguish any two countries are pertinent to explaining the differences we find in their social structures or in how these social structures affect people's lives. I do not contend that cross-national differences cannot be lawfully explained—quite the contrary—but only that the lawful explanation of cross-national differences requires more explicit consideration of historical, cultural, and political-economic particularities than does the lawful explanation of cross-national similarities.

Ultimately, the distinction between cross-national similarities and differences breaks down, and the issues cannot be so simply and neatly dichotomized. Nonetheless, it is a useful way to think about these issues. Therefore, I shall discuss the two types of cross-national research findings separately, beginning with cross-national similarities. I use the U.S.-Polish and U.S.-Japanese comparisons that my collaborators and I have carried out as my principal illustrations of both cross-national similarities and differences, my substantive concern in this part of the essay being the relationship between social structure and personality.[3] The conclusions I draw are by no means limited to this substantive area.

Cross-National Similarities

Over the course of three decades of research in the United States, Carmi Schooler and I, in collaboration with Joanne Miller,

Karen A. Miller, Carrie Schoenbach, and Ronald Schoenberg, have intensively studied the psychological impact of social stratification—by which we mean the hierarchical distribution of power, privilege, and prestige (Kohn 1969; Kohn and Schooler 1983). We interpret the consistent relationships that we have found between social stratification and such facets of personality as values, orientations to self and others, and cognitive functioning as the product, in large part, of the intimate relationship between social stratification and particular job conditions. People of higher social-stratification position (as indexed by educational attainment, occupational status, and job income) enjoy greater opportunities to be self-directed in their work—that is, to work at jobs that are substantively complex, free from close supervision, and not highly routinized. The experience of occupational self-direction, in turn, is conducive to valuing self-direction, both for oneself and for one's children, to having self-conceptions and social orientations consonant with such values, and to effective intellectual functioning. It is even conducive to seeking out opportunities for engaging in intellectually active leisure-time pursuits (K. Miller and Kohn 1983). All this is true both for employed men and for employed women (J. Miller, Schooler, Kohn, and K. Miller 1979; Kohn and Schooler 1983; Kohn, Slomczynski, and Schoenbach 1986).

Structural-equation analyses of longitudinal data have enabled us to confirm even that part of the interpretation that posits a causal impact of job conditions on personality (Kohn and Schooler 1978, 1982). These analyses show the relationships to be reciprocal, with job conditions both affecting and being affected by personality. Moreover, analyses of housework (Schooler, Kohn, K. Miller, and K. Miller 1983) and of education (J. Miller, Kohn, and Schooler 1985, 1986) demonstrate that the experience of self-direction, not only in paid employment, but also in housework and schoolwork, decidedly affects people's self-conceptions, social orientations, and cognitive

functioning. The interpretation has considerable generality.

In the absence of appropriate cross-national evidence, though, there would be no way of knowing whether this (or any other) interpretation applies outside the particular historical, cultural, and political contexts of the United States. No analyses based solely on U.S. data could tell us whether the relationships between social stratification and personality are an integral part of the social-stratification system typical of industrial societies, or are to be found only in the United States, or only in countries that have capitalist economies, or only in countries characterized by Western culture, with its purportedly higher valuation of self-direction. Replications of our research by colleagues in other countries (for a review, see Kohn and Schooler 1983, chap. 12), particularly the comprehensive replications that have been carried out by our Polish and Japanese colleagues (Slomczynski et al. 1981; Naoi and Schooler 1985), have made possible tests of the generality of the U.S. findings and of the validity of our interpretation. In the main, these findings are highly consistent with those for the United States, thus greatly enlarging the power of the interpretation.

Of pivotal importance here are the Polish-U.S. comparisons, particularly the comparative analyses of men, for whom the Polish study contains more complete occupational data. The principal issue to which these analyses are addressed is the specificity or generality of the U.S. findings about the linkages of social stratification to job conditions, and of job conditions to personality. Are these linkages specific to the economic and social structures of capitalist society, or do they obtain as well in socialist society?

We have found, for Poland as for the United States, that higher social-stratification position is associated with valuing self-direction, with holding social orientations consonant with such a value—namely, a nonauthoritarian, open-minded orientation, personally responsible standards of morality, and trustful-

ness (Slomczynski et al. 1981)—and with effective intellectual functioning (Slomczynski
and Kohn in press). We have further found a
strong reciprocal relationship, for Poland as for
the United States, between social-stratification
position and occupational self-direction (Slomczynski et al. 1981). Finally, insofar as possible
with cross-sectional data, we have shown for
Poland, too, a causal impact of occupational
self-direction on values, social orientations,
and intellectual functioning (Slomczynski et al.
1981; Slomczynski and Kohn in press). Self-
direction in one's work leads to valuing self-
direction for one's children, to having a more
open, flexible orientation to society, and to effective intellectual functioning. Lack of opportunity for self-direction in one's work leads to
valuing conformity to external authority for
one's children, to viewing social reality as hostile and threatening, and to diminished intellectual flexibility. The effects of social stratification on job conditions, and of job conditions on
personality, are much the same in socialist
Poland as in the capitalist United States.

This does not mean that these processes are
necessarily the same in all socialist and all capitalist societies, but it does mean that the U.S.
findings are not restricted to capitalist countries. There is solid evidence, instead, that the
interpretive model developed for the United
States applies to at least one socialist society.[4]

The United States and Poland, of course,
are both Western societies. Are the processes
similar in non-Western societies? The Japanese
study provides an excellent test of whether our
interpretation of the U.S. and Polish findings
applies as well to a non-Western industrialized
society. In the main, the findings for Japan are
markedly consistent with those for the United
States and Poland. Social-stratification position is related to values, to social orientations,
and to cognitive functioning in the same way,
although perhaps not to quite the same degree,
as in the United States and Poland (Kohn et al.
1987). Occupational self-direction has markedly similar effects on psychological functioning in Japan as in the West (Naoi and Schooler

1985). Thus, despite pronounced cultural differences, and despite the sharper division between the primary and secondary sectors of the
economy in Japan, the linkages of social stratification to occupational self-direction, and of
occupational self-direction to personality, are
much the same in Japan as in the United States
and Poland. The U.S. and Polish findings are
not limited to Western society. Here, again, a
single cross-national comparison yields immense benefits for our ability to test the generality of a set of empirical relationships and
their interpretation.

Moreover, since the United States, Poland,
and Japan are such diverse societies, the set of
three studies provides prima facie evidence
that the psychological impact of social stratification is much the same, and for much the
same reasons, in *all* industrialized societies.
Admittedly, negative evidence from research
in *any* industrialized society would require a
modification of this hypothesis or a restriction
of its generality. Admittedly, too, the interpretation speaks only to existing societies. We can
say nothing from this evidence as to whether it
would be possible to have an industrialized society in which one or another link in the explanatory chain is broken—a society with a
less pronounced system of social stratification;
a society in which social-stratification position
is not so intimately linked with opportunities
for occupational self-direction; even a society
where occupational self-direction has less impact on personality.[5] Nevertheless, the Polish
and Japanese studies do tell us that in decidedly diverse societies—arguably, in all industrialized societies—social stratification is associated with values, social orientations, and
cognitive functioning, in large part because
people of higher position have greater opportunity to be self-directed in their work.

Whether or not this interpretation is
correct, it does illustrate my central point:
Where one finds cross-national similarities,
then the explanation need not, indeed should
not, be focused on the particular histories, cultures, or political or economic circumstances

of each of the countries, but instead should focus on social-structural regularities common to them all.

In studying social stratification, I am of course dealing with a feature of social structure that is notably similar in all industrialized societies (Treiman 1977). I would like to extend the argument a bit, to suggest that even where some feature of social structure is not "identical" in all the countries being compared, but only "equivalent," it is still possible to find cross-nationally consistent relationships between contemporaneous social structure and personality. More than that, it is still appropriate to interpret these consistent relationships in terms of contemporaneous social structure, however much that feature of social structure has been shaped by the particular histories and cultures of those countries.

My illustration here comes from our analysis of position in the class structure and personality in the United States, Japan, and Poland (Kohn et al. 1987). For all three countries, we have adapted the same basic idea—that social classes are to be distinguished in terms of ownership and control of the means of production, and control over the labor power of others—to the particular historical, cultural, economic, and political circumstances of the country. (For Poland, where ownership of the means of production is not a primary desideratum of class, *control* over the means of production and over the labor power of others is our primary criterion of class position.) The guiding hypothesis is that social class would bear a similar relationship to personality as does social stratification. Hence, we hypothesized that, in all three countries, those who are more advantageously situated in the class structure are more self-directed in their values and orientations, and are more intellectually flexible, than are those who are less advantageously situated. Our further hypothesis, again paralleling what we have learned for social stratification, is that, in all three countries, the explanation lies mainly in the greater opportunities for occupational self-direction enjoyed by those who are more ad-

vantaged in class position. The hypotheses, then, are simple extrapolations to social class from what we have consistently found to be the psychological impact of social stratification; the new element is the much greater country-to-country variability of class structures than of stratification systems.

Both hypotheses are confirmed. All three countries can be meaningfully thought to have class structures; class position has similar effects on cognitive functioning, values, and orientation in all three countries; and class affects these facets of psychological functioning for essentially the same reason—because of the intimate relationship between position in the class structure and opportunities afforded for occupational self-direction. Hence, to extrapolate, it is no bar to structural interpretation that social structures have been shaped by distinctly different historical processes.

Cross-National Differences

Interpreting differences, as I said earlier, is where things become much less certain and much more difficult. The key, of course, is the truism that if consistent findings have to be interpreted in terms of what is common to the countries studied, the inconsistent findings have to be interpreted in terms of how the countries—or the studies—differ. This truism, unfortunately, gives no clue as to which of the many differences between countries or between studies lies at the heart of the differences in findings. Prudence dictates that the first hypothesis one entertains is that the inconsistent findings are somehow a methodological artifact. As Bernard Finifter noted:

There is a curious inconsistency in the way researchers interpret results from attempted replications when discrepancies crop up. Failure to reproduce a finding in the *same* culture usually leads the investigator to question the reliability, validity, and comparability of the research procedures used in the two studies for possible method artifacts. But failure to corroborate the same finding in a *different* culture often leads to claims of having discovered "cultural" differences, and substantive interpretations are promptly devised to account for the apparent differences. (1977, p. 155)

Issues of Method The most fundamental methodological issue is whether the concepts employed in the analyses are truly equivalent. Stefan Nowak posed the issue with characteristic clarity:

How do we know we are studying "the same phenomena" in different contexts; how do we know that our observations and conclusions do not actually refer to "quite different things," which we unjustifiably include into the same conceptual categories? Or if they seem to be different, are they really different with respect to the same (qualitatively or quantitatively understood) variable, or is our conclusion about the difference between them scientifically meaningless? (1976, p. 105) (See also Almond and Verba 1963, pp. 57–72; Scheuch 1967, 1968; Smelser 1968; Nowak 1977; Marsh 1967; and Armer 1973).

The issue is so complex that a thorough treatment would require quite another essay. In this essay, instead, I simply assume equivalence of concepts and go on to consider more mundane methodological differences.

In principle, methodological differences between studies could produce either consistent or inconsistent findings (Finifter 1977). Still, when one finds cross-national similarities despite differences in research design, even despite defects in some of the studies, it is unlikely that the similar findings were actually produced by the methodological differences. Substantive similarity in the face of methodological dissimilarity might even argue for the robustness of the findings. But when one finds cross-national differences, then dissimilarities and defects in research design make for an interpretive quagmire—there is no way to be certain whether the apparent cross-national differences are real or artifactual.

It can be terribly perplexing not to know whether an apparent cross-national difference is merely a methodological artifact. I know, for example, of two studies of the interrelationship of social stratification, occupational self-direction, and personality in less than fully industri-

alized societies, neither of which shows the pattern that has been consistently found in fully industrialized societies. One study was conducted in Taiwan before that island became as industrialized as it is today (Stephen Olsen 1971), the other in Peru (Scurrah and Montalvo 1975). In Taiwan, the relationship between social stratification and parental valuation of self-direction was essentially the same as has been found in more industrialized societies, but occupational self-direction fails to explain this relationship. In Peru, the correlations of social stratification with such aspects of personality as fatalism, trust, and anxiety are similar to those found in more industrialized societies, but occupational self-direction explains only a modest portion of these correlations.

Should we therefore restrict the interpretation that occupational self-direction is of central importance for explaining the psychological impact of social stratification to apply only to fully industrialized societies? Perhaps we should, and one can readily think of reasons why the interpretation might not apply to partially industrialized societies—for example, the link between social stratification and occupational self-direction may be weaker in such societies. But, since neither the Taiwan nor the Peru study is truly comparable to those done in industrialized societies (see the discussion in Kohn and Schooler 1983, pp. 293–94), the issue is very much in doubt. The Taiwan and Peru studies leave us in a quandary: They raise doubts as to whether the interpretation does apply to partially industrialized societies, but they do not provide convincing evidence that it does not.

To obviate the possibility that differences in findings are merely an artifact of differences in method—in the nature of the samples, in the meaning of the questions asked, in the completeness of data, in measurement—one tries to design the studies to be comparable, to establish both linguistic and conceptual equivalence in questions and in coding answers, and to establish truly equivalent indices of the underlying concepts (Scheuch 1968). Edward Suchman (1964, p. 135) long ago stated the matter with elegant simplicity: "A good design for the collection of comparative data should permit one to assume as much as possible that the differences observed ... cannot be attributed to the differences in the method being used." Unfortunately, one can never be certain. The best that is possible is to try to establish damage control, to present whatever evidence one can that methodological incomparables are not so great as to explain the differences in findings. Short of that, it remains a gnawing doubt.

My colleagues and I have written extensively about the technical issues in achieving true cross-national comparability, particularly those involved in interviewing and in index construction (J. Miller, Slomczynski, and Schoenberg 1981; Slomczynski et al. 1981; J. Miller et al. 1985; Kohn et al. 1986). So, too, have many other scholars (see, in particular, Scheuch 1968; Przeworski and Teune 1970; Armer 1973; Elder 1976; Kuechler 1986). Therefore, I do not discuss these issues further here. Instead, I assume comparability of methods (as well as comparability of concepts) and go on to the equally perplexing substantive issues in interpreting cross-national differences.

The Substantive Interpretations of Cross-National Differences Finding a cross-national difference often requires that we curtail the scope of an interpretation, by limiting our generalizations to *exclude* implicated variables or relationships or types of countries from a more encompassing generalization. Ultimately, though, we want to *include* the discrepant findings in a more comprehensive interpretation by reformulating the interpretation on a more general level that accounts for both similarities and differences. Thus, although the discovery of cross-national differences may initially require that we make a less sweeping interpretation, in time and with thought, it can lead to more general and more powerful interpretations.

I wish that I could offer from my research an example of a powerful reinterpretation derived from coming to terms with cross-national differences. Instead, I can only share with you my dilemma in still not fully understanding some differences that I have been struggling to understand for some years. I may not convince you that discovering cross-national differences necessarily leads to new understanding, but I shall certainly convince you that the discovery of such differences forces one to question generalizations made on the basis of studying only one country. To illustrate, I use the most perplexing cross-national inconsistencies that we have found in the U.S.-Polish-Japanese comparisons (Kohn et al. 1987).

Quite in contrast to our consistent findings about the relationship of social stratification to other facets of personality, we have found a decided inconsistency in the relationship between social stratification and a principal underlying dimension of orientations to self and others—a sense of well-being *versus* distress. In the United States, higher stratification position *decreases* feelings of distress; in Japan, there is virtually *no* relationship between social stratification and feelings of distress; and in Poland, higher stratification position *increases* feelings of distress.[6] The magnitude of the correlation is not great in any country, but the inconsistency in direction of relationship is striking. Similarly for social class: In the United States, members of more advantaged social classes, managers in particular, have a greater sense of well-being; members of less advantaged social classes, blue-collar workers in particular, have a greater sense of distress. In Poland, quite the opposite: It is the managers who are more distressed, the blue-collar workers who have a greater sense of well-being. In Japan, as in the United States, managers have a strong sense of well-being, but it is the white-collar—not the blue-collar—workers who are most distressed.

Why don't advantaged positions in the stratification and class systems have cross-nationally consistent effects on the sense of distress? On one level, this question is readily answered: Our analyses show that stratification and class matter for psychological functioning primarily because people of more advantaged position have greater opportunity to be self-directed in their work. But we find, in causal models of the reciprocal effects of occupational self-direction and distress, that although occupational self-direction has a statistically significant effect (negative, of course) on the sense of distress for the United States and Japan, it has no effect at all for Poland. This is in marked contrast to the cross-nationally consistent effects of occupational self-direction on intellectual flexibility, values, and self-directedness of orientation. One can, in fact, incorporate the cross-national inconsistency into an encompassing generalization: Where occupational self-direction has cross-nationally consistent effects on psychological functioning, so too do social stratification and social class; where occupational self-direction fails to have consistent effects, stratification and class also have inconsistent effects.

On another level, though, the question persists: *Why* doesn't occupational self-direction mitigate against distress in Poland, as it does in the United States and Japan? Moreover, occupational self-direction does not provide as effective an explanation of the relationships of stratification and class with distress in *any* of the three countries as it does for their relationships with other facets of personality in *all* three countries. Given the rather substantial effect of occupational self-direction on distress for the United States, we might well expect a higher correlation of social stratification with distress than the -0.18 that we actually do find. We should *certainly* expect a higher correlation than the -0.01 that we actually do find for Japan. We should expect *no* relationship, not a positive relationship, for Poland. Clearly, more than occupational self-direction is involved in explaining the relationships of stratification and class to distress. My formulation, which implies that occupational self-direction, and therefore also stratification and class, would have an impact on feelings of distress consistent with its impact on values, self-

directedness of orientation, and cognitive functioning, must be revised.

It is not at all certain from the evidence at hand, though, whether the interpretation requires minor revision or extensive overhaul. I am reasonably certain that the cross-national differences are not merely a methodological artifact, for example in the conceptualization or measurement of distress. In particular, the cross-national differences are found, not only in analyses using the "higher-order" concept, distress, but also in analyses using the "first-order" concepts, notably self-confidence and anxiety (see note 6). The issues are substantive, not methodological.

In any reformulation, it is essential that we not lose sight of the fundamental principle that any explanation of cross-national *differences* must also be consistent with the cross-national *similarities*. To be valid, any explanation has to explain why we find cross-national inconsistencies *only* for the sense of distress, not for values, for self-directedness of orientation, or for cognitive functioning. Explanations so broadly framed as to lead one to expect Polish or Japanese men of more advantaged position to value conformity for their children, to have a conformist orientation to self and society, or not to be intellectually flexible, could not be valid. Nor would it make any sense to explain the findings in terms of a weaker linkage of social stratification or of social class to occupational self-direction in Poland or in Japan than in the United States, or in terms of occupational self-direction being any less important for Polish or Japanese men than for U.S. men.

As I see it, there are at least five ways that my interpretation might be reformulated:

The simplest reformulation would be to limit the scope of the interpretation to exclude the sense of distress; for as-yet unknown reasons, an interpretation that does apply to cognitive functioning, values, and self-directedness of orientation seems not to apply to the affective realm. This reformulation simply curtails the scope of my interpretation, until such time as we are able to develop a more general interpretation that incorporates cross-national differences along with cross-national similarities.

A second type of reformulation would posit that the psychological mechanisms by which job conditions affect distress may be different from those by which job conditions affect cognitive functioning, values, and self-directedness of orientation. Such a reformulation might or might not emphasize job conditions different from those that I have emphasized; it certainly would posit different *processes* by which job conditions affect personality. Mine is a learning-generalization model: People learn from their job experiences and apply those lessons to nonoccupational realms of life (Kohn 1985). One could argue that the inconsistent effects of occupational self-direction on the sense of distress raise questions as to whether a learning-generalization model applies to this facet of personality. Perhaps, instead, one should employ some other model of psychological process—a "stress" model is the obvious candidate—for understanding the effects of job on the sense of distress. The "stress" model posits that job conditions affect personality, in whole or in part, because they induce feelings of stress, which in turn have longer-term, off-the-job psychological consequences, such as anxiety and distress. Clearly "stress" is a plausible link from job conditions to distress. But I think the evidence for a "stress" model, even when applied only to anxiety and distress, is less than compelling (Kohn 1985); moreover, positing different mechanisms for different facets of personality would be, at best, inelegant.

A related possibility, one that is much more to my liking, retains the learning-generalization model but expands the range of pertinent job conditions. This reformulation begins with the U.S. finding that job conditions other than those directly involved in occupational self-direction are more important for distress than for other facets of personality (Kohn and Schooler 1982; 1983, chapter 6). *Some* of these

job conditions are related to stratification and class, hence might explain the effects—or lack of effects—of stratification and class on distress. The crux of this reformulation is the hypothesis that the effects of these other job conditions on distress may be at odds with, and perhaps more important than, those of occupational self-direction. We have some pertinent, albeit limited, evidence that lends credence to this possibility (Kohn et al. 1987). In the United States, for example, job protections (such as seniority provisions in union contracts) mitigate against distress. Nonetheless, the very people who at the time of our interviews enjoyed the greatest job protections—the blue-collar workers—were also the most distressed. Blue-collar workers were distressed *because* they lacked opportunities for occupational self-direction and *despite* the job protections that many of them, particularly union members, enjoyed. Occupational self-direction and job protections seem to have countervailing effects, which may account for the relatively modest relationships of both social stratification and social class with distress, even in the United States.

For Japan, we find that believing that one works under considerable pressure of time, and believing that people in one's occupation are at risk of being held responsible for things outside of their control, are both related to distress. Although these findings may merely reflect a propensity of distressed people to overestimate the pressures and uncertainties of their jobs, it is at least a plausible hypothesis that such job conditions do increase distress. Our causal models suggest as well that either education itself, or job conditions related to education, increases distress. The countervailing effects of occupational self-direction, education, and other job conditions correlated with them both, may help explain why stratification and class have so little net effect on distress in Japan.

For Poland, we lack information about job conditions other than those directly pertinent to occupational self-direction. We do, however, have one fascinating bit of information that may help explain what it is about the conditions of life experienced by Polish *managers* that makes them more distressed than members of other social classes, quite in contrast to the situation of managers in the United States and Japan. We find that one segment of the Polish managerial class is particularly distressed — those managers who are not members of the Polish United Workers (Communist) Party. There are too few non-Party managers for this finding to be definitive, but I think it suggestive that the non-Party managers have decidedly higher levels of distress, compared not only to managers who are members of the Party, but also compared to members of any other social class, Party members or not. The implication, I think, is that being a non-Party manager in the Polish system of centralized planning entails uncertainties, risks, and insecurities greater than those experienced by managers in the less centralized systems of capitalist countries. The Polish system may hold these managers responsible for accomplishments they have neither the leeway nor the resources to achieve. By the same token, the U.S. and Japanese systems may lead managers to feel more in control of the conditions of their lives than they really are.

Our evidence suggests, then, that not only does occupational self-direction fail to have the cross-nationally consistent effect on distress that it has on other facets of psychological functioning, but also, that other job conditions associated with stratification and class may have countervailing effects. What is lacking is adequate information about these other job conditions.

A fourth type of reformulation would take greater account of the processes by which people attain their occupational positions and of the meaning these positions have to them. Slomczynski, Miller, and Kohn (1981) speculated at length about the implications of post–World War II historical developments that resulted in differences between the United States and Poland in structural mobility, job-selection processes, and the symbolic importance attached to class position — differences that might explain why social stratification bears a different relationship to distress in the two countries. These speculations still seem to me to be plausible and they are certainly potentially testable. One could similarly point to differences between Japan and the West in the structure of industry, particularly in the sharper division in Japan between primary and secondary sectors of the economy, that might be pertinent to explaining why stratification has so little relationship to distress in Japan, and why Japanese white-collar workers are more distressed than are members of other social classes.

Finally, one could broaden the scope of the interpretation even more, by taking account of conditions of life other than those involved in job and career. It might be, for example, that cross-national differences in family structure, or in religious belief, or in whether the urban population is primarily rural in origin, or in "national culture" bear on the sense of distress. The pivotal questions, though, are not whether family, religion, rural origins, or culture account for differences in Polish, Japanese, and American men's sense of distress, but whether such nonoccupational conditions help explain why *social stratification* and *social class* bear different relationships to the sense of distress in Poland, Japan, and the United States.

We do not have the evidence to test any of these interpretations. Each type of reformulation (other than simply limiting the scope of the interpretation to exclude distress) would require a different type of data. To test a "stress" formulation would require more information about the relationship between objective job conditions and the subjective sense of "stress" in one's work, and about the relationship between job *stress* and off-the-job *dis*tress. Similarly, to test any other model of psychological process would require data directly pertinent to that formulation. To test the hypothesis that job conditions other than those involved in occupational self-direction help explain the relationships of social stratification and social class to distress would require that we obtain much fuller information in all three countries about those job conditions thought to be productive of a sense of distress. To test the hypothesis that different processes of educational and occupational attainment account for the differential effects of stratification and class on the sense of distress would require information of yet another type: historical information about the impact of changes in the educational and occupational structures of Poland, Japan, and the United States since World War II as they impinged on particular cohorts of Polish, Japanese, and American workers. And then, finally, to test the rather vaguely formulated hypothesis that nonjob conditions explain the cross-nationally inconsistent relationships of both class and stratification with distress would require information about the interrelationship of stratification and class with these other lines of social and cultural demarcation, in all three countries.

In any case, on the basis of presently available evidence, I still do not have a fully adequate explanation of why social stratification and social class have cross-nationally inconsistent effects on the sense of distress. Perplexed though I am, I value the cross-national evidence for making clear where my interpretation applies and where it does not, thus defining what is at issue. Were it not for the Polish and Japanese findings, there would have been little reason to doubt that my interpretation applies, albeit not quite as well, to the sense of distress, just as it clearly does to values, self-directedness of orientation, and cognitive functioning.

Some General Considerations

I can now address some more general issues about cross-national research that I deliberately deferred until I had offered some concrete examples. These remarks are primarily addressed to research in which nation is treated as context.

1. In whose interest is cross-national research? This seemingly innocuous question contains a range of serious ethical and professional issues. At its worst, as in the infamous Camelot affair (Horowitz 1967), cross-national research has been used in the service of political oppression. In a less dramatic way, cross-national research has too often been a mechanism by which scholars from affluent countries have employed scholars in less affluent countries as data gatherers, to secure information to be processed, analyzed, and published elsewhere, with little benefit either in training or in professional recognition for those who collected the data (Portes 1975; Scheuch 1967). These are complex issues, where surface appearances may be misleading. But, certainly, the history of cross-national research has not been entirely benign.

Past sins and mistakes notwithstanding, cross-national research need not be employed in the service of academic or other imperialisms. My own research is again illustrative. As a matter of historical record, it was not I but Wlodzimierz Wesolowski (1975, p. 98) who proposed the Polish-U.S. comparative study. He did so for precisely the same reason I found the prospect so attractive when he suggested it to me: to see whether the U.S. findings would apply to a socialist society. The study was funded and carried out by the Polish Academy of Sciences, who thought the issues important for Polish sociology and Polish society. The extension of the U.S.-Polish comparison to encompass Japan came about because Ken'ichi Tominaga, his Japanese colleagues, and the Japanese universities and foundations that funded this research were as interested as were the Americans and the Poles in seeing whether these phenomena are similar in that non-Western society.

The opportunities for genuine cross-national collaboration today, when there is a thriving, highly professional sociology in many parts of the world, are much greater than they were only a few years ago. Today it is quite possible, and advantageous for all concerned, for sociologists of many countries to collaborate effectively. The theoretical and policy issues to be addressed in cross-national research can be—in principle, ought to be—equally important for sociologists of all the countries concerned.

2. Is cross-national research distinctly different from research that compares social classes, or ethnic groups, or genders in a single country? I see cross-national research as one type of comparative research. In many discussions, though (see, for example, Armer and Grimshaw 1973), the term "comparative research" is treated as synonymous with cross-national research, as if the only possible comparison were *inter*-national comparison; this I regard as hubris on the part of the internationalists. In other discussions (e.g., Hopkins and Wallerstein 1967) the term "comparative" is used more broadly and "cross-national" is limited to what I consider to be only one type of cross-national research, transnational research. And in still other discussions (e.g., Ragin 1982), comparative research is seen as that particular type of cross-national research where "society" is used as the explanatory unit.[7] These varying usages seem to me to impede meaningful discourse. I think it best to use the commonsense meanings of both "comparative" and "cross-national."

My own research shows that cross-national research is no different in principle from other comparative research, although in practice it is likely to be more complex, especially as one tries to interpret cross-national inconsistencies. What makes it worth distinguishing cross-national research from other types of comparative research is that a much broader range of comparisons can be made: comparisons of political and economic systems, of cultures, and of social structures. Any comparisons we make within a single country are necessarily limited to the one set of political, economic, cultural, and historical contexts represented by that particular country. I simply cannot imagine any study of the psychological impact of class and stratification, done entirely within the United

States, that could have extended the scope of our knowledge, or the power of our interpretation, as greatly as did the Polish and Japanese studies.

3. Why put the emphasis on cross-national? Why not cross-cultural or cross-societal or cross-systemic? Doesn't the term cross-national *ascribe a greater importance to the nation-state than it deserves?* I use the term *cross-national* mainly because *nation* has a relatively unambiguous meaning. *Cross-cultural* can mean anything from comparing subcultures within a single nation, for example, comparing Mexican-American and Anglo-American subcultures in the Southwest region of the United States, to comparing very large groupings of nations that share broadly similar cultures, as in William Goode's (1963) comparative analyses of historical changes in family patterns in "the West," Arabic Islam, sub-Saharan Africa, India, China, and Japan. Similarly, as Charles Tilly (1984) cogently argues, it is extremely difficult to define what is a "society." And the term *cross-systemic* is so vague as to have little research utility.

I do not think that this usage of *nation* necessarily implies anything about the importance of nation, or the nation-state, as such, any more than cross-cultural implies (or, at any rate, should imply) that *culture* is the explanatory desideratum. Furthermore, we learn something about the importance or lack of importance of the nation-state by discovering which processes transcend national boundaries and which processes are idiosyncratic to particular nations or to particular types of nations. In choosing which nations to compare, sometimes we do mean to compare nation-states; how could Theda Skocpol (1979) have done differently in her analyses of revolutions? When we deal with governments, laws, and legally regulated institutions, the nation-state is necessarily a decisive context. But sometimes we use nation as a way of comparing cultures; in this case, we would choose nations with distinctly different cultures, for example, by comparing the United States to Japan, not the Federal Republic of Germany to Austria. Sometimes we mean to compare political and economic systems, as in comparing the United States and Japan to Poland, or if one wanted to minimize cultural differences while contrasting political systems, in comparing the German Democratic Republic to the Federal Republic of Germany. Cross-national research is flexible, offering the advantage of making possible multiple types of comparison within one general analytic framework.

This flexibility, it must be recognized, comes at a price: When one finds cross-national differences, it may not be clear whether the crucial "context" that accounts for the differences is nation or culture or political or economic system (Scheuch 1967). Still, one can at least try to assess which of these contexts might logically be pertinent to explaining a particular cross-national difference. And, for many types of research, one can then proceed to design new studies to differentiate among the contexts.

4. How many nations are needed for rigorous cross-national analysis, and how should they be chosen? For some purposes, particularly when using secondary data to establish cross-national generalities, it is desirable to include all countries for which pertinent data can be secured. Thus, Alex Inkeles's pioneering paper, "Industrial Man," (1960) gained considerably from its demonstration that the relationship between social stratification and many facets of values and beliefs is consistent for a wide array of countries. Seymour Martin Lipset's argument in "Democracy and Working Class Authoritarianism" (1959), that the working class is more "liberal" than the middle class on economic issues, but illiberal on issues of civil liberties and civil rights, was the more forceful because he marshalled evidence from several countries. Donald Treiman's (1977) comprehensive analysis of the similarity of social stratification systems throughout the industrialized world effectively utilized data from many countries and was enriched as well by information about the historical past. Janet

Chafetz and Anthony Dworkin's (1986) analysis of the size and range of ideologies of women's movements gained scope and power from their use of data from a considerable diversity of countries. With similar intent, I have searched for all extant studies to establish the "universality" of a self-direction/conformity dimension to parental values in industrialized societies (Kohn and Schoenbach 1980). I have also searched for evidence in studies conducted in many countries for cross-national tests of one or another link in my explanatory scheme (Kohn 1977, 1981; Kohn and Schooler 1983, Chapter 12). And, as recently as the July, 1987 issue of the *American Journal of Sociology,* Alejandro Portes and Saskia Sassen-Koob demonstrated anew the usefulness of a broad comparative sweep, in showing that, contrary to all theoretical belief, the "informal," "underground" sector of the economy is not merely a transitional phenomenon of Third World development, but is instead a persistent and integral part of the economies of even advanced capitalist nations. In doing secondary analyses it is highly advantageous to utilize data from all countries for which pertinent information can be secured.

Moreover, even in collecting primary data, there can be considerable advantage to assessing the consistency of findings across a range of nations, cultures, and political systems, as Inkeles and Smith showed in *Becoming Modern* (1974) and as Erik Olin Wright and his colleagues are demonstrating anew, in a very different type of research endeavor, in their multination studies of social class.

Yet, it is expensive, difficult, and time-consuming to collect data in many countries. We are rarely able to collect reliable data about enough nations for rigorous statistical analysis. Nor are we ordinarily able to study many countries in sufficient depth for intensive comparison. It is not necessarily true that the more nations included in the analysis, the more we learn. There is usually a tradeoff between number of countries studied and amount of information obtained. In this tradeoff, investigators can certainly disagree about the relative importance of number of countries and depth of information. And the same investigator might make different choices for different substantive problems. By and large, though, I would opt for fewer countries, more information.

My own preferred strategy is the deliberate choice of a small number of nations that provide maximum leverage for testing theoretical issues. One may begin with a study in one country, with subsequent extensions of the inquiry to other countries, as my collaborators and I have done in using Poland to learn whether U.S. findings are applicable to a socialist society and Japan to learn whether such findings apply to a non-Western, industrialized society. Alternatively, one can select pivotal countries that provide maximum opportunity to test some general hypothesis, as Theda Skocpol (1979) did in selecting France, Russia, and China for her study of the causes and consequences of social revolutions, or as John Walton (1984) did in selecting the Philippines, Colombia, and Kenya for his comparative analysis of national revolts in underdeveloped societies. Whether one starts with one country and then extends the inquiry to others, or begins with a small set of countries, does not seem to be crucial. Either way, the deliberate choice of a small number of countries for *systematic, intensive study* offers maximum leverage for testing general propositions about social process.

How, then, does one decide which countries to compare? The only rule of thumb I know is that cross-national research is most useful when it can resolve a disputed question of interpretation. It follows that what is a strategic comparison at one stage of knowledge may be overly cautious or overly audacious at another.

At an early stage of my own research, for example, when I had established little more than that white middle-class parents in Washington, DC valued self-direction for their children more highly than did white working-class parents in that same city at that one time, the focal issue was Washington's atypicality. Was the Washington finding peculiar to the times and circumstances of this relatively affluent, economically secure, mainly nonindustrialized city in the late 1950s, or did that finding reflect a more general relationship between social stratification and parental values? Leonard Pearlin (1971; Pearlin and Kohn 1966) resolved this question by demonstrating a similar relationship of social stratification to parental values in Turin, Italy—an industrial city, less affluent and less economically secure than Washington, and with a much less conservative working-class tradition. A more cautious choice of locale would have been an industrial city in the United States or perhaps in English-speaking Canada or in Australia. A more audacious choice would have been an industrial city in a non-Western country or in a socialist country. Turin, to my mind, was neither too cautious nor too audacious a choice: different enough from Washington that if the findings proved to be similar, the increment to our knowledge would be considerable, but not so different from Washington that if the findings had proved to be dissimilar, we would have been at a complete loss to know why. Turin was not the only city that could have served our purposes; several other Western European cities might have served as well. In that state of our knowledge, though, I do not think that Warsaw or Tokyo would have been optimal choices. It would have been too difficult to interpret dissimilar findings.

Later, when we had solid evidence about the generality of our findings in Western, capitalist societies, studies in Poland and Japan became especially useful. The issue was no longer Washington's atypicality, but whether the relationship among social stratification, job conditions, and psychological functioning were peculiar to capitalist society or to Western society. Here, again, we could have chosen other countries that might have served our purposes as well: perhaps Hungary instead of Poland, or if it had been possible to do such research there at that time, the Soviet Union; perhaps South Korea instead of Japan. It is often the case that no one country is uniquely appropriate for cross-national comparison. Other considerations—research feasibility, the availability of potential collaborators, funding, happenstance—may then legitimately enter in.

Were I to embark on a new comparative study today, the considerations would again be different, mainly because of what we now know from the Polish and Japanese studies, and because of new interpretive problems that have arisen from these studies. It would now be useful to study another socialist country and another non-Western industrialized country. It would also be useful to study a less than fully industrialized country, I think preferably (for the nonce) a capitalist country with a predominantly Western culture, perhaps a Latin American country. The possibilities for fruitful comparison do not shrink as one learns more, but actually grow.

The choice of countries should always be determined by asking whether comparing these particular countries will shed enough light on important theoretical issues to be worth the investment of time and resources that cross-national research will certainly require (Galtung 1967, p. 440). One must always ask: If I find cross-national consistencies, will this particular cross-national comparison extend the scope of my interpretation enough to have made the venture worthwhile? And if I find differences, will this particular cross-national comparison shed light on crucial interpretive problems? Cross-national research is always a gamble; one might as well gamble where the payoff is commensurate with the risk.[8]

5. *What are the costs of doing cross-national research?* If, as I have argued throughout this essay, the advantages of cross-national research are considerable, so too are the costs. These costs are considerably greater than most investigators realize, great enough to make a rational person think twice about doing cross-national research when it is not needed or when it is premature.

Securing funds is always problematic, even (as in my own research) when financial support is obtained in the countries that are participating in the research. This, however, is only the first and by no means the most serious difficulty. Establishing collaborative relationships that can be sustained and will develop throughout the course of what can be counted on to be difficult research is much more problematic (Hill 1962; Sarapata 1985). Both the greatest benefits and the most difficult problems of cross-national research come from the collaborative relationships. If a good collaboration is like a good marriage, rewarding yet difficult, then a good cross-national collaboration is akin to a cross-cultural marriage that manages to succeed despite the spouses living much of the time in different countries, sometimes with considerable uncertainty about passports, visas, and the reliability and timeliness of mail delivery, and despite working in different institutional settings with conflicting demands and rewards. And still, it's far preferable to the alternatives. More than that, without good collaboration, many types of cross-national research are simply not possible.

The methodological pitfalls are another set of obstacles to good cross-national research; I have touched on some of them earlier in this essay. It would be hard to exaggerate the amount of time, thought, and analysis that must go into the effort to achieve comparability of methods, concepts, and indices. There are also issues in the standards of research employed in different countries. Sometimes these issues become acutely problematic when one least expects them. As a simple yet telling example: The reason why we do not have Polish data about some of the job conditions that may be pertinent to distress is that the survey research specialists at the Polish Academy of Sciences refused to include questions about job conditions that did not meet their criteria of objectivity in a survey for which they were professionally responsible. Even when we appealed to them that cross-national comparability required their repeating the defects of the earlier U.S. study, they would not yield. They were as zealous in imposing their justifiable, yet irrelevant professional standards as were the clearance officers of the U.S. Department of Health, Education, and Welfare, and of the Office of Management and the Budget, in imposing their not nearly so justifiable requirements.

And still, there are yet more difficult problems, problems of interpretation. Particularly when one finds cross-national differences, an expert knowledge of all the countries is essential—a knowledge most easily achieved, of course, by collaborators who have expert knowledge of their own countries (see Kuechler 1986). Even when such collaboration exists, though, sharing knowledge, interpreting within a common framework, even having enough time together to think things through at the crucial junctures, does not come easily.

Unless one has a good reason why research *should* be cross-national, it generally isn't worth the effort of making it cross-national. Operationally, this means that one should do cross-national research either when a phenomenon cannot be studied in just one country (for example, the causes of revolutions) or else when some phenomenon has been well substantiated in one country and the next logical questions have to do with the limits of generality of what has been learned. In principle, but rarely in practice, it may be worth embarking on a cross-national study of a less well researched problem if you have good a priori reason to believe that important theoretical issues can be more effectively addressed by conducting the research in more than one country. I remain a strong proponent of cross-national research, but I would not wish to mislead anyone into thinking that its very considerable advantages do not come at equally considerable cost.

6. *Finally, to return to a question that has pervaded this essay: What role does history play in cross-national interpretation?* In posing this question, I most decidedly do not mean to cast doubt on the utility of historical analysis as a *method* for doing cross-national research. I regard the persistent debate about the relative merits of historical and quantitative methods in cross-national research as a wasteful distraction, addressed to a false dichotomy.[9] Each method is appropriate for some research purposes and inappropriate for others. Best of all, as Jeffery Paige (1975) demonstrated in his analysis of the relationship between agricultural organization and social movements in seventy developing nations, is to combine the two. My question concerns, not historical analysis as method, but history as explanation. At issue, of course, are the competing merits of idiographic and nomothetic explanation. I can hardly do justice to this complex question in the closing paragraphs of this essay, but I would at least like to point out that the issues are somewhat different when analyzing cross-national similarities from what they are when analyzing cross-national differences.

As I have argued throughout this essay, the interpretation of cross-national *similarities* should not focus on the unique historical experiences of each of the countries. One seeks to discover, instead, social-structural regularities that transcend the many differences in history, culture, and experience that occur among nations. This is true even in inquiries—Walton's (1984) *Reluctant Rebels* is a good example—where the evidence is mainly historical but the analysis searches, not for historical idiosyncrasies, but for historical commonalities. The intent in all analyses of cross-national similarities is to develop generalizations that transcend particular historical experiences in a search for more general explanatory principles. In short, the method may be historical, the interpretation should be sociological.

In a broader sense of history, of course, cross-national analysis, just as any other type of sociological analysis, cannot be ahistoric, even when much about history is only implicit in the interpretation (Sztompka 1986). To compare the impact of social stratification on personality in the United States and Poland, for example, assumes that we are comparing industrialized states that have shared much of Western history. That one is a capitalist state and the other a socialist state can be viewed, depending on how you read the broad sweep of history, as a comparison of different economic-political systems or as a comparison of different levels of political development. In either case, even though history is not treated explicitly, historical considerations are certainly there implicitly. And when one compares fully industrialized to partially industrialized societies, historical issues are necessarily at least implicit. Nevertheless, in interpreting cross-national similarities, history need not be at the forefront of attention.

In interpreting cross-national *differences,* by contrast, historical considerations cannot be merely implicit; history must come to the forefront of any interpretation. For example, after demonstrating remarkable parallels in both the causes and consequences of the French, Russian, and Chinese revolutions, Skocpol (1979) had to explain differences, particularly in revolutionary outcomes, in terms of historically unique circumstances. Similarly, when I find that social stratification and social class do not have the same impact on the sense of distress in the United States, Poland, and Japan, I have to look to the separate historical developments of the three countries, to try to discover what may explain the inconsistent findings. I maintain, though, that even in interpreting cross-national differences, explanation cannot consist merely in explicating pertinent historical differences. The object is not an understanding of history just for history's sake, but the use of history for understanding more general social processes. The interpretation must be historically informed, but sociological interpretations, even of cross-national differences, are quintessentially transhistorical.

Epilogue

In the preface to *Class and Conformity,* I made a declaration of faith: "The substance of social science knowledge comes from the process of speculation, testing, new speculation, new testing—the continuing process of using data to test ideas, developing new ideas from the data, doing new studies to test those ideas" (Kohn 1969, p. xii). I take this occasion to reaffirm this fundamental tenet of my scientific faith. Its relevance to this essay is, I trust, obvious: In the process of speculating, testing, and speculating anew, cross-national research, properly employed, provides uniquely valuable evidence. There is no other evidence so useful for confirming social-structural interpretations, or for discovering their limitations. Either way, cross-national research is of pivotal importance for the development and testing of sociological theory.

Notes

* From the *American Sociological Review* 52, no. 6 (1987): 713–31, by permission of the author and the American Sociological Association. Copyright 1987 by the American Sociological Association.

† I am indebted to my collaborators in cross-national research: Carmi Schooler, Kazimierz M. Slomczynski, Joanne Miller, Carrie Schoenbach, Atsushi Naoi, and (some years ago) Leonard I. Pearlin; to the sponsors of the Polish and Japanese studies: Wlodzimierz Wesolowski and Ken'ichi Tominaga; and to colleagues who have critiqued one or another version of this paper: Stephen G. Bunker, Christopher Chase-Dunn, Andrew J. Cherlin, Bernard M. Finifter, William Form, Jonathan Kelley, Janet G. Kohn, Tadeusz Krause, John W. Meyer, Joanne Miller, Jeylan T. Mortimer, Alejandro Portes, Carrie Schoenbach, Carmi Schooler, Theda Skocpol, Kazimierz M. Slomczynski, Katherine Verdery, and Wlodzimierz Wesolowski.

1. Similarly for the United States: Armer and Grimshaw (1973, pp. xi–xii) point out that several of the early presidents of the American Sociological [Association], among them, William Graham Sumner, W. I. Thomas, E. A. Ross, and Robert E. Park, "exhibited substantial interest in the comparative study of other societies." Between the 1930s and 1950s, these concerns seemed marginal to American sociologists; here they again use ASA presidents as their

index, noting that, of the twenty presidents from 1931 to 1950, not one is known primarily or substantially for (cross-national) comparative work. Leaving aside the obvious question of the validity of using the interests of ASA presidents as an index of the substantive concerns of U.S. sociology, I would agree with their generalization and I am intrigued with their explanation. They see the "shift toward parochialism" in U.S. sociology of the 1930s and 1940s as resulting from a combination of concern with scientific status, constricting resources, attention to immediate social problems (primarily the Depression and World War II), and the political isolationism of American society during that time. From the vantage point of 1973, Armer and Grimshaw saw a strong revival of cross-national research occurring in the 1960s. So, too, did William Evan (1975), and not only in the United States. In a fascinating analysis, Evan documented the growth of cross-national collaborations and of the "internationalization" of sociology, demonstrating as well the important role of the International Sociological Association in this process.

2. I make no claim that this classification is theoretically superior to other classifications of cross-national research, only that it serves my analytic purposes better than others do. Compared to Tilly's (1984) well-known classification, my "nation as object" category corresponds roughly to his "individualizing comparisons;" my "nation as context" category encompasses both his "universalizing" and his "variation-finding comparisons" (what he sees as two distinct *strategies* of research I see as attempts to interpret two distinct types of findings); my "nation as unit of analysis" category is ignored in his classification; and my "transnational" category may be a little broader than his "encompassing comparisons," which are limited to studies that see nations as components of encompassing international systems. (For other useful classifications of cross-national research, see Hopkins and Wallerstein 1967; Marsh 1967; Elder 1976; and Nowak 1977; see also Hill 1962.)

3. My concern is not with cross-national similarities or differences in *personality* but with cross-national similarities or differences in the *relationship* between social structure and personality. I do not believe that current methods are adequate for assessing whether Poles are more or less intellectually flexible than are Americans, or whether Japanese value self-direction more or less highly than do Americans. Methodological experts whom I greatly respect disagree with this judgment. They believe that if you construct confirmatory factor-analytic models of the same concept for representative samples of two countries, using not only the same indicators of the concept, but also the same reference indicator to establish the metric in both countries, you can compare, e.g., the mean level of authoritarian conservatism for U.S. and Polish adults (Schoenberg 1982). This assumes not only an exact equivalence of meaning, an issue about which confirmatory factor analysis does give us considerable confidence, but also exact equivalence in the frames of reference that people employ in answering questions. I doubt, though, that "strongly disagree" has the same connotations in a Polish interview as in an American interview; the survey specialists of the Polish Academy of Sciences believe that it is difficult for Polish respondents to overcome their cultural tendency to be polite to their guest, the interviewer. We do not have a zero-point for our scales, nor any other basis for mean comparisons. This, however, in no way prevents us from accurately assessing whether, for example, the relationship between social stratification and authoritarian beliefs is of the same sign and of roughly the same magnitude for the United States, Poland, and Japan. And this, I believe, is in any case the more important question for cross-national analysis.

4. The Polish study provides many further examples of cross-national similarity. We have found, for example, that in both Poland and the United States, occupational self-direction not only affects intellective process, but does so consistently for younger, middle-aged, and older workers (J. Miller, Slomczynski, and Kohn 1985). We have further found that, in both the United States and Poland, the social-stratification position of the parental family has a considerable impact on the values of its adolescent and young-adult offspring (Kohn et al. 1986).

The family's stratification position affects both father's and mother's occupational self-direction; each parent's occupational self-direction affects that parent's values; the parents' values affect their children's values. For present purposes, these findings are important primarily because they show how cross-national evidence strengthens the argument that the processes by which social stratification affects values and orientation, even into the next generation, are essentially the same for a socialist and a capitalist society.

5. Michael Burawoy's (1979, p. 13) warning is pertinent, even though our research transcends capitalist society: "By taking the particular experiences of capitalist society and shaping them into universal experiences, sociology becomes incapable of conceiving of a fundamentally different type of society in the future; history is endowed with a teleology whose realization is the present."

6. In our original comparative analysis of the United States and Poland (Slomczynski et al. 1981), we put the issue somewhat differently: Social stratification has similar effects in the United States and Poland on *all* aspects of social orientation, but affects *some* aspects of self-conception differently. In particular, in the United States, higher stratification position is associated with greater self-confidence and less anxiety; in Poland, quite the opposite.

   "Social orientation" and "self-conception," however, are merely convenient rubrics; they are not underlying *dimensions* of orientation. Schooler and I (Kohn and Schooler 1982; 1983, chapter 6) subsequently did a second-order confirmatory factor analysis of the several first-order dimensions of orientation, using U.S. data, to demonstrate that there are two underlying dimensions: self-directedness of orientation versus conformity to external authority, and a sense of well-being versus a sense of distress. Self-directedness of orientation implies the beliefs that one has the personal capacity to take responsibility for one's actions and that society is so constituted as to make self-direction possible. It is reflected in not having authoritarian conservative beliefs, in having personally responsible standards of morality, in being trustful of others, in not being self-depracatory, in

not being conformist in one's ideas, and in not being fatalistic. Distress is reflected in anxiety, self-deprecation, lack of self-confidence, nonconformity in one's ideas, and distrust. We have since shown that these same two dimensions underlie the several facets of orientation in Poland and in Japan (Kohn et al. 1987). The basic parameters of the Polish and Japanese models, in particular the relationships between second-order and first-order factors, are quite similar to those for the U.S. model. In all three countries, there is a strong positive relationship between social stratification and self-directedness of orientation. The relationship between social stratification and the sense of distress, however, is neither strong nor cross-nationally consistent: the correlations are -0.18 for the United States, -0.01 for Japan, and $+0.15$ for Poland.

7. The issues in distinguishing cross-national research from other comparative research are discussed thoughtfully and at length by Grimshaw (1973), who, inter alia, reviews and summarizes pertinent earlier discussions by Erwin Scheuch and Neil Smelser. See also Marsh (1967) and Zeldtich (1971).

8. A corollary is that, if one wants to gamble audaciously, do so where the payoff will be considerable. A splendid example is provided by Nancy Olsen (1974). She not only extended to Taiwan the scope of our U.S. findings about the relationship between closeness of supervision and parents' values for their children, but also extended the scope of generalization about the institution in which close supervision is experienced, from paid employment to the family itself.

9. The methodological debate takes place on two levels: the type of analysis used *within* each nation and the type of analysis used for *comparing* nations. I see nothing of value in the first part of the debate; one uses whatever methods are appropriate to the task. The second part of the debate deals with real issues, for example, the meaningfulness of using "samples" of nations, the utility of statistical tests when basing one's analysis on the entire set of existing countries, and the difficulties of having to test multiple interactions on a necessarily small number of "cases" (see, e.g., Ragin 1982). This

literature, despite its antiquantitative bias, offers some useful cautions.

References

Allardt, Erik and Wlodzimierz Wesolowski, eds. 1978. *Social Structure and Change: Finland and Poland–Comparative Perspective.* Warsaw: Polish Scientific Publishers.

Almond, Gabriel A. and Sidney Verba. 1963. *The Civic Culture: Political Attitudes and Democracy in Five Nations.* Princeton, NJ: Princeton University Press.

Armer, Michael. 1973. "Methodological Problems and Possibilities in Comparative Research." Pp. 49–79 in *Comparative Social Research: Methodological Problems and Strategies,* edited by Michael Armer and Allen D. Grimshaw. New York: Wiley.

Armer, Michael and Allen D. Grimshaw, eds. 1973. *Comparative Social Research: Methodological Problems and Strategies.* New York: Wiley.

Blumberg, Rae Lesser and Robert F. Winch. 1972. "Societal Complexity and Familial Complexity: Evidence for the Curvilinear Hypothesis." *American Journal of Sociology* 77:898–920.

Bornschier, Volker and Christopher Chase-Dunn. 1985. *Transnational Corporations and Underdevelopment.* New York: Praeger.

Bunker, Stephen G. 1985. *Underdeveloping the Amazon: Extraction, Unequal Exchange, and the Failure of the Modern State.* Urbana, IL: University of Illinois Press.

Burawoy, Michael. 1979. *Manufacturing Consent: Changes in the Labor Process under Monopoly Capitalism.* Chicago: University of Chicago Press.

Burawoy, Michael and Janos Lukacs. 1987. "Mythologies of Work: A Comparison of Firms in State Socialism and Advanced Capitalism." *American Sociological Review* 50:723–37.

Burton, Michael G. and John Higley. 1987. "Elite Settlements." *American Sociological Review* 52:295–307.

Cardoso, Fernando Henrique and Enzo Faletto. 1979. *Dependency and Development in Latin America.* Berkeley, CA: University of California Press.

Chafetz, Janet Saltzman and Anthony Gary Dworkin. 1986. *Female Revolt: Women's Movements in World and Historical Perspective.* Totowa, NJ: Rowman & Allanheld.

Chase-Dunn, Christopher K. 1979. "Comparative Research on World-System Characteristics." *International Studies Quarterly* 23:601–23.

———. 1982. "The Uses of Formal Comparative Research on Dependency Theory and the World-System Perspective." Pp. 117-137 in *The New International Economy,* edited by Harry Makler, Alberto Martinelli, and Neil Smelser. London: Sage.

Chase-Dunn, Christopher K., Aaron M. Pallas and Jeffrey Kentor. 1982. "Old and New Research Designs for Studying the World System: A Research Note." *Comparative Political Studies* 15:341–56.

Chirot, Daniel and Charles Ragin. 1975. "The Market, Tradition and Peasant Rebellion: The Case of Romania in 1907." *American Sociological Review* 40:428–44.

Elder, Joseph W. 1976. "Comparative Cross-National Methodology." Pp. 209–230 in *Annual Review of Sociology,* vol. 2, edited by Alex Inkeles. Palo Alto, CA: Annual Reviews, Inc.

Ellis, Godfrey J., Gary R. Lee and Larry R. Petersen. 1978. "Supervision and Conformity: A Cross-cultural Analysis of Parental Socialization Values." *American Journal of Sociology* 84:386–403.

Evan, William M. 1975. "The International Sociological Association and the Internationalization of Sociology." *International Social Science Journal* 27:385–93.

Finifter, Bernard M. 1977. "The Robustness of Cross-Cultural Findings." *Annals New York Academy of Sciences* 285:151–84.

Form, William H. 1976. *Blue Collar Stratification: Autoworkers in Four Countries.* Princeton, NJ: Princeton University Press.

———. 1979. "Comparative Industrial Sociology and the Convergence Hypothesis." Pp. 1–25 in *Annual Review of Sociology,* vol. 5, edited by Alex Inkeles. Palo Alto, CA: Annual Reviews, Inc.

Galtung, Johan. 1967. *Theory and Methods of Social Research.* Oslo: Universitetsforlaget.

Goode, William J. 1963. *World Revolution and Family Patterns.* New York: The Free Press of Glencoe.

Grimshaw, Allen D. 1973. "Comparative Sociology: In What Ways Different from Other Sociologies?" Pp. 3–48 in *Comparative Social Research: Methodological Problems and Strategies,* edited by Michael Armer and Allen D. Grimshaw. New York: Wiley.

Hill, Reuben. 1962. "Cross-National Family Research: Attempts and Prospects." *International Social Science Journal* 14:425–51.

Hopkins, Terence K. and Immanuel Wallerstein. 1967. "The Comparative Study of National Societies." *Social Science Information* 6:25–58.

Horowitz, Irving L. 1967. *The Rise and Fall of Project Camelot.* Cambridge, MA: MIT Press.

Inkeles, Alex. 1960. "Industrial Man: The Relation of Status to Experience, Perception, and Value." *American Journal of Sociology* 66:1–31.

Inkeles, Alex and David H. Smith. 1974. *Becoming Modern: Individual Change in Six Developing Countries.* Cambridge, MA: Harvard University Press.

Kelley, Johathan and Herbert S. Klein. 1981. *Revolution and the Rebirth of Inequality: A Theory Applied to the National Revolution in Bolivia.* Berkeley, CA: University of California Press.

Kohn, Melvin L. 1969. *Class and Conformity: A Study in Values.* Homewood, IL: Dorsey Press. (2nd ed. 1977, published by the University of Chicago Press.)

———. 1977. "Reassessment, 1977." Pp. xxv–lx in *Class and Conformity: A Study in Values,* 2nd ed. Chicago: University of Chicago Press.

———. 1981. "Personality, Occupation, and Social Stratification: A Frame of Reference." Pp. 267–97 in *Research in Social Stratification and Mobility: A Research Annual,* vol. 1, edited by Donald J. Treiman and Robert V. Robinson. Greenwich, CT: JAI Press.

———. 1985. "Unresolved Interpretive Issues in the Relationship Between Work and Personality." Paper presented at the annual meeting of the American Sociological Association, Washington, DC, August.

Kohn, Melvin L., Atushi Naoi, Carrie Schoenbach, Carmi Schooler and Kazimierz Slomczynski. 1987. "Position in the Class Structure and Psychological Functioning: A Comparative Analysis of the United States, Japan, and Poland. Paper presented at a plenary session of the Southern Sociological Society, Atlanta, April, 1987, and at a USSR-US Symposium on the Social Organization of Work, Vilnius, USSR, July 1987.

Kohn, Melvin L. and Carrie Schoenbach. 1980. "Social Stratification and Parental Values: A Multi-National Assessment." Paper presented to the Japan-U.S. Conference on Social Stratification and Mobility, Hawaii, January.

Kohn, Melvin L. and Carmi Schooler. 1978. "The Reciprocal Effects of the Substantive Complexity of Work and Intellectual Flexibility: A Longitudinal Assessment." *American Journal of Sociology* 84:24–52.

———. 1982. "Job Conditions and Personality: A Longitudinal Assessment of Their Reciprocal Effects." *American Journal of Sociology* 87:1257–86.

———. 1983. "Class, Stratification, and Psychological Functioning." Pp. 154–89 in *Work and Personality: An Inquiry Into the Impact of Social Stratification.* Norwood, NJ: Ablex.

———. With the collaboration of Joanne Miller, Karen A. Miller, Carrie Schoenbach, and Ronald Schoenberg. 1983. *Work and Personality: An Inquiry Into the Impact of Social Stratification.* Norwood, NJ: Ablex.

Kohn, Melvin L., Kazimierz M. Slomczynski, and Carrie Schoenbach. 1986. "Social Stratification and the Transmission of Values in the Family: A Cross-National Assessment." *Sociological Forum* 1:73–102.

Kuechler, Manfred. 1986. "The Utility of Surveys for Cross-National Research." Paper presented to the XI World Congress of Sociology, New Delhi, August.

Lipset, Seymour Martin. 1959. "Democracy and Working-Class Authoritarianism." *American Sociological Review* 24:482–501.

Marsh, Robert M. 1967. *Comparative Sociology: A Codification of Cross-Societal Analysis.* New York: Harcourt, Brace & World.

Meyer, John W. and Michael T. Hannan, eds. 1979. *National Development and the World System: Educational, Economic, and Political Change, 1950–1970.* Chicago: University of Chicago Press.

Miller, Joanne, Carmi Schooler, Melvin L. Kohn, and Karen A. Miller. 1979. "Women and Work: The Psychological Effects of Occupational Conditions." *American Journal of Sociology* 85:66–94.

Miller, Joanne, Kazimierz M. Slomczynski, and Melvin L. Kohn. 1985. "Continuity of Learning-Generalization: The Effect of Job on Men's Intellective Process in the United States and Poland." *American Journal of Sociology* 91:593–615.

Miller, Joanne, Kazimierz M. Slomczynski and Ronald J. Schoenberg. 1981. "Assessing Comparability of Measurement in Cross-National Research: Authoritarian-Conservatism in Different Sociocultural Settings." *Social Psychology Quarterly* 44:178–91.

Miller, Karen A. and Melvin L. Kohn. 1983. "The Reciprocal Effects of Job Conditions and the Intellectuality of Leisure-time Activities." Pp. 217–41 in *Work and Personality: An Inquiry into the Impact of Social Stratification,* by

Melvin L. Kohn and Carmi Schooler. Norwood, NJ: Ablex.

Miller, Karen A., Melvin L. Kohn, and Carmi Schooler. 1985. "Educational Self-Direction and the Cognitive Functioning of Students." *Social Forces* 63:923–44.

— — —. 1986. "Educational Self-Direction and Personality." *American Sociological Review* 51:372–90.

Naoi, Atsushi and Carmi Schooler. 1985. "Occupational Conditions and Psychological Functioning in Japan." *American Journal of Sociology* 90:729–52.

Nowak, Stefan. 1976. "Meaning and Measurement in Comparative Studies." Pp. 104–132 in *Understanding and Prediction: Essays in the Methodology of Social and Behavioral Theories.* Dordrecht, Holland: D. Reidel.

— — —. 1977. "The Strategy of Cross-National Survey Research for the Development of Social Theory." Pp. 3–47 in *Cross-National Comparative Survey Research: Theory and Practice,* edited by Alexander Szalai and Riccardo Petrella. Oxford: Pergamon Press.

Olsen, Nancy J. 1974. "Family Structure and Socialization Patterns in Taiwan." *American Journal of Sociology* 79:1395–1417.

Olsen, Stephen Milton. 1971. "Family, Occupation and Values in a Chinese Urban Community." Ph.D. diss., Cornell University.

Paige, Jeffery M. 1975. *Agrarian Revolution: Social Movements and Export Agriculture in the Underdeveloped World.* New York: Free Press.

Pearlin, Leonard I. 1971. *Class Context and Family Relations: A Cross-National Study.* Boston: Little, Brown.

Pearlin, Leonard I. and Melvin L. Kohn. 1966. "Social Class, Occupation, and Parental Values: A Cross-national Study." *American Sociological Review* 31:466–79.

Portes, Alejandro. 1975. "Trends in International Research Cooperation: The Latin American Case." *American Sociologist* 10:131–40.

Portes, Alejandro and Saskia Sassen-Koob. 1987. "Making It Underground: Comparative Material on the Informal Sector in Western Market Economies." *American Journal of Sociology* 93:30–61.

Przeworski, Adam and Henry Teune. 1970. *The Logic of Comparative Social Inquiry.* New York: Wiley-Interscience.

Ragin, Charles. 1982. "Comparative Sociology and the Comparative Method." *International Journal of Comparative Sociology* 22:102–20.

Ragin, Charles and David Zaret. 1983. "Theory and Method in Comparative Research: Two Strategies." *Social Forces* 61:731–54.

Rokkan, Stein. 1964. "Comparative Cross-National Research: The Context of Current Efforts." Pp. 3–25 in *Comparing Nations: The Use of Quantitative Data in Cross-National Research,* edited by Richard L. Merritt and Stein Rokkan. New Haven, CT: Yale University Press.

Sarapata, Adam. 1985. "Researchers' Habits and Orientations as Factors Which Condition International Cooperation in Research." *Science of Science* 5:157–82.

Scheuch, Erwin K. 1967. "Society as Context in Cross-Cultural Comparisons." *Social Science Information* 6:7–23.

— — —. 1968. "The Cross-Cultural Use of Sample Surveys: Problems of Comparability." Pp. 176–209 in *Comparative Research Across Cultures and Nations,* edited by Stein Rokkan, Paris: Mouton.

Schoenberg, Ronald. 1982. "Multiple Indicator Models: Estimation of Unconstrained Construct Means and Their Standard Errors." *Sociological Methods and Research* 10:421–33.

Schooler, Carmi, Melvin L. Kohn, Karen A. Miller, and Joanne Miller. 1983. "Housework as Work." Pp. 242–60 in *Work and Personality: An Inquiry into the Impact of Social Stratification,* by Melvin L. Kohn and Carmi Sholler. Norwood, NJ: Ablex.

Scurrah, Martin J. and Abner Montalvo. 1975. "Clase Social y Valores Sociales en Peru [Social Class and Social Values in Peru]. Lima, Peru: Escuela de Administracion de Negocios Para Graduados (Serie: Documento de Trabajo No. 8).

Skocpol, Theda. 1979. *States and Social Revolution: A Comparative Analysis of France, Russia, and China.* Cambridge: Cambridge University Press.

Slomczynski, Kazimierz M. and Melvin L. Kohn. In press. *Sytuacja Pracy I Jej Psychologiczne Konsekwencje: Polsko-Amerykanskie Analizy Porownawcze [Work Conditions and Psychological Functioning: Comparative Analyses of Poland and the United States].* Warsaw: Ossolineum Publishing Co.

Slomczynski, Kazimierz M., Joanne Miller, and Melvin L. Kohn. 1981. "Stratification, Work, and Values: A Polish-United States Comparison." *American Sociological Review* 46:720–44.

Smelser, Neil J. 1968. "The Methodology of Comparative Analysis of Economic Activity." Pp.

62–75 in *Essays in Sociological Explanation.* Englewood Cliffs, NJ: Prentice-Hall.

Suchman, Edward A. 1964. "The Comparative Method in Social Research." *Rural Sociology* 29:123–37.

Sztompka, Piotr. 1986. "The Renaissance of Historical Orientation in Sociology." *International Sociology* 1:321–37.

Tilly, Charles. 1984. *Big Structures, Large Processes, Huge Comparisons.* New York: Russell Sage Foundation.

Treiman, Donald J. 1977. *Occupational Prestige in Comparative Perspective.* New York: Academic Press.

Wallerstein, Immanuel. 1974, 1980. *The Modern World System.* 2 vols. New York: Academic Press.

Walton, John. 1984. *Reluctant Rebels: Comparative Studies of Revolution and Underdevelopment.* New York: Columbia University Press.

Wesolowski, Wlodzimierz. 1975. *Teoria, Badania, Praktyka. Z Problematyki Struktury Klasowej* [Theory, Research, Practice: Problems of Class Structure]. Warsaw: Ksiazka i Wiedza.

Williams, Robin M., Jr. 1985. "The Use of Threats in US/USSR Relations." *Research in Social Movements, Conflicts, and Change,* vol. 8, pp. 1–32. Greenwich, CT: JAI Press.

Zelditch, Morris, Jr. 1971. "Intelligible Comparisons." Pp. 267–307 in *Comparative Methods in Sociology: Essays on Trends and Applications,* edited by Ivan Vallier. Berkeley, CA: University of California Press.

Methods

In the field of comparative social research the line between theory and method is not sharply drawn. In the theory papers presented in section I we were already introduced to a number of methodological distinctions. For example, Melvin Kohn stressed that his research used the nation-state only as *context* for studying the relation of self-direction on the job and certain values such as open-mindedness. A different kind of analysis takes the nation-state not as context but treats it in itself as the unit of analysis. Neil Smelser's paper in this section gives as an example the effort to explain the different rates of growth in gross national product (GNP) by reference to certain cultural and political characteristics of the nations under study.

In our first selection Erwin Scheuch, although himself an expert in doing studies that take the nation as the unit of analysis, sees many dangers in uncritically accepting the nation-state as an obviously meaningful entity for comparative research. He urges us to look more systematically into this "black box" to better understand what is really there and thus make our comparisons more sensitive and meaningful. In the course of elaborating these methodological cautions, he gives us a concise guide to some of the most important comparative studies that have been done. He tells us that these studies have made us "data-rich" but, to close the circle, suggests that we may still be "theory-poor."

Charles Ragin goes much further than Scheuch, seeing so many problems in using the nation as the unit of study by the correlational method that it becomes for him an unaccept-

able approach. Instead, he favors the case method, in which one does not seek a large number of cases, all measured on a small set of variables, but instead works with a small set of nations especially selected because of their relevance for one's problem. The analysis then takes into account the characteristics of each nation as a whole, following the rules of inductive inquiry developed by John Stuart Mill. This approach, Ragin feels, is in no way inferior to the statistical method.

Neil Smelser finds similar challenges and faces comparable hard choices when he seeks, in our third selection, to use the comparative method for studying the social aspects of economic life. What we mean by the "economic" aspect of social organization is likely to vary as we move from one society and culture to another. The example Smelser uses is that of a "market," which is a simple and basic idea for most economists but may not be so simple or obvious when approached from the perspective of the anthropologist or sociologist who knows a certain society in depth. Yet if we go too far in following the perspective of a given culture, we may lose the ability to compare its economic activity with any other. In this paper Smelser ends up favoring what he called "the method of systematic observation," which is similar to the method favored by Ragin. At a later point in time Smelser moved more to support of the correlational method, a move that provided Ragin the platform for launching his defense of the more qualitative method. That we are not unsympathetic to this approach is reflected in the fact that we have included in our set of readings a number of studies that utilize the qualitative method. But we also recognize the virtues of the correlational method. Rather than an absolute commitment to one method or another, we favor allowing each method to do the best it can, depending on the requirements and potentialities of the particular problem under investigation.

Theoretical Implications of Comparative Survey Research: Why the Wheel of Cross-Cultural Methodology Keeps on Being Reinvented*

Erwin K. Scheuch[†]

The real problem is not the methodology per se, but it is methodological in its consequences: what can be done to make methodological advances and practical experiences in comparative research more cumulative? Or phrasing the question both more realistically and more depressingly: how can we make knowledge in this area cumulative at all?

Some seventeen and twenty-five years ago, respectively, two major international conferences attempted to summarize the state of the art in comparative research both with respect to methodology *strictu sensu* but also for research technology. In 1964 at Yale the leading spirit was Sandor Szalai, and the proceedings concentrated on macrostudies such as *The World Handbook, The Yale Political Data Program* and the *Human Relations Area File* (cf. Merritt and Rokkan 1966). In general the accent was on research philosophy, including the interrelation between research design and the objective of comparison.

In the second of the conferences, 1972 in Budapest, many of the same researchers came together again. The main agenda was a postmortem on five large-scale comparative studies (Szalai and Petrella 1977): "The Time Budget Project"; "Juvenile Delinquency and Development"; "Images of the World in the Year 2000"; the Jacobs and Jacobs study on leadership values; and the Verba and Nie Project on political participation.[1] All of these projects were based on survey research. This second time, basic discussions on design alternated with ex-

changes of management experiences in actually carrying out comparative research, and on technological devices.[2]

The proceedings of both conferences have been published, and these books can still be considered as major compendia. Other creditable books have been published, such as in 1984 *How to Compare Nations* by Mattei Dogan and Dominique Pelassy, and in the same year Manfred Niessen, Jules Peschar, and Chantal Kurilsky (eds.), *International Vergleichende Sozialforschung*[3]—both books remaining quite unknown in the United States. It is my considered judgment that for the time being, in terms of methodology *in abstracto* and on issues of research technology, most of all that needed to be said has already been published. As an example of the methodological refinement already reached by the late sixties, see the internationally comparative study for the WHO on the utilization of medical care facilities 1968–1969, with 48,000 interviews in twelve research sites (Kohn and White 1976, especially Chapter 3).

The problems that are encountered in practical research are not due to a lack of available methodological knowledge. In view of this appraisal of the state of the available methodological knowledge as against the state of the art in practical research, we set ourselves three modest goals:

(a) To spread the message that methodological discussions are often reinventing what has been forgotten and influence actual research very little. Only in so far as they are included in text-book teachings do they have an imprint on a later generation of scholarship.

(b) To help with the *ex post* interpretation of data from cross-national survey research. This is especially necessary for the elementary unit of the analyses in this research: the implications of using "country," "nation," "society," or "culture," respectively.[4]

(c) To use the experiences with difficulties and payoffs in the use of cross-cultural surveys as opportunities for substantive insights.

This is an opportune time to attempt this. This does not result, however, from new basic insights in the methodology of comparative research. There are none. There are two other conditions though, which make this attempt here not only timely but urgent.

(1) With a generational change among comparativists under way, there is the danger of a second case of collective amnesia in methodology. Toward the end of the sixties and the beginning of the seventies the methodological literature on comparativism had grown to such proportions that international institutions commissioned major bibliographies. The International Sociological Association requested Robert Marsh to prepare an overview of the literature since 1950 (1966). The International Social Science Council had asked Elina Almasy for such a bibliography limited to survey research, and subsequently the Vienna Center of UNESCO issued a contract for an update (Rokkan et al. 1969; Almasy et al. 1976). Limiting himself to English language journals only and also somewhat in the scope of subject matter, Frederick W. Frey from the MIT's Center of International Studies compiled an annotated bibliography with 1,600 individual entries (Frey et al. 1969).

Significantly, the first major undertaking in this area was missing in these sources. As early as the fifties the Division of Applied Social Science of UNESCO gave a contract to the World Association for Public Opinion Research (WAPOR) to prepare a survey of journal articles on cross-cultural research between 1925 and 1955. Stuart C. Dodd and Jiri Nehnevajsa com-

piled 1,103 entries, and unlike Fred Frey not limiting themselves to one language.[5]

The comparativists of the late sixties and early seventies are probably largely ignored by the current younger American methodologists, as the center of cross-cultural methodology had by then shifted to Europe (Szalai and Petrella 1977).[6] In turn, during this Europeanization it was largely overlooked that there had been a sudden blossoming of comparative social research immediately after 1945. A high point in this development was the nine-country study by Buchanan and Cantril (1953), and the development of standardized tests for international surveys (such as the self-anchoring scale by Cantril, culture-free intelligence tests, and cross-culturally applicable versions of the MMPI and the n-achievement testing). As an example of a sophisticated discussion of measurement, see Cantril and Free (1962: 4–30). A complete presentation of the issues in developing a culture-free scale can be found in Cantril (1965). Of the many areas of specialization in which cross-cultural research at that time led to important advances, see Glock (1954). At that time the center of discussion was the North American continent, and a major forum for methodological contributions was the Mexico-based *International Journal of Opinion and Attitude Research.*

Then interest in comparative data waned in the United States in the later fifties. The *International Journal* ceased publication for lack of funds, and the *US Public Opinion Quarterly* dropped its section on World Polls. Hadley Cantril's attempt at a worldwide collection of public opinion material 1935–1946 found no successor (Cantril and Strunk 1951).[7] All of these initiatives were largely forgotten by the midsixties when a new generation with different experiences dominated the methodological scene, spearheaded by Stein Rokkan and later Sandor Szalai.[8]

As this is a time of another generational shift, this paper (and its notes) are an attempt to prevent yet another instance of reinventing the wheel in cross-cultural methodology.

(2) Comparative research, insofar as it meant data collection in several countries, was an expensive and administratively difficult undertaking (Sarapata 1985: 157–82). This meant that as a rule the researcher was an experienced social scientist. Nowadays, comparative data are available to the less experienced and underfunded, even to the moneyless graduate student. Two such resources will be mentioned toward the end of this paper: ISSP and the EUROBAROMETER. Data from these sources are easily obtainable but difficult to analyze properly. Nonetheless, I hope to stimulate interest in secondary analysis with cross-cultural data. It is done with the conviction that even faulty comparative research has its merits.

Pitfalls in Using Country as a Black Box

During the first spell of popularity that comparative research enjoyed following the end of World War II, the preferred tool was the survey—if possible representative for a country. The purpose of comparisons was to demonstrate numerically a uniqueness of the countries surveyed. What accounts for the aberrant political developments of industrialized Germany and modern Japan was a repeated topic of such comparisons using nationally representative surveys.[9]

In such surveys, countries were treated as objects known in their peculiarities. Thus, in their study of "political culture," Almond and Verba assumed they knew that properties that could be shown as being peculiar to the United States could be used to define a democratic political culture, those peculiar to Mexico as denoting an incompletely integrated system, and those specific for (Western) Germany as an indication of a nondemocratic milieu (Almond and Verba 1963; see also Verba 1965). Of course, in each of the countries compared one obtained some percentage points for each response possibility; a perfect uniqueness in responses being out of the question in survey work. Percentage point differences, in the case

of Almond and Verba mostly between the marginals compared, were treated as evidence.

This logic and procedure are still quite frequent in internationally comparative surveys. Examples are the *Readers Digest* studies on consumers in Europe, the Shell International youth studies, and in comparative surveys on youth commissioned by the Japanese prime minister—all rather recent and well-funded projects. In comparing practices in these studies, one can see that they imply the following:

> *Implication 1:* A mere aggregation of individual responses makes sense.
> *Implication 2:* For purposes of explanation, individual questions can be used as variables.
> *Implication 3:* Percentages are taken at face value, even though they may only indicate rank orders.
> *Implication 4:* If data from several countries are compared, they are compared as though they were regions within one country.

It is characteristic in this use of surveys as a tool of comparison that a country is merely used as a dummy variable for all of the individual cases collected in that area. To proceed in this way appeals to common sense, but it is objectionable in principle and will often lead to research artifacts. The Almond and Verba book on *The Civic Culture* was based on such analyses, not controlling for third factors. Undoubtedly, many statements in that text, widely used for instructional purposes, have to be included in the disturbing list of our research artifacts turned into required knowledge for students.

The most elementary precaution when using country as a dummy variable is correcting the marginals for variables that are later used as independent variables—such as the demography. Thus, in comparing Mexico with the United States by way of two-way tables— as in Almond and Verba—one should normalize through weighting operations the differences in age distribution and in occupational structure plus education, before interpreting differences in political participation as the result of differences in civic culture—or rather the verbal commitment to participation—

showing that the United States is a participatory political culture, while Mexico is not.

This example was chosen with two considerations in mind: in all likelihood the differences cited by Almond and Verba for the global property "participatory political culture" are in this particular instance real and not artifacts — but still the procedure is not adequate to prove the point. And, of principal importance, correcting marginal distributions by weighting may destroy the usefulness of having survey data from more than one country. Let us suppose that the purpose of our comparison were to demonstrate the changes in volume and style of participation as a function of high levels of education and high percentages of adults, then the differences between the United States and Mexico in these respects are just what was needed to clarify the issue.[10]

Before continuing with this point — that the methodological criteria in comparative work differ depending on the use that is made of the countries as contexts (see Hyman 1964: 153–88) — there are two more objections to be considered against this most naive use of cross-cultural material — namely imputing observed differences by way of black-box argumentation to the countries: the stability of properties measured, and the pitfalls of the "individualistic fallacy."

Decades of survey research should have taught the social science community that many of the percentages reported cannot be replicated. They were the property of a moment in time only. In 1973 representative samples in the United Kingdom, the United States, and in France had been asked "What is the most important problem facing this country to-

day?"[11] The rank order of the three problem areas at that time is given in Table 5.1.

The differences between countries made intuitive sense as they conformed to national stereotypes: the French are self-centered, showing little interest in the world around them; the British are mercenary; and the United States are internationally hawkish. However, in 1962 among French voters, international and defense affairs had first priority by a large margin. And a measurement in 1978 revealed the very same rank order of concern in all three countries compared.

The data from the cross-polity survey are a case in point for developing countries (Banks and Textor 1963). In a decade-long labor-of-love the authors had coded information about developing countries — much in the spirit of *The Human Relations Area File*. Significantly, they used the subdivisions of Africa that the former colonial powers had left behind as entities in the sense of Thailand and Ceylon. Proudly they reported as proven causal nexus: former British possessions are characterized by democratic structures and independent legal systems; former French colonies are not. A few decades saw those differences fade away.

Are the Germans industrious? In a time series spanning thirty years, the result for questions referring to attitudes toward work differ by 30 percentage points (Scheuch 1988a). However, according to behavioral data, there cannot have been a major change. What measurements of attitudes showed as change was in all likelihood a mere change in the *façon de parler*. In general, we tend to overestimate the stability of measurements. Test-retest studies have demonstrated the merely approximate na-

T A B L E 5 . 1 Rank Order of the Three Problem Areas		
France	**United States**	**United Kingdom**
Domestic political	International and defense	Economic
Economic	Economic	Domestic political and social
International and defense	Domestic political and social	International and defense

ture of measurements especially for attitudinal and opinion items.[12] Cross-cultural surveys are especially demanding for the reliability and validity of observations. It is then a very risky undertaking to treat individual percentage point differences between countries as evidence. Only a configuration (a "gestalt") of results can be trusted.

Observation under differing conditions is the high road of social research. Sociology is an observational science in the sense of John Stuart Mill. This accepted, it is necessary to consider the central difference between observational data and data from experiments. In experiments "third factors" intervening between the assumed dependent and independent variables are controlled *ex ante* through design. For observational data this control is largely *ex post* through appropriate statistical techniques. Data from comparative survey research are thus more difficult to analyze and interpret than experimental data.

The Many Meanings of Comparisons

The prevailing kind of comparative survey research is in practice a cross-level design with an unsatisfactory understanding of the highest of the levels. To understand this better, and to gain insight into what this means for analysis and interpretation, it is useful to recall a distinction proposed by Stein Rokkan (1970): cross-national, cross-cultural, and cross-societal comparisons.[13]

Usually the nation-state is the geographical frame for sampling. Subsequently, the data collected in various nation-states are used as though that would also mean that the comparisons were cross-cultural and cross-societal as well. Whether the three meanings the geographical sampling frame could have—namely, nation, culture and society—do in fact coincide is in any particular case a substantive issue.

"Juan Linz delineated eight Spains, Erik Allardt four Finlands, and Stein Rokkan as many Norways. Anyone knows that there are three Belgiums, four Italys, and five or six Frances" (Dogan and Pelassy 1984: 15). Whether the nation-state as a relatively recent form of political aggregation did in fact succeed in integrating social structures and neutralizing older mediating levels differs by country and also by domain. This was controversially debated in the seventies under the umbrella of "governability" of Western states. P. Schmitter led the partisans of corporatism—that is, those who understood the survival of medieval structures during the process of nation building as a great advantage to a polity, and not at all as a liability as is usually argued.

In the frequent comparative surveys, including the four Scandinavian countries, the most important one is the "Welfare Survey," directed by Erik Allardt—Finland is often the odd case. This proved to be true again in an investigation of the incidence of various illnesses. In particular, coronary heart disease has a much higher incidence in Finland than in neighboring Sweden. An analysis of the survey data by subregion, rather than only by country, showed that this high incidence was entirely due to the concentration of that ailment in the northern, much more rural, half of Finland; values for the southern, more developed, part—where one would otherwise expect higher incidences—were identical with rates for Sweden, Denmark, and Norway. The currently accepted explanation for the concentration of coronary heart disease in rural northern Finland is the combined effect of life under stressful conditions for farmers, and especially lumber workers, and the fantastic levels of alcohol abuse in these dismal settings. It was not "Finland" as a nation-state, culture, or society that could account for the odd values, but Finland as an administrative unit included a setting with aberrant living conditions (see also Allardt 1966).

The reverse problem, that the causative element is part of a much larger geographical context, is just as frequently overlooked. In this case the unit society, or nation-state, or culture, is incorrectly used in sampling and as a frame in analyses. Thus, in *The Human Relations Area File* one speaks of "samples" that are drawn from "cultures." Maybe that is permissible for some ethnographic units, but not for the file as a worldwide collection. That issue had been debated in ethnology already at the turn of the century as "Galton's problem." "Galton's problem" is the issue whether a given culture can be thought of as "causing" something, or whether that something is instead the result of diffusion across cultures. The issue is given the name "Galton's problem" as it was first raised by him during a meeting of the Royal Anthropological Institute in 1889. Galton, at that time already a famous statistician, is quoted as having remarked in discussing a paper by Tylor: "It was extremely desirable for the sake of those who may wish to study the evidence for Dr. Tylor's conclusion, that full information should be given as to the degree in which the customs of the tribes and races which are compared together are independent. It might be that some of the tribes had derived them from a common source, so that they were duplicate copies of the same original" (Tylor 1961 [1889]: 23).

The Human Relations Area File is the most ambitious effort so far at comparative social research. Here, "cultures" are treated as units in explanation—within-culture variation (as is frequent in cross-cultural comparisons) being bypassed as an irritant.[14]

With worldwide communication systems, unprecedented levels of international trade, and a volume of cross-border travel exceeding the level of 400 million movements per year, international diffusion is evidently a major factor in cultural change.[15] However, while the volume may be something unique, the phenomenon is not new at all. A case in point are eating habits, and presumably national cuisines, in Western Europe.[16] Before a social scientist attributes the dominant position of the potato in the German cuisine to a German pref-

erence to dig deep, he should consider another causation: the combined effect of a climate disadvantageous to very many agricultural products, and the efficiency with which authorities in an area, that was later named Prussia, could force the population to accept this then new vegetable of the American Indians.

"Galton's problem" is everywhere! In comparative work it is fraught with the danger to use a stochastic approach in selecting study areas in the whole Western world if one looks for explanations of differences in consumer styles, leisure behavior, or food preferences. Differences between, for example, Scandinavia, Germany, and France, in their preferences for housing and interior equipment were considerable twenty years ago, and they were usually attributed to "culture." Differences still exist, but the kind of changes since then have to be largely attributed to national housing policies and the different policies of the respective industries (as long as these were protected by customs barriers and administrative chicaneries). While in many respects a Western European society is emerging with a strong "family likeness" between the countries, quite a bit of descriptive knowledge, including historical information, is required before remaining country differences can be attributed to black boxes called Spain or Britain.

Since the midsixties, protest movements have become a routine element in the politics of Western Europe.[17] There are cross-national differences and similarities but the factors explaining differences are primarily not national but cultural. Those movements have become an as yet uninstitutionalized parallel to institutionalized politics—and as such are a characteristic of Protestant Europe, and within that context weaker in Lutheran areas. Maybe that is true only as description, and to turn the descriptive correlations into an explanation is premature. Is it really something in Protestantism as a religious culture? Or is it at least in part the consequence of its younger clergy? Or is it mainly the consequence of a tension between the desire for individual moral/religious commitment, and the waning of institutionalized religion in a society with high functional differentiation? Or is it an interrelation of all those factors? All this is currently unclear. What is clear is the fact that the explanandum cuts across the administrative boundaries of nation-states. States that enclose both Protestant and Catholic territories—that is the case in Western Germany—offer an opportunity for a check as to which factor is the stronger: religious culture or nation-state. Both are relevant, but religious culture appears to be the much stronger one (Scheuch forthcoming).

While nation-states, culture, or society, may be too large a unit for a causal attribution (e.g. the Finnish example) or too small (as in the case of protest movements), it may also be too weak a context to account for differences observed with individual data. True, in its most ideological form the nation-state assumes a basic sameness among its citizens. However, all industrial societies are pluralistic—and if material well-being and the political system permit this, they are so pluralistic that often within-country differences are larger than between-country differences.

Since the seventies, the High Commission for the Common Market has comparative surveys carried out in all member states several times a year, the EUROBAROMETER.[18] One does observe differences in percentage distributions; some of them remain consistent even over time. An example are levels of dissatisfaction in various countries, where satisfaction levels are consistently below average in Italy, average in Western Germany, and above average in Denmark. However, variations for such attitudinal data rarely exceed 10 percent between the countries high and low on a measurement. Obviously when between-country variances are smaller than within-country variations, then it is quite improbable that references to countries can be understood as explanations. In such pluralistic societies, survey research can usually be treated as observation

under differing conditions and not as a test of the meanings and effects of a culture, a society, or a polity.

The many difficulties, and as a consequence the many errors in an attribution when using units such as Japan, or Australia, or Hungary as black-box explanation, should lead us to two conclusions:

1. Very often we do not really know what we are talking about when we use nation names.
2. One needs a great store of descriptive knowledge before one can use nation names as explanans in comparative work.

Nation Names in Global Studies

In the discussion of the ecological fallacy, a distinction between aggregate and global properties of higher-order units—such as regions or nation-states—gained currency (Scheuch 1969).

It is not uncommon in comparative survey research to use aggregated properties, and that can lead to a fallacy that is specific for that mode of procedure: the "individualistic fallacy" of incorrectly imputing to the higher-order unit the aggregation of values for individuals. Using responses by the same individuals to characterize nations or cultures, and also as an explanandum, one is in danger of circular reasoning. Beyond that, many of the aspects of a nation or a culture are global properties in the sense that Lazarsfeld uses the term. By definition global properties are those characteristics of a collective that cannot be explained by the composition of the individual units.[19]

One influential type of comparative research can be labeled "global studies." This approach is characterized by using the largest number of countries possible—as is true for ethnological research for *The Human Relations Area File,* and the *Cross-Polity Survey*—treating the countries as black boxes being simultaneously congruent with societies, cultures, and nations. Survey data are only part of the empirical base but, by treating a very large number of societies as global entities, it is here that the use of surveys is often improper on logical grounds.

These global studies are especially instructive for the country-as-black-box approach in comparative work. Beginning with the *Yale Political Data Handbook,* global studies attained a certain importance, especially in political sociology (Russett et al. 1964). Even though the use of countries in the *YPDH* was already severely criticized in the early sixties, that argument had absolutely no effect on this project, nor on other global studies.[20] Ted Gurr and David Singer started a "school" relating incidences of violence—a typical aggregate property for within-nation violence but certainly not so for between-nation violence—to global properties of nations (Singer and Small 1972; Wallace and Singer 1973; Gurr 1968, 1974).[21] More central for sociology has been the world systems approach by Immanuel Wallerstein. It became a veritable research paradigm, possibly because of its ideological appeal (Wallerstein 1974, 1980, 1984; see also Bollen 1983; Haman and Carrol 1981).[22] A related "school" started by Peter Heintz (the late president of the *"Weltgesellschaft"* foundation in Switzerland) understands this comparison of the largest feasible number of nation-states as an attempt to test propositions in a quasi-experimental design (Heintz 1969, 1973, 1982).

In all these cases the nations compared are treated as black boxes. In just correlating an input variable, such as foreign investment, with an output variable, such as per capita income, all structural properties of nation-states are ignored. True, by using partial regressions for the largest possible number of countries to establish relations between input and output variables of countries treated as systems, one eliminates all third factors as in an experiment. But it is just this that makes this "largest number of black-box countries" approach unsociological. If theoretically sounding terms are used, as by the Wallersteiners with their terms "center," "periphery," or "dependencia" or "world system," they are undefined and/or used metaphorically.[23] Taken as an approach, global stud-

ies are probably more responsible for research artifacts than any other comparative approach.

The so-called "world models" can be considered intellectually as a spin-off from global studies. World models that strongly influenced public discussion, such as those of the Club of Rome (important in Western Europe), Global 2000 (of primary interest in the United States), or the Bariloche model (oriented to the public of Latin America) were really designed as education (or propaganda) tools. Their authors meant them to be self-destroying prophecies. Frightened by the picture of a future as sketched in the world model, the public would pressure for action to avoid the predicted fate. Such models are easy to design: in an equation predicting growth that includes many factors, one merely has to postulate that at least one factor will have a slower growth rate than the other factors; then that one factor will create the bottleneck causing the system to come to a grinding halt.

"To compare two events or two things is always a process of matching. . . . No two events are all alike in everything, but we compare them in those aspects that matter for the purpose at hand. We also therefore compare things which in other aspects are not comparable," writes Karl W. Deutsch (1985: 5), one of the pioneers of comparativism in social research. From this perspective it becomes obvious how hazardous an approach the use of countries as black boxes is. Deutsch proceeds in arguing that in comparative research countries should be treated as systems with internal transactions that decline—gradually or abruptly at system boundaries—while other processes, therefore termed outer processes, ". . . may be more frequent or more powerful outside the boundaries of the system than inside of it" (ibid.). Properties of systems are not simply additive; within systems the properties are reactive. This systemic character of the units compared is characteristically ignored in global studies, and global studies even fail in the first consideration quoted here by not testing the rationale for comparing properties.

Deutsch proceeds to propose three catalogs of basic functions to be used as common yardsticks in comparisons across many countries.

(a) In the *General Theory of Action,* Talcott Parsons delineates in his AGIL-scheme four BASIC FUNCTIONS OF SYSTEMS:
   —Pattern maintenance;
   —Adaptation;
   —Goal attainment;
   —Integration.
   To this Karl W. Deutsch adds—he claims "ultimately" with the consent of Parsons, but that is here of secondary relevance only—two more basic functions:
   —Goal change;
   —Self-transformation (transformation in some dimensions, while maintaining continuity in others—as in revolutions).
   With the two additional functions, Deutsch attempts to make Parsonian functionalism more useful for analyzing systems changes.

(b) A set of eight POLITICAL NEEDS OF MODERN POPULATIONS—a set that comes in four pairs, one of the poles denoting tangibles, the opposite intangibles.[24]
   —Maintenance of physical equipment . . . and of the authority system
   —Increase of physical capital . . . ethics of performance (*Leistungsethik*)
   —Communication equipment . . . readiness for communication
   —Preservation of environment . . . need for spontaneity

(c) On the level of STATE FUNCTIONS, Deutsch postulates seven characteristic ones, five of which are important in the present world already, two more to become decisive within the next hundred years:
   —Internal order;
   —International power;
   —Increase wealth;
   —Promote common welfare;
   —Mobilization of relevant populations;
   —Adaptive learning (new);
   —New initiatives (just emerging).

Several objections against such catalogs—specifically the one for populations and the one for the state—are obvious. The one for population, worked out jointly with Rudolf Wildenmann and Bruno Fritsch (another *Weltgesellschaft* social scientist from Switzerland), is indebted to the spirit of the time ("Zeitgeist"), and has no rationale save its appeal to plausibility. An ad-hoc-ishness is even more evident for the list of functions of the state. One is reminded of the twenties when lists of basic needs, or drives, or levels of personality were being proposed by psychologists. However, while none of these suggestions of the twenties was empirically "proven," they were useful milestones in making psychology more cumulative.

Thus, it might indeed be preferable to continue with Deutsch's hypothesis that these needs will be important in all industrialized countries organized as pluralistic democracies. "Comparative research on the twenty or thirty industrial democracies in the world would tell us whether this is in fact the case or not" (Deutsch 1985: 8). Survey procedures would have an important part in the research design for such a project. It would still belong to the tradition of global studies, and yet avoid the black-box treatment—the latter meaning by implication excluding a contribution to sociological theory.

Countries as Unstable Aggregates and Stable Configurations

When using nation-states as sampling frames, then proceeding to compare as observations under differing conditions, the use of countries presents no problem of a principal nature. There is merely the practical problem whether the researcher is sufficiently well informed about the conditions in a country. However, countries are also chosen as units in comparison because one wants to relate their unique (?) configuration of properties, including global properties, to the dependent variables. In doing this, several problems occur that are frequently not seen at all.

It is usual in comparing values for some variables between several countries to take for granted what the countries stand for. Most often this is identical to the stereotypes current in intellectual circles in one's home country. After all, everyone knows what France stands for. But does one really even in an elementary sense? The process of nation-building penetrated with varying degrees into the social structure of current countries—as is now becoming apparent even in nation-states as classical as those of England and France. The monopolization of functions at the national level is a variable, not a defining constant of every nation-state.

The present-day nation-states in Europe and America could be understood, according to this perspective, as unique aggregates of properties which do not coincide with the domain of state. The Federal Republic may on occasions be described as "capitalistic" as is Japan; in another perspective, however, as "European" in contrast to Japan, and jointly so with the GDR. The GDR may as a political system regard itself as part of a socialist world, together with Tanzania and Vietnam, but it is also an industrial society and as such more dissimilar to Bulgaria than to the Federal Republic.

There exists a German culture, and this does not, nor ever did, coincide with the political boundaries of any one political entity. For village life, insofar as this still exists today in central Europe, there is something like an Alpine village life in contrast to the village life of the North German lowlands. In the demography and fertility patterns the Federal Republic and the GDR are, compared with developing countries, part of an aggregate of "old societies."

Internationally comparative surveys among industrialized and affluent democracies already show outlines of a common civic culture. The results of the 1985 International Social Survey Programme are an example.[25] Among a whole battery of questions relating to the role of government, it was asked:

"All systems of justice make mistakes, but which do you think is worse—
To convict an innocent person?
To let a guilty person go free?"

The differences cluster in two groups: an Anglo-Saxon variant of the civic culture, and a continental variation (Table 5.2). And between the two there is a distinctive family likeness. For a methodologist this is a nightmarish confirmation of the fear that Galton's problem lurks everywhere. For the social scientist motivated by substantive interests it is a suggestion that Deutsch is most likely right in assuming a common culture for industrialized affluent democracies.

Sometimes differences are quite substantial, and yet they are obviously response distributions following the same pattern. To give an example from the same ISSP survey 1985:

"It is the responsibility of the government to reduce the differences in incomes between people with high incomes and those with low incomes."

Here the countries line up along a different axis from before (Table 5.3). Going by welfare state indicators, the correlation appears to be: the larger the public sector and the welfare state apparatus, the smaller the acceptance of income inequalities.[26] Of course, this is merely a first diagnosis which needs to be tested for

	Australia (%)	West Germany (%)	Great Britain (%)	U.S. (%)	Austria (%)	Italy (%)
TABLE 5.2						
Convict innocent	77.1	85.3	76.7	75.2	82.6	82.0
Guilty goes free	22.9	14.7	23.3	24.8	17.4	18.0

T A B L E   5 . 3

	Australia (%)	West Germany (%)	Great Britain (%)	U.S. (%)	Austria (%)	Italy (%)
Agree strongly	15.1	29.5	22.5	12.5	36.7	30.5
Agree	27.8	26.9	29.7	17.0	29.6	36.5
Neither	16.3	23.5	24.0	20.5	21.4	18.3
Disagree	24.3	10.0	17.5	30.7	7.3	12.4
Disagree strongly	16.5	10.1	6.2	19.4	4.9	2.2

contextual effects. Historical factors need to be considered as to whether there could be a common causal agent for both variables: size of public sector and rejection of income inequality.

However, the more important lesson from both examples is: in our explanations we are here not really dealing with countries as distinct entities but with different locations as sets of conditions. Given nation-states of the "First" and of the "Second" World, one may safely assume that in most instances of cross-cultural surveys these countries are not the causative entities in their global or "cultural" peculiarities. In most instances of actual survey research countries affect the explanandum as a set of conditions.

Immediately after World War II, whenever surveys showed a difference—especially among American social scientists—the usual interpretation was a reference to "culture."[27] For the already mentioned aberrant political developments in Japan and Germany, "culture" was even habitually referred to as causative. Thus, B. H. Schaffner (1948) explained the successes of Nazism in Germany with the conditioning to authoritarianism in a specific "German" family tradition. There was no proof offered, nor even looked for, whether there was indeed a specific German family tradition—different from bourgeois family traditions in France or England. By way of contrast, in the very same year, 1948, another research report by David Rodnik

argued that German families were overly warm in their socialization practices. On the descriptive level the contradiction between the two reports was probably due to an emphasis on different strata in German society.

In referring to whole societies, such as Poland and or the Federal Republic, one is plagued by doubts that our characterization of such whole societies lacks criteria for what is important and what is ephemeral. There is a continuity in Polish society, unaffected by the great changes in the territory of the state, even unaffected by the reduction of the Poles to the status of national minorities within the borders of other states, but what is this—partly latent—continuity? In this twentieth century, "the Germans" were the population of an imperial domain (*Kaiserreich*), which was simultaneously conservative and yet modernizing rapidly; afterward they lived with a rather liberal republic (Weimar), and subsequently with a quite efficient form of totalitarianism. Since the Second World War the Germans exist side by side as the populations of two political systems of a totally different kind, in their respective "Western" and "Eastern" contexts which are relatively equally successful. What constitutes continuity in constant change? The attempted partial and ad hoc answer for Germany was: (a) elements of the stratification system and the work orientation, distinct features of the leadership subculture, and the exclusion of ideological cleavages from whole domains of life;

(b) the corporatistic network of intermediation between the level of the state and the private worlds (cf. Scheuch 1988b).

In the United States, Japan, and the countries of continental Western Europe, both aspects of a modernized country are apparent: social change is common and rapid but at the same time there is strong continuity as countries in comparison with one another—despite the complaints of cultural critics about universal Americanization. This is less true for many parameters which are emphasized in the description of social systems as global collectives: the value of the GNP, living standards, distribution of income, even occupational structures and types of housing. Differences in housing are one of the most obvious distinctions between the United States, Britain, France, Germany, Denmark and Italy. However, surveys have shown that differences in housing preferences in the respective populations are much smaller by far than differences on the supply side. Primarily, these obvious differences were the consequence of a shortage of urban housing on the Continent for generations plus regulatory policies of governments. Thus, they cannot be used as expressions of popular culture—rather they are indicators of differences between economies and polities.

Differences which, toward the end of the fifties, seemed to social scientists to be characteristic of countries—such as variations in the value of the GNP and in living standards—are viewed over time as quite unreliable indicators distinguishing, for example, between England and Italy. These properties are, however, of key importance to mark the position of the "trilateral" countries (Japan, USA/Canada, Western Europe, Australia/New Zealand) vis-à-vis the entire world. The "affluent society" can in many respects—lifestyles, marriage patterns, orientation toward work—be regarded as a distinct social type. Affluent society means a new priority of values, it means a shift of apprehensions from economics to events in one's private world, implies a higher degree of institutional differentiation, and, as a consequence,

a greater need for integrative processes and institutions. On the basis of a more intuitive recall of survey results we feel certain that these affluent countries have a strong family likeness as social systems. Unfortunately we lack a theoretical rationale, empirically supported, for this judgment.

After decades of reading results from comparative surveys we feel encouraged to suggest that a more sociological characteristic of a society may be its mode and degree of differentiation. Central for modern societies appears to be the acceptance of sectorial autonomy, combined with domain-specific rationalities (*Eigengesetzlichkeit*). Phrased in Parsonian language this means that diffuse orientations turn into functionally specific ones. That we are identifying central and distinctive elements of societies is suggested by signs of disorientation that visitors from less differentiated societies display with this very aspect of everyday life in an economically and socially modern society. Historically and worldwide, multifunctionality of behavior and institutions has been prevalent, and a minimum of multifunctionality and functional diffuseness may be crucial for social stability. Was Durkheim right in suspecting that societies characterized by sheer mechanical solidarity were untenable in the long run? (Hence Durkheim's plea for corporatism.)

A Central Lesson from Comparative Survey Research

Viewed over a period of nearly three decades, there are two dominant experiences:

1.   Comparisons that include both modern and developing countries produce differences that are very hard to interpret—if they make sense at all. An example: in youth surveys one observes young people in developing countries reacting with high degrees of optimism that are factually completely inappropriate—such as in India. By way of contrast, young people in Sweden or in the Netherlands exude gloom in the wake of incomparably greater opportunity. In appraisals of parent-child relations there ap-

pears to be a zero correlation, if not a negative one, between differences in restrictiveness of behavior and differences in expressed evaluation. Of course, that should not be read as a "no" to comparative survey research but it points to a need for intensive consideration of intervening and contextual factors before differences between countries can be "explained." In routine research such comparisons are advisable only for the "most different" designs in testing universals.[28]

2. Comparisons between countries with similar levels of modernity are frustrating and stimulating at the same time: most of the time the differences at the level of individual measurement do not account for differences at an institutional level, especially not for the behavior of formal organizations, and hardly at all for differences between polities. Hence one has to introduce substantive assumptions about system features for the polities between which comparisons are attempted. One needs theory—and usually middle-level theory—to make sense of data.

Comparative research in its very frustrations, using countries as part of reality and not mere data collection frames, can be a major stimulant for a theoretically guided description, and an empirically grounded macrosociological theory. Two developments should help to attract researchers, especially younger ones, to such comparisons:

(a) Since the early seventies the European Community has four times a year conducted representative surveys in all of its member countries–twelve countries by now. This material of the EUROBAROMETER allows both comparisons—a time series analysis and a cross-national comparison. The demographic section permits tests as to how important the level of the nation is relative to other integrative institutions. It is easy to relate these survey data to masses of nonsurvey data produced by institutions.

(b) The "General Social Surveys" of several countries have developed internationally comparative modules, the ISSP (International Social Survey Programme). These are the topics of international modules:[29]

—1985 Role of government
—1986 Social networks and support systems
—1987 Social stratification
—1988 The family
—1989 World of work

All of the participating countries are of the highly modern variety, making comparisons at the level of countries less hazardous with respect to research artifacts.

Now that we are data-rich, the limiting condition in advancing knowledge is our poverty in not having a theory of society.

Notes

* From *International Sociology* 4, no. 2 (1989): 147–67, by permission of the author and Sage Publications. Copyright 1989 by the International Sociological Association.

† This paper takes off from a presentation at the President's session, convener Melvin Kohn, during the ASA meetings in Chicago, August 1987.

1. Of course, not all of the five projects discussed had the same impact, but some became landmarks of the comparative approach. See Szalai et al. (1972); Verba and Nie (1973); Jacobs and Jacobs (1971).

2. Of special importance here is the chapter by Szalai in Szalai and Petrella (1977: 49–93). A brilliant postmortem of the Jacobs and Jacobs project is Przeworski and Teune (1970).

3. Instructive especially for practical problems in comparative survey work. These are the proceedings of a conference by the Vienna Center of UNESCO, bringing together social scientists from Eastern and Western Europe.

4. This distinction and its implications were first introduced into the methodological discussion by Rokkan (1970).

5. This was the "Project Demoscopes" of which a final report was submitted to UNESCO in 1956. To the best of this author's knowledge, the volume circulated only in mimeographed form (Dodd and Nehnevajsa 1956).

6. Two essays of that period afford an instructive overview of the issues already debated and often clarified: Wiatr (1970/71, 1971); Scheuch (1968: 176–209).

7. The closest to this endeavor was Kurt Baschwitz's "Poll Index project 1947–1955" for WAPOR—which remained unpublished.

8. The organizational nuclei had changed as well to the then active International Social Science Council (ISSC), and later to some of the newly installed Research Committees of the International Sociological Association.

9. The attempts to explain the political developments in Japan and Germany attributed a deterministic quality to (presumably) specific and single traits of the respective countries. Thus, Ruth Benedict (1946) related the political development of Japan to socialization practices, by which a certain code of honor is installed which then prevents the development of a democratic culture. Using additional material from survey search, Jean Stoetzel (1954) later refutes this argument on empirical grounds. The more basic objection to the type of argumentation used by Ruth Benedict is the doubtfulness of relating political development to one factor (be it socialization or culture) as both a necessary and a sufficient condition. However, if one were to use "country" only as a necessary but not a sufficient condition (e.g., developments in Germany made possible by an X-tradition plus triggered by Y-circumstances) one would be forced to abandon the naive use of country as a black-box cause.

10. A more detailed criticism of the Almond and Verba report can be found in Scheuch (1967).

11. The surveys were carried out by the Gallup organization. The example is taken from Douglas A. Hibbs (1985: 63–74).

12. For a recent study based on the German equivalent of the General Social Survey, the *Allbus,* see ZUMA-Nachrichten (1987).

13. The taxonomy was in part inspired by Talcott Parsons's distinction between a social system, a cultural system, and the polity.

14. The official presentation of the program is George P. Murdock (1949). The most important methodologist of this approach is Raoull Naroll (1961, 1965). A discussion of the various proposals to neutralize the effects of diffusion, and consequently being able to treat "cultures" as statistically independent units, can be found in Thomas Schweizer (1978, especially Ch. 5).

15. On tourism as a vehicle of international diffusion, see Scheuch (1981, especially p. 1109 ff.). Also Eric Cohen (1979); T. Hamer (1979); K. Hudson (1972); H. Matthews (1978); C. G.

Varley (1978). A case in point for the increasing internationalization of tourism is Western Germany. Here, the share of vacations spent abroad rose from 15 percent in 1954, to 50 percent in 1967, and to 69 percent in 1987; cf. Franz Dundler (1988, Table 4).

16. The famous French cuisine of the late eighteenth century was an import from northern Italy; the Italian noodle was brought to that country by Marco Polo as an import from China. Consequently, an attempt to develop a sociology of food could not use countries of Western Europe in a naive way as a collective variable in explanation, and any sociology of food for that area would lead to grievous errors if it were to lack a historical dimension.

17. An analysis of this development—using data from five countries—will be found in Samuel H. Barnes and Max Kaase (1979).

18. The data and machine-readable code books are available to the social science community directly through the Zentralarchiv at the University of Cologne, or indirectly through data archives that are members of the International Federation of Data Archives (IFDO).

19. Apart from physical characteristics, for social characteristics that are global in nature Robert K. Merton has given a theoretical rationale; the "principle of emergence." For nation-states there are hardly any attempts to specify such "emergences."

20. Richard L. Merritt and Stein Rokkan (1966) is largely a detailed methodological critique of the black-box approach of the global studies as exemplified by the YPDH.

21. An elaborate and critical review of the Singer-Gurr school is Ekhard Zimmermann (1977).

22. The ideological commitment to something that in French is [characterized] as *tiers mondism* is quite evident in Wallerstein's follower Volker Bornschier (1980); also with Christopher Chase-Dunn (1985). When critics pointed to the obvious problem of all global studies, that countries in various parts of the world are different as social entities, and that the social problems of Africa were quite unlike those of Latin America, Bornschier maintained: the correlates of underdevelopment were the same the world over (1980: 170). For a criticism of the "school," and an empirical refutation of the

contention by Bornschier, see Carl Olivia (1987: 531); also Erich Weede (1986: 421–41).

23. Michael Hester points to this in his review (1975: 217–22). The lack of distinctiveness in using the term "world system" is criticized by Arthur L. Stinchcombe in a review (1982: 1389–95).

24. The labels subsequently used in the taxonomies are in part inferred by us, as Deutsch sometimes uses sentences instead of phrases for traits. This is especially true when he incorporates elements of Zeitgeist discussion. Specifically for the function of the state, the responsibility for a possible mislabeling would be mine.

25. The ISSP is a loose federation of organizations carrying out a variant of the General Social Survey of the United States. Each year a common module of fifteen minutes of questions is fielded internationally. Data and machine-readable code books are available from the archive of the ISSP, the Zentralarchiv at the University of Cologne.

26. For the methodological problems in computing an indicator for the size of the public sector and growth of governments, see Tom W. Rice (1986: 233–57). The historical dimension of differences between Western European developments is characterized in Peter Flora, Jens Alber, and Jürgen Kohl (1977: 707–22); Peter Flora and Arnold J. Heidenheimer (1981).

27. The emphasis on "culture" as causative for an explanandum was a characteristic, anyway, of the "Chicago School" since Robert Park, and to a large part of American sociology.

28. The distinction between the two designs "most similar systems" and "most different systems" in using countries was proposed by Adam Przeworski and Henry Teune (1970). The most similar design is the preferred design in specifying time-space coordinates for a nonuniversal relationship or factor. On implications in choosing and using countries in the comparative approach, see also Mattei Dogan and Dominique Pelassy (1984, Part 3, especially pp. 117–32). The considerations seem to be strongly related to John Stuart Mill's rules of evidence in causal attribution.

29. A large number of these surveys is already available through member institutes of the International Federation of Data Organizations (IFDO) in Germany at the Zentralarchiv of the University of Cologne.

References

Allardt, E. 1966. "Implications of Within-Nation Variations and Regional Imbalances for Cross-National Research," in Merritt, R. and Rokkan, S. (eds.), *Comparing Nations: The Use of Quantitative Data in Cross-National Research.* New Haven: Yale University Press.

Almasy, E., Balandier, A., and Delatte J. 1976. *Comparative Survey Analysis—An Annotated Bibliography 1967–1973.* Beverly Hills, Calif.: Sage.

Almond, G. and Verba, S. 1963. *The Civic Culture.* Princeton, NJ: Princeton University Press.

Banks, A. S. and Textor, R. B. 1963. *A Cross-Polity Survey.* Cambridge, Mass.: MIT Press.

Barnes, S. H. and Kaase, M. eds. 1979. *Political Action.* Beverly Hills, Calif.: Sage.

Benedict, R. 1946. *The Chrysanthemum and the Sword.* Boston, Mass.: Houghton Mifflin.

Bollen, K. 1983. "World System Position, Dependency, and Democracy." *American Sociological Review* 48: 468–78.

Bornschier, V. ed. 1980. *Multinationale Konzerne, Wirtschaftspolitik und nationale Entwicklung im Weltsystem.* Frankfurt/Main: Campus.

Bornschier, V. and Chase-Dunn, C. 1985. *Transnational Corporations and Underdevelopment.* New York: Praeger.

Buchanan, W. and Cantril, H. 1953. *How Nations See Each Other.* Urbana, Ill.: University of Illinois Press.

Cantril, H. 1965. *The Pattern of Human Concerns.* New Brunswick, NJ: Rutgers University Press.

Cantril, H. and Free, L. A. 1962. "Hopes and Fears for Self and Country." *American Behavioral Scientist* 6 (2) (Suppl.): 4–30.

Cantril, H. and Strunk, M. eds. 1951. *Public Opinion 1935–1946.* Princeton, N.J.: Princeton University Press.

Cohen, E. ed. 1979. "Sociology of Tourism." *Annals of Tourism Research* 6 (Special issue/Jan. & April).

Deutsch, K. W. 1985. "The Systems Theory Approach as a Basis for Comparative Research." *International Social Science Journal* 37.

Dodd, S. C. and Nehnevajsa, J. 1956. "Techniques for World Polls—A Survey of Journal Articles on Cross-Cultural Polling, 1925–1955." Mimeo. Paris.

Dogan, M. and Pelassy, D. 1984. *How to Compare Nations.* Chatham, N.J.: Chatham House.

Dundler, F. 1988. *Urlaubsreisen 1954–1987.* Starnberg: Studienkreis für Tourismus.

Flora, P., Alber, J., and Kohl, J. 1977. "Zur Entwicklung des westeuropäischen Wohlfahrtsstaates." *Politische Vierteljahresschrift* 4: 707–22.

Flora, P. and Heidenheimer, A. J. eds. 1981. *The Development of Welfare States in Europe and America.* New Brunswick, N.J.: Transaction Books.

Frey, F. W., Stephenson, P., and Archer Smith, K. 1969. *Survey Research on Comparative Social Change.* Cambridge, Mass.: MIT Press.

Glock, C. V. 1954. "The Comparative Study of Communication and Opinion Formation," in Schramm, W. (ed.), *The Process and Effects of Mass Communication.* Urbana, Ill.: University of Illinois Press.

Gurr, T. R. 1968. "A Causal Model of Civil Strife— A Comparative Analysis Using New Indices." *American Political Science Review* 62:1104–24.

Gurr, T. R. 1974. "The Neo-Alexandrians—A Review Essay on Data Handbooks in Political Science." *American Political Science Review* 68: 243–52.

Haman, M. T. and Carrol, G. R. 1981. "Dynamics of Formal Political Structure." *American Sociological Review* 46: 19–35.

Hamer, T. 1979. *Tourismus und Kulturwandel.* Starnberg: Studienkreis für Tourismus.

Heintz, P. 1969. *Ein soziologisches Paradigma der Entwicklung.* Stuttgart: Enke.

Heintz, P. 1973. *The Future of Development.* Bern: Huber.

Heintz, P. 1982. *Ungleiche Verteilung, Macht und Legitimität.* Dissenhofen: Rüegger.

Hester, M. 1975. Review. *Contemporary Sociology* 4: 217–22.

Hibbs, D. A. 1985. "Macro-Economic Performance, Policy and Electoral Politics in Industrial Democracies." *International Social Science Journal* 37 (103): 63–74.

Hudson, K. 1972. *Air Travel—A Social History.* Bath, England: Adam and Dart.

Hyman, H. 1964. "Research Design," in Ward, R. E. (ed.), *Studying Politics Abroad.* Boston: Little, Brown, pp. 153–88.

Jacobs, P. and Jacobs, B. 1971. *Values and the Active Community.* New York: Free Press.

Kohn, R. and White, K. L. eds. 1976. *Health Care.* Oxford: Oxford University Press.

Marsh, R. 1966. "Comparative Sociology 1950– 1963." *La sociologie contemporaine* 14 (2), special issue.

Matthews, H. 1978. *International Tourism—A Political and Social Analysis.* Cambridge, Mass.: Schenkmann.

Merritt, R. L. and Rokkan, S. eds. 1966. *Comparing Nations. The Use of Quantitative Data in Cross-National Research.* New Haven: Yale University Press.

Murdock, G. P. 1949 [1966]. *Social Structure.* New York: Free Press.

Naroll, R. 1961. "Two Solutions to Galton's Problem." *Philosophy of Science* 28: 15–39.

Naroll, R. 1965. "Galton's Problem: The Logic of Cross-Cultural Research." *Social Research* 32: 428–51.

Niessen, M., Peschar, J., and Kurilsky, C. eds. 1984. *International Vergleichende Sozialforschung.* Frankfurt: Campus Verlag.

Olivia, C. 1987. "Die Vernachlässigung der Bedeutung internationaler Regionen in Datenanalyse und Theoriebildung." *Kölner Zeitschrift für Soziologie und Sozialpsychologie* 39.

Przeworski, A. and Teune, H. 1970. *The Logic of Comparative Social Inquiry.* New York: Wiley.

Rice, T. W. 1986. "The Determinants of Western European Government Growth 1950–1980." *Comparative Political Studies* 19 (2): 233–57.

Rodnik, D. 1948. *Postwar Germans—An Anthropologist's Account.* New Haven: Yale University Press.

Rokkan, S. 1970. "Cross-Cultural, Cross-Societal, and Cross-National Research," in *Main Trends of Research in the Human and the Social Sciences.* Paris: UNESCO.

Rokkan, S., Verba, S., Viet, J., and Almasy, E. 1969. *Comparative Survey Analysis.* Paris: Mouton.

Russett, B. M., Alker, H. R., Deutsch, K. W., and Lasswell, H. D. 1964. *World Handbook of Political and Social Indicators.* New Haven: Yale University Press.

Sarapata, A. 1985. "Researchers' Habits and Orientations as Factors Which Condition International Cooperation in Research." *Science of Science* 5 (3/4): 157–82.

Schaffner, B. H. 1948. *Fatherland—A Study of Authoritarianism in the German Family.* New York: Columbia University Press.

Scheuch, E. K. 1967. "Society as Context in Cross-Cultural Comparisons." *Social Science Information* 6 (5), Oct. Republished in: *Guru Nanak Journal of Sociology* 1 (1–2).

Scheuch, E. K. 1968. "The Cross-Cultural Use of Sample Surveys: Problems of Comparability," in Rokkan, S. (ed.), *Comparative Research across Cultures and Nations.* Paris/The Hague: ISSC/Mouton, pp. 176–209.

Scheuch, E. K. 1969. "Ökologischer Fehlschluss," in Bernsdorf, W. (ed.), *Wörterbuch der Soziologie.* Stuttgart: Enke Verlag.

Scheuch, E. K. 1981. "Tourismus," in: *Die Psychologie des 20. Jahrhunderts.* Zurich: Kindler Verlag.

Scheuch, E. K. 1988a. *Arbeitszeit contra Freizeit? Die Einstellung der Bundesbürger im Laufe der Zeit.* Cologne: Arbeitgeberverband der Metallindustrie.

Scheuch, E. K. 1988b. "Continuity and Change in German Social Structure." *Historical Social Research* 13: 31–121.

Scheuch, E. K. Forthcoming. *Die Volkszählung 1987 als Gegenstand von Kontroversen.*

Schweizer, T. 1978. *Methodenprobleme des interkulturellen Vergleichs.* Cologne: Böhlau.

Singer, D. and Small, M. 1972. *The Wages of War 1816–1965.* New York: Wiley.

Stinchcombe, A. L. 1982. Review. *American Journal of Sociology* 87: 1389–95.

Stoetzel, J. 1954. *Jeunesse sans chrysanthéme ni sabre.* Paris: Plon-UNESCO.

Szalai, A. et al. eds. 1972. *The Use of Time.* The Hague: Mouton.

Szalai, A. and Petrella, R. eds. 1977. *Cross-National Comparative Survey Research.* Oxford: Pergamon Press.

Tylor, E. B. 1961 [1889]. "On a Method of Investigating the Development of Institutions Applied to Laws of Marriage and Descent," in Moore, F. W. (ed.), *Readings in Cross-Cultural Methodology.* New Haven: Yale University Press.

Varley, C. G. 1978. *Tourism in Fiji—Some Economic and Social Problems.* Cardiff: University of Wales Press.

Verba, S. 1965. "Comparative Political Culture," in Pie, L. and Verba, S. (eds.), *Political Culture and Political Development.* Princeton, N.J.: Princeton University Press.

Verba, S. and Nie, N. 1973. *Participation in America.* New York: Harper.

Wallace, M. D. and Singer, D. 1973. "Large Scale Violence in the Global System." Paper presented at the American Political Science Association meeting, Montreal.

Wallerstein, I. 1974 [1984]. *The Modern World System.* New York: Academic Press.

Wallerstein, I. 1980. *The Modern World System II.* New York: Academic Press.

Weede, E. 1986. "Rent-Seeking or Dependency as Explanations of Why Poor People Stay Poor." *International Sociology* 1: 421–41.

Wiatr, J. J. 1970/71. "Problems of Theory and Methodology in Cross-National Comparative Research," in *The Polish Round Table* IV; also 1971, in *Indian Journal of Politics* No. 1.

Zimmermann, E. 1977. *Soziologie der politischen Gewalt.* Stuttgart: Enke Verlag.

ZUMA-Nachrichten 1987. "Wie stabil sind Umfragedaten?" No. 20, May.

CHAPTER SIX

The Distinctiveness of Comparative Social Science*

Charles C. Ragin

"Thinking without comparison is unthinkable. And, in the absence of comparison, so is all scientific thought and scientific research" (Swanson 1971: 145). Most social scientists today would agree with this observation, although some might be tempted to substitute the phrase *variables and relationships* for the word *comparison*. Virtually all empirical social research involves comparison of some sort. Researchers compare cases to each other; they use statistical methods to construct (and adjust) quantitative comparisons; they compare cases to theoretically derived pure cases; and they compare cases' values on relevant variables to average values in order to assess covariation. Comparison provides a basis for making statements about empirical regularities and for evaluating and interpreting cases relative to substantive and theoretical criteria. In this broad sense, comparison is central to empirical social science as it is practiced today. Lieberson (1985: 44) states simply that social research, "in one form or other, is *comparative* research."

While virtually all social scientific methods are comparative in this broad sense, in social science the term *comparative method* typically is used in a narrow sense to refer to a specific kind of comparison—the comparison of large macrosocial units. In fact, the comparative method traditionally has been treated as the core method of comparative social science, the branch of social science concerned with cross-societal differences and similarities (Easthope 1974). Despite this tradition, there is substantial disagreement today concerning the distinctiveness of comparative social science in general and the comparative method in particular. Several comparativists have objected to the idea that comparative social science is distinctive in any important respects from social science in general (Grimshaw 1973: 18).

Smelser (1976: 2–3), for example, claims that comparative social scientific inquiry is not a "species of inquiry independent from the remainder of social scientific inquiry" and that "the analysis of phenomena in evidently dissimilar units (especially different societies or cultures) should have no methodological problem unique to itself." According to Smelser (1976: 5), this continuity between comparative and noncomparative work exists because their respective goals are identical—to explain social phenomena by establishing controls over the conditions and causes of variation. (See also Armer 1973: 50). Any technique that furthers the goal of explaining variation, according to this reasoning, is a comparative method. This includes virtually all analytic methods used by social scientists (see Bailey 1982).

This position, that there is nothing truly distinctive about comparative social science and that virtually all social scientific methods are comparative methods, is sound, and it is attractive because it suggests that social science subdisciplines are united by their methods. The argument is favored by many comparativists, in fact, because the emphasis on continuities between comparative and noncomparative work supports the idea that comparative social science is as scientific as its siblings. This position overlooks the fact, however, that there are important differences between the *orientations* of most comparativists and most noncomparativists and these differences have important methodological consequences. While it is true that the logic of social science is continuous from one subdiscipline to another, the peculiarities of comparative social science make it an ideal setting for an examination of key issues in methodology. In fact, I argue that a lot can be gained from exaggerating the distinctive aspects of comparative work and that these lessons can be applied to other social science subdisciplines as well.

The most distinctive aspect of comparative social science is the wide gulf between qualitative and quantitative work. It is wider in comparative social science than in perhaps any other social science subdiscipline. In part this is because its qualitative tradition is dominant, the opposite of the situation in most other fields. Over the last twenty years, some of the most celebrated works in the social sciences (from Moore's *Social Origins of Dictatorship and Democracy* to Wallerstein's *Modern World System*) have come out of this tradition, making it appear continuous with the grand theorizing of such classical scholars as Durkheim and Weber.

More fundamental to the gulf, however, is the fact that several other divisions coincide with the qualitative/quantitative split in comparative social science and reinforce it. Qualitative researchers tend to look at cases as wholes, and they compare whole cases with each other. While cases may be analyzed in terms of variables (for example, the presence or absence of a certain institution might be an important variable), cases are viewed as configurations—as combinations of characteristics. Comparison in the qualitative tradition thus involves comparing configurations. This holism contradicts the radically analytic approach of most quantitative work.

Not only is the qualitative tradition oriented toward cases as wholes, as configurations, but it also tends to be historically interpretive. The term *interpretive* is used in a

restricted sense here. Often, the term is used to describe a type of social science that is only remotely empirical and concerned primarily with problems of meaning or hermeneutics. In this book, interpretive work is treated as a type of empirical social science: historically oriented interpretive work attempts to account for specific historical outcomes or sets of comparable outcomes or processes chosen for study because of their significance for current institutional arrangements or for social life in general. Typically, such work seeks to make sense out of different cases by piecing evidence together in a manner sensitive to chronology and by offering limited historical generalizations that are both objectively possible and cognizant of enabling conditions and limiting means—of context. This definition of interpretive work leans heavily on Weber (1949, 1975, 1977) but makes more allowance for the possibility of historical generalization based on examination of comparable cases. In this chapter I discuss these distinctive characteristics and sketch the implications of these features for comparative methodology. I begin by delineating the field.

The Boundaries and Goals of Comparative Social Science

There have been several attempts to delineate the boundaries of comparative social science. Yet, there is still little agreement today concerning its domain. Most attempts to delineate the field have emphasized its special data or its special types of data. For reasons detailed below, this is a poor starting point. I argue that comparative social science is better defined by its distinctive goals.

It is common to define comparative research as research that uses comparable data from at least two societies. This definition emphasizes the fact that the data of comparative social science are cross-societal. (See Andreski 1965: 66; Armer, 1973: 49.) While this is an acceptable working definition of comparative social science, most comparativists would find this definition too restrictive. It excludes, for example, comparatively oriented case studies. Tocqueville's *Democracy in America* is excluded, as is Durkheim's *Elementary Forms of the Religious Life*. Many area specialists are thoroughly comparative because they implicitly compare their chosen case to their own country or to an imaginary but theoretically decisive ideal-typic case. Thus, to define comparative social science in terms of its special data is a misleadingly concrete way to delineate its boundaries.

Others have attempted to differentiate comparative social science by emphasizing its multilevel character (as in Rokkan 1966: 19–20). According to Przeworski and Teune (1970: 50–51), comparative work proceeds at two levels simultaneously—at the level of systems (or macrosocial level) and at the within-system level. According to their argument, any analysis that is based only on macrosocial similarities and differences is not truly comparative, even if this analysis includes an examination of aggregations of within-system characteristics. For example, if an investigator uses system-level variables (such as GNP per capita) to explain variation in a dependent variable based on aggregations of individual-level data within each system (such as literacy rates), the study would not qualify as a comparative study according to Przeworski and Teune. Ideally, system-level variables should be used to explain variation across systems in within-system relationships.

Alford's (1963) study of international variation in class voting qualifies as a comparative study by these criteria because he uses system-level variables (degree of industrialization and urbanization) to explain differences among countries in within-system relationships (the strength of the relationship between social class and party support). Walton's (1984) study of national revolts in the Third World also conforms to this definition of comparative work. He uses degree of incorporation into the world economy, a system-level variable, to account for variation in the degree to which popular

protests and state reactions to protest contributed to the coalescence of revolutionary situations in six countries (see especially Walton 1984: 188–97). Few studies traditionally thought of as comparative, however, conform to these strictures. Comparatively oriented case studies are excluded, as are quantitative cross-national studies that use only aggregate, national-level data. (Note that quantitative cross-national studies focus directly on cross-societal similarities and differences.) Przeworski and Teune's definition of comparative inquiry as multilevel research is much more restrictive than even the first definition considered here.

Both definitions are inadequate. Yet they suggest a tentative solution to the problem of delineating comparative work. One level that invariably plays a big part in definitions of comparative work is the macrosocial level. It appears in the first definition offered above in its emphasis on data from two societies and in the second's emphasis on multilevel analyses, with one level the macrosocial. The boundaries of comparative social science, therefore, must be coterminous with a specific usage of macrosocial units.

It is not as a data category that macrosocial units are important to comparativists, but as a metatheoretical category. What distinguishes comparative social science is its use of attributes of macrosocial units in explanatory statements. This special usage is intimately linked to the twin goals of comparative social science—both to explain and to interpret macrosocial variation.

The importance of macrosocial units to explanation in comparative social science is best understood by example. Consider an investigation which concludes that a strong relationship between social class and party preference exists in Great Britain because "Great Britain is an industrial society." This conclusion concretizes the term *society* by providing an example (Great Britain) and by implying that there are other societies, some of which are industrial and some of which are not. If the investigator had concluded instead that the relationship exists because "citizens vote their pocketbooks" or because "the relations of production shape political consciousness," then he or she would have avoided concretizing any macrosocial unit and thereby would have avoided engaging in comparative social science.

This direct, empirical implementation of abstract, macrosocial units is a metatheoretical act, and it separates comparativists from noncomparativists. In order to compare societies or any other macrosocial unit, the comparativist must identify them by name. The comparativist thus assumes, at least implicitly, that macrosocial units are real and then defines them, sometimes by default, in the course of research. The fact that the difference between comparativists and noncomparativists is a metatheoretical difference based on the special goals of comparative social science has been obscured by the tendency of all social scientists to claim that they study societies or that social science is the study of society. For the noncomparativists, however, macrosocial units tend to remain abstractions. Noncomparativists can assure themselves that the patterns and processes they study exist in a society; the concept need not be operationalized explicitly. For the comparativists, however, macrosocial units impinge on their work in a fundamental manner.

Rarely are these large, encompassing units defined. (Parsons 1977 and Marsh 1967 are exceptions.) In his discussion of the distinctiveness of comparative work, for example, Grimshaw (1973: 4) states, "I will defer discussion of what constitutes a [macrosocial] system." This reluctance is not uncommon; most comparativists are more interested in making comparisons than in defining the objects of their comparisons (see Andreski 1965: 66). The fact remains, however, that comparativists compare macrosocial units; they must be operationalized in the course of comparative work.

At a very general level, comparativists are interested in identifying the similarities and differences among macrosocial units. This knowledge provides the key to understanding, explaining, and interpreting diverse historical outcomes and processes and their significance for current institutional arrangements. Cross-societal similarities and differences for many social scientists constitute the most significant feature of the social landscape, and, consequently, these researchers have an unmistakable preference for explanations that cite macrosocial phenomena. This tendency is reinforced by the fact that the goals of comparative social scientists typically extend beyond an interest in simply cataloging and explaining cross-societal similarities and differences. Most comparativists, especially those who are qualitatively oriented, also seek to interpret specific experiences and trajectories of specific countries (or categories of countries). That is, they are interested in the cases themselves, their different historical experiences in particular, not simply in relations between variables characterizing broad categories of cases. This interest reinforces the tendency to use macrosocial attributes in explanatory statements.

The decision to study macrosocial variation and to use explanatory statements citing macrosocial properties is, of course, a conscious choice, shaped in large part by the enduring reality of countries, nations, states, and other large (and imposing) political entities. As long as social scientists continue to be influenced by their social and historical contexts and continue to try to interpret them, they will use macrosocial attributes in their explanations of social phenomena. It is possible to imagine a social science devoid of explanatory statements citing macrosocial phenomena. A totally psychologized social science, for example, might attempt to disavow such explanations. It is unlikely, however, that social scientists will lose interest in interpreting national and international events and processes and thereby divorce themselves from significant features of their social contexts. (In any event, to do so would be to deny the social origins and bases of social science.) Thus, macrosocial units are central to the practice of comparative social science because they are an essential ingredient of the explanations comparativists offer.

A Note of Caution on Units of Analysis

It would be wrong at this point to conclude simply that comparativists differ from non-comparativists in their "chosen unit of analysis." The example supplied previously suggests that any data unit can be used in comparative research. All that matters is how the results of research are understood. The fact that the explanations of comparative social science tend to be cross-societal and cite macrosocial phenomena, however, implies that the question of units is relevant.

Very little continuity exists, however, in discussions of units of analysis offered by comparatively oriented social scientists. An important source of this lack of continuity is the simple fact that the term *unit of analysis* is used to describe two very distinct metatheoretical constructs. Sometimes unit of analysis is used in reference to data categories. In a quantitative cross-national study of economic dependency and economic development, for example, an investigator might state that the unit of analysis is the nation-state because the data are collected at that level. At other times, however, the term *unit of analysis* is used in reference to theoretical categories. Wiener (1976), for example, in a review of Barrington Moore's *Social Origins of Dictatorship and Democracy* (1966), states that Moore's unit of analysis is "class." Wallerstein (1974, 1979, 1980, 1984) argues in various works that there is only one valid unit of analysis in comparative social science: the "world system." Upon closer examination, however, one finds that Moore's cases are different countries and Wallerstein's discussion of the modern world system is rife with references to nation-states and comparisons of, for example, core countries and peripheral countries.

The fact that the term *unit of analysis* has been used in reference to both data categories

and theoretical categories has created a great deal of confusion in the field of comparative social science. Some followers of Wallerstein, for example, have attacked those who use the nation-state as a unit of analysis in the data category sense, arguing that this practice violates world-systems theory and results in meaningless tests of its propositions. (See, for example, Bach 1977.) Other researchers have attempted to use the modern world system as a unit of analysis in the data category sense and have examined cycles and trends in the world economy as a whole. (See, for example, Bergesen 1980 and McGowan 1985.) It is clear from Wallerstein's discussion and from his actual analyses of the world system, however, that his argument is that the world system is the only valid explanatory unit, not the only valid data unit.

This tension between the two meanings of unit of analysis has bedeviled the comparative social science literature at least since the early 1960s. Issues associated with the aggregation problem have compounded the terminological difficulties and confusion. Allardt (1966: 339–41), for example, attempted to draw a distinction between "data units" and "analytical units," arguing that the latter are more theoretically relevant. In a similar vein, Scheuch (1966: 164) argued that comparativists should distinguish between "units of observation" (see also Walton 1973: 176) and "units of inference." In an early attempt to formulate a methodological position, Hopkins and Wallerstein (1970: 183) contrasted "research sites" and "theoretical units." Several researchers attempted to clarify the situation by limiting their comments to "units of comparison" (Eisenstadt 1966: 86; Etzioni and Dubow 1970: 7; Czudnowski 1976: 27). Finally, Przeworski and Teune (1970: 8, 49–50) attempted to distinguish between "levels of observation" and "levels of analysis."

Most of these discussions were stimulated by the ambiguity associated with the term *unit of analysis*. For most noncomparative social scientists, the term presents no special problems. Their analyses and their explanations typically proceed at one level, the individual or organizational level. This is rarely the case in comparative social science, where the analysis often proceeds at one level (perhaps the individual level, as in the preceding example) and the explanation is couched at another level (usually the macrosocial level). Of course, this duality exists in other types of social science, and the methodological issues raised here apply to these areas as well. The duality is most pronounced, however, in comparative social science, which is one of the features that makes it an ideal arena for methodological discussion.

To clarify the unit of analysis question in comparative social science, it is necessary to distinguish between observational units and explanatory units. This distinction follows my discussion concerning the two meanings of unit of analysis—as a data category and as a theoretical category. *Observational unit* refers to the unit used in data collection and data analysis; *explanatory unit* refers to the unit that is used to account for the pattern of results obtained. In the class voting example mentioned above, the observational unit is the individual (the relationship is based on individual-level data) and the explanatory unit is societal.

Methodological Consequences

The explanation that there is a strong relationship between social class and party preference in a sample of British voters because "Great Britain is an industrial society" implies that societies can be identified, that they can be classified as either industrial or not industrial, and that in industrial societies there is a strong relationship between social class and party preference, while in nonindustrial societies there is no such relationship. Because societies are (at least apparently) identifiable, an investigator conceivably could draw up a list of them, classify them as industrial and not industrial (or at least measure the degree to which each society is industrial), and then examine the degree to which the more industrial societies agree in manifesting a consistent relationship between social class and party choice and also the degree to which the less industrial societies agree in manifesting a weaker relationship. If these two patterns of agreement can be established, then the general statement (that in industrial societies there is a strong relationship between social class and party preference) used to explain the particular instance (the relationship observed in Great Britain) is supported.

Unfortunately, social scientific investigation is rarely this simple. There are many practical problems associated with establishing cross-societal demonstrations such as the one described above. Most of these practical problems concern the comparability of relatively dissimilar societies. This concern for comparability derives ultimately from the fact that the cases (say, countries) which comparativists study have known histories and identities. They are not anonymous, disembodied observations. In the preceding investigation, for instance, a researcher familiar with the relevant cases might have doubts about the cross-societal comparability of measures of class positions or about the identification of parties with social classes. An investigator might also have doubts about the classification of societies as industrial and not industrial or about ordinal and interval measures of degree of industrialization. These measurement problems are very important, and they have absorbed the attention of comparative social scientists for some time. In fact, many discussions of comparative methods have concerned these issues almost exclusively.

At a more basic level, it is difficult to evaluate explanatory statements of comparative social science because the number of relevant units available for such assessments is often limited by empirical constraints. Even the investigator who claims that he or she is interested in all societies, and defines societies as all contemporary nation-states, encounters serious statistical problems if a quantitative analysis of these cases is attempted. A seemingly large set of more than one hundred nation-states can be reduced by half if there are problems with missing data. Often, the remaining cases are not representative of the original hundred-plus nation-states, much less of all societies (or all macrosocial systems). This problem is apparent in the hypothetical research described above. There are many societies, both industrial and nonindustrial, that are not democratic. Thus, any attempt to assess the strength of the relationship between social class and party preference in these countries would be questionable, if not misguided. Furthermore, the definition of democratic society is problematic and ideologically charged.

Theoretical strictures also may reduce the number of relevant cases. In the hypothetical analysis of more and less industrial societies discussed above, for example, it is possible that the general statement (that social class shapes party preference only in industrial societies) is theoretically meaningful only when applied to democratic countries with a feudal past. If this were the case, then the investigator would first draw up a list of democracies with a feudal past and then distinguish between more and less industrial countries within this set. Generally speaking, the greater the theoretical or empirical specificity, the smaller the number of cases relevant to the investigation. The smaller the number of relevant cases, the greater the likelihood that the investigator will find it difficult to evaluate an explanatory statement in a way that conforms to the standards of mainstream social science, especially its quantitative branch.

Sometimes there are more explanations of a certain phenomenon than there are examples of it because these strictures reduce the number of relevant cases to a mere handful. In such investigations it is impossible to adjudicate among competing explanations. In the language of the statistical method, the use of societies in explanatory statements often presents serious degrees-of-freedom problems, for the number of relevant explanatory variables may far exceed the number of cases. From the perspective of mainstream social science, therefore, com-

parative social science is severely deficient in the opportunities it presents for testing theory.

But many comparativists, especially those who are qualitatively oriented, are not often involved in "testing" theories per se. Rather, they *apply* theory to cases in order to interpret them. Because the explanatory statements of comparative social science cite attributes of macrosocial units, objects with known identities and histories figure prominently in the conduct of inquiry. Thus, it is very difficult to treat these units simply as the undifferentiated raw material of empirical social science. There is an ever present pressure to take into account and to explain the particularity of specific cases, which in turn requires the use of case-oriented methods sensitive to time, place, agency, and process.

Recall also that one of the distinctive goals of comparative social science is to interpret significant historical outcomes. From the perspective of mainstream social science this goal imposes very restrictive boundaries on social research, dramatically reducing the number of relevant observations. In essence, when a comparativist interprets significant historical outcomes, he or she selects extreme values on a more general dependent variable (for instance, social revolution is an extreme value on a general measure of social turmoil) and studies the cases with these extreme values exclusively. This practice is justified by the qualitative break that exists between extreme values and lesser values on what might be viewed by some as a continuum and also by the cultural importance and historical significance of these extreme cases. Thus, the problem of having too few societies on which to test theory is compounded by the fact that the interests and goals of comparative social science (and scientists) often dictate the design of studies with a small number of cases—too few to permit the application of any technique of statistical comparison.

Most comparativists, in fact, are interested in questions that are limited, substantively and historically. The questions they ask usually are much more circumscribed than the abstract research question posed above concerning the effect of industrialization on the strength of the relationship between social class and party preference. In the typical comparative study, only a small set of cases may provide the basis for empirical generalization. Instances of social revolution, at least as defined by Skocpol (1979), for example, are few. There are also only a few instances of successful antineocolonial revolt. There are more cases of dependent industrial development in the Third World today, but not so many that they can be studied easily with quantitative cross-national techniques. Yet these and related topics demand the attention of comparative social scientists. The fact that there are few relevant instances of each phenomenon and that these instances have known identities and histories (that is, known particularity) has a powerful impact on the character of the research process.

Enter the Comparative Method

As the number of relevant observations decreases, the possibility of subjecting arguments to rigorous statistical testing diminishes. Other methods must be used. Smelser (1976: 157) argues that the method of "systematic comparative illustration" (a method he portrays as a crude approximation of more sophisticated statistical methods) must be used when the number of relevant cases is small: "This method is most often required in the comparative analysis of national units or cultures." Smelser provides as one example of the method of systematic comparative illustration Tocqueville's three-way comparison of American, French, and English customs. Tocqueville argued simply that the conditions these collectivities share (such as language in the case of the English and the Americans) could not be used to explain their differences and that differences could not be used to explain similarities (Smelser 1976: 158). In general, the technique of systematic comparative illustration involves applications of Mill's (1843) method of agreement and his indirect method of difference.

In an earlier work, Smelser (1973) called this systematic analysis of similarities and differences the comparative method and contrasted it with the statistical method. In his more recent *Comparative Methods in the Social Sciences* (1976), however, Smelser argues that, broadly speaking, virtually all social scientific methods are comparative and that the method of systematic comparative illustration is inferior to the statistical method as a comparative method. It is inferior, according to Smelser, because it must be used when the number of relevant cases is small and the possibility of establishing systematic control over the sources of variation in social phenomena is reduced. The possibilities for social scientific generalization are reduced.

In fact, the method that Smelser calls "the method of systematic comparative illustration" is what social scientists traditionally have called the comparative method. It forms the core of the case-oriented strategy and is quite different from correlational methods which form the core of the variable-oriented strategy. It is proper to call this method the comparative method because it follows directly from asking questions about empirically defined, historically concrete, large-scale social entities and processes—the kinds of questions that comparative social scientists tend to ask. Questions that necessarily lead to detailed analyses of relatively small numbers of cases are asked in other types of social science, as well, but this type of investigation is most common in comparative social science.

Once it is admitted that the comparative method derives its distinctiveness from the special goals of comparative social science and that it is most often a direct consequence of engaging in this enterprise, the special features of the comparative method can be delineated.

The Logic of the Comparative Method

"It is surprising, for all that has been said about the value of comparison, that a rigorous comparative methodology has not emerged. The reason for this lack may be the great difficulties that a rigorous comparative methodology would impose" (Porter 1970: 144). Smelser might argue that a rigorous comparative method is a contradiction in terms because, by definition, the comparative method is used only when the number of relevant cases is too small to allow the investigator to establish statistical control over the conditions and causes of variation in social phenomena. While the number of cases relevant to an analysis certainly imposes constraints on rigor, often it is the combinatorial nature of the explanations of comparative social science and the holistic character of the comparative method that militate against this kind of rigor.

Most comparativists, especially those who are qualitatively oriented, are interested in specific historical sequences or outcomes and their causes across a set of similar cases. Historical outcomes often require complex, combinatorial explanations, and such explanations are very difficult to prove in a manner consistent with the norms of mainstream quantitative social science. When causal arguments are combinatorial, it is not the number of cases but their *limited variety* that imposes constraints on rigor.

When qualitatively oriented comparativists compare, they study how different conditions or causes fit together in one setting and contrast that with how they fit together in another setting (or with how they might fit together in some ideal-typic setting). That is, they tend to analyze each observational entity as an interpretable combination of parts—as a whole. Thus, the explanations of comparative social science typically cite convergent causal conditions, causes that fit together or combine in a certain manner.

A simple example illustrates this practice. A comparativist might argue that social class and party preference are strongly related to each other in a sample of British voters not *simply* because Great Britain is an industrial society but also because it has a long history of class mobilization and conflict which coincided with the development of its current political system. In effect, this explanation cites three convergent conditions: (1) a history of class struggle (2) coinciding with polity maturation (3) in a country that has been industrialized for a long time. It is their combined effect that explains the enduring individual-level relationship between social class and party preference. The argument would be that this configuration of causes explains the observed association.

To evaluate this argument rigorously, it would be necessary to find instances (among democratic countries) of all the logically possible combinations of the three conditions and then to assess the relationship between social class and party preference in each combination. Each logically possible combination should be examined because the argument is that it is the coincidence of these three conditions that explains the association. If the expected relationship is obtained only when these three conditions coincide, and if all instances of such concurrence manifest the predicted relationship, then the general statement would be supported.

It would be difficult to evaluate this argument because instances of all logically possible combinations of conditions are not available. A completely rigorous assessment would require the identification of democratic countries with eight different combinations of characteristics. (There are eight different logically possible combinations of three dichotomies.) Each different combination is conceived as a different situation, a different totality, not simply as a different collection of values on three variables. Some of these combinations, however, while logically possible, do not exist. At best, the investigator would be able to examine the combinations that do exist and assess the relationship between class and party within each of these configurations.

While this simple example shows the limitations placed on the comparative method as a consequence of its holistic nature, it also illustrates key features of the method. As already noted, the comparative method attends to configurations of conditions; it is used to determine the different combinations of conditions associated with specific outcomes or processes. Moreover, the comparative method is based on "logical methods" (see Gee 1950); it uses two of Mill's methods of inductive inquiry: the method of agreement and the indirect method of difference (Mill 1843; see also Skocpol 1979: 36; Skocpol and Somers 1980; Zelditch 1971; Ragin and Zaret 1983). These methods use all available and pertinent data concerning the preconditions of a specific outcome and, by examining the similarities and differences among relevant instances, elucidate its causes.

Because the comparative method has this character, statistical criteria are less important to this approach. This means that the comparative method does not work with samples or populations but with all relevant instances of the phenomenon of interest and, further, that the explanations which result from applications of the comparative method are not conceived in probabilistic terms because every instance of a phenomenon is examined and accounted for if possible. Consequently, the comparative method is relatively insensitive to the relative frequency of different types of cases. For example, if there are many instances of a certain phenomenon and two combinations of conditions that produce it, both combinations are considered equally valid accounts of the phenomenon regardless of their relative frequency. If one is relatively infrequent, an application of the statistical method to this same set of data might obscure its existence. The comparative method would consider both configurations of conditions relevant since both result in the phenomenon of interest.

Smelser's argument implies that the comparative method is inferior to the statistical method. Is it? The comparative method is superior to the statistical method in several important respects. First, the statistical method is not combinatorial; each relevant condition typically is examined in a piecemeal manner. Thus, for example, the statistical method can answer the question: what is the effect of having a history of class struggle net of the effect of industrialization? But it is difficult to use this method to address questions concerning the consequences of different combinations of conditions (that is, to investigate situations as wholes). To investigate combinations of conditions, the user of the statistical method must examine statistical interactions. The examination of a large number of statistical interactions in variable-oriented studies is complicated by collinearity and by problems with scarce degrees of freedom, especially in comparative research where the number of relevant cases is often small. An exhaustive examination of different combinations of seven preconditions, for example, would require a statistical analysis of the effects of more than one hundred different interaction terms.

Second, applications of the comparative method produce explanations that account for every instance of a certain phenomenon. True, these explanations may contain interpretive accounts of the particularity of one or more deviating cases, but at least the comparative method automatically highlights these irregularities and requires the investigator to propose explanations of them. This concern makes the comparative method more consistent with the goal of interpreting specific cases and addressing historical specificity. This feature of the comparative method also makes it especially well suited for the task of building new theories and synthesizing existing theories.

Third, the comparative method does not require the investigator to pretend that he or she has a sample of societies drawn from a particular population so that tests of statistical significance can be used. The boundaries of a comparative examination are set by the investigator (see Walton 1973: 174–75); they are not coterminous with the boundaries of an arbitrarily defined or (more typically) undefined population of societies or points in time or events in societies.

Finally, the comparative method forces the investigator to become familiar with the cases relevant to the analysis. To make meaningful comparisons of cases as wholes, the investigator must examine each case directly and compare each case with all other relevant cases. The statistical method, by contrast, requires the investigator only to disaggregate cases into variables and then to examine relationships among variables, not to conduct a direct examination of the differences and similarities among cases considered as configurations of characteristics (that is, as meaningful wholes).

In short, the comparative method is not a bastard cousin of the statistical method. It is qualitatively different from the statistical method, and it is uniquely suited to the kinds of questions that many comparativists ask.

The Qualitative/Quantitative Split in Comparative Social Science

As outlined here, the comparative method is essentially a case-oriented strategy of comparativist research. The focus is on comparing cases, and cases are examined as wholes—as combinations of characteristics (Ragin and Zaret 1983). This orientation distinguishes it from mainstream statistical methodology. Of course, not all social scientists who call themselves comparativists use the comparative method as presented in this chapter. Many use a variable-oriented strategy which conforms to the methodological norms of mainstream social science with its emphasis on variables and their interrelationships. The usual goal of variable-oriented investigations is to produce generalizations about relationships among variables, not to understand or interpret specific historical outcomes in a small number of cases or in an empirically defined set of cases. Combined strategies also exist, but close examination usually shows that studies using combined strategies tend to fall into one of the two camps. Examples of combined strategies include variable-oriented analyses supple-

mented with case studies (as in Paige 1975 and Stephens 1979) and case studies reinforced with quantitative analyses (as in Shorter and Tilly 1974).

The dichotomized nature of comparative work (case-oriented comparative study versus variable-oriented analysis) makes it an ideal setting for examining methodological issues—especially the gap between qualitative and quantitative orientations and how this gap might be bridged. Comparative work is the one branch of contemporary American social science that accords high status to the qualitative analysis of a small number of cases. In comparative social science, the variable-oriented strategy poses a challenge to traditional qualitative approaches. In other social science research areas, by contrast, the opposite is true. Thus, in comparative social science there is an established case-oriented tradition that can be directly contrasted with a growing variable-oriented tradition.

In comparative social science the qualitative tradition is strong because other methodological divisions coincide with the qualitative/quantitative split. As the preceding discussion of the logic of the comparative method shows, qualitative researchers tend to ask historically and empirically defined questions and typically answer these questions historically, in terms of origins. Thus, qualitative comparative researchers are both holistic and interpretive in their approach to comparative materials.

The split between qualitative and quantitative work in comparative social science is further aggravated by the fact that all comparativists are concerned with questions of direct relevance to macrosocial units with meaningful social identities (nation-states, for example). These identities are crucial to qualitative researchers, whereas they sometimes confound the work of those who do quantitative cross-national work. (For example, Kuwait is always a troublesome outlier in studies of economic dependence and development.) This aspect of comparative social science magnifies its value as an arena for addressing methodological issues. Contrasts between research strategies are exaggerated and the (often political) implications of methodological decisions are readily apparent.

Development, for example, is an outcome that has attracted the attention of social scientists for some time. Yet it can be defined in a variety of ways. To define it in terms of gross national product per capita makes Western Europe, the United States, and a few oil-rich countries appear to be the most developed. Defining it in terms of satisfaction of basic human needs, however, shuffles the development hierarchy and Eastern European countries occupy more of the prominent positions. Alternatively, development can be defined politically and qualitatively in terms of the emergence of a national political culture supported by a stable central government which, in turn, is acknowledged as legitimate by its subjects. This third definition reshuffles the hierarchy (Mexico, for example, is among the more advanced countries according to this definition) and suggests a complete rethinking of issues surrounding the causes of development.

Thus, methodological decisions that might seem minor in other research areas have unavoidably political implications in comparative work. These implications are especially salient to researchers who do qualitative work.

Note

* From *The Comparative Method: Moving beyond Qualitative and Quantitative Strategies,* by Charles C. Ragin (Berkeley: University of California Press, 1987), 1–18, 173–79, by permission of the author and the University of California Press. Copyright 1987 by the Regents of the University of California.

References

Alford, Robert. 1963. *Party and Society.* Chicago: University of Chicago Press.

Allardt, Erik. 1966. "Implications of Within-Nation Variations and Regional Imbalances for Cross-National Research." In *Comparing Nations,* ed. Richard Merritt and Stein Rokkan, 333–48. New Haven: Yale University Press.

———. 1979. *Implications of the Ethnic Revival in Modern Industrialized Society.* Helsinki: Societas Scientarium Fennica.

Andreski, Stanislav. 1965. *The Uses of Comparative Sociology.* Berkeley: University of California Press.

Armer, Michael. 1973. "Methodological Problems and Possibilities in Comparative Research." In *Comparative Social Research,* ed. Michael Armer and Allen Grimshaw, 49–79. New York: Wiley.

Armer, Michael, and Allan Schnaiberg. 1972. "Measuring Individual Modernity: A Near Myth." *American Sociological Review* 37: 301–16.

Bach, Robert. 1977. "Methods of Analysis in the Study of the World-Economy: A Comment on Rubinson." *American Sociological Review* 42: 811–14.

Bailey, Kenneth. 1982. *Methods of Social Research.* New York: Free Press.

Barton, Allen. 1955. "The Concept of Property Space in Social Research." In *The Language of Social Research,* ed. Paul Lazarsfeld and Morris Rosenberg, 40–53. New York: Free Press.

Bendix, Reinhard. 1977. *Nation-Building and Citizenship: Studies of Our Changing Social Order.* Berkeley: University of California Press.

———. 1978. *Kings or People: Power and the Mandate to Rule.* Berkeley: University of California Press.

Bergesen, Albert. 1980. "From Utilitarianism to the World-System: The Shift from the Individual to the World as a Whole as the Primordial Unit of Analysis." In *Studies of the Modern World-System,* ed. Albert Bergesen, 1–12. New York: Academic Press.

Bonnell, Victoria. 1980. "The Uses of Theory, Concepts and Comparison in Historical Sociology." *Comparative Studies in Society and History* 22: 156–73.

Bornschier, Volker, Christopher Chase-Dunn, and Richard Rubinson. 1978. "Cross-National Evidence of the Effects of Foreign Investment and Aid on Economic Growth and Inequality: A Survey of Findings and a Reanalysis." *American Journal of Sociology* 84: 651–83.

Bradshaw, York. 1985. "Dependent Development in Black Africa: A Cross-National Study." *American Sociological Review* 50: 195–207.

Burawoy, Michael. 1979. *Manufacturing Consent: Changes in the Labor Process under Monopoly Capitalism*. Chicago: University of Chicago Press.

Butler, David, and Donald Stokes. 1969. *Political Change in Britain*. New York: St. Martin's Press.

Campbell, Donald, and Julian Stanley. 1966. *Experimental and Quasi-Experimental Designs for Research*. Chicago: Rand McNally.

Cardoso, Fernando Henrique. 1973. "Associated-Dependent Development: Theoretical and Practical Implications." In *Authoritarian Brazil: Origins, Policies, and Future,* ed. Alfred Stepan, 142–76. New Haven: Yale University Press.

———. 1977. "The Consumption of Dependency Theory in the United States." *Latin American Research Review* 12: 7–24.

Chase-Dunn, Christopher, Aaron Pallas, and Jeffrey Kentor. 1982. "Old and New Research Designs for Studying the World-System: A Research Note." *Comparative Political Studies* 15: 341–56.

Chirot, Daniel, and Charles Ragin. 1975. "The Market, Tradition, and Peasant Revolt." *American Sociological Review* 40: 428–44.

Cohen, Lawrence, and James Kluegel. 1978. "Determinants of Juvenile Court Dispositions: Ascriptive and Achieved Factors in Two Metropolitan Juvenile Courts." *Social Forces* 58: 146–61.

Cook, Thomas, and Donald Campbell. 1979. *Quasi-Experimentation: Design and Analysis Issues for Field Settings*. Boston: Houghton Mifflin.

Cox, Kevin. 1967. "Regional Anomalies in the Voting Behavior of the Populations of England and Wales: 1921–1951." Unpublished Ph.D. dissertation, University of Illinois.

———. 1970. "Geography, Social Contexts, and Voting Behavior in Wales, 1861–1951." In *Mass Politics,* ed. Erik Allardt and Stein Rokkan, 117–59. New York: Free Press.

Cressey, Donald Ray. 1953. *Other People's Money*. Glencoe, Ill.: Free Press.

Czudnowski, Moshe. 1976. *Comparing Political Behavior*. Beverly Hills: Sage.

Delacroix, Jacques, and Charles Ragin. 1978. "Modernizing Institutions, Mobilization, and Third World Development: A Cross-National Study." *American Journal of Sociology* 84: 123–50.

Diesing, Paul. 1971. *Patterns of Discovery in the Social Sciences*. Chicago: Aldine.

Drass, Kriss, and J. William Spencer. 1986. "Accounting for Presentencing Recommendations: Typologies and Probation Officers' Theory of Office." Unpublished manuscript. Department of Sociology, Southern Methodist University.

Drass, Kriss, and Charles Ragin. 1986. *QCA: A Microcomputer Package for Qualitative Comparative Analysis of Social Data*. Evanston: Center for Urban Affairs and Policy Research, Northwestern University.

Dumont, Louis. 1970. *Homo Hierarchicus: The Caste System and Its Implications*. Chicago: University of Chicago Press.

Duncan, Otis Dudley. 1984. *Notes on Social Measurement: Historical and Critical*. New York: Russell Sage Foundation.

Dunham, H. Warren. 1966. "The Juvenile Court: Contradictory Orientations in Processing Offenders." In *Juvenile Delinquency: A Book of Readings,* ed. Rose Giallombardo, 381–98. New York: Wiley.

Durkheim, Emile. [1915] 1961. *The Elementary Forms of the Religious Life*. Reprint. New York: Collier.

Easthope, Gary. 1974. *A History of Social Research Methods*. London: Longman.

Eisenstadt, Shmuel. 1966. *Problems in Sociological Theory*. Jerusalem: Academon.

Erikson, Patricia. 1974. "The Defense Lawyer's Role in Juvenile Court: An Empirical Investigation into Judges' and Social Workers' Points of View." *University of Toronto Law Review* 24: 126–48.

Etzioni, Amitai, and Fredric Dubow, eds. 1970. *Comparative Perspectives: Theories and Methods*. Boston: Little, Brown.

Evans, Peter. 1979. *Dependent Development: The Alliance of Multinational, State, and Local Capital in Brazil*. Princeton: Princeton University Press.

Fienberg, Stephen. 1985. *The Analysis of Cross-Classified Categorical Data*. Cambridge: MIT Press.

Frank, André Gunder. 1967. *Capitalism and Underdevelopment in Latin America: Historical Studies of Chile and Brazil*. New York: Monthly Review.

———. 1969. *Latin America: Underdevelopment or Revolution*. New York: Monthly Review.

———. 1972. *Lumpenbourgeoisie, Lumpendevelopment: Dependence, Class, and Politics in Latin America*. New York: Monthly Review.

Gee, Wilson. 1950. *Social Science Research Methods*. New York: Appleton.

Geertz, Clifford. 1963. *Old Societies and New States: The Quest for Modernity in Asia and Africa*. New York: Free Press.

Gellner, Ernest. 1969. *Thought and Change*. Chicago: University of Chicago Press.

Giddens, Anthony. 1973. *The Class Structure of the Advanced Societies*. London: Hutchinson.

Goffman, Erving. 1974. *Frame Analysis: An Essay on the Organization of Experience*. Cambridge: Harvard University Press.

Grimshaw, Allen. 1973. "Comparative Sociology: In What Ways Different from Other Sociologies?" In *Comparative Social Research: Methodological Problems and Strategies,* ed. Michael Armer and Allen Grimshaw, 3–48. New York: Wiley.

Gurr, Ted Robert. 1970. *Why Men Rebel*. Princeton: Princeton University Press.

———. 1974. "Persistence and Change in Political Systems, 1800–1971." *American Political Science Review* 68: 1482–1504.

Hage, Jerald. 1975. "Theoretical Decision Rules for Selecting Research Designs: The Study of Nation-States or Societies." *Sociological Methods and Research* 4(2): 131–65.

Handler, Joel. 1965. "The Juvenile Court and the Adversary System: Problems of Form and Function." *Wisconsin Law Review* (Winter): 7–51.

Hannan, Michael. 1979. "The Dynamics of Ethnic Boundaries in Modern States." In *National Development and the World System: Educational, Economic, and Political Change, 1950–1970,* ed. Michael Hannan and John Meyer, 253–77. Chicago: University of Chicago Press.

Harris, Marvin. 1978. *Cannibals and Kings: The Origins of Cultures*. New York: Vintage.

———. 1985. *Good to Eat: Riddles of Food and Culture*. New York: Simon & Schuster.

Hawley, Amos. 1981. *Urban Society: An Ecological Approach*. New York: Wiley.

Hechter, Michael. 1975. *Internal Colonialism: The Celtic Fringe in British National Development*. London: Routledge & Kegan Paul.

Hopkins, Terence, and Immanuel Wallerstein. 1970. "The Comparative Study of National Societies." In *Comparative Perspectives: Theories and Methods,* ed. Amitai Etzioni and Fredric Dubow, 183–204. Boston: Little, Brown.

Inkeles, Alex, and David Smith. 1974. *Becoming Modern: Individual Change in Six Developing Countries*. Cambridge: Harvard University Press.

Jenkins, J. Craig. 1983. "Resource Mobilization Theory and the Study of Social Movements." *Annual Review of Sociology* 9: 527–53.

Johnson, Stephen. 1967. "Hierarchical Clustering Schemes." *Psychometrika* 32: 241–54.

Kidron, Michael, and Ronald Segal. 1981. *The State of the World Atlas*. New York: Simon & Schuster.

Lenski, Gerhard. 1966. *Power and Privilege*. New York: McGraw-Hill.

———. 1974. *Human Societies*. New York: McGraw-Hill.

Lieberson, Stanley. 1985. *Making It Count: The Improvement of Social Research and Theory*. Berkeley: University of California Press.

Lindesmith, Alfred. 1968. *Addiction and the Opiates*. Chicago: Aldine.

Lipset, Seymour, and Stein Rokkan. 1967. *Party Systems and Voter Alignments*. New York: Free Press.

McCarthy, J. D., and M. N. Zald. 1977. "Resource Mobilization and Social Movements: A Partial Theory." *American Journal of Sociology* 82: 1212–39.

McDermott, Robert. 1985. *Computer-Aided Logic Design*. Indianapolis: Howard W. Sams.

McGowan, Pat. 1985. "Pitfalls and Promise in the Quantitative Study of the World-System: A Reanalysis of Bergesen and Schoenberg's 'Long Waves' of Colonialism." *Review: Journal of the Fernand Braudel Center* 8: 477–500.

McHale, Vincent, and Sharon Skowronski. 1983. *Political Parties of Europe*. Westport, Conn.: Greenwood Press.

McKinney, John. 1965. *Constructive Typology and Social Theory*. New York: Appleton-Century-Crofts.

Mann, Michael. 1973. *Consciousness and Action among the Western Working Class*. London: Humanities.

Marsh, Robert. 1967. *Comparative Sociology: A Codification of Cross-Sectional Analysis*. New York: Harcourt Brace Jovanovich.

Mendelson, Elliot. 1970. *Boolean Algebra and Switching Circuits*. New York: McGraw-Hill.

Merton, Robert. 1973. *The Sociology of Science: Theoretical and Empirical Investigations*. Chicago: University of Chicago Press.

Mill, John Stuart. [1843] 1967. *A System of Logic: Ratiocinative and Inductive*. Toronto: University of Toronto Press.

Moore, Barrington, Jr. 1966. *The Social Origins of Dictatorship and Democracy: Lord and Peasant in the Making of the Modern World*. Boston: Beacon.

Nagel, Ernest. 1961. *The Structure of Science*. New York: Harcourt.

Nagel, Joane, and Susan Olzak. 1982. "Ethnic Mobilization in New and Old States: An Extension of the Competition Model." *Social Problems* 30: 127–43.

———, eds. 1986. *Competitive Ethnic Relations.* New York: Academic Press.

Nielsen, Francois. 1980. "The Flemish Movement in Belgium after World War II: A Dynamic Analysis." *American Sociological Review* 45: 76–94.

———. 1985. "Toward a Theory of Ethnic Solidarity in Modern Societies." *American Sociological Review* 50: 133–49.

Nielsen, Francois, and Michael Hannan. 1977. "The Expansion of National Educational Systems: Tests of a Population Ecology Model." *American Sociological Review* 42: 479–90.

Nisbett, Richard, and Lee Ross. 1980. *Human Inference: Strategies and Shortcomings of Social Judgment.* Englewood Cliffs, N.J.: Prentice-Hall.

Olzak, Susan. 1982. "Ethnic Mobilization in Quebec." *Ethnic and Racial Studies* 5: 253–75.

———. 1983. "Contemporary Ethnic Mobilization." *Annual Review of Sociology* 9: 355–74.

Paige, Jeffrey. 1975. *Agrarian Revolution: Social Movements and Export Agriculture in the Underdeveloped World.* New York: Free Press.

Parsons, Talcott. 1975. "Some Theoretical Considerations on the Nature and Trends of Change of Ethnicity." In *Ethnicity: Theory and Experience,* ed. Nathan Glazer and Daniel Moynihan, 56–71. Cambridge: Harvard University Press.

———. 1977. *The Evolution of Societies.* Englewood Cliffs, N.J.: Prentice-Hall.

Petersen, William. 1975. "On the Subnations of Western Europe." In *Ethnicity: Theory and Experience,* ed. Nathan Glazer and Daniel Moynihan, 177–208. Cambridge: Harvard University Press.

Porter, John. 1970. "Some Observations on Comparative Studies." In *Stages of Social Research,* ed. Dennis Forcese and Stephen Richer, 141–54. Englewood Cliffs, N.J.: Prentice-Hall.

Przeworski, Adam, and Henry Teune. 1970. *The Logic of Comparative Social Inquiry.* New York: Wiley-Interscience.

Ragin, Charles. 1977. "Class, Status, and 'Reactive Ethnic Cleavages': The Social Bases of Political Regionalism." *American Sociological Review* 42: 438–50.

———. 1979. "Ethnic Political Mobilization: The Welsh Case." *American Sociological Review* 44: 619–35.

———. 1983. "Theory and Method in the Study of Dependency and International Inequality." *International Journal of Comparative Sociology* 24: 121–36.

———. 1985. "Knowledge and Interests in the Study of the Modern World-System." *Review: Journal of the Fernand Braudel Center* 8: 451–76.

———. 1986. "The Impact of Celtic Nationalism on Class Politics in Scotland and Wales." In *Competitive Ethnic Relations,* ed. Joane Nagel and Susan Olzak, 199–219. New York: Academic Press.

Ragin, Charles, and Daniel Chirot. 1984. "The World-System of Immanuel Wallerstein: Sociology and Politics as History." In *Vision and Method in Historical Sociology,* ed. Theda Skocpol, 276–312. Cambridge: Cambridge University Press.

Ragin, Charles, and Ted Davies. 1981. "Welsh Nationalism in Context." *Research in Social Movements, Conflicts and Change* 4: 215–33.

Ragin, Charles, and David Zaret. 1983. "Theory and Method in Comparative Research: Two Strategies." *Social Forces* 61: 731–54.

Ragin, Charles, Susan Meyer, and Kriss Drass. 1984. "Assessing Discrimination: A Boolean Approach." *American Sociological Review* 49: 221–34.

Rokkan, Stein. 1966. "Comparative Cross-National Research: The Context of Current Efforts." In *Comparing Nations,* ed. Richard Merritt and Stein Rokkan, 3–26. New Haven: Yale University Press.

———. 1970. *Citizens, Elections, Parties.* New York: McKay.

Roth, Charles. 1975. *Fundamentals of Logic Design.* St. Paul: West.

Rubinson, Richard, and Deborah Holtzman. 1981. "Comparative Dependence and Economic Development." *International Journal of Comparative Sociology* 20: 86–101.

Scheuch, Erwin. 1966. "Cross-National Comparisons Using Aggregate Data: Some Substantive and Methodological Problems." In *Comparing Nations,* ed. Richard Merritt and Stein Rokkan, 131–68. New Haven: Yale University Press.

Shorter, Edward, and Charles Tilly. 1974. *Strikes in France, 1830–1968.* Cambridge: Cambridge University Press.

Simon, Julian. 1969. *Basic Research Methods in Social Science.* New York: Random House.

Skocpol, Theda. 1979. *States and Social Revolutions: A Comparative Analysis of France, Russia, and China.* Cambridge: Cambridge University Press.

Skocpol, Theda, and Margaret Somers. 1980. "The Uses of Comparative History in Macrosocial

Inquiry." *Comparative Studies in Society and History* 22: 174–97.

Smelser, Neil. 1973. "The Methodology of Comparative Analysis." In *Comparative Research Methods,* ed. Donald Warwick and Samuel Osherson, 45–52. Englewood Cliffs, N.J.: Prentice-Hall.

———. 1976. *Comparative Methods in the Social Sciences.* Englewood Cliffs, N.J.: Prentice-Hall.

Snyder, David. 1975. "Institutional Setting and Industrial Conflict: Comparative Analyses of France, Italy, and the United States." *American Sociological Review* 40: 259–78.

Stapleton, Vaughn, and Lee Teitelbaum. 1972. *In Defense of Youth: A Study of the Role of Counsel in American Juvenile Courts.* New York: Russell Sage Foundation.

Stapleton, Vaughn, David Aday, and Jeanne Ito. 1982. "An Empirical Typology of American Metropolitan Juvenile Courts." *American Journal of Sociology* 88: 549–64.

Stephens, John. 1979. *The Transition from Capitalism to Socialism.* London: Macmillan.

Stinchcombe, Arthur. 1961. "Agricultural Enterprise and Rural Class Relations." *American Journal of Sociology* 67: 165–76.

———. 1965. "Social Structure and Organizations." In *Handbook of Organizations,* ed. James G. March, 142–93. Chicago: Rand McNally.

———. 1978. *Theoretical Methods in Social History.* New York: Academic Press.

Swanson, Guy. 1971. "Frameworks for Comparative Research: Structural Anthropology and the Theory of Action." In *Comparative Methods in Sociology: Essays on Trends and Applications,* ed. Ivan Vallier, 141–202. Berkeley: University of California Press.

Tappan, Paul. 1976. "The Nature of Juvenile Delinquency." In *Juvenile Delinquency: A Book of Readings,* ed. Rose Giallombardo, 5–24. New York: Wiley.

Tilly, Charles. 1975. *The Formation of National States in Western Europe.* Princeton: Princeton University Press.

———. 1978. *From Mobilization to Revolution.* Reading, Mass.: Addison-Wesley.

———. 1984. *Big Structures, Large Processes, Huge Comparisons.* New York: Russell Sage Foundation.

———. 1986. *The Contentious French.* Cambridge, Mass.: Belknap Press.

Tocqueville, Alexis de. [1835] 1945. *Democracy in America.* Reprint: New York: Knopf.

Walker, Henry, and Bernard Cohen. 1985. "Scope Statements: Imperatives for Evaluating Theory." *American Sociological Review* 50: 288–301.

Wallerstein, Immanuel. 1974. *The Modern World System: Capitalist Agriculture and the Origins of the European World Economy in the Sixteenth Century.* New York: Academic Press.

———. 1979. *The Capitalist World-Economy.* Cambridge: Cambridge University Press.

———. 1980. *The Modern World-System II: Mercantilism and the Consolidation of the European World-Economy 1600–1750.* New York: Academic Press.

———. 1984. *The Politics of the World-Economy: The States, the Movements and the Civilizations.* Cambridge: Cambridge University Press.

Walton, John. 1973. "Standardized Case Comparison: Observations on Method in Comparative Sociology." In *Comparative Social Research,* ed. Michael Armer and Allen Grimshaw, 173–88. New York: Wiley.

———. 1984. *Reluctant Rebels.* New York: Columbia University Press.

Weber, Max. 1946. *From Max Weber: Essays in Sociology.* Ed. H. H. Gerth and C. Wright Mills. New York: Oxford University Press.

———. 1949. *The Methodology of the Social Sciences.* New York: Free Press.

———. 1975. *Roscher and Knies: The Logical Problems of Historical Economics.* New York: Free Press.

———. 1977. *Critique of Stammler.* New York: Free Press.

———. 1978. *Economy and Society.* Ed. Guenther Roth and Claus Wittich. Berkeley: University of California Press.

Wiener, Jonathan. 1976. Review of Barrington Moore Jr., "Social Origins of Dictatorship and Democracy." *History and Theory* 15: 146–75.

Wolf, Eric. 1969. *Peasant Wars of the Twentieth Century.* New York: Harper & Row.

Zelditch, Morris, Jr. 1971. "Intelligible Comparisons." In *Comparative Methods in Sociology: Essays on Trends and Applications,* ed. Ivan Vallier, 267–307. Berkeley: University of California Press.

Zimmerman, Ekkart. 1983. *Political Violence, Crises, and Revolution: Theory and Research.* Cambridge, Mass.: Schenkman.

CHAPTER SEVEN

The Methodology of Comparative Analysis of Economic Activity*

Neil J. Smelser†

The objective of this essay is to throw light on a number of difficult and unresolved methodological issues that have plagued the comparative analysis of economic institutions and behavior—as well as other types of comparative analysis—for many decades. I shall first outline the issues, then mention a few efforts that scholars have made to solve them, and finally outline my own views on a methodological perspective and some research strategies that may improve on these suggested solutions.

The Issues

The issues I shall address take the following forms:

1. In what ways is it appropriate to regard comparative economic analysis as the search for features of economic life that are universal in their incidence and in what ways as a study of variations? For example: Is the psychological propensity to economize to be considered universal? Is it profitable to search for similar institutional forms (e.g., the market) from society to society? Is it appropriate to ascertain the degree to which industrialization is correlated with the isolated nuclear family? In one respect the answers to these questions are empirical; however, I am posing them in terms of their methodological appropriateness.

2. How is it possible to compare economic institutions and activities in diverse sociocultural contexts? This issue, which might be termed "the problem of comparability," arises at three distinct levels: (a) How can we be certain that the *events* and *situations* we

wish to explain are comparable from one sociocultural context to another? How, for example, can we compare production rates a century ago with production rates today? Were not recording procedures different then from now? Was not the social meaning of a product different then from now? More generally, are not "the [economic] activity and the income . . . inseparable and . . . both embedded together in the customs and ways of thought which mold the social life of the community as a whole?"[1] (b) How can we be certain that the general *dimensions* used to compare societies cross-culturally do not do violence to the events and situations we wish to study? In what sense is it appropriate to apply the concept "economic" to both the role of an African subsistence farmer and to that of a member of the board of directors of a large American corporation? In what sense are both roles economic? Certainly it appears that *some* general dimensions are necessary to engage in comparative analysis; otherwise the investigator would seem to be committed to a radical relativism that prohibits him from moving beyond the confines of a single social unit. But the truth of this general point does not solve the problem of what particular comparative dimensions do least violence to the distinctive sociocultural meaning of events and situations, yet at the same time provide a genuinely general basis for comparison. (c) How is it possible to compare very different *social units* (or social systems) with one another? Does it make any sense to compare a highly complex economy like those of the modern West or the Soviet Union with hunting-and-gathering tribes in Australia, when it is obvious that these economies differ from one another in almost every conceivable respect?

3. Should economic activity in different societies be described in terms of its meanings to the members of the societies themselves, or should it be measured by some objective index? Should we, at one extreme, be prepared to regard as economic any kind of activity that any culture happens to regard as economic? Or should we, at the other extreme, search for indices such as dollar equivalents to describe all economic activity everywhere, no matter what its sociocultural context?[2]

4. If, indeed, we wish to investigate economic life in different contexts, how are we to define the various concepts to be used—concepts such as "economic" and "noneconomic" themselves, "capital," "savings," "production," and so on?

These several issues are closely interrelated. The degree of universality of a phenomenon depends in part on the way this phenomenon is defined. "Marketplace," which refers to a physical location at which exchange takes place, for example, is more nearly universal than "market," which in the economist's definition would involve not only exchange but also some generalized medium of exchange such as money, equilibrating mechanisms such as supply and demand, and perhaps some notion of economic rationality attributed to buyers and sellers.[3] Moreover, the degree of comparability of different units also depends on the choice and definition of concepts. To choose a noneconomic example, the concept of civil service is so intimately linked with a bureaucratic form that it is literally useless in connection with societies without a formal state or governmental apparatus. The concept of administration is somewhat superior, since it is not so closely tied to particular forms of bureaucracy, but even this term is quite culture-bound. Weber's concept of staff is even more helpful, since it can encompass, without embarrassment, various political arrangements based on kinship

and other forms of particularistic loyalties.[4] Staff is more satisfactory than administration, then, and administration more satisfactory than civil service, because the former allow for a wider range of instantiation in principle. The questions of definition of concepts, adequacy of comparability, and universality of occurrence, then, appear to rest in large part on a single master question: how adequately does the investigator choose and use his comparative categories? To this question this essay is devoted.

Approaches to the Issue of Comparability

In the area of comparative economics existing solutions to the master question I have posed tend to fall between two extremes—phenomenological subjectivism (and relativism) on the one hand, and positivistic objectivism on the other. With respect to the former, the investigator, conscious of the vast ranges of variability in economic activity and in meanings assigned to it in different sociocultural contexts, is pulled toward the position of representing the "economic" differently for each culture. This position is well stated by Marcel Mauss, who characterized his own comparative methodology as follows:

Since we are concerned with words and their meanings, we choose only areas where we have access to the *minds of the societies* through documentation and philological research. This further limits our field of comparison. Each particular study has a bearing on the systems we set out to describe and is presented in its logical place. In this way we avoid that *method of haphazard comparison in which institutions lose their local colour and documents their value.*[5]

Presumably the research method most appropriate to this kind of definition is ethnographic work in the field, on the basis of which the investigator records the values, beliefs, and other cultural items as faithfully and accurately as possible. If pressed to its extreme, however, this position leaves the investigator in a state of paralysis. He soon ends in a position of radical relativism, at which he must treat everything as "economic" that any group happens to define thus; and, respecting "local color" in this way, he loses his grasp on any general concept of the economic whatsoever, and hence loses any ability to engage in comparative analysis.

The first rule of thumb in comparative analysis, then, is to avoid concepts that are so particularly tied to single cultures or groups of cultures that no instance of the concepts, as defined, can be found in other cultures. Some more general definition of the economic is required—for example, a definition based on the fact that all societies face the problem of scarcity of natural resources and human resources and skills, and that they must come to term in some institutionalized way with this problem. Such a definition would appear to have comparative potential, since all societies can be said to have a scarcity problem and display economic behavior; moreover, the definition would appear to avoid the conceptual paralysis associated with the extreme of phenomenological subjectivism. But it is necessary to proceed further and ask how economic behavior, defined thus, is identified empirically in different sociocultural contexts.

One convenient and widely used way of identifying the economic is to limit the empirical referents of the term, as did Alfred Marshall, to those aspects of men's attitudes and activities which are subject to measurement in terms of money.[6] From the standpoint of empirical precision, this monetary index has clear advantages. From the standpoint of encompassing economic behavior on a uniform and universal basis, however, it is severely limited. Even in our own society, many activities that are economically significant—housewives' labor, lending a hand to a friend, and so forth— are seldom expressed in monetary terms. In the case of economies based on subsistence farming and domestically consumed household manufacture, the limitations of the monetary index are even more marked, since the most fundamentally economic kinds of behavior—

such as the production, distribution, and consumption of foodstuffs—never become monetized. In addition, the monetary index is limited from the standpoint of comparing a growing economic system with its own past, since one of the concomitants of economic growth is the entry of an increasing proportion of goods and services into the market context—and hence their increasing monetization; this means that if the monetary definition of *economic* is used, the rate of growth will be artificially inflated by the fact of the transformation of nonmonetized economic activity into monetized economic activity.[7] When used for international comparisons of wealth, such indices suffer not only from the fact of differential levels of monetization, but also from the frequent practice of translation of various currencies into dollar or some other equivalencies, usually on the basis of current international exchange ratios. Since many of these ratios are pegged artificially and do not represent true economic exchange ratios, additional bias creeps into the comparative estimates.

Another objective definition has been suggested in the work of Polanyi, Arensberg, and Pearson.[8] Reacting negatively to the tradition of formal economics—which distorts comparisons by imposing a market bias on nonmarket economies—they suggest that economic activity be defined as that instituted process which results in a "continuous supply of want-satisfying *material* means." This materialistic definition introduces a bias precisely opposite to that of the monetary definition of economic activity—a bias in favor of the primitive and peasant societies. In such societies, it appears (but is not necessarily the case) that economic activity is devoted to a sort of material subsistence based on food, clothing, and shelter. In advanced market societies, however, in which expressive behavior, ideas, personalities, and other nonmaterial items have economic value, the formula of the economic as the "supply of want-satisfying material means" collapses as an adequate comparative tool. It is as illegitimate to try to force a physical or material bias on all economic activity as it is to impose a fully developed model of the market on all economic activity.[9]

How, then, is the comparative analyst to steer a course between the Scylla of paralysis associated with culture-specific definitions and the Charybdis of distortion associated with more general definitions?[10] No ready solution exists in the literature, from my reading, and the approach I now propose is put forth as an indication of the general direction to be taken rather than as a final solution to this difficult dilemma.

Any encompassing definition and measure of economic activity must involve more than some convenient index of monetized activity, physical production, or some other objective phenomenon. It must involve a definition of the production, distribution, and consumption of scarce goods and services *in relation to individual and social goals.* Economists have long recognized this relational quality of economic activity in their preoccupation with the notion of utility as the basis of value. Yet their preoccupation has been predominately with the wants of individuals, despite the tradition of welfare economics that has pursued questions of interindividual comparability and community welfare.[11] Furthermore, economists have generally tended to treat wants as given and stable, and therefore subject to no further analysis. But in comparative analysis the question of wants as the ultimate defining basis for economic activity and measurement cannot be taken as a parametric given;[12] it must be treated in relation to variable societal values and goals.

To arrive at an appropriate comparative definition of economic activity, therefore, we first recognize that a society possesses a value system that defines certain goals as desirable for members and groups of the society at various levels. By a process of institutionalization, the appropriate channels for realizing these goals are specified. It is apparent, however, that all societies exist in an environment that does not guarantee automatically the complete and instantaneous realization of these goals.

Hence an important part of the societal situation is that certain institutionalized attention be given to the supply of various facilities to attain the valued goals. Part of this attention is economic activity. The goals—and the institutionalized means for attaining them—may vary considerably; they may concern perpetuation of kinship lines, attainment of a state of religious bliss, territorial expansion, or maximization of wealth. Economic activity in any society is defined as a *relation* between these goals and the degree of scarcity of goods and services. Indeed, the definition of the economic in any given society—and the structure of its economy—will be in large part a function of both the institutionalized values and goals and the availability (or scarcity) of human and nonhuman resources.

The investigator of comparative economic activity, then, must allow cultural values and meanings to intervene between his most general concept ("the economic") and its specific measurements. He must begin by comparing systematically the value systems of different societies, then identify and measure—using a different set of operational rules in each society—what classes of activity are economic (scarce) in relation to these values. This difficult and prolonged method of research is certainly more plagued with problems of operationalization than the simple comparison of market transactions. The difficulties of the comparative analysis of cultural values are only too well appreciated by anthropologists and comparative sociologists. But I am convinced that comparative analysis—both of economic activity in particular and social behavior in general—cannot proceed far without striving to introduce social values and meanings into the comparative identification and measurement of general constructs; if it does not undertake this task, it will be bedeviled by uncorrectable distortions from the very outset of study.

From a methodological point of view, I am suggesting that some of the sources of cultural variability (values and goals) that obscure a neat correspondence between universal concept (the economic) and its specific manifestations (items of behavior) *be themselves systematically classified and brought to bear on the measurement process.* As I have indicated, past solutions to this methodological issue have tended either to ignore these sources of variability by treating them as given and nonvariable or to be discouraged from comparative analysis and driven into isolated case studies by them. The type of solution suggested here would incorporate the sources of cultural variability into the very process of comparative analysis. I see this solution as in keeping with the general method of scientific analysis, namely, to make determinate those sources of variation that have hitherto been assumed to be so simple as to be nondeterminate or so complex as to be indeterminate.

Some Research Strategies for Comparative Analysis

Thus far the discussion has concerned primarily general and conceptual means of coming to terms with the problems of sociocultural variability and complexity. In addition, there are a number of more concrete and specific strategies to be observed in posing research questions and conducting research—strategies also directed toward the problems of variability and complexity. In the remainder of this essay I shall outline these strategies, again using mainly the comparative study of economic activity for illustration.

Let us begin with a specific comparative problem: why does the gross national product of some societies grow at a faster rate than that of others? (Assume for the moment that adequate comparative measures for GNP have been devised.) The factors contributing to the answer to such a question are obviously very numerous. In the first instance, the several factors of production—land, labor, capital, and organization—and the characteristics of demand determine the level of production. Each of these determinants is, however, itself conditioned by a vast array of sociocultural

factors—the kinship system, the educational framework, the stratification system, the political structure, and so on. How does the investigator deal with this array of determinants?

In general, the social scientist imposes some sort of conceptual organization on the conditions, for example, by distinguishing among independent, intervening, and dependent variables. In the illustration at hand, the supply of the various factors of production are considered to be dependent variables in relation to the sociocultural factors, independent with respect to the level of the gross national product, and intervening with respect to the relations between the sociocultural factors and the GNP.[13] Further conceptual organization is often imposed on the conditions by combining them into various forms of explanatory models.[14]

Another fundamental way of organizing conditions is found in the distinction between conditions treated as *parameters* and conditions treated as *operative variables.* As indicated above,[15] parameters are conditions that are known or suspected to influence the dependent variable, but which, in the investigation at hand, are made or assumed not to vary. Operative variables are conditions that are known or suspected to influence the dependent variable and which, in the investigation at hand, are made or allowed to vary in order to assess this influence. By making variables into parameters for purposes of analysis, most of the potentially operative conditions are made not to vary, so that the operation of one or a few conditions may be isolated and examined.

The distinction between parameters and operative variables is a relative one. What is treated as a parameter in one investigation may become a variable condition in another. Suppose, for example, it is known that foreign trade is important in the determination of the national income of a society, but that calculation of the impact of foreign trade on the domestic economy is impossible unless certain internal relations—say, between private investment, government investment, and consumption—are already known. The economist may proceed by assuming that foreign trade is a parameter—that it does not exist, or that it occurs at a constant rate throughout the time period in question—and, by thus simplifying the picture of the determinants of income, may proceed to establish national income as some function of private investment, government investment, and current consumption. Having established these relations, he may then "relax" the restricting assumption about foreign trade, and "allow" it to vary, thus tracing its impact on the known relations internal to the economy. In the same operation he may very well have transformed domestic investment into a parameter—assumed it not to vary—in order to pinpoint the impact of foreign trade more precisely.

The several methods of inquiry in the social sciences may be characterized in terms of the ways in which parameters and operative variables are controlled, manipulated, combined, and recombined into explanatory accounts.[16] In this essay I am particularly concerned with the comparative method—or the method of systematic comparative illustration—which is employed for the scientific analysis of historical data which cannot be controlled experimentally and the number of cases of which is too small to permit statistical analysis. I have showed elsewhere how Durkheim's analysis of suicide rates employed this method of systematic comparative illustration.[17] Max Weber's studies on religion and rational bourgeois capitalism provide another illustration.

Weber's starting point was those societies in northwest Europe and North America that had developed rational bourgeois capitalism. He wished to establish the essential characteristics that these societies had in common. In doing so he was using the *positive* comparative method—identifying similarities in conditions associated with a common outcome. Then, turning to societies that had not developed this kind of economic organization (e.g., classical India, classical China), he asked in what respects they differed from the former societies. In so doing he was using the *negative* compara-

tive method—identifying conditions associated with divergent outcomes. By thus manipulating the conditions and the outcomes, Weber built his case that differences in religious systems were crucial in accounting for the different economic histories of the various societies.[18] Translating Weber's comparative method into the language of scientific inquiry, we see that Weber was making parameters of those general features shared by both the West and his Oriental examples (for instance, he ruled out the influence of merchant classes by pointing out that both China and the West had these classes prior to the development of capitalism in the West); and he was making operative variables of those religious features in which they differed.

The comparative method as just outlined is a systematic attempt to come to grips with the methodological issues raised at the beginning of this essay. It takes cognizance of the variability in sociocultural context but attempts to control it by the method of systematic illustration, and by continuous transformation of parameters into operative variables and vice versa. Viewing the comparative problem in this way, it is possible to suggest a few specific research strategies that are advisable at the present state of the art of comparative analysis.

First, while it is in principle possible, given the appropriate comparative categories, to compare economies so different as the American urban-industrial complex and hunting-and-gathering tribes, it is more fruitful to compare economic variations in societies that are much closer to one another in many respects. For example, it would be a fruitful exercise to compare the different paths of development of socialist economic policies in Denmark, Norway, Sweden, Finland, and Iceland, which are similar but not identical in cultural traditions and social structure. It would be less fruitful to compare the socialism of Denmark with the socialism of emerging African countries, whose cultural traditions and social structures are vastly different. The reason for adopting this research strategy can be stated in terms of the distinction between parameters and operative variables. If two societies share some important conditions in common, it is relatively more permissible to treat these common conditions as parameters, and proceed to examine the operation of other variables as if these common conditions were not operative, because their operation is presumably similar in both cases. By contrast, if two social units that differ in almost every respect are chosen for comparison, the investigator is in the disadvantaged position of having to consider all sources of difference as operative variables, because he is unable to "control" them by considering them to be similar. The more similar two or more societies are with respect to crucial variables, in short, the better able is the investigator to isolate and analyze the influence of other variables that might account for the differences he wishes to explain.[19]

Second—and related to the first—it is fruitful to replicate comparisons *between* social units by means of comparisons *within* social units. Let me illustrate this method first by reference to a noneconomic example. Durkheim's most thoroughly analyzed case of altruistic suicide was the military case. His general interpretation was that military personnel, in comparison with civilians, are more involved in a collective code of honor, and therefore are more likely to sacrifice themselves through self-destruction in the name of this code. On this basis he predicted higher rates of suicide among military personnel than among civilians. The available suicide statistics tended to support his hypothesis. Even after he corrected for marital status, the differences between military and civilian personnel stood. Still, it might be argued, it is not clear that Durkheim had isolated the salient differences between military and civilian personnel; after all, they differ in many other circumstances than in degree of commitment to a code of honor, and on the basis of the gross comparison between military and civilian personnel alone it is impossible to know that the differential value-commitment is

the operative variable. By way of attempting to support his own interpretation, Durkheim turned to the analysis of *intramilitary* differences in suicide rates. First he compared those with limited terms of service with those of longer duration, finding that the latter—presumably more imbued with the military spirit than the former—showed higher suicide rates; next he compared officers and noncommissioned officers with private soldiers, finding that the former—again more involved in the military life—showed higher rates; finally, he found a greater tendency for suicide among volunteers and reenlisted men, that is, those who chose the military life freely. Summarizing these intramilitary findings, Durkheim concluded that "the members of the army most stricken by suicide, are also those who are most inclined to this career. . . ."[20] By this replication at the intraunit level Durkheim rendered more plausible the interunit relation (between military and civilian).[21]

The main advantage of replication at different analytic levels is to increase or decrease the investigator's confidence in a suspected association between conditions and the phenomenon to be explained. In some cases intraunit comparisons may prove more fruitful than interunit comparisons. The logic behind this assertion is the same that lies behind the assertion that it is more fruitful to compare social units that are similar to one another in important respects. Suppose we wish to carry out certain investigations on societies that differ from one another in terms of level of industrialization. Suppose further that Germany, a highly industrialized country, and Italy, a less industrialized country, are the two societies chosen for comparison. For many purposes it would be more fruitful to compare northern Italy with southern Italy, and the Ruhr with Bavaria, than it would be to compare Germany as a whole with Italy as a whole. These two countries differ not only in level of industrialization but also in cultural traditions, type of governmental structure, and so on. From the standpoint of interunit comparison these differences are not controllable as parameters. If the investigator were instead to pursue intraunit comparisons between those parts of Italy and Germany that are industrialized and those parts that are not, it is more nearly possible to hold these interunit differences constant, and thus pinpoint the factors lying behind differential industrialization more precisely. Then, having located what appear to be operative factors in the intraunit comparisons, it is possible to move to the interunit comparisons to see if the same differences hold in the large.

Important and advantageous as are the methods of comparison of similar cases and of replication at different levels for the establishment of comparative findings, the investigator must proceed judiciously in their use. He must attempt to establish empirically—not merely assume—that those conditions he treats as parameters are indeed based on similarities and continuities between and within social units. Otherwise his study will suffer from the methodological weaknesses that arise when incomparable units are analyzed.

I shall conclude with a few comments—ventured in the light of the methodological approach I have outlined—on the first issue I introduced: the appropriateness of asking to what degree empirical phenomena and association are universal and to what degree variable. So long as this question is posed with the understanding that the extent of empirical occurrence of a phenomenon and its associations is a necessary preliminary to comparative explanation, it is a legitimate question. Insofar as the search for empirical universals becomes an end in itself, however, it can lead to relatively unproductive research and unnecessary controversy. I shall illustrate this point by referring to the familiar issue of the relations between the urban-industrial complex and the isolated nuclear family.

The argument for the universal association between these two social phenomena—an argument presented by the Chicago school of the interwar period[22]—runs roughly as follows: The traditional farm or peasant family is given a shock by the development of a commercial market structure, by the development of industry, or by the development of cities—usually, in fact, by some great social force involving an undifferentiated combination of all three. The immediate effects of this shock are to draw one or more family members into wage labor (separated from the household), thereby destroying the traditional division of labor, making the family more mobile socially and geographically, placing the family in a generally anonymous social environment, and perhaps destroying its economic base further by flooding the market with cheap, mass-produced commodities that compete with those previously produced in the domestic setting. The result is the small nuclear family that is mobile, neolocal, and isolated from many of its previous social connections and functions. Once this assertion of the universality of the connection between the urban-industrial complex and the isolated nuclear family is made, the research problem quite appropriately becomes one of establishing the empirical strength of the relation by examining different societies at different stages of economic and urban development.

If the research question remains at this level, it is likely to lead to two unhelpful preoccupations. First, research on the degree of universality of some occurrence or association may degenerate into controversy over the precise degree of "universality" that exists. With respect to the association between the urban-industrial complex and the family, "negative findings" have begun to accrue and attacks have been launched on the formulation just outlined.[23] These findings tend to show that the isolated nuclear family sometimes antedates urbanization and industrialization and that various kinds of extended family structures persist into urban-industrial development. While such findings are valuable, the research does little to specify, in a systematic way, any new conditions by which we can account for differences in the relations between urban-industrial variables and family structure. This limitation stems, I submit, from an exaggerated preoccupation with the empirical universality—or lack of it—of the association.

Second, if a sociocultural occurrence or association is to be described as genuinely universal, its characterization may have to be so general as to compress many important sources of variation into very global concepts. Certainly the variables of industrialization and urbanization should be separated from one another at the very outset for purposes of assessing their impact on the family. Furthermore, neither urbanization nor industrialization constitutes an irreducible whole; several subtypes of each should be identified before any adequate statement of the relations between each and the family can be formulated. In addition, the "isolation of the nuclear family" is not a single entity; it also displays a variation that demands classification and separate description of subtypes. If we introduce these kinds of complexity in relating the variables—though limiting the subclassification on both sides to avoid falling into mere historical description—we are in a more advantageous position for establishing the specific conditions under which urban and industrial variables will influence family variables than if we remain at the level of highly nonspecific universals. Of course, to refine variables in this way means to sacrifice some "universals" and "invariants" in the meantime, but in this case I consider the sacrifice to be an advantage for the program of comparative analysis.

Notes

* From *Essays in Sociological Explanation,* by Neil J. Smelser (Englewood Cliffs, N.J.: Prentice-Hall, 1968), 62–75, by permission of the author and Prentice-Hall, Inc. Copyright 1968 by Prentice-Hall, Inc.

† Revised version of a paper delivered at the annual meetings of the American Sociological Association, Miami Beach, August 1966; and prepared for the Sixth World Congress of Sociology, Evian, September 1966. The paper was originally published in the *Transactions of the Sixth World Congress of Sociology* (Louvain: Éditions Nauwelaerts, 1968), Vol. 2, pp. 101–17.

1. S. Herbert Frankel, *The Economic Impact on Under-Developed Societies* (Cambridge: Harvard University Press, 1959), pp. 41–42.

2. Claude Lévi-Strauss has presented this distinction in terms of its relation to consciousness. "[The anthropologist] may have to construct a model from phenomena the systematic character of which has evoked no awareness on the part of the culture. . . . Or else the anthropologist will be dealing, on the one hand, with raw phenomena and, on the other, with the models already constructed by the culture to interpret the former." See "Social Structure," reprinted in Sol Tax, ed., *Anthropology Today: Selections* (Chicago: University of Chicago Press, 1962), p. 324.

3. For a discussion of the distinction between marketplace and market, and the empirical occurrence of both, see Paul Bohannan and George Dalton, "Introduction," in *Markets in Africa* (Evanston: Northwestern University Press, 1962), pp. 1–12.

4. Max Weber, *The Theory of Social and Economic Organization,* trans. A. M. Henderson and Talcott Parsons (New York: Oxford University Press, 1947), pp. 329 ff.

5. *The Gift: Forms and Functions of Exchange in Archaic Societies,* trans. Ian Cunnison (New York: Free Press, 1954), pp. 2–3. Emphasis added.

6. Alfred Marshall, *Principles of Economics,* 8th ed. (New York and London: Macmillan, 1920), Book I, Chapter 2.

7. It should be added that some definitions of economics do not limit economic activity to monetized activity. Thus Samuelson's textbook definition is ". . . the study of how men and society choose, *with or without the use of money,* to employ scarce productive resources to produce various commodities over time and distribute them for consumption, now and in the future, among various people and groups in society." Paul A. Samuelson, *Economics: An Introductory Analysis,* 5th ed. (New York: McGraw-Hill, 1961), p. 6. Emphasis added.

8. Karl Polanyi, Conrad M. Arensberg, and Harry W. Pearson, *Trade and Market in the Early Empires* (New York: Free Press and Falcon's Wing Press, 1957).

9. For further development of this point, and further criticism of the formulation developed by Polanyi et al., cf. Neil J. Smelser, "A Comparative View of Exchange Systems," *Economic Development and Cultural Change* 7 (1959): 173–82.

10. This tension between culture-specific and general measures has made its appearance in the general theoretical discussions of structural-functional analysis, in particular in the discussion of the "postulate of indispensability." In general terms, this postulate holds that there are certain universal functional exigencies (such as the socialization of the young, the integration of diverse groups in society) which society faces, *and* that there are *specific* social-structural forms which *alone* serve these functions (structural forms such as the nuclear family for socialization and organized religion for integration, for instance). Thus the postulate of indispensability links specific institutional or behavioral indices with general social functions, just as the monetary definition of economic activity links "measurement in terms of money" to the general concept of "economic." The formulations are parallel. Objecting to the postulate of indispensability, Merton has asserted that "just as the same item may have multiple functions, so the same function may be diversely fulfilled by alternative items. Functional needs are . . . taken to be permissive, rather than determinant, of specific social structures." Robert K. Merton, *Social Theory and Social Structure,* revised and enlarged ed. (New York: Free Press, 1957), pp. 33–34. In line with this position, Merton goes on to insist on the importance of concepts like "functional alternatives," "functional substitutes," and "functional equivalents." Here Merton is opting for general comparative concepts (functions) that encompass a wide variety of empirical manifestations (items).

11. See, for example, I. M. D. Little, *A Critique of Welfare Economics* (Oxford: Clarendon Press, 1950); Jerome Rothenberg, *The Measurement of Social Welfare* (Englewood Cliffs, N.J.: Prentice-Hall, 1961).

12. Joseph S. Berliner, an economist, commenting on the anthropological method, states: "Economists do not as a rule search for regularities between the economic system and the kinship system or religious or political systems; the latter are assumed to be 'given'. . . . The application of the cultural anthropological method . . . would involve the replacement of the shift parameter by a series of variables. . . . The economist's assumption of the stability of consumer preferences, at least with respect to cultural variables in the short run, is probably valid. For long-run prediction, however, the use of cultural variables may significantly improve the results." "The Feet of the Natives Are Large: An Essay on Anthropology by an Economist," *Current Anthropology* 3, no. 1 (February 1962): 53–54.

13. For further illustrations of the use of independent, intervening, and dependent variables, Neil J. Smelser, *Essays in Sociological Explanation* (Englewood Cliffs, N.J.: Prentice-Hall, 1968), pp. 12–13.

14. Smelser, *Essays,* pp. 14–16 and pp. 209–16.

15. Smelser, *Essays,* p. 16.

16. Smelser, *Essays,* pp. 16–20.

17. See Smelser, *Essays,* pp. 18–19.

18. Relevant works include *The Protestant Ethic and the Spirit of Capitalism,* trans. Talcott Parsons (London: George Allen & Unwin, 1948); *The Religion of China,* trans. Hans H. Gerth (New York: Free Press, 1951); *The Religion of India,* trans. Hans H. Gerth and Don Martindale (New York: Free Press, 1958).

19. For an example of a comparative study of "close" cases, see Lipset's comparisons of differences in political structure among the four English-speaking democracies of Australia, Canada, Great Britain, and the United States. Seymour M. Lipset, "The Value Patterns of Democracy: A Case Study in Comparative Analysis," *American Sociological Review* 28 (1963): 515–32.

20. Emile Durkheim, *Suicide,* trans. by John A. Spaulding and George Simpson (New York: Free Press, 1951), p. 233.

21. For a discussion of Durkheim's study, with special reference to the problems of replication and statistical significance, cf. Hanan C. Selvin, "Durkheim's *Suicide* and Problems of Em-

pirical Research," *American Journal of Sociology* 63 (1958): 607–19.

22. Relevant works are Ernest W. Burgess and Harvey J. Locke, *The Family: From Institution to Companionship,* 2nd ed. (New York: American Book Company, 1953); W. F. Ogburn and M. F. Nimkoff, *Technology and the Changing Family* (Boston: Houghton Mifflin, 1955); Ernest R. Mowrer, *Family Disorganization: An Introduction to a Sociological Analysis* (Chicago: University of Chicago Press, 1927).

23. For example, Gideon Sjoberg, "Family Organization in the Pre-industrial City," *Marriage and Family Living* 18 (1956): 30–36; John Mogey, "Introduction" to "Changes in the Family," *International Social Science Journal* 14 (1962): 417; Eugene Litwak, "Occupational Mobility and Family Cohesion," and "Geographic Mobility and Extended Family Cohesion," *American Sociological Review* 25 (1960): 9–21 and 385–94; Sidney M. Greenfield, "Industrialization and the Family in Sociological Theory," *American Journal of Sociology* 67 (1961–62): 312–22. See also the brief but informative discussion by William J. Goode, in *The Family* (Englewood Cliffs, N.J.: Prentice-Hall, 1964), pp. 108–16.

Social Stratification

Social stratification, the study of equality and inequality across a broad spectrum of social contexts in which differential positions can be manifested, has been a major focus of sociological inquiry since the discipline's inception. Originally, interest in social stratification began as the study of social classes, sparked by the observations of Marx and others about the differentiations in social hierarchies in socialist and nonsocialist environments. Study then came to encompass occupational hierarchies and perceptions regarding differing occupational and class positions, as well as potential mobility between strata. In more recent times the study of social stratification has also focused attention on its expression in countries of differing levels of economic development (and dependency), as well as the role of a country's political position in determining the creation, elaboration, perpetuation, or diminution of social inequalities.

From a comparative perspective there are several contexts in which international differences in equality are pursued. One approach is to study differing perceptions of stratification, in class and occupation, for example, among nations. Are these perceptions the result of traditional attitudes (the culturalist position) or of structural characteristics? What determines the presence of inequalities? Of equalities? Political institutions, demographic patterns, labor market characteristics, elites, power over the resource allocation system—all these and many more impact the presence or absence of, and attitudes toward, social inequalities.

Our first selection, by Inkeles and Rossi, sets out to explore perceptions of occupational prestige across six industrial nations, asking specifically how these statuses are evaluated. The countries examined exhibit some noticeable variations in the maturity of industrialization that appear to stem from differentiations in their sociocultural systems. Also, the six studies examined by Inkeles and Rossi suffered from marked heterogeneity in their research designs. Nevertheless, the authors find predominantly for the structuralist position and suggest that there is a "relatively invariant hierarchy of prestige associated with the industrial system."

The next selection, by Treiman and Terrell, explores status attainment in the United States and Great Britain, especially with respect to father's occupation and the subject's education. Census data and materials from sociological research are used for the United States, and the British data are drawn from an independent study. Despite the two countries having quite different educational systems, the impact of education in both countries proves to be similar. As expected, Great Britain exhibits less intergenerational mobility than does the United States.

Initiated in 1977, Wright's Comparative Project on Class Structure set out to "create a systematic cross-national data set on class structure and class consciousness which incorporates Marxist and non-Marxist approaches to class." Taking a relational rather than a gradational approach to inequality, Wright presents an illustrative matrix and reviews several studies growing out of the project. His main argument is in favor of a Marxist approach to the definition of class position rather than the standard sociological approach.

National Comparisons of Occupational Prestige*

Alex Inkeles and Peter H. Rossi†

During the latter part of the nineteenth and the first half of the twentieth centuries the factory system of production was introduced, at least on a small scale, to most areas of the world. The factory has generally been accompanied by a relatively standard set of occupations, including the factory manager (sometimes also owner) and his administrative and clerical staff, engineering and lesser technical personnel, foremen, skilled, semiskilled, and unskilled workers. In the factory, authority and responsibility are allocated largely according to the degree of technical or administrative competence required for the job. In addition, the allocation of material and social rewards, the latter generally in the form of deference, is closely adjusted to levels of competence and degrees of authority and responsibility. The pattern of differentiation of authority is undoubtedly functionally necessary to the productive activity of the factory, and it may be that the associated pattern of reward differentiation is also functionally necessary.

There is, however, no clear-cut imperative arising from the structure of the factory as such which dictates how the incumbents of its typical statuses should be *evaluated* by the population at large. One possibility is that in popular esteem the typical occupations will stand relative to one another in a rank order strictly comparable to their standing in the formal hierarchy of competence, authority, and reward in the factory. It is also possible, however, that the popular evaluation of these occupations will be quite different. Indeed, where the factory system has been introduced into societies like those of Spain or Japan, with well-established values based on tradition and expressive of the

culture, one might expect significant differences between an occupation's standing in the formal hierarchy of the industrial system and its position in the popular ranking scheme.

Thus the interaction of the two systems—the standardized modern occupational system and the individual national value pattern for rating occupations—presents an interesting and important problem in comparative sociology.

We may posit two extreme positions in this interaction, while granting that it might be difficult to find live exponents of either. The extreme "structuralist" would presumably insist that the modern industrial occupational system is a highly coherent system, relatively impervious to influence by traditional culture patterns. Indeed, he might go so far as to insist that the traditional ranking system would in time have to be subsumed under, or integrated into, the industrial system. Consequently, his argument would run, even such occupations as priest, judge, provincial governor, not part of the modern occupational system and often given unusual deference, would come in time to have roughly the same standing relative to one another and to other occupations, no matter what their national cultural setting.

By contrast, an extreme "culturalist" might insist that within each country or culture the distinctive local value system would result in substantial—and, indeed, sometimes extreme—differences in the evaluation of particular jobs in the standardized modern occupational system. For example, he might assume that in the United States the company director would be rated unusually high because of our awe of the independent businessman and large corporations or that in the Soviet Union the standing of industrial workers would be much higher relative to managerial personnel than in Germany, with its emphasis on sharply differentiated status hierarchies. Furthermore, he might argue that the more traditional occupational roles assigned special importance in particular cultures would continue to maintain their distinctive positions in the different national hierarchies. Indeed, he might hold that the characteristic roles of the modern industrial system would come to be subsumed within the traditional rating system, each factory occupation being equated with some traditional occupation and then assigned a comparable rank.

A systematic test of these contrasting positions is not beyond the capacity of contemporary social research. A standard list of occupations—say thirty or forty in number—might be presented for evaluation to comparable samples from countries presenting a range of culture types and degrees of industrialization. The list should contain both standard industrial occupations and the common, but differentially valued, traditional roles (e.g., priest, legislator).

Data are available which, though far from completely adequate, will carry us a long way beyond mere speculation on these matters. In the postwar years studies of occupational ratings have been conducted in and reported on five relatively industrialized countries: the United States, Great Britain, New Zealand, Japan, and Germany.[1] In addition, the authors have available previously unpublished data for a sixth country, the Soviet Union.

Since these six studies[2] were, on the whole, undertaken quite independently, our ideal research design is clearly far from being fulfilled. Nevertheless, the data do permit tentative and exploratory cross-national comparisons.

The Comparability
of Research Designs

The elements of similarity and difference in the six studies may be quickly assessed from the following summary of their essential features:

Population Studied

United States. National sample of adults fourteen years and over; 2,920 respondents

Japan. Sample of males twenty to sixty-eight years of age in the six large cities of Japan; 899 respondents

Great Britain. Written questionnaires distributed through adult-education centers and other organizations; 1,056 returns (percentage returned unspecified)

U.S.S.R. Sample of displaced persons, mostly in DP camps near Munich, Germany, and some former DP's now residing on Eastern Seaboard of the United States; 2,100 written questionnaires

New Zealand. Sample collected mainly by interviews with inhabitants of town of 2,000, partly by mailed questionnaires (12 percent returns) sent out to town of 4,000; 1,033 questionnaires and interviews used

Germany. 1,500 Schleswig-Holsteiners: vocational-school students, university students, and male adults (not otherwise specified); adult sample only used here

Overlap among
Occupations Studied

Each study involved a different number of occupations, ranging from eighty-eight in the case of the National Opinion Research Center American study to thirteen in the Soviet research. Only the New Zealand and the British groups studied exactly the same occupations. Each of the remaining four studies used a different, but partially overlapping, set of occupations.

In order to make comparisons between pairs of countries, each occupation studied in each research was matched, when possible, with an occupation in the data gathered in the other country. In many cases it was necessary to disregard the information about an occupation in one of the paired countries because no comparable occupation was studied in the other. In other instances, in order to increase the number of occupations which could be compared for any given pair of countries, occupations were matched which were only very roughly comparable, for example, Buddhist priest and minister, or collective farm chairman and farm owner and operator. In most cases, however, a direct correspondence characterizes the pairs of occupations which are being equated. The reader is invited to turn to Table 8.5 (below), where the lists of occupations used from each of the researches are printed. The occupations listed on any row or line were matched. The number of pairs of similar or identical occupations for each cross-national comparison is shown in Table 8.1.

Nature of Rating Task

United States. Respondents were asked: "... Please pick out the statement that best gives your own *personal opinion* of the *general standing* that such a job has. Excellent standing, good standing, average standing, somewhat below average, poor standing."

Japan. Respondents were given a set of thirty cards and asked: "... Think of the general reputations they have with people, and sort them into five or more groups, from those which people think highly of to those which are not thought so well of."

Great Britain. Respondents were told: "We should like to know in what order, *as to their social standing,* you would grade the occupations in the list given to you. [Rate them] ... in terms of five main social classes ... ABCDE."

U.S.S.R. Respondents were asked: "Taking everything into consideration, how desirable was it to have the job of (———) in the Soviet Union? Very desirable? Desirable? So-so? Undesirable? Very undesirable?"

New Zealand. Same as in Great Britain.

Germany. The source is unfortunately not very specific about the rating task assigned. The respondents were apparently asked to rank-order a list of thirty-eight occupations presented as one slate.

Computing Prestige Position

With the exception of the German study, each research presents a "prestige score" for each of the occupations studied. These scores, computed variously, represent in each case the "average" rating given to each of the occupations by the entire sample of raters used. The German study presented only the rank-order positions of the occupations.

One is not sure whether differences between nations are generated by the differences in the questionnaires or the differences in the nations themselves. However, similarities in the prestige hierarchies, particularly when they are striking, are somewhat strengthened by the same lack of comparability in research designs and in the occupations matched to one another. Similarities may be interpreted as showing the extent to which design and other differences

T A B L E 8 . 1 Number of Identical or Similar Occupations Rated between Six Countries

	U.S.	Great Britain	U.S.S.R.	Japan	New Zealand	Germany
United States	—	24	10	25	24	20
Great Britain	—	—	7	14	30	12
U.S.S.R.	—	—	—	7	7	8
Japan	—	—	—	—	14	19
New Zealand	—	—	—	—	—	12
Total occupations studied	88	30	13	30	30	38

are overcome by the comparability among the prestige hierarchies themselves.

Comparability of Occupational Prestige Hierarchies

Since each study included some occupations used in another study, it is possible to compare the prestige hierarchies of occupations in pairs of countries by computing correlation coefficients for the scores (or ranks) of occupations. The fifteen correlation coefficients which result are presented in Table 8.2.[3] It will be seen immediately that the levels of correlation are considerably higher than the magnitude to be expected if there were only rough agreement on placement in the top and bottom halves of the prestige hierarchy. Indeed, twelve of the fifteen coefficients are above .9, and only one is below .8. The three coefficients below .9 all concern the Soviet ratings, which, it will be recalled, involve only a very small number of occupations, maximizing the chances for lower correlations arising from merely one or two "mismatches."

For most of the comparisons, furthermore, the findings go beyond establishing mere comparability of rank orders. With the exception of the correlations involving Germany, each coefficient represents the relationships between prestige *scores* given to the same occupations in

two different nations. Hence there is a high relationship between the relative "distance" between occupations, as expressed in score differences, as well. In other words, if, of two occupations, one is given a much lower score than the other by the raters in one country, this difference in prestige scores and not merely crude rank order also obtains in another country.

It should also be noted that these high correlations were obtained by using samples of occupations which were not strictly identical from country to country, including such very crude comparisons already mentioned as that of collective farm chairman and farm owner and operator. One may anticipate that if the occupations studied were more uniform, the similarities of prestige hierarchies from country to country would be even higher.

In other words, *despite the heterogeneity in research design, there exists among the six nations a marked degree of agreement on the relative prestige of matched occupations.* To this extent, therefore, it appears that the "structuralist" expectation is more nearly met than is the expectation based on the culturalist position.

Each of the six nations differs in the extent to which its prestige hierarchy resembles those of other nations. The average of the correlations for each nation, contained in the bottom row of Table 8.2, expresses these differences

T A B L E 8 . 2*   Correlations between Prestige Scores (or Ranks) Given to Comparable Occupations in Six National Studies

	U.S.S.R.	Japan	Great Britain	New Zealand	U.S.	Germany[†]
U.S.S.R.	—	.74	.83	.83	.90	.90
Japan	—	—	.92	.91	.93	.93
Great Britain	—	—	—	.97	.94	.97
New Zealand	—	—	—	—	.97	.96
United States	—	—	—	—	—	.96
Av. correlation	.84	.89	.93	.93	.94	.94

*See Table 8.1 for numbers of occupations involved in each comparison.
†All coefficients are product-moment correlations, with the exception of those involving Germany, which are rank-order coefficients.

among nations quantitatively. Thus we may see that the American and German occupational prestige hierarchies are most similar to those of other nations, while the Soviet and Japanese hierarchies are most dissimilar. When we consider that the Soviet Union and Japan are, of the six, the more recently industrialized cultures, we may see there some small degree of evidence for the culturalist position.

Furthermore, if we examine the correlations among the three nations which have the closest cultural ties and which share a common historical background and language—Great Britain, the United States, and New Zealand—we find these coefficients to be among the highest in Table 8.2. Again, the evidence to some extent supports the interpretation of a small "cultural" effect. However, the coefficients in question are not sufficiently distinguished in size from those involving Germany[4] and the three Anglo-Saxon nations to allow much weight to be given to the influence of the common Anglo-Saxon culture. In other words, whatever the national differences between the six, they do not greatly affect the general pattern of the prestige hierarchy.

National Patterns of Occupational Prestige

Although the relationships among the six occupational hierarchies are very high, they do not indicate one-to-one correspondences among the national ranks of occupations. Each nation shows some variation from every other, and the international discrepancies may perhaps throw further light on the relationships between social structure, culture, and occupational prestige.

One possibility is that unique aspects of the culture or social structure of a particular country determine distinctive appraisals of a certain type or types of occupation. National differences are thus to be interpreted in a unique fashion for each country.

A second possible explanation is that it is the type of occupation which engenders dis-

agreement, some occupations being similarly rated everywhere and others yielding no consistent rating. To some extent these contrasting explanations are similar, respectively, to the culturalist and structuralist positions discussed earlier.

Here again the available data place marked limits on the possibility of a definitive answer, but it is nevertheless feasible for us to go some distance in exploring the problem. In order to obtain some means by which to assess the presence or absence of disagreement among nations, regression equations were computed to predict the prestige positions of the occupations in one country as against the prestige positions of the comparable occupations in each other country. Ten such equations were computed, interrelating the prestige hierarchies in the United States, Japan, Great Britain, New Zealand, and the Soviet Union but excluding Germany, since the published data on that country indicated only the rank order of occupations. Those occupations which lay more than one standard deviation of the estimate off the regression lines were arbitrarily characterized as occupations over which there was a disagreement between the two nations involved.

Applying this criterion, we have, in Table 8.3, presented the discrepancies in ratings between all the relevant pairs of nations. The columns show the occupations rated higher by a given country in relation to each of the other countries represented in the rows. Reading the table by rows, we find the occupations rated lower by one country than by other nations, not forgetting that each comparison of a pair of countries involves a somewhat different set of occupations from the comparison of ratings for any other two countries. Only a few occupations, such as farmer, teacher, doctor, factory manager, and some form of industrial worker, were rated in all five countries and therefore appear in all the pairs of comparisons. Some occupations, such as judge, were rated in only two countries and therefore appear in only one paired comparison.[5]

Table 8.3 serves to highlight the special positions held by certain occupations in particular countries. For example, the Japanese Buddhist priest rates lower than a minister in each of the three available comparisons, and this undoubtedly reflects the cultural differences in structure and role between the Buddhist religion in Japan and the Judeo-Christian religion in the three Anglo-Saxon countries. Equally notable is the consistently lower position of farm manager as rated by displaced persons from the Soviet Union. While the occupation collective farm chairman is not strictly comparable to those with which it is matched, there can be no doubt that the displaced persons regard that occupation with a special ambivalence arising out of the position of agriculture in the Soviet economy during the last three decades.

Despite the clarity with which a particular occupation may stand out, it is difficult to find any definite *pattern* characterizing the disagreements expressed by any one country. Of course, such a pattern, if it does exist, may be obscured in our data by the modest number of occupations rated by each country. There are seldom more than one or two occupations of a given type in each of the comparisons, and it is hazardous to assume from the fact, for example, that since the Japanese rate the occupation newspaper reporter higher than Americans, Britishers, or New Zealanders, they would rate occupations *of this type* higher than the other two countries. Nevertheless, it will be noticed that in the country with the largest number of comparisons, the instances of disagreement involve a wide variety of quite disparate occupa-

T A B L E   8 . 3   Discrepancies in the Rating of Matched Occupations by Pairs of Nations*

	Rated Higher in Japan	**Rated Higher in U.S.**	**Rated Higher in Great Britain**	**Rated Higher in New Zealand**	**Rated Higher in U.S.S.R.**
Rated lower in Japan		Minister, farmer, insurance agent, carpenter	Minister, farmer, insurance agent	Minister, farmer, insurance agent	Accountant
Rated lower in U.S.	Company director, labor leader, reporter (news), street sweeper, shoe shiner		Accountant, chef, street sweeper	Accountant, farmer, truck driver, street sweeper	Engineer, worker
Rated lower in Great Britain	Reporter (news), street sweeper	Civil servant, truck driver, minister, building contractor, electrician		Truck driver	Worker
Rated lower in New Zealand	Reporter (news), street sweeper	Civil servant, building contractor, bookkeeper, electrician, dock worker	Chef, bartender		Worker
Rated lower in U.S.S.R.	Factory manager, farmer	Scientist, farmer	Farmer	Farmer	

*We consistently designate any cited occupation by the title closest and most familiar to Americans. For example, we used minister in preference to Buddhist priest, electrician rather than fitter (electrical). For the exact titles see Table 8.5.

tions. Those rated higher in the United States, for example, range from building contractor to farmer and from scientist to dock worker and appear to have little in common. The same range and absence of a common denominator are shown by the occupations rated lower in the United States. Furthermore, the discrepancies do not consistently appear in all the relevant comparisons: farm owner is out of line in only two out of four comparisons; as to truck driver, the two recorded disagreements go in opposite directions, that occupation being rated higher in comparison with Britain and lower in comparison with New Zealand.

International Comparability of Types of Occupation

If there is no clear-cut pattern of deviance by country, is there perhaps a tendency for certain types of occupation to be foci of disagreement? Perhaps if we classify occupations according to the features of social structure or culture to which they are most closely related, we may gain further insight into the interaction between culture, social structure, and occupational prestige hierarchies. To explore this question, we grouped all the occupations into seven basic types: industrial, clerical and commercial, professional, political, traditional crafts, agricultural and service occupations.[6] In Table 8.4 we have indicated the number of international comparisons between pairs among the five countries, again excluding Germany, which could be made involving the occupations in each class of occupations. We have also indicated the proportions of those comparisons which yielded disagreements. Disagreements were recorded on the same basis as in the preceding table, that is, on the basis of predictions from regression equations.

Because our findings so far have so strongly supported the structuralist expectation concerning the influence of industrialization in producing uniformity, our initial expectation may well be that occupations closely allied to the industrial system will enjoy highly compa-

rable standings from country to country, while occupations more remotely connected would be the focus of international discrepancies. Table 8.4 indicates that industrial occupations do enjoy comparable standing in all five countries. Nevertheless, the *lowest* proportion of disagreements is shown by the professions. In addition, other occupational types, such as the political occupations and the traditional crafts, which are not necessarily closely allied to the industrial system, manifested levels of disagreement as low as that enjoyed by the industrial occupations. Only the agricultural and service occupations yield a degree of disagreement which sets them apart from the other occupational groups.

Accounting for these discrepancies appears to require a combination of arguments. In the first place, some types of nonindustrial occupations are easily assimilated to the industrial system. The traditional crafts serve as the prime example here, since the skills involved in such occupations as bricklayer, carpenter,

T A B L E 8 . 4   Discrepancies in Prestige Position according to Type of Occupation

Occupation Types*	Proportion of Discrepancies (Percent)	No. of Comparisons
Professional	16	31
Industrial	24	29
Political	25	16
Traditional crafts	27	11
Clerical and commercial	32	37
Agricultural	50	16
Service	63	20

*Examples of occupations included in each type are as follows: *Professional:* doctor, minister, teacher, etc.; *industrial:* industrial worker, company director, factory manager, engineer; *political:* judge, civil servant, etc.; *traditional crafts:* bricklayer, carpenter, fisherman; *clerical and commercial:* accountant, bookkeeper, salesman, small entrepreneur, etc.; *agricultural:* farm owner and operator, farm hand; *service:* shoe shiner, barber, porter, streetcar conductor, etc.

TABLE 8.5

Occupation	Score	Occupation	Rank	Occupation	Score	Occupation	Score	Occupation	Score	Occupation	Score
United States		*Germany*		*Great Britain*		*New Zealand*		*Japan*		*U.S.S.R.*	
Physician	93	Doctor	2	Medical officer	1.3	Medical officer	1.4	Doctor	7.0	Doctor	75
State governor	93		1					Prefectural gov.	3.8		
College professor	89	Univ. professor						Univ. professor	4.6	Scientific worker	73
Scientist	89										
County judge	87							Local court judge	4.7		
Head of dept. in state government	87	High civil servant (Regierungsrat—höherer Beamter)	4	Civil servant	6.0	Civil servant	7.0	Section head of a government office	7.2		
Minister	87	Minister (Pfarrer)	6	Nonconformist minister	6.4	Nonconformist minister	5.9	Priest of a Buddhist temple	12.5		
Architect	86	(Elec. engineer)*	10	Country solicitor	2.6	Country solicitor	3.8	(Architect)	9.5		
Lawyer	86										
Member of board of directors of large corporation	86	Factory director (Fabrikdirektor)	5	Company director	1.6	Company director	3.6	Officer of a large company	5.5	Factory manager	65
Civil engineer	84	Elec. engineer	10					(Architect)†	9.5	Engineer	73
Owner of factory that employs about 100 people	82							Owner of a small or medium-sized factory	10.2		
Accountant for a large business	81			Chartered accountant	3.2	Chartered accountant	5.7	(Company office clerk)‡	16.1	Bookkeeper	62
Captain in regular army	80	Major (in armerd forces)	8							Officer in the armed services	58
Building contractor	79			Jobbing master builder	11.4	Jobbing master builder	10.7				
Instructor in public schools (teacher)	78	Elementary-school teacher (Volksschullehrer)	11	Elementary-school teacher	10.8	Elementary-school teacher	10.3	Elementary-school teacher	11.7	Teacher	55
Farm owner-and-operator	76	Farmer (Bauer—mittelgrosser Betrieb)	13	Farmer	7.3	Farmer	8.1	Small independent farmer	16.4	Chairman of collective farm	38
Official of international labor union	75							Chairman of national labor federation	10.8		
Electrician	73										
Trained machinist	73	Skilled industrial worker (Industrie facharbeiter)	24	Fitter (elec.)	17.6	Fitter (elec.)	15.8				
Reporter on daily newspaper	71			News reporter	11.8	News reporter	13.8	Newspaper reporter	11.2		
Bookkeeper	68	Bank teller (bookkeeper in bank)	19	Routine clerk	16.1	Routine clerk	16.4	Company office clerk	16.1	(Bookkeeper)§	62
Insurance agent	68	Insurance agent	20	Insurance agent	14.6	Insurance agent	16.1	Insurance agent	20.2		

Traveling salesman for wholesale concern — 68		Commercial traveler — 12.0	Commercial traveler — 14.1	Commercial traveler — 14.1	
Policeman — 67	Postman — 23	Policeman — 16.1	Policeman — 15.5	Policeman — 16.4	
Mail carrier — 66	Carpenter — 18	Carpenter — 18.6	Carpenter — 17.0	Carpenter — 20.2	
Carpenter — 65	Noncommissioned officer — 31				
Corporal in regular army — 60	Machine operator (Maschinenschlosser-Geselle) — 26	(Composite of fitter, carpenter, bricklayer, tractor driver, coal hewer)‖ — 20.5	(Composite of fit-ter, carpenter, bricklayer, tractor driver, coal hewer)‖ — 20.9	Latheman — 21.1	Rank-and-file worker — 48
Machine operator in factory — 60	Barber — 16	Shop assistant — 20.2	Shop assistant — 20.2	Barber — 20.5	
Barber — 59	Store clerk (Verkäufer im Lebensmittel geschäft) — 28			Department-store clerk — 19.8	
Clerk in a store — 58				Fisherman — 22.0	Rank-and-file collective farmer — 18
Fisherman who owns own boat — 58	Conductor — 33	Chef — 13.8	Chef — 21.8	Bus driver — 20.9	
Streetcar motorman — 58		Carter — 25.8	Carrier# — 20.2		
Restaurant cook — 54	Farm laborer (worker) — 36	Agricultural laborer — 25.5	Agricultural laborer — 24.4	Coal miner — 23.7	
Truck driver — 54		Coal hewer — 23.2	Coal hewer — 24.7		
Farm hand — 50	Waiter (Kellner) — 30	Dock laborer — 27.0	Dock laborer — 28.3	Road worker — 24.8	
Coal miner — 49		Barman — 26.4	Barman — 28.3	Shoe shiner — 26.9	
Restaurant waiter — 48	(Unskilled laborer)** — 38	Road sweeper — 28.9	Road sweeper — 28.9		
Dock worker — 47	Bricklayer — 27	Bricklayer — 20.2	Bricklayer — 19.3	Owner of a retail store — 15.3	
Bartender — 44	Clothing-store owner — 12	Business manager — 6.0	Business manager — 5.3	Tailor — 17.7	
Street sweeper — 34	Tailor — 14	Works manager — 6.4	Works manager — 7.9	Street-stall keeper — 24.9	
Shoe shiner — 33	Street peddler — 35	News agent and tobacconist — 15.0	News agent and tobacconist — 15.4		
		Tractor driver — 23.0	Tractor driver — 22.8		
		Railway porter — 25.3	Railway porter — 25.3		

*Used here only for comparison with Japan. For comparison with other countries, see beginning "United States civil engineer."

†Architect is the only occupation of a technical nature in Japan and was used here as a comparison only with the Soviet Union.

‡Used here only for comparison with the Soviet Union. For comparison with other countries, see line beginning "United States bookkeeper."

§Used here only for comparison with Japan. For comparison with other countries, see line beginning "United States accountant for a large business." ‖

‖Used here only for comparison with the Soviet Union. For comparison with other countries, see individual occupations as they appear later in the table.

#As there was no comparable occupation in New Zealand, the occupation substituted was carrier.

**Used here only for comparison with Japan.

and plumber have a close resemblance to the skills of industrial workers. Indeed, some crafts have been partly incorporated into the industrial system, and, it may be argued, such occupations are easily placed within the hierarchy of industrial occupations and may tend to assume roughly the same position vis-à-vis industrial occupations. Likewise, some professions, such as engineering and applied scientific research, have a most immediate connection with the industrial system, and others, such as architecture, are easily equated with it.

However, closeness or assimilability to the industrial system will not suffice to explain the relatively stable position of other professions, such as doctor. Nor will it serve to explain the low proportion of disagreement concerning the political occupations. We must recognize that the nations being compared have certain structural and cultural features in common, in addition to the presence of industry. For example, they share certain needs, as for socialization, and values, such as health and systematic knowledge, which ensure relatively comparable standing to doctors, teachers, and scientists. Furthermore, all the countries compared have in common the national state, with which is associated a relatively standardized occupational structure ranging from ministers of state to local bureaucrats. In addition, both the professions and the political occupations are highly "visible," and agreement as to their standing is probably facilitated by the relatively objective and easily perceived indexes of power, knowledge, and skill manifested by their incumbents.

The types of occupation which generate the greatest amount of disagreement are highly variant and unstandardized or difficult to assimilate to the industrial structure. Agriculture may be conducted, as in Japan, on relatively small holdings, on collective farms as in the U.S.S.R., or, as in the western plains of the United States, in "agricultural factories." Being a farmer means very different things in each of the five countries, quite unlike the standardized image of the machinist or the factory

manager. It can be anticipated, however, that as agriculture tends to be similarly organized in different countries, agricultural occupations will achieve more uniform standing.

The "service" occupations—barber, shoe shiner, chef, street sweeper—show the greatest amount of variation. Many of them antedate the industrial system and are in agrarian as well as industrial societies. They have no fixed position relative to the industrial order, nor are they similar to typical industrial occupations, as are many of the traditional crafts. They therefore appear to be most easily evaluated according to the traditional culture. Personal service in countries like Japan and Great Britain, in which a servant class was historically well developed and benefited from intimate association with an aristocratic upper class, may still be regarded as not so degrading as in the more democratic societies, such as the United States and New Zealand. In fact, the greatest discrepancy to be found among all the comparisons involves the differences in prestige position accorded to chef in Great Britain as compared with either the United States or New Zealand, although in the case of the former the match was poor, since the comparable occupation was "restaurant cook." As these services come to be organized and mechanized—as in modern laundries or restaurants—they will become more thoroughly integrated into the larger economic order and may in time achieve more strictly comparable status from country to country.

All told, it would appear from this examination of international discrepancies that a great deal of weight must be given to the cross-national similarities in social structure which arise from the industrial system and from other common structural features, such as the national state. The greatest incidence of discrepancies occurs for occupations which are hardest to fit into either the one or the other structure. To this extent the structuralist position which we outlined earlier seems to be more heavily borne out in these data.

Summary and Conclusions

To sum up, our examination of occupational ratings in six modern industrialized countries reveals an extremely high level of agreement, going far beyond chance expectancy, as to the relative prestige of a wide range of specific occupations, despite the variety of sociocultural settings in which they are found. This strongly suggests that there is a relatively invariable hierarchy of prestige associated with the industrial system, even when it is placed in the context of larger social systems which are otherwise differentiated in important respects. In addition, the fact that the countries compared also have in common the national state and certain needs or values, such as interest in health, apparently also contributes to the observed regularity of the ratings, since both professional and political occupations are foci of agreement. Perhaps the most striking finding is the extent to which the different classes of occupation have been woven together into a single relatively unified occupational structure, more or less common to the six countries. At the same time, there is strong evidence that this relatively standardized occupational hierarchy does not apply without major exception to all occupations in all large-scale industrialized societies. In some instances, important disagreement may arise from the distinctive role of a single occupation in a particular country. In the majority of cases, however, the disagreement appears to involve certain classes of occupation, notably agricultural and service, about which there is only modest agreement. Disagreement probably reflects differences in the length and "maturity" of industrialization in various countries but also clearly results from differentiations in sociocultural systems which may well be relatively enduring.

Notes

*   From the *American Journal of Sociology* 61, no. 4 (1956): 329–39, by permission of the University of Chicago Press. Copyright 1956 by the University of Chicago Press.

†   We wish to express our appreciation to Edward A. Tiryakian for his voluntary services as research assistant and to Alice S. Rossi for a critical reading.

1.   Additional studies of occupational prestige are available for the United States and for Australia. The authors decided to restrict the United States data to the most comprehensive study available. The Australian case (Ronald Taft, "The Social Grading of Occupations in Australia," *British Journal of Sociology* 4, no. 2 [June 1953]) was not included in this report because it was felt that little was to be gained by the inclusion of another Anglo-Saxon country.

2.   (1) A. A. Congalton, "The Social Grading of Occupations in New Zealand," *British Journal of Sociology* 4, no. 1 (March 1953) (New Zealand data); (2) John Hall and D. Caradog Jones, "The Social Grading of Occupations," *British Journal of Sociology* 1, no. 1 (January 1950) (Great Britain); (3) National Opinion Research Center, "Jobs and Occupations: A Popular Evaluation," in Reinhard Bendix and S. Martin Lipset, *Class, Status, and Power* (Glencoe, Ill.: Free Press, 1953) (United States data); (4) the Schleswig-Holstein data are taken from an article published in *Der Spiegel,* June 30, 1954, reporting a study by Professor Karl-Martin Bolte, of Christian-Albrecht University, in Kiel, Germany, to be published early in 1955; (5) Research Committee, Japan Sociological Society, "Report of a Sample Survey of Social Stratification and Mobility in the Six Large Cities of Japan" (mimeographed; December 1952) (the authors are grateful to Professor Kunio Odaka, of the University of Tokyo, for bringing this valuable study to their attention); and (6) the Soviet materials were collected by the Project on the Soviet Social System of the Russian Research Center at Harvard University. The authors plan to publish several articles dealing with the special features of the occupational ratings secured from former Soviet citizens.

3.   Note that the correlation coefficients are all product-moment correlations, with the exception of the five coefficients involving the German study, which are rank-order correlations.

With the exception noted, these coefficients represent the degree of similarity between the prestige *scores* given to the occupations.

4. Since the correlations involving Germany are rank-order correlations, it is difficult to make comparisons of such coefficients with others in Table 8.1. However, the relationship between rank-order correlations and product-moment correlations is rather high in the upper ranges, and it can be taken for granted that if prestige scores were available for the German ratings, the analysis shown in Table 8.2 would not be materially altered.

5. Table 8.5 will be found a useful aid in this connection, since by reading across the rows of that table one can tell quickly how many times a particular occupation was evaluated and by which national samples.

6. See note to Table 8.4 for examples of occupations included in each type.

CHAPTER NINE

The Process of Status Attainment in the United States and Great Britain*

Donald J. Treiman and Kermit Terrell†

The belief that societal values influence social stratification systems is so intuitively comfortable that it has hardly been tested. A case in point is the comparative work on the stratification systems of the United States and Great Britain. The two countries are typically characterized as highly similar in structure but substantially different in value orientations. For example, Lipset (1966, pp. 162–64) asserts that "though the United States and Great Britain are both urbanized, industrialized, and have stable, democratic political systems, they are integrated around different values and class relations. . . . The United States, more than any other modern non-Communist industrial nation, emphasizes achievement, equalitarianism, universalism, and specificity. . . . The [British] *social class* system [by contrast] retains many elements of ascription, elitism, particularism, and diffuseness." Turner (1960), like Lipset, suggests that the two countries display toward upward mobility distinctive normative orientations that shape their respective educational systems. According to Turner, the British educational system is characterized by "sponsored" mobility, the American by "contest" mobility, and each form of educational mobility reflects national norms regarding social mobility in general.

These theoretical discussions, however, have failed to specify at the empirical level how the pattern and process of social mobility might be expected to vary in the two societies, if at all. While one might infer from the discussions of Lipset and Turner that a system of sponsored mobility implies a closer connection between educational achievement and subsequent status attainment than does a system of contest mobility (because sponsorship implies early recruitment and socialization to role requirements), no ready prediction is possible regarding the social origins of those recruited into various positions. This is especially true since the British system, as characterized by both Turner and Lipset, is a meritocracy in which recruitment into the elite educational system is based on talent. Lipset, citing Tocqueville, notes that the British system is "an 'open aristocracy,' which can be entered by achievement but which confers on new entrants many of the diffuse perquisites of rank enjoyed by those whose membership stems from their social background" (1966, p. 164).

Yet if these distinctions between normative orientations have any utility in helping us to understand differences between the British and American stratification systems, they must be reflected in the actual experiences of the respective populations—that is, they must create differences in the pattern of mobility and the process of status attainment. To date, there is no believable evidence on the question. We simply do not know whether and in what ways the mobility regimes of Britain and the United States differ. While studies of social mobility and of the role of education in mobility have been conducted in both countries (most notably Blau and Duncan [1967] in the United States and Glass [1954] in Great Britain), differences in analytic procedures and definitions of variables have precluded valid comparisons.[1] This difficulty has, in fact, been common to all attempts at comparative research on social mobility and the process of status attainment, with the result that it has heretofore been impossible to distinguish between true differences in social structure and differences resulting from variations in measurement procedures (Treiman 1975b). However, recently completed work in the comparative study of occupational structures (Treiman 1975a) has yielded a standardized procedure for scaling occupational status—a procedure which permits truly comparable cross-national comparisons. In addition, using the standard occupational scale as an "anchor," it is now possible to compare the role of education in status attainment for countries where educational systems differ markedly. This paper will demonstrate the utility of these procedures in the context of a substantive comparison of the process of status attainment in two such countries, the United States and Great Britain. We will consider a model which relates father's occupational status, son's educational attainment, son's occupational status, and son's annual income.

Data

The American data are from the representative national sample of 20,700 males aged 20–64 collected by the Current Population Survey of the U.S. Bureau of the Census in conjunction with the study of Occupational Changes in a Generation (OCG) (Blau and Duncan 1967, p. 13). The British data are from a representative sample of the adult population of England, Scotland, and Wales surveyed in 1963; data are available for 908 males (Butler and Stokes 1969, pp. 449–62). This survey has one major shortcoming: no information is available on father's education, a variable of substantial interest. But the omission does not present as great a difficulty as would appear at first glance. Data for the United States indicate that the effects of father's education and occupation on educational attainment overlap to a large extent, owing to the intercorrelation between these two variables. Blau and Duncan

(1967, pp. 169, 174) found that the two variables together account for 26 percent of the variance in educational attainment, while either variable alone accounts for approximately 20 percent.

Our analysis is restricted to white male heads of households aged twenty-five to sixty-four in the civilian labor force. The restrictions are based on the following considerations: (1) For the United States, data are available only for males and, in any event, the process of status attainment cannot be assumed to be similar for men and women.[2] (2) Age is restricted to avoid problems created by the facts that many younger men are still in school or in the military and most older men are retired. (3) In the British sample, income data are available only for heads of households. (4) Racial differences in the process of status attainment are known to be so substantial in the United States (Duncan 1968; Treiman and Terrell 1975) that we thought it best to restrict our comparison to the majority populations of the two countries. In addition, we have utilized only those cases for which complete data are available. This results in effective sample sizes of 10,479 for the United States and 536 for Great Britain. The American data were weighted to adjust for variations in response rates, following the normal practice of the U.S. Bureau of the Census. However, weights were chosen to yield a weighted N identical to the actual sample size to permit interpretable tests of significance.

One issue which does not receive as much attention as it deserves from survey analysts is the quality of the data generated by relatively small sample surveys based on stratified sampling procedures. While the British survey is a model of careful sampling procedures, it is nonetheless useful to check the distributions of data available for analysis against census distributions on the key variables, especially because complete interviews were obtained in only about four-fifths of the cases (79.4 percent—see Butler and Stokes [1969, pp. 452–57] for a detailed discussion of response rates). Accordingly, we compared the distributions of school-leaving age, occupation (by twenty-seven categories), and age for male respondents or main earners against the corresponding distributions of the 1961 British census, and computed an index of dissimilarity in each case (Duncan and Duncan 1955). In general, the distributions proved to be gratifyingly similar: in no case did the index of dissimilarity rise above 10; this is quite small as such figures go. Considering that the sample survey was conducted two years after the census with which we compared it (so that some true change in population characteristics could have occurred), the correspondence between census and sample distributions appears to be satisfactorily close.[3] Since the OCG data have been shown elsewhere to be of extremely high quality (Blau and Duncan 1967, pp. 451–55; U.S. Bureau of the Census 1963), we can proceed with confidence in the adequacy of our samples.

Comparability of Data

A major requirement of comparative analysis is to render the variables under consideration precisely comparable in each of the populations being studied. In the present instance we have three variables to consider—education, occupational status, and income. Income presents no problem, since in both countries data were collected on the annual income of respondents precoded into fairly small intervals. Simply scoring each interval by its midpoint and making appropriate estimates for the open-ended upper intervals produces an interval variable. Application of the appropriate exchange rate then yields a precisely comparable variable for the two countries. Occupational status and education, by contrast, are not amenable to such a straightforward approach.

Fortunately, however, it is possible to solve completely the problem of comparability in the measurement of occupational status by means of a Standard International Occupational Prestige Scale (hereafter referred to as the Standard Scale) (Treiman 1975a). Based on a collation of data from occupational prestige studies conducted in fifty-five countries around the world, the scale provides prestige scores for each of 509 occupations, classified according to the *International Standard Classification of Occupations* (International Labour Office 1969). Evidence of the Standard Scale's validity for measuring the occupational prestige hierarchy in any country can be found in the fact that the average correlation between the Standard Scale scores and scores derived from occupational prestige studies conducted in each of fifty-five countries is .91. For both the United States and Great Britain the correlations exceed .96 (Treiman 1975a, chap. 8). Since these correlations are far higher than those between scales which are normally treated as interchangeable, the Standard Scale can, in full confidence, be used to assign status scores to the occupational data for each country. Thus, through the use of the Standard Scale, the crucial requisite of coding comparability is fulfilled.

The recoding procedure for the occupational variables was carried out in a straightforward way. Standard Scale scores were assigned to each of the detailed census codes into which the data were initially coded (U.S. Bureau of the Census 1960; Great Britain Register General 1960). There was little difficulty in matching code categories between the classifications of either census and the Standard Scale categories. For the U.S. data, the matching procedure was carried out twice; the correlation between the scores assigned by the two coders exceeded .98.

The remaining variable of concern is educational attainment. Although differences between the British and American educational systems make it impossible to match directly levels or types of schooling in the two countries, it is nonetheless possible to compare them. To do so, we scale educational attainment by two different procedures, each of which provides comparability, and then assess the results of each approach.

The first procedure simply compares school-leaving age in Great Britain with years of school completed in this country. Both measures are in standard use in the countries in question. The British data include explicit information concerning school-leaving age; the American data are coded into educational attainment categories which are conventionally transformed into years of school completed. Both variables, then, school-leaving age and years of completed schooling, can be expressed as interval level measures.

We wished, however, to develop an alternative procedure, because it is not certain that school-leaving age is related in a linear manner to occupational attainment. In both the United States and Great Britain a year of schooling may well vary in its effect on occupational status depending upon where in the educational career it comes. For Britain, the matter is still more complex. Disparate schooling experiences of children of the same age often lead to different careers. For example, a child who drops out of grammar school at the age of fourteen is probably destined for some sort of white-collar employment, whereas one who drops out of secondary modern school at the same age is likely to end up in a manual job.

In view of these contingencies, it is necessary to explore the relationship between occupational attainment and types and amounts of educational experience. Table 9.1 presents a tabulation of mean occupational status for each category of education appearing in the American data.[4] Table 9.2 presents a similar tabulation for Great Britain. It is evident from Table 9.1 that in the United States additional years of schooling do not result in equal increments in occupational status. The importance of each additional year is greatest at the highest levels of educational attainment.

The educational picture in Britain is substantially more complicated. Whereas American education is essentially unidimensional— what counts is how long one has gone to school, not what sort of school one has attended[5]—in Great Britain the kind of schooling one receives, as well as school-leaving age, is of crucial importance. The basic tracking deci-

sion in Britain occurs at a very early age (approximately eleven years). Students are channeled into radically different types of schools on the basis of their academic records and their performances on the 11+ examinations (Floud, Halsey, and Martin 1956). A minority gain admission to grammar schools, which leads ultimately to university admission or at least to white-collar jobs. The majority enter secondary modern schools, which leads mainly to blue-collar jobs. Once routed to a secondary modern school, it is practically impossible to shift to a grammar school. Moreover, for some individuals additional schooling can have a substantial impact upon occupational attainment. Table 9.2 presents mean occupational attainment by type of school attended when the respondent initially left school and, for those categories containing enough cases, further breakdowns by school-leaving age and nature of subsequent schooling. Type of school attended, school-leaving age, and probability and type of subsequent schooling are, for the most part, so closely related that a complete cross-tabulation of these variables would produce a table consisting largely of empty cells.

At first glance, the homogeneity of British education is striking; over 80 percent of the sample attended secondary modern or similar schools. However, both delayed school-leaving age and subsequent schooling enhance occupational attainment. Technical college and teacher training have the greatest impact; but night school, by far the most popular form of continuing education, also contributes to occupational status attainment. *Type* of schooling is of substantial importance regardless of school-leaving age. For each age, those with grammar school educations have jobs of higher status than those with secondary modern educations. Grammar school can lead to very high status occupations if one stays long enough. Those leaving at age sixteen or later, have, on the average, jobs roughly equivalent in prestige to professional, technical, and higher administrative occupations (the mean Standard Scale score for "professional, technical, and related"

T A B L E   9 . 1   Mean and Standard Deviation of Occupational Prestige Scores by Level of Educational Attainment, for U.S. Males Aged 25–64

Level of Education	School-leaving Age	Occupational Prestige		
		M	**SD**	*N*
None	8	29.5	10.0	39
Elementary:				
1–4	10	34.5	9.9	308
5–7	12	36.3	9.3	951
8	14	38.1	10.3	1,564
High school:				
1–3	16	39.3	9.8	1,977
4	18	42.5	10.0	3,022
College:				
1–3	20	46.9	10.2	1,099
4	22	54.2	9.2	859
5 or more	24	62.1	11.1	660
Total		43.1	12.1	10,479

Note: School-leaving ages were estimated by adding six to the midpoint of years of school completed. However, the two lowest categories were assigned slightly different scores in order to conform to Blau and Duncan's coding of education (1967, pp. 165–66). As it turns out, the Blau-Duncan scoring produces a slightly higher education-occupation correlation than that produced when the education categories are scored with their midpoints.

occupations is 58 while that for "administrative and managerial" occupations is 64 [Treiman 1975a]). The scores for late grammar school leavers are similar to those for individuals attending public schools, technical colleges, and universities.[6]

In view of the complicated relationship between education and occupational attainment in Great Britain and the moderate nonlinearity in the relationship between years of school completed and occupational status in the United States, we sought an alternative procedure for scaling education which would permit a fully comparable analysis of the connection between schooling and subsequent status attainment in the two countries.[7] The strategy we adopted was to construct "effect-proportional scales" of educational attainment, based on the average occupational attainment of individuals in each education category (Lyons 1971). The basic procedure is to compute the mean on the criterion variable, in this case oc-

cupational status, for each category of the variable to be scaled and then simply to assign the mean scores as scale values. Such a method produces a scale which has the maximum correlation with the criterion variable of any possible scaling of the original categories. Since the educational systems of the two countries are so manifestly different, no direct comparison of educational outcomes can be made (except, as above, to consider the average effect of each additional year of schooling). What can be determined is whether the *dependence of occupational status on education* is greater or less in one place than in the other (or, possibly, the same in both places). This is precisely what effect-proportional scales measure: the extent to which an individual's score on an interval variable is dependent upon his placement in a category of an associated nominal variable.[8]

The choice of occupational status as the criterion variable is dictated by the primacy of the functional connection between education and

TABLE 9.2 Mean and Standard Deviation of Occupational Prestige Scores by Level of Educational Attainment, for British Males Aged 25–64*

	Type of Schooling and School-leaving Age										
	Elementary, Secondary Modern, etc.				Grammar, Senior Secondary, etc.				Commercial, etc.	Public School	Technical College
Subsequent Schooling	13 or Earlier	14	15	16 or Later	14	15	16	17 or Later			
Means											
None	32.1	34.3	33.2	36.4	41.6	36.3	43.8	47.0	41.8	46.8	—
Night School	35.3	36.5	42.0	50.7	38.0	34.5	49.6	63.0	—	—	57.7
Technical, etc	36.0	41.2	44.9	47.7	54.0	44.0	57.5	52.0	51.5	61.7	78.0
Total†	32.8	35.5	38.1	44.1	42.5	36.9	51.3	53.3	47.2	56.3	59.9
Standard Deviations											
None	9.5	7.8	10.5	9.7	7.0	14.6	5.9	5.8	4.6	10.4	—
Night school	5.9	8.7	9.1	8.7	7.6	7.1	7.7	0.0	—	—	7.6
Technical, etc.	0.0	12.0	10.9	12.4	8.5	11.3	12.1	11.0	14.5	15.9	0.0
Total†	8.5	8.7	11.2	11.1	8.6	12.0	11.1	10.9	10.7	14.2	9.1
Cases (N)											
None	32	192	39	8	5	10	6	5	5	4	—
Night school	9	65	25	7	5	4	5	1	—	—	9
Technical, etc.	1	19	7	3	2	2	6	8	4	3	1
Total†	45	283	79	21	13	17	22	22	10	9	11

*Four cases are excluded from the table, three for whom type of schooling is unknown and the lone individual in our sample who entered university directly from grammar school.

†Includes other subsequent schooling.

occupational attainment. In modern industrial societies—if not in all societies—the main purpose of schooling is to prepare individuals to perform roles in the occupational world. This is just as true when schooling is not specifically vocational as when it is; indeed, the characteristic feature of elite education is that it prepares persons to function effectively in a wide variety of circumstances and positions. In this study the questions of interest regarding educational attainment are: (1) How closely is it related to occupational attainment in the United States and in Great Britain? (2) To what extent does education serve as a vehicle for status maintenance or alternatively as a vehicle for social mobility? (3) To what extent does education affect income, either directly or indirectly through occupational achievement? To answer each of these questions, the appropriate scaling of education is precisely that which we have proposed here, because each question concerns the occupationally relevant aspects of educational attainment.

For the American data, respondents in each education category were simply assigned the mean occupational status scores presented in Table 9.1. For Britain we needed to account for three education variables: type of school attended, school-leaving age, and type of subsequent schooling. We therefore computed the regression of occupational status on a set of dummy variables corresponding to each of the categories of the three education variables and used this equation to derive predicted occupational status scores for each combination of variables. This procedure assumes that there are no interactions among these variables with respect to their effect on occupational attainment: Table 9.2 indicates that the assumption is probably reasonable.

Status Attainment in the United States and Great Britain

The first step in comparing the process of status attainment in the two countries is to compare the distribution of status attributes

(see Table 9.3). It is often assumed that the two occupational systems differ markedly, Britain's being much more working-class. There is, however, only limited support for this assumption. The mean occupational status of the male labor force is slightly higher (about 4.5 points) here than in Britain, but the standard deviations hardly differ.[9] In contrast, the educational structures are not at all similar, even when attention is restricted to school-leaving age. Americans spend about three more years in school than do the British,[10] and they exhibit much more variability in extent of schooling. Income differences are also substantial: annual income is far larger, on the average, and far more variable in the United States than in Britain.[11] As we shall see, these differences have important implications for the process of status attainment in the two countries.

The correlations reported in Table 9.3 allow us to draw a number of inferences regarding both the extent of social mobility and the degree of crystallization of the stratification systems in the two countries. First, there appears to be substantially less intergenerational occupational mobility in Britain: the British correlation is about 10 points higher. Since the correlations are based upon data scaled in identical ways, the difference between them must be attributed to a true difference in the mobility patterns of the two countries. Moreover, it does not simply reflect the substantial downward mobility of sons of farmers in the United States, since the difference in correlations is nearly as great for the nonfarm-origin population (the corresponding correlations are, respectively, .281 and .361, for the United States and Britain). Second, in Great Britain income is much more closely associated with education, occupational status, and father's occupation than it is here. Third, while the association between education and occupational status is stronger in the United States when school-leaving age is considered, it is stronger in Britain when type of schooling is taken into account via effect-proportional scaling. Taken together, these correlations indicate that the British strat-

TABLE 9.3   Correlations, Means, and Standard Deviations for Males Aged 25–64 in the United States* and Great Britain†

	School-leaving Age	Effect-proportional Education Scale	Occupa-tional Status	Income	*M*	SD
Father's occupational status:‡						
United States	.266	.293	.255	.157	41.0	10.3
Great Britain	.254	.335	.352	.305	35.3	10.5
School-leaving age:						
United States	—	.931	.532	.418	11.1	3.4
Great Britain	—	.716	.451	.491	14.5	1.3
Effect-proportional education scale:						
United States	—	—	.571	.406	43.1	6.9
Great Britain	—	—	.630	.585	38.8	7.3
Occupational status:‡						
United States	—	—	—	.393	43.1	12.1
Great Britain	—	—	—	.622	38.8	11.5
Annual income ($):						
United States	—	—	—	—	6,397	3,659
Great Britain	—	—	—	—	2,541	1,238

* $N = 10,479$.

† $N = 536$.

‡ Standard scale.

ification system is considerably more crystallized than our own; the various forms of advantage are more tightly intermeshed in Britain, creating a more unitary status hierarchy.

To examine how the greater crystallization of the British stratification system affects the opportunities of individuals, we estimate a model of status attainment for both the United States and Britain (Table 9.4). In this model, educational attainment is presumed to depend upon father's occupation; occupational status to depend upon educational attainment and father's occupation; and income to depend upon education, occupational status, and father's occupational status. In addition, each variable in the model is assumed to depend upon other unmeasured factors, which are assumed to be mutually uncorrelated.

Obviously, it would be useful to compare models containing many more of the variables known to affect the process of status attainment (see Duncan, Featherman, and Duncan 1972), but the limitations of available data do not permit this. However, even the limited set of variables under consideration can take us a substantial way toward understanding the British and American stratification systems. Table 9.4 presents estimates of the model based on both codings of the education variable (school-leaving age and the effect-proportional scale), presented in both metric and standardized form.

Consider first the influence of father's occupation on educational achievement. Turner (1960, pp. 861–62) has suggested that, because of the meritocratic character of the British edu-

TABLE 9.4	Coefficients for Alternative Versions of a Model of the Process of Status Attainment in the United States and Great Britain

	Dependent Variables					
	United States			Great Britain		
Independent Variables	**Education**	**Occupation**	**Income**	**Education**	**Occupation**	**Income**
	Effect-proportional Education Scale					
Metric coefficients:						
Father's occupation	.028*	.113	6.79	.032*	.174	6.90
	(.001)	(.010)	(3.25)	(.004)	(.038)	(4.09)
Education	—	6.57†	969†	—	6.65†	383†
		(.101)	(39.5)		(.403)	(51.8)
Occupation	—	—	71.4	—	—	43.6
			(3.22)			(4.53)
R^2	.086	.334	.204	.112	.420	.451
Standardized coefficients:						
Father's occupation	.293	.096	.019	.335	.159	.059
Education	—	.543	.265	—	.577	.309
Occupation	—	—	.237	—	—	.406
	School-leaving Age					
Metric coefficients:						
Father's occupation	.089	.143	7.28	.032	.278	8.31
	(.003)	(.010)	(3.21)	(.005)	(.042)	(4.09)
Education	—	1.76	305	—	3.38	241
		(.030)	(11.0)		(.336)	(34.1)
Occupation	—	—	70.8	—	—	51.7
			(3.11)			(4.04)
Intercept	7.47	17.6	−343	13.3	−20.0	−3,253
R^2	.071	.296	.216	.064	.274	.447
Standardized coefficients:						
Father's occupation	.266	.122	.021	.254	.254	.071
Education	—	.499	.287	—	.387	.257
Occupation	—	—	.235	—	—	.481

Note: Numbers in parentheses = standard errors.

*A semimetric coefficient, derived by dividing the corresponding standardized coefficient by the standard deviation of father's occupation. This indicates the expected difference on the educational scale, *expressed in standard deviations,* associated with a one *unit* difference in father's occupational status.

†A semimetric coefficient, derived by multiplying the corresponding standardized coefficient by the standard deviation of the dependent variable. This indicates the expected difference on the dependent variable *in metric units* associated with a 1 SD difference on the education scale.

cational system, educational attainment might depend less upon social origins in Britain than in the United States. However, this prediction fails to take account of several important factors. First, there is a well-documented correlation between social class and intelligence scores (Jensen 1969, pp. 75–78) which implies that, compared with middle-class children, working-class children start school at a disadvantage. Their disadvantage gradually increases at least up to age eleven (Plowden Report 1967, p. 31). As a result, class is highly associated with admission to grammar school even though the selection process is "objective" (Westergaard and Little 1967, pp. 53–55). Second, the British system is not as pure a meritocracy as the 11+ system would imply. For while the 11+ examination opens doors to children of all classes who do well, it also closes the same doors to working-class children who perform less well. There are, however, fewer limitations for the less competent children of the well-to-do; "public" schools (private secondary schools) admit children from financially and socially appropriate families even if they have performed poorly on the 11+ examinations (Baron 1965, p. 139; Banks 1968, p. 47). In fact, fully 22 percent of the boys aged eleven to thirteen from professional or managerial families attended public schools in 1950 in contrast with 4 percent of the sons of other nonmanual workers and fewer than 1 percent of the sons of manual workers (Westergaard and Little 1967, p. 54). Thus, in Britain as well as in the United States (Sewell and Shah 1967), educational attainment is not exclusively a matter of academic performance: one may succeed also on the basis of proper origins.[12]

In fact, as we have already seen when studying the correlations, the association between social origins and educational attainment is about the same in the two countries: in both places there is a modest tendency for the sons of high-status fathers to stay longer in school and to obtain the sort of schooling which leads to a high-status job. Both the standardized and semimetric[13] coefficients relating father's occupation to the effect-proportional education scale are substantially similar for the two countries. These coefficients provide empirical evidence that opportunities for occupational mobility through education are no more and no less restricted in Britain than in the United States.[14] But in both countries education is largely independent of social origins and thus serves mainly as a channel of social mobility rather than as an instrument of status maintenance.

If we accept Turner's (1960) characterization of the British educational system as fostering sponsored mobility by early selection on the basis of academic promise and subsequent socialization for elite or routine roles, we would predict a closer association between type of schooling and occupational attainment in Britain than in the United States. Once again, the theoretical prediction is not supported by the evidence. Although the occupational return for each additional year of schooling completed is clearly larger in Britain than in the United States (the metric coefficients are, respectively, 3.38 and 1.76), the standardized coefficient relating school-leaving age and occupational status is substantially smaller (.387, compared with .499 for the United States), demonstrating once again that the school-leaving-age variable misses much that is important in the British educational system. When the effect-proportional education scale is utilized, the connection between educational attainment and occupational status appears to be equally strong in the two countries: both the standardized and the semimetric coefficients are about the same. A difference of one standard deviation in educational attainment yields slightly more than half a standard deviation, or close to seven points, in expected occupational status in both countries. Thus, despite radical differences in the social organization of education and in the presumed normative structures supporting it (Turner 1960; Lipset 1966), the role of education in the intergenerational transmission of occupational status appears to be very similar in the two countries. In both, appropriate schooling is by far the most important means to occupational success.

The two countries do differ noticeably in the strength of the direct influence of father's on son's occupational status, that is, the tendency among those with a given amount of education to acquire occupations similar in prestige to those of their fathers. While this effect is not very strong in either country, in all comparisons of corresponding coefficients the coefficient for Britain is substantially larger than that for the United States. Since the effect of education is about the same in the two countries, this is the principal source of the stronger determination of occupational status in Great Britain than in this country. It would be worthwhile to consider how occupational opportunities are transmitted from one generation to the next in each of the two countries other than through educational attainment. We might ask to what extent the transmission of occupational status is direct, in the sense that fathers actually secure specific jobs for their sons. To what extent is it instead a consequence of opportunities and constraints which are created by such factors as variations among local labor markets; occupationally specific patterns of residence, contacts, lines of credit, and other advantages and disadvantages; and occupationally specific information, skills, and attitudes (see Ridge 1974, p. 34)? Unfortunately, data with which to conduct such an analysis are not available in the surveys utilized here. But this line of attack should be given high priority in future work.

Finally, we note that income is much more strongly determined by other status attributes in Great Britain than in the United States. Inspection of the coefficients in Table 9.4 indicates that this is primarily a consequence of the far stronger dependence of income on occupational status in Britain. Keith Hope, in a private communication, has suggested that this may reflect the fact that substantial numbers of British workers, both public and private, manual and nonmanual, work under nationally negotiated wage and salary agreements. But unpublished data for the Toro of Uganda (Kelley 1971) and for several Latin American cities (Sheets 1973) are more consistent with the British than with the American results, suggesting that ours may be the deviant society in this respect.[15] Obviously, this is a matter worthy of more detailed attention when better data become available.

In any event, the stronger connection between occupational status and income in Britain may account for the marked class differences in consumption patterns and other aspects of lifestyle which many observers have noted (e.g., Goldthorpe et al. 1969, pp. 1–29; Abrams 1968, pp. 138–42). Insofar as income depends upon the sort of work one does, occupation—the primary basis of both objective and subjective class position—comes to play a central role in setting both the standard and style of existence, in creating opportunities and imposing constraints. This relationship, then, may be the principal source of the widely assumed greater salience of class in British than in American life.[16]

Summary and Conclusions

The recent development of a Standard International Occupational Prestige Scale has permitted a uniquely precise comparison of the process of status attainment in the United States with that in Great Britain. In particular, comparisons have been made concerning the role of education in status attainment. Taking advantage of our ability to scale occupational status in an identical way for the two countries, we developed a scaling procedure which assesses educational attainment by scaling educational categories on the basis of their occupational effects as well as in terms of school-leaving age. We were also able to develop a comparable set of correlations involving income.

With these newly scaled data we have shown (1) that there is less intergenerational occupational mobility in Britain than in the United States, (2) that this difference is apparently due to the stronger direct effect of father's occupational status on son's occupational status in Britain, since (3) the effect of father's occupation on son's education and that of son's education on son's occupation are about equally strong in the two countries when an effect-proportional educational scale is used (but weaker in Britain when school-leaving age is used, because this variable fails to reflect the greater complexity of the British educational system), and (4) that income is more heavily dependent upon occupational attainment in Britain.

These results point to the existence of a somewhat more closed stratification system in Britain than in the United States. But they also suggest clearly that, despite large differences in educational systems, the role of educational attainment in occupational mobility is highly similar in the two countries. In particular, distinctions between sponsored and contest mobility are not reflected in differences in the general processes of occupational attainment in the two countries, although they may be somewhat more pertinent to the process of recruitment to the elite, a topic we could not consider here. Further research will need to focus on the means by which occupational opportunities and propensities for success are transmitted from father to son outside the educational system, since it is principally here that the difference in the extent of social mobility in the United States and Great Britain is to be found.

Appendix

Evidence that American education is essentially unidimensional is surprisingly hard to come by, but we have pulled together data from several sources which collectively demonstrate that, once years of schooling are taken into account, type of schooling adds little or nothing to the prediction of occupational status. First, for American youth there is little variation in

the type of primary and secondary education: about 90 percent attend public schools, and about 90 percent of those attending nonpublic schools attend Catholic parochial schools (Ferriss 1969, pp. 21, 376–77). Thus, at the precollege level the only important distinction in school type is between public and Catholic parochial schooling. But this distinction is of no consequence for occupational status attainment, once amount of schooling is taken into account. Computations provided by Richard Alba from a representative national sample of Catholic men (the data reported in Greeley and Rossi 1966) show a squared multiple correlation of .332 between a set of dummy variables representing amount of schooling completed and occupational status (measured by the Duncan index) and a squared multiple correlation of .346 between occupational status and amount of school plus type of schooling (all, some, or no Catholic schooling at the primary, secondary, and college levels).

It is still possible, however, that differences among public schools are important. Some evidence against this possibility is to be found in a comparison of "expected occupation," measured one year after high school graduation, between those who had completed an academic curriculum and those who had completed other curricula. From material published in Spaeth and Greeley (1970, p. 139) based on a sample of high school seniors surveyed as part of the Project Talent study, we computed the correlation of expected occupational status (coded in HSR-NORC occupational prestige scores [see Siegel 1971]) with a dichotomous variable scored one for those who had gone on to college and zero otherwise. We then computed the multiple correlation of occupational status with college attendance and a dichotomous variable distinguishing academic from other high school curricula. The squared correlations are, respectively, .335 and .351, indicating that curriculum makes virtually no difference in expected occupation once college attendance is taken into account.

Second, two studies of college differences support our claim. (1) Alwin (1973), using data from Sewell's representative sample of Wisconsin 1957 high school graduates, but restricting his sample to males who had had some college experience by 1964 and were no longer in school or in the military, explicitly addressed the question of whether type of college has any effect on occupational attainment. His conclusion is basically negative. Computations we performed with his results (Alwin 1973, p. 219) show that introduction of a set of dummy variables representing twelve types of colleges adds virtually nothing to the variance in occupational status (coded in Duncan scores) explained by years of school completed: the squared correlations are, respectively, .297 and .316. (2) Spaeth and Greeley (1970, p. 153) report correlations among years of graduate school completed, undergraduate college quality (Astin's "selectivity" index), and occupational status in 1968 (coded in HSR-NORC prestige scores), for a representative national sample of June 1961 college graduates. Once again the evidence is clear: quality of college has no effect on occupational status once years of postgraduate schooling are taken into account (the squared zero order and multiple correlations are, respectively, .230 and .240).

Finally, the OCG data themselves show that type of schooling has no independent effect in occupational attainment for the adult male labor force as a whole. The OCG questionnaire includes a question about whether respondents attended public, parochial, or other private schools, or various combinations of these. From the resulting data we computed a squared multiple correlation of .339 between a set of dummy variables representing amount of schooling completed and occupational status (measured by the Standard Scale) and a squared multiple correlation of .341 between occupational status and amount of schooling plus type of schooling. Thus, in sum, it is overwhelmingly obvious that type of schooling has virtually no effect on occupational attainment in the United States independent of its influence on amount of schooling obtained.

Notes

* From the *American Journal of Sociology* 81, no. 3 (1975): 563–83, by permission of the University of Chicago Press. Copyright 1975 by the University of Chicago Press.

† This is a revised version of a paper presented at the Annual Meeting of the American Sociological Association, New Orleans, August 1972. Preparation of the paper was supported by a grant from the National Science Foundation to Columbia University (no. 28050, "Societal Development and Social Mobility"). We are grateful to Robert Althauser, Vincent Covello, Otis Dudley Duncan, Jane Ferrar, Robert Hauser, Keith Hope, Jonathan Kelley, Alan Kerckhoff, and Judah Matras for their very helpful comments on earlier drafts.

1. Comparisons of mobility rates and patterns in the United States and Great Britain have been attempted by, among others, Hall and Ziegel (1954, pp. 260–65), Miller (1960), Lipset and Bendix (1959), Svalastoga (1965), Blau and Duncan (1967, pp. 432–35), Hope (1972), and Kerckhoff (1974). But the comparisons have been based either on noncomparable occupational classifications or on extreme aggregations of the data (into manual and nonmanual categories) designed to overcome differences in classification schemes. Moreover, various analysts have drawn contradictory conclusions from the same data, a fact which underscores the point that numerical results may depend as much on measurement procedures as on social reality and that standardized measurement procedures are therefore a necessary prerequisite to the valid attribution of observed differences to differences in social reality. To be sure, standardized measurement procedures may mask as well as reveal true differences, but this problem is best resolved by refining measurement, not by muddling it.

2. For the United States there is evidence indicating that the level and process of educational and occupational attainment are nearly identical for men and women but that the level and process of income attainment differ substan-

tially for the two sexes (Treiman and Terrell 1975).

3. There is no systematic bias in the sample, with the possible exception of school-leaving age. Those leaving school at age nineteen or older constitute 1.3 percent of the sample and 4.7 percent of the census distributions, indicating a possible underrepresentation of the highest levels of educational attainment in the sample. However, differences in the wording of the school-leaving-age questions in the census and survey could easily account for this discrepancy, since the census question encouraged and the survey question discouraged inclusion of schooling subsequent to initial school leaving, and such schooling is common in Britain (see Table 8.2). In any event, this difference and other differences between the sample and survey distributions are not large enough to have any notable effect on the coefficients we report.

4. Like most other American data sets, the OCG data available to us contained information, not on single years of schooling, but on levels of educational attainment which often encompass more than one year. Fortunately, however, there is some evidence that such aggregation is of little consequence. Data collected by the Bureau of the Census for the *Longitudinal Study of the Labor Market Experience of Women* (Parnes et al. 1970) include education coded in single years. From the original data we computed two multiple correlations, one between occupational status and a set of dummy variables corresponding to the education categories in the OCG data; another between occupational status and dummy variables for single years of schooling. (The occupational data are for husbands of a representative sample of married women aged thirty to forty-four). The squared correlations for the two relationships are .340 and .363. This indicates that the finer coding of educational attainment makes very little difference in predicting occupational status.

5. See Appendix for evidence supporting this claim.

6. Oddly, we have only one man out of 532 who indicates that he went straight through a university, and only 14 with a university education (2.6 percent of the sample). This is fewer than would be expected on the basis of esti-

mates of the proportion of the British population with university education. Floud (1954, p. 137) found that 2.8 percent of the adult population had a university education in 1949; today the figure must be higher. We suspect that the pattern in our sample of dropping out of school for a while before entering a university is not typical either, but we cannot confirm this suspicion.

7. While it might have been desirable to carry out separate analyses for individuals attending the various types of educational institutions in Britain, our data are not sufficient for this procedure. Of the 536 cases available for analysis, 428 attended elementary or secondary modern schools, leaving too few cases in any other category to support a separate analysis.

8. Note that the resulting correlation coefficient is identical to that obtained by computing the correlation ratio of occupation on education.

9. In fact, the shape of the distributions is remarkably similar. They are both unimodal and quite symmetrical about the mean. Of course, similarity in the occupational status distribution does not in itself imply that the British and Americans do the same *kinds* of work. However, as it turns out, both the industrial and occupational distributions of the labor force are substantially similar in the United States and Britain. From data (for 1960 and 1961) coded into the major group classifications of the International Labour Office (1967), we obtained an index of dissimilarity of 14.3 between the industrial distributions of the two countries and one of 16.2 between their occupational distributions. The manufacturing sector is slightly larger and the commercial sector slightly smaller in Britain than in the United States, and this difference is reflected in a larger proportion of the labor force in manual jobs and a smaller proportion in administrative jobs in Britain. No other differences are worthy of note.

10. School-leaving age is computed for the United States by adding six years to highest grade completed.

11. The British income data were converted into dollars at the 1963 official exchange rate: £1 = $2.80.

12. Because the British educational system was radically reorganized in 1944 in an attempt,

among other things, to create greater equality of opportunity, it would be of considerable interest to assess the effect of the changes on the process of status attainment. Unfortunately, our sample is both too old and too small to permit such an analysis. Only the youngest men in it began school after the reorganization; these men are still near the beginning of their work lives and hence cannot validly be compared with older men with respect to current occupational status. In any event, we have too few cases in our British sample to permit intercohort comparisons. Recently there have been two attempts to assess trends in rates and patterns of mobility in Great Britain and the United States; both concluded that no systematic trends are to be found. These studies (Hope 1974; Hauser et al. 1975), which are models of analytical excellence, must be taken as the definitive statements to date on this question.

13. One limitation of effect-proportional scales is that they have no intrinsic metric. Yet often, as in the present instance, it is useful to be able to interpret the connections between variables scaled in this way and variables which do have an intrinsic metric. Our present solution to this problem is to utilize what we have called "semimetric coefficients," in which regression coefficients are expressed in terms of the standard deviations of change in the effect-proportional scale associated with a unit of change in the metrically scaled variables, or vice versa. An alternative solution which we considered but rejected as beyond our ability to interpret would be to transform the effect-proportional scale for each country so as to give it a mean and standard deviation identical to the corresponding school-leaving-age (or years-of-school-completed) variable for that country. The resulting coefficients could then, perhaps, be interpreted as indicating the effect of an additional "year's worth" of schooling, taking account of the fact that some years are worth more than others depending on when in the educational career and in what type of school they occur. We invite others to consider the general problem of appropriate procedures for quantitative comparisons of the type we have attempted here.

14. Of course, variations in father's occupational status do produce greater variations in school-leaving age in the United States than in Britain (the metric coefficients are, respectively, .089 and .032). But this simply reflects the fact that the variance in school-leaving age is far smaller in Britain than in the United States. The standardized coefficients relating father's occupational status to school-leaving age (which are of course just the correlation coefficients) are nearly identical in the two countries.

15. In this connection it is interesting to note that American blacks of both sexes and white American women are much more similar to British males than to white American males with respect to income determination. For the three former groups income is well predicted by education and occupational status, just as it is for British males (Treiman and Terrell 1975).

16. Whether this assumption is in fact valid must be regarded as problematic in the absence of comparative data on class differences. Despite the sociological commonplace that British society is more class bound than American society, to our knowledge no systematic evidence exists regarding this question.

References

Abrams, Mark. 1968. "Some Measurements of Social Stratification in Britain." Pp. 133–44 in *Social Stratification,* edited by J. A. Jackson. Sociological Studies 1. Cambridge: Cambridge University Press.

Alwin, Duane F. 1973. "College Effects on Educational and Occupational Attainments." *American Sociological Review* 39 (April): 210–23.

Banks, Olive. 1968. *The Sociology of Education.* New York: Schocken.

Baron, G. 1965. *Society, Schools and Progress in England.* London: Pergamon.

Blau, Peter M., and Otis Dudley Duncan. 1967. *The American Occupational Structure.* New York: Wiley.

Butler, David, and Donald Stokes. 1969. *Political Change in Britain.* New York: St. Martin's.

Duncan, Otis Dudley. 1968. "Inheritance of Poverty or Inheritance of Race?" Pp. 85–110 in *On Understanding Poverty,* edited by Daniel P. Moynihan. New York: Basic.

Duncan, Otis Dudley, and Beverly Duncan. 1955. "A Methodological Analysis of Segregation Indexes." *American Sociological Review* 20 (April): 210–17.

Duncan, Otis Dudley, David L. Featherman, and Beverly Duncan. 1972. *Socioeconomic Background and Achievement.* New York: Seminar.

Ferriss, Abbott L. 1969. *Indicators of Trends in American Education.* New York: Russell Sage Foundation.

Floud, Jean. 1954. "The Educational Experience of the Adult Population of England and Wales as of July 1949." Pp. 98–140 in *Social Mobility in Britain,* edited by D. V. Glass. London: Routledge & Kegan Paul.

Floud, Jean, A. H. Halsey, and F. M. Martin. 1956. *Social Class and Educational Opportunity.* London: Heineman.

Glass, D. V., ed. 1954. *Social Mobility in Britain.* London: Routledge & Kegan Paul.

Goldthorpe, John H., David Lockwood, Frank Bechhofer, and Jennifer Platt. 1969. *The Affluent Worker in the Class Structure.* Cambridge: Cambridge University Press.

Great Britain Register General. 1960. *General Register Officer's Classification of Occupations, 1960.* London: Her Majesty's Stationery Office.

Greeley, Andrew M., and Peter H. Rossi. 1966. *The Education of Catholic Americans.* Chicago: Aldine.

Hall, J. R., and W. Ziegel. 1954. "Appendix 3: A Comparison of Social Mobility Data for England and Wales, Italy, France, and the U.S.A." Pp. 260–65 in *Social Mobility in Britain,* edited by D. V. Glass. London: Routledge & Kegan Paul.

Hauser, Robert M., John N. Koffel, Harry P. Travis, and Peter J. Dickinson. 1975. "Temporal Change in Occupational Mobility: Evidence and Hypotheses for Men in the United States." *American Sociological Review* 40 (June): 279–97.

Hope, Keith. 1972. "Quantifying Constraints on Social Mobility: The Latent Hierarchies of a Contingency Table." Pp. 121–90 in *The Analysis of Social Mobility: Methods and Approaches,* edited by Keith Hope. Oxford Studies in Social Mobility. Working papers 1. Oxford: Clarendon.

— — —. 1974. "Trends in the Openness of British Society in the Present Century." Paper presented at the Conference on Measurement and Models in Social Stratification, Toronto, August 14–16.

International Labour Office. 1967. *1967 Yearbook of Labour Statistics.* Geneva: International Labour Office.

— — —. 1969. *International Standard Classification of Occupations.* Rev. ed. Geneva: International Labour Office.

Jensen, Arthur R. 1969. "How Much Can We Boost IQ and Scholastic Achievement?" Pp. 1–124 in *Environment, Heredity, and Intelligence.* Harvard Educational Review Reprint Series no. 2. Cambridge, Mass.: Harvard Educational Review.

Kelley, Jonathan. 1971. "Social Mobility in Traditional Society: The Toro of Uganda." Ph.D. dissertation, University of California, Berkeley.

Kerckhoff, Alan C. 1974. "Stratification Processes and Outcomes in England and the United States." *American Sociological Review* 39 (December): 789–801.

Lipset, Seymour Martin. 1966. "Value Systems, Class, and the Democratic Polity: The United States and Great Britain." Pp. 161–71 in *Class, Status, and Power,* edited by Reinhard Bendix and Seymour Martin Lipset. 2nd ed. New York: Free Press.

Lipset, Seymour Martin, and Reinhard Bendix. 1959. *Social Mobility in Industrial Society.* Berkeley: University of California Press.

Lyons, Morgan. 1971. "Techniques for Using Ordinal Measures in Regression and Path Analysis." Pp. 147–74 in *Sociological Methodology 1971,* edited by Herbert L. Costner. San Francisco: Jossey-Bass.

Miller, S. M. 1960. "Comparative Social Mobility: A Trend Report and Bibliography." *Current Sociology* 9 (1): 1–89.

Parnes, Herbert S., John R. Shea, Ruth S. Spitz, Frederick A. Zeller, et al. 1970. *Dual Careers: A Longitudinal Study of the Labor Market Experience of Women.* Vol. 1. Washington, D.C.: Department of Labor.

Plowden Report. 1967. *Children and Their Primary Schools.* Vol. 1. *The Report.* London: Her Majesty's Stationery Office.

Ridge, J. M. 1974. "Fathers and Sons." Pp. 27–45 in *Mobility in Britain Reconsidered,* edited by J. M. Ridge. Oxford Studies in Social Mobility. Working papers 2. Oxford: Clarendon.

Sewell, William H., and Vimal P. Shah. 1967. "Socioeconomic Status, Intelligence and the Attainment of Higher Education." *Sociology of Education* 40 (Winter): 1–23.

Sheets, Betty. 1973. "The Process of Industrialization and Occupational Stratification in Three Latin American Cities: A Comparative Perspective." Unpublished manuscript, Center for Policy Research, New York.

Siegel, Paul M. 1971. "Prestige in the American Occupational Structure." Ph.D. dissertation, University of Chicago.

Spaeth, Joe L., and Andrew M. Greeley. 1970. *Recent Alumni and Higher Education: A Survey of College Graduates.* New York: McGraw-Hill.

Svalastoga, Kaare. 1965. "Social Mobility: The Western European Model." *Acta Sociologica* 9 (1–2): 175–82.

Treiman, Donald J. 1975a. *Occupational Prestige in Comparative Perspective.* New York: Academic.

———. 1975b. "Problems of Concept and Measurement in the Comparative Study of Occupational Mobility." *Social Science Research* 4 (September): 183–230.

Treiman, Donald J., and Kermit Terrell. 1975. "Sex and the Process of Status Attainment: A Comparison of Working Women and Men."

American Sociological Review 40 (April): 174–200.

Turner, Ralph H. 1960. "Sponsored and Contest Mobility and the School System." *American Sociological Review* 25 (December): 855–67.

U.S. Bureau of the Census. 1960. *Alphabetical Index of Occupations and Industries.* Rev. ed. Washington, D.C.: Government Printing Office.

———. 1963. *The Current Population Survey: A Report on Methodology.* Technical paper no. 7. Washington, D.C.: Government Printing Office.

Westergaard, John, and Alan Little. 1967. "Educational Opportunity and Social Selection in England and Wales: Trends and Policy Implications." Pp. 215–32 in *Social Objectives in Educational Planning.* Paris: OECD. (Reprinted in *Family, Class and Education,* edited by Maurice Craft. London: Longman, 1970.)

CHAPTER TEN

The Comparative Project on Class Structure and Class Consciousness: An Overview*

Erik Olin Wright

General Objectives of the Research

The Comparative Project on Class Structure and Class Consciousness began in 1977 as an attempt to remedy what I felt was a serious shortcoming in the Marxist tradition of research within sociology. Until very recently empirical investigations within the Marxist tradition have been almost exclusively restricted to historical and qualitative research. This is to be explained by a variety of factors: the general hostility of radical scholars in general to "positivism"; the particular substantive concerns of Marxists with broad historical dynamics; the general hostility of academic programs that stress quantitative methods to the kinds of theoretical concerns and political commitments of Marxist students. Whatever the explanation, however, Marxist intellectuals have generally not pursued quantitative strategies of research.

As a graduate student in sociology in the early 1970s I decided that it was important for Marxism to engage in serious and systematic quantitative research. On the one hand, I felt that if Marxism was to be taken seriously within U.S. sociology, it was necessary to demonstrate its explanatory power on the central terrain of academic sociology, which is clearly quantitative research. This does not mean that quantification should preempt other lines of research, nor that it should be treated as some kind of privileged basis for developing and reconstructing theoretical arguments. But simply to abandon that terrain completely risked perpetuating the marginality of Marxism within the academy. On the other hand, quite

apart from problems of strengthening the academic legitimacy of Marxism, I felt that Marxism itself had much to gain from statistical research, both because of the conceptual discipline it imposes on the clarification of arguments (so that they can be operationalized), and because at least some of the important questions which are traditionally asked by Marxists can be illuminated through multivariate empirical strategies.

One problem faced by an aspiring "multivariate Marxist," however, was the lack of suitable data for such research. All of the already existing data sets of which I was aware had been gathered by scholars working in other theoretical traditions, and thus in general the categories embedded in the data reflected non-Marxist conceptual frameworks. The Comparative Project on Class Structure and Class Consciousness was therefore conceived initially as a way of remedying this deficit. The aspiration was to create a set of data which as rigorously as possible tried to operationalize and measure a range of core Marxian concepts, particularly around the problems of class structure and class consciousness.

The kind of survey research on which this project is based is very expensive, and an agenda of empirical research directed entirely within Marxism was not likely to win great support among funding agencies. It was therefore necessary to defend the project by pointing to intellectual gains beyond Marxist theory itself. To accomplish this task I argued that the Comparative Project would help to remedy two significant gaps between theoretical debates and empirical research in sociology. The first of these concerns the role of Marxism in sociology, particularly in theories of class and inequality. It would not be an exaggeration to say that the debate between Marxism and various non-Marxist approaches has been the central preoccupation of abstract theoretical discussions of class in Western sociology. And yet, remarkably, there is virtually no empirical research which attempts systematically to operationalize Marxist and non-Marxist class concepts and examine their respective empirical properties. One of the basic objectives of the Comparative Project was to develop a survey questionnaire which would effectively measure a variety of alternative class concepts and thus allow for such cross-paradigm research on class.

The second gap between theory and research which the project hoped to remedy concerns the relationship between macrostructural theory and empirical data analysis. Even though the heart of many sociological theories centers on the causes and consequences of the macrostructural properties of societies, systematic macrocomparative empirical investigations have played a relatively marginal role in contemporary sociological research. Most empirical research continues to take the macrostructural societal context of the problems under investigation for granted, and even fewer studies treat that macrostructural context as the object of investigation itself.

The reasons for this disjuncture between classical theory and contemporary research are twofold. First of all, there is simply the practical difficulty of conducting systematic comparative research of either a historical or quantitative cross-sectional character. In historical sociological research, comparative analyses require the mastering of historical material from several countries; in quantitative cross-sectional research, societal comparisons typically involve gathering survey data simultaneously from several countries, which, if nothing else, is usually financially prohibitive. Secondly, and perhaps ultimately more impor-

tantly, the ascendancy of survey research as the central technology of data gathering in contemporary sociology has tended to push sociologists into less macrostructural ways of understanding problems. Survey data are necessarily tagged on to individuals, and the use of survey data tends to encourage a kind of micropreoccupation in the practice of sociological research even where the announced theoretical concerns of the researcher are with social structure.

As a result of these factors, while there are literally tens of thousands of social surveys that have been carried out on national or local samples, there are relatively few which have been replicated systematically across countries. When sociologists do attempt comparative analyses, therefore, they are usually forced to rely on sets of data that are similar across national samples, but not strict replications. If careful and systematic macrocomparative research is to be carried out in ways that will advance our understanding of the differences among contemporary societies, it is essential that rigorously comparable detailed data be available for a range of countries. The Comparative Project on Class Structure and Class Consciousness has generated one of the most extensive sets of survey data of this kind.

The central objective of the Comparative Project, therefore, has been to create a systematic, cross-national dataset on class structure and class consciousness which incorporates as rigorously as possible a variety of measures of Marxist and non-Marxist approaches to class. In practice this has meant developing questions capable of tapping what is sometimes called the *relational* dimensions of inequality, particularly property relations, authority relations, and market relations. Much sociological work on stratification deploys exclusively *gradational* concepts of class. In such concepts, classes are envisioned as being rungs on a ladder, with one class being "above" or "below" another; thus the names of classes—upper, upper middle, middle, lower, and so on. In *relational* concepts, in contrast, classes are defined by specific kinds of social relations which bind them together, and the names of classes, accordingly, are derived from the relations which constitute them: lords and serfs within feudal relations, capitalists and workers within capitalist relations. One of the basic innovations of the Comparative Project was to attempt to develop a set of measures of such relational properties of classes.[1]

These relational class questions were then combined in a large questionnaire with a wide range of other kinds of questions on such things as class biography (class origins, occupational history, unemployment history), social networks, family structure, the sexual division of labor in the household, and a variety of social and political attitudes.

Theoretical Orientation

The conceptual problem which has animated much recent development in Marxist class theory, and has certainly motivated much of my own research, is what might be termed the "embarrassment" of the middle class. For all of their disagreements, all Marxists share a basic commitment to a polarized abstract concept of class relations, and yet the concrete class structures of contemporary advanced capitalist societies look anything but polarized. The basic conceptual problem, then, is to figure out how to accommodate such people as professionals, managers, teachers, and so on, within a Marxist class structural framework.

In the course of this project, my own theoretical orientation has undergone a considerable evolution. My initial work on the concept of class structure can be viewed as one possible solution to the problem of the middle class.[2] I argued that the positions aggregated under the popular rubric "middle class" should not be treated as *a* class at all. Rather, they should be viewed as locations which are simultaneously in more than one class, positions which I called "contradictory locations within class relations" (Wright 1976, 1978; see also Carchedi 1977).

Managers, for example, should be viewed as simultaneously in the working class (insofar as they are wage laborers dominated by capitalists) and in the capitalist class (insofar as they control the operation of production and the labor of workers).

In the course of my research in the Comparative Project I grew increasingly dissatisfied with this solution, on both empirical and theoretical grounds. At the heart of this dissatisfaction was the category "semiautonomous employees," positions which I had argued occupied a contradictory class location which combined working class and petty bourgeois (i.e., self-employed without employees) locations. Empirically, regardless of what specific criteria were used to operationalize "semiautonomous employees," there were always anomalous classifications. In the United States survey, for example, there is a janitor in an elementary school who performs a variety of "handyman" tasks and thus ended up being considerably more autonomous than an airline pilot in the sample. Of course this could be regarded as a profound discovery—that contrary to appearances, the pilot of a commercial jet is more firmly in the working class than a janitor. On the other hand, such results could indicate that autonomy itself should not be treated as a class criterion. Furthermore, even if I was willing to ignore the empirical anomalies, I was finding it increasingly difficult to defend theoretically the claim for nonanomalous cases that the class location of semiautonomous employees was indeed a "contradictory" fusion of working class and petty bourgeois classes.

In spite of these difficulties, I continued to use the framework of contradictory locations within class relations because I neither had a coherent diagnosis of its theoretical limitations nor a constructive idea about how to forge an alternative. I subsequently believed that I had reached a diagnosis and at least the basic ingredients for a reconceptualization.

My diagnosis was that in developing the concept of contradictory locations I had inadvertently shifted the basis for the concept of class from the concept of *exploitation* to the concept of *domination*. In spite of the fact that I generally affirmed the importance of exploitation for class analysis, in practice the concept of contradictory locations within class relations rested almost exclusively on relations of domination rather than exploitation. Managers, for example, were basically defined as a contradictory location because they were simultaneously dominators and dominated. Domination relations were also decisive in defining the class character of "semiautonomous employees" since "autonomy" defines a condition with respect to domination. In neither case did the concept of exploitation enter explicitly into the definition of these class locations.

For some people, of course, marginalizing the concept of exploitation is a virtue, not a sin. My own view, however, is that this is a serious weakness for two reasons. First, the shift to a domination-centered concept of class weakens the linkage between the analysis of class locations and the analysis of objective interests. The concept of "domination" does not in and of itself imply any specific interests of the actors. Parents dominate small children, but this does not imply that they have intrinsically opposed interests to their children. What would make those interests antagonistic is if the relation of parents to children were exploitative as well. Exploitation intrinsically implies a set of opposing material interests. Secondly, domination-centered concepts of class tend to slide into what can be termed the "multiple oppressions" approach to understanding society. Societies, in this view, are characterized by a plurality of oppressions each rooted in a different form of domination—sexual, racial, national, economic, and so on—none of which have any explanatory priority over any other. Class, then, becomes just one of many oppressions, with no particular centrality to social and historical analysis.[3] Again, this displacement of class from the center stage may be viewed as an achievement rather than a problem, but if

one wants to retain the traditional centrality Marxism has accorded to the concept of class, then the domination-centered concept of class does pose real problems.

Given this diagnosis of the problem with the concept of contradictory class locations, the question becomes: Can the concept of exploitation be elaborated in such a way that it enables us to theorize coherently the "middle class" and thus generate concrete class maps of contemporary capitalist societies? Such an elaboration, I believe, can be found in the recent innovative work by the economist John Roemer (1982, 1982 et al.). While Roemer himself has not been particularly concerned with problems of empirical investigation or the elaboration of concrete maps of class structures, nevertheless his work does provide a rich foundation for such endeavors.

Roemer's critical contribution for sociological problems of class analysis has been to disentangle in a rigorous manner the concept of exploitation from the Marxian labor theory of value and elaborate a general set of conceptual tools for distinguishing different forms of exploitation. The intuition behind his technical arguments is as follows. We observe inequalities in the distribution of incomes, the real consumption packages available to individuals, families, groups. The concept of exploitation is a particular way of analyzing such inequalities. To describe an inequality as reflecting exploitation is to make the claim that there exists a particular kind of causal relationship between the incomes of different actors. More concretely, we will say that X exploits Y when it can be established that the welfare of X causally depends upon the deprivations of Y — X benefits at the *expense* of Y. In particular, in the case of *class* exploitation, X benefits by virtue of appropriating at least part of the social surplus produced by Y. The analysis of different forms of class exploitation, then, revolves around analyzing the specific *mechanisms* through which such appropriation occurs.

The central message of Roemer's approach to the analysis of exploitation is that the material basis of exploitation is inequalities in distributions of productive assets, or what is usually referred to as property relations. On the one hand, inequalities of assets are sufficient to account for transfers of surplus; on the other hand, different forms of asset inequality specify different systems of exploitation. Classes are then defined as positions within the social relations of production derived from these relations of exploitation.

In Roemer's own explicit formulation, only two kinds of assets are formally considered: physical assets (alienable assets in his terminology) and skill assets (inalienable assets). Inequalities in the former generate capitalist exploitation; inequalities in the latter, "socialist" exploitation.

I have extended Roemer's analysis by considering two additional productive assets: assets in people and assets in organization. Inequalities in the distribution of assets in people, or perhaps, more precisely, labor power assets, constitute the basis of *feudal* exploitation and the accompanying feudal class relations. Labor power is a productive asset (Cohen 1978: 40–41). In capitalist societies everyone owns one unit of this asset, namely themselves. In feudalism, on the other hand, ownership rights over labor power are unequally distributed: feudal lords have more than one unit, serfs have less than one unit. Feudal exploitation is thus exploitation (transfers of labor) which results from inequalities in the distribution of assets in labor power; feudal classes are defined by the social relations of production corresponding to feudal exploitation.

The second productive asset which I want to add to Roemer's analysis is more problematic. I will term it "organization assets." As both Adam Smith and Marx noted, the technical division of labor among producers was itself a source of productivity. The way the process of production is organized is a productive resource independent of the expenditure of labor power, the use of means of production, or the skills of the producer. Of course there is an interdependence between organization and these other assets, just as there is an interdependence between means of production and skills. However, organization—the conditions of coordinated cooperation among producers in a complex division of labor—is a productive resource in its own right. Inequalities in the distribution of this asset provide the basis for the distinctive forms of exploitation and the accompanying class relations of "state socialist" societies.

Concrete societies are always complicated combinations of different kinds of exploitation relations, and this generates a particularly complex map of corresponding class relations. Specifically, in most societies there will be many positions in the class structure which are *simultaneously* exploiters and exploited along different dimensions of exploitation relations. To be able to specify the class structures of concrete societies, therefore, we have to be able to define the range of possible exploitation relations in that society and the different ways in which these exploitation relations may be concretely combined.

In capitalist society, as I have reformulated Roemer's analysis, there are three principle types of exploitation: capitalist exploitation, based on unequal control over the means of production; bureaucratic or organization exploitation, based on unequal control over organization assets; and skill or credential exploitation, based on unequal control over scarce skills.

On the basis of these three forms of exploitation, the class structure of capitalist society can be mapped in the way illustrated in Table 10.1. For the purposes of the research in this project, the critical part of the table is the typology of class locations among nonowners of the means of production (wage earners). If the only relations of exploitation in capitalist society were capitalist—exploitation based strictly on ownership of the means of production—all of these positions would be firmly

TABLE 10.1   Basic Typology of Exploitation and Class

Assets in the Means of Production

Owners		*Nonowners (Wage Laborers)*			
1. Bourgeoisie U.S. 1.8% Sweden 0.7%	4. Expert manager U.S. 3.9% Sweden 4.4%	7. Semicredentialed manager U.S. 6.2% Sweden 4.0%	10. Uncredentialed manager U.S. 2.3% Sweden 2.5%	+	Organization assets
2. Small employers U.S. 6.0% Sweden 4.8%	5. Expert supervisors U.S. 3.7% Sweden 3.8%	8. Semicredentialed supervisors U.S. 6.8% Sweden 3.2%	11. Uncredentialed supervisor U.S. 6.9% Sweden 3.1%	>0	
3. Petty bourgeoisie U.S. 6.9% Sweden 5.4%	6. Expert nonmanager U.S. 3.4% Sweden 6.8%	9. Semicredentialed workers U.S. 12.2% Sweden 17.8%	12. Proletarian U.S. 39.9% Sweden 43.5%	−	
+	>0	−			

Skill/credential assets

Note: United States: N = 1,487. Sweden: N = 1,179. Distributions are of people working in the labor force, thus excluding unemployed, housewives, pensioners, and so on. For operationalizations, see Wright (1985: 303–17).

within the working class. The internal class divisions among wage earners, then, should be viewed as the result of the operation of two noncapitalist mechanisms of exploitation. The "middle class" of capitalist societies, in these terms, consists of those positions among wage earners which are also exploiters through bureaucratic mechanisms of exploitation and/or skill/credential mechanisms of exploitation. The working class, then, is defined as positions exploited along all three dimensions of exploitation.

Class structure defined in this way should be viewed as a structure of relations which determines a matrix of material class interests. "Exploitation" is an interest-generating concept, since it defines a social relation within which one party materially benefits at the expense of another. The map of class locations in Table 10.1 is therefore a map of exploitation-based interests, with some positions having rather complex, perhaps contradictory, interests with respect to exploitation since they are simultaneously exploiters and exploited.

The conceptual map of class locations illustrated in Table 10.1 constitutes the basic framework within which I am currently pursuing my comparative studies of class structure and its effects on class consciousness and other variables. Nevertheless, this new concept, like its predecessor, has significant internal, conceptual problems.[4] Among other things, the characterization of state-socialist societies as class systems based on organization exploitation is not entirely persuasive, nor is the implication of this view that managers in capitalism, by virtue of being organization exploiters, have an "objective" interest in statism. Furthermore, while it might be plausible to see ownership of skills as the basis for a kind of exploitation, it is less easy to see a specific class *relation* existing between the skill-owner and the unskilled, thus undermining the strong sense in which Marxist concepts of class structure attempt to be relational.

As a result of these and other conceptual issues, I continue to work on the basic problem of producing a concept of class structure which is at the same time theoretically coherent and empirically useful. However, since I do not believe that empirical research should wait until all conceptual problems are solved, I have embarked upon a series of studies which deploy this existing conceptual framework.

Preliminary Empirical Results of the Research

These data are being used to address a wide range of theoretical and empirical problems. The following examples illustrate some of the recent data analyses conducted within the American project.

Description of the American Class Structure (Wright et al. 1982; Wright 1985: Chapter 6)

Wright et al. (1982) was the first empirical study produced from the project, and was completed using my early model of class structure analysis (Wright 1978). Nevertheless, all of the major generalizations in that paper were confirmed in the subsequent work on class structure using the framework I elaborated in my 1985 book, *Classes.* Four general results in these analyses were particularly important:

1. The working class is by far the largest class in the U.S. class structure. Depending upon the details of the operationalization of the different dimensions of the class structure matrix, somewhere between 40 and 45 percent of the U.S. labor force is in the working class. If we add uncredentialed supervisors and semi-credentialed workers to this category, the figure rises to about 55–60 percent of the labor force.
2. Between 40 and 50 percent of all locations in the class structure have a "contradictory character": that is, in the multiple exploitations approach to class structure, they are simultaneously exploited and exploiting. The U.S. class structure cannot therefore be represented by any simple scheme of class polarization.
3. Lower-status white-collar *occupations* are virtually as proletarianized as manual occupations. It therefore makes little sense to consider such occupations as part of the "middle class."

4. Women and blacks are considerably more proletarianized than white males. Whereas among white males, 44 percent of the labor force falls into the semicredentialed workers and proletarianized workers categories combined (which might be termed the enlarged working class), the figure is nearly 57 percent for white women, 69 percent for black men, and 78 percent for black women. The result is that a sizable majority of the U.S. working class—close to 66 percent—is composed of women and minorities.

Comparative Analysis of the Swedish and U.S. Class Structures (Ahrne and Wright 1983; Wright 1985: Chapter 6)

These analyses attempt to accomplish two things: first, describe the basic similarities and differences between the class structures of Sweden and the United States, and second, decode the structural roots of the observed differences. The basic descriptive conclusions are as follows. While the overall class distributions in these two countries are not dramatically different, the working class is somewhat larger in Sweden than in the United States, and the supervisory "class" category considerably larger in the United States than in Sweden. The analysis then explores the extent to which the differences between the class structures of Sweden and the United States can be attributed to differences in the distribution of the labor force into industries, occupations, and state employment in the two countries, or to differences in the class distributions within industries, occupations, and the state. The findings unequivocally indicate that the overall differences between the two class structures cannot be attributed to different distributions across sectors, occupations, or state employment; they must be attributed directly to differences in the class relations themselves. In these terms, two facts are particularly striking: first, that in the United States, authority is much more closely linked to autonomy (in the 1983 paper) and credentials (in the 1984 chapter) than in Sweden, and, second, that there is much more supervision in general in the U.S. labor force. These results were interpreted in terms of the different roles and strategies of the labor movement in the two countries and the accompanying effects on the problem of social control within production.

Empirical Adjudications of Contending Class Definitions (Wright 1985: Chapter 5)

One of the general purposes for developing the class structure data in this project was to intervene in various kinds of theoretical disputes over the concept of class. In particular, I wanted to be able to provide an empirical strategy for adjudicating between contending definitions of the working class. The presupposition of such empirical intervention, of course, is that the debate in question is not simply over the use of words but rather consists of disputed *definitional criteria* for an agreed-upon theoretical *object.*

The basic strategy of this analysis is to cross-classify two definitions of the working class, and then examine the differences between, on the one hand, the cells in the table in which both definitions agree on the classification (agreed-upon workers and agreed-upon "middle class"), and the cells in which there are disputed classifications. Let us suppose, for example, that we are comparing two Marxist definitions of the working class. The issue then becomes: on some criterion variable which is supposedly affected by class location (income, attitudes, and so on) are those respondents classified as workers in definition 1 but classified as "middle class" in definition 2 more like the individuals classified as workers by both definitions or more like the individuals classified as nonworkers by both? If they are more like the agreed-upon workers, then this provides empirical support for the first definition.

Using this basic strategy, I compared my definition of the working class with two others—a simple manual labor definition and the more complex productive labor definition pro-

posed by Nicos Poulantzas. In both cases the results indicate that the exploitation-centered concept elaborated above was more consistent with the data than its rivals.

Class Structure and Class Consciousness (Wright 1985, Chapter 7; 1984b)

These papers explore the relationship between class structure, defined in terms of exploitation mechanisms, and class consciousness. If this conceptualization of class structure is correct, then one would expect an essentially monotonic relationship between location within that structure and class ideologies: as one moves along each of the dimensions of the class structure matrix in Table 10.1 from the "expert manager" corner of the wage-earner class structure to the working-class corner, ideological orientation should become increasing pro–working class.

Class consciousness, in these analyses, is measured by a very simple scale going from −6 (consistently pro-capitalist) to +6 (consistently pro–working class), based on an aggregation of six Likert items (items which register the strength of agreement/disagreement with various statements) from the survey. The basic results are presented in Table 10.2.

Several generalizations can be drawn from the results of this analysis: First, the essential patterning of class consciousness is basically the same in both Sweden and the United States: as you move along every dimension of the matrix from the proletarian corner of the table to the expert-manager corner, ideological orientation monotonically becomes more procapitalist. This adds considerable credibility to the proposed conceptualization of class. Secondly, there is virtually no difference between capitalists in the United States and Sweden on the class attitudes in the study, whereas Swedish workers are far more anticapitalist than U.S. workers. The degree of ideological polarization thus differs considerably across the two countries. Thirdly, while the overall shifts in

TABLE 10.2   Class Consciousness by Location in the Class Structure

I. The United States

Assets in the Means of Production

Owners		Nonowners (Wage Laborers)		
1. Bourgeoisie −1.31	4. Expert manager −1.46	7. Semi-cred. manager −0.34	10. Uncred. manager −0.29	+
2. Small employers −0.87	5. Expert supervisors −0.78	8. Semi-cred. supervisors −0.24	11. Uncred. supervisor +0.54	>0 Organization assets
3. Petty bourgeoisie −0.09	6. Expert nonmanager −0.09	9. Semi-cred. workers +0.78	12. Proletarian +0.78	−
+		>0	−	

Skill/credential assets

II. Sweden

Assets in the Means of Production

Owners		Nonowners (Wage Laborers)		
1. Bourgeoisie −2.00	4. Expert manager −0.70	7. Semi-cred. manager +1.03	10. Uncred. manager +1.81	+
2. Small employers −0.98	5. Expert supervisors +0.07	8. Semi-cred. supervisors +0.74	11. Uncred. supervisor +1.98	>0 Organization assets
3. Petty bourgeoisie −0.46	6. Expert nonmanager +1.29	9. Semi-cred. workers +2.81	12. Proletarian +2.60	−
+		>0	−	

Skill/credential assets

Note: Entries in the table are means on a simple pro–working class attitude scale. The values on the scale range from +6 (pro–working class on every item) to –6 (pro–capitalist class on every item). See Wright (1985: 146–47, 252–54) for details.

ideology are similarly patterned in the two countries, the critical ideological lines of demarcation between class locations are quite different: in the United States nearly 40 percent of the labor force is ideologically part of the "bourgeois coalition" whereas in Sweden this figure is less than 10 percent. Finally, none of these results appear to be artifacts of demo-graphic or biographical variables; the similarities and differences between the countries remain essentially the same when a wide range of controls are added to the analysis.

How should these findings be interpreted? At the most general level I think that these results indicate that individual class consciousness can be viewed as shaped by two general dynamics: on the one hand, individual consciousness is directly affected by class location insofar as that location determines a set of interests and experiences faced by the individual; on the other hand, consciousness is shaped by politics, insofar as the strategies of parties, unions, and other political actors determine the ways in which people interpret those experiences and act on their interests. In terms of the patterns discussed above, this implies that the basic similarities in underlying class structure in the two countries explain why the overall contours of the relationship between class structure and class consciousness are the same in the two countries; while the significant political differences explain the different types of class formations that are constructed on this common terrain.

Class Structure and Class Formation in Sweden and the United States (Wright et al. 1989)

This paper extends the analysis of the relationship between individual class location and attitudes to a more macroanalysis of the relationship between class structure and what we call "ideological class coalitions" in the United States and Sweden. The paper is based on the general theoretical argument that class structures impose limits of possibility on class formations, but do not determine unique patterns of class formations. A class structure imposes obstacles and opportunities on any political actor's attempt to organize people into class formations, and these obstacles and opportunities make certain class formations easy to create and stable once created, others difficult to create and precarious if formed, and still others virtually impossible to create.

The study of the empirical relationship between class structure and class formation, therefore, involves exploring the way actual class formations are produced within these limits. The central finding of the analysis in this paper is that Sweden is characterized by three distinct ideological coalitions, whereas in the United States there are only two clear ideological coalitions. At first glance this was quite a surprising result, since it might suggest that the United States was more ideologically polarized (two blocks) than Sweden (two blocks with an intermediary "buffer" coalition). On closer inspection, what became clear was that what is missing in the United States is a clearly differentiated working-class coalition: on the one hand the bourgeois coalition penetrates much deeper into the various middle-class "contradictory class locations," and on the other the working class is essentially absorbed into the middle-class ideological formation.

These differences in patterns suggest that in the process of class formation, two collective differentiations have occurred in Sweden which have been muted in the United States: on the one hand, the middle class has been able to differentiate itself ideologically from the bourgeoisie to a greater extent in Sweden than in the United States, and on the other, the working class has been able to differentiate itself ideologically more consistently from the middle class. We argue in the paper that the massive importance of state employment for the Swedish middle class provides a material basis for the first of these ideological differentiations, whereas the strength of the Swedish labor movement and the division between blue-collar and white-collar unionism provides a basis for the latter differentiation. Overall, then, the paper illustrates the argument that class structures generate limits on processes of class formation, but within those limits a variety of political and historical factors shape the actual patterns that emerge.

Temporality and Class Structure (Wright and Shin 1988)

This paper looks at the effects of class location and class mobility on class identity and class interest consciousness in Sweden and the United States. The paper argues that subjective understandings of identity and interest have different temporal structures: the former is rooted in one's biographical past, the latter in one's anticipated future. This implies that class mobility patterns should be more important in predicting class identities than in predicting subjective understandings of interests, whereas class locations should be better predictors of interest consciousness. These basic predictions hold for both the United States and Sweden. The most striking difference between the two countries is that both class mobility and class location have much more powerful effects on consciousness for Swedish men than for any other category in the analysis.

Women in the Class Structure (Wright 1989)

This paper examines the effects of family class composition on the class identities of married women in the United States and Sweden. The analysis is used to address the general problem of how to understand the class location of married women when their own jobs have a different class character from the jobs of their husbands. This issue has become particularly salient in recent years, both because of the large increase in the labor force participation of women and because of a range of debates sparked by feminism over the relationship between class and gender. More specifically, there has been considerable debate over the problem of defining the class location of married women in the labor force: should it be identified with their own class or with that of the "head of household," which is usually their husband's?[5]

In the paper I argue that if the class location of women is largely derived from that of their husband's, then their subjective class identity should be more systematically determined by the class location of their husband's jobs than of their own. The most striking finding of the study is that for U.S. married women, class identity is not at all affected by their own jobs once the class of their husband's job is taken into consideration, whereas for Swedish women, their own and their husband's jobs have roughly equal impact on their class identities. This suggests that the interconnection be-

tween individuals, families, and the class structure is quite different in the two countries. This might be due to the lower degree of economic dependence of Swedish women on their husbands due to redistributive policies of the state and greater labor-market equality, or it might be due to the ways in which class formation in Sweden is more closely linked to the workplace (thus enhancing the effects of everyone's own jobs on their identity) than in the United States.

The Degree of Openness of Class Boundaries (Wright, Western and Shin, paper unpublished)

This paper examines the patterns of friendship ties within and across class boundaries in the United States, Canada, Sweden, and Norway. While the data analysis is not yet complete, there are three basic preliminary findings in the analysis worth noting:

1. The basic class patterns of friendship ties are virtually identical in all four countries.
2. The boundary between workers and managers is much more permeable in all four countries than is the boundary between workers and experts. This result holds whether we merge supervisors and managers into a composite category or separate them.
3. The one case in which there seems to be significant difference across countries centers on the boundary between the working class and small employers: this boundary seems to be much less permeable in the United States than in the other countries.

Conclusion

"Multivariate Marxism" runs a number of significant risks. By proposing to operationalize and measure a range of central concepts within the Marxist tradition, it risks reducing the complexity of those concepts to a few simple empirical categories. By deploying these empirical measures in statistical models, it risks losing the "dialectical" and dynamic character of the explanations Marxists generally advocate. And by suggesting that Marxian arguments can be formulated as "testable hypotheses" within multivariate equations, it encourages empiricist attacks which may frequently do more to confuse than clarify the issues.

The underlying assumption of the Comparative Project on Class Structure and Class Consciousness has been that these risks are worth taking. While the new empirical insights generated by the research have, to date, been relatively modest, the very attempt at operationalizing abstract concepts and formulating precise arguments about the interconnections among these concepts has done much to clarify a range of dilemmas within the Marxist theory of class structure, class formation, and class consciousness. Now, with the full eleven-country data tape finally ready to be released, we will be able to see if these theoretical clarifications can be translated into enlightening new empirical analyses.

Notes

* From *Acta Sociologica* 32, no. 1 (1989): 3–16, by permission of the Scandinavian University Press. Copyright 1989 by the Scandinavian University Press.

1. The contrast between relational and gradational approaches to class is a familiar one in the sociological literature. For an early formulation, see Ossowski (1963). I discuss this contrast at some length in Chapter 1 of my book *Class Structure and Income Determination* (Wright 1979).

2. For a detailed review of the range of alternative conceptualizations within the Marxist tradition to the problem of understanding the middle class, see Wright (1980). For views of class within the Marxist tradition which differ significantly from my own, see Johnson (1982); Poulantzas (1975); Mallet (1975); Ehrenreich and Ehrenreich (1977); and Gouldner (1979).

3. This view is characteristic of what is sometimes called "post-Marxist" radical theory. Some of the leading proponents include Albert and Hahnel (1978, 1981), Cohen (1982), and Aaronowitz (1981).

4. These difficulties have been raised in a number of critical discussions of my book *Classes* (Wright 1985). See especially the collection appearing in the journal *Critical Sociology* (formerly *The Insurgent Sociologist*), Summer 1988, edited at the Sociology Department, University of Oregon.

5. See Goldthorpe (1983) for a recent statement of the conventional view that the class of married women should be derived from that of their husbands.

References

Aaronowitz, S. 1981. *The Crisis of Historical Materialism.* South Hadley, Mass.: J. F. Bergin Publishers.

Ahrne, G. and Wright, E. O. 1983. "Classes in the United States and Sweden: A Comparison." *Acta Sociologica* 26 (November): 211–35.

Albert, M. and Hahnel, R. 1978. *Unorthodox Marxism.* Boston: South End Press.

Carchedi, G. 1977. *The Economic Identification of Social Classes.* London: Routledge & Kegan Paul.

Cohen, G. A. *Karl Marx's Theory of History: A Defense.* Princeton, N J.:Princeton University Press.

Cohen, J. 1982. *Class and Civil Society: The Limits of Marxian Critical Theory.* Amherst, Mass.: University of Massachusetts Press.

Ehrenreich, B. and Ehrenreich, J. 1977. "The Professional-Managerial Class." *Radical America* 11(2): 7–31.

Goldthorpe, J. 1983. "Women and Class Analysis: In Defense of the Conventional View." *Sociology* 17(4): 465–88.

Gouldner, A. 1979. *The Future of Intellectuals and the Rise of the New Class.* New York: Seabury Press.

Johnson, D. (ed.) 1982. *Class and Social Development: A New Theory of the Middle Class.* Beverly Hills: Sage.

Mallet, S. 1975. *Essays on The New Working Class.* St. Louis: Telos Press.

Ossowski, S. 1963. *Class Structure in the Social Consciousness.* London: Routledge & Kegan Paul.

Poulantzas, N. 1975. *Classes in Contemporary Capitalism.* London: New Left Books.

Roemer, J. E. 1982. *A General Theory of Exploitation and Class.* Cambridge: Harvard University Press.

Roemer, J. E. et al. 1982. "Marxism, Functionalism, Game Theory: The Case for Methodological Individualism," *Theory and Society* 11(4) (July): 453–482

Wright, E. O. 1976. "Class Boundaries in Advanced Capitalist Societies." *New Left Review* 98.

Wright, E. O. 1978. *Class, Crisis and the State.* London: NLB/Verso.

Wright, E. O. 1979. *Class Structure and Income Determination.* New York: Academic Press.

Wright, E. O. 1980. "Varieties of Marxist Conceptions of Class Structure." *Politics and Society* 9(3): 323–70.

Wright, E. O. 1984. "A General Framework for the Analysis of Class Structure." *Politics and Society* (13): 383–423.

Wright, E. O. 1985. *Classes.* London: Verso.

Wright, E. O. 1989. "Women in the Class Structure." *Politics and Society* 17 (March): 35–66.

Wright, E. O., D. Hachen, J. Sprague, and, C. Costello. 1982. "The American Class Structure." *American Sociological Review* 47 (December): 709–26.

Wright, E. O., C. Howe, and, D. Cho. 1989. "Class Structure and Class Formation in Sweden and the United States." In M. Kohn (ed.), *Comparative Sociology.* Beverly Hills: Sage.

Wright, E. O., and Kwang-Yeong Shin. 1988. "Temporality, Class and Consciousness." *Sociological Theory* 6(1) (Spring): 58–83.

Family

Sociological studies of the family lend themselves well to comparative analysis. Indeed, the earliest such studies, though leaning heavily toward the anthropological perspective, are among the most famous sociological work. These early studies, focusing on such comparative phenomena as traditional kinship networks, matrilineal and patrilineal patterns, and matriarchal and patriarchal family systems, have given way to comparative studies exploring, for example, the impact of industrialization on the family. Here the nuclear family is seen as a consequence of the rise of industrialism, and that subject has been explored to great depth in recent years.

Today the family is also studied as an economic unit, a household, which is subject to many external forces dictated by economic reality, leading to inequalities and shifting forms and patterns of employment. Many such studies are couched in comparative terms as data become more widely available and comparable.

Our opening selection in this section by Höllinger and Haller takes up the question of whether or not kin ties are weakening in the social networks in the modern industrial societies of Europe and the New World. They find this to be more true of Americans and Australians than of Britons, Italians, or Hungarians. Level of economic development helps to explain these differences, although some clearly go back in time and have deep cultural roots. While there may have been some decline in the importance of kinship, however, it is not true that modern industrial societies have largely undermined close kin ties. On the contrary, most people in modern societies name close kin, along with friends, as being the most important persons in their lives.

Parental socialization values are explored in our second selection by Ellis, Lee, and Petersen. Using data from the Human Relations Area Files (122 cultures) and the Standard Cross-Cultural Sample (186 cultures), they tested to see how generally applicable might be the model developed in industrial societies indicating that the routinized and closely supervised quality of blue-collar work leads to attitudes and values on the part of blue-collar families emphasizing conformity in the socialization of children. In their larger sample of cultures they measured closeness of supervision in the economic, familial, and political domains, to see if such cultural qualities would lead to emphasizing conformity rather than self-reliance in child rearing. Although there were the inevitable complications and reservations, the evidence clearly supported the model.

Our final selection by Bridgeland, Smith, and Duane compares and contrasts child care for preschoolers in the United States and Sweden. Whereas Sweden is seen to have made a major national commitment to make preschool programs available to all children, the author notes that there is "no equivalent U.S. commitment to equal the child-care efforts in Sweden." Bridgeland and coauthors compare the political contexts of child-care policy in these two nations by examining not only the policies themselves but also the policymakers.

CHAPTER ELEVEN

Kinship and Social Networks in Modern Societies: A Cross-Cultural Comparison among Seven Nations*

Franz Höllinger and Max Haller

Introduction
Dissolution of Kin Networks in Modern Societies?

The transition from preindustrial, rural society to modern, industrial society led to new forms of personal social relationships. In preindustrial society, social networks were determined almost exclusively by primary groups of kin and village-community. In the course of industrialization and urbanization (which have not always gone together, however) the traditional production and living unit of the "houseful" ("Das Ganze Haus," Brunner, 1968) has been dissolved. Economic demands for increased geographic mobility led people to live at growing distance from their kin. Contacts with extended kin were reduced, while emotional bonds within the nuclear family became closer (Shorter, 1975; Rosenmayr, 1986).

In modern society, which typically is also a much more urbanized society, the individual can shape an increasing part of his personal network himself and change it during his life (Schulz, 1978). This is true for the more casual relations to acquaintances as well as for more enduring relations to friends and kin. Even the relationships toward close kin are no longer necessarily a lifelong commitment. Among those who marry more than one-third dissolve their marriage in most Western nations. Cohabitation without marriage and single-parent families are more and more legally recognized and accepted as equivalent options to the traditional marriage and complete family.

Until the 1940s and 1950s it was commonly held that in modern society primary groups lose their importance for people's social networks. It was assumed that tasks of socialization and social support, hitherto provided by kin and small communities, would gradually be taken over by social institutions. In fact, the local separation of household and workplace has led people to spend an increasing part of their lifetime not with the family but with peer groups of schoolmates and workmates. Many old people live alone[1] or spend their twilight years with other pensioners in old people's homes. Thus, secondary group relations form an increasing part of people's social networks.

Litwak and Szelenyi (1969) were among the first to argue that the structural changes of primary group relations must not necessarily reduce the importance of these groups. Modern means of transport and communication facilitate maintaining contacts with kin and friends even at larger distances. Even if some aspects of social support (help for sick, unemployed, old people) are provided by social institutions, primary groups of kin, friends, and neighborhood do still play a major role in providing help for immediate emergencies and emotional assistance with personal problems. Litwak and Szelenyi conclude that the definition of primary groups as permanent, face-to-face, affective, and noninstrumental relationships has to be modified. They argue that today regular face-to-face contact is not any more a definitional criterion of primary group relationships. According to their redefinition, Litwak and Szelenyi consider kin, friends, and neighbors as the three main primary groups. When speaking of primary groups in this article we will refer to this terminology. We think, however, that in modern society not only has there been a structural change in primary group relations (less face-to-face contact), but that relations to extended kin and neighbors no longer meet the requirements of primary group relations (permanence, affectiveness, noninstrumentality). In our interpretation, thus, the latter were primary groups in former times, but are not so today.

The dissolution of traditional family structures has also transformed the earlier, patriarchal, and authoritarian relations between parents and children. Today, parents view their children much more as equals. Reduced face-to-face contact with kin, particularly between parents and grown-up children, does not rule out the possibility that these relations can be even more satisfactory than in previous times (Shorter, 1975). Furstenberg (1987) has even argued that the emergence of new forms of living together (such as "conjugal succession") will lead to an increasing importance of kin relations in the future as children in such cases form part of two or more families. This argument, however, seems rather questionable to us. Having various "fathers" and "mothers" and consequently many grandparents does not imply that these family ties will be held up during all one's life.

Methods for Measuring Social Networks

In the past decades, various methods have been developed to record the structural changes in social networks. In this context, the most relevant model is the "ego-centered social network" (Marbach, 1986). It covers an individual's social relations and allows for quantifiable statements on the number of relations maintained, the frequency of contact, as well as on the functions of these relations. This model is used for the analysis of contacts with kin as well as non-kin. Up to now, the contact patterns in large cities (Pfeil, 1970; Schulz, 1978), differences between rural and urban populations (Fischer, 1982a; Ward-Crowe, 1978), and between social classes (Bott, 1957; Pearlin, 1971) have been the topics most frequently studied. In the past few years, the concept of ego-centered social networks has also been adopted by some national surveys, as for instance by the ALLBUS Survey in West Germany (1984), by the General Social Survey 1985 in the United States, or by the Austrian Microcensus "Contacts with Kin and Non-Kin" (ÖStZ, 1975). Findings from various studies on social networks, available for several Western countries, basically agree that the assumption that close kin relations have lost their importance today cannot be confirmed (Schenk, 1983). Close relatives, especially parents, do still hold center stage in personal networks. There are, however, differences between rural and urban populations and between social strata in the importance of extended kin as compared to friends and acquaintances. In larger cities as well as in middle classes, relations with extended kin become looser, while those with friends and acquaintances gain in importance (Fischer, 1982a; Höllinger, 1987). Overall, the crucial significance of an intact social support network for the individual's mental and physical health has been proved (Lin, et al., 1986).

There exist only few cross-national studies on this topic and they are limited to comparisons of two countries. Litwak and Szelenyi (1969) compared primary group structures in the United States and Hungary; Pearlin (1971) carried out a cross-national study on "Class Structure and Family Relations in the United States and Italy." Both these studies, however, have used different questionnaires in the two countries compared, which is not satisfactory from the viewpoint of a reliable method. The ALLBUS and General Social Survey studies, which involve a comparison of core social networks in Germany and the United States using a network instrument developed by R. S. Burt, meet higher methodological standards.

In the present paper, we are presenting an analysis from the 1986 survey of the International Social Survey Program (ISSP) on "Social Relations and Social Support" (another has been presented by Finch, 1989). This survey was a first attempt to provide data for a more extensive cross-national comparison.[2] In this survey, seven countries were included: Australia, Austria, Britain, West Germany, Hungary, Italy, and the United States. As in many other comparative studies, the inclusion of these countries was not to aim at a systematic comparison of different culture areas but arose from the participation of these countries in the ISSP. The countries can, however, be subdivided into several groups according to their socioeconomic development and their affiliation to specific cultures. Thus, our study is both concerned with "cross-cultural" comparisons of nations belonging to different culture areas and with "cross-national" comparisons of nation states belonging to the same culture area (Boh, 1989; Haller, 1990).

Hypotheses

The selection of countries included in the study allows us to test in a relatively systematic way several hypotheses on the relations between macrostructural, societal characteristics and the patterns of social networks and support. In this regard, we think that the following aspects have to be taken into account:

(1) *The takeoff of the Industrial Revolution and the present state of socioeconomic development:* According to modernization theories, in countries with an earlier industrialization and higher socioeconomic development the structural change of primary group relations will also be more pronounced. This implies that people will rely more on nuclear family relations than on those of extended kin. Secondary group relations have become more important in social support networks.

(2) *Degree of urbanization:* Living conditions in large cities exert a major influence on social relations (Pfeil, 1970; Fischer, 1982a). Thus, in countries with a higher degree of urbanization, relations with kin should have less and non-kin relations should have more importance as it is the case in countries with a lower degree of urbanization.

(3) *Geographic mobility:* Geographic mobility often leads to large distances between family members. It is quite obvious that the maintenance of contacts over such distances becomes more difficult. Consequently, also, the personal relevance of such contacts might decrease. The same might apply to neighborhood relations which are directly affected by geographic mobility (Sampson, 1988). The fact that geographic mobility is higher in North America (United States, Canada) as compared to Europe (Long, 1970), might also be combined with loosened family bonds and more flexible social networks in these countries.

(4) *Sociocultural factors:* Modern historical family research (Laslett and Wall, 1972; Mitterauer and Sieder, 1977, 1982) has disproved convincingly the earlier assumption of the predominance of the extended "stem" family (Le Bon) in preindustrial Europe. In preindustrial times, family structures differed considerably within the "European cultural areas" (Jordan, 1988). Simplifying somewhat, preindustrial Europe can be categorized into three areas. In northwestern and Central Europe, that is, in Britain, the northern parts of France and in the German-speaking countries, the two-generation family with parents and children only was widespread as early as in the sixteenth century. This phenomenon can be attributed to people marrying relatively late which had the consequence that (given the low life expectancy of that time) the period during which three generations overlapped was very short. Moreover, those children who did not hold any hereditary title to the farm of their parents had to work as servants on other farms. These characteristics of rural economy led to the members of a family living at growing dis-

tances. In Eastern and southeastern Europe, the Slavic language area, complex family structures, both three-generation families as well as living and production communities of brothers with their wives and children, were more common. In contrast to northwestern Europe, in this region the old farmer remained the head of the household until he died. People married earlier, more than one married son was allowed to stay on his father's farm with his family, and no nonfamily workers were hired. In the third area, southern Europe, extended family patterns were not very common. However, family bonds were a lot tighter than in northwestern Europe. The children stayed in their parents' house until they got married and the old farmer remained "pater familias" until his death.

While modernization theory holds that industrialization led to the disintegration of kin relations, these findings of historical family research suggest another interpretation: The lower cohesion of kin relationships was not only a result, but also a precondition for the earlier industrial development of northwestern Europe. Relatively weak kin ties and a rural economy based on nonfamily servant workers allowed for higher geographical mobility, one of the requirements for the Industrial Revolution.

After the transformation of the agricultural to an industrial and—in recent times—in a postindustrial society, these sociocultural differences of family patterns have become less important. The specific living conditions of the working-class family, on the one hand, and the bourgeois family, on the other hand, (Weber-Kellerman, 1974; Rosenbaum, 1981) have led to new class-specific types of families which are, however, on a supraregional level, relatively similar. Today the nuclear family is the dominant family type in all advanced industrialized countries. Nevertheless, the resistance against the liberalization of divorce laws in southern Europe could probably be explained by the fact that traditional close family structures are still alive. This can not only be attributed to an economic lag of these countries or to

the influence of Catholic norms but also to the old tradition of close family relations. On the other hand, the early liberalization of divorce laws and the historically very high divorce rate in the United States indicate that in America the change of family structures has begun earlier than in Europe (Furstenberg jun, 1987).

Socioeconomic Structure and Sociocultural Characteristics of the Countries in the Study

In our opinion these factors, that is, industrialization, urbanization, mobility, and sociocultural family patterns, and their mutual interaction, are crucial to explain international differences in social networks. In Table 11.1 we present some basic figures in this regard from which a rough classification of the countries results. For the time being, we do not want to tackle these economic and social indicators in detail. We want to point out only that different aspects of family structures in the various nations do not necessarily follow one single pattern; there exists also no specific pattern of "modern" family structures in the more developed countries as contrasted to "traditional" family structures in the economically less developed countries of our example. West Germany and Italy, for example, both have low birth rates and a high marriage age. Italy, however, in contrast to West Germany has a very low divorce rate. In both Australia and in Hungary—differing from each other considerably in terms of economic development—the marriage age was relatively low in 1983, whereas in (highly developed) West Germany marriage age was much higher. Thus, the distinction between "modern" and "traditional" family structures can be maintained, if at all, only within a given national or cultural context (Wurzbacher, 1987).

The distinction between a more traditional "community" and a more modern "society" orientation (to use Tönnies's distinction) is relevant not only from the chronological, but also from a geographic and sociocultural point of view. In his study of "national characteristics,"

TABLE 11.1 Selected Indicators of Socioeconomic and Demographic Structure for Seven Countries

	Australia	United States	Great Britain	Federal Republic of Germany	Austria	Hungary	Italy
GNP per capita (US$ 1000s) (1983)	10.7	14.1	9.1	11.4	9.2	2.1	6.3
Labor force in agriculture (1983)	5%	3%	3%	6%	9%	22%	12%
Labor force in agriculture (1900)	20%	21%	6%	29%	32%	52%	47%
Rural population (1983)*	10%	15%	25%	12%	37%	42%	20%
Divorce rate (1983)†	38	47	40	33	26	38	4
Birth rate (1983)‡	16	15	13	10	12	12	11
Married males, 20–24-year-old (1981)§	33%	28%	25%	16%	19%	34%	12%
Married females, 20–24-year-old (1981)§	60%	47%	46%	40%	43%	69%	44%

*Rural population: Towns of less than 5,000 inhabitants (see Table 11.2).
†Divorce rate: Number of divorces per 100 marriages.
‡Birth rate: Number of live-births per 1,000 population.
§Married males and females: Data for Italy: 1973; Australia: 1976.
Sources: Fischer Weltalmanach, 1986; *Demographic Yearbook of the United Nations, 1985;* Peter Flora: *State, Economy and Society in Western Europe 1815–1975*, Frankfurt–London–Chicago, 1983.

Peabody (1985) has categorized nations according to the prevalence of "community" or "society" values. The study of Peabody is based on Parsons's and Lipset's differentiation of the dichotomy of community and society into the scheme of pattern variables (Parsons, 1954). This allows for a more exact characterization of the relative prevalence of "private" versus "public" virtues in different nations. Private virtues correspond to affective, collective, particularistic, diffused, and ascribed orientation in social relations, public virtues correspond to the opposite orientation (affective neutrality, self-orientation, universalism, achievement, and specificity). Peabody concludes that Americans and Britons are more public-oriented, that among Germans and French private and public virtues are balanced, whereas Russians and Italians are mainly private-oriented (Greeley, 1989 shows that this dichotomy is closely related to the difference between the Protestant and

Catholic ethic; see also Haller, 1990). If we assume that private orientation means social networks consisting mainly of primary group relations and public orientation means social networks with more secondary relations, this classification is in accordance with historical family research, showing that in the southern and East European culture area primary-group ties are closer than in Northwestern Europe and that the Anglo-Saxon nations have gone even further in the dissolution of kin ties. Taking up Litwak and Szelenyi's argument that primary groups maintain their importance even in the most developed Western nations, cultural differences should be interpreted as "structural changes" of primary group relations. In this interpretation, primary group relations in public-oriented nations have only lost their character as permanent face-to-face relations, but still maintain their function of providing affective and instrumental support; in private-oriented nations, however, primary group relations still retain the character of permanent face-to-face relations.

Empirical Results

As mentioned earlier, the method of measuring social networks in the ISSP project was to present a questionnaire to representative samples of the population in each of the participating countries. In this way, a total of about 10,000 persons over eighteen years of age was interviewed. The size of the sample varied between 1,000 and 2,800 in the several countries. As in Italy the upper age limit was set at seventy-five years, people over seventy-five were excluded also in all other countries. In this context, it is worth noting that the age distribution of the sample population is of major importance because social contact patterns depend strongly on the life cycle. When comparing the age distribution in three groups (18–34, 35–54, 55–75-year-olds), the results varied only slightly between the countries.

The questionnaire consists of two parts. The first part investigates the spatial distance between and the frequency of contacts with parents, children, brothers and sisters, and other relatives as well as the number of friends and the frequency of contact with the respective best friend. These questions should give information on the structural differences of primary group relations in various countries, but they do not allow conclusions on the (emotional) quality of contacts. In the second part, the respondents were asked to select from a list of professional associations) those whom they would ask for help in certain emergency situations. We consider the provision of social support in such situations as an indicator of emotionally close personal relationships.

Frequency of Contact with Kin

We have started from the assumption that in all advanced industrial societies the nuclear family, consisting of parents and unmarried children, is the predominant family type. The findings show that this does basically apply to all countries of our sample. Nevertheless, some differences are already to be seen. In Italy, 12 percent of married children still live in their parents' household, in Austria and Hungary, the rate is 10 percent whereas in West Germany, the United States, Australia, and Britain it is only 3 to 5 percent. The different degree of maintaining close relations with the family becomes more apparent when comparing the percentage of unmarried young people over eighteen who live in their parents' household. In Italy, the proportion of children living in their parents' house until they get married is still very high. This is the case for 92 percent of singles. Even in Hungary (85 percent) and—surprisingly enough—in Britain (75 percent), only a small percentage of young people set out to live alone before they get married. In West Germany, the United States, and Australia, however, only one-third of unmarried youth live with their parents.[3]

Intercultural variations in the spatial closeness of relations between parents and children remain the same even after children have moved out from the parents' house. The percentage of those settling in the immediate neighborhood of their parents (at a walking distance of fifteen minutes) seems to be a good indicator of the importance which spatial propinquity to the parents may have when setting up house (Figure 11.1).[4] Again Italians (57 percent) and Hungarians (43 percent) most frequently settle close to their parents while Australians and Americans are the least "family-bound": here, only 25 percent live at a distance of fifteen minutes from their parents.

Does the different closeness of relations with kin have an impact on the varying frequency of contact at a given distance? Differences between the respective countries are not marked: 75 to 80 percent of Italians and Hungarians as well as 60 to 70 percent of Austrians, West Germans, and Americans who live very close to their parents, that is, at a distance of fifteen minutes, report that they see their parents every day or at least several times a week.

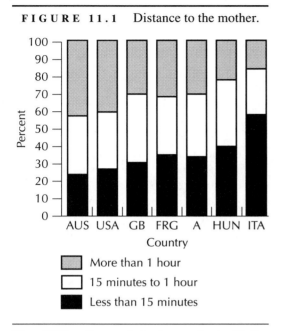

FIGURE 11.1   Distance to the mother.

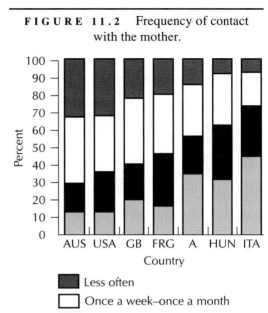

FIGURE 11.2   Frequency of contact with the mother.

(*Note:* 100% = all respondents whose mother is still alive but who do not live in the same household.)

However, only 50 percent of Australians and Britons see their parents that frequently.[5] We will return to the Australians' and Britons' reserved social contacts, which also apply to close relatives, at a later stage.

Considering together the cross-cultural variety of the frequency of children living in their parents' house, the typical distance from the parents' house when setting up one's own house, and the frequency of contact at a given spatial distance, the following result for the closeness of relations with parents in the individual countries is established (Figure 11.2): While approximately three-quarters of adult Italians with parents still alive either live in their house or go to visit them at least some days a week, only a quarter of Australians have comparably intense contacts. In Italy and Hungary, less than 10 percent indicate that they meet their parents only a few times a year or even less frequently. The corresponding figure for America and Australia is about 30 percent.

When talking about "contacts," we have up to now been referring to personal encounters. The questionnaire has also included items on other contacts with the parents, be it telephone calls or letters. Two-thirds of those meeting their parents only a few times a year or less frequently indicate that they write to or call up their parents at least once a month. These results apply to all countries except Hungary which can be attributed to the much less dense telephone network in this country. Thus, when taking into account these phone calls, the percentage of Australians and Americans who have hardly any contacts with their parents is reduced to about 10 percent. This confirms Litwak and Szelenyi's findings that the loss in permanent face-to-face contact with relatives does not mean a breakdown of social contact. Modern means of communication allow people to maintain personal relations even at larger distances.

What about contacts with other grown-up relatives? The questionnaire also asked for the frequency of contact and the spatial distance between the homes of the respondents and their children, brothers and sisters over eighteen, and one other relative. When a person had several children, brothers or sisters, or other relatives, he was to refer to the person he had the most frequent contact with. The frequency of contact with the parents compared with that with brothers and sisters or the one other relative is more or less the same in all countries (Figure 11.3 presents the respective contact patterns for three countries, Australia, West Germany, and Italy). The respondents stated that they see their brothers or sisters only half as often as their parents; the frequency of contact with the one other relative is more or less the same as with the parents. This result which, at first glance, seems rather surprising, can be explained as follows. In many cases, an interviewee's place of residence is nearer to the house of his spouse's parents, which has the consequence that this person meets his parents-in-law more often than his own parents.[6] This result means that most respondents have at least one relative they maintain close contact with. It does not indicate that their contact to all extended kin is as close as to their own parents. Therefore, our results do not falsify the thesis, often the subject of empirical studies, that in modern societies only the distant and not the close relatives lose importance in social networks. However, this thesis has to be modified. As can be seen in Figure 11.3, contact with extended kin declines in the proportion as the contact with close relatives is reduced.

Let us now try to explain these significant cross-cultural differences concerning family relations. As to European countries, the closeness of relations with kin increases gradually, moving from Britain to the Federal Republic of Germany, Austria and Hungary to Italy. Thus, earlier or later economic modernization goes hand in hand with more or less marked loosening of social contacts with the family. The findings established by historical family research mentioned in the introduction seem to make it plausible, however, that the lower frequency of contacts with kin in northwestern and Central Europe is

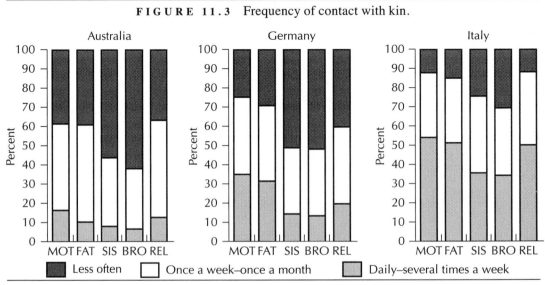

FIGURE 11.3   Frequency of contact with kin.

(*Note:* MOT = mother; FAT = father; SIS = sister; BRO = brother; REL = relative one sees most frequently; 100% = all respondents who do not live in the same household with the respective person.)

not only a consequence of economic modernization but also of the existence of specific kin structures dating back to preindustrial times.

In Italy, the tradition of close kin contacts which has deep sociocultural roots is still maintained to a high degree today. This can be demonstrated effectively by breaking down the data by regions within Italy. It turns out, then, that even in the northern parts of Italy where economic development has reached the levels prevailing in Central and northwestern Europe, the custom of children living with their parents until they get married is still alive. Our data indicate that there are hardly any differences between northern and southern Italy in this regard. The existence of close family ties in Italy has frequently been attributed to the strong impact of Roman Catholic family morality which does not allow for premarital cohabitation or for divorce (Finch, 1989). Austria and southern Germany are Catholic as well, but their traditional view of family life did not forbid premarital cohabitation (Mitterauer, 1983) and the rate of divorce has been relatively high in Austria since the 1920s (Haller, 1977). Thus, the Roman Catholic influence on family life in Italy can be explained only in connection with the sociocultural patterns of close kin ties in southern Europe.

Hungarians also maintain very close contacts with their family of procreation and their extended kin. In this case, the higher cohesion of families might be attributed to the fact that industrialization began later here than in other countries and is not yet that advanced. The scarcity of adequate housing might also "force" young Hungarians (often even couples) to live in their parents' household for a longer time (Finch, 1989). Studies of preindustrial family structures in Hungary indicate, however, that Hungary constitutes a transitional area between the family-centered Slavic and the more individualistic German culture area. This is why as early as in preindustrial times, basic conditions were quite different from those in Central and Western Europe (Farago, 1986). Unlike in

Italy, where close family ties are also reflected in low labor force participation of women and a low divorce rate, for some decades now the Socialist system in Hungary has established preconditions (encouragement of employment of women, relief of working mothers by introducing day-care centers, liberalization of divorce legislation) which could well hasten the erosion of close family structures.

The loosened kin ties in America and Australia compared with Europe can be explained by various factors. Although neither belonged to the early industrialized nations, they have caught up and even overtaken some of the highly industrialized European nations in this century. In both New World countries, however, other factors probably play a more important role. In America, as early as in the eighteenth century, the two-generation family, consisting of parents and children, was almost the only family pattern whereas, at that time, even in northwestern Europe extended forms of family organization were more frequent (Laslett and Wall, 1972). The inexhaustible land resources in America might have contributed to the fact that the establishment of new farms had not to be regulated by restrictive systems of heritage. Thus economic conditions stimulated the nuclear family's separation from extended kin (Parsons, 1954; Haller, 1989).

The structure of kin relations in Australia and the United States might be influenced by family traditions of the immigrant's nation of origin as well. The lasting cultural impact on kin relations is confirmed by an Australian study (Kendig and Rowland, 1983), showing that three-generation families are more common still nowadays among descendants of Southern and East European immigrants than among descendants of British immigrants, while both groups were exposed to the same modernization process. Thus, loosened kin relations in Australia can also be seen as a continuation of family traditions in Britain where most of Australian immigrants came from. For Americans, having similar kin-contact patterns as Australians, this argument cannot be upheld. White Anglo-Saxon Protestants (WASPs) contributed a major share to the shaping of American society but this nation is composed of natives from almost all European (and many extra-European) countries.[7]

The geographic size of America and Australia is certainly also a reason for the very high percentage of persons (more than 30 percent) who see their family only a few times a year. When Americans or Australians move, they will settle more often than Europeans at a spatial distance which makes it almost impossible to see their parents often. Almost 25 percent of Americans and Australians live more than five hours' traveling time away from their parents; in Europe it is only 10 percent. Geographic size, however, is not the only reason for the larger distance to the relatives. It is also the higher mobility of Americans and Australians compared to Europeans. According to our data, 28 percent of Americans but only 17 percent of West Germans and 6 percent of Austrians have changed residence within the past five years (in the other countries, this variable was, unfortunately, not included in the questionnaire). It is likely that Australians would show a mobility similar to Americans, whereas Italians, Hungarians, and British would probably have produced results similar to West Germans or Austrians. The less marked geographic mobility in Europe can, among other things, be ascribed to the fact that personal and social identity here is determined to a larger degree by regional affinities. So, even in small European countries like Austria or Switzerland, different subregions have developed and maintain rather specific sociocultural identities. These are reinforced by local dialects or even languages which linguistically make of Europe one of the most complex areas of the world (Jordan, 1988). Thus, a Sicilian would probably consider moving to northern Italy a more significant upheaval than an American moving from the East to the West Coast. Closer relations with kin in Europe must, therefore, also be seen in the context of the fact that Europeans

are more rooted in small regions bearing the imprint of a specific history and culture.

Urbanization and Contacts with Kin

We now want to have a closer look at the impact of urbanization on contact with kin. Previous network studies confirmed the assumption that in rural areas people meet their relatives, especially their extended kin, more frequently than do their fellow countrymen in urban areas (Fischer, 1982a; ÖStZ, 1975).[8] On the international level, this means that the higher the degree of urbanization of the respective countries, the larger the spatial distance from relatives and the less frequent are contacts with kin (with Australia as top of the list, declining then from the United States to Britain, the FRG, Austria, Hungary, and Italy).

It is rather difficult to measure the degree of urbanization in the respective countries in a reliable way, because national statistics use different category systems. The same problem arises when referring to the "urban-rural" variable in our data set. Australian, Austrian, and Italian statistics only categorize the size of the place of residence. In the United States and the FRG a compound variable, combining the size of the place of residence and the variable "metropolitan agglomerations" (suburbs of big cities), was used. Hungarian statistics do only distinguish between three categories, that is, "large city, "medium-size city," and "village/town." The British data record from the 1986 network questionnaire does not include an "urban-rural" variable, but the 1987 British Social Attitudes Survey uses a five-category scale, similar to the Hungarian classification. Taking the Hungarian categories as the basis for comparison, defining "large city" as a community with more than 100,000 inhabitants, "medium-size city" as a community with 5,000 to 100,000 inhabitants, and "village/town" as communities with fewer than 5,000 inhabitants, leads to the following Table 11.2, showing the degree of urbanization in the respective countries.

Among the seven countries studied, Australia has the largest percentage of metropoli-

TABLE 11.2 Degree of Urbanization

	Australia	United States	Great Britain	Federal Republic of Germany	Austria	Hungary	Italy
Larger cities (more than 100,000 inhabitants) %	61	30	38	40	30	36	29
Medium-size cities (5,000 to 100,000 inhabitants) %	30	55	37	48	32	22	51
Towns and villages (less than 5,000 inhabitants) %	9	15	25	12	37	42	20

Note: The following deviations from the categories used in the table arise due to different category systems in the individual counties. Australia: towns and villages, less than 1,000 inhabitants; United States: large cities, more than 50,000 inhabitants; medium-size cities, 2,500 to 50,000 inhabitants plus suburbs of large cities; towns and villages, less than 2,500 inhabitants; Federal Republic of Germany: medium-size cities, 5,000 to 100,000 inhabitants plus suburbs of large cities.

tan population (61 percent).[9] In all other countries, this percentage fluctuates between 30 to 40 percent. When adding the percentage of people living in suburbs of large cities to the metropolitan population, the percentage of the latter rises to more than 60 percent in the United States and the FRG. This method would also increase the percentage of urban population in other countries. Austria and Hungary, however, having 40 percent of rural population, are markedly less urbanized than the other countries.

When comparing the countries two by two, it becomes apparent that the supposed association between a higher degree of urbanization and a declining frequency of contact with relatives cannot be upheld in several cases. The United States and the FRG, for example, show a comparable degree of urbanization although the frequency of contact with relatives is much higher in West Germany than in the United States. From the comparison of Italy and Austria a negative association even emerges. Although Italy is more urbanized than Austria, Italians see their relatives more frequently than Austrians. Does this lead to the conclusion that the association between place of residence of the respondents (urban or rural), spatial distance, and frequency of contact with relatives differs cross-culturally?

We have calculated the strength of this association for the individual countries by means

TABLE 11.3 Association between Type of Residence ("Urban-Rural") and Spatial Distance/Frequency of Contact to the Mother

		Australia	United States	Federal Republic of Germany	Austria	Hungary	Italy
Urban-rural by spatial distance	tau-b	0.03	−0.02	0.14	0.23	0.19	0.16
	sign	n.s.	n.s.	s.s.	s.s.	s.s.	s.s.
Urban-rural by frequency of contact	tau-b	0.08	0.05	0.08	0.10	0.06	0.10
	sign	s.	n.s.	s.s.	s.	n.s.	s.

Notes: Positive coefficients signify an association between urban-rural and larger-smaller spatial distance/less-more frequent contacts with the mother. n.s. = not significant; s.s. = sign. <0.01; s. = sign <0.05.

of Kendall's tau-b.[10] In the United States and Australia, there is practically no association between the place of residence of interviewed persons and the distance to their mother's house. In Germany, Austria, Hungary, and Italy there is a significant association, that is, the larger the place of residence of the respondents the larger the distance to the mother's house. The association between size of the hometown and the frequency of contact with the mother corresponds to the expectation, that is, persons living in urban areas see their mothers more rarely. The strength of this association, however, is quite small in all countries (the respective tau-b values vary between 0.05 and 0.10).

Taking into account the major differences between countries with regard to frequency of contact mentioned above, this means that Americans and Australians both in urban and rural areas have a relatively low frequency of contact with kin. The data for the FRG and Austria suggest that in urban area loosened family contact is as widespread as in the United States although in small towns and villages close relations with kin are still somewhat more frequent. In Hungary and Italy, however, close kin relations are quite common both in rural and urban areas although in the latter relatives tend to live further away from each other.

The size of a settlement, measured by the number of inhabitants of an administrative unit, is only one aspect of urbanization. In this context, we should like to mention another factor which seems to be important. The seven countries studied differ more in the prevailing types of housing and, thus in types of settlement than in the degree of urbanization. Several sources of information disclose that approximately 80 percent of Americans, Australians, and British have their own houses (one-family dwellings or semidetached houses). In Austria this proportion is 57 percent, in West Germany 46 percent, and in Italy only 36 percent.[11] While in these three countries about half or more of the population lives in densely built-up housing estates, the Americans', Australians', and Britons' affection for their own

houses leads to widely scattered settlements. Even in large cities, the relatively small densely populated center is surrounded by huge housing belts consisting of thousands of single-family houses.

The Britons', Americans', and Australians' affection for their own houses may be attributed to their high standard of living as well as—in the case of the United States and Australia—to the low population density. The cross-cultural difference in patterns of living, however, points at a sociocultural factor as well, which is reflected by the British saying "My home is my castle." Family houses, in present-day America, very often contain a large array of fixtures, including air-conditioned rooms, a tightly filled refrigerator, a house bar, a swimming pool in the garden, making of the family house a self-sufficient unit. In this regard, the housing individualism in Britain and in the countries of the New World is an expression of the individualistic lifestyle in general (see also Willi, 1966; Münch, 1986). One aspect of this individualism is the importance ascribed to the privacy of the nuclear family. The fact that people distance themselves from their parents and other relatives is relevant also in the geographic sense. The vast settlements arising from the tradition of living in one-family houses have the consequence that members of a family live quite far apart even within one single town. The predominance of closed, densely built-up types of settlements in small-town and rural areas in Italy might help us to explain why the percentage of those living quite near their mother's house in rural areas is far higher here than in other countries (Italy 70 percent, Hungary, Austria, and Germany about 50 percent, United States 32 percent, Australia 23 percent).

Relations with Friends

Given the methodological restriction of the ISSP project (fifteen minutes for a self-administered questionnaire), relations with friends were examined only in a summary way. The questionnaire asked for the number of friends

	Australia (%)	United States (%)	Great Britain (%)	Federal Republic of Germany (%)	Austria (%)	Hungary (%)	Italy (%)
No friend	6	5	13	20	23	34	15
1–4 friends	38	44	45	50	48	44	53
5–9 friends	29	28	42*	19	18	12	18
10 or more friends	27	23		11	11	10	15
Total	100	100	100	100	100	100	100

TABLE 11.4   Number of Friends

*Great Britain: 5 or more friends.

as well as for the frequency of contacts with the best friend. Concerning the "number of friends" it has to be taken into account that the subjective approach to the question "who qualifies as a friend?" in different social strata and cultures depends on varying criteria (Duck and Perlmann, 1985). Thus, this question probably also measures sociocultural differences on the understanding of the term "friend" and not only the size of the network of friends, as it has been examined in methodologically more refined network studies (Fischer, 1982; see also note 14).

Let us first look at the overall results on the number of friends in cross-national perspective. Table 11.4 shows significant differences between the various countries. About 20 percent of West Germans and Austrians, and 34 percent of Hungarians state that they have no friend at all; in Australia and America the corresponding figure is only 5 percent. On the other hand, approximately 25 percent of Americans and Australians but only 10 percent of West Germans, Austrians, and Hungarians answered that they had more than ten friends. Eight percent of Americans and Australians hold that they even have more than twenty friends (whereas in other countries these levels were, by no means, reached). As mentioned above these differences have to be viewed as results of different sociocultural concepts of "friendship." As early as in 1936, Kurt Lewin considered the different meanings of

friendship as central in his classical comparison between Americans and Germans: "Compared with Germans, Americans seem to make quicker progress towards friendly relations in the beginning, and with many more persons. Yet this development often stops after a certain point; and the quickly acquired friends will, after years of relatively close relations, say goodbye as quickly as after a few weeks of acquaintance" (quoted in Peabody, 1985: 171). Similar observations can be found in de Tocqueville's book on "Democracy in America" (1976). Americans, and evidently Australians as well, define the concept of "friend" in a wider and more casual way than other nations (see also Fischer, 1982b). West Germans, Austrians, and Hungarians have fewer but probably more lasting friendships. The high number of people in West Germany, Austria, and Hungary stating that they had no friends at all suggests, however, that a sense of social isolation is more common in these countries. This might apply particularly to old people, who most frequently have no friends. More than 30 percent of over fifty-five-year-olds in West Germany and Austria and 55 percent in Hungary responded that they had no friends at all whereas only some 20 percent of Italians and Britons, and 10 percent of Americans and Australians gave the same answer.

With regard to the number of friends, Britons and Italians lie between Americans and Australians, on the one hand, and West Germans, Austrians, and Hungarians on the other hand. Similar results on this question, however, do not imply the same type of friendship in these countries. In his book on "National Characteristics," Peabody (1985) quoting various other authors describes the British as rather formal and reserved in their social relations. He holds that this applies to their closest social reference group as well. Italians, however, do not separate themselves from "others" in their privacy, they maintain informal and familiar relations not only with their relatives but also with their close friends. Our study underpins this assumption by the finding that Italians meet their best friend more frequently than the British (56 percent of Italians as compared to 37 percent of Britons meet their best friend several times a week). The same difference arises when we compare Australians and Americans. Although the average number of friends is the same in America and Australia, Australians are more reserved with their close friends than Americans. Twenty-five percent of Australians as opposed to 42 percent of Americans replied that they called on their best friends several times a week. The reserved form of personal relations, which can be shown also for the contact with close kin (controlling for the spatial distance, Australians and Britons see their parents less frequently than the other nationalities) can be attributed to sociocultural similarities between Australians and Britons. It is exactly this sociocultural aspect which also distinguishes Australians and Americans although in the rest of our study they are, in the most part, very similar.

Previous network studies found that the number of friends depends on the stage in the life cycle. The older the person the smaller the number of friends. In particular, the founding of one's own family usually leads to a reduction of contacts with friends (Fischer, 1982a; Schulz, 1978; a more specific recent study of Belsky and Rovine, 1984 found, however, that this generalization cannot be maintained). The number of friends depends largely on social class. This is less obvious among young people. Although the peer group structure varies from one social class to the other, peer group friendships are important for all young people. Class-specific differences become apparent mainly among older people. Persons with a higher educational level tend to have larger social friendship networks (Höllinger, 1987). As stated by the thesis of an increase on non-kin and secondary relations under urban living conditions, an extension of relations with friends and acquaintances in urban areas was empirically confirmed (Fischer, 1982a; ÖStZ, 1975).

Let us now try to investigate whether these assumptions and findings, which have been repeatedly asserted and tested within English- and German-speaking countries, will also be confirmed on the international level. When comparing the average number of friends according to age cohort (Figure 11.4),[12] there are only minor differences between the several countries in the youngest age-group (eighteen to twenty-four years). Differences become more marked in older age-groups. Data for Hungary, West Germany, and Austria confirm the assumption that the number of friends declines gradually in the course of one's life. (It has to be recalled that our statements on change of friendship networks in the life cycle are not based on longitudinal data.) The average number of friends reported by Italians and Australians hardly varies from age-group to age-group. In America, surprisingly enough, the average number of friends even increases in the older age cohorts.

The association between education and number of friends in our data confirms the findings of previous network studies. In all countries, respondents with a higher educational level report a larger number of friends.[13] The data do not confirm, however, the finding that the average number of friends is higher in urban areas. Only in Austria and Hungary did respondents living in cities name more friends than those living in rural areas. In the FRG and Australia, there are no differences between urban and rural areas, in the United States and

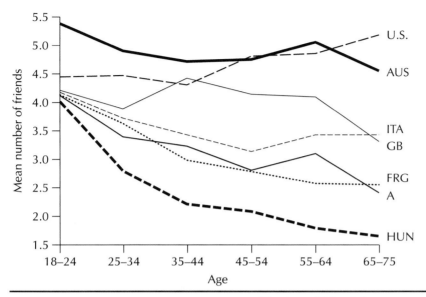

FIGURE 11.4 Number of friends by age.

Italy people living in rural areas replied that they had more friends.

Our results concerning friends do not correspond, in particular, to the American study carried out by Fischer (1982a). The Austrian microcensus survey (ÖStZ, 1975), however, produced similar results as the ISSP question on the number of friends. These partly inconsistent results are due to the use of different network instruments.[14] The validity of our question concerning the number of friends is depreciated only insofar as (in some countries more than in others) it cannot be used to measure the "actual" number of friends according to criteria which are the same for all respondents. However, when highlighting the subjective aspect, this question produces quite relevant findings for the cross-cultural comparison.

Social Support Provided by Kin, Non-Kin and, Professional Associations

The ISSP questionnaire included six hypothetical situations on this topic. The question was the following:

"Who would you turn to if . . .

1. You needed help for work in your house or garden
2. You had the flu and had to stay in bed for some days
3. You had to borrow a large sum of money
4. You had problems with your partner and could not talk with him/her about it
5. You were depressed
6. You had to make an important decision and needed advice"

For all these situations the respondents had to choose from a list of persons (father, mother, friend, neighbor, physician, etc.) the one they would turn to first and second for help. In order to make the abundance of data more accessible, we will limit ourselves to the two first and the two last questions, which go together.[15] "Help in the house" and "help during illness" might be called instrumental assistance which requires immediate neighborhood. "Help during depressions" and "advice with an important decision" involve emotional assistance, which might depend less on the distance between the persons involved. As the proportion of certain persons (categories) being named is quite similar in all countries, we will present the results of the accumulated data record for all countries.

TABLE 11.5   Who Do You Expect Help from in Emergency Situations*

	Instrumental Assistance (Household and Sickness)	Emotional Assistance (Depression and Important Decision)
Partner	29.7	27.9
Mother	8.8	8.7
Father	3.9	3.7
Daughter	9.5	7.2
Son	9.8	6.0
Sister	3.7	4.9
Brother	3.6	2.7
Other kin	5.7	3.5
Friend	10.5	18.1
Neighbor	7.8	1.0
Parish priest		1.1
Physician		1.7
Psychologist		0.7
Others, none	7.1	12.8
Total	100.0	100.0

*Percentages of the persons named first and second in the accumulated data record of all countries.

This first overview serves only as a rough weighting of the importance of certain relations in various situations requiring help because the results of such instruments depend largely on the offered categories (Litwak and Szelenyi's study, using similar "emergency" situations, but offering only the three response categories "neighbors," "friends," and "kin," produced quite different results). Respondents named their partner by far the most frequently both for instrumental and emotional assistance (approximately 30 percent of all answers). They expected help from their mothers roughly twice as often as from their fathers, who also did badly compared to other relations. People turn to their sons and daughters more frequently for instrumental than for emotional help. Compared to the closest relatives, that is, the partner, the mother, and children (not the father!), brothers and sisters as well as other

relatives are turned to far more seldomly. Friends are expected to provide emotional support (18 percent of all namings) rather than instrumental help (10 percent). Apart from the partner, friends were named most frequently in case of emotional assistance. Neighbors are only asked for instrumental help (8 percent) but hardly at all for support with personal problems (1 percent).

These ratios, for example, that the mother is asked for help twice as often as the father, that friends are of higher importance for emotional than for instrumental support and so forth do not vary from country to country. We take this as a proof for the gross structure of social support networks being relatively similar in our sample of countries.

Analyzing the data in detail, we find additional cross-national similarities, but also some important differences in social support networks. It seems logical that spatial distance to a person plays a major role when one is in need of instrumental assistance (illness, help in the house). Fifty-three percent of respondents in all countries who live within a distance of fifteen minutes to their mother's house name her as the person they would turn to in at least one of these two situations. If they live at a distance of more than one hour, the proportion is only 11 percent in the cumulated data set. Cross-national differences in this regard are not significant. Consequently, in those countries where the spatial distance between parents and children is smaller, instrumental assistance is more often granted by the closest relatives.

As far as emotional assistance is concerned, spatial distance is not that relevant. Table 11.6 shows the percentage of respondents who have named their father or mother in at least one of the two situations. When controlling for differences in spatial distance, the mother is named equally often in all countries. At a distance of less than fifteen minutes, about 45 percent name their mother, at a distance of more than one hour, the proportion is still 25 percent. The father is named more rarely in all countries, but particularly in Italy and Hun-

T A B L E 1 1 . 6 Mother and Father as Persons of Confidence in Case of Personal Problems, Depending on Spatial Distance to Parents*

	Australia	United States	Great Britain	Federal Republic of Germany	Austria	Hungary	Italy
Distance to mother:							
Up to 15 minutes	46	47	44	43	38	49	46
15 minutes to 1 hour	35	40	38	34	39	47	28
More than 1 hour	20	26	26	23	27	28	23
Distance to father:							
Up to 15 minutes	33	30	30	27	42	15	21
15 minutes to 1 hour	22	33	25	19	24	13	6
More than 1 hour	21	22	16	15	15	10	8

*Percentage of respondents who would turn to their mother/father in case of depression or need of advice, for all respondents who do not live in the same household with their parents.

gary. This could be interpreted as an indicator that father-child relations in these countries are still rather patriarchal while in the other countries fathers are somewhat more actively involved in close family relationships. However, a study carried out with eleven- to fifteen-year-old pupils in ten European countries (Eder, 1988) showed that mother-child relations of today's rising generation are still closer than father-child relations. When asked which of their parents they could talk to more freely and easily, young people in all countries named their mother twice as often as their father.

Italians and Hungarians also differ from the rest of the countries in how often they name their partner as "Number One Helper." Eighty to 85 percent of Australians, West Germans, Britons, and Austrians who are married and/or live with a partner named their partner at least in three out of four situations. In Hungary the figure is down to 72 percent and in Italy to 63 percent. This difference can either imply that the set of persons Italians and Hungarians can turn to is larger due to closer kin ties and that they feel less obliged to turn to their partner. It can also mean that in these countries marriage is seen as a partnership to a lesser degree than in northwestern Europe.

The percentage of brothers and sisters and other relatives being named (Table 11.7) corresponds largely to the differences we found with regard to frequency of contact and spatial distance from relatives. In Italy, brothers and sisters and other relatives are named by 17 percent, in Hungary and Austria by 13 percent, in the FRG, Britain, and Australia by about 10 percent. In the United States, however, brothers and sisters and other relatives were named in 14 percent of the responses although the spatial distance would have implied a lower percentage.

With the exception of Italy, the frequency of friends being named (in the average of the four mentioned support situations) is inversely proportional to the distance to kin. The larger the distance from kin, the more frequent people turn to friends for help. In America and Australia, where spatial distance from kin is largest, friends are named in 20 percent of the cases, in Britain and West Germany the figure is 13 percent to 14 percent, and in Austria and Hungary, where distance from kin is relatively small, friends are named only in 10 percent of the cases.

The frequency of "neighborly help" hardly varies from country to country. This may be

TABLE 11.7   Extended Kin and Friends Providing Help*

	Australia	United States	Great Britain	Federal Republic of Germany	Austria	Hungary	Italy
Extended kin	9	14	10	10	13	13	17
Friends	18	20	13	14	10	9	14

*Percentage of extended kin (brothers, sisters and other relatives) and friends named in the four situations "help in the house," "illness," "depression," and "decision."

a methodological artifact: since respondents could only name two persons for each situation, relatives and friends were named most frequently, and were included in the list in several categories; neighbors were consequently reduced to a small percentage. Thus our results cannot be directly compared with those of Litwak and Szelenyi (1969). Offering a choice of only three categories (neighbors, friends, and relatives), they found that both in the United States and Hungary neighbors are of equal importance to relatives and even more important than friends in cases of emergency (help for one-day stomachache).

Let us now turn to the importance of professional assistance (Figure 11.5). On the aggregate level of the various nations this analysis demonstrates again a correlation between reduced kin contacts and an extension of the social network to non-kin relations. Americans and Australians go for professional assistance most frequently, Italians and Hungarians most rarely. These results can, however, only partly be explained by the transition from a primary to a secondary group orientation in the course of modernization. What comes as a surprise is the varying frequency of the "parish priest" being named as an important contact person. Americans name him four times, and Australians twice as frequently as Europeans. This result, rather striking at first glance, has to be put into context. Unlike in Europe, in America and Australia the church plays a more active role in society. Right from the beginning of colonization, freedom of religion and the separation of church and state were main character-

istics of these nations. The large number of denominations and sects which were founded in due course have preserved the active involvement of religious communities in social life more effectively than the highly institutionalized, large churches in Europe (Lipset, 1979). This might explain why in America and Australia the parish priest is more often mentioned as an important contact person. The fact that in America and Australia, where according to our findings personal network structures proved to be the most "modern," the traditional field of religion plays a more important role than in Europe shows once more that the historical change of patterns of living and value orientations by no means follows a unilinear trend.

FIGURE 11.5   Importance of professional assistance in personal problems.

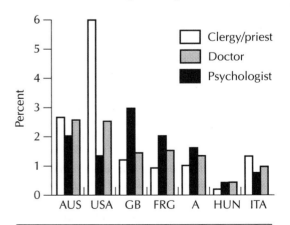

(*Note:* Percentage of professional assistance being named concerning the 3 questions "problem with partner," "depression," and "important decision.")

The results concerning the question of social support only lend themselves to cautious interpretation. Unlike the data on frequency of contact and spatial distance, these results reflect subjective evaluations. When asked whom they would turn to in case of emergency, respondents do not only respond according to their experiences but also to wishful thinking. It must be assumed that the reactions of the respondents contain a certain amount of "social desirability" implied in the fixed answer scheme of the questionnaire. Answers will, thus, not always reflect the behavior in situations of emergency but also stereotypes about social behavior which are probably similar in all countries. "If one has to make an important decision, one should ask one's partner for advice."[16]

Summary

At this point we will briefly restate the main hypotheses related to the cross-cultural comparison of primary group relations and social support networks.

(1) According to the thesis of the transition from "community" to "society" (Tönnies), in the course of modernization a shift occurs from primary to secondary group relations. Concerning kin relations, this theory has to be specified: it is the extended kin which lose in importance, while emotional bonds within the nuclear family become even closer than in premodern society (Shorter, 1975). Urbanization and high geographic mobility inherent in industrial development are the main factors explaining larger spatial distance and thus reduced face-to-face contact with kin. Higher-developed nations are expected to have gone further in this restructuring of social networks.

(2) Litwak and Szelenyi (1969) have argued that these structural changes of primary group relations do not imply a loss in their importance for the individual's social support network. Even if geographic mobility leads to reduced face-to-face contacts with kin and friends, modern means of transport and communication allow close relations to be maintained at greater distances. According to this thesis, higher-developed nations are expected to differ from lower-developed nations in the spatial distance and frequency of contact with kin and friends but not in the social support provided by these primary relations.

(3) Modernization theories assume that specific levels of development will be connected with corresponding forms of family structures and social networks. We have hypothesized, on the contrary, that in advanced industrial societies the structure of social networks is significantly influenced by sociocultural factors and in particular, that there exist differences both within Europe (here, we have distinguished between the Northwest and Central, and the Southeast culture areas) and between Europe and the nations of the New World. Family patterns rooted in preindustrial rural society (Laslett and Wall, 1972; Mitterauer and Sieder, 1982) and national cultural characteristics related to the degree of prevalence of "public" versus "private" virtues (Peabody, 1985) play an important role for the structuring of social networks. Even geographic mobility and its implications for social relations have to be considered not only as the (inevitable) consequence of economic development but also as an independent sociocultural factor.

Our analysis has shown that the frequency of face-to-face contacts with kin is much higher in Italy and Hungary than in the United States and Australia. Austria, West Germany, and Britain are at an intermediate position, with Austria being closer to the Italian/Hungarian pattern, Britain closer to the American/Australian pattern. The fact that Hungary and, to a less marked degree, Italy are lagging behind the other nations economically and that they are both representatives of the South-East European as contrasted to the Northwest-European culture area, makes our results compatible both with the hypothesis of a "modernization" effect and with that of sociocultural differences. There is some evidence, however, that sociocultural factors are outweighing the influence of modernization. Even in the highly industrialized northern parts of Italy kin relations are much more similar to the overall Italian pattern of close kin contacts than to the loosened kin contacts of people in Northwestern Europe. On the other hand, contacts with kin are considerably less frequent in America and Australia than in the comparably developed nations of West Germany and Britain. Higher geographic mobility in the countries of the New World is a main factor explaining this difference. Concerning the effect of urbanization on social networks, we have found that in cross-national perspective the degree of urbanization is of little importance. However, sociocultural differences in the prevailing type of housing are important. The dominance of single-family houses in Britain, the United States, and Australia leads to widespread settlements both in urban and rural areas and to larger distances between different parts of a family even within one town. The preference for one's own house can be seen as expressing a more individualistic lifestyle in these countries, leading people to separate themselves from their kin as well as from their neighborhood.

In the second part of this article, we have examined social support networks. In accordance with previous network studies, it has been shown that close kin do play an important role in emergency situations even in advanced industrial societies. Although in the English- and German-speaking countries spatial distance from parents is larger than in Italy and Hungary, the data suggest that relations with parents and children do not lose their emotional strength. Emotional assistance within the nuclear family, between husband and wife, father and children is even more frequent in the English- and German-speaking countries than in Italy and Hungary. Family structures in these countries seem still to be closer to the patriarchical type. Consistently with this, extended kin relations are more important in the two latter than in the former countries. With the exception of Italy, the importance of friends in people's social support networks is inversely

proportional to the importance of extended kin. Italians expect social support from both relatives and friends. This result agrees with Peabody's argument that Italians maintain close relations not only with their relatives but also with their friends.

Our results on cross-cultural differences in the friendship networks have to be interpreted, on the one hand, by sociocultural differences in the meaning of the term "friendship." Americans and Australians consider many persons as friends, which Europeans would at best call close acquaintances. Geographic mobility has to be considered again as a main factor for a higher "friendship turnover" in the countries of the New World. On the other hand, the result that the frequency of contact with the best friend is lower in Britain and Australia than in America and Italy might be taken as an indicator of social relations being more formal and reserved in the former in contrast with the informal and familiar social relations in the latter countries. Austrians and Hungarians stand out because a high percentage of respondents say that they had no friends at all and because they quite rarely expect friends to provide social support. Differences in the concept of friendship, as we have been arguing in the case of America, might explain this result. There is, however, another possible explanation for this phenomenon (see also Höllinger, 1987). The Austrians' limited friend network can also be attributed to their social characteristics. Both writers and sociologists have described the Austrians, in contrast with a widespread national stereotype, as introverted, taboo-loving, and conflict-avoiding (Magris, 1966; Johnston, 1972). This tendency not to communicate about one's personal problems has repeatedly been associated with the high suicide rate in Austria (Gaspari and Millendorfer, 1973; Ringel, 1984). By coincidence, Hungarians, who in international suicide statistics rank even higher than Austrians, also rarely name friends as persons of confidence. A positive association between suicide and social isolation as pointed out by Durkheim (1966) seems plausible. Nevertheless, we do not have an explanation of why Austrians and Hungarians should be more socially isolated than people in other nations.

Summarizing our results we may state that they are in agreement with Peabody's (1990) typology of "national characteristics." On the sociocultural continuum of private-oriented versus public-oriented values (more versus less permanent face-to-face contacts with kin and friends; less versus more instrumental professional assistance in case of personal emergencies), America, Australia, and Britain are clearly on the side of the public-oriented societies. West Germany and Austria are in an intermediate position, and Italy and Hungary correspond to the type of private-oriented societies.

As confirmed recently by Inkeles (1989), there might exist in fact enduring "national characters" connected with specific ways of estimating the value of human life, of modal happiness of a population, and so on. We think that our results suggest an interpretation of these characters not only from a sociopsychological but also from a genuine sociological perspective. As pointed out by Durkheim (1966) in his seminal work on suicide, only sociological interpretations are able to account for the often astonishing differences between nations in the incidence of social phenomena. In this regard, our analysis has also given some indications about possible macrostructural and cultural preconditions which determine kin relations and social networks in the several societies under consideration. Further research along these lines aiming at a more precise recording of social networks as well as at a more comprehensive consideration of the macrostructural and cultural preconditions of these networks promises to be quite fruitful.

Notes

* From the *European Sociological Review* 6, no. 2 (1990): 103–24, by permission of the Oxford University Press. Copyright 1990 by the Oxford University Press.

1. In 1981, approximately 40 percent of sixty- to seventy-five-year-old Austrian women and 50 percent of over seventy-five-year-olds lived alone.

2. The International Social Survey Program (ISSP) is a continuing, annual program of cross-national collaboration. It brings together preexisting national social science surveys and coordinates research goals by adding a cross-national perspective to the individual national studies. Since its establishment in 1984–85, ISSP has grown to include eleven nations in 1990. The 1986 survey was developed on the basis of the project proposal worked out by Max Haller (1984).

3. The percentage of eighteen- to twenty-four-year-olds being married is more or less the same in Britain, Australia, and the United States. Approximately 20 percent of under twenty-five-year-olds are married. In Italy, Germany, and Austria, this percentage is significantly lower (10 percent), in Hungary it is highest (35 percent). The varying frequency of young people living in their parents' houses until they get married in the individual countries cannot be associated with the percentages quoted above.

4. Spatial distance and frequency of contact do not differ between father and mother in any country. Therefore, the following discussion of the issue is restricted to data for contact with the mother.

5. The association tau-b between spatial distance and frequency of contact with the mother amounts to the following figures in the several countries (categories correspond to Figure 11.1 and Figure 11.2): Australia 0.73; USA 0.71; GB 0.50; FRG 0.62; Austria 0.51; Hungary 0.60; Italy 0.68. The frequency of contact with kin is thus strongly associated with spatial distance. Respondents living at a distance of several hours from their mother meet her only a few times a year or less and thus increase the tau-b values. When excluding those respondents who live at a distance of more than five hours from their mother from the calculations, tau-b coefficients diminish most significantly in America and Australia (because the percentage of those living far away from their mother is far higher than in Europe). Cross-national differences in the association between spatial distance and frequency of contact with the

mother become rather insignificant when applying this method: Australia 0.61; USA 0.58; GB 0.52; FRG 0.57; Austria 0.47; Hungary 0.56; Italy 0.60.

6. Approximately 50 percent of respondents in all countries replied that the relative they maintain closest contact with is a member of the family-in-law (mother-in-law, father-in-law, brother-in-law or sister-in-law).

7. From 1820 to 1971, natives of the following European countries emigrated to the United States: England and Ireland approximately 5 million each, FRG 7 million, rest of Central Europe 4.5 million, Italy 5 million, Scandinavia and rest of Northwestern Europe 4 million (Source: Fischer Weltgeschichte: Die Vereinigten Staaten von Amerika, Frankfurt, 1977). The cumulated data set of the American General Social Survey (1972–87) gives the following data on the questions. "What countries did your ancestors come from?; which of these countries do you feel closest to?": Great Britain and Ireland 30 percent, Germany 20 percent, Africa 10 percent, Italy and Spain 10 percent, East- and Southeast-European countries 8 percent, Scandinavia 5 percent, Mexico and Latin America 4 percent.

8. It is not the urban living conditions per se which lead to a reduction of relations with kin but the demographic composition of the urban population, that is, a higher percentage of people with a higher educational level or the larger spatial distance to kin among the urban population. A previous analysis of Austrian social network data suggested that at a constant distance from relatives, the urban and rural populations showed the same frequency of contact with their closest relatives (Höllinger, 1987).

9. According to Meyers Enzyklopädisches Lexikon (Vol. 3, 1972), in Australia 70 percent of the population is urban; 60 percent of Australians live in five cities with more than 500,000 inhabitants.

10. "Urban-rural" was subdivided according to Table 11.1. Spatial distance and frequency of contact were categorized according to Figures 11.1 and 11.2. Tests for several types of relatives produced more or less the same results. Therefore, we will limit the analysis to the data for the mother.

11. Sources: ALLBUS 1986 for the FRG, GSS 1987 for the USA, BSA Survey 1987 for Britain, ISSP-87 for Austria, Meyers Enzyklopädisches Lexikon for Australia.

12. As the British data record coded "8 or more friends" as "8," we recorded the categories for all other countries accordingly. This has the methodological advantage that mean values were not distorted by individual namings of a very high number of friends.

13. Differences between urban and rural areas were calculated on the basis of the category system in Table 11.2. Education of respondents was coded into three levels: "primary education" (eight to ten years depending on the respective country), "secondary education" and "higher education" (twelve years in all countries). The dependent variable "number of friends" was submitted to a multiple classification analysis according to the size of the place of residence, education and age cohort. This analysis produced the following eta-, beta- and multiple r^2 values:

Association between "Number of Friends" and "Age," "Education," "Urban-Rural"							
	AUS	U.S.	GB	FRG	A	HUN	ITA
Age:							
eta	0.06	0.09	0.09	0.21	0.15	0.25	0.09
beta	0.04	0.11	0.09	0.16	0.13	0.17	0.06
Education:							
eta	0.10	0.03	0.14	0.21	0.13	0.27	0.13
beta	0.10	0.07	0.15	0.17	0.10	0.19	0.13
Urban–rural:							
eta	0.02	0.11		0.01	0.11	0.10	0.05
beta	0.03	0.11		0.01	0.08	0.05	0.07
Multiple r^2	0.012	0.024	0.026	0.068	0.040	0.099	0.027

The amount of variance explained by these three variables is very small in the three English-speaking countries and Italy (r^2 between 0.012 and 0.027). Only in West Germany, Austria, and Hungary a somewhat larger amount of variance is explained.

14. Fischer used a name generator in this study. The respondents had to indicate with which person they spent their leisure time, discussed their personal problems, and so forth. This pro-

cedure which defined criteria for "close relations," more exactly resulted in a smaller number and probably a more realistic estimation of the number of friends. In the Austrian Microcensus (ÖStZ, 1975) the method was to ask for "the number of acquaintances, one had met on purpose in the last month."

15. Results on the question of "borrowing a large sum of money" showed national characteristics very different from the rest of the questions. This suggests the need for separate analysis. The question "whom would you turn to if you had a problem with your partner?" was not put in the same way in all countries, thus the results cannot directly be compared.

16. The following result demonstrates that the validity of answers to such questions is questionable: in Austria and West Germany, respondents were also asked when was the last time they were faced with such situations. Forty percent of Austrians and West Germans indicated that they had never in their life been depressed and that they had never had to ask someone for advice. In the other countries, these additional questions were not included in the questionnaire.

References

Belsky J., Rovine A. (1984): "Social Network Contact, Family Support, and the Transition to Parenthood." *Journal of Marriage and Family* 46: 426–55.

Boh K. (1989): "Besondere Probleme der kulturvergleichenden Familienforschung," in Nave-Herz R, Marefka M, *Handbuch der Familien —und Jugendforschung*. Neuwied/Frankfurt; Luchterhand, pp. 163–75.

Bott E. (1957): *Family and Social Network*. London: Tavistock.

Brunner O. (1968): *Neue Wege der Verfassungs— und Sozialgeschichte*. Göttingen: Vandenhoeck & Ruprecht.

De Tocqueville A. (1976): *Über die Demokratie in Amerika*. München: Deutscher Taschenbuch Verlag.

Duck S., Perlmann D. (1985): *Understanding Personal Relationships*. London/Beverly Hills/New Delhi: Sage.

Durkheim E. (1966): *Suicide: A Study in Sociology*. Glencoe, Ill.: Free Press (orig. publ. 1897).

Eder A. (1988): *Risikofaktor Einsamkeit: Analysen zum Zusammenhang zwischen sozialer Isola-tion, Lebens—und Schulzufriedenheit, und Gesundheit bei 11-, 13- und 15-jährigen Schülern aus 10 Ländern*. Wien: Bundeskanzleramt.

Farago T. (1986); "Formen bäuerlicher Haushalts— und Arbeitsorganisation in Ungarn um die Mitte des 18. Jahrhunderts," in Ehmer J, Mitterauer M, *Familienstruktur und Arbeitsorganisation in ländlichen Gesellschaften*. Wien: Böhlau, pp. 103–84.

Finch J. (1989): "Kinship and Friendship," in Jowell R, Witherspoon S, Brook L, *British Social Attitudes: Special International Report*. Aldershot/Brookfield: Gower Publishing Company, pp. 87–104.

Fischer C. S. (1982a): *To Dwell among Friends*. Chicago: University of Chicago Press.

——— (1982b): "What Do We Mean by 'friend': An Inductive Study." *Social Network* 3: 287–306.

Furstenberg F. Jun. (1987): "Fortsetzungsehen: Ein neues Lebensmuster und seine Folgen." *Soziale Welt,* 38: 29–40.

Gasperi C., Millendorfer H. (1973): *Prognosen für Österreich*. München: Oldenburg.

Goode W. J. (1979): *World Revolution and Family Patterns*. London/New York: Free Press.

Greeley A. (1989): "Protestant and Catholic: Is the Analogical Imagination Extinct?" *American Sociological Review* 54: 485–502.

Haller M. (1977): "Austria," in Chester R., (ed.), *Divorce in Europe*. Leiden: M. Nijhoff, pp. 211–51.

——— (1984): "Patterns of Social Relations in Advanced Industrial Societies: Proposal for a Comparative Survey in England, West Germany and the United States." Mannheim: ZUMA (mimeo).

——— (1989): *Klassenstrukturen und Mobilität in fortgeschrittenen Gesellschaften*. Frankfurt/New York: Campus.

——— (1990): "The Challenge for Comparative Sociology in the Transformation of Europe." *International Sociology* 5: 183–204.

Höllinger F. (1987): "Familie und außerfamiliäre Netzwerke als Basis für soziale Beziehungen und Hilfeleistungen," in Haller M., Holm K., (eds.), *Werthaltungen und Lebensformen in Österreich*. München/Wien: Oldenbourg/Verlag für Geschichte und Politik, pp. 111–40.

Inkeles A. (1989): "National Character Revisited," in Haller M., Hoffman H. J., Zapf W., (eds.), *Kultur und Gesellschaft*. Frankfurt/New York: Campus, pp. 98–112.

Johnston W. M. (1972): *The Austrian Mind: An Intellectual and Social History 1848–1938.* University of California Press.

Jordan T. G. (1988): *The European Culture Area: A Systematic Geography.* New York: Harper & Row.

Laslett P., Wall R. (1972): *Household and Family in Past Time.* Cambridge: Cambridge University Press.

Lin N., Dean A., Ensel W. (1986): *Social Support, Life Events and Depression.* Orlando, Fla.: Academic Press.

Lipset S. M. (1979): "The Third Century: America as a Postindustrial Society," in Inkeles A., (ed.), *Continuity and Change in the American National Character.* New York/London: W. W. Norton, pp. 390–454.

Litwak E., Szelenyi I. (1969): "Primary Group Structures and Their Functions: Kin, Neighbours, and Friends." *American Sociological Review* 34: 465–81.

Long L. H. (1970): "On Measuring Geographic Mobility." *Journal of the American Statistical Association* 65: 1195–1203.

Magris, C. (1966). *Der habsburgische Mythos in der osterreichischen Literatur.* Salzburg, Austria: O. Müller.

Marbach J. (1986): "Familie und soziales Netzwerk." München: Deutsches Jugendinstitut (mimeo).

Mitterauer M. (1983): *Ledige Mütter: Zur Geschichte unehelicher Geburten in Europa.* München: Beck.

Mitterauer M., Sieder R. (1977): *Vom Patriarchat zur Partnerschaft.* München: Beck.

——— (1982): *Historische Familienforschung.* Frankfurt: Suhrkamp.

Münch R. (1986): *Die Kultur der Moderne, Band I: Ihre Grundlagen und Entwicklung in Enland und Amerika.* Frankfurt: Suhrkamp.

Österreichisches Statistisches Zentralamt (ÖStZ) (1975): *Kontakte im Verwandten—und Bekanntenkreis: Ergebnisse des Mikrozensus 1975.* Wien: ÖStZ, Beiträge zur Österreichischen Statistik, Heft 484.

Parsons T. (1954): "The Kinship System of the Contemporary United States," in *Essays in Sociological Theory.* Glencoe, Ill.: Free Press.

——— (1951): *The Social System.* London: Routledge & Kegan Paul.

Peabody D. (1985): *National Characteristics.* Cambridge: Cambridge University Press.

Pearlin L. I. (1971): *Class Context and Family Relations: A Cross-National Study.* Boston: Little, Brown.

Pfeil E. (1970): "Die Großstadtfamilie." *Kölner Zeitschrift für Soziologie und Sozialpsychologie,* SH 14: 411–32.

Ringel E. (1984): *Die österreichische Seele.* Wien/Köln/Graz: Böhlau.

Rosenbaum H. (1981): *Formen der Familie.* Frankfurt: Suhrkamp.

Rosenmayr L. (1986): *Familie—Tatsachen, Probleme, Perspektiven, Sonderveröffentlichung aus Anlaß des 71. Deutschen Fürsorgetages.* München: Heft 2–4 des Archivs für Soziale Arbeit.

Sampson R. J. (1988): "Local Friendship Ties and Community Attachment: A Multilevel Model." *American Sociological Review* 53: 766–79.

Schenk M. (1983): "Das Konzept des sozialen Netzwerks." *Kölner Zeitschrift für Soziologieund Sozialpsychologie,* SH 25: 88–105.

Schulz W. (1978): *Sozialkontakte in der Großstadt.* Wien: Institut für Stadtforschung.

Shorter E. (1975): *The Making of the Modern Family.* New York: Basic Books.

Tönnies F. (1979): *Gemeinschaft und Gesellschaft.* Darmstadt: Wissenschaftliche Buchgesellschaft.

Ward-Crowe P. (1978): "Good Fences Make Good Neighbourhood: Social Networks at Three Levels of Urbanisation in Tirol." Dissertation, Williamsburg, USA.

Weber-Kellermann I. (1974): *Die deutsche Familie: Versuch einer Sozialgeschichte.* Frankfurt: Suhrkamp.

Willi V. J. (1966): *Grundlagen einer empirischen Soziologie der Werte und Wertsysteme.* Zürich: Orell Füssli.

Wurzbacher G. (1987): "Zur bundesdeutschen Familien—und Sozialisationsforschung in den Nachkriegsjahren." *Zeitschrift für Soziologie* 16: 323–31.

Supervision and Conformity: A Cross-Cultural Analysis of Parental Socialization Values[*]

Godfrey J. Ellis, Gary R. Lee, and Larry R. Petersen[†]

Social Class and Parental Values

Sociologists have long been interested in the association between socioeconomic status and parental values in the socialization process. Kohn's work (1959a, 1959b, 1963, 1969; Kohn and Schooler 1969, 1973; Pearlin and Kohn 1966), pointing to a negative relationship between socioeconomic status and a parental value on conformity in children, has been of particular interest (see also Gecas and Nye 1974; Wright and Wright 1976; Gecas 1978).

The interpretation of this relationship is often couched in terms of class differences between blue- and white-collar workers. Briefly, a part of the argument is that members of these strata operate under differing reward structures in the pursuit of occupational (and thus economic) success.[1] Blue-collar workers are typically subjected to a high degree of supervision on the job. Their tasks are likely to be routinized, adherence to established procedures is required, and there is little need for innovation. Satisfactory performance is largely defined by conformity to external authority. Blue-collar parents, so the interpretation goes, generalize this value to other arenas of behavior and thus value the trait of conformity in their children.[2] White-collar workers, on the other hand, achieve success largely by virtue of individual initiative. They are less closely supervised and must often exercise independent judgment. The reward structure in white-collar occupations is likely to place a premium on autonomy and self-reliance. Since these traits are perceived

as conducive to success, white-collar parents value them in their children.

In support of this theory, Kohn and others have consistently found that American blue-collar parents value conformity in children over self-reliance,[3] while the opposite is true of white-collar parents. In addition, these findings have been supported in several studies outside the United States (see Kohn [1977, introduction] for a summary of this literature). Pearlin (1971, pp. 58–70) demonstrates, with data from both Italy and the United States, that class differences in parental values are due largely to class-related differences in the nature of occupational experiences. There are three relevant types of differences: differences in the closeness of supervision, in the major component of work (things, people, or ideas), and in the requirement of self-reliance in work. White-collar occupations are characterized by low supervision, an emphasis on people or ideas rather than objects, and a relatively high degree of self-reliance. Each of these factors is negatively related to the value placed on conformity in children and thus contributes to the explanation of class differences in socialization values.

Extensions of the Theory

Kohn's theory has most frequently been interpreted as a theory of the effects of social class on socialization values, with dimensions of occupational experience serving as intervening variables. Olsen (1974), however, has demonstrated that the implications of the theory may be considerably broader than this. She generalizes the theory by concentrating on the supervision dimension and noting that closeness of supervision is a general concept which pertains to many behavioral domains other than occupation.[4] One of these domains is the family. Olsen reasons that mothers in patrilocal extended families are closely supervised in the performance of family roles by the husband's mother. She hypothesizes that ". . . mothers in three-generational households should resemble working-class men in the high value they place upon conformity and obedience in children, while mothers in nuclear families should place more emphasis on autonomy and self-reliance" (1974, p. 1396). This hypothesis was supported on a Taiwanese sample. Olsen concludes that the effects of closeness of supervision in extended families may be interpreted according to the logic developed by Kohn for the explanation of occupational stratum differences in parental values. Closeness of supervision of the parent, whether in the occupational or familial role, causes the parent to value the traits of conformity and obedience in children.

Anthropologists have also investigated antecedents of socialization values via cross-cultural research and have employed similar conceptualizations of the dependent variables. Barry, Child, and Bacon (1959) distinguish between "compliance" and "assertion" as socialization values.[5] Their dependent variable is actually a composite of four separate measures, including emphasis on responsibility and obedience (which define the "compliance" pole of the continuum) and emphasis on achievement and self-reliance (which define "assertiveness"). They discover that, where economic systems permit the accumulation and storage of food (pastoral and agricultural economies), the culture tends to emphasize the value of compliance. But in hunting, gathering, or fishing economies food cannot usually be stored or accumulated. Here the value structure places a higher premium on individual achievement and self-reliance.

The explanation offered for the association between socialization values and type of econ-omy is that economic systems which permit the accumulation of food generally require routinized, cooperative, and organized labor. This implies supervision and "faithful adherence to routines" (Barry et al. 1959, p. 62). Individual innovativeness in method may threaten the organization and functional effectiveness of the work group. Hunting and gathering, though, are usually more individualistic activities. Aggressiveness and autonomy are prerequisites for success; cooperation and adherence to routines are not so clearly required. Since parents value traits in their children which they perceive to be instrumental in their own activities, self-reliance is valued in hunting and gathering societies, obedience (conformity) in pastoral and agricultural societies.

The logic employed by Barry et al. (1959) may be integrated with a part of Kohn's theory. In cross-cultural terms, type of economy may be conceived as an indirect measure of closeness of supervision in subsistence activities. Where adult workers are closely supervised (i.e., in high-accumulation technologies), they value conformity in their children. Where their work is more autonomous, self-reliance is the more valued outcome of socialization.

A second anthropological observation on sources of variation in socialization values implicates the political structure. Stephens (1963, p. 372) shows that societies with autocratic political states tend to be characterized by relatively "severe" socialization practices, including clear-cut power and deference relationships and strong emphasis on obedience. Tribal societies, which have no centralized or autocratic political structure, require less obedience and conformity of their children. To the extent that autocratic political structures imply close supervision of adults, this relationship may be interpreted using the same general logic. Barry et al. (1976), in another study employing societies contained in the Standard Cross-cultural Sample, report that complexity of political structure is positively related to a measure of socialization for obedience and negatively related to socialization for self-reliance. However, they offer no explanation for these associations. Aberle (1961) also suggests that degree of political supervision is correlated with inhibition of aggression. Finally, Bronfenbrenner (1970) points out that socialization in the Soviet Union is much more oriented toward producing conformity than is the case in the United States; this difference is consistent with Stephens's (1963) observation on the effects of autocratic political systems (see also Ellis 1977).

From this brief view, it is apparent that anthropologists and sociologists have actually been employing a very similar basic theory in their attempts to explain parental values in socialization (see Lee [1977, pp. 258–74] for a more detailed explication of this point). The theory has been applied to different behavioral domains by the two disciplines, thus implicating different independent variables. However, each set of empirical relationships can be at least partially interpreted through the more abstract concept of closeness of supervision and the requirement of self-reliance. Where adults are closely supervised in their economic, political, or family roles, they tend to value conformity in their children; where they are more autonomous in these roles, self-reliance becomes a primary socialization value. This similarity of theory is not the result of interdisciplinary exchange, since the correspondence has rarely been recognized (for a partial exception, see Olsen 1973). Instead, the theory appears to have been independently generated within each discipline.

The central proposition of this general theory is that parental valuation of conformity relative to self-reliance in children is positively related to the extent to which adults are themselves closely supervised in the performance of their own roles. If this is true we may deduce hypotheses about the effects of supervision of adults on socialization values in areas of social life which have not yet been explored from this perspective.

One such behavioral domain is religion. Perceptions of the supernatural may vary along a continuum corresponding to an abstract conceptualization of supervision over human affairs. At one extreme, the god or gods may be culturally endowed with great powers over human destiny which they exercise for human benefit or detriment according to the morality of human behavior. Deviation from culturally defined moral behavior may be believed to invoke negative sanctions from the supernatural forces. In this situation, the supernatural constitutes an external authority, conformity to which is perceived as crucial to human well-being. At the other extreme, the supernatural may be endowed with insufficient power to enforce behavioral standards. Also, in many cultures the deities are believed to be quite arbitrary in their administration of positive and negative sanctions; there is little that human beings can do to influence their fate. Here, conformity to the perceived wishes or prescriptions of the supernatural is much less of a virtue; human fate is largely independent of one's relationship with the deity or deities.

If the relationship between supervision and socialization values is generalizable beyond the occupational domain, we would expect closeness of supervision by the supernatural to influence these values.[6] Consistent with the basic theory, we hypothesize that closeness of supervision by the supernatural is positively related to conformity relative to self-reliance as a value in socialization of children.

In summary, a considerable body of research and theory in several disciplines suggests that parental values in socialization are responsive to variation in the criteria of success for adults. These criteria pertain to diverse behavioral domains, including the family, politics, and religion, as well as the economic or occupational realm. In each case, adult experience may be arrayed along a continuum representing closeness of supervision or, alternatively, self-reliance. The central proposition of this study, which results from a partial synthesis of theory in both sociology and anthropology, is that parents value conformity over self-reliance in children to the extent that conformity supersedes self-reliance as a criterion for success in their own endeavors. The importance of conformity in adult behavior may be estimated by indirect measures of closeness of supervision in the various behavioral domains discussed above; these provide multiple measures of the value of conformity in adult life.

Methods

Sampling

The empirical objective of this study is to bring cross-cultural data to bear upon the theory developed above.[7] Accordingly, the Standard Cross-cultural Sample (Murdock and White 1969) was employed as one source of data. The sample ($N =186$) is representative of all geographic and cultural regions in the world; furthermore, the societies which constitute the sample were selected in such a way as to minimize proximity between members of the sample. This reduces the probability that correlations between cultural traits observed on this sample are attributable to "cultural borrowing" or diffusion (see Marsh 1967, pp. 274–303; Naroll 1968, pp. 258–62; Lee 1977, pp. 44–47).

Most of the independent variables implicated by the theory are available in the Standard Cross-cultural Sample (SCS). These data do not, however, contain satisfactory indices of parental values in socialization or closeness of supervision in the religious domain. These variables were therefore coded from the Human Relations Area Files (HRAF; see measurement section below for coding procedures). The HRAF consists of classified ethnographic data in verbal form. Of the 186 societies in the SCS, 122 also appear in the available microfiche version of the HRAF. Since both data sets were required for this study, the actual sample consists of the 122 societies which are included in both.

This sample is not random, nor can it be considered representative of all cultures in the world. However, it is impossible to obtain a random or representative cross-cultural sample (Lee 1977, pp. 22–23). Nonetheless, with the exception of industrial societies, the sample contains a complete range of societal types and is fully appropriate for testing hypotheses regarding relationships between supervision and socialization values. It is also notably larger than the samples of other cross-cultural studies requiring primary coding of ethnographic data.

Measurement

Five indicators of closeness of supervision were obtained from the precoded data in the SCS. They are intended to index closeness of supervision in the economic, familial, and political domains.

The first independent variable, closeness of supervision in the economic sphere, is indexed by type of economy. The various primary subsistence bases represented in our cross-cultural data sets may be ranked along a continuum ranging from highly individualistic activities, in which group cooperation is minimal, to highly structured and routinized cooperative endeavors. The cooperative activities require greater interpersonal coordination, planning, and therefore supervision. As Barry et al. (1959, p. 52) point out, activities such as fishing and hunting are more likely to yield immediate rewards for individual initiative. In accord with this logic, the various types of subsistence economies were ranked in rough order of increasing supervision as follows: fishing, hunting, gathering, animal husbandry, incipient agriculture, extensive agriculture, and intensive agriculture.[8] There are undoubtedly many instances in which this ordering does not precisely conform to a continuum of closeness of supervision; for example, fishing and hunting may occasionally be done in large groups which require coordination, leadership, and therefore supervision. However, it is reasonable to contend that cooperative group activities requiring supervision are more essential to and frequent in agricultural economies than fishing or hunting (see Steward 1955; Barry et al. 1959; Nimkoff and Middleton 1960; Blumberg and Winch 1972; Lee 1977).

Furthermore, group cooperation and interpersonal coordination are more clearly required in the more complex forms of agriculture (such as intensive agriculture, which implies permanent fields, the use of rudimentary mechanical devices, and often irrigation) than in extensive or, particularly, incipient agriculture. In this order, the scale corresponds roughly to an index of economic complexity (the complexity of the collective technology, not of individual tasks) and will be labeled as such. More complex technologies require greater coordination, supervision, and conformity to established routines.

Three variables are available in the SCS as measures of closeness of supervision in the familial domain. The first is a simple index of the dominant family structure, categorized as nuclear, stem, small extended, and fully extended. In this order, the categories represent increasing structural complexity of the family in terms of the number of social positions contained in the family structure (see Nimkoff [1965, p. 19] and Lee [1977, pp. 112–15] for detailed definitions of each type). In any of the three types of extended families the parental generation is not the senior generation and is subject to the supervision of its own parents or in-laws. The extent of supervision, then, is presumed to increase as the structural complexity of the family increases.

A second family-related variable measures the dominant mode of tracing descent. Societies with bilateral descent systems have no corporate kin groups; individual families are autonomous with respect to kinship structure. We therefore take bilateral descent as indicative of low supervision and any form of unilineal descent as reflective of higher supervision. It is also possible, however, to distinguish between patrilineal and matrilineal systems along this dimension. In virtually all cultures, the mother is the primary agent of socialization (Minturn and Lambert 1964; Olsen 1973, p. 513). The mother is clearly more subject to supervision by senior members of kin groups in patrilineal systems than in the matrilineal case.

The wife-mother in a patrilineal group is an "outsider," at least until she attains some seniority over other in-marrying females such as daughters-in-law. But in matrilineal systems the wife-mother retains membership in her natal kin group throughout her life. If she is subject to supervisory control, it is the control of senior members of her own kin group. This is likely to be much less strict and rigorous than in the patrilineal case. Furthermore, the matrilineal mode of tracing descent cannot be combined with any single custom of postmarital residence in a manner which produces localized kin groups (see Aberle 1961; Fox 1967; Lee 1977, pp. 161–62). This reduces the potential for supervision of parents by senior members of their kin groups. Therefore, supervision of the primary socializing agent is highest in patrilineal kinship systems, lowest in bilateral, and intermediate in matrilineal.

A third measure of familial supervision has to do with cultural control over mate selection. This variable indexes cultural rules regarding community endogamy and exogamy. Some cultures require that communities be strictly endogamous or exogamous, others have rules that are similar but loosely enforced, while still others have no effective custom on the matter. We posit that strict rules requiring either community endogamy or community exogamy are indicative of high degrees of supervision over the mate-selection process, while the absence of such rules indicates low supervision. Societies with flexible customs were classified as intermediate on this variable.

Finally, an index of supervision in the political realm is given by the complexity of the political structure, measured in terms of number of distinct jurisdictional levels. We assume that political structures increase in complexity as the need for control and organization above the local level increases. A highly differentiated political system exercises more control and supervision than a less differentiated or nonexistent structure. A five-point scale is employed as a measure of political supervision, which ranges from stateless societies where authority is not centralized even at the local level to societies with three or more administrative levels above the local community. This scale was used by Barry et al. (1976, p. 101) and is consistent with Stephens's (1963) logic, but is much more discriminating than the "kingdom" versus "tribe" dichotomy he employed.

Satisfactory measures of supervision in the religious domain were not available in the SCS and were thus coded from the HRAF. Two variables were employed. The first indexes religious taboos, or the extent to which supernatural forces are believed to negatively sanction certain behaviors, thereby directing the behavior of human beings.[9] This variable was coded independently by two judges on a five-point scale, ranging from no supernaturally sanctioned behaviors to the existence of taboos pertaining to virtually every aspect of daily life. The Pearson product-moment correlation between the two coders' ratings was determined to be +.662, based on 115 cases for which sufficient information was available.[10] To assign a final score on this variable to each society, the two coders' ratings were summed, creating a nine-point scale; higher scores indicate closer supervision.

A second measure of religious supervision indexed the presence or absence of ancestor worship. We were specifically interested in the extent to which the ancestors are believed to play a part in the affairs of the living by controlling their fate, rewarding good behavior, punishing immorality, and so forth. This variable was originally coded as a simple dichotomy differentiating between the presence and absence of ancestor worship. There was, however, substantial disagreement between coders in the application of this dichotomy, as indicated by an intercoder correlation coefficient of +.614, based on 120 cases. The disagreements uniformly represented cases where the religion stipulated the existence of ancestral spirits but accorded them minimal influence over human affairs. It was therefore decided to employ cases of coder disagreement as an intermediate category on a three-point scale,

created by summing the two codes for each society. A high score on this variable represents a clear belief in ancestors who have the power, and the proclivity, to control the outcomes of human endeavors according to their approval or disapproval of human behavior; a low score indicates the absence of ancestor worship.

The dependent variable, emphasis on conformity relative to self-reliance in socialization, was also coded from the HRAF. This variable was coded on a seven-point scale, with high scores indicating a greater emphasis on conformity (obedience, compliance) than self-reliance and low scores a greater emphasis on self-reliance (independence, self-sufficiency) than conformity. The emphasis in coding this variable was upon the kinds of behaviors for which children were rewarded or punished. High scores (representing conformity) were assigned where children were encouraged to be cooperative and obedient to parental authority, or were punished for failure to follow parental directives or group norms involving compliance and responsibility to others. Low scores (indicative of a value on self-reliance) were assigned to cases where children were encouraged to be independent, self-sufficient, or autonomous. This is perhaps most clearly exemplified by initiation rites which require individual survival under arduous conditions. These codes were, of course, made in the absence of any knowledge of the independent variables from either the SCS or from other sections of the HRAF. The two coders for each case worked independently at all times. The current conceptualization of this variable is compatible, although not identical, with those of Kohn (1969, p. 24), Pearlin (1971, p. 57), Barry et al. (1959, p. 58; 1967), and Olsen (1974, p. 1405).

Separate ratings were made for the socialization of males and females, since we anticipated that many societies would differentiate strongly between the traits deemed appropriate for each sex. However, the original correlations between socialization codes for boys and girls were in excess of +.9, and the two variables behaved in virtually identical fashion in relation to each of the independent variables. This paper therefore reports only the correlates of socialization values for boys; however, the results for the socialization of girls are identical for all relevant purposes. The intercoder correlation for socialization values was +.503, based on one hundred analyzable cases.[11] Final scores were assigned by summing the two coders' ratings.

The data were analyzed by means of partial correlation techniques. This method produces readily interpretable estimates of the correlation between the dependent variable and each independent variable net of the effects of other independent variables. In addition, an estimate of total variation explained by all independent variables was obtained from a regression analysis. Methods of causal modeling, including path analysis, are not employed here since we are interested solely in the extent to which socialization values may be explained by the multiple indices of closeness of supervision over adults. The theory to be tested does not require specification of a causal order among the independent variables.

Findings

Pearson product-moment correlation coefficients between all possible pairs of variables in our model are reported in Table 12.1.[12] Cor-

relations between conformity versus self-reliance in socialization and the independent variables are reported in column 8. At the bivariate level each hypothesis except one is clearly supported. Conformity relative to self-reliance as a value in socialization is positively related to economic complexity ($r = .479$), political complexity ($r = .411$), mode of descent ($r = .360$), ancestor worship ($r = .335$), control over mate choice ($r = .322$), and religious taboos ($r = .313$); each of these relationships was predicted by the theory. One hypothesis is not supported: conformity relative to self-reliance is unrelated to family complexity ($r = .016$).

Since the independent variables are intercorrelated to varying degrees, it is possible that they account for some of the same variation in the dependent variables. To determine the correlation between each independent variable and the dependent variable net of all other independent variables, partial correlation analysis was employed. Table 12.2 reports the sixth-order partial correlations between conformity/self-reliance and each independent variable controlling for all other independent variables. In most cases the relationships are attenuated by the multivariate controls; however, in each case a substantial association remains.

Family complexity, as in the bivariate analysis, is uncorrelated with conformity ver-

Variable	1	2	3	4	5	6	7	8	X	SD	N
1. Economic complexity		.598	.204	.190	.099	.367	.178	.479	5.03	1.99	121
2. Political complexity			.035	.029	.057	.272	.124	.411	2.03	1.18	122
3. Religious taboos				.345	.109	.193	.094	.313	6.64	2.15	115
4. Ancestor worship					.183	.248	.112	.335	3.43	.82	120
5. Family complexity						.055	.112	.016	2.37	1.17	122
6. Mode of descent*							.232	.360	2.07	.92	108
7. Control over mate choice								.322	2.01	.73	122
8. Conformity/self-reliance†									8.00	2.74	100

TABLE 12.1 Bivariate Correlations and Univariate Distributions

*High scores are assigned to patrilineal systems, low scores to bilateral systems. Matrilineal systems are intermediate.
†High scores indicate emphasis on conformity.

TABLE 12.2   Bivariate and Sixth-Order Partial Correlations between Independent Variables and Conformity versus Self-Reliance

Independent Variable	Bivariate Correlation	Partial Correlation	N
Economic complexity	.479	.193	82
Political complexity	.411	.225	82
Religious taboos	.313	.188	82
Ancestor worship	.335	.213	82
Family complexity	.016	.009	82
Mode of descent*	.360	.114	82
Control over mate choice	.322	.239	82

*See Table 12.1 for variable metric.

Note: High scores indicate an emphasis on conformity. Multiple $R = .635$; $R^2 = .403$

sus self-reliance when the other variables are controlled ($r = .009$). Also, the correlation between mode of descent and conformity is reduced to a nonsignificant level ($r = .114$) by controlling for the other independent variables.[13] However, the remaining partial correlations are significant in both statistical and substantive terms. The magnitudes of these partial correlations are similar, ranging from .188 (religious taboos) to .239 (control over mate choice). The seven independent variables in the analysis yield a multiple correlation coefficient of .635 and collectively explain 40.3 percent of the variation in the dependent variable.

These results support the proposition that an emphasis on conformity over self-reliance in the socialization process is fostered by recurring structured situations in economic, political, religious, and familial domains which require adults to conform to external authority. Where the behavior of adults is more autonomous in these areas, self-reliance is more highly valued in children.

Discussion

Of the seven hypotheses relating closeness of supervision to emphasis on conformity over self-reliance in socialization, five were clearly supported. The two variables which do not be-

have according to the predictions of the theory are both family related. Family complexity is simply uncorrelated with socialization values, and the correlation between mode of descent and socialization values is greatly reduced when the effects of the other independent variables are removed.

The ineffectiveness of family complexity as an antecedent of socialization values is particularly surprising, since it is clearly implicated by the theory and since Olsen (1974) found marked differences in socialization values between nuclear and extended families in her Taiwanese sample. Her results supported the theory in this respect; ours do not. The relevant question here is whether the problem lies with the theory or the measurement—that is, the fit between the abstract concept of closeness of supervision and the empirical indicator, family complexity.

Olsen (1974) compared the values of mothers in nuclear families with those of mothers in extended families. However, the extended families in her sample were actually of only one specific type: patrilocal stem families. Our measure of family complexity distinguishes between nuclear, stem, small extended (lineal), and fully extended family systems, without regard to postmarital residence patterns. Mean conformity scores by family complexity and postmarital residence are shown in Table 12.3.

TABLE 12.3 Conformity versus Self-Reliance by Family Complexity and Postmarital Residence

| Residence | Family Complexity | | |
	Nuclear	Small Extended*	Fully Extended
Nonpatrilocal	7.7	6.7	7.2
	(15)	(12)	(9)
Patrilocal	7.9	8.8	8.4
	(21)	(23)	(11)

*Includes both stem and lineal family types.
Note: High mean scores indicate greater relative emphasis on conformity; *N*s in parentheses.

The difference observed by Olsen between nuclear and small extended families in patrilocal societies is clearly replicated by these cross-cultural data: in patrilocal systems socialization for conformity relative to self-reliance is highest in small extended families and lowest in nuclear family systems. However, societies with fully extended patrilocal families place *less* emphasis on conformity than those with small extended families. In societies with residence systems other than patrilocal (neolocal, bilocal, matrilocal, or avunculocal), conformity scores are uniformly lower and do not covary with family structure in any systematic fashion predictable from the theory.

The problem here may well be one of measurement—that is, the epistemic correlation between our abstract construct (supervision) and our empirical indicator (family complexity). The relevant variable appears to be the extent to which the mother is directly and immediately supervised by senior members of her husband's family, particularly her mother-in-law. In nonpatrilocal residence systems the mother-in-law and the daughter-in-law are members of different households and families, regardless of family structure. In nuclear family systems, patrilocal postmarital residence usually means that the couple resides in the same community as the husband's parents, but not in the same household. The implications of this for supervision of the mother by her husband's mother are, it appears, minimal. In fully extended families, several daughters-in-law may be simultaneously present, and family size is also likely to be quite large. This may reduce the immediacy of the supervision of each mother by senior females. Thus, while our logic was not sufficiently refined to predict the pattern shown in Table 12.3, these results are not necessarily contrary to the general theory. Supervision of the mother may well be highest in small, extended, patrilocal families. The nonlinear relationships and interaction effects observable in this table also show why no linear relationship is observed between family complexity and socialization values. Our results do not contradict those of Olsen (1974) but rather show that the relationship becomes much more complex when the range of the independent variable (family complexity) is expanded (see also Minturn and Lambert 1964).

It is also important to consider here the fact that our measurement of the properties of family complexity, as in any cross-cultural study, pertains solely to the cultural level of analysis. That is, system properties reflected in the measurement of family complexity are indicative of ideal or preferred family types. As Levy (1965) and others have shown, extended family systems are not uniformly populated by extended families; there are many conditions (such as low life expectancy) which inhibit the general attainment of this ideal by individual families. This means that, in any given extended family system, only a variable proportion of families are in fact extended (see Goode 1963). Thus there is considerable slippage between the variable of family complexity and the abstract concept of supervision by family elders. This may account, in part, for the small correlation between family complexity and socialization values.

This study provides further evidence that, at least in terms of selected parameters, Kohn's theory of social class and socialization values may be generalizable beyond the bounds of American and Western cultures. But more important, the range of independent variables implicated by this theory has been expanded. The seven independent variables employed here are admittedly rough indicators of the extent to which adults are subject to requirements for conformity in several aspects of their daily lives; alternatively, they may be viewed as inverse indicators of the utility of self-reliance or autonomy. Collectively, they explain approximately 40 percent of the variation in socialization values along a dimension of conformity/self-reliance. The findings of this study support the proposition that adults value in their children traits or qualities which they have found to be instrumental to their own success in a variety of behavioral domains, including the familial, religious, and political, as well as the economic.

This study is obviously not a replication or extension of Kohn's complete theory. Instead, we have concentrated on certain aspects of this theory which relate most directly to previous theoretical formulations in anthropology and comparative sociology. However, the fact that hypotheses pertaining to many areas of social life may be derived from only a small portion of Kohn's theory, and were supported on a cross-cultural sample such as this, indicates that the scope and explanatory utility of the theory may be much broader than we have previously believed.

An ability to explain a significant proportion of the variation in socialization values is, however, of little theoretic utility unless these values themselves have demonstrable conse-quences for either parental behaviors or the outcomes of the socialization process. Possible connections between socialization values and parental behaviors in the child-rearing process are currently being investigated through cross-cultural research and will be the subject of a subsequent paper.

Notes

* From the *American Journal of Sociology* 84, no. 2 (1978): 386–403, by permission of the University of Chicago Press. Copyright 1978 by the University of Chicago Press.

† This is a revised version of a paper presented at the annual meetings of the National Council on Family Relations, San Diego, California, October 1977. The authors are listed in alphabetical order; no other priority ranking is implied. The authors wish to extend their appreciation to Lorene Stone and Mindy Kezis for their assistance in coding the ethnographic data and to Nancy Olsen for her comments on an earlier draft of this manuscript.

1. For more detailed summaries of this theory, see Kohn 1969; Pearlin 1971; Lee 1977; and Gecas 1978.

2. This is not intended to imply that blue-collar children are actually more conforming than others; in fact, the opposite may well be true (see Devereaux, Bronfenbrenner, and Rodgers 1969; Devereaux 1970, 1972; Lee 1977). The relevant point here is that blue-collar parents appear to value conformity in children more than white-collar parents do.

3. A great number of terms have been employed by Kohn and other researchers working with similar ideas (see below) to refer to the general trait which we label here as self-reliance. The terms have included self-direction, autonomy, independence, and even assertiveness. We do not wish to confuse conceptual clarity with labeling decisions; consequently we employ the term "self-reliance" throughout this paper. Our intention is to refer to the essential common properties of the terms noted above as the concepts have been employed by previous researchers. It is not our intention to replicate precisely the conceptualization of any previous researcher, singly or collectively. Our opera-

tional definition of self-reliance is given in the Methods section below.

4. Pearlin (1971) and others have measured closeness of supervision and the requirement of self-reliance in work separately, and Olsen (1974) uses only the concept of supervision as the basis for her generalization of the theory. However, these two variables appear to be closely related on the conceptual level and are also negatively correlated empirically (Pearlin 1971, p. 65). A high degree of self-reliance in work implies a low degree of supervision, almost by definition. These two concepts will thus often be employed interchangeably or in combination in the present analysis.

5. For related studies, see Barry 1969; Barry et al. 1976; Berry 1967; Draper 1975; and Munroe, Munroe, and Daniels 1973. The basic logic of each of these studies is similar to that of Barry, Child, and Bacon (1959); see also Barry et al. (1967) and Inkeles (1968).

6. Lambert, Triandis, and Wolf (1959) found that a belief in aggressive (as opposed to benevolent) gods is positively related to socialization for independence and self-reliance. However, aggressiveness by the deities is not the same as closeness of supervision and is not clearly related to the theory discussed here.

7. By "cross-cultural" data we mean, in this case, information gleaned from ethnographic reports. Such data provide one observation per variable for each society, or culture included in the sample. For a more detailed explication of the nature, potentials, and limitations of cross-cultural data in sociological research, see Lee (1977, pp. 10–11, 22–24, and 31–34.)

8. Our ordering of subsistence types is similar to but not identical with that of Barry et al. (1959). The differences are attributable to the fact that their order was intended to index ability to store and accumulate food, while ours is an attempt to tap closeness of supervision. These two abstract concepts should be positively, but not perfectly, correlated.

9. Space precludes the presentation of complete coding procedures and instructions here.

10. This estimate of coder reliability, while acceptable according to standards of cross-cultural research, nonetheless indicates a substantial amount of code disagreement. As a check for the effects of coder error, all cases in which

coders disagreed by more than two points on the five-point scale were dropped from the analysis. This resulted in the loss of 14 cases; the intercoder correlation coefficient for the remaining 101 societies was +.808. All analyses reported below were then run with only these 101 cases; however, no differences occurred in the behavior of the religious-taboo variable when compared to analyses employing all 115 cases. Therefore the results reported below were obtained by using the entire sample for which sufficient data are available.

11. As a check for the effects of coder error, 11 cases on which coder disagreement exceeded two points on the seven-point scale were temporarily dropped from the analysis. The intercoder correlation for the remaining 89 cases was +.751. All analyses were then performed for these 89 societies, and results compared with those obtained from the 100 cases with nonmissing data on this variable. Again, there were no significant differences in the behavior of the socialization-values variable. In the interest of maximizing sample size, we therefore report results obtained from the total sample for which data are available in spite of the relatively low intercoder correlation.

12. All correlations were originally computed using both listwise and pairwise deletion of missing values (Nie et al. 1975, pp. 312–13). The results obtained with each option were essentially identical. Consequently the analysis with pairwise deletion is reported here. This has the advantage of utilizing as much of the data as possible. In addition, an analysis-of-variance test for nonlinearity was conducted for all possible bivariate relationships (Blalock 1972, pp. 411–12). No significant violations of the linearity assumption were detected. However, see Table 12.3 in the Discussion section below.

13. This partial correlation has a probability of .148 (one-tailed test) and is, therefore, not significant at conventional levels. All other partial correlations are significant beyond the .05 level, and all bivariate correlations are significant beyond the .001 level. However, tests of significance have limited meaning, given the nature of cross-cultural data. While the societies included in the Standard Cross-cultural sample and the Human Relations Area Files are generally considered to be fairly representative

of known nonindustrial societies, they do not constitute a probability sample. Hence significance levels are not reported in the tables.

References

Aberle, David. 1961. "Culture and Socialization." Pp. 381–99 in *Psychological Anthropology,* edited by Francis L. K. Hsu. Homewood, Ill.: Dorsey.

Barry, Herbert III. 1969. "Cross-Cultural Research with Matched Pairs of Societies." *Journal of Social Psychology* 79 (October): 25–33.

Barry, Herbert III, Margaret Bacon, and Irvin Child. 1967. "Definitions, Ratings, and Bibliographic Sources for Child Training Practices of 110 Cultures." Pp. 293–331 in *Cross-Cultural Approaches,* edited by Clellan Ford. New Haven, Conn.: HRAF.

Barry, Herbert III, Irvin Child, and Margaret Bacon. 1959. ''Relation of Child Training to Subsistence Economy." *American Anthropologist* 61 (February): 51–63.

Barry, Herbert III, Lili Josephson, Edith Lauer, and Catherine Marshall. 1976. "Traits Inculcated in Childhood: Cross-Cultural Codes." *Ethnology* 15 (January): 83–114.

Berry, J. W. 1967. "Independence and Conformity in Subsistence Level Societies." *Journal of Personality and Social Psychology* 7 (December): 415–18.

Blalock, Hubert M., Jr. 1972. *Social Statistics.* 2nd ed. New York: McGraw-Hill.

Blumberg, Rae Lesser, and Robert F. Winch. 1972. "Societal Complexity and Familial Complexity: Evidence for the Curvilinear Hypothesis." *American Journal of Sociology* 77 (March): 898–920.

Bronfenbrenner, Urie. 1970. *Two Worlds of Childhood: U.S. and U.S.S.R.* New York: Russell Sage Foundation.

Devereux, Edward C., Jr. 1970. "Socialization in Cross-Cultural Perspective: Comparative Study of England, Germany, and the United States." Pp. 72–106 in *Families in East and West,* edited by Reuben Hill and Rene Konig. Paris: Mouton.

———. 1972. "Authority and Moral Development among German and American Children: A Cross-National Pilot Experiment." *Journal of Comparative Family Studies* 3 (Spring): 99–124.

Devereux, Edward C., Jr., Urie Bronfenbrenner, and Robert R. Rodgers. 1969. "Childrearing in England and the United States: A Cross-National Comparison." *Journal of Marriage and the Family* 31 (May): 257–70.

Draper, Patricia. 1975. "Cultural Pressure on Sex Differences." *American Ethnologist* 2 (November): 602–16.

Ellis, Godfrey. 1977. "Parent-Adolescent Conflict in the United States: Some Societal and Parental Antecedents." *Family Perspective* 2 (Spring): 13–27.

Fox, Robin. 1967. *Kinship and Marriage.* Baltimore: Penguin.

Gecas, Victor. 1978. "The Influence of Social Class on Socialization." In *Contemporary Theories about the Family,* edited by Wesley R. Burr, Reuben Hill, F. Ivan Nye, and Ira L. Reiss. New York: Free Press.

Gecas, Victor, and F. Ivan Nye. 1974. "Sex and Class Differences in Parent-Child Interaction: A Test of Kohn's Hypothesis." *Journal of Marriage and the Family* 36 (November): 742–49.

Goode, William J. 1963. *World Revolution and Family Patterns.* New York: Free Press.

Inkeles, Alex. 1968. "Society, Social Structure, and Child Socialization." Pp. 73–129 in *Socialization and Society,* edited by John Clausen. Boston: Little, Brown.

Kohn, Melvin L. 1959a. "Social Class and the Experience of Parental Authority." *American Sociological Review* 24 (June): 352–66.

———. 1959b. "Social Class and Parental Values." *American Journal of Sociology* 64 (January): 337–51.

———. 1963. "Social Class and Parent-Child Relationships: An Interpretation." *American Journal of Sociology* 68 (January): 471–80.

———. 1969. *Class and Conformity: A Study in Values.* Homewood, Ill.: Dorsey.

———. 1977. *Class and Conformity: A Study in Values.* 2nd ed. Chicago: University of Chicago Press.

Kohn, Melvin L., and Carmi Schooler. 1969. "Class, Occupation and Orientation." *American Sociological Review* 34 (October): 659–78.

———. 1973. "Occupational Experience and Psychological Functioning: An Assessment of Regional Effects." *American Sociological Review* 38 (February): 97–118.

Lambert, W. W., Leigh Triandis, and Margery Wolf. 1959. "Some Correlates of Beliefs in the Malevolence and Benevolence of Supernatural Beings: A Cross-Cultural Study." *Journal of Abnormal and Social Psychology* 58 (September): 162–69.

Lee, Gary R. 1977. *Family Structure and Interaction: A Comparative Analysis.* Philadelphia: Lippincott.

Levy, Marion J. 1965. "Aspects of the Analysis of Family Structure." Pp. 1–64 in *Aspects of the Analysis of Family Structure,* by Ansley J. Coale, Lloyd A. Fallers, Marion J. Levy, David M. Schneider, and Sylvan S. Thompkins. Princeton, N.J.: Princeton University Press.

Marsh, Robert M. 1967. *Comparative Sociology.* New York: Harcourt, Brace & World.

Minturn, Leigh, and William Lambert. 1964. *Mothers of Six Cultures: Antecedents of Child-rearing.* New York: Wiley.

Munroe, Robert, Ruth Munroe, and Robert Daniels. 1973. "Relation of Subsistence Economy to Conformity in Three East African Societies." *Journal of Social Psychology* 89 (February): 149–50.

Murdock, George Peter, and Douglas R. White. 1969. "Standard Cross-Cultural Sample." *Ethnology* 8 (October): 329–69.

Naroll, Raoul S. 1968. "Some Thoughts on Comparative Method in Cultural Anthropology." Pp. 236–77 in *Methodology in Social Research,* edited by Hubert B. Blalock, Jr., and Ann B. Blalock. New York: McGraw-Hill.

Nie, Norman, C. Hull, J. Jenkins, K. Steinbrenner, and D. Bert. 1975. *Statistical Package for the Social Sciences.* 2nd ed. New York: McGraw-Hill.

Nimkoff, Meyer F. 1965. *Comparative Family Systems.* Boston: Houghton Mifflin.

Nimkoff, Meyer F., and Russel Middleton. 1960. "Type of Family and Type of Economy." *American Journal of Sociology* 66 (November): 215–25.

Olsen, Nancy J. 1973. "Family Structure and Independence Training in a Taiwanese Village." *Journal of Marriage and the Family* 35 (August): 512–19.

———. 1974. "Family Structure and Socialization Patterns in Taiwan." *American Journal of Sociology* 79 (May): 1395–1417.

Pearlin, Leonard I. 1971. *Class Context and Family Relations: A Cross-National Study.* Boston: Little, Brown.

Pearlin, Leonard I., and Melvin L. Kohn. 1966. "Social Class, Occupation, and Parental Values: A Cross-National Study." *American Sociological Review* 31 (August): 466–79.

Stephens, William N. 1963. *The Family in Cross-Cultural Perspective.* New York: Holt, Rinehart & Winston.

Steward, Julian. 1955. *Theory of Culture Change: The Methodology of Multilinear Evolution.* Urbana: University of Illinois Press.

Wright, James, and Sonia Wright. 1976. "Social Class and Parental Values for Children: A Partial Replication and Extension of the Kohn Thesis." *American Sociological Review* 41 (June): 527–37.

CHAPTER THIRTEEN

Child-Care Policy Arenas: A Comparison between Sweden and the United States*

William M. Bridgeland, Philip R. Smith, and Edward A. Duane

In most societies, the responsibility for the young child historically has belonged to the family. However, as nations have industrialized and urbanized, some degree of extrafamily child care has emerged in many places. In the past decade or so, both Swedish and American child-care arrangements have become a notable public policy issue and in large part because of the increasing numbers of mothers with young children who have joined the workforce in both countries. Our objective in this paper is to compare the political arenas in which the child-care policies of the United States and Sweden have evolved. We will discuss briefly some of the major child-care programs of the two countries, synthesize the policy culture underlying Swedish and American child-care programs, identify the policy framers who interact to determine the child-care policies of each country, and evaluate the relative advantages and disadvantages of Swedish and American child-care policy.

Why compare the child-care policy processes of the United States and Sweden? Both countries are at a similar stage of advanced industrial development as evidenced by per capita income, life expectancy, and other socioeconomic measures. In addition, the countries share a common background of European civilization, constitutional government, and quasi-market economies. Beyond their similarities, they also present an interesting study in contrasts. Sweden has a small, highly compact population (less than 5 percent of the United States) characterized by stability and

homogeneity. The United States has been distinguished by its large, dispersed, and culturally heterogeneous population. The dominant American cultural themes of relevance stress individual competitiveness and private, voluntary-group efforts. In contrast, Swedish society has valued social deference and group consensus-seeking which promote public responsibility for the quality of social life. It is the contention of the authors that these differences in orientation also manifest themselves in contrasting patterns of public policies for child care.

Child-Care Programs—The Programmatic Dimension

In the United States, at least prior to the Reagan administration, public funding or subsidies as well as guidelines and support for child-care programs have come largely from the federal government (e.g., Title XX–Child Care).[1] However, circumstances in the United States, given its large population and federal system, encourage fragmentation of services for child care. As a consequence, a plethora of state and local health, education, and social services agencies administer and supervise these programs, with little apparent coordination. In Texas, for example, Grubb and Brody (1982) found substantial intrastate inequalities in nonschool programs for children including Title XX, Aid to Families with Dependent Children (AFDC), and so forth. Other states exhibit a similar pattern, for example, California (Kirst, unpublished), Michigan (Duane and Bridgeland, 1978), and New York (Garms, unpublished).

Sweden, as a relatively small centralized society, has an integrated child-care system of center-based arrangements; the development of children is an important and publicized national goal (Dodge, 1979, p. 255). First, and parallel to but not as extensive as the American kindergarten, Swedish national law requires that municipalities provide all six-year-old children with a year of "part-time nursery school" with a direct fee (Melsted, 1979, p. 4). Second, there has been much expansion of "day nurseries," which offer services to children between six months and seven years, five days a week between 6:30 A.M. and 7:00 P.M. (Fact Sheets, 1982). The ratio of children to staff in these Swedish child-care centers is four or five to one (Fact Sheets, 1982, p. 3). Because of the wide variation between states and communities in the United States, comparable figures are difficult to determine. However, in a major study of American day-care centers, Coelen et al. (1979, p. 28) found the "average actual child/staff ratio in the U.S. [to be] 6.8 children per adult." The Swedish public policy objective is to ensure, by about 1990, openings for all children (Melsted, 1979, p. 4). Third, and in response to the "inadequate supply of day nurseries, local authorities have been subsidizing 'child minders' to provide day care in homes" (Fact Sheets, 1982, p. 1).

In Sweden, local authorities also set a scale of user charges. The proportional share borne by each of the funding sources (national and municipal government expenditures and parent fees) varies from community to community according to ability to pay. Moreover the nature of the preschool expenditure may change the mix of funding responsibility. For example, the national government may fund a larger proportion of the "start-up" costs for a preschool program, but subsequently reduce the proportion of funding for program operation or maintenance. Funding proportions for preschool ex-

penditures from each source have varied some over the years, but are approximately national government = 57 percent, municipal government = 32 percent, and parental fees = 11 percent (Jaffe, 1979, p. 3). Fourth, and in clear contrast with the United States, there is a close linkage between the local and national levels among service areas affecting preschool children (Adams and Winston, 1980, pp. 50–55; Kahn and Kamerman, 1977, p. 15).

Differences between Swedish and American early childhood programs carry over into support for the family purchase of child care. Since 1975, the comprehensive Swedish approach is clearly reflected in its national "parental insurance system" which contains substantial benefits including paid parental leaves for child care at birth, and help in special situations such as the serious illnesses of children (Trost, 1983). In the United States, in contrast, there is a more limited role of child-care support from the federal government. This is divided into two types, a maternal child-care allowance for those on public assistance while seeking jobs or in training and a parental income tax deduction (income to $35,000) for a fixed sum spent on child care (Kahn and Kamerman, 1977, p. 20).

Another area of contrast is the estimated need for child care versus actual availability. In Sweden, 31 percent of preschool children were in day nurseries or family day nurseries in 1980 (Fact Sheet, 1982, p. 2). And center-based programs are slated to expand to include all children of working and student parents and, eventually, all children of parents who desire to utilize full-time or part-time child-care programs. In the United States, on the basis of much less reliable data, it is estimated that approximately 6 million or 29 percent of American children under six years of age were in some out-of-home care arrangement in 1974 (Kahn and Kamerman, 1977, p. 28). The quality of these arrangements seems to vary widely from outstanding to many rated as poor (Adams and Winston, 1980, p. 66). One estimate placed the need at upward of 3 million licensed child-care places in the United States (Kahn and Kamerman, 1977, p. 28). By 1982, not quite 50 percent of American mothers with children under six worked or were seeking work outside the home (*U.S. News,* 1983). Given the increase in working mothers, the need for help has clearly risen. Nonetheless, there seems to be no governmental commitment in the United States equivalent to that in Sweden to meet the demand for child care.

Policy Values—The Cultural Dimension

A basic difference between the United States and Sweden is that they have alternative rationales for public involvement in child care. An examination of these rationales will ensure not only a better understanding of current policy, but also an improved conception of probable policy directions in both societies.

Elazar's (1972) typology of American policy subcultures is useful in comparing Swedish and American political cultures. Elazar isolated three basic ideological types: the individualistic with strong private concerns, the moral which emphasizes selective public intervention, and the traditional where emphasis is placed on received values and the social hierarchy. In Elazar's terms, the United States most nearly represents a predominantly individualistic thrust mitigated to some extent by moralism, whereas Sweden exhibits a moral orientation tinged with traditional deference especially to "functional experts" (Castles, 1978, p. 447).

Also relative to early childhood policy values, Dunlop (1980 and unpublished) found three types of rationale for governmental involvement: maintenance, reform, and revolution. Within the maintenance category, public involvement is characteristically thought legitimate only in response to wartime needs, to economic crises, or to children in crisis. Reform rationales are incremental, where governments typically supplement and support the

family as it undergoes social change. Within the revolutionary perspective, governments operate as a vehicle for fundamentally recasting the basic social institutions, including the ongoing child-rearing patterns. If the Dunlop typology were applied to the United States and Sweden, it is highly unlikely that revolutionary orientations would be significant in either country. Rather they are almost certain to have a mix of the other two rationales, with Sweden favoring greater public involvement or reform, and the United States tending toward a somewhat minimal approach or maintenance (Dunlop, unpublished).

The American emphasis on individualism has accented family self-help mitigated by occasional public assistance in individual cases. Nonetheless, there have also been vocal people both inside and outside government who have in the last two decades employed reform rationales for child care. Such reform proposals emphasized child care as a vehicle for enhancing child development, increasing parental competence, and maximizing women's opportunities (Dunlop, 1980). Thus far such objectives seem to have had relatively little impact on actual policy.

In Sweden, "[e]xpansion of child care facilities was regarded . . . as the most important family policy issue of the 1970s. This expansion has enjoyed high priority" (Fact Sheet, 1982, p. 1). In practice, Swedish child-care centers may provide more parental "convenience . . . than [act] as an educational experience for their children" (Adams and Winston, 1980, p. 54). It is believed in Sweden, however, that child care acts as a developmental stage where contact with both peers and trained personnel can make a vital contribution to child development (Bergstrom, 1978).

Although some American politicians (e.g., Senator Mondale in the mid-1970s) have argued for a more extensive role in child-care funding, neither the Democratic nor the Republican Party has supported it. Most American policymakers are reluctant to place child care on the public agenda. Insofar as they have done so, their actions appear to be governed by private concerns, that is, for "maintenance." In contrast most Swedish political parties (the powerful Social Democrats, the Center Party and the Liberal Party; all except the Communists) have long advocated child-care subsidies. The most clear-cut reform orientation comes quite expectedly from the socialists, whose leader has demanded that:

Children must be allowed to grow up under calm, secure conditions. This requires that parents and children have more time to spend with each other. It affects the child-care system and the expansion of parental insurance, and it requires higher children allowances and housing allowances. (Melsted, 1979, p. 6)

And in a 1979 parliamentary motion on family policy, the party stated:

For the Social Democrats, family policy is part of an overall policy aimed at bringing greater social equality and creating a better society. (Melsted, 1979, p. 6)

Policy Actors—The Structural Dimension

Power structures, including decision makers and advocate groups, contrast rather markedly in the two countries. Sweden has a consensus-building and highly integrated political system. This integration verges on union or fusion (Castles, 1978, p. 51). That is to say, the Swedes are represented by interest groups that are highly centralized, well-disciplined, and closely affiliated with the political parties. In the United States, in contrast, there are many more interest groups which tend to be smaller and less formal. The American political process is therefore competitive, but structurally fragmented. Interest groups in the United States try to have influence on specific factions within the political parties or upon the separate units of government. Swedish interest groups, on the other hand, enjoy institutionalized participation in the policy process. In part, this stems from the overall role that such groups

play in Sweden's system of multiparty proportional representation. The Swedish political parties are more clearly an embodiment of particular social classes than the rather heterogeneous socioeconomic mix of America's two-party system (Castles, 1978, p. 453). Secondly and more formally, interest groups have institutionalized policy involvement through a procedure called "remiss," where government ministries and appointed commissions are obliged to consult all interest groups affected by a given policy proposal (Castles, 1978, p. 452).

The structural dimensions which are useful for comparison in the child-care arena include: public actors (elected and nonelected governmental officials), and private actors (interest groups and unorganized publics). In the United States, there is a wide array of diverse categorical programs under several government jurisdictions. Consequently, policy making for the young child is scattered across a multitude of legislative committees and executive agencies at the federal, state, and local levels of government. At the state level, policy-making coordination is limited by jurisdictional and financial competition and attempts at coalition building. For instance, in the states of Michigan, California, and New York, Duane, Bridgeland, and Stern (1982) found some interagency conflict over control of childhood programs, with occasional efforts at agency co-optation of child-oriented interest groups in these struggles. The structural configuration differs in Sweden, where responsibility for formulating and administering preschool policy is located in the Ministry of Health and Social Affairs while the supervisory function is under the National Board of Health and Welfare (Jaffe, 1979, p. 3). These national agencies primarily provide supervision, training, research, and technical assistance to local governmental units that implement and administer day-to-day preschool policy (Jaffe, 1979, p. 3).

At the local governmental level in Sweden, preschool programs are under the auspices of a municipal council, an elected body that reflects the political party composition of the community. In particular, early childhood programs are administered by the Central Board of Welfare Services in conjunction with the Municipal Education Committee. At this level there is considerable coordination with the other welfare services (for example, care for the aged). Thus, Sweden's administrative structure tends to respond to the dominant cultural imperative of compromise and to produce coherent and functional child-care programs.

As noted above, American political parties have no clear party policy initiatives in the early childhood area. By contrast, Sweden's political parties constitute brokers in national preschool politics. While Swedish interest groups play a major role, this is primarily accomplished by influencing party leaders and ultimately party platforms. Dodge (1979, p. 260) argues that there is a "Swedish preference (after Erikson and Piaget) for an open preschool classroom [to instill] . . . respect of one individual for another. . . ." Certainly, this seems to be an important mode in Sweden. The authors found, however, at the local level, child-care philosophy and policy tend to mirror the preferences of the political party or parties that dominate in the community. Thus in a municipality that has, for example, a large faction critical of the core institutions, there is often considerable debate over the socialization of preschool children. As might be expected, then, these programs are sometimes influenced by class-conflict values (Marx) rather than values that emphasize individual development or cooperation (Erikson).

American early childhood people have been, in large part, atomized into small, competitive, and often isolated groups. They are often "inexperienced in understanding the political process and in using political strategy" (Sponseller and Fink, 1982, p. 20). Moreover, there are extensive divisions along organizational lines including public (e.g., Head Start), voluntary (e.g., Montessori), and proprietary (e.g., Kindercare) child-care organizations often with wide differences in philosophies and thrusts. Therefore, informal and intermittent

requests by local child-care practitioners and parents of clients to municipal and state agencies are the most frequent way interests are made known, especially over a controversial issue like licensing. There are, however, a few broadly based interest groups, such as the National Association for the Education of Young Children (NAEYC) or the Children's Defense Fund (CDF). Such organizations have had some policy influence in transmitting research to policymakers, orchestrating responses to actual or proposed policy changes, and making demands on the policymakers. The CDF, especially, has been a vigilant "watchdog" on the recent federal and state cuts and as an advocate for children (Blank, 1983). For example, among other recent proposals, they are asking Congress for "a federally funded Information and Referral system that would help maximize existing child care resources" (Blank, 1983, p. 12).

Swedish interest groups, in contrast, are quintessential political bureaucracies with formalized input in preschool policy making. Unlike the American labor movement, the Swedish Trade Union Confederation (LO) has been an important lobby for the rapid expansion of publicly supported preschool facilities and programs. The LO has advocated, for example, public operation of preschool and free-time activities for children whose parents work at inconvenient hours (Schyl-Bjierman, 1977, pp. 3–4).

Not unexpectedly, early childhood unions and associations are a key force in Sweden's preschool politics. Preschool administrators, professionals, and teachers are represented by their respective unions and associations. While there is a real potential for conflict among such people, interest group involvement in the context of consensus building usually leads to accommodation rather than conflict.

Parents, as parents, are largely unrepresented in Swedish preschool interest groups. A combination of tight bureaucratic hierarchies, political party dominance in policy making, and the cultural propensity to defer to expertise or credentials have discouraged individuals and small groups of child-care practitioners. This translates into little meaningful input by consumers on policy (Jaffe, 1979, pp. 3–4). In clear contrast, the American tradition of parental involvement and the recent accountability movement has led to an array of formalized processes for regular parental participation in policy on many levels and in many types of child-care programs. Parental involvement includes parental advisory groups, parental representation on boards of directors, and the inclusion of parents on committees for hiring staff.

Conclusions and Projections

The "policy arena" frame of reference employed in the present paper provides an overview of the setting and facilitates the separate analyses of the major policy dimensions: programs, values, and actors. This three-way differentiation permits us to uncover more readily similarities and differences between the two countries.

Within each society, the underlying cultural and population differences are reflected in the programs, values, and actors of the early childhood area. Congruent with the general "welfare state" pattern in Sweden are the developed and coordinated child-care programs that are derived in many cases from American early childhood research and experiences. In contrast, these programmatic ideas have not been extensively applied in the United States though there are many specific instances of much utilization in a wide array of alternative programs. In large and heterogeneous American communities (e.g., those with universities), affluent parents may choose programs from numerous child-care centers with differing developmental thrusts (Baumrind, 1973). Even so, the more general American pragmatic-custodial pattern contrasts markedly with the strong commitment found generally in Sweden. Swedish political parties, for example, publicly sponsor child care with a developmental thrust. Finally, while high levels of political integration characterize Sweden, political fragmentation is typical of the United States. These patterns have had some immediate consequences for the relevant configurations among child-care policy people. Even as coordination of policy making in Sweden readily increases program effectiveness, it tends to lead to self-perpetuating elites, with parents having limited access to policy. In the United States, fragmentation not only means programmatic weakness, but also small-sized groups of practitioners deplete their scarce resources through infighting. Occasionally they are co-opted and dominated by governmental agencies (Duane, Bridgeland, and Stern, 1982). Clearly, a very important feature of the rather unstructured American system is that it puts up fewer barriers to the entrance of emergent groups into the arena than exist in Sweden.

But what is the future? The recent deep and sustained recession in the industrial economies lends credence to the assertion that there is a trend away from postwar growth, perhaps even to a no-growth economy (Sederberg and Taylor, 1981). Concurrently, there is an emergent political movement of "antistatism" in many Western industrial societies most clearly evidenced in Anglo-American politics (the Reagan and Thatcher governments). These leaders appeal to the general disillusionment with the administrative state and the insistence on its retrenchment.

The twin forces of economic scarcity and antistatism are likely to lead to additional differential responses in Swedish and American societies on the issue of public involvement in child care. Conditions of accelerated economic constraint and political alienation could result in a "radicalization" of child-care policy. Both countries could shift sharply away from reform to mostly maintenance in the United States and to more revolutionary intervention in Sweden. In the United States, there could be near abandonment of any public commitment to child-care support for lower income groups. Simultaneously, there could be an increase of some indirect subsidies to profit-oriented child-care providers in the name of "free enterprise" and the granting of more tax relief for child care (a middle-class subsidy). In any case, the net impact may well be to increase structural inequality in child-care usage.

In Sweden, with its paternal traditions, the reemergence of economic scarcity could lead to redoubled efforts at redistributing scarce resources in order to soften the blow on those people least able to meet their own child-care needs. Indeed, rather than curbing big government, there may be more potential for national planning.

It might be expected that both countries, while tending to revert to traditional national responses, might do so with significant differences from the past. In the United States, the citizenry might not be willing to accept the harsh consequences of full governmental retrenchment after having enjoyed a variety of entitlements since the 1930s. In Sweden, a now better educated and possibly more sophisticated, assertive public might be unwilling to tolerate traditional control from the top and demand greater citizen participation in the operation of public policy, for example, through advisory councils (Schyl-Bjierman, 1977). In both countries, the desire to avoid the extremes of individual self-help and state collectivism could spawn an era of voluntarism in child-care arrangements. As a consequence, we should look for the growth of local cooperatives and collectives in Sweden, and nonprofit voluntary organizations in the United States.

Notes

* From the *International Journal of Comparative Sociology* 26, nos. 1 and 2 (March–June 1985): 35–44, by permission of E. J. Brill, Publisher. Copyright 1985 by E. J. Brill.

1. Actually, both federal and state support on Title XX have declined about 14 percent since the Reagan administration took office (Blank, 1983, p. 5).

References

Adams, C. T., and K. T. Winston. 1980. *Mothers at Work: Public Images in the United States, Sweden, and China.* New York: Longman, Inc.

Baumrind, D. 1973. "Will a Day Care Center Be a Child Development Center," *Young Children* 28: 154–169.

Bergstrom, A. 1978. Staff psychologist, Danderyd, Sweden Child Care Centers, Interview, Summer.

Blank, H. 1983. "Children and Federal Child Care Cuts: A National Survey of the Impact of Federal Title XX Cuts on State Child Care Systems, 1981–83." *Children's Defense Fund.*

Bridgeland, W. M., and E. A. Duane. 1980. "State Politics of Pre-Kindergarten Education: An Inquiry in Three States." *Education and Urban Society* 2: 211–26.

Castles, F. G. 1978. "Scandinavia: The Politics of Stability," in Roy C. Marcridis, (ed.) *Modern Political Systems.* Englewood Cliffs, N.J.: Prentice-Hall.

Coelen, C., F. Glantz, and D. Calore. 1979. *Day Care Centers in the U.S.: A National Profile, 1976–1977.* Cambridge, Mass.: Abt Books.

Dodge, M. K. 1979. "Swedish Programs for Children: A Comprehensive Approach to Family Needs." *Child Care Quarterly* 4: 254–65.

Duane, E. A., and W. M. Bridgeland. 1980. "Children's Services in Michigan: A First Look." ERIC ED 171 414.

Duane, E. A., W. M. Bridgeland, and M. E. Stern. 1982. "Relationships between Early Childhood Groups in Three States." *The Annals of The American Academy of Political and Social Science* 461: 43–52.

Dunlop, K. H. 1980. "Child Care and Parent Education: Reformist Rationales for Governmental Intervention." *Education and Urban Society* 12: 175–91.

Dunlop, K. H. "Rationales for Governmental Intervention into Child Care and Parent Education." Unpublished paper.

Elazar, D. 1972. *American Federalism: A View from the States,* 2nd edition. New York: Thomas Y. Crowell, 94–102.

— — —. 1982. *Fact Sheets on Sweden,* "Child Care Programs in Sweden," Oct., F.S. 86.

Garms, W. 1977. "New York State Programs for Children." Unpublished paper.

Grubb, W. N., and J. G. Brody. 1982. "Spending Inequalities for Children's Programs in Texas." *The Annals of the American Academy of Political and Social Science* 461: 53–62.

Jaffe, K. 1979. "The Politics of Child-Care." *Social Change in Sweden* 11.

Kahn, A. J., and S. B. Kamerman. 1977. *Child Care Programs in Nine Countries.* Washington, D.C.: United States Department of Health, Education and Welfare, Office of Human and Child Development.

Kirst, M. W. 1977. "Children's Services in California: A First Look." Unpublished paper.

Melsted, L. 1979. "Swedish Family Policy." *Swedish Information Service* 4.

Schyl-Bjierman, G. 1977. "Areas of Development in the Swedish Pre-School System." *Current Sweden* 175.

Sederberg, P. C., and M. W. Taylor. 1981. "The Political Economy of No-Growth." *Policy Studies Journal* 2: 735–55.

Sponseller, D. B., and J. S. Fink. 1982. "Public Policy toward Children: Identifying the Problems." *The Annals of the American Academy of Political and Social Science* 461: 14–20.

Trost, J. 1983. "Parental Benefits—A Study of Men's Behavior and Views." *Social Change in Sweden,* October, 28.

U.S. News and World Report. 1983. "Mothers and Young Children," June 27, p. 67.

Women, Gender, and Feminism

Most of the world's societies can be characterized as exhibiting rampant gender inequality. Ironically, in some societies in the past, and even in a few so-called primitive societies, such inequality was minimal or even nonexistent. And, in the 1990s, trends evidence a shift back toward gender equality in many societies, but certainly not all. These pervasive inequalities express themselves in nearly all realms of life—education, the labor market and occupations, and attitudes, to name only a few.

With the recognition of the nearly universal and insidious character of gender inequality, sociologists have, of course, turned attention to the issue and studied it from many points of view, including, among others, social power, male dominance, religion, stratification hierarchies, and role duality. Much of this work has been spurred on by the many national women's movements that have arisen since the 1960s to bring about recognition of the problems and, in turn, to take positive steps to achieve lasting solutions.

Our first selection is by Schlegel, who first notes, from a socioanthropological perspective, that women have traditionally been viewed as being mainly "reproductive specialists," with their social power thereby limited solely to the domestic sphere. In this essay, her presidential address to the Society of Cross-Cultural Research, Schlegel cites recent history's monotheistic tradition as one source of the problem. She also details some specific methodological implications and reviews other recent comparative works in the field.

Davis and Robinson explore gender inequality from a number of perspectives in four different nations. They tested ten independent demographic variables against perceptions of gender inequality and support for efforts to reduce such inequality, treated as dependent variables. Several hypotheses with varying theoretical underpinnings were tested. In almost all instances women were more likely than men to perceive inequality and to support efforts to combat it. Perhaps unexpectedly, especially disadvantaged women perceived no greater levels of gender inequality, and better-educated women are less supportive of efforts to combat inequality. Interestingly, the authors found only limited support for the generalizability of findings from the United States.

The third selection in this section, by Roos, explores the dual career theory as a subset of human capital theory and puts it in competition with the institutionalist or internal labor market theory. At issue is the question: Are women disadvantaged in job access and earnings because they fail to invest in job-related education and work shorter hours, which the dual role theory emphasizes, or is their disadvantage due to prejudice and similar workplace barriers? Roos explores this issue in twelve industrialized countries and finds that never-married women, while faring better in the job market than other women, still do not get either the same kinds of jobs or the same pay as men. Consequently, the disadvantage of women, in general, in the labor market cannot be explained solely by the fact that they put family over work in their "dual careers."

CHAPTER FOURTEEN

Gender Issues and Cross-Cultural Research*

Alice Schlegel†

There is nothing more fundamental to social organization than gender. It is a commonplace in the study of human life that all societies recognize at minimum the age categories of infant, child, adolescent (at least for boys), and adult. Sex categories are even simpler, for there are only two, female and male. (I will discuss later the question of transvestites.) Margaret Mead can be credited with challenging the assumption that maleness and femaleness are more or less equivalent across cultures by claiming that the behavior and personality attributed to one's sex vary markedly. While the fieldwork on which she based this claim has been questioned, and one might even posit that there are universal properties underlying culturally specific concepts of femaleness and maleness, no one today assumes that the attributes associated with one's sex are culturally invariant. Nevertheless, all societies recognize as normal at birth only two types of infants, these with female and those with male genitals.

I have been careful to use the words *maleness* and *femaleness,* because I want to distinguish between sex—or the biological features of the individual that are manifested in the genitals and the secondary sexual characteristics—and gender—the appropriate behaviors and attributes that are associated with sex. There are two reasons for doing so. One is the recognition that while sex is unlikely to be culturally variant, since we are all members of the same species, gender assuredly is. The second reason is that currently we sometimes hear one of those arguments that raises emotions and spills ink but has little to recommend it logically or empirically. That is the position that there are multiple genders in some societies, with the corollary that ours is restrictive in recognizing only two. The supporting evidence that is offered is usually the existence of the transvestite, the transsexual, and the berdache (see Kessler and McKenna [1978], two psychologists who treat this subject). Since in these cases, every effort is made by the individual to appear and act like a person of the opposite sex, rather than some intermediate type, these cases of gender-crossing only reinforce the position that all cultures recognize only two genders.

Some confusion has arisen from the fact that in many societies individuals who exhibit, under certain circumstances, the characteristics of the opposite gender are socially acceptable. Perhaps the most widely known example is the berdache, the male or female transvestite who is well known from Plains tribes in North America and who appears in some other Indian societies as well. To a more limited degree, the "manly-hearted woman" of the Plains was also somewhat of a gender anomaly, a woman who went to battle and counted coup along with other warriors. (This individual was often a woman who led a party to avenge the death of a son or other close kinsman.) Another case of limited gender-crossing is that of the female "husbands" of West Africa and among the Bantu—women whose behavior in every other respect is feminine, but who establish independent households by marrying other women and becoming socially recognized fathers to these women's children. Even societies as rigid in their division of gender behavior as the Islamic societies of the Middle East permitted women under exceptional circumstances to take up the male pursuit of religious scholarship and to become masculine within that domain, as manifested in the proverb: "A woman on the path of God becomes as man." Nevertheless, no society to my knowledge socializes children for more than two genders.

Despite the cultural variability of gender attributes—which is too well known to merit discussion here—and the tolerance of some societies for gender anomalies, the division of human societies into two genders seems to be as pervasive as the division into the two sexes to which the gender attributes are attached. Whatever else they may be, the genders are firmly grounded in the biological reality of sex difference. It is no more likely that we can achieve a totally gender-free, culturally androgynous society than that we can evolve one that is biologically androgynous. This is not to claim that gender differences cannot be minimized or that gender difference entails sexual inequality—I have gone on record many times to assert the falsity of that proposition—but rather that gender is inescapable, because it is grounded in biology, as a social and cultural elaboration of a biological construct.

The culturally variable nature of gender lends itself to cross-cultural comparisons. Many writings of the first wave of recent feminist studies in anthropology responded to the appeal of comparative research, attempting to answer a question that is central to feminist thinking, that is, is male dominance universal? I addressed this question in my doctoral dissertation of 1970, later published as *Male Dominance and Female Autonomy* (Schlegel 1972). This was a study of domestic authority patterns in matrilineal societies. At that time I assumed, following Schneider (1962), that authority in the descent group would be held by men, saying: "We can take it for granted that authority in the descent group sphere is of necessity in the hands of the men of the matrilineage" (Schlegel 1972: 6). I would not make that assumption today. In 1974, the influential collec-

tion *Women, Culture, and Society* (Rosaldo and Lamphere 1974) was published. It contained three systematic comparisons that dealt with female status. In a controlled comparison of two Ijaw villages, Leis (1974) called for a "detailed cross-cultural study" to test her hypotheses about the factors that predict the presence or absence of women's groups. Sacks (1974), in a more or less controlled comparison (i.e., her four societies are all located in sub-Saharan Africa), developed a Guttman scale for indexes of female status. Sanday (1974) also constructed a Guttman scale of somewhat different indexes based on a selected sample of eleven societies and then plotted them on a graph to show the relation between status and contribution to subsistence. While we might have some quarrel with the methods that Sacks and Sanday employed, we note that these researchers, as well as the editors of the collection, took for granted the comparability of gender attributes across cultures, as I had done in my cross-cultural study.

The mid-1970s saw a spate of collections of papers about women in particular parts of the world: Africa, Asia, Latin America, the Middle East (cited in Lamphere 1987). Collections of the late 1970s and early 1980s had a different focus, such as the continuation of interest in gender status (Schlegel 1977), the nature-culture dichotomy and its application to the female-male dichotomy (MacCormack and Strathern 1980), a redefinition of some of the questions regarding gender differences (Reiter 1975), and a search for the meaning of gender differences (Ortner and Whitehead 1981). Many of these collections were primarily intended to reveal more information on women specifically, while others, notably Schlegel (1977) and Ortner and Whitehead (1981), contained a majority of papers that regarded the relations of the sexes or the perception of both genders as central. The regional collections, in particular, are implicitly comparative. They provide a rich source of data on underreported aspects of society and culture and provide fresh material for both coding and analysis.

Problems Addressed

The consequences of research done about women, much of it by women, are far greater than merely adding to our stockpile of codable variables. In focusing on women, and by necessity on relations between women and men, researchers have been compelled to think about old problems in new ways. I will mention some of these.

Social Power

The old way of thinking about women was as reproductive specialists, whose impact on society did not extend much beyond their families, since they were concerned mostly with domestic activities. Anthropologists looking at women's lives and at their relations to men have called into question the assumptions about female status and roles that had been almost universally accepted among social scientists: first, that women were confined to the domestic as contrasted to the public domains; and second, that women are universally subordinate to men. These assumptions were, in fact, initially held by some of the feminists discussed above: Rosaldo, Lamphere, and Ortner took this position in *Women, Culture, and Society* and attempted to give culturally based explanations for it. Others, however, disputed it: Eleanor Leacock (cf. 1981) had for many years been a lone voice, claiming from her Marxist perspective that foragers were sexually egalitarian before a class system imposed inequality on the sexes. Even non-Marxists like myself (Schlegel 1977), drawing on my evidence from the Hopi, denied the universality of female subordination. My point was and continues to be that the indicators for equality or subordination are not necessarily the same everywhere. To be specific, Lamphere and others claim that community-level decision making—when to hold ceremonies, when to go to war, and the settlement of certain kinds of disputes—is the primary indicator of social power. Since in most societies, most formal community decision makers are men, this indeed would seem to indicate universal male dominance. My position is that community-level decisions are not necessarily primary in determining people's actions; in small societies, where power is not centralized but is dispersed, decision making at other levels—for example, those of the household or the descent group—may well be just as important. It is in such societies that women's social power can equal men's, if indeed they control decision making in certain central institutions.

If I am right, then the comparativist's job becomes much more difficult. To conduct cross-cultural studies of gender status, not only is it necessary to develop measures of women's status within the central institutions of a society but it is also necessary to have some scale of these institutions. As one example, female control of the domestic economy is much different in a foraging band or a subsistence horticultural village, where the domestic economy is the only one there is, from what it is in a complex tribe or state, where domestic production is secondary to production for trade. In the first instance, control over domestic production and distribution indicates female social power; in the second, it may or may not, as it may be overridden by many other activities or areas of decision making, which men control.

Another example is the uncritical assumption that distributing goods leads to social power. When it became apparent that female participation in production did not lead to high female status, an alternative explanation was that participation in distribution was the central economic activity related to social power. For instance, it is well recognized that among animal-keeping peoples—whether they are the pastoralists of the arid zones of Africa and Eurasia, the pig raisers of Oceania, or the equestrian hunters of the Great Plains—animal owners can acquire clients through the gift or loan of animals, thus raising their own power and prestige. This power to allocate has been, I believe mistakenly, applied to foragers by Friedl (1975) and possibly by others, who assert that males are always dominant because they bring in the prized economic good—meat—and distribute it. What this position neglects to take into account is that the ability to distribute leads to social power only if the distributor has the power to withhold. Otherwise, it simply gains prestige for the distributor. In many foraging societies, goods cannot be withheld. Therefore, as comparativists, we have to be sensitive to the question of ownership of goods and what ownership means before we can assume that an indicator of economic power in one society has its equivalent in another.

I suggest that it is this lack of sensitivity to the contextual difference among indicators of status that led to the disappointing results of Whyte's (1978) attempt to develop a worldwide understanding of female status, although on specific cultural features he did reach some interesting findings. It is not surprising that without any well-developed theoretical base from which to draw hypotheses, and without any attempt to conceptualize measures of status, Whyte came to no conclusions about gender status other than to say that it is difficult to measure.

Reproduction

Feminism does not stand alone in influencing a new interest in reproduction, and also in marriage—the institution through which reproduction primarily occurs in human society. French structuralism puts reproduction—specifically the incest taboo and the necessity of marrying outside the family—at the core of kinship and of social organization in kin-based societies. Ethology and sociobiology alert us to the centrality of reproductive strategies in understanding animal social organization and thereby providing models for one means of

understanding our own. Marxists and those influenced by them have always recognized reproduction as inherently tied to production, for example, the reproduction of labor or, more recently, the family as both a productive and a reproductive unit. Sociobiology and Marxism offer strong theoretical positions and analytical procedures for the study of reproduction. Since it is an undeniable fact that women are reproductive specialists (along with many other things), feminist scholars should be friendly to this new and strong interest in reproduction.

However, feminist scholars can alert their colleagues to the danger of old wine in new bottles: of assuming along with Lévi-Strauss that men exchange women in order to form social alliances, thus making women the pawns in men's political games; of taking the male-dominant baboon troop as a model for terrestrial primate behavior, including humans; of uncritically assuming that men always seek to control reproduction through control over women; of assuming that because male apes grab more bananas than females do at the feeding station, they necessarily dominate them and thus demonstrate that male dominance is a higher-primate characteristic. It has taken feminist anthropologists and primatologists to point out these lurking assumptions and to provide the cross-cultural or cross-species data that are needed to discredit them.

Sexuality

Related to reproduction is the question of human sexuality in all its varieties. Feminists have been eager to demolish the view of the passive female and have welcomed studies of sexuality in other cultures (cf. Broude [1976] and Frayser [1985]), which provide evidence for the variability of sexual expressiveness. Feminists have also joined forces with those who have conducted research into homosexuality, for such studies help to destroy the stereotypes that do us all a disservice. A wealth of new or rediscovered data on both heterosexuality and homosexuality across cultures has challenged psychologists and other social scientists to revise their definitions of what is normal, what is alternative, and what is pathological.

Gender Principles in Expressive Culture

A fourth broad area where feminist research has altered our view of society is in the study of feminine and masculine principles in the way people conceive of their world. Coming from a tradition of androcentric monotheism, it is easy to overlook the importance of the feminine in other cultures' cosmogonies. The first step was to take women's ceremonies seriously, an undertaking by male anthropologists (e.g., Victor Turner) as well as by their female counterparts. More recently, there has been an explosion of interest in gender as a ground theme in symbols and rituals of all sorts. In hindsight, it seems obvious that the fact of male-female differences and the joys, difficulties, and ambiguities of relations between these two classes of beings should provide major themes for rituals that are expressive of social concerns. The information was always there: we just were not asking the right questions to be able to interpret or even to notice it.

These are, as I see it, the broad areas in which feminist scholarship has had its major impact in anthropology. No doubt there are others as well, and I would welcome a discussion of them. The point is that feminist scholarship, by insisting on the study of the other half of humanity and by taking seriously the implications of that study, has challenged the assumptions, acknowledged or unrecognized, that have been made about human society and has broken down ethnocentric stereotypes about normal female and male behavior. Thus, feminist scholarship has benefited comparative research in two ways, by providing more information on neglected topics and by asking fresh questions.

The major impact of feminist thinking has been on the assumptions made about gender. Women per se have not been neglected by the social sciences. There has certainly been considerable interest on the part of psychology and psychological anthropology in women as mothers—often as mothers who inhibit their sons' masculine identity. Also, a great many studies have been made in which women and men were contrasted—this has been standard fare in sociology and psychology for many years. However, there has been a tendency to assume that men represented the "normal" and women the "deviant." I exaggerate, of course; nevertheless, in a culture that values attributes more commonly ascribed to men, such as activity (with its negative value of passivity) and strength (as against weakness), men become the unmarked category, as against women the marked, in social science research. Feminism has put the spotlight on this tendency, and most researchers today are careful not to interpret any differences between male and female behavior as invidious.

Then there is the questioning of what component of behavior is gender specific and what is due to women's and men's positions within structures. A shining example of this is Kantor's review (1976) of Tiger and Shepher (1975), *Women in the Kibbutz*. The authors of that book regretfully conclude that kibbutz women's failure to achieve equality lies in female nature. Kantor succinctly demolishes this conclusion by showing that both the values and the structure of the kibbutzim favor men. The kibbutz women's adaptation to this situation is similar to that of any people in a structurally subordinate position.

A third important questioning of assumptions is the result of the flood of information on women's lives that anthropologists and historians have been collecting. All of this information shows the great variability of gender across time and space and cautions us against taking any gender ascriptions for granted.

Cross-Cultural Studies with Gender as a Central Issue

Gender is both a social and a cultural construct. As a social construct, gender is a set of expectations about behavior and the assignment of status and roles by sex. As a cultural construct, gender as interpreted by a society is the more or less consistent set of beliefs, evaluative statements, and representations in myth, ritual, and folklore that has developed regarding the sexes. While in any society, the two types of construct are operant at any given time or in any given situation, it is important to distinguish them for the purpose of analysis.

Gender as a Social Construct

Most cross-cultural studies of gender as a social construct in one way or another involve that most critical distinction between the sexes, reproduction. Although gender was not his topic, Murdock (1949), in *Social Structure,* identified reproductive tasks and constraints as the primary cause of division of labor by sex. Wittingly or not, he established a tradition for future researchers. While he would probably rather be known as a follower of Durkheim than of Marx, the concept of reproductive differences in establishing gender roles is compatible with both Marxist and Durkheimian social theory. Specifically, it is women's reproductive activities as constraining them, rather than men's strength as giving them an advantage, that is frequently the focus of these studies. While a man's greater upper body strength might be seen as giving him the advantage in hunting and warfare, most recent researchers have paid less attention to this advantage than to the need to protect reproductive women and the constraints of pregnancy and lactation on women's energy and mobility. The logical conclusion of this argument is that if fertility were not socially promoted, and if women could thus be largely freed from the restrictions of reproduction, then women would be doing the same tasks as men. This is perhaps overestimating the similarities between the sexes,

when one considers that the upper body strength required to shoot a longbow, hurl a spear, club an enemy, steer the heavy wooden plow of Asia, or manage pack animals and wagons may be better suited to the musculature of the average man than to that of the average woman. Nevertheless, much primitive technology is within the physical capacities of women, so female constraint rather than male advantage seems the likelier explanation for the origins of most sex differences in the most basic types of division of subsistence labor. The occupational androgyny that is the trend in the modern world is the consequence of two unprecedented phenomena: technological advances that make human muscle power irrelevant and a negative value on fertility—in itself an indirect consequence of advanced technology—which reduces the proportion of time that women spend on reproduction in their increasingly longer lives.

White, Burton, and Dow (1981) address the question of allocation of tasks by sex in their study of African agriculture, using constraints on women as an explanatory feature, along with slavery. In a cross-cultural study, they demonstrate that root crops, which require less secondary processing, are more likely to be cultivated by women; whereas cereal crops, which require more of such processing, are likely to be cultivated by men, with the women being responsible only for the secondary processing activities that can be done within the home. Ember and Ember (1971) and Ember (1983) contribute to this discussion by showing that war is more likely to interrupt the agricultural cycle in areas where root crops are grown, that is, the tropics, than where cereal crops are grown, that is, the temperate zone. It appears that men must be freed from day-to-day subsistence labor in order to be prepared to fight. Where war is conducted by specialized armies, however, men are enabled to work full-time in agriculture, even in the tropics (e.g., the Azande). It is now time to conduct a study that pulls together the various hypotheses to determine those conditions that explain sex biases in the major survival activities of economic production and war.

If gender roles and relations are determined by survival activities, the next step is to show how the specific features of production, reproduction, and war affect gender as a social construct. White, Burton, and Dow (1981) find an association of female labor with polygyny, as do Schlegel and Barry (1986). Schlegel and Barry also find an association between female contribution to production and to both behavior—for example, premarital freedom of girls—and ideology, for example, evaluation of children by sex.

For all of the concern that there is with male dominance and with male political control as its indicator, little systematic research has been done on women's involvement in political activities beyond the early papers by Sanday (1974) and Sacks (1974). A more recent exception is the paper by Ross (1986), in which he tests the presence of female participation and of female organizations with other variables. One important finding is that participation and the presence of sororities are separate variables and should not be conflated. The mere presence of female sodalities is not, in itself, an indication of high female status or power. The major finding of this paper, to me, is the exposition of the inverse relation between the centralization of power and female participation: where power is centralized, as in complex societies or—at the kin group and community level—in fraternal interest groups, women do not participate much; where it is dispersed, they have a better chance. But why? We still have not discovered the origins of male dominance. If we were inhabitants of tribal New Guinea or the Amazon Basin, we could turn to myth: in these regions, men say that they gained power by stealing the sacred flutes from the women. We have no such tales to enlighten us and must create our own explanations (myths?) of the origin of male dominance.

Taking women seriously has resulted in a massive amount of research on the reasons for sex differences. While this interest is probably more characteristic of psychology than of the other social sciences, it has been felt in anthropology as well. Notable among cross-cultural studies are those by the Whitings (e.g., Whiting and Whiting 1975), whose attention in recent years has been on the situational causes of behavior, in contrast to endogenous causes or those arising from infantile experiences (Whiting 1980).

One of the most imaginative cross-cultural studies relating to the social organization of gender is by Paige and Paige (1981), *The Politics of Reproductive Ritual,* in which the reproductive capacities of both sexes become a central feature of the organization of the society. Men's claims over the reproductive capacity of others—their wives, their children—become, in the view of these authors, the basis for political statements. Reproductive rituals, those of menarche, circumcision, birth, and menstruation, are the form that these political statements take. I find the arguments as applied to the menarche and the circumcision ritual particularly convincing. They have the advantage of locating the explanation for social rituals within the social process rather than within some assumed psychological state, and they see the "cause" of ritual to lie in the advantage to those who control it, rather than in the advantage to those for whom it is conducted. Thus, we do not have to attribute altruism or even more complicated motives, such as castration anxiety, to those who organize the ceremonies, although there is nothing in the theory that precludes such additional interpretations.

Gender as a Cultural Construct

If gender is a social construct, defining behavior and position within social structures, it is also a cultural or symbolic construct. It has meaning for those who share a common culture. This fact complicates matters: the meanings attached to gender must fit with other meanings ascribed to features of the social, natural, and supernatural domains as constructed by a culture. Male and female as symbolic categories do not stand alone or outside the totality of symbolic categories that make up a culture's symbolic system; on the contrary, they must be coordinated with other categories. This causes the cultural analysis of gender to be fraught with ambiguity—any representation of gender within the symbolic repertoire might be a reflection of some other category, rather than a mirroring of gender relations. For example, derogatory representations of women in men's rituals might be expressing structural fractures in the patrilineage or ambivalence between sisters and brothers, rather than attitudes toward women per se (cf. Schlegel n.d. [1]). Is gender as a cultural construct thus not amenable to cross-cultural studies? It is one thing to measure prestige, or polygyny, or female contribution to subsistence; it is another to transform culture-specific meanings into generalized statements that can be coded across cultures. It is not impossible, however, and it is essential if symbolic anthropology is to go beyond interpretation to explanation.

Explanation looks for causes, even if we use more relaxed terms like "causal influences" or "determining conditions." The studies to which I refer attempt to link culture to social organization by locating the causes of gender meaning in social processes. While others have tied culture to social structure, from Durkheim to Guy Swanson (1960) in his *The Birth of the Gods,* only a few cross-cultural studies have dealt with gender and culture. One of these studies is by Zelman (1977), who regards reproductive rituals as measures of female-male similarity or dissimilarity, thus relating them to cultural constructs, rather than to social processes, as do Paige and Paige (1981). Zelman finds that couvade, which brings men into the act of birth, occurs where male and female separateness is less culturally emphasized. Menstruation rituals, which emphasize the difference between the sexes, tend to occur where the social distance between the sexes is greatest. There is, of course, no necessary incompatibility between these two differing interpretations of gender rituals, in which Zel-

man sees gender as a causal factor of rituals, while Paige and Paige emphasize the political use to which gender rituals are put.

The couvade has been related to a gender issue of a different sort by John W. M. Whiting and by the Munroes, that is, gender identity (cf. Munroe 1980 for a discussion of this relationship). These scholars have related the couvade to cross-sex identity, and they treat it as a milder manifestation of the same dynamic that underlies male transvestism. Gray and Ellington (1984) expand the argument by including male homosexuality as coexisting with male transvestism and as absent from societies that practice the couvade. Papers such as these indicate the comfortable fit between feminist concerns about the construction of gender and psychogenic interpretations, so long as they are free from the sexist assumptions of earlier analytic psychology.

A recent cross-cultural study on the cultural construction of gender is Sanday's (1981) *Female Power and Male Dominance.* The underlying thesis of the book is that men's orientation is outward, manifested in hunting, killing, and seeking power, and that women's is inward, as in giving birth and containing power. She proposes that the nature of a society's environment plus its technology—that is, whether the society is animal/outward-oriented or plant/inner-oriented—is what conditions its behavior. This behavior in turn is reflected in origin symbolism—masculine for the first type, feminine for the second. Thus, ideology is linked to the material base by means of behavior.

Studies such as these encourage us to do further research on the meaning of gender across cultures. An additional study of meaning that has relevance for the cross-cultural construction of gender comes from the field of psycholinguistics, in a paper by Osgood (1976), which analyzes meaning across languages. Words from thirty languages were scaled by factor analysis into clusters whose factors emerged as Potency, Evaluation, and Activity. As an aside, Osgood remarks that in the kinship and male-female categories of all the languages, male concepts are more potent than female, that is, they cluster with other potent words. (However, see Parker [1988] on the variations of gender-word clusterings within a single language.) Osgood's analysis suggests that there may be widespread, even universal, properties of gender that underlie the varying cultural constructions. Cross-cultural research on language and symbols is the only way I know of to test this suggestion.

Conclusion

Explanations of culture, as the concepts and understandings out of which cross-cultural hypotheses are drawn, change over time. If earlier feminist studies have a faintly old-fashioned air, it is because we now have a more sophisticated understanding of the dialectic between reproduction and production in determining the social relations between men and women in preindustrial societies. We also know about the variability of gender construction across cultures.

Future studies of the roles and statuses of the sexes will have to tie reproduction and its control in with production and its control. It will not be enough just to look at female contribution to subsistence, although this is a good place to start and has provided some significant results. Production alone is not sufficient, even for preindustrial societies, where the household is for the most part the unit of both production and reproduction. Men's and women's places in the household are also linked to the accumulation of goods by means other than household production—such as bridewealth and dowry (Schlegel and Eloul 1988), female and male inheritance, wages or earnings through trade, and usufruct in collective property—and they are related to how these goods are controlled and by whom. Studies like these call out for multivariate statistical methods, as being more appropriate for studying a multivariate world. However, I am painfully aware of the limitations that lack of data places on the use of mul-

tivariate techniques, so this proclamation is offered more in hope than in expectation.

I can think of a number of widespread cultural features that need explanation as well as interpretation: the value placed on female virginity (cf. Schlegel n.d. [2]); the vagina dentata myth; the myth of men stealing power from women along with the theft of the sacred flutes or bullroarers or whatever; beliefs about pollution by menstrual blood or semen (but never, so far as I know, by human milk); the fact that some societies celebrate marriage—the joining of the sexes—with elaborate weddings, while others with equal amounts of time and disposable goods do not; and also the fact that in some societies females are associated with nature, whereas in others, such as medieval and early modern Europe, it is males who have this symbolic value—the list goes on and on.

Whiting and Child (1953) explored the relation between personality and culture; it is time to extend the existing studies of the culture of gender relations and to provide systematic psychological and social explanations for the cultural features that, so far, have received mainly idiographic interpretations. (Carol Ember's [1989] paper on the sex of ogres in myths is an example of what I mean.) Our findings should prove interesting and useful to the interpretive anthropologists, who stand in danger of collecting masses of individual interpretive studies with little to integrate them. In turn, we can learn from the idiographic studies what the contexts of gender representations and behavior are, so that the variables we test can have meaning in the societies to which they are being applied—the sample. In this way, we can fulfill the hope that the case study and the cross-cultural study will be mutually enriching in our quest for the causes of human behavior.

Notes

* From *Behavior Science Research* 23, no. 2 (1989): 265–80, by permission of the Sage Periodicals Press. Copyright 1989 by the Human Relations Area Files.

† First presented as the Presidential Address at the Society for Cross-Cultural Research, February 1989.

References

Broude, Gwen J. 1976. "Cross-Cultural Patterning of Some Sexual Attitudes and Practices." *Behavior Science Research* 11: 227–62.

Ember, Carol R. 1983. "The Relative Decline in Women's Contribution to Agriculture with Intensification." *American Anthropologist* 85: 285–304.

———. 1989. "Why Are Ogres in Folktales Male or Female?" Paper delivered at the Society for Cross-Cultural Research, Annual Meeting, New Haven.

Ember, Melvin, and Carol R. Ember. 1971. "The Conditions Favoring Matrilocal versus Patrilocal Residence." *American Anthropologist* 73: 571–94.

Frayser, Suzanne G. 1985. *Varieties of Sexual Experience.* New Haven: HRAF Press.

Friedl, Ernestine. 1975. *Women and Men: An Anthropologist's View.* New York: Holt, Rinehart, and Winston.

Gray, J. Patrick, and Jane E. Ellington. 1984. "Institutionalized Male Transvestism, the Couvade, and Homosexual Behavior." *Ethos* 12: 54–63.

Kantor, Rosabeth Moss. 1976. "Interpreting the Results of a Social Experiment." *Science* 192: 662–63.

Kessler, Suzanne J., and Wendy McKenna. 1978. *Gender: An Ethnomethodological Approach.* Chicago: University of Chicago Press.

Lamphere, Louise. 1987. "Feminism and Anthropology: The Struggle to Reshape our Thinking about Gender." In *The Impact of Feminist Research in the Academy.* Farnham Christie, ed., pp. 11–33. Bloomington: Indiana University Press.

Leacock, Eleanor. 1981. *Myths of Male Dominance.* New York: Monthly Review Press.

Leis, Nancy B. 1974. "Women in Groups: Ijaw Women's Associations." In *Women, Culture, and Society.* M. Z. Rosaldo and L. Lamphere, eds., pp. 223–42. Stanford: Stanford University Press.

MacCormack, Carol, and Marilyn Strathern. 1980. *Nature, Culture, and Gender.* Cambridge: Cambridge University Press.

Munroe, Robert L. 1980. "Male Transvestism and the Couvade: A Psycho-Cultural Analysis." *Ethos* 8: 49–59.

Murdock, George P. 1949. *Social Structure.* New York: Macmillan.

Ortner, Sherry, and Harriet Whitehead. 1981. *Sexual Meanings.* Cambridge: Cambridge University Press.

Osgood, Charles E. 1976. "Probing Subjective Culture." *Studies in Language Learning* 1: 325–57.

Paige, Karen E., and Jeffery M. Paige. 1981. *The Politics of Reproductive Ritual.* Berkeley: University of California Press.

Parker, Seymour. 1988. "Rituals of Gender: A Study of Etiquette, Public Symbols and Cognition." *American Anthropologist* 90: 372–84.

Reiter, Rayna, ed. 1975. *Toward an Anthropology of Women.* New York: Monthly Review Press.

Rosaldo, Michelle Z., and Louise Lamphere, eds. 1974. *Women, Culture, and Society.* Stanford: Stanford University Press.

Ross, Marc H. 1986. "Female Political Participation: A Cross-Cultural Explanation." *American Anthropologist* 88: 842–58.

Sacks, Karen. 1974. "Engels Revisited: Women, the Organization of Production, and Private Property." In *Women, Culture, and Society.* M. Z. Rosaldo and L. Lamphere, eds., pp. 207–22. Stanford: Stanford University Press.

Sanday, Peggy R. 1974. "Female Status in the Public Domain." In *Women, Culture, and Society.* M. Z. Rosaldo and L. Lamphere, eds., pp. 189–206. Stanford: Stanford University Press.

———. 1981. *Female Power and Male Dominance.* Cambridge: Cambridge University Press.

Schlegel, Alice. 1972. *Male Dominance and Female Autonomy.* New Haven: HRAF Press.

———. n.d. (1) "Gender Meanings, General and Specific." Manuscript.

———. n.d. (2) "Status, Property, and the Value on Virginity." Manuscript.

———. 1977. *Sexual Stratification.* New York: Columbia University Press.

Schlegel, Alice, and Herbert Barry III. 1986. "The Cultural Consequences of Female Contributions to Subsistence." *American Anthropologist:* 142–50.

Schlegel, Alice, and Rohn Eloul. 1988. "Marriage Transactions: Labor, Property, and Status." *American Anthropologist* 90: 291–309.

Schneider, David M. 1962. "Introduction: The Distinctive Features of Matrilineal Descent Groups." In *Matrilineal Kinship.* David M. Schneider and Kathleen Gough, eds., pp. 1–29. Berkeley: University of California Press.

Swanson, Guy. 1960. *The Birth of the Gods.* Ann Arbor: University of Michigan Press.

Tiger, Lionel, and Joseph Shepher. 1975. *Women in the Kibbutz.* New York: Harcourt Brace Jovanovich.

White, Douglas R., Michael L. Burton, and Malcolm M. Dow. 1981. "Sexual Division of Labor in African Agriculture: A Network Autocorrelation Analysis." *American Anthropologist* 83: 824–49.

Whiting, Beatrice B. 1980. "Culture and Social Behavior: A Model for the Development of Social Behavior." *Ethos* 8: 95–116.

Whiting, Beatrice B., and John W. M. Whiting. 1975. *Children of Six Cultures.* Cambridge: Harvard University Press.

Whiting, John W. M., and Irvin L. Child. 1953. *Child Training and Personality: A Cross-Cultural Study.* New Haven: Yale University Press.

Whyte, Martin K. 1978. *The Status of Women in Preindustrial Societies.* Princeton: Princeton University Press.

Zelman, Elizabeth C. 1977. "Reproduction, Ritual, and Power." *American Ethnologist* 4: 714–33.

Men's and Women's Consciousness of Gender Inequality: Austria, West Germany, Great Britain, and the United States*

Nancy J. Davis and Robert V. Robinson†

Nearly a quarter of a century has passed since the feminist movement began a resurgence in the United States in the mid-1960s. Within a few years, second-wave feminist movements had sprung up throughout Europe. Although the specific causes underlying these movements differed from country to country, a common factor was a growing awareness of gender inequalities in the workplace and home and a growing belief that these inequalities were sufficiently unjust that they should be eliminated.

In studies of U.S. women and men, attitudes toward gender inequality have been associated with employment and family structure (Mason and Bumpass 1975; Cherlin and Walters 1981; Thornton, Alwin, and Camburn 1983; Smith 1985; Plutzer 1988). However, because these studies have not been replicated in other countries, it is unknown whether findings for the United States apply to other societies. We propose a model of consciousness of gender inequality based, in part, on hypotheses derived from prior research in the United States, then test its generalizability using national survey data of women and men in four Western societies—the United States, Great Britain, West Germany, and Austria.

Theoretical Background

Drawing on models of class awareness or consciousness (e.g., Giddens 1973, pp. 112–16), we assume that individuals must first perceive that inequality exists, and then decide that this inequality is sufficiently unfair that some corrective action is warranted. Consciousness of inequality includes the self-awareness of subordinate groups as well as awareness of inequality on the part of those who are not disadvantaged. By this definition, men who favor action to reduce discrimination against women are conscious of gender inequality. We propose further that perceptions of the extent of gender inequality and support for efforts to combat it arise from (1) location in gender and other stratification hierarchies, (2) educational and labor experiences, (3) family situation, and (4) the historical conditions prevailing when social and political attitudes were formed.

Gender, Socioeconomic Status, Education, and Age

We begin with several hypotheses that explain consciousness of inequality *in general* and then proceed to hypotheses that apply more specifically to consciousness of *gender* inequality. Our general hypotheses concern the effects of gender, socioeconomic status, education, and age on consciousness.

Gender and Socioeconomic Status. The *underdog thesis* predicts that individuals who are disadvantaged by the distribution of opportunities, treatment, and conditions will be more conscious of inequality than individuals who are advantaged (Robinson and Bell 1978; Robinson 1983). According to this thesis, women will be more conscious of gender inequality than men. The underdog thesis also predicts that individuals with low-prestige jobs and/or low incomes will be more conscious of gender inequality.[1] An alternative to this thesis, the *threat hypothesis* (Husbands 1979), can be derived from the study of race relations. Men with less prestigious occupations or low incomes may tend to view women as a threat in the competition for jobs, and perhaps as responsible for their own disadvantaged positions. As a result, these men may deny the existence of gender inequality and oppose efforts that they see as elevating women at their expense.

Education. We test two somewhat contradictory hypotheses regarding the effects of education. According to the *enlightenment thesis,* education produces a greater awareness of inequality in society by familiarizing individuals with experiences different from their own (including those of the other sex) and inculcates Enlightenment ideals that promote equal treatment for all. Thus, highly educated individuals will be more likely to perceive inequality than individuals with less education and to favor efforts to reduce inequality.

The *reproduction thesis* contends that education increases awareness of inequality while encouraging its acceptance (thus "reproducing" inequality). Education, through its competitive evaluation system, pedagogical content, and hierarchical structure, promotes the idea that inequality is meritocratic, that is, it results from individual differences in talent, effort, and educational credentials rather than from discrimination on the basis of ascribed group characteristics (Bowles and Gintis 1977). Education rewards and stresses *individualistic* striving and self-improvement, which may reduce support for government intervention as a solution to group disadvantage. From the reproduction thesis, we hypothesize that highly educated individuals will be more likely to perceive inequality than individuals with less education, but will be *less* favorable to intervention to reduce inequality.

Age. According to the *egalitarian Zeitgeist thesis,* individuals' attitudes toward inequality are strongly affected by the historical context when they were coming of age politically (Lipset and Ladd 1971, p. 654). In the United States, the 1960s and early 1970s were a period of "rediscovery" of inequalities of class, race, and gender that saw the rise of movements (New Left, civil rights, feminist) to eliminate these inequalities (Gans 1973). Many European countries also experienced strong New Left movements in the 1960s pressing for a greater role for students in the educational process and for greater equality and democracy in the larger society. The resurgence of feminism in Europe began in the late 1960s and early 1970s, a few years later than in the United States (Chafetz and Dworkin 1986, pp. 171–90). More recently, the emergence of grass-roots peace and ecology movements in the late 1970s and the formation of Green political parties with explicit feminist stances have politicized another generation in West Germany, Austria, and Great Britain (Kolinsky 1989; Spretnak and Capra 1986, p. 5).[2]

From the egalitarian Zeitgeist thesis, we expect young people to be more conscious of gender inequality than older people, reflecting their coming of age in the 1960s through the early 1980s. In the United States, however, individuals who came of age politically after the mid 1970s when the direct activism of the U.S. feminist movement had subsided (Kitschelt 1985, pp. 283–84) and an antifeminist backlash was on the upswing (Ferree and Hess 1985, pp. 132–39) may have been less affected by the feminist movement than the preceding generation. Whereas the feminist-oriented environmental and peace movements activated many young people in Europe during the 1980s, the issues that mobilized the young in the United States during the Reagan years (South Africa, campus racism, peace, Central America) were, with few exceptions (e.g., pornography, abortion), not feminist issues. We are uncertain whether an egalitarian Zeitgeist effect in the United States would be limited to individuals who came of age during the most active phase of the American feminist movement (making the middle generation more conscious of gender inequality than older or younger generations), or whether it would also include younger persons who came of age during a time of less dramatic, more institutionalized feminism and the rise of antifeminism (making the younger and middle generations more conscious of gender inequality than the older generation). Therefore, we also test the hypothesis that age is related curvilinearly to gender consciousness in the United States and, for comparability, in the other three countries.

Intervention to Reduce Inequality. Our model of consciousness of inequality also assumes that individuals first perceive the existence of inequality and then may proceed to support efforts to reduce it. We hypothesize that individuals who perceive sizable gender inequalities will be more likely to favor efforts to combat inequality than those who perceive little or no inequality.

Additional Factors

In addition to these general hypotheses, which might explain consciousness of inequality on any dimension, we test several hypotheses that apply specifically to consciousness of *gender* inequality.

Employment. Most U.S. studies have found that women's labor force participation is an important factor in their support of feminist principles.[3] Work outside the home gives women direct experience with sex disparities in earnings, promotion, and work conditions that are not faced by women who work in the unpaid domestic economy. Employed women also have a clear economic interest in gender equality in the workplace. Nonemployed women who depend on a male wage earner and who face rising divorce rates and the declining status of housewifery may have an interest in maintaining traditional gender roles and their attendant sex disparities (Gerson 1987). It has also been argued that women's support for

feminist goals depends more on their current employment status than on past employment statuses (Gerson 1987). We hypothesize that the greater a woman's attachment to the labor force, the more likely she will be to perceive gender inequality and the more favorable toward intervention to reduce it. Specifically, we hypothesize that women who are currently employed will be more conscious of gender inequality than women who are not currently but were employed, and that the latter, in turn, will be more conscious of gender inequality than women who have never been employed. Furthermore, we hypothesize that the more hours per week spent in paid employment, the more conscious of gender inequality a woman will be (Plutzer 1988). We offer no corresponding hypotheses for men because employment is the overwhelming norm for men.

Marital Status and Spouse Employment. Previous research on U.S. women points to the importance of family situation in feminist orientations (Luker 1984; Gerson 1987). We expect that marital status and spouse's employment status interact with sex: Women who are single, divorced, widowed, or married to a man who is not employed are harder hit by women's lower average wages than women whose family includes a male wage earner. We expect such women to be more conscious of gender inequality than married women with employed spouses.[4]

In contrast, we hypothesize that men whose wives are employed will be more conscious of gender inequality than single, separated/divorced, widowed, or married men whose wives are not employed (Smith 1985). Men with employed wives may receive more information about discrimination faced by their wives or other women in the labor market that increases their awareness of gender inequality. The effect of wives' employment on husbands' attitudes toward efforts to reduce gender inequality is less clear. Men with employed wives may have an economic interest in gender equality because their family income is reduced to the extent that their wives face discrimination. However, to the extent that equity in employment and earnings increases wives' marital power and increases the amount of housework expected of husbands (Ross 1987), men with employed wives may oppose greater equality in the workplace. On balance, however, we believe that the economic interest of men with employed wives will predominate and they will be more supportive of efforts to reduce gender inequality than men in other family situations.

Gender/Age Interaction. Finally, we assume that movements that support feminist principles have had a greater impact on women's attitudes than men's. Although feminism is often directed at men and women, the movement has had a greater following among women than among men. As a corollary of the egalitarian Zeitgeist thesis, we expect that the effect of age on consciousness of gender inequality is stronger for women than for men.

Are U.S. Findings Generalizable?

We test the generalizability of our model using survey data from four societies: the United States, Great Britain, West Germany,

and Austria. These countries differ in the extent of objective gender inequality, though the differences are not always consistent (see Table 15.1). The percentage of women who are employed is much greater in the United States than in the three European countries. U.S. women are also more likely to be employed full-time than women in Austria, West Germany, or Great Britain. The United States is also distinctive in women's opportunities for college education: Women are just over one-half of college students compared to about two-fifths in the other three countries. The index of dissimilarity, which indicates the percentage of women (or men) who would have to be shifted among occupations in order for the occupational distributions to be the same for both sexes, shows that the United States and Great Britain are more segregated than West Germany and Austria (Roos 1985, pp. 50–52).[5] Comparing women's earnings relative to men's earnings, Austrian and British women do better relative to men than do women in West Germany and the United States. The four countries present diverse treatments of women. As such, they afford an opportunity to test whether find-

TABLE 15.1   Selected Indicators of Gender Inequality: Austria, West Germany, Great Britain, and the United States

Indicator	Austria	West Germany	Great Britain	United States
Percent women employed	47.8	49.4	49.9	66.0
Percent women employed full-time	35.1	35.0	29.7	49.8
Percent married women employed	42.0	44.8	46.3	59.9
Percent college students who are female	41.1	41.9	37.3	51.7
Index of dissimilarity between men's and women's occupations*	37.6	42.6	51.1	46.8
Women's annual earnings as percent of men's for full-time only	71.5	59.9	64.0	61.9

*High scores indicate more sex segregation.
Sources: Percent of women employed, percent of women employed full-time (35 hours or more), percent of married women employed (computed from ISSP samples); percent of college students who are female (UNESCO 1985, pp. 310–13, Table 3.12); index of dissimilarity between men's and women's occupations (Roos 1985, pp. 50–52, Table 3.3), women's annual earnings as a percentage of men's (ISSP samples).

ings for the United States apply to other advanced industrial societies.

Data and Measures

In each country, data were collected by leading academic research organizations participating in the *International Social Survey Program* (ISSP).[6] The program aims to collect comparable data on social attitudes, values, and politics using items developed by representatives of the member countries of the ISSP, pretested in each country, and revised. We analyze the "Role of Government" survey, which was collected in Great Britain, the United States, and West Germany in 1985 and in Austria in 1986. Each sample is a multistage, stratified random national sample of individuals age eighteen and over. The samples are weighted as suggested by the original investigators to ensure representativeness and limited to an upper age of sixty-four. The resulting sample sizes are 548 in the United States, 1,265 in Great Britain, 855 in West Germany, and 781 in Austria.

Independent Variables

Employment experience is measured by two dummy variables:

Currently employed—whether the individual is currently employed (coded 1) versus previously employed or never employed (coded 0).

Previously employed—whether the individual was once employed (coded 1) versus currently employed or never employed (coded 0).[7] For these variables, the omitted category is "never employed." Previous employment status is not available for Austria.

Income—respondents' yearly job earnings before taxes and deductions, in categories, with midpoints representing each category. National currencies in Austria, West Germany, and Great Britain are reported in thousands of U.S. dollars.

Occupational prestige—coded in Treiman's (1977) Standard International Prestige Units.

Hours worked—the number of hours worked at all occupations during the previous week.

Missing values on income, occupational prestige, and hours worked were recorded to the mean for employed persons of each sex in each country so that in the regression equations distinctions are made among employed persons only.

Education—years of school completed. Analyses using educational categories unique to each country yielded essentially similar results (available on request).

Married, spouse employed—a dummy variable coded 1 for men or women with currently employed spouses and 0 for married with non-employed spouses and single, divorced/separated, or widowed individuals.

Married, spouse not employed—a dummy variable coded 1 for men and women with spouses not currently employed and 0 for married with employed spouses and single, divorced/separated, or widowed individuals. For these two variables, the omitted category is "single, divorced/separated, and widowed."

Age—measured in years.

(Age −39)[2]—captures a possible curvilinear effect of age (thirty-nine is the approximate mean age in the four samples; Blalock 1979, pp. 489–91). The continuous measure models the gradual growth of the New Left, feminist, and Green movements in the European countries, while the parabolic term models the gradual growth and subsequent decline in direct action of the U.S. feminist movement. The gradual rise (and fall) of these movements makes it nearly impossible to identify affected cohorts. Moreover, to the extent that affected cohorts differ among countries, this would necessitate the use of age cohorts that are not comparable across countries.

Dependent Variables

Perceptions of Gender Inequality—measured by a three-item index. Respondents were asked: (a) "Would you say that opportunities for a *university* education are, in general, better or worse for women than for men?"; (b) "How about *job* opportunities for women—do you think they are, in general, better or worse than job opportunities for men with similar education and experience?"; and (c) "And how about *income and wages*—compared with men who have similar education and jobs—are women, in general, paid better or worse than men?" Response categories and their scores were: much better for women (1); better for women (2); no difference, can't tell (3); worse for women (4); and much worse for women (5). The index ranges from 3 to 15 with high scores indicating a perception of greater inequality to the disadvantage of women.

Because only the single item on income and wages was asked in Austria, we are unable to analyze perceptions of inequality for Austria, but we include the single perception item as a proxy for the perception index in the analysis of efforts to reduce gender inequality in Austria. (Scores on the one perception item for Austria were multiplied by three to give the variable the same range as the index in the other countries.[8]

Support for Efforts to Reduce Gender Inequality—measured with a three-item index. Respondents were asked whether (a) "The government should increase opportunities for women in business and industry"; (b) "The government should increase opportunities for women to go to university"; and (c) "Women should be given preferential treatment when applying for jobs or promotions." Responses and their scores were: strongly against (1); against (2); neither for nor against (3); in favor (4); and strongly in favor (5). The index ranges from 3 to 15 with high scores indicating support for efforts to reduce gender inequality.[9]

A favorable response to the third item indicates a willingness to reduce the gap between men and women in job opportunities, although some respondents may have felt such action was inegalitarian in the sense of being "reverse discrimination." This item is positively correlated with the other two items in the index, correlates with independent variables like the other two items, and loads on the same factor, sug-

gesting that respondents interpreted the item as an attempt to equalize job opportunities for men and women.

Factor analyses of the three perception items with the three items measuring support for intervention to reduce gender inequality revealed two clear factors in the three countries where all six measures are available, suggesting that they are distinct dimensions of consciousness of gender inequality. Cronbach's alpha, a measure of reliability, is .60 for the index measuring perceptions of inequality in West Germany, .58 in Great Britain, and .60 in the United States. Cronbach's alpha for the index measuring support for efforts to reduce inequality is .71 in Austria, .69 in West Germany, .70 in Great Britain, and .79 in the United States.

Statistical Analysis

The effects of independent variables are estimated using OLS regression techniques. Employment status, hours worked, income, occupational prestige, education, age, and marital status/spouse employment affect perceptions of gender inequality. These variables, together with perceptions, affect support for efforts to reduce inequality. We must assume that individuals' objective characteristics determine their attitudes. Lacking longitudinal data, we cannot determine the direction of causality among these variables, but there is probably some two-way causality. For example, Thornton, Alwin, and Camburn (1983), using longitudinal data, found that women's employment affects and is affected by gender attitudes.

We estimate regression models separately for men and women because several of our hypotheses assume different effects for the two sexes. Hypotheses that predict the same effects for men and women can also be tested with the separate regressions. The significance of sex interactions is tested using a difference of slopes test between the coefficients for a particular variable in these separate equations. This is equivalent to testing the significance of the interaction term of the variable with sex (Kmenta 1971, pp. 419–23).

Results

From the underdog thesis, we hypothesized that women would perceive more gender inequality than men and would be more favorable toward efforts to combat such inequality. The means for the two indices of consciousness of inequality, shown in Table 15.2, strongly support this hypothesis. In every country, women are significantly more likely to perceive inequality than men and to support efforts to reduce inequality. Controlling for independent variables has little effect on the gap between men and women in perceptions of inequality and support for efforts to combat it and all sex differences remain significant. Although these sex differences may not seem surprising, many earlier U.S. studies found little or no difference between men and women in support for women's rights (e.g., Cherlin and Walters 1981; Schreiber 1978; Ferree 1974; Roper Organization 1980).

The remaining hypotheses are tested with separate regressions for women and men (Tables 15.3 and 15.4). The underdog thesis receives little support in its assumption that the occupationally or economically disadvantaged will be more conscious of gender inequality. Only three of twenty-eight coefficients for income and occupational prestige on perceptions of gender inequality and support for its reduction across these countries are significant in the predicted direction.[10] An earlier study of consciousness of racial inequality among U.S. and English respondents found no tendency for individuals with low incomes or low occupational prestige to be more likely to perceive racial inequality than higher-status individuals (Robinson 1983). Sex is the only determinant of attitudes toward gender inequality, suggesting that the underdog thesis applies only when the disadvantaged group has a direct interest in the inequality under study.

Nor is there any support for the threat hypothesis that economically disadvantaged men are more likely to deny the existence of gender inequality and oppose efforts to reduce it. In no

T A B L E 1 5 . 2   Means and Adjusted Means for Indices of Perceptions of Gender Inequality and Support for Efforts to Reduce Gender Inequality, by Sex: 1985–86

Index	Austria		West Germany		Great Britain		United States	
	Men	**Women**	**Men**	**Women**	**Men**	**Women**	**Men**	**Women**
Perceptions of gender inequality:								
Mean	—	—	11.24	11.62	10.15	10.47	10.05	10.35
			(1.32)	(1.36)	(1.34)	(1.39)	(1.46)	(1.53)
Adjusted mean*	—	—	11.26	11.62	10.06	10.53	10.03	10.38
Support for efforts to reduce gender inequality:								
Mean	10.08	10.95	9.67	10.72	8.78	9.88	8.48	9.89
	(2.46)	(2.15)	(2.23)	(2.16)	(2.13)	(1.96)	(2.43)	(2.38)
Adjusted mean*	10.24	10.80	9.74	10.62	8.85	9.82	8.66	9.74
Number of cases	377	404	450	405	595	670	249	299

*Based on a multiple classification analysis with controls for current and previous employment, hours worked, income, occupational prestige, education, age, (age − 39)^2, and marital status.

Note: Standard deviations in parentheses. All sex differences are significant at $p < .05$. The indices can range from 3 to 15. The index for perceptions of gender inequality is not available for Austria.

country does occupational prestige or income have a significant positive effect on men's perceptions of gender inequality or support for efforts to reduce this. We suspect that sex segregation of the labor market limits direct competition between men and women for low-status jobs, making it unlikely that disadvantaged men perceive women as a threat.

The effect of education on perception is generally positive, as predicted by both the enlightenment and reproduction theses, although this is significant only for men in West Germany and women in the United States. The enlightenment thesis prediction that education produces greater support for efforts to reduce inequality is rejected, as none of the coefficients for education is significantly positive. Instead, there is considerable support for the reproduction thesis that education leads to acceptance of inequality; seven of the eight effects of education on support for efforts to reduce gender inequality are negative and five of these are significant. This negative effect may be due to education's emphasis on individual striving and accumulation of credentials rather than government intervention as the solution to group disadvantage.

From the egalitarian Zeitgeist thesis, we hypothesized generational differences reflecting the dominant political themes when people were coming of age politically. In the three European countries, we expected young people to be more conscious of gender inequality, reflecting the influence of the New Left, feminist, and Green movements of the 1960s through the 1980s. In the United States, we wondered whether the egalitarian Zeitgeist effect would be limited to middle-generation respondents who came of age during the period of greatest activism of the feminist movement and before the antifeminist backlash, or would also include the youngest generation. The negative coefficients for age in Table 15.3 indicate that young women perceive more gender inequality than older women in West Germany and Great Britain, but the effect is significant only in West Germany (it falls just short of signifi-

cance in Britain, $p = .054$). The significant negative coefficient for the squared age term for U.S. women in Table 15.3 indicates that the middle generation perceives more inequality than either older or younger women.[11] Our data also show that young U.S. women are significantly more likely to favor efforts to reduce gender inequality than older women (indicated by the negative effect of age in Table 15.4), perhaps because these women realize that they have much of their working lives ahead of them and want to see recent gains protected by government intervention. Contrary to expectation, the significant negative coefficients for the squared age term in Table 15.4 indicate that the middle generation of Austrian and West German women is more likely to favor efforts to reduce inequality. Possibly the feminist movements in these countries had their greatest effects on support for efforts to reduce inequality on women who were coming of age during the early years of resurgence of these movements in the late 1960s and early 1970s, before these movements were to some extent eclipsed by the peace and ecology movements (Chafetz and Dworkin 1986, p. 179; Altbach 1984, p. 3). Although sometimes the middle generation of women is most conscious of gender inequality and other times young women, in no country are older women the most likely to perceive inequality or to favor intervention to reduce this, a result that would be inconsistent with the Zeitgeist thesis.

A corollary to the Zeitgeist thesis predicted weaker age differences among men than among women, reflecting the greater appeal to women of feminist movements. Other than a weak tendency for the middle generation of German men to be more likely to perceive gender inequality, age has no effect on consciousness of gender inequality among men in our samples. An earlier study of U.S. data also found greater change over time in women's attitudes toward the position of women than in men's (Davis and Robinson 1988).

There is little support for the hypothesis that labor market experience leads women to

TABLE 15.3 Unstandardized Regression Coefficients for the Relationship between Perceptions of Gender Inequality and Selected Independent Variables, by Sex: 1985

Independent Variable	West Germany		Great Britain		United States	
	Men	Women	Men	Women	Men	Women
Currently employed	−.614*†	.493*†‡	−.101	−.001	.305	−.369
	(.280)	(.217)	(.256)	(.212)	(.691)	(.375)
Previously employed	−.448†	.510*†‡	−.635*‡	−.211	.311	−.475
	(.321)	(.224)	(.275)	(.213)	(.749)	(.388)
Hours worked	.0004‡	−.0063	.0004	−.0005	.014*†	−.015†
	(.0064)	(.0065)	(.0074)	(.0106)	(.007)	(.009)
Income (in U.S. $1000s)	−.0176	−.0184	.0144	.0249	−.0049	−.0071
	(.0098)	(.0231)	(.0111)	(.0256)	(.0076)	(.0121)
Occupational prestige	.003	.003	.0117	.002	.002	.016
	(.007)	(.011)	(.0061)	(.007)	(.009)	(.009)
Education	.069*	.021‡	−.003	.052‡	.056	.128*
	(.023)	(.031)	(.039)	(.037)	(.039)	(.037)
Age	−.009‡	−.014*‡	.001‡	−.0075‡	.016	.019
	(.007)	(.007)	(.005)	(.0047)	(.010)	(.008)
$(Age - 39)^2$	−.0009*	.000001‡	.00053†	.00003‡	−.00036†	−.00257*†
	(.0005)	(.000542)	(.00036)	(.00038)	(.00073)	(.00059)
Spouse employed	.098	−.102	.177	.149‡	.192†	−.242†
	(.187)	(.189)	(.160)	(.143)	(.222)	(.175)
Spouse not employed	.403*‡	.258	.229	.089	−.051	.490
	(.176)	(.264)	(.159)	(.183)	(.268)	(.353)
Constant	11.553	11.852	9.370	9.923	7.755	8.847
R^2	.089	.039	.048	.026	.057	.163
Number of cases	440	398	586	660	249	299

*$p < .05$ (one-tailed tests for all variables except occupational prestige, income, education, spouse not employed, and, for men only, employment and hours worked).
†Differences between slopes for men and women are significant at $p < .05$
‡Slope is significantly different from that for the corresponding sex in the United States at $p < .05$
Note: Standard errors in parentheses. The index measuring perceptions of gender inequality is not available for Austria.

greater consciousness of gender inequality. Employed women in West Germany are more likely to perceive inequality than women who have never been employed, and employed women in the United States are more likely to support intervention than women who have never been employed. Otherwise, women's employment has no significant effect on their perceptions of gender inequality or support for

its reduction. Even in these two exceptions, whether women are currently employed or are not currently employed but have some work experience makes no difference, contrary to Gerson's (1987) argument that attitudes depend on current status. In addition, hours worked is not significant in any country.

The hypothesis that men with employed wives would be more conscious of gender in-

TABLE 15.4 Unstandardized Regression Coefficients for the Relationship between Support for Efforts to Reduce Gender Inequality and Selected Independent Variables, by Sex: 1985–86

Independent Variable	Austria		West Germany		Great Britain		United States	
	Men	Women	Men	Women	Men	Women	Men	Women
Currently employed	.055‡	−.120‡	−.868	−.117‡	−1.168*†	−.206†‡	−2.015†	1.351*†
	(.350)	(.220)	(.454)	(.294)	(.384)	(.289)	(1.086)	(.605)
Previously employed	—	—	−.524	−.435‡	−.853*	−.291‡	−.912†	1.519*†
			(.518)	(.304)	(.416)	(.290)	(1.176)	(.628)
Hours worked	−.004	−.008	−.021*	−.003	−.003	.001	−.015	.006
	(.010)	(.008)	(.010)	(.009)	(.011)	(.014)	(.010)	(.014)
Income (in U.S. $1000s)	−.0075†	−.1157*†‡	−.0085	−.0233	−.0293	−.0301	−.0240*	−.0136
	(.0341)	(.0484)	(.0159)	(.0311)	(.0167)	(.0348)	(.0119)	(.0195)
Occupational prestige	−.005	.011	−.020†	−.048*†‡	−.016	−.013	−.006	.006
	(.015)	(.014)	(.012)	(.014)	(.009)	(.009)	(.015)	(.015)
Education	−.066	−.090	−.075*	.025‡	−.209*	−.109*	−.167*	−.201*
	(.081)	(.061)	(.038)	(.042)	(.059)	(.050)	(.061)	(.062)
Age	.002	−.008‡	.028	.012†	−.0008	−.0057‡	.010†	−.034*†
	(.012)	(.009)	(.011)	(.009)	(.0074)	(.0063)	(.016)	(.012)
$(\text{Age} - 39)^2$	.0002†	−.0022*†‡	−.00097	−.00190*‡	.00054‡	.00027	−.00130	−.00001
	(.0010)	(.0007)	(.00074)	(.00073)	(.00056)	(.00052)	(.00115)	(.00010)
Spouse employed	.669*†‡	−.515*‡	.097†	−.756*†	−.089	−.461*	−.037†	−.733*†
	(.356)	(.263)	(.301)	(.254)	(.241)	(.194)	(.350)	(.283)
Spouse not employed	−.349	−.213	−.642*†	.618*†	.073	−.300	−.120	.206
	(.344)	(.410)	(.286)	(.355)	(.239)	(.249)	(.421)	(.572)
Perceptions of gender inequality	.391*	.324*‡	.615*†‡	.764*†‡	.384*	.382*‡	.260*†	.015†
	(.068)	(.051)	(.078)	(.068)	(.063)	(.053)	(.102)	(.095)
Constant	6.441	9.818	5.555	4.229	9.420	8.489	11.351	12.399
R^2	.122	.140	.181	.305	.139	.102	.164	.103
Number of cases	377	404	440	398	586	660	249	299

*$p < .05$ (one-tailed tests for all variables except occupational prestige, income, education, spouse not employed, and, for men only, employment and hours worked).

†Differences between slopes for men and women are significant at $p < .05$

‡Slope is significantly different from that for the corresponding sex in the United States at $p < .05$

Note: Standard errors in parentheses. Previous employment is not available for Austria.

equality than other men receives little support in our data. Austrian men with employed wives are significantly more likely to support efforts to reduce inequality than single, divorced/separated, or widowed men (the omitted category) and men whose wives are not

employed ($p < .05$). German men with employed wives differ significantly from those whose wives are not employed ($p < .05$), but not from single, divorced/separated, and widowed men. Otherwise, there is no tendency for men with employed wives to be more conscious of gender inequality. Because higher wages for their wives may mean a reduction in men's marital power and greater pressure to share in housework, it is possible that these factors cancel out the economic interest of men with employed wives in greater equality for women in the workplace.

Family situation has a much stronger effect on women's attitudes than on men's. We expected women with employed husbands to perceive less gender inequality and be less favorable toward efforts to combat inequality than women without a male wage earner. This hypothesis differs from the more common hypothesis that married women are less feminist than women who are single, divorced, or widowed. Our dummy variables for "married, spouse employed" and "married, spouse not employed" (with single/divorced/widowed as the omitted category) allow us to see whether the crucial distinction in attitudes is among married women based on spouse's employment or between married women generally and other women. U.S. women with employed husbands are significantly less likely to perceive gender inequality than women whose husbands are not employed ($p < .05$), but not less likely compared to single, divorced/separated, and widowed women. With regard to support for efforts to reduce inequality, women with employed husbands in all four countries are significantly less favorable than single, divorced/separated, and widowed women (only in West Germany do women whose husbands are not employed differ significantly from nonmarried women). In additional analyses in which the omitted category combined women whose husbands were not employed with single, separated/divorced, and widowed women, women with employed husbands were significantly less supportive than other women of efforts to reduce gender inequality in all four countries (details available from authors). Surprisingly, husband's employment has a more consistent effect on women's support for efforts to reduce gender inequality than does women's own employment.

As studies of attitudes toward inequality in the United States have found (Kluegel and Smith 1982; Form and Hanson 1985; Knoke, Raffalovich, and Erskine 1987), the percentage of variance explained in consciousness of gender inequality by objective characteristics is quite low. Generally we explain less of the variance in perceptions of how much gender inequality exists than in support for efforts to combat inequality, probably because perceptions of gender inequality have an objective referent. For example, there is an objective answer to the question of whether opportunities for a university education are worse for women. The mass media in all of these countries report figures on the wage gap between men and women, the extent to which women are moving into traditionally male-dominated occupations or are still largely absent from others, and college enrollment rates of women and men. But there is no objective answer to the question of what, if anything, should be done about gender inequality. Not surprisingly, as the standard deviations of the two indices (see Table 15.2) and the effects of independent variables suggest, respondents generally disagree more on what should be done about gender inequality than on how much there is.

Discussion and Conclusions

Are the findings of U.S. studies of attitudes toward gender roles and inequality over the past decade generalizable to other Western countries? Our analysis of survey data in the United States, Great Britain, West Germany, and Austria revealed several patterns that hold in most of these countries. Women consistently perceive more gender inequality than men and are more supportive of efforts to combat this inequality. Well-educated people tend to be less favorable toward intervention to reduce gender inequality than less well educated people. Married women whose husbands are employed are less supportive of efforts to combat gender inequality than other women. Women's employment status and hours worked generally have little effect on their consciousness of gender inequality.

These findings are not those commonly reached by U.S. researchers. Generally, U.S. studies have found little or no difference between men and women in support for feminist goals (e.g., Cherlin and Walters 1981; Schreiber 1978; Ferree 1974; Roper Organization 1980, but see Huber, Rexroat, and Spitze 1978) whereas we find significant sex differences in all four countries.

In U.S. studies, education tends to be positively related to feminist orientations (e.g., Huber et al. 1978; Thornton et al. 1983; Plutzer 1988) whereas we find that education tends to be positively related to perceptions of gender inequality but is more consistently negatively related to support for efforts to reduce inequality.

Some U.S. studies have found that divorced women are somewhat more feminist than married women (Huber et al. 1978; Plutzer 1988), but few studies have tested the hypothesis that women with employed spouses are less feminist than women, married or not, whose family income does not include a male wage earner. We found that the critical division in attitudes was not between married and nonmarried (i.e., divorced, single, widowed) women but between women with a male wage earner present and women without a male wage earner.

U.S. studies consistently find that employment is a key factor in women's support of feminist principles (Smith 1985). In these countries, neither current nor previous employment has a consistent effect on perceptions of gender inequality or support for efforts to combat it. Nor is there any tendency for currently employed women to be more conscious of gender inequality than previously employed women or for the number of hours per week spent in the labor force to affect women's consciousness of inequality.

Are U.S. Women Unique? Although it could be argued that women in each of these four countries are distinctive in important respects, the fact that most prior research on attitudes toward feminism has been conducted in the United States suggests that it is important to consider whether U.S. women are unique. We focus on U.S. women because they differ more from European women than U.S. men differ from their European counterparts. U.S. women are most distinctive in the influence of background factors on support for efforts to combat gender inequality—the higher state of consciousness of gender inequality.

First, U.S. women who perceive considerable gender inequality are no more favorable toward efforts to reduce it than women who perceive little inequality (all country differences are significant at $p < .05$). Consider the effects of the most important determinants of gender consciousness—education and age. Among U.S. women, both education and age affect perceptions of gender inequality differently from support for efforts to combat inequality, which helps explain why there is no strong positive link between perceptions and support for intervention. Well-educated women perceive more gender inequality than less well educated women but are less supportive of government intervention to reduce inequality. Perhaps well-educated U.S. women adopt more individualistic solutions to women's disadvantaged position because of the U.S. educational system, which may emphasize personal effort and achievement more than systems in Britain and other European countries (Turner 1960). The extensive self-help literature in the United States, including popular magazines (e.g., *Working Woman, New Woman, Self*) directed at career women, also promotes individual avenues to advancement, such as dressing for success, networking, learning to talk "like a man," and organizing one's time. Not surprisingly, the tendency for education to increase perceptions of inequality but decrease support for efforts to combat inequality is more pronounced among U.S. women than among their European counterparts. Other things being equal, these contradictory effects of education among U.S. women decrease the likelihood of a strong positive association between perceptions and support for intervention that we find among women in the European countries.

Age also has contradictory effects among U.S. women. Young U.S. women perceive less gender inequality than the middle generation of women but are more supportive of efforts to reduce gender inequality than middle-generation or older women. Young U.S. women, having grown up in a period of less dramatic feminist activism than the preceding generation, may face less discrimination than older generations or may not yet have experienced the difficulties of balancing career and domestic responsibilities (Steinem 1984), and for these reasons perceive less inequality. At the same time, these young women, who expect to work outside the home for much of their lives and who have an entire lifetime ahead of them in which to reap the benefits of greater gender equality, may favor government intervention to guarantee equality. As in the case of education, the contradictory effects of age on perceptions of inequality and support for efforts to reduce inequality decrease the likelihood of a strong positive association between perceptions of inequality and support for intervention among U.S. women.

Second, U.S. women are also unique in the significant effect of employment on support for efforts to combat gender inequality (all country differences are significant at $p < .05$). Although we cannot analyze the possible objective bases for this finding here, our data suggest that greater discrimination in education and the labor market cannot explain the effect of employment among U.S. women (see Table 15.1). Even if there were greater discrimination in education and employment in the United States, there is no tendency for employed women to perceive more inequality than women who have never been employed.

In a country like the United States where labor market participation for women has rapidly expanded and is now the norm, women who are in the unpaid domestic economy may oppose efforts to increase gender equality in the workplace, viewing such efforts as devaluing and threatening their status as full-time homemakers and possibly eroding their husbands' earnings (Gerson 1987). In our U.S. sample, women who have never been employed are outnumbered by currently employed women nearly twelve to one, but only about six to one in Great Britain and four to one in West Germany. Moreover, the increase in women's employment has been far more dramatic in the United States than in the other countries, perhaps making women who have never worked outside the home more defensive. From 1966 to 1986, the percentage of women aged fifteen to sixty-four who were employed increased by nearly 20 percent in the United States, compared to roughly 11 percent in Britain and only 2 percent in West Germany (and 3 percent in Austria from 1970 to 1986; Becker 1989, p. 23).

Although several determinants of consciousness of gender inequality are common to the four Western societies considered, they are not the determinants that have been highlighted in prior U.S. research. Moreover, there are some respects in which Americans, and U.S. women in particular, seem to be distinctive, calling into question the generalizability of U.S. studies and emphasizing the importance of cross-national research.

Notes

* From the *American Sociological Review* 56, no. 1 (1991): 72–84, by permission of the authors and the American Sociological Association. Copyright 1991 by the American Sociological Association.

† This paper was presented at the XII World Congress of Sociology, Madrid, July 1990. We thank our respective universities for sabbatical leaves in Vienna, Austria, and Freiburg, West Germany, during which this paper was written. We also thank Michael Braun, Heinz-Herbert Noll, and *ASR*'s editor and anonymous referees for helpful comments on earlier drafts.

1. Regrettably, the data do not include measures of race or class (e.g., ownership of a business or the exercise of authority) in every country, so our hypotheses are limited to income and occupational prestige.

2. The Greens received 5.6 percent of the vote in the West German Bundestag elections of 1983, the national election immediately preceding the year our data were gathered (1985). In Austria, the Left and Right branches of the Greens together garnered 3.3 percent of the Nationalrat vote in 1983 (Rossi and McCrea 1985, p. 176; Kohl and Stirnemann 1984, p. 32). In Britain, the Ecology Party (the British Green Party) has not yet established itself on the national political scene (Spretnak and Capra 1986, p. 176).

3. Only three of fourteen U.S. studies found no relationship between women's employment and support for women's rights (Smith 1985, p. 501).

4. We do not include the number of children in our analyses despite the fact that previous U.S. research has found this to be an important factor in attitudes toward abortion (Luker 1984; Plutzer 1988, p. 644). While this variable may be associated with attitudes toward abortion, it is not clear that family size should affect attitudes toward gender inequality.

5. The index of dissimilarity is based on a fourteen-category occupational classification coded similarly in the four countries (Roos 1985, pp. 50–52).

6. The organizations are the National Opinion Research Center (NORC) of the University of Chicago in the United States; Zentrum für Umfragen, Methoden und Analysen (ZUMA) in Mannheim, West Germany; Institut für Soziologie of Graz University in Austria; and Social and Community Planning Research in London, England.

7. Respondents who indicated that they were not currently employed but who reported an occupation that they "normally do" (United States) or reported a "last" occupation (West Germany and Great Britain) are classified as previously employed.

8. Additional analyses using only the one perception item available in all countries yielded essentially similar results (details available from authors).

9. Although the third item asks respondents to compare women with men, the first two items do not explicitly mention men as a referent. Thus it is possible that someone might agree that government should increase opportunities for women, but feel that it should increase opportunities equally for men. Nonetheless, the positioning of these questions immediately after the questions on perceptions which introduced a clear comparison of women with men appears to have supplied a context that encouraged respondents to compare men and women. The item on opportunities for a university education, which referred specifically to women and men, is correlated only .25 across all samples with a later item on whether opportunities for a university education should be increased for all young people, suggesting that few respondents misinterpreted the item in our index.

10. We found no evidence of multicollinearity among occupational prestige, income, education, and hours worked. Most correlations among these variables were well below .50 and the largest for either sex in any country was .58, well below the .70 level suggested as grounds for concern by Hanushek and Jackson (1977, p. 90). Additional analyses excluding one or more variables at a time also suggested little evidence of multicollinearity.

11. A recent *New York Times* survey also found strong curvilinear effects of age on perceptions of gender inequality among U.S. women in response to the question: "All things considered, there are more advantages in being a man in America today," and in the ability to name obstacles to women's progress (Belkin 1989, p. 16).

References

Altbach, Edith Hoshino. 1984. "The New German Women's Movement." *Signs* 9:454–69.

Becker, Uwe. 1989. "Frauenerwerbstätigkeit: Eine vergleichende Bestandsaufnahme" [Women's Employment: A Comparative Assessment] Pp. 22–33 in *Aus Politik und Zeitgeschichte*. Trier, West Germany: Das Parlament.

Belkin, Lisa. 1989, August 20. "Bars to Equality of Sexes Seen as Eroding, Slowly." *New York Times*, pp. 1, 16.

Blalock, Hubert M., Jr. 1979. *Social Statistics* (2nd ed.). New York: McGraw-Hill.

Bowles, Samuel, and Herbert Gintis. 1977. *Schooling in Capitalist America*. New York: Basic.

Chafetz, Janet, and Anthony Dworkin. 1986. *Female Revolt: Women's Movements in World and Historical Perspective*. Totowa, NJ: Rowman and Alexander.

Cherlin, Andrew, and Pamela Barnhouse Walters. 1981. "Trends in U.S. Men's and Women's Sex-Role Attitudes: 1972 to 1978." *American Sociological Review* 46:453–60.

Davis, Nancy J., and Robert V. Robinson. 1988. "Class Identification of Men and Women in the 1970s and 1980s." *American Sociological Review* 53:103–12.

Ferree, Myra Marx. 1974. "A Woman for President?: Changing Responses, 1958–1972." *Public Opinion Quarterly* 38:390–99.

Ferree, Myra Marx, and Beth B. Hess. 1985. *Controversy and Coalition: The New Feminist Movement*. Boston: Twayne Publishers.

Form, William, and Claudine Hanson. 1985. "The Consistency of Stratal Ideologies of Economic Justice." Pp. 239–69 in *Research in Social Stratification and Mobility,* vol. 4, edited by Robert V. Robinson. Greenwich, CT: JAI.

Gans, Herbert J. 1973. *More Equality*. New York: Vintage.

Gerson, Kathleen. 1987. "Emerging Social Divisions among Women: Implications for Welfare State Politics." *Politics and Society* 15:213–21.

Giddens, Anthony. 1973. *The Class Structure of the Advanced Societies*. New York: Barnes and Noble.

Hanushek, Eric A., and John E. Jackson. 1977. *Statistical Methods for Social Scientists*. New York: Academic.

Huber, Joan, Cynthia Rexroat, and Glenna Spitze. 1978. "A Crucible of Opinion on Women's Status: ERA in Illinois." *Social Forces* 57:549–65.

Husbands, Christopher T. 1979. "The 'Threat' Hypothesis and Racist Voting in England and the United States." Pp. 147–83 in *Racism and Political Action in Britain,* edited by R. Miles and A. Phizacklea. London: Routledge & Kegan Paul.

Kitschelt, Herbert. 1985. "New Social Movements in West Germany and the United States." *Political Power and Social Theory* 5:273–324.

Kluegel, James R., and Eliot R. Smith. 1982. "Whites' Beliefs about Blacks' Opportunity." *American Sociological Review* 47:518–32.

Kmenta, Jan. 1971. *Elements of Econometrics*. New York: Macmillan.

Knoke, David, Lawrence E. Raffalovich, and William Erskine. 1987. "Class, Status, and Economic Policy Preferences." Pp. 141–58 in

Research in Social Stratification and Mobility, vol. 6, edited by Robert V. Robinson. Greenwich, CT: JAI Press.

Kohl, Andreas, and Alfred Stirnemann. 1984. *Österreiches Jahrbuch für Politik, 1983* [*Austrian Yearbook of Politics, 1983*]. Munich, West Germany: Oldenbourg Verlag.

Kolinsky, Eva. 1989. "Generation and Gender." Pp. 248–66 in *Developments in West German Politics,* edited by G. Smith, W. E. Peterson and P. H. Merkl. London: MacMillan.

Lipset, Seymour Martin, and Everett C. Ladd, Jr. 1971. "College Generations and Their Politics." *New Society* 16:652–58.

Luker, Kristin. 1984. *Abortion and the Politics of Motherhood*. Berkeley: University of California Press.

Mason, Karen O., and Larry Bumpass. 1975. "U.S. Women's Sex-Role Ideology, 1970." *American Journal of Sociology* 80:112–19.

Plutzer, Eric. 1988. "Work Life, Family Life, and Women's Support of Feminism." *American Sociological Review* 53:640–49.

Robinson, Robert V. 1983. "Explaining Perceptions of Class and Racial Inequality in England and the United States of America." *British Journal of Sociology* 35:344–66.

Robinson, Robert V., and Wendell Bell. 1978. "Equality, Success, and Social Justice in England and the United States." *American Sociological Review* 43:125–43.

Roos, Patricia A. 1985. *Gender and Work: A Comparative Analysis of Industrial Societies*. Albany, NY: State University of New York Press.

Roper Organization. 1980. *The 1980 Virginia Slims American Women's Opinion Poll: A Survey of Contemporary Attitudes*.

Ross, Catherine E. 1987. "The Division of Labor at Home." *Social Forces* 65:816–33.

Rossi, Ernest E., and Barbara P. McCrea. 1985. *The European Political Dictionary*. Santa Barbara, CA: ABC-Clio.

Schreiber, E. M. 1978. "Education and Change in American Opinions on a Woman for President." *Public Opinion Quarterly* 42:171–82.

Smith, Tom W. 1985. "Working Wives and Women's Rights: The Connection between the Employment Status of Wives and the Feminist Attitudes of Husbands." *Sex Roles* 12:501–8.

Spretnak, Charlene, and Fritjof Capra. 1986. *Green Politics*. Santa Fe: Bear and Company.

Steinem, Gloria. 1984. *Outrageous Acts and Everyday Rebellions*. New York: New American Library.

Thornton, Arland, Duane F. Alwin, and Donald Camburn. 1983. "Causes and Consequences of

Sex-Role Attitudes and Attitude Change." *American Sociological Review* 48:211–27.

Treiman, Donald J. 1977. *Occupational Prestige in Comparative Perspective*. New York: Academic Press.

Turner, Ralph H. 1960. "Sponsored and Contest Mobility and the School System." *American Sociological Review* 25:855–67.

United Nations Educational, Scientific, and Cultural Organization. 1985. *Statistical Yearbook, 1985*. New York: United Nations Educational, Scientific, and Cultural Organization.

Marriage and Women's Occupational Attainment in Cross-Cultural Perspective[*]

Patricia A. Roos[†]

One explanation for why women and men are concentrated in different types of jobs is that dual demands on women's time place them at a disadvantage in the competition for jobs, relative to their male counterparts. According to dual career theory, actual (or in the case of single women, anticipated) family responsibilities affect the kinds of jobs women enter by limiting their investment in education and/or on-the-job training, the number of hours they work, the continuity of their labor force attachment, and their ability to pursue opportunities for advancement. Human capital theorists (e.g., Mincer and Polachek, 1974; Polachek, 1975), the strongest proponents of the dual career explanation, attribute sex differences in occupational distribution and attainment to individualistic criteria, that is, to characteristics of women themselves that place them in an inferior wage-bargaining position relative to men. These sex-correlated characteristics are viewed as deriving from sex differences in socialization, in the accumulation of human capital and hence productivity on the job, and/or in household responsibility.

An alternative explanation for occupational sex segregation posits the existence of barriers institutionalized in the organization of work that hinder women's access to, and mobility into, higher-prestige, higher-paid employment. One such institutional explanation, internal labor market theory (Doeringer and Piore, 1971), argues that (1) various classes of workers (e.g., women and men) have differential access to occupational opportunities, and (2) the productivity of individual workers is a function not

only of their personal characteristics (e.g., amount of labor force experience), but also of the characteristics of occupations and firms in which they labor. Hence, factors outside an individual's control are presumed to have important consequences for the kinds of jobs in which men and women work, and hence the earnings they receive for that employment (see Roos, 1981a, for a detailed review of the dual career and institutional explanations).

The present analysis evaluates the efficacy of the dual career (or human capital) explanation for predicting differential occupational locations of women with varying amounts of family responsibilities. Although the data do not permit an explicit test of the institutionalist view, the failure of human capital theory to account for differential occupational locations would increase the plausibility of such a view as an explanation of occupational sex segregation. In previous tests of human capital theory, researchers have focused on *gender* differences in occupational behavior. Gender comparisons, however, assume that since most men and women are married, and most women and not their husbands have primary responsibility for home and child care, the effect of differing family responsibilities on occupational attainment will be reflected in gender differences in occupational outcomes. The purported negative effects of home and child-care responsibilities, however, should be important not for all women, but only for those employed women who must contend with such responsibilities (i.e., married women and women with children). Since never-married women do not face the same home and child-care demands as married women, and because their total amount of labor force experience more closely approximates that of men (Treiman and Terrell, 1975), they should (according to the human capital view) be more likely than married women to pursue nontraditional work options and to optimize income-producing activities, that is, to be more like men in their occupational choice and attainment patterns.

This analysis goes beyond a comparison of gender differences to a more stringent test of dual career theory by comparing the occupational distributions and attainments of married and never-married women in twelve industrial societies. If dual career theory is an important explanation for observed gender differences in occupational distribution, there should exist sharp differences in the distributions and attainment patterns of married and never-married women. A finding that never-married women closely approximate the occupational distribution and attainment of men would support the notion that women's economic disadvantage depends in large measure on the responsibilities associated with marriage. If we find minimal or no differences in the attainment of ever- and never-married women, other more fundamental features of the organization of work are likely responsible for the sex-segregated occupational structure.

The comparative aspect of the analysis is particularly important. Previous research on occupational sex segregation has been conducted almost entirely on U.S. data (noteworthy exceptions include Galenson, 1973; Organisation for Economic Co-operation and Development (OECD), 1975, 1979; Gaskin, 1979). In attempting to account for sex differences in occupational distribution in the United States, it is useful to consider whether such occupational patterns emerge out of the historical circumstances of this country or whether they derive in part from more general structural features common to all industrial societies. The comparative perspective permits a determination of whether patterns of occupational attainment observed in

this country are idiosyncratic or whether they can be generalized to other cultural contexts. A similar pattern of sex and/or marital differences in attainment across industrial societies would imply that the sex-segregated occupational structure is quite firmly entrenched and that progress toward integration requires major changes in the way work is organized.[1]

Data and Methods
Data

The twelve data sets are national representative samples of the adult populations of Austria (1974), Denmark (1972), Finland (1972), West Germany (1976), Great Britain (1974), Israel (1974), Japan (1967), Netherlands (1974), Northern Ireland (1968), Norway (1972), Sweden (1972), and the United States (1974–77). Only industrial societies were selected since it is in these countries that reconciling family and work responsibilities should be most difficult for women. There are three major reasons for this. First, the historical shift to an industrial economy changed the productive role of women—they now had to leave home to continue their economic role (Boserup, 1970; Tilly and Scott, 1978; Degler, 1980). Second, the potential effect of women's marriage and child-rearing responsibilities on their occupational outcomes has substantially increased in recent years as more (especially married) women have entered the paid workforce in the United States as well as in other industrial societies. Notably, the greatest increase in labor force participation in recent years has been among married women with small children (Sweet, 1975; OECD, 1975). Third, time-use studies conducted in various industrialized countries have documented that wives bear the primary responsibility for child rearing and home work regardless of whether they work outside the home (Szalai, 1972; Walker and Woods, 1976).[2]

The selection of the economically active population utilizes an employment variable that includes all full-time and part-time workers (of any age) as comprising the "employed" population. For the attainment analyses, the sample is further restricted to the most economically active portion of the population—employed persons aged twenty to sixty-four working full- or part-time. This restriction is necessary due to cross-cultural variability in the age cutoffs used in the samples as well as in the ages at which people generally start work.

Description of Variables

Two measures of occupation are used. For a nominal measure of occupation, the seven-category International Standard Classification of Occupations (ISCO) is employed. This makes the usual "type of work" distinction between large occupational sectors such as professional, clerical, and production (International Labour Office [ILO], 1969). Sample size limitations precluded the use of a more detailed classification. In order to have a summary measure of occupational attainment for use in multivariate analysis, also used is an "occupational wage rate scale," designed to reflect the gender differentiation of the occupational structure. The raw data on which this scale is based are the average earnings of men within each of the categories of Treiman's (1977:204) fourteen-category classification in the ten countries for which earnings data were available.[3] These average occupational earnings were then converted to a common metric, averaged across the ten countries, and converted to a 0- to 100-point scale. The resulting metric scale represents a cross-cultural standard earnings hierarchy of occupations, with 0 assigned to the occupation group with the lowest average male earnings (low-prestige agricultural occupations) and 100 to the occupation group with the highest average male earnings (administrative and managerial occupations).[4]

Three determinants of occupation are identified—*father's occupation,* as a measure of social origins, age, and educational attainment, is operationalized using the occupational wage rate scale. *Age* is measured in years and, in the present context, is a crude proxy for experience. In addition, an age-squared term is added

to allow for the possibility that the relationship between age and occupational attainment is curvilinear, which tests for whether workers move into less-demanding (and hence less income-producing) jobs prior to their moving out of the labor force altogether. Since age and age-squared are highly collinear, a constant (equal to the mean of age) was subtracted from age before squaring it, in order to reduce the correlation between the two variables and hence improve the stability of the coefficients. Finally, *educational attainment* is measured in years of school completed. (For additional details on the sample characteristics, the selection of the employed population, and the measurement of variables, see Roos, 1981a: chapter 2.)

Analytic Strategy

The "ever-married" group in each country includes women who are presently married, separated, divorced, or widowed; the "never-married" group includes only women who never married. The distinction between the ever and never married is used rather than that between the currently and not currently married, because women who have been married are more likely to have child-care and other home responsibilities left over from their marriage that may affect their occupational choice and advancement.[5]

The problem with making comparisons between married and single women is that many single women are really "premarried" women; that is, their occupational preferences may be affected by an anticipated assumption of the traditional responsibilities of marriage.[6] Never-married women are also younger on the average than those who have married, and younger workers are generally occupied in different jobs than older workers. Because of these factors, age must be carefully controlled. To make the best possible test of the dual career explanation, one should select never-married women whose current labor force behavior and occupational choice are not affected by an anticipation that their stay in the workplace may be temporary. To approximate this group, a sample of women older than the average age at which women in the particular country first marry was chosen for comparison purposes (calculated from United Nations, 1977).[7] The resulting sample of "older" or "committed" never-married women provides an approximation (albeit crude) of a group of women whose labor force decisions should be most similar to those of men.

The subsequent analyses first compare the labor force behavior and occupational distribution patterns of ever- and never-married women in all twelve countries. The distribution of the marital groups on each of the variables included in the attainment analyses is then described. Finally, occupation models are estimated separately for employed ever- and never-married women twenty to sixty-four in each country. The results for "committed" never-married women are compared with those for all women and are described in the text where appropriate but are not provided in tabular form.

Analysis
Labor Force Behavior

As is evident in Table 16.1, marriage responsibilities affect the labor force behavior of women in industrial societies in ways consistent with dual career theory. With the exceptions of Finland, Japan, and Sweden, where the two marital groups are about equally likely to be employed, never-married women are more likely to work than ever-married women. In addition, excepting Finland and Sweden, never-married women are substantially more likely than their married counterparts to work full-time.

The anomalous results for Finland and Sweden may be in part a consequence of the high participation rates of women in those countries: 77 percent of Finnish women twenty to sixty-four, and 70 percent of Swedish women, were employed full- or part-time (Roos, 1981a: Table 3.1). Thus, in societies where a high rate of female participation is the norm, marital re-

sponsibilities may not play as important a role in explaining differences in participation.

There is an alternative explanation for these anomalous results. Since never-married women are on the whole younger than ever-married women, it may be that a large portion are still in school, and hence not full-time labor force members. For this reason, comparing all never-married women with all ever-married women is not, strictly speaking, the best possible comparison. To test for this possibility, the percentage employed and the percentage employed full-time of all never-married women were compared with comparable figures for "older" never-married women (i.e., never-married women older than the average age at which women in their country first marry). Selecting "older" never-married women substantially increases the percentage employed, as well as the percentage employed full-time, in each of the countries with anomalous results: the percentage of *never-married* women employed increases from 72 to 89 percent in Finland, from 42 to 80 percent in Japan, and from 68 to 83 percent in Sweden.[8] The percentages of never-married women employed full-time in Finland and Sweden (anomalies in Table 16.1) also increase markedly when age is controlled (from 46 to 82 percent in Finland and from 29 to 62 percent in Sweden).

In addition to Sweden (discussed above), unexpectedly low rates of full-time participation of never-married women were shown in Table 16.1 for Israel and Norway. As above, restricting the analysis to "older" never-married women results in substantial increases in the percentage working full-time (from 24 to 48 percent in Israel and from 33 to 74 percent in Norway). Although the case base is small in some of the countries (particularly the Scandinavian countries), the magnitude and consistency of the increases provide strong evidence that the anomalous results observed in Table 16.1 are primarily attributable to the large number of young (and hence school-age) women included in some of the samples. Overall, the more "committed" the never-married

TABLE 16.1   Employment Status of Women (All Ages), by Marital Status, for Twelve Industrialized Countries (in Percentages)

Country	Employment Status			Total (%)	N
	Full time	**Part time**	**Not at work**		
Austria					
Ever married	27.3	9.5	63.2	100.0	741
Never married	56.3	6.7	37.1	100.1	125
Denmark					
Ever married	32.0	22.9	45.1	100.0	463
Never married	43.4	20.2	36.4	100.0	99
Finland					
Ever married	58.7	12.6	28.7	100.0	373
Never married	45.5	26.1	28.4	100.0	134
Germany (Fed. Rep.)					
Ever married	13.2	16.2	70.6	100.0	1127
Never married	54.5	10.3	35.2	100.0	171
Great Britain					
Ever married	19.7	20.2	60.1	100.0	628
Never married	61.8	4.1	34.1	100.0	100
Israel					
Ever married	13.4	14.6	71.9	99.9	11283
Never married	23.8	10.4	65.8	100.0	3726
Japan					
Ever married		42.1*	57.9	100.0	865
Never married		41.9*	58.1	100.0	253
Netherlands					
Ever married	13.2	10.8	76.0	100.0	353
Never married	60.3	4.6	35.2	100.1	118
Northern Ireland					
Ever married		28.2*	71.9	100.1	497
Never married		73.3*	26.7	100.0	109
Norway					
Ever married	19.0	21.6	59.5	100.1	385
Never married	32.9	23.7	43.4	100.0	76
Sweden					
Ever married	27.7	37.4	34.9	100.0	455
Never married	28.6	39.8	31.6	100.0	98
United States					
Ever married	28.0	11.8	60.2	100.0	2755
Never married	49.4	11.5	39.0	99.9	327

*Full-time/part-time status not available.

women, the more their labor force behavior resembles men's.

Occupational Distribution

Table 16.2 presents the occupational distributions of ever- and never-married women for all twelve countries, using the seven-category ISCO classification (ILO, 1969). Given the small case base in Denmark, Norway, and Sweden, these data should be viewed as suggestive. The indexes of dissimilarity presented in Table 16.2, ranging from a very low 9.6 percent in West Germany to an unusually high 43.4 percent in Japan, indicate the existence of small to moderate marital differences in major occupation group. The twelve-country average is 21.2, suggesting that on average 21 percent of married women would have to change occupations to make their distribution equal to that of never-married women. Although not so large as *gender* differences in occupational distribution—the twelve-country average for gender differences is 39.1 (based on the seven-category ISCO classification and calculated from Roos, 1981a: Table 6.4)—the indexes are sufficiently large in most countries to merit serious consideration.

Japan is the one exception to the general rule. In that country marital differences in occupation are substantially *larger* than gender differences (43 and 26 percent, respectively). The relatively *low* gender index in Japan is most likely due to the large proportion of the female population engaged in agricultural employment. In 1967, the date of the survey, 37 percent of the Japanese women were employed in agriculture. By 1978, that percentage had decreased to 15 percent (calculated from ILO, 1979: Table 2B). Similar logic can explain the relatively *high* Japanese marital index. As Table 16.2 documents, the large number of Japanese women employed in agriculture is composed almost entirely of married women. Nearly half of the *never-married* women (but only 8 percent of the married women) are employed in clerical jobs. In contrast, 45 percent of *married* women, compared with only 4 percent of never-married

women, are employed in agriculture. These women are undoubtedly family-farm workers: 77 percent of the women engaged in agriculture in Japan in 1972 were "family helpers" (OECD, 1975:23). Never-married Japanese women, with their lesser marital and child-rearing responsibilities, have evidently been better able than married women to move into the newly emerging service occupations (e.g., clerical, sales, and service jobs) that accompanied the relatively late emergence of industrialization in Japan (Singelmann, 1978). Similar factors may also be at work in Finland, where nearly a third of ever-married women labored in agricultural employment. Notably, Finland has an index of marital dissimilarity second only to that of Japan.

Because single women are on the average much younger than married women, one might expect that these indexes are conservative estimates of the difference in the occupational distributions of ever- and never-married women. To investigate this possibility, the indexes presented in Table 16.2 were compared with those calculated for ever- and never-married women older than the average age at which women in the particular country first marry (data not shown). In nine of the twelve countries, the marital index increases, although in only five is the increase as large as five percentage points. This finding appears to be due to an increase in the proportion of the never-married labor force engaged in professional and technical employment, reflecting "older" never-married women's employment in the female professions while their younger counterparts enter the labor force in clerical, sales, service, and production jobs.[9]

The U.S. pattern of marital differences reflected in Table 16.2 is fairly typical of all the countries. With two exceptions (Israel and Sweden), never-married women are more likely than married women to work in professional and technical jobs (although only in Denmark, Great Britain, Netherlands, and the United States is the difference as large as five percentage points). When the sample is restricted to post-marriage-age women, the percentage of

TABLE 16.2 Occupational Distribution of Employed Women (All Ages), by Marital Status, for Twelve Industrialized Countries (in percentages)

Occupational Category*	Austria		Denmark		Finland		Germany (Fed. Rep.)		Great Britain		Israel	
	Ever married	Never married	Ever married	Never married	Ever married	Never married	Ever married	Never married	Ever married	Never married	Ever married	Never married
1. Professional and technical	6.3	10.8	15.5	27.9	12.6	15.7	14.2	15.4	12.2	25.9	31.8	22.9
2. Administrative and managerial	0.7	0.0	0.0	0.0	1.2	1.4	0.0	0.0	1.1	0.0	1.2	0.6
3. Clerical and related	21.4	30.1	27.7	23.3	17.3	27.1	39.0	46.4	27.5	38.8	25.5	36.7
4. Sales	12.3	10.8	10.2	2.3	10.6	5.7	16.3	16.7	12.9	7.9	9.9	4.6
5. Service	17.9	14.5	18.4	23.3	14.6	28.6	12.5	5.5	25.9	9.4	17.8	13.6
6. Agricultural	23.2	13.3	18.9	11.6	30.7	11.4	3.2	0.6	1.3	1.4	3.2	1.4
7. Production and related	18.2	20.5	9.2	11.6	13.0	10.0	14.8	15.4	19.0	16.5	10.6	20.3
Total	100.0	100.0	99.9	100.0	100.0	99.9	100.0	100.0	99.9	99.9	100.0	100.1
N	264	77	232	49	250	69	292	93	249	64	3143	1264
Index of dissimilarity	15.5		19.6		27.2		9.6		25.1		20.8	

Occupational Category*	Japan		Netherlands		Northern Ireland		Norway		Sweden		United States	
	Ever married	Never married	Ever married	Never married	Ever married	Never married	Ever married	Never married	Ever married	Never married	Ever married	Never married
1. Professional and technical	6.7	9.9	21.1	28.1	16.8	17.6	18.7	21.9	24.8	13.9	21.3	27.6
2. Administrative and managerial	0.9	1.1	0.9	0.0	1.3	1.2	1.4	6.3	0.4	0.0	3.4	0.9
3. Clerical and related	7.6	45.8	31.2	35.4	13.4	30.6	21.6	25.0	29.0	50.0	32.7	35.9
4. Sales	11.0	12.4	20.2	9.4	8.1	9.4	14.4	12.5	12.6	5.6	6.9	6.5
5. Service	11.3	8.8	18.3	18.8	31.5	14.1	15.8	28.1	23.5	25.0	19.1	19.8
6. Agricultural	45.4	4.5	3.7	0.0	2.7	4.7	19.4	6.3	1.3	0.0	0.5	0.0
7. Production and related	17.1	17.5	4.6	8.3	26.2	22.4	8.6	0.0	8.4	5.6	16.1	9.2
Total	100.0	100.0	100.0	100.0	100.0	100.0	99.9	100.1	100.0	100.1	100.0	99.9
N	354	97	85	75	140	80	126	29	259	39	1095	204
Index of dissimilarity	43.4		15.4		21.3		23.7		22.4		10.2	

*International Standard Classification of Occupations (ISCO) major groups (International Labour Office, 1969).

never-married women in professional positions increases even further in ten of the twelve countries. While never-married women are indeed more likely to work in professional jobs than married women, a more detailed classification system shows that these are low-prestige and low-paying professional jobs such as primary school teacher and nurse (Roos, 1981a: chapters 3, 6).

With the exception of Japan (as described above), large portions of both ever- and never-married women in each country work in clerical occupations. Where an economy has a large agricultural component (Austria, Denmark, Finland, Japan, and Norway), ever-married women are more likely than never-married women to be agricultural workers. Given the nature of agricultural work, with the location of work close to the home, married women can more easily contribute to the productive effort. Consistent with this interpretation, the concentration of ever-married women in clerical occupations is somewhat less in these five countries (at least when age is controlled). Finally, in most but not all of the countries, ever-married women are more likely to be employed in sales and service work than never-married women, at least when young single workers (who are more likely to work in such jobs) are eliminated from the sample.

In sum, these effects, though small, are consistent with previous U.S. literature on marital differences in occupational distribution (Sewell et al., 1980) and in the direction predicted by dual career theory: marriage reduces the likelihood that women work in the better-paid and more prestigious jobs. Never-married women's greater representation in the (semi) professions reflects the greater investment in training and stronger labor force commitment required for these jobs. Intermittent labor force attachment for workers in these occupations would lead to depreciation of skills and a loss of bargaining power for those who wanted to reenter them later in life. This is less true for other occupations in which married (as well as never-married) women work.

Occupational Attainment

While many investigators have studied the occupational attainment patterns of men and women, few have investigated whether the process of attainment differs by marital status (exceptions include Treiman and Terrell, 1975; Hudis, 1976; McClendon, 1976; Sewell et al., 1980). These studies found that the small marital differences in occupational distribution described above translate into a prestige and status advantage for never-married women on the order of five to fourteen points. Despite these marital differences in occupational prestige and status, previous research found no marital differences in occupational returns to personal characteristics and investments (i.e., the process of occupational allocation), a result inconsistent with dual career theory (Treiman and Terrell, 1975; McClendon, 1976; but see Sewell et al., 1980).

As suggested above (note 4), one reason previous studies failed to find *gender* differences in the process of occupational attainment was because occupation was measured in such a way as to mask sex differences in "type of job" performed. Before accepting previous research on marital attainment patterns as refuting dual career theory, the occupational wage rate scale was used to test the possibility that *marital* differences in the process of occupational attainment are also masked in studies using prestige or status as a measure of occupation.

Distribution of Variables by Marital Status.
Table 16.3 presents the means and standard deviations of all variables for each marital group. To simplify comparisons, for the most part the discussion includes only those differences significant at the .05 level. Ever- and never-married women in most of the countries come from similar social origins. In the three exceptions (Denmark, Germany, and Japan), never-married women have the advantage with respect to social origins, reflecting the possibility that women from higher-status backgrounds in these countries are relatively less likely to

marry, or perhaps to marry later (see Waite and Spitze, 1981, who found similar results for the United States).

As expected, the means for age show that never-married women are on average significantly younger than married women in each country except Norway, where given the small sample size the result is of doubtful reliability. Corroborating past research on U.S. data, never-married women complete more years of education than married women in all the countries, significantly so in eight. Part of this differential is probably due to the younger average age of the single women, and the fact that educational attainment is negatively correlated with age. When post-marriage-age women are selected, never-married women remain significantly younger and more educated than married women.

Despite their age and educational advantages, however, never-married women in most countries are unable to translate age and schooling into higher prestige or occupational wages. In only three of the countries (Denmark, Great Britain, and Japan) do the prestige *and* wage rates of ever- and never-married women differ significantly. In the United States, never- and ever-married women work in jobs of significantly different prestige (corroborating past research), but these jobs do not differ in average wage rate.[10]

Marital Differences in Attainment. Table 16.4 presents the coefficients of a model of occupational attainment for each of the countries, separately for the two marital groups. The results generally replicate those of previous analyses based on U.S. data that used prestige and status as measures of occupation (Treiman and Terrell, 1975; McClendon, 1976; although see Sewell et al., 1980). Hence, even with a measure of occupational attainment sensitive to gender differences in occupational distribution, the dual career expectation of marital differences in the process of occupational attainment is not supported. Interestingly, with the exception of the education effect, the small differences that do occur are often in the direction opposite that predicted by dual career theory.

Dual career theory predicts that because of their lesser home responsibilities, never-married women should, like men, be better able to capitalize on their *social origins* than married women. Although evidence indicates that men accrue significant occupational advantages from their social origins in each of the included countries except Sweden (Roos, 1981a: chapter 5), there is little support in the present data for the hypothesis that never-married women receive similar benefits. The effect of social origins on occupational attainment is significant for never-married women in only two countries, Finland and West Germany, and only in Finland is it significant in the expected positive direction. On the other hand, social origins significantly benefit married women in three countries (Austria, Japan, and the United States).[11] Thus, with few exceptions, coming from higher-status social origins does not apparently affect the occupational outcomes of women, married or single.

With respect to the occupational return to *age,* dual career theory predicts it should be less for married women, who spend a greater proportion of their lives out of the labor force and work part-time when they do work. As with social origins, there is little support for this expectation. Only in the United States is age significantly associated with never-married women's occupational wage rate and even that association loses significance in the post-marriage-age comparison. Moreover, in half the countries the relationship is unexpectedly negative. Age is a significant predictor of married women's occupational position only in Finland, Israel, and the United States (although in Israel the coefficient is unexpectedly negative). Interestingly, Finland and to a lesser extent the United States are the countries in which women's age pattern of participation comes closest to approximating the inverted U-shape pattern characteristic of men (Roos, 1981a: Chapter 3). Hence, women in these countries are more likely to have continuous labor force

TABLE 16.3 Means and Standard Deviations for Models of Occupational Attainment for Currently Employed Women 20–64 (by Marital Status)

	Austria		Denmark		Finland		Germany (Fed. Rep.)		Great Britain		Israel	
	Ever married	Never married	Ever married	Never married	Ever married	Never married	Ever married	Never married	Ever married	Never married	Ever married	Never married
Mean												
Father's occupation—prestige	37.3	39.0	37.8 *	44.2	39.0	38.8	41.2 *	44.8	46.3	50.5	41.1	41.8
Father's occupation—wage rate scale†	28.3	30.2	27.9	37.3	28.3	27.4	31.6 *	37.7	—	—	43.1	42.9
Age	42.6 *	34.7	40.2 *	32.5	40.7 *	34.6	41.8 *	28.8	44.1 *	31.7	39.3 *	24.4
$(Age^m)^2$	114 *	195	146 *	208	139 *	221	135 *	210	159 *	224	172 *	142
Years of schooling	9.13	9.53	7.98 *	9.43	8.20 *	9.33	10.2 *	11.2	10.1 *	11.5	10.6	11.1
Respondent's occupation—prestige	35.7	35.6	37.8 *	43.6	37.8	39.8	40.3	41.4	37.5 *	43.8	42.4	41.7
Respondent's occupation—wage rate scale	27.1	28.0	31.8 *	39.6	30.1	33.4	35.1	35.1	32.0 *	40.9	39.5	38.6
Standard Deviation												
Father's occupation—prestige	10.0	12.1	10.0	13.1	8.37	8.29	11.8	9.82	21.6	20.0	12.8	15.8
Father's occupation—wage rate scale†	18.2	19.0	18.9	26.1	17.5	16.5	16.2	16.3	—	—	24.7	28.2
Age	10.6	12.5	12.1	12.9	11.8	13.3	10.7	11.9	11.7	12.9	12.0	6.95
$(Age^m)^2$	123	165	140	126	133	147	164	124	148	119	199	82.3
Years of schooling	1.57	1.74	1.64	2.62	2.67	3.01	1.96	2.19	1.82	2.14	4.33	3.15
Respondent's occupation—prestige	11.2	11.5	10.1	11.3	11.8	12.4	11.8	10.4	12.8	10.8	13.5	12.9
Respondent's occupation—wage rate scale	16.6	16.1	16.9	20.2	18.8	20.5	17.4	15.2	19.5	14.7	21.1	18.8
N‡	232	60	219	34	232	50	286	79	228	42	2571	82

	Japan		Netherlands		Northern Ireland		Norway		Sweden		United States	
	Ever married	Never married	Ever married	Never married	Ever married	Never married	Ever married	Never married	Ever married	Never married	Ever married	Never married
Mean												
Father's occupation—prestige	34.2	* 36.5	40.9	41.0	36.9	39.8	39.8	42.5	39.1	41.7	40.0	41.5
Father's occupation—wage rate scale[†]	16.5	* 27.3	36.6	37.5	26.3	31.9	31.3	37.6	32.6	37.4	36.3	40.0
Age	42.8	* 25.4	36.0	* 27.6	42.1	* 33.8	39.8	40.7	40.4	* 33.3	40.6	* 28.8
$(Age^m)^2$	118	* 259	173	110	139	* 181	143	163	129	* 205	146	* 207
Years of schooling	10.0	* 11.1	9.97	10.5	10.3	* 11.1	8.64	9.09	8.66	* 9.77	12.3	* 13.5
Respondent's occupation—prestige	35.8	* 39.3	39.3	41.9	36.4	39.4	38.6	42.9	39.8	39.2	41.3	* 44.7
Respondent's occupation—wage rate scale	28.5	38.1	35.4	39.5	31.7	34.0	32.2	39.9	34.9	35.2	37.7	40.9
Standard Deviation												
Father's occupation—prestige	7.49	8.71	13.8	12.9	13.3	13.8	9.71	12.9	10.6	12.1	11.6	11.9
Father's occupation—wage rate scale[†]	24.1	25.3	26.0	25.5	19.9	25.2	21.6	25.7	22.0	25.6	27.4	28.5
Age	10.3	8.22	12.0	10.1	11.4	12.5	12.0	13.0	11.3	13.3	11.9	10.5
$(Age^m)^2$	136	99.6	247	166	154	128	126	145	129	126	148	117
Years of schooling	2.47	1.72	2.48	2.33	2.00	1.94	2.61	2.62	2.60	2.94	2.62	2.51
Respondent's occupation—prestige	9.57	8.73	14.0	12.1	13.7	12.5	12.7	11.2	12.9	10.4	12.8	12.7
Respondent's occupation—wage rate scale	20.0	18.2	21.9	19.9	23.1	21.6	21.5	25.6	20.6	17.9	21.5	20.5
N[‡]	297	68	80	52	129	70	125	20	257	32	899	147

Note: For details of scoring see text. Age^m = Age − mean of age.

*Difference in ever married and never married mean is significant at .05 level, two-tailed test.

[†]The father's occupational wage rate variable could not be constructed for Great Britain, due to the way father's occupation was measured.

[‡]Missing cases deleted pairwise, lowest number of cases reported.

TABLE 16.4 Coefficients of a Model of Occupational Wage Rate Attainment, for Currently Employed Ever- and Never-Married Women, 20–64

		Metric coefficients				
		Father's occupation*	Age	$(Age^m)^2$	Years of schooling	Intercept
Austria	Ever married	.165†	−.026	.007	4.47†	−18.1
	Never married	−.055	−.075	.004	6.52†	−30.7
Denmark	Ever married	−.002	−.034	−.000	4.83†	−5.24
	Never married	.151	−.245	.009	4.72†	−4.46
Finland	Ever married	.058	.239†	−.002	4.90†	−21.2
	Never married	.224†	.227	−.028†	5.29†	−23.8
Germany	Ever married	.091	−.035	−.011	3.15†	2.83
(Fed. Rep.)	Never married	−.231†	−.040	−.012	4.41†	−1.85
Great Britain	Ever married	−.027	.162	−.008	4.70†	−20.2
	Never married	−.062	−.119	−.001	3.10†	12.5
Israel	Ever married	.022	−.080†	−.008†	3.09†	10.4
	Never married	−.002	.259	.011	3.86†	−12.2
Japan	Ever married	.218†	.162	−.021†	2.90†	−8.63
	Never married	−.054	.394	.031	3.29†	−15.1
Netherlands	Ever married	.062	.264	−.002	4.00†	−16.0
	Never married	.035	−.018	.029	4.45†	−11.2
Northern	Ever married	.009	.104	.005	7.35†	−49.3
Ireland	Never married	.126	.077	−.019	7.34†	−50.6
Norway	Ever married	−.014	−.017	.007	6.02†	−19.8
	Never married	.261	.385	.013	4.36	−27.3
Sweden	Ever married	.063	.085	−.002	4.61†	−10.2
	Never married	−.254	−.330	−.014	5.04†	9.39
United States	Ever married	.068†	.155†	.001	3.91†	−19.2
	Never married	.067	.317†	−.013	3.41†	−14.2

attachment, and are thus better able to benefit from increasing seniority. Finally, in only three countries is the age-squared variable significant (never-married women in Finland and ever-married women in Israel and Japan), indicating that these workers move into less income-producing jobs prior to their moving out of the labor force altogether.

The lack of support for the human capital expectation with respect to age suggests the plausibility of an alternative hypothesis: that age returns little in the way of occupational wage benefits to women regardless of their

marital status. Thus even never-married women with their more consistent labor force attachment fail to gain in occupational wages from seniority (as indexed by age). These results are consistent with Barrett's (1979:37) finding that women have a flatter age-earnings profile than men even when they have the same achieved education, and Sawhill's (1973) evidence that this flat age-earnings profile is characteristic of never-married as well as married women. In addition, it also verifies Rosenfeld's (1980:603) finding that although continuous employment returns oc-

TABLE 16.4   *Continued*

		Standardized coefficients				
		Father's occupation*	Age	$(Age^m)^2$	Years of schooling	Intercept
Austria	Ever married	.181[†]	−.016	.051	.423[†]	.280
	Never married	−.065	−.058	.041	.707[†]	.477
Denmark	Ever married	−.002	−.024	−.004	.469[†]	.226
	Never married	.196	−.157	.056	.613[†]	.528
Finland	Ever married	.054	.150[†]	−.017	.697[†]	.500
	Never married	.181[†]	.147	−.201[†]	.775[†]	.714
Germany	Ever married	.084	−.022	−.101	.356[†]	.187
(Fed. Rep.)	Never married	−.248[†]	−.032	−.099	.635[†]	.395
Great Britain	Ever married	−.030	.098	−.058	.436[†]	.174
	Never married	−.085	−.104	−.009	.451[†]	.243
Israel	Ever married	.026	−.046[†]	−.078[†]	.633[†]	.454
	Never married	−.003	.096	.050	.645[†]	.416
Japan	Ever married	.262[†]	.083	−.142[†]	.357[†]	.260
	Never married	−.075	.178	.168	.312[†]	.089
Netherlands	Ever married	.074	.144	−.017	.453[†]	.232
	Never married	.045	−.009	.241	.519[†]	.323
Northern	Ever married	.008	.052	.035	.639[†]	.410
Ireland	Never married	.147	.044	−.111	.661[†]	.543
Norway	Ever married	−.014	−.009	.043	.731[†]	.538
	Never married	.263	.196	.074	.447	.457
Sweden	Ever married	.067	.047	−.011	.582[†]	.369
	Never married	−.364	−.247	−.100	.831[†]	.619
United States	Ever married	.086[†]	.086[†]	.004	.476[†]	.249
	Never married	.094	.162[†]	−.076	.418[†]	.230

*For Great Britain only, father's occupation = prestige of father's occupation; for all other countries, father's occupation = wage rate scale.

[†]Metric coefficient is twice its standard error.

Note: Age^m = Age − mean of age. Means and standard deviations for all variables are provided in Table 16.3.

cupational status to women, there is no comparable *wage* increase.

Dual career theory predicts that women with strong labor force commitment would invest more in *education* than women who have left or anticipate leaving the labor force to raise a family. Hence, never-married women should experience a greater return to educational investment than married women. Education is the primary determinant of occupational wage rate for both ever- and never-married women,

as the relatively larger standardized coefficients for this variable attest.[12] Greater educational achievement is thus always associated with incumbency in jobs with higher wage rates, regardless of marital status. There is some support for the dual career hypothesis that never-married women receive the larger return to educational attainment. In seven of the twelve countries, the return to education is slightly greater for never-married women, in one country it is the same, and in four countries it is less than that of ever-married women. When post-marriage-age women are compared, the never-married return is slightly greater in eight countries. For those societies where the results are in the expected direction, the ratio of the married to never-married return ranges from a low of .69 in Austria to a high of .93 in Finland, with a seven-country average of .83. In those countries where the return to education is greater for married women, the four-country average is .81.

Discussion

The present study tests the dual career explanation for occupational sex segregation by investigating marital differences among women in labor force behavior, occupational composition, and occupational attainment. If dual career responsibilities are an important factor affecting the employment and occupational outcomes of women, they should affect married women more than women who have never married. Never-married women should be more like men in pursuing nontraditional work options and optimizing income-producing activities.

What do these data tell us about the occupational positions and employment outcomes of women and what do they say about the adequacy of the dual career theory in explaining occupational sex segregation? On the whole, the data suggest that never-married women are more like men in their *labor force behavior,* in the sense that they are more likely than married women to participate in the labor force and to work full-time when they are employed. At the same time, however, despite their greater labor force commitment, never-married women are concentrated in very different jobs from those in which men are employed, working in the female professions rather than in higher-paying male employment. As we know from previous analyses (Roos, 1981a: chapter 3), the female professions do not differ very substantially in average pay from clerical, sales, and service work. These findings thus suggest that although

marital responsibilities affect the kinds of jobs in which women work, these differences are not large and for the most part do not translate into differences in prestige or wage rate. The one benefit accruing to never-married women (in seven of the countries) is a relatively greater occupational return to educational investment. Married women in these countries evidently catch up in other ways, however, since in six of these seven countries the occupational attainments of ever- and never-married women (measured by either prestige or the wage rate scale) do not differ significantly. This is all the more surprising when one considers the higher achieved education of never-married women.[13]

Dual career theory is thus useful in explaining certain differences in labor force and occupational behavior of married and never-married women. However, it is not particularly useful in explaining why never-married women, similar in many ways to men in their labor force behavior and occupational commitment, are still limited in their occupational outcomes and differ little from married women in their returns to background factors and personal characteristics. Women's economic disadvantage, relative to men, cannot be attributed solely, or even in large measure, to differential marital responsibilities. Never-married women, who have no immediate marital responsibilities, do not fare much better than married women in their occupational attainment.

Findings such as those reported here cast doubt on the traditional human capital assumption that men and women have equivalent *access* to occupational opportunities. If in fact women's dual responsibilities are not the primary factor accounting for their differential occupational placement relative to men, researchers need to concentrate on further delineating the institutional and societal mechanisms that operate to perpetuate sex-typical employment. Some have begun recently to address these issues, taking an institutionalist perspective for the most part in investigating barriers to women's access to, and mobility into, nontraditional employment (for an overview, see Roos and Reskin, forthcoming). However, much more theoretical and empirical work remains to be done.

Notes

* From the *American Sociological Review* 48, no. 6 (December 1983): 853–64, by permission of the author and the American Sociological Association. Copyright 1983 by the American Sociological Association.

† A previous version of this paper was presented at the Annual Meetings of the Population Association of America, Washington, D.C., March 1981. The research was funded by a grant from the U.S. Department of Labor, Employment and Training Administration (Grant #DD–06–80–003). I wish to thank Lee Clarke, Valerie Oppenheimer, Michael Sobel, Donald Treiman, Wendy Wolf, Glenn Yago, and the Sociology Workshop at SUNY–Stony Brook for their helpful comments on an earlier draft. The data were made available by Donald Treiman and the Inter-University Consortium for Political and Social Research (ICPSR), University of Michigan.

1. The assumption underlying this discussion is that a woman's decision to work, and her occupational outcome, are dependent upon her marital and child-rearing responsibilities, and not vice versa. I have thus ignored the likelihood that a decision regarding marriage and/or children, especially how many children, depends on one's labor force/occupational choices or expectations. The relationship between occupational attainment and marital status is obviously more complicated than the one I am able to test here. Presumably, labor force and fertility expectations affect one's initial job choice, which usually occurs prior to marriage and childbearing; this initial job choice in turn affects whether one marries, age at marriage, whether one has children, and how many children one has. Initial job choice and subsequent marital and child-rearing choices both, in turn, affect one's occupational options later in life. Unfortunately, lack of appropriate data, especially measures of the presence and age of children, precludes the possibility of testing this more complicated model. With the cross-section data I have, I can test only a small piece of

this more complicated process of occupational attainment: the effect of current marital status on current occupational position. These limitations of the data should be borne in mind in the interpretation of results.

2. Selecting only industrialized countries also tends to minimize the amount of noncomparability that arises from varying definitions and measurements of the "economically active" population across countries, a factor that affects the enumeration of female more so than male workers.

3. Treiman's fourteen-category occupational classification is based on the seven-category ISCO classification. In addition to the "type of work" distinction between large occupational sectors, the fourteen-category classification also differentiates between prestige groupings within major categories.

4. I also used prestige as a metric measure of occupation but space constraints preclude full presentation of these results. I chose to present the occupational wage rate results because the use of prestige is not sufficient when exploring gender differences in occupational attainment patterns (see Roos, 1981b, for documentation of this point). What is needed is an occupational classification that takes account of the kinds of work men and women do, that is, one that reflects to a greater extent than prestige the gender differentiation of the labor market. The occupational wage rate scale was designed for just this purpose.

5. Sample size limitations preclude separating a "previously married" or an "ever married with children" group, either of which would be preferable theoretically to the "ever-married" group.

6. Even without this expectation of marriage, however, never-married women would probably not exactly approximate the attainments of men—most men have traditionally had the responsibility for assuring their family's as well as their own financial security, while unless they have children, single women generally need only be concerned with their own welfare. Although this "male" responsibility has been mitigated somewhat in recent years as more married women work for pay outside the home, it is still the case that men on average contribute the larger share of the household

income, if for no other reason than they are typically older than their wives and generally work in jobs that pay more. Smith (1979:12), in fact, estimated that working wives in the United States contribute on average one-quarter of their family's total income; the comparable figure for wives employed full-time year-round was 38 percent. This is not to suggest that wives' income is unnecessary for the family's financial security. To the contrary, Oppenheimer (1977) found that wives' economic role is an important one, especially when their husbands are in poorly paid occupations. Women's added earnings, according to Oppenheimer, are often a functional substitute for upward occupational mobility on the part of the husband.

7. The average age at first marriage was based on 1974 or 1975 data (United Nations, 1977). The ages were: Austria, 22.6; Denmark, 23.3; Finland, 23.1; West Germany, 22.3; Great Britain (England and Wales), 22.3; Israel, 21.5; Japan, 24.5; Netherlands, 21.9; Northern Ireland, 22.6; Norway, 22.5; Sweden, 24.8; United States, 21.4. Although conceptually it would have been desirable to use a more stringent criterion (perhaps the age by which 75 percent of all women had married), the potential loss of cases made such a choice unacceptable. As it was, deriving a conceptually more "pure" definition of the never-married group resulted in a loss of a large number of cases, and hence a reduction in the stability in the estimates of the percentage employed.

8. Mention should be made of the three exceptions to this general finding—in Germany, Great Britain, and Northern Ireland, "older" never-married women are somewhat less likely to work than all never-married women.

9. Israel is the only truly anomalous result—the index of marital dissimilarity decreases by ten percentage points when age is controlled. As in the remaining countries, controlling for age substantially increases the percentage of never-married women engaged in professional employment. Unlike in other countries, however, the increase in the percentage of professional workers among "older" never-married women in Israel brings these women to parity with married Israeli women, rather than increasing the marital difference. Notably, the percentage

of married women working in professional employment in Israel is the highest of any of the included countries. These findings may reflect the overrepresentation of women from higher-status social origins in the Israeli labor force (Roos, 1981a: chapter 5).

10. "Older" ever- and never-married women work in jobs of significantly different prestige in Denmark, Great Britain, Northern Ireland, and the United States (table not shown). Only in Great Britain and the United States, however, do "older" never-married women work in jobs of significantly higher wages than married women.

11. This pattern of results holds even when "older" women are compared, with the one exception that the father's occupation coefficient for Finland loses significance.

12. The only situation in which education is not significant is for never-married women in Norway, and this finding is probably unreliable due to the small sample size.

13. These findings are consistent with those of Hill (1979), who found no evidence of a detrimental wage effect of marriage among women (but a strong positive wage effect for married men). Hill concluded that while number of children is an appropriate proxy for labor force experience, marital status per se is not.

References

Barrett, Nancy. 1979. "Women in the Job Market: Occupations, Earnings, and Career Opportunities." Pp. 31–61 in Ralph E. Smith (ed.), *The Subtle Revolution: Women at Work.* Washington, D.C.: Urban Institute.

Boserup, Ester. 1970. *Woman's Role in Economic Development.* London: Allen and Unwin.

Degler, Carl N. 1980. *At Odds: Women and the Family in America from the Revolution to the Present.* New York: Oxford University Press.

Doeringer, Peter G., and Michael J. Piore. 1971. *Internal Labor Markets and Manpower Analysis.* Lexington: D. C. Heath.

Galenson, Marjorie. 1973. *Women and Work: An International Comparison.* ILR Paperback No. 13. New York: New York State School of Industrial and Labor Relations.

Gaskin, Katharine A. 1979. "Occupational Differentiation by Sex: An International Comparison." Ph.D. dissertation, Department of Sociology, University of Michigan.

Hill, Martha S. 1979. "The Wage Effects of Marital Status and Children." *Journal of Human Resources* 14:579–93.

Hudis, Paula M. 1976. "Commitment to Work and to Family: Marital-Status Differences in Women's Earnings." *Journal of Marriage and the Family* 38:267–78.

International Labour Office. 1969. *International Standard Classification of Occupations.* Revised edition. Geneva: International Labour Office.

———. 1979. *Yearbook of Labour Statistics.* Geneva: International Labour Office.

McClendon, McKee J. 1976. "The Occupational Status Attainment Processes of Males and Females." *American Sociological Review* 41:52–64.

Mincer, Jacob, and Solomon Polachek. 1974. "Family Investments in Human Capital: Earnings of Women." *Journal of Political Economy* 82: Supplement 76–108.

Oppenheimer, Valerie K. 1977. "The Sociology of Women's Economic Role in the Family." *American Sociological Review* 42:387–406.

Organisation for Economic Co-operation and Development. 1975. *The Role of Women in the Economy.* Paris: OECD.

———. 1979. *Equal Opportunities for Women.* Paris: OECD.

Polachek, Solomon W. 1975. "Discontinuous Labor Force Participation and Its Effect on Women's Market Earnings." Pp. 90–122 in Cynthia B. Lloyd (ed.), *Sex, Discrimination, and the Division of Labor.* New York: Columbia University Press.

Roos, Patricia A. 1981a. "Occupational Segregation in Industrial Society: A Twelve-Nation Comparison of Gender and Marital Differences in Occupational Attainment." Ph.D. dissertation, Department of Sociology, University of California, Los Angeles.

———. 1981b. "Sex Segregation in the Workplace: Male-Female Differences in Economic Returns to Occupation." *Social Science Research* 10:195–224.

Roos, Patricia A., and Barbara F. Reskin. Forthcoming. "Institutional Factors Contributing to Sex Segregation in the Workplace." In Barbara F. Reskin (ed.), *Sex Segregation in the Work-place: Trends, Explanations, and Remedies.* Washington, D.C.: National Academy Press, 1984.

Rosenfeld, Rachel A. 1980. "Race and Sex Differences in Career Dynamics." *American Sociological Review* 45:583–609.

Sawhill, Isabel V. 1973. "The Economics of Discrimination Against Women: Some New Findings." *Journal of Human Resources* 8:383–96.

Sewell, William H., Robert M. Hauser, and Wendy C. Wolf. 1980. "Sex, Schooling, and Occupational Status." *American Journal of Sociology* 86:551–83.

Singelmann, Joachim. 1978. "The Sectoral Transformation of the Labor Force in Seven Industrialized Countries." *American Journal of Sociology* 83:1224–34.

Smith, Ralph E. 1979. "The Movement of Women into the Labor Force." Pp. 1–29 in Ralph E. Smith (ed.), *The Subtle Revolution: Women at Work.* Washington, D.C.: Urban Institute.

Sweet, James A. 1975. "Recent Trends in the Employment of American Women." Working Paper 75–14, Center for Demography and Ecology, University of Wisconsin, Madison.

Szalai, Alexander (ed.). 1972. *The Use of Time: Daily Activities of Urban and Suburban Populations in Twelve Countries.* The Hague: Mouton.

Tilly, Louise A., and Joan W. Scott. 1978. *Women, Work, and Family.* New York: Holt, Rinehart and Winston.

Treiman, Donald J. 1977. *Occupational Prestige in Comparative Perspective.* New York: Academic Press.

Treiman, Donald J., and Kermit Terrell. 1975. "Sex and the Process of Status Attainment: A Comparison of Working Women and Men." *American Sociological Review* 40:174–200.

United Nations. 1977. *Demographic Yearbook, 1976.* New York: United Nations.

Waite, Linda J., and Glenna D. Spitze. 1981. "Young Women's Transition to Marriage." *Demography* 18:681–94.

Walker, Kathryn E., and Margaret E. Woods. 1976. *Time Use: A Measure of Household Production of Family Goods and Services.* Washington, D.C.: American Home Economics Association, Center for the Family.

Deviance and Control

The study of deviance and control as a sociological subdiscipline encompasses a broad range of topics centered around crime—its manifestations, etiology, behavioral expressions, and theoretical explanations. Topics of particular interest over the years and recently include suicide, homicide, youth and adult crime, juvenile delinquency, divorce, and child abuse. Criminological theories have until now been an almost exclusively American domain. Comparative researchers have come to see these theories as culture bound and thus not operationally relevant in other than American social contexts. As a consequence, comparative work in deviance and control has begun to reexamine the generalizability of previous American work.

The study of deviance and control goes beyond the topics mentioned above in that researchers are naturally searching for explanations for deviant behavior. Motivational, and "control and opportunity" explanations have garnered much attention, as have the "routine activity" approach and the "material deprivation" approach. Additionally, the roles of industrialization and modernization have been extensively examined. Comparative work has traditionally been hampered by nearly incomparable cross-national data. A United Nations survey begun in 1975, and now conducted every five years, is attempting to bring about a new level of data standardization that will contribute to improved comparative work in the coming years.

Norman L. Farberow's essay here on the "Cultural History of Suicide" traces the shifting attitudes and values toward suicide across cultures and throughout recent history. The author focuses not only on nation-states as a unit of analysis but also on the world's major religions. The latter are seen to have substantial impact on attitudes toward suicide. Among Farberow's other observations, he dichotomizes suicide: social or institutional suicide, on the one hand, and individual or personal suicide, on the other. He also cites many of the world's famous philosophers and writers who have commented on the subject.

In Paul Friday's broad assessment of the evolution and state of juvenile crime and delinquency throughout the world, we revisit the contention that criminological theories, with their American origins, are too culture-bound to apply cross-nationally. In looking at youth crime and delinquency, Friday finds that industrialization definitely plays a key role by shunting youth out of labor market opportunities, thereby creating a lengthened period of isolation from the mainstream that is all too often expressed in delinquent and criminal behaviors, with gangs being an important form of expressing peer-group solidarity. Friday concludes by identifying several structural factors at work.

Rosemary Gartner studied homicide victim rates in eighteen developed democratic countries between 1950 and 1980. Important risk factors identified in this longitudinal, cross-national survey include divorce, economic stress (though not inequality per se), material deprivation, weak social integration, exposure to official violence, and welfare spending. Other risk factors applied differentially to specific victim groups. For example, the presence of a death penalty was, contrary to popular expectation, *positively* associated with increased homicide rates for adult female and young child victims.

Cultural History of Suicide[*]

Norman L. Farberow

Suicide has been known to man as long as recorded history. However, the word *suicide* is of relatively recent vintage. It does not appear in the Bible nor in the famous pamphlet by John Donne (1644) on self-homicide. One possible derivation is the word "suist," meaning a selfish man, and "suicism," meaning selfishness. In 1671, the third edition of Phillips's *New World of Words* protested against the word "suicide." The index to Jackson's *Works,* published two years later in 1673, used the word "suicidium." However, the *Oxford Dictionary* states that suicide was first used in English in 1651, just six years after Donne's *Biathanatos,* and is derived from the modern Latin "suicidium," which in turn stems from the Latin pronoun for "self" and verb "to kill."

Viewing suicide from the perspective of its sociocultural history allows a more comprehensive understanding of the phenomenon. Two main threads of self-destruction appear, each present in varying proportions depending on the era. These threads are: (1) social or institutional suicide and (2) individual or personal suicide. The relative degree and importance of each vary in the successive epochs, but both are always present in some degree.

Institutional suicide is self-destruction that society demands of the individual as part of his identification with the group. Institutional suicide has taken many forms, with some existing to this day. Thus, a general attitude of approval arises when the act conforms to the ideals of the society, for example, sacrificing one's life for another. Those institutional suicides that have disappeared did so because they were specific for the age and were felt no longer to serve any good purpose. Not only did institu-

tional suicide prescribe the *occasion* in which the self-destruction was to occur but frequently the *form* it was to take. There were, for example, sacrifices of widows and servants of a great lord or king, or even the sacrifice of the king himself after a prescribed period. One form of institutional suicide was practiced in a country where there were food shortages, and the old and the sick were expected to sacrifice themselves for the good of their group. Among some primitive cultures, suicide was a way of expressing anger and revenge, highly personal motives, but for which the form for expression was nevertheless rigidly prescribed. Thus, in a primitive tribe described by Malinowski (1908), when an individual was accused of having transgressed one of the taboos of the tribe, he climbed to the top of a palm tree, declared his hurt at having been so charged, named who it was that had insulted him, and then plunged headfirst to his death.

On the other hand, personal suicide was an individual act of protest or declaration against either interpersonal hurts or transgressions against society. The motives were preservative of honor and dignity, expiation of pusillanimity or cowardice, avoidance of pain and ignominy by old age and/or disease, preservation of chastity, escape from personal disgrace by falling into the hands of the enemy, unwillingness to bear the hurt of separation or loss of love, and others.

The overview of suicide also makes it clear that the rate of suicide has been high or low in particular eras in direct relationship with variations in social controls and different emphases on the value of the individual in comparison with the state, such as idealization of reason, rationality, individuality, and democratic processes. Where the controls were greatest the rate was lower; where the individual was more free, the rate was higher. In those eras of greatest social control, the attitudes toward suicide were usually lodged in the emotional, nonrational aspects. For example, in primitive and precivilized areas characterized by a highly structured society, the attitudes could be found in the beliefs of magic and superstitions developed to control social behavior. In more civilized cultures the attitudes became lodged in the beliefs and faith of religion, often incorporating the magical elements from the primitive heritage into the canonical regulations. In the society led by the dictator the attitudes were integrated into the tightly organized, strictly controlled political ideology needed to develop the required loss of self and overidentification with the state. The concepts are similar to those of Bayet (1922), who posited two kinds of morality. The first, *morale simple,* was a primitive morality for the common people developed from religion and superstition; the second, *morale nuancée,* was the morality of the intellectual and had its roots in reason and awareness of the complexities of any human act.

Most of the early writers on suicide were concerned with the rightness or wrongness of the act. Although our interest is divorced from such moralistic evaluations, the early writers reflected the psychocultural history of suicide, providing insights into its extent, form, and characteristics over time. On the one hand, suicide has been strongly condemned. As mentioned above, one has to go back to the early magic of the primitive in order to determine the source of the irrational attitude toward the suicide (Fedden, 1938). It is this irrational attitude that has surrounded the act with horror and antagonism. In primitive societies death has always been a highly tabooed subject; taboos were accumulated around suicide by its very nature, many to ward off the possible evil from a self-inflicted death. Thus, Baganda women were especially fearful of ghosts of suicides

who might possibly "impregnate" them, and they threw grass or sticks on the place where the suicide had been buried. The later English custom of burial at a crossroads was directly linked to the primitive custom of burying at a crossroads a child who had been born feet first and so was considered unclean. The taboos later became rituals, practiced for the purpose of purification; the original act became a moral and religious sin.

There were two other reasons for the growth of the strong feeling of revulsion around suicide. First, the fact that a man was rejecting all of the things he prized showed a contempt for society, compelling society to question everything it valued. The second reason was an economic one, for a suicide deprived the tribe of a useful warrior or a potential mother.

Among the earliest of the great cultures, Oriental sacred writings contained many contradictions about suicide. Although it was encouraged in some parts, it was vigorously condemned in others. Brahmanism institutionalized and sanctioned suttee, a ceremonial sacrifice of widows that was as common in China as in India. The Brahman doctrine was sympathetic to suicide, for it was consonant with denial of the flesh, a common objective in philosophies of the Orient. One goal in Oriental mysticism was to divorce the body from the soul so that the soul might occupy itself only with supersensual realities. Buddhism emphasized that through extinction of craving or passion life's chief purpose of acquisition of knowledge could be achieved. Both Brahmanism and Buddhism are religions of resignation and despair. In Japan, suicide became embedded in the national tradition and eventually developed the highly traditionalized rituals of *seppuku* and *hara-kiri.* On the other hand, Muhammadanism always condemned suicide with the utmost severity, for one of the cardinal teachings of Mohammed was that the Divine Will was expressed in different ways and man must submit himself at all times.

Suicide among the Jews was generally rare. The Old Testament expressed the value of life for the Jew. A Jew was permitted to transgress every religious commandment to save his life with the exception of three things: murder, the denial of God, and incest. Suicide in Jewish law was wrong. As a result, when the act did occur, the victim and his family were punished by denial of a regular burial and the customary rituals of mourning. However, suicide was acceptable under extreme conditions, such as apostasy, ignominy, disgrace of capture, or torture. At least four instances of suicide appear in the Old Testament, those of Samson, Saul, Abimelech, and Ahitophael. Samson (Judges 16:28–31) killed himself and the Philistines by pulling the pillars of the temple down; Saul (Samuel 31:1–6) slew himself after defeat in battle to avoid the ignominy of capture; Abimelech (Judges 9:54) killed himself after being mortally wounded by a woman so that it could not be said he had been killed by a woman; and Ahitophael (Samuel 17:1) hanged himself when his betrayal of David to Absalom failed. Talmudic times (A.D. 200 to 500) reported an increasing number of suicides, with a condemnatory tone appearing for the first time.

The most notable instance of mass suicide in Jewish history is probably that of the Zealots who took refuge in Masada on the western shore of the Dead Sea. When capture was inevitable, Eleaszar Ben Jair, the leader, urged his followers to kill themselves rather than to fall in the hands of the enemy. Several versions of the story then occur: one is that each committed suicide; the other, that a plan was drawn to determine for each person to kill one other person, which they all did, including the women and children. There were additional outbursts of suicide among Jews when persecution became intense during the Middle Ages and the early Renaissance. Suicides were also noted in more recent periods of persecution, such as in Nazi Germany, although the records are unclear about this.

In the Greek and Roman periods, the primitive and religious forces weakened. While the attitudes of horror and condemnation for suicide were preserved in the lower classes, the upper classes seemed to develop a different religion and different morals, expressing tolerance and acceptance. Contributing to the latter were the international philosophies that appeared with the establishment of the Roman Empire. This replaced the old city-states of Athens and Sparta with their stricter, more localized codes of mores and ethics. The number of suicides grew throughout these periods, mainly from four motivations: (1) to preserve honor, (2) to avoid pain and ignominy, (3) to express bereavement from loss of a loved one, and (4) suicide for the state or for a patriotic cause.

Examples of bereavement suicide are Dido, who preferred to stab herself on her husband's funeral pyre rather than to marry again; Portia, who swallowed red-hot coals when she learned of Brutus's death at Philippi; and Paulina, who tried to follow Seneca in death after he had killed himself on Nero's order.

Patriotic suicide is exemplified by Decius Mus, a consul of Rome, who learned that an oracle had proclaimed the battle could be won only by the sacrifice of a Roman noble, and who met certain death by dashing into the ranks of the enemy far ahead of his own troops.

Suicide to avoid pain of sickness or old age was considered quite acceptable. Pliny the Elder considered the existence of poisonous herbs as proof of a kindly Providence because it allowed man to die painlessly and quickly. Seneca says: "I will not relinquish old age if it leaves my better parts intact, but if it begins to shake my mind, if it destroys its faculties one by one, if it leaves me not life but breath, I will depart from the putrid or tottering edifice. I will not escape by death from disease so long as it may be healed and leaves my mind unimpaired. I will not raise my hand against myself on account of pain, for so to die is to be conquered. But if I know that I must suffer without hope of relief, I will depart, not through fear of pain itself, but because it prevents all for which I would live." Zeno, the founder of Stoic philosophy, preached the above doctrine all the way to age ninety-eight, apparently without meeting a situation serious enough to warrant his taking his life. At ninety-eight, however, he fell down and put a toe out of joint and he was disgusted enough to go home and hang himself.

The death of Cato of Utica was an example of a cool, reasoned death to preserve honor and express patriotism. Cato killed himself out of a concern for his country and for his own principles. When he tried to rally the Republican party at Utica in Libya, he might have been successful except for Scipio's defeat. As Caesar, defeat, and certain slavery approached, he felt he had no other recourse except to kill himself.

The Cynic, Stoic, and Epicurean philosophies of this world fostered an acceptance of suicide while two main lines of thought were in opposition. One was from Pythagoras, who viewed life as a discipline imposed by the gods to which man must submit himself. His theory of numbers lent itself to his position, for he hypothesized there were just so many souls available for use in the world in any given moment. With a suicide the spiritual mathematics were upset, for it might well be that no other soul was ready to fill the gap in the world caused by the sudden exit. The Aristotelians considered suicide an act against the best aims of the state and therefore an act that must be punished. Plato's position was in the middle. In the *Phaedo,* he has Socrates state his position on suicide. Because man is God's child, he is not merely the property but also the soldier of the gods. Suicide is therefore tantamount to desertion. However, in certain cases, such as incurable illness or when God had summoned the soul, suicide is acceptable.

The laws formulated about suicide in this period, primarily among the Romans, became more and more economically oriented. The suicide of a slave or a soldier represented a considerable financial loss to the master or a weakening of the effective force of the Roman armies. Punishments began to be named in the laws, detailing terms of forfeiture and confiscation of estates. A suicide when under arrest robbed the treasury of goods it might have been able to obtain. This loss in revenues was stopped by decreeing that those who killed themselves to escape conviction were without legal successors and their goods were to go to the state.

The advent of Christianity about this time brought with it, at the beginning, a marked indifference to martyrdom. There was pessimism, longing for a better life, a struggle for redemption, and a desire to come before God and live there forever. As a result, suicides occurred in great numbers. A quick halt was brought about by Saint Augustine's "City of God" in the fourth century A.D. in which the first codification of the Church's official disapproval of suicide spread. In all of the Middle Ages from about the fourth century to the twelfth or thirteenth, while the Catholic Church held great sway in Europe, suicide became practically unknown.

Until A.D. 250, the attitude toward suicide was the same as before the birth of Christ. Suicide was common, especially among the early Christians. The courage of these martyrs and their disregard of pain was amazing and at times frightening. It was as if nothing could deter them in their active seeking out of death. As the fourth century began, changes appeared, with the Church adopting a hostile attitude that progressed from tentative disapproval to severe denunciation and punishment. Antagonism toward suicide developed. Suicide became proof that the individual had despaired of God's grace, or that he lacked faith and was rejecting God by rejecting life, God's gift to man. As Rome's civilization and influence declined, starting about the third century, the intellectual aspects and characteristics of society also began to dissipate and suicide again became a social crime. These attitudes were not, however, incorporated into the Church from its authorities and intellectuals and then handed down to the people; they were, instead, morals that came from below—a transference of the popular pagan idea into the semi-Christianized world.

Saint Augustine produced four arguments to justify the Church's antisuicide stance: (1) no private individual may assume the right to kill a guilty person; (2) the suicide who takes his own life has killed a man; (3) the truly noble soul will bear all suffering from which the effort to escape is an admission of weakness; and (4) the suicide dies the worst of sinners because he is not only running away from the fear of temptation but also any possibility of absolution. The Council of Arles in A.D. 452 repeated Rome's legislation against suicide by exercising forfeiture of estate, and the Council of Braga in A.D. 563 ordered no religious rites for the suicide.

Three kinds of suicide continued to be accepted: voluntary martyrdom, self-inflicted death of the ascetic, and death of the virgin or married woman to preserve chastity. The Circumcelliones in North Africa almost seemed to enjoy killing themselves (they did in great numbers) when threatened with persecution. Some of the young monastics who chose celibacy and solitary seclusion killed themselves by extreme privation or by a starvation diet. Saint Augustine's arguments were used to prevent the rush of women to kill themselves to preserve their chastity by arguing that no woman can lose her chastity by violation, since real virginity was an attribute of the soul and not of the body.

The Antisidor Council of A.D. 590 added for the first time a system of penalties to the condemnation of suicide, and in 1284 the Synod of Nimes invoked the Church's final weapon for prevention, denial of Christian burial. Suicides were buried outside of the church or close beneath the wall. Desecration of the corpse occurred as the body was dragged through the streets and buried at the crossroads, often with a stake through the heart. Odd customs appeared, such as in Danzig when the body of a suicide was not permitted to go out through the door but rather had to be taken out through a window. Sometimes a hole had to be knocked in the wall when there was no window.

There was only one period in the Middle Ages when there was a change from the suicide-horror attitudes that characterized this time. This was the brief era of Charlemagne's rule (A.D. 768 to 814) when intellectual aristocracy and respect for learning and reason flowered. This period saw the first occasion for the use of "suicide because of insanity" as an excuse, an explanation that continues to be used even today as subterfuge to evade antisuicide legislation without an open breach with popular prejudice. After Charlemagne's premature civilization broke up, the old attitudes of absolute condemnation returned.

Outside of the framework provided by the Church during the Middle Ages, there were two main groups where suicide was common: (1) the heretics and (2) the Jews. The most famous suicide martyrs of the Middle Ages were the Albigenses in southern France. In 1218, some five thousand were put to death as heretics. There were also many pogroms against the Jews in England, especially in the early years of Richard the Lion-Hearted. On more than one occasion there were mass suicides, such as at York in 1190 when six hundred died to escape oppression.

There were still people, however, who attempted suicide out of personal and individualistic motives. One, for example, was Joan of Arc, who attempted suicide while in prison at Beaurevoir. In her trial the bishops used this suicide attempt against her, finding in it one more proof of her susceptibility to the Spirit of Evil.

In the thirteenth century, Thomas Aquinas in his *Summa Theologiae* formulated the authoritative Church position on suicide for that time. Suicide was absolutely wrong for these reasons: (1) it was unnatural, (2) every man was a member of some community and suicide was therefore antisocial, and (3) life was a gift of God and was not at the disposal of man. About this time the *Inferno* appeared, in which Dante illustrated the current attitudes toward the suicide by condemning him to eternal unrest in the woods of self-destruction.

The Renaissance and the Reformation that followed, however, facilitated a shift in the attitudes toward suicide. The individual began to emerge and values in religion began to change. Luther became the representative of orthodox Protestantism. His ideas caused a shift from absolutism and obedience to personal inquiry and a sense of personal responsibility. The contrast with the rigidified framework of the Middle Ages led man to questions, doubts, and challenges of what had formerly been taken for granted. Along with these, however, came a sense of isolation and self-consciousness. Luther at first fostered reason as a challenge to the principles of the Catholic Church but later became distrustful of the rapidity with which reason spread and he began to condemn it.

Calvinism also appeared about this time, starting first in Switzerland and sweeping across France (Huguenots) to England, while Lutheranism in general became firmly entrenched in Scandinavia. Calvin's opposite approach exalted God and tended to remove him to a plane of inaccessible superiority. In this way, he tended to minimize and humble man even more and thus raise indirectly the question of the value of the individual human soul. Italy saw a revival of learning and resurrection of ideas that began to diminish the strong feeling of suicide-horror. In France, where Montaigne's writings appeared about this time, the absolute condemnation of suicide disappeared from the enlightened classes but not from among the common people. In England, Sir Thomas More displayed a reasonable attitude toward suicide in his *Utopia,* writing in an unemotional way about euthanasia and certain types of suicide.

As the Renaissance spread and man began to find life more and more intolerable because of his awareness of poverty and lack of a future, he also became more melancholy. Although Death had been an important figure in the concern of the Catholic Church during the Middle Ages, the Renaissance saw a marked intensification of preoccupation with death, with many editions of the *Danse Macabre,* or scenes illustrated by the presence of a skeleton. Literature also began to reflect the melancholy of the time and to show an increasing awareness of psychological complexity. In this period we find Shakespeare producing in-depth psychological studies with such characters as Hamlet, Lear, and Prospero. In his eight tragedies may be found no less than fourteen suicides. Two other important literary figures—Burton in 1621 and Donne in 1644—wrote on melancholy and suicide. Burton's *Anatomy of Melancholy* broke sharply with church dogma of the time and questioned the eternal damnation of suicide. Donne's *Biathanatos* dealt with suicide from a practical angle and stated openly that because circumstances alter the cases of suicide, each must be judged individually. Donne's work is the first defense of suicide in English.

Although suicide was now readily tolerated by the educated group, among the lower classes the powerful Church was still staunchly against suicide. Its influence was strong enough to produce reactionary secular legislation in 1670, in which suicide was not merely murder but high treason and heresy. One additional important cultural element appeared about this period, the stigma associated with poverty. In medieval times being poor had not been associated with any moral position; indeed poverty in some groups had acquired a certain mystical importance, mostly from religious association. However, with the rise of commercialism and the advent of Protestantism, there was a drastic change in the attitude of society toward the poor. Social relationships were evaluated from purely economic standards. Puritans talked about rewarding good with prosperity and meting out poverty to evil. Economic failure became a mark of sin. The poor now became both social and moral outcasts and as a result suffered as never before. It was, however, more the change of fortune, a decline from prosperity to poverty, rather than the fact of poverty itself, that accounted for most suicides at that time. The man who was impoverished suddenly found added to his sad lot contempt and damnation.

The eighteenth century saw further changes in suicide with opposition arising to the prejudice and penalties against suicide. Most activity appeared in France where the liberal currents of criticism and skepticism were expressed by such men as Voltaire (1766), who brought a reasonable approach toward suicide, Rousseau (1761), a romanticized approach, and Montesquieu (1721), for the first time, a criticism of suicide from the point of view of the survivors. Rousseau's work was incorporated into the *Declaration of the Rights of Man,* which inaugurated the French Revolution in 1789.

England developed attitudes of greater tolerance somewhat more slowly than France. The most significant publication at this time was David Hume's *Essay on Suicide* (1783) in which he argued that suicide, if it were to be abhorred, had to be proved a crime against God, neighbor, or self. He pointed out that first it was not a crime against God because he gave man the power to act and therefore death at one's own hands was as much under the control of the deity as if it had proceeded from any other source. Second, suicide was not a breach against neighbor and society, "For a man who retires from life does no harm to society, he only ceases to do good and which, if it is an injury, is of the lowest kind." Third, Hume stated that suicide cannot be a crime against self because he believed that no man ever threw away a life while it was still worth keeping. Poverty continued to be a significant cause of suicide. In 1732, Richard Smith and his wife killed their infant daughter, hanged themselves, and left a long letter addressed to the public describing the hopelessness of poverty and complaining that life was not worth living.

Of those who continued to write against suicide, an important new argument offered by Merian (1763) became equivalent to the first medical theory and separated the arguments from moral theory. Merian stated that suicide

was not a crime but an emotional illness. All suicides were therefore in some degree deranged and so did not run counter to the law of nature, a rationalization that led to the Church's use of "suicide while of unsound mind" in later years as a way of skirting Church laws against suicide.

Madame de Staël (1814), writing against suicide in France, argued that living through pain and crisis makes a person a better man so that it was folly to commit suicide. The opinion that crisis may be a turning point in life with positive potentialities is used by some writers today (Morley, 1965). She stated that since God never deserted man, the individual need never feel he was completely alone. Finally, she offered the interesting argument that suicide was against the moral dignity of man, an argument that placed suicide in the opposite camp of the Stoics and Epicureans who felt that suicide helped preserve man's dignity and self-concept.

In England, Bishop Charles Moore (1790) continued the criticism of suicide but was much more lenient, stating that each case of suicide had to be judged on its own merit. In Germany, Immanuel Kant (1797) wrote about the sacredness of human life which therefore must be preserved at all costs. On the opposite side, Goethe's *Sorrows of Werther* (1774) swept across Europe at this time and precipitated an epidemic of suicide. Goethe himself, however, weathered his own emotional traumas and later wrote about the value of work as the one great means toward grace and health.

The nineteenth century saw Schopenhauer (1851) giving explicit expression to the pessimism characteristic of so much of this era. He has often erroneously been considered an advocate of suicide but actually he ruled against it. His theory is that moral freedom, the highest ethical ideal, can be obtained only by the denial of the will to live. Suicide is not such a denial, for the essence of negation lies in shunning the joys, not the sorrows, of life. The suicide is willing to live but is dissatisfied with the conditions under which life is offered to him.

The greatest change brought about by the nineteenth century was the introduction and emphasis of the word "disgrace," a social value. This contrasted markedly with the principal words associated with suicide heard in the century preceding, "crime" and "sin." Disgrace was now associated with the feelings of the survivors, the status of the family, friends, and neighbors who remained. This theme was related to an emerging characteristic of this century, that is, the development of a strong family and middle-class status in society. Because it was essential for the family to maintain status within the community, suicide became secretive and hidden, especially for the upper class, as it grew more and more to be associated with insanity.

Another reflection on the social versus the individual aspects of suicide was voiced by Bonser in 1885, who came out strongly against any kind of state interference with suicide. For him these are rights which the individual does not give to society and therefore cannot be taken away from him. Life has been given value primarily by society; actually, in nature it is valueless. Society has no right to demand that others should suffer because it considers life sacred.

During the nineteenth century the old religious and social groupings, which were the strongest bulwarks against suicide, began to lose effectiveness. Capitalism with its insistence on purely material values added to the difficulties of the suicide, as it exerted a disintegrating force on social life. Capitalism made people more interdependent economically but isolated them socially; cities grew larger and individuals grew more solitary.

Scientific writing on suicide began to appear. Medical theories of the time attempted to fit suicide into the current theories of physiological medicine. For example, it was hypothesized that the act of suicide occurred in people with thick craniums or that it resulted from excess phosphorus in the brain. Esquirol (1838)

claimed all suicides were insane, although later Kraepelin (1917) stated that only 30 percent showed symptoms of insanity. Statisticians gathered factual data and investigated quantitative and medical aspects. Writers of this period, such as Lisle (1856), Bertrand (1857), and Brierre de Boismont (1865), felt that suicides had to be judged on their own merits. The last quarter of the century saw researches by Morselli in Italy (1882), O'Dea in America (1882), Legoyt in France (1881), and Strahan in England (1893).

Durkheim's *Le Suicide* in 1897 was one of the most important books to appear with the viewpoint that suicide as a collective phenomenon was influenced by specific factors characterizing the society in which it appeared. Essentially, the theme was that where social solidarity was strong there would be little suicide, where it was weak there would be more.

Legal changes saw abolishment of the laws prescribing desecration of the corpse and forfeitures for penal offenses. In 1882, the maximal sentence for attempted suicide was reduced to two years. By the end of the century the law punished only attempted suicide and aiding and abetting suicide. In France, the attitude toward suicide followed the fluctuations of French politics. When the liberal legislation of the Code Napoleon was overthrown, suicides and their survivors were punished; when liberty and democratic government reappeared, the rights of the suicides were respected.

In 1897, William James wrote his famous essay, "Is Life Worth Living?", in which he concluded that man did not commit suicide primarily because of his religious faith. For James, religion was belief in the existence of an unseen order in which one believed only because of faith, not our incomplete knowledge based on science. It was faith that helped man to believe, even in deep depression, that life was still worth living.

The attitudes toward suicide today are reflected in the laws of the various countries of the world. Suicide continues to be a sin in canonical law, especially of the Catholic

Church. However, the practical attitude is one of leniency and frequent use of the terminology, "suicide while of an unsound mind." A study of Roman and Greek priests in their parishes in Los Angeles, dealing with suicides and their survivors, indicated that rarely was burial denied or opprobrium attached to the family (Demopolous, 1968). To some degree, the attitude toward suicide of predominantly Catholic countries is reflected in their unusually low rates, such as in Italy, Spain, and Ireland. However, studies have shown that in many instances suicides are certified under another mode, such as "accident" or "natural." Paradoxically, in some Catholic countries, such as Austria, the opprobrium does not exist and the rate of suicide is high. Personal communications with investigators from Austria have indicated that Catholicism as practiced in Austria today is considered neither strict nor intense.

In many of the Middle European countries, secular law continues to hold attempted suicide a crime. Usually this results in registration of suicide attempts, probably permitting better statistics; Austria, the Soviet Union, and Hungary are examples. England abolished the statute against attempted suicide in 1961. American law retains a statute against attempted suicide in seven of its fifty states but considers aiding and abetting suicide a crime in eighteen of them. Likewise, abetting suicide is still punishable in Germany, Hungary, Russia, Holland, Japan, and Italy. In most laws today the presumption is almost always against suicide and in favor of death from natural causes. Suicide is not generally found unless the evidence excludes every other reasonable hypothesis.

In the past, accusations have been made that the extensive social welfare programs in Scandinavian countries have contributed to the higher suicide rates. Social welfare is an important characteristic of Scandinavian culture. These countries in comparison with others represent probably the most advanced level of concern of a state for its citizens through all as-

pects of their lives. Dr. Ruth Ettlinger, a prominent investigator of suicides in Sweden, found in her 1964 follow-up of attempted suicides a significant excess of social-minus factors among people who later committed suicide versus those who died a natural death or who were still alive. Suicide was found, in other words, to be related to people whose social contacts were characterized more by "incomplete welfare" than by loss of contact or interest in society.

Ruth Link (1969) in a popular article in *Sweden Now* explained Sweden's higher suicide rate by pointing out that Sweden has the world's most reliable statistics, that autopsies are performed routinely, that there are fewer moral and religious taboos against suicide, that Sweden has a very low birth rate and a predominance of older people, and that if unpredicted deaths are viewed as a whole (including accidents and homicides), Sweden's figures are similar to those of most other Western countries.

The above comments on Sweden illustrate the value of knowing the cultural background in which suicide appears. Cultural history provides a perspective for viewing suicide as it has been influenced by religion, law, philosophies, and thought. Deeper understanding permits more reasonable reactions and, especially, improvement in treatment approaches.

Note

* From *Suicide in Different Cultures,* edited by Norman L. Farberow, (Baltimore: University Park Press, 1975), 1–15, by permission of the author and the University Park Press. Copyright 1976 by the University Park Press.

References

Aquinas, T. 1947. *Summa Theologiae,* reprint of the first edition. New York: Benziger Brothers.

Augustinus, A. 1950. *De Civitate Dei* (The City of God, Books I–VII), reprint, Vol. 8. New York: Fathers of the Church.

Bayet, A. 1922. *Le Suicide et La Morale*. Paris: Librairie Felix Alcan.

Bertrand, L. 1857. *Traite du Suicide, Considere dans ses Rapports avec la Philosophie, la Theologie, la Medecine et la Jurisprudence*. Paris: J. B. Bailliere.

Bohannan, P. et al. 1960. *African Homicide and Suicide*. Princeton, N.J.: Princeton University Press.

Bonser, T. O. 1885. *The Right to Die*. A paper read before the Dialectical Society of London, the Richmond Athenaeum and the Deptford Branch of the NSS. London: Freethought Publishing Company.

Brierre de Boismont, J. F. 1865. *Du Suicide et de le Folie Suicide*. Paris: Librairie Germer Bailliere.

Burton, R. 1621. *The Anatomy of Melancholy*, reprint of the first edition, 1881. London: Chatto and Windus.

Demopolous, H. 1968. "Suicide and Church Canon Law." Unpublished doctoral dissertation, Claremont School of Theology, California.

De Staël (Staël von Holstein), G. S. 1814. *Reflexions sur le Suicide*. Paris: H. Nicolle.

Devereux, G. *Mohave Ethnopsychiatry and Suicide. The Psychiatric Knowledge and the Psychic Disturbances of an Indian Tribe*. Washington, D.C.: Smithsonian Institution, Bureau of American Ethnology, Bulletin 175, U.S. Government Printing Office.

Donne, J. 1930. *Biathanatos*, reprint of the first edition, 1644. New York: Facsimile Text Society.

Durkheim, E. 1897. *Le Suicide*. Paris: Librairie Felix Alcan. (Reprint 1912, J. S. Spaulding and G. Simpson, Translators. New York: The Free Press of Glencoe, 1951).

Esquirol, J. E. D. 1838. *Mental Maladies: A Treatise on Insanity* (Translated by E. K. Hunt) Philadelphia: Lea and Blanchard, 1845; New York: Hefner, 1965.

Ettlinger, R. 1964. Suicides in a Group of Patients Who Had Previously Attempted Suicide. *Acta Psychiatrica Scandinavica* 40:363, 378.

Fedden, R. 1938. *Suicide: A Social and Historical Study*. London: Peter Davies.

Goethe, J. W. von. 1774. *Die Leiden des Jungen Werther*. Leipzig: In the Weggandschen Bookstore.

Hume, D. 1929. *An Essay on Suicide*, reprint of the first edition, 1783. Yellow Springs, Ohio: Kahoe and Company.

James, W. 1927. Is Life Worth Living? In: *The Will to Believe*, p. 27, reprint of the first edition, 1897. New York: Longmans, Green and Company.

Kant, I. 1871. *The Metaphysic of Ethics* (Translator J. W. Semple). Edinburgh: T. and T., Clark, 1871.

Kraepelin, E. 1917. *Lectures on Clinical Psychiatry* (Authorized translation from the 2nd German edition, revised and edited by Thomas Johnstone, 3rd English edition. New York: Wood.

Kraus, H. H. 1970. A Cross-Cultural Study of Suicide. *Journal of Cross-Cultural Psychology* 1, no. 2: 159, 167.

Legoyt, A. 1881. *Le Suicide Ancien et Moderne. Etude Historique, Philosophique, Morale et Statistique*. Paris: A Drouin.

Link, R. 1969. Suicide: The Deadly Game. *Sweden Now* 12: 40–46.

Lisle, P-E. 1856. *Du Suicide: Statistique, Medecine, Historie et Legislation*, Paris: J. B. Bailliere.

Malinowski, B. 1908. Suicide: A Chapter in Comparative Ethics. *Sociology Review* 1: 14.

Merian, 1763. *Sur la Crainte de la Mort, Sur le Mepris de la Mort, Sur le Suicide, Memoire*. In volume (tome) XIX of the Histoire de l'Academie Royale des Sciences et Belles-Lettres de Berlin, pp. 385, 392, and 403.

Montesquieu, C. L. 1721. *Persian Lettres (Letter LXXVI)*. Paris: John Davidson, (Trans. George Routledge and Sons, Ltd., London).

Moore, C. 1790. *A Full Enquiry into the Subject of Suicide*. London: Rivington.

Morley, W. E. 1965. Treatment of the Patient in Crisis. *Western Medicine* 3: 77.

Morselli, E. A. 1882. *Suicide: An Essay on Comparative Moral Statistics*. New York: D. Appleton and Company.

Noyes, R., Jr. 1968. "The Taboo of Suicide." *Psychiatry* 31 No. 2: 173–83.

O'Dea, J. J. 1882. *Suicide: Studies on Its Philosophy, Causes and Prevention*. New York: G. P. Putnam's Sons.

Pretzel, P. W. 1968. Philosophical and Ethical Considerations of Suicide Prevention. *Bulletin Suicidology* July.

Rousseau, J. J. 1761. *La Nouvelle Heloise:* Lettres 21 et 22, Paris.

Schopenhauer, A. 1851. On Suicide. In: *Complete Essays of Schopenhauer*. New York: T. B. Saunders.

Strahan, S. A. K. 1893. *Suicide and Insanity*. London: S. Sonnenschein & Company.

Voltaire, F. M. A. 1766. *De Caton, du Suicide, et du Livre de l'Abbe de Saint-Cyran qui Legitime le Suicide*.

Westermarck, E. 1908. *Origin and Development of the Moral Ideas*, Vol. II, pp. 229–64. London: Macmillan and Company.

CHAPTER EIGHTEEN

International Review of Youth Crime and Delinquency*

Paul C. Friday

While crime may be considered ubiquitous, its manifestation varies by time, region, country, and state. There is, therefore, a natural curiosity about the circumstances and conditions which appear to foster crime and delinquency in one area and inhibit their development in another. This curiosity is the basis for comparative research, for it involves the search for commonalities upon which to base meaningful comparisons.

Yet, criminological theory as dominated by the Americans has emerged through time as culture-bound with limited, if any, power to actually explain the etiology of the criminal act. Despite the historical emphasis on "social facts" (Durkheim, 1938), theory as it developed in the United States has focused on the individual actor within the unique cultural context of American society.

During the 1960s there was an upsurge in interest in comparative research and cross-cultural theory testing. Unfortunately, such attempts were of limited utility.

What was done comparatively was limited to testing American delinquency models. When transported abroad, however, such theories tended to be inappropriate. Thus, after her attempt to test delinquency gang theories in Argentina, DeFleur (1969) attacked the "uncritical application" of U.S.-based delinquency theories and proposed instead the development of culture-specific explanations. Downes (1966) was unable to support differential opportunity theory in the East End of London, and Friday (1972) found none of the American models to be applicable to Sweden. However, more generalized theories such as Sutherland's differential association model did find some basic support in such diverse cultural contexts as Ghana (Weinberg, 1964), Sweden (Friday, 1972), Belgium (Junger-Tas, 1977), Mexico (Rosenquist and Megargee, 1969), and India (Rad, 1967). The result of attempts to verify the limited propositions was to reduce criminological theory to a set of diverse and often conflicting probability statements which lacked integration and synthesis or widespread applicability.

While Americans struggled with the applicability of their models abroad, European scholars, in developing their own legalistic and systems models of analysis, rejected the search for cause as futile and irrelevant. Törnudd (1971), for example, suggested the need to abandon "cause" and formulated research to provide estimates or predictions of fluctuations in the level of criminality or the process of selection within the criminal justice system.

Emerging from this development has been an emphasis on the study of crime and deviance within political, historical, and economic contexts. More explicitly, Phillipson (1971) suggests that, instead of looking for the causes of delinquency, one needs to look at the significance of the act. To him it becomes important to try to determine the process by which actors arrive at their specific conduct and the legal and structural determinants by which some actors are selected for legal sanction and others are not.

Comparative research is thus at a new point, in that it is sensitive to the failure of culture-bound theories to explain involvement, unwilling to accept as necessity the social psychological factors affecting individual pathology, and searching for more general structural and historical commonalities.

If criminology is to develop theory it needs to focus on *process,* not dichotomies or nominal legal classifications. Crime is not a dichotomy; it is not an either/or situation, it is not simply that a crime is committed or not committed. Instead, crime is an act which is a product of time and experience of the actor. It becomes necessary, then, to view the act in terms of its emergence, transmission, perpetuation, and modification within the historical context of the social system in which the actor lives. Comparative research within the context of the sociology of deviance returns criminology to analysis of "social facts" rather than "individual facts."

Delinquency Rates and Trends

The terms *juvenile delinquency* and *juvenile delinquent* are legal categories whose meaning and context vary considerably between and within societies. The terms are very much contingent upon the artificial age of responsibility. Legally, a juvenile is under 18 in parts of the United States, 15–17 in Sweden, 14–17 in England and Wales, and 14–20 in Japan. In Cuba the age of responsibility was reduced from 18 to 16 in 1973. One of the primary reasons for this was the belief that psychological maturity would be reached by age 15 and that the new economic conditions required 16-year-olds to assume adult responsibilities (Salas, 1978). In all societies juvenile delinquency tends to reflect special concerns. On the one hand, it represents society's failure to integrate, co-opt, or socialize its young into its accepted ways. On the other hand, it represents the failure of youth to live up to or abide by the idealized conception the society has of its young. Thus, delinquency tends to incorporate two different conceptualizations—violations of expectations held only for youth (status offenses) and violations of codified norms required for all members of society (crime).

It is not easy, therefore, to draw a clear international picture of the problem of youth crime and delinquency. While the Second United Nations Congress on the Prevention of Crime and the Treatment of Offenders recommended in 1960 that the meaning of juvenile delinquency be restricted as far as possible to violations of criminal law (Lopez-Rey, 1978), antisocial behavior of youth is often viewed as a precursor to more serious acts. Consequently, much of the available research tends to operationally define delinquency as youth crime, but draws etiological generalizations from prior antisocial activity.

In most parts of the world (and there are important exceptions) both delinquency and youth crime tend to show a rapid and systematic increase. The Council of Europe (1978) recently expressed concern over the increased criminal activity of youth and the trend in urban delinquency to manifest violent behavior, drugs, alcohol, and vandalism. Lopez-Rey (1978) conservatively estimates that on the average of 10 of every 100 young males commit at least one criminal offense between the ages of 15 and 20.

In Sweden, arrests of young persons aged 15 to 17 for serious crimes have increased nearly 10 times per 100,000 population since 1920 and an especially strong increase is evident since 1965 (Tham, 1978). In Israel the popular press reports an increase in juvenile arrests of about 25 percent over the past two years (Kotler, 1979), while other reports suggest an increasing concern with youth delinquency in the Soviet Union and China (Shipler, 1978; Butterfield, 1979). In Cuba it was estimated that by 1967 41 percent of all crimes were committed by minors (Salas, 1978). Even in Japan, where the general rate of crime is decreasing, those committed by 14 to 15-year-olds have increased (Clifford, 1976).

Not only has there been concern over the extent of youth involvement in crime, but also the age of peak involvement. Using official statistics, Sweden's peak age-group is 15–17 (Tham, 1978), while Sveri et al. (1966), utilizing records for the under-15 age-group, found the single most active age for registration of legal code violation was 14 years. This was reinforced recently by a self-report study of 519 school boys in Sweden. Ninety-six percent said they had committed at least one of twenty-two offenses, and the highest-risk age-group was 13–15 (Olofsson, 1976). In an older cohort study in Norway, Christie (1960) found initial registration to be within the 14 to 17-year-old group. Even between the 1960s and 1970s the age of peak involvement in Scandinavia appeared to be declining. In Montreal it was found to be around 13–15 (Frechette and Le-Blanc, 1978), but this varies with whether the acts being considered are status offenses or statutory violations. There is some indication, however, that the peak age varies with the legal school-leaving age (McKissach, 1973).

In general, delinquency and crime have statistically increased with urbanization and industrialization. While this generalization varies by the type of crime, time, and social conditions of the larger society, the association is found more frequently than not.

In studies in the United States and abroad (in Iowa in 1942 and Sweden in 1960), Clinard (1974) found that the greater the degree of urbanism in a community, the higher the rate of property offenses. In the United States there has been a significant positive relationship between city size and violence (Barlow, 1978). The pattern has been demonstrated in studies worldwide: it is seen in the United States (Clinard, 1974), in industrialized Europe (Christiansen, 1960; Mościskier, 1969; Szabo, 1960), the Far East (Lopez-Rey, 1978; United Nations, 1958), Latin America (Hauser, 1960), and Africa (Clifford, 1964; Clinard and Abbott, 1973).

Important exceptions to this pattern are evident, however. Japan reports a steady decrease in juvenile involvement in crime (Ministry of

Justice, 1970) and studies of youth crime in the German Democratic Republic also show a steady decline and a substantially lower rate than in the Federal Republic of Germany (Freiburg, 1975). Poland is another country where the rate of delinquency is seen to be declining (Mościskier, 1976). Between 1960 and 1974 there has been nearly a twofold decrease in crime in Poland both in the country and in the towns (Michalski, 1976). However, with Poland the urban centers still have slightly higher rates characterized by property-type offenses. The rate of delinquency convictions between 1971 and 1973 in Warsaw, for example, was 128.6 per 10,000 inhabitants between the ages of 10 and 16, while the average for all towns was only 89.5 (Kossowska, 1976). Gödöny (1976), after reviewing the industrial growth and urban migration patterns in the socialist countries, concluded that the number of criminal offenses dropped by 7 to 13 percent. Looking at trends, he concludes:

> Whereas for the Western countries the high rates of delinquency and the rapidly growing trend of delinquency are characteristic, in the socialist countries even the relatively lower rates of delinquency and delinquency as a whole tend to decrease. (Gödöny, 1976:98)

In the Ivory Coast where urban development has been especially pronounced, Brillon (1973) demonstrated that despite a 24 to 31 percent increase in the urban population, there has not been a noticeable increase in general crime. LeBlanc (1977) indicated that delinquency in Quebec, after an enormous increase at the end of the 1960s, decreased or at least stabilized.

The different conclusions about the association between delinquency and urbanization on the one hand and industrialization on the other are significant. They suggest that what has often been taken as a universal law (cause) of crime has meaningful variances. However, these conclusions are based on statistics, and anyone who has worked with statistics realizes the difficulty inherent in comparing rates between countries. Such statistics are based on different legal definitions, arrest priorities and procedures, as well as different national characteristics. For this reason, the statistics themselves are less important than the trends they reflect. In this sense there *is* a difference in delinquency between societies which cannot be understood independently of the structure of the state, and especially the role of youth in the society.

The Role and Status of Youth

From a sociological perspective, then, it is important to look at the dynamics of the urban-industrial condition as it affects youth development in crime. Much of the difference between societies is reflected in the relative position on both the degree of urbanization and the level of industrialization. Christiansen (1976) suggests that while Japan has demonstrated a steady growth in the proportion of the population living in urban areas, it has not shown the development of urbanism or the urban way of life characterized by impersonality and anonymity. This he asserts is a primary factor in the lower rates of delinquency and crime.

Since urbanization and industrialization are in some way associated with crime, and since the conventional crime that does occur in these areas is disproportionately committed by the young males of the population, what, if any, factors are involved? To answer this question one must first deal with the changing status of youth in industrial societies. For while many of the traditional theories of crime and delinquency have focused on the individual, a more fruitful approach would be to assess the process by which the urban-industrial society differentially affects the probability of youths committing criminal acts.

Looking at the role and role expectations of youth, there has been a marked change in the attitudes toward children and their role as well

as toward the perception of the role of the state in dealing with them since the middle of the nineteenth century. As the industrial economies develop, age in and of itself becomes a central factor. If one were to classify societies according to technological development or level of industrialization, there would clearly be seen a gradual extension of the period of time considered "youth" or childhood.

In the early stages of industrial development, youths, like women, play important economic roles; their labor is vital. But production can develop only to a certain level before a reduction in the labor force, and especially the unskilled, is required (Bell, 1973). To incorporate everyone into the labor force would result in a tremendous increase in production, production which in turn would require consumption. It is not clear if any single society can consume all it is capable of producing. In addition, increasing industrialization brings increased levels of technical competence required for participation in the economy.

The result of this is the systematic (though not necessarily conscious) exclusion of youth, women, the aged, and at times minorities from participation in the core activities of the society—work. During the Industrial Revolution in Western Europe women and children were "protected" by law from the burden of manual labor. This, in essence, isolated them from primary involvement in the society as a whole. In the United States many child labor laws and compulsory education laws were passed between 1870 and 1920. These had an effect on youths' commitments to the system itself. After the Depression the teenage labor force further decreased and the school-leaving age was increased (Greenberg, 1977). While exemption from hard labor may be considered benevolent, it may also be considered a mechanism of restricting access to the rewards of the society.

With the change in economic level also came a change in the age distribution of crime. During the nineteenth century in the United States when the peak age was higher than at present, criminal involvement tended to decline with age (Greenberg, 1977). Peak age for official contact in nineteenth-century Europe showed higher rates for agrarian countries than for industrialized England (Tobias, 1967). More recent data suggest the same decline in age with economic development (McClintock et al., 1968; Lopez-Rey, 1970).

Simultaneous with the development of the principle of exclusion based on age came an ideology of youth with slogans such as "Youth are our most valuable asset." The result was the development of status offenses which tended to reify the ideal behavior of youth. Consequently, the concern with delinquency per se tends to center the cause of crime on the psychological and interpersonal dynamics of the child rather than the structural conditions surrounding his exclusion from full participation in the society. By making delinquency an all-embracing concept with arbitrary age limits below which a person is assumed to lack maturity, rationality, or social responsibility, theories of delinquency tend to focus on individual pathology. Review of the age limits used to define delinquency shows the internationally pervasive influence of a variety of theories of psychological and physical development. Consequently, the upper age limit of 18 has been adopted by countries as diverse as Sweden, Turkey, Ghana, Iran, Switzerland, Colombia, Malaysia, France, and Mexico.

The upper limits of delinquency reflect an extension of childhood into what has commonly been referred to as adolescence. During this period of time youths are expected to acquire the educational prerequisites to integration into the economic system and are excluded primarily on the basis of age. As Christie (1975) points out, in industrial societies youngsters are becoming older. The consequence of this is an increased segregation by age and a systematic isolation from the mainstream of the society, particularly work, and subsequently a greater involvement in and adherence to subgroups or countercultures. This isolation increases the risk for conflicts with the formal system of control.

When socially integrated, one develops commitments to the status quo. As Durkheim (1933:401) suggested,

The individual becomes cognizant of his dependence upon society; from it come the forces which keep him in check and restrain him. In short since the division of labor becomes the chief source of social solidarity, it becomes at the same time the foundation of the moral order.

The nature of the work and the ability of the work situation to facilitate meaningful relationships are crucial.

Work, having a job, and earning an income are important parts of male social identity. Preparing for a technical career may be a structural equivalent to being employed, but being in school simply because it is required is not. It is this loss of work, defined as being unemployed or seeing no future potential for work, that probably most deeply affects the adolescent's sense of powerlessness (Marwell, 1966).

The impact of the work situation on delinquent behavior is illustrated by a study of the stages of industrialization in Poland (Mościskier, 1969). While industrialization per se did not affect delinquency rates, certain stages of industrial development—such as rapid growth and mobility in the development of the work situation—temporarily facilitated delinquency, while in situations where youths were part of the workers' councils and developed what is referred to as socialist social relations, delinquency rates did not increase.

The importance of the work situation for youths is also seen in studies from Japan. Kiefer (1970:71) concluded that

responsible behavior is secured in Japan by developing the allegiance of the individual to the work group in such a way as to legitimate its disciplinary claims on him and intensify his feelings of obligation not to offend against it.

Since the work group seems to dominate personal life in Japan, criminality is reduced to the extent that one is integrated behaviorally into the group.

The relationship of youth to employment patterns has been shown in a variety of countries. Unemployment has been shown to correlate highly with delinquency. Hellberg (1977) suggests that in Sweden youth unemployment, criminality, school problems, and alcohol and narcotic problems show a parallel increase over the years. Most notably has been the increase in youth unemployment. In the fall of 1977, 40,000 youth were unemployed (Hellberg, 1977); by August 1978 the figure had increased to 64,000 (*Aftonbladet,* 1978). While the society as a whole has made considerable technological and social progress, the young have seemed to be left behind or isolated (Daun et al., 1974). In Sweden Toby (1967) also emphasized the economic relations, as has Christie (1975) in Norway.

Sveri (1978) suggests that during the 1930s youths of 14 or 15 who finished the folk-school classes of study went directly into the labor market, helped support their families, and naturally grew into the adult role. Rapid industrialization after World War II changed the economic prerequisites, requiring longer periods of time in training, so that today in Sweden only a fraction of the youth under 18 are in the labor force. He suggests that youths in such an industrial society have become "tolerated parasites."

This economic isolation has in essence lengthened childhood to the point that the social realities of integration are in conflict with the individual's physical and psychological development.

Bottoms and McClintock (1973), in an extensive assessment of the institutional adoption of adolescent offenders in England, concluded that 40 percent of the offenders had records of lengthy periods of unemployment while others had intermittent and unstable work patterns. Interestingly, violent offenders had more stable work records than property offenders. Soviet researchers suggest that unemployed youths are twenty-four times more likely than secondary school students to be convicted of an offense (Gertsenzon, 1976).

Throughout Western Europe, youth unemployment has become a major problem. Figures from the nine Common Market nations show approximately 1.8 million jobless youths; they make up 37 percent of all unemployed in the region. In Britain the figure is 35 percent, 37.6 percent for France, and in Italy youth unemployment is estimated to be between 65 and 80 percent (*Time,* 1977).

In West Africa unemployment and crime is described by Brillon (1973) within the context of education. He states,

After very little schooling, the young people from the countryside flock to the cities. Since they are not sufficiently trained to take on a well-paying job, they merely swell the ranks of the unemployed, and hence find themselves in a highly criminogenic situation. (1973:22)

The meaning of the unemployment statistics and the general pattern in Western Europe to extend adolescence is the creation of extended periods of leisure for youth. In Belgium, Racine (1966) found that the role of increased leisure in juvenile delinquency is inseparable from the problems of education, mental hygiene, and social integration. This study suggests that purely restrictive measures to combat delinquency which do not account for leisure needs are dubious. Junger-Tas' (1977) study in Belgium found leisure time variables highly (and statistically significantly) related to delinquency. Most important were spending free time with delinquent friends, spending free time away from home, and feelings of boredom.

Within the Soviet Union there is a conscious attempt to deal with the problems of increasing leisure. These include after-hours music schools, chess clubs, and hobby centers with supervised model building, chemistry experiments and photography. However, these formal activities appear insufficient, as evidenced by news accounts of youths wasting time at restaurants and in impromptu groups in building entrances (Shipler, 1977).

The variance in patterns of youth crime and delinquency reflect less the absolute change in industrialization and urbanization than the internal mechanisms to reduce the isolation of youth and in turn create attachments to the established system.

Social Institutions and Delinquency

The social isolation of youth is not simply a function of the individual's personal desires or even the economic system. It is a function of the integrating institutions in the society to effectively co-opt youth. The bulk of the literature on delinquency tends to look at it in relation to specific social institutions such as the family, school, or community activity.

Family and Delinquency

The family is considered important because of its early socialization role in shaping values, morality, and, consequently, behavior. The family has almost exclusive contact with children when they are most dependent and influenced, and has continued intimate contact over a subsequent period of several years. It is the first social institution to affect behavior and to provide knowledge of and access to the goals, means, and social expectations of the wider society. But there may be deficiencies in the integration process between parent and child so that the child fails to learn appropriate behaviors (Bredemeier and Stephenson, 1962:126). On the other hand, socialization may be inadequate for dealing with societal expectations, as youths often do not learn clear definitions of appropriate norms (Toby, 1974).

Homes from which delinquent children come are frequently characterized by one or more of the following conditions: (1) other members of the family are criminalistic, immoral, or alcoholic; (2) one or both parents are absent by reason of death, divorce, or desertion; (3) there is a lack of parental control because of ignorance, indifference, or illness; (4) home uncongeniality exists, as evidenced by domination by one member, favoritism, oversolicitude, overseverity, neglect, jealousy, crowded housing conditions, or interfering relatives; (5) religious or other cultural differences, or differences in conventions and standards are present; (6) economic difficulties exist, such as unemployment, poverty, both parents working, or poor arrangement of financial affairs (Davies and Day, 1974).

The family may affect crime directly by imparting delinquent behavior. MacKay and McDonald in *Brothers in Crime* (1966) indicated that older siblings taught younger ones to steal. The Gluecks (1950) found that 70 percent of their delinquents had at least one parent with a criminal record. According to the Gluecks, drunkenness, crime, or immorality was found in 90 percent of the homes of delinquents but in only 54 percent of the control group. The McCords found that the sons of offenders had higher rates of criminality than the sons of others (McCord and McCord, 1958).

After looking at family structure and delinquency in England, Wilson (1975) found delinquency correlated with parental criminality. Children whose parents were major offenders had about twice the offense rate of those from families where the parents had no record or had only committed minor violations. Farrington et al. (1975) specifically studied the familial transmission of criminality. They searched for the records of nearly four hundred males born in 1951 and found that nearly half of the boys with criminal fathers had records, while less than one-fifth of those without criminal fathers had records. Viewed another way, of the criminal fathers, 62.8 percent had one or more delinquent sons, whereas only 27 percent of the noncriminal fathers had delinquent sons (Farrington et al., 1975). This study also revealed that certain families were criminogenic. Eleven percent of the families studied accounted for almost half of all convictions within the four hundred families studied. Regardless of family size, Farrington and his associates concluded, the risk of an individual acquiring a criminal record increases considerably if another member of the family has a conviction. In Poland, 31 percent of the fathers of delinquents were considered to be themselves delinquent, while 9 percent of the mothers were suspected of prostitution (Strzembosz, 1974).

The probability of recidivism is also substantially increased (Farrington et al., 1975; Buikhuisen and Hoekstra, 1974) if family members have criminal careers. Severy (1973) studied delinquent and law-abiding high school students over a four-year period. Among these youths, if there had been low exposure in early years to the deviance of family members, greater exposure during adolescence led to increasing deviance. On the other hand, when family exposure had originally been high, increasing exposure led to rejection of delinquency.

Other perspectives dealing with the family and crime have stressed the role of the "broken home." In a controversial study, the Gluecks (1950) concluded that such a family pattern was a major cause of delinquency. Several studies have tended to confirm this conclusion, but others have suggested that the broken home is but one of a number of variables that act together to generate illegal conduct. Studies demonstrating a relationship between broken homes and delinquency may be biased, since most have sampled only lower-class delinquents. On the other hand, Toby (1957) found the broken home to be more significant if the family controls were traditionally strong; if family controls were weak, the broken homes had little direct effect.

As early as 1929, Burt found no difference between delinquent and nondeliquent groups as a result of the father's death, but was of the opinion that divorce, separation, and desertion had a marked influence on delinquency. Subsequent research conducted during the decades of 1950 and 1960 revealed that while the broken

home played a major role in delinquency, the effect differed considerably among children. In the working class, the effect was greater than in other social classes, and it was also greater for girls than boys.

In Norway, Christie (1960) studied all males born in 1933 and found that 5 percent had become registered offenders by 1958. Comparing home structure for offenders and others, he found that the home was broken 17 and 13 percent of the time, respectively, a difference which is not statistically significant. From this, one would conclude that broken homes are not necessarily linked with delinquency for adolescent males. Another study in Sweden showed a positive relationship between broken homes and delinquency only among working-class boys where other criminogenic factors were also present (Olofsson, 1971). The differential effect on females was investigated by Monahan (1957), who found that broken homes appeared to have a greater effect in generating delinquency for females and for blacks than for white males.

The structure and interaction patterns of the home are considered important factors in determining how conducive the family is to crime. West's (1969) study in Britain found that boys from backgrounds which investigators characterized as "socially handicapped" (that is, poor income, poor housing, large family, or welfare support), were more likely to be in trouble. Although these families comprised only one-eighth of the study population, they included half of the boys with "unstable" mothers, nearly half of those coming from homes with "lax rules," and over one-fourth of the homes with marital disharmony (1969:136). In Nigeria, Oloruntimehin (1973) confirmed the importance of the family interaction patterns. She found a statistically significant relationship between delinquency and the "cordiality" between parent and child. In essence, cordiality is affection and interaction which directly affects the youth's self-concept and willingness to use parental figures as role models. Likewise, Bottoms and McClintock (1973) found familial conflict in 74 percent of the serious delinquents they studied.

In general, the family may have a positive impact in insulating individuals from criminal patterns, providing it retains its ability to control rewards and effectively maintain positive attachments within the family unit. Commitments to family, or what Hirschi (1969) calls attenuated attachments, reduce the probabilities of involvement in acts of deviance. Research by Hindelang (1973) reaffirms the importance of family interaction and attachment. Delinquency is highest when family interaction and controls are weak (Rodman and Grams, 1967). Some parents do not supervise their children's recreational activities, do not enforce bedtimes, and do not perform activities as a group with their children or even eat meals together with them (Nye, 1958). For the delinquent, it is a life free of restraint, but also without guidance. Studies have shown that these weak controls and low-frequency interaction patterns are more common in low-income and ethnic minority families (Lewis, 1965). Vaz and Casparis (1971) reached a similar conclusion in their comparison of Canadian and Swiss youth. They indicate that the Canadian sample tended to be more peer-oriented and also more deviant, while the Swiss favored their parents and engaged in fewer criminal acts. Further, the Swiss boys interacted more frequently with adults than with their peers.

Kobal (1965), studying delinquency in Yugoslavia and England, concluded that there tended to be more openness and communication and general contacts between youth and adults in Slovenia than in London.

Clinard and Abbott (1973) found crime rates higher in Africa in areas less likely to have stable family relationships. A report on living conditions of delinquents, prepared by the criminological institute at Ljubljana, Yugoslavia, states that one of the characteristics of families producing juvenile delinquents is a lack of emotional ties between parents. Mack-

owiak and Ziembinski report a study in Poland which stressed the importance of socially positive role models (1971:27), and Bandura and Walters (1963) in the United States reported that behavior copying is more frequent when a positive relationship exists.

The importance of family role models and behavior modeling can be seen in the effects of migration in Israel (Schichor and Kirschenbaum, 1977). When a family migrates and the father, because of lack of skills, is unable to find employment consistent with his status in his home country, his status and image within the family is seen to suffer and with it control over children. This condition was seen in Israel to operate particularly in families migrating from Moslem countries. This disintegration of the family means a reduction in the parents' ability to effectively control the behavior of their children. The Soviets, subscribing to the importance of family control, attribute 80 percent of the juvenile problems to a lack of supervision by parents (Juviler and Forschner, 1978).

The family is thus seen as important as an immediate origin of crime; not because it causes crime per se, but because relationships within the family effectively influence the exposure and importance of other norm-defining reference groups. The important point of these studies, and the issue stressed by Friday and Hage (1976), is that isolation from the family is likely to increase the child's associations with peers and/or deviant associations.

Schools and Crime

In our highly technical, industrial society, education and schools play a key role in determining the eventual placement of the individual in society. In terms of length and intensity of exposure, education is considered, next to the family, the major force shaping youths' lives. The most general societal function of schools is to transmit knowledge, norms, and values along with their orientational and motivational underpinnings (Clausen, 1968:

153). In essence, Durkheim maintained that the school functions as the primary regulator of moral education for a nation and that it is "the sole moral environment where the child can learn methodically to know and to love" (1963:67).

Domestic and international literature are replete with references to and analysis of the relationship between school performance and crime. As a primary socializing agent, school can have a positive or negative impact on youths. At its best, it can work to counteract a harmful family situation. At its worst, it can act as a stumbling block for those who have had a positive upbringing.

Studies have shown that low achievement in school is directly related to delinquent behavior (Empey and Lubeck, 1971; Gold, 1963; Polk and Halferty, 1966; Polk and Schafer, 1972; Reckless and Dinitz, 1972). Low achievers are prone to feel themselves outsiders, which in turn can decrease the probability of meaningful relationships and informal controls within the school (Olofsson, 1971). Delinquency was uniformly low among boys of all social classes who were doing well in school, while it was uniformly high among those doing poorly. In another study, Elliot and Voss (1974) found the school to be the most critical institution in affecting patterns of delinquent behavior. In Ghana, Weinberg (1964) found that 83 percent of the male delinquents who had been enrolled in school did poorly and were frequently truant. At times the truancy preceded the delinquency; at other times it was concomitant with the total pattern of behavior.

Studies elsewhere show a similar pattern. The Ministry of Interior in Cuba found that 90 percent of the juvenile offenders in juvenile homes were more than three academic grades behind their peers. These studies found school truancy and poor performance to be closely related to all forms of antisocial acts (Salas, 1978). Statistics from Poland show the same pattern. As many as half of the one hundred boys aged 10 to 11 charged with theft were poor academically. At least 36 percent were

poor readers and 80 percent of them were considered by teachers to be "difficult pupils" (Zabczynska, 1974). Seventy-seven percent of older youths who were delinquent were at least two years behind their peers in academic performance (Strzembosz, 1974).

Such statistics, however, do not demonstrate a causal relationship. Failure at school is often interpreted as a failure of the pupil to respond. However, it could also be interpreted as a failure of the school to stimulate interest and develop a commitment to conformity.

School performance is dependent both upon the home and the neighborhood from which children come to school and upon the way they are treated once they get there, as well as individual talents and innate abilities and temperaments. Recent teacher-writers argue that lower-class "culturally disadvantaged" children are eager to learn and are excited by the initial experience of school, but that the schooling process, reliance on IQ tests that are social-class biased, "tracking," and the physical conditions of the school and the attitudes of teachers soon deplete the initial motivation.

Schafer and Polk (1967), in a report for the Presidential Task Force on Delinquency and Youth Crime, comment that "delinquent commitments result in part from adverse or negative school experiences" and that there are "fundamental defects within the education system, especially as it touches lower-income youth" that contribute to delinquency. Students who fail are progressively excluded by individual teachers and by other achieving students. Failure and rejection in turn make the school experience increasingly unsatisfying and frustrating.

Brusten (1974) suggests from his research in Germany that the system of tracking, in a sense, establishes a class system within a school. The ability and behavior of a child are to a certain extent determined by his social background and family class position. The school, on the other hand, represents middle-class values; and it is on these that students are evaluated. Middle-class values carry with them certain expectations of those from lower social classes; that is, teachers might expect lower-class youths to underachieve and exhibit deviant behavior (Hackler, 1971; Brusten, 1974). The result is that youths from lower social classes will end up in lower tracks which provide fewer opportunities for achievement. Those in lower tracks are likely to perceive themselves as underachievers. This has a large impact on the self-concept of students in these tracks.

School performance and delinquency cannot be viewed independently of the role youths are expected to play. School is the place where the problems of status and competition are visible for this crime-prone age-group. Problems in school may be seen as a continuation of the problem created by extending the period of adolescence and keeping youths out of the labor force.

The effects of competition and strain in school on delinquency are shown in a study by Elliot (1966). He hypothesized that if school adjustment and experience are causally related to delinquency, then the latter will be lower among out-of-school than in-school youths. His findings indicate that the highest delinquency rate was among lower-SES dropouts *prior* to their leaving school (1966). He also found that the same boys had the *lowest* rate after dropping out of school. Their out-of-school rate was less than one-third their in-school rate. Elliot thus concluded that the school experience contributed to and sustained delinquency. The same conclusion was reached in New Zealand; McKissach (1973) postulated that the age variations in the level of property theft parallel the school-leaving age. Delinquency is tied to "life-style" needs legitimately unattainable while in school. As the school-leaving age is raised, the probability of delinquency in the final compulsory year is also raised.

The impact of increased educational requirements to meet the technological demands of the industrial state is clearly seen in the problems faced by the emerging states in Africa. Cusson (1972) states:

The rapid development of the school, made necessary to prepare the youth to live in a modern society, is not without its drawbacks. Many are the young people who fail in school and who must abandon their studies. These children run the risk of becoming socially maladjusted on two counts: they are unable to adapt to the traditional life of the village because the school gave them other aspirations, and they cannot adapt to the demands of modern life because they are inadequately prepared. (1972:51)

Even in the villages, the school may not be the integrating force it is expected to be. Brillon (1973:13) states:

In the Villages, the school often indirectly plays a negative role, in that it widens the cultural gap that separates the young generation from the old, and also tends to uproot the child from his milieu. On the one hand, the children believe less and less in "fetishes," that is, the ancient customs, beliefs and values, and on the other hand, as soon as they have acquired a modicum of schooling, they refuse to do any manual or farm labour.

The school is seen internationally as an important factor in delinquency causation, since it is both a socializing and integrating element and ultimately the source of economic rewards. A person's anticipation of success in either deviant or conforming activities is in part a function of the degree of prior success. Rewards for conforming behavior in school compete with rewards for deviant activities, and often a child can more realistically anticipate deriving feelings of competence, self-esteem, and support from delinquent peers than from conforming adults. If rewards are greater out of school, truancy will increase. The interaction process and reward structure in school are therefore critical in understanding delinquency and help to explain why truancy is one of the best statistical predictors of later delinquency (Glaser, 1962).

Underlying Dimensions of Delinquency

Whether one discusses youth unemployment, the school, or family conditions as a precipitator of delinquency, the issue ultimately involves the position or role of youth. For delinquency is a temporary condition and there is reason to suggest that youths "outgrow" it as they find stable roles in the wider society. Sveri (1978) suggests that in Sweden the peak of criminal activity has already ended during the ages 16 to 18. Frechette and LeBlanc (1978) reached a similar conclusion from their study in Montreal; they found that only about 13 percent of their sample seemed to be capable of maintaining a significant pattern of delinquency over time. This longitudinal study suggests that few youths maintain their delinquent behavior over time.

The temporary nature of delinquency tends to correspond with the ability of the wider social structure to effectively integrate the young people. Delinquency tends to depend upon the manner in which young persons assume the statuses available to them (LeBlanc et al., 1978). That is, if positive or conforming roles are available through work, family, or school, the saliency of isolated peers is reduced (Friday and Hage, 1976).

Employment, school, family, and peers should not be considered independent factors in the causation of crime. Each contributes to a process which increases the probability that a given individual will engage in crime. The process involves the development of commitments to deviant versus normative patterns and to the groups that transmit those patterns. Hirschi (1969:200) argues that attachment to parents generates a wider concern for the approval of other authority figures and ultimately a belief that societal norms bind one's conduct. Hindelang (1973) empirically demonstrates an inverse relationship between attachments to parents, teachers, school, and school-related activities on the one hand and delinquency on the other. Attachment to peers, however, is related directly to involvement in crime. In essence, this is what Sutherland's differential association theory implies: delinquency increases with isolation from conventional norms. When isolation, rejections, and alienation decrease, there is a general reduction in

criminality. Karacki and Toby (1962) indicate that lack of commitment to the adult way of life is at the root of delinquency. When they examined the shift of many delinquent gang members of law-abiding behavior, it appeared that these erstwhile delinquents tended to be boys who had moved from participation in the youth culture to adult roles and who successfully returned to school or work. Akers (1973) contends that a lack of attachment to conventionality means that youths are isolated from or unable to obtain sufficient rewards for conformity in the family, school, and peer groups. The lack of ties with major socializing institutions is seen to precede deviance.

Friday and Hage (1976) suggest that the family, school, community, work, and peer group interactions must be considered as a whole or totality rather than as independent factors. In so doing, the types of activities and groups tend to reinforce conforming norms. Integration is fostered when individuals interacting within a role set (such as the school) know individuals from another role set (such as the community). This tends to increase interdependence and conformity. In other words, the greater youths' meaningful or significant role relationships within all integrating institutions (family, school, community, work), the less the probability of their becoming involved in crime (Friday and Hage, 1976). Thus, it is not the significance of being unemployed, out of school, or having a broken home, but the number and importance of compensating relationships. In this sense, the important factor is not only the socialization of norms, but the controls facilitated by interaction in a variety of overlapping role sets.

The degree of overlap in relationship is a function of community. Clinard (1953) discusses the importance of neighborhood or community to integration. He refers to communicative integration as the extent to which contacts permeate the group. Neighborhood integration is seen to operate on both individual and organizational levels. On the individual level, integration involves the extent to which relationships are limited to the community, that is, across role sets—the commitments individuals have to others in the community, and the number of acquaintances one has in the community. These community relationships decrease as family and school relationships become more alienating or as they disappear due to migration. In Africa, Clinard and Abbott (1973) found the low-crime area of their study to have less mobility, more tribal homogeneity, more visiting of relatives, more stable family relationships, and less individual isolation than in the high-crime area. The study suggests that internal and overlapping relations within the local community are more important with respect to norm adherence than integration into the wider society. Relationships, then, tend to have a structural basis.

Another example of the importance of looking at the integrating function across sets of relationships rather than simply within the school, family, or community comes from Israel. Schichor and Kirschenbaum (1977) reviewed delinquency patterns in "new" towns where the majority of residents were immigrants to Israel after 1968. They found four major variables to explain best the differential rates of crime: extent of unemployment, quality of elementary education, year the settlement was founded, and proportion of natives born in the town. The authors suggest an explanation that confirms Clinard's findings and supports the overlapping role thesis: The more isolated the community and the more socially cohesive and more integrated the diverse socializing institutions, the more informal social control there appears to be.

Dizon (1978) in the Philippines tested the importance of overlapping role relationships. Using several measures of integration, he found that the less youngsters were integrated in the family, the school, and work situation, the higher they scored on frequency and seriousness of self-reported offenses. Youngsters with delinquent friends reported more as well as more serious offenses than those without such friends. In the Philippines peer attach-

ment had a significant inverse relationship with adult attachment or involvement in other roles. In Belgium Junger-Tas (1977) also found a lack of social integration in such important subsystems as the family and the school, which seemed to lead to attachment to other marginals, who then tended to support and reinforce deviant norms.

Other studies have also supported the thesis that the pattern of interaction across socializing institutions is as significant as the pattern within any single structure. Shoham et al. (1970) found the length of stay in Israel to be significantly more highly associated with delinquency than urban-rural differences. This implies that the shorter the stay, the less is the likelihood of integration into diverse social groups. Weinberg (1964) concluded that the extracultural effects of family, school, and peers were effectively interrelated in Ghana. The study found that not only did delinquents experience more familial stress than nondelinquents, but they were also more alienated at school and isolated from other community or integrating activities.

Factors facilitating overlapping role sets must not be viewed as a function of the individual, but a product of the wider political, economic, and demographic societal characteristics. Rahav (1978) conducted an ecological study of delinquency in Israel and found that the major explanatory variable was the number of youths in a particular community. This suggests that a "critical mass" is needed before the development of the process which led to the formation of subcultures of youth. The study concludes:

Delinquency, as a systematic response to structural strains, appears only when the local juvenile groups is large enough to develop a delinquent subculture. When the group is too small social control is too tight to allow any systematic deviation. (Rahav, 1978:14)

The implication of this finding is that the larger the cohort of juveniles, the less the probability that any one group—work, school, or community—can integrate individuals or in turn provide consistent reinforcement of norms or overlapping social controls. The crime rate in turn will vary by the amount of time required before all of the members of the large cohort can become part of integrated role sets. Thus, cessation of criminal activity most frequently corresponds in time to the development of employment, marriage, and other social responsibilities. Even large cohorts of youth may be easily integrated if the economic and social conditions of a society are in a growth phase. One subsequently finds lower rates of criminality under such conditions, as is evident in many of the socialist countries; that is, when either the economic or social conditions absorb rather than isolate youths. When segregated from meaningful participation and a variety of responsible roles, youths will tend to deviate.

Criminality is not reduced simply by the formation of attachments to a given set of relationships, but by a function of the interaction of attachment and control by the overlap of groups themselves. Internationally, then, when delinquency and youth crime are high, youths tend to have an isolated pattern of role relationships which is created and fostered by external, structural conditions in the society.

Note

* From *Crime and Deviance! A Comparative Perspective,* edited by Graeme R. Newman (Vol. 4 of Sage Publications' *Annual Review of Studies in Deviance* Series; Beverly Hills: Sage Publications, 1980, 100–129), by permission of the author and Sage Publications. Copyright 1980 by Sage Publications.

References

Aftonbladet. 1978. August 18: 1.

Akers, R. 1973. *Deviant Behavior: A Social Learning Approach.* Belmont, CA: Wadsworth.

Bandura, A., and R. A. Walters. 1963. *Social Learning and Personality Development.* New York: Holt, Rinehart and Winston.

Barlow, H. D. 1978. *Introduction to Criminology.* Boston: Little, Brown.

Bell, D. 1973. *The Coming of Postindustrial Society: A Venture in Social Forecasting.* New York: Basic Books.

Bottoms, A. E., and F. H. McClintock. 1973. *Criminals Coming of Age.* London: Heinemann.

Bredemeier, H. C., and R. M. Stephenson. 1962. *The Analysis of Social Systems.* New York: Holt, Rinehart and Winston.

Brillon, Y. 1973. "The Evolution of Crime in the Ivory Coast," in *Urban and Rural Crime and Its Control in West Africa.* Abidjan: Abidjan Institute of Criminology.

Brusten, M. 1974. "Soziale Schichtung, selbstberichtete delinquenz und prozesse der stigmatisierung in der schule." *Criminologisches Journal* 6: 29–46.

Buikhuisen, W., and H. A. Hoekstra. 1974. "Factors Related to Recidivism." *British Journal of Criminology* 14: 63–69.

Burt, C. 1929. *The Young Delinquent.* London: University of London Press.

Butterfield, F. 1979. "Peking Is Troubled about Youth Crimes." *New York Times* March 11: 13.

Christiansen, K. O. 1960. "Industrialization and Urbanization in Relation to Crime and Juvenile Delinquency." *International Review of Criminal Policy* 16: 3–8.

———. 1976. "Industrialization, Urbanization and Crime," pp. 46–37 in *Crime and Industrialization.* Stockholm: Scandinavian Research Council for Criminology.

Christie, N. 1960. *Unge norske lovovertredere.* Oslo: Universitetsforlaget.

———. 1975. *Hvor tett et samfunn?* Oslo: Universitetsforlaget.

Clausen, J. (ed.) 1968. *Socialization and Society.* Boston: Little, Brown.

Clifford, W. 1964. "Crime and Criminology in Central Africa," pp. 210–32 in T. Grygier, H. Jones, and J. C. Spender (eds.) *Criminology in Transition.* London: Tavistock.

———. 1976. *Crime Control in Japan.* Lexington, MA: D. C. Heath.

Clinard, M. B. 1953. "Urbanization and Crime," pp. 238–46 in C. B. Vedder (ed.) *Criminology: A Book of Readings.* New York: Drydon.

———. 1974. *The Sociology of Deviant Behavior.* New York: Holt, Rinehart and Winston.

———, and D. J. Abbott. 1973. *Crime in Developing Countries.* New York: John Wiley.

Council of Europe. 1978. *Information Bulletin on Legal Activities.* Strasbourg: Council of Europe (June).

Cusson, M. 1972. "Observations on the Problem of Juvenile Delinquency: The Case of Abidjan," pp. 49–66 in *First West African Conference in*

Comparative Criminology. Abidjan: Abidjan Institute of Criminology.

Daun, A., B. Borjesen, and S. Åhs. 1974. *Samhallsförändringar och brottslighet.* Stockholm: Folksam.

Davies, L., and E. C. Day. 1974. "The Criminal and Social Aspects of Families with a Multiplicity of Problems." *Australian and New Zealand Journal of Criminology* 7: 197–213.

DeFleur, L. B. 1969. "Alternative Strategies for the Development of Delinquency Theories Applicable to Other Cultures." *Social Problems* 17: 30–39.

Dizon, D. P. 1978. "Explaining Youth Crime: A Proposal for a Crosscultural Perspective." Presented at the World Congress of Sociology, Uppsala, Sweden, August.

Downes, D. 1966. *The Delinquent Solution.* New York: Free Press.

Durkheim, E. 1933. *The Division of Labor in Society* (George Simpson, trans.). New York: Free Press.

— — —. 1938. Les Regles de la methode sociologique (S. A. Solvay and J. H. Mueller, trans.), in G. E. G. Catlin (ed.) *The Rules of Sociological Method.* Chicago: University of Chicago Press.

— — —. 1963. *Education and Sociology.* New York: Free Press.

Elliot, D. S. 1966. "Delinquency, School Attendance and Dropouts." *Social Problems* 3: 307–14.

Elliot, D. S., and H. L. Voss. 1974. *Delinquency and Dropouts.* Lexington, MA: D. C. Heath.

Empey, L. T., and S. G. Lubeck. 1971. *Explaining Delinquency.* Lexington, MA: D. C. Heath.

Farrington, D. P., G. Gundry, and D. J. West. 1975. "The Familial Transmission of Criminality." *Medicine, Science and the Law* 15: 117–86.

Frechette, M., and M. LeBlanc. 1978. *La Delinquance Cachee des Adolescents Montrealais,* vol. 1. Montreal: G.R.S.I.J., University of Montreal.

Freiburg, A. 1975. "Zur jugendkriminalität in der DDR." Kölner Zeitschrift zur Soziologie und Sozialpsychologie 27: 489–537.

Friday, P. C. 1972. "La verifica delle teorie della struttura differenziale delle opportunità delle associazioni differenziali nella societa Svedese" (The applicability of differential opportunity and differential association theory in Sweden). *Quanderni di Criminologia Clinica* (September) 14: 279–304.

Friday, P. C., and J. Hage. 1976. "Youth Crime in Postindustrial Societies: An Integrated Perspective." *Criminology* 14: 347–68.

Gertsenzon, A. A. 1976. *Kriminologiia.* Moscow.

Glaser, D. 1962. "The Differential Association Theory of Crime," in A. M. Rose (ed.) *Human Behavior and Social Processes.* Boston: Houghton Mifflin.

Glueck, S., and E. Glueck. 1950. *Unraveling Juvenile Delinquency.* New York: Commonwealth Fund.

Gödöny, J. 1976. "Criminality in Industrialized Countries," pp. 91–109 in *Crime and Industrialization.* Stockholm: Scandinavian Research Council for Criminology.

Gold, M. 1963. *Status Forces in Delinquent Boys.* Ann Arbor: University of Michigan, Institute for Social Research, 1963.

Greenberg, D. 1977. "Delinquency and the Age Structure of Society." *Contemporary Crisis* 1: 189–223.

Hackler, J. C. 1971. "A Development Theory of Delinquency." *Canadian Review of Sociology and Anthropology* 8: 61–75.

Hauser, P. (ed.) 1960. *Urbanization in Latin America.* New York: International Documents Service, Columbia University Press.

Hellberg, I. 1977. "Ungdomsarbetslöshet och Kriminalitet." *Bra Apropa* No. 3: 3–10.

Hindelang, M. J. 1973. "Causes of Delinquency: A Partial Replication and Extension." *Social Problems* 20: 471–87.

Hirschi, T. 1969. *Causes of Delinquency.* Berkeley: University of California Press.

Junger-Tas, J. 1977. "Hidden Delinquency and Judicial Selection in Belgium," pp. 70–94 in P. C. Friday and V. L. Stewart (eds.) *Youth Crime and Juvenile Justice.* New York: Praeger.

Juviler, P., and B. E. Forschner. 1978. "Juvenile Delinquency and the Soviet Union" (unpublished).

Karacki, L., and J. Toby. 1962. "The Uncommitted Adolescent: Candidate for Gang Socialization," *Sociological Inquiry* 32: 203–15.

Kiefer, C. W. 1970. "The Psychological Interdependence of Family, School, and Bureaucracy in Japan." *American Anthropologist* 72: 66–75.

Kobal, M. 1965. *Delinquent Juveniles from Two Different Cultures.* Ljubljana: Reviga za Kriminalisto in Kriminologijo.

Kossowska, A. 1976. "Delinquency in the Warsaw Area," pp. 141–264 and 347–57 in *Polska Akademia Nauk. Archiwum Kryminologii* (vol. VII). Wroclaw: Zakland Narodowy im Ossolinskich.

Kotler, Y. 1979. "Israel's Juvenile Crime War." *Atlas World Press Review* (February): 53.

LeBlanc, M. 1977. *La Delinquance Juvenile au Quebec.* Montreal: Ministere des Affaires Sociales.

LeBlanc, M., L. Biron, G. Cote, and L. Pronovost. 1978. La delinquance juvenile: Son developpement en regard du developpement psychosocial durant l'adolescence. Montreal: Groupe de Recherce Sur L'Inadaptation Juvenile. (unpublished)

Lewis, H. 1965 "Child Rearing among Low Income Families," pp. 342–53 in L. A. Ferman, J. L. Kornbluh, and A. Harber (eds.) *Poverty in America: A Book of Readings.* Ann Arbor: University of Michigan Press.

Lopez-Rey, M. 1970. *Crime: An Analytical Appraisal.* London: Routledge and Kegan Paul.

———. 1978. "Youth and Crime in Contemporary and Future Society." UNAFEI Resource Material Series No. 14.

Mackay, H. D., and J. F. MacDonald. 1966. *Brothers in Crime.* Chicago: University of Chicago Press.

McCord, J., and W. McCord. 1958. "The Effects of Parental Role Model on Criminality." *Journal of Social Issues* 14: 66–75.

McLintock, F. H., N. H. Avison, and G. N. C. Rese. 1968. *Crime in England and Wales.* London: Heinemann.

McKissach, I. J. 1973. "Property Offending and the School Leaving Age." *International Journal of Criminology and Penology* 1: 353–26.

Mackowiak, P., and S. Ziembinski. 1971. "Social Aspects of Sources of Criminality and Its Prevention and Control." *International Review of Criminal Policy* 29: 25–31.

Marwell, G. 1966. "Adolescent Powerlessness and Delinquency." *Social Problems* 14: 35–47.

Michalski, W. 1976. "Phenomena in the Field of the Dynamics and Structure of Crime in Poland," pp. 129–35 in *Crime and Industrialization.* Stockholm: Scandinavian Studies in Criminology.

Ministry of Justice. 1970. *The Trends of Juvenile Delinquency and Procedures for Handling Delinquents in Japan.* Tokyo: Ministry of Justice.

Monahan, T. P. 1957. "Family Status and the Delinquent Child: A Reappraisal and Some New Findings." *Social Forces* 35: 250–58.

Mosćiskier, A. 1969. "Delinquency in Regions under Intensified Industrialization and the Relation between the Dynamics of Delinquency and the Dynamics of Socioeconomic Processes (1958–1960 and 1964–1968)." *Archives of Criminology* 4: 223–28.

———. 1976. "Delinquency in Poland and the Processes of Industrialization and Urbanization." *Polish Sociological Bulletin* 33: 53–63.

Nye, I. F. 1958. *Family Relationships and Delinquent Behavior.* New York: John Wiley.

Olofsson, B. 1971. *Vad var det vi sa!* Stockholm: Utbildningsforlaget.

———. 1976. "On Delinquency and Conformity among School Boys," pp. 1–15 in *National Council for Crime Prevention. Swedish Studies on Juvenile Delinquency.* Stockholm: Brottsforebyggande Radet.

Oloruntimehin, O. 1973. "A Study of Juvenile Delinquency in a Nigerian City." *British Journal of Criminology* 13: 157–69.

Phillipson, M. 1971. *Understanding Crime and Delinquency.* Chicago: AVC.

Polk, K., and D. Halferty. 1966. "Adolescence, Commitment and Delinquency." *Journal of Research in Crime and Delinquency* 3: 82–96.

Polk, K., and W. E. Schafer. 1972. *Schools and Delinquency.* Englewood Cliffs, NJ: Prentice-Hall.

Racine, A. 1966. "Role des loisirs dans l'etiologie de la delinquance juvenile," pp. 41–45 in *Loisirs et Delinquance Juvenile,* Publication No. 15. Bruxelles: Centre d'Etude de la Delinquance Juvenile.

Rad, S. V. 1967. *Facets of Crime in India.* Bombay: Allied.

Rahav, G. 1974. *Middle-Class Juvenile Delinquency in Israel.* Ann Arbor, MI: University Microfilms.

———. 1978. "Culture Conflict, Urbanization and Delinquency: An Ecological Study." Presented at the American Society of Criminology Meeting, Dallas, Texas, November.

Reckless, W., and S. Dinitz. 1972. *The Prevention of Juvenile Delinquency.* Chicago: University of Chicago Press.

Rodman, H., and P. Grams. 1967 "Juvenile Delinquency and the Family: pp. 188–221 in *LEAA U.S. Task Force Report: Juvenile Delinquency and Youth Crime.* Washington, DC: U.S. Government Printing Office.

Rosenquist, C. M., and E. I. Megagree. 1969. *Delinquency in Three Cultures.* Austin: University of Texas Press.

Salas, L. P. 1978. "Juvenile Delinquency in the Revolution: Cuba's Response." (unpublished)

Sarnecki, J. 1978. Vad skall vi gora at ungdomsbrottsligheten? *Bra Apropa,* No. 3.

Schafer, W. E., and K. Polk. 1967. "Delinquency and the Schools," pp. 227–77 in *LEAA Task Force Report: Juvenile Delinquency and Youth*

Crime. Washington, DC: U.S. Government Printing Office.

Severy, L. J. 1973. "Exposure to Deviance Committed by Valued Peer Groups and Family Members." *Journal of Research in Crime and Delinquency* 10: 35–46.

Schichor, D., and A. Kirschenbaum. 1977. "Juvenile Delinquency and New Towns: The Case of Israel," pp. 95–108 in P. C. Friday and V. L. Stewart (eds.) *Youth Crime and Juvenile Justice: International Perspectives.* New York: Praeger.

Shipler, D. K. 1977. "A Problem for Soviet's Young: What to Do with Leisure." *New York Times* December 16: A2.

———. 1978. "Rising Youth Crime in Soviet Troubles Regime and Public." *New York Times* March 5: 1.

Shoham, S., N. Shoham, and A. Abd-El-Razek. 1970. "Immigration, Ethnicity, and Ecology as Related to Juvenile Delinquency in Israel," pp. 77–97 in S. Shoham (ed.) *Israel Studies in Criminology,* vol. 1. Tel-Aviv: Gomeh Publishing.

Strzembosz, A. 1974. "Extent of Recidivism among Juvenile Delinquents and Their Later Careers," pp. 149–55 and 220–24 in *Polskiej Akademii Nauk, Archiwum Kryminologii,* vol. VI. Wroclaw: Zaklad Narodowy im Ossolinskich.

Sveri, K. 1978. "Ungdomsbrottsligheten i perspektiv." *Bra Apropa* No. 3: 30–36ff.

———, G. Rylander, T. Eriksson, and A. Asp. 1966. *Kriminaliteten och samhallet.* Stockholm: Aldus/Bonniers.

Szabo, D. 1960. *Crime et Villes: Etude Statistique de la Criminalite Rurale en France et en Belgique.* Paris: Editions Cujas.

Tham, H. 1978. "Ungdomsbrottsligheten engligt den officiella statistiken." *Bra Apropa,* No. 3.

Time. 1977. "Danger: Not Enough Young at Work." May 30: 64–65.

Tobias, J. J. 1967. *Crime in Industrial Society in the 19th Century.* London: B. J. Batsford.

Toby, J. 1957. "The Differential Impact of Family Disorganization." *American Sociological Review* 22: 505–12.

———. 1967. "Affluence and Adolescent Crime," pp. 136–37 in *LEAA U.S. Task Force Report: Juvenile Delinquency and Youth Crime.* Washington, DC: U.S. Government Printing Office.

———. 1974. "The Socialization and Control of Deviant Motivation," pp. 85–100 in D. Glaser (ed.) *Handbook of Criminology.* Chicago: Rand, McNally.

Törnudd, P. 1971. "The Futility of Searching for Causes of Crime," pp. 23–33 in N. Christie (ed.) *Scandinavian Studies in Criminology.* Oslo: Universitetsforlaget.

United Nations. 1958. *Urbanization in Asia and the Far East. Proceedings of the Joint U. N./UNESCO Seminar, Bangkok, August 8–18, 1956.* New York: United Nations—55.57.V7A.

———. 1966. Report on the Inter-regional Meeting on Research on Criminology: Denmark, Norway, Sweden, 18 July–7 August, 1965. New York: United Nations.

Vaz, E. W., and J. Casparis. 1971. "A Comparative Study of Youth Culture and Delinquency: Upper Class Canadian and Swiss Boys." *International Journal of Comparative Sociology* 12: 1–23.

Weber, M. 1949. "Social Science and Social Policy," in *The Methodology of Social Sciences* (E. Shils and H. Finch, trans. and eds.). New York: Free Press.

Weinberg, S. K. 1964. "Juvenile Delinquency in Ghana: A Comparative Analysis of Delinquents and Non-delinquents," *Journal of Criminal Law, Criminology, and Police Science* 55: 471–81.

West, D. J. 1969. *Present Conduct and Future Delinquency.* New York: International Universities Press.

Wilson, H. 1975. "Juvenile Delinquency, Parental Criminality, and Social Handicap." *British Journal of Criminology* 15: 241–50.

Zabczynska, E. 1974. "The Follow-up Studies of 100 Boys Charged with Theft at the Age of 10–11," pp. 128–39 and 216–20 in *Polskiej Akademii Nauk. Archiwum Kryminologii.* Wroclaw: Zaklad Norodowy im Ossolinskich.

The Victims of Homicide: A Temporal and Cross-National Comparison*

Rosemary Gartner[†]

Nations and eras vary widely in the extent to which they facilitate or inhibit criminal violence. Homicide rates in Western societies appear to have declined over the last several hundred years, but more recently, they experienced sharp, short-term upsurges in the early nineteenth century and in the last two decades (Gurr 1981). Even over relatively brief periods, the risk of violent death can vary greatly: homicide rates in developed democracies averaged 60 percent higher in the late 1970s than in the late 1950s (World Health Organization, various years). Despite this general upward trend in criminal violence, there are substantial cross-national differences in the risk of being murdered. Throughout this period, homicide rates were 40 percent higher for Australians than for New Zealanders, 50 percent higher for Italians than for Swiss, three times greater in Norway than in Finland, and four times greater in the United States than in Canada.

In this study, I attempt to account for both recent trends and cross-national differences in homicide rates in developed democracies. Drawing on motivational, control, and opportunity explanations of homicide, I argue that a nation's homicide rate is shaped by four structural and cultural contexts: material, integrative, demographic, and cultural. Some aspects of these four contexts are relatively enduring and stable features of nations and are expected to account for cross-national differences in homicide rates, while others vary over time within nations and are expected to account for trends in homicide rates. Testing these expectations using data from eighteen nations for the period 1950–80 allows me to examine the generality of relationships derived from more limited studies.

Because the risk of murder varies not only across time and space, but also across subgroups of a population, I analyze homicide rates disaggregated by the sex and age of the victim. In the United States, where most models of variation in homicide rates have been tested, young adult males are substantially more likely to be murdered than females or children. This pattern varies somewhat among developed democracies, raising the possibility that existing models of the social causes of homicide may not account well for the murders of females or children.

Theory and Research on Homicide Rates

Traditional Approaches: The Motivation and Control of Homicide

Traditional explanations of variation in rates of violent crime have emphasized one of two possible mechanisms: motivations or controls. Motivational approaches focus on social conditions or processes that engender homicidal inclinations in a population. Examples include strain theories, such as Merton's anomie theory (1938), and cultural theories, such as that of Wolfgang and Ferracuti (1967). Motivational concepts drawn from strain theories have received considerable support in macrolevel research. For instance, Blau and Blau (1982) found that economic inequality, both between and within races, is a significant predictor of homicide rates across metropolitan areas. They suggest that economic inequality "engenders alienation, despair, and pent-up aggression, which find expression in frequent conflicts, including a high incidence of criminal violence" (Blau and Blau 1982, p. 126). A cultural orientation to violence is suggested by the finding that the prevalence of legitimate or official violence is associated with both cross-sectional and temporal variation in homicide rates (Williams and Flewelling 1988; Landau and Pfefferman 1988; Archer and Gartner 1984).

Control explanations focus on social conditions or processes that weaken informal and formal social controls. In Shaw and McKay's social disorganization theory (1942), communities with attenuated social networks cannot adequately supervise or socialize their members, leaving them free to engage in crime. With the recent reemergence of community-level analyses of crime (e.g., Reiss and Tonry 1986), the control dimension of social disorganization theory is again framing numerous ecological studies. For example, Sampson has successfully used it to explain variation among communities in violent crime rates in England and the United States (Sampson 1986; Sampson and Groves 1989).

Opportunity Models of Homicide Victimization

Both motivational and control models are primarily concerned with explaining the behavior of offenders. Recent research on criminal victimization has shifted focus to the circumstances under which violent crimes are carried out. The most systematically formulated model of ecological variation in victimization is Cohen and Felson's (1979) routine activity approach. They argue that the homicide rate is a function of the opportunities for victimization, defined as the convergence of motivated offenders and suitable targets in the absence of capable guardians. Because this convergence is expected to occur more often where people spend much time outside the home or away from family members, they pre-

dict homicide rates will be higher where daily activities are more dispersed. They found an indicator of dispersion (the residential population density ratio) to be related to postwar trends in the U.S. homicide rates, net of the effects of traditional measures of motivations and controls (Cohen and Felson 1979).

Social control is the mechanism linking social structure to homicide rates in the routine activity approach (Cohen and Land 1987b). This perspective explains how the organization of daily activities allows criminal motivations to be realized, rather than how these motivations are generated within a population.[1] Thus, a routine activity model can account for increases in violent crimes in the United States during a period when many of the social conditions thought to foster violence were not worsening.

Recent Empirical Applications

The most recent efforts at modeling the distribution of homicide rates are concerned with the social production of motivations, controls, and opportunities (Cohen and Land 1987a; Devine, Sheley, and Smith 1988; Fiala and LaFree 1988). For example, in Williams and Flewelling's (1988) model, three exogenous constructs—social disintegration, resource deprivation, and violent cultural orientation—influence homicide rates indirectly through social controls and the intensity of interpersonal conflict. Measures of each of these constructs (divorce rate, percent living below the poverty line, and justifiable homicide rate, respectively) predict the homicide rate across 168 American cities during the early 1980s.

Noteworthy in the Williams and Flewelling study is their analysis of homicide rates disaggregated by victim-offender relationship and type of conflict. Similar to an earlier study (Parker and Smith 1979), they demonstrate that social conditions assumed to shape the control of and motivation to homicide vary in their effects by type of homicide. While this should not preclude the search for a general model, it argues for greater attention to the heterogeneity of acts comprising the total homicide rate.

Only one cross-national analysis has attended to this issue. Fiala and LaFree (1988) test a model explaining child homicide rates that incorporates the traditional perspectives of social disorganization, culture of violence, economic distress, and opportunity. Only measures of economic distress predict variation in child murders in developed nations, leading them to favor a motivational model. However, because their model is restricted to children, it is not informative about whether social characteristics associated with the total homicide rate are also associated with rates for subgroups.

Implications for the Present Study

Macrolevel research on homicide shows appreciable consensus about the causes of variation in homicide rates over time and place, despite a tendency in the literature to emphasize the inconsistencies in empirical findings or incompatibilities in theoretical approaches. Several elements of the social and cultural environment have consistently been implicated in the study of homicide. Each is assumed to have an indirect effect on homicide by raising motivations, lowering controls, and/or increasing opportunities for homicide.

However, this consensus is limited because most systematically formulated and tested models are based on the experience of the United States. The homicide rate in the United States is unique in that it is substantially higher, and its composition different from that in other developed nations. According to data from the Federal Bureau of Investigation, the majority of homicides in the United States involve strangers or acquaintances (rather than relatives), and the typical murder occurs between young males away from their households. In other developed democracies, homicides are more likely to be home-centered, and victims are more likely to be family members or females (Curtis 1974). Consequently, the indicators of motivations, controls, and opportunities derived from the U.S. experience may have quite different effects in other countries. For

this reason, I analyze homicide rates disaggregated by sex and age of the victim, two characteristics highly correlated with homicide rates in the United States.

How might the sex or age of the victim have implications for existing models? Some have argued that murders of women and children are more pathological, because they are less likely to be instrumentally motivated (Gelles and Cornell 1983). Homicide data suggest that women and children are more likely than adult males to be killed by family members or by someone dissimilar in sex or age (Curtis 1974; Gelles and Cornell 1983).[2] The social inequality between female or child victims and their offenders may render such violence distinctly different from violence between adult males. This point is emphasized in feminist literature on family violence (e.g., Guberman and Wolfe 1985) and is supported by the finding that, in the United States, rates of family homicide appear to have a somewhat different etiology than rates of nonfamily homicide (Williams and Flewelling 1988; Parker and Smith 1979).

Identifying the full range of differences underlying the motivation and control of male homicides and female or child homicides is an important task, but one beyond the scope of this paper. In the analysis that follows, I consider only how characteristics usually associated with total homicide rates vary by sex and age of the victim.

A Model of Variation in Sex- and Age-Specific Homicide Rates

The characteristics of a population commonly associated with the homicide rate can be grouped into four categories, which constitute the exogenous structural and cultural contexts for homicide in my model. These include (1) the distribution of economic resources, (2) the integration of social networks and institutions of control, (3) the composition and activities of the population, and (4) exposure to official, legitimated violence. In combination, these factors structure the control of, and motivation and opportunities for, homicide in a population.

The Material Context

According to perspectives as diverse as evolutionary psychology (Daly and Wilson 1988), Marxism (Bonger 1916), and anomie theory (Durkheim 1951), economic stress resulting from the inadequate or unequal distribution of resources is a major contributor to high rates of interpersonal violence. While economic inequality has consistently been associated with cross-national variation in total homicide rates (Krahn, Hartnagel, and Gartrell 1986; see also Messner 1989), the inadequacy of resources may be a more general risk factor. Absolute deprivation increases the risks of various types of family homicide, including infanticide, as well as nonfamily homicide (Daly and Wilson 1988; Williams and Flewelling 1988). Government efforts to alleviate deprivation are associated with lower homicide rates for the population in general (DeFronzo 1983), and children in particular (Fiala and LaFree 1988).

Economic inequality, on the other hand, may have particularly strong effects on certain types of homicides. Typically, economic inequality is assumed to generate diffuse aggression and hostility that is expressed in irrational or "unrealistic conflicts" (Coser 1968). In contrast, and similar to Daly and Wilson (1988), I view these heightened motivations as rationally targeted. People typically kill those they feel most directly competitive with or threatened by, and for the relatively deprived this will be similarly situated others. Since most killers are adults, I expect that in conflicts between adults the sense of relative deprivation will be most likely to lead to homicide. This leads to the following predictions:

Where government efforts to provide a minimum living standard are more limited, and where income inequality is greater, homicide rates will be greater for both females and males, adults and children.

However, I expect that:

The effects of income inequality will be most pronounced on the homicide rates of adults.

The Integrative Context

The capacity of a nation to provide control and protection against violence should be greater the more prevalent and interdependent are individuals' ties to social institutions, and social institutions' ties to each other. Japan's success at avoiding a post-1960s crime wave frequently is attributed to the strength of its group ties, made possible by the homogeneity of its population (Bayley 1976). In aggregate-level research on homicide, a high rate of family dissolution is assumed to weaken interindividual ties, while extensive ethnic or linguistic cleavages in a population are assumed to weaken interinstitutional ties. The former has been associated with intranational variation (Williams and Flewelling 1988; Sampson 1986), and the latter predicts cross-national variation (Hansmann and Quigley 1982, McDonald 1976) in homicide rates.

Weakened social integration lessens social control and should increase most types of homicide. Divorce, for example, by reducing guardianship and control of both potential victims and offenders, will raise risks for everyone, rather than simply for members of disrupted families. Williams and Flewelling (1988) found that cities with high divorce rates have significantly higher rates of both family and nonfamily homicides. Weak intergroup integration, however, may be a stronger risk factor for murders of adults, compared to murders of children. If cultural heterogeneity taps the potential for conflict and an absence of control among groups (Blau 1977), murders of adults ought to be affected most, since they engage in more intergroup interactions than children. If cultural heterogeneity, like economic inequality, incites perceptions of threat and competitive hostility (Hansmann and Quigley 1982), this too may be channeled largely toward adults. Consequently, I predict:

Divorce rates and ethnic-linguistic heterogeneity will be associated with higher homicide rates for females and males, adults and children.

The effects of heterogeneity will be strongest for the homicide rates of adults.

The Demographic Context

Two demographic aspects of a population, its composition and its daily movements, are particularly important for the homicide rate. The younger a population and the more widely dispersed its activities, the less effective are social controls and the more extensive are opportunities for homicide. The post-1960s wave of violent crime that engulfed most Western nations has been attributed, in part, to the aging of the postwar baby boom cohort into their late teens and early twenties (Gurr 1981). This account has received empirical support in time-series analyses of U.S. homicide rates (e.g., Cohen and Land 1987a). The same analysis found that the shift of productive and consumptive activities away from traditional-family households was related to higher homicide rates.

The effects of these demographic changes may be confined to certain types of victims, however. A population skewed toward the teen and young adult years typically is assumed to have higher homicide rates by increasing "the relative frequency of interactions between motivated offenders and individuals leading highly victim-prone lifestyles" (Cohen and Land 1987a, p. 174). If this opportunity mechanism links age structure and homicide rates, it seems unlikely to affect murders of children.

A second implication of the opportunity hypothesis is that the shift away from household activities will have its strongest effects on homicide rates for women and children. The most significant change in activity patterns is the movement of women into the labor force. The resulting reduction in guardianship should make women and children more vulnerable to murder.[3] Because the activities of adult males will also be less closely supervised, their risks of murder also are likely to increase, though to a lesser degree. This leads to two predictions:

A higher percentage of teens and young adults in a population will significantly increase the homicide rate for adults, but children will be negligibly affected.

A higher percentage of households with working women will be associated with higher homicide rates for all persons, but women and children will be more strongly affected than men.

The Cultural Context

At the cross-national level, evidence of co-variation between a variety of types of violence (Russell 1972; Archer and Gartner 1984) lends support to cultural explanations of differences in homicide rates. Some explanations assume that these associations reflect an underlying system of norms prescribing, or failing to proscribe, violence as a response to conflict (Straus 1983). Others contend that exposure to violence (whether direct or indirect) generates violence, either through modeling, habituation, or desensitization (e.g., Bandura 1973). According to modeling theories, exposure to violence that is legitimate, intentional, and real is most likely to elicit aggression (Comstock 1975).

The claims of normative and modeling approaches are consistent with evidence that officially approved violence, such as wars and executions, is often followed by elevated rates of illegitimate, interpersonal violence (Bowers 1984; Archer and Gartner 1984; Landau and Pfefferman 1988), and that rates of justifiable homicide covary with rates of criminal homicide (Williams and Flewelling 1988). The habituation argument is supported by Archer and Gartner's finding that postwar increases in homicide occurred most often in nations suffering large numbers of combat deaths during wars.

Differences in causal mechanisms aside, this literature agrees that where officially approved violence is prevalent, rates of criminal violence are higher. However, neither theory nor research provides a strong rationale for predicting different effects for different subgroups, therefore I predict:

Homicide rates will be higher for both sexes and all ages where the death penalty is legally sanctioned, and where involvement in wars has been more frequent and more deadly.

Sample and Variables

Sample

The sample is eighteen economically developed democracies observed at five-year intervals from 1950 to 1980. The unit of analysis is a nation-time period. The nations include Canada, New Zealand, Australia, Japan, the United States, and thirteen Western European nations. The analysis is confined to these nations because most macrolevel models of homicide refer to the United States experience and are formulated in terms of social processes that characterize developed nations in modern times. Developed democracies provide a context for testing the generality of these models. These nations also present relatively few measurement problems.[4]

Variables

The Dependent Variables. The World Health Organization reports annual sex-specific rates of death "due to injury purposely inflicted by others" for the years 1951–1984, and annual age-specific rates beginning in 1965 (WHO, various years).[5] The age-groups analyzed are infants under 1 year, 1- to 4-year-olds, 5- to 14-year olds, and those over 14. Because the time-varying independent variables in the analysis are available only at five-year intervals, mean sex-specific rates were calculated at seven time points and mean age-specific rates at five time points. Each mean death rate is based on data from the year for which the independent variables were available and the subsequent four years (with the exception of the first sex-specific rates which are based on data for 1951–1954). The timing of observations on the independent and dependent variables, then, is consistent with the causal ordering presumed by existing models. Averaging the rates also

corrects for yearly fluctuations due to the small number of homicides in some nations.

The Independent Variables. Measures of the material context include indicators of both absolute and relative deprivation. The former is measured by social security expenditures as a percentage of GNP (International Labour Office).[6] Relative deprivation is measured by the Gini index of household income inequality (Weatherby, Nam, and Isaac 1983). The integrative context is represented by two indicators. The number of divorces per thousand marriages (U.N. Demographic Yearbook) measures intragroup integration, and the percentage of significant ethnic and linguistic groups in the population (Taylor and Hudson 1972) measures intergroup integration. The demographic context is characterized by percentage of the population aged 15–29 (U.N. Demographic Yearbook), and by an approximation of the residential population density ratio, the ratio of the total number of female labor force participants (International Labour Office 1977) to the total households (U.N. Demographic Yearbook).[7] The cultural context is represented by three variables tapping the existence, extent, and severity of official violence: a dummy variable indicating the existence of the death penalty (U.N. Economic and Social Council 1985), the number of international and civil wars in which the nation participated between 1900 and 1980, and the total battle deaths (per million prewar population) incurred during these wars (Small and Singer 1981).[8]

Social security expenditures, divorce rates, the ratio of female labor force participants to households, the percentage of the population aged 15–29, and the death penalty vary through time and among nations, and are expected to account for both national and time-period differences in homicide rates. The remaining variables vary only among nations. The measures of income inequality and of ethnic and linguistic diversity are available for only one year, in most cases near the midpoint of the period.

Along with the measures of the number of wars and battle deaths, income inequality and ethnic heterogeneity are assumed to tap relatively enduring patterns that distinguish advanced democracies from each other. Note that none of these four can account for variations through time in homicide rates.

Variation in Sex- and Age-Specific Homicide Rates

Descriptive data on postwar trends and cross-national differences in homicide rates that the model is expected to explain are presented in Table 19.1. These data challenge conclusions of other analysts concerning the lack of covariation between female and male victimization rates, and between adult and child victimization rates.

Female and Male Homicide Rates, 1950–84

According to Verkko's (1951) "universal static and dynamic laws of homicide," homicide rates for females are relatively invariant over time and place. For these eighteen nations and three decades, this is clearly not the case (columns 1 and 2). For both sexes, homicide rates (averaged over nations) declined from the early 1950s to the early 1960s, then increased continuously to their highest levels by the 1980s. The zero-order correlation between the rates is .90. From a low point in the early 1960s to a high point in 1980, the average homicide rate for females for all eighteen nations increased by almost 50 percent, compared to 62 percent for males. (Among the nations, only Italy and Japan had lower homicide rates after 1967 compared to pre-1967 rates.) Regarding variation among nations, females in the United States were nine times as likely to be murdered as females in Ireland during this period. Contrary to Verrko's predictions, females do not universally enjoy a protective advantage over males. Females in Australia, Canada, Finland, and the United States were between two and three times more likely to be murdered than

males in Denmark, England and Wales, and the Netherlands.

Despite substantial changes in homicide rates over time, the relative ranking of nations remained quite stable from 1950 to 1980. The rank-order correlation between the total homicide rate in 1950 and 1980 for the sixteen nations with increasing rates (excluding Japan and Italy) is .92. The correlation is .65 when Japan and Italy are added. Similar to the delinquent neighborhoods in Shaw and McKay's (1942) portrayal, this group of nations appears to have enduring propensities to violence despite changes in the composition of their populations.

Child and Adult Homicide Rates, 1965–80

Previous cross-national studies have found little association between annual rates of child homicide and total homicide (Fiala and LaFree 1988; Christoffel, Liu, and Stamler 1981). My data suggest a different conclusion, possibly because they are drawn from several years, rather than a single year.[9] Paralleling the trend for total homicide rates, average homicide rates for the different age-groups (except infants) increased between 1965 and 1980 (bottom panel of Table 19.1). Similarly, international stability is seen in the rankings over nations of the homicide rates for the different age-groups. Correlations over nations, shown in Table 19.2, are moderately strong for the comparison between adult females and children aged 1–14 as contrasted with the comparison between adult males and children. One reason for the stronger relationships between rates for adult females and children is their predominantly primary-group character (Daly and Wilson 1988).

Comparing age-groups, homicide rates for children are consistently lower than those for adults or infants. In seventeen of the eighteen nations (Japan is the exception), children aged 1–14 are less likely to be murdered than persons over 14 or infants. Homicide rates for infants are notable both for their level and their

T A B L E   1 9 . 1   Mean Sex- and Age-Specific Homicide Rates*

Country/Year	1950–80		1965–80				
	Males (1)	Females (2)	Males > 14 (3)	Females > 14 (4)	Children 5–14 yrs (5)	Children 1–4 yrs (6)	Infants < 1 yr (7)
Australia	2.12	1.34	2.30	1.41	.51	1.06	3.00
Austria	1.54	1.15	1.67	1.20	.48	.89	6.81
Belgium	1.30	1.01	1.53	1.13	.33	.73	.98
Canada	2.83	1.49	3.28	1.55	.58	1.04	3.17
Denmark	.76	.85	.75	.78	.65	.83	2.21
England and Wales	.89	.72	.88	.71	.28	.99	4.30
Finland	4.03	1.37	4.89	1.51	.55	.89	6.92
France	1.18	.70	1.39	.79	.26	.48	1.92
West Germany	1.43	1.03	1.48	1.03	.56	1.03	5.59
Ireland	.93	.40	1.09	.43	.10	.18	2.05
Italy	2.03	.61	2.45	.69	.24	.22	.80
Japan	1.50	.94	1.34	.74	.80	2.26	7.64
Netherlands	.91	.47	1.00	.51	.21	.43	1.63
New Zealand	1.50	1.00	1.46	.83	.38	1.71	4.49
Norway	1.03	.56	1.20	.59	.23	.35	1.80
Sweden	1.33	.82	1.41	.83	.44	.84	1.36
Switzerland	.95	.82	1.04	.81	.51	.75	4.57
United States	14.05	3.83	14.92	4.18	.99	2.11	5.40
All 18 Nations:							
Mean	2.00	.97	2.45	1.10	.45	.93	3.65
Standard deviation	2.54	.67	3.24	.83	.24	.62	2.85
1950	1.79	.88	—	—	—	—	—
1955	1.63	.82	—	—	—	—	—
1960	1.59	.81	—	—	—	—	—
1965	1.67	.88	1.93	.88	.41	.81	4.34
1970	2.24	1.05	2.54	1.09	.43	.96	3.90
1975	2.46	1.13	2.67	1.16	.46	.96	3.56
1980	2.58	1.19	2.65	1.25	.49	.97	2.81

*Note: All rates are calculated per 100,000 persons per year in the appropriate sex or age-group, except rates for infants, which are calculated per 100,000 live births per year.
Source: World Health Organization, various years.

TABLE 19.2 Zero-Order Correlations between Adult and Child Homicide Rates, 1965–80*

Age-group	(1)	(2)	(3)	(4)
(1) Males > 14	—			
(2) Females > 14	.91	—		
(3) Children 5–14	.52	.66	—	
(4) Children 1–4	.41	.56	.75	—
(5) Infants < 1	.22	.33	.51	.61

*Correlations are based on five-year mean rates (shown in Table 19.1) that have been log transformed (base 10).

trend. Rates for infants are highest of all the age-groups in each nation, except the United States, Sweden, and Italy. The rate for infants, unlike the other age-groups, decreased markedly between 1965 and 1980.[10]

Results of a Multivariate Analysis
The Data Set and Methods of Estimation

Observations on the dependent and independent variables are pooled for the multivariate analysis. For the analysis of sex-specific homicide rates, pooling across eighteen nations and seven time points yields a sample size of 126. For the age-specific analysis, the sample size is 72 (eighteen nations at four time points). Analyzing pooled data has the advantage of allowing a more stringent test of the generality of the model, because the model must account for variation through time and among nations in homicide rates. Moreover, the effects of idiosyncratic events or processes are minimized in a pooled analysis.

The model is estimated with a modified generalized least squares (MGLS) procedure that corrects for both serial correlation and heteroskedasticity, and assumes a single, first-order autoregressive process.[11] The procedure calculates an autocorrelation coefficient and a cross-sectional correlation from the residuals of an OLS regression. These estimates are used to remove the autoregressive component and reweight the final MGLS estimates. I estimated both linear-additive models and models on log-transformed data. Log transformation adjusts for the skewed distributions of some of the variables, and is a common procedure in tests of other models (e.g., Cohen and Land 1987a). Since results are similar for both models, only results for the logged data are reported here. To determine whether the results are sensitive to the inclusion of particular nations, each model was reestimated excluding a different nation from the sample each time. The results are robust across different samples.

Postwar trends in three of the five time-varying indicators of the structural and cultural contexts predicting homicide rates follow a u-shaped curve similar to that for homicide rates (Table 19.3). Divorce rates, the ratio of female workers to households, and the relative size of the 15 to 29-year-old population declined to a low point in 1960 and increased thereafter to 1980. In contrast, mean welfare spending increased and the number of nations with the death penalty decreased. The multivariate analysis combines these time-varying measures with the time invariant measures (income inequality, ethnic heterogeneity, and battle deaths)[12] in separate analysis of sex- and age-specific rates.

Results for Female and Male Homicide Rates, 1950–80

The risk factors predicting homicide rates do not appear to vary by the sex of the victim (columns 1 and 2, Table 19.4). Given the extremely high correlation between female and male rates, these results are not surprising. The model explains a substantial amount of the variance in homicide rates of both females and males ($R^2 = .72$). As predicted, the indicators of material deprivation, weak social integration, and exposure to official violence are associated with significantly higher risks of homicide for both sexes. For both sexes, the divorce rate is by far the most important risk factor, as indicated by the standardized coefficients.

T A B L E   1 9 . 3   Descriptive Data for Independent Variables Predicting Homicide Rates, Eighteen Developed Democracies

Independent Variable	All Years		1950	1955	1960	1965	1970	1975	1980
	Mean	**S.D.**							
Material Context									
Welfare spending	12.21	5.78	6.93	8.93	7.07	10.95	12.66	16.86	19.39
Income inequality*	38.33	3.38							
Integrative context									
Divorce rate	1.25	.93	.87	.78	.78	.93	1.41	1.88	2.11
Ethnic heterogeneity*	23.70	21.71							
Demographic context									
Female workers/ households	45.04	11.61	45.47	44.69	43.49	43.86	44.00	45.62	49.97
Percent aged 15–29	22.57	2.12	22.86	21.22	20.99	22.39	23.01	23.73	23.82
Cultural context									
Battle deaths*	14,407	17,890							
Death penalty	.46	.50	.56	.56	.56	.44	.39	.39	.33

*These measures vary only among nations, not over time.
Note: Data are not log transformed. S.D. = standard deviation.

Among the demographic indicators, the effect of the ratio of the female labor force to households, though positive for both sexes, is significant only for females. The postwar shift in routine activities away from households appears to put women at a greater risk of homicide. Contrary to prediction and previous research, the percentage of the population aged 15–29 has no effect on the homicide rates of either sex. (Alternative specifications of the age range did not alter this conclusion.)

Results for Child and Adult Homicide Rates, 1965–80

The relative importance of risk factors varies between children and adults, and a number of these relationships coincide with expectations (columns 3 through 7, Table 19.4). The results for females and males aged 14 and older for 1965–80 essentially replicate those for females and males of all ages for 1950–80. In the more recent period, however, the difference between the sexes in the effect of the ratio of female workers to households is significant, providing even stronger support for the notion that the dispersion of activities away from family households has put women at greater risk.

Looking at the two indicators of the material context, welfare spending appears as the only variable with significant effects for all age-groups. This effect, which is strongest at the youngest ages, follows predictions and is consistent with Fiala and LaFree's (1988) cross-national analysis of child homicide rates. Also consistent with predictions, income inequality is associated with high homicide rates of adults but not children. Apparently absolute deprivation is a more general risk factor than is relative deprivation.

Turning to the integrative context, the prediction that weak intergroup integration, here measured by ethnic and linguistic heterogene-

TABLE 19.4 MGLS Estimates from Models of Sex- and Age-Specific Homicide Rates, Eighteen Developed Democracies

Independent Variable		1950–80		1965–80				
		Males All Ages (1)	Females All Ages (2)	Males > 14 (3)	Females > 14 (4)	Children 5–14 yrs (5)	Children 1–4 yrs (6)	Infants < 1 yr (7)
Material Context								
	b	−.22***	−.12***	−.27**	−.10*	−.13**	−.25**	−.64***
Welfare spending	s.e.	.06	.03	.10	.05	.04	.07	.14
	B	−.22	−.22	−.21	−.14	−.33	−.35	−.52
Income	b	1.77***	.68**	2.16***	.66*	.34	.39	.72
inequality	s.e.	.43	.24	.56	.32	.23	.60	.73
	B	.32	.22	.36	.20	.19	.08	.12
Integrative context								
	b	.83***	.45***	1.01***	.47***	.15*	.17	−.03
Divorce rate	s.e.	.11	.07	.15	.08	.07	.11	.22
	B	.53	.51	.56	.47	.27	.16	−.02
Ethnic	b	.06*	.06***	.08*	.08***	.01	.01	.06
heterogeneity	s.e.	.03	.02	.04	.02	.02	.03	.05
	B	.13	.26	.17	.32	.04	.05	.14
Demographic context								
Female	b	1.14	1.75**	−.20	1.34*	2.15***	4.33***	4.93**
workers/	s.e.	.98	.57	1.29	.65	.60	.98	1.86
households	B	.08	.21	−.01	.14	.41	.45	.30
Percent	b	−.02	.00	−.35	−.09	−.03	.64	−.54
aged 15–29	s.e.	.25	.15	−.43	.21	.20	.33	.64
	B	−.00	.00	−.05	−.02	−.02	.17	−.08
Cultural context								
	b	.03***	.01*	.03*	.02*	.00	.02*	.04*
Battle deaths	s.e.	.01	.00	.01	.01	.01	.01	.02
	B	.24	.16	.19	.20	.01	.27	.26
	b	.11*	.06*	.12	.09*	.02	.06*	−.12
Death penalty	s.e.	.05	.03	.08	.04	.03	.03	.12
	B	.12	.11	.12	.14	.07	.13	−.12
R^2 (OLS)		.72	.72	.70	.73	.51	.59	.51
d.f.		117	117	61	61	61	61	61

*p < .05   **p < .01   ***p < .001

Note: Data are log transformed (base 10). b = unstandarized coefficient; B = standarized coefficient; s.e. = standard error; d.f. = degrees of freedom; and OLS = ordinary least squares.

ity, is a significant risk factor for adults but not for children is supported. A similar but unanticipated pattern emerges for divorce rates. While adults and older children face significantly higher risks where divorce rates are higher, this is not the case for children under the age of five. This runs counter to the prediction that family disruption is associated with higher rates of homicide at all ages. It also challenges popular conceptions and the predictions of evolutionary psychology (Daly and Wilson 1988) concerning the dangers to young children posed by divorce. The strongest effects of the shift away from nuclear family-based activities appears among children. The greater the ratio of women in the labor force to households, the greater the rates of child homicide, a result also found by Fiala and LaFree (1988). The second indicator of the demographic context, the relative size of the young adult population, is not associated with child homicide rates, as was predicted.

Finally, a cultural orientation to violence is associated with higher homicide rates among adults and children, though the effects are less general than predicted. Nations with a high number of wartime battle deaths tend to have higher homicide rates for infants, young children, and adults of both sexes. The presence of a death penalty is associated with higher homicide rates for adult females and young children. These results, as well as previous research, suggest that legitimate and illegitimate acts of violence may be part of a common cultural desensitization to or tolerance of violence.

Comparing the standardized coefficients in Table 19.4 (columns 3 through 7) reveals that the most important risk factors for children 14 and younger are welfare spending and the ratio of female workers to households. Nations in which spending on social programs is more limited and in which more women work outside the home tend to have higher homicide rates for children. For persons over 14, family dissolution is by far the greatest risk factor.

Discussion

The foregoing analysis suggests that the four structural and cultural contexts explaining total homicide rates in the United States are also important in other developed democracies. At one level, then, the model tested appears quite general, rather than being limited to homicide rates of young males. Although the strength of effects varies, the direction of the effects of seven of the eight explanatory variables is the same, and consistent with predictions, for the homicide rates of adults and children. Only infanticides depart from this pattern. Nations with greater material deprivation, more cultural heterogeneity, more family dissolution, higher female labor force participation, and greater exposure to official violence generally have higher homicide rates.

At another level, some limits to the international generality of some well-accepted explanations of variations in homicide rates are evident. In particular, the demographic context of homicide is less general than suggested by prior research. A disproportionate number of teens and young adults was not associated with higher homicide rates for any age-group, among these eighteen nations. This is surprising since demographic explanations of trends in violent crime have been given considerable attention (e.g., Wilson and Herrnstein 1985) and have garnered substantial empirical support in the United States (but see Gartner and Parker 1988).[13]

Modifications of existing perspectives are suggested by the results found for female employment. The growth in female employment, a driving force in the movement of activities away from family-households according to the routine activity model, appears to be a less general risk factor since this variable was not associated with male homicide rates. This suggests that female labor force participation may influence homicide by raising the motivations for female and child homicide, rather than by weakening controls. Both microlevel research on family violence (Brown 1980) and macrolevel research on child homicide (Fiala and LaFree 1988) apply motivational interpretations to the relation between women's employment and homicide.

Some differences from previous research in the effects of explanatory variables require cautious interpretation. The measures of income inequality and weak social integration—including divorce rates—are not strong risk factors for children. This indicates the etiology of child homicide may differ in ways that traditional sociological perspectives on homicide have not fully developed.[14] Alternatively, the weak effects of some of the explanatory variables on child homicide could result from greater measurement error in child homicide rates. Homicides of young children may be more easily disguised or misclassified than homicides of adults. This possibility needs to be explored before ruling out the importance of some of the explanatory variables for child homicides.[15]

Conclusion

Explanatory variables derived from previous research were able to account for changes through time and among nations in homicide rates, supporting the basic generality of the model. This is the first evidence that homicide rates are related to divorce rates and spending on social programs between time periods, and that the ratio of female labor force participants to households and national war experiences are related to differing national homicide rates.

The model is general only within obvious limits: it appears to account well for variation in the aggregate risks of homicide in postwar developed democracies. It cannot speak to the importance of structural and cultural characteristics that are relatively constant in this group of nations during these years, such as level of economic development, democratic political structure, or value systems of postindustrial, secular society. Such characteristics may be crucial for explaining both differences in homicide rates between these and other nations, and changes in rates within these nations over longer periods of time. These are questions for future research.

The microlevel implications of the aggregate patterns revealed in this and other macrolevel studies need to be explored in future research. Are all persons in populations with high divorce rates or unequal income distributions at higher risk of homicide, or are these risks borne primarily by members of disrupted families or by persons in the lower economic strata? Where more women work outside the home, do all women and children, or only working women and their children, face higher risks? From whom do these enhanced risks emanate—family members, strangers, the relatively deprived, the unattached? Answers to these questions would help identify the motivational and/or control mechanisms linking aggregate social characteristics to homicide rates.

Finally, researchers typically have allowed political boundaries to define the unit of analysis in macrolevel research, and have ignored "Galton's problem"—the fact that political units (nations, states, cities) are not independent, as assumed by methods for estimating covariation. The boundaries for the different structural and cultural processes on which models of homicide rates are based also rarely coincide. Critiques of analyses that treat political units as distinct, autonomous, internally coherent entities (e.g., Tilly 1984) are especially relevant to phenomena linked to cultural variation, such as homicide. This argues for reconceptualizing the unit of analysis in macrolevel research on homicide, as has happened in world-systems approaches in political sociology. Such reconceptualization can build on the considerable evidence about homicide risks from traditional macrolevel research.

Notes

*   From the *American Sociological Review* 55, no. 1. (February 1990): 92–106, by permission of the author and the American Sociological Association. Copyright 1990 by the American Sociological Association.

†   This research was partially funded by a grant-in-aid from the Society for the Psychological Study of Social Issues, and by an Old Gold Fellowship from the University of Iowa. I thank Bill McCarthy, Barry Wellman, and two anonymous ASR reviewers for comments on an earlier draft of this paper. Kathryn Baker and Fred Pampel provided invaluable insights at various stages of this project.

1. Similar to other control theories of crime (e.g., Hirschi 1969) the routine activity approach assumes motivations to crime in a population are constant and "at least partially explained by the lack of external restraints" (Cohen and Land

1987b, p. 51). Thus, while a pool of motivated offenders is a minimal element in homicide, explaining the existence of this pool is unnecessary.

2. This suggests that the principal of homogamy developed in the victimization literature (Cohen, Kluegel, and Land 1981), and derived from U.S. experience should be qualified when considering murders of females and children.

3. One could argue that this shift away from household activities reduces the opportunities for homicides within the family, and thus should reduce the homicide rates of women and children relative to those for males, since a larger proportion of the former are family homicides. This seems to me to strain the concept of opportunity. Even were this the case, one would have to argue that the risks of family homicide have decreased enough to counterbalance the increased risk of nonfamily murders of females and children. Since there is evidence to suggest that female labor force participation may increase motivations for the murder of women and children (Brown 1980; Fiala and LaFree 1988), this, too, seems unlikely.

4. The United Nations typically cautions that the infant mortality rates reported for many less developed countries (LDCs) are based on incomplete civil registers of unknown reliability. Since similar registers are the source of the WHO death rates, it seems likely that statistics on the purposeful killing of infants and children from many LDCs are unreliable. An examination of WHO data for LDCs reveals, for example, that in 1968 the Philippines reported twenty homicides of infants less than a year old, and fifty-nine child homicides; four years later, there were no recorded infanticides, and only two recorded homicides of young children. Such unreliability probably contributes to the absence of effects of explanatory variables in Fiala and LaFree's (1988) analysis of child homicide in LDCs. Even in developed nations, inaccurate reporting of infant and child homicides may make these rates less reliable than rates for adults.

5. Rates are calculated per 100,000 persons in the appropriate sex or age-group, except infant rates, which are calculated per 100,000 live births. WHO changed its homicide measure during this thirty-year period, but this does not appear to result in significant changes in the data. Prior to the 1960s, the measure included "deaths by legal intervention (which includes killings by police, but not legal execution) and deaths due to war." However, a comparison of the WHO homicide data for young males with estimates of battle deaths (Small and Singer 1981) for those nations involved in wars in the 1950s indicates that war deaths apparently were not included in the homicide data with the exception of France during the Algerian War. Results were unchanged after adjusting the French data for these casualties. No adjustment was made for police killings in early years. I assume the number of such killings is small, and their inclusion has not biased the observed estimates. Other sources of measurement error in the homicide data, to the extent the error is random, will attenuate observed relationships, and lessen support for the predicted effects.

6. This measure includes benefit expenditures (cash and in-kind) for a diverse array of programs, including pensions, sickness/maternity, and public health, as well as means-tested public assistance, unemployment compensation, and family allowances, though these latter three receive less than a third of social security expenditures in most developed democracies (Pampel and Williamson 1988). Thus, the population benefiting from social security expenditures is broader than found in most studies of welfare dependence. I also examined the effects of more disaggregated measures of spending on social programs, including a measure of cash transfer payments per GNP, and family allowance payments per GNP. Both include a larger proportion of payments to needy populations than do social security expenditures. Their effects are similar to, though somewhat lower than, the effects of the social security measure, a finding that parallels Fiala and LaFree's (1988).

7. This measure differs from that used by Cohen and Felson (1979). They use the ratio of the number of female labor force participants with husbands present plus the number of non–husband-wife households to the total number of households.

8. The 1900–1980 time period was used because war was a rare event in recent years and these measures would have been highly skewed as a result.

9. In several of these eighteen nations, annual homicides in certain age-groups is quite small. In 1974, for example, ten of the nations had fewer than five infant homicides, and twelve had fewer than five homicides of children aged 1 to 4. Even after aggregating data over five-year periods, some age-specific rates are based on less than twenty-five victims.

10. There is nothing in WHO publications to suggest reporting practices for infant homicides changed over time so as to produce this unique trend. If reporting of infant homicides improved over time—a more plausible hypothesis given the growing attention to child abuse in developed nations during this period—precisely the reverse trend would be expected.

11. In the first-order autoregressive model, the residuals are a function of values at only the previous time point and an autoregressive component unique to each nation. The autocorrelation function declines approximately geometrically and approaches zero by the fourth lag, which is consistent with a first-order process.

12. Multicollinearity precluded including both number of wars and battle deaths in the same model. Furthermore, the effect of number of wars, while positive, was trivial for most homicides. Consequently, only the results for battle deaths are reported. A cultural orientation to violence may be better tapped by the costliness of war (in terms of lives lost) rather than the number of wars.

13. Nevertheless, age structure may have important effects on trends in homicide rates in some nations. Japan and Italy, the only two nations in the sample with lower homicide rates in the 1970s than the 1950s, are two examples. Along with West Germany, they were the only nations in which the percentage of the population aged 15–29 decreased during this period. Although variations in age structure do not predict variations in homicide in my model, it may be that a decrease in the percentage of young persons in the population was a necessary condition for a decrease in the homicide rate after the 1960s. In West Germany, the average homicide rate for males after 1967 was only 4 percent higher than the average rate prior to 1967, the smallest increase in the sample. These patterns suggest age structure may in fact be an important determi-nant of homicide rates in some nations, but in more complex ways than has been considered.

14. Other perspectives provide insights into risk factors that may be particularly important for child homicide. See Daly and Wilson (1988) and Fiala and LaFree (1988) for a review of risk factors featured, respectively, in evolutionary perspectives on infanticide and in the literature on child abuse.

15. The possibility of systematic measurement error in the reporting of child and infant homicide rates cannot be ruled out. If errors in reporting are systematically associated with the explanatory variables, observed estimates will be biased. The absence of effects for divorce rates or ethnic heterogeneity in child homicide could result if nations with high divorce rates or greater ethnic diversity consistently underenumerated child homicides. It seems less plausible that the significant effects for welfare spending, ratio of female workers to households, and battle deaths could be due to such systematic error, however, given the robustness of these effects across age-groups.

References

Archer, Dane, and Rosemary Gartner. 1984. *Violence and Crime in Cross-National Perspective.* New Haven: Yale University Press.

Bandura, Albert. 1973. *Aggression: A Social Learning Analysis.* Englewood Cliffs, NJ: Prentice Hall.

Bayley, David H. 1976. "Learning about Crime: The Japanese Experience." *Public Interest* 44:55–68.

Blau, Peter M. 1977. *Inequality and Heterogeneity.* New York: Free Press.

Blau, Judith R., and Peter M. Blau. 1982. "Metropolitan Structure and Violent Crime." *American Sociological Review* 47:114–28.

Bonger, Willem Adrian. 1916. *Criminality and Economic Conditions.* Boston: Little, Brown.

Bowers, William J. 1984. *Legal Homicide.* Boston: Northeastern University Press.

Brown, Bruce. 1980. "Wife-Employment, Marital Equality, and Husband-Wife Violence." Pp. 176–87 in *The Social Causes of Husband-Wife Violence,* edited by M. A. Straus and G. T. Hotaling. Minneapolis: University of Minnesota Press.

Christoffel, Katherine K., Kiang Liu, and Jeremiah Stamler. 1981. "Epidemiology of Fatal Child

Abuse: International Mortality Data." *Journal of Chronic Diseases* 34:57–64.

Cohen, Lawrence E., and Marcus Felson. 1979. "Social Change and Crime Rate Trends: A Routine Activity Approach." *American Sociological Review* 44:588–607.

Cohen, Lawrence E., James Kluegel, and Kenneth Land. 1981. "Social Inequality and Predatory Criminal Victimization: An Exposition and Test of a Formal Theory." *American Sociological Review* 46:505–24.

Cohen, Lawrence E., and Kenneth Land. 1987a. "Age Structure and Crime: Symmetry versus Assymetry and the Projection of Crime Rates through the 1990s." *American Sociological Review* 52:170–83.

———. 1987b. "Sociological Positivism and the Explanation of Criminality." Pp. 43–55 in *Positive Criminology,* edited by M. R. Gottfredson and T. Hirschi. Beverly Hills: Sage.

Comstock, George. 1975. *Television and Human Behavior: The Key Studies.* Santa Monica, CA: Rand Corporation.

Coser, Lewis A. 1968. "Conflict: Social Aspects." Pp. 232–36 in *International Encyclopedia of the Social Sciences,* Vol. 3, edited by David L. Sills. New York: Macmillan.

Curtis, Lynn. 1974. *Criminal Violence: National Patterns and Behavior.* Lexington, MA: D. C. Heath.

Daly, Martin, and Margo Wilson. 1988. *Homicide.* New York: Aldine de Gruyter.

DeFronzo, James. 1983. "Economic Assistance to Impoverished Americans: Relationship to Incidence of Crime." *Criminology* 21: 119–36.

Devine, Joel A., Joseph Sheley, and M. Dwayne Smith. 1988. "Macroeconomic and Socio-Control Policy Influences on Crime Rate Changes, 1948–1985." *American Sociological Review* 53:401–20.

Durkheim, Emile. 1951. *Suicide.* Translation by John A. Spaulding and George Simpson. Glencoe, IL: Free Press of Glencoe.

Fiala, Robert, and Gary LaFree. 1988. "Cross-National Determinants of Child Homicide." *American Sociological Review* 53:432–45.

Gartner, Rosemary, and Robert Nash Parker. 1988. "Cross-National Evidence on Homicide and the Age Structure of the Population." Paper presented at the annual meetings of the American Sociological Association.

Gelles, Richard J., and Claire Pedrick Cornell. 1983. *International Perspectives on Family Violence.* Lexington, MA: D. C. Heath.

Guberman, Connie, and Margie Wolfe. 1985. *No Safe Place: Violence against Women and Children.* Toronto: The Women's Press.

Gurr, Ted Robert. 1981. "Historical Trends in Violent Crime: A Critical Review of the Evidence." Pp. 295–353 in *Crime and Justice: An Annual Review of Research,* Vol 3, edited by Michael Tonry and Norval Morris. Chicago: University of Chicago Press.

Hansmann, Henry B., and John M. Quigley. 1982. "Population Heterogeneity and the Sociogenesis of Homicide." *Social Forces* 61:206–24.

Hirschi, Travis. 1969. *Causes of Delinquency.* Berkeley: University of California Press.

International Labour Office. Various years. *Yearbook of Labour Statistics.* Geneva: International Labour Organization.

———. 1977. *Labour Force: 1950–2000.* Geneva: International Labour Organization.

———. Various years. *The Cost of Social Security.* Geneva: International Labour Organization.

Krahn, Harvey, Timothy F. Hartnagel, and John W. Gartrell. 1986. "Income Inequality and Homicide Rates: Cross-National Data and Criminological Theories." *Criminology* 24:269–95.

Landau, Simcha, and Danny Pfefferman. 1988. "A Time-Series Analysis of Violent Crime and Its Relation to Prolonged States of Warfare: The Israeli Case." *Criminology* 26:489–504.

McDonald, Lynn. 1976. *The Sociology of Law and Order.* Montreal: Book Centre.

Merton, Robert. 1938. "Social Structure and Anomie." *American Sociological Review* 3:672–82.

Messner, Steven. 1989. "Economic Discrimination and Societal Homicide Rates: Further Evidence on the Cost of Inequality" *American Sociological Review* 54:597–611.

Pampel, Fred C., and John B. Williamson. 1988. "Welfare Spending in Advanced Industrial Democracies, 1950–1980." *American Journal of Sociology* 93:1424–56.

Parker, Robert Nash, and M. Dwayne Smith. 1979. "Deterrence, Poverty, and Type of Homicide." *American Journal of Sociology* 85:614–24.

Reiss, Albert J., Jr., and Michael Tonry (editors). 1986. *Communities and Crime.* Chicago: University of Chicago Press.

Russell, E. W.. 1972. "Factors of Human Aggression: A Cross-Cultural Factor Analysis of Characteristics Related to Warfare and Crime." *Behavior Science Notes* 7:275–312.

Sampson, Robert J. 1986. "Neighborhood Family Structure and the Risk of Personal Victimization." Pp. 25–46 in *The Social Ecology of*

Crime, edited by James M. Byrne and Robert J. Sampson. New York: Springer-Verlag.

Sampson, Robert J., and W. Byron Groves. 1989. "Community Structure and Crime: Testing Social Disorganization Theory." *American Journal of Sociology* 94:774–802.

Shaw, Clifford, and Henry McKay. 1942. *Juvenile Delinquency and Urban Areas.* Chicago: University of Chicago Press.

Small, Melvin, and J. David Singer. 1981. *Resort to Arms: International and Civil War, 1816–1980.* Beverly Hills: Sage.

Straus, Murray. 1983. "Societal Morphogenesis and Intrafamily Violence in Cross-Cultural Perspective." Pp. 27–43 in *International Perspectives on Family Violence,* edited by R. J. Gelles and C. P. Cornell. Lexington, MA: D. C. Heath.

Taylor, Charles L., and M. Hudson. 1972. *World Handbook of Political and Social Indicators,* 2nd edition. New Haven: Yale University Press.

Tilly, Charles. 1984. *Big Structures, Large Processes, Huge Comparisons.* New York: Russell Sage Foundation.

United Nations. 1985. "Social Development Questions: Capital Punishment." Report 85-12176 of the Economic and Social Council, 26 April.

United Nations. Various years. *Demographic Yearbook.* New York: United Nations.

Verkko, Veli. 1951. "Are There Regular Sequences in Crimes against Life Which Can Be Formulated as Laws?" *Homicides and Suicides in Finland and Their Dependence on National Character.* Scandinavian Studies in Sociology #3. Copenhagen: C. E. S. Gads Forlag.

Weatherby, Norman L., Charles B. Nam, and Larry W. Isaac. 1983. "Development, Inequality, Health Care, and Mortality at Older Ages: A Cross-National Analysis." *Demography* 20:27–43.

Wolfgang, Marvin, and Franco, Ferracuti. 1967. *The Subculture of Violence.* London: Tavistock.

World Health Organization. Various years. *World Health Statistics Annual: Vital Statistics and Causes of Death.* Geneva: WHO.

Williams, Kirk R., and Robert L. Flewelling. 1988. "The Social Production of Criminal Homicide: A Comparative Study of Disaggregated Rates in American Cities." *American Sociological Review* 53:421–31.

Wilson, James Q., and Richard J. Herrnstein. 1985. *Crime and Human Nature.* New York: Simon and Schuster.

Education

Research on comparative education has been particularly useful for educational practitioners throughout the world, though these comparative studies have not always yielded popular results. Indeed, much of the research in comparative education has identified flaws not only in educational systems themselves but also in the attempts made by educators to bring about reform. And, of course, this has meant a rethinking of the traditional theoretical underpinnings of education.

What all this means is that educators must once again reexamine the educational process in order to diagnose its problems and come up with new solutions. One approach, stemming from findings which indicate that only the student matters in the educational process—not teachers, not educational policies, not bricks and mortar—is to shift emphasis to more qualitative evaluative means. These qualitative approaches would enhance the many quantitative measures already in use. A second tactic involves a reevaluation of the theories which traditionally have been used in comparative educational research. "Conflict" and "legitimation" theories have been suggested, and even adoption of a more Marxist-oriented perspective.

Gail P. Kelly and Philip G. Altbach wrote our first selection in this section exploring comparative education. They review much of the major work in the field between the field's major reevaluations of itself in 1979 and 1986.

They stress the need to go beyond the focus on school outcomes to revise theory and to adopt more and better qualitative assessment methods. Given that educational reforms have been "less than successful," they stress the need to transform education into a means to the end of social equality.

The chief finding conveyed in the work by Aaron Benavot and colleagues is that a common core curriculum has emerged worldwide. Drawing on international compendiums of curricula as their principal source, the authors also queried 120 ministries of education for information on primary school curricula during the period 1920 to 1986. Modern curricular emphases, they stress, are not closely related to variations in national levels of development. This apparent standardization across all nations is further linked to an emerging world cultural system or world polity.

In the selection by Harry G. Judge, teaching as a profession is explored in the United States and the United Kingdom through systematic exposition of these two countries' similarities and differences in attitudes toward teaching. The author raises the question whether teaching really is, technically speaking, a profession, and reaches a rather surprising conclusion. In exploring the issues, the author identifies significant differences between the secondary educational systems in the two nations.

CHAPTER TWENTY

Comparative Education: Challenge and Response[*]

Gail P. Kelly and Philip G. Altbach[†]

Comparative education is characterized today by a wide diversity of views, lively debates, and varying theoretical perspectives. Since *Comparative Education Review* and *Comparative Education* published their retrospective "state-of-the-art" issues in 1977, the field has changed. In this essay, we will discuss some of these changes and the debates and research trends that have arisen since that time. Our interest is in the challenges posed to the field and the field's response.

It is our view that since 1977 many of the approaches that underlay the field, articulated so perceptively in the British and American appraisals in *Comparative Education* and the *Comparative Education Review,* have come under criticism. Some have questioned the national comparisons that have traditionally characterized research and have argued cogently for world systems and regional analyses. Others have challenged the field to move beyond quantitative studies of school outcomes to qualitative research on educational processes. The theoretical assumptions that had guided the field, especially in the United States and particularly structural functionalism, have also emerged as subjects of intense debate. Some scholars have begun to explore alternative perspectives such as conflict theory, legitimation theory, and Marxism. Simultaneously, scholars challenged the field to consider subjects of inquiry that it had hitherto ignored. Among these are women's education, the concrete study of social and political institutions, and the question of how knowledge is disseminated, produced, and used. In the past decade, scholars in

comparative education have also turned to reconsidering old questions, especially the role of education in bringing about modernization and social change.

The pages that follow first consider the new challenges posited to the field since 1977 and then look at the field's response. Our discussion is based on an analysis of research that has appeared in the major journals in the field, such as *Comparative Education Review,* the *International Review of Education, Compare,* and *Comparative Education,* as well as in some of the major books published on the field in the United States and Great Britain, including those in the series issued by Pergamon and Praeger. Our discussion is limited to the English-language literature, which, for the most part, is a British and North American literature. We make no pretenses of representing the developments in the field in Third World nations or anywhere but in the United States, Great Britain, and, to a lesser extent, Canada.

Our focus here is on new directions in the field. We will not dwell at length on traditional approaches or modes of analysis, which continue to dominate comparative education. Our purpose is to highlight challenges and to direct the field's attention to perspectives that have yet to be fully considered and that we believe are important to its vitality.

Challenges and New Directions

Since 1977, four kinds of challenges to established research traditions in comparative education have emerged. These are (1) those that question the nation-state or national characteristics as the major parameter in defining comparative study; (2) those that question the use of input-output models and exclusive reliance on quantification in the conduct of comparative research; (3) those that challenge structural functionalism as the major theoretical premise undergirding scholarship; and (4) those that direct attention to new subjects of inquiry. Some of these challenges began prior to 1977; however, before that time they scarcely entered the discourse of the field and were not promoted through the major journals or texts in comparative education. After 1977, they were increasingly and more directly articulated.

Although we have grouped the challenges to the field into four categories, we are aware that there is some overlap among them. For example, world systems analysis, which looks at international inequalities between nation-states in examining educational expansion, is guided by conflict theory and, in some instances, by Marxism. This is also the case with research that has arisen on women and sex differences in education cross-nationally, on knowledge distribution and control, and on the politics of educational planning. Regardless of the overlap, we believe it useful to discuss the challenges.

Challenges to the Nation-State as the Exclusive Research Framework

Until recently, most research in comparative education focused on the nation-state, and/or characteristics of nation-states, treated as an autonomous unit. Indeed, much of the field consisted of studies that applied a method derived from the social sciences to the study of education in a particular nation or that simply described education in a specific country. Often research asked how education contributed to the development and maintenance of social structures within that nation-state and compared education's role in one country with its role in another.[1] When the focus was on individual attitudes, research was situated in the context of school systems in a single nation presumed to be autonomous and coequal with

others. This framework predominated region-wide studies that, while dealing with Southeast Asia, Africa, Latin America, or Eastern Europe, focused on education in individual nation-states within that region that presumably shared similar cultures, histories, and economic or political structures. Topically based studies also were situated in national frameworks, asking for example, if one national school system was more conducive to economic growth than another.

Scholars such as John Meyer, John Boli-Bennett, Francisco Ramirez, Mathew Zachariah, Martin Carnoy, Robert Arnove, and Philip Altbach challenge the use of the nation-state as the dominant category guiding comparative research. They argue that educational systems in one country are often affected more by factors outside that country than they are by factors inside it and urge research to focus on identifying these external forces. Martin Carnoy's 1974 book, *Education as Cultural Imperialism,* marked the beginning of such scholarship in the field. After 1977, the number of works of this nature in comparative education increased markedly.[2]

In 1979, John Meyer and Michael T. Hannon published *National Development and the World System.*[3] They point out that educational expansion in the post–World War II period could not be explained by reference to a single nation-state or its political structure, to the way in which it organized power, to how its economy was controlled, or to its peculiar social structure. The drive for universal primary education and the unparalleled expansion of education on the secondary and tertiary levels had little to do with national educational policies, either. Meyer and Hannon maintain that given changes in technology and communications and the internationalization of the labor market, education functions within a transnational context. They call on the field to reorient its inquiry by looking at what they call the world system rather than merely at the nation-state.

Meyer and his colleagues, as well as other scholars who focus on world systems analysis, use a range of perspectives in their work. Meyer, and his coauthors, for example, argue that an individual nation's political and economic systems have relatively little to do with either how education is organized and distributed or its content. Immanuel Wallerstein, on the other hand, discusses the nature of the world system by using Marxian frameworks, although his work is not directly dealing with education.[4] Most of the scholars directly in the field of comparative education utilize a range of explanatory frameworks in their work on specific aspects of how relationships between nations, regions, classes, or group within and among societies affect schooling and its social, economic, and political outcomes. Altbach, Arnove, Carnoy, Zachariah, and Silva all argue that national school systems exist within the context of unequal power relations among nations.[5] They argue that either through design, historical circumstance, or the contemporary distribution of resources, including intellectual resources, the Western industrialized capitalist nations dominate the economic and educational systems of the less industrialized countries. Silva argues that educational dominance patterns parallel trading blocs. Altbach discusses how the knowledge that schools distribute in the Third World is generated, controlled, and distributed by the United States, Great Britain, and France. Carnoy contends that such controls seek to maintain existing international inequalities and keep the Third World dependent.

World systems analysis challenges comparative education to go beyond the nation-state as the major analytical category guiding research and to look at regional variations, racial groups, classes, and others that are not necessarily bound to the nation. Other scholars who have not used the world systems approach have come to similar conclusions, frequently based on microanalytic research. Notable among these are those scholars who have focused on regional variation.

Research in comparative education before 1977 focused on schooling within a nation-state; rare was the scholar whose work centered on regional variation beyond urban/rural distinctions that were applied to Third World nations and, in the case of a few studies of African nations, beyond ethnically based distinctions. Comparative work took the nation-state as the boundary for comparison and referred to it in tracing school/society relations. Comparative research did not inquire as to whether there were major regional variations in the pattern of educational diffusion or in the determinants of educational access and outcomes within a nation-state. Proponents of the analysis of regional variation argue that comparison among regions within nation-states is as significant as comparison between nations. The challenge to pursue such a line of analysis was developed by John Craig and Margaret Archer in their works tracing the spread of education in the nineteenth century.[6] It was also advanced by Mary Jean Bowman, Phyllis Goldblatt, and David Plank.[7] All of these scholars showed that educational variance often is as great, if not greater, between regions within a nation as between nations. The determinants of women's education, for example, are not the same in northeast Brazil as in the dominant south of that country; class and ethnicity may not operate similarly in regard to educational access and outcome throughout a single nation. They have pointed to the obvious—the necessity of looking at regional variation given growing trends to decentralization of education and deconcentration of educational decision making in much of the world.

Although scholars working in the newly emergent tradition of world systems analysis and analysis of regional variation challenge established research traditions, their questions represent but one kind among those to emerge since 1977.

Challenges to Input/Output Models and Dominant Reliance on Quantification

Much research in comparative education tended to focus almost exclusively on the quantitative analysis of educational inputs and outcomes, mostly the outcomes. Research assumed that the outcomes—such as modern attitudes or mathematics achievement levels—could be attributed to whatever schools taught. With some exceptions, research—following Sadlerian traditions—assumed that whatever went on in the school was unimportant and not worthy of study. The only studies of school processes—if one could call them that—were descriptions of curricular guides, analyses of texts, and a few ethnographic studies—considered anthropology—that treated the classroom as part of the broader social order, reflecting a social consensus.

Before 1977, there were some criticisms of the field for presuming that school processes were unimportant. More recently, this criticism was extended to research such as the international achievement studies (IEA) that focused only on the quantitative measurement of outcomes and inputs (such as test scores, number of hours in the classroom, years of teacher training, and the like) to stand for the study of the educational process. Scholars such as Masemann, Weis, Heyman, and Pfau argued cogently that reliance on school outcome data failed to relate outcomes to the processes of schooling and suggested that only through qualitative methods could the nature of educational processes and their outcomes be understood.[8] They pointed out that what schools teach cannot be reduced only to the formal curriculum texts and teacher attributes; rather, student and teacher interaction, the structure of educational institutions, and the "lived culture" of the schools represented a very powerful element in producing the social, cultural, and political outcomes of schooling. Their call was for the use of qualitative means of research that focused on educational processes.

Heyman and Pfau urge comparative education to adopt ethnomethodological techniques derived exclusively from anthropology; Masemann and Weiss, in their respective works, challenge the field to go beyond anthropological traditions and to relate educational processes to broader theories of school/society relations. Weis points out that such scholarship could adopt varying theoretical perspectives, including either structural functionalism or Marxism.[9]

Although the challenge to engage in qualitative research on educational processes in light of social theory does not necessarily entail a paradigm shift for the field, parallel interest in such studies has increased questioning of the dominance of structural functionalism in guiding research in comparative education.

Challenges to Structural Functionalism

Until the 1970s, comparative education in North America was largely influenced by structural functionalism. This is not surprising given the domination of this perspective in many of the social sciences. The "state-of-the-art" volumes of *Comparative Education Review* and of *Comparative Education* are largely in this tradition.[10] The field asked either how education functioned to maintain the social fabric or how it could be made to function, in the case of the Third World, to develop a nation-state generally along Western models. It was assumed that what was good for the nation also benefited all of society. In this context, conflict, as John Bock and Rolland Paulston so aptly point out, was considered dysfunctional at best.[11] Although many questions about functionalism were raised outside comparative education before 1977, few within the field paid much attention to debates in sociology and political science. Kazamias and Schwartz, in their essay that prefaces *Comparative Education Review*'s state-of-the-art issue, note the dominance of structural functionalism in the field and urge that scholars inform their works with different perspectives.[12] Other voices joined them. Martin Carnoy, Philip Altbach, Robert Arnove, Michael Apple, and Henry Levin began to look at how educational systems serve societal groups differentially and how social inequalities are played out at the regional and international levels.[13] Carnoy, Apple, and Levin emphasize the relationship between education and the development of capitalist relations and argue that the nature of economic systems and of state control make a difference as to what schools teach and as to the outcomes of education.

Rolland Paulston argues that reliance on functionalism has led the field away from correctly analyzing education in most social settings and places too much stress on the national setting and not on the roles that education might play in society and its myriad institutions.[14] John Bock makes a similar point.[15] He asserts that most developing societies are plural societies characterized by conflict, where dominant groups seek to legitimize their control over the state. At the same time, minorities attempt to use education to assert themselves and sometimes to unseat the dominant groups. Bock shows us that education assumes contradictory roles—it is at once oppressive and liberating. Paulston and Bock and, more recently, Hans Weiler see alternatives to functionalism in conflict theory and in legitimation theory;[16] others have adopted a classical Marxian perspective.

It is not our intention in this essay to explore in depth these alternative theories; rather, our point here is to show that alternatives to structural functionalism have been articulated in the field. These alternatives have also led to changes in research concerns, as we will now explore.

The Emergence of New Research Concerns

Comparative education until recently was a field that focused mainly on issues of education and development, on educational planning, on the individual outcomes of schooling in the context of the nation-state, and on a range of descriptive analyses and discussions of educational systems and issues. Most of the research was informed by structural functionalism or was basically atheoretical and descriptive. Few qualitative studies appeared in the field's journals that sought to understand what schools taught and that related educational processes to outcomes of education. Over the past decade the field has been challenged to study subjects that it had hitherto ignored. These ranged from including women both as a category in and as a central concern of research; to looking at the ways in which knowledge was disseminated, produced, and used; to new ways of looking at educational institutions and their relation to society. A major research challenge in all instances has been to reorient study away from preoccupation with individual outcomes and attitudes toward looking at institutions ranging from schools to the state to international agencies and finally to the relationships among them. The research challenge that emerged was to chart institutional content— that is, how institutions such as schools, planning agencies, the government, and so forth are organized and controlled and what the effect is that these institutional arrangements have on educational outcomes. We will discuss some of these challenges that have arisen in the past decade in the form of an interest in how education is planned and controlled, how educational contents are structured and distributed, and how schools shape the social reality of their pupils.

Although comparative education has a substantial literature on educational planning, much of that literature focuses on the technical aspects of planning and its outcomes—whether goals were or were not fulfilled. New scholarship has appeared that looks at the institutional context of planning—who plans what in whose interests and the relation between planning and structured inequality. Studies like Urwick's on Nigeria; McGinn, Schiefelbein, and Warwick's on planners in Chile; and Salvador's and McGinn and Street's on Mexico are in this vein.[17] Others have looked at institutional capacity to plan, the mechanisms by which plans are put into practice, and the role of political parties with distinctly different ideologies in planning. Some of these institutional studies have focused on the roles of international agencies in forming and implementing national plans—for example, Linda Dove's research on Universal Primary Education in Bangladesh.[18] These works challenge the field to look at institutional processes in the context of national and international politics.

While much scholarship to emerge since 1977 has called the field's attention to the institutional processes of planning, related research has emerged on how knowledge is generated and used in educational systems to make educational policy and shape society. Much of this research—but by no means all of it—stems from world systems or conflict analysis. Some scholars have been concerned with knowledge distribution systems. Altbach's work on transnational publishing, for example, focuses on how books are produced and distributed internationally and the implications for educational and knowledge systems within specific countries.[19] Others have been concerned with knowledge generation and control. Edward Berman's research on the role of philanthropic foundations is an example of a concern with the factors that influence research and development.[20] Other scholars have been concerned with knowledge utilization. Fry, among others, studies how educational planners use research to guide policy.[21] James Coleman has considered the role of U.S.-trained political scientists in Africa and has written on the impact of foundation assistance in Asia and Africa.[22] Hans Weiler and others have written of the impact of foreign study on education and development in the Third World. This research has looked at student flows and the students' impact on host institutions and on the students' country of origin.[23] These studies, and many others, have focused on the nature of knowledge transfer and its impact on the Third World.[24]

There has also been an interest in what kind of knowledge enters the classroom and how that knowledge is communicated. Heyneman's research on the role, availability, and effectiveness of textbooks in Third World nations is an example of such scholarship. There is also a growing body of research that seeks to understand the nature of social reality conveyed in textbooks used in the Third World and the relationship of this reality to development and culture.[25]

Although comparative education has traditionally been concerned with school outcomes, there has been a new concern with the detailed study of the content of schooling and with the internal workings of the school. Some of these studies have used ethnographic and participant observation research tools to search deeply into the internal life of educational institutions. Paul Willis's study of British education is an example of this trend.[26] Other studies have looked at the interaction between the formal and the "hidden" curriculum in schools in an effort to understand school cultures.[27] Some researchers have looked at a range of variables to obtain a broad picture of the impact of education on students and on society. William Cumming's work on Japan takes such an approach.[28] Susan Shirk and Jonathan Unger analyze education in China during the Cultural Revolution from this perspective.[29] The originality of this research is its concern with the internal culture of the school, the "in-school" outcomes of education, and the effect of the relationship between these factors on society.

Another important and new stream of scholarship has been gender studies. The field in the 1980s has been challenged to look at women in the context of educational and social structures that have resulted in gender-based inequalities. This scholarship has pointed out that research can no longer assume that findings based on the study of male populations are necessarily relevant for females as well. The 1980 special issue of *Comparative Education Review* challenged the field not only to include gender as a background variable in research—something almost totally neglected in comparative education—but also to make women a central research focus.[30] The field was also challenged to ask how education changed women's lives in the family and in the workforce and not confine itself to asking whether educational outcomes for males and females were the same.

We have thus far detailed currents new to the field since 1977. We have by no means represented all currents in the field. Our goal has been to call attention to innovations in the field, not to the field's mainstream. Much research in the field continues to presume the autonomous nation-state and is guided by structural functionalism and its correlates like human capital theory. Research still focuses on development and on the outcomes of schooling and, as in the past, is predominantly quantitative, centered around primary through higher education.

The challenges to the field that we have outlined have, for the most part, generated some debate. They have appeared in the major journals and texts in the field; they have been presented at conferences; some have been the themes of world yearbooks of education. The last part of this essay asks how the field has responded to these challenges—what kinds of debates, if any, have they generated, and how have they affected the mainstream of the field?

Response

It is always difficult to gauge the response of a field of inquiry to challenges that it reexamine its theoretical assumptions or study phenomena through the lens of theories that contradict those that the field has traditionally used. We now ask if there have been any changes in the research published in the major journals and texts in comparative education that reflect the new challenges we have outlined thus far. Is there, for example, a greater emphasis on qualitative research that seeks to understand educational processes? Are there more studies focusing on women or on education in the context of the world system or on institutional behaviors? Has there been less reliance on structural functionalism and a greater diversity of theoretical orientations?

We will show that there have been three types of responses to the new research challenges. In many instances the field has tended to ignore new challenges. Such a response, we believe, is basically a sign of weakness in comparative education. A second response has been to confront new challenges and to attempt to refute them. In some instances scholars have contested the validity of new trends and sought to end the debates that they engendered. The third response has been to co-opt the challenges. This has led to some changes in what scholars study but not necessarily in how they study it or in the theoretical assumptions that underlie inquiry. We will discuss these three types of responses separately.

Ignoring the Challenges

A common response to new trends is to ignore them. Comparative education is no different in this regard from other fields of inquiry. Many of the challenges we noted appeared in the field's major journals as "think pieces." For example, Vandra Masemann and Douglas Foley urged the field to engage in qualitative research that seeks to understand educational processes.[31] No debate followed, nor for that matter did much research of a qualitative nature on school processes. The field neither accepted nor rejected the challenge; it simply acted as if it were never made. *Comparative Education Review* continued to publish a very small number of ethnographies, but they, by and large, were in the tradition of anthropologically based works that did not seek to relate classroom phenomena to social theory. Journals in Great Britain like *Compare* carried no such material; the recent *International Encyclopedia of Education* fails to mention this work as even a part of the field, although there is substantive coverage given to ethnography and to the anthropology of education.[32]

The tendency to ignore new trends extends also to challenges to attend to gender both as a variable in research and as a focus of research. Two of the major journals in the field published special issues on women's education and sex differences in education, and the *World Yearbook of Education* in 1984 focused on women.[33] Despite this, some journals in the field have yet to run research articles on either women's education or sex differences in education. The few articles that acknowledge gender that find their way into the field's journals have women as the subject of study and are written by women as well. Very rarely does research use gender as a significant background variable, even when that research does deal with other variables like class, ethnicity, and urban/rural residence. This occurs even when scholarship focuses on inequality or the determinants of academic achievement, despite the clear-cut evidence that gender is both a basis for structural inequality and a predictor of educational outcomes. At the same time that the field has tended to ignore the sizable body of research on women and gender effects that has appeared in women's studies journals, UNESCO publications, and special issues in the field, there has also been little debate about the validity of such scholarship. Gender often becomes a nonissue, neither incorporated nor debated and then rejected.[34]

The field's reaction to the challenges to engage in the qualitative study of school processes or to make women a focus of research and gender a variable in scholarship has parallels in the case of regional analysis. A few scholars have called on the field to consider such work, and their calls so far have landed on deaf ears.

Although comparative education has ignored some new currents that have arisen since 1977, this is not the case with all new scholarship. The field has hotly debated scholarship that has directly challenged the theoretical premises underlying research. In the case of world systems analysis, the field has debated and co-opted some challenges by accepting parts of the research foci commended by such scholarship while discarding the theory that led to these very concerns. Before discussing co-optation, however, we will trace the debates that the new challenges have engendered.

Debate

Although many recent commentaries on the field have ignored the challenges posed by world systems analysis to comparative education,[35] others have attacked it on the basis of the association of world systems analysis with a Marxist problematic. Harold Noah and Max Eckstein have dubbed this approach the "new simplicitude."[36] They claim that such an approach, deriving from dependency theory and focusing on the unequal power relations between Third World and industrialized nations, has tended to look on Third World nations as passive victims of the industrialized nations and to blame the current economic hardships of these Third World nations on former colonial rulers. Noah and Eckstein deny that there is any evidence of attempts on the part of Western industrialized nations to maintain economic domination that would explain either the poverty or the evolution of school systems in much of Africa, Asia, and Latin America. Rather, they attribute the problems of the Third World solely to underdevelopment, which predated colonialism and which industrialized nations are, through their aid programs, seeking to remedy. Additionally, Noah and Eckstein point out that if world systems analysis had any validity, it would be impossible to explain social revolutions in parts of the Third World or development in other parts.

Attacks on world systems analysis, similar to those initiated by Noah and Eckstein, were mounted by Keith Watson and Jon Lauglo in British journals.[37] Watson does not dispute the existence of the international ties documented by Arnove, Altbach, and others. He simply disagrees with world systems analysts' interpretation of what these ties mean. Watson, for one, sees dependency as a stage in the development of autonomous nation-states.

The debates over world systems analysis do not only concern the interpretation of underdevelopment. One study has attempted to generate data to refute world systems analysis and the application of dependency theory to the evolution of schooling in the Third World. Sica and Prechel ask if there is any relation between the spread of Western-style education and economic dependency (they note the lack of relation between educational expansion and economic development).[38] They find no significant relation between measures of educational enrollments and dependency. Whether such a statistical analysis has validity is open to question—the authors themselves point out that the fact that they have found no statistically significant relation cannot be taken to mean that no relation at all exists.

The debates surrounding world systems analysis are related to those that challenges to structural functionalism have generated. Not only have scholars working in the tradition of world systems analysis questioned structural functionalism but so also have some scholars who focus their studies on education and inequality and on the role of education as an institution in maintaining existing social and political injustice. These scholars have been openly critical of structural functionalism and have applied conflict, Marxist, and/or other nonmainstream theories to the study of education. Within comparative education there have been few, if any, outright defenses of structural functionalism; rather, there have been critiques of alternative approaches, especially those identified as Marxist. Some scholars have dismissed such approaches out of hand as ideological and "biased."[39] Others, like Erwin Epstein, have tried to moderate the debate and strive for consensus in the field. In his presidential address to the Comparative and International Education Society, Erwin Epstein implied that the strident debates that Marxist and conflict theories had brought to the field put comparative education's future at risk.[40] He claimed that "neo-Marxism," "neo-positivism"

(which he identified with functionalism), and "neo-relativism" (which he associated with Brian Holmes and his "problem approach" first articulated in the 1960s) divided the field into hostile camps. Each position generated its own data sets, none of which were comparable. Because of this, the field had reached a point where it was unable to provide "objective" evidence to guide policy. Epstein felt that comparative education would be better off if theoretical divisions were muted and attention focused on generating a knowledge base that all could use.

Epstein did not directly attack Marxian theory—his plea was one for greater consensus in the field. Paulston, in his article that outlines the divergent theories in the field, also argues for consensus.[41] He suggests that Marxian theories could be used to "diagnose" educational problems and consensual functionalist theories to arrive at reform strategies. Whether such a strategy is viable is open to question.

Not only has the application of conflict and Marxist theories been criticized for being divisive but there have also been some works that seek to disprove empirically the findings of such studies. Among these is William Cummings's book, *Education and Equality in Japan.*[42] Cummings characterizes Marxist-based theories of social/cultural reproduction as refusing to posit the possibility of social transformation other than through a revolution that drastically alters the way production is organized and the ownership of the means of production. Despite a highly differentiated system of higher education and evidence that socioeconomic status closely predicts educational levels and future income, Cummings contends that the schools are making Japanese society more egalitarian than is the case in any other country, including those countries that have undergone socialist revolutions. He bases this on an analysis of attitudes of students and corporate employees, which are egalitarian. He argues that because students and corporate executives place little emphasis on social mobility and show sympathy toward income equalization, the transformation of Japanese society will soon occur. He maintains that such a change is inevitable, since individual attitudes shape social structures. He interprets his study as refuting Bowles and Gintis and other Marxist scholars of education who argue that without structural transformation there can be no social change.

Cummings's study and the other critiques of conflict and Marxist alternatives to structural functionalism represent a set of responses to the scholarship generated in recent years. Debate, however, has not been the only active response. In some instances the field has co-opted some of the recent challenges.

Co-optation

Although the field has debated and ignored many of the new currents, some have been co-opted into the field. This co-optation has followed a distinct pattern. For example, world systems analysis has suggested a research agenda that includes study of international aid agencies and linkages among Third World and industrialized nations with a view toward understanding the mechanisms through which the world system is maintained. A host of studies have appeared on topics suggested by world systems analysis; most are devoid of the theoretical frames from which they initially arose. For example, the journals in the field have devoted considerable coverage to the activities of international aid agencies, most recently to the World Bank.[43] This work has, for the most part, described the policies of these agencies and changes in them over time. Some of this scholarship has not sought to explain the impact of such policies. More often than not, the assumption is that these institutions exist outside the frame of international politics and serve simply to develop Third World nations.

Another example of co-optation of world systems analysis is renewed interest in "institutional transfers." The British journal *Compare,* for example, ran a special issue on this topic in 1980.[44] The studies that it included, aside from Robert Arnove's on the Ford Foundation, attacked the very concept of world systems analysis and focused on transfers instead. The articles, by implication, likened educational borrowing between Great Britain and the United States to that between the United States and Latin America or between Great Britain and Africa. They criticized the presumption that educational borrowing takes place within the context of either international politics or unequal relations between nation-states.

World systems analysis is not the only new challenge to be co-opted in comparative education and transformed in the process. This is also the case for research emanating from scholarship on women. We pointed out earlier that the field for the most part has ignored the challenge to focus on women as a central concern and a variable in research. However, the field has begun to focus to some extent on issues raised by this challenge. Such research has not focused on women as such or on the social construction of gender. Rather, it has centered on issues presumed to be the province of women—fertility, nutrition, health, and the generation of basic needs for poor families in which the male is not able to be the sole provider.[45] The focus of this research is on women in the narrowly defined roles of child bearers and child rearers in the family. Women are not the center of study or necessarily the subject of research so much as its object. In the process of co-optation the very issues initially raised about the necessity of studying women and their education have disappeared.

The ways in which the field has co-opted world systems analysis and, to an almost unrecognizable degree, the study of women stand as examples of how the field has responded to new challenges that it has not attacked or totally ignored. These forms of co-optation exemplify the approaches that the field has taken to other issues and theoretical challenges posited over the past decade. What we have suggested about world systems analysis and the study of women's education also extends to the field's treatment of the challenge to study educational institutions and their processes.

Conclusion

We understand that our discussion of new currents and comparative education's response to them is far from complete. We have attempted in this essay to provide an overview of recent challenges and to outline the ways in which the field has responded. We hope that the reluctance with which the field has greeted many of these challenges is but a temporary phase. We do not believe it is healthy for a field of inquiry to ignore questioning about the frameworks, theories, and methods that it has used to generate research or to dismiss challenges out of hand. To do so is to consign the field to stagnation and to rehashing old questions.

Although our focus in this essay has been on new challenges, comparative education has, as a field of study, shown considerable continuity both in its approaches to research and in the theory underlying such research. Since 1977, however, this continuity has also shown some signs of change. The optimism that education could be a force for social equality, which pervaded the field in the 1960s and 1970s, has been muted by years of not always successful attempts to reform both schools and society. This sober mood has especially appeared in the scholarship on comprehensive school reforms in Western Europe, on the Chinese experiments during the Great Proletarian Cultural Revolution, and on evidence drawn from the Soviet Union, Eastern Europe, and the Third World.[46] The thought that expanded enrollments and common schooling would change social structures or the effects of parental education and income, gender, and race on children's life chances has become a subject of debate.

Much of this discussion was stimulated by a radical critique of structural functionalism that assumed that over time the transformation of society could occur without changes in social structures. The radical critique was clearly articulated, for example, by Weis in her study of Ghanaian secondary schools. Levin, in his study of Western Europe, argued that without changes in social structures the schools could only reproduce existing social relations and the inequalities currently structured into them. Others in comparative education maintained that inequality was difficult, indeed almost impossible, to eradicate, even if basic social structures were changed. Such was the argument made by Court's study of educational expansion and inequality in Kenya and Tanzania, Morrison's work on Tanzania, and Dobson's studies of the Soviet Union.[47]

Comparative educators have, to some extent become more pessimistic—some would say realistic—about the role of education in shaping social change and in contributing to economic development and modernization. This "new realism" has been stimulated to a considerable degree by the insights of radical critics of the past decade as well as by the failure of many of the educational efforts of the 1960s and 1970s. The fiscal crisis of the 1980s as well as the lowered expectations of the current period have stimulated further critique and analysis, this time from a more conservative stance. Scholars like Philip Coombs, George Psacharopoulos, and Mateen Thobani have questioned the viability and, to some extent, even the desirability of the vision of universal, free primary education and total literacy for Third World nations.[48] Some have argued that not only is universal primary education a luxury but in some cases it may be harmful to economic development and to social well-being, since it discourages the efficient use of resources. In the 1980s, some scholars in the field have turned increasingly to the concept of privatization as a means to improve economic efficiency in the provision of education and to enhance educational quality.[49] The recent debates on educational vouchers and on the imposition of school fees represent a return to some of the debates of the 1950s.

The field has recently reconsidered with increasing frequency the role of education of any sort—formal or nonformal, vocational or general—in development. In the 1960s and 1970s, many hoped that given the proper form and content of education and its widespread diffusion, Third World countries would industrialize and become modern, and the poverty and accompanying ills that were associated with underdevelopment would be eradicated. The vision was development, and the field assumed that no matter how poor a country was, education would lead to the creation of human capital, which in turn would develop the nation to the levels of most Western countries.[50] Much empirical research has shifted its major focus from modernization to education's relation to the provision of basic needs: to crop production, small-scale technology, marketing, and family health and nutrition. Education is increasingly being looked to for survival or as a means of stemming a demographic and ecological disaster. In short, the vision of what it means to develop human capital is undergoing modification.

In this essay we have been critical of the field for the ways in which it has responded to new ways of thinking about comparative education and treated alternative theories. Unlike some who have openly attacked some of the new challenges for their divisiveness, we believe that the new strains are a sign of vitality for the field of comparative education. It strengthens the field to have more than one way of viewing the role of education in society and to debate alternatives for studying education and its context. To ignore new challenges, many of which arise from changing contexts and advances in scholarship both in comparative education and sister disciplines, is to consign the field to irrelevance in the long run. It is commendable that the field has taken time to reflect on issues that it considered in the past. Nonetheless, it is important that it explores new ones. The challenge of the next decades

will be not only to explore the issues raised in the field since 1977 and to take them seriously but also to identify new areas for investigation that will bring continuing debate and vitality to research in comparative education.

Notes

* From the *Comparative Education Review* 30, no. 1 (1986): 89–107, by permission of the University of Chicago Press. Copyright 1986 by the University of Chicago Press.

† The authors wish to thank Joseph Farrell and Stephen Klees for their criticism on an earlier draft of this article.

1. For a more complete discussion see Gail P. Kelly and Philip G. Altbach, "Comparative Education: A Field in Transition," in *International Bibliography of Comparative Education,* ed. P. G. Altbach, G. P. Kelly, and D. H. Kelly (New York: Praeger, 1981). See also, "Comparative Education: Its Present State and Future Prospects," *Comparative Education* 13 (June 1977): 75–150; and "The State of the Art: Twenty Years of Comparative Education," *Comparative Education Review* 21 (June/October 1977): 151–416.

2. John W. Meyer et al., "The World Educational Revolution, 1950–1970," *Sociology of Education* 50 (October 1971): 242–58; John Meyer and Michael T. Hannon, *National Development and the World System* (Chicago: University of Chicago Press, 1979); Robert Arnove, "Comparative Education and World Systems Analysis," *Comparative Education Review* 24 (February 1980): 48–62; Philip G. Altbach, "Servitude of the Mind: Education, Dependency and Neocolonialism," *Teachers College Record* 79 (December 1977): 188–204; Mathew Zachariah, "Comparative Educators and International Development Policy," *Comparative Education Review* 23 (October 1979): 341–54; Martin Carnoy, "Education for Alternative Development," *Comparative Education Review* 27 (June 1982): 160–77; and Martin Carnoy, *Education as Cultural Imperialism* (New York: McKay, 1974).

3. Meyer and Hannon.

4. Immanuel Wallerstein, *The Modern World System* (New York: Academic Press, 1974).

5. Philip G. Altbach, Robert F. Arnove, and Gail P. Kelly, eds., *Comparative Education* (New York: Macmillian, 1982); Carnoy, *Education as Cultural Imperialism;* Zachariah; Edward T. Silva, "Cultural Autonomy and Ideas in Transit: Notes from the Canadian Case," *Comparative Education Review* 24 (February 1980): 63–72.

6. Margaret Archer, ed., *The Sociology of Educational Expansion: Take-Off Growth and Inflation in Educational Systems* (Beverly Hills, Calif.: Sage, 1982).

7. See Mary Jean Bowman, "An Integrated Framework for Analysis of the Spread of Schooling in Less Developed Countries," *Comparative Education Review* 28 (November 1984): 563–83; David N. Plank, "The Determinants of School Enrollment Rates in Brazil, 1940–1980" (Ph.D. diss., University of Chicago, 1983).

8. Vandra Masemann, "Critical Ethnography in the Study of Comparative Education," *Comparative Education* 26 (February 1982): 1–15; Lois Weis, "Educational Outcomes and School Processes: Theoretical Perspectives," in Altbach, Arnove, and Kelly, eds.; Richard Heyman, "Comparative Education from an Ethnomethodological Perspective," *Comparative Education* 15 (October 1979): 241–49; Richard H. Pfau, "The Comparative Study of Classroom Behaviors," *Comparative Education Review* 24 (October 1980): 400–414.

9. Those that incorporate a Marxian approach include Paul Willis, *Learning to Labour: How Working Class Kids Get Working Class Jobs* (Westhead, England: Saxon House, 1977); and Pierre Bourdieu and Jean-Claude Passeron; *Reproduction in Education, Society and Culture* (London: Sage, 1977). Those who do not include John U. Ogbu, *Minority Education and Caste: The American System in Cross-Cultural Perspective* (New York: Academic Press, 1978); John U. Ogbu, "Minority Status and Schooling in Plural Societies," *Comparative Education Review* 27 (June 1983): 168–90; and Karen Coffyn Biraimah, "Different Knowledge for Different Folks: Knowledge Distribution in Togolese Secondary School," in Altbach, Arnove, and Kelly, eds.

10. See Andreas M. Kazamias and Karl Schwartz, "Intellectual and Ideological Perspectives in Comparative Education: An Interpretation," *Comparative Education Review* 21 (June/October 1977): 153–76; and Robert Koehl, "The Comparative Study of Education: Prescription and Practice," *Comparative Education Review* 21 (June/October 1977): 177–94.

11. John C. Bock, "Education and the Meaning of Development: A Conflict of Meaning." in Altbach, Arnove, and Kelly, eds. (n. 5 above); Rolland Paulston, "Conflicting Theories of Educational Reform," in *Better Schools: International Lessons for Reform,* ed. John Simmons (New York: Praeger, 1983).

12. Kazamias and Schwartz.

13. See, e.g., Carnoy, *Education as Cultural Imperialism;* Robert F. Arnove, "The Ford Foundation and 'Competence Building' Overseas: Assumptions, Approaches and Implications." *Studies in Comparative International Development* 12 (Fall 1977): 100–126; Robert F. Arnove, ed., *Philanthropy and Cultural Imperialism: The Foundations at Home and Abroad* (Boston: G. K. Hall, 1980); Philip G. Altbach, "Servitude of the Mind" (n. 2 above); Henry M. Levin, "The Dilemma of Comprehensive Secondary School Reforms in Western Europe," *Comparative Education Review* 22 (October 1978): 434–51; Michael Apple, "Ideology, Reproduction and Educational Reform," *Comparative Education Review* 22 (October 1978): 367–87.

14. Paulston.

15. Bock.

16. See, e.g., Hans N. Weiler, "Legalization, Expertise and Participation: Strategies of Compensatory Legitimation in Educational Policy," *Comparative Education Review* 27 (June 1983): 259–77; Hans N. Weiler, "Educational Planning and Social Change: A Critical Review of Concepts and Practices," in Altbach, Arnove, and Kelly, eds. (n. 5 above).

17. See, e.g., Noel McGinn, Ernesto Schiefelbein, and Donald P. Warwick, "Educational Planning as Political Process: Two Case Studies from Latin America," *Comparative Education Review* 23 (June 1979): 218–39; James Urwick, "Politics and Professionalism in Nigerian Educational Planning," *Comparative Education Review* 23 (October 1983): 323–40; Noel McGinn and Susan Street, "The Political Rationality of Resource Allocation in Mexican Public Education," *Comparative Education Review* 26 (June 1982): 178–98; Weiler, "Legalization,

Expertise, and Participation"; E. Mark Hanson, "Administrative Development in the Columbia Ministry of Education: A Case Analysis of the 1970s," *Comparative Education Review* 27 (February 1983): 89–107.

18. McGinn, Schiefelbein, and Warwick. See also Linda Dove, "The Political Context of Education in Bangladesh, 1971–80," in *Politics and Educational Change,* ed. P. Broadfoot, C. Brock, and W. Tulasiewicz (London: Croom Helm, 1982).

19. Philip G. Altbach, "The Distribution of Knowledge in the Third World," in *Higher Education in the Third World: Themes and Variations,* by P. G. Altbach (Singapore: Maruzen, 1982).

20. Edward Berman, "Foundations, United States Foreign Policy and African Education, 1945–1975," *Harvard Educational Review* 49 (May 1979): 145–79.

21. Sippandondha Ketudat and Gerald Fry, "Relations between Educational Research, Policy, Planning and Implementation: The Thai Experience," *International Review of Education* 27 (1981): 141–52.

22. James S. Coleman, "Professional Training and Institution Building in the Third World: Two Rockefeller Foundation Experiences," *Comparative Education Review* 28 (May 1984): 180–202.

23. Hans Weiler, "The Political Dilemma of Foreign Study," *Comparative Education Review* 28 (May 1984): 168–79. See also Philip G. Altbach and Y. G.-M. Lulat, "International Students in Comparative Perspective: Toward a Political Economy of International Study," in *Research on Foreign Students and International Study,* ed. P. G. Altbach, D. H. Kelly, and Y. G.-M. Lulat (New York: Praeger, 1985).

24. Thomas O. Eisemon, "Scientific Life of Indian and African Universities: A Comparative Study of Peripheriality in Science," *Comparative Education Review* 25 (June 1981): 164–82; and Arnove, "The Ford Foundation and 'Competence Building' Overseas" (n. 13 above).

25. Stephen P. Heyneman, *Textbooks and Achievement: What We Know* (Washington, D.C.: World Bank, 1978). Also see Karen Coffyn Biraimah, "The Impact of Western Schools in Girls' Expectations," *Comparative Education Review* 24 (June 1980): 196–208.

26. Willis (n. 9 above).

27. See, e.g., Biraimah, "Different Knowledge for Different Folk" (n. 9 above).

28. William Cummings, *Education and Equality in Japan* (Princeton, N.J.: Princeton University Press, 1980), esp. chap. 5.

29. Susan Shirk, *Competitive Comrades: Career Incentives and Student Strategies in China* (Berkeley and Los Angeles: University of California Press, 1982); Jonathan Unger, *Education under Mao: Class and Competition in Canton Schools, 1960–1980* (New York: Columbia University Press, 1982).

30. See, esp., Carolyn M. Elliott and Gail P. Kelly, "Perspectives on Women's Education," *Comparative Education Review* 24 (June 1980): S1–S12. See also Gail Kelly, "Women's Access to Education in the Third World: Myths and Realities," in *World Yearbook of Education 1984: Women in Education,* ed. S. Acker (New York: Kogan Page, 1984). For a complete bibliography of recently generated works, see David H. Kelly and Gail P. Kelly, "Women and Schooling in the Third World: A Bibliography," in *Women's Education in the Third World: Comparative Perspectives,* ed. G. P. Kelly and C. Elliott (Albany: SUNY Press, 1982).

31. Masemann (n. 8 above). See also Douglas Foley, "Anthropological Studies of Schooling in Developing Countries: Some Recent Findings and Trends," *Comparative Education Review* 21 (June/October 1977): 311–28.

32. Torsten Husen and T. Neville Postlethwaite, eds., *International Encyclopedia of Education* (Oxford: Pergamon, 1985), 10 vols.

33. See G. P. Kelly and Carolyn Elliott, eds., "Women and Education in the Third World," *Comparative Education Review* 24 (June 1980, part 2): S1–S266. See also Acker, ed.

34. Husen and Postlethwaite. See also Keith Watson and Raymond Wilson, eds., *Contemporary Issues in Comparative Education: A Festschrift in Honor of Professor Emeritus Vernon Mallinson* (London: Croom Helm, 1985).

35. Watson and Wilson.

36. Harold Noah and Max Eckstein, "Dependency Theory in Comparative Education: The New Simplicitude," *Prospects* 15, no. 2 (1985): 213–25.

37. Keith Watson, "Dependence or Independence in Education: Two Cases from Post-colonial Southeast Asia," *International Journal of Educational Development* 5 (1985): 83–94. See also Jon Lauglo, "Mass Schooling: A Tool of Capitalist Domination?" *Compare* 15, no. 1 (1985): 21–27.

38. Alan Sica and Harland Prechel, "National Political-Economic Dependency in the Global Economy and Educational Development," *Comparative Education Review* 25 (October 1981): 384–402.

39. See Brian Holmes, *Comparative Education: Some Consideration of Method* (London: Unwin Educational, 1981).

40. Erwin Epstein, "Currents Right and Left: Ideology in Comparative Education," *Comparative Education Review* 27 (February 1983): 3–27.

41. Paulston (n. 11 above).

42. Cummings (n. 28 above), esp. chap. 1.

43. See Wadi D. Haddad, "The World Bank's Education Sector Policy Paper: A Summary," *Comparative Education* 17 (June 1981): 127–39; Milagros Fernandez, "The World Bank and the Third World: Reflections of a Sceptic," *Prospects* 11 (1981): 294–301; Martin Carnoy, "International Institutions and Educational Policy: A Review of Education-Sector Policy," *Prospects* 10 (1980): 265–83; Seth Spaulding, "The Impact of International Assistance Organizations on the Development of Education," *Prospects* 11 (1981): 421–33; Paul Hurst, "Aid and Educational Development: Rhetoric and Reality," *Comparative Education* 17 (June 1981): 117–25; A. R. Thompson, "How Far Free: International Networks of Constraint upon National Education Policy in the Third World," *Comparative Education* 13 (October 1977): 155–68; George Psacharopoulos, "The World Bank in the World of Education: Some Policy Changes and Some Remnants," *Comparative Education* 17 (June 1981): 141–46.

44. Ronald Goodenow, "To Build a New World: Toward Two Case Studies on Transfer in the 20th Century," *Compare* 13, no. 1 (1983): 43–60. See also "Educational Transfer" (special issue), *Compare* 13, no. 1 (1983): 1–88.

45. See, e.g., Susan Cochrane, *Education and Fertility: What Do We Really Know?* (Baltimore: Johns Hopkins University Press, 1979).

46. Henry Levin (n. 13 above); Lois Weis, "Education and the Reproduction of Inequality: The Case of Ghana," *Comparative Education Review* 23 (February 1979): 41–50; Torsten Husen, *The School in Question* (New York: Oxford University Press, 1979); Joseph P. Farrell, "Educational Expansion and the Drive for Social Equality," in Altbach, Arnove, and Kelly, eds. (n. 8 above); Gail Lapidus, *Women in Soviet Society* (Berkeley and Los Angeles: University of California Press, 1981); Joseph R. Fiszman, "Education and Equality of Opportunity in Eastern Europe," in Altbach, Arnove, and Kelly, eds. (n. 5 above); W. D. Halls, "A Comparative Political and Sociological Analysis of Educational Opportunity in Western Europe, 1960–80," in Watson and Wilson, eds. (n. 34 above).

47. David Court, "Education as Social Control: The Response to Inequality in Kenya and Tanzania," in *Education and Politics in Tropical Africa,* ed. V. C. Uchendu (Owerri and New York: Conch, 1979); Richard Dobson and Michael Swafford, "The Educational Attainment Process in the Soviet Union: A Case Study," *Comparative Education Review* 24 (June 1980, part 1): 252–69; David Morrison, *Education and Politics in Africa: The Tanzanian Case* (Montreal: McGill-Queens University Press, 1967).

48. See George Psacharopoulos, "The Perverse Effects of Public Subsidization of Education, Or How Equal if Free Education?" *Comparative Education Review* 21 (February 1977): 69–90; Mateen Thobani, "Charging User Fees for Social Services: Education in Malawi," *Comparative Education Review* 28 (August 1984): 402–23; Steven J. Klees, "The Need for a Political Economy of Educational Finance: A Response to Thobani," *Comparative Education Review* 28 (August 1984): 424–40; and W. Van Vliet and J. A. Smyth, "A Nineteenth Century French Proposal to Use School Vouchers," *Comparative Education Review* 26 (February 1982): 95–103.

49. Estelle James, "Benefits and Costs of Privatized Public Services: Lessons from the Dutch Educational System," *Comparative Education Review* 28 (November 1984): 605–24. See also Thobani.

50. See Philip H. Coombs, *The World Crisis in Education: The View from the Eighties* (New York: Oxford University Press, 1985); Irvin Sobel, "The Human Capital Revolution in Economic Development," in Altbach, Arnove, and Kelly, eds. (n. 5 above); Hans Weiler, "Educational Planning and Social Change" (n. 16 above); Hans Weiler, "Towards a Political Economy of Educational Planning," *Prospects* 8 (1978): 247–67; George Psacharopoulos, "The State of Educational Planning Revisited," *Prospects* 11 (1981): 154–58.

CHAPTER TWENTY-ONE

Knowledge for the Masses: World Models and National Curricula, 1920–86[*]

Aaron Benavot, Yun-Kyung Cha, David Kamens, John W. Meyer, and Suk-Ying Wong[†]

Classical theorists in the sociology of knowledge such as Marx, Durkheim, Mannheim, and Scheler sought to establish that the content and validity of ideas are ultimately tied to the social and economic interests in society (Mannheim 1936; Durkheim [1912] 1954; for reviews, see Coser 1968; Kuklick 1983; Eisenstadt 1988). Subsequent research has focused on how sociohistorical conditions influence the production, validation, and justification of different types of knowledge. Few scholars have examined an important corollary: *how knowledge is selected, organized, and transmitted by social forces* (see Wuthnow 1987).

This neglect was forcefully stated by British sociologists of education (Young 1971). Sociologists, they argued, should treat "the knowledge ('transmitted' in education) as neither absolute, nor arbitrary, but as 'available sets of meanings' which in any context do not merely 'emerge' but are collectively 'given'" (Young 1971, p. 3). "How a society selects, classifies, distributes, transmits and evaluates the educational knowledge it considers to be public, reflects both the distribution of power and the principles of social control. From this point of view, differences within and change in the organization, transmission and evaluation of educational knowledge should be a major area of sociological interest" (Bernstein 1971, p. 47).

National educational institutions—which presently enroll about one-fifth of the world's inhabitants (United Nations Educational Social and Cultural Organization 1987)—have be-come the most important mechanism for organizing and transmitting knowledge to the young. Although sociologists have shown great interest in the expansion, improvement, and equalization of educational opportunity, they have had little to say about the nature and social basis of the formal knowledge transmitted by these institutions, especially from a comparative vantage point. The types of socially approved knowledge taught in mass and elite educational institutions and the official endorsement of that knowledge as reflected in national school curricula deserve more attention from sociologists.

We tackle these issues by analyzing, from a longitudinal and cross-national perspective, the changing nature of knowledge intended to be transmitted by schools to the mass population. We examine official primary school curricula and their relationship to national differences in political, economic, and social structure. We use a new data set that pulls together information on national curricular policies around the world since the 1920s. We first describe the school subjects that have been required in primary school curricula and how these required subjects vary across time and country. Such information should fill a major gap in the literatures on comparative education and world mass culture.

Our main goal, however, is to rethink previous hypotheses about the rise and nature of the modern curriculum. In previous work, the educational curriculum has been viewed either as the product of the functional requirements of society (e.g., the economies of advanced, industrialized countries require more instruction in mathematics and science) or as a reflection of existing power relations in society (e.g., an emphasis on academic subjects such as classical language, literature, or laboratory science serves the political and economic interests of the "dominant classes" or powerful elites). School curricula, according to these views, are nationally patterned collections of socially approved knowledge that, if compared cross-nationally, should show considerable diversity.

We propose a different view: The content of school curricula—especially mass curricula—is closely linked to the rise of standardized models of society (see Meyer 1980; Thomas, Meyer, Ramirez, and Boli 1987) and to the increasing dominance of standardized models of education as one component of these general models (see Boli, Ramirez, and Meyer 1985; Ramirez and Boli 1987). These modern models of society and education, and their interrelation, are similar around the world and generate educational systems and school curricula that are strikingly similar. As a result, a new culture or set of cultures is being promulgated by mass educational institutions. If we are to understand this emergent world cultural system, the mass educational curriculum is an important place to start.

Many characteristics of societies or time periods can affect the content of school curricula, but their characteristics do not predict the rapid worldwide expansion of primary education (Meyer, Ramirez, Rubinson, and Boli-Bennett 1977; Boli et al. 1985; Meyer, Ramirez, and Soysal 1990). World educational expansion has outpaced most national indicators of political or economic development and is rather poorly predicted by such variables. Thus, the same worldwide processes that were involved in the spread of primary education may also have generated similarity in its content. This theme is useful for understanding both the character and the stability of curricular

policies in primary education during the twentieth century.

Background

The formal content of the school curriculum was a more central sociological concern in earlier historical periods. Durkheim ([1938] 1977), in his penetrating analysis of French educational history, highlighted the succession of political battles over the officially prescribed curriculum during the nineteenth century (see Lukes 1985, pp. 379 ff.). Waller discussed the social and psychological consequences for teachers and students of the parceling out of human knowledge into school subjects and "nicely graded" courses ([1932] 1965, pp. 335 ff.).

In the early reports of educational leaders, issues of content—the textbooks used, the questions asked on tests, and classroom pedagogical practices—were a primary focus (e.g., see Barnard 1854; Klemm 1897; Prince 1897). Later, academics debated which languages to teach, at what age to introduce new topics in the natural or social sciences, and whether to allot instructional time to physical or aesthetic education.

In recent decades, however, the basic outline of the curriculum has become surprisingly uncontroversial. Conflicts arise, but they center on specialized issues (e.g., teaching of evolution, gender biases in textbook illustrations, bilingual instruction). These "controversies" bespeak the taken-for-granted character of the basic structure.

The issue of curricular content has almost disappeared from social theory. Durkheim's examination of legitimate school knowledge in France was replaced by Mannheim's more abstract assumptions and Parsons' completely abstract discussion of the presumed functions of the content of schooling (Mannheim 1952; Parsons 1959). Indeed, in the sociology of education, the term "curriculum" now seems to have two meanings unrelated to content. First, it means "track," or academic program—a structural feature of schools that is linked to past, present, or future inequalities. Second, it often refers to the "hidden curriculum"—the implicit knowledge and values conveyed to students by the schooling experience itself (see Schubert 1986, pp. 105 ff.; Apple 1979).

Hypotheses

There is little comparative historical research on school curricula. Springer (1977) noted the paucity of comparative studies in the area of pedagogy and the curriculum (see also Benavot and Kamens 1989). Lacking basic comparative descriptions, there has been a tendency to apply general theories about the origins and significance of mass education to questions about the curriculum.

Early theoretical statements on the sources of educational expansion were functionalist in character, with ideological variations. The modern differentiated society (or its elites) created and required primary education to equip the masses with technical skills and hegemonic culture and to enhance their integration into society. Ideological variations revolved around who benefits from the system rather than the origins of mass education. Recent comparative and historical research underscores the problematic status of fundamental propositions in functionalist thought: comparisons in the United States, both within states (Kaestle and Vinovskis 1980) and between states (Meyer, Tyack, Nagel, and Gordon 1979; Guest and Tolnay 1985), and cross-national comparisons, both between particular countries (Maynes 1985; Ramirez and Boli 1987) and across a range of countries (Meyer et al. 1977), cast doubt on the idea that urbanization or industrialization are good predictors of the expansion of mass education (se Boli et al. 1985 for a review).

Since the modern functionalist literature offers few specific hypotheses on curricular content, we suggest several taken from the classic literature:

H_1: The more developed a society, the greater the emphasis in the curriculum on modern skills and values. Instruction in mathematics, the natural sciences, social science, and a national language will be stressed more in developed societies than in less developed societies. Instruction in local languages, the arts, physical education, and vocational subjects like agriculture, manual training, and domestic science, will be emphasized less.

H_2: With increased modernization and development around the world, modern subjects like mathematics, natural science, and social science will be increasingly emphasized.

H_3: Because international differences in socioeconomic development are relatively stable, national curricular differences will also be relatively stable.

In reaction to the failures of functionalism and its variants, a growing body of curriculum research has moved toward descriptive studies of individual nations that emphasize case-specific historical explanations (e.g., Young 1971; Goodson 1987; Goodson and Ball 1984). Much of this historical work traces the spread of mass education and curricular content to competition among different status and political groups (Collins 1979; Archer 1979). The changing content of curricula and the definition of what is legitimate knowledge for the schools are issues fundamentally affected by the complex matrix of interactions, primarily in the political realm, among local and national group interests (Whitty and Young 1976; Goodson 1983; Kliebard 1986; Labaree 1986). In some arguments, the content of the curriculum is seen as reflecting the interests and advantages of dominant status groups (e.g., professionals, political elites, capitalist social classes); in others, the content is less important than the competitive advantages groups may gain through particular curricular arrangements (Collins 1979).

The historicist perspective argues that the interactions of conflicting forces in particular settings—rather than general functional imperatives—best explain the nature and development of school curricula. This view highlights the diversity of national school curricula and the inadequacy of general explanations in contrast to interpretive ones (Ragin 1987). Considerable heterogeneity between nations is predicted: Each nation-state—or perhaps family of nation-states descending from a common imperial metropole or sharing a common religious or cultural tradition—is seen as having its own curricular trajectory. Moreover, because the political battle tends to be fought over the inclusion of specific subjects rather than the emphasis placed on a subject once it has been officially incorporated, this perspective predicts that a nation's curricular emphasis will be fairly consistent over time. Two basic hypotheses follow:

H_4: Considerable curricular diversity exists among national educational systems.
H_5: National educational systems, each with its own trajectory, show consistent curricula over time.

Neither historicist approaches nor the variants of functionalism have come to terms with the rapid spread of standardized mass education. To account for this, arguments about the importance of a wider world polity have developed. Two related ideas are involved: First, despite societal variability, world models of society have standardized around the nation-state principle (Meyer 1980; Thomas et al. 1987). If, despite variation, models of society incorporating standard goals like national progress and social justice are widespread, institutional standardization might follow. Mass education, which is closely linked to the goals of national development, economic progress, and the formal integration of individuals in the collectivity, would be a likely candidate (Fiala and Lanford 1987). Second, even if models of society vary, but means to achieve them are uncertain, we might expect less developed countries to copy institutions such as education from more successful nations. This would be aided by the portrayal of the value of education for national development by the world's professionals and scientists, by the pressures of international

agencies and relations, and by local aspirations for successful development (DiMaggio and Powell 1983).

We apply these themes to the study of the curriculum: If mass education is a worldwide model, or one component of a larger standardized nation-state model, its curricula should also evidence standardization at the world level. The institutionalized ideologies of society, and the specific ideologies of education as socializing individuals for society, should carry institutionally standardized content. Thus:

H_6: National primary curricula will generally reflect modern values, independent of national development.
H_7: Primary curricula in national societies will exhibit increasing similarity.
H_8: National differences in curricular emphases will show little consistency over time because all national systems derive from prevailing world conventions.

Data

Given the paucity of academic research comparing curricula across countries and over time, we began our search for data with limited expectations. However, it quickly became clear that data were available. Many groups, frequently linked to UNESCO, have attempted to bring together standard descriptions of national school curricula. In earlier periods, this was done with enthusiasm and flair, whether in the published accounts of foreign educational systems by comparative educators or in international conferences and educational yearbooks. But throughout the twentieth century, education has been seen as an important national enterprise—one that should be publicized and compared with other nations. As a consequence, curricular standards and policies in sovereign states and dependent territories have been explicitly formulated and collected in a great many comparative reports.

Our main sources of curricular information are international media rather than national case reports. Perhaps surprisingly, comparative accounts of educational matters have been geared to an international audience. As was true with enrollment data on primary education (Benavot and Riddle 1988), curricular discourse has a universalistic and worldwide character rather than a local and primordial one. Thus our data were easily organized into general categories—they were, so to speak, written to be coded. Although the easy interpretability suggests the importance of transnational processes in the development of school curricula, it raises some methodological and substantive questions.

Curricular information was derived from diverse sources, including historical and contemporary accounts of national school systems, comparative histories of educational development, international educational compendia, and encyclopedias. In 1986, we sent queries to over 120 ministries of education requesting information on curricular timetables. We received usable responses from over one-half of the countries.[1]

From each official curricular timetable, we coded two items of information: the required subjects to be taught during the elementary school cycle (usually a five- to six-year period), and the number of periods (or hours) to be devoted to each subject during a typical week. This information was transformed into two dependent variables: one indicating the presence or absence of basic school subjects in the official curriculum and the second indicating the relative emphasis on each subject.

Specific subjects were classified into general categories according to the following scheme: *Language* (national, local, official, and foreign languages); *Mathematics* (arithmetic, geometry); *Natural Sciences; Social Sciences* (history, geography, civics, social studies); *Religious and Moral Education* (religion, moral education); *Aesthetic Education* (art, handicrafts, singing, dance); *Physical Education; Hygiene/Health Education; Vocational Education/Practical Subjects* (manual training, agriculture, domestic science, industrial arts, gardening); and *Other* (recreation, extracurricular activities, miscellaneous subjects, recess, and elective subjects). National language refers to an indigenous language, spoken by over 50 percent of the population, that is also an official language. Official language refers to a metropolitan or world language that is given national standing but is not indigenous in origin or use. Local language is spoken by a minority of the population and not given official standing. Foreign languages are those that are neither official nor indigenous.

Subjects listed in official timetables and allocated instructional time usually fit into one of these categories. Subjects that did not clearly fit into one of these categories were coded as "other." Most nations organize primary education in a six-year cycle (UNESCO 1987). In countries where the primary cycle was longer than six years, we considered the official curriculum for the first six years only; where the cycle was shorter, we included information for the first year or two of the secondary cycle where possible. These coding decisions had very little impact on our results. Some national timetables combined topics we preferred to code separately (e.g., mathematics and science). In such cases, we coded both subjects as taught, and split the allotted instructional time equally.

Data Frame and Coverage

The data refer primarily to nations with state-administered educational systems. However, each period also includes a small number of self-governing dependent territories with official school curricula. (See note 5 for differences between these two types of polities.) Curricular information was assigned to one of three historical periods: the interwar period, 1920–44; the decolonization period, 1945–69; and the current period, 1970–86. When we had more than one timetable for a country during a period, we recorded data nearest the target years of 1935, 1960, and 1985. Data coverage for each period, while extensive, does not constitute a representative sample. Data coverage is sparsest for the interwar period (1920–44) and tends to overrepresent countries in Europe and the Americas, whereas the sample of countries for the 1970–86 period is more complete.

Limitations of the Data

Our curricular measures indicate which subjects are required in the official curriculum and their relative emphasis, that is, the percentage of total curricular time devoted to each subject. However, we have little information on how many school periods or instructional hours each subject was supposed to be taught during the annual school term. Preliminary analyses show a slight tendency for average annual hours of instruction to be lower in developing countries, newer educational systems, and in the distant past (Benavot and Kamens 1989). Weighting our curricular measures by variations in annual hours of instruction would alter the results presented below very little (Kamens and Benavot 1991).

We have no information on the specific content of the subjects taught. Differences among countries or over time in such categories as "history" or "social studies" may or may not represent real differences in curricula. Similar general categories may mask national variability in intended content. The lack of detail in our data makes it difficult to directly address these issues. However, categories like "social studies" increasingly denote standard sets of expectations, materials, and topics. Therefore, changes in these categories seem likely to signify real changes, at least in intent.

Apart from the intrinsic gap between general curricular categories and actual curricular content, certain organizational processes may widen this gap (Meyer and Rowan 1977). This is especially true of educational systems in developing countries and in less centralized educational systems (Stevenson and Baker 1991). Policy and practice respond to different resource constraints. For example, great curricular visions may not be attainable by teachers and students with few educational resources;

policymakers may wish to impress national and international audiences more than teachers and local administrators do; or local educators may have to adapt to local requirements, and so on. Such processes might generate official curricula in greater conformity to world models than local practice is, and produce some distortions in our results.[2]

Actual instructional practices in schools and classrooms cannot be inferred from official policy, but official definitions of what children should study are of interest in their own right. In a world in which education is usually a creature of the nation-state, official policies affect the formal organization of schooling by specifying the content of instruction throughout the schooling cycle according to relatively explicit goals. They also indicate what types of classes will be offered to students and establish boundaries around certain bodies of knowledge deemed appropriate.

Results

Table 21.1 reports basic trends in the percent of countries offering instruction in specified subjects. To permit comparisons across historical periods, Table 21.1 is based on a constant set of countries for adjacent time periods. (Because data coverage is more complete in the recent period, information on the middle period is included twice.)

A core of subjects—language, mathematics, natural science, social science, the arts, and physical education—have appeared in most official curricula through the time periods studied, and have become even more widespread over time. A few countries, for instance, adopted science instruction only during the periods covered by our study (Kamens and Benavot 1991). But by the most recent period, the core subjects appear in practically all curricula, and may suggest the operation of processes of world educational standardization.

Little change occurred in the prevalence of religious or moral education and in health education. These subjects are not part of a universal core. Vocational education is declining through the period (as fewer countries treat primary education as a terminal stage).

Within two core areas, some changes appear. Instruction in official (or foreign, more rarely) languages is more common in the later periods, a finding that turns out to reflect the development of primary educational systems in former colonies (Cha 1991). And within the general social science category, there has been a strong trend toward instruction in a general social studies subject and away from instruction allocated to history, geography, and civics. This trend may reflect the recent hegemony of liberal or American educational doctrines (Wong 1991).

The most important finding in Table 21.1 is the rise to universality of a set of core subjects across the diverse countries of the world. This result provides some support for ideas that educational curricula reflect standardizing world processes. And it runs against the predictions

of more diversity by functional or historicist arguments.

Table 21.2 presents the average percentage of instructional time allocated to each subject during the primary school cycle, along with the standard deviation around the average. Overall, there is a good deal of consistency over time in the allocation of instructional time to the subjects. For the universally required subjects, standard deviations are relatively small and tend to decline over time, indicating more standardization in the time devoted to the subjects. The other subjects—religious education, health education, and vocational education, as well as subcategories of the core subjects—show more variation (distributions, in addition, tend to be more skewed).

Language instruction—reading, writing, and grammar—is the dominant activity in primary education. In each time period, about one-third of total curricular time is devoted to language education. Variation is relatively small, and

TABLE 21.1   Percentage of Countries Offering Specified Subjects in the Primary School Curriculum: 1920–86

Subject	Panel A			Panel B		
	1920–44	**1945–69**	*N*	**1945–69**	**1970–86**	*N*
Language:	100.0	100.0	43	100.0	100.0	73
National, local	97.7	97.7	43	92.0	92.0	75
Official, foreign	18.8	47.9	48	59.5	60.8	74
Mathematics	100.0	100.0	48	100.0	100.0	82
Natural science	81.3	93.8	48	92.3	100.0	78
Social sciences:	97.9	97.9	47	96.1	100.0	76
History, geography, civics	91.5	85.1	47	76.3	52.6	76
Social studies	10.9	28.3	46	28.9	60.5	76
Aesthetic education	86.4	97.7	44	97.4	98.7	76
Religious or moral education	77.8	73.3	45	77.3	74.7	75
Physical education	89.4	95.7	47	97.4	96.1	76
Hygiene/health education	34.8	28.3	46	38.2	42.1	76
Practical subjects/ vocational education	86.4	75.0	44	72.0	68.0	7

Note: Each panel refers to a constant set of countries for which data were available for the two time periods.

TABLE 21.2   Average Percentage of Total Instructional Time Allocated to Subjects in the Primary School Curriculum: 1920–86

Subject	Panel A			Panel B		
	1920–44	1945–69	N	1945–69	1970–86	N
Language:	35.3 (9.2)	36.4 (7.9)	31	36.0 (9.2)	33.9 (8.3)	70
National, local	31.0 (9.4)	32.4 (9.6)	31	26.0 (12.4)	25.1 (10.2)	72
Official, foreign	3.5 (9.3)	4.6 (8.2)	45	9.5 (13.3)	8.3 (11.6)	73
Mathematics	15.4 (4.2)	17.3 (4.6)	37	16.5 (4.0)	18.2 (3.3)	80
Natural science	5.2 (4.0)	7.0 (4.3)	42	7.1 (4.6)	7.9 (3.7)	75
Social sciences:	8.8 (4.0)	8.6 (4.0)	36	8.1 (4.0)	8.1 (3.7)	73
History, geography, civics	8.0 (4.3)	6.2 (4.1)	37	5.9 (4.5)	3.2 (3.9)	74
Social studies	0.5 (2.4)	2.5 (4.6)	45	2.1 (4.2)	4.8 (5.2)	74
Aesthetic education	9.2 (5.9)	10.5 (4.5)	39	10.0 (3.9)	10.2 (4.4)	71
Religious or moral education	6.9 (7.5)	5.2 (4.9)	37	6.1 (6.0)	5.2 (5.3)	68
Physical education	6.0 (4.2)	7.2 (3.3)	39	6.9 (2.7)	7.1 (3.3)	72
Hygiene/health education	0.9 (1.9)	1.0 (2.6)	40	1.4 (2.8)	1.2 (1.9)	70
Practical subjects/ vocational education	6.2 (4.8)	5.8 (5.5)	34	6.3 (6.9)	5.1 (5.3)	73

Note: Standard deviations in parentheses. Each panel refers to a constant set of countries for which data were available for the two time periods.

tends to decline. Almost all language instruction is in national or official languages (Cha 1991); very little is in local or tribal languages. There has been a slight increase in the amount of instruction in foreign languages or in official languages that are exogenous in origin, resulting from the addition of more developing countries to the data set (and to the world of primary education). These patterns support functionalist or worldly polity theories, which emphasize the primacy of the nation-state, and run against historicist perspectives. The unimportance of local languages, however, provides little support for functionalist theories, which emphasize the importance of these languages in peripheral economies and societies.

There have been slight increases in the percentage of time that is to be devoted to mathematics education, and some movement toward increased similarity among countries in this measure. The percentage of instructional time devoted to natural science increased during the period under study, and (the rather low) variability declined overall. Similarly, there are modest increases in time allocated to aesthetic and physical education. Variability here is also fairly low, but does not show consistent declines.

The percentage of time allocated to combined social science instruction shows little change over the period of the study. Variation is low, but unchanged over the period. Within this category, the percentage of time devoted to history, geography, or civics declines sharply, while that devoted to "social studies" increases sharply. This striking worldwide trend toward a more integrated notion of society could have a functionalist interpretation, for example, greater public involvement in and control over social life produced a stronger conception of society as a "social system." It could also result from worldwide cultural changes—perhaps reflecting a dominant American model of proper curricular content that became institutionalized in the 1960s (Wong 1991).

Aside from the common core of subjects, the main finding in Table 21.2 is the low percentage of time allocated to the less universal ones. Religious or moral education is still required in primary schools in about three-fourths of the countries, but the time allocated to it is low and declining. This is also true of practical or vocational subjects. Health or hygiene receives very little time. The fact that such less universal subjects are not more prevalent in primary school curricula speaks against historical theories of educational development, which predict a wide range of distinctive patterns.

Overall, Tables 21.1 and 21.2 suggest that an increasingly similar world curriculum takes up most of the instructional time. These findings suggest that during much of the twentieth century a standard world curriculum for primary education has been in operation. They provide some support for functionalist arguments suggesting that primary school curricula should move in a "modern" direction over time. But they call into question the assumptions of historicist theories, which tend to view the evolution of national school curricula in terms of distinctive national trajectories.

An important corollary of historicist conceptions of the curriculum predicts distinctive educational systems at a regional level as a result of common cultural, political, or religious traditions, rather than at a national level. Table 21.3 presents the average percentage of instructional time devoted to subjects for major world regions for the most recent period (1970–86). Results for other periods (not shown) are similar. Countries are classified in the following world regions: Sub-Saharan Africa; the mainly Islamic countries of the Middle East and North Africa; Asia; Latin (Iberian) America; the non-Iberian Caribbean; Eastern Europe; and "West" (which includes the United States and the former British dominions of Canada, Australia, and New Zealand).

Latin American countries allocate significantly less instructional time to language education (in total) than countries in other world regions. One explanation is that because Latin America experienced a long colonial period during which indigenous populations were decimated by disease and warfare, Spanish became the dominant language and the need to teach several languages was minimized. Also, many newly independent Third World nations, especially in sub-Saharan Africa and the Caribbean, have kept the language of their former colonizers as an official language of instruction in primary schools. Other former colonies in the Middle East/North Africa and Asia teach the former metropolitan language as a required foreign language. In general, however, regional differences in the time devoted

TABLE 21.3 Average Percentage of Total Instructional Time Allocated to
Subjects in the Primary School Curriculum, by World Region: 1970–86

Subject	Sub-Saharan Africa	Mideast North Africa	Asia	Latin America	Caribbean	Eastern Europe	West*
Language:	38.2	36.8	36.7	24.4	34.7	37.4	34.1
	(29)	(15)	(18)	(14)	(9)	(9)	(19)
National, local	13.5	31.8	27.3	18.1	18.1	30.3	27.7
	(29)	(15)	(18)	(16)	(9)	(9)	(19)
Official	24.2	0.0	7.0	3.8	14.2	1.9	3.5
	(29)	(15)	(18)	(16)	(10)	(9)	(22)
Foreign	0.5	4.9	2.4	0.4	0.7	5.1	2.2
	(29)	(15)	(18)	(16)	(10)	(9)	(21)
Mathematics	17.7	16.6	17.5	18.6	20.7	20.5	18.5
	(32)	(18)	(20)	(18)	(10)	(9)	(21)
Natural science	7.0	6.7	8.1	11.3	7.5	7.5	6.4
	(32)	(17)	(19)	(18)	(9)	(9)	(19)
Social sciences:	7.8	6.4	8.7	13.1	12.0	6.3	9.0
	(29)	(15)	(18)	(15)	(9)	(9)	(19)
History, geography, civics	4.5	2.6	2.6	4.3	4.3	6.3	3.3
	(29)	(15)	(18)	(15)	(10)	(9)	(20)
Social studies	3.3	3.8	6.0	8.7	7.2	0.0	5.0
	(29)	(15)	(18)	(15)	(9)	(9)	(19)
Aesthetic education	8.5	7.7	9.5	8.0	7.4	10.4	13.5
	(28)	(15)	(18)	(14)	(9)	(9)	(19)
Religious or moral education	4.6	12.0	6.1	3.4	2.5	0.0	5.0
	(29)	(13)	(17)	(14)	(9)	(9)	(18)
Religious education	3.8	11.8	3.0	2.2	2.2	0.0	4.7
	(29)	(15)	(18)	(14)	(9)	(9)	(18)
Moral education	0.8	0.7	2.9	1.0	0.8	0.0	0.2
	(29)	(13)	(17)	(16)	(10)	(9)	(20)
Physical education	5.9	6.3	5.8	7.4	5.3	9.4	9.2
	(28)	(15)	(18)	(15)	(9)	(9)	(19)
Hygiene/health education	0.9	1.8	1.5	2.5	2.9	0.3	0.5
	(28)	(15)	(18)	(17)	(10)	(8)	(21)
Practical subjects/ vocational education	7.3	2.4	4.1	9.5	3.2	6.6	0.7
	(28)	(15)	(17)	(15)	(10)	(9)	(22)

*West includes Western Europe, North America, Australia, and New Zealand.
Note: Number of cases in parentheses.

to language education are small: most regions allocate, on the average, about one-third of total curricular time to some type of language instruction.

In the other core areas of the curriculum—mathematics, natural science, and social science—curricular emphases are rather similar across regions. Mathematics receives slightly more emphasis in Caribbean and Eastern European nations (a pattern that predates the establishment of socialist regimes). Emphasis on natural science and social science is stronger in Latin American countries (perhaps reflecting Enlightenment rationalism and the sharp separation of church and state); emphasis on social science is also strong in Caribbean nations.

The percentage of time allocated to religious or moral education exhibits considerable regional variation. Muslim countries in the Middle East/North Africa region place great emphasis on the teaching of the Koran and the religious principles of Islam in the elementary schools. This is reflected in their relatively high average percentage of instructional time devoted to religious education. Western countries, some of which maintain a state religion, also allocate more time to religious instruction than do countries in other regions. Among Asian countries, many of which lack an established national religion, moral education receives more emphasis than elsewhere. Instruction in religion or moral education is allocated no instructional time in Eastern Europe under socialist regimes—this is also the case in the constitutionally radical American educational system (Cha, Wong, and Meyer 1988).

Eastern European and Western countries devote more time, on the average, to aesthetic education and physical education than other regions—but the differences are not marked. Instruction in practical subjects such as farming, industrial arts, manual training, and domestic science receives relatively more time in Latin American countries, and relatively less time in Western and Islamic countries.

Overall, interregional variation in the amount of time allocated to different subject areas appears, but this variation does not suggest radically different notions of appropriate subject matter for primary school children.[3] Apart from the differences noted, regional variations in the allocation of curricular time are small. The similarity of emphasis in the primary curriculum, especially in the core subjects of language, mathematics, natural science, social science, and the arts, is the dominant feature of the regional breakdown.

Curriculum Stability

Historicist theories of the development of school curricula predict high correlations over time in the allocation of instructional time. Early battles over the inclusion of particular school subjects tend to dissipate over time. Once subjects are incorporated into the official curriculum, the amount of time devoted to them should change slowly. Functionalist theories lead to similar predictions because, if national levels of development determine curricular emphases, the former do not change dramatically. On the other hand, the idea that national curricula reflect worldwide influences suggests low correlations in curricular emphases because countries are drawing from increasingly standardized global models rather than from their own unique history or developmental requirements.

Table 21.4 presents Pearsonian interperiod correlations within curricular categories. These correlations indicate the degree of stability over time in the percentage of curricular time allocated to these subjects. All but five of the thirty-three correlations are below .50. Two of the exceptions concern the inclusion of imperial or metropolitan languages as official curricular languages in newly independent countries—the group of countries requiring instruction in a nonindigenous official language remained stable in the post–World War II period. Two relatively high correlations occur for religious and moral education; further analysis shows that this result is due to religious education (Cha et al. 1988). Whether religious instruction is included in the school curriculum depends on whether church and state are institutionally and politically separated and tends to be stable over time. Apart from these two subject areas, the results suggest considerable volatility over time. Correlations between the

two postwar periods tend to be a bit higher, but this may be due to the shorter time span and the greater number of cases for these periods.

These generally low correlations support the view that national curricula are shaped more by worldwide processes than national ones. They seem to result from a system in which country curricular decisions reflect world standards rather than national educational history.

National Development and Curricular Emphases

Are nations' official curricula affected by national variations in political, economic, and social structure? For each period, several measures of socioeconomic development were correlated with the percentage of instructional time devoted to particular subjects in the primary school curricula. The three measures were: (1) Log of per capita energy consumption (United Nations 1952, 1984). This measure, for which relatively complete information is available for each time period, tends to be highly correlated with other measures of economic development. (2) Urbanization, measured as the percent of the population living in cities larger than 100,000 (World Bank 1987). Due to insufficient data for the 1920–44 period and the fact that this variable orders counties consistently over time, 1950 data for this measure were employed for the earliest period. (3) The proportion of the school-age population enrolled in primary school (Benavot and Riddle 1988; UNESCO 1987). This variable is widely available, is positively related to other development measures, and reflects the expansion and perhaps modernization of the mass educational system (which may have modernizing effects on the curriculum over and above effects of development in general).

The correlations presented in Table 21.5 lend limited support to functionalist theories. Such theories tend to predict that national curricula are highly patterned: a group of "modern" subjects are linked together in the curriculum and given greater shares of instructional

TABLE 21.4 Pearsonian Interperiod Correlations between Percentages of Total Instructional Time Allocated to Subjects in the Primary School Curriculum: 1920–86

Subject	1920–44 vs. 1945–69	1920–44 vs. 1970–86	1945–69 vs. 1970–86
National, local language	.45*	.25	.62*
	(31)	(27)	(72)
Official, foreign language	.34*	.27	.80*
	(45)	(39)	(73)
Mathematics	.45*	.14	.34*
	(39)	(32)	(81)
Natural science	.16	.27	.33*
	(44)	(36)	(76)
History, geography, civics	.36*	−.04	.14
	(37)	(31)	(74)
Social studies	.52*	−.02	.36*
	(45)	(40)	(74)
Religious or moral education	.67*	.47*	.76*
	(37)	(32)	(68)
Aesthetic education	.29	.34*	.30*
	(39)	(31)	(71)
Physical education	.22	.26	.28*
	(39)	(32)	(72)
Hygiene/health education	.09	.12	.19
	(40)	(35)	(70)
Practical subjects/ vocational education	.18	.45*	.44*
	(34)	(29)	(73)

*p < .05.

Note: Number of cases in parentheses.

TABLE 21.5 Zero-Order Correlations between Measures of National Development and Percentage of Instructional Time Allocated to Subjects in the Primary School Curriculum: 1920–86

Subject	1920–44			1945–69			1970–86		
	Energy Consumption per Capita	Urbanization	Primary School Enrollment	Energy Consumption per Capita	Urbanization	Primary School Enrollment	Energy Consumption per Capita	Urbanization	Primary School Enrollment
Language:	-.02 (29)	-.14 (36)	.09 (36)	.03 (84)	.03 (89)	-.06 (87)	.06 (109)	.00 (115)	-.03 (106)
National, local	.13 (29)	-.05 (36)	.24 (36)	.27* (84)	.22* (89)	.21* (87)	.33* (111)	.15* (117)	.12 (108)
Official, foreign	-.10 (29)	-.03 (36)	-.06 (36)	-.23* (89)	-.21* (94)	-.25* (92)	-.29* (113)	-.16* (119)	-.15 (110)
Mathematics	.39* (31)	.13 (38)	.11 (38)	.22* (90)	.06 (94)	.30* (93)	.11 (123)	-.03 (129)	.16* (120)
Natural science	.23 (33)	.19 (45)	.13 (42)	-.12 (90)	-.01 (94)	.03 (93)	-.07 (118)	-.02 (123)	-.01 (115)
History, geography, civics	.12 (31)	.06 (39)	.10 (38)	.14 (89)	.05 (94)	.13 (92)	-.12 (112)	.10 (118)	-.07 (109)
Social studies	.05 (38)	-.04 (50)	.01 (47)	-.18* (89)	-.07 (94)	-.07 (92)	-.02 (110)	.02 (118)	.03 (109)
Religious or moral education	-.10 (32)	.18 (41)	-.11 (40)	.01 (86)	.06 (91)	-.23* (90)	-.04 (104)	.04 (110)	.18* (101)
Aesthetic education	.13 (31)	.38* (42)	.36* (40)	.22* (87)	.16 (92)	.27* (91)	.25* (108)	.22* (114)	.03 (105)
Physical education	.08 (32)	.16 (43)	.10 (40)	.16 (88)	.06 (93)	.13 (92)	.21* (109)	.18* (115)	.09 (106)
Hygiene/health education	-.22 (35)	-.10 (42)	-.25* (42)	-.12 (86)	-.01 (91)	-.13 (89)	-.06 (113)	.01 (119)	-.02 (110)
Practical subjects/ vocational education	.15 (28)	-.07 (35)	.10 (35)	-.24* (88)	-.17* (93)	-.14 (91)	-.34* (112)	-.23* (118)	-.04 (109)

*p < .05.

Note: Number of cases in parentheses. Measures pertain to 1930 for the 1920–44 period (1950 for urbanization); 1960 for 1945–69; and 1980 for 1970–86.

time as a result of modernization and national development. If mathematics, natural science, and, to a lesser degree, social studies constitute an interrelated nexus of "modern" subject matter, the results show that socioeconomic development is not strongly correlated with an emphasis on "modern" subjects in twentieth-century curricula. Some positive correlations along this line appear (e.g., between mathematics instruction and energy consumption in the first period), but they are not consistent and do not remain in the current period.[4]

By contrast, socioeconomic development in the post–World War II periods is positively associated with an emphasis on national languages and negatively associated with an emphasis on official or foreign language instruction. This has more to do with changing models of nationhood and nationalism in different historical periods than with development per se (Kamens, Cha, and Wong 1988). The amount of time devoted to language education of all types in primary curricula is unrelated to socioeconomic development.

Socioeconomic development is also positively correlated with the share of time devoted to aesthetic education. This may reflect broader values and socialization patterns of modern societies. However, such an effect of development is not central to functionalist theories. In the post–World War II periods, socioeconomic development is negatively related to an emphasis on practical or vocational education. This reflects two phenomena: the "adapted" colonial curriculum of the pre-independence era has not been fully replaced in many former colonies and "practical" knowledge relating to agriculture, farming, and household work is emphasized by many agrarian nations during the primary school cycle—in part because primary education in these countries is often a terminal educational phase. This effect, while generally compatible with functionalist thinking, is once again not a central prediction. Our main conclusion is that "modern" curricular emphases are not closely related to variation in national levels of devel-

opment—a core idea in most functionalist thought about educational development.[5]

Summary and Discussion

Functionalist theory suggests that national curricula vary by level of socioeconomic development, increasingly incorporate modern subject matter, and are slow to change. Few relationships with development were found: the fact that developed countries devote relatively more time to physical education and the arts and less to vocational subjects is of marginal significance since these relationships do not reflect core functionalist ideas. There is a weak trend toward "modernity" in the expansion of instructional time for natural science, social science, and mathematics. Furthermore, there is little national stability over time in the allocation of instructional time. Thus, it is difficult to make a case for tight linkages between official curricular emphases and variation in functional societal requirements.

Historicist theories suggest diversity in national curricula among countries or world regions and a substantial degree of stability over time. Again, these predictions are not substantially supported by the data, aside from some long-term consistency in the time devoted to religious instruction.

The idea that the curricula of mass education are closely tied to standardized worldwide models of social and educational progress suggests that instruction in such "modern" topics as mathematics, natural science, and social science will diffuse throughout the world, that national primary curricula will be increasingly similar, and that stability over time will be modest. Most of our findings support this line of argument. While there is some variation concerning minor subjects—whether they are taught and how much time they are allocated—instruction in core subject areas appears in practically all national curricula and there is a great deal of similarity in the amount of time devoted to these core categories. National characteristics are only weakly related to curricular emphases. Only the expectation of sharply increased similarity over time receives limited support; change is modest, though most countries include all the standard subjects in the curriculum.

The notion that official primary curricula reflect a world educational order modifies rather than eliminates functionalist and historicist hypotheses. Theorists can retain the notion of the modern curriculum as functional: they need simply to understand that functionalist models hold at the world level and are often adopted in peripheral areas as models rather than as responses to changed national political or social realities. Similarly, a historical perspective can still view the curriculum as a contested historical product, but the history involved in, say, the shift from geography and history studies to social studies may be better viewed as the playing out of hegemonic forces in a global arena. Most scholarship in this camp sees history as a product of specific interactions, but there is no logical reason to insist that these intersections be primarily local or national. The knowledge being selected, organized, and transmitted by different elementary school systems has a good deal of worldwide standardization. The modern pattern—much of it already in place at the beginning of our study—seems to involve the expansion of a language-focused curriculum to include mathematics, natural science, social science, and physical and arts education. The spread of this curricular pattern around the world—mostly independent of regional and developmental factors—effectively incorporates modern functionalist theory as a broad ideological base and as a general legitimizing system.

We have no information on the processes by which this curricular standardization is achieved. The nation-state is the dominant form of societal organization in the modern period—preferred by political elites and advanced by all sorts of social groups (Thomas et al. 1987). To some extent, this model carries implications for desirable knowledge for the population, from a shared national culture to

aspects of modern technical rationalism—perhaps these implications become obvious in each nation-state, producing overall similarity. Also, the prescription of mass education is endemic, encouraged by international organizations, by professional elites, and by the dominant powers throughout the modern period. To some extent, the logic of mass education carries implications for a common cultural content (again emphasizing shared national culture and a good deal of rationalism). Finally, to some extent the mass curriculum is directly defined and prescribed through the influence of international organizations (e.g., the World Bank and United Nations organizations), through the models provided by dominant nation-states, and the education professionals who operate on a worldwide basis. All these influences (which are difficult to distinguish empirically) find receptive audiences in national societies and states eager for legitimacy and progress. As with individual identity in Tocqueville's vision of America, national identity in the modern world system is achieved through conformity to the institutionalized ideals.

In one respect, the standardization of national school curricula is not a complete surprise. Our period is one in which local and primordial cultures are undergoing wholesale destruction, in part as a result of mass education. Local languages die out or are circumscribed, as are local gods and spirits. Local political divisions are undercut, usually in the name of a national polity, along with parochial technologies and customs. Every aspect of the modern world system builds conformity of economic, or political, or familial and cultural rules to regional, ethnic, or national standards (Thomas et al. 1987). Similarly, schools claim to be laid out in standard ways at national levels regardless of gender, class, tribe, region, and locality. (In practice, however, there may be curricular variation across such subgroups that is not acknowledged in the official rules of mass educational systems.)

The real surprise of our findings lies not in the unimportance of local influences, but in the relative unimportance of national influences on curricular structure. Similarities clearly outweigh differences. The few differences observed tend to be unstable and seem to arise as a matter of chance in national societies differing dramatically in wealth, political structure, and cultural and religious tradition. We may speak with some confidence about a relatively standard world curriculum.

Future research should examine trends in national curricula to analyze the world flow of curriculum changes, and the importance of particular paths (e.g., particular international organizations, dominant powers, or professional groups). Data on the intended content of subjects would study whether the widespread shift from history and geography instruction to social studies is a change in content or in label. Data on the content of actual classroom instruction would indicate whether official policy actually penetrates to this level. For example, how much local "resistance" is there? How aware are local educators of worldwide curricular trends apart from the particular policies of their authorities?

Our study suggests the value of direct independent measures of world curricular standards over time, since these appear to influence national policies. What preferences are found in the discussions of the educational professionals, the policies of the dominant powers in the world stratification system, and the organizational stances of the important international organizations?

Finally, if so much of educational content is established at a global level, it is important to study the forces that produce it. Is there a substantive cultural logic or is it simply the exercise of accidental or systematic patterns of international dominance?

Notes

*   From the *American Sociological Review* 56, no. 1 (February 1991): 85–100, by permission of the authors and the American Sociological Association. Copyright 1991 by the American Sociological Association.

†   Authors' names are in alphabetical order. This research was supported by a National Science Foundation grant (#SES-8512561); the Stanford Center for the Study of Families, Children and Youth; and the University of Georgia Research Foundation. We have benefited from the comments and suggestions of John Boli, Connie McNeely, Francisco Ramirez, Yasemin Soysal, Marc Ventresca, and other members of the Stanford Comparative Education Seminar. Earlier versions of this paper were presented at seminars at the University of Chicago and the World Bank and at meetings of the American Sociological Association and the American Educational Research Association.

1.   For the contemporary period (1970–86), we coded data for approximately 125 countries and colonies, though for about 15 the information indicates only whether a given subject is to be taught. The data come from UNESCO's International Bureau of Education (microfiche); the UNESCO Regional Office for Education in Asia and the Pacific (1984); Massialas and Jarrar (1983); Fafunwa and Aisuku (1982); al-Misnad (1985); and from responses to our survey of national ministries of education. For 1945–69, we coded curricular data for 105 countries and had relatively complete information for about 95 countries. The main sources for this period are the UNESCO survey (UNESCO 1958) and Dottrens's (1962) study which was prepared under UNESCO auspices using data published by the International Bureau of Education (1958). Supplementary sources were also used: Europe (Schultze 1968–70), Central America (Waggoner and Waggoner 1971), Asia (National Institute for Educational Research 1970; Ministry of Education, Japan 1964), and Africa (Sasnett and Sepmeyer 1966; Hawes 1979).

For the interwar period (1920–44) we have data on about 65 countries, with relatively complete data for 45. Data come from the Educational Yearbook (1924–44); UNESCO (1958); Kandel (1933); and individual country reports based on responses to our survey.

2.   It is a mistake, however, to *assume* that while national officials seek to comply with international educational models, local school teachers and principals follow curricular standards that, by and large, reflect local constituencies

and constraints. Given the growth of national and international networks, of teacher-training institutes and professional associations, it is hard to imagine that teachers and school administrators in developing countries follow distinctive curricular conventions. It is also difficult for local interests to develop distinct curricular themes. It is much more likely that they drew from similar curricular content frames, though in a less effective manner, as their national bureaucratic elites. In any case, it is interesting to see whether the official statements of national educational leaders reflect world standards of educational policy.

3. Several nations in each historical period have official primary school curricula in which particular subject areas are allotted significantly more (or less) curricular time than is the averages reported in Tables 21.2 and 21.3. However, in supplemental analyses, we find that the number of countries that maintain an extreme emphasis (or lack of emphasis) on a particular subject over time is very small (Kamens 1990). Typically, one of two processes occurs: (1) a country doesn't require a particular subject—science, for example—in one time period but does in the next period, usually allotting curricular time to that subject at a level similar to world norms; or (2) a country continues to require a subject—vocational education, for example—that has gone out of fashion in much of the world. Delay in requiring new subjects or dropping old subjects that have lost their value accounts for many of the "deviant" curricular patterns.

The one subject area in which we noted a distinctive curricular pattern is religious and moral education. A few countries, mainly Islamic, allot a substantial part of the curriculum to religious instruction. For example, Saudi Arabia (1945–69; 1970–86), Egypt (1920–44), Yemen (1970–86), and Palestine (1920–44) devote more than one-fourth of the primary curriculum to religious instruction.

Apart from religious and moral education, there is little evidence of distinctive elementary school curricula, a striking finding in view of the fact that many countries—for example, China, Korea, Japan, Islamic countries—had unique systems of instruction entirely outside the modern world educational system. At least

in terms of official policies, the rich and diverse cultural traditions of these countries are minimally reflected in the elementary curriculum.

4. Socioeconomic development may be related to the development of a modern curriculum in the nineteenth century. In a supplemental historical analysis of our data, Cha (1989) found that in European countries the modern curriculum—which included science, industrial and physical education, the arts, and expanded social science—began to replace the traditional classical and language-oriented curriculum by the late nineteenth century. Our results, which begin around World War I, seem to capture the tail end of this process. By the interwar period, the outlines of the modern curriculum were already in place (Kamens and Benavot 1991).

5. Another prediction from both functionalist and historical theories is that national independence itself has a substantial effect on curricular policies and practices, perhaps generating a more aggressively modern orientation. In analyses not reported here, we contrasted the curricular emphases of independent countries versus dependent colonies and dominions for each time period. Dependent colonies devoted greater proportions of curricular time to language instruction, and less to most other subjects (although they distributed the time among these other subjects in ways that roughly parallel independent countries). On the average, language education was allocated 39.8 percent of the total curriculum time in the 1920–44 period, 43.8 percent in the middle period, and 44.0 percent in the 1970–86 period in dependent colonies. The respective percentages for independent nations were: 34.5, 35.7, and 34.9. Clearly, in many dependent educational systems, extra time was devoted to the language of the colonial metropole, which was likely to be alien to most of the population. With independence, the pressure to devote this time to what had become a foreign language was eliminated or reduced (Cha 1991). Beyond this single effect, there is little evidence that dependent polities followed radically different curricular trajectories in most subject areas.

References

Apple, Michael. 1971. *Ideology and Curriculum*. London: Routledge and Kegan Paul.

Archer, Margaret. 1979. *Social Origins of Educational Systems.* London: Sage Publications.

Barnard, Henry. 1854. *National Education in Europe.* (2nd ed.). Hartford, CT: Frederick Perkins.

Benavot, Aaron, and David Kamens. 1989. *The Curricular Content of Primary Education in Developing Countries.* Policy, Planning and Research Working Papers, Education and Employment Working Paper 237, Washington, D.C.: World Bank.

Benavot, Aaron, and Phyllis Riddle. 1988. "The Expansion of Primary Education, 1870–1940: Trends and Issues." *Sociology of Education* 61:191–210.

Bernstein, Basil. 1971. "On the Classification and Framing of Educational Knowledge." Pp. 47–76 in *Knowledge and Control,* edited by Michael Young. London: Collier MacMillan.

Boli, John, Francisco O. Ramirez, and John W. Meyer. 1985. "Explaining the Origins and Expansion of Mass Education." *Comparative Education Review* 29:145–70.

Cha, Yun-Kyung. 1989. "The Origins of Expansion of Primary School Curricula in the West: 1800–1920." Unpublished manuscript, Stanford University, School of Education, Stanford, CA.

———. 1991. "Effect of the Global System on Language Instruction, 1850–1986." *Sociology of Education* 64:19–32.

Cha, Yun-Kyung, Suk-Ying Wong, and John Meyer. 1988. "Values Education in the Curriculum: Some Comparative Empirical Data." Pp. 11–28 in *The Revival of Values: Education in Asia and the West,* edited by W. Cummings, S. Gopinathan, and Y. Tomoda. London: Pergamon Press.

Collins, Randall. 1979. *The Credential Society.* Orlando, FL: Academic Press.

Coser, Lewis. 1968. "Sociology of Knowledge." Pp. 428–34 in *International Encyclopedia of the Social Sciences.* New York: Macmillan and Free Press.

DiMaggio, Paul, and Walter Powell. 1983. "The Iron Cage Revisited." *American Sociological Review* 48:147–60.

Dottrens, Robert. 1962. *The Primary School Curriculum.* Paris: UNESCO.

Durkheim, Emile. [1912] 1954. *The Elementary Forms of the Religious Life.* Glencoe, IL: Free Press.

———. [1938] 1977. *The Evolution of Educational Thought.* London: Routledge and Kegan Paul.

Educational Yearbook. 1924–1944. New York: Teacher's College, Columbia University.

Eisenstadt, S. N. 1988. "Explorations in the Sociology of Knowledge." Pp. 1–71 in *Cultural Traditions and Worlds of Knowledge: Explorations in the Sociology of Knowledge,* vol. 7, edited by S. N. Eisenstadt and Ilana Friedrich Silber, New Haven: JAI Press.

Fafunwa, A., and J. Aisuku (eds.). 1982. *Education in Africa.* London: George Allen and Unwin.

Fiala, Robert, and A. Gordon-Lanford. 1987. "Educational Ideology and the World Educational Revolution, 1950–1970." *Comparative Education Review* 31:315–32.

Goodson, Ivor. 1983. *School Subjects and Curriculum Change.* London: Croom Helm.

———. 1987. *The Making of Curriculum: Essays in the Social History of Schooling.* Barcombe: Falmer Press.

Goodson, Ivor, and Stephen Ball (eds.). 1984. *Defining the Curriculum: Histories and Ethnographies.* London: Falmer Press.

Guest, Avery, and Stewart Tolnay. 1985. "Agricultural Organization and Educational Consumption in the U.S. in 1900." *Sociology of Education* 58:201–12.

Hawes, Hugh. 1979. *Curriculum and Reality in African Primary Schools.* Briston, UK: Longman.

International Bureau of Education. 1958. *Preparation and Issuing of the Primary School Curriculum,* no. 194. Paris: UNESCO.

Kaestle, Carl, and M. Vinovskis. 1980. *Education and Social Change in Nineteenth Century Massachusetts.* New York: Cambridge University Press.

Kamens, David. 1990. "Variant Forms: Countries with Distinct Primary Curricula." Unpublished manuscript, Northern Illinois University, Department of Sociology.

Kamens, David H., and Aaron Benavot. 1991. "Elite Knowledge for the Masses: The Origins and Spread of Mathematics and Science Education in National Curricula." *American Journal of Education* 99:137–180.

Kamens, David, Yun-Kyung Cha, and Suk-Ying Wong. 1988. "On the Shoulders of Children: Building a National Community via the Primary School in the 19th and 20th Centuries." Paper presented at the annual meeting of the American Sociological Association, Atlanta, Georgia.

Kandel, I. L. 1933. *Comparative Education.* New York: Houghton Mifflin.

Klemm, Louis. 1897. *European Schools.* New York: Appleton and Company.

Kliebard, Herbert. 1986. *The Struggle for the American Curriculum, 1893–1958.* Boston: Routledge and Kegan Paul.

Kuklick, Henrika. 1983. "The Sociology of Knowledge: Retrospect and Prospect." *Annual Review of Sociology* 9:287–310.

Labaree, David. 1986. "Curriculum, Credentials and the Middle Class." *Sociology of Education* 59:42–57.

Lukes, Steven. 1985. *Emile Durkheim.* Stanford, California: Stanford University Press.

Mannheim, Karl. 1936. *Ideology and Utopia.* New York: Harcourt, Brace and World.

———. 1952. *Essays on the Sociology of Knowledge.* London: Routledge and Kegan Paul.

Massialas, B. G., and S. A. Jarrar. 1983. *Education in the Arab World.* New York: Praeger.

Maynes, Mary Jo. 1985. *Schooling in Western Europe: A Social History.* Albany, NY: State University of New York Press.

Meyer, John W. 1980. "The World Polity and the Authority of the Nation-State." Pp. 109–37 in *Studies of the Modern World System,* edited by A. Bergesen. New York: Academic Press.

Meyer, John W., Francisco O. Ramirez, R. Rubinson, and John Boli-Bennett. 1977. "The World Educational Revolution, 1950–1970." *Sociology of Education* 50:242–58.

Meyer, John W., Francisco O. Ramirez, and Yasemin Soysal. 1990. "World Expansion of Mass Education, 1870–1980." Department of Sociology, Stanford University.

Meyer, John W., and Brian Rowan. 1977. "Institutionalized Organization: Formal Structure as Myth and Ceremony." *American Journal of Sociology* 83:340–63.

Meyer, John W., David Tyack, J. Nagel, and A. Gordon. 1979. "Public Education as Nation-Building in America." *American Journal of Sociology* 85:591–613.

Ministry of Education, Japan. 1964. *Education in Asia.* Tokyo: Ministry of Education.

al-Misnad, Sheikha. 1985. *The Development of Modern Education in the Gulf.* London: Ithaca.

National Institute for Educational Research and UNESCO. 1970. *Asian Study of Curriculum.* Tokyo: NIER.

Parsons, Talcott. 1959. "The School Class as a Social System." *Harvard Educational Review* 29:297–318.

Prince, John. 1897. *Methods of Instruction and Organization of the Schools of Germany for the Use of American Teachers and Normal Schools.* Boston: Lee and Shepard.

Ragin, Charles. 1987. *The Comparative Method.* Berkeley: University of California Press.

Ramirez, Francisco O., and John Boli. 1987. "The Political Construction of Mass Schooling: European Origins and Worldwide Institutionalization." *Sociology of Education* 60:2–18.

Sasnett, Martena, and I. Sepmeyer. 1966. *Educational Systems of Africa.* Berkeley, CA: University of California Press.

Schubert, William. 1986. *Curriculum: Perspective, Paradigm, and Possibility.* New York: Macmillan.

Schultze, Walter (ed.). 1968–1970. *Schools in Europe.* Berlin/Weinheim: Verlag Julius Beltz.

Springer, Ursula. 1977. "Education, Curriculum, and Pedagogy." *Comparative Education Review* 21:358–70.

Stevenson, David H., and David Baker. 1991. "State Control of the Curriculum and Classroom Instruction." *Sociology of Education* 64:1–10.

Thomas, George, John W. Meyer, Francisco O. Ramirez, and John Boli. 1987. *Institutional Structure: Constituting State, Society, and the Individual.* Beverly Hills, CA: Sage Publications.

United Nations Educational Scientific and Cultural Organization. 1958. *World Survey of Education,* vol. 2. Paris: UNESCO.

United Nations Educational Scientific and Cultural Organization, Regional Office for Education in Asia and the Pacific. 1984. *Towards Universalization of Primary Education in Asia and the Pacific.* Bangkok: UNESCO.

United Nations Educational Scientific and Cultural Organization. 1987. *Statistical Yearbook.* Paris: UNESCO.

United Nations. 1952. *World Energy Supplies 1929–1950.* New York: United Nations.

United Nations. 1984. *Energy Statistics Yearbook.* New York: United Nations.

Waggoner, George, and B. Waggoner. 1971. *Education in Central America.* Lawrence, KS: University Press of Kansas.

Waller, Willard. [1932] 1965. *The Sociology of Teaching.* New York: John Wiley.

Whitty, Geoff, and Michael Young (eds.). 1976. *Explorations in the Politics of School Knowledge.* Nafferton, England: Nafferton Books.

Wong, Suk-Ying. 1991. "The Evolution of Social Science Instruction, 1900–86: A Cross-National Study." *Sociology of Education* 64:33–47.

World Bank. 1987. *World Tables, 1987* (4th ed.). Washington: World Bank.

Wuthnow, Robert. 1987. *Meaning and Moral Order.* Berkeley: University of California Press.

Young, Michael (ed.). 1971. *Knowledge and Control.* London: Collier MacMillan.

CHAPTER TWENTY-TWO

Cross-National Perceptions of Teachers[*]

Harry G. Judge[†]

Public perceptions of teachers and of their place in society vary, sometimes in dramatic ways, between one country and another. A study of such variations is likely to generate new insights into social attitudes—not simply to teachers and teaching but also to education itself and to the values that it embodies. A comparative methodology may serve, as some have argued powerfully that it should, to formulate transnational rules.[1] Equally, and this is the direction of this article, such a methodology may help to clarify—by analogy, analysis, and contrast—intranational factors, affecting the culture and coherence of one society. Comparative education may legitimately choose to emphasize either the general or the particular, the scientific or the cultural.[2]

What is attempted, in an effort to illustrate the potentialities of such a method, is a systematic discussion of the similarities and differences—static and historic, as well as dynamic—between perceptions of teachers in the United States and the United Kingdom. From that examination I will distill some central and coherent characteristics of the case in the United States. These characteristics will be shown to be structurally related to one another and, I argue, to be further clarified by being placed alongside the example of France. The implied claim is that useful comparative work can and should be done by concentrating on a limited range of issues—in this case, teachers and, especially teacher education—in a limited number of countries—in this case, three.

A common, and not wholly discredited, method of locating perceptions of the role and status of the teacher in any given society is to apply the test of "professionalism." Is teaching, within the country in question, acknowledged as a professional activity? What does that word mean within that society? Are some groups of teachers viewed as members of a professional class, and others not? Do the categories of "minor profession" and "semiprofession" illuminate these and similar questions? How do the criteria of professionalism refer to the structures and procedures of education and training and, in particular, to the mainstream of higher education? Does the answer to the key question, and to those derived from it, change over time, and, if so, in what senses and at what speed? These are not trivial questions, and addressing them as preliminaries to a more subtle series may be useful.[3] The usefulness of these questions is nevertheless limited and becoming more so. The growing diversification and specialization of high-status activities within developed societies is eroding the traditional territory of the concept of professionalism. Nothing very precise or impressive is represented by the public insistence that airline pilots should be professionals (rather than enthusiastic amateurs) or by the corporate insistence of advertising agents that they should be regarded as professionals (rather than unlicensed charlatans). Relatively few of the traditional criteria apply in such cases as these. Accompanying this loosening of traditional definitions of professionalism (erudition, autonomy, public service) is an enlarging and probably healthy disenchantment with the tendency of professional groups within society to employ the techniques of mystification in order to claim power, wealth, or freedom from public accountability.

Some serviceable generalizations, however, can be derived from even a cursory application of the criteria of professionalism to teachers in both the United States and the United Kingdom. It is certainly not difficult to parade the reasons that would generate, in both countries, a negative response to the question, Is teaching a profession?

In both countries the reasons for that negative response are intuitive but nonetheless powerful, given that the issue is one of public perceptions. In the United States there are over 2 million teachers and only about half a million doctors: the number of doctors in the United States is comparable with the number of teachers in the United Kingdom, whereas the population of the former country is some ten times greater than the latter. In the past, professions have defined themselves in terms of membership of an elite minority; that claim is not tenable for teachers in developed society. Equally widespread is the general sense that—however varied and numerous the qualifications and exceptions—members of a profession are expected to receive fees rather than salaries or, even more obviously, wages.

The symbol and reality of the fee is important in that it identifies and honors the contractual relationship between the parties. Members of a profession relate to a client rather than to a customer or an undifferentiated mass of persons entitled to some publicly provided service, and their overriding duty is to protect and promote the best interests of that client. But, for most teachers in most schools, who is that client? There is a wonderful confusion of competitors, both in the United States and in the United Kingdom: the parent or parents, the community, the school board, the local education authority, the national government, or, even in reified form, society itself or the economy. Any identification of the student himself or herself as the client is uncomfortable since it seems to impose on the teacher a professional duty to promote solely the interests of that student, if

necessary, at the expense of others competing for attention or resources.

These factors—the size of the relevant workforce, the fee relationship, the tight link of that relationship to client status—are unlikely to be fundamentally modified in either the United States or the United Kingdom.[4] The bid by teachers for recognition as professionals is rooted in powerful aspirations to improve their status and to dignify the tasks that they perform. The consideration of other relevant factors—rules for admission to the ranks of teachers, formal licensing, the control of standards—leads to a similar conclusion. These are matters over which control has not been, and in no conceivable future will be, handed over to teachers.

There is, then, a dispiriting sameness in the answers proffered on either side of the Atlantic to well-rehearsed questions about whether teaching is or could be a profession. The similarity of the answers emphasizes the characteristics *common* to perceptions of teaching in the United States and the United Kingdom, and from it may be derived a transnational rule: teaching cannot be perceived in those countries as a profession insofar as it incorporates a large and unwieldy occupational group, is not client based, enjoys little corporate autonomy, and so on. There are, however, some important characteristics, much less frequently discussed, which elicit *differences* of perception in the two nations. Five of them are identified below. An analysis of these characteristics dissolves the crude homogeneity of public perceptions and also demonstrates that significant contemporary changes can be observed when the two societies are compared. The differences between the two countries taken together with the movement within each of them provide an exemplary natural laboratory within which to test more subtle hypotheses.

The five characteristics are labeled as:

1. *Nationality.* The questions at issue here turn on the extent to which the teaching force in a society (for the moment, the United

States and the United Kingdom) is perceived as being national in character, rather than regional or local. The secondary, but important, question relates to the speed at which and the direction in which such a perception is currently being modified (the dynamic element in this analysis). The United States, therefore, earns a low rating with regard to this first characteristic of nationality. It is, for example, a source of some legitimate pride to each of the fifty states that they should control standards of admission to licensed teacher status and, in turn, to the local school boards that they should be the employers of the teachers and set their conditions of service. Superannuation and other benefits are rarely transferrable from one district to another, even within one state.[5]

The contrast with the United Kingdom is striking. Since the end of the First World War, salary scales and conditions of service have been settled nationally.[6] The secretary of state for education and science determines the conditions under which status as a qualified teacher may be given or withdrawn and controls the mechanisms for giving effect to such policies. Teachers move freely, within the general limitations of job opportunities, from one employer to another.

So much is obvious. In each case, however, there is at present an important shift of perception, and in each case that shift is "upward" on the nationality characteristic. Within the United States, the states have become more active in setting the rules within which the school districts must operate: the setting of minima for teachers' salaries is an obvious example. More recently, and at a national (albeit not a federal) level, an authoritative report from the Carnegie Corporation has stressed the importance of establishing national standards validated by a national examination for certification, an emphasis that is specifically linked to the systematic pursuit of professional status.[7]

At the same time within the United Kingdom, a high score on the characteristic here being discussed is being driven even higher by well-coordinated efforts by the government in London. After painfully long and unsuccessful negotiations, the secretary of state, Kenneth Baker, has intervened decisively to introduce nationwide conditions of service for teachers. His predecessor, Sir Keith Joseph, had already published the criteria to be satisfied by programs of teacher education and created a body to ensure that those criteria were duly respected.[8] Baker has more recently made clear his determination to introduce a national curriculum defining the limits within which teachers must teach, as well as a national program for the testing of students to ensure that the required standards are achieved by those teachers.[9]

The virtues or vices of such policies are not under discussion here. Their only relevance is to illuminate the differences in perceptions of teachers between the two countries and, more particularly, the ways in which such perceptions are being changed. The conclusion at this point is that with regard to nationality the United States has a low score and the United Kingdom a high one, but that in both countries there is a marked movement upward on this particular scale.

2. *Stratification.* An interestingly different conclusion emerges from a review of the second characteristic, which relates to the importance for teachers of formal and informal hierarchies. For this characteristic the U.S. score is again low. There is little differentiation of a formal kind among teachers within a school: the principal is regarded not as a teacher but as an administrator, and salary scales are not designed to reflect or reward differences of responsibility within a largely bureaucratized workforce. The only way upward for a teacher is away from teaching itself into the other branches of the so-called education professions.[10]

In the United Kingdom, however, and especially in secondary schools, a high degree of stratification has developed and is faithfully mirrored in salary scales and related payments.

School principals, whatever they may be called, are styled as head teachers and would generally resent being classified as administrators. Departments within a school are strong, and their heads are formally designated and given considerable responsibility for the management of other teachers.[11]

In each country, however, the readings for this second characteristic (stratification) can be shown to be changing. In the United States there has been a wide but by no means universal movement toward such concepts and practices as merit pay and the career ladder (certainly a significant metaphor in this context). Two influential reports published in 1986 stressed the desirability of making firm and, indeed, hierarchical distinctions among teachers based on differing levels of responsibility, expertise, and qualifications.[12] Here the movement is up this particular scale.

In the United Kingdom a good deal of smoke still lies over the battlefield. The whole issue of stratification and its relation to salaries is contentious, with some protagonists asserting the need for greater differentiation and others praising the virtues of a relatively uniform structure with a "main professional grade" of salaries for teachers. Whatever the outcome of these lively and continuing debates, it is at least clear that there will be movement on this particular scale and that its direction and pace will be closely related to the rhetoric of professionalism and to the realities of political and trade union power. One powerful crosscurrent may indeed push the system away from nationally agreed salary scales with all that they imply, thereby driving down the U.K. reading on characteristic 1 (nationality). Indeed, movements of emphasis within several of the characteristics will prove to be closely linked.

3. *Syndicalism.* There is often, within groups enjoying or aspiring to professional status and rewards, a profound conflict between the use of trade union tactics to achieve immediate goals and the rejection of such methods and styles as inappropriate to the dignity and sense of vocation of a respected group within society. The more threatening to life or welfare such action is, and the more vulnerable (sick or young) those who must suffer from it are, the more inappropriate such action becomes. Such tensions raise important questions about the analysis of the behavior of organized groups of teachers.[13]

Readings for this characteristic assessed for the early 1960s would be low in both the United States and the United Kingdom. In the United States, strikes by teachers were in many places formally outlawed, and collective bargaining unheard of, while the National Education Association (NEA) in particular behaved in a nonconfrontational manner and covered a wide range of potentially divergent interests, including those of the administrators or managers within the school system.[14] There was a strong parallelism in the United Kingdom, where the polite consensus of the 1950s had not yet been broken by the bitter salary disputes that arose a few years later.[15] Strikes were, for most teachers as for the public at large, rejected as unsuitable behavior for a group claiming professional status. There had indeed been heroic action of this kind in the past, but it was important only in the folk memory of teachers and not as a guide to policy in the modern world.

A simple description of these circumstances evokes a sense of the rapidity of change since the early 1960s: in both countries the movement has been up the scale for this third characteristic. Collective bargaining has become in the United States the commonplace procedure and is now technically illegal in only two of the states, whereas strikes of greater or lesser severity are taken for granted among the predictable hazards of life.[16] The world of teaching was permanently changed by the events in New York in the 1960s. In the United Kingdom, the contrasts over time are even more salient, if only because of the high score in that country under characteristic 1 (nationality). Action by teachers' unions is usually nationwide and for that reason highly visible and certain to generate public attention and concern. The precedents for trade union–type activity were set in the later 1960s, and conflict between teachers, their employers, and the government in London achieved new levels of recrimination in the period between 1985 and 1987.

4. *Autonomy.* Trade union–type activity of the kind that is now common among teachers in the United States and the United Kingdom is generally perceived as conflicting with the traditional claim of a professional group to be trusted to eschew actions calculated to damage the interests of the client or patient. Some would, of course, argue that such claims are in fact rhetorical (and often employed to consolidate the power or monetary advantage of the organized group) and that trade union–type activity may in any case be necessary as a short-term means to achieve the long-term goal represented by professional status. Once again, my concern is not with the virtues and vices of the case but only with the attempt to clarify the differences and tendencies across the two societies under review.

A quarter of a century ago—and the links with characteristic 3 (syndicalism) are as obvious as they are important—the U.K. readings for the autonomy characteristic were dramatically different from those in the United States. In Britain the score was high, even if it turns out on examination to be higher in perceptions than in reality. The centrally orthodox view then was that teachers, like other professionals in this respect, knew best and should be entrusted with educational decisions, including the choice of curriculum, textbooks, teaching methods, internal school organization, and methods of discipline.[17] This prevailing orthodoxy was about to acquire a novel form with the foundation in 1963 of the Schools Council, a body that for most of its uneasy life canonized the notion that teachers should be in charge of the curriculum, much as doctors saw themselves as being in charge of medicine.[18] This development did, however, represent a mutation of the belief that teachers (individually) should have control into the doctrine that the teachers (collectively) should be so empowered. This mutation was caused, in my view, by the corresponding rise in the U.K. score for characteristic 3 (syndicalism) and contributed in its turn to the rise in the score for characteristic 1 (nationality).

At the same period, the U.S. score for the perception of teachers as autonomous professionals was very low. The schools belonged not to the teachers (an excusable exaggeration of the U.K. perception) but to the community—a perception tidily linked to the low score on characteristic 1 (nationality). Teachers were, therefore, accountable to that community through administrators acting as managers. Nor is it clear that this perception has been fundamentally modified. The model is unashamedly industrial with an emphasis, going back at least to the beginning of this century, on efficiency and control and the limited delegation of carefully specified tasks. This important and historic characteristic has been particularly well analyzed in the literature.[19]

So much for the (static) perceptions of the early 1960s. For the United Kingdom, the shift in these perceptions (the dynamic in this analysis) has been dramatic and unambiguous. Consider only some of the indices of that change. The Schools Council, the epitome of syndicalist autonomy, has been abolished as part of an effort to establish a national curriculum, defined for, and not by, teachers.[20] Two successive and very different governments have made clear their discontent with the performance of the educational system and in particular with the unacceptably wide range of diversity within it. The machinery for negotiating teachers' salaries has broken down under considerable strain, and the secretary of state for education and science has felt himself obliged to use his powers to prescribe a settlement and to associate with it novel arrangements for the appraisal of teachers—a clear sign of the application of the classical U.S. view of teachers as functionaries within a system or even, in some exaggerated forms, as workers within a factory. It is not a coincidence that this sharp fall in the U.K. score for characteristic 4 (autonomy) is associated with equally clear rises for 3 (syndicalism) and 1 (nationality).

Comparably clear conclusions do not emerge from a study of the U.S. case, where the reactions are more confused and contradictory. On the one hand, it can be argued from much of the evidence that the score for characteristic 4 (autonomy) is falling even lower. Many of the policy initiatives within the so-called educational reform movement of recent years emphasize the desirability of exercising even greater control over teachers: subjecting them to tests of basic competency, motivating them by the inducements of merit pay, requiring them to work longer hours, specifying their duties in greater detail, measuring their performance by recording and evaluating the test results of their students, and so on. This is probably the prevailing tendency and obviously suggests a declining score for the characteristic being discussed in this section.[21]

Running contrary to this prevailing tendency is evidence of disenchantment with the top-down model clearly implied by that tendency. It may be better to describe this countervailing evidence as one theme in the literature of educational reform, rather than to search for a set of observable changes in the operation of the system itself. The 1986 reports of the Carnegie task force and of the Holmes Group at least gesture toward the hope that teachers (or, more precisely, the genuine professionals among them) will be allowed a great deal more autonomy within a reconstructed framework of teaching as a high-level activity. In such proposals, and particularly in the Carnegie version, there is a marked stress on accountability for the attainment of agreed goals as a necessary restraint on such autonomy.

In 1979, Arthur E. Wise deployed a lucid critique of the limitations of educational policies that took for granted and reinforced models of educational efficiency by incorporating a belief that if schools and teachers were more firmly controlled they would produce better results.[22] More recently, Linda McNeil, in an empirical study of great importance exploring the contradictions within the educational reform movement, has succeeded in demonstrating the lowering effects on teacher attitudes that ensue when collegial styles of decision making and action are abruptly supplanted by the prevailing orthodoxies of control.[23] Her work suggests that, in such circumstances, to specify is, in effect, to limit. Underlying these works are the scholarly and imaginative explorations of teachers and teaching by Dan Lortie and Philip Jackson.[24] Arguments for greater freedom and flexibility for teachers might also be supported by attempts to redefine good management techniques. Some recent studies suggest that, even within the world of business itself, older versions of how to improve performance and manage large systems are themselves coming under attack.[25] At some point, the powerful emphasis within the United States on the importance of controlling from above and outside the daily life of schools will collide with the growing conviction, at least among teachers and those who write about them, that, if teachers are to perform effectively as professionals in some kind of new order, they need to be freed from much of that control.

5. *Unity.* The discussion of this last characteristic of perceptions of teachers, analyzed cross-nationally, will focus on the extent to which teachers are perceived as belonging to a single and relatively homogeneous group within either of the countries, without regard to the type of school in which those teachers work or to the ages or abilities of those whom they teach. Until recently, the score for the United Kingdom, by these criteria, would be low. The structures of teacher education reflected this, with the training colleges (renamed as colleges of education in the 1960s) producing the teachers for the elementary schools while the universities provided those for the academic secondary schools, whether private or public.[26] This symmetry was, of course, disrupted first by the introduction, after the 1944 Education

Act, of universal secondary schooling and, perhaps even more fundamentally, by the evolution over the past two decades of the secondary comprehensive school. These developments have softened the distinction between the schoolmaster or schoolmistress, who was a graduate and may not have received any professional training before teaching older and more academic pupils, and the elementary school teacher, who attended a college for teachers for two years, taught younger pupils, and had no degree.

Although the lines of such a distinction are still quite clear in some other European countries, they have effectively disappeared in the United Kingdom. It is, nevertheless, still a widely shared prejudice that teachers in secondary schools teach subjects, while those in primary schools teach children. Such a perception is much less prevalent in the United States. There have, for example, never been two separate unions or associations for teachers in the two categories of school. Junior high and middle schools occupy an influential position at the heart of the system. The American rejection of the selective academic school makes it improbable that a clear line will ever be drawn between two distinct categories of teacher. The score for the United States under this characteristic is therefore high, and it is not obvious that there is at present any noticeable movement. In the United Kingdom, however, the score is low with a tendency to rise over time as a result of the reorganization of secondary schooling, itself reflecting powerful social movements.

Five characteristics defining the modes in which teachers as a group are perceived—nationality, stratification, syndicalism, autonomy, and unity—have now been examined cross-nationally alongside the earlier assertion that differences between and among societies may prove at least as illuminating as similarities. The most obvious of those similarities between the United States and the United Kingdom were illustrated by a rehearsal of the reasons for which professional status in both countries is commonly denied to teachers. The discussion was then carried forward into an examination of five dimensions along which perceptions would be differently placed in the two countries. Such a discussion points toward the crucial task of *explaining* these differences. The discussion was at several points complicated and illuminated by the factor of change: if a perception is changing in either or both of the countries under review, and if that change is in the same or in a different direction, what conclusions follow? What, finally, might be learned from the relations between the readings for different characteristics?

One example may be resumed: for the United Kingdom, a rise in the score for characteristic 1 (nationality) may be linked, at least speculatively, with a matching rise for characteristic 3 (syndicalism) and a fall for characteristic 4 (autonomy). The claim being made is that both the initial (static) readings and the (dynamic) changes in them become more readily visible when viewed alongside the U.S. case in a cross-national perspective.

Harold Noah and Max Eckstein suggest that the main purpose of comparative study is to generate supranational laws.[27] I would prefer to argue that, while that should indeed be one of the main purposes, alongside it and generated by the same techniques of cross-national comparison is an equally respectable task, namely, the clarification of what is peculiar to a culture. The methodological point is that such intranational perceptions are often best clarified by cross-national analysis. This becomes a necessary stage in the task and distinguishes such efforts as are attempted here from the earlier preoccupation with culture as an explanatory device in comparative education. A second methodological point is that there should be concentration on a particular issue or theme. Taken together, these two points on method indicate a further stage of analysis or, more correctly, of synthesis. It is not the case that the varied readings and shifts noted for the five characteristics just happen to happen. They cohere. They are structurally related. They are historically determined. They are, above all, culturally embedded.

Reflection in this spirit on the U.S. example leads, therefore, to a synthesis in which national perceptions of teaching are pulled into focus by a shared national view of what schooling is and should be. For that reason, the readings could not logically be other than they are and changes in them are similarly indicative of wider and more deep-rooted changes.

From the analysis of the five characteristics the outlines of a synthesis for the United States (as, although the example is not pursued here, for the United Kingdom) emerge. One of the most powerful American educational traditions relates to the common school.[28] In marked contrast to developments in the United Kingdom and elsewhere, the high school developed as an outgrowth of the elementary school. The colonial example of the Latin school did not become the national model for the secondary school; in the United Kingdom the medieval example of the grammar school and the nineteenth-century ideal of the independent boarding school did become a model.[29]

Nationally, therefore, the high school came to be regarded (and correctly so) as the property in every sense of the local community and its school board, rather than as a colony planted by the university. A community that, in every sense, owned such a school would of course require of those who staffed it that they should reflect the character and ambitions of that community, and teachers would be hired in order to work toward those ends. Their autonomy would be limited, they would be perceived as a local rather than a national resource, they would not be expected or even allowed to unionize, they would not be encouraged to form quasi-professional hierarchies among teachers within the school, and they would not be divided in the public mind into one group (elementary), which extended the functions of the family, and another (secondary), which imported the purposes of an external academic community. With the growth of big city sys-

tems and a parallel emphasis on the importance of efficiency narrowly defined, such powerful ideas were given a new but entirely predictable force. The role of the principal and, even more, that of the superintendent (a profoundly significant term) was distanced from that of the teacher; teachers themselves were bureaucratized, and measurement and testing became the appropriate methods of evaluation and control. Such tightly linked perceptions will be shifted with difficulty if at all.

These perceptions, tightly linked and deeply rooted as they are, may be thrown into even sharper relief when displayed against the example not only of the United Kingdom but also of a third country. Consider for a moment the case of France, taken as an example of a tentatively proposed third component in a cross-national study leading to intranational synthesis. A presentation as brief as this runs the obvious risk of collapsing into parody, but the generalizations about to be hazarded are nevertheless worthy of further serious investigation; at the moment, there do not appear to be enough firm empirical data against which to test them. At a number of strategic points the French case contrasts with that of either the United States or the United Kingdom, or both, while at others it is comparable with either the United States or the United Kingdom, or, more rarely, with both.[30]

In the perception of teachers in France, nothing is more clear than the separation of those who teach in the lower schools from those who teach in the higher: the separate terms of *instituteur* and *professeur* persist as symbols of that distinction, as do quite different patterns of teacher education for the two categories. Repeated but incomplete efforts at the comprehensive reorganization of the schools have complicated but not destroyed that traditional distinction. The *professeur* in the *lycée*, especially if he teaches the *classes préparatoires,* is perceived as belonging to the same group (and there is little doubt of its professional status) as the university professor, and careers often overlap in the two sectors. Preparation for teaching in the more academic forms of secondary education is the same as that for a university career: the status of *agrégé* and the power of the *École Normale Supérieure* effectively guarantee this. Similarly, the *baccalauréat* in France is the first university degree, as in the United States and the United Kingdom, but is, of course, taken at the end of the secondary cycle of education. Teachers in France, at whatever level, do not "belong" to a local community but are, in much more than the formal sense, civil servants who receive from the state a salary, even while they are still in training.

The organization of elementary and secondary education is on a regional basis of academies based on universities and operates under the general oversight of the rector. The systems of examination and of inspection are national and strong, reflecting much of the authoritarian spirit of the Napoleonic reform. Even these brief comments may be sufficient to suggest some highly provisional scoring for France on the five characteristics discussed above. More significantly, they suggest an agenda for further research: for example, on the role of the trade unions, the effects of efforts directed toward administrative devolution, the pattern of relationships between administrators and teachers within schools, the careers of those teachers and administrators in the Fifth Republic, the realities as distinct from the rhetoric of prescription from Paris and its effect on teacher autonomy, the working conditions for teachers, the results in practice of the reorganization of lower secondary education, and the planning and delivery of teacher education.

Teacher education may indeed prove to be a particularly illuminating theme through which to approach cross-national studies, and the U.S./U.K./France grouping can serve as a useful case. The case for bringing teacher education itself into sharp focus is adapted from the work of those historians who (especially in France) have shown that one of the most effective ways of arriving at a sense of cultural and

historical reality is by drilling deeply into one carefully defined theme and set of data. That case is strengthened by the fact that, in most if not all countries, teacher education is changing rapidly and (as argued above), such change provides opportunities for analysis that are lacking in static systems. The argument, as adapted to the purposes being explored here, is that teacher education is embedded in each nation within the cultures of teaching, just as teaching is contained within schooling, while schooling is located as one part (but by no means the only one) of education, which itself reflects, transmits, and modifies the values of the whole society.[31]

Such a thesis implies, of course, a belief in the value of studying small things rather than large.[32] But that is, properly understood, no more than a statement of temperamental and methodological preference. Too much energy has been wasted among comparative educationists in making or refuting exclusive claims— on the importance of "theory," for example. In this underpopulated field there is more than enough room for both big enders and little enders. This article has attempted to show that there is no inconsistency in arguing the case for a supranational approach alongside a plea for the intranational, provided always that the comparative imperative is respected as it deserves to be. Moreover, there are some cases (and France may possibly prove to be one of them) where more empirical work first needs to be done within the country before comparative questions can begin to be addressed. It is, of course, on grounds such as these that one-country studies are often to be welcomed in comparative education, provided only that there is an intention to carry them forward at some stage in a comparative framework.

Work of this kind, and that bearing on teacher education, seen as a point of entry into descriptions and analyses of the cultures of teaching, would contribute to both categories of inquiry—the supranational and intranational—or perhaps even help to redefine the relation between them. This discussion will therefore be closed with an attempt to indicate some of the organizing questions that might be formulated to guide such work.

Cross-national studies of teacher education would bring into sharp relief issues related to each society's view of what constitutes the desirable knowledge that schools are to transmit. A low-level version of this question relates to the subject-matter knowledge that teachers are required or expected to have. To what extent is the definition of that desirable minimum the same for teachers of younger students as it is for teachers of older students? It will be important to establish whether there is in place a consensual view of a *culture générale,* whether knowledge is shaped and schematized in ways that reveal hierarchies of status, and whether the emphasis is on specialization or breadth.[33] It will be impossible to raise such questions or to develop them adequately without exploring contentious issues related to the multicultural emphasis so marked in many modern societies or to nationwide attempts (whether officially sponsored or not) to give operational effect to such notions as a national curriculum or cultural literacy.

Another range of epistemological questions bears more directly on the professional component in the education of teachers. What can be learned about and from the differences among nations in the ways in which they perceive the relevance and—equally important and unexamined—define the content of studies in sociology or psychology as they are deployed in the professional formation of the teacher? It seems probable that, to take the case of sociology, such variations will reflect systemic differences in the degree of autonomy assumed to be appropriate to the teacher or in perceptions of the relation between the school and social change (or a desired absence of it). In the case of psychology, it may be that the variations would reflect significantly different views of motivation or of human nature itself. Of particular interest here will be a study of changes over recent time in the consensual or formally established definition of what constitutes a

proper social science base for teacher education programs. In some countries the base will be large; in others, it may not even exist.

Other variations could be explored through a review of the wide differences, within nations as well as between them, in the importance attached to more precisely pedagogical studies. Where and why is it assumed that the "mastery" of a subject (mathematics, e.g., or a foreign language) is all that is required as preparation for the teaching of that subject? Is the mathematics taught in the university indeed the same "subject" as that which is learned in the elementary school? Questions of this type will overlap with explorations of the relations between the world of practice, as represented by the real schools and their teachers and their unions, and that of theory, represented by the universities and other establishments of teacher education. What can these relations tell us of public perceptions of teachers and of higher education?

It was argued above that, in the case of the United States, the perceptions of teachers, as organized around five characteristics, were linked to one another and rooted in a common set of assumptions. Teacher education, it may be supposed, will faithfully reflect those same perceptions and assumptions. Given the lay ownership of schooling in the United States, the vulnerability of teachers to administrative inspection and control, the absence from the school site of teacher hierarchies, the demystification of the tasks of teaching, the modest financial and status rewards for teachers, it is not surprising that access to courses of teacher education should be wide and flexibly defined. Teacher education programs are dispersed over a great number and variety of institutions and embedded within undergraduate education.[34] They are so fragmented that parts of them can be taken in different places and at different times and frequently are. Standards of admission to the ranks of teaching are neither high nor nationally consistent. Contrast with such "open" programs, offered in multipurpose institutions and mirroring the openness of American education itself, the closed type of program of a highly specialized kind extending over a continuous and considerable period of time and often available only within an institution exclusively dedicated to specific preparatory tasks— for teaching in some countries outside the United States, for example, as for medicine within that country. It is likely that such differences do indeed reflect important national differences in the perceptions of teachers. It is even more clear that the relation of teacher education programs and institutions to the whole structure of higher education has varied across time and still varies across national frontiers. To understand those relations, to decode the intellectual and social values they express, to appreciate them as manifestations of a culture, to identify the pace and direction of change within them—these efforts exemplify the value of studying cross-nationally small questions that generate larger questions and, perhaps, even some answers.

Notes

* From the *Comparative Education Review* 32, no. 2 (1988): 143–58, by permission of the University of Chicago Press. Copyright 1988 by the Comparative and International Education Society.

† This article is an abbreviated and revised version of the Eggertsen Lecture given at the meeting of the Comparative and International Education Society in Washington, D.C., in March 1987.

1. Harold Noah and Max Eckstein, *Metropolitanism and Education: Teachers and Schools in Amsterdam, London, Paris, and New York,* Teachers College Institute of the Philosophy and Politics of Education, Occasional Paper no. 1 (New York: Teachers College Press, 1973).

2. Vernon Mallinson, *An Introduction to the Study of Comparative Education,* 4th ed. (London: Heinemann, 1975), chap. 1.

3. Glenn Langford, *Teaching as a Profession* (Manchester: Manchester University Press, 1978), pp. 20–21.

4. Harry Judge, "Teaching and Professionalism: An Essay in Ambiguity," in *World Yearbook of Education 1980,* ed. Eric Hoyle and Jacquetta

Megarry (London: Kogan Page, 1980), pp. 340–42.

5. Emily Feistritzer, *The Condition of Teaching* (New York: Carnegie Foundation for the Advancement of Teaching, 1983).

6. P. H. J. H. Gosden, *The Evolution of a Profession* (Oxford: Basil Blackwell, 1972), p. 37.

7. *A Nation Prepared: Teachers for the 21st. Century* (New York: Carnegie Corporation, 1986), p. 65.

8. United Kingdom, Department of Education and Science, *Initial Teacher Training: Approval of Courses* (London: Her Majesty's Stationery Office, 1984).

9. United Kingdom, Department of Education and Science, *The National Curriculum 5–16* (London: Her Majesty's Stationery Office, 1987).

10. Harry Judge, *American Graduate Schools of Education: A View from Abroad* (New York: Ford Foundation, 1982), p. 37.

11. Charles Handy and Robert Aitken, *Understanding Schools as Organizations* (Harmondsworth: Penguin, 1986), p. 79.

12. See n. 7 above; and *Tomorrow's Teachers: A Report of the Holmes Group* (East Lansing, Mich.: Holmes Group), p. 64.

13. Martin Lawn, ed., *The Politics of Teachers Unions* (London: Croom Helm, 1985).

14. Edgar B. Wesley, *N.E.A., the First Hundred Years: The Building of the Teaching Profession* (New York: Harper, 1957).

15. Maurice Kogan, *The Politics of Educational Change* (London: Fontana, 1978), p. 79.

16. Bruce S. Cooper, *Collective Bargaining, Strikes and Financial Costs in Public Education: A Comparative Review* (Eugene, Oreg.: ERIC Clearinghouse, 1982).

17. Frank Musgrove and Philip H. Taylor, *Society and the Teacher's Role* (London: Routledge and Kegan Paul, 1969), p. 7.

18. Tony Becher and Stuart Maclure, *The Politics of Curriculum Change* (London: Hutchinson, 1978), p. 41.

19. Raymond E. Callahan, *Education and the Cult of Efficiency* (Chicago: University of Chicago Press, 1962), p. 244; David Tyack and Elisabeth Hansot, *Managers of Virtue: Public School Leadership in America, 1820–1980* (New York: Basic, 1982), p. 218.

20. John Mann, "Who Killed the Schools Council?" in *Life and Death of the Schools Council,*

ed. Maurice Plaskow (Lewes: Falmer, 1985), pp. 179–93.

21. Gary Sykes, "Contradictions, Ironies and Promises Unfulfilled," *Phi Delta Kappan* 65 (October 1983): 87–93.

22. Arthur E. Wise, *Legislated Learning: The Bureaucratization of the American Classroom* (Berkeley and Los Angeles: University of California Press, 1979).

23. Linda M. McNeil, *Contradictions of Control: School Structure and School Knowledge* (New York: Routledge and Kegan Paul, 1986).

24. Dan C. Lortie, *Schoolteacher: A Sociological Study* (Chicago: University of Chicago Press, 1986); Philip Jackson, *Life in Classrooms* (New York: Holt, Rinehart and Winston, 1968).

25. Thomas J. Peters and Robert H. Waterman, Jr., *In Search of Excellence* (New York: Warner, 1982), p. 201.

26. H. C. Dent, *The Training of Teachers in England and Wales, 1800–1975* (London: Hodder and Stoughton, 1977), p. 33.

27. Harold Noah, "The Use and Abuse of Comparative Education," in *New Approaches to Comparative Education,* ed. Philip G. Altbach and Gail Kelly (Chicago: University of Chicago Press, 1986), pp. 153–66; Max Eckstein, "The Comparative Mind," in Altbach and Kelly, eds., pp. 167–78.

28. Lawrence A. Cremin, *American Education: The National Experience, 1783–1876* (New York: Harper and Row, 1982), p. 390.

29. Olive Banks, *Parity and Prestige in English Secondary Education* (London: Routledge and Kegan Paul, 1955), p. 17.

30. For what follows, see in particular John Ardagh, *France in the 1980's* (Harmondsworth: Penguin, 1982); Ida Berger, *Les instituteurs d'une génération à l'autre* (Paris: Presses Universitaires de France, 1979); Michael Crozier, *Le phénomène bureaucratique* (Paris: Editions du Seuil, 1963); Émile Durkheim, *L'évolution pédagogique en France,* vol. 2 (Paris: Alcan, 1938); W. R. Fraser, *Reform and Restraints in Modern French Education* (London: Routledge and Kegan Paul, 1971); W. D. Halls, *Education, Culture and Politics in Modern France* (Oxford: Pergamon, 1976); H. D. Lewis, *The French Education System* (London: Croom Helm, 1985); Gaston Mialaret, *La formation des enseignants* (Paris: Presses Universitaires de France, 1983); Guy Neave, "France," in *The School and the University,* ed. Burton R. Clark (Berkeley and Los Angeles: University of California Press, 1985); Antoine Prost, *L'enseignement en France, 1800–1967* (Paris: Armand Colin, 1968).

31. There have been few attempts at cross-national studies of teacher education. Notable among them is James Lynch and Dudley Plunkett, *Teacher Education and Cultural Change: England, France, West Germany* (London: Allen and Unwin, 1973). See also Donald Lomax, ed., *European Perspectives in Teacher Education* (London: Wiley, 1976). In the collection by Richard Goodings, Michael Byam, and Michael McPartland, eds., *Changing Priorities in Teacher Education* (London: Croom Helm, 1982), there is an important chapter by William Taylor, entitled "Changing Priorities in Teacher Education," pp. 16–30, asserting the importance of initiating cross-national studies in teacher education.

32. See Clifford Geertz, *Local Knowledge* (New York: Basic, 1983).

33. See Basil Bernstein, *Class, Codes and Control* (London: Routledge and Kegan Paul, 1975).

34. Gary Sykes, "Teacher Education in the United States," in Clark, ed., chap. 10.

Welfare and Social Services

One of the most pervasive and profound changes in the pattern of social life introduced in a century full of massive change has been the process whereby governments have taken over responsibility for all manner of fundamental life activities which previously were the responsibility of the family and the individual. The provision of education for the young and of medical care for all, the arrangements for dealing with the contingency of joblessness and for later retirement from employment, the care of the elderly, and the responsibility for dealing with the impoverished and destitute—all have moved in the same direction. The result is considered a new phenomenon in human experience, called the welfare state, and to understand it has been a major challenge to contemporary social scientists.

A general review of these challenges and the efforts to respond to them is offered by Jens Alber, Gösta Esping-Andersen, and Lee Rainwater. They discuss the difficulties of defining exactly what is meant by the welfare state, review efforts to explain its rise and its consequences, and assess research seeking to explain the seemingly wide variation observed in the welfare policies of different nations. These authors express strong concerns about the adequacy of the data in this field and of the methods used to analyze them. They thus provide a useful supplement to the discussion of the methods of comparative analysis presented in section II of this book.

John B. Williamson and Jeanne J. Fleming use the welfare system to test a more general proposition, namely, the assumption that the industrial nations of the world, although having started with very different cultural and historical legacies, are all converging on a common model of social organization. Their conception of "the welfare system" is very broad, ranging from expenditures for old age assistance, through the provision of health care, to issues of income equality. Their methodological contribution lies in the use of longitudinal rather than onetime cross-sectional data, and in the application to that data of a simple but important coefficient of variation to measure convergence. They find that the evidence supports the theory of convergence in all respects except that of income equality.

To better understand this exception, that is, why income inequality responds as it does in the welfare state, is the special concern of Vincent A. Mahler and Claudio J. Katz. They focus, in particular, on the question of how far income maintenance programs actually affect the distribution of income in advanced industrial countries. What they help us understand is that the effects depend on which kind of program one observes. Money spent on family allowances and on unemployment insurance, positive as such expenditures may be in other respects, does not seem to have a marked effect on the distribution of income nationwide. By contrast, old age insurance programs do indeed reduce the proportion of people living at or near the poverty level. Japan, however, is a striking exception, spending little on government income maintenance programs but nevertheless manifesting a notable degree of equality in the overall distribution of income. The uniqueness of Japan is not fully explained here, but the identification of its special status is a good example of the challenges with which comparative research can confront us.

CHAPTER TWENTY-THREE

Studying the Welfare State: Issues and Queries*

Jens Alber, Gösta Esping-Andersen, and Lee Rainwater

Over the past two decades social scientists have discovered the welfare state. A careful review of the research reveals a large and unwieldy literature which spans the disciplines of sociology, political science, history, social administration, and public policy analysis, documenting how diverse and multifaceted the broad subject of social policy in the modern state is. Different researchers focus on different kinds of question and with different theoretical and practical goals. The dominant focus of most of the research to date has been on the social, political, and economic determinants of social policy development, but scholars have also been concerned with the developmental patterns of particular programs, the effects of social policy on the economy and on national politics, and the effects of social policy on the level and distribution of well-being in welfare societies.

Taking stock of this broad area of research has also revealed that the work to date does little more than start a serious political sociology of the welfare state. Much more remains to be done to provide a solid basis for understanding the causes and consequences of the rapid growth of social protection institutions in modern societies. Results of work to date are highly problematic on the basis of theoretical, substantive, and methodological concerns. The early studies of welfare-state development had to invent methods of systematic comparative and historical macrosociology. The shortcomings of those pioneering databases and methods have set the stage for methodological innovations.

The social policy literature encompasses three basic perspectives which make it difficult to integrate results. However, work done with one goal in mind may provide a critical appraisal of the other approaches.

The welfare-state perspective is part of the tradition of classical macrosociology and seeks to study the welfare state as an element in the development of modern capitalist and democratic societies. The social policy perspective emphasizes assessing the effectiveness of social programs in realizing the goals set by the policymakers. The welfare-distribution perspective focuses on the distribution and levels of actual well-being among the population. Within this general framework the question becomes how to conceptualize the welfare state. Two important aspects of this problem are, first, what is the essence of the welfare state: security as the stabilization of social status, or the government provision of minima and redistribution? and second, should we consider only state programs or the mix of private, occupational, associational, and state schemes?

What Causes the Welfare State?

The welfare state has been an attractive subject for many investigators as a testing ground for general theory concerning macrosocial processes—theories of power, the state, industrialization, or more broadly, modernization. Major theoretical controversies in the social sciences have been tested by studying the welfare state and its development. In these studies the central problem has been the independent variable—economic development, class power, state development, and so forth—with little attention to a precise specification of the dependent variable, the welfare state. Because the welfare state was conceived, if only for reasons of research expediency, as a unitary institution, much of the research in this tradition has relied on simple measures of expenditure as the sole operationalization of the complex of institutions known as the welfare state.

Wilensky et al. (1978) conclude that "economic level and its bureaucratic and demographic correlates" are the root causes of welfare-state effort and an even stronger cause of per capita expenditures. Thus, economic development is thought to push toward convergence. Within the limits specified by basic economic forces, the authors conclude that the process of democratization as well as ideologies and power blocs within societies (especially the strength of Catholicism) are important factors to explain variations among nations in welfare achievements and in the vulnerability of those achievements to "backlash."

However, the root cause is generally traced to a society's economic level and its correlates, regardless of regime type. If effort is measured in terms of social expenditure as a percentage of GDP, the research of Esping-Andersen and Korpi (1985) suggests that economic level is less important than political variations to explain the growth trends of the last fifty years. More generally, the accumulated research is characterized by its inability to reach any commonly shared generalization regarding the causal influence of economic level, power variables, bureaucratic variables, ideologies, or, for that matter, any root cause.

Perhaps the absence of theoretical consensus can be traced to the diversity of research approaches. Detailed comparative case histories (Rimlinger 1971; Heclo 1974; Skocpol and Ikenberry 1983) are contrasted by broad generalizations across many nations based on the isolation of a few key variables. These two approaches tend to portray starkly different realities. The former approach often refuses to pinpoint any single, or set of, core explanatory variables; the latter, due perhaps to properties of its design, usually singles out a handful of key causes. Regardless, the lack of consensus on root causes will most likely remain for the

simple reason that too many variables must be tested with too few cases for genuinely quantitative comparisons; and the case-history approach is unable to handle more than a few nations simultaneously.

While the debate on causality may never be resolved, some agreement must be reached on what constitutes the object of explanation. If, for example, the goal of research is to compare welfare-state development, what constitutes the existence of a welfare state? The essence of the welfare state has been defined as government-protected minimum standards of income, nutrition, health and safety, education, and housing assured to every citizen as a right. While this is a widely shared definition, few studies systematically address the basic question of which cases qualify as welfare states. For example, almost all comparative studies include laggards such as Australia, without assessing its conformity to the definition above. Indeed, how many nations guarantee a minimum standard of housing as a right? Furthermore, the key term "minimum standards" has proved unacceptable to some who insist on a definition based on "adequate" or even "optimal" standards. These questions are crucial to comparative research.

Disaggregating the Welfare State

Confronting the macrosociological literature on the welfare state with the "social policy" perspective raises at least two new critical issues. First, the boundaries of the welfare state must be described in terms of the kinds of programs it includes. Second, should variations in the character of social programs as well as their extensiveness be measured by expenditures?

With respect to the boundary issue, Strümpel and Scholz (1978) demonstrate that most research has focused on the "core area" of government-operated income-maintenance programs. But as Heimann (1929) and many other early social democrats have argued, the labor movement's basic social policy goal was to push forward the boundaries of "democracy." Social policy encompassed a very broad arena of the labor movement's struggle to replace market and employer authority with citizen rights. From this perspective welfare-state research should seek to develop a measure which encompasses the replacement of commodified resources. The range of resources subject to this process is one measure of an enlargement of the welfare state; the degree of replacement is another. Although a broad political consensus has emerged around the core programs of social policy, in recent years the real battles have been fought over social policy extensions in such areas as housing, labor-market rights, economic citizen rights, and enterprise ownership rights. If the social dynamics driving these struggles are those which during earlier periods produced more traditional welfare-state programs, it makes little sense to exclude them from the area of research. As an empirical matter, the extent to which dynamics are the same can only be tested if these border areas are included within the definition of the welfare state.

Recent debates in the field also call into question the limitation of the traditional social policy perspective on state programs. Boundaries between state and nonstate functions are problematic in ways that confound comparative research. Further, the interplay of public and private institutions around issues of social protection has become so complex that the isolation of state welfare expenditures as the object of study makes little sense theoretically (Rein and Rainwater 1985).

The vast majority of studies employ highly aggregative measures such as social spending levels, date of program introduction or program coverage. These are easily quantifiable, amenable to correlational analyses, and presumably capture welfare effort. Since many of these comparative studies seek to test propositions derived from fields outside social policy per se, no particular attention is given to the more detailed and complex issues within social policy. Only rarely do conceptualizations bear any relationship to the classics of social policy,

such as T. H. Marshall's concept of social citizenship or Titmuss's social division of welfare. The validity of convergence (or other theoretical) arguments may disappear in comparisons of the institutional character of welfare states, such as status differentiation, degree of universalism, and the like. While few researchers examine institutional features, these were central to the concepts of welfare states developed by Titmuss, Marshall, and Heimann. Do the empirical generalizations accumulated in past research remain sufficiently valid from the "social policy" perspective? Future comparative social policy research must devote more attention to the question of what is to be explained. In particular, much more attention must be given to the "qualities" of the welfare state: the strength and scope of citizens' rights should be central to research efforts.

The validity of any study depends on whether it explains what it purports to explain. Most of the continuing controversy among comparative welfare-state researchers concerning the causes of international variations could be resolved if more attention were given to the measurement and operationalization of the dependent variables. Comparative case histories uncover a myriad of details of social reforms, their administrative properties, coverage, financial agreements, distributive logic, and so forth. In the correlational approach, the welfare state is often reduced to one or two highly aggregated indices. Social security expenditure as a percentage of GDP is the most widely adopted indicator. Others like Castles (1982) include total public consumption. Flora et al. (1983) attempt to trace the dynamics of social policy evolution by using year of program introduction. Aggregate indices have their advantages; they are easily available, roughly comparable across very diverse nations, and quantifiable. But the choice of such aggregated variables may lead to theoretical conclusions that do not necessarily apply if welfare effort is disaggregated and specific institutional features of welfare states are studied. Perhaps the most pressing basic issue facing comparative social policy research is how to measure "welfare effort."

Aggregate expenditure indices are problematic because one must assume that more spending reflects some kind of greater political will to optimize welfare. But can this be assumed? The Thatcher government explicitly desires to reduce public welfare commitments; yet the level of spending has actually risen. High spending levels can reflect an unusually high incidence of social problems. High spending may also reflect an inability to prevent social problems from occurring. Also questionable is Castles's choice of total public consumption, which includes defense spending.

Aggregate indices camouflage underlying differences in spending patterns. If, for example, the usual eighteen nations are ranked by level of social spending during the 1930s, the United States ranks comparatively high. Yet most of this spending was on civil servant benefits and targeted poor relief. Effort variables should bear a closer relationship to, for example, the distributional qualities of social policy, the strength and scope of social entitlements, the degrees of universalism, the comprehensiveness and range of social policy, and financial arrangements. As noted, indicators such as waiting days for cash benefits may be much more sensitive to crucial international variations in efforts.

A closer cross-fertilization between case-study material and correlational approaches is sorely needed. Operationalizing welfare-state effort along these lines would more closely reflect the real concerns of social policy as such, yielding considerably greater validity to research in this area. but more importantly, the basic theoretical concerns would be linked more closely. Convergence theory's empirical support, for example, may be reduced sharply if a general comparison of spending and program introduction is modified by the specific institutional features of welfare programs. And since most of the literature directly or indirectly tests political power hypotheses, the object of study must be something that has been

politically decisive in history. Clearly, social classes and political parties never struggled over spending volumes per se; they fought over eligibility rules, coverage principles, targeting versus universalism, financial burdens, benefit levels, and perhaps most importantly, the boundaries of social citizenship rights.

If these more ambitious requirements regarding the "dependent variables" are accepted, less confidence can be placed in the generalizations that have accumulated thus far simply because too few studies of this kind exist. Probably future investigations will require a thorough redefinition of the scope of research.

Perhaps a major reorientation is already under way. Myles's (1984) comparative study of the quality of pension systems, the welfare-state comparisons of Therborn et al. (1978), the Epsing-Andersen and Korpi research on the institutional aspects of social policy systems, and the Flora et al. (1983) survey of European welfare-state development in the postwar period represent significant departures from previous work in the field. However, the process of historical change requires considerably more research, and many key components of the welfare state have been virtually ignored; "fiscal welfare" and welfare-state finances are two glaring examples.

An "institutional" approach to the conceptualization and operationalization of the dependent variables might compel researchers to examine a much broader field of policy arenas, including housing, labor markets, education, working conditions, and perhaps even regional policies because issues of citizens' rights and distributional concerns cut across conventionally defined policy fields. In this view, the study of social policy becomes the study of societal policy (Ferge 1980).

The majority of existing theory and research concerns growth processes and typically departs from linear assumptions of change. To what degree is the current theoretical baggage equipped to handle the contraction and reversals presently under way in many nations? To what extent has the literature been sensitive to sharp historical breaks? Few comparative studies have employed dynamic models and designs. Notable exceptions include the work of Peters (1972), Flora and Heidenheimer (1981), and Therborn et al. (1978). These, bolstered by the historical case studies, do seem to identify—repeatedly—decisive historical breaks. Again, the correlational approaches suffer from the problem of too few cases and therefore cannot provide adequate tests for interaction effects and historical shifts in the relative weight of contending causal variables. Is there sufficient evidence, for example, to conclude that economic level is a more important causal influence in certain historical periods than in others, or to conclude that the role of the left (or Catholic parties) is more decisive in certain periods? Has the possible existence of threshold effects on the impact of party power been confirmed? In short, more research effort might fruitfully be devoted to the investigation of nonlinear growth processes, welfare-state decline, and threshold effects.

The Effects of the Welfare State

Although the literature on the effects of welfare states is sparse, in recent years "result" studies have made important strides. Due to their intimate connection to social policy and to their holistic approach to welfare, the Nordic Level of Living Studies represent a watershed in comparative social policy research (for example, Nordic Council 1984). These studies analyze the distribution of a very broad range of resources among citizens, and thus permit the identification of not only lingering poverty in the traditional sense but also accumulated deprivation among the entire population. The selection of variables, furthermore, permits the linkage of policy intents with outcomes to a greater degree than most other research. Allardt's (1976) study of "Having, Loving, and Being" is even more ambitiously cast along parallel lines, since its corruption of welfare and distribution merged both "subjective" and "objective" properties of human welfare. Pre-

cisely because such studies transcend conventionally imposed boundaries of the welfare state, they are at the vanguard of comparative social policy research. Thus they encompass both health resources, political resources, and working conditions, making explicit links between private life and public citizenship; and they permit assessments of the ways in which the totality of peoples' welfare is derived from state, market, and family. The Scandinavian Level of Living approach stands in sharp contrast to most past and current research which has centered exclusively on either one policy domain (e.g., health) or on specific target populations (typically the poor).

Problems of Adequacy of Data and Methods

Three methodological issues have emerged which require attention: the merits of cross-sectional versus longitudinal studies; the relative advantages of aggregate comparisons of a large number of countries versus more detailed case studies; and the most appropriate operationalization of the "welfare state."

Most researchers agree that the prevailing cross-sectional studies need to be complemented by longitudinal comparisons. Most of the present assumptions about the development of the welfare state are based on cross-country comparisons which on closer analysis may prove misleading. Thus the finding that countries with long periods of government control by "left-wing" parties tend to spend generously on welfare does not preclude that expenditure increases occurred predominantly under "right-wing" or "centrist" governments. The relative merits of more intensive case studies of few countries as opposed to more sweeping comparisons was discussed in various contexts. Some argue that extending the number of countries is the best way to deal with problems of overdetermination. Others argue that discrimination according to the explanatory power of different variables is also possible by extending the number of observations over time in historical case studies. A second argument in favor of case studies is that they allow for the identification of politically controversial aspects of welfare programs, and thus help to determine in more detail the nature and impact of political processes.

The substantive issues concerning the specification of the welfare state as multidimensional in ways that reflect the diversity of its patterns of growth and operation in different countries, noted in the previous sections, have quite direct methodological implications for the kinds of data that must be gathered in order to yield an empirical description of these institutions in any particular society at any particular time. And to the extent that research is to be comparative across historical periods or countries, or both, methods must be developed to ensure that descriptions of the welfare state in different times and places are generated by comparable methods.

The project for advancement of comparative social policy research suggested by these considerations, in summary, will require the conceptualization of social policy as a five-dimensional object of study. Future research must be (1) cross-national; (2) historical, using, for example, time-series methods; (3) focused on social expenditure as part of the dependent variable; (4) addressed to the issue of coverage, that is, research needs to take into account who in the nation receives these resources; and (5) attentive to programs and their defining characteristics such as the type of institution providing the resource (public or private), bases of entitlements (citizen right, means-tested), type of resource provided (e.g., cash or kind), type of need being met (e.g., health, housing, retirement, etc.).

Particular studies have concentrated on some of these dimensions and ignored others. For example, the core of welfare-state studies is composed of cross-national explorations of the correlates of total expenditure at one time. Other strategies offer promise of further development of understanding—by extension to a third dimension (nation by expenditure by time, or nation by time by program characteristics) or with sufficient resources, to all five dimensions. The argument for single-country studies ("case study" is perhaps implicitly pejorative) generally assumes that they will deal with all four dimensions within that country and thus contribute depth of understanding to cross-national studies. Useful contributions to knowledge may probably come from many different combinations of these dimensions in the specification of the units of observation.

The research review surveys an enormous literature on the determinants of welfare-state variations. Since cross-national samples are of such limited size the research design clearly imposes severe limitations. If the theoretical model specifies multiple relations and interaction effects, it is not possible to test it statistically. Alternative designs must be adopted to resolve the main theoretical controversies. This is most clearly evidenced in recent developments concerning the impact of parties. To gauge their role, researchers must first control for economic variables and their "bureaucratic and demographic correlates," and then identify the proper "power" variable, for example, left-wing party power. Yet Catholic parties are also believed to play a role in some nations. Political divisions among rightist and leftist parties may be influential. And trade union centralization and unity may be crucial to the rise of welfare-state provisions. If these forces are believed to interact in a way that is decisive, researchers will require much larger samples than the usual eighteen to twenty nations in order to test the relative influence of these variables empirically.

In short, the cross-sectional correlation approach does not permit the researcher to test fully the theoretical propositions that many agree must be tested. One solution is to shift toward a time-series approach, but this requires a heavy investment in data collection and validation. But it can be done.

Another attractive possibility is to approximate the panel-type study, as Therborn et al. (1978) do in their twelve-nation study. Here they attempt to identify the relative influence of "social democracy" by a comparison of the cross-national variance in welfare performance in the 1930s and again in later periods. Aside from the advantage of operating with more independent variables, these kinds of dynamic designs also permit the identification of critical historical conjunctures, cycles, or shifts in the causal influence of diverse variables.

A second limitation with the prevailing cross-sectional approach is its general inability to identify processes. We correlate such variables as left-wing party strength (measured as cabinet shares, for example), economic level, demographic distribution, and the like, with welfare effort. But in reality these variables stand for black boxes. On the basis of empirical evidence it can be concluded that "social security growth . . . is hastened by the interplay of political élite perceptions, mass pressures and welfare bureaucracies," but the real curiosity centers on the question of how. How do these variables hasten social security growth? Comparative social policy research should therefore address the possibility of a closer synthesis between the correlational and case-history approach. If the impact of political parties is to be assessed, researchers will need to know the objects of their struggles as well as the obstacles they met. In other words, the plausibility of existing generalizations must rest on more than a willingness to infer complex sociopolitical processes from cross-section-based correlations between highly aggregated variables. To give a grotesque example, Esping-Andersen reports that the correlation between social spending levels and the number of miles a nation's capital is from Stockholm is stronger than with either economic level or left-wing party power.

A third related misgiving is that the specification of a causal variable is always linked to some assumption about its "historical mission" or basic impact. But the connection between a variable as specified and historical processes is not always so straightforward. Diffusion theory has not been very successful in specifying

the path of causality. This may be due to the choice of assumptions regarding diffusion; perhaps the issue is not whether some countries pioneer and others follow, but that communication flows between historical political forces. For example, the socialist parties (and conservatives) learned from one another in a very direct way, in some cases directly importing each others' proposals and plans. More attention to the actual historical process of program diffusion should help uncover such phenomena. A second example entails the properties assumed to characterize left-wing parties. Including the American Democratic Party in this category requires the assumption that its historical objectives are reasonably similar to those of European labor parties. Are they? Is convergence or divergence of party objectives a criterion for confident classifications? Referring to the "conventional left-wing wisdom of the welfare state," Wilensky et al. (chapter 12) suggest that "in the cause of fairness and redistribution, taxes should be visible, progressive, and heavily based on incomes and property, and benefits should be based on need and concentrated on the poor." A more common reading of socialist parties' social policy objectives suggests (except for progressive taxation) opposite welfare goals. Their emphasis on universalism and the rejection of targeting has been especially pronounced. The issue is not so much which interpretation is accurate, but rather the need to establish a stronger intellectual consensus as to the assumed motives applied to "variables."

The Organization of Comparative Social Policy Research

Just like the participant observer in field research, the social policy analyst must find the narrow path between the two evils of "going native" and "going naive." Case studies tend to run the first risk. Although the researcher may become more sensitive to the meaning of the data, he or she will easily confound nationally specific and general aspects of welfare-state development and may fail to achieve the social science goal of general explanation. Sweeping comparisons, on the other hand, easily fall prey to the second risk. As noted, they encounter equivalence problems in the operationalization of variables, and given the large masses of data, they may fail to detect statistical artifacts.

Two strategies to cope with this persistent dilemma in the organization of research seem indicated. First, comparisons of a large number of countries could be limited to specific sectors of welfare-state provisions such as health or pension policy, which would allow for sufficient expertise to shield against the risk of "going naive." Second, comparative projects of a new type could bring country specialists together in order to analyze their countries in a common theoretical and comparative framework. This type of organization would probably safeguard against both risks.

Future Steps in Comparative Social Policy Research

Five goals seem to emerge from the debates on the above-mentioned topics. First, work for improvement must be conducted simultaneously on three fronts: databases, analytic methods, and theory development. Improvement of the database calls for the systematic collection of quantitative and institutional data which would allow us to map similarities and differences in the national path of welfare-state development. Improvement of theory implies the development of propositions on the bases and functions of welfare-state development, specifying which properties are inherent in all capitalist and democratic, or even all modern, societies, and which are the result of particular historical circumstances or constellations of variables.

Second, cross-country comparisons based on aggregate data analysis must be enhanced with detailed longitudinal analyses and case studies. Third and similarly, the prevailing studies of core social programs (i.e., social security) must be complemented by research on the boundaries of the welfare state (public goods,

fiscal welfare, etc.) Fourth, the study of state schemes must be accompanied by analyses of the specific national mixes of welfare production in the state, the associational and the private sectors. Finally, studies on the determinants of welfare-state development must be brought together with analyses of its effects on the level of system integration (welfare growth, political stability, external security), the level of social integration (cleavage structures, strike patterns, etc.) and the distribution of well-being (levels of living) in societies.

Note

*   From *Comparative Policy Research: Learning from Experience,* edited by Meinolf Dierkes, Hans N. Weiler, and Ariane B. Antal (New York: St. Martin's Press, 1978), 458–69, by permission of St. Martin's Press, Inc. Copyright 1978 by M. Dierkes, H. N. Weiler, and A. B. Antal.

References

Allardt, E. 1976. *Att Ha, at Alska, att Vara: Om Valfard i Norden.* Lund: Argos.

Castles, F. 1982. *The Impact of Parties.* London and Beverly Hills: Sage.

Esping-Andersen, G., and W. Korpi. 1985. "From Poor Relief to Institutional Welfare States" in R. Eriksson et al., eds. *The Scandinavian Model.* New York: M. E. Sharpe.

Ferge, S. 1980. *A Society in the Making.* New York: M. E. Sharpe.

Flora, P., and A. Heidenheimer. 1981. *The Development of Welfare States in Europe and America.* New Brunswick: Transaction Books.

Flora, Peter et al. 1983. *State, Economy, and Society in Western Europe, 1815–1975: A Data Handbook in Two Volumes.* Frankfurt: Campus; Chicago: St. James.

Heclo, H. 1974. *Social Politics in Britain and Sweden.* New Haven: Yale University Press.

Heimann, E. 1929. *Soziale Theorie des Kapitalismus.* Frankfurt: Suhrkamp (reprinted 1980).

Myles, J. 1984. *Old Age in the Welfare State.* Boston: Beacon Press.

Nordic Council. 1984. *Level of Living and Inequality in the Nordic Countries.* Stockholm: Nordic Council.

Peters, B. Guy. 1972. "Public Policy, Socioeconomic Conditions and the Political System: A Development Analysis." *Polity* 5: 277–84.

Rein, M., and L. Rainwater. 1985. *The Private/Public Interplay in Social Protection.* New York: M. E. Sharpe.

Rimlinger, G. 1971. *Welfare and Industrialization in Europe, America and Russia.* New York: Wiley.

Skocpol, T., and J. Ikenberry. 1983. "The Political Formation of the American Welfare States." Unpublished manuscript, University of Chicago.

Strümpel and Scholz. 1978. Chapter 10 in Dierkes et al. *Comparative Policy Research: Learning from Experience.* New York: St. Martin's Press.

Therborn, G. et al. 1978. "Sweden before and after Social Democracy." *Acta Sociologica,* supplement.

Wilensky et al. 1978. Chapter 12 in Dierkes et al. *Comparative Policy Research: Learning from Experience.* New York: St. Martin's Press.

Convergence Theory and the Social Welfare Sector: A Cross-National Analysis*

John B. Williamson and Jeanne J. Fleming

Convergence theory proposes that industrial nations are becoming more and more alike despite different cultural and historical legacies and diverse political and economic systems. The idea of convergence is implicit in the work of such disparate nineteenth-century theorists as Marx and Spencer. Maine (1964), de Tocqueville (1952), and Töennies (1963) were also among those who supported the idea that diverse societies would become increasingly similar, but de Maistre (1964) and Comte argued against it. As Weinberg (1969) points out, consideration of convergence thesis issues was common among nineteenth-century social scientists. Twentieth-century theorists have continued the convergence debate, arguing both for and against convergence among industrial nations in such areas as economic life, political systems, personality development, and stratification systems (Meyer et al., 1975; Baum, 1974).

This paper examines the convergence thesis as it relates to the social welfare sector. The term "social welfare" as it is used here refers both to social welfare effort by national governments and to social welfare outcome as reflected in "quality-of-life" measures. At issue is whether or not the politically and culturally diverse industrial nations are, as convergence theory predicts, becoming more and more alike with regard to social welfare.

A number of recent studies support the convergence thesis as it relates to social welfare by illustrating the relative importance of economic development rather than political or historical variables in determining social welfare

levels. Wilensky (1975) argues that welfare-state development is only weakly related to political system and ideology. He found that economic development, through its effect on the age structure of the population, is a more powerful determinant of social welfare progress than either political system or political ideology. In a comparison of seven market economies with seven centrally planned economies, Pryor (1968) showed that economic development is a considerably more important factor in health and welfare expenditures and total education expenditures than is economic system. Similarly, Cutright's (1967) analysis showed that extent of industrialization is a better predictor of social security coverage than is level of political representativeness.

In a longitudinal study more explicitly testing the convergence thesis, Mishra (1973) found that industrial societies are becoming more similar with regard to social welfare as they reach advanced levels of industrial development. He found that (1) statutory programs of social security and education tend to develop in all industrial nations; and (2) the trend to increasing similarity is more pronounced in aspects of social welfare that are close to technology. Analyzing longitudinal data from twenty Western industrial societies, he argued that there was a stronger convergence trend for provision of compulsory education than for social security program enactment. Compulsory education, he hypothesized, is an aspect of welfare that is closer to technology than social security program enactment because industrial development requires skilled, literate workers;

thus the "logic of industrialization" (Kerr et al., 1964) requires mass education.

Most quantitative research on the convergence thesis to date has been based on cross-sectional data. This research has typically found support for convergence with respect to the social welfare sector. However, the convergence theory is actually a statement about trends over time and for this reason it is more appropriate to test it using longitudinal data.

Of the various aspects of social welfare, none has been of greater interest to the sociologist than the distribution of income. The most thorough analysis to date on the topic is that carried out by Jackman (1975: 27–43) using cross-sectional data from sixty countries. He regresses his measure of income inequality on a linear measure of level of economic development and is able to account for 36 percent of the variance in income inequality (Jackman, 1975: 37). This evidence is interpreted as supporting the linear specification of convergence theory implicit in the work of Kerr et al., (1964), Lenski (1966), and Cutright (1967).

Another interpretation of convergence theory specifies that with increasing industrialization there will come a point at which the trend toward increased economic equality begins to level off at higher levels of industrial development (Pryor, 1968: 181; Wilensky, 1975: 18–19). Such a model is implicit in the theorizing of Goldthorpe (1969) and is supported by the logarithmic specification of Jackman's model in which he is able to account for 42 percent of the variance in income inequality (Jackman, 1975: 38).

The research of Jackman and others leaves no doubt as to the support for convergence with respect to income inequality which can be obtained on the basis of cross-sectional data. However, as we have mentioned earlier, the convergence theory describes a longitudinal process and is more accurately assessed on the basis of longitudinal data. As the first step in the present analysis we examine the longitudinal evidence on convergence with respect to income inequality. As it turns out the evidence

does not point to convergence in this sphere. This raises doubts about the generalizability of cross-sectional studies on other aspects of social welfare too. In view of this we examine longitudinal evidence on social security, education, unemployment, birth rates, and health care. In each case the evidence points to convergence. This leaves us with the question as to why income inequality is different. We conclude with a discussion of several possible explanations for the discrepancy.

Methodology
Sampling

The present study is based on national level aggregate data for twenty-six countries. We use only countries which can be considered "industrial"; others have referred to them as "rich." A variety of alternative (and very highly correlated) indicators such as GNP, GNP per capita, and energy consumption per capita are available. We have selected GNP per capita and have restricted the sample to countries with a GNP per capita of $850 and over in 1965, a figure roughly comparable to the "rich" nations used by Wilensky (1975: 121) and the "industrial" nations used by Mishra (1973). The requirement that comparable data be available for at least two points in time separated by ten or more years considerably restricts our sample size. To make maximum use of the available data, our tables are based on all countries for which the data on that particular variable are available. The number of countries represented ranges from ten to twenty-four depending on the variable; for each table we indicate which countries are being considered.

Measuring Convergence

In the present analysis convergence is measured using the coefficient of variation (the ratio of the standard deviation to the mean, expressed as a percent) rather than the more common alternatives such as the standard deviation or variance because the coefficient of variation is adjusted for shifts in the mean (i.e., a 10-point spread is likely to have a different interpretation around a mean of 150 than around a mean of 15). The greater the decrease in the coefficient of variation over a specified period of time, the greater the convergence. Since our data are available for different time periods, we also present a measure of the mean convergence per year.[1]

Results

Income Inequality

Considering the evidence from previous studies based on cross-sectional data, we would be led to hypothesize a convergent trend with respect to income inequality.

Our measure of income inequality is intersectoral income inequality rather than individual income inequality. Recently (Rubinson, 1976; Paukert, 1973) data on individual income inequality has become more available, but the longitudinal data are still too scant to be of use for our present purposes. Until very recently efforts to compare a substantial number of countries have relied on intersectoral income inequality as a proxy for individual income inequality.[2] The measure was developed by Kuznets (1963). It is computed by first dividing the percentage of total domestic product produced in each of eight sectors (e.g., manufacturing, agriculture, mining) by the number of workers in that sector. A Gini coefficient is then computed to measure the degree to which per worker product is unequal across sectors.

The data for the trend in income inequality between 1950 and 1960 are presented in Table 24.1. The coefficient of variation is 41 percent in 1950 and still 41 percent in 1960. There is no evidence of convergence. This is in marked contrast to the results based on cross-sectional data.

The discrepancy between the results in Table 24.1 and the results for previous cross-sectional studies (e.g., Jackman, 1975: 37–41) raises the question as to whether the cross-sectional evidence for convergence will hold up when we look at longitudinal data for other

TABLE 24.1   Trend in Intersectoral Income Inequality for Ten Industrial Nations between 1950 and 1960*

	1950	1960
$\overline{X}$	.11	.17
SD	.05	.07
CV	41%	41%
Mean convergence = 0% per year		

*Or nearest year
Note: Countries include: United Kingdom, Netherlands, Belgium, United States, Austria, Canada, Italy, Norway, Ireland, Finland. CV = Coefficient of variation; $\overline{X}$ = mean (average); and SD = standard deviation.
Source: For 1950, Kuznets (1963: 70–71); for 1960, Taylor and Hudson (1972: 263–64).

spheres of social welfare. To answer this question we next consider indicators of trends with respect to social security, unemployment, education, birth rates, and health care.

Social Security Expenditure

On the basis of the convergence theory we would hypothesize a convergent trend in social security expenditure. Social security expenditure as a percent of GNP can be interpreted as a measure of a nation's social welfare effort. The measure includes compulsory social insurance, family allowances, public health services, public assistance (welfare), as well as other related programs such as benefits granted to war victims (see Wilensky, 1975: 122–28).

The data for the trend between 1949 and 1966 are presented in Table 24.2. The coefficient of variation is 35 percent in 1949 and 31 percent in 1960; this averages out to a .67 percent decrease per year. The trend is not strong, but it is in the direction of convergence.

Number of Social Security Programs

This variable is simply a count of the number of five social security programs (work injury compensation, old age pension, sickness benefits, unemployment benefits, family allowance) that a given country has in effect. The data for the trend between 1900 and 1967 are

TABLE 24.2 Trend in Social Security Expenditure as a Percentage of Gross National Product at Factor Cost in Eighteen Industrialized Nations between 1949 and 1966

	1949	1966
$\overline{X}$	8.1	14.0
SD	2.8	4.3
CV	35%	31%
Mean convergence = .67% per year		

Note: Countries include: Switzerland, Canada, Ireland, New Zealand, Norway, Finland, Denmark, United Kingdom, Italy, Sweden, France, Netherlands, Belgium, West Germany, Austria, Israel, Australia, United States. CV = coefficient of variation; $\overline{X}$ = mean (average); and SD = standard deviation.
Source: Wilensky (1975: 30–31).

TABLE 24.3 Trend in Social Security Programs Available in Twenty Industrial Nations between 1900 and 1967

	1900	1967
$\overline{X}$	.75	4.78
SD	.95	.54
CV	127%	11%
Mean convergence = 1.36% per year		

Notes: Programs included: Work injury compensation, old age pensions, sickness benefit, unemployment benefits, and family allowance. Countries include: Canada, Israel, Australia, New Zealand, Austria, Belgium, Denmark, Finland, France, West Germany, Iceland, Italy, Luxembourg, Netherlands, Norway, Sweden, Switzerland, United Kingdom. CV = coefficient of variation; $\overline{X}$ = mean (average); and SD = standard deviation.
Source: Mishra (1973: 544); U.S. Department of Health, Education, and Welfare (1967).

presented in Table 24.3. The coefficient of variation is 127 percent in 1900 and 11 percent in 1967; this averages out to a 1.36 percent decrease per year. These results offer strong support for the convergence theory.

Duration of Compulsory Education

On the basis of convergence theory we would hypothesize a convergent trend in duration of compulsory education. This variable measures variations in the number of years of school that are required.[3] It does not differentiate between varying proportions of the population reached.

The data for the trend between 1900 and 1969 are presented in Table 24.4. The coefficient of variation is 40 percent in 1900 and 7 percent in 1969; this averages out to a 1.20 percent decrease per year. Again the data strongly support the convergence thesis.

Unemployment Rates

On the basis of convergence theory we would hypothesize a convergent trend in unemployment rates. Note that this trend can occur even if there is substantial year-to-year fluctuation in unemployment rates, as long as

the trend is toward increasingly similar rates between countries in any given year.

In Table 24.5 relevant data are presented for 1950 and for the 1970–74 period. The coefficient of variation is 76 percent in 1950 and 64 percent for the 1970–74 period. This averages out to a .72 percent decrease per year. Again the trend is in the direction of convergence.

So far we have considered indication of trends with respect to convergence in the areas

TABLE 24.4 Trend in Duration of Compulsory Education in Ten Industrial Nations between 1900 and 1969

	1900	1969
$\overline{X}$	6.1	8.7
SD	2.4	.67
CV	40%	7%
Mean convergence = 1.20% per year		

Note: Countries include: Germany, Italy, Japan, New Zealand, Norway, Sweden, United Kingdom, Austria, Belgium, France. CV = coefficient of variation; $\overline{X}$ = mean (average); and SD = standard deviation.
Source: Mishra (1973: 550); UNESCO (1958); Beck (1970).

TABLE 24.5 Trend in Unemployment in Eleven Industrial Nations between 1950* and 1970–74*

	1950	1970–74
$\overline{X}$	4.7	3.4
SD	3.6	2.2
CV	76%	64%
Mean convergence = .72% per year		

*Or nearest year.
Note: Countries include: Austria, Australia, Sweden, Denmark, Belgium, United States, Canada, Ireland, Norway, West Germany, Japan. CV = coefficient of variation; $\overline{X}$ = mean (average); SD = standard deviation.
Source: for 1950, United Nations (1951: 10); for 1970–74, International Labor Organization (1974: 390–93).

of income inequality, social security, education, and unemployment. We now turn to four indicators in the health area: birth rates, number of physicians, infant mortality, and life expectancy. We find that for all four of these measures the evidence supports the convergence theory.

Health Indicators

In Table 24.6 we present data for the trend in crude birth rate; that is, births per 1,000 population. The coefficient of variation drops from 24 percent in 1930 to 16 percent in 1965 which averages out to a .95 percent decrease per year.

Data for number of physicians per million inhabitants are presented in Table 24.7. The coefficient of variation decreases from 32 percent in 1948 to 22 percent in 1965 which averages out to a 1.84 percent decrease per year.

Data for infant mortality rate (i.e., deaths of infants under one year old per 1,000 live births) are presented in Table 24.8. The coefficient of variation decreases from 42 percent in 1930 to 34 percent in 1965 which averages out to a .54 percent decrease per year.

Data on life expectancy for females at age one year are presented in Table 24.9. The coefficient of variation decreases from 6 percent in 1955 to 2 percent in 1965. This averages out to a 6.67 percent decrease per year.

TABLE 24.6 Trend in Crude Birth Rate in Twenty-Three Industrial Nations between 1930 and 1965*

	1930	1965
$\overline{X}$	22	18.8
SD	5.2	3.0
CV	24%	16%
Mean convergence = .95% per year		

*Or nearest year.
Note: Countries include: Hungary, Czechoslovakia, Luxembourg, Belgium, Sweden, Poland, Finland, France, Austria, Denmark, United Kingdom, Norway, Japan, United States, Italy, Switzerland, Netherlands, Australia, Canada, Ireland, New Zealand, Iceland, and Israel. CV = coefficient of variation; $\overline{X}$ = mean (average); SD = standard deviation.
Source: for 1930, United Nations (1951;34–41); for 1965, Taylor and Hudson (1972: 249–52).

Discussion

To date most efforts to test the convergence theory have been based on cross-sectional data. When such data have been used to test for convergence with respect to income inequality, the evidence has supported the convergence thesis.

TABLE 24.7 Trend in Number of Physicians per Million Inhabitants in Nineteen Industrial Nations between 1948* and 1965*

	1948	1965
$\overline{X}$	939	1,303
SD	297	282
CV	32%	22%
Mean convergence = 1.84% per year		

*Or nearest year.
Note: Countries include: Finland, Luxembourg, Sweden, Japan, France, Canada, Netherlands, Norway, Poland, Denmark, Iceland, Australia, Belgium, United States, Switzerland, New Zealand, Czechoslovakia, Austria, Hungary. CV = coefficient of variation; $\overline{X}$ = mean (average); SD = standard deviation.
Source: for 1948, United Nations (1951; 539–45); for 1965, Taylor and Hudson (1972: 259–62).

T A B L E   2 4 . 8   Trend in Infant Mortality Rates in Twenty-Two Industrial Nations between 1930* and 1965*

	1930	1965
$\overline{X}$	82	23
SD	34	8
CV	42%	34%
Mean convergence = .54% per year		

*Or nearest year.

Note: Countries include: Sweden, Norway, Australia, Japan, Finland, Switzerland, New Zealand, Denmark, United Kingdom, France, Canada, Belgium, Luxembourg, United States, Czechoslovakia, Ireland, Austria, Italy, Hungary, Poland, Norway, Iceland. CV = coefficient of variation; $\overline{X}$ = mean (average); and SD = standard deviation.

Source: for 1930, United Nations (1951; 50); for 1965, Taylor and Hudson (1972: 253–55).

In the present study we have used longitudinal data because the convergency theory is basically a theory about trends which occur over time as a consequence of industrialization. We have found that when the trend in income inequality is examined using longitudinal data, the evidence does not support the conver-

T A B L E   2 4 . 9   Trend in Life Expectancy for Females at Age One Year in Twenty-Four Industrial Nations between 1955* and 1965*

	1955	1965
$\overline{X}$	63	75
SD	3.9	1.3
CV	6%	2%
Mean convergence = 6.67% per year		

*Or nearest year.

Note: Age 0 for Austria, USSR, Czechoslovakia, and Hungary. Other nations include: Ireland, Finland, West Germany, Belgium, New Zealand, East Germany, Australia, Poland, Italy, United Kingdom, Switzerland, United States, Japan, Canada, Denmark, Iceland, France, Netherlands, Norway, and Sweden. CV = coefficient of variation; $\overline{X}$ = mean (average); and SD = standard deviation.

Source: for 1955, United Nations (1951; 62–74); for 1965, United Nations (1973: 336–56).

gence theory.[4] However, when we look at other aspects of social welfare such as social security, education, unemployment, and health the evidence tends to be consistent with the theory.

This suggests the possibility that when data on income inequality do become available for a large sample of nations and over a longer period of time, it may turn out that there is at least a weak trend toward convergence with respect to the distribution of income too. However, even if longitudinal evidence for convergence with respect to income inequality can eventually be found, the results of the present study suggest that the trend will be substantially weaker than in other sectors such as health and education. Why is this so? While there is no single answer to this question, there are a number of factors which are undoubtedly of some importance.

Mishra (1973) has argued that highly industrialized nations are converging more in areas close to technology than in areas less directly linked to technology. Thus in industrial society we can expect convergence in the education sector because it is tied to the needs of a technologically based system. In contrast, any relationship between the distribution of income and the needs of a technological system is less direct. For this reason we would expect the push toward convergence in this area to be weaker. A limitation of this explanation is that in practice it turns out to be very difficult to rank various indicators of social welfare with respect to how directly they relate to technology.

A second possible explanation for the difference between the rate of convergence for income inequality compared to other aspects of social welfare is implicit in the "logic of industrialization" thesis (Kerr et al., 1964). According to this thesis industrialization leads to an increase in the proportion of the labor force in various middle-level occupations such as technicians, bureaucrats, and lower-level managers. This shift in the occupational structure leads to an expansion in the middle classes. We would then expect convergence with respect to measures which can be linked to the needs and demands of this increasingly powerful middle class. This explanation works well in accounting for convergence with respect to health care and social security, areas the middle classes can be counted on to take an interest in. However, we would also expect this group to push for a more equal distribution of income. This explanation does not adequately account for the lack of convergence with respect to the distribution of income.

For yet another explanation we turn to conflict theory. From this perspective it follows that the resistance to social change will be greatest in those spheres which most directly threaten the existing class structure and the relationships of property which underlie it. Thus we would expect considerable resistance to change in the distribution of income related as it is to the distribution of wealth and property. On the other hand, innovation in the health care sector can be made without any serious threat to existing class relationships. Thus substantially more convergence would be expected in the health care area and in other areas not directly threatening the existing class structure than would be expected with respect to income inequality. While this third explanation does not by itself account for all our results, it does seem to go further than either of the previous two explanations.

Where do we go from here? One potentially fruitful line of investigation would be to take into consideration the role a nation plays in the world economy. A case can be made that the issue of convergence needs to be considered in the context of an evolving world society (Hopkins and Wallerstein, 1967; Meyer et al., 1975). For example, Rubinson (1976) argues that the distribution of income within a country can be substantially influenced by the role the country plays in the capitalist world economy. To the extent that income inequality within a nation is a function of the relative power of that nation in the world economy, we would not expect convergence in income inequality unless there is convergence with re-

spect to economic power. Thus we would want to determine whether nations are converging or diverging with respect to economic power. Finally, we would want to assess the extent to which the economic power of transnational corporations diminishes the relevance of findings from studies in which the nation is the unit of analysis.

Notes

*　　From the *International Journal of Comparative Sociology* 18, nos. 3–4 (1977): 242–53, by permission of the authors and the publisher. Copyright 1977 by the *International Journal of Comparative Sociology.*

1.　The mean convergence per year can be expressed symbolically as follows:

$$MC/\text{year} = \left[\frac{(CV_{t_1} - CV_{t_2})}{CV_{t_1}} \times 100 \right] \div (t_2 - t_1)$$

where MC/year = mean convergence per yer, CV_{t1} = coefficient of variation at the earlier date, CV_{t2} = coefficient of variation at the later date, t_1 = the earlier date, and t_2 = the later date. Implicit in this statistic is the simplifying assumption that any ten-, or twenty-, or thirty-year period is equivalent to another. Some such statistic is needed when comparing convergence trends for different length time spans, but clearly there will be at least some variation in the rate of convergence from one era to another.

2.　One reason for this is that data on individual income inequality were available for only a very limited number of countries. In addition, what data on individual income inequality were available tended to be of poor quality.

3.　The variables *duration of compulsory education* and *number of social security programs* were both proposed by Mishra (1973); we have drawn our data from his study.

4.　Since we were only able to obtain data on ten nations, it is quite possible that we would have found a convergent trend for the decade considered were the necessary income distribution data available for more nations. It is also quite possible that we would have found convergence had a longer time span been considered. There is evidence to suggest that a trend toward more equal distribution of income in some countries such as the United States (Miller,

1966; Kravis, 1962) and Norway (Soltow, 1965) when we consider a time span of fifty or one hundred years.

References

Baum, Ramer. 1974. "Beyond Convergence: Toward Theoretical Relevance in Quantitative Modernization Research." *Sociological Inquiry* 44: 225–40.

Beck, Carlton E., ed. 1970. *Perspective on World Education.* Dubuque, Iowa: William C. Brown.

Cutright, Phillips. 1967. "Inequality: A Cross-National Analysis." *American Sociological Review* 32: 562–78.

De Maistre, Joseph. 1964. *On God and Society.* Chicago: Regnery.

Goldthorpe, John H. 1969. "Social Stratification in Industrial Society." Pp. 452–65 in Celia A. Heller (ed.), *Structural Social Inequality.* New York: Macmillan.

Hopkins, Terence K., and Immanuel Wallerstein. 1967. "The Comparative Study of National Societies." *Social Science Information* 6: 25–58.

International Labour Organization (ILO). 1974. *ILO Statistical Yearbook.* Geneva: ILO.

Jackman, Robert. 1975. *Politics and Social Equality: A Comparative Analysis.* New York: Wiley.

Kerr, Clark, John T. Dunlop, Frederic Harbison, and Charles Meyers. 1964. *Industrialism and Industrial Man: The Problems of Labor and Management in Economic Growth.* New York: Oxford University Press.

Kravis, Irving. 1962. *The Structure of Income.* Philadelphia: University of Pennsylvania Press.

Kuznets, Simon. 1963. "Quantitative Aspects of the Economic Growth of Nations, VIII: The Distribution of Income by Size." *Economic Development and Cultural Change* 11: 1–80.

Lenski, Gerhard. 1966. *Power and Privilege.* New York: McGraw-Hill.

Maine, Henry Sumner. 1964. *Ancient Law.* Boston: Beacon Press.

Meyer, John, John Boli-Bennett, and Chris Chase-Dunn. 1975. "Convergence and Divergence in

Development." Pp. 223–46 in Alex Inkeles (ed.), *Annual Review of Sociology,* Volume 1. Palo Alto: Annual Reviews Inc.

Miller, Herman P. 1966. *Income Distribution in the United States.* Washington, D.C.: U.S. Government Printing Office.

Mishra, Ramesh. 1973. "Welfare and Industrial Man." *Sociological Review* 21: 535–60.

Paukert, Felix. 1973. "Income Distribution of Different Levels of Development: A Survey of Evidence." *International Labour Review* 108: 97–125.

Pryor, Frederic. 1968. *Public Expenditures in Communist and Capitalist Nations.* Homewood, Ill.: Irwin.

Rubinson, Richard. 1976. "The World-Economy and the Distribution of Income within States: A Cross-National Study." *American Sociological Review* 41: 638–59.

Soltow, Lee. 1965. *Toward Income Equality in Norway.* Madison: University of Wisconsin Press.

Taylor, Charles L., and Michael Hudson. 1972. *The World Handbook of Political and Social Indicators.* New Haven, CT: Yale University Press.

Tocqueville de, Alexis. 1952. *Democracy in America.* London: Oxford University Press.

Töennies, Ferdinand. 1963. *Community and Society.* New York: Harper Torchbook.

United Nations. 1951. *Statistical Yearbook.* New York: United Nations.

— — —. 1973. *Demographic Yearbook.* New York: United Nations.

United Nations Education, Scientific and Cultural Organization (UNESCO). 1958. *World Survey of Education.* Vol. 2, *Primary Education.* Paris: UNESCO.

U.S. Department of Health, Education, and Welfare (HEW). 1967. *Social Security Programs throughout the World.* Washington, D.C.: U.S. Government Printing Office.

Weinberg, Ian. 1969. "The Problem of Convergence of Industrial Societies: A Critical Look at the State of a Theory." *Comparative Studies in Societies and History* 11: 1–15.

Wilensky, Harold. 1975. *The Welfare State and Equality.* Berkeley: University of California Press.

Social Benefits in Advanced Capitalist Countries: A Cross-National Assessment*

Vincent A. Mahler and Claudio J. Katz

One of the most striking characteristics of the state in the advanced capitalist democracies is the role it plays in the allocation of disposable income. Government policy has, of course, always influenced income distribution through regulation and the provision of public goods, but redistribution is a by-product of such activity, which seeks primarily to accomplish other ends. In contrast, a distinguishing feature of the modern welfare state is its deliberate effort to ameliorate the distribution of income generated by the market.

Contemporary states perform this function in two ways, through tax policy and income transfer programs. These are clearly linked, and a comprehensive study of the redistributive consequences of the welfare state would require an examination of their combined impact. Yet income transfers are important in their own right.[1] They have, indeed, been among the fastest-growing components of government activity and, unsurprisingly in an era of economic constraints, among the most controversial.

The sharp differences characteristic of contemporary assessments of income transfer policy follow from divergent interpretations of the causes of inequality and of the government's role in addressing it. Supporters of an active welfare state favor more ambitious public redistributive efforts because they regard poverty and insecurity as structural problems inherent in the operation of the market, and they maintain that a measure of social security should be treated almost as a right of citizenship. Moreover, they contend that an active welfare state

need not be achieved at the expense of economic growth; indeed, they see income security and distributive equity as important preconditions of a productive workforce. Critics of public welfare programs, on the other hand, are suspicious of wide-ranging government transfers because they view most forms of poverty as reflecting a lack of individual effort, and they argue that welfare programs only exacerbate the problem by creating disincentives for individuals to work and save. They reserve their sharpest criticism for programs aimed at the working-aged poor: these efforts, in their view, foster a dependence on government that erodes the self-reliance necessary for a permanent escape from poverty. But even such programs as pensions and health benefits are subject to criticism, if only because they are seen as diverting resources from a productive private sector to an inherently unproductive public sector.[2]

Indicators

Our paper offers a cross-national perspective on this debate by examining the relationship between, on the one hand, benefit expenditures for major social programs and, on the other, patterns of income distribution, social dislocation, and economic growth in nineteen advanced market economy countries. In contrast to more general analyses which consider welfare expenditures as a whole, we have assessed separately the impact of the major types of public social programs in OECD countries, focusing on old age and disability pensions, means-tested public assistance benefits, sickness and maternity programs, unemployment insurance, and family allowances.[3] Although all countries use the same basic tools to address social needs, they combine them in quite different ways, yielding a distinct policy profile for each nation. It is our intention to explore some of these differences, on the assumption that the "welfare state" is not of one piece and that the impact of different types of programs can be expected to differ.[4]

There are two major sources of detailed cross-national data on income support and social welfare programs. One, the International Labour Office publication, *The Cost of Social Security,* focuses in considerable detail on receipts and expenditures of national social programs.[5] A second, the United States Department of Health and Human Services publication, *Social Security Programs throughout the World,* offers detailed descriptions of the nature and coverage of social programs in a wide range of countries.[6] Both of these compendia are employed in this study, the former as a source of comparative data on the magnitude of public expenditures for social benefits, the latter as a source of descriptive information on the coverage of individual national programs.[7]

The basic data on benefit expenditures have been computed from figures presented in *The Cost of Social Security.*[8] Data have been assembled for 1980 for the following OECD countries: Australia, Austria, Belgium, Canada, Denmark, Finland, France, the Federal Republic of Germany, Ireland, Italy, Japan, the Netherlands, New Zealand, Norway, Spain, Sweden, Switzerland, the United Kingdom, and the United States (see Table 25.1).[9] The poorest OECD countries, Turkey, Greece, and Portugal, have been excluded from the analysis, as has Luxembourg, with a population of less than 1 million.

Our major indicator of income distribution derives from figures assembled by the World Bank for the distribution of disposable household income accruing to quintiles of households in each country.[10] These data are available for eighteen of the nineteen countries of our analysis (all but Austria) for a single date in the late 1970s or early 1980s. Although the World Bank considers the figures to offer the best available cross-national data on income distribution, it warns that they must be interpreted with caution. The main reason is that figures on distribution in individual countries are not always completely consistent definitionally. In particular, the figures reported have not been adjusted to account for differences among countries in the distribution of household size. The problem is that household size tends to be systematically related to household income. As a result, a country with many large households may appear to demonstrate less inequality than a country with fewer large households simply because its poor households have more members and thus more total income. In order to address these problems we have also conducted all analyses using income distribution figures that are adjusted for household size, but data are available for only twelve countries of our sample for an earlier date.[11] Findings based on the latter data are consistent with findings for the larger World Bank data set.[12]

Although income differentials are important, it must be recognized that economic well-being is not entirely a relative matter. Thus, even if a period of general economic growth fails to improve the overall shape of distribution, it can hardly be said that low-income groups are no better off at the end of the period than they were at the beginning. As critics of welfare programs insist, if government initiatives equalize income and yet reduce general living standards by impairing the investment underlying economic growth, they can hardly be considered successful.[13] To explore this possibility, we will examine the relationship between countries' expenditures on income maintenance programs and the level of gross domestic savings/GDP in 1980 as well as between the growth of income maintenance expenditures/GDP between 1960 and 1980 and the growth of gross domestic savings/GDP and the growth of real GDP over the same period.[14]

TABLE 25.1   Benefits in Five Major Areas as a Percent of GDP, 1980

	Total	Pensions	Health Benefits	Public Assistance	Family Allowances	Unemployment Benefits
Canada	13.7	3.7	4.1	3.0	1.2	1.7
United States	9.6	3.9	2.1	3.0	0	0.6
Austria	16.3	8.8	3.7	0.7	2.5	0.6
Belgium	19.8	6.6	6.3	0.7	2.6	3.6
Denmark	24.9	7.9	6.7	6.3	0.8	3.2
Finland	15.0	6.2	5.1	2.3	0.8	0.6
France	22.6	7.7	7.0	4.0	2.7	1.2
Germany	18.8	9.5	5.8	0.9	1.2	1.4
Ireland	17.8	5.2	9.1	0.5	1.0	2.0
Italy	12.8	6.2	5.4	0.7	NA	0.5
Netherlands	24.1	11.5	7.7	1.7	2.1	1.1
Norway	18.7	7.5	8.1	1.7	1.0	0.4
Spain	13.6	9.3	3.3	0.5	0.4	0.1
Sweden	28.3	9.7	11.4	5.2	1.6	0.4
Switzerland	11.4	7.5	2.6	1.1	0.1	0.1
United Kingdom	15.1	5.6	4.9	2.7	1.5	0.4
Japan	7.5	2.3	3.5	1.2	0.1	0.4
Australia	8.1	4.3	2.5	0.5	NA	0.8
New Zealand	11.9	6.7	4.9	0	NA	0.3

Note: NA = not available.
Source: Calculated from ILO, *The Cost of Social Security*.

In examining the impact of one particular mode of social expenditure, public assistance to the working-aged population, it is necessary to go beyond the distribution of income per se to consider its impact on people's social behavior. Perhaps most pernicious, in the view of critics, is the way in which means-tested public assistance threatens the family. Aid to female-headed households has attracted particular attention: welfare payments, its critics argue, contribute to divorce and desertion and foster illegitimacy. Social dislocation of this sort is related to but extends beyond poverty and is very difficult to eliminate because the traditional social structures for dealing with it have been undermined.[15] Defenders of welfare pro-grams respond that properly designed programs reinforce family structures.[16] In their view, the most serious source of dislocation is to be found not in public efforts to ameliorate poverty but rather in an economic system that effectively excludes a significant segment of the population.

To explore these propositions, we gathered data on two additional variables. These are intended to tap, in an admittedly crude way, family stability. The first of these is the illegitimacy rate, a measure of the number of out-of-wedlock births as a proportion of total live births. The second is the divorce rate, the number of divorces in a country per 1,000 population.[17]

Benefit Levels and Income Distribution

Before exploring empirically the relationship between income maintenance programs and patterns of income distribution and social dislocation, it is useful to describe briefly overall trends in social coverage and distributive equity in the nineteen countries we are examining. The level of expenditures in 1980 for the five major social benefits we discuss ranged considerably among OECD countries, from lows of 7.5 percent of GDP in Japan, 8.1 percent in Australia, and 9.6 percent in the United States, to highs of 28.3 percent in Sweden, 24.9 percent in Denmark, and 24.1 percent in the Netherlands. The ratio of expenditures to GDP has been growing rapidly over the last two decades in the countries of our sample, from an average of about 6 percent of GDP in 1960 to over 16 percent in 1980.

Despite these substantial efforts, widespread relative poverty and inequality are continuing problems in the developed capitalist economies. In the eight OECD member countries for which data are available, an average of about 8 percent of the population falls below a standardized poverty line developed by the OECD, ranging from France and the United States, where the poor account for 16 percent and 13 percent of the population, respectively, to West Germany and Sweden, where roughly 3 percent of the population lives in poverty.[18] In the eighteen OECD countries for which comparable data are available, the upper-income quintile on average receives *after* transfers 6.35 times the share of national income of the lowest quintile.[19]

One explanation for the persistence of widespread poverty and distributive inequality, despite sizable expenditures for income maintenance, is that not all government social programs benefit the poor or redistribute income. Different programs embody different policy goals, and each has potential unintended consequences alien to its design. In the following sections some of these differences will be ex-

plored with reference to individual social programs.[20]

Pensions

Among the most important income maintenance programs in every advanced country are public old age and disability pensions. Pensions alone accounted for an average of 6.8 percent of GDP in 1980 in the nineteen countries we have examined. Moreover, pensions have been among the most rapidly growing types of social expenditure over the last two decades: pension disbursements as a proportion of GDP in these countries on average more than doubled between 1960 and 1980. This rapid growth is in part a reflection of the fact that the over-sixty-five population in the OECD countries has increased rapidly over the period, from an average of 9.8 percent in 1960 to 12.6 percent in 1980 in our countries.[21]

The expected impact of benefits depends in large measure on the design of pension programs. A majority of OECD countries organize pensions according to social insurance principles. Other countries (including Britain and the Scandinavian nations) have historically provided mainly flat rate basic benefit plans, while Australia and New Zealand offer substantially means-tested benefits. Most of the latter countries, however, introduced supplementary social insurance plans between 1959 and 1966, bringing them closer to the social insurance model. Indeed, there has been something of a convergence among the Western democracies in old age pension schemes: countries offering flat rate or means-tested plans have supplemented them with contributions-related schemes, while countries providing social insurance plans have supplemented them with flat rate minimum benefits. The main reason for this convergence is probably the perceived weaknesses in the two plans. Social insurance programs inadequately address the problem of poverty: the poor are not able to contribute much to the program and hence draw insufficient benefits to lift them out of poverty. In contrast, flat rate and means-tested plans suffer from a weak political base: they tend to offer limited protection to the middle classes, who see little reason to support them.[22]

Given these differences in program design, the expected relationship between old age pensions and income distribution is somewhat uncertain. A widely held view maintains that social insurance pension schemes have at best a limited redistributive impact. Redistribution is, after all, not their main objective; rather, the key principle underlying social insurance is income security, the protection of individuals and families against precipitous reductions in their standard of living over the course of a lifetime. There is, indeed, a potential tension between the principles of security and equality: since social insurance is employment-related and aims to maintain an individual's customary living standard over a lifetime, the result of social insurance schemes may well be to stabilize or reinforce income differences generated by the market.[23]

An alternative view holds that pensions do make a significant contribution to income equality. To begin, flat rate benefits are obviously intended to have a redistributive impact. Even social insurance schemes, however, may modify inequality, since the low-income population, especially the elderly and the disabled among them, tends to be economically the most vulnerable. Furthermore, as has been noted, state policy in most countries has relaxed the strictly insurance-based link between contributions and benefits, concentrating instead on the adequacy of benefits and often establishing a minimum benefit. (In each of nine countries for which estimates are available, pension benefits are more equally distributed than overall household income.)[24] The actual level of minimum benefits, however, varies widely across countries. In the United States, for example, the minimum old age pension level in 1972–73 was only 44.3 percent of a standardized poverty level developed by the OECD, compared with 70.9 percent in West Germany, 77.0 percent in

the United Kingdom, and 117.3 percent in Sweden.[25]

Old age pensions are typically financed by special contributions divided between employers and employees, although in some instances general public revenues may finance all or part of a particular program. (In all cases, of course, the government is the ultimate guarantor of benefits.) Most employee contributory schemes would be expected to have a limited, perhaps slightly regressive, impact on income distribution because they are assessed at a fixed rate and incorporate an upper income limit. It is indeed possible that even employer contributory schemes will have regressive consequences for the primary distribution of income, at least to the extent that employers shift the burden of the tax to employees or consumers.[26] On the other hand, it is evident that special contributions tend to make social insurance programs more palatable politically. The idea of "getting what you pay for" makes covering the growing cost of social security much easier in many countries, and it is doubtful whether income support programs detached from their special contributions could successfully compete with other spending programs for a share of general revenues.[27]

To explore these issues we have conducted a cross-national statistical analysis examining the relationship between pensions—as well as other benefit expenditures—and patterns of distribution and economic growth in OECD countries.[28] The coefficients reported are beta weights of a bivariate regression relating benefit expenditures to the various dependent variables (which is to say, Pearson product-moment correlations). Levels of statistical significance are one-tailed on the assumption that various benefits either have a redistributive effect or do not and that one would not expect higher benefit levels to be associated with a *less* egalitarian distribution.

There is always a danger in cross-national statistical analysis that findings will be dominated by outliers. One indicator of the extent to which this is true is the statistic Cook's distance, which reflects changes in the residuals of all cases when the *i*th case is deleted. In none of our regressions was Cook's distance statistically significant at even the .25 level, indicating that none of our regressions is severely affected by any single influential case. On the other hand, Cook's distances are very useful, in conjunction with a careful examination of scattergrams, in identifying cases which, if not extremely atypical, do affect the findings substantially. As will be seen, Cook's distance will be employed for this purpose as well.

The correlation between pension benefits and income equality is weakly positive for the entire sample.[29] The scattergram reveals, however, that Japan is an anomalous case: it enjoys the most egalitarian income distribution of any OECD country and yet devotes one of the smallest shares of GDP to public pensions (see Figure 25.1), which is no doubt a product of Japan's long-standing tradition of family responsibility for the elderly.[30] When Japan is excluded from the analysis the correlation between expenditures and the income share of the

poorest 20 percent of households is +.60 ($p < .005$), a pattern which is also in evidence for the next poorest quintile, +.53 ($p < .01$). The impact of pensions on the income shares of the poorer classes is reflected in the overall shape of income distribution across the countries of the sample: benefits/GDP, excluding Japan, are negatively related to the Gini index of income inequality, $-.42$ ($p < .02$).[31]

One might argue that relationships may differ when one considers the absolute rather than the relative level of benefits provided.[32] Here too, however, the findings are quite similar to those for expenditures as a proportion of GDP: per capita pension expenditures for seventeen OECD countries (less Japan) are correlated +.46 ($p < .03$) and +.56 ($p < .01$) with the income shares of the lowest and the next lowest quintiles of the population, respectively, and $-.49$ ($p < .02$) with the Gini index of household income distribution.

In sum, aside from the anomalous case of Japan, the relationship between pension expenditures and a relatively egalitarian distribution

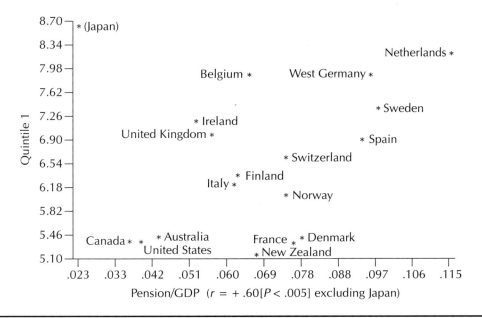

FIGURE 25.1 Scattergram relating pension expenditures/GDP (1980) to income quintile I (poorest 20 percent of households).

of income is rather strongly positive. Such modestly progressive aspects of most old age pension programs as minimum benefit guarantees, coupled with the sheer magnitude of these programs and the fact that they are directed at a segment of the population whose earning power is limited, appear to result in programs that have a significant egalitarian impact on income distribution. The importance of social security pensions in alleviating poverty has long been conceded in the case of the United States.[33] Our analysis indicates, with the obvious proviso that the findings are necessarily at a general level of analysis, that it is also the case across countries.

Does any egalitarian impact associated with pension benefits come at the expense of economic performance? Conservatives in particular maintain that the rapidly growing costs of pensions, their compulsory nature, and the bureaucratization that inevitably accompanies them syphon resources away from the private economy, impairing its inherent dynamism.[34] Quite simply, our analysis failed to confirm this expectation.[35] We found no significant relationship in either direction between pensions and gross domestic savings in 1980, nor was the increase in the level of pensions/GDP between 1960 and 1980 related to the percentage increase in the level of gross domestic savings/GDP or real GDP as a whole over the same period.[36]

Public Assistance Programs

Unlike social insurance programs, means-tested public assistance programs are specifically designed to alleviate poverty. Eligibility for benefits is usually determined by comparing measures of individual or family resources to a minimum living standard, with the size and type of benefits administratively determined.

The most important means-tested programs in OECD countries are those classified by the ILO as public assistance and assimilated schemes.[37] These are much less prominent in relative amount of expenditures (although not always in the public debate) than the pension programs just discussed: in our nineteen countries, public assistance benefits in 1980 averaged 1.9 percent of GDP. Public assistance benefits have, however, been growing fairly rapidly over the last two decades in most developed countries (about as rapidly as social benefits as a whole): the average of public assistance as a proportion of GDP increased nearly 150 percent between 1960 and 1980 in the countries under consideration.

Perhaps the strongest argument in support of means-tested programs is their target efficiency: they are designed explicitly to concentrate the greatest share of welfare expenditures on the poor. Given the trade-offs that must take place when various spending programs compete for a share of limited revenues, it is often argued that the poor may best be served by programs designed to benefit them alone.[38]

Are these expenditures in practice associated with significant poverty relief? Critics have pointed out that the high target efficiency of means testing does not necessarily mean that poor-specific programs will be successful. Their actual impact depends on how many people are covered and how much is spent. Clearly, even very efficient programs may do little to reduce poverty if too many poor are ineligible and little is spent, while inefficient programs can still alleviate poverty if they are sufficiently comprehensive and enough is spent. Means-tested programs, critics argue, are at a decided disadvantage in securing funding. They have a very restricted constituency, one which, moreover, tends to be relatively inactive politically. Given the general public dissatisfaction with means-tested benefits, programs directed specifically at the poor are often the first to suffer in periods of budget constraints. As a result, it may be expected that, despite its target efficiency, means testing makes a limited contribution to poverty relief. Thus, for example, in comparing Australia and Belgium, Beckerman found that Australia's highly target efficient but relatively meager means-tested benefits largely failed to reduce poverty, whereas Belgium's inefficient but extensive universal benefits were far more successful in doing so.[39] In a similar vein, Heidenheimer et al. found, in a comparison of programs to aid single women with children in the United States and Sweden, that the United States' more target-efficient program was less successful than Sweden's less efficient universal program in reducing the incidence of poverty within this economically vulnerable segment of the population.[40]

Perhaps for these reasons, we found no significant relationship between expenditures for public assistance and patterns of income distribution (and, in particular, the income share of the poorest quintile). Whatever the combination of factors that might help to push or keep individuals or families above the poverty line, it appears that, at least across the countries of our sample, public assistance benefits are not prominent among them.[41]

The negative public perceptions of means-tested welfare programs are in large measure a result of their perceived deleterious consequences on society's moral fabric. We assessed this perception by considering the argument that public assistance programs tend to create a system of perverse incentives that undermine the family. Our analysis indicates, however, that relative expenditures for public assistance are not significantly related (at the .05 level) to the divorce or illegitimacy rates in the countries we examined.[42] At least at the level of broad aggregates covering countries as a whole, the family disintegration said to be associated with public assistance programs does not appear to be in evidence.[43]

Are public assistance programs economically efficient, or do they tend to impair national economic performance? Means-testing in effect imposes high marginal tax rates on the poor by reducing benefits as their earnings rise.[44] The economic impact of public assistance programs depends on the effect of these tax rates on the propensity of the low-income population to work and save as well as on the effect of a larger public sector on national productivity as a whole.[45] Our analysis indicates no significant relationship in either direction

between public assistance expenditures and the rate of gross domestic savings in 1980 or between the rate of increase in public assistance expenditures between 1960 and 1980 and the increase in gross domestic savings or real gross domestic product over the same period. Clearly, a finding at this level does not necessarily suggest that means-tested programs do not create any economic disincentives among the poor, but it does indicate that any such disincentives are not so great that they seriously affect the savings rate of the nation as a whole.

Sickness and Maternity Benefits

Public sickness and maternity benefits in our nineteen countries in 1980 averaged 5.5 percent of GDP, ranging from 11.4 percent in Sweden to 2.1 percent in the United States.[46] Moreover, health care expenditures have been growing rapidly in the developed countries, although generally not as rapidly as expenditures for pensions: over the last two decades public health care expenditures in our nineteen countries on average nearly doubled.

The redistributive impact of sickness and maternity programs depends on how benefits affect different income groups' ability to obtain medical attention and on the value of the savings to recipients in different income classes from reductions in their medical expenses. Two alternative hypotheses can be formulated. A first is that health care benefits are substantially redistributive. One of the main aims of public health care programs is to break the link between health and wealth, making quality medical attention accessible to the entire population. If benefits represent substantial reductions in all groups' medical expenses, these savings are clearly worth more to lower- than to higher-income groups, since benefits constitute a larger proportion of their income.

On the other hand, it can be argued that public health care programs have little or no redistributive impact. One reason is that sickness and maternity benefits are designed to protect people against what are normally temporary episodes in their lives; they are not intended to address the more permanent causes of poverty and, indeed, most recipients are not poor when they require assistance. Moreover, it is sometimes argued that the advantages of access to health care are to some extent unrelated to monetary income: the major benefits of health care have an intangible "quality of life" character that, while very real, may not be directly reflected in monetary income.[47] Finally, it can be argued that the need for and benefit from access to medical services are more randomly distributed among groups in the population than many of the other social needs addressed by governments; this is particularly true in developed countries, where, in contrast to Third World countries, major diseases that affect *only* the poor are largely a thing of the past.

Our findings suggest that the first hypothesis is the more valid: across the countries of our sample health care programs appear progressive, although the relationship is not as strong as was the case for pension expenditures. There is only a weak redistributive relationship between health expenditures as a proportion of

GDP and overall income distribution measured by the Gini index of household income inequality, $-.25$ ($p < .16$). A clearer pattern emerges, however, when the anomalous case of Japan is omitted.[48] Excluding Japan, the correlation between health expenditures and the income share of the poorest income quintile is $+.42$ ($p < .05$) (see Figure 25.2). Once again, findings are not affected substantially when one focuses on per capita expenditures rather than expenditures as a proportion of GDP.

Is there a trade-off between the public provision of health care and economic performance? Compared to other sectors of the economy, health care delivery is a labor-intensive industry, and it is argued that, as public health care expenditures rise and more workers shift to a lower productivity field, the economy as a whole is adversely affected.[49] These arguments are not supported by our findings: there is no significant relationship between public health care expenditures and gross domestic savings in 1980 and no relationship between the rate of growth of health care expenditures/GDP and

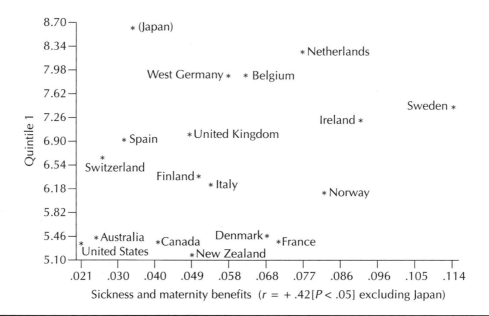

FIGURE 25.2   Scattergram relating sickness and maternity benefits/GDP (1980) to quintile I (poorest 20 percent of households).

the percentage change in the savings rate/GDP or the rate of growth of real GDP as a whole between 1960 and 1977.[50]

Unemployment Benefits

Temporary benefits for the unemployed represent a relatively modest share of GDP in the developed capitalist countries, although they have been among the most rapidly growing of any mode of public expenditure. In the nineteen OECD countries under consideration, unemployment benefits averaged slightly less than 1 percent of GDP in 1980. This figure, however, represented a rapid increase in recent years: expenditures for unemployment benefits as a share of GDP increased marginally from an average of 0.33 percent to 0.35 percent of GDP between 1960 and 1970, but then tripled to about 1.0 percent in 1980. This increase was obviously related to a sharp rise in unemployment during the 1970s: on average, the unemployment rate in the developed countries of our sample more than doubled between 1960 and 1980.[51]

The provisions of unemployment programs in OECD countries would not lead one to expect them to be markedly redistributive. In the first place, programs typically impose a minimum qualifying period of contribution to insurance funds to become entitled to benefits. This requirement means that a worker must have been a regular member of the labor force before receiving benefits, a link which is reinforced by programs which tie the duration of benefits to length of employment. (Programs in all OECD countries, however, impose a time limit during which a worker can continue to draw benefits.) Moreover, benefit levels are usually related to the level of past earnings, although some countries provide flat rate unemployment benefits and many have special provisions for poor workers, large families, and older workers. Finally, the source of funds for unemployment insurance may limit its redistributive impact: contributions ordinarily constitute a fixed percentage of wages, shared by the employer and the employee, although in

most cases the government also contributes a subsidy from its general revenues.[52] In sum, unemployment insurance may be necessary to alleviate the danger of temporary unemployment for workers, but it clearly is not intended to address the problem of structural unemployment or to alter the overall shape of income distribution.

Accordingly, unemployment benefits were not found to be substantially redistributive: relative benefit levels were not significantly related to the Gini index of household income distribution or to the income share of any quintile, nor were there any obvious anomalous cases whose exclusion would result in a clearer pattern. Similarly, unemployment benefits in 1980 were not significantly related to gross domestic savings in the same year, nor was the increase in the proportion of GDP devoted to unemployment benefits between 1960 and 1980 significantly related in either direction to the increase in gross domestic savings or gross domestic product over the same period.[53]

Family Allowances

Like unemployment benefits, family allowances do not loom large in the overall amount of benefit expenditure in developed market economy countries: family allowances as a proportion of GDP averaged just over 1 percent in OECD countries in 1980, having increased only marginally between 1960 and 1980.[54]

The methods of allocating family allowances in the OECD countries lead one to expect a redistributive program. The majority of programs are funded from general revenues; most provide a flat benefit for all citizens; and benefits generally increase with family size and sometimes with the age of children.

However, no doubt because of the limited amounts of expenditures involved in family allowances, this expected redistributive impact is not borne out by our analysis: family allowances are not significantly related to the posttransfer income shares of any population quintile.[55] Perhaps for the same reason, no relationships are found between relative family allowance benefits and the measures of economic performance.

Conclusion

Are public social expenditures associated with a relatively egalitarian distribution of income? The answer to this question appears to depend on the particular program in question. The two largest income maintenance programs, old age and disability pensions and sickness/maternity benefits, do appear to be positively related to income equality, in particular to the income share of the poorer classes. Although universal and social insurance benefits such as these may indeed be primarily supported by the middle class, their size and the fact that the benefits they offer typically represent a larger share of the income of poorer than of wealthier persons indicate that their redistributive impact may be considerable. This progressive character does not, however, appear to extend to such programs as means-tested public assistance, family allowances, and unemployment benefits. Across the countries of our sample expenditures for these programs are not related to national patterns of income distribution, perhaps because of contradictory effects on work incentives and family structures, perhaps simply because of their relatively small size. In any event, our paper offers some empirical support for the thesis that large-scale comprehensive social programs, in particular those which provide benefits as an entitlement, are more closely associated with redistribution than programs which concentrate benefits only on the poor.

Do public expenditures for transfer programs, whatever their redistributive impact, exact a cost in terms of economic performance? Based on our analysis, the answer appears to be negative, at least at the level of such broad macroeconomic indicators as GDP growth rate and the level and rate of growth of gross national savings.

In recent years the welfare state has come under increasing pressure throughout the democratic West. Critics of social policies have become ever bolder in their indictment of the public sector as almost inherently inefficient, while even the architects of the welfare state appear to be on the defensive about social programs created to rectify shortcomings in the private sector that seemed all too evident at the time major programs were inaugurated. We would suggest that a greater willingness of social scientists to assess empirically the role of the state in a wide range of modern capitalist democracies would help to inform this debate, rescuing it from the broad and ideologically charged generalizations that all too commonly inform the public discourse in this area.

Notes

* From *Comparative Politics* 21, no. 1 (October 1988): 37–53, by permission of the authors and *Comparative Politics.* Copyright 1988 by City University of New York.

1. It has been estimated that transfer payments account on average for 77.4 percent of direct fiscal redistribution in OECD countries; see Alexander Hicks and Duane H. Swank, "Governmental Redistribution in Rich Capitalist Democracies," *Policy Studies Journal* 13 (December 1984): 279–81.

2. Contrast Norman Furniss and Timothy Tilton, *The Case for the Welfare State: From Social Security to Social Equity* (Bloomington: Indiana University Press, 1977), pp. 22–49, 192–204, with Charles Murray, *Losing Ground: American Social Policy 1950–1980* (New York: Basic Books, 1984), pp. 192–204.

3. This paper focuses on public social benefits. Protection comparable to that offered publicly in some developed countries may be offered privately in others, particularly in the areas of pensions and private health insurance. See Martin Rein and Lee Rainwater, eds., *Public/Private Interplay in Social Protection: A Comparative Study* (Armonk: M. E. Sharpe, 1986).

4. A major review of the literature on these topics, relating primarily to the United States, is offered in Sheldon Danziger, Robert Haveman, and Robert Plotnick, "How Income Transfer Programs Affect Work, Savings and the Income Distribution: A Critical Review," *Journal of*

Economic Literature 19 (September 1981): 975–1028. See also Wilfred Beckerman, *Poverty and the Impact of Income Maintenance Programmes* (Geneva: International Labour Office, 1979).

5. International Labour Office, *The Cost of Social Security: Eleventh International Inquiry, 1978–1980* (Geneva: ILO, 1985), and *The Cost of Social Security: Eleventh International Inquiry, Basic Tables* (Geneva: ILO, 1985).

6. United States Department of Health and Human Services, *Social Security Programs throughout the World* (Washington, D.C.: 1983).

7. A valuable description of these sources is offered in Richard M. Coughlin and Philip K. Armour, "Methodological Issues in the Comparative Study of Social Security: Quantitative vs. Qualitative Analysis and the Appropriate Use of Data," *International Review of Modern Sociology* 10 (July–August 1983): 25–48.

8. The International Labour Office's definition of public social security programs is relatively wide-ranging, encompassing all benefits intended (1) to maintain income in case of involuntary loss of earnings or of an important part of earnings, (2) to grant curative or preventive medical care, and (3) to grant a supplementary income to persons having family responsibilities. Data are provided for receipts and expenditures of "all public, semi-public and autonomous" agencies addressing these needs which have been created by public legislation and which administer the programs they are charged with overseeing. (Even these fairly comprehensive figures do, of course, exclude a number of potentially redistributive programs, including housing allowances, education, and various social services.) Of the programs covered by this definition, we do not focus on figures for public employee benefits—the most important of which are civilian and military pensions—because from a beneficiary's point of view they correspond more closely to employee benefits in the private sector than to social benefits available to the population as a whole. Nor do we focus on the two smallest social programs, employment injury and war victims' benefits, which account for only a tiny proportion of GDP in OECD countries.

9. For the purposes of this paper, the figures reported by the ILO have been recalculated as a proportion of GDP, using benefits/GDP figures supplied in the source. The per capita figures reported at various places in the paper are derived by multiplying by an estimate of GDP per capita from United Nations, *Yearbook of National Accounts Statistics,* vol. 2 (New York: 1983). Figures for per capita benefits and benefits/GDP are correlated +.89.

10. *World Development Report 1986* (Washington, D.C.: Oxford University Press for World Bank, 1986), table 24. Gini indexes have been computed from the raw data presented in the source.

11. Malcom Sawyer, "Income Distribution in OECD Countries," *OECD Economic Outlook, Occasional Studies* (July 1976), pp. 3–36, supplemented (for Denmark) by Wouter van Ginneken and Jong-goo Park, eds., *Generating Internationally Comparable Income Distribution Estimates* (Geneva: International Labour Organization, 1984).

12. In every instance, the direction of relationships based on the Sawyer figures is the same as those we report, although the coefficients and significance levels differ somewhat. Similar findings were expected: the correlation between the income share of the poorest quintile reported by Sawyer and that reported by the World Bank is +.75 ($p < .004$). According to data on household size assembled for a handful of countries by the United Nations Statistical Office, Ireland and Spain have a larger proportion of larger households than other countries of the sample; see U.N., *National Accounts Statistics: Compendium of Income Distribution Statistics* (New York: Statistical Papers, Series M, Number 79, 1985). Scatterplots confirm that Spain is a somewhat anomalous case in the correlation reported above (Ireland is not included in Sawyer's study); without Spain the correlation between the two estimates is an even stronger +.88 ($p < .003$).

13. See Arthur M. Okun, *Equality and Efficiency: The Big Trade-off* (Washington, D.C.: Brookings Institution, 1975).

14. Figures for program growth are from ILO, *The Cost;* data are available for all countries except Spain. Figures for growth are from World Bank, *World Development Report, 1982.* The variables for increase in various expenditure models/GDP and gross domestic savings/GDP

are calculated according to the formula: (1980 share − 1960 share)/1960 share. Figures for GDP growth are for average annual real growth rate. William D. Berry and David Lowery, "The Measurement of Government Size: Implications for the Study of Government Growth," *Journal of Politics* 46 (November 1984): 1193–1206, argue that diachronic figures for public expenditures/GDP can be misleading if the cost of providing goods and services differs between the public and the private sectors. Lewis-Beck and Rice, however, respond that such figures may actually be preferable in that they "give a better indication of government scope and power vis-à-vis the national economy" and that there is in any event no clear alternative. Michael S. Lewis-Beck and Tom W. Rice, "Government Growth in the United States," *Journal of Politics* 47 (February 1985): 5–6.

15. Murray, *Losing Ground,* pp. 9, 155–91.

16. Alfred J. Kahn and Sheila B. Kamerman, *Not for the Poor Alone: European Social Policies* (Philadelphia: Temple University Press), p. 172.

17. Data are from Organization for Economic Co-operation and Development [OECD], *Child and Family: Demographic Developments in the OECD Countries* (Paris: OECD, 1979), and United Nations, Department of Economic and Social Affairs, *Demographic Yearbook, 1982* (New York: 1984).

18. OECD, *Public Expenditures on Income Maintenance Programmes,* Studies in Resource Allocation no. 3 (Paris: OECD, 1976), pp. 66–67.

19. World Bank, *World Development Report 1986,* table 24.

20. It is often argued that relatively egalitarian patterns of income distribution are associated with development level. While this is undoubtedly true across all nations, it does not appear to be the case for the limited range of development levels represented by the advanced capitalist countries. For our countries the level of gross domestic product in 1980 is not significantly correlated (at the .05 level) to the Gini index of income inequality or to the income shares of low- or high-income groups. We constructed a series of multiple regression analyses that included GDP level as a control variable along with our benefit expenditure variables, but, as would be expected, the findings were very sim-

ilar to those for the bivariate model reported here.

21. OECD, *Child and Family,* p. 16, for 1960; United Nations, *Demographic Yearbook, 1982,* for 1980.

22. Peter Flora and Jens Alber, "Modernization, Democratization, and the Development of Welfare States in Western Europe," in Peter Flora and Arnold J. Heidenheimer, eds., *The Development of Welfare States in Europe and America* (New Brunswick: Transaction, 1981), p. 53; Beckerman, pp. 14–17; U.S. Department of Health and Human Services, table 30.

23. Peter Flora and Arnold J. Heidenheimer, "The Historical Core and Changing Boundaries of the Welfare State," in Flora and Heidenheimer, eds., pp. 17–32; Benjamin I. Page, *Who Gets What from Government* (Berkeley: University of California Press, 1983), p. 66.

24. OECD, *Public Expenditures,* p. 24.

25. Ibid., p. 36.

26. A great deal of information is available on the effects of social security taxes; see, for example, International Social Security Association, *Methods of Financing Social Security: Their Economic and Social Effects* (Geneva: 1979). In order to limit the scope of this paper we have not discussed this aspect of social programs in any detail.

27. Arnold J. Heidenheimer, Hugh Heclo, and Carolyn Teich Adams, *Comparative Public Policy: The Politics of Social Change in Europe and America,* 2nd ed. (New York: St. Martin's Press, 1983), p. 225.

28. The part of our analysis relating public benefits to income distribution is of necessity cross-sectional, since data covering patterns of income distribution in more than a handful of our countries are available for only a single point in time. Although we would have preferred to examine diachronic figures were they available, this does not mean that findings based on cross-sectional analysis are inherently "inferior" to findings based on time series. As put by Douglas Hibbs, in reference to a study of political violence: "There is no reason . . . to be apologetic about having used cross-sectional data in this research. In many ways cross-section-based models are superior to those estimated against time series, since typical time series, especially those available to social scientists, are

of relatively short duration. Short-duration time series simply cannot pick up the effects of [a wide range of variables that] have important effects . . . [but] do not change much in the short run; and without variance estimation precision and causal inference are not feasible." Douglas A. Hibbs, Jr., *Mass Political Violence: A Cross National Causal Analysis* (New York: Wiley, 1973), pp. 201–2.

29. Data are available for about a dozen countries on the *direct* impact of all transfer programs together on income shares, with reference to the difference between pre- and posttransfer income. Focusing on these figures, however, requires one to assume that "the observed post-transfer income-sharing unit and the period of income receipt are not affected by the transfer," which, among other things, makes the household size problem mentioned earlier even more difficult (Danziger et al., p. 983). Moreover, one must assume that "transfers elicit no behavioral responses that would cause income without transfers to deviate from observed post-transfer income" (ibid.). These effects are crucial in that, while critics of the welfare state do not deny that the direct effects of transfers are positive, they argue that they are offset by negative effects on economic and social behavior. While the posttransfer figures we report do not discriminate between direct and indirect effects, they have the obvious benefit of tapping the latter. In any event, pre-minus-post-transfer income shares disaggregated to the level of individual programs, which is the primary focus of this paper, are unavailable for more than a tiny handful of countries.

30. See T. J. Pempel, *Policy and Politics in Japan* (Philadelphia: Temple University Press, 1982), p. 136.

31. The Cook's distance associated with Japan is 1.28, which, while only associated with a statistical significance level of .31, is substantially higher than the next highest Cook's distance, 0.28 ($p < .76$), confirming the visual evidence of the scattergrams presented in Figure 25.1. For similar reasons Japan was also excluded from the cross-national statistical analysis of advanced countries' welfare efforts reported in John D. Stephens, *The Transition from Capitalism to Socialism* (Urbana: University of Illinois Press, 1986), pp. 89–90.

32. See Richard Rose, *How Exceptional Is American Government?* (Glasgow: Center for the Study of Public Policy, University of Strathclyde, Studies in Public Policy number 150, 1985).

33. See Samuel H. Preston, "Children and the Elderly in the U.S.," *Scientific American* 251 (December 1984): 44–49.

34. This paper does not pretend to contribute to the vast literature examining the impact of pensions on private savings, most of it relating to the United States. See Henry J. Aaron, *Economic Effects of Social Security* (Washington, D.C.: Brookings Institution, 1982); and Selig Lesnoy and Dean R. Leimer, "Social Security and Private Saving: Theory and Historical Evidence," *Social Security Bulletin* 48 (January 1985): 14–30.

35. Our findings must be offered with the obvious qualification that analysis at the level of whole countries taps the net effect of what may be simultaneous positive and negative relationships between benefit expenditures and various aspects of economic growth as mediated by work incentives, labor supply, and savings. See Danziger et al., pp. 978–82.

36. Japan, whose pensions increased some fifteen-fold over this period from an almost nonexistent base in 1960, is a clear outlier in the latter analysis and is excluded.

37. As we have noted, the ILO has classified noncontributory pension benefits with pension programs even though payment of benefits may to some extent be subject to a means test; see ILO, *The Cost of Social Security,* p. 9.

38. Irwin Garfinkel, "Conclusion," in Irwin Garfinkel, ed., *Income-Tested Transfer Programs: The Case For and Against* (New York: Academic Press, 1982), p. 503.

39. Beckerman, pp. 57–58, 70–71.

40. Heidenheimer et al., pp. 226–28.

41. Although some countries adopt public assistance as an *alternative* to more comprehensive programs, this is not generally the case. Thus, the two countries with the largest means-tested programs, Sweden and Denmark, also make the strongest general public commitment to income maintenance. Even excluding these two countries, there is no statistically significant correlation between public assistance and more comprehensive programs.

42. Sweden and Denmark, with illegitimacy rates so much higher than those of any other OECD country as to be obvious outliers, are omitted from this analysis. See, on the topic of Scandinavian exceptionalism in this area, Furniss and Tilton, *The Case for the Welfare State,* pp. 145–46.

43. A more detailed analysis that examines public assistance recipients alone is necessary for a comprehensive review of this issue. See, for a review of the literature concerning the United States, John H. Bishop, "Jobs, Cash Transfers and Marital Instability: A Review and Synthesis of the Evidence," *Journal of Human Resources* 15 (Summer 1980): 301–34.

44. Edgar K. Browning and Jaquelene M. Browning, *Public Finance and the Price System,* 2nd ed. (New York: Macmillan, 1983), pp. 251–89.

45. See Danziger et al., pp. 993–95, for a more detailed discussion referring to the United States.

46. In almost all cases health care programs are universal in coverage. The one major exception is the United States' means-tested Medicaid program.

47. Robert J. Maxwell, *Health and Wealth: An International Study of Health Care Spending* (Lexington: Lexington Books, 1981), pp. 51–57.

48. The Cook's distance associated with Japan is 0.25 ($p < .78$), which is considerably less than that of the next highest case, 0.10 ($p < .91$).

49. Organization for Economic Development and Cooperation, OECD Policy Studies, *Social Expenditure 1960–1980: Problems of Growth and Control* (Paris: OECD, 1985), p. 58.

50. The analysis extends only to 1977 because for its current survey covering 1978–80 the ILO omitted coverage of services provided by public health agencies that were not provided "as a statutory right ... under social security schemes covering the entire population" (pp. 2–3). The ILO series for sickness and maternity benefits is thus not completely consistent over time beyond 1977.

51. OECD, *Economic Outlook: Historical Statistics 1980–1982* (Paris: OECD, 1984), Table 2.15.

52. Information on individual programs is from U.S. Department of Health and Human Services, *Social Security.*

53. As might be expected, there was a modest nonsignificant positive relationship between unemployment benefits/GDP and gross domestic savings, no doubt related to the economic downturns associated with higher unemployment rates.

54. At least part of this slow growth is a reflection of demographic factors: the average proportion of the population in our nineteen countries under five years of age declined from 9.3 percent in 1960 to 7.9 percent in 1977, and the average proportion between five and fourteen years declined from 17.8 percent to 16.9 percent over the same period; see OECD, *Child and Family,* p. 16.

55. Figures for family allowances alone may to some extent understate the family assistance offered in OECD countries. Children and families, for example, are among the primary beneficiaries of education and housing programs, which are not discussed in this paper. Moreover, some countries offer tax credits for families with children, which in some cases are larger than cash assistance (see OECD, *Public Expenditures,* p. 27). The redistributive effect of cash transfers is, however, probably greater than that of tax credits since low-income families are not normally liable for substantial tax payments in the first place.

Organizations

Researchers have been analyzing, and occasionally comparing, social organizations for much of the twentieth century. Social organizations, of course, include a diverse variety of institutions, from profit-making corporations to not-for-profit churches, schools, hospitals, political parties, labor unions, and so on. Characterized as consisting of a professional "staff," a clientele, and some kind of governing body (e.g., board of directors), their study tends to focus on the dynamics and interplay of these three groups.

In the case of comparative studies of organizations, much of the work has taken place in the corporate environment as multinational firms continually analyze their management approaches in an effort to optimize their efficiency in foreign countries. Comparative studies extend beyond the private environment to include cross-national comparisons of most of the institutions mentioned above.

Our first selection in this section is an essay by Karlene H. Roberts and Nakiye A. Boyacigiller in which, in 1984, they called for a moratorium on cross-national research on social organizations. During this moratorium re-

searchers would construct a new and better paradigm within which to work. As with other researchers, they see the inadequate conceptualization and operational definition of "culture" as a serious hindrance to advances in the field.

Geert Hofstede has studied the influence of national cultures on management styles and practices. In the 1950s, management across nations was seen as converging on the Western model, but subsequent observation proved this to be incorrect. Culture—a nation's "collective mental programming"—does matter. Hofstede shows this to be the case through the elaborate empirical study he describes in this section.

Noting that what he sets out to do is to compare the incomparable, Erhard Blankenburg studies employment agencies in five Western European nations. Drawing on data from a large study of local labor market administrative agencies, the author finds that there are few similarities among the agencies studied, making generalization difficult if not impossible. Blankenburg introduces the concept of "administrative culture" to typologize the findings.

Cross-National Organizational Research: The Grasp of the Blind Men*

Karlene H. Roberts and Nakiye A. Boyacigiller

One mechanism for assessing progress is to examine existing investigations across the gamut of comparative organizational research from micro to macro and to ask whether they meet these criteria. However, it is impossible to examine all existing research or even that completed in the last few years in this regard because of the sheer volume of research activity in this area.

Our perusal of the literature indicated that, as is true of single-nation organizational research, cross-nation investigations fall into two categories. There are surveys and interviews that provide cursory snapshots of organizational life and there are ethnomethodological studies that provide thick description (Geertz, 1973) and questionable generalization. It is difficult, if not impossible, to integrate these two kinds of investigations. The kinds of nets they cast and the kinds of fish these nets are likely to trap are as different as sharks and bluegills. While both are fish, we have as yet found no recipe for an adequate stew composed of the two. Again, as is true in single-nation organizational research, the majority of the comparative investigations fall into the snapshot category. Consequently, a set of these investigations are examined in some depth.

Among the structural systematic comparative studies, we selected five for in-depth examination which by no means exhausts the population of such studies. They were selected for two reasons: they received widest "press" among such investigations and they represent research efforts conducted over rather long periods of time and usually by teams of researchers. That

is, they are the "Big Macs" (Multi-Attribute Cultural Studies) in the area. . . .

Prior to discussing what might be learned from examining the investigations together, we offer brief summaries of what was done and indicate some inherent problems in each of the studies. In our summary of the studies taken together we will attempt to differentiate those problems particularly crucial to cross-national organizational research from those common also to single-nation studies. At the outset it is important to keep in mind that although each study is flawed, they all represent Herculean efforts at conceptualizing and implementing large-scale comprehensive research programs.

The Manager and His Values

England's (1975) five-nation, ten-year study is the most micro of the investigations here. It is an investigation of managerial values. England's value construct is derived from and builds on existing theory about values (for example, Allport and Vernon, 1931; Rokeach, 1968). One wonders why England chose to go cross-national, and this issue is never adequately answered. The author does not discuss how organizational, industrial, national, or cultural aspects might be expected to influence values and in fact, makes it clear that he is not studying organizations, industries, nations, or cultures (p. 4). . . .

England developed a scale (the Personal Values Questionnaire—PVQ) to measure value importance and value orientation along three dimensions (pragmatic, ethical, and affective).

PVQ development is based entirely on United States–based research, building ethnocentrism into the study at its outset. It is entirely possible that this set of values is incomplete for managers from any nation and irrelevant for some. While England considers the issue of relevance in his conceptualization, the instrument itself is of such a nature that it probably cannot uncover irrelevance. Values are judged as high-medium-low importance, but any respondent would probably feel compelled to report that at least some of the sixty-six stated values are important.

The major theoretical notion underlying this investigation is that to the extent that individual behavior is a function of values, it is a joint function of the concepts important to that individual and his or her personal orientation. Concepts making up a person's operative values have the greatest impact on behavior. Intended and adopted values are less central and have less impact on behavior. Value profiles can be constructed for individual managers by listing concepts in the PVQ that are operative, intended, adopted, and weak (irrelevant) for that individual. Conditional probabilities are used to obtain individual value profiles. This rather complex scoring procedure may mask true similarities and differences within individual cognitions.

Individual responses can be aggregated for any group. Aggregation shows for each of the sixty-six concepts the number of individuals as a proportion of the group for which the concept is operative, intended, adopted, and weak. High proportion implies high behavioral relevance. A concept is viewed as "operative" if it fits his primary orientation (pragmatic, ethical, or affective); as "intended" if it is important but does not fit the primary orientation; as "adopted" if it fits the primary orientation but is average or low in importance; and as "weak" if it is neither important nor fits a primary orientation. Sixty-six scores derived this way are a bit difficult to compare across groups.

One behavioral relevance summary score for a group is generated by using a weighting scheme for all sixty-six concepts that weights the four value categories in descending order from operative to weak values. Behavioral relevance scores derived this way range from 0 to 100. Thus:

$$\text{Behavioral relevance of a construct for a group} = \frac{3(\text{operating value score}) + 2(\text{intended value score}) + 1(\text{adopted value score})}{3}$$

A second summary behavioral relevance score is simply the percentage of the total group for whom the concept is operative. This score varies from 0 to 100. The two summary scores correlate .97 to .99 across constructs.

While the data can generate a large number of comparisons across groups, it would be foolhardy to think any group of people can be described adequately with a minimal set of concepts, even only within the value domain. Yet, even this large number of comparable concepts is derived from a set of only three value orientations, suggesting the model itself may yet be too simplistic.

England investigates within-country variance among the concepts and cross-nation similarities and differences. Both similarities and differences are found within and between nations. As we might expect, possibly due to cultural homogeneity and nation size, Japanese managers have the most homogeneous values. Considerable variation exists among primary orientation of managers within the five countries. Again, it is difficult to know what this means if the PVQ does not tap a relatively full set of managerial values, or if to some managerial group the set tapped is largely irrelevant. The basic argument for these two criticisms has to do with constraints due to the way the instrument was developed. However, England's results are largely consistent with those of other studies of values, which supports this approach (see, for example, Cummings, Harnett, and Stevens, 1971; Hayashi, Harnett, and Cummings, 1973; Whiteley, 1979).

England next examines relationships of values of "behavior." Behavior, however, is assessed in only two countries by providing managers with critical incidents requiring decisions about budgeting, a morally questionable procedure with regard to research and development funds, selection of an assistant, and delegation of authority. Managers are asked what they would do with regard to each incident. This strategy offers a strong possibility for obtaining correlated response error.

Managerial values are also related to success, age, job satisfaction, organizational size, organizational level, and organizational type (manufacturing versus nonmanufacturing). An interesting measure of success is used—pay relative to age. The age categories are decade intervals. There is some question as to whether managerial age is appropriately chopped at decades. Might one expect to see managers spurt to success somewhere in their thirties or somewhere between twenty-five and thirty-five? In addition, if time is handled differently in different nations, would a spurt toward managerial excellence in one age-group in one country be at all relevant for managers in another country?

Many similarities emerged across the four countries used in relating values to success, leading England to suggest the use of the PVQ in making selection and placement decisions. More successful, as opposed to less successful, managers had values "seated in High Productivity, Profit Maximization, Managers, My Subordinates, Labor Unions, Ability, Aggressiveness, Prejudice, Achievement, Creativity, Success, Change, Competition, and Liberalism" (p. 69).

Job satisfaction is assessed using four items from the Hoppock Job Satisfaction scale. Managers in all five countries are fairly well satisfied. PVQ scores and job satisfaction are moderately and similarly related across the five countries. Interestingly, a different set of values is related to job satisfaction than to managerial success. Value profiles of different-age managers show many significant differences and no consistent patterns across nations.

Relationships among values and organizational characteristics are highly country-specific, and form no overall international pattern or convergence. Job level is used as one organizational characteristic. We question, however, whether it is truly an organizational or an individual difference characteristic. It is important that researchers provide the theoretical rationale for categorizing their variables.

In regard to studies such as this, it is difficult not to slip into causal language. Do values cause job success? Does job success cause values? What else might a relation between values and success mean? If the measurement problems contribute to correlated response error, one might obtain results found here—except those concerning relationships of values to success. That is, values are highly and similarly related across nations to variables measured similarly to the way values are measured. Values are less similarly and consistently related across nations to variables measured differently than the values are measured. At the very least it is difficult to know what the relationships mean because the summary value scores tend to entangle whatever the primary measures contributing to them mean. Then, too, managers may feel compelled to call relevant what is not and wonder why they are not confronted with the value most relevant to them.

More optimistically, one might say that managerial values appear most highly related to more proximal variables (other cognitions like job satisfaction, their own success, etc.) and not as related to more distal stimuli (organizational size, etc.) and that these relations are consistent across nations, suggesting managers are managers are managers. This argues for looking for micro cultural factors (such as norms about various things, individual religious orientations, etc.) to explain individual differences and macro cultural aspects (for example, political or legal systems) in relation to more macro organizational aspects (size, differentiation, etc.).

Competence and Power in Managerial Decision Making

Heller and Wilpert and their colleagues (1981) report a four-year, eight-nation investigation of organizational decision making designed by a multinational team of researchers. The research had three purposes. First it "throws light on the process of decision making, participation, and power sharing in 129 successful companies as seen from the policy making senior two levels of the organization" (p. xiii). A second objective was to link up with other research, and a third objective was to link with current controversial debate about employee participation and industrial democracy.

These authors avoid dealing with culture at all.

We avoid [the term] culture for two reasons. First, it has strong emotional implications and secondly any reasonable definition of "culture" refers to deep set characteristics of personality, habit and value patterns, tradition, and the social heritage of a community transferred from generation to generation. (p. 41)

Heller and his colleagues examine five methods of managerial decision making (making own decision without explanation, own decision with explanation, prior consultation, joint decision making, and delegation). They call the range of choices across these methods the influence power continuum (IPC).

The model on which the research is based is derived from the American-made human resources approach (Miles, 1965). These authors argue that they are in search of relative truths, of relationships between two or more variables that are assumed to exist only under certain circumstances. Thus, they indirectly indicate their interest in extending variance on some independent setting characteristics and examining the impact of those on decision making.

They predict that successful managers in successful companies do not use the same decision-making methods in all or most situations. Successful managers are predicted to use relatively autocratic strategies when decisions affect their organizations broadly and are immediately important to subordinates. When an issue is of great immediate importance to a subordinate but is not critical organization-wide, it tends to be shared between boss and subordinate. A second aspect of the model is that the outcome of power sharing is better use of human resources. The third aspect is that circumstances influence choice, particularly those in closest psychological proximity to the decision maker.

In each of the eight countries in the sample, organizations were selected to match for products, technologies, and managerial level. Thus, 129 organizations contributed 1,600 managers to the study. Managers were assembled in groups, the research was explained, and fourteen short questionnaires were administered. The research team then compiled questionnaire results and fed them back to the managers. The discussions that followed were tape-recorded, resulting in a second round of data collection (group feedback analysis).

In addition to asking how decisions are made generally, the questionnaires included items about job satisfaction, similarities and differences in level-one and level-two jobs, the time and skills a subordinate would need to learn the incumbent's job, job constraints, environmental turbulence, skill utilization, skill qualifications, and education. Thus, the majority of the data discussed were obtained by paper-and-pencil techniques, and the study suffers all the problems of these techniques. An interesting measure of managerial success takes into account managerial age relative to the mean managerial age in an industrial sector at a particular level and the variability of age within that sector. This measure is favorably compared to England's measure of success.

A decision centralization score was obtained by multiplying by another number the percentage of time managers responded to each of the five IPC dimensions with regard to a particular decision, adding the five resulting numbers together, and dividing by 100. As in work previously discussed, convoluted methods of arriving at scores mask the meaning of these scores. Factor and cluster analyses were used to assess internal consistency of the forms. Correlational, analysis of variance, and regression analyses procedures were used along with nonparametric techniques to analyze relationships posited.

Heller and Wilpert et al. are strong advocates of group feedback analysis as both a potential data collection device and as a tool for organizational development. Their book, however, focuses much more on statistical analyses than on process data. This may illustrate the severe difficulties involved in combining structural and process approaches to studying a problem. While these authors did not develop a process approach as extreme as ethnomethodology, it is still difficult to think about how to analyze appropriately and interpret group feedback analysis data. One might have expected at least some content analyses that could have been compared to the more rigid statistical data.

The results of the study showed managers used more than one decision-making method, depending on the circumstances. Managers bring subordinates into the process considerably more frequently than they do colleagues at the same level. Participation is apparently used to improve the quality of decision making and to improve communication. However, group feedback analysis showed that managers had serious reservations about engaging in group decision making. Participation increases with perceived environmental uncertainty, size of the work group, the age of the manager-subordinator dyad, and managerial skill. There were more similarities across nations than differences in managerial decision making, one form of convergence. In some industries (representing different technologies), there is considerably more participation than in others. A num-

ber of other findings, many of which are not directly relevant to decision making, are discussed. The authors discuss implications of their findings for managers; the level of analysis at which their theory is discussed.

The major problem with this study, other than failure to diverge as much as it appears they had promised from a paper-and-pencil approach, is in the level of sophistication of theory. The authors feel they provide theoretical advancement. We feel many of the findings are commonsensical. One suspects that a good review of American managerial decision-making research would show many of the same kinds of findings produced by these authors, and in addition, the weaving together of a more theoretically tight set of variables.

Organization and Nation

Hickson and McMillan's book (1981) is a collection of cross-national extensions of the original Aston studies (Pugh, Hickson, Hinings, and Turner, 1968, 1968, 1969b). The papers are about organizations in such diverse societies as Poland, the United States, West Germany, Jordan, Egypt, Britain, Canada, Japan, Sweden, and India. The specific hypotheses addressed differ somewhat from chapter to chapter, but the overwhelming concern is to enlighten the fundamental question first posed by Hickson, Hinings, McMillan, and Schwitter (1974): "Are societal differences overwhelming or are there stable relationships between such contextual factors and structures of work organizations, relationships which hold whatever the society in which the organizations are situated" (p. 66). This question is a microanalytic approach to the convergence hypothesis. All the studies utilize the methodology and measures of the Aston group (Pugh et al., 1969, 1968; Hickson, Pugh, and Pheysey, 1969; Inkson, Pugh, and Hickson, 1970; McMillan, Hickson, Hinings, and Schneck, 1973).

Sampling strategies differed in the various studies, but because the Aston works are interested in the influence of organizational size on the structure of bureaucracies, the organizations sampled are primarily large ones. Even in countries in which firms tend to be small, the authors preferred to focus on the largest organizations. (Ayoubi states that in Jordan only 55 firms out of 589 have more than thirty employees, yet these are the ones he sampled.) Still, compared to the original Aston samples with a mean size of 3,379 employees per organization (Pugh et al., 1968) and 1,542 employees per organization (Child, 1972), much more variation in firm size is achieved here. The organizations range in size from very small (30 employees) to very large (23,000 employees). The status of the organizations, measured by the dependence score, varies from independent organizations to branches or subsidiaries of larger organizations.

It is difficult to assess the veracity of these studies without voluminous debate over the measures and methodology of the original Aston work. These debates already exist (Aldrich, 1972; Crozier, and Friedberg, 1980; Pugh and Hickson, 1972; Scott, 1981; Starbuck, 1981). Our particular concern is with problems conceptualizing and measuring size, technology, and dependence that seems evident in this research.

Kimberly (1976) reviewed eighty comparative studies of size and organizational structure, and detailed the theoretical and methodological problems with the construct of size. He cites Child's study showing a range of intercorrelations of various measures of size (e.g., physical capacity, personnel, organizational inputs) which suggests that different ways of conceptualizing size have different implications for structuring organizations. Another oft-cited problem with size is that it is not independent of other aspects of organizing; operations can and are divided at managerial discretion.

As a technology measure, the authors use the yardstick for automation developed by Amber and Amber, "an estimate of the automaticity of the bulk of the equipment used by the or-

ganization in its workflow activities—'bulk' meaning the modal or most frequently occurring piece of equipment" (Hickson and McMillan, 1981, p. 203). As Hickson et al. (1974) explain, due to problems of inconsistency in the interrelationships among scales of technology used in the original Aston studies, they focused on the single automaticity mode (p. 69). Theoretical justification for focusing on automaticity is not given. The authors simply indicate that "its inclusion in this paper is due to its being common to all the studies analyzed and does not imply that it alone is an adequate measure of technology" (Hickson et al., 1974, p. 69). This represents the strength and the weakness of building on previous research; the research begins to take on a reality of its own.

The original Aston studies have been criticized for taking a too narrow view of technology (Fry, 1982; Gerwin, 1979; Kmetz, 1978; Scott, 1975) by focusing only on operations rather than materials or knowledge, two other aspects of technology. Further, there is a level of analysis problem with technology. It may mean different things and have vastly different repercussions depending on the unit of focus. In most of the Aston studies, the chief executive provides all information. It is questionable whether top management has the same perspective of technology as someone working on the line.

The final independent variable, organizational dependence, measures the degree to which an organization is tied to others in its environment. Hickson et al. (1974) use three of the original seven scales assessing dependence. They justify this by noting the high intercorrelations among scales (Inkson et al., 1970). Thus, they obtain data on origin (foundation), status (independent principal unit or branch), and relative size of the unit. Other studies in the book also measure organizational representation on the policy makeup body and public accountability of the group as aspects of dependence.

The data were collected via structured interviews with chief executives. For the most part, confirmatory data were not collected. Thus the major source of information in all the studies were the perceptions of one or two individuals. As questions are asked on nonpersonal aspects of the organization, the use of perceptual measures is not too detrimental. Yet evaluating an organization's key attributes with the input of so few individuals is a definite weakness. Organizations may look decidedly different depending on whether one's vantage point is that of a chief executive officer or a foreman.

Scales are constructed for dependence, automaticity, functional specialization, formalization, and centralization. The authors state that the unidimensionality of the scales was established by Pugh et al. (1968, 1969) and Inkson et al. (1970). "Organizations are scored either 1 or 0 depending on whether a firm possesses each item, and the scores are added without differential weighting" (p. 69). Each organization gets an overall score for each scale which is then used to determine country-level scores, the mean of all the organization-level scores in a country. These studies are superior to the earlier Aston work in one important aspect. By handling structural measures separately, the authors avoid the theoretically vacuous construct "structuring of activities," which was arrived at through factor analysis and which lost the theoretical veracity of the original measures.

A problem that surfaces throughout the book is that of explaining differences which were found between countries. The better studies in the volume couple the Aston measures with a sufficiently well-versed interpretation of the cultural, economic, and sociopolitical milieu of the country. For example, although Child and Kieser (chapter 4), in their study of German and English organizations, find the magnitude and direction of the relationships between context and structure to be in line with the contingency thesis, they did find that German firms tend toward greater centralization. They explained this difference by examining German culture and analyzing the differences

in managerial roles between German and English managers.

Alternative hypotheses posited are the late development effect (Dore, 1973) which states that countries which industrialize late will have more developed bureaucracies from the start or that the particular political economic regime will have an effect on organizational characteristics. An example of the latter is given in Badran and Hining's study of Egyptian organizations (chapter 7). The authors state that Egypt's planned economy requires "considerable information for producing plans, targets, monitoring and evaluation" which influences the level of specialization and formalization (p. 131).

Kuc, Hickson, and McMillan (chapter 5), in their comparative study of Poland, Britain, Japan, and Sweden, find an especially high level of centralization in Poland that they associate with the role of the state in organizational decision making and the influence of central planning. They also find Poland has a higher level of specialization (focusing on the mean and range of scores). This, they suggest, may be a reflection of the late development effect.

One problem alluded to by the editors stems from changing the scales to fit the research aims in a particular country. This prevents comparison with results from other countries. Yet a researcher must make his or her own choices within a given study; and the Aston scales are not perfect. This is an issue warranting debate among the "Aston" scholars. There are certain problems with the constructs (automaticity not being a complete technology score; dependence being relatively narrowly defined) and with the method of data collection. Yet a vast database of relatively comparable measures has been developed in ten countries. Given the paucity of comparable data to date, this in itself is no mean achievement.

As for results, what is the relationship between context and structure and is it stable across societies? Although product moment correlations for the most part show constancy of direction and magnitude, there are enough discrepancies for Hickson and McMillan to be cautious in their concluding chapter. Use of nonequal interval scales limits the comparisons of the numerical scores that can be made. As a result, both researchers and readers are left asking, "How close is similar enough?" It is necessary to eyeball correlations between certain factors to try to discern where there are significant differences. Although several of the authors allude to these problems and to the fact that causality cannot be inferred from correlations, there is an overwhelming suggestion that size as a "contextual variable" has an inordinate effect on the structuring of organizations.

Size is viewed as having a much greater impact than operations technology, which is viewed as being "little, if at all, related to structural features beyond those directly linked with the workflow itself" (p. 16). We believe this to be an overstatement.

First, technology was measured in a much less encompassing manner than was size. That is, the conceptual "size" of the two variables as measured is not the same and consequently comparisons of their correlations with other variables are suspect. While most of the work in the Aston tradition points to the ubiquity of size as having an important effect on structure, technology too has been found to have significant effects in other studies (see Fry 1982 for a comprehensive review). Pfeffer and Leblebici (1973) found the relationship between technology and structure to vary, given the level of competition in the environment. Unfortunately no assessment is made of this aspect of the environment. In the final analysis, the relationships among technology, size, and environment are interactive. Overall, Hickson and McMillan (chapter 12) suggest that the following conclusions in Table 26.1 be taken "with a pinch of salt" (p. 193).

While most of the studies did corroborate the relations indicated by Hickson and McMillan, the tone of their book suggests that cultural and nation-state variables are important. The "bold hypothesis" of the early cross-national Aston studies (Hickson et al., 1974) that states that context-structure relations are stable across societies is somewhat muted. In their concluding chapter Hickson and McMillan are content to say, and rightly so, that similarities in work organization across societies seem to outweigh differences. But why?

Hierarchy in Organization

Tannenbaum and his colleagues (1974) explore the general proposition that certain conditions, the abolition of private ownership, a high degree of formal participation and egalitarianism, reduce, if not eliminate, the unintended and dysfunctional effects of hierarchy. This work is a cross-national extension of *Control in Organizations* (Tannenbaum, 1968), which presented a research agenda for the study of control. Its approach is a social psychological one, in the tradition of Likert, based on the underlying tenet that hierarchy and organizational characteristics have profound psychological implications for organizational members (1974).

T A B L E 2 6 . 1 Relationships between Organizational Structure and Organizational Context

	Formalization	Specialization	Centralization
Size	+	+	−
Size of parent organization	+	+	
Dependence	+ usually		+

Note: + = positive correlation; − = negative association; and a blank = unstudied or indeterminate.
Source: Hickson and McMillan, 1981, chapter 12, p. 193.

The study was conducted in five countries: Israel, Yugoslavia, Austria, Italy, and the United States. The countries were chosen for differentiation along the dimensions of private ownership, degree of formal participation, and egalitarianism. The kibbutz in Israel and the plants in Yugoslavia were organized ostensibly in a Marxist socialist manner, whereas the plants in the United States, Austria, and Italy, in free enterprise countries, presumably were organized in the traditional nonparticipative bureaucratic pattern. The underlying theoretical argument is that these differences in conditions of society lead to differences in the gradient of distribution of control, which in turn lead to differences in the reactions and adjustments of organizational members.

The authors begin by presenting short discussions of the management systems in the five countries. These provide excellent introductions for the uninitiated and a common starting point for all readers. More important, they clarify the justifications for the various hypotheses presented. All cross-national work would benefit from similar exposition.

Ten plants are sampled in each country and matched on size (number of employees) and type of industry (five industries: plastics, nonferrous foundry, food canning, metal works, and furniture). Tannenbaum et al. collect their data with survey instruments (translated and back-translated) administered to thirty-five people in each plant. They oversample the upper levels of the organization to maximize the uninterrupted chains of authority that are selected. One should note that Tannenbaum and his colleagues are careful to distinguish between large and small plants. They indicate that while their hypotheses are valid in the smaller plants, the larger plants may more closely support the Kerr et al. (1960) "logic of industrialism" argument.

The researchers ask questions grouped into three categories: decision making and control, hierarchy, and gradients of reaction and adjustment. Several of the decision-making control items are on participation; in fact, this book may tell us more about participation than it does control. Data are also collected on the official hierarchical position each person holds (two measures of distance from the top and bottom of the organization), as well as information about the length of the reporting chain the respondent is in.

Through their analysis of control graphs, Tannenbaum et al. state that hierarchy exists in all societies, although the kibbutz and Yugoslavian plants have flatter gradients than the plants in the other nations. This is substantiated by the fact that kibbutz and Yugoslav plants have less steep gradients of control than do plants in the other nations. Authority and influence increase with hierarchy regardless of nation. In the power-equalized plants of Yugoslavia and the kibbutz, managers have less control compared to other countries. There is also a moderately high amount of control in these plants.

While the Yugoslav plants were high on formal participation, members did not have favorable attitudes or open communication. Satisfaction with one's job and salary, a sense of responsibility, motivation, and initiative, tend to increase with hierarchy while psychological adjustment and alienation do not. In all countries, organizations have distributions of sex that were hierarchical; even the egalitarian organizations were sexist! The interaction between superior and subordinate is characterized by informal participation in the American and kibbutz plants but not in the Yugoslav, Italian, or Austrian ones. Thus, "differences between the two systems [Marxist and capitalist] are not consistent on all criteria; differences occur within the two systems as well as between them" (1974, p. 211).

While most of these findings make sense, we have problems with methodology used by Tannenbaum et al. that render our acceptance of them problematic. The conceptualization of power and control which they use is quite narrow, especially given current developments. Even if evaluated in terms of the level of theoretical theory development in 1974, they would have been better off with some structural measures of power and control. In order to accept these results, one must accept reputational perceptual measures of control, influence, and power. The authors feel their large sample sizes ensure their measures are valid. We do not consider this sufficient.

Tannenbaum et al. use the mean average of all respondents, managers, workers, and executives to determine control and participation. Surely managers and workers view distribution of control differently; difference scores would have been useful. Means of individual responses are plotted for control graphs and country-level inferences are made from these aggregated, individual-level scores. The concept "total amount of control" is difficult to understand. If the question on control had been divided into substantive areas, it might be easier to make sense of it. A better measure might be to ask who makes decisions about budgets, vacations, schedules, hiring, adjustment of machines, and so forth.

Finally, we question the use of control graph methodology which is not a graph in the mathematical sense. And while a picture is said to be worth a thousand words, in this case it appears to lend more veracity to the measures than is warranted. A few more statistical measures, especially measures of dispersion around means, would have been helpful.

Summary

Many of our criticisms of the studies reviewed here are true of single-nation as well as cross-national research. Frequently, however, these faults are writ large when research goes cross-national. For example, the world is filled with criticisms of the original Aston work (see, for example, Aldrich, 1972; Crozier and Friedberg, 1980; Scott, 1981; Starbuck, 1981) and when these same issues and methods are taken abroad, further problems abound. We can, though, limit our view solely to the cross-national arena and evaluate these studies in two ways.

First, we can ask whether they meet their own stated goals. Generally they fail to do so for two primary reasons. The first is that linkages between construct and operation are weak and/or the aggregations and analyses are so convoluted that the meanings of the inputs to them are lost. Second, in one form or another, these studies stack the cards in favor of desired outcomes.

Alternatively, we can look more intensely at the problems identified that may be more important to cross-national organizational research than to single-nation studies. The most severe problems in these investigations are weak conceptualization and poor linkage from concept to operation. When one varies setting characteristics, which is the entire reason for cross-national research, the weakness of setting concepts influences the inferences that can be drawn, and the weakness of other constructs is highlighted to a greater degree than in single-nation work. All of the studies reviewed are subject to this criticism. Also falling into this domain are issues concerning ethnocentrism, treating environments too narrowly, questioning the relevance of certain variables in certain settings, the correlation of culture with aspects very similar to culture, lack of clear conceptualization and justification of constructs, and the use of indirect questioning that makes assumptions about respondents' frames of reference.

The second most severe problem in these studies is the way measures are obtained, aggregated, and analyzed. This problem is surely more severe in cross-nation than single-nation studies because problems of meaning are inherently more difficult in the former than the latter. When one weights survey data in complex ways, assumes responses from people at different organizational levels are equivalent, derives scores in complex ways, and analyzes data using complex techniques, inferences become problematic.

Level-of-analysis problems are also inherent in a number of these studies. As one illustration, technology may mean different things at different levels of the organization. Another example is the use of country-level data to inform policy relevant to individuals in organizations. By definition, in cross-national research one adds a level of construct (environment) in addition to what is usually seen in single-nation work. Greater care must be taken with regard to consistency across theory, measurement, analysis, interpretation, and application of results than in investigations involving few levels of concern (Roberts, Hulin, and Rousseau, 1978).

Related to levels of analyses are problems concerning time. We see several here, including lack of justification for time intervals over which data in any one investigation are collected, attempts to integrate studies in which data are collected over considerable ranges of time (lacking in synchrony) or are collected using very different "envelopes" of time, and lack of attention to time at all.

This set of investigations, as is true of the gamut of cross-national investigations, is not inclusive of organizational life. For example, the Aston studies fail to think about the role of people in organizations though their respondents are all people. In studies such as Tannenbaum's and Hofstede's, important dimensions of organizational life are ignored and severe problems in aggregation are exposed.

There is, also, a slavish adherence to paper-and-pencil measures, resulting in static pictures of organizational life. Even in the one situation in which some process data were collected, little use was made of them. Similarly, to all contingency approaches these investigations

cast organizational life in rigid deterministic terms. In an extreme form variables like technology, organizational structure, task, or turbulence may be introduced as straightjackets allowing little freedom of choice and strategy. People . . . emerge as puppets in a network of contingency relations. (Crozier and Friedberg cited in Heller and Wilpert, 1981, p. 57)

Given these circumstances, it is not surprising that we have not developed a cumulative

research base or any overarching worldview of organizational life. We made no attempt here to fully review cross-national organizational research and the issue of cumulation cannot be addressed on the basis of a few studies. However, our review of cross-national work published in major academic journals during the last ten years (Roberts and Boyacigiller, in press) comes to the same conclusion. That the studies looked at here are almost nonintegratable is a more serious problem in terms of pushing forward future research.

Finally, as a set these studies are representative of most cross-national organizational research in that they fail to take advantage of the strengths of the basic social science disciplines from which they emerge. For example, Heller and Wilpert and their colleagues do not really provide a thick description as would an anthropological ethnomethodologist, though they flirt around it. England and Hofstede derive their respective work from a dominant psychological approach to attitudes. Because attitude research is one of the oldest aspects of social psychology, sufficient time has passed for it to be brought into the mainstream of cross-national research. However, current social psychology attitude research is considerably more sophisticated than is this work. In the more macro areas that should be informed by the sociological literature, as for example participation, we do not see much borrowed from that literature either in the work of Heller and Wilpert and their colleagues or in the research of Tannenbaum and his colleagues.

Generally, then, we do not see the strengths of anthropology contributing either to cultural identification (Hofstede's is the only investigation that takes anthropology seriously) or methodology in this kind of research. Neither the important organizational constraints generated by political science and economics nor the theories developed in sociology and psychology are incorporated into this research. All in all, the studies reviewed here do not sufficiently meet the criteria set out for an adequate paradigm of cross-national organizational research. Is the elephant too large or the researcher too blind?

Note

* From *Research in Organizational Behavior*. Vol. 6, (Greenwich, CT: JAI Press, 1984), 433–35; 444–46; 450–62, 473–75, by permission of the JAI Press, Incorporated. Copyright 1984 by the JAI Press, Inc.

References

Aldrich, H. "Technology and Organization Structure: A Reexamination of the Findings of the Aston Group." *Administrative Science Quarterly,* 1972, *17,* 26–43.

Allport, G. W., and Vernon, P. T. *A Study of Values.* Boston: Houghton Mifflin, 1931.

Barnet, R. J., and Müller, R. *Global Reach.* New York: Simon & Schuster, 1974.

Benedict, R. *Patterns of Culture.* New York: Houghton Mifflin, 1934.

Beres, M. E., and Portwood, J. D. "Sociological Influences on Organizations: An Analysis of Recent Research." In A. R. Negandhi and B. Wilpert (Eds.), *The Functioning of Complex Organizations.* Cambridge, MA: Oelgeschlager, Gunn and Hain, 1981.

Bhagat, R. S., and McQuaid, S. J. "Role of Subjective Culture in Organizations: A Review and Directions." *Journal of Applied Psychology,* 1982, *67,* (5), 653–85.

Brown, W., and Jacques, E. *Glacier Project Papers.* London: Heinemann, 1975.

Campbell, D. T. "Ethnocentrism of Disciplines and the Fish-Scale Model of Omniscience." In M. Sherif and C. W. Sherif (Eds.), *Interdisciplinary Relationships in the Social Sciences.* Chicago: Aldine, 1969.

Child, J. "Organization Structure and Strategies of Control: A Replication of the Aston Study." *Administrative Science Quarterly,* 1972, *17,* 163–76.

———. "Culture, Contingency, and Capitalism in the Cross-National Study of Organizations." In L. L. Cummings and B. M. Staw (Eds.), *Research in Organizational Behavior* (Vol. 3). Greenwich, CT: JAI Press, 1981.

Child, J., and Kieser, A. "Organization and Managerial Roles in British and West German Companies: An Examination of the Culture-Free Thesis." In C. J. Lammers and D. J. Hickson (Eds.), *Organizations Alike and Unlike.* London: Routledge and Kegan Paul, 1979.

Cohen, M. D., March, J. G., and Olsen, J. P. "A Garbage Can Model of Organizational Choice." *Administrative Science Quarterly,* 1972, *17,* 1–25.

Crozier, M. *The Bureaucratic Phenomenon.* Chicago: University of Chicago Press, 1964.

Crozier, M., and Friedberg, E. *Actors and Systems: The Politics of Collective Action.* Chicago: University of Chicago Press, 1980.

Cummings, L. L., Harnett, D. L., and Stevens, O. V. "Risk, Fate, Conciliation and Trust: An International Study of Attitudinal Differences among Executives." *Academy of Management Journal,* 1971, *14,* 285–304.

Cyert, R. M., and March, J. G. *A Behavioral Theory of the Firm.* Englewood Cliffs, NJ: Prentice-Hall, 1963.

Dachler, H. P. "Constraints on Current Perspectives for the Cross-Cultural Study of Organizations." Presented at 39th annual meeting of the Academy of Management, Atlanta, 1979.

Demsetz, H. "Antitrust: Problems and Proposals." In J. F. Weston and M. E. Granfield (Eds.), *Corporate Enterprise in a New Environment.* New York: K. C. G. Productions, 1982.

Dixon, K. "Is Cultural Relativism Self-Refuting?" *British Journal of Sociology,* 1977, *28,* 75–88.

Doob, L. W. "The Inconclusive Struggles of Cross-Cultural Psychology." *Journal of Cross-Cultural Psychology,* 1980, *11,* 59–73.

Dore, R. *British Factory—Japanese Factory: The Origins of National Diversity in Industrial Relations.* Berkeley, CA: University of California Press, 1973.

Ekehammar, B. "Interaction in Personality from a Historical Perspective." *Psychological Bulletin,* 1974, *81,* 1026–48.

England, G. W. *The Manager and His Values: An International Perspective from the United States, Japan, Korea, India, and Australia.* Cambridge, MA: Ballinger, 1975.

England, G. W., Negandhi, A. R., and Wilpert, B. *Organizational Functioning in a Cross-Cultural Perspective.* Kent, OH: Kent State University Press, 1979.

Evan, W. M. "Measuring the Impact of Culture on Organizations." *International Studies of Management and Organization,* Spring 1975, *5,* 91–113.

Farmer, R. N., and Richman, B. M. *Comparative Management and Economic Progress.* (2nd ed.). Bloomington, IN: Cedarwood Press, 1970.

Ferrari, S. "Cross-Cultural Management Literature in France, Italy, and Spain." *Management International Review,* 1974, *14*(4–5), 17–23.

Fry, L. W. "Technology-Structure Research: Three Critical Issues." *Academy of Management Journal,* 1982, *25,* 532–52.

Galbraith, J. K. *The New Industrial State.* Boston: Houghton Mifflin, 1967.

Geertz, C. *The Interpretation of Cultures.* New York: Basic Books, 1973.

Gergen, K. J. "Social Psychology as History." *Journal of Personality and Social Psychology,* 1973, *26, 309–20.*

Gerwin, D. "The Comparative Analysis of Structure and Technology: A Critical Appraisal." *Academy of Management Review,* 1979, *4,* 41–51.

Glaser, B. G., and Strauss, A. L. *The Discovery of Grounded Theory.* London: Weidenfeld and Nicolson, 1968.

Graham, R. J. "The Role of Perception of Time in Consumer Research." *Journal of Consumer Research,* 1981, *7,* 335–42.

Haire, M., Ghiselli, E., and Porter, L. W. *Managerial Thinking: An International Study.* New York: Wiley, 1966.

Hall, E. T. *The Silent Language.* New York: Anchor Press/Doubleday, 1973.

———. *Beyond Culture.* Garden City, NY: Anchor Press, Doubleday, 1981.

Harbison, F., and Myers, C. A. *Management in the Industrial World: On International Analysis.* New York: McGraw-Hill, 1959.

Harris, M. *Cultural Materialism: The Struggle for a Science of Culture.* New York: Random House, 1979.

Hayashi, K., Harnett, D. L., and Cummings, L. L. *Personality and Behavior in Negotiations: An American-Japanese Empirical Comparison.* Working paper, Institute for International Studies and Training, Fujinomuya, Japan, 1973.

Heller, F. A., Wilpert, B., Docherty, P., Fourcade, J. M., Fokking, P., Mays, R., Roig, B., Weinshall, T., and t'Hooft, W. *Competence and Power in Managerial Decision-Making: A Study of Senior Levels of Organization in Eight Countries.* New York: Wiley, 1981.

Hickson, D. J., and McMillan, C. J. *Organization and Nation: The Aston Programme IV.* Westmead, England: Gower, 1981.

Hickson, D. J., Pugh, D. S., and Pheysey, D. C. "Operations Technology and Organization Structure: An Empirical Reappraisal." *Administrative Science Quarterly,* 1969, *14,* 378–97.

Hickson, D. J., Hinings, C. R., McMillan, C. J., and Schwitter, J. P. "The Culture-Free Context of Organization Structure." *Sociology,* 1974, *8,* 59–80.

Hofstede, G. *Culture's Consequences: International Differences in Work-Related Values.* Beverly Hills: Sage Publications, 1980.

Hydebrand, W. V. *Comparative Organizations: The Results of Empirical Research.* Englewood Cliffs, NJ: Prentice-Hall, 1973.

Inkson, J. H. K., Pugh, D. S., and Hickson, D. J. "Organization Context and Structure: An Abbreviated Replication." *Administrative Science Quarterly,* 1970, *15,* 318–29.

Kenny, D. A. "Cross-Lagged Panel Correlation: A Test for Spuriousness." *Psychological Bulletin,* 1975, *82,* 887–903.

Kerr, C. *The Future of Industrial Societies: Convergence or Continuing Diversity?* Cambridge, MA: Harvard University Press, 1983.

Kerr, C., Dunlop, J. T., Harbison, F. H., and Myers, C. A. *Industrialism and Industrial Man: The Problems of Labor and Management in Economic Growth.* Cambridge, MA: Harvard University Press, 1960.

Kimberly, J. "Organizational Size and the Structuralist Perspective: A Review, Critique, and Proposal." *Administrative Science Quarterly,* 1976, *21,* 571–97.

Klausner, S. Z. *On Man in His Environment.* San Francisco: Jossey-Bass, 1971.

Kluckhohn, C. "The Study of Culture." In D. Lerner and H. D. Lasswell (Eds.), *The Policy Sciences.* Stanford, CA: Stanford University Press, 1951.

Kmetz, J. "A Critique of the Aston Studies and Results with a New Measure of Technology." *Organization and Administrative Sciences,* 1977/1978, *8,* 123–44.

Kroeber, A., and Kluckhohn, C. *Culture: A Critical Review of Concepts and Definitions.* Cambridge, MA: Peabody Museum, 1952.

Kuhn, T. S. *The Structure of Scientific Revolutions* (2nd ed.). Chicago: University of Chicago Press, 1970.

March, J. G., and Olsen, J. P. *Ambiguity and Choice in Organizations.* Bergen: Universitelsforlaget, 1976.

March, J. G., and Simon, H. A. *Organizations.* New York: Wiley, 1958.

McGrath, J. E., and Rotchford, N. L. "Time and Behavior in Organizations." In B. Staw and L. Cummings (Eds.), *Research in Organizational Behavior* (Vol. 5). Greenwich, CT: JAI Press, 1983.

McMillan, C. J., Hickson, D. J., Hinings, C. K., and Schneck, R. E. "The Structure of Work Organizations across Societies." *Academy of Management Journal,* 1973, *16,* 555–69.

Meyer, A. G. "Theories of Convergence." In C. Johnson (Ed.), *Change in Communist Systems.* Stanford, CA: Stanford University Press, 1970.

Meyer, J. W., Boli-Bennett, J., and Chase-Dunn, C. "Convergence and Divergence in Development." *Annual Review of Sociology,* 1975, *1,* 233–46.

Meyer, J. W., and Rowan, B. "Institutionalized Organizations: Formal Structure as Myth and Ceremony." *American Journal of Sociology,* 1977, *83,* 340–63.

Miles, R. E. "Human Relations or Human Resources?" *Harvard Business Review,* 1965, *43,* 148–63.

Morgenstern, O. *On the Accuracy of Economic Observations.* Princeton, NJ: Princeton University Press, 1973.

Mulder, M. "Reduction of Power Differences in Practice: The Power Distance Reduction Theory and Its Applications." In G. Hofstede and M. S. Kassem (Eds.), *European Contributions to Organization Theory.* Assen, Neth.: Van Gorcum, 1976.

Negandhi, A. R. "Cross Cultural Management Studies: Too Many Conclusions, Not Enough Conceptualization." *Management International Review,* 1974, *14*(6), 59–67.

Pfeffer, J. "Merger as a Response to Organizational Interdependence." *Administrative Science Quarterly,* 1972, *17,* 382–94.

Pfeffer, J., and Leblebici, H. "The Effect of Competition on Some Dimensions of Organizational Structure." *Social Forces,* 1973, *52,* 268–79.

Platt, J. R. "Strong Inference." *Science,* 1964, *46,* 347–53.

Pugh, D. S., and Hickson, D. J. "Causal Inference and the Aston Studies." *Administrative Science Quarterly,* 1972, *17,* 273–76.

Pugh, D. S., Hickson, D. J., Hinings, C. R., and Turner, C. "An Approach to the Study of Bureaucracy." *Sociology,* 1968, *1,* 61–72.

———. "Dimensions of Organizational Structure." *Administrative Science Quarterly,* 1968, *13,* 121–34.

———. "The Context of Organization Structures." *Administrative Science Quarterly,* 1969, *14,* 91–114.

Roberts, K. H. "On Looking at an Elephant: An Evaluation of Cross-Cultural Research Related to Organizations." *Psychological Bulletin,* 1970, *74,* 327–50.

Roberts, K. H., and Boyacigiller, F. N. "A Survey of Cross-National Organizational Researchers:

Their Views and Opinions." *Organization Studies,* in press.

Roberts, K. H., Hulin, C. L., and Rousseau, D. M. *Developing an Interdisciplinary Science of Organizations.* San Francisco: Jossey-Bass, 1978.

Rokeach, M. *Beliefs, Attitudes and Values: A Theory of Organization and Change.* San Francisco: Jossey-Bass, 1968.

Schell, J. *The Fate of the Earth.* New York: Knopf, 1982.

Scott, W. R. "Organizational Structure." *Annual Review of Sociology,* 1975, *1,* 1–20.

———. *Organizations: Rational, Natural and Open Systems.* Englewood Cliffs, NJ: Prentice-Hall, 1981.

Starbuck, W. H. "A Trip to View the Elephants and Rattlesnakes in the Garden of Aston." In A. H. Van de Ven and W. F. Joyce (Eds.), *Perspectives on Organization Design and Behavior.* New York: Wiley, 1981.

Stinchcomb, A. L. "Social Structure in Organizations." In James G. March (Ed.), *Handbook of Organizations.* Chicago: Rand McNally, 1965.

Tannenbaum, A. S. *Control in Organizations.* New York: Basic Books, 1968.

Tannenbaum, A. S., Kavcic, B., Rosner, M., Vianello, M., and Wieser, G. *Hierarchy in Organizations.* San Francisco: Jossey-Bass, 1974.

Triandis, H. *Some Dimensions of Intercultural Variation and Their Implications for Interpersonal Behavior.* Technical report. Department of Psychology, University of Illinois at Urbana-Champaign, 1981.

Udy, S. H., Jr. "Technical and Institutional Factors in Production Organization: A Preliminary Model." *American Journal of Sociology,* 1961, *67,* 247–54.

von Alemann, H. "International Contacts of University Staff Members: Some Problems in the Internationality of Science." *International Social Science Journal,* 1974, *26,* 445–57.

Weick, K. *The Social Psychology of Organizing* (2nd ed.). Reading, MA: Addison-Wesley, 1979.

Whiteley, W. "A Cross-National Test of England's Model of Managers' Value Systems and Their Relationship to Behavior." In G. W. England, A. R. Negandhi, and B. Wilpert (Eds.), *Organizational Functioning in a Cross-Cultural Perspective.* Kent, OH: Kent State University Press, 1979.

Zucker, L. G. "The Role of Institutionalization in Cultural Persistence." *American Sociological Review,* 1977, *42,* 726–43.

CHAPTER TWENTY-SEVEN

The Cultural Relativity of Organizational Practices and Theories*

Geert Hofstede

Introduction

Management and National Cultures

A key issue for organization science is the influence of national cultures on management. Twenty or even ten years ago, the existence of a relationship between management and national cultures was far from obvious to many, and it may not be obvious to everyone even now. In the 1950s and 1960s, the dominant belief, at least in Europe and the United States, was that management was something universal. There were principles of sound management, which existed regardless of national environments. If national or local practice deviated from these principles, it was time to change local practice. In the future, the universality of sound management practices would lead to societies becoming more and more alike. This applied even to the poor countries of the Third World, which would become rich as well and would be managed just like the rich countries. Also, the differences between management in the First and Second World (capitalist and socialist) would disappear; in fact, under the surface they were thought to be a lot smaller than was officially recognized. This way of thinking, which dominated the 1950s and 1960s, is known as the "convergence hypothesis."

During the 1970s, the belief in the unavoidable convergence of management practices waned. It was too obviously in conflict with the reality we saw around us. At the same time supranational organizations like the European Common Market, which were founded very much on the convergence belief, had to recognize the stubbornness of national differences. Even within existing nations, regional differences became more rather than less accentuated. The Welsh, the Flemish, the Basques, the Bangladeshi, the Quebecois defended their own identity, and this was difficult to reconcile with a management philosophy of convergence. It slowly became clear that national and even regional cultures do matter for management. The national and regional differences are not disappearing; they are here to stay. In fact, these differences may become one of the most crucial problems for management—in particular for the management of multinational, multicultural organizations, whether public or private.

The Importance of Nationality

Nationality is important to management for at least three reasons. The first, very obviously, is political. Nations are political units, rooted in history, with their own institutions: forms of government, legal systems, educational systems, labor and employer's association systems. Not only do the formal institutions differ, but even if we could equalize them, the informal ways of using them differ. For example, formal law in France protects the rights of the individual against the state much better than formal law in Great Britain or Holland. However, few French citizens have ever won court cases against the state, whereas this happens quite regularly in Holland or Britain. Such informal political realities are quite resistant to change.

The second reason why nationality is important is sociological. Nationality or regionality has a symbolic value to citizens. We all derive part of our identity from it; it is part of the "who am I." The symbolic value of the fact of belonging to a nation or region has been and still is sufficient reason for people to go to war, when they feel their common identity to be threatened. National and regional differences are felt by people to be a reality—and therefore they are a reality.

The third reason why nationality is important is psychological. Our thinking is partly conditioned by national culture factors. This is an effect of early life experiences in the family and later educational experiences in schools and organizations, which are not the same across national borders. In a classroom, I can easily demonstrate the process of conditioning by experience. For this purpose I use an ambiguous picture: one that can be interpreted in two different ways. One such picture represents either an attractive young girl or an ugly old woman, depending on the way you look at it. In order to demonstrate the process of conditioning, I ask one half of the class to close their eyes. To the other half, I show for five seconds a slightly changed version of the picture, in which only the young girl can be seen. Then I ask the other half to close their eyes, and to the first half I show, also for five seconds, a version in which only the old woman can be seen. After this preparation, I show the ambiguous picture to everyone at the same time. The results are amazing: the vast majority of those "conditioned" by seeing the young girl first, now see only the young girl in the ambiguous picture; and most of those "conditioned" by seeing the old woman first can see only the old woman afterward.

Mental Programming

This very simple experiment shows that, as a teacher, I can in five seconds condition a randomly taken half of a class to see something else in a picture than would the other half. If this is so, how much stronger should the differences in perception of the same reality be between people who have been "conditioned" by different educational and life experiences not for a mere five seconds, but for twenty, thirty, or forty years? Through our experiences we become "mentally programmed" to interpret new experiences in a certain way. My favorite definition of "culture" is precisely that its essence is *collective mental programming:* it is that part of our conditioning that we share with other members of our nation, region, or group but not with members of other nations, regions, or groups.

Examples of differences in mental programming between members of different nations can be observed all around us. One source of difference is, of course, language and all that comes with it, but there is much more. In Europe, British people will form a neat queue whenever they have to wait; not so, the French. Dutch people will as a rule greet strangers when they enter a small, closed space like a railway compartment, doctor's waiting room, or lift; not so, the Belgians. Austrians will wait at a red pedestrian traffic light even when there is no traffic; not so the Dutch. Swiss tend to become very angry when somebody—say, a foreigner—makes a mistake in traffic; not so the Swedes. All these are part of an invisible set of mental programs which belongs to these countries' national cultures.

Such cultural programs are difficult to change, unless one detaches the individual from his or her culture. Within a nation or a part of it, culture changes only slowly. This is the more so because what is in the minds of the people has also become crystallized in the institutions mentioned earlier: government, legal systems, educational systems, industrial relations systems, family structures, religious organizations, sports clubs, settlement patterns, literature, architecture, and even scientific theories. All these reflect traditions and common ways of thinking, which are rooted in the common culture but may be different for other cultures. The institutions constrain and reinforce the ways of thinking on which they are based.

One well-known mechanism by which culturally determined ways of thinking perpetuate themselves is the self-fulfilling prophecy. If, for example, the belief is held that people from a certain minority are irresponsible, the institutions in such an environment will not admit these people into positions of responsibility; never being given responsibility, minority people will be unable to learn it, and very likely they will actually behave irresponsibly. So, everyone remains caught in the belief—including, probably, the minority people themselves. Another example of the self-fulfilling prophecy: if the dominant way of thinking in a society is that all people are ultimately motivated by self-interest, those who do not pursue self-interest are considered as deviant. As it is unpleasant to be a deviant, most people in such an environment will justify whatever they want to do with some reference to self-interest, thereby reinforcing the dominant way of thinking. People in such a society cannot even imagine motives that cannot be reduced to self-interest.

National Character

This paper shall be limited to national cultures, excluding cultural differences between groups within nations; such as, those based on regions, social classes, occupations, religion, age, sex, or even families. These differences in culture within nations, of course, do exist, but for most nations we can still distinguish some ways of thinking that most inhabitants share and that we can consider part of their national culture or national character. National characters are more clearly distinguishable to foreigners than to the nationals themselves. When we live within a country, we do not discover what we have in common with our compatriots, only what makes us different from them.

Statements about national culture or national character smell of superficiality and false generalization. There are two reasons for this. First, there is no commonly accepted language to describe such a complex thing as a "culture." We meet the same problem if we

want to describe someone's "personality": we risk being subjective and superficial. In the case of "personality," however, psychology has at least developed terms like intelligence, energy level, introversion-extroversion, and emotional stability, to mention a few, which are more or less commonly understood. In the case of "culture," such a scientific language does not exist. In the second place, statements about national character have often been based on impressions only, not on systematic study. Such statements can indeed be considered false generalizations.

A Research Project across Fifty Countries

My own research into national cultures was carried out between 1967 and 1978. It has attempted to meet the two objectives I just mentioned: to develop a commonly acceptable, well-defined, and empirically based terminology to describe cultures; and to use systematically collected data about a large number of cultures, rather than just impressions. I obtained these data more or less by accident. From 1967 to 1971 I worked as a psychologist on the international staff of a large multinational corporation. As part of my job I collected data on the employees' attitudes and values, by means of standardized paper-and-pencil questionnaires. Virtually all employees of the corporation were surveyed, from unskilled workers to research scientists in many countries around the globe. Then from 1971 to 1973 the surveys were repeated once more with the same group of employees. All in all the corporation collected over 116,000 questionnaires which were stored in a computerized data bank. For forty countries, there were sufficient data for systematic analysis.

It soon appeared that those items in the questionnaires that dealt with employee values rather than attitudes showed remarkable and very stable differences between countries. By an attitude I mean the response to a question like "how do you like your job?" or "how do you like your boss?" By a value I mean answers to questions of whether people prefer one type of boss over another, or their choice of factors to describe an ideal job. Values indicate their desires, not their perceptions of what actually went on. These values, not the attitudes, reflect differences in mental programming and national character.

These differences, however, were always statistical in nature. Suppose people were asked whether they strongly agreed, agreed, were undecided, disagreed, or strongly disagreed with a certain value statement. In such a case we would not find that all employees in country A agreed and all in country B disagreed; instead we might find that 60 percent of the employees in country A agreed, while only 40 percent in country B agreed. Characterizing a national culture does not mean that every individual within that culture is mentally programmed in the same way. The national culture found is a kind of average pattern of beliefs and values, around which individuals in the country vary. For example, I found that, on average, Japanese have a greater desire for a strong authority than English; but some English have a greater desire for a strong authority than quite a few Japanese. In describing national cultures we refer to common elements within each nation, but we should not generalize to every individual within that nation.

In 1971 I went as a teacher to an international business school, where I asked the course participants, who were managers from many different countries, to answer the same values questions we used in the multinational corporation. The answers revealed the same type of pattern of differences between countries, showing that we were not dealing with a phenomenon particular to this one company. Then in my later research, from 1973 to 1979, at the European Institute for Advanced Studies in Brussels, I looked for other studies comparing aspects of national character across countries. I found about forty such studies comparing five or more countries which showed differences confirming the ones found in the

multinational corporation. All this material together forms the basis for my book *Culture's Consequences* (Hofstede 1980). Later, supplementary data became available for another ten countries and three multicountry regions, thereby raising the total number of countries to fifty (Hofstede 1983).

Four Dimensions of National Culture

My terminology for describing national cultures consists of four different criteria which I call "dimensions" because they occur in nearly all possible combinations. They are largely independent of each other:

1. Individualism versus collectivism;
2. Large or small power distance;
3. Strong or weak uncertainty avoidance; and
4. Masculinity versus femininity.

The research data have allowed me to attribute to each of the forty countries represented in the data bank of the multinational corporation an index value (between 0 and about 100) on each of these four dimensions.

The four dimensions were found through a combination of multivariate statistics (factor analysis) and theoretical reasoning. The cases analyzed in the factor analysis were the forty countries; the variables were the mean scores or answer percentages for the different value questions, as produced by the multinational corporation's employees within these countries. This factor analysis showed that 50 percent of the variance in answer patterns between countries on the value questions could be explained by three factors, corresponding to the dimensions 1 + 2, 3, and 4. Theoretical reasoning led to the further splitting of the first factor into two dimensions. The theoretical reasoning meant that each dimension should be conceptually linkable to some very fundamental problem in human societies, but a problem to which different societies have found different answers. These are the issues studied in primitive, nonliterate societies by cultural anthropologists, such as the distribution of power, or the distribution of roles between the sexes. There is no reason why such issues should be relevant only for primitive societies.

Individualism-Collectivism

The first dimension is labeled "individualism versus collectivism." The fundamental issue involved is the relation between an individual and his or her fellow individuals. At one end of the scale we find societies in which the ties between individuals are very loose. Everybody is supposed to look after his or her own self-interest and maybe the interest of his or her immediate family. This is made possible by a large amount of freedom that such a society leaves individuals. At the other end of the scale we find societies in which the ties between individuals are very tight. People are born into collectivities or in-groups which may be their extended family (including grandparents, uncles, aunts, and so on), their tribe, or their village. Everybody is supposed to look after the interest of his or her in-group and to have no other opinions and beliefs than the opinions and beliefs in their in-group. In exchange, the in-group will protect them when they are in

trouble. We see that both the individualist and the collectivist society are integrated wholes, but the individualist society is loosely integrated, and the collectivist society tightly integrated.

All fifty countries studied can be placed somewhere along the individualist-collectivist scale. On the basis of the answers obtained on the questionnaire in the multinational corporation, each country was given an individualism index score. The score is such that 100 represents a strongly individualist society and 0 a strongly collectivist society: all fifty countries are somewhere between these extremes.

It appears that the degree of individualism in a country is statistically related to that country's wealth. Figure 27.1 shows the list of countries used, and Figure 27.2 shows vertically the individualism index scores of the fifty countries, and horizontally their wealth, expressed in their gross national product per capita at the time the surveys were taken (around 1970). We see evidence that wealthy countries are more individualist and poor countries more collectivist. Very individualist countries are the United States, Great Britain, the

ARA	Arab countries (Egypt, Lebanon, Libya, Kuwait, Iraq, Saudi-Arabia, United Arab Emirates)	GER	Germany	PAN	Panama
		GRE	Greece	PER	Peru
		GUA	Guatemala	PHI	Philippines
ARG	Argentina	HOK	Hong Kong	POR	Portugal
AUL	Australia	IDO	Indonesia	SAF	South Africa
AUT	Austria	IND	India	SAL	Salvador
BEL	Belgium	IRA	Iran	SIN	Singapore
BRA	Brazil	IRE	Ireland	SPA	Spain
CAN	Canada	ISR	Israel	SWE	Sweden
CHL	Chile	ITA	Italy	SWI	Switzerland
COL	Colombia	JAM	Jamaica	TAI	Taiwan
COS	Costa Rica	JPN	Japan	THA	Thailand
DEN	Denmark	KOR	South Korea	TUR	Turkey
EAF	East Africa (Kenya, Ethiopia, Zambia)	MAL	Malaysia	URU	Uruguay
		MEX	Mexico	USA	United States
EQA	Ecuador	NET	Netherlands	VEN	Venezuela
FIN	Finland	NOR	Norway	WAF	West Africa (Nigeria, Ghana, Sierra Leone)
FRA	France	NZL	New Zealand		
GBR	Great Britain	PAK	Pakistan	YUG	Yugoslavia

F I G U R E   2 7 . 1   The countries and regions.

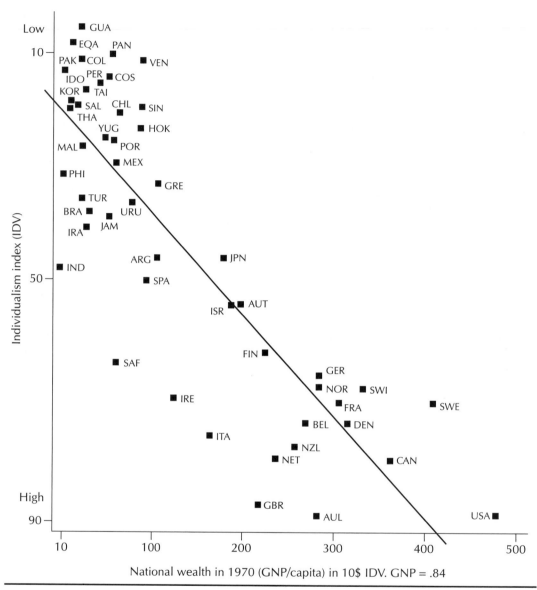

FIGURE 27.2   The position of the fifty countries on their individualism index (IDV) versus their 1970 national wealth.

Netherlands; very collectivist are Colombia, Pakistan, and Taiwan. In the middle we find Japan, India, Austria, and Spain.

Power Distance

The second dimension is labeled "power distance." The fundamental issue involved is how society deals with the fact that people are

unequal. People are unequal in physical and intellectual capacities. Some societies let these inequalities grow over time into inequalities in power and wealth; the latter may become hereditary and no longer related to physical and intellectual capacities at all. Other societies try to play down inequalities in power and wealth as much as possible. Surely, no society has ever reached complete equality, because there are strong forces in society that perpetuate existing inequalities. All societies are unequal, but some are more unequal than others. This degree of inequality is measured by the power distance scale, which also runs from 0 (small power distance) to 100 (large power distance).

In organizations, the level of power distance is related to the degree of centralization of authority and the degree of autocratic leadership. This relationship shows that centralization and autocratic leadership are rooted in the "mental programming" of the members of a society, not only of those in power but also of those at the bottom of the power hierarchy. Societies in which power tends to be distributed unequally can remain so because this situation satisfies the psychological need for dependence of the people without power. We could also say that societies and organizations will be led as autocratically as their members will permit. The autocracy exists just as much in the members as in the leaders: the value systems of the two groups are usually complementary.

In Figure 27.3 power distance is plotted horizontally and individualism-collectivism vertically. The Philippines, Venezuela, India, and others show large power distance index scores, but also France and Belgium score fairly high. Denmark, Israel, and Austria score low. We see that there is a global relationship between power distance and collectivism: collectivist countries always show large power distances, but individualist countries do not always show small power distances. The Latin European countries—France, Belgium, Italy, and Spain, plus marginally South Africa—show a combination of large power distances plus individualism. The other wealthy Western countries all combine smaller power distance with individualism. All poor countries are collectivist with larger power distances.

Uncertainty Avoidance

The third dimension is labeled "uncertainty avoidance." The fundamental issue involved here is how society deals with the fact that time runs only one way; that is, we are all caught in the reality of past, present, and future, and we have to live with uncertainty because the future is unknown and always will be. Some societies socialize their members into accepting this uncertainty and not becoming upset by it. People in such societies will tend to accept each day as it comes. They will take risks rather easily. They will not work as hard. They will be relatively tolerant of behavior and opinions different from their own because they do not feel threatened by them. Such societies can be called "weak uncertainty avoidance" societies; they are societies in which people have a natural tendency to feel relatively secure.

Other societies socialize their people into trying to beat the future. Because the future remains essentially unpredictable, in those societies there will be a higher level of anxiety in people, which becomes manifest in greater nervousness, emotionality, and aggressiveness. Such societies, called "strong uncertainty avoidance" societies, also have institutions that try to create security and avoid risk. We can create security in three ways. One is technology, in the broadest sense of the word. Through technology we protect ourselves from the risks of nature and war. We build houses, dikes, power stations, and ICBMs which are meant to give us a feeling of security. The second way of creating security is law, again in the broadest sense of the word. Through laws and all kinds of formal rules and institutions, we protect ourselves from the unpredictability of human behavior. The proliferation of laws and rules implies an intolerance of deviant behaviors and opinions. Where laws cannot be made because the subject is too fuzzy, we can create a feeling of security by the nomination of experts. Experts are people whose word we accept as a kind of law because we assume them to be beyond uncertainty. The third way of creating a feeling of security is religion, once more in the broadest sense of the word. This sense includes secular religions and ideologies, such as Marxism, dogmatic capitalism, or movements that

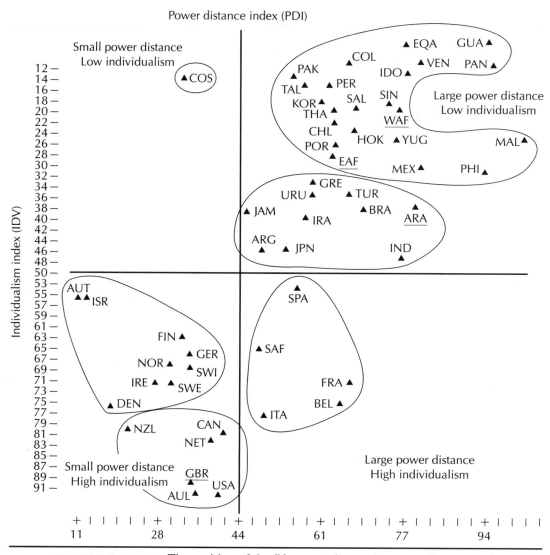

FIGURE 27.3 The position of the fifty countries on the power distance and individualism scales.

preach an escape into meditation. Even science is included. All human societies have their religions in some way or another. All religions, in some way, make uncertainty tolerable, because they all contain a message that is beyond uncertainty, that helps us to accept the uncertainty of today because we interpret experiences in terms of something bigger and more powerful that transcends personal reality. In strongly un-

certainty-avoiding societies we find religions which claim absolute truth and which do not tolerate other religions. We also find in such societies a scientific tradition looking for ultimate, absolute truths, as opposed to a more relativist, empiricist tradition in the weak uncertainty avoidance societies.

The uncertainty avoidance dimension, thus, implies a number of things, from aggressiveness

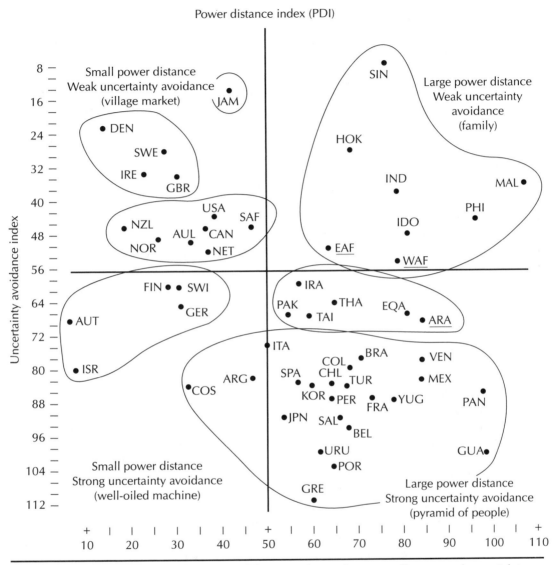

FIGURE 27.4   The position of the fifty countries on the power distance and uncertainty avoidance scales.

to a need for absolute truth, that we do not usually consider as belonging together. They appear to belong together in the logic of culture patterns, but this logic differs from our own daily logic. Without research we would not have found that, on the level of societies, these things go together.

Figure 27.4 plots the uncertainty avoidance index for fifty countries along the vertical axis,

against the power distance index on the horizontal axis. We find several clusters of countries. There is a large cluster of countries with strong uncertainty avoidance and large power distance. They are: all the Latin countries, both Latin European and Latin American; Mediterranean countries, such as Yugoslavia, Greece, and Turkey; and Japan plus Korea.

The Asian countries are found in two clusters with large power distance and medium to weak uncertainty avoidance. Then we find a cluster of German-speaking countries, including Israel and marginally Finland, combining small power distance with medium to strong uncertainty avoidance.

Both small power distance and weak uncertainty avoidance are found in Denmark, Sweden, Great Britain, and Ireland, while the Netherlands, the United States, Norway, and the other Anglo countries are in the middle.

Masculinity-Femininity

The fourth dimension is labeled "masculinity versus femininity." The fundamental issue involved is the division of roles between the sexes in society. All societies have to deal with the basic fact that one half of mankind is female and the other male. The only activities that are strictly determined by the sex of a person are those related to procreation. Men cannot have babies. Human societies, however, through the ages and around the globe, have also associated other roles to men only, or to women only. This is called social, rather than biological, sex role division.

All social role divisions are more or less arbitrary, and what is seen as a typical task for men or for women can vary from one society to the other. We can classify societies on whether they try to minimize or to maximize the social sex role division. Some societies allow both men and women to take many different roles. Others make a sharp division between what men should do and what women should do. In this latter case, the distribution is always such that men take the more assertive and dominant roles and women the more service-oriented and caring roles. I have called those societies with maximized social sex role division "masculine," and those with a relatively small social sex role division "feminine." In masculine societies, the traditional masculine social values permeate the whole society—even the way of thinking of the women. These values include

the importance of showing off, of performing, of achieving something visible, of making money, of "big is beautiful." In more feminine societies, the dominant values—for both men and women—are those more traditionally associated with the feminine role: not showing off, putting relationships with people before money, minding the quality of life and the preservation of the environment, helping others, in particular the weak, and "small is beautiful." In a masculine society, the public hero is the successful achiever, the superman. In a more feminist society, the public sympathy goes to the antihero, the underdog. Individual brilliance in a feminine society is suspect.

Following the procedure used for the other dimensions, each of the fifty countries was given an index score on the masculinity-femininity scale: a high score means a more masculine, a low score a more feminine country. Figure 27.5 plots the masculinity index score horizontally and the uncertainty avoidance index again vertically. The most masculine country is Japan; also quite masculine are the German-speaking countries: Germany, Austria, and Switzerland. Moderately masculine are a number of Latin countries, such as Venezuela, Mexico, and Italy; also the entire cluster of Anglo countries including some of their former colonies: India and the Philippines.

On the far end toward the feminine side we find the four Nordic countries and the Netherlands. Some Latin and Mediterranean countries like Yugoslavia, Chile, Portugal, Spain, and France are moderately feminine.

Some Consequences for Management Theory and Practice

The naive assumption that management is the same or is becoming the same around the world is not tenable in view of these demonstrated differences in national cultures. Consider a few of the ideas about management which have been popularized in the Western literature in the past fifteen years; in particular,

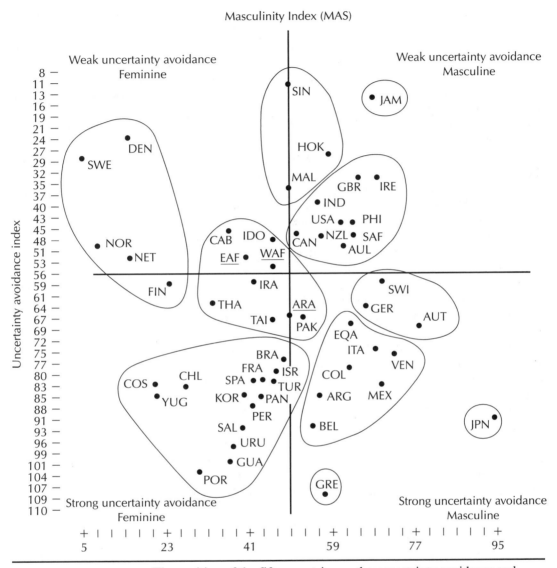

FIGURE 27.5 The position of the fifty countries on the uncertainty avoidance and masculinity scales.

about leadership, about models of organization, and about motivation. These theories were almost without exception made in the United States; in fact, the post–World War II management literature is entirely U.S.-dominated. This reflects the economic importance of the United States during this period, but culturally the United States is just one country among all others, with its particular configuration of cultural values which differs from that of most other countries.

Leadership

The most relevant dimensions for leadership are individualism and power distance. Let us look at Figure 27.3 again. We find the

United States in an extreme position on the individualism scale (50 out of 50) and just below average on the power distance scale (16 out of 50). What does the high individualism score mean? U.S. leadership theories are about leading individuals based on the presumed needs of individuals who seek their ultimate self-interest. For example, the word "duty," which implies obligations toward others or toward society, does not appear at all in the U.S. leadership theories.

Leadership in a collectivist society—basically any Third World country—is a group phenomenon. A working group which is not the same as the natural in-group will have to be made into another in-group in order to be effective. People in these countries are able to bring considerable loyalty to their job, providing they feel that the employer returns the loyalty in the form of protection, just like their natural in-group does.

Let us now look at the power distance dimension, in terms of participative leadership. What does participative leadership U.S. style mean?

Individual subordinates are allowed to participate in the leader's decisions, but these remain the leader's decisions; it is the leader who keeps the initiative. Management prerogatives are very important in the United States. Let us remember that on power distance, the United States is more or less in the middle zone. In countries with higher power distances—such as many Third World countries, but also France and Belgium—individual subordinates as a rule do not want to participate. It is part of their expectations that leaders lead autocratically, and such subordinates will, in fact, by their own behavior make it difficult for leaders to lead in any other way. There is very little participative leadership in France and Belgium. If the society is at the same time collectivist, however, there will be ways by which subordinates in a group can still influence the leader. This applies to all Asian countries.

Let us take some countries on the other side, however: Denmark, Sweden, or Israel. In this case, subordinates will not necessarily wait until their boss takes the initiative to let them participate. They will, for example, support forms of employee codetermination in which either individuals or groups can take initiatives toward management. In these cultures there are no management prerogatives that are automatically accepted; anything a boss does may be challenged by the subordinates. Management privileges in particular are much more easily accepted in the United States than in some of the very low power distance countries. A similar difference is found in the ratios between management compensation and subordinate compensation.

Organization

In organizations the decisive dimensions of culture are power distance and uncertainty avoidance. Organizations are devices to distribute power, and they also serve to avoid uncertainty, to make things predictable. So let us look at Figure 27.4 again. My former colleague, Professor James Stevens from *INSEAD,* once gave the same description of an organizational problem to separate groups of French, West German, and British management students. The problem described a conflict between two departments. The students were asked to determine what was wrong and what should be done to resolve the problem. The French in majority referred the problem to the next higher authority level. The Germans suggested the setting of rules to resolve such problems in the future. The British wanted to improve communications between the two department heads, perhaps by some kind of human relations training. My colleague concluded that the dominant underlying model of an organization for the French was a pyramid, a hierarchical structure held together by the unity of command (larger power distance) as well as by rules (strong uncertainty avoidance). The model for the Germans was a well-oiled machine; the exercise of personal command was largely unnecessary because the rules settled everything (strong uncertainty avoidance, but smaller power distance). The model for the British was a village market: no decisive hierarchy, flexible rules, and a resolution of problems by negotiating (small power distance and weak uncertainty avoidance). These models left one corner in the diagram of Figure 27.4 unexplained, but a discussion with an Indian colleague led me to believe that the underlying model of an organization for the Indians is the family: undisputed personal authority of the father-leader but few formal rules (large power distance and weak uncertainty avoidance). This should also apply in the Chinese culture city-states of Hong Kong and Singapore (see Figure 27.4).

The United States is close to the center of the diagram of Figure 27.4 and so are the Netherlands and Switzerland. This may explain something of the success of U.S., Dutch, and Swiss multinationals in operating in a variety of cultures; in the U.S. literature and practice, all four models of organization—the pyramid, the well-oiled machine, the village market, and the family—can be found, but none of them can be considered dominant.

Motivation

The theories of motivation (what makes people act) and the practices of motivating people can both be related to the individualism-collectivism dimension. In the United States, the highest motivation is supposed to stem from the individuals' need to fulfill their obligations toward themselves. We find terms like "self-actualization" and "self-respect" on the top of the list of motivators. In a more collectivist society, however, people will try primarily to fulfill their obligations toward their in-group. This may be their family, but their collective loyalty may also be directed toward some larger unit: their enterprise, or their country. Such people do not seek self-actualization or self-respect, but they primarily seek "face" in their relationships with in-group members. The importance of face as a motivator does not appear in the U.S. motivation literature at all. The distinction between "face" cultures and

"self-respect" cultures is similar to the distinction between "shame" and "guilt" cultures identified by the anthropologist Ruth Benedict (1974).

Other dimensions relevant to motivation are uncertainty avoidance and masculinity-femininity. Let us look at Figure 27.5 again. The dominant theme of the U.S. literature of the past twenty years is that people are basically motivated by a desire to achieve something. We should, therefore, allow our people to achieve: give them challenge, and enrich their jobs if they do not contain any challenge. The idea of "achievement" and "challenge," U.S. style, implies two things: a willingness to take some risks (weak uncertainty avoidance) and a need to perform, to assert oneself (masculinity). It is therefore no wonder that in the diagram of Figure 27.5 we find the United States in the weak uncertainty avoidance, masculine corner. It shares this position with the other Anglo countries. Let us take the case of some other countries, however: Japan or Germany. These are also masculine countries but with stronger uncertainty avoidance. This means that in these countries there is less willingness to take risks: security is a powerful motivator. People are very willing to perform if they are offered security in exchange. Interestingly, these security-seeking countries seem to have been doing better economically in the past twenty years than the risk takers; but the management theories that tell us that risk taking is a good thing were made in the United States or Great Britain, not in Japan or Germany.

If we go to the other corner of Figure 27.5, we find the Netherlands and the Nordic countries combining weak uncertainty avoidance with a more feminine value system. Here, the maintenance of good interpersonal relations is a strong motivator, and people frown at competition for performance. In these countries we meet a powerful interpersonal motivation which is missing in the U.S. theories. There is a striking difference in the forms of "humanization of work" proposed in the United States and in

Sweden: a stress in the United States on creating possibilities for individual performance, but a stress in Sweden on creating possibilities for interpersonal solidarity. In the fourth corner of Figure 27.5, we find both security and interpersonal motivation; Yugoslav worker self-management contains both elements. We are far away here from the motivation to achieve according to the U.S. style.

Conclusion: The Cultural Relativity of Management and Organization Practices and Theories

Both management practitioners and management theorists over the past eighty years have been blind to the extent to which activities like "management" and "organizing" are culturally dependent. They are culturally dependent because managing and organizing do not consist of making or moving tangible objects, but of manipulating symbols which have meaning to the people who are managed or organized. Because the meaning which we associate with symbols is heavily affected by what we have learned in our family, in our school, in our work environment, and in our society, management and organization are penetrated with culture from the beginning to the end. Practice is usually wiser than theory, and if we see what effective organizations in different cultures have done, we recognize that their leaders did adapt foreign management ideas to local cultural conditions. This happened extremely effectively in Japan, where mainly U.S. management theories were taken over but in an adapted form. This adaptation led to entirely new forms of practice which in the Japanese case were highly successful. An example is the quality control circle, originally based on U.S. impulses but adapted to the Japanese uncertainty-avoiding, semicollectivist environment. The quality control circle has been so effective in Japan that now the Americans are bringing it back to the United States,

but it is doubtful whether most of its present U.S. protagonists realize the role that Japanese educational and social conditions play in the ability of Japanese workers to function effectively in a quality control circle.

Not all other countries have been as fortunate as Japan in that a successful adaptation of American management theories and practices could take place. In Europe but even more often in Third World countries, foreign management methods and ideas were indiscriminately imported as a part of "technology transfer." The evident failure of much of the international development assistance of the 1960s and 1970s is at least partly due to this lack of cultural sensitivity in the transfer of management ideas. It has caused enormous economic losses and human suffering. Free-market capitalism as practiced in the United States, for example, is an idea which is deeply rooted historically and culturally in individualism. "Everybody for himself" is supposed to lead to the highest common good, according to Adam Smith [1970]. If this idea is forced upon a traditionally collectivist society, it means that work organizations will be created which do not offer to employees the protection which they expect to get in exchange for their loyalty. The system itself in such a society breeds disloyal, irresponsible employees. Japan has not taken over this aspect of capitalism and has maintained a much higher level of protection of employees by their organization. Many U.S. managers and politicians have great problems with recognizing that their type of capitalism is culturally unsuitable for a more collectivist society. It is for good cultural reasons that various forms of state capitalism or state socialism are tried in Third World countries.

Most present-day management theories are "ethnocentric," that is, they take the cultural environment of the theorist for granted. What we need is more cultural sensitivity in management theories; we could call the result "organizational anthropology" or "management anthropology." It is unlikely to be the product of one single country's intellectual effort; it needs by definition a synergy between ideas from different sources. The fact that no single country now enjoys a degree of economic dominance as the United States once did will certainly help: economic power is all too often related to intellectual influence. In a world in which economic power is more widely spread, we can more easily hope to recognize truth coming from many sources. In this process, the contribution of Japanese and Chinese scholars, for example, will be vital, because they represent sources of practical wisdom and ideas which complement practices and ideas born in Europe and the United States.

The convergence of management will never come. What we can bring about is an understanding of how the culture in which we grew up and which is dear to us affects our thinking differently from other peoples' thinking, and what this means for the transfer of management practices and theories. What this can also lead to is a better ability to manage intercultural negotiations and multicultural organizations like the United Nations, which are essential for the common survival of us all.

Note

* From the *Journal of International Business Studies* 14, no. 2 (Fall 1983): 75–89, by permission of the author and R. R. Bowker, Inc., for the Academy of International Business and Rutgers University. Copyright 1983 by the Academy of International Business.

References

Benedict, Ruth. 1974 (1946). *The Chrysanthemum and the Sword: Patterns of Japanese Culture.* New York: New American Library, p. 222.

Hofstede, Geert. 1980. *Culture's Consequences: International Differences in Work-Related Values.* Beverly Hills/London: SAGE Publications.

———. 1983. "Dimensions of National Cultures in Fifty Countries and Three Regions." In *Expiscations in Cross-Cultural Psychology,* edited by J. Deregowski, S. Dziurawiec, and R. C. Annis. Lisse, Netherland: Swets and Zeitlinger.

Smith, Adam. 1970 (1776). *The Wealth of Nations.* Harmondsworth, UK: Penguin.

CHAPTER TWENTY-EIGHT

Comparing the Incomparable— Study of Employment Agencies in Five Countries*

Erhard Blankenburg

West European industrial countries are facing similar problems of unemployment, and they have agreed on a common concept of "active labor market policy" as an attempt to fight long-term unemployment. However, the administrative setup to implement this policy is different from one country to another.

This paper reports on some of the results of the comparison of local labor market administration in the Federal Republic of Germany, England, France, Italy, and Sweden. Differences are analyzed as far as legal rules and authority are concerned, and they are followed into the organizational setup of placement services. Results are reported only insofar as this is necessary to give a rationale for the methodological approach of the study. Since there is no correspondence of organizational boundaries of labor market agencies in the respective countries, comparison has to start with task definitions and the analysis of task contingencies. The explanation of national differences lies in a configuration of variables extending beyond the organizational boundaries of labor market administration. In order to integrate explanatory variables, the typological concept of "administrative culture" is introduced.

Because of the incomparabilities of the organizational structures, standardized methods are infeasible. Therefore, the paper argues that the comparison of national institutions should be based on a "methodology of Verstehen."

Object, Methodology, and Paradigmatic Tradition of Cross-Cultural Organizational Comparison

Social science in our age has grown with exponential speed. One of the organizing principles of this growth is that differentiation leads to ever-new specialized fields. Hardly have comparisons of organizations within one cultural context been developed as a subfield of organization sciences, when a new subfield emerges: that of intercultural comparison of organizations. At first glance, it may appear as if "culture" has been introduced as just another variable. But this holds true only as long as intercultural comparisons stay within the methodological and theoretical paradigm of "comparative organizations." This field has assembled a specific set of methods from the traditions of business administration, sociopsychology and sociology, and developed a limited number of research questions. The emergence of a field of "intercultural comparison of organizations" stays within this consensus on object and methodology of organizational research as long as "culture" is treated as just another variable. If the concept of "organization" is conceived in formal terms irrespective of historical patterns and task contingencies, very little variance is likely to be found in the "cultural" variable.

Continuing such paradigmatic traditions into intercultural comparisons, the question is asked whether generalizations found in a number of organizations in one country hold true in others as well. While most comparative organizational studies have been developed in a culturally homogeneous environment, comparison across countries now tests whether the generalization of such studies holds true in different cultural environments. Thus, one may ask whether the achievement motive of managers in steel companies in India is as pronounced as that in Australia or the United States. Or, one may ask whether there are more levels of hierarchy in the French factory than can be found in Great Britain or Germany. Such studies fit into the paradigmatic tradition of sociopsychological or sociological research on organizations trying to arrive at generalizations about "how organizations work." Here research follows the operationalization of formal characteristics with an attempt to formulate these at a level so general as to be applicable to a large variety of organizations. The result will tell whether standardized indicators of behavior patterns of formal organizational characteristics undergo cultural variation or not. "Culture" in this understanding is reduced to a variable in a set of standardized indicators, as they have been developed in a culturally homogeneous environment (largely in the Anglo-Saxon tradition of instrumental pragmatism).

It should not be surprising that such research disproves that much cultural variation exists (England and Negandhi, 1979). Such a finding is the result of a specific set of methods and a limited number of research questions. If we compare steel factories in different countries, and translate achievement scales into another language, we might indeed find behavior regularities across countries. However, this is due to the imitation of technology as well as the limited scope of reality which we measure by our indicators. What is specific about different "cultures" is largely outside of the differences regarded by formal explanatory models.

Cultural differences might be such that the units of analysis have to be defined differently for each country; that standardized indicators do not fit into other cultural contexts; and that the meanings of questionnaire responses vary with language and traditions (Brossard and Maurice, 1976).

Therefore, this study does not follow the paradigmatic tradition of studies in "comparative organizations." Many of these studies treat organizations as boundary-defined entities. This is not a self-evident assumption since the boundaries of an organization are very often not clearly marked. The persons who are included on the payroll might not be identical with those in the organization chart. Different goal orientations might lead to a number of subdivisions and overlaps. Changing task descriptions might shift the boundary of an organization altogether. The ambiguity of boundary definitions might be less in economic organizations, where production goals are relatively well defined. This study, however, looks at agencies of public administration, which derive their authority from complex legal prescriptions. Here the goals of agencies are very often multifunctional. The boundaries might be different from one country to another; what is called an "employment agency" in one country, might be under the authority of several agencies in another. Many agencies in the government bureaucracy are part of a chain of decisions and implementation processes with rather complicated legal boundary definitions. Therefore, they can much better be understood as part of "organizational networks" which as a whole fulfill the tasks which we want to study.

Our organization comparison therefore starts with an analytical definition of its units of analysis. How this definition is arrived at is a consequence of the goals of the study: as we are trying to explain the implementation process of "labor market policy," we chose a functional definition of a certain set of tasks, and then tried to find the agencies which are responsible for them. Analytically, the focus is on "task contingencies" rather than on formal organizational contingencies. This approach enables us to better grasp the contextual quality of what "culture" is about.

In this paper we do not try to give a comprehensive summary of the study of labor administration. Rather, we want to develop the reasons for a methodological approach to cross-cultural comparison away from established explanatory paradigms. As has already been outlined, the analysis starts with the tasks of labor administrations and its contingencies. We then compare the different institutional arrangements, concentrating here on the placement activities and on three of the five nations compared. The summary fashion in which this is presented is meant to give an exemplification of the methodological approach. The analytical concepts which developed from the comparison are then outlined.

This attempt at not following established explanatory models has consequences on the methodology (which are outlined in the concluding remarks). The restrictions of using only those variables which allow for standardized operationalization are not accepted. Therefore a descriptive approach in trying to discover a wide range of data is used. The attempt to describe complex configurations which make "culture" distinguishable leads to description rather than measurement; the number of characteristics to be taken into consideration at the same time leads to a methodology of discovery rather than to one of testing theories.

Organizational Study of Implementation

There have been a number of studies of employment agencies at the local level. These include the classical studies by Blau (1955) and Francis (1956). Both studies criticized models of formal organizations, such as the ideal-type construction of Max Weber's "bureaucracy." Both studies analyzed interactions among placement officials as well as their encounters with

the agencies' clients. The behavior patterns found were labeled as informal organizations and they led to an incorporation of behavioral data into general models of bureaucracy. This might be called a process of "paradigmatic enrichment" as any model-building involves a selection of variables from complex reality; every critique of such models will follow the path of enriching them. Both studies developed aspects of a general theory of organization. Their conceptual level is so general as to be applicable to all bureaucratic organizations in general. Blau explicitly states, in his methodological epilogue, that he initially intended to study a set of different organizations but problems of access happened to lead to a study of employment agencies.

In a later study of Blau and Schönherr (1971) the process of paradigmatic reduction which followed can be observed. Trying to formulate a general theory of the structure of organizations, Blau and Schönherr followed the standards of scientific measurement. They used structural variables as their main indicators which can be coded from organization charts, thus reducing their reality to formal characteristics. The tasks of the organizations under comparison are mentioned only as a matter of courtesy. The analysis aims at general conclusions about organizational size, structural differentiation, and decentralization irrespective of what organizations do and with which environment they interact.

Studies of interaction of employment agencies with what we call core actors form another extension of the paradigmatic limits of what is operationalized as the structure of organizations. Schmidt and Kochan (1976) do not accept placement agencies as organizationally bounded to be their unit of analysis. Rather, they take exchanges between employment services and employers as units of their analysis. Aldrich (1976) uses frequency of interaction as a measurement to define a more inclusive unit of analysis which he calls organizational network. These studies still reduce reality in taking "interaction" rather formally, and in not giving much information on the characteristics of the units at both ends of interaction. Nevertheless, these studies are nearer to the type of problem definition which is needed in cross-national research, because they do not take organizational boundaries as self-evident, but rather define them according to task definitions and interaction patterns.

In a study of this type, organizations have different task descriptions from one country to another. The tasks and scope of authority of a German *Arbeitsamt* includes processing unemployment claims as well as placement and job counseling; these are located in different agencies in England, France, and Sweden. Training facilities, which are at the core of labor market policy, are organized privately according to the subsidiary principle in Germany; they are integrated into the general school system and intrafirm training in Sweden; they are organized as a unitary, centralized service in France; and there is an attempt to organize them similarly in England. Thus, the unit of analysis of comparison is an analytical construction. It is defined by a set of tasks which are the basis for labor market policy. Thus, we start by defining these tasks, then stating general task contingencies of labor market policy in order to finally compare the different solutions which national administrations choose in order to overcome them.

This does not imply taking employment agencies as purely instrumental. Organizations are instrumental as one facet among many, such as trying to survive, maintaining the support of staff and of environmental forces, and pursuing long-term and short-term goals. Introducing "policy implementation" as the explanandum of this study, we cannot be satisfied by measuring a few output indicators. Policy definitions are complex in nature: they contain general statements of intent on a very abstract, sometimes symbolic level; they might be operationalized in terms of political programs, always including standards for the performance of routine tasks as well as goals for special measures. Only by looking at the combined effect of the different tasks which employment agencies perform can we understand the way labor market policy is implemented.

A Cross-Cultural Study of Employment Agencies

Employment agencies are peculiar among public administration institutions in that they have to mediate more than they can govern. Since their task is to achieve a match between the supply and demand for labor, they have simultaneously two types of clients with partly opposing interests: job seekers and employers. This explains some of the contingencies of labor administration. Its penetration of labor markets is only partial and its means of implementation are rendering services and providing subsidies rather than making authoritative and binding decisions. Employment agencies act in an interorganizational network where their policy is determined by general economic conditions and the climate of industrial relations.

Limitations on the effectiveness of labor market policies, which stem from the contingencies of employment agencies, can hardly be overcome by political "fiat." Nevertheless, politicians have raised their expectation of labor administration due to the pressure of unemployment problems. With economic and technological change in western industrial societies proceeding at a rapid pace, all European countries are experiencing a rise in unemployment independent of the business cycles. This has had long-term effects. During the 1960s and early 1970s (before the recession following 1973), European countries provided their labor market administrations with increased power to interfere in the labor market. The formulation of a policy normatively labeled "active labor market policy" was stimulated and coordinated by OECD experts. Comparisons of the measures of labor market policies used in northern European countries show that the OECD exchange of their international "mandarins" led to highly congruent policy recommendations.

All countries which took part in this mutual imitation process introduced major changes in their administrative structures. Some countries (like France and England) built up new, autonomous organizations separate from the traditional agencies of the department of labor. Some (like Germany and Sweden) shifted the goals and capacities of their traditional administrative structures. A comparison in these four countries—some results of which are reported here—analyzes the implementation of institutional change on a local level. A parallel project is being undertaken in Italy, where the traditional pattern of the labor bureaucracy (relative style, combining unemployment insurance and bureaucratic placement procedures) still prevails.

Conceptually, the study starts out with task contingencies of labor market policy and the resulting limits to labor market administration. The next step is to define the actors in the field. In a comparative study, this can be done only by functionally defining the boundaries of the policy system. Those agencies are defined as *core actors* which provide placement services, unemployment insurance, further training and target programs for improving the labor market structure. *Relevant actors* are those with whom the core agencies have to interact continuously in order to achieve their goals. As one of the contingencies of this policy field is high interdependence with employers, trade unions and local government, all countries have some sort of institutionalized participation by relevant actors in the management of labor market agencies.

In this study, representatives of core actors and relevant actors were interviewed about their perception of labor market problems, their own goals and the goals of the other actors. As information in such interviews is complex, they cannot be standardized interviews. Interpretation has to take into consideration the gaps between the formulation of abstract goals and actual activities. In addition, the different interviewees may have different perceptions of the same problem. By confronting them, the re-

searchers are trying to interpret formal structures as well as informal relations.

The study's findings show that, despite the congruent policy statements and the similar goals of labor market agencies in the 1960s, actual implementation has led to quite different administrative structures. Intra-agency traditions, as well as institutional differences in the relevant environment, lead to a number of national differences. Analyses of these differences, however, can only be undertaken on the level of descriptions. When comparing (five) cases of organizational change, quantification does not seem to be appropriate. Rigid measurement of indicators which could be used in all countries alike would lead to a substantive loss in information. Therefore, the aim is analytical description, making use of a case study approach and a rather pragmatic compromise between comparative intention and adaptation to the peculiarities of each national case. This leads to a methodological point with theoretical consequences. Comparing functionally equivalent institutions cross-nationally has to take into account what one might call "national administrative cultures," a typological label for dealing simultaneously with more variables than we have cases to compare.

The Concept of "Active Labor Market Policy"

The term "active labor market policy" has been a very successful label, even though its meaning has been manifold and often not spelled out at all. In 1964, the OECD Manpower and Social Affairs Committee formulated its "Recommendation on an Active Manpower Policy" which suggested the following means of implementation:

1. Offering retraining and further training for those skills which became obsolete by production changes and sectorial changes in the economy;
2. Offering subsidies for regional mobility to move the labor force from backward regions to those of high labor demand;
3. Integrating handicapped groups into the labor force;

4. Reintegrating women into the labor force; and
5. Providing for higher mobility of capital to areas where a supply of labor can be found.

It is quite obvious that this program was aimed at a situation with a generally high level of employment, and with a small, but hard core of unemployed. These could not easily be placed in jobs in their regions or with the qualifications they offered. In those days, the general demand for labor was high, so the main tasks of labor policy were to activate labor market resources and to reduce the mismatch of demand and supply on the labor market by encouraging mobility. Under such favorable conditions, labor market problems were somewhat marginal to the issues of day-to-day policies. Full employment has been a favorable condition for concepts of "active labor market policies" to be designed. There was a consensus about the goal of full employment: there was a shared understanding that the main obstacles were to be found in maladaptations of demand and supply in the labor market; and there was a coordinated set of means of implementation to meet these problems by increasing the mobility of the workforce across regional, sectorial, and occupational skill barriers. The term "active" emphasizes two aspects of its general philosophy: that labor market policy should no longer leave market mechanisms to themselves as the classical "human capital" approach to manpower policy would have done, and that labor administration should no longer see its role in merely reacting to changes on the labor market, but rather seek to "actively" monitor such changes in a desired direction.

However, the 1960s were a time of limited labor market problems and a time of basic optimism in many policy fields. This caused politicians to create an expectation level as high as is indicated by the label "active labor market policy." The impact of their Zeitgeist becomes apparent if we look at the parliamentary debates which accompany the passing of the Labor Promotion Act (AFG) in the Federal Republic of Germany in 1969. These debates were praised to the effect that through an "active labor market policy" the goal of full employment was very near to being realized. Unemployment risks, at that time, were seen as resulting solely from imbalances of labor markets by regions and by economic sectors. Matching job seekers to existing vacancies was the main problem rather than the creation of jobs. This optimism was based on fifteen years of experience with overall high employment and demand for foreign labor, which was only clouded by regional development problems and crises in individual sectors such as unemployment resulting from the decline of mining in the Ruhr-area. The very mild recession in 1967–68 led only to a temporary rise in unemployment figures and stabilized the optimistic mood even more.

Six years later, labor market problems changed completely. A worldwide recession following the oil crisis in 1973 showed that any labor market policy is limited as soon as global demand is lacking. But even if the priority is placed on general economic policy and its effect on the level of employment, recent experience casts doubt on the effectiveness of existing methods of implementing policy with respect to matching the supply of labor over the long term with the qualification criteria of its demand. Today, job creation is in operation and at the same time there are job offers which cannot be filled. Plans for further training are being put into effect at the same time as some of the most highly trained individuals, that is, academics, are threatened by unemployment. Thus, we now are faced with problems of global demand, as well as with problems of change in the structures of labor demand and supply. Labor market problems have increased to a degree which had not been foreseen by legislators at the end of the 1960s.

Even if the expectations of labor market policy in the late 1960s are now regarded as having been unrealistically high, the use of the concepts of "active labor market policy" can nevertheless be seen as a remarkable success story. In a number of countries, among them Germany, France, and England, a process of major organizational changes was enacted. While in Germany this was done by revising the statutes and enlarging the existing National Labor Agency, in France and in the United Kingdom a new institutional infrastructure was built. Due to the common stimulus of the OECD Committee on Manpower Policy (which was then headed by Gösta Rehn from Sweden), there is a high similarity of the guidelines for this process of organizational change. Its main postulates are:

1. Increasing the penetration rate of placement by labor administration, and getting away from the "dole" image of unemployment benefit offices;
2. Improving statistical information about and scientific services for ongoing changes and future trends in labor market developments;
3. Empowering administrative bodies to implement measures for guiding labor market developments such as further training/retraining, mobility inducements, job creation, and so forth; and
4. Integrating conflicting social interests into the administrative setup by offering trade unions, as well as employer organizations, some forms of participation.

Based on the experiences of Swedish labor market policy, which had been formed along these lines in 1949, the German *Bundesanstalt für Arbeit* revised and enlarged its administrative setup; the *Agence Nationale pour l'Emploi* in France was founded in 1967 and took over the former unemployment administration; and the English Manpower Services Commission was founded in 1973 taking over the placement services of the Department of Labor and changing its setup completely.

In all cases a strategy of organizational change was followed. In some countries this was done by founding new institutions, in others by changing the laws, regulations, and organizations from within. There was a constant information exchange about the developments in the other countries, communications being provided by the OECD and by direct links. But, in each of the cases, the institutional result of this reform movement took a different shape. With basically similar concepts in mind and the same means of implementation at hand, the labor market administration in each country was shaped by legal and political tradition and by the strategy of organizational change chosen.

Contingencies of Labor Market Policy

From the period of the 1960s (when the institutional infrastructure of "active labor market policy" was designed) to the 1970s (when it was put into operation) the scope of labor market problems has changed considerably. The rapid environmental change is one of the contingencies faced by all the labor market administrations. This is due to two major reasons. Labor market policy, more than other policy fields, is characterized by constant and very quick changes in the scope of problems and in the feasibility of measures. Questioning labor agencies about their current main concerns leads to an enormous variety of regional differentiation; half a year later the researcher might be faced with a complete change in priorities in the targets of administrative action. This is one of the features of labor market policy; that its problems vary not only according to local conditions but also within short time periods. The best "policy" in such a situation must be to create an infrastructure of agencies and options for action which can react in a flexible way. In such a policy field, legal regulations can provide authority for measures, but they should leave open when and to what degree that authority is used.

Such a task description does not fit into the traditional thinking of administrators, who perceive themselves as simply executing directives while the responsibility for their underlying policy rests with the legislative bodies. Labor policy needs institutions which can handle political decisions within the framework of general goals rather than an executing body which implements clearly prescribed operations. Its administration therefore needs a high degree of discretion in determining whether and when to use the means of implementation available to it. The use of such discretion presupposes a constant flow of information on current labor market developments. Therefore, information gathering forms a considerable part of the work of all labor administration. Central evaluation facilities are a necessary tool of labor market policy.

Labor market developments are also highly dependent on general economic policy. Any decision in the national or regional economy affects labor market problems, and very often such effects are felt more strongly than any action undertaken explicitly under the label "labor market policy." On the national level, labor market problems derive from the fluctuations of global demand. On the regional level, the maintenance of existing jobs and the creation of new ones are the major determinants of the scope of labor market problems, but neither keeping nor attracting industries is within the scope of influence of labor administrations.

Placement activities and the impact of administrative actions only partly penetrate labor markets. Most labor mobility takes place without the aid of administrative agencies, because:

1. On internal labor markets within big firms, internal careers and firm-run training programs are offered, especially for further training;
2. On segmented job markets specialized search procedures are used to obtain highly skilled and professional employees. The higher the skill level needed for a job, the scarcer such a skill is on the labor market and the more likely it is that placement will be handled outside of the public agencies; and
3. On all labor markets, for all skill levels, informal search procedures, advertising, and other direct attempts are used to fill jobs.

Even though it is true that in all countries a sifting out of jobs and job seekers occurs, leaving the less desirable to the public agencies, there are differences in the degree of penetration of labor markets by different placement agencies. There are differences, too, in the degree of involvement of labor market administration in the politics of maintaining and creating jobs. Starting from an analysis of their traditional tasks, hypotheses need to be formulated as to which of the institutional setups is

most apt to overcome the contingent limitations of employment administration.

Typology of Employment Administration Tasks

There are marked differences from country to country in whether and how the different tasks of employment administration are distributed over several institutions. In all countries, the employment administration includes the traditional tasks of making regulations and processing unemployment insurance claims and it is centered around the services of placing people into jobs. To these traditional tasks the objectives of an active labor market policy, such as furthering occupational mobility, maintaining and creating workplaces are related. Thus, we have to include regulatory, service-oriented, and goal-oriented activities as the core of employment administration.

Unemployment Insurance

Traditionally, labor administrations were predominantly institutions for handling the unemployed and processing insurance claims. Whenever there is much unemployment, this task is of primary importance; in times of full employment, personnel capacities are free for other tasks. Handling claims for unemployment benefits is an activity governed by rules and burdened by paperwork. As with any insurance, the prerequisites for a claim have to be checked, the amount of the claim has to be computed, payments have to be handled, and the main prerequisite (that of being unemployed) has to be continuously checked. Handling such claims is *regulation-oriented* and is handled by a strict legal program.

Regulatory Tasks vis-à-vis Employers

In some countries (like France and Italy) labor inspectors are perceived as being a part of labor administration. Labor inspectors have to survey all laws applicable to employers regarding safety regulations, minimum working conditions, employment restrictions, and so on. A similar *regulatory orientation* is involved in the process of granting loan subsidies, apprentice subsidies, and so forth, in almost all countries. Even if its powers are generally considered to be very weak, labor administration is found to have a norm-control task in the studies of all countries.

Mediating Tasks

One of the prerequisites to claim unemployment benefits is that the claimant be a job seeker and be willing to accept any adequate job which is offered. While related to regulatory decisions discussed above, this is a situation which is basically service- and client-oriented; matching job seekers to existing job offers requires a consulting situation where neither side withholds information for tactical reasons. Placement, as well as job counseling, make up a large part of the activity of labor market agencies and can best be dealt with in a supportive atmosphere with a minimum of legal regulations.

Policy Tasks

Within the same administrative frame, goal-oriented instruments have to be applied: facilities for training and retraining have to be set up; jobs for the handicapped have to be created; relief work and subsidized positions have to be organized. Such policy-implementing tasks are clearly related to placement and to the information gathered by registering the unemployed. Training and retraining proposals can be the result of unsuccessful placement attempts. Job creation measures or loan subsidies can be the result of having too many long-term benefit claimants. If unemployment is high, placement and counseling activities can aim at reducing the workforce by discouraging marginal workers. In times of full employment attempts may focus on activating potential members of the labor force. Any such measures are dependent on information obtained from unemployment and placement statistics, and are implemented in placement and job counseling. The policy, however, is determined on a more

general level as a result of negotiating with potential employers and mobilizing financial resources.

In the German case, all three administrative activities are combined within one administrative agency. In Sweden, insurance tasks are separated from client-oriented and goal-oriented activities while the means for accomplishing the latter is wider than in any other country. In France and England, all three activities are handled by separate organizations which operate in close cooperation. In all countries these *core actors* are linked by relationships—partly formal, partly informal—to trade unions, chambers of commerce, employers' associations, local governments and regional administrative bodies. This environment of *relevant actor* relationships is more important the more we get into policy-oriented activities. Providing places for further training and retraining, creating workplaces, and providing apprenticeships for the young are activities of vital importance for an active labor market policy, but these activities transcend the authority of administrative core actors; thus the dependence on cooperation with a wide range of relevant actors.

Apart from the limitation of authority on a horizontal basis, local labor market administration faces a number of national and regional interdependencies. Here again, boundaries are defined by interpreting the perceptions of actors. It is useful to distinguish three "games" in which labor market policy is involved.

Game I is the national level of formulating overall goals which are related to general fiscal and economic policy. All countries which explicitly aim at a more active labor market policy (that is, four of the countries being studied, Italy being the exception) have a separate administrative body outside of the federal ministries which acts as the top hierarchical level of employment administration; its offices on the local level are under bureaucratic control. However, in some countries, the core actors are

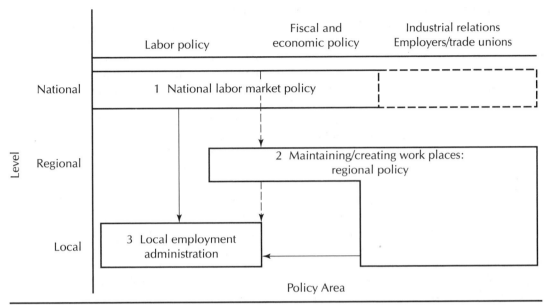

FIGURE 28.1

dispersed over separate organizations with separate agencies and independent lines of hierarchy. Nevertheless, in all cases employers and trade unions exert a strong influence on labor market policy.

The network of relevant actors is repeated on the local level. Trade unions and employers' organizations, regional and local government, schools and training institutions all belong to the set of actors in local labor market policy. Local networks, however, are very often too limited in size to plan and implement strategies for industrial settlements and commercial development. Thus, a number of links are imbedded in a regional network referred to here as "Game II." From the viewpoint of local actors, Game II is mainly concerned with creating and maintaining jobs. A number of persons are present in more than one game, very often the boundaries between games are not distinct. Employment administrations as well as interest groups are institutionalized on all three levels with predominantly hierarchical patterns of communication within each of their own setups.

Institutional Arrangement of the Placement Situation

Nobody would assume that the level of unemployment in a country could be explained by the methods and quality of placement services of the employment agencies. However, it is certainly observable that under high unemployment the behavior patterns of placement agencies are different from those during times of full employment. One must ignore the differences in the level of employment in order to better serve the purpose of comparing institutional arrangements. The focus is on the national differences in the institutional arrangements of placement which are independent of the employment situation. In the following section placement procedures are compared in England, Italy, and the Federal Republic of Germany. Data on Sweden and France are left out because these would lead to a detailed discussion of national peculiarities of employment administrations. We here describe only parts of the data in three countries and to the extent necessary for showing how much variance national administrative cultures show in spite of the task contingencies outlined above. The differences analyzed are a result of legal and administrative traditions, the characteristics of which recur in other public administrations in these countries.

Italy

Placement in Italy is governed by strict legal regulations which date back to the fascist laws of 1938, and were not significantly changed (in 1949) following the war. They require that placement in any job be solely under the control of the public labor administration. Except for the cases excluded by law, all placement has to be carried out by public administration which is bound by rules designed to provide a nondiscriminatory, strictly legal treatment. Job seekers are placed according to their qualifications when they register with the employment administration. They are also assigned a priority for placement which can be changed according to social criteria (the number of children, exceptional need, etc.). Following these ranks, job seekers are assigned to the next employer, who has previously registered his need for labor. Further restrictions are the result of labor protection laws. Dismissals are governed by legal restrictions, while trade unions seek to preserve the status quo of employment in their firms. Even if dismissals for economic reasons were legally possible, the trade unions would react to any such attempts by going on strike. Therefore, employers complain that neither reducing the number of jobs nor dismissing any workers holding a job in their firm is possible. The only exception is that new employees do not have to be kept if after the first month it becomes apparent that their qualifications do not meet the requirements of the job.

There is no doubt that legal regulations directly restrict the employers' alternatives. However, a number of informal practices allow them to succeed in gaining some leeway. The employer may seek a number of unskilled workers through advertisement. These persons, who are hired for short-term employment, are recruited from outside neighboring regions and they are not registered with the local employment agency. After learning something about their qualifications, the employer recommends to those whom he wants to keep on the job that they register with the local employment agency for a particular certification. Then he asks the agency for placement of the desired number of workers, indicating that they are desired for "confidential jobs," under which condition he is allowed to name specific people to fill the jobs. As a result, the administration does not raise any objections to hiring "confidential personnel" because they are glad to have any placement.

Another form of circumventing the ranks set by the placement administration is by calling for qualifications which are rarely available. For example, a machine operator with good knowledge of Rumanian can be requested. Since this combination of skills is very rare, somebody who meets the requirement will bypass all other machine operators who have been ranked on the list. (Since academic unemployment is rising, this usage has become risky, however. Often students are clever enough to meet even extraordinary qualification criteria, and can thus spoil the arrangements between employers and certain job seekers. In such cases, the student who is placed usually takes the job for a month, and then the original game may be repeated).

Big firms have another way of avoiding the risk involved by taking workers based on their ranks on the lists. By law, small firms with up to three employed persons may hire people without consulting placement services. Big firms therefore subcontract with a greater number of small firms and, after a certain period of subcontracting they are allowed to take their labor into the firm. Since this way of circumventing the law was used to a considerable extent, it was restricted in 1970 by requiring a clearance certificate for taking labor from small firms into bigger firms. However, the labor administration rarely withholds such a clearance, as this would cause conflicts not only with some of the powerful employers, but with the workers holding jobs as well.

In a strictly regulated system, the placement situation reduces client contacts by the placement agent to a minimum. Decisions are made on the basis of written forms, the allocation of job is carried out with lists in a bureaucratic manner. Client contacts are reduced to the calling up of persons to be placed and to the allocation of vacancies. An important role for handling conflicts which might arise and for correcting the output of this bureaucratic placement process lies with an administrative board at the local employment agency. Here employers' associations and trade unions, as well as administration representatives, discuss complaints. This provides informal means for the rank order to be changed. It enables job seekers to increase their chances for placement without having an arrangement with one of the employers. Members of the board favor their clientele, be this on the basis of family relations, or by affiliation to trade unions, church, or political parties.

It was not difficult for our interviewer to get interviewees to talk about the informal ways of circumventing the bureaucratic and legal rules of the placement administration. In general, employers as well as trade unionists and even administrators share the perception that the legally prescribed system "cannot work" and that an attempt to implement it strictly would lead to a further reduction of mobility and to an even lower employment level. The attitude toward the administrative system of placement is fatalistic and clever at the same time—there is a general accusation of the inflexibility to the address of the political system which cannot be changed. On the level of personal interaction, ever-new ways of circumventing the system are found.

The Federal Republic of Germany

In the Federal Republic of Germany, public agencies have a placement monopoly as well; only the employment administration is allowed to run placement activities on a continuous basis, and exceptions have to be authorized by the national employment agency. However, this does by no means prevent employers from looking for labor on their own initiative, either by informal recruitment or by public advertisement. It is not even mandatory to register any new employment contracts with the labor administration, a condition which makes it hard to guess to what degree the labor administration is actually involved in influencing labor mobility. Employment administration, according to the goals of active labor market policy, tries to increase its penetration rate and can only do so by making its services attractive enough to induce employers and job seekers to use them voluntarily. This rise in the penetration rate of labor markets has been achieved by employment agencies in the previous years. This is due partly to a higher level of unemployment, which has involved all levels of qualifications, and partly to public relations attempts to get away from the image of an "administration for unemployment compensation." Nevertheless, the majority of employers interviewed still share the perception that employment agencies offer rather unqualified workers and that those who are placed by the administration are not the most able ones. Correspondingly, job seekers feel that being placed by the employment administration might be seen as an indication of inferior ability, so they consider it preferable to find a job by other means.

These disadvantages of the "dole" image are reinforced by the combination of placement activities and decisions on unemployment compensation within one administrative agency. If a placement agent offers a job to an unemployed person, and if the person refuses the job without giving good reasons, his unemployment compensation may be canceled or temporarily discontinued. The decision depends on an evaluation of whether the job offered is adequate and the conditions are acceptable. It is up to the discretion of the placement officer to judge whether job seekers can be considered as being willing to work.

The placement officers in the German placement administration exert considerable power over job seekers who claim unemployment compensation. Furthermore, placement is organized in a way which maximizes the delimiting power of the placement agent. Each agent is assigned an area of responsibility based on qualifications, for which he administers a file where vacancies as well as job seekers are registered. He is the only person who has access to information both on the qualifications needed and offered. The ranking of candidates for placement is determined by his own judgment of whether and to what extent the two sides match. As a result, a placement agent may indicate to an employer, for example, that he "might have to pay a little more" in order to get a qualified person or that a high turnover "might be due to certain deficiencies in the labor conditions." Similarly, he can put pressure on job seekers to change their expectations by declaring that "the desired kind of position" or "that a certain salary level" is "not available anywhere." Implicit in such mediation is the threat that a placement might not be feasible under certain desired conditions; for the unemployed this includes the potential reprisal of withholding unemployment compensation.

In the description of the placement situation it is important to remember that the disciplinary power of the officer toward employers is minimal compared to that toward the job seekers. It is significant that contact to employers occurs usually by telephone, while job seekers have to pay personal visits to the placement office. While matching information from both sides the placement agent has a considerable delimiting power, he has no authority to compel any party to sign an employment contract. Decisions on contracts remain with employers and job seekers; the role of the placement agent is strictly one of mediation.

The consolidation of information in one person means that the agency has to divide labor by defining the authority of each agent based on specific qualifications and economic sectors. The consequence is that within the agency the service provided to white-collar and blue-collar workers differs. Furthermore, in spite of many qualifications cutting across economic sectors, they may end up in the files of only one agent. For example, there may be vacancies for car drivers in different sectors, but as vacancies are scarce, each agent keeps those he receives to himself. The overall effect—due to the specialization of placement officers by qualification—is a decrease of potential mobility across sectors. A special problem arises in the placement of unqualified young people, as they have no previous classification and thus fall under the authority of a specialized youth placement officer. However, he does not have a continuous clientele of employers and thus depends on colleagues to provide him with a share of vacancies. Thus, the consolidation of mediation in one person and the consequent division of labor according to qualifications and economic sectors increases the difficulties in integrating newcomers into the labor force.

England

The dysfunctions of the "mediating monopoly" have led many countries to introduce self-service into the general placement activity. Trying to reach a higher level of mobility in the labor market, the Manpower Services Commission in the United Kingdom increased the availability of access and decreased some of the barriers. Local employment agencies were decentralized and access was eased by introducing "job shops" where vacancies are openly displayed. The shops can be entered easily and can be left without any embarrassment. If the job seeker finds a vacancy he is interested in, he can get the address at a placement agency nearby. Usually the agent checks with a telephone call to the employer whether the opening still exists and this provides an opportunity for a minimum of mediating interaction. If a job seeker's situation is more complicated, or if he wants to register as unemployed, he is sent to a "second tier," a personalized placement service. Here placement interaction comparable to that of a German *Arbeitsamt* is possible. The agent, however, does not have his own file of vacancies, but can only consult a central file for the entire office. This seems to be an unavoidable consequence of the self-service model; registration of vacancies is separated from placement and there is a special division which files the qualification criteria of vacancies and forwards these to the self-service and the personalized placement offices, and sometimes even to job shops in the neighborhood as well. Service is oriented toward processing vacancies as rapidly and widely as possible without an individual placement officer gaining first priority on a new vacancy. Only positions requiring very specialized qualifications or vacancies which have been set aside for disabled job seekers are excluded from this open availability of information.

In England there is no monopoly on placement for public administration. Certain occupations (such as office personnel) are handled through private placement agencies, which display their offers in openly accessible shops similar to those in the public sector. There is also competition in some parts of the labor market, even among separate public agencies. For example, besides job shops there is a separate organization called "Careers" which provides counseling and placement service for persons leaving school. Competition for the scarce vacancies is demonstrated by the attempts of both agencies to market vacancies and to stimulate employers to create jobs and training positions. It is doubtful whether such activities increase the overall demand for labor, but they do increase the speed of announcing vacancies because there are several agencies trying to register them "before the others get a hold of them."

A certain amount of further competition arises between the job shops and a specialized public agency, entitled "Professional and Exec-

utive Register" (PER), which caters to professionals and executives. This is a specialized part of the public employment administration for job seekers with higher qualifications. The separation of qualifications is not always clear—there is an overlap of medium-level positions which could be registered by a job shop as well as by PER. Registration for unemployment compensation should be done, however, at only one of these organizations, which gives rise not only to competition but also to conflicts in jurisdiction. PER charges a fee of a month's salary from employers, which is about half the price of commercial agencies. The orientation of PER officials, however, is influenced very much by the motive of at least covering the costs of the services. Being primarily interested in placement success, they place the better-qualified first, in order to keep employers from consulting other agencies. In their orientation, if not in their actions, general employment services give more consideration to social conditions. Disabled and needy job seekers would never have a chance if the pressure for successful placement were increased by the motive of covering the costs of the agency.

In England (as everywhere) the legal claim for unemployment compensation depends on the unemployed person's being available for employment. However, the processing of forms and payments is under the authority of a separate agency, the "benefit offices." The prerequisite for compensation is registration with the employment services, and "no objection" with respect to availability. However, in reality, objections due to "unavailability" are rarely made. This cannot be ascribed solely to the separation of placement and unemployment insurance, for even in a single agency like the German *Arbeitsamt* there is a similar role separation between the placement officer who gives his evaluation, and a separate division which implements the nonpayment of benefits. The permissive practice in English employment administration seems to be rooted mainly in the orientation of placement agents who, in contrast to their German colleagues, do not like to use the power of reprisal which is available to them, and who do not perceive themselves as public officials using their authority. It would be hard to differentiate between the effects of organizational separation and of the ideological orientation of agents. The remarkable fact is that they correspond in being more permissive in England, and more authority-oriented in Germany.

Analytical Criteria for Comparison

Observation of the institutional arrangements of job placement and its operational link to unemployment insurance shows the central and traditional tasks of employment administration. To these, more and more policy tasks have been added. Expectations of politicians as to the range of goals which should be achieved by employment administration largely neglected the relative lack of power which the mediating situation creates for the employment agents. Under the market conditions of unemployment, vacancies are scarce. Thus, inducing employers with incentives and good service to use the facilities offered is the main way to increase the administration's mediating authority. Also, to a limited degree, sanctioning power can be used by withholding payments of permits.

After characterizing the institutional arrangements of regulatory and service-oriented tasks, we can now proceed to the analysis of policy goals. It is on the basis of routine activities that the administration has to develop policy-oriented activity. Structural conditions for performing policy tasks vary as much as the institutional arrangements of placement services do. Here, many of the traditional concepts of organizational sociology help in the analysis. However, this does not imply adopting the operationalization which is common for these concepts. Having defined the unit of analysis by comparable tasks forces us to seek new operationalizations for these concepts. The standardized measurement of organizational variables very often leads to a point that cannot be

strictly compared. By finding the reasons for these incomparabilities we discover the essential aspects in the cultural comparison of institutions.

Decentralization versus Centralization

It is not astonishing that a great deal of organizational literature is concerned with the issue of centralization and decentralization. It is one of the recurring problems of intra-agency disputes about organizational design. In a comparison of agencies in different countries the issue becomes more complex, because the boundaries of organizational tasks are not uniformly defined. In addition to differences about centralization of control versus local autonomy and the incorporation of tasks within one organization, there are different ways to attribute these tasks to the individual administration agencies. The regional extension of labor markets varies with scarcity and level of qualifications, while professional and executive jobs usually require a large degree of regional mobility. Thus, part of the placement activities need a national exchange of information, and part of them can be satisfied in local labor market regions.

The same holds true for the difficult tasks centering around maintaining and creating workplaces. Industrial location decisions certainly consider the basic economic conditions which cannot be influenced by regional incentives. Local authorities tend to compete for investors by offering similar favors and incentives, and, in the course of negotiations, they often withhold information for tactical reasons. Local employment administration in most countries does not participate in this game. Being part of a hierarchy of national agencies limits their activity in industrial settlement. It is of secondary importance compared to that of local governments, chambers of commerce, and regional political bodies. Employment administrators could only then participate in this game if they became part of the local power structure.

Confronted with the alternative of giving authority to administrators to integrate economic settlement policies and considerations of employment structure into the local policy networks, or to have a separate employment agency with rather narrow tasks but nationally integrated policies, none of the five countries under comparison chose the first alternative of local autonomy and of a decentralized broad range of competence.

There is a feedback, however, because decentralized data gathering caters to the centralized decision-making process. Data on the employment level, on employment structures, and on mobility, are gathered by the local administrative agencies in all European countries. This statistical information is forwarded along hierarchical channels and evaluated by central agencies. Their policy recommendations and guidelines are based on the data of the individual employment agencies and on scientific research. These guidelines are then fed back down the hierarchy of control. However, universal as this model may be in general terms, the pattern of central coordination differs very much according to the range of competence and uniformity of employment services. Unemployment insurance, for example, is linked to a separate chain of organizational control as is the case in France and Sweden; it has recently been separated at the local and regional level in England; and is part of the encompassing service in Germany and Italy. Special policy targets such as relief work or youth unemployment programs in England are delegated to separate task force organizations with field offices of their own besides those of the general employment administration; they are pursued by regional offices in France and from there more closely linked to the local political game than to the employment administration on the local level; they are tightly integrated into the day-to-day placement operations of the Swedish agencies; and the German administration leaves parts of the special policy measures with regional offices and has decentralized other parts to the local level, keeping them organizationally separated from placement activities. Without going into further details a general point concerning comparability should be made: the allocation of tasks varies along vertical and along horizontal lines, and with these the boundaries vary of what is nationally regarded as the core of the employment administration. The degree of centralization and decentralization can be different with regard to different tasks, thus forming complex patterns which, as a whole, should be compared.

The challenge for coordination of employment policies is too great for any one organization to master. Not only should there be an integration of economic, fiscal, educational, and employment policies, but also of the diverging needs for coordination on national, regional, and local levels. In the cases studied here this matrix of coordination has been recognized at the national policy level, with more or less fragmented structures at the local level.

Patterns of Organizational Control

The description of placement in Germany and Italy has served as an example of how bureaucratic activity is controlled by legal regulations. As we have seen, there is a plausible correlation between the attempt to control the abuse of unemployment insurance and the concentration of placement information on the desks of placement agents. This attempt prevents the German and Italian administration from introducing self-service into placement (in contrast to the three others). Again, the attempt to control is correlated to the degree of legalistic prescription, but with remarkable differences between German and Italian administration. How can a high degree of legalism be made compatible with policy tasks? The German AFG may serve as an example. It does not leave much discretion to the administration to decide on the policy relevance of further training measures, for example. While, in Italy, legalism implies the absence of goal-oriented activities of employment administrations, the German *Bundesanstalt für Arbeit* formulates its policy in the form of laws, regulations, and continuous amendments thereof. The labor promotion act (AFG = *Arbeitsförderungsgesetz*) is an encompassing codification of organization and policy measures of employment administration. Every member of the unemployment insurance has the right to claim a subsidization of further training. The agencies are therefore legally bound, if the individual prerequisites are given. This is not directly a consequence of the text of the law which prescribes that a claim for subsidization can be made, if the further training measure is considered "in accordance with improving the chances of the applicant on the job market." While this general clause would leave some discretion in less legally oriented cultures, German courts ruled in a number of cases that rejection of a claim for further training has to be very well founded in order to be legally sustained. Thus, the indicator for the degree of legal binding has to include the handling of legal rules on the level of administrator as well as on the level of the interpretation.

Strict binding of administration by legal regulations causes problems of flexibility in a rapidly changing task environment. This is demonstrated by the greater number of amendments which the AFG underwent since having been enacted eight years ago. Less legalized bureaucracies adapt to task changes by issuing guidelines or allocating funds within the administrative hierarchy. Clearly this increases the speed of adaptation. The degree of legalism can then be measured by finding the level at which the rules for recurring activities and the decisions for special policy measures are made. However, the concept of "levels" can be attached to quite different meanings according to the legal culture of the respective country. Institutional alternatives may perform equivalent tasks, legal terminology may hide actual behavior patterns. Therefore, measurement of legalism has to be validated by several related indicators, such as "amount of procedural rules," and the "degree of precision of binding rules versus discretion."

One of the functional alternatives to legal rules are central administration guidelines. They are formulated at the national level and forwarded to the local employment agencies. In Germany, in addition to the legal prescriptions, guidelines are so numerous and detailed as to fill a bookcase in the office of a placement agent. Standard letters suggesting a polite form of addressing clients, and even the amount of time to be spent on the counseling of each client are prescribed in detail. It is not astonishing that many of the placement agents become disoriented in the mass of prescriptions and their constant amendments, and finally tend to neglect many of them altogether.

Studying an administration in only one country normally provides some data of internal control for the researcher to work with. On cross-national comparison, however, these often do not match from one country to another. Again, the German case shall serve as an illustration. When new guidelines are issued, reports on their implementation are fed back to the national offices, preparing future adaptations of guidelines with respect to their feasibility. These hierarchical feedback mechanisms provide some data on the performance of the German administration. However, there are no equivalent performance indicators available in other countries which would make cross-national comparisons possible. While in the German labor administration the individual agent's performance can be measured by the number of his successful placements, the self-service section of English, Swedish, and French labor administrations does not allow for such statistics because there is no way of accounting for placements actually made with the help of the services.

These examples illustrate that it is rarely possible to compare the same type of decisions across all five countries. If only those indicators are used for which there are comparable data in all countries, the major cultural characteristics of the control patterns in each of the administrations under study might be missed. In the light of the incomparabilities of national traditions, different indicators often have to be used from one case to another, in order not to miss the essentials of cultural differences altogether.

Organizational Networks

The employment administrations serve two types of clients with partly opposing interests. Collective bargaining and labor disputes engage them in one of the most crucial organized conflicts of society. Therefore, being dependent on a complex political environment, employment agencies gain some autonomy from general administration. At the same time they attempt to establish institutional links with trade unions and employers' associations as these are the most powerful organizations in their political environment. The major variable for the feasibility of such participation is the degree of cooperation in industrial relations. In some countries (like Italy, France, and England) institutionalized participation is restricted to the national level and is mainly concerned with policy recommendations. In Germany, tripartite boards exist at the national, regional, and local level, and have the authority to accept or reject guidelines at the national level, to pass the budget, and to control personnel decisions at each level. The competence of these boards is not restricted to controlling the management of agencies. It could rather be described as a quasi-legislative body making management decisions. At the local level the range of budgetary and personnel decisions is limited by the framework which is given within the hierarchical setup of the administrative structure. The activity of local boards varies from one agency to the next; regular meetings take place about four times a year. As could be expected, agency heads present their management proposals generally without giving alternatives. They use their boards for legitimizing decisions, and they use board members as multiplicators in order to get collaboration with the interest organizations of their clients.

While the German system of management by participation involves participation bodies only in decisions on the agencies' general policies, Swedish administration uses a model of participation at the operational level. In addition to boards for general policy recommendations, the interaction of the agency with its environment takes place by placement agents. Department heads participate in personnel decisions of big employers, in training schools, and in regional policy committees. Operational participation works best with bigger firms which have a separate personnel department and, thus, a bureaucratic counterpart for designing a coherent employment policy. Here the administrative agents take part in consultations on decisions about the employment structure, about dismissals and the creation of workplaces. Legal means, like prescribing a certain structure of employment, are rarely used. In most cases, participation itself leads to mutual information and agreement on general employment decisions. The difference of participation at the operational level can best be exemplified with respect to the integration of the disabled into the labor force. While in Germany there is a legal prescription on the percentage of disabled persons to be employed (which can be lowered by paying a certain sum for any such workplace), the Swedish model of participation institutionalizes "adaptation groups" in bigger firms in which management, labor unions, and employment administration are represented. They look into the possibilities of creating workplaces for disabled persons and work out firm-specific plans for such employment. Participation is used as a functional equivalent to legal rulings, being much nearer to operational feasibility, more flexible for matching workplace offers to local needs, and more informative, thus giving administration better means of control.

In the countries compared, employment agencies generally try to establish institutional participation of their relevant environment. Linking the activities of an employment administration to its environment can be seen as one of the contingencies of an administration which is mainly mediating between two types of clients. The forms of such organizational networks, however, vary with the degree of social contact in the conflict between trade unions and employers. What the term "organizational network" means is something quite different in each of the five administrations studied.

This again leads to the point that a specific feature of employment administrations can only be understood by putting it into the context of wider cultural data. The organization which trade unions follow and the degree of cooperation in industrial relations determine the limits and the possibilities of employment administrations to integrate their policies with those of their political environment. The data which enter into the comparison of the relations among the core actors of employment administrations, as well as their relations with relevant actors of their environments, are so manifold that one cannot do more than describe them and give plausible explanations for the elements of which each national configuration is composed.

Verstehen as a Method for Comparing the Incomparable

We have been talking of understanding patterns and configurations which can be described as administrative culture. This outline does not present all of the findings. Rather, it demonstrates the kind of results desired: which features of the context of societal institutions are relevant for the way in which employment administration is set up; and the way employment administrations implement what is labeled as "active labor market policy." To answer these questions we first had to elaborate on the task contingencies which are inherent in what labor market policy wants to achieve: mediating between two types of clients; adapting to changing employment situations; performing bureaucratic tasks such as the red tape of unemployment insurance together with more client-oriented tasks such as counseling and placing job seekers. These contingencies limit

the possibilities of employment administration in meeting the expectations which policymakers raised when formulating the goals of an active labor market policy.

However, in spite of the features of employment administration which are contingent on their tasks, there are great differences between the different European countries in the way administration is set up. In order to describe these differences fairly unstandardized methods were used. Even when comparing agencies in one country, there might be some questions concerning the validity of indicators (for example, the critique of using indicators for hierarchical levels which Argyris [1972] put forward). These difficulties are increased if cross-national comparisons are attempted. Societal meaning of hierarchical levels can be so different that a comparison of such formal indicators might lead into understanding different cultures, but would mislead if results are interpreted without taking configurative variables into consideration (Brossard and Maurice, 1976). In this study one step further toward incomparability has been taken. With regard to policy goals and their implementations, functional equivalents which can only be understood in the context of a structural configuration, called administrative culture, have been considered.

When talking of "culture" (in analogy to "political culture" as used by Almond and Verba [1963]) typologies for comparison are used. While Almond and Verba relied on surveys which at least guarantee a comparable data basis, and while they interpret attitudes and behavior patterns which uniformly relate to individuals as unit of analysis, the use of the term "culture" in this paper refers to a configuration of institutions and to the laws and links which rule their interactions. The range of authority of an organization was found to be culture-bound, just as the way agencies are directed by political programs and environmental pressures, the degree of their legalistic orientation, the range of their discretionary power, and their patterns of intraorganizational control. The term "administrative culture" in employment agencies includes their relations to relevant actors such as trade unions, employers, local government, and regional planning. Employment administration is dependent on the way labor relations are constituted in a country and these change with the type of trade union which prevails. Administrative culture is a term summarizing patterns of behavior and configurations of societal institutions.

What is an adequate method to use in the study of administrative culture? Structural configurations can be described; their relation to the implementation to policy goals can be made plausible, but they cannot be measured in any strict sense. The methods used here for data gathering have been analyses of policy statements, organization charts, and internal documents. These, given some knowledge of formal organizational structures, were used in order to design focused interviews, which were aiming at reconstructing the self-perception of the actors in the field of study. Not even the samples of persons to be interviewed could be standardized. As the number and competence of institutions concerned varies from one country to another, our researchers had to follow the task descriptions of what was analytically defined as "employment administration," and had to identify the core actors as well as those of the relevant environments with the "snowball-technique" of the reputational method.

Our interviews aimed at reconstructing the logic of action in which the actors see themselves (Crozier and Friedberg, 1977). Such information can be contradictory. The self-perceptions of interviewees are not always consistent, nor do they always fit together. Contradictions and different perceptions from the point of view of different actors are ubiquitous elements of any institutional configuration. Understanding culture implies understanding the contradictions which it entails. Thus, understanding means more than just following the information given by interviewees. It includes the confrontation of different points of view, making contradictions "meaningful"

from the point of view of an outside analyst. For comparison, a further step is needed. Some heuristic device is needed in order to distinguish relevant data for the description of what makes for the national differences of administrative cultures from irrelevant data. The descriptive data were ordered along the lines of analytical criteria such as "patterns of centralization," "patterns of control," and "patterns of linkage with relevant organizations of the environment."

Trying to understand such configurational structures in several countries leads to case studies as a basis for comparison. The number of variables which is necessary to describe these configurations will always be bigger than the number of cases to be compared. Epistemologically, administrative cultures are singular events. They form unique configurations. Certainly, in characterizing such configurations analytical criteria of general applicability such as can be tested in deductive-nomological models of explanation are used. But we resist standardization of their measurement, as the use of standardized indicators would overly restrict the reality we want to focus on.

It could be argued that such an understanding of culture is the first step for designing more strictly comparable research. It is a necessary step. Only if proceedings are free from measurement technology will we be able to discover which features are relevant for cultural comparison. If we put these into a testable "model," we will again have to reduce reality to indicators which can be measured in a standardized way. The more standardized, the more comparison is narrowed down. The more complex the concept of culture gets, the more we have to reconstruct the logic of a system using what one might call a methodology of *verstehen*. This methodological paradigm is not to be confounded with the "operation" of "verstehen." Abel (1948) criticized that understanding does not add to our store of knowledge, but rather "consists of the application of knowledge already validated by personal experience." However, used as a method of successive steps in describing and comparing, each of the many operations of *verstehen* in the course of an accumulative process of research adds to our knowledge and to the validity of our concept of "culture."

Note

* From *Organizational Functioning in a Cross-Cultural Perspective,* edited by George W. England, Anan R. Negandhi, and Bernard Wilpert (Kent, OH: Kent State University Press, 1979), 273–97 by permission of the author and Kent State University Press, for the Comparative Administration Research Institute. Copyright 1979 by Kent State University Press.

References

Abel, Theodore. 1948. "The Operation Called *Verstehen*." *American Journal of Sociology* 54:211–18.

Aldrich, Howard. 1976. "Resource Dependence and Interorganizational Relation." *Administration and Society* 4:419–53.

Almond, Gabriel, and Sidney Verba. 1963. *The Civic Culture.* Princeton: Princeton University Press.

Argyris, Chris. 1974. *The Applicability of Organizational Sociology.* London: Cambridge University Press.

Blau, Peter. 1955. *The Dynamics of Bureaucracy.* Chicago: University of Chicago Press.

Blau, Peter, and Richard Schönherr. 1971. *The Structure of Organizations.* New York and London: Basic Books.

Brossard, Michel, and Marc Maurice. 1976. "Is There a Universal Model of Organizational Structure?" *International Journal of Sociology* 6:41–75.

Crozier, Michel, and Erhard Friedberg. 1977. *L'Acteur et le Systeme.* Paris: Éditions de Seuil.

England, George, and Anant Negandhi. 1979. *National Context and Technology as Determinants of Employer's Perceptions.* Kent, OH: Kent State University Press.

Francis, R. G. 1956. *Service and Procedure in Bureaucracy.* Minneapolis, Minn.: University of Minnesota.

Schmidt, Stuart, and Thomas Kochan. 1976. "An Application of a 'Political Economy' Approach to Effectiveness." *Administration and Society* 4:455–73.

Politics

Comparative politics, in the context of sociology, centers on the analysis of the social institutions involved in the political process. These institutions are nearly all-encompassing, and thus in this brief introduction the breadth of the topic cannot be sufficiently addressed. Unquestionably, culture plays a major role in shaping the character of political institutions, but this model must compete with others which stress economic and class interest, and the differential distribution of power internal and external to any polity.

Today, the world faces an unusual configuration of political positioning in that over half the world's nations are enjoying or actively striving to develop democratic political structures. Whether this condition will endure remains, of course, to be seen. Sociologists and political scientists now have an unprecedented opportunity to explore the many and varied cultural expressions of democracy, and to seek explanations for this exceptional rise to prominence of a single political form.

Our first selection, by Gabriel A. Almond and Sidney Verba, is from a study that has become a classic, influencing a generation and more of detailed research in politics. It presents "profiles and illustrative case histories," through a "configurative and clinical method of exposition," of five countries' "political cultures." Italy is described as an alienated political culture characterized by social isolation and distrust; Mexico as one of alienation and aspiration; Germany as having the most aware and

well-informed but passive and formal political culture, with a degree of hostility prevailing between its political parties. The United States and Great Britain are both described as "civic cultures," though the former has "participant" as a qualifier, while the latter has "deferential" as a qualifier (i.e., deferential to the independent authority of the government).

In our second selection, Seymour Martin Lipset's 1993 presidential address to the American Sociological Association, Lipset revisits his earlier work and describes in very contemporary terms the so-called third wave of democracy, in which democratic political systems have suddenly found themselves nearly in the majority worldwide. Lipset explores this phenomenon in terms of the cultural and economic variables that act as factors and processes affecting the prospects for democracy.

Our last selection is the work of S. N. Eisenstadt, another scholar of great eminence in comparative studies. In this historical sociological essay he describes and analyzes in some detail the necessary conditions for the outbreak of revolutions. Some of these include interelite and interclass struggles, new social groups and economic forces that are denied access to power, and economic turbulence. How these conditions will produce their effects, however, will depend on the specific historical circumstances, such as a period of early modernity, as well as on the *context* of civilizational premises, and of extant political regimes and economies.

CHAPTER TWENTY-NINE

Five Political Cultures*

Gabriel A. Almond and Sidney Verba

In [our book *The Civil Culture*], we presented our data dimension by dimension. We began with knowledge and awareness of the various aspects of government and politics in our five countries; then we turned to political emotion and involvement, the sense of political obligation and competence, and social attitudes and experiences in other authority contexts that might have effects on political attitudes. Our concern was, not only to describe differences among our countries, but to discern what relations existed among these attitude dimensions.

An analytical procedure such as this tends to obscure the wholeness of individual countries and the reality of the human beings who constitute them. We turn now to a configurative and clinical method of exposition, presenting summary country profiles and illustrative case histories. For each nation we shall briefly summarize the pattern of attitudes found. In the next chapter we shall attempt to relate these patterns of attitudes to a theory of the functioning of democratic government. The cases of individual respondents are, like all individual cases, unique; and they do not lend themselves easily to generalization. They are presented here as illustrations of patterns of attitudes analyzed in other chapters in our book.

Italy: An Alienated Political Culture

The picture of Italian political culture that has emerged from our data is one of relatively unrelieved political alienation and of social isolation and distrust. The Italians are particularly low in national pride, in moderate and open partisanship, in the acknowledgment of the obligation to take an active part in local community affairs, in the sense of competence to join with others in situations of political stress, in their choice of social forms of leisure-time activity, and in their confidence in the social environment.

If we consider Italian political history, these tendencies are not surprising. Before unification Italy had experienced centuries of fragmentation and external tyranny in which allegiant subject and citizen could not develop. In the brief century of her national history Italians have learned to associate nationalism with humiliation, and constitutionalism and democracy with ineffectiveness. Her liberating experiences—the risorgimento and the resistance to Fascism in World War II—were incomplete and deeply divisive in their effects. Thus Italians tend to look upon government and politics as unpredictable and threatening forces, and not as social institutions amenable to their influence. The political culture of Italy does not support a stable and effective democratic system; but these characteristics are quite understandable in the light of her political history.[1]

We may add two more features to this description of the Italian political culture. Italian national and political alienation rests on social alienation. If our data are correct, most Italians view the social environment as full of threat and danger. Thus the social fabric sustains neither an allegiant political culture nor an allegiant pattern of political participation. And perhaps as sobering is the fact that the Italians are the most traditional of our five peoples in their attitudes toward family participation. The norms of the patriarchal family still persist among a large proportion of Italians. Though the younger age-groups have experienced participatory family socialization patterns more frequently than have the older groups, these differences between generations are of a smaller order than in the United States, Britain, and Germany.

The striking economic improvements in recent years in Italy hold out some prospect of changes in social structure and political culture. Rapid industrial development will certainly weaken traditionalism, and rising standards of living, assuming equitable distribution, may increase social trust and confidence in the political system. But the present pattern is of a predominantly alienated political culture.

This alienation may or may not be accompanied by belief in some revolutionary alternative to the present Italian political system. Italian Communists may, by our definition, be viewed as participants: they are aware of and involved in politics and they have an active sense of their own political competence—this despite the fact that they would cease being participants in the same sense if their political party came into power. This is also true of the supporters of the Fascist right, insofar as they take an active part in public affairs. It is paradoxical that the majority of politically involved and informed Italians are opposed to the contemporary constitutional and democratic regime, and that the bulk of the support for this regime comes from Italians who are oriented as subjects or as parochials. Italy's largest political party, from which her governments have been drawn since World War II, rests in considerable part on the votes of politically uninvolved Catholic women.

Mexico: Alienation and Aspiration

What have been most striking in the Mexican pattern of political culture are the imbalances and inconsistencies. Mexico is lowest of all five countries in the frequency with which impact and significance are attributed to government and in its citizens' expectations of equal and considerate treatment at the hands of the bureaucracy and police. At the same time, the frequency with which Mexicans express pride in their political system is considerably higher than that of the Germans or Italians. And the objects of this pride tend predominantly to be the Mexican Revolution and the presidency. Furthermore, what sense of participation there is appears to be relatively independent of a sense of satisfaction with governmental output. Those Mexicans with a high sense of subjective competence are no more likely than those with low competence to evaluate specific governmental performance favorably, though they are more likely to express general system affect. In Mexico, then, participant orientation appears to have outrun subject orientation, and the role of participant tends to be isolated from a sense of allegiance in the subject sense.

Much of this isolation and imbalance may be explained by Mexican political history. Before 1910 the Mexican political system was primarily an exploitative, extractive one. Prerevolutionary parochialism was based on tradition; more, it represented a protective reaction against an exploitative central regime, and against predatory local chieftains and guerrilla bands. Thus historical experience and personal memory sustain an alienation from governmental authority, and these specific memories are consistent with contemporary authority trends in the various institutions of Mexican society.

The Mexican Revolution of 1910 represented a break with the past, for the government began to affect the population materially and favorably. But corruption and authoritarianism persist. The result, according to Scott, is an ambivalence in authority reactions. Mexicans have had direct experience with bureaucratic authority, and they reject that authority as corrupt and arbitrary. At the same time, there exists the myth of the benign Revolution and *presidencialismo,* the institutional charisma that the Mexican presidency has acquired in recent decades.[2]

There is another striking inconsistency in the Mexican data: high frequencies in subjective political competence are coupled with the lowest frequencies of all five countries in political performance (as measured by political information scores, voluntary association membership, and political activity). On the one hand, Mexicans have been exposed to a revolutionary ideology that places a high value on political participation. Exposure to these norms may create a tendency toward overestimating the competence of the self; a tendency to confuse aspiration with performance. On the other hand, the high rate of social mobility in Mexico, the discontinuous patterns of socialization associated with it, and the value conflicts that result from it create a high incidence of personal-identity crises comparable to the situation described by Pye in his Burmese study.[3] The personality aspects of this mobility are value conflict and a fragile self-esteem that typically produces over- and underestimation of the self. This may account for the inconsistency in Mexican responses: high self-appraisal of competence, coupled with cognitive inadequacy and political inexperience.

Nevertheless, these civic aspirational tendencies in Mexican political culture are important evidence that the democratic aspiration of the Mexican Revolution and the political elite is meaningful to the population. The norms have begun to take root among large numbers of Mexicans. And increasingly the Mexican political system offers opportunities for political experience that may begin to consolidate these aspirations.

Germany: Political Detachment and Subject Competence

Germany is a technologically advanced nation with a highly developed and widespread educational and communications system. It had a bitter and traumatic political history before the founding of the present republic: a hu-

miliating defeat in World War I, an abortive experiment in democracy, the Nazi dictatorship, the devastation and national division at the end of World War II. Both her technological advance and her traumatic history are reflected in Germany's political culture.

The high level of development in the communications and educational fields is reflected in the fact that most Germans are aware of and well informed about politics and government. In a number of ways they take part in the political system. The frequency of voting is high, as is the belief that voting is an important responsibility of the ordinary man. And their level of exposure to political material in the mass media of communications is high. Furthermore, German political culture is characterized by a high level of confidence in the administrative branches of government and a strong sense of competence in dealing with them.

Yet the contemporary political culture also reflects Germany's traumatic political history. Awareness of politics and political activity, though substantial, tend to be passive and formal. Voting is frequent, but more informal means of political involvement, particularly political discussion and the forming of political groups, are more limited. Germans are often members of voluntary associations, but rarely active within them. And norms favoring active political participation are not well developed. Many Germans assume that the act of voting is all that is required of a citizen. And Germany is the only nation of the five studied in which a sense of administrative competence occurs more frequently than a sense of political competence. Thus, though there is a high level of cognitive competence, the orientation to the political system is still relatively passive—the orientation of the subject rather than of the participant.

Germany's traumatic political history affects other important characteristics of the political culture. Though there is relatively widespread satisfaction with political output, this is not matched by more general system affect. Germans tend to be satisfied with the performance of their government, but to lack a more general attachment to the system on the symbolic level. Theirs is a highly pragmatic—probably overpragmatic—orientation to the political system; as if the intense commitment to political movements that characterized Germany under Weimar and the Nazi era is now being balanced by a detached, practical, and almost cynical attitude toward politics. And the attitudes of the German citizen to his fellow political actors are probably also colored by the country's political history. Hostility between the supporters of the two large parties is still relatively high and is not tempered by any general social norms of trust and confidence. And the ability of Germans to cooperate politically also appears to have serious limitations.

The United States: A Participant Civic Culture

The pattern of political culture found in the United States approximates what we have labeled the civic culture. There are several significant components of this cultural pattern. In the first place, the role of the participant is highly developed and widespread. As our data show, respondents in the United States, compared with those in the other four nations, are very frequently exposed to politics. They report political discussion and involvement in political affairs, a sense of obligation to take an active part in the community, and a sense of competence to influence the government. They are frequently active members of voluntary associations. Furthermore, they tend to be affectively involved in the political system: they report emotional involvement during political campaigns, and they have a high degree of pride in the political system. And their attachment to the political system includes both generalized system affect as well as satisfaction with specific governmental performance.

The civic culture, though, is a mixed and incorporative culture. The participant role is highly developed, but the more passive roles of subject and parochial persist, and are fused with the political system. That these other orientations temper the performance of the participant role can be shown by the fact that primary affiliations are important in setting the political style of participation in the United States. They are both an influence resource, providing individuals with what we have called a reserve of influence, and an important link in the political communications process. Moreover, the ability to cooperate with one's fellow citizens, which the use of informal groups as a political resource reflects, appears to depend upon a more general social trust and confidence that permeate the political system. This social trust is also seen in the "open" pattern of partisanship in the United States. Though there is emotional involvement in the outcome of elections, this does not mean complete rejection of one's political opponent.

The civic culture, then, is characterized by balance among the parochial, subject, and participant roles. But though the American political culture comes close to this balance, the data suggest that there is some imbalance in the direction of the participant role . . . Participant orientation in the United States appears better developed than subject orientation and to some extent dominates it. Subject competence seems to depend upon political competence; those Americans who feel competent in bureaucratic authority contexts are likely to be those who feel competent in political contexts. In the specific measures of subject competence—expectations of consideration by bureaucratic and police authority—the Americans drop to third place among our five countries, below Britain and Germany. This cultural imbalance, we have suggested, is the result of American historical experience with governmental and bureaucratic authority—an experience that began with distrust and revolution against the British Crown, and that has been consolidated by the American tendency to subject all governmental institutions, including the judiciary and bureaucracy, to direct popular control.

Great Britain: A Deferential Civic Culture

The political culture in Great Britain also approximates the civic culture. The participant role is highly developed. Exposure to politics, interest, involvement, and a sense of competence are relatively high. There are norms supporting political activity, as well as emotional involvement in elections and system affect. And the attachment to the system is a balanced one: there is general system pride as well as satisfaction with specific governmental performance.

Furthermore, the British political culture, like the American, fuses parochial and subject roles with the role of participant. Primary groups are relatively open to the political process and available as influence resources, and the political culture is permeated by more general attitudes of social trust and confidence. Open patterns of partisanship predominate. To some extent, the British political culture represents a more effective combination of the subject and participant roles. . . . The development of the participant orientation in Britain did not challenge and replace the more deferential subject orientations, as was the tendency in the United States. Despite the spread of political competence and participant orientations, the British have maintained a strong deference to the independent authority of government. Thus the British political culture, like the American, approximates the balanced civic culture; but the balance is weighted somewhat differently from that in the United States. If in the latter country there tends to be too much weight placed on the participant role, in Britain the deferential subject role is more strongly developed and widespread.

Notes

* From *The Civic Culture: Political Attitudes and Democracy in Five Nations,* by Gabriel Almond, and Sidney Verba (Princeton, NJ: Princeton University Press, 1963), 402–3, 414–15, 429, 440–41, 455–56, by permission of the Princeton University Press. Copyright 1963 and renewed 1991 by Princeton University Press.

1. For a detailed discussion of Italian political culture, see the study of Joseph G. La Palombara, *Interest Groups in Italian Politics,* Princeton, NJ: Princeton University Press, 1964: 103–125.

2. Robert E. Scott, *The Modernization of Political Culture in Mexico,* a paper prepared for the Summer Institute on Political Systems and Political Development, Committee on Comparative Politics, Social Science Research Council, 1962. On the basis of social psychological and anthropological studies, Scott argues that the majority of Mexicans are oriented to the political system as subjects. But the Mexican subject orientation is ambivalent: it is characterized by both strong dependency needs and rejective and rebellious tendencies. Scott describes this ambivalence as one that pervades all authority relations in Mexican society—family, school, work group, and governmental-political system. The authority syndrome involves an exploitative and dominative exercise of power by those in authority positions, and a rebellious-dependency reaction by those in subordinate roles.

3. Lucian W. Pye, *Politics, Personality, and Nation Building: Burma's Search for Identity,* New Haven, CT: Yale University Press, 1962.

CHAPTER THIRTY

The Social Requisites of Democracy Revisited*

Seymour Martin Lipset†

The recent expansion of democracy, what Huntington (1991) has called "the third wave," began in the mid-1970s in southern Europe. Then, in the early and mid-1980s, it spread to Latin America and to Asian countries like Korea, Thailand, and the Philippines, and then in the late 1980s and early 1990s to Eastern Europe, the Soviet Union and parts of sub-Saharan Africa. Not long ago, the overwhelming majority of the members of the United Nations had authoritarian systems. As of the end of 1993, over half, 107 out of 186 countries, have competitive elections and various guarantees of political and individual rights—that is more than twice the number two decades earlier in 1970 (Karatnycky 1994:6; *Freedom Review* 1993:3–4, 10). Democracy is weakest in Islamic countries (where, as I will discuss later, few nations are democratic) and in parts of Africa. However, though not fully democratic, "more than 30 African countries are in the process of transition from an authoritarian civilian or military government to one that is more pluralistic" (Schneidman 1992:1; Diamond 1992b:38–39; Diamond, 1993b:3–4). The move toward democracy is not a simple one. Countries that previously have had authoritarian regimes may find it difficult to set up a legitimate democratic system, since their traditions and beliefs may be incompatible with the workings of democracy.

In his classic work *Capitalism, Socialism, and Democracy,* Schumpeter (1950) defined democracy as "that institutional arrangement for arriving at political decisions in which individuals acquire the power to decide by means of a competitive struggle for the people's vote"

(p. 250).[1] This definition is quite broad and my discussion here cannot hope to investigate it exhaustively.[2] Instead, I focus here on such things as cultural and economic variables, the debate about electoral systems, constitutional arrangements (e.g., presidents versus parliaments), the importance of a participatory civil society, and the methods through which political parties should be structured to set up and maintain stability—in short, the factors and processes affecting the prospects for the institutionalization of democracy.

How Does Democracy Arise?
Politics in Impoverished Countries

In discussing democracy, I want to clarify my biases and assumptions at the outset. I agree with the basic concerns of the Founding Fathers of the United States—that government, a powerful state, is to be feared (or suspected, to use the lawyer's term), and that it is necessary to find means to control governments through checks and balances. In our time, as economists have documented, this has been particularly evident in low-income nations. The "Kuznets curve" (Kuznets 1955; 1963; 1976), although still debated, indicates that when a less developed nation starts to grow and urbanize, income distribution worsens, but then becomes more equitable as the economy industrializes (Olson 1963; Weede and Tiefenbach 1981; Todaro 1981:134; Bollen and Jackman 1985b; Muller 1988; Chan 1989; Weede 1993).[3] Before development, the class income structure resembles an elongated pyramid, very fat at the bottom, narrowing or thin toward the middle and top (Lipset 1981:51). Under such conditions, the state is a major, usually *the* most important, source of capital, income, power, and status. This is particularly true in statist systems, but also characterizes many so-called free-market economies. For a person or governing body to be willing to give up control because of an election outcome is astonishing behavior, not normal, not on the surface a "rational choice," particularly in new, less stable, less legitimate polities.

Marx frequently noted that intense inequality is associated with scarcity, and therefore that socialism, which he believed would be an egalitarian and democratic system with a politically weak state, could only occur under conditions of abundance (Marx 1958:8–9). To try to move toward socialism under conditions of material scarcity would result in sociological abortions and in repression. The Communists proved him correct. Weffort (1992), a Brazilian scholar of democracy, has argued strongly that, although "the political equality of citizens . . . is . . . possible in societies marked by a high degree of [economic] inequality," the contradiction between political and economic inequality "opens the field for tensions, institutional distortions, instability, and recurrent violence . . . [and may prevent] the consolidation of democracy" (p. 22). Contemporary social scientists find that greater affluence and higher rates of well-being have been correlated with the presence of democratic institutions (Lipset, Seong, and Torres 1993:156–58; see also Diamond 1992a). Beyond the impact of national wealth and economic stratification, contemporary social scientists also agree with Tocqueville's analysis, that social equality, perceived as equality of status and respect for individuals regardless of economic condition, is highly conducive for democracy (Tocqueville 1976: vol. 2, 162–216; Lipset 1981:439– 50; Dahl 1971:85–104; Sartori 1987:343–45; Dogan 1988:11–12). But as Weffort (1992) emphasized, "such a 'minimal' social condition is absent from many new democracies, . . . [which can] help to explain

these countries' typical democratic instability" (p. 18).

The Economy and the Polity

In the nineteenth century, many political theorists noted the relationship between a market economy and democracy (Lipset 1992:2). As Glassman (1991) has documented, "Marxists, classical capitalist economists, even monarchists accepted the link between industrial capitalism and parliamentary democracy" (p. 65). Such an economy, including a substantial independent peasantry, produces a middle class that can stand up against the state and provide the resources for independent groups, as many twentieth-century scholars such as Weber (1906:346 ff.), Schumpeter (1950), Moore (1966), Skocpol (1979), and Berger (1986; 1992) have also concluded. Schumpeter (1950) held that, "modern democracy is a product of the capitalist process" (p. 297). Moore (1966), noting his agreement with the Marxists, concluded, "No bourgeois, no democracy" (p. 418).

Berger (1992), from the conservative side, noted that while there "has been no case of political democracy that has *not* been a market economy, . . . [t]here have been numerous cases of *non*democratic market economies" (p. 9). That is, capitalism has been a necessary, but not sufficient, condition (Diamond 1993a). As reported earlier (Diamond, Linz, and Lipset 1988:xxi), those democracies "most advanced in their capitalist development (size of market sector of the economy, autonomy of their entrepreneurial class) are also those that have been most exposed to pressures for democracy."

Waisman (1992:140–55), seeking to explain why some capitalist societies, particularly in Latin America, have not been democratic, has suggested that private ownership of the means of production is not enough to foster democracy. He has argued that a strong market economy is necessary. Where the state limits the market, where it fosters autarchy (a self-sufficient economy that limits competition), it spawns authoritarianism. A free market needs democracy and vice versa.

But while the movement toward a market economy and the growth of an independent middle class have weakened state power and enlarged human rights and the rule of law, it has been the working class, particularly in the West, that has demanded the expansion of suffrage and the rights of parties (Therborn 1977; Rueschemeyer, Stephens, and Stephens 1992: 59, 97–98, 140–43). As John Stephens (1993) noted, "Capitalist development is associated with the rise of democracy in part because it is associated with a transformation of the class structure strengthening the working class" (p. 438).

Corruption, a major problem of governance, is inherent in systems built on poverty (Klitgaard 1991:86–98). The state must allocate resources it controls, such as jobs, contracts, and investment capital. When the state is poor, it emphasizes particularistic, personalistic criteria. The elimination of personal "networking" on resources controlled or influenced by the state is obviously impossible. Formulating laws and norms to reduce the impact of personal networks, rules that require the application of impersonal meritocratic standards, is desirable; but doing so has taken a long time to institutionalize in the now-wealthy countries, and has usually gone against the traditions and needs of people in less affluent ones. Hence, as Jefferson, Madison, and others argued in the late eighteenth century, the less the state has to do the better; the fewer economic resources the state can directly control, the greater the possibilities for a free polity.

Therefore, a competitive market economy can be justified sociologically and politically as the best way to reduce the impact of nepotistic networks. The wider the scope of market forces, the less room there will be for rent seeking by elites with privileged access to state power and resources. Beyond limiting the power of the state, however, standards of propriety should be increased in new and poor regimes, and explicit objective standards should be applied in allocating aid, loans, and other sources of capital from outside the state. Doing this, of course, would be facilitated by an efficient civil service selected by meritocratic standards. It took many decades for civil service reforms to take hold in Britain, the United States, and various European countries (Johnston 1991:53–56). To change the norms and rules in contemporary impoverished countries will not be achieved easily, although South Korea appears unique in having done so in a relatively short period (Seung-Soo 1992; Macdonald 1992).

The Centrality of Political Culture

Democracy requires a supportive culture, the acceptance of the citizenry and political elites of principles underlying freedom of speech, media, assembly, religion, of the rights of opposition parties, of the rule of law, of human rights, and the like (Almond 1956:34–42; Pye 1965:3–26; Dahl 1971:1–16; Bobbio 1987: 63–78; Diamond, Linz, and Lipset, 1990:16–18). Such norms do not evolve overnight. Attempts to move from authoritarianism to democracy have failed after most upheavals from the French Revolution in 1789 to the February Revolution in Russia in 1917, from those in most new nations in Latin America in the nineteenth century to those in Africa and Asia after World War II. Linz (1988) and Huntington (1991) noted that the two previous waves of democratization were followed by "reverse waves" which witnessed the revival of authoritarianism. "Only four of the seventeen countries that adopted democratic institutions between 1915 and 1931 maintained them throughout the 1920s and 1930s. . . . [O]ne-third of the 32 working democracies in the world in 1958 had become authoritarian by the mid-1970s" (Huntington 1991:17–21).

These experiences do not bode well for the current efforts in the former Communist states of Eastern Europe or in Latin America and Africa. And the most recent report by Freedom House concludes: "As 1993 draws to a close, freedom around the world is in retreat while violence, repression, and state control are on the increase. The trend marks the first increase in five years ..." (Karatnycky 1994:4). A "reverse wave" in the making is most apparent in sub-Saharan Africa, where "9 countries showed improvement while 18 registered a decline" (p. 6). And in Russia, a protofascist movement led all other parties, albeit with 24 percent of the vote, in the December 1993 elections, while the Communists and their allies secured over 15 percent.

Almost everywhere that the institutionalization of democracy has occurred, the process has been a gradual one in which opposition and individual rights have emerged in the give-and-take of politics (Sklar 1987:714). As I, and my then-students Martin Trow and James Coleman, wrote almost forty years ago:

Democratic rights have developed in societies largely through the struggles of various groups— class, religious, sectional, economic, professional, and so on—against one another and against the group which controls the state. Each interest group may desire to carry out its own will, but if no one group is strong enough to gain complete power, the result is the development of tolerance. In large measure the development of the concept of tolerance, of recognition of the rights of groups with whom one disagrees to compete for adherents or power, arose out of conflicts among strong and indestructible groups in different societies. There were a number of processes through which tolerance became legitimate. In some situations groups such as the Catholic and the Protestant churches attempted to destroy the opposing faction, but finally recognized that the complete victory of one group was impossible or could occur only at the risk of destroying the very fabric of society. In these conflicts minority or opposition groups developed a democratic ideology, an insistence on specific minority rights, as a means of legitimating their own right to exist. These groups might then force the dominant power group to grant these rights in order to prevent a revolutionary upsurge or achieve power themselves. For them to reject their own program may then mean a considerable loss of support from adherents who have come to hold the democratic values. (Lipset, Trow, and Coleman 1956:15–16)

As a result, democratic systems developed gradually, at first with suffrage, limited by and linked to property and/or literacy. Elites yielded

slowly in admitting the masses to the franchise and in tolerating and institutionalizing opposition rights (Almond and Verba 1963:7–8; Rustow 1970:357). As Dahl (1971:36–37) has emphasized, parties such as the Liberals and Conservatives in nineteenth-century Europe, formed for the purpose of securing a parliamentary majority rather than to win the support of a mass electorate, were not pressed to engage in populist demagoguery.

Comparative politics suggest that the more the sources of power, status, and wealth are concentrated in the state, the harder it is to institutionalize democracy. Under such conditions the political struggle tends to approach a zero-sum game in which the defeated lose all. The greater the importance of the central state as a source of prestige and advantage, the less likely it is that those in power—or the forces of opposition—will accept rules of the game that institutionalize party conflict and could result in the turnover of those in office. Hence, once again it may be noted, the chances for democracy are greatest where, as in the early United States and to a lesser degree in other Western nations, the interaction between politics and economy is limited and segmented. In northern Europe, democratization let the monarchy and the aristocracy retain their elite status, even though their powers were curtailed. In the United States, the central state was not a major source of privilege for the first half century or more, and those at the center thus could yield office easily.

Democracy has never developed anywhere by plan, except when it was imposed by a democratic conqueror, as in post–World War II Germany and Japan. From the United States to northern Europe, freedom, suffrage, and the rule of law grew in a piecemeal, not in a planned, fashion. To legitimate themselves, governmental parties, even though they did not like it, ultimately had to recognize the right of oppositions to exist and compete freely. Almost all the heads of young democracies, from John Adams and Thomas Jefferson to Indira Gandhi, attempted to suppress their opponents.

As noted before, most new democracies are soon overthrown, as in France prior to 1871, in various parts of Europe after 1848, in Eastern, Central, and Southern Europe after World War I, and repeatedly in Latin America and Africa. Democratic successes have reflected the varying strengths of minority political groups and lucky constellations, as much or more than commitments by new officeholders to the democratic process.

Cross-national historical evaluations of the correlates of democracy have found that cultural factors appear even more important than economic ones (Lipset et al. 1993:168–70; see also Huntington 1991:298–311). Dahl (1970:6), Kennan (1977:41–43), and Lewis (1993:93–94) have emphasized that the first group of countries that became democratic in the nineteenth century (about twenty or so) were Northwest European or settled by Northwest Europeans. "The evidence has yet to be produced that it is the natural form of rule for peoples outside these narrow perimeters" (Kennan 1977: 41–43).[4] Lewis (1993), an authority on the Middle East, has reiterated Kennan's point: "No such [democratic] system has originated in any other cultural tradition; it remains to be seen whether such a system transplanted and adapted in another culture can long survive" (pp. 93–94).

More particularly, recent statistical analyses of the aggregate correlates of political regimes have indicated that having once been a British colony is the variable most highly correlated with democracy (Lipset et al. 1993:168). As Weiner (1987) has pointed out, beyond the experiences in the Americas and Australasia in the nineteenth century, "every country with a population of at least 1 million (and almost all the smaller countries as well) that has emerged from colonial rule and has had a continuous democratic experience is a former British colony" (p. 20). The factors underlying this relationship are not simple (Smith 1978). In the British/non-British comparison, many former British colonies, such as those in North America before the revolution or India and Nigeria

in more recent times, had elections, parties, and the rule of law before they became independent. In contrast, the Spanish, Portuguese, French, Dutch, and Belgian colonies, and former Soviet-controlled countries did not allow for the gradual incorporation of "out-groups" into the polity. Hence democratization was much more gradual and successful in the ex-British colonies than elsewhere; their preindependence experiences were important as a kind of socialization process and helped to ease the transition to freedom.

Religious Tradition

Religious tradition has been a major differentiating factor in transformations to democracy (Huntington 1993:25–29). Historically, there have been negative relationships between democracy and Catholicism, Orthodox Christianity, Islam, and Confucianism; conversely Protestantism and democracy have been positively interlinked. These differences have been explained by (1) the much greater emphasis on individualism in Protestantism and (2) the traditionally close links between religion and the state in the other four religions. Tocqueville (1976) and Bryce (1901) emphasized that democracy is furthered by a separation of religious and political beliefs, so that political stands are not required to meet absolute standards set down by the church.

Scholars from Tocqueville's time to the mid-1970s have observed that, among European countries and their overseas offspring, Protestant countries have been more likely to give rise to democratic regimes than Catholic ones (Lipset 1981:57–58; Lipset [1970] 1988: 90; Bollen 1979:83; Huntington 1991:79–82). Pierre Trudeau (1960), writing as a political scientist in the late fifties, noted that Catholics have been closely linked to the state, adhering to a church which has been hierarchical, and "authoritarian in spiritual matters, and since the dividing line between the spiritual and the temporal may be very fine or even confused, they are often disinclined to seek solution in temporal affairs through the mere counting of heads" (p. 245). Protestants, particularly the non–state-related sects, have been less authoritarian, more congregational, participatory, and individualistic. Catholic countries, however, have contributed significantly to the third wave of democratization during the 1970s and 1980s, reflecting "the major changes in the doctrine, appeal, and social and political commitments of the Catholic Church that occurred . . . in the 1960s and 1970s" (Huntington 1991:281, 77–85). The changes that have occurred are primarily a result of the delegitimation of so-called ultrarightist or clerical fascism in Catholic thought and politics, an outgrowth of the defeat of fascism in Europe, and considerable economic growth in many major Catholic lands in postwar decades, countries such as Italy, Spain, Quebec, Brazil, and Chile.

Conversely, Muslim (particularly Arab) states have not taken part in the third wave of democratization. Almost all remain authoritarian. Growth of democracy in the near future in most of these countries is doubtful because "notions of political freedom are not held in common . . . ; they are alien to Islam" (Vatikiotis 1988:118). As Wright (1992) has stated, Islam "offers not only a set of spiritual beliefs, but a set of rules by which to govern society" (p. 133). Gellner (1991) noted that "Muslim societies in the modern world present a picture which is virtually a mirror image of Marxist ones. They are suffused with faith, indeed they suffer from a plethora of it . . ." (p. 506). In elaborating on the past and present relationship of Muslim beliefs to the polity, Lewis (1993) noted:

The Islamic state was in principle a theocracy—not in the Western sense of a state ruled by the Church and the clergy, . . . but in the more literal sense of a polity ruled by God. . . . In principle, the state was God's state, ruling over God's people; the law was God's law. . . .

Not surprisingly, . . . the history of Islamic states is one of almost unrelieved autocracy. (pp. 96, 98)

Kazancigil (1991) has offered parallel explanations of the weakness of democracy in Is-

lam with those for Orthodox Christian lands as flowing from their failures "to dissociate the religious from the political spheres" (p. 345). In Eastern Europe, particularly Russia, the Orthodox Church has closely linked the two. As Guroff and Guroff (1993) emphasized: "The Church has always been an organ of the Russian state, both under the Tsar and under the Soviet Union. . . . Neither in Tsarist Russia, nor in the Soviet Union has the Orthodox Church played an active role in the protection of human rights or religious tolerance" (pp. 10–11).

Noting that in Confucian China "no church or cultural organization . . . existed independently of the state" (p. 25), and that "Islam has emphasized the identity between the religious and political communities," Eisenstadt (1968) stressed the resultant "important similarity between the Chinese and Islamic societies" (p. 27). Huntington (1993) reported that "no scholarly disagreement exists regarding the proposition that traditional Confucianism was either undemocratic or antidemocratic" (p. 15; see also Whyte 1992:60). Lucian Pye (1968; see also Pye with Pye 1985) has pointed to the similarities between Confucian and Communist beliefs about "authority's rights to arrogance . . . both have been equally absolute . . . upholding the monopolies of officialdom. . . . It is significant that . . . both Confucianism and Maoism in ideological content, have explicitly stressed the problems of authority and order" (Pye 1968:16). Though somewhat less pessimistic, He Baogang's (1992) evaluation of cultural factors in mainland China concluded that "evidence reveals that the antidemocratic culture is currently stronger than the factors related to a democratic one" (p. 134). Only Japan, the most diluted Confucian country, "had sustained experience with democratic government prior to 1990, . . . [although its] democracy was the product of an American presence" (Huntington 1991:15). The others— Korea, Vietnam, Singapore, and Taiwan—were autocratic. As in the other less democratic cultures, "Confucianism merged society and the state and provided no legitimacy for autonomous social institutions at the national level" (p. 301). The situation, of course, has changed in recent years in response to rapid economic growth, reflecting the ways in which economic changes can impact on the political system undermining autocracy.

But India, a Hindu country that became democratic prior to industrialization, is different:

The most salient feature of Indian civilization, from the point of view of our discussion, is that it is probably the only complete, highly differentiated civilization which throughout history has maintained its cultural identity without being tied to a given political framework. . . . [T]o a much greater degree than in many other historical imperial civilizations politics were conceived in secular forms . . . . Because of the relative dissociation between the cultural and political order, the process of modernization could get underway in India without being hampered by too specific a traditional-cultural orientation toward the political sphere (Eisenstadt 1968:32)

These generalizations about culture do not augur well for the future of the third wave of democracy in the former Communist countries. The Catholic Church played a substantial role in Poland's move away from Soviet Communism. But as noted previously, historically deeply religious Catholic areas have not been among the most amenable to democratic ideas. Poland is not troubled by conflicts flowing from increasing Church efforts to affect politics in Eastern Europe even as it relaxes its policies in Western Europe and most of the Americas. Orthodox Christianity is hegemonic in Russia and Belarus. The Ukraine is dominated by both the Catholic and Orthodox Churches. And fascists and Communists are strong in Russia and the Ukraine. Muslims are a significant group in the central Asian parts of the former Soviet Union, the majority in some—these areas are among the consistently least democratic of the successor Soviet states. Led by the Orthodox Serbians, but helped by Catholic Croats and Bosnian Muslims, the former Yugoslavia is being torn apart along ethnic and religious lines with no peaceful, much less

democratic end in sight. We are fooling ourselves if we ignore the continuing dysfunctional effects of a number of cultural values and the institutions linked to them.

But belief systems change; and the rise of capitalism, a large middle class, an organized working class, increased wealth, and education are associated with secularism and the institutions of civil society which help create autonomy for the state and facilitate other preconditions for democracy. In recent years, nowhere has this been more apparent than in the economically successful Confucian states of East Asia—states once thought of as nearly hopeless candidates for both development and democracy. Tu (1993) noted their totally "unprecedented dynamism in democratization and marketization. Singapore, South Korea, and Taiwan all successfully conducted national elections in 1992, clearly indicating that democracy in Confucian societies is not only possible but also practical" (p. viii). Nathan and Shi (1993), reporting on "the first scientifically valid national sample survey done in China on political behavior and attitudes," stated: "When compared to residents of some of the most stable, long-established democracies in the world, the Chinese population scored lower on the variables we looked at, but not so low as to justify the conclusion that democracy is out of reach" (p. 116). Surveys which have been done in Russia offer similar positive conclusions (Gibson and Duch 1993), but the December 1993 election in which racist nationalists and pro-Communists did well indicate much more is needed. Democracy is not taking root in much of the former Soviet Union, the less industrialized Muslim states, nor many nations in Africa. The end is not in sight for many of the efforts at new democracies; the requisite cultural changes are clearly not established enough to justify the conclusion that the "third wave" will not be reversed. According to the Freedom House survey, during 1993 there were "42 countries registering a decline in their level of freedom [political rights and civil liberties] and 19 recording gains" (Karatnycky 1994:5).[5]

Institutionalization

New democracies must be institutionalized, consolidated, and become legitimate. They face many problems, among which are creating a growing and more equalitarian economy; reducing the tensions with, and perhaps replacing, the old civil and military elites; and formulating workable democratic electoral and administrative systems that rest on stable political parties (Linz and Stepan 1989; Whitehead 1989; Di Palma 1990:44–108; Huntington 1991:208–79). To deal with all the issues inherent in the institutionalization of democracy requires a book, so I limit myself here to: legitimacy, executive and electoral systems, civil society and political parties, and finally, the rule of law and economic order.

Legitimacy

Political stability in democratic systems cannot rely on force. The alternative to force is legitimacy, an accepted systemic "title to rule."[6] Most of the northern European and British Commonwealth nations, for example, developed democratic institutions while retaining what is known as traditional legitimacy derived from a continuing monarchy. Without these institutions and traditions already present, democracy might not have developed as it did, if at all.

Weber (1946), the fountainhead of legitimacy theory, named three ways by which an authority may gain legitimacy. These may be summarized:

1. *Traditional*—through "always" having possessed the authority, the best example being the title held in monarchical societies.

2. *Rational-legal*—when authority is obeyed because of a popular acceptance of the appropriateness of the system of rules under which they have won and held office. In the United States, the Constitution is the basis of all authority.

3. *Charismatic*—when authority rests upon faith in a leader who is believed to be endowed with greater personal worth, either from God, as in the case of a religious prophet, or

simply from the display of extraordinary talents. The "cult of personality" surrounding many leaders is an illustration of this (pp. 78–79).

Legitimacy is best gained by prolonged effectiveness, effectiveness being the actual performance of the government and the extent to which it satisfies the basic needs of most of the population and key power groups (such as the military and economic leaders) (Lipset [1960] 1981:64–70; Lipset 1979:16–23; Linz 1978: 67–74; Linz 1988:79–85; Diamond et al. 1990: 9–16). This generalization, however, is of no help to new systems for which the best immediate institutional advice is to separate the source and the agent of authority.

The importance of this separation cannot be underestimated. The agent of authority may be strongly opposed by the electorate and may be changed by the will of the voters, but the essence of the rules, the symbol of authority, must remain respected and unchallenged. Hence, citizens obey the laws and rules, even while disliking those who enforce them. This happened in post-Franco Spain where the monarchy was successfully and usefully restored, although few, if any, countries today could do the same thing. After World War II, Japan, thanks to MacArthur, made dramatic changes under the aegis of the Emperor, avoiding the error made by the Allies at the end of World War I. Following the first World War, the Allies deposed the German monarchy and supported what became the Weimar Republic. Winston Churchill strongly opposed this action, correctly anticipating that the new democratic system would be opposed by adherents of the old empire and would not command their allegiance.

Rational-legal legitimacy is weak in most new democratic systems, since the law had previously operated in the interests of a foreign exploiter or domestic dictator. Efforts to construct rational-legal legitimacy necessarily involve extending the rule of the law and the prestige of the courts, which should be as independent from the rest of the polity as possible.

As Ackerman (1992:60–62) and Weingast (1993) noted, in new democracies, these requirements imply the need to draw up a "liberal" constitution *as soon as possible.* The constitution can provide a basis for legitimacy, for limitations on state power, and for political and economic rights. Establishing stable legitimacy, of course, takes time.

The postwar democratic regimes of the formerly fascist states, created, like the Weimar Republic, under the auspices of the conquerors clearly had no legitimacy at their outset. But they had the advantage of the subsequent postwar "economic miracles" which produced jobs and a steadily rising standard of living. These new regimes have been economically viable for over four decades. The stability of these democratic systems is also linked to the discrediting of antidemocratic right-wing tendencies—these forces were identified with fascism and military defeat.

To reiterate, if democratic governments which lack traditional legitimacy are to survive, they must be effective, or as in the example of some new Latin American and post-communist democracies, may have acquired a kind of negative legitimacy—an inoculation against authoritarianism because of the viciousness of the previous dictatorial regimes.

Weber (1946:232–34) noted that an autocrat is often less powerful than a democratic ruler. He suggested that because of the restrictions on freedom of information, the dictator may not know when his orders are ignored by bureaucrats or interest groups that oppose them. He cited as an example the failure of Frederick the Great's land reforms. The Prussian state bureaucracy and local authorities linked to the landed aristocracy simply disobeyed the new laws. And no one told Frederick. In a democracy, by contrast, the opposition and/or the press usually exposes such sabotage.

At least twice in his first few years in office, Mikhail Gorbachev made speeches noting the dysfunctional consequences of one-party regimes. In terms similar to Weber's, he pointed out that the bureaucracy ignored orders and reforms they opposed. He said this could not happen in a multiparty system. He, of course, did not advocate more parties. Rather, he called on the Soviet press and intelligentsia to fulfill the functions of communication and finger-pointing that are handled in democratic countries by the opposition (Gorbachev 1987: R24; 1988:33).

Executive and Electoral Systems

Democracy can be recommended not only on moral grounds, but as ultimately facilitating systemic stability. Democracy enables the citizenry to see the polity as including all societal elements, not only those in power. The electorate becomes part of the legitimating structure. It, rather than the government, holds the ultimate authority. Members of the electorate are encouraged to work for changes in government while remaining loyal to the system. However, efforts to institutionalize freedom in low-income countries face severe difficulties inherent in the fact that new democratic rights encourage demands and actions that destabilize the economy.

As Canadian sociologist Metta Spencer (1991) has emphasized, an equally important concern is "the protection of the rights of minorities from infringement by *the majority*." Where minorities, particularly ethnic-linguistic-religious ones, feel they cannot share power (i.e., that they will be "invariably out voted under the conditions of majority rule"), and where they form majorities in prescribed areas, they may try to gain local autonomy or secede as a way of turning a cultural minority into a majority. This has happened in parts of former Yugoslavia and the former Soviet Union (p. 427). Democracies will lack legitimacy in the eyes of minorities who feel excluded from power. Hence, transition to electoral regimes will often destabilize multicultural polities, as the situation in many post-Communist states has demonstrated. Calhoun's (1947) early nineteenth-century theory of concurrent majority and Lijphart's (1977) contemporary notion of consociational systems suggest similar solutions to this problem. They proposed constitutional structures that give minorities veto power in the policy development process when their interests are affected. Efforts to do this in Cyprus and Lebanon have failed. Switzerland has apparently been successful. Canada and South Africa are currently looking for comparable arrangements. Ironically, Lani Guinier (1993:1589–1642, especially 1625–42) proposes reforms similar to Calhoun's; however, Calhoun's proposal aimed to preserve the interests of the masters, and Guinier's was intended to facilitate the demands of the descendants of their slaves.

Federalism, of course, is the oldest and in many ways the most satisfactory means to manage such conflicts between ethnic or other groups and define regional political boundaries. As Horowitz (1985:598) argued, federalism permits five different conflict-reducing mechanisms to operate: (1) taking "heat off a single focal point;" (2) devolving power and office among ethnic lines; (3) offering inducements for ethnic coalitions; (4) encouraging intraethnic conflict within provinces, thus allowing for cross-cutting cleavages; and (5) promoting efforts to "reduce disparities between groups." But clearly federalism is no panacea. It has its failure as well as successes.

Civil Society and Political Parties
Civil Society as a Political Base

More important than electoral rules in encouraging a stable system is a strong civil society—the presence of myriad "mediating institutions," including "groups, media, and networks" (Diamond 1993b:4), that operate independently between individuals and the state. These constitute "subunits, capable of opposing and countervailing the state" (Gellner 1991:500). Forty years ago, my first major effort to analyze "the conditions that favor democracy" (Lipset, Trow, and Coleman 1956: 15) focused on civil societies, noting that "in a large complex society, the body of the citizenry

is unable to affect the policies of the state. If citizens do not belong to politically relevant groups, if they are atomized, the controllers of the central power apparatus will completely dominate the society" (p. 15).

Citizen groups must become the basis of—the sources of support for—the institutionalized political parties which are a necessary condition for—part of the very definition of—a modern democracy. As Merkl (1993) reiterating Schumpeter (1950) correctly emphasized, "The major device for facilitating the formation of the popular will, its generation of meaningful choices and its impact upon government, have been political parties" (pp. 257–58). Or as Weffort (1992) puts it: "Democracy-building is a process of . . . institutionalizing conflict" (p. 111).

We owe our awareness of the importance of civil society to Tocqueville (1976) who, in the early nineteenth century, saw in the widespread existence of civil associations the secret to why Americans did so well politically and economically when compared to the European nations of his day.[7] He noted that people

cannot belong to these associations for any length of time without finding out how order is maintained among a large number of people and by what contrivance they are made to advance, harmoniously and methodically, to the same object. . . . Political associations may therefore be considered as large free schools, where all the members of the community go to learn the general theory of association. . . .

In their political associations the Americans, of all conditions, minds, and ages, daily acquire a general taste for association and grow accustomed to the use of it. . . . [T]hey are mutually stimulated to all sorts of undertakings. They afterwards transfer to civil life the notions they have thus acquired and make them subservient to a thousand purposes. (vol. 2:116, 119)

A fully operative civil society is likely to also be a participant one. Organizations stimulate interests and activity in the larger polity; they can be consulted by political institutions about projects that affect them and their members, and they can transfer this information to the citizenry. Civil organizations reduce resistance to unanticipated changes because they prevent the isolation of political institutions from the polity and can smooth over, or at least recognize, interest differences early on.

In a twist on Schumpeter's (1950) definition of political parties as the basis of democracy, certain democratic values and rights have evolved primarily through conflict among groups in society. Instead of struggling to attain elite political power, various groups—class, religious, economic, professional, and the like—compete with one another and the state for popular attention, for the power to carry out their own agendas. As noted earlier, such opposition groups must legitimate themselves by encouraging the rights of other groups to oppose them, thus providing a basis for democracy. Through these conflicts and their differing ideologies, these groups form an alternative to the state and its control of society.

Totalitarian systems, however, do not have effective civil societies. Instead, they either seek to eliminate groups mediating between the individual and the state or to control these groups so there is no competition. And while by so doing they may undermine the possibility for *organized* opposition, they also reduce group effectiveness generally, and reduce the education of individuals for innovative activities (i.e., Tocqueville's "civil partnerships" [1976, vol. 2:124]). In the West, polities are based on a wide diversity of groups that form the basis for parties (e.g., unions, ethnic and religious groups, farm associations, veterans' organizations). Fortunately, most of the new democracies outside of the ex-Communist bloc, such as Argentina, Chile, South Korea, Taiwan, and Spain, were not totalitarian and had institutionalized some of the pluralistic institutions of civil society while under autocratic rule (Scalapino 1989). The new democracies must be encouraged to form more of these civil groups. Yet the "newly created" leaders of these interest groups more often

than not only have "become . . . [favorable to democracy] during the transition period" (Weffort 1992:12).

The countries of Eastern Europe and the former Soviet Union, however, are faced with the consequences of the absence of modern civil society, a lack that makes it difficult to institutionalize democratic polities. These countries have not had the opportunity to form the civil groups necessary to coalesce into stable political parties, except through churches in some nations, such as Poland, and assorted small autonomous illegal networks (Sadowski 1993:171–80). Instead, they have had to create parties "from scratch." Ideologically splintered groups must oppose the former Communists, who have been well organized for many years and have constructed their own coalitions. "Instead of consolidation, there is fragmentation: 67 parties fought Poland's most recent general election, 74 Romania's" (*Economist* 1993a:4). As a result, the former Communists (now "socialists") have either been voted in as the majority part in parliament, as in Lithuania, or have become the largest party heading up a coalition cabinet, as in Poland. In January 1992, the Communist-backed candidate for president in Bulgaria garnered 43 percent of the vote (Malia 1992:73). These situations are, of course, exacerbated by the fact that replacing command economies by market processes is difficult, and frequently conditions worsen before they begin to improve.

Recent surveys indicate other continuing effects of forty-five to seventy-five years of Communist rule. An overwhelming majority (about 70 percent) of the population in nearly all of the countries in Eastern Europe agree that "the state should provide a place of work, as well as a national health service, housing, education, and other services" (*Economist* 1993a:5). The success of democracy in these countries depends in large part on their populations' ability to adapt to freedom, to break away from their former views on the role of the state, and their willingness to accept the cyclical nature of the free-market system, and of course, on successful economic performance. Garton Ash (1990), Kohák (1992), and Di Palma (1991) have written eloquently on the persistence of Communist structures and mindsets, as has Hungarian politician and scholar Tamás (1992) when he noted:

All the surveys and polling data show that public opinion in our region rejects dictatorship, but would like to see a strong man at the helm; favors popular government, but hates parliament, parties, and the press; likes social welfare legislation and equality, but not trade unions; wants to topple the present government, but disapproves of the idea of a regular opposition; supports the notion of the market (which is a code word for Western-style living standards), but wishes to punish and expropriate the rich and condemns banking for preying on simple working people; favors a guaranteed minimum income, but sees unemployment as an immoral state and wants to punish or possibly deport the unemployed (p. 73)

Political Parties as Mediators

Political parties themselves must be viewed as the most important mediating institutions between the citizenry and the state (Lipset 1993). And a crucial condition for a stable democracy is that major parties exist that have an almost permanent significant base of support. That support must be able to survive clear-cut policy failures by the parties. If this commitment does not exist, parties may be totally wiped out, thus eliminating effective opposition. The Republicans in the United States, for example, though declining sharply in electoral support, remained a major opposition party in the early 1930s, despite the fact that the Great Depression started under their rule and reached severe economic depths in unemployment, bankruptcy, and stock market instability never seen before.

If, as in new democracies, parties do not command such allegiance, they can be easily eliminated. The Hamiltonian Federalist Party, which competed in the early years of the American Republic with the Jeffersonian Democra-tic-Republicans, declined sharply after losing the presidency in 1800 and soon died out (Lipset 1979:40–41; Dauer 1953). In more recent postauthoritarian European polities, early democratic movements that appeared to have mass support—the Party of Action in Italy, the Union of the Democratic Center in Spain which formed a majority government in the first post-Franco election, the Civic Union in East Germany, Solidarity in Poland—were eliminated or declined greatly in early elections. As mentioned earlier, the same pattern has occurred in a number of former Soviet countries. It may be argued, then, that having at least two parties with an uncritically loyal mass base comes close to being a necessary condition for a stable democracy. Democracy requires strong parties that can offer alternative policies and criticize each other. Historically, the cross-cutting cleavages of impoverished India linked to allegiances of caste, linguistic, and religious groupings have contributed to the institutionalization of democracy by producing "strong commitment to parties" on the part of a large majority (Das Gupta 1989:95; Diamond 1989b:19). More recently, volatility and decay in the party system has been associated with a decline in the quality and stability of democracy in India (Kohli 1992).

The Rule of Law and Economic Order

Finally, order and predictability are important for the economy, polity, and society. The Canadian Fathers of Confederation, who drew up the newly unified country's first constitution in 1867, described the Constitution's objective as "peace, order and good government" (Lipset 1990b:xiii). Basically, they were talking about the need for the "rule of law," for establishing rules of "due process," and an independent judiciary. Where power is arbitrary, personal, and unpredictable, the citizenry will not know how to behave; it will fear that any action could produce an unforeseen risk. Essentially, the rule of law means: (1) that people and institutions will be treated equally by the institutions administering the law—the courts, the police, and the civil service; and (2), that people and institutions can predict with reasonable certainty the consequences of their actions, at least as far as the state is concerned. As the World Bank (1991) has emphasized: "The rule of law is a key element of predictability and stability where business risks may be rationally assessed, transaction costs lowered, and governmental arbitrariness reduced" (p. iii). Here, once again, we see the needs of the polity and economy as joined.

In discussing "the social requisites of democracy," I have repeatedly stressed the relationships between the level of economic development and the presence of democratic government. As noted, a host of empirical studies has continued to find significant correlations between socioeconomic variables (such as GNP, educational attainments, level of health care) on the one hand, and political outcomes (such as free polities and human rights) on the other. (Lipset et al. 1993; Diamond 1992a; Inkeles 1991; Bollen and Jackman 1985a; Bollen and Jackman 1985b; Bollen 1979; 1980; Flora 1973; Flanigan and Fogelman 1971; Olsen 1968; Neubauer 1967; Cutright 1963).

Some of the countries that have moved toward democracy in recent years exemplify the implications of the economic development model (e.g., Chile, Spain, South Korea, and Taiwan). Prior to democratization, they moved up rapidly on economic and human welfare measures. But the relationship between the economy and human welfare is far from consistent (Lipset et al. 1993). The characteristics of the most populous democracy in the world, India, contradict this relationship, as do those of Botswana, Papua New Guinea, and Sri Lanka. The diffusion of democracy to some poor less-developed countries in recent years also undermines the correlation, although this has happened in large part due to the end of a bipolar world—Third World dictators can no longer take advantage of the tension between

the Soviet Union and the West (on diffusion, see Di Palma 1990:15–21).

Clearly, socioeconomic correlations are merely associational, and do not necessarily indicate cause. Other variables, such as the force of historical incidents in domestic politics, cultural factors, events in neighboring countries, diffusion effects from elsewhere, leadership and movement behavior can also affect the nature of the polity. Thus, the outcome of the Spanish Civil War, determined in part by other European states, placed Spain in an authoritarian mold, much as the allocation of Eastern Europe to the Soviet Union after World War II determined the political future of that area and that Western nations would seek to prevent the electoral victories of Communist-aligned forces. Currently, international agencies and foreign governments are more likely to endorse pluralistic regimes.

Karl and Schmitter (1991:270–71) argued that the search for democratic prerequisites is misguided. They accounted for democratic transitions by observing the pact-making process of political regimes and parties. Karl contended, "Rather than engage in a futile search for new preconditions, it is important to clarify how *the mode of regime transition (itself conditioned by the breakdown of authoritarian rule) sets the context within which strategic interactions can take place because these interactions, in turn, help to determine whether political democracy will engage and survive . . ."* (Karl 1990:19).

Karl and Schmitter (1991) viewed the analysis of the behavior of elites in constructing pacts as mutually exclusive from the study of democratic prerequisites. I disagree. Social requisite analysis is concerned with the foundations for successful democratic consolidation. Since pacts are one means of institutionalizing democracy, whether they emerge or hold is linked to probabilities associated with the presence or absence of these requisites. As Weffort (1992) emphasized, *"The minimal procedural working of a political democracy implies certain minimal social conditions"* (p. 18). Thus, it is not necessary to make an "either-or" choice between the study of democratic conditions and pact building—they are complementary.

Conclusion

Democracy is an international cause. A host of democratic governments and parties, as well as various nongovernmental organizations (NGOs) dedicated to human rights, are working and providing funds to create and sustain democratic forces in newly liberalized governments and to press autocratic ones to change (*Economist* 1993c:46). Various international agencies and units, like the European Community, NATO, the World Bank, and the International Monetary Fund (IMF), are requiring a democratic system as a condition for membership or aid. A diffusion, a contagion, or demonstration effect seems operative, as many have noted, one that encourages democracies to press for change and authoritarian rulers to give in. It is becoming both uncouth and unprofitable to avoid free elections, particularly in Latin America, East Asia, Eastern Europe, and to some extent in Africa (Ake 1991:33). Yet the proclamation of elections does not ensure their integrity. The outside world can help, but the basis for institutionalized opposition, for interest and value articulation, must come from within.

Results of research suggest that we be cautious about the long-term stability of democracy in many of the newer systems given their low level of legitimacy. As the Brazilian scholar Francisco Weffort (1992) has reminded us, "In the 1980s, the age of new democracies, the processes of political democratization occurred at the same moment in which those countries suffered the experience of a profound and prolonged economic crisis that resulted in social exclusion and massive poverty. . . . Some of those countries are building a political democracy on top of a minefield of social apartheid . . ." (p. 20). Such conditions could easily lead to breakdowns of democracy as have already occurred in Algeria, Haiti, Nige-

ria, and Peru, and to the deterioration of democratic functioning in countries like Brazil, Egypt, Kenya, the Philippines, and the former Yugoslavia, and some of the trans-Ural republics or "facade democracies," as well as the revival of antidemocratic movements on the right and left in Russia and in other formerly Communist states.

What new democracies need, above all, to attain legitimacy is efficacy—particularly in the economic arena, but also in the polity. If they can take the road to economic development, it is likely that they can keep their political house in order. But as I have tried to show, the strains flowing from economic growth may undermine democratic stability. As Diamond (1992b) noted in his writings on Africa, comments that apply to much of the former Communist lands as well: "How can structural adjustment [in the economy], which imposes so much short-term pain . . . , be reconciled with democracy?" (p. 41). And some argue that *perestroika* (economic and social reform) *must precede glasnost* (political freedom). They contend that *perestroika* is more possible without the latter, in impoverished lands.

The profusion of empirical, historical and comparative work since World War II, and especially the research in recent years, has added considerably to our understanding of the conditions for democracy. There are a number of assertions we can now advance with considerable confidence, about the structural, cultural, and institutional factors that are conducive to the development of democracy. But specific outcomes depend on particular contexts: on whether the initial electoral and other political institutions are appropriate to the ethnic and cleavage structures of the given country, on the current state of the economy, as well, of course, on the abilities and tactics of the major actors. For example, Washington and Lincoln, Lenin and Gorbachev, Nehru and DeGaulle, each had a profound effect on the prospects for democracy in his time and country.

Clearly then, we cannot generalize by a formula. The various factors I have reviewed here do shape the probabilities for democracy, but they do not determine the outcomes. The record of social scientists as futurologists is not good. Dahl (1971:208) and Huntington (1984), two of the leading explicators of the structural conditions approach, were extremely pessimistic about the prospects for more polyarchies or democracies prior to Gorbachev's rise to power. This is very similar to the failure of most Sovietologists to anticipate the collapse of the USSR (Lipset and Bence forthcoming). Whether democracy succeeds or fails continues to depend significantly on the choices, behaviors, and decisions of political leaders and groups.

Notes

* From the *American Sociological Review* 59, no. 1 (February 1994): 1–8, 9–10, 12–14, and 15–22, by permission of the author and the American Sociological Association. Copyright 1994 by the American Sociological Association.

† This paper was written with assistance provided by the Hoover Institution of Stanford University and the Woodrow Wilson Center for International Scholars. It incorporates and extends my earlier work on the social requisites of democracy over three decades (Lipset [1960] 1981; Lipset, Seong, and Torres 1993). I am indebted to Chris Winters and Scott Billingsley for research assistance and to Larry Diamond for intellectual commentary. An earlier version was presented as a Stein Rokkan Memorial Lecture at the University of Bergen in November 1992.

1. For elaborations, see Lipset (1981:27); Dahl (1970:78; 1971:150–62; 1982:11); Huntington (1991:5–13); and Schmitter and Karl (1993: 40–46).

2. For a discussion of the way definitions affect analyses of democracy, see Sartori (1983:28–34; 1987:257–77).

3. These generalizations do not apply to the East Asian NICS, South Korea, Taiwan, and Singapore.

4. That evidence, of course, has emerged in recent years in South and East Asia, Latin America, and various countries descended from Southern Europe.

5. In the Freedom House survey, a country may move up or down with respect to measures of freedom without changing its status as a democratic or authoritarian system.

6. See Dogan (1988) for recent writings on legitimacy. See also Lipset ([1963] 1979:17).

7. Gramsci, a leading Marxist scholar, writing in the twenties, also emphasized the need for a "dense civil society" arising out of capitalism, which made democratic discourse possible (Stephens 1993:414), as more recently did Lipset (1981:52–53) and Huntington (1984:202–3).

References

Ake, Claude. 1991. "Rethinking African Democracy." *Journal of Democracy* 2(1):32–47.

Ackerman, Bruce. 1992. *The Future of Liberal Revolution.* New Haven, CT: Yale University Press.

Almond, Gabriel. 1956. "Comparative Political Systems." Pp. 34–42 in *Political Behavior: A Reader in Theory and Research,* edited by H. Eulau, S. J. Eldersveld, and M. Janowitz. Glencoe, IL: Free Press.

Almond, Gabriel, and Sidney Verba. 1963. *Civic Culture: Political Attitudes and Democracy in Five Nations.* Princeton, NJ: Princeton University Press.

Amalrik, André. 1970. *Will the Soviet Union Survive Until 1984?* New York: Harper and Row.

Berger, Peter. 1986. *The Capitalist Revolution.* New York: Basic Books.

———. 1992. "The Uncertain Triumph of Democratic Capitalism." *Journal of Democracy* 3(3):7–17.

Bobbio, Norberto. 1987. *The Future of Democracy: A Defense of the Rules of the Game.* Minneapolis, MN: University of Minnesota Press.

Bollen, Kenneth. 1979. "Political Democracy and the Timing of Development." *American Sociological Review* 44:572–87.

———. 1980. "Issues in the Comparative Measurement of Political Democracy." *American Sociological Review* 45:370–90.

Bollen, Kenneth, and Robert Jackman. 1985a. "Economic and Noneconomic Determinants of Political Democracy in the 1960s." *Research in Political Sociology* 1:27–48.

———. 1985b. "Political Democracy and the Size Distribution of Income." *American Sociological Review* 50:438–57.

Bryce, James. 1901. *Study in History and Jurisprudence.* New York: Oxford University Press.

Calhoun, John. 1947. *A Disquisition on Government.* New York: Political Science Classics.

Chan, Steve. 1989. "Income Inequality among LDCs: A Comparative Analysis of Alternative Perspectives." *International Studies Quarterly* 33:45–65.

Cutright, Phillips. 1963. "National Political Development: Measurement and Analysis." *American Sociological Review* 28:253–64.

Dahl, Robert. 1970. *After the Revolution: Authority in a Good Society.* New Haven, CT: Yale University Press.

———. 1971. *Polyarchy: Participation and Opposition.* New Haven, CT: Yale University Press.

———. 1982. *Dilemmas of Pluralist Democracy.* New Haven, CT: Yale University Press.

Das Gupta, Jyotirindra. 1989. "India: Democratic Becoming and Combined Development." Pp. 53–104 in *Democracy in Developing Countries: Asia,* edited by L. Diamond, J. Linz, and S. M. Lipset. Boulder, CO: Lynne Rienner.

Dauer, Manning. 1953. *The Adams Federalists.* Baltimore, MD: Johns Hopkins University Press.

Diamond, Larry. 1989a. "Beyond Authoritarianism and Totalitarianism: Strategies for Democratization." *The Washington Quarterly* 12(1):141–63.

———. 1989b. "Introduction: Persistence, Erosion, Breakdown and Renewal." Pp. 1–52 in *Democracy in Developing Countries: Asia,* edited by L. Diamond, J. Linz, and S. M. Lipset. Boulder, CO: Lynne Rienner.

———. 1992a. "Economic Development and Democracy Reconsidered." Pp. 93–139 in *Reexamining Democracy: Essays in Honor of Seymour Martin Lipset,* edited by G. Marks and L. Diamond. Newbury Park, CA: Sage.

———. 1992b. "The Second Liberation." *Africa Report* 37:38–41.

———. 1993a. "Economic Liberalization and Democracy." The Hoover Institution, Stanford University, Stanford, CA. Unpublished manuscript.

———. 1993b. "Ex-Africa, a New Democratic Spirit Has Loosened the Grip of African Dictatorial Rule." *Times Literary Supplement,* 2 July (no. 4709), pp. 3–4.

Diamond, Larry, Juan Linz, and Seymour Martin Lipset, eds. 1988. *Democracy in Developing Countries: Africa.* Boulder, CO: Lynne Rienner.

Diamond, Larry, Juan Linz, and Seymour Martin Lipset, eds. 1990. *Politics in Developing Countries, Comparing Experiences with Democracy.* Boulder, CO: Lynne Rienner.

Di Palma, Giuseppe. 1990. *To Craft Democracies. An Essay on Democratic Transitions.* Berkeley, CA: University of California Press.

———. 1991. "Legitimation from the Top to Civil Society: Politico-Cultural Change in Eastern Europe." *World Politics* 44(1):49–80.

Dogan, Mattei, ed. 1988. *Comparing Pluralist Democracies: Strains on Legitimacy.* Boulder, CO: Westview.

Economist. 1993a. "Survey on Eastern Europe." March 13:1–22.

Economist. 1993b. "Russia Into the Swamp." May 22:59–60.

Economist. 1993c. "Aid for Africa: If You're Good." May 29:46.

Eisenstadt, Shmuel N. 1968. "The Protestant Ethic Theses in the Framework of Sociological Theory and Weber's Work." Pp. 3–45 in *The Protestant Ethic and Modernization: A Comparative View,* edited by S. N. Eisenstadt. New York: Basic Books.

Feshbach, Murray. 1978. "Population and Manpower Trends in The U.S.S.R." Paper presented at the Conference on the Soviet Union Today, sponsored by the Kennan Institute for Advanced Russian Studies, Woodrow Wilson International Center for Scholars, April, Washington, DC.

———. 1982. "Issues in Soviet Health Problems." Pp. 203–27 in *Soviet Economy in the 1980s: Problems and Prospects, Part 2.* U.S. Congress, Joint Economic Committee. 97th Cong., 2d sess., 31 Dec. Washington, DC: Government Printing Office.

———. 1983. "Soviet Population, Labor Force and Health." Pp. 91–138 in *The Political Economy of the Soviet Union.* U.S. Congress, Joint Hearings of the House Committee on Foreign Affairs and Joint Economic Committee. 98th Cong., 1st sess., 26 July and 29 Sept. Washington, DC: Government Printing Office.

Flanigan, William H., and Edwin Fogelman. 1971. "Patterns of Political Development and Democratization: A Quantitative Analysis." Pp. 441–74 in *Macro-Quantitative Analysis: Conflict, Development, and Democratization,* edited by J. Gillespie and B. Nesvold. Beverly Hills, CA: Sage.

Flora, Peter. 1973. "Historical Processes of Social Mobilization: Urbanization and Literacy: 1850–1965." Pp. 213–59 in *Building States and Nations: Models and Data Resources,* vol. 1, edited by Shmuel N. Eisenstadt and S. Rokkan. Beverly Hills, CA: Sage.

Freedom Review. 1993. "Freedom around the World." *Freedom Review.* 24(1)(Special Issue):3–67.

Garton Ash, Timothy. 1990. "Eastern Europe: The Year of Truth." *New York Review of Books,* 15 Feb., pp. 17–22.

Gellner, Ernest. 1991. "Civil Society in Historical Context." *International Social Science Journal* 43:495–510.

Gibson, James L., and Raymond M. Duch. 1993. "Emerging Democratic Values in Soviet Political Culture." Pp. 69–94 in *Public Opinion and Regime Change,* edited by A. A. Miller, W. M. Reisinger, and V. Hesli. Boulder, CO: Westview.

Gladish, Ken. 1993. "The Primacy of the Particular." *Journal of Democracy* 4(1):53–65.

Glassman, Ronald. 1991. *China in Transition: Communism, Capitalism and Democracy.* Westport, CT: Praeger.

Gorbachev, Mikhail. 1987. Text of Report delivered to plenary meeting of CPSU Central Committee. *Foreign Broadcast Information Service Daily Report: Soviet Union,* 28 Jan., pp. R2–R48.

———. 1988. Text of Report delivered to CPSU Central Committee at 19th All-Union CPSU Conference. *Foreign Broadcast Information Service Daily Report: Soviet Union,* 28 June (Suppl), pp. 1–35.

Guiner, Lani. 1993. "Groups, Representation, and Race-Conscious Districting: A Case of the Emperor's Clothes." *Texas Law Review* 71:1589–642.

Guroff, Gregory, and A. Guroff. 1993. "The Paradox of Russian National Identity." (Russian Littoral Project, Working Paper No. 16). College Park and Baltimore, MD: University of Maryland–College Park and The Johns Hopkins University SAIS.

He, Baogang. 1992. "Democratization: Antidemocratic and Democratic Elements in the Political Culture of China." *Australian Journal of Political Science* 27:120–36.

Horowitz, Donald. 1985. *Ethnic Groups in Conflict.* Berkeley, CA: University of California Press.

———. 1990. "Comparing Democratic Systems." *Journal of Democracy* 1(4):73–79.

Huntington, Samuel. 1968. *Political Order in Changing Societies.* New Haven, CT: Yale University Press.

———. 1984. "Will More Countries Become Democratic?" *Political Science Quarterly* 99:193–218.

———. 1991. *The Third Wave: Democratization in the Late Twentieth Century.* Norman, OK: University of Oklahoma Press.

———. 1993. "The Clash of Civilizations." *Foreign Affairs* 72(3):22–49.

Inglehart, Ronald. 1990. *Culture Shift in Advanced Industrial Society.* Princeton, NJ: Princeton University Press.

Inkeles, Alex, ed. 1991. *On Measuring Democracy: Its Consequences and Concomitants.* New Brunswick, NJ: Transaction.

Johnston, Michael. 1991. "Historical Conflict and the Rise of Standards." *Journal of Democracy* 2(4):48–60.

Karatnycky, Adrian. 1994. "Freedom in Retreat." *Freedom Review* 25(1):4–9.

Karl, Terry Lynn. 1990. "Dilemmas of Democratization in Latin America." *Comparative Politics* 23:1–21.

Karl, Terry Lynn, and Philippe C. Schmitter. 1991. "Modes of Transition in Latin America: Southern and Eastern Europe. *International Social Science Journal* 43:269–84.

Kazancigil, Ali. 1991. "Democracy in Muslim Lands: Turkey in Comparative Perspective." *International Social Science Journal* 43:343–60.

Kennan, George. 1977. *Clouds of Danger: Current Realities of American Foreign Policy.* Boston, MA: Little, Brown.

Klitgaard, Robert. 1991. "Strategies for Reform." *Journal of Democracy* 2(4):86–100.

Kohák, Erazim. 1992. "Ashes. Ashes . . . Central Europe after Forty Years." *Daedalus* 121(2):197–215.

Kohli, Atul. 1992. "Indian Democracy: Stress and Resilience." *Journal of Democracy* 3(1):52–64.

Kuznets, Simon. 1955. "Economic Growth and Income Inequality." *American Economic Review* 45:1–28.

———. 1963. "Quantitative Aspects of the Economic Growth of Nations: VIII, The Distribution of Income by Size." *Economic Development and Cultural Change* 11:1–80.

———. 1976. *Modern Economic Growth: Rate, Structure and Spread.* New Haven, CT: Yale University Press.

Lee, Stephen J. 1987. *The European Dictatorships. 1918–1945.* London: Methuen.

Lewis, Bernard. 1993. "Islam and Liberal Democracy." *Atlantic Monthly.* 271(2):89–98.

Lijphart, Arend. 1977. *Democracy in Plural Societies: A Comparative Exploration.* New Haven, CT: Yale University Press.

———. 1984. *Democracies, Patterns of Majoritarian and Consensus Government in Twenty-One Countries.* New Haven, CT: Yale University Press.

Linz, Juan J. 1978. *The Breakdown of Democratic Regimes: Crisis, Breakdown, and Reequilibrium.* Baltimore, MD: Johns Hopkins University Press.

———. 1988. "Legitimacy of Democracy and the Socioeconomic System." Pp. 65–97 in *Comparing Pluralist Democracies: Strains on Legitimacy,* edited by M. Dogan. Boulder, CO: Westview.

———. 1990a. "The Virtues of Parliamentarianism." *Journal of Democracy* 1(4):84–91.

———. 1990b. "The Perils of Presidentialism." *Journal of Democracy* 1(2):51–69.

Linz, Juan J., and Alfred Stepan, eds. 1987. *The Breakdown of Democratic Regimes.* Baltimore, MD: Johns Hopkins University Press.

———. 1989. "Political Crafting of Democratic Consolidation or Destruction: European and South American Comparisons." Pp. 41–61 in *Democracy in the Americas: Stopping the Pendulum,* edited by R. A. Pastor. New York: Holmes and Meier.

Lipset, Seymour Martin [1960] 1981. *Political Man: The Social Bases of Politics.* Expanded ed. Baltimore, MD: Johns Hopkins.

———. [1963] 1979. *The First New Nation.* Expanded ed. New York: Norton.

———. [1970] 1988. *Revolution and Counterrevolution: Change and Persistence in Social Structures.* Revised ed. New Brunswick, NJ: Transaction.

———. 1985. *Consensus and Conflict: Essays in Political Sociology.* New Brunswick, NJ: Transaction.

———. 1990a. "The Centrality of Political Culture." *Journal of Democracy* 1(4):80–83.

———. 1990b. *Continental Divide: The Values and Institutions of the United States and Canada.* New York: Routledge.

———. 1991. "No Third Way: A Comparative Perspective on the Left." Pp. 183–232 in *The Crisis of Leninism and the Decline of the Left: The Revolutions of 1989,* edited by D. Chirot. Seattle, WA: University of Washington.

———. 1992. "Conditions of the Democratic Order and Social Change: A Comparative Discussion." Pp. 1–14 in *Studies in Human Society: Democracy and Modernity,* edited by S. N. Eisenstadt. New York: E. J. Brill.

———. 1993. "Reflections on Capitalism, Socialism and Democracy." *Journal of Democracy* 4(2):43–53.

Lipset, Seymour Martin, and Gyorgy Bence. Forthcoming. "Anticipations of the Failure of Communism." *Politics and Society.*

Lipset, Seymour Martin, and Stein Rokkan. 1967. "Cleavage Structures, Party Systems and Voter Alignments." Pp. 1–64 in *Party Systems and Voter Alignments,* edited by S. M. Lipset and S. Rokkan. New York: Free Press.

Lipset, Seymour Martin, Kyoung-Ryung Seong, and John Charles Torres. 1993. "A Comparative Analysis of the Social Requisites of Democracy." *International Social Science Journal* 45:155–75.

Lipset, Seymour Martin, Martin Trow, and James Coleman. 1956. *Union Democracy: The Inside Politics of the International Typographical Union.* New York: Free Press.

Macdonald, Donald S. 1992. "Korea's Transition to Democracy." Pp. 19–28 in *Democracy in Korea: The Roh Tae Woo Years* (papers published from the June 22, 1992 Merrill House conference), edited by C. Sigur. New York: Carnegie Council on Ethics and International Affairs.

Malia, Martin. 1992. "Leninist Endgame." *Daedalus* 121(2):57–75.

Mann, Michael. 1993. "The Struggle between Authoritarian Rightism and Democracy: 1920–1975" (Working Paper 1993/45). Juan March Institute, Center for Advanced Study in the Social Sciences, Madrid, Spain.

Marx, Karl. 1958. *Capital.* Vol. 1. Moscow, Russia: Foreign Languages Publishing House.

Merkl, Peter H. 1993. "Which Are Today's Democracies?" *International Social Science Journal* 45:257–70.

Moore, Barrington. 1966. *Social Origins of Dictatorship and Democracy: Lord and Peasant in the Making of the Modern World.* Boston, MA: Beacon.

Muller, Edward N. 1988. "Democracy, Economic Development, and Income Inequality." *American Sociological Review* 53:50–68.

Nathan, Andrew J., and Tao Shi. 1993. "Cultural Requisites for Democracy in China: Findings from a Survey." *Daedalus* 122:95–124.

Neubauer, Deanne. 1967. "Some Conditions of Democracy." *American Political Science Review* 61:1002–9.

Olsen, Marvin E. 1968. "Multivariate Analysis of National Political Development." *American Sociological Review* 33:699–712.

Olson, Mancur, Jr. 1963. "Rapid Growth as a Destabilizing Force." *Journal of Economic History* 23:453–72.

Pye, Lucian W. 1965. "Introduction: Political Culture and Political Development." Pp. 3–26 in *Political Culture and Political Development,* edited by L. Pye and S. Verba. Princeton, NJ: Princeton University Press.

———. 1968. *The Spirit of Chinese Politics.* Cambridge, MA: Massachusetts Institute of Technology.

Pye, Lucian, with Mary W. Pye. 1985. *Asian Power and Politics. The Cultural Dimensions of Authority.* Cambridge, MA: Harvard University Press.

Riggs, Fred. 1993. "Fragility of the Third World's Regimes." *International Social Science Journal* 45:199–244.

Rueschemeyer, Dietrich, Evelyne Huber Stephens, and John D. Stephens. 1992. *Capitalist Development and Democracy.* Chicago: IL: University of Chicago Press.

Rustow, Dankwart. 1970. "Transitions to Democracy." *Comparative Politics.* 2:337–66.

Sadowski, Christine M. 1993. "Autonomous Groups as Agents of Democratic Change in Communist and Post-Communist Eastern Europe." Pp. 163–95 in *Political Culture and Developing Countries,* edited by L. Diamond. Boulder, CO: Lynne Rienner.

Sartori, Giovanni, ed. 1983. *Social Science Concepts: A Systemic Analysis.* Beverly Hills, CA: Sage.

———. 1987. *The Theory of Democracy Revisited.* Chatham, NJ: Chatham House.

Scalapino, Robert H. 1989. *The Politics of Development. Perspectives on Twentieth Century Asia.* Cambridge, MA: Harvard University Press.

Schmitter, Philippe C., and Terry Lynn Karl. 1993. "What Democracy Is . . . and Is Not." Pp. 39–52 in *The Global Resurgence of Democracy,* edited by L. Diamond and M. F. Plattner. Baltimore, MD: Johns Hopkins University Press.

Schneidman, Witney, W. 1992. "Africa's Transition to Pluralism: Economic and Investment Implications." *CSIS Africa Notes* (Nov.):1–7.

Schumpeter. Joseph. 1950. *Capitalism, Socialism, and Democracy.* 3d ed. New York: Harper and Row.

Seung-Soo, H. 1992. "Democracy and Economic Development: An Economic Historical Perspective." Pp. 79–90 in *Democracy in Korea: The Roh Tae Woo Years* (papers from the June 22, 1992 Merrill House conference), edited by C. Sigur. New York: Carnegie Council on Ethics and International Affairs.

Sklar, Richard. 1987. "Developmental Democracy." *Comparative Studies in Society and History* 29:686–714.

Skocpol, Theda. 1979. *States and Social Revolutions.* Cambridge, England: Cambridge University Press.

Smith, Tony. 1978. "A Comparative Study of French and British Decolonization." *Comparative Studies in Society and History* 20(1):70–102.

Spencer, Metta. 1991. "Politics beyond Turf: Grassroots Democracy in the Helsinki Process." *Bulletin of Peace Proposals* 22(4):427–35.

Stephens, John D. 1993. "Capitalist Development and Democracy: Empirical Research on the Social Origins of Democracy." Pp. 409–47 in *The Idea of Democracy,* edited by D. Copp, J. Hampton, and J. Roemer. Cambridge, England: Cambridge University Press.

Tamás, Gáspár M. 1992. "Socialism, Capitalism, and Modernity." *Journal of Democracy* 3:60–74.

Therborn, Göran. 1977. "The Rule of Capital and the Rise of Democracy." *New Left Review* 103:3–41.

Tocqueville, Alexis de. 1976. *Democracy in America.* Vols. 1 and 2. New York: Knopf.

Todaro, Michael P. 1981. *Economic Development in the Third World.* New York: Longman.

Todd, Emanuel. 1979. *The Final Fall: Essays on the Decomposition of the Soviet Sphere.* New York: Karz.

Trudeau, Pierre. 1960. "Some Obstacles to Democracy in Quebec." Pp. 241–59 in *Canadian Dualism,* edited by M. Wade. Toronto, Ontario: University of Toronto Press.

Tu, Wei-ming. 1993. "Introduction: Cultural Perspectives." *Daedalus* 122:vii–xxii.

Vatikiotis, Panayiotis J. 1988. *Islam and the State.* London: Croom Helm.

Waisman, Carlos. 1992. "Capitalism, the Market and Economy." Pp. 140–55 in *Reexamining Democracy,* edited by G. Marks and L. Diamond. Newbury Park, CA: Sage.

Weber, Max. 1906. "Zur Lage der bürgerlichen Demokratie in Russland." *Archiv für Sozialwissenschaft und Sozialpolitik* 22:234–353.

———. 1946. *From Max Weber: Essays in Sociology.* Edited and translated by H. H. Gerth and C. W. Mills. New York: Oxford University Press.

Weede, Erich. 1993. "The Impact of Democracy or Repressiveness on the Quality of Life, Income Distribution, and Economic Growth Rates." *International Sociology* 8:177–95.

Weede, Erich, and Heinrich Tiefenbach. 1981. "Some Recent Explanations of Income Inequality." *International Studies Quarterly* 25:255–82.

Weffort, Francisco C. 1992. "New Democracies, Which Democracies?" (Working Paper #198). The Woodrow Wilson Center, Latin American Program, Washington, DC.

Weiner, Myron. 1987. "Empirical Democratic Theory." Pp. 3–34 in *Competitive Elections in Developing Countries,* edited by M. Weiner and E. Ozbudun. Durham, NC: Duke University Press.

Weingast, Barry. 1993. "The Political Foundations of Democracy and the Rule of Law." The Hoover Institution, Stanford, CA. Unpublished manuscript.

Whitehead, Lawrence. 1989. "The Consolidation of Fragile Democracies: A Discussion with Illustrations." Pp. 79–95 in *Democracy in the Americas: Stopping the Pendulum,* edited by R. A. Pastor. New York: Holmes and Meier.

Whyte, Martin King. 1992. "Prospects for Democratization in China." *Problems of Communism* 42(3):58–70.

World Bank. 1991. *Managing Development: The Governance Decision.* Washington, DC: World Bank.

Wright, Robin. 1992. "Islam and Democracy." *Foreign Affairs* 71(3):131–45.

CHAPTER THIRTY-ONE

Frameworks of the Great Revolutions: Culture, Social Structure, History, and Human Agency*

S. N. Eisenstadt

1

The past two decades have witnessed the reemergence of comparative historical sociological studies after a period of relative neglect. These have raised some of the basic questions of macrosociological analysis, especially those of the relations between structure and history and between social structure, history, and human agency, between culture and social structures as well as problems of the validity of the evolutionary perspectives predominant in many of the classical studies as in those of modernism and the consequences of industrial societies conducted in the 1950s.

The crux of this great debate is whether human activities and the course of history are shaped by "deep" rules which regulate human activity, either those of the human mind (as claimed by the structuralists) or those governing social relations and the modes of production (as the Marxists claim). If so, what about human creativity? What about the individual as an autonomous agent? A closely related problem is whether laws or patterns of change common to all human societies exist, or whether different societies or civilizations develop in their own ways.

More recently, studies of relations between human agency and structure and between structure and history have focused on the controversy between emphasis on deep structure versus negotiated order as the key to understanding social interaction and institutional formation.

This question arises from the theoretical controversies in contemporary sociology, especially those related to the structural-functional school. They stressed that the institutional contours of any social group or setting of social interaction or institutional formation should not be taken for granted, neither can these contours be explained in terms of systemic needs or levels of structural differentiation, but instead should be investigated as to the conditions and processes through which such contours emerge, function, are reproduced and change.[1]

Two major theoretical orientations have emerged out of the discussions. The first is an attempt to analyze how such frameworks are constructed, either through the activities of different social actors—through some process of negotiation, struggle, and conflict between them—or, to use Anthony Giddens' term, through "structuration" rather than "structure."[2]

The second approach—because it removes the active subject from the picture—has developed above all among the structuralists, starting with Lévi-Strauss[3] and continuing in other approaches, especially Marxist ones, as in the work of Althusser and semiotic and semiological writers. All these approaches stressed that any institution or pattern of behavior must be explained as a manifestation of some principle of deep structure of the human mind, of forces of production or the like.[4]

Closely related is the problem of how to conceive relations between culture and social structure. Above all it was related to the classic problem of the order-maintaining as against the order-transforming functions of culture, as well as the degree to which social structure determines culture, or vice-versa—that is, the extent of mutual determination of culture, social structure, and social behavior. As Renato Rosaldo (1985)[5] has put it, what is the degree to which culture is a cybernetic feedback mechanism controlling behavior and social structure, or is there a possibility of choice and inventiveness in the use of cultural resources?

Here also two opposing trends can be distinguished. One, found mostly among structuralists, tends to emphasize a rather closed static and homogeneous view of these relations, with heavy emphasis on culture as programming human behavior or social organization.

On the other hand, recent social science discourse has thrown up the opposite view, presenting the relations between culture and social structure as a process of almost endless reconstruction and reinterpretation of cultural visions and symbols of meaning concomitantly with changing patterns of behavior, structure, power, and other resources.

In its extreme formulation such a view can be interpreted as presenting the culture of a society (as suggested for instance by Ann Swidler), as a reservoir or toolbox of strategies[6] of action, which can be activated in different situations according to the interests— "material" and "ideal"—of social actors.

A different but closely related set of problems, rooted in the evolutionary perspective of large parts of classical sociology—and of the studies of modernization and of the emergence of industrial societies—was thrown up in the 1940s and 1950s. The most important problem here was whether any directions of change are inherent in the development of societies, to what extent such directions may be common to all human societies and what is the role of historical contingencies, different ecological conditions, intersocietal relations, and human actors.

2

All these problems have informed the recent comparative and historicosociological studies, and most works share many common analytical themes arising out of recent major theoretical controversies, at the same time as they differ from each other with respect to certain central theoretical issues.[7]

First of all, these works do not accept any simple evolutionist view, a criticism often made of the earlier studies of modernization and convergence of industrial societies, although some of the problems posed by that view (especially what may be called the expansive capacities, whether in the cultural, political, or economic spheres of societies or civilizations) are addressed in many of them. Second, most of these works do not accept the "closed systemic" view of societies so heavily emphasized by the structural-functional school. Third, all of them place a very strong emphasis on civilizations as important arenas of macrosociological analysis and on intersocietal or intercivilizational relations. They not only attempt to analyze different societies in isolation, but also combine such an analysis with that of certain major patterns of intersocietal dynamics as they interconnect through population movements, wars and conquests, the encounter of nomad peoples with settled ones, migrations, trade, and cultural and religious movements. Moreover, these works lay heavy emphasis on the importance of broader civilizational units or frameworks—Judaism, Islam, medieval Europe—not just of apparently self-centered (political) societies, as the major focus or arena of comparative sociological analysis. In most of these works the combination of an antievolutionist attitude with a strong emphasis on historical, institutional, and intercivilization perspectives is connected with great emphasis on the importance of various contingent historical trends to explain the evolution of different institutional formations.

The major theoretical or analytical differences among these works are centered in the relationship between culture and society, or as it has often and not very felicitously been put, on the "role of ideas" in institutional dynamics.

3

In the following discussion, we shall take up these problems as related to historical and comparative analysis by a reexamination of the characteristics and conditions of the "great," "classical" revolutions: the English Civil War, the American and French Revolutions, and later, the Chinese and Russian ones, also others such as the Turkish or the Vietnamese Revolutions. These were closely connected with the emergence of the modern world, of modern civilization; since revolutionary ideologies, the revolutionary image, and movements have become a basic component of the modern perspective.[8]

Revolutions or revolutionary change, have become the epitome of "real" social change, and the revolutionary phenomenon has become a central topic and a focus of great interest and fascination in modern intellectual, ideological, and scholarly discourse.

Large portions of the literature on revolutions and social change have assumed that revolutions are true, pristine, "real" social change, other processes being judged or scaled according to their proximity to some ideal type of revolution. In this way the specificity of both these "great" revolutions and of other processes and types of change was often lost.

Accordingly, we shall first attempt to indicate the specific characteristics of these revolutions as distinct from other processes of change, especially of drastic changes of political regimes. Second, we shall turn to the perennial question of the causes of revolutions and reexamine the wide-ranging literature on this subject. Throughout our analysis we shall attempt to understand the specificity of revolutions by comparison with other, somewhat similar cases of political and social change.

4

Revolutions, of course, denote first of all radical change in the political regime far beyond the deposition of rulers or even the replacement of ruling groups. They denote a situation in which such deposition and change—usually very violent—results in a radical transformation of the rules of the political game and the symbols and bases of legitimation, a change closely connected with novel visions of political and social order.[9] It is this combination that is distinctive of revolutions. In other words, such revolutions tend to spawn (to use Said Arjomand's term) certain distinct cosmologies, certain very marked cultural and political programs.[10]

The combination of violent changes of regime with a very strong ontological and political vision happened not only in "great" revolutions. The crystallization of the Abbasid caliphate, often called the Abbasid revolution, is a very important—even if possibly only partial—illustration of such a combination in an earlier historical period. What is characteristic of modern revolutions is the nature of their ontologies or cosmologies; certain central aspects of the revolutionary process that developed within them and the relations between the changes and regimes and in major institutional arenas of the affected societies.[11]

The cosmologies promulgated in these revolutions were characterized first of all by an emphasis on themes of equality, justice, freedom, and the participation of the community in the political center. These were combined with "modern" themes such as the belief in progress, and with demands for full access to the central political arenas and participation in them. Second, what was new was the combination of all these themes with an overall utopian vision of the reconstruction of society and of political order, not just with millenarian visions of protest.

Third, in all these revolutions, society was seen as an entity to be remolded through political action according to the visions. These also entailed the reconstruction of society, including far-reaching institutional change, radical restructuring of class and status relations, doing away with traditional ascriptive criteria of stratification, unseating or destroying old and upper classes, and shifting the relative hegemony to new ones, be it the bourgeoisie or the proletariat.

Fourth, these visions emphasized dissociation from the preceding historical background of societies, a denial of the past, an emphasis on a new beginning, and the combination of such discontinuity with violence.

The fifth major characteristic of these revolutions was their universalistic and missionary vision. Although each set up a new regime in a certain country, a regime which, especially in its later stages, proclaimed strong patriotic themes, and although such regimes always bore an ineradicably national stamp yet the revolutionary visions were projected in different degrees, as universal, extendable in principle to all of humanity. This universal message became most strongly connected with a missionary zeal reminiscent, as Maxine Rodinson has shown, of the expansion of Islam. As in the case of Islam, the spread of this vision was supported by revolutionary armies ready to carry it abroad. As in the case of Islam, again, such missionary zeal did not necessarily make for greater tolerance or "liberalism" but certainly bore an unmistakably universalistic stamp.[12]

The specifically "national," primordial, or patriotic revolutionary themes were usually secondary to the more general, universalistic ones which constituted the core of the revolutionary vision and of nations as bearers of their universalistic relevance.

5

The central institutional change was, as Michael Walzer has pointed out, that in the first revolutions (the English and the French and, in a different, less personal way, in the American one) the rulers were not just driven out, exiled or killed, but deposed through a legal procedure.[13] Even if the rulers themselves did not accept its legality or legitimacy, the fact that such a legal procedure was undertaken at all is of immense significance; it indicated very serious attempts to find a new institutional grounding for the accountability of rulers.

This idea itself was not new. It was part and parcel of the basic premises of the Axial civilizations within whose frameworks these revolutions occurred, though it became transformed in very far-reaching ways.

Closely related were the distinct characteristics of the political process that arose out of these revolutions, first, as Eric Hobsbawm[14] has shown, the direct impact on the central political struggle of popular uprisings through their movement into the center.

Second was the continuous interweaving of several types of political action (such as rebellions, movements of protest, and struggles at the center) previously to be found in many, sometimes in all, societies within certain common frameworks of political action and a common ideology, however fragile and intermittent. Such currents were contingent on a new type of leadership, one which appealed to various sectors of the population.

Third, and possibly the most distinctive feature of the political processes was the role of autonomous cultural, religious, or intellectual groups: heterodox religious or secular groups like the English (and to an even greater extent American) Puritans, the French intellectual clubs analyzed by A. Cochin and later by F. Furet, the Russian intelligentsia, and the like.[15]

They constituted the crucial element which, to no small degree, shaped the whole revolutionary political process. It is impossible to understand these revolutions without taking account of the ideological, propagandist, and organizational skills of such intellectuals or cultural elites. Without them the entire revolutionary movement as it crystallized would probably not have occurred.

Yet another aspect of this revolutionary process was the transformation of the liminal aspects and symbols, especially of peripheral movements of protest. In most cases, the central political arena became, for relatively long periods, shaped in a liminal mode. The center itself became, perhaps temporarily, a quasi-liminal situation or arena, a series of such situations, or the arena in which liminality was played out. These dimensions are closely connected to the centrality of violence, to its very sanctification, as can be seen in the rise and sanctification of terror.

6

Thus these revolutions were characterized not only by three distinct characteristics—their cosmologies and political programs, novel overall cultural agendas, and the political processes that developed within them—but perhaps above all by their combination, not to be found, even incipiently, in all social transformations.

This can perhaps best be illustrated by a brief consideration of one radical change which has often been compared with "great" revolutions, the so-called Meiji Restoration of 1868 in Japan.[16] It has often been compared with the "great" revolutions because, like them, it gave rise to far-reaching processes of social, economic, and political transformation and because it spawned a new cultural and political agenda which, for all its "traditionalist" components, constituted a radical break with the preceding Tokugawa shogunate.

And yet, with respect to certain crucial features, especially revolutionary ideology and the nature of the political process generated by it, the Meiji Restoration differed greatly from "great" revolutions.

As before the revolutions, three types of political movements—rebellions (especially of peasants), movements of protest, and political struggle at the center—abounded in the pre-restoration setting and in the process leading to restoration as well as in the first two decades of the new regime.

Many ad hoc contacts were forged naturally between these groups and between them and certain urban groups and rebellious peasants; they all constituted a very important background to the toppling of the Tokugawa regime but were not a basic component of the political aspect of the restoration.

Significantly enough, however, in the process which toppled the Togukawa regime no new patterns of political organization crystallized in which such groups would combine for common political action. Nor was there any political leadership which attempted to mobilize disparate social forces for the more central political struggle.

The Meiji Restoration, unlike the "great" revolutions, was characterized by an almost total absence of autonomous, distinct religious or secular intellectual groups as politically active elements.

It was above all samurai, some of them learned in Confucian lore, and the shishi, who were most active in the restoration, but they did not act as autonomous intellectuals bearing a new Confucian vision. They acted as members of their respective social and political groups bearing a distinct political vision.

But this vision differed greatly from that of the "great" revolutions: they were in a way the mirror images of those of the latter. The restoration was presented as a renovation of a previous archaic system, which in fact never existed, not as a revolution aimed at directing the social and political order in an entirely fresh direction. There were almost no utopian elements in the vision. The whole reversion to the emperor could be seen, as Hershel Webb has pointed, as an "inverted utopia." The message of the Meiji Restoration was addressed to the renovation of the Japanese nation; it had no basic universalistic or missionary dimensions.[17]

Similar processes of radical change in modern times arose in such countries as India, Thailand, and the Philippines. Most Latin American countries evolved in ways markedly different from the classical revolutions, with but certain of the distinctive characteristics of the "great" revolutions.

7

How can we then explain this specific combination of such characteristics in the classical "great" revolutions? Here we come to the analysis of the causes of revolution, a problem of central importance for historical and comparative sociology.

Several broad types of cause have been analyzed in the literature. The first concerns structural conditions, the second, the sociopsychological preconditions of revolutions, and the third, special historical causes.

Several structural conditions have been singled out. One concerns aspects of internal struggles, such as those between the major classes predominant in prerevolutionary societies, or interelite struggles between components of the ruling or upper class as leading to revolution.[18]

A special subtype of such analyses is the emphasis (to be found in the work of Theda Skocpol and other scholars, building on the earlier work of Barrington Moore) on the more general relations between the state and the major social strata, especially the aristocracy and the peasantry.[19]

Second and closely related to such explanations are those which emphasize the weakening or decay of the prerevolutionary political regimes from internal causes such as economic or demographic trends or through the impact of international forces such as economic trends, through wars, or some combination thereof.[20]

Earlier studies were also devoted to the contribution to revolutionary situations of broad economic factors or trends like economic fluctuations and rising inflation with the resulting impoverishment of large sectors of society, not only of the lower strata but also of wide sectors of the middle and even upper classes.

In some of the Marxist literature such economic explanations, together with those of class struggle, were elevated into ineluctable contradictions between old and newly emerging forces of production.

Such studies have often been connected with the third type of explanation, the sociopsychological one. Often, following Toqueville's brilliant analysis, these have emphasized the importance of relative deprivation and frustration arising in bad times following good ones, when the aspirations of large sectors of the population were raised, in generating widespread dissatisfaction which could give rise to rebellions or revolutionary predispositions.

Thus it was interclass and interelite struggles, demographic expansion, the domestic (above all fiscal) and international weaknesses of the state, economic imbalances and sociopsychological frustrations attendant on worsening economic conditions, that constituted the most important items in the causes of revolutions.

The exploration of how these "causes" coalesce, their relative importance, and their actual constellations in different revolutions should and will continue. But in themselves such analyses, important as they are, will not provide an adequate answer to the search for "the causes" of revolution.

It is not that the answers to the questions posed in this literature are sometimes unsatisfactory or controversial, which, of course, is inherent in any scholarly enterprise. What is more important is that the questions asked are not sufficient for the analysis of some of the most important aspects of the problem. For a very simple reason: these causes are not specific to revolutions. The same causes, in different constellations, have been singled out in the vast literature on the decline of Empires.

The fact that these causes can be found in all prerevolutionary societies, but not only in them, should not be surprising. Revolutions are, after all, first and foremost synonymous with decline or breakdown of regimes and with the results thereof.

Jack Goldstone has recently summarized very accurately the combination of these processes leading to the breakdown of regimes:

The four related critical trends were as follows. (1) Pressures increased on state finances as inflation eroded state income and population growth raised real expenses. States attempted to maintain themselves by raising revenues in a variety of ways, but such attempts alienated elites, peasants, and urban consumers, while failing to prevent increasing debt and eventual bankruptcy. (2) Intra-elite conflicts became more prevalent, as larger families and inflation made it more difficult for some families to maintain their status, while expanding population and rising prices lifted other families, creating new aspirants to elite positions. With the state's fiscal weakness limiting its ability to provide for all who sought elite positions, considerable turnover and displacement occurred throughout the elite hierarchy, giving rise to factionalization as different elite groups sought to defend or improve their position. When central authority collapsed as a result of bankruptcy or war, elite divisions came to the fore in struggles for power. (3) Popular unrest grew, as competition for land, urban migration, flooded labour markets, declining real wages, and increased youthfulness raised the mass mobilization potential of the populace. Unrest occurred in urban and rural areas and took the various forms of food riots, attacks on landlords and state agents, and land and grain seizures, depending on the autonomy of popular groups and the resources of elites. A heightened mobilization potential made it easy for contending elites to marshal popular action in their conflicts, although in many cases popular actions, having their own motivation and momentum, proved easier to encourage than to control. (4) The ideologies of rectification and transformation became increasingly salient.[21]

These causes of decline and breakdown of regimes, especially of imperial or imperial-feudal ones, are also necessarily causes or preconditions of revolutions. But they do not explain the specific revolutionary outcome of the breakdown of regimes. Certainly, they constitute necessary conditions of revolutions, but by themselves are not sufficient. For the sufficient causes we must look beyond the breakdown of regimes.

8

One possible direction in the search for such sufficient conditions is the specific historic "timing" or historical contexts of revolutions. All have taken place in the early modern (though chronologically varying) phases of societies, within the framework of modernizing autocracies, of modern absolutist regimes which created the early modern territorial, often bureaucratic states (Poggi), and provided the strong impetus toward economic modernization, the development of early mercantile and even the beginnings of industrial capitalist economies, and of the rise of a market-based political economy.

It was the internal contradictions in the political systems of early absolutism, situated between traditional monarchical, semiaristocratic legitimation and new economic cultural and ideological currents challenging such legitimation as well as between these groups and the more traditional ones that provided the motor forces for the breakdown of such regimes. The ideological or symbolic components of revolutions were to no small degree fed by contradictions in the ideological legitimation of absolutist monarchies, especially between traditional or semitraditional legitimation and components of enlightenment bearing the seeds of a new cultural agenda.[22]

And yet, even this combination is not yet the end of our exploration of the causes of revolutions. Not all such combinations causing the decline of regimes within the historical framework of early modernity have generated revolution and revolutionary outcomes. India, or in a somewhat different mode Thailand, and many provinces of the Ottoman Empire—with the possible exception of Turkey itself where the establishment of the Kemalist regime was sometimes called a revolution (even if one from above) and possibly of Algeria—are among cases of nonrevolutionary outcomes in situations of early modernity. Another such "negative" illustration is provided by the Latin American countries, where the wars of independence were not revolutionary in the sense of promulgating an entirely new sociopolitical order, and where many of the crucial aspects of the revolutionary process were very weak, especially the continuous interweaving between political actors and the liminal characteristics of the central revolutionary struggle.[23]

But perhaps the most important case is once again Japan—the downfall of the Tokugawa regime, and the Meiji Ishin.[24]

The Tokugawa regime was characterized by some of the major structural features of early modernity and of its contradictions; by the rise of vibrant new economic (merchant and peasant) forces, by the undermining of older aristocratic "traditional" forces; by the breakdown of the regulatory economic policies of the older regime. It was also characterized by a very wide spread of education apparently making Japan the most literate preindustrial society in the world, and by the emergence of a very intensive political discourse.

The Togukawa regime was weakened by these internal processes as well as by the impact of external forces. It also faced a crisis of legitimization, but one not couched in the ideological terms characteristic of the prerevolutionary "ancien régimes" of Europe and China.

9

Note that the explanations referred to above do not address themselves to what is probably the most important distinctive element in the revolutionary process; new ontological visions or cosmologies and bearers of such visions, the autonomous cultural or intellectual groups which, as we have seen, constitute one of the most important reservoirs of new political leadership and organizations most characteristic of revolutions. Indeed, in large parts of the literature the ideological factors (new ideologies, religious beliefs, ideologies, and the like) are rarely analyzed as causes of revolution. Usually, even among non-Marxist historians, with the exception of Albert Cochin and Francois Furet,[25] they are seen more as epiphenomena of the "deeper" social processes or as a general background to revolutionary processes.

It may therefore be worth inquiring under what conditions, or in what societies, such ideologies or cosmologies and the groups which bear them and which unlike rebellions, movements of protest, class and interelite struggle are not to be found in all societies, become so central. They tend to develop in very specific civilizations, the so-called Axial civilizations.[26] By this term, we mean those civilizations that crystallized during the period from 500 B.C. to the first centuries of the Christian era, within which new ontological visions, including conceptions of basic tension between the transcendental and mundane orders emerged and were institutionalized in many parts of the world—in ancient Israel, later in Second-Commonwealth Judaism and Christianity, in ancient Greece, very partially in Zoroastrian Iran, in early imperial China under Hinduism and Buddhism, and, beyond the Axial Age proper, under Islam.

These conceptions were developed and articulated by a relatively new social element: elites that carried models of a cultural order, particularly intellectual elites, ranging from the Jewish prophets and priests, Greek philosophers, Chinese literati, Hindu brahmins, to Buddhist sanha or Islamic ulema. Their activities were centered on belief in the creation of the world according to some transcendental vision or command.

The successful institutionalization of such conceptions and visions resulted in the internal restructuring of these societies and of the interrelations between them.

Thus, there developed first a high level of distinctiveness of societal centers and their perception as symbolic and organizational entities, and a continuous interaction between center and periphery. Further, there was the rise of distinct collectivities, especially cultural or religious ones with a very high symbolic component as well as the somewhat ideological structuring of social hierarchies.

Third, and most important for our analysis, there took place a far-reaching restructuring of the relationship between the political and transcendental orders. The political order, as the central locus or framework of the mundane order, was usually conceived of as being subordinated to the transcendental order and so had to be restructured according to the precepts of the latter, above all according to the perception of the right way of overcoming the tension between the transcendental and the mundane orders of "salvation." The rulers were usually responsible for structuring the political order.

At the same time, the nature of the rulers was greatly transformed. The king-god—the embodiment of both the cosmic and the earthly orders—disappeared and a secular ruler emerged in principle accountable to some higher order; hence the possibility of calling a ruler to account before a higher authority, be it God or divine law. The first and most dramatic appearance of this conception occurred in ancient Israel, in priestly, especially prophetic, pronouncements. A different conception of such accountability to the community and its laws occurred on the northern shores of the eastern Mediterranean in ancient Greece. The notion of accountability occurred in all these civilizations in different ways.

Fourth is the development of relatively autonomous primary and secondary elites, especially of cultural, intellectual, and religious ones which continuously struggled with each other and with political elites.

It was such elites in general—the religious or intellectual ones in particular, many of which were also carriers of strong utopian visions with universalistic orientations—that constituted the most crucial elements in different heterodoxies and in political struggles and movements of protest.

10

These distinctive ideological and structural components of the political process characteristic of the Axial civilizations gave rise, within their regimes to very specific political dynamics, in which many kernels of the "great" revolutions could be found, but not to such revolutions themselves.

The basic cultural orientations and civilizational premises prevalent in them inspired visions of new social orders with very strong utopian and universalistic orientations, while the organization and structural characteristics provided the frameworks within which certain aspects of these visions could be institutionalized. The two became combined through the activities of the different elites analyzed above.[27]

The combination of all these characteristics gave rise in these usually imperial or imperial-feudal regimes to a relatively higher degree of coalescence than in other Axial Age civilizations between movements of protest, institution building, articulation and ideological levels of political struggle, and changes in the political system.

In some extreme cases such as, for instance, the transition from the Ummayad to the Abbyside Caliphate this could merge into what may seem like revolutionary processes and the establishment of the Abbyside Caliphate has indeed sometimes been defined in modern scholarship as a revolution. It rode on the wave of a strong sectarian-tribal movement which emphasized the universalistic component of Islamic ideals and in the name of this ideology, in conjunction with the interests of broader sectors, toppled the Ummayad rulers. But the ideologies of these movements of protest and political upheaval did not contain those components which characterized the modern ones; they were usually oriented to past visions and not to certain crucial future agendas. Nor did they spawn very stable constitutional and institutional formations. The Abbyside revolutions can, in many ways, be seen as one point in the Khaldounian cycles of Islamic political dynamics.[28]

In parallel, although of course greatly differing in details, distinctive dimensions of political process could also be found in other Axial civilizations, by comparison with seemingly similar political regimes which emerged in (sometimes neighboring) non-Axial civilizations.

But only when these ideological and structural components coincided in periods of early modernity did they generate revolutionary processes in the sense used here. It was only in these historical contexts that the elective affinities between the political process which developed in the Axial civilizations and the core ideological and organizational characteristics of revolutions were achieved that the major components of change in general and of the political process in particular became transformed in the revolutionary direction.

Such transformation of ideological components and cultural or symbolic themes did not, especially in the first revolutions—the English, American, and French ones—usually emerge at the very beginning of the rebellions and upheavals destined to topple various "ancient" regimes. It was only with the intensification of the revolutionary dynamic that such transformation evolved. But this does not mean, as proposed by Goldstone, that ideology became important only in the outcome of revolutions. The comparison between revolutionary dynamics in Axial and non-Axial civilizations, as well as between Japan on the one hand and China and the revolutions in the realm of Christianity of the other, indicates that ideological elements, in combination with their institutional settings, were of crucial importance, from relatively early stages, in the transformation of both the ideological and the political process in a revolutionary direction.[29]

Some of the characteristics of the Meiji-Ishin which distinguish it from "great" revolutions especially its predominantly "inverse-utopian" components, the restriction of the Ishin vision to Japan, and the lack of universalistic missionary components, are indeed very closely related to certain aspects of the Japanese historical experience. It is especially notable that, throughout its history, structural-institutional formations and dynamics arose in Japan, including, for instance, feudalism and very strong semiautonomous cities similar to those of western Europe, together with basic non-Axial ontological conceptions. On the other hand there were no autonomous religious and intellectual groups—Buddhist monks and other priests and Confucian scholars became embedded in small "familial" groups—which

explains their absence as a factor in the Meiji-Ishin.[30]

11

The close elective affinity between the political process in many of the Axial civilizations and the central characteristics of the revolutions does not mean (as the cases of India, South Asia, or most Islamic societies clearly indicate) that revolutions occurred with the onset of modernity in *all* Axial civilizations. How can we explain this?

Two additional factors have to be taken into account. One, which applies especially to India and to the Buddhist countries of South Asia, is the nature of the basic ontological visions, especially of conception of salvation within the Axial civilizations.[31] The second factor, which attaches to most Islamic states (and even some European ones) and also to India and the Theravada Buddhist societies, is the nature of their political regimes and political economies.

With respect to the first factor, the major distinction is—to adopt Weber's terminology—that between other-worldly and this-worldly conceptions of salvation. In the other-worldly civilizations the political arena did not constitute a basic focus of salvation, of the implementation of the vision of the civilization and proper ways of religious salvation did not constitute a focus of political struggle. Significantly enough no wars of religion broke out in India until the age of Axial Age civilizations or in the Buddhist countries until the contemporary era. The numerous sects and potential heterodoxies in these civilizations did not aim at the reconstruction of the political centers but rather at the redefinition of the boundaries between basic ascriptive collectivities.[32]

12

It was mainly in those Axial civilizations in which the basic ontology of salvation was this-worldly or one which contained a mixture of this-worldly and other-worldly orientations that free resources generated within social sectors could be channeled by the elites into "this-worldly" political or economic arenas. But the generation of such free resources was not always naturally secured under these regimes. Quite often, historical and politicoecological conditions, such as relative isolation from major international markets, impeded it. In such cases more patrimonial regimes (whether tribal or centralized kingdoms) tended to be established.

Sometimes, patrimonial regimes could spread especially into distant regions, as in the case of Islam, but can also be identified in the expansion of Christianity to relatively "undifferentiated" societies by the expansion of an Axial civilization.

Thus in the case of Islam, it was only at the core of the Ottoman Empire—and even there, only to a very limited extent—that the kernels of an autonomous civil society and the concomitant revolutionary potential arose.[33]

At the same time, however, given the basic premises of Islamic tradition, there developed throughout the realm of Islam, after the establishment of the first caliphates, especially after the downfall of the Abbyside Empire, a strong predisposition to revolutionary ideologies and to the rise of autonomous elites, often rooted in tribal traditions. Only rarely could such elites mount a fully revolutionary process or found a revolutionary regime.[34]

A rather important difference exists between those Axial civilizations with patrimonial political systems and political economies, mainly because of the basic characteristics of the elites and the ontological conceptions borne by them, and those in which such patrimonial tendencies were due above all to contingent historical, structural, or ecological conditions.

In the former case the basic structure and orientations of the elites restricted social movements aiming to reconstruct the political arena, although certainly not the participation of the religious elites in the patrimonial political arena.

In the second type of patrimonial regime there existed strong, even if for a long time only latent, orientations toward the reconstruction of the political arena so that, as in the case of Islam, protorevolutionary tendencies or, as in Russia or China, prerevolutionary ones could arise.

Thus there exists a close elective affinity between "this-worldly" (or a combination of this- and other-worldly) Axial civilizations and imperial and imperial-feudal regimes. Although only very rarely did feudal or feudal-imperial regimes develop into Axial civilizations, it did sometimes happen. The most important instance is, again, Japan, in which, as we have seen, a feudal-absolutist regime did arise within the framework of a non-Axial civilization. Yet, unlike feudal-imperial regimes in the Axial civilizations, above all the absolutist regimes of early modern Europe, in Japan, as we have seen no autonomous religions or intellectual groups promulgating a universal utopian vision existed. This is the crucial difference between the Meiji-Ishin and the "great" revolutions.

13

Not all revolutionary attempts under conditions similar to those of the accomplished revolutions have succeeded. Spain, Italy, and Germany are probably the most important locations of failed revolutions, along with those of Central Eastern Europe in 1848. How can we explain such failures?[35]

Some scholars attribute these failures to the predominance within the "ancien régimes" of Spain, Italy, and the Eastern European countries of many patrimonial components explaining the relatively low levels of free resources and weak autonomous elites.

But this is not the whole story, for it certainly does not apply to Germany. At least two additional sets of factors must be taken into account when discussing "failed" revolutions. The first is the simple fact that all revolutions result from civil war with many contestants and participants and that their success depends on both coherent and efficient behavior of the revolutionary groups, as well as on the relative weakness of the rulers, on a failure of their nerve or their will. Neither of these conditions is naturally given in a revolutionary situation. In some cases, as in Eastern Europe in 1848, where the autocratic rulers showed a marked strength of will which was reinforced by international circumstances—a sort of "autocratic international"—revolutionary attempts failed.

Failure was reinforced by divisions within would-be revolutionary forces, above all, in the case of Germany, between the rising bourgeoisie and the lower class, the former being afraid, after the experience of the French Revolution, of the latter. Further divisions arose between sectors of the intelligentsia or cultural elites bearing different visions, especially between "liberals" and constitutionalists, different groups of "patriots" and nationalists and incipient socialists.

Another factor to be taken into account was the absence of a unified German (or Italian) state and very strong aspirations to the creation of such a state by national movements among many sectors of German and Italian society. Unlike in England, France, or Russia, such national entities had yet to be constructed, which competed with the revolutionary agendas. Above all, such agendas could be subsumed, as in Germany and to a lesser extent in Italy, by certain groups and leaders (like Bismarck) closely allied with the ancien régime.

14

We have thus come full circle in our analysis of the causes or conditions of revolutions. As revolutions are, by definition, equivalent to the breakdown of regimes, it is the causes of such breakdowns, the constellations of interelite and interclass struggles, the rise of new social groups and economic forces which are blocked from access to power; the weakening

of regimes through such struggles, through economic turbulence and the impact of international forces that constitute the necessary conditions for the outbreak of revolutions.

But it is only insofar as such processes take place under specific historical circumstances, and within the frameworks of specific civilizational premises and political regimes, as well as of specific political economies that they may trigger revolutionary conditions and outcomes.

The specific historical circumstances are those of early modernity when the autocratic modernizing regimes faced the contradictions inherent in their own legitimation and policies and confronted the rise of new economic strata and "modern" ideologies.

The civilizational frameworks are those of "this-worldly" or combined this- and other-worldly Axial civilizations and Imperial or feudal-imperial regimes. If, for various historical reasons, such regimes are not thrown up in these civilizational frameworks the processes of change tend to be deflected from the revolutionary path.

The concrete outcome of these processes further depends greatly on the balance of power between revolutionary and counterrevolutionary forces and their cohesion.

15

The combination of civilizational and structural conditions and historical contingencies that generated the "great" revolutions has been rather rare in the history of mankind. With all their dramatic importance, these revolutions certainly do not constitute the only, or even the major or most far-reaching types of change, whether in premodern or modern times. Where other combinations of structural and institutional factors exist, for instance, in Japan, India, South Asia, or Latin America, they give rise to other processes of change and novel political regimes. These are not just "failed" would-be revolutions. They should not be measured by the criteria of the "great" revolutions;

rather they represent different patterns of social transformation, just as "legitimate" and meaningful, and should be analyzed in their own terms.

Accordingly, this analysis also indicates the relations between culture and social structure, history and structure, human agency and structure, as well as between order-maintaining versus order-transforming dimensions of culture.

Beliefs and cultural visions are basic elements of the social orders, of crucial importance in shaping their institutional dynamics. Beliefs or visions become such elements by the assimilation of their content into the basic premises of patterns of social interaction, that is, into clusters of regulative principles governing the major dimensions of social roles. These were classified by the "founding fathers of Sociology" as the social division of labor, the building of trust (or solidarity), the regulation of power, and the construction of meaning.[36]

One of the most important processes through which beliefs or visions are transformed into such regulative principles is the crystallization of models of cultural and social order and of codes. This closely resembles Weber's concept of "economic ethics" which specify how to regulate the frameworks of concrete social organizations and institutional settings, the patterns of behavior, and the range of major strategies of action appropriate to different arenas.[37]

Such transformations of religious and cultural beliefs into "codes" or "ethics" for a social order is effected through the activities of visionaries, themselves transformed into elites and who then form coalitions and countercoalitions with other elites. Such dynamics are not limited to the exercise of power in the narrow political or coercive sense. As even the more sophisticated Marxists, especially Gramsci,[38] have stressed, they are pervasive and include many relatively autonomous symbolic aspects; they represent different combinations of "ideal" and "material" interests. Such measures of control, as well as the challenges to them among elites and broader strata, shaped class relations and modes of production.

The institutionalization of such cultural visions, through the social processes and mechanisms of control, as well as their "reproduction" in space and time, necessarily generates tensions and conflicts, movements of protest and processes of change which offer certain opportunities to reconstruct the premises themselves.

Thus, in principle, the order-maintaining and order-transforming aspects of culture are but two sides of the same coin. Not only is there no basic contradiction between the two; they are part and parcel of the symbolic dimensions in the construction of social order.

The potential of change and transformation is not accidental or external to the realm of culture. It is inherent in the basic interweaving of culture and social structure as twin elements of the construction of social order. Precisely because the symbolic components are inherent in the construction and maintenance of social order they also bear the seeds of social transformation.

Such seeds are indeed common to all societies. Yet the actual ways in which they work out, the configurations of liminal situations, of different orientations and movements of protest, of modes of collective behavior and their impact on societies within which they develop, vary greatly between societies giving rise to contrasting social and cultural dynamics.

But new civilizational settings and social organizations, whether the Axial civilizations, those that ushered in capitalism in the West, or the great revolutions, are not "naturally" brought about by the basic tenets of a religion. Rather, they arise out of a variety of economic and political trends, as well as ecological conditions, all interrelated with the basic civilizational premises and with specific institutions.

Many general historical changes, especially the constructions of novel institutional orders, were probably the outcome of factors listed by J. G. March and John Olsen (1984).[39] These are the combination of basic institutional and normative forms; processes of learning and accommodation and types of decision making by individuals in appropriate arenas of action in response to a great variety of historical events.

As Said Arjomand has pointed out, the crystallization of any pattern of change is the result of history, structure, and culture, with human agency bringing them together.[40] It is also human agency, as manifested in the activities of institutional and cultural entrepreneurs, and their influences on different sectors of society, that shapes actual institutional formations. The potential for the crystallization of such formations is rooted in certain general societal conditions, such as degrees of structural differentiation or types of political economy. But these are only potentials, the concretization of which is effected through human agency.

It is the real constellations or configurations of these factors that are the major objects of comparative historicosociological analysis and discourse.

Notes

* From the *International Social Science Journal* 44, no. 3 (1992): 385–92, 394–401, by permission of UNESCO. Copyright 1992 by UNESCO.

1. S. N. Eisenstadt and M. Curelaru, *The Form of Sociology: Paradigms and Crises* (New York: Wiley, 1976).

2. A. Giddens, "Functionalism—après la lutte?" *Studies in Social Political Theory* (London: Hutchinson, 1979), pp. 96–129.

3. C. Lévi-Strauss, *Structural Anthropology* (New York: Basic Books, 1963); idem, *The Savage Mind* (London: Weidenfeld and Nicholson, 1966).

4. See Rossi, *From the Sociology of Symbols to the Sociology of Signs: Towards a Dialectical Sociology* (New York: Columbia University Press, 1983).

5. R. Rosaldo, *Culture and Truth* (Boston: Beacon Press, 1989); idem, "While Making Other Plans," *Southern California Law Review*, 1985, no. 58, pp. 19–28.

6. A. Swidler, "Culture in Action: Symbols and Strategies," *American Sociological Review*, 1986, no. 51, pp. 273–86.

7. See, for greater detail, S. N. Eisenstadt, "Macro-Sociology and Sociological Theory— Some New Directions," *Contemporary Sociology*, vol. 16, no. 2, September 1987, pp. 602–9.

8. S. N. Eisenstadt, *Revolutions and the Transformation of Societies* (New York: Free Press, 1978). On the image of revolution in modern social thought, see M. Lasky, "The Birth of a Metaphor: On the Origins of Utopia and Revolution," *Encounter*, vol. 34, no. 2, 1970, pp. 35–45, and no. 3, 1970, pp. 30–42; idem, *Utopia and Revolution* (Chicago: University of Chicago Press, 1976); K. Marx, *On Revolution*, S. K. Padover (ed.) (New York: McGraw-Hill, 1971); G. Landauer, *Die Revolution* (Frankfurt am Main: Rutten, 1912); A. T. Hatto, "Revolution: An Enquiry into the Usefulness of an Historical Term," *Mind*, vol. 58, no. 232, 1949, pp. 495–517; idem, "The Semantics of Revolution," in P. J. Vatikiotis (ed.), *Revolution in the Middle East* (London: Allen and Unwin, 1972). Among useful surveys of the literature on revolutions, see H. Wassmund, "Revolutionforschung," *Neue Politische Literatur*, vol. 18, no. 4, 1973, pp. 421–29; idem, "Revolutionforschung," ibid., vol. 20, no. 4, 1975, pp. 425–33; K. Lenk, *Theorien der Revolution* (Munich: Wilhelm Fink, 1973); C. Lindner, *Theorien der Revolution* (Munich: Wilhelm Goldmann, 1972); G. P. Meyer, "Revolutionstheorien Heute: Ein kritischer überblick in historischer Absicht," in H. U. Wehler (ed.), *200 Jahre amerikanische Revolution und modern Revolutionsforschung* (Gottingen: Vandenhoeck & Ruprecht, 1976), pp. 122–76; T. Skocpol, *State and Social Revolutions* (Cambridge: Cambridge University Press, 1979).

9. S. N. Eisenstadt, 1978, op. cit.

10. S. Arjomand, "History, Structure and Revolution in the Shi'ite Tradition in Contemporary Iran," *International Political Science Review*, vol. 10, no. 2, April 1989, pp. 111–21.

11. M. Lasky, "The Birth of a Metaphor on the Origins of Utopia and Revolution," *Encounter*, vol. 34, no. 2, 1970, pp. 35–45; S. N. Eisenstadt, op.

cit.; A. Seligman (ed.), *Order and Transcen-dence—The Role of Utopias and the Dynamics of Civilizations* (Leiden: E. J. Brill, 1989); J. A. Goldstone, "Révolutions dans l'histoire et histoire des révolutions," *Revue Française de Sociologie,* 1983, pp. 405–30.

12. M. Rodinson, *Marxism and the Muslim World.* (London: Lend Press, 1979); *Europe and the Mystique of Islam* (London: I. B. Tauris, 1989).

13. M. Walzer, *Regicide and Revolution* (Cambridge: Cambridge University Press, 1974).

14. E. Hobsbawm, *The Age of Revolution* (London: Weidenfeld and Nicholson, 1964).

15. A. Cochin, *La Révolution et la libre pensée* (Paris: Plon-Nourrit, 1924); A. Cochin, *L'esprit du Jacobinisme* (Paris: Presses Universitaires de France, 1979); F. Furet, *French Revolution* (New York: Macmillan, 1970); idem, *Interpreting the French Revolution* (Cambridge: Cambridge University Press, 1981); A. Cochin, 1979, op. cit.; F. Furet, 1981, op. cit.; V. C. Nahirny, *The Russian Intelligentsia: From Torment to Silence* (Rutgers, N.J.: Transaction Publications).

16. On the Meiji Restoration and its background, see P. Akamatsu, *Meiji,* 1868. (New York: Harper and Row, 1972); H. Norman, *Japan's Emergence as a Modern State* (New York: Institute of Pacific Relations, 1940); A. M. Craig, *Choshu in the Meiji Restoration* (Cambridge: Harvard University Press, 1961); J. Arnasson, *Paths to Modernity—The Peculiarities of Japanese Feudalism,* in G. McCormack and Y. Sugimoto (eds.), *The Japanese Trajectory: Modernization and Beyond* (Cambridge: Cambridge University Press, 1988); H. D. Haroutounian, "Late Tokugawa Culture and Thought," in M. Jansen, *Cambridge History of Japan,* vol. 5, *The Nineteenth Century* (Cambridge: Cambridge University Press, 1989), pp. 168–258; James W. White, "State Building and Modernization: The Meiji Restoration," in G. Almond, S. Flanagan, and R. Mundt *Crisis, Choice, and Change: Historical Studies of Political Development* (Boston: Little, Brown, 1973); James W. White, "State Growth and Popular Protest in Tokugawa Japan," *Journal of Japanese Studies,* vol. 14, no. 1, 1988, pp. 1–27; Thomas M. Huber, *The Revolutionary Origin of Modern Japan* (Stanford: Stanford

University Press, 1981); M. B. Jansen and G. Rozman (eds.), *Japan in Transition from Tokugawa to Meiji* (New York: Princeton University Press, 1986); M. B. Jansen, "The Meiji Restoration," in *The Cambridge History of Japan,* Vol. V., *The Nineteenth Century* (Cambridge: Cambridge University, 1989), pp. 308–67; T. Najita and J. V. Koschmann (eds.), *Conflict in Modern Japanese History* (Princeton, N.J.: Princeton University Press, 1982). On the outcomes of the Meiji Restoration see Akamatsu, *Meiji,* 1868; Norman, *Japan's Emergence;* R. A. Scalapino, "Japan between Traditionalism and Democracy," in S. Neumann (ed.), *Modern Political Parties* (Chicago: University of Chicago Press, 1965), pp. 305–53; Fairbank et al., *East Asia,* pp. 408–42; R. P. Dore (ed.), *Aspects of Social Change in Modern Japan* (Princeton: Princeton University Press, 1967); R. Ward (ed.), *Political Development in Modern Japan* (Princeton: Princeton University Press, 1968); W. W. Lockwood (ed.), *The State and Economic Entrepreneurs in Japan* (Princeton: Princeton University Press, 1965); A. E. Barshay, *State and Intellectuals in Imperial Japan—The Public Man in Crisis* (Berkeley, Los Angeles: University of California Press, 1980); W. Davis, "The Civil Theology of Inoke Tetsuriro," *Japanese Journal of Religious Studies,* vol. 5, no. 3(1), 1978; Peter Duus, *The Rise of Modern Japan* (Boston: Houghton Mifflin, 1976); S. C. Garon, "State and Religion in Imperial Japan 1912–1945," *Journal of Japanese Studies,* vol. 12, no. 2, 1986, pp. 273–302; C. Gluck, *Japan's Modern Myths—Ideology in the Late Meiji Period* (Princeton: Princeton University Press, 1985); T. C. Smith, *The Agrarian Origins of Modern Japan* (Stanford: Stanford University Press, 1959).

17. H. Webb, *The Japanese Imperial Institution in the Tokugawa Period* (New York: Columbia University Press, 1968).

18. The literature on the causes of revolutions is too vast to be cited here. A good overview can be found in the readers cited in note 4 above and in L. Stone "Theories of Revolution," *World Politics,* vol. 18, no. 2, 1966, pp. 159–76; L. Kramnick, "Reflections on Revolution: Definition and Explanation in Recent Scholar-

ship," *History and Theory,* vol. 11, no. 1, 1972, pp. 26–63; and K. Kumar, Introduction to *Revolution,* pp. 1–90; C. Tilly, "Revolutions and Collective Violence," in F. I. Greenstein and N. Polsby (eds.), *Handbook of Political Science* (Reading, Mass.: Addison-Wesley, 1975), pp. 483–555; C. Tilley, "Does Modernization Breed Revolution?" *Comparative Politics,* vol. 5, no. 3, 1973, pp. 425–47.

19. T. Skocpol, 1979, op. cit.; Barrington Moore, *The Social Origins of Dictatorship and Democracy* (Boston: Beacon, 1960).

20. Skocpol, 1979, op. cit.; J. B. Gillis, "Political Decay and the European Revolutions, 1789–1818," *World Politics,* vol. 22, no. 3, 1970, pp. 344–70.

21. J. A. Goldstone, *Revolution and Rebellion in the Early Modern World* (Berkeley, Los Angeles: University of California Press, 1991).

22. S. N. Eisenstadt, 1978, op. cit.; F. Furet, 1981, op. cit.

23. T. Halperin-Donghi, *The Aftermath of Revolution in Latin America* (New York: Harper and Row, 1971); J. Malloy (ed.), *Authoritarianism and Corporation in Latin America* (Pittsburgh, Penn.: University of Pittsburgh Press, 1977); H. J. Wiarda, *Politics and Social Change in Latin America: The Distinct Tradition* (Amherst: University of Massachusetts Press, 1974).

24. See the references in note 16.

25. A. Cochin, 1979, op. cit.; F. Furet, 1981, op. cit.; V. Nahirny, op cit.

26. S. N. Eisenstadt (ed.), *The Origins and Diversity of Axial Age Civilizations* (Albany, N.Y.: State University of New York Press, 1986).

27. A. Seligman, 1989, op. cit.

28. M. A. Shaban, *The Abbasid Revolution* (Cambridge: Cambridge University Press, 1970); M. Sharon, *Black Banners from the East* (Jerusalem: Magnes Press, 1983); E. Gellner, *Muslim Society* (Cambridge: Cambridge University Press, 1981), especially pp. 1–185; A. S. Ahmed, *Millenium and Charisma among Pathans* (London: Routledge and Kegan Paul, 1979).

29. See Goldstone, 1991, op. cit.; S. N. Eisenstadt, op. cit., chap. 9.

30. M. Jansen, "The Meiji Restoration," in idem (ed.), *The Cambridge History of Japan,* op. cit.,

pp. 308–61; H. D. Haroutounian, "Late Tokugawa Culture and Thought," in M. Jansen (ed.), *Cambridge History of Japan,* op. cit., pp. 168–258.

31. S. N. Eisenstadt, 1986, op. cit. On certain basic elements of Indian politics, see L. Dumont, *Religion, Politics and History in India;* J. C. Heesterman, *The Ancient Indian Royal Consecration: The Rajasuya Described According to the Yajus Texts,* annotated by J. C. Heesterman (Paris: Mouton, 1957); idem, *The Inner Conflict of Tradition* (Chicago: University of Chicago Press, 1985); D. C. C. Ingalls, "Authority and Law in Ancient India," *Journal of the American Oriental Society* (supp.), no. 74, 1954, pp. 34–45; H. N. Sinha, *Sovereignty in Ancient Indian Polity* (London: Luzac, 1938).

32. On the impact of sectarian religious groups, see J. Bunnag, *Buddhist Monk. Buddhist Layman: A Study of Urban Monastic Organization in Central Thailand* (Cambridge: Cambridge Studies in Social Anthropology, no. 6, 1973); E. B. Harper (ed.), *Religion in South Asia* (Seattle: University Washington Press, 1964); M. Nash, G. Obeyesekere, H. M. Ames et al., *Anthropological Studies in Theravada Buddhism* (New Haven: Yale University, Southeast Asia Studies Cultural Report Series, no. 13, 1966); P. Mus, "Traditions anciennes et bouddhisme moderne," *Eranos Jarhbuch,* vol. 32, 1968, pp. 161–275; P. Mus, "La Sociologie de Georges Gurvitch et L'Asie," *Cahiers Internationaux de Sociologie,* vol. 43, December 1967, pp. 1–21; B. Smith, *Religion and Legitimation of Power in Sri Lanka* (Chambersburg, Penn.: Anima Books, 1978); B. Smith, *Religion and Political Power in Thailand, Laos and Burma* (Chambersburg, Penn.: Anima Books, 1979); R. Thapar, *Ancient Indian Social History: Some Interpretations* (New Dehli, 1978); S. C. Malik (ed.), *Dissent, Protest and Reform in Indian Civilization* (Simla: India Institute of Advanced Study, 1973); see also M. S. A. Rao, in S. N. Eisenstadt, R. Kahane, and D. Shulman (eds.), *Social Movements in India* (New Delhi: Mahonar, 1982).

33. S. Mardin, "Power, Civil Society, and Culture in the Ottoman Empire," *Comparative Studies in Society and History,* no. 11, June 1969,

pp. 258–81; K. H. Karpat (ed.), *The Ottoman State and Its Place in World History* (Leiden: E. J. Brill, 1974); I. M. Lapidus, *A History of Islamic Societies* (Cambridge: Cambridge University Press, 1988); I. M. Lapidus, *Islam, Politics and Social Movements* (Berkeley: University of California Press, 1988); A. Kazançigil, "Democracy in Muslim Lands—Turkey in a Comparative Perspective," *International Social Science Journal,* no. 128, May 1991, pp. 343–63.

34. B. Lewis, *The Arabs in History* (New York: Harper and Row, 1966); idem, "Islamic Concepts of Revolution," in idem, *Islam in History* (London, Alcore Press, 1985), pp. 253–66.

35. See G. Mann, *The History of Germany since 1783* (London: Chatto and Windus); V. Valentin, *Geschichte der Revolution von 1948–9* (Berlin: Herder); A. Dorpalen, *Die Revolutionen von 1848;* T. Schneider (ed.), *Revolution der Gesselschaft* (Freiburg, 1973), pp. 97–116; A. W. Salomone (ed.), *Italy from the Risorgimento to Fascism* (Garden City, N.Y.: Doubleday, 1970); R. Carr, *Spain 1808–1939* (New York: Oxford University Press, 1966).

36. Eisenstadt and Curelaru, op. cit.

37. M. Weber, *Religion of China* (Glencoe, Ill.: Free Press, 1951); idem, *Religion of India* (Glencoe, Ill., Free Press, 1958); S. N. Eisenstadt, "Some Observations on Structuralism in Sociology, with Special and Paradoxical Reference to Max Weber," in P. M. Blau and R. K. Merton (eds.), *Continuity in Structural Inquiry* (Beverly Hills, Cal.: Sage, 1981).

38. A. Gramsci, *The Modern Prince* (London: Lawrence and Wishart, 1957).

39. J. G. March and J. Olsen, "The New Institutionalism: Organizational Factors in Political Life," *American Political Science Review,* vol. 78, no. 3, 1984, pp. 734–49.

40. S. Arjomand, *History, Structure and Revolutions,* op. cit.

The Study of National Development

The fascination of contemporary social scientists with the rise of the welfare state is equaled, indeed often exceeded, by their preoccupation with the problem of national development and underdevelopment. Just as there are great gaps in the income and power of nations, so there are profound divisions among social scientists as to the nature and causes of that condition. In this section we present three contrasting views of the forces which make for underdevelopment and the possible and likely ways out. They vary in tone and style of discourse almost as much as they diverge in their analysis and conclusion.

Samuel Huntington is the author of a classic work on the politics of national development, a book which is a point of reference for almost any and all discussions of the problem. In our selection he sets out five universally acknowledged goals for "the Good Society," assesses how far these have been achieved in the less developed countries of the world, and examines explanations for the relative success or failure of nations in achieving those goals. We see that the main theories offered by students of the problem stress the conflict and tension between the goals of development, as between economic growth on the one hand and equity and stability on the other, or between rapid economic growth and democracy. Ideas about how to reconcile these differences abound, and these are also evaluated here. As his more personal contribution to the dialogue, Huntington suggests more attention should be given to the role of culture and religion, and to the combinations of these factors in influencing the course of development in different regions of the world such as sub-Saharan Africa and Latin America.

While analysts such as Huntington assign considerable importance to forces *internal* to a nation, those who adhere to other schools of thought give little weight to such factors, and assign responsibility for development and non-development to forces *external* to each nation. For Immanuel Wallerstein the key lies in recognizing that there has been a world system in operation since at least 1450, and that system's most important characteristic is that it has been a capitalist world system following laws of development unique to capitalism. A main element of the Wallersteinian view is that the capitalist world system has always involved a *core* set of capitalist states, and others that were *peripheral,* and that this pattern of inequality is intrinsic to the system so long as it remains a capitalist system. His review of the history of national development presented here stresses two different stages. The first involved the struggle against colonialism and for national independence which dominated the period up to the end of World War II. In interpreting this period Wallerstein offers the novel view that the objectives of Woodrow Wilson and V. I. Lenin were basically similar! In the second stage, in full swing by 1968, we were, in Wallerstein's opinion, caught up in a world revolution against the liberalism and developmentalism which the core and its dominant ideology had all along been offering the less developed world. Wallerstein pursues his sweeping summary of hundreds of years of social, political, and economic history in a style much more prophetic than that which most social scientists would permit themselves, concluding that the capitalist system "will perhaps be no more by 2050."

The world as imagined by the so-called dependency school is also one deeply divided into two mutually exclusive sets, one made up of nations that are "dominant," and can expand and sustain themselves, and another that is "subjected" and whose development is therefore dependent on the control exercised by the dominant nations and the system of interrelations they develop and operate. In Dos Santos's words, the controls which inhibit the less favored nations are "terrible chains imposed by dependent development." And the idea that the less developed nations have somehow *themselves* been the source of failure because they did not adopt more advanced models of production and did not modernize, all that is, in Dos Santos's opinion, "nothing more than ideology disguised as science."

The Goals of Development*

Samuel P. Huntington

By the mid 1970s, substantial bodies of literature existed elaborating the importance of growth, equity, democracy, stability, and autonomy for developing societies and analyzing the ways in which those societies might best make progress toward those goals. Implicit in the widespread acceptance of these goals was also the acceptance of an image of the Good Society: wealthy, just, democratic, orderly, and in full control of its own affairs, a society, in short, very much like those found in Western Europe and North America. A backward society was poor, inequitable, repressive, violent, and dependent. Development was the process of moving from the latter to the former.

Individual scholars, of course, valued these individual goals differently and devoted their energies to analyzing and promoting different goals. They also, quite independently, had different ideas as to the relations that existed among these goals and the extent to which progress toward one goal helped or hindered progress toward another. In general, three broad approaches dominated the thinking about these relations. The first approach assumed the inherent compatibility among the goals. The second approach emphasized the intractable conflicts among the goals. The third approach stressed the imperative need for policies to reconcile those contradictions.[1]

The Compatibility Assumption

Compatibility theories in American social science essentially had their roots in the concept, elaborated by Karl Deutsch, Daniel Lerner, and Cyril Black, among others, of modernization as a comprehensive, systemic process in which societies changed fundamentally and across the board from an approximation of the traditional model to an approximation of the modern model. The various components of modernization were associated together, and changes from tradition to modernity in one sector or dimension were related to and reinforced by comparable changes in other sectors. To social scientists such as Deutsch, Lerner, and Black, it was perfectly clear that while modernization might be all of a piece, it was not necessarily all of a *good* piece; inevitably it involved stresses, strains, dislocations, upheavals. It was very easy for others, however, to move from the concept of modernization as a coherent process to the concept of development as a coherent process to a concept of the coherence and compatibility of the widely accepted goals of development. A society could and, indeed, almost had to make progress toward all these goals simultaneously; they were not only compatible with one another but also, in many cases, supportive of one another. This viewpoint, of course, had its roots in the fact that the societies of Western Europe and North America were, by and large, modern across the board; it may also have rested on the conclusion from a too-cursory survey of Western history that the progress of these societies toward wealth, equity, stability, democracy, and autonomy had been generally harmonious and linear.

This assumption that "all good things go together" is generally wrong and easy to criticize. It clearly does not describe developments in the Third World between 1955 and 1985. Yet it would also be wrong to dismiss it entirely. Some countries, indeed, are good cases of what could be called "negative compatibility": that is, they equally failed to make progress toward any of the goals of development. A much smaller number of countries, less than a handful, recorded significant progress toward achievement with respect to all five goals. In Asia, Japan obviously did so, but was it a developing country or a recovering country after World War II? Of countries whose developmental status cannot be questioned, perhaps Costa Rica was the most obvious case of substantial success with respect to all five goals. Following their 1948 revolution, Costa Ricans established a stable democratic regime that endured for decades. From the 1960s through the mid-1970s, their country achieved a very high rate of economic growth that brought it into the "upper middle class" of Latin American countries.[2] Land ownership was, comparatively speaking, relatively equal. From the 1960s to the 1970s, the proportion of the population living in absolute poverty declined dramatically, and overall equality in income distribution increased. At the same time, however, the relative position of the poorest 20 percent in terms of income shares also decreased, as did that of the richest 10 percent, reflecting the gains of the middle class (a phenomenon that in a democracy could have been predicted). In terms of autonomy, Costa Rica was heavily dependent on international trade, but during the 1960s and 1970s its agricultural exports expanded and diversified. All in all, Costa Rica comes close to being a success story in terms of both progress toward and achievement of the goals of development.

Other success stories undoubtedly exist. There are not, however, many of them. The compatibility thesis, at least in its positive version, has not been borne out by events. Under one circumstance, however, the compatibility assumption may be more valid than it is otherwise, that is, when societies are at war or under the sustained imminent threat of war. Setting apart the physical destruction that may be caused by war, wars are generally periods of extremely intense economic growth. They are also, as Albert Hirschman pointed out, "fre-

quently the condition for achieving a *peaceful* redistribution of income within the country."[3] This was certainly the case with Great Britain in World Wars I and II and with the United States in World War II. While antiwar dissent will be ruthlessly suppressed, political participation often expands in a variety of ways. Crime rates and civil disorder decline, unless it becomes clear that the war is being lost. National autonomy, of course, becomes identical with the pursuit of the war. It is, consequently, easy to understand why both Russians and Americans look back to World War II as "the best years of our lives"[4] and perhaps also why developing countries like South Korea, Taiwan, and Israel that confront an immediate and continuing security threat may have greater success than other countries in making simultaneous progress toward two or more developmental goals. The proponents of compatibility do not, however, argue for war as the engine of developmental progress, and, as the example of Vietnam demonstrates vividly, sustained war is in itself no guarantee of such progress.

Despite its dubious validity, the compatibility assumption has, as Robert Packenham showed, informed much of U.S. policy, particularly in economic aid, toward the Third World.[5] It surely provided the central core of the Alliance for Progress, with its triple commitment to economic growth, structural reform and political democratization. "These goals were, in theory," Arthur Schlesinger has observed, "mutually dependent. Structural change and political democratization were deemed indispensable in order to assure more equitable distribution of the gains of growth. The implication was that U.S. economic assistance would be conditioned on, or at least associated with, performance in social and political reform." Five years after the alliance was inaugurated, Senator Robert Kennedy similarly defined its goals as involving "economic progress, . . . social justice, political freedom, and democratic government." Eventually, however, even the alliance's most devoted advocates had to admit that the relations among these goals had not worked out as they had hoped. "We understood," concluded Schlesinger, "that in the short run there might well be conflict among these objectives. We also supposed, or hoped, that in the long run they were mutually reinforcing. This was evidently, in the middle run at least, an illusion."[6]

The impetus to assume the compatibility of these goals, however, remained present in U.S. policy toward Latin America. In 1984 the Kissinger Commission on Central America argued that "the requirements for the development of Central America are a seamless web" and defined U.S. goals for Central America in almost the identical words used two decades earlier in the Alliance for Progress:

- Elimination of the climate of violence and civil strife,
- Development of democratic institutions and processes,
- Development of strong and free economies with diversified production for both external and domestic markets,
- Sharp improvement in the social conditions of the poorest Central Americans, and
- Substantially improved distribution of income and wealth.[7]

The assumption that political democracy was compatible with social reform was concretely evident in the policies the Carter administration and the Reagan administration pursued in El Salvador. Both administrations pushed both for land reform and for early elections to a national legislative assembly, apparently oblivious to the well-documented fact that elected legislatures in developing countries are almost invariably hostile to land reform. The 1982 legislative election in El Salvador, a product in part of the policies of both administrations, once again demonstrated that point, with voters returning a legislature dominated by opponents of the land reform that both U.S. administrations had been supporting.

The compatibility assumption is undergirded by two very natural human inclinations. The first is to believe that all good things will, in some way, go together and hence that it will be possible to avoid a difficult choice, such as

that between democratic legislative elections and effective land reform. The second natural inclination is to believe that the elimination of one obvious, clear-cut evil will automatically lead to the elimination of the other principal social evils. Phrased another way, it is easy to see a particular goal as the critical one and progress toward that goal as performing a "locomotive" function and bringing progress toward other goals in its train. In the 1950s and early 1960s, for instance, it was widely assumed by some African nationalists and sympathetic Westerners that the granting of independence would usher in a new era in which the other goals of development could be relatively quickly achieved. "See ye first the political kingdom," as Kwame Nkrumah put it, "and all things will be added unto it."

In the postindependence world, three "locomotive" theories played major roles. One theory assumed that economic growth would perform the locomotive function and make possible a more equitable distribution of income and wealth, provide an indispensable precondition to the development of democratic institutions, reduce social conflict and hence undergird political order, and enable the society to stand independently on its own. This set of assumptions, which might be termed the liberal model of development, implicitly underlay much American scholarly and official thinking on the problems of development.[8] For a traditional Marxist, the revolutionary overthrow of the existing social-political order in an underdeveloped society and its replacement by a more equitable system would lead to economic growth, true democracy, social harmony, and real independence. The dependency theorist, on the other hand, expected to achieve the same result by starting on the international scene, breaking the chains of dependence drastically, and freeing the society from the international capitalist order. Once this was achieved, democracy, equity, growth in the sense of true development, and social stability would necessarily follow. In effect, each of these theories focused on one single source of evil—poverty, injustice, dependency—the removal of which would almost inevitably lead to the elimination of other evils that flowed from it. Significantly, perhaps, all three theories—liberal, Marxist, and dependency—identified the preeminent evil as economic. No significant body of development theory argued that the replacement of dictatorial regimes by democratic ones or the achievement of political order (however desirable these might be in themselves) was likely to produce the wondrous effects resulting from the elimination of poverty, inequity, or dependency.

Conflict Theories

By the 1970s, the demonstrated limits of the compatibility assumption generated increased awareness that good things often did not and could not go together. A new body of literature emerged, sobering and somber in its message and emphasizing the necessity for choice among goals. The works of the 1960s on development usually had words like "development," "nation-building," or "modernization" in their titles, which conveyed a sense of hopeful movement: *The Passing of Traditional Society* (1958), *The Politics of the Developing Areas* (1960), *The Politics of Modernization* (1965), *The Dynamics of Modernization* (1966), *The Stages of Economic Growth* (1960), *Nation-Building and Citizenship* (1964), *Nation-Building* (1963). The titles of the new wave of the 1970s conveyed a different message: *The Cruel Choice* (1971), *Pyramids of Sacrifice* (1976), *No Easy Choice* (1976), *Choice and the Politics of Allocation* (1971), *Crisis, Choice, and Change* (1973), *The Cruel Dilemmas of Development* (1980). As these titles suggest, the analyses of the 1970s were couched in terms of dilemmas, choices, trade-offs, crises, and even vicious circles. They particularly stressed the conflicts between growth and equity and between growth and freedom. In the mid-1980s, one scholar could quite legitimately conclude that "the conventional wisdom of the sixties and early seventies held that, except in the very

long run, rapid development and human rights are competing concerns."[9]

At the simplest level, ten bilateral relationships can be conceived as possible among the five goals of development. In the 1960s and 1970s, significant bodies of thought and writing developed that saw at least six of these relations as at least in part conflictual. Four of these conflicts involved the relations of economic growth to social-economic equity, political stability, political democracy, and national autonomy. Other conflicts were identified between democracy and equity and between stability and equity.

In various forms, the growth versus equity conflict had, of course, been a staple of economics for some while. Simon Kuznets focused the attention of mid-twentieth-century developmental economists on it, however, with his 1950s argument that a U-shaped curve relationship existed between level of economic development and income inequality. Based on cross-sectional analysis, this argument implied, of course, that, as countries moved from the low to middle levels of economic development, economic inequality would initially increase before decreasing as still higher levels of economic development were reached. Subsequent evidence has borne out this relationship.[10] Other economists carried the argument further. Not only was there a curvilinear relationship between the levels of wealth and equity, there also was a significant negative relationship between the rate of economic growth and income equality. "Higher rates of industrialization, faster increases in agricultural productivity, and higher rates of growth all tend to shift income distribution in favor of the higher income groups and against the low income groups. The dynamics of the process of economic development tend to work relatively against the poor; the major recipients of the rewards of economic development are consistently the middle class and the highest income groups."[11] Standard economics texts made the same point. A sizable literature on the "Green Revolution" emphasized how the benefits from increased agricultural productivity accrued primarily to well-off peasants rather than to the poor and landless. Some writers saw the contrast between growth and equity strategies epitomized in the cases of Brazil and China. "In the dichotomy of capitalist and socialist models of development, Brazil and China regularly appear as polar opposites. . . . Brazil is today the largest and most dynamic case of capitalist development in the Third World, as China is the most important case of socialist alternative . . . each model has been deemed a success *in its own terms. . . . Both . . . models assume the sacrifice of at least a generation for the achievement of their respective goals.*"[12]

The liberal model of development assumed that political instability was associated with poverty. A whole series of studies soon showed, however, that the relationship between level of economic development and political instability was a curvilinear one, like that between wealth and equity. The highest levels of instability are associated with middle levels of development. The causes of instability were similarly found in the processes of economic growth. The conflict between these goals was summed up in the title of an early article by Mancur Olson, "Rapid Growth as a Destabilizing Force."[13] This and other works challenged the assumption of the liberal model of development that poverty was the source of instability. Political instability and civil violence were instead seen as the result of economic and social modernization and development. In some cases, it was argued, simple growth itself destabilized. In other cases, the culprit was seen as the slackening or ending of growth, which left unfulfilled expectations (the "J-shaped curve" hypothesis). In still other cases, imbalanced development, such as social mobilization (narrowly defined) outpacing economic development (narrowly defined), was held to be the source of instability. In still others, economic growth was the ultimate source of instability, but the proximate source was the heightened economic inequality produced by growth.[14] In virtually all these cases,

efforts were made to establish a general relationship between some aspect or consequence of economic growth and one or more forms of political instability.

In the two conflict theories just discussed, economic growth is seen as undermining equity and stability. It is not clear that rapid economic growth would necessarily have deleterious effects on democracy, except insofar as it tended to produce instability. It could then be argued, however, that a democratic system might be better able than an authoritarian one to cope with and moderate such instability. The conflicts between growth and democracy are of a somewhat different sort. In the first place, it was argued, and some evidence exists, that rapid economic growth and social change may complicate and even undermine the democratization of an undemocratic political system. As one analyst argued with respect to two indices of economic change: "Successful attempts to introduce democracy are accompanied by more moderate change in urbanization and agricultural employment, while unsuccessful attempts are accompanied by more rapid change."[15] More basically, Guillermo O'Donnell's theory of bureaucratic authoritarianism challenged the proposition set forth in the late 1950s by Seymour Martin Lipset and others that higher levels of economic development were associated with the prevalence of democratic political systems. At least in Latin America, O'Donnell argued, beyond a certain point a conflict existed between economic development and democracy; democracy was associated with intermediate levels of economic development; and "the higher levels of contemporary South American modernization are not associated with political democracies."[16]

In a more general sense the conflict between growth and democracy is seen in terms of what Jack Donnelly calls "the liberty trade-off."[17] The argument is that if a less developed country is going to achieve higher rates of economic growth, it will have to have a development-oriented authoritarian government. Democratic governments will simply be too "soft" and hence unable to mobilize resources, curtail consumption, and promote investment so as to achieve a high growth rate. Many analyses have probed the relations between political system and economic development and come up with varying answers. In general, however, it appears that democratic states almost never achieve very high rates of economic growth, while authoritarian states may have extremely high growth rates, moderate growth rates, and abysmally low growth rates. One careful analysis of ninety-eight countries did come to the conclusion that "among the poor nations, an authoritarian political system increases the rate of economic development, while a democratic political system does appear to be a luxury which hinders development."[18] In 1979 Soedjatmoko could sadly come to the conclusion that "a majority of western development theorists seem to have come to accept, with some regrets to be sure, the seeming inevitability of development to be accompanied by authoritarian government."[19] Interestingly enough while those analysts concerned with the growth versus equity conflict focused on Brazil and China, those concerned with growth versus democracy have tended to zero in on India.

The conflicts between growth, on the one hand, and equity, stability, and democracy, on the other, tended to undermine the harmony assumptions underlying liberal theories of development. The harmony among goals posited by the dependency theorists also was challenged. One such challenge involved the high correlation existing between political stability and the absence of autonomy, this, of course, resulting from the fact that foreign investment and manifestations of dependency blossom under conditions of political stability. A more serious conflict involves the relation between various forms of dependency and economic growth. This issue has been explored in numerous studies focused in large part on Latin America that have come up with differing results. One of the more careful analyses came to the cautious conclusion that "there was a positive relationship between dependency and economic

growth in Latin America in the 1960s."[20] It was still possible, however, that this economic growth might, as some dependency theorists argued, be distorted, and that in the longer run more-dependent states might grow at slower rates than less-dependent ones.

The prevailing Western approaches to development tended to see a mutually reinforcing relationship between equity and democracy. The creation of a democratic political system depended, in some measure, on the absence of great social-economic inequalities, and, once created, the functioning of that system would tend to produce movement toward greater equality. Data on nineteenth-century western Europe tended to support these propositions. Yet one could also raise the question as to whether the movement toward greater equality in income distribution was produced primarily by higher levels of economic development or by the functioning of democracy. Conflict theorists could also point to the extent to which major inequalities in economic wealth persisted in democratic societies. More specifically, conflict theorists could and did make two arguments. First, the creation of a democratic political system, in a country at a fairly low level of social mobilization, and hence with political participation effectively limited to a fairly small middle class, was likely to promote less economic equality. Second, while at higher levels of social mobilization democratic political systems might promote greater income equality, democratic political systems at any level of development were generally unable to bring about significant redistribution of economic assets. Hence at lower levels of development in particular, when issues such as land reform are likely to be more salient and any democratic system would involve political participation by only a limited portion of the population, an authoritarian system is more likely than a democratic one to be compatible with greater economic equality.

Finally, challenging liberal and reformist models of development, radical theorists argued that a high level of instability—that is, revolution—may be necessary in order to achieve a minimum degree of equity. Revolutionary theorists are, in this respect, generally right, at least in the short run. A major revolutionary upheaval will normally produce greater equality in income and wealth, at least among those whom the revolution neither exiles nor executes. In time, however, new patterns of inequality are likely to emerge, not necessarily any less inequitable than those that were destroyed by the revolution.[21]

The four conflictual relationships between economic growth and equity, stability, democracy, and autonomy exemplify what can perhaps best be termed the "rate/level paradox," that is, the condition in which a high level of Variable A is associated with a high level of Variable B but a high rate of increase in Variable A is associated with no increase or a negative rate of increase in Variable B. Globally high levels of economic wealth are associated with high levels of equity, stability, democracy, and autonomy. Yet, seemingly, high rates of economic growth also have negative consequences for movement toward these other goals. If this relationship existed in the past, one has to confront the following question: How did the developed countries of Western Europe and North America arrive at their present benign position blessed with high levels of all five good things?

One plausible answer to this question is that the rate/level paradox did not operate in Western development as it does now because the rate of economic change was so much lower then. During the years 1870–1913, for instance, the gross national products of the major European countries grew at annual rates varying from 1.4 percent for Italy to 2.8 percent for Germany. Among Western industrializing countries, only the U.S. economy, with an annual rate of 4.3 percent grew at more than 3 percent a year. The average growth rate for current developing countries, on the other hand, was 4.8 percent in the 1950s, 5.2 percent in the early 1960s, and 5.9 percent in the late 1960s. Many individual countries, of course, achieved

growth rates of 7 to 10 percent, which in some cases were sustained for several years. The relative success of the current developing countries in achieving historically high rates of economic growth may thus be the source of the rate/level paradox. The relatively slow processes of development in the West may have made possible their current high levels of goal achievement. Rapid economic growth in the presently developing countries may be the principal reason for the relevance of the conflict theories to the relations among developmental goals.

Reconciliation Policies

The conflict theories posited general relationships between goals: the opposition between growth and equity, for instance, was conceived to be a universal one. At time, also, some conflict theorists seemed almost to revel in the difficulty and unpleasantness of the choices and dilemmas that they saw as unavoidable. Inevitably, however, the elaboration of these "cruel" alternatives generated a third body of development literature, devoted to exploring the ways in which development goals could be reconciled with one another. Assumed compatibility, in short, was undermined by the perceived pervasiveness of conflicts, which in turn gave birth to the psychological and political desire to resolve these conflicts. Emphasis on the cruel necessity for choice was replaced by emphasis on the urgent need for reconciliation. The issue became this: through what policies can developing societies expect to make progress toward two or more developmental goals? In varying ways, attention seemed to focus on policies concerning *sequences* in the choice of development goals, institutional *structures* for reconciling development goals, and governmental *strategies* to promote the simultaneous achievement of development goals.

If simultaneous progress toward several development goals is difficult or impossible, conceivably progress could be made toward them sequentially by first emphasizing one goal and then another. In one sense, some form of sequencing is inevitable: no government could hope to pursue all five goals simultaneously with equal intensity. The imperatives of politics and the requirements of bureaucratic implementation, at the least, would lead some goals to get priority over others. Beyond this, however, there is the question from a developmental viewpoint as to whether progress toward all goals will be affected by the sequence in which goals are pursued. Some sequences, conceivably, may be more productive than others and, conversely, giving early priority to one goal could conceivably preclude subsequent progress toward other goals. Or, to state the issue more formally: If progress toward goal A at time T_1 is incompatible with progress toward goal B at time T_1, does progress toward goal A at time T_1 aid or obstruct progress toward goal B at time T_2 and, conversely, does progress toward goal B at time T_1 aid or obstruct progress toward goal A at time T_2?

Much has been written on developmental sequences. By and large, consensus seems to exist on the most appropriate sequence to maximize achievement of political goals but not economic ones. Dankwart Rustow sums up much of the thinking when he says that "the most effective sequence" is the pursuit of national unity, governmental authority, and political equality, in that order. Eric Nordlinger and Samuel Huntington emphasize the importance of developing effective governmental institutions before the emergence of mass participation in politics. Robert Dahl similarly highlights the desirability of establishing patterns of contestation before expanding political participation.[22] Overall, the political science literature tends to urge the temporal priority of order over democracy.

In contrast, no agreement seems to exist among economic analysts as to whether growth or equity should have priority. Some argue that a heavy emphasis on rapid growth is essential to expand the economic pie to the point where some measure of equity becomes possible. This was, of course, the articulated policy of Delfim Neto during the years of the Brazilian "economic miracle." It was also explicitly followed in other countries. "In my view," a top Korean official said in 1975, "the first stage is getting the economy going; the next stage is to consider [social] welfare. First growth and efficiency, then equity."[23] Others, of course, argue the contrary view that a growth-first strategy will not work and that skewed patterns of income distribution that become fixed during periods of rapid growth are very resistant to subsequent change. Or, as one writer put it, if the "trickle down" theory were valid, in the early 1980s in Brazil the benefits of development "should be not merely trickling, but cascading, down to the poor. They are not. Likewise, according to the conventional wisdom, income inequality should be declining. It is not."[24] To the contrary, such analysts argue, redistribution should come first, particularly the more equitable distribution of assets, such as land, and then rapid economic growth will follow. By and large this view seems to prevail among academic analysts while practitioners often espouse the opposing sequence.

Policy choices can also promote or obstruct the development of particular institutional structures that may facilitate the reconciliation of goals. A strong two-party political system rather than a multiparty system, for instance, may be better able to reconcile expanded political participation with political stability, and both of these with the institutional means for promoting national autonomy. Limitation of the role of the state sector in the economy may encourage both economic growth and the development of an indigenous bourgeoisie supportive of democracy, although it may also obstruct progress toward greater social-economic equity. In the mid 1970s, economists also were increasingly publishing books with titles like *Redistribution with Growth,* analyzing the conflict between growth and equity, and setting forth strategies that would reconcile these goals.[25] Among the strategies frequently mentioned were extensive investment in education to develop human capital on a broad basis, promotion of labor-intensive rather than capital-intensive industries, priority to agriculture over industry, and early redistribution of economic assets, particularly land reform. Economists also identified strategies that did not seem to work: progressive taxation, expanded political participation, government ownership of productive enterprises. In their efforts to find out how growth and equity could be reconciled, economists rushed to analyze the experiences of those countries where, in some measure, it had been achieved: Japan, Costa Rica, Singapore, Israel, South Korea, Taiwan. The two latter countries, indeed, became the favorite cases of the reconciliation economists. They showed how to escape the cruel choice between Brazil and China posed by the conflict theorists.

As this brief discussion suggests, the efforts at reconciliation tended to involve either political scientists attempting to reconcile stability and democracy or economists attempting to reconcile equity and growth. Rarer were cross-disciplinary efforts to show how the achievement of economic goals might be reconciled with the achievement of political ones. One such effort was that by Ikuo Kabashima to show how democracy, growth, and equity could be reconciled. Joan Nelson and I had argued that more advanced developing countries often had to choose between (1) a populist "vicious circle," involving expanded political participation, more socioeconomic equality, slower economic growth, and intensifying class conflict leading to a military coup and a participation "implosion," and (2) a technocratic "vicious circle," often starting with a military coup, and involving suppression of political participation, rapid economic growth, and increased socioeconomic inequality, leading to mounting popular discontent and a participation "explosion" against the regime. "Not necessarily so," said Ilua Kabashima. Japan, he argued, was a case where "supportive" political participation enhanced the stability of the government, which in turn made possible rapid economic growth, which in turn made possible redistribution of income from more privileged to less privileged, which in turn reinforced the supportive participation. The "primary implication" of the Japanese case "for theories of development," he said, "is that political participation by the have-nots is not *necessarily* a cost to economic development, as Huntington and Nelson have argued." Japan may or may not be unique, but it does show that "participation by have-nots, rapid growth, and economic equality *can be* compatible. . . ."[26] The question, however, is: Can they be compatible outside Japan? If not, why not?

The Cultures of Development

The conflict theorists effectively disposed of the assumption of universal or even general harmony among goals. The proponents of reconciliation showed that conflicts among goals were not necessarily unresolvable. They did not demonstrate, however, that any particular reconciliation policies could be successfully applied on a universal basis. Like harmony and conflict, reconciliation is not inevitable. Through some combination of sequencing, structural innovations, and appropriate strategies, some countries could and did make progress toward two or more goals. Other countries did not. What worked in Korea did not work in Brazil. What was possible in India was not possible in Nigeria. By the 1980s, for instance, economists were arguing that "there seems to be no clear relationship between the rate of economic growth and either (a) the degree of inequality at a point in time or (b) the trend of inequality over time. Fast growers include both equal and unequal societies; they also include societies that have been growing more, and less, unequal. The same is true, also, of slow growers."[27]

The question thus becomes: How can these and other differences in progress, achievement, and reconciliation be explained? Why were Korea and Taiwan but so few other countries able to make simultaneous progress toward growth, equity, and stability? Why was Japan able to achieve not only these goals but democracy and autonomy also? Why did Brazil do well first at growth and then at democratization but not so well in terms of equity, stability, and autonomy? Why, generally, did South American countries seem to oscillate between democracy and authoritarianism? How was Sri Lanka able to reconcile equity and democracy for so long? Why did so many African countries record so little progress toward any goals? Why did India develop a stable democracy while no Islamic country did? How can one explain, as Lawrence Harrison asked, the contrasts in political and economic development between Costa Rica and Nicaragua, Haiti and Barbados, Argentina and Australia?[28] As one economist observed, the differences among countries in achieving growth, equity, both, or neither depend on "the environment in which growth occurs and the political decisions taken."[29] To explain why reconciliation, like harmony and conflict, is not universal, one is forced back to things unique to the particular countries. These include natural resources, geographical location, character of the population, and, of course, historical experience. In terms of explaining different patterns of political and economic development, however, a central independent variable is culture—that is, the subjective attitudes, beliefs, and values prevalent among the dominant groups in the society.

The concept of culture is a tricky one in social science because it is both easy and unsatisfying to use. It is easy (and also dangerous) to use because it is, in some sense, a residual category. If no other causes can plausibly explain significant differences between societies, it is inviting to attribute them to culture. Just exactly how culture is responsible for the political and economic differences one is attempting to explain is often left extraordinarily vague. Cultural explanations are thus often imprecise or tautological or both, at the extreme coming down to a more sophisticated rendering of "the French are like that!" On the other hand, cultural explanations are also unsatisfying for a social scientist because they run counter to the social scientist's proclivity to generalize. They do not explain consequences in terms of relationships among universal variables such as

rates of economic growth, social mobilization, political participation, and civil violence. They tend, instead, to speak in particulars peculiar to specific cultural entities.

Culture can be thought of at a variety of levels. Within nations significant cultural differences may exist among regions, ethnic groups, and social classes. Even greater differences in culture usually exist among nations, and the nation and the nation-state are probably the most important units for the analysis and comparison of culture and its effect on development. Beyond the nation, however, exist a number of broad cultural families or groupings, often including several nations that often share much in terms of common race and ethnicity, language, religion, and history. At least nine such cultural families can be identified (see Table 32.1).

These nine cultural groupings do not, obviously, encompass all the world's countries. Some national societies may include groups reflecting two or more traditions (e.g., Malaysia, South Africa). Some countries may not fit neatly into any of these categories; consider, for instance, Hungary, Poland, Rumania, Israel, Turkey, Iran, Pakistan, Afghanistan, Burma, Sri Lanka, Thailand, Cambodia, Laos, Bolivia, and Guatemala. At least 85 percent of the world's population, however, is in national societies that fit reasonably well into one of these categories. It consequently makes sense to ask whether each of these cultural groupings may not have its own particular pattern of political and economic development and of goal achievement. If one wanted to predict the probable pattern of development of a country X and could be given only one piece of information concerning X, would not its cultural identity be the information to ask for? Would not that be the single most important factor in predicting the extent to which X was likely to achieve growth, equity, democracy, stability, and autonomy?

Major differences obviously exist among countries within particular cultural groupings; often one country may deviate strongly from the prevailing cultural pattern (e.g., Costa Rica

TABLE 32.1 Cultures and Regions

Culture	Principal Religion	Region/Countries
Nordic	Protestantism	Northwest Europe, British settler countries
Latin	Catholicism	Southern Europe, Latin America
Arab	Islam	North Africa, Middle East
Slavic	Orthodox	Eastern Europe, Soviet Union
Indian	Hinduism	India
Sinic	Confucianism	China, Taiwan, Korea, Singapore, Vietnam
Japanese	Confucianism/Buddhism/Shinto	Japan
Malay	Islam/Buddhism/Catholicism	Malaysia, Indonesia, Philippines
African	Christianity/Paganism	Africa south of the Sahara

in Latin America). Yet by and large significant differences do exist among these cultural groupings in terms of the extent to which their countries have made progress toward their developmental goals. The fact of the matter, as we all know, is that Islamic, Sinic, African, Latin, and other societies have developed in very different ways. It is hard to see much convergence among them in their patterns of development between the 1950s and the 1980s or between any one of them and the commonly accepted Western pattern (which is largely a Nordic pattern). In 1962, for instance, Ghana and South Korea had virtually identical economies in terms of per capita GNP, sector sizes, and exports. Twenty years later they could hardly have been more different.[30] Looking at the economic and political variables in those countries in 1962, one could never have predicted that divergence. If one had thought at that point in terms of the differences between West African and Korean cultures, however, that divergence in development might not have been so surprising.

Widespread agreement appears to exist among scholars and practitioners on the desirability of societies becoming wealthy, equitable, democratic, stable, and autonomous. These goals, however, emerge out of the Western and particularly the Nordic experience. They are Western goals, as is, indeed, the concept of development itself. The articulated

support for them by political and intellectual elites throughout the world may simply be tribute to the intellectual dominance of Western ideas, the extent to which non-Western elites have been indoctrinated in Locke, Smith, Rousseau, Marx, and their twentieth-century disciples. These ideas may find little support in the indigenous culture. In contrast to the Western model, another culture's image of the good society may be of a society that is simple, austere, hierarchical, authoritarian, disciplined, and martial.

The image of the developed Western society—wealthy, equitable, democratic, stable, autonomous—thus may not constitute a meaningful model or reference group for a modern Islamic, African, Confucian, or Hindu society.[31] Throughout the non-Western world, societies have judged themselves by Western standards and have found themselves wanting. Maybe the time has come to stop trying to change these societies and to change the model, to develop models of a modern Islamic, Confucian, or Hindu society that would be more relevant to countries where those cultures prevail. In some measure, of course, this process has been under way for some time as Third World intellectuals have spun out theories of "African socialism" and "Islamic democracy." The useful models, however, are less likely to come from the normative theorizing of intellectuals than from the historical experience of societies. The need is to generalize from the East Asian experience and derive from that experience a developmental model of a society that is authoritarian, stable, economically dynamic, and equitable in its income distribution. The South American model might be one of class stratification, inequality, moderate growth, political conflict, economic penetration, and alternating democratic and authoritarian regimes. Obviously, future development may change the model, and any theorist must be sensitive to that. Yet the construction of a Latin American model of development and the explanation of why in terms of culture and other variables Latin American experience approximates that model surely is a worthy scholarly undertaking. O'Donnell's theory of bureaucratic authoritarianism was a first approximation of such a model and is, in a sense, a prototype of the sort of region- and culture-specific theoretical model that is desirable. O'Donnell's theory threw needed light on the Latin American experience, and, interesting to note, efforts to apply it outside Latin America to East Asia or elsewhere have not been notably successful.

The relevance of culture to explaining different patterns of development may also be enhanced by once again emphasizing the distinction between modernization and Westernization. In theory these concepts were always distinguishable; in application, however, they seldom were distinguished. In many respects they overlapped. With respect to the non-Western world, the two usually went together no matter how much non-Western elites might attempt to differentiate technology and material processes, on the one hand, from basic values and norms, on the other. More recently, however, in a variety of ways in many different circumstances, non-Western values, attitudes, beliefs (religious and otherwise) have reasserted themselves. As Western colonial rule fades into history, as elites are increasingly the product of their own culture rather than that of Paris, London, or New York, as the masses in their soci-

eties, never much exposed to Western culture, play an increasingly important role in politics, as the global influence of the principal Western powers continues its relative decline, the indigenous cultures naturally become more important in shaping the development of these societies. The partnership between modernization and Westernization has been broken. While continuing to pursue modernization, the Third World is also, in some measure, deeply involved in and committed to a process of de-Westernization.

In the 1950s, the systematic study of comparative politics developed apart from and partly in opposition to area or regional studies. Area specialists believed the explanation lay in the particular, that in order to understand and explain what happened politically in a society one had to have deep knowledge of its history, language, culture, and social institutions. The comparative politics scholars, on the other hand, believed the explanation could be found in empirical generalizations, that in order to understand and explain what happened politically in a society one had to have a broad knowledge of how social, economic, and political variables interacted generally and then had to apply the appropriate generalizations to the particular case. Area specialists and comparative scholars thus went their separate ways. In the late 1950s and 1960s, the study of comparative politics tended to subdivide further, as those specializing in development and developing countries became detached from those specializing in industrial societies. (Those specializing in the principal Communist societies, the Soviet Union and China, never fully escaped being area specialists.) The "developmentalists" and the "industrialists," with a few exceptions (e.g., corporatism), employed different concepts and had different foci of interest. The industrialists also worked fairly closely with the more traditional area specialists dealing with Western Europe. The developmentalists were more likely to be distant from and at odds with traditional specialists on the Middle East, Latin America, and East Asia.

The scholars of comparative politics would gain nothing by going back to the extreme parochialism of the traditional area specialists, in many cases so totally blind to any way in which the phenomena they studied might be illuminated by comparative generalizations. If, however, the study of development leads back to a focus on culture and the differences among major cultural traditions and country cultures, then the time is perhaps appropriate for closer links between the comparative politics scholars (developmentalist subbranch) and area specialists. If the differences in the present and future development and goal achievement of East Asia, Latin America, and sub-Saharan Africa are to be found in the different values and beliefs of East Asians, Latin Americans, and Africans, then surely a primary place has to be accorded the comparative analysis of culture, how and why it develops, how it is transmitted, what patterns it forms, how its various dimensions can be defined and measured, and how and under what circumstances it changes. For those who wish to explain the extent to which different countries have made differing progress toward achieving the goals of development, such an approach becomes almost indispensable. Culture and its impact on development cry out for systematic and empirical, comparative and longitudinal study by the scholars of political development.

Notes

  * From *Understanding Political Developments: An Analytic Study,* edited by Samuel P. Huntington and Myron Weiner (Boston: Little, Brown & Co. Series in Comparative Politics, 1987), 6–32, by permission of the author and Little, Brown & Company.
  1. At the simplest level, each of the five goals of development can be conceived as possibly having a relationship with the other four, for a total of ten bilateral relationships. The picture can be further complicated, however, if these are thought of in terms of relations in which each goal could be either the independent variable or the dependent variable. This would multiply the number of possible relations to twenty. Finally, if a distinction is made between relations involving the *level* of each variable and the *rate* of change of each variable, eighty possible relations exist between pairs of variables. Many of these potential relationships would be meaningless or totally unascertainable. For purposes of discussion here, we will focus on the ten simple relationships, incorporating whatever references seem to be appropriate to the direction of the flow of influence and to the components of rate and level.

In evaluating Third World evolution, it is also desirable to distinguish between progress and achievement with respect to these five goals. Progress is measured by the rate of change of conditions with respect to that goal; achievement, by the level obtained or the extent to which the goal is realized. To take a simple example, if Country A increases its literacy from 10 percent to 30 percent of the population in five years, while Country B increases its literacy from 30 percent to 40 percent, clearly Country A has a higher rate of progress with respect to literacy, but Country B has a higher level of achievement. The distinction between progress and achievement, between rates and levels, of course, is particularly important in economic development, where progress is normally measured by rates of growth of GNP and of GNP per capita and achievement is measured by GNP per capita. Similar distinctions between rates and levels are at times useful with respect to other goals of development. The distribution of income in a society can be measured at a particular point in time and changes in that distribution over time, if reliable data are available (which is not often the case). In a similar manner, levels of stability (or, more likely, instability) can be measured and perhaps in some measure rates of change in stability can be identified over time. Countries can also be compared as to how democratic they are, and where democratization (or its opposite) takes place over time at least some qualitative measurement can be made of rates of change. The more common phenomenon, however, is a discontinuous break involving a rapid change of regime in a short period of time. Thus one speaks far more frequently of levels of democracy than of rates of democratization or its reverse. With respect to national autonomy, on the other hand, quantitative data as to some indices of both rates and levels are available, most notably with respect to trade, investment, loans, and foreign aid.

2. Gary S. Fields, *Poverty, Inequality, and Development* (Cambridge: Cambridge University Press, 1980), 185.

3. Albert O. Hirschman, *Journeys toward Progress: Studies of Economic Policy-making in Latin America* (New York: Twentieth Century Fund, 1963), 137.

4. See Geoffrey Perrett, *Days of Sadness, Years of Triumph* (Baltimore, Md.: Penguin, 1974); Mark Jonathan Harris, Franklin D. Mitchell, and Steve J. Schechter, *The Homefront: America during World War II* (New York: Putnam, 1984); John Morton Blum, *V Was for Victory: Politics and American Culture during World War II* (New York: Harcourt Brace Jovanovich, 1976); and, on the Russians, Hedrick Smith, *The Russians* (New York: Quadrangle/New York Times, 1976), 302–3. The extent to which crime and civil violence increase or decrease during war is in dispute. See Arthur A. Stein, *The Nation at War* (Baltimore, Md.: Johns Hopkins University Press, 1980), and Michael Stohl, *War and Domestic Political Violence: The American Capacity for Repression and Reaction* (Beverly Hills, Calif.: Sage, 1976).

5. Robert A. Packenham, *Liberal America and the Third World: Political Development Ideas in Foreign Aid and Social Science* (Princeton, N.J.: Princeton University Press, 1973), 123–29.

6. Arthur Schlesinger, Jr., "The Alliance for Progress: A Retrospective," in *Latin America: The Search for a New International Role,* edited by Ronald G. Hellman and H. Jon Rosenbaum (New York: Wiley, 1975), 57–92.

7. *The Report of the President's National Bipartisan Commission on Central America* (New York: Macmillan, 1984), 48, 60 ff.

8. See Packenham, *Liberal America,* passim, and Samuel P. Huntington and Joan M. Nelson, *No Easy Choice: Political Participation in Devel-*

oping Countries (Cambridge, Mass.: Harvard University Press, 1976), 17–21.

9. Jack Donnelly, "Human Rights and Development: Complementary or Competing Concerns?" *World Politics* 36, no. 2 (January 1984), 255.

10. Simon Kuznets, "Economic Growth and Income Inequality," *American Economic Review* 45, no. 1 (March 1955):1–28; Fields, *Poverty, Inequality, and Development,* 59–77, 122; David Morawetz, *Twenty-Five Years of Economic Development 1950–1975* (Washington, D.C.: World Bank, 1977), 38–40.

11. Irma Adelman, "Summary, Conclusions, and Recommendations," Part I, Final Report, Grant AID/csd/2236, Northwestern University, Evanston, Ill., (12 February 1971), 6.

12. Peter L. Berger, *Pyramids of Sacrifice: Political Ethics and Social Change* (Garden City, N.Y.: Doubleday Anchor, 1976), 151. See also Sylvia Ann Hewlett, *The Cruel Dilemmas of Development: Twentieth-Century Brazil* (New York: Basic Books, 1980), 215–18.

13. Mancur Olson, Jr., "Rapid Growth as a Destabilizing Force." *Journal of Economic History* 23, no. 4 (December 1963):529–52, and, for a summary of the early conflict literature on this point, Samuel P. Huntington, *Political Order in Changing Societies* (New Haven, Conn.: Yale University Press, 1968), 39–59.

14. For a general review of research on the causes of instability, see Ekkart Zimmerman, *Political Violence, Crises, and Revolutions: Theories and Research* (Cambridge, Mass.: Schenkman, 1983).

15. William Flanigan and Edwin Fogelman, "Patterns of Democratic Development: An Historical Comparative Analysis," in *Macro-Quantitative Analysis: Conflict, Development, and Democratization,* edited by John V. Gillespie and Betty A. Nesvold (Beverly Hills, Calif.: Sage, 1971), 487.

16. Guillermo A. O'Donnell, *Modernization and Bureaucratic-Authoritarianism: Studies in South American Politics* (Berkeley: Institute of International Studies, University of California, 1973), 49–52, 114.

17. Donnelly, "Human Rights and Development," 257–58.

18. Robert M. Marsh, "Does Democracy Hinder Economic Development in the Latecomer Developing Nations?" *Comparative Social Research* 2 (1979):244.

19. Soedjatmoko, "Development and Freedom," Ishizaka Memorial Lectures, unpublished manuscript, 2–3.

20. James Lee Ray and Thomas Webster, "Dependency and Economic Growth in Latin America," *International Studies Quarterly* 22, no. 3 (September 1978): 432.

21. See Jonathan Kelley and Herbert S. Klein, *Revolution and the Rebirth of Inequality* (Berkeley: University of California Press, 1981), especially chaps. 1 and 8.

22. Dankwart A. Rustow, *A World of Nations: Problems of Political Modernization* (Washington, D.C.: Brookings Institution, 1967), 120–32, 276; Eric A. Nordlinger, "Political Development: Times Sequences and Rates of Change," *World Politics* 20, no. 3 (April 1968):494–520; Huntington, *Political Order in Changing Societies,* 78–92; and Robert A. Dahl, *Polyarchy: Participation and Opposition* (New Haven, Conn.: Yale University Press, 1971). 33 ff. See also Leonard Binder et al., *Crises and Sequences in Political Development* (Princeton, N.J.: Princeton University Press, 1971).

23. Deputy Prime Minister Nam Duck Woo, *Time* 106 (22 December 1975):40.

24. Donnelly, "Human Rights and Development," 260.

25. Hollis Chenery et al., *Redistribution with Growth* (New York: Oxford University Press, 1974). It is striking how often efforts to reconcile growth and equity were spoken of as "strategies." See, for example, Irma Adelman, "Growth, Income Distribution and Equity-Oriented Development Strategies," in *The Political Economy of Development and Underdevelopment,* edited by Charles K. Wilber, 2d ed.

(New York: Random House, 1979), 312–23, and Francis Stewart and Paul Streeten, "New Strategies for Development: Poverty, Income Distribution, and Growth," in Wilber, *Political Economy of Development and Underdevelopment,* 390–411.

26. Ikuo Kabashima, "Supportive Participation with Economic Growth: The Case of Japan," *World Politics* 36, no. 3 (April 1984):309–38.

27. Morawetz, *Twenty-Five Years of Economic Development,* 41.

28. See Lawrence E. Harrison, *Underdevelopment Is a State of Mind: The Latin American Case* (Cambridge, Mass.: Center for International Affairs, Harvard University, and University Press of America, 1985). Harrison makes the argument that the differences in development within Latin America can be explained only in cultural terms.

29. Fields, *Poverty, Inequality, and Development,* 94.

30. Keith Marsden, "Why Asia Boomed and Africa Busted," *Asian Wall Street Journal,* 11 June 1985, 8.

31. For a succinct statement from a slightly different perspective of similar argument, see Howard J. Wiarda's stimulating essay, *Ethnocentrism in Foreign Policy: Can We Understand the Third World?* (Washington, D.C.: American Enterprise Institute, 1985).

32. For a superb study of the cultural bases of power and authority in Asian societies, combining the approaches of area specialists and comparative politics scholars, see Lucian W. Pye, *Asian Power and Politics: The Cultural Dimensions of Authority* (Cambridge, Mass.: Harvard University Press, 1985).

CHAPTER THIRTY-THREE

National Development and the World System at the End of the Cold War*

Immanuel Wallerstein

The Concept of National Development, 1917–1989: Elegy and Requiem

Since at least the sixteenth century, European thinkers have been discussing how to augment the wealth of the realm, and governments have sought or were adjured to take steps to maintain and enhance this wealth. All the debates about mercantilism centered around how to be certain that more wealth entered a state than left it. When Adam Smith wrote *The Wealth of Nations* in 1776, he was concerned to attack the notion that governments could best enhance this wealth by various restrictions on foreign trade. He preached instead the notion that maximizing the ability of individual entrepreneurs to act as they deemed wisest in the world market would in fact result in an optimal enhancement of the wealth of the nation.

This tension between a basically protectionist versus a free trade stance became one of the major themes of policy-making in the various states of the world system in the nineteenth century. It often was the most significant issue that divided the principal political forces of particular states. It was clear by then that a central ideological theme of the capitalist world economy was that every state could, and indeed eventually probably would, reach a high level of national income and that conscious, rational action would make it so. This fit in very well with the underlying Enlightenment theme of inevitable progress and the teleological view of human history that it incarnated.

By the time of the First World War, it was also clear that a series of countries in Western Europe plus the white settler countries in the rest of the world had indeed become, in our contemporary parlance, "developed," or at least were well on their way to doing so. Of course, by the standards of 1990, all of these countries (even Great Britain) were far less "modern" and wealthy than they became later in the century, but by the standards of the time they were doing magnificently. The First World War was the shock it was precisely because, among other things, it seemed a direct menace to this generalized prosperity of what we today call the core zones of the world economy.

The year 1917 is often taken to be an ideological turning point in the history of the modern world system. I agree that it was this, but not quite in the way it is usually argued to be. On April 2, 1917, President Woodrow Wilson addressed the Congress of the United States and called for a declaration of war against Germany. He argued: "The world must be made safe for democracy." That same year, on November 7, the Bolsheviks assaulted the Winter Palace in the name of the workers' revolution. The great ideological antinomy of the twentieth century, Wilsonianism versus Leninism, may be said to have been born in 1917. I shall argue that it died in 1989. I shall further argue that the key issue to which both ideologies addressed themselves was the political integration of the periphery of the world system. And finally, I shall argue that the mechanism of such integration was, both for Wilsonianism and for Leninism, "national development," and that the essential dispute between them was merely about the path to such national development.

Wilson, Lenin, and National Sovereignty

Wilsonianism was based on classical liberal presuppositions. It was universalist, claiming that its precepts applied equally everywhere. It assumed that everyone acted on the basis of rational self-interest and that therefore everyone in the long run was reasonable. Hence peaceful and reformist practice was plausible. It placed great emphasis on legality and on form.

Of course, none of these precepts were new. In 1917, in fact, they seemed quite old-fashioned. Wilson's innovation (not invention) was to argue that these precepts applied not only to individuals within the state but to nation-states or peoples within the international arena. The principle of self-determination, the centerpiece of Wilsonianism, was nothing but the principle of individual freedom transposed to the level of the interstate system.

The transposition of a theory that had been intended to apply only at the level of individuals to the level of groups is a very tricky proposition. A harsh critic, Ivor Jennings (1956), said of Wilson's doctrine of self-determination: "On the surface it seemed reasonable: let the people decide. It was in fact ridiculous because the people cannot decide until somebody decides who are the people" (p. 56). Ay, there's the rub, indeed!

Still, it was obvious that, when Wilson was talking about the self-determination of nations, he was not worrying about France or Sweden. He was talking about the liquidation of the Austro-Hungarian, Ottoman, and Russian Empires. And when Roosevelt picked up the same theme a generation later, he was talking about the liquidation of the British, French, Dutch, and other remaining imperial structures. The self-determination of which they were speaking was the self-determination of the peripheral and semiperipheral zones of the world system.

Lenin pursued very similar policy objectives under the quite different slogans of proletarian internationalism and anti-imperialism. His views were no doubt based on other premises. His universalism was that of the world working class, the soon-to-be singular class that was slated to become literally identical with the "people." Nations or peoples had no long-run place in the Marxian pantheon; they were supposed eventually to disappear, like the states. But nations or peoples did have a short-run, even middle-run reality that not only could not be ignored by Marxist parties but was potentially tactically useful to their ends.

The Russian Revolution denounced the Russian Empire in theory and provided for the same self-determination of nations/peoples that did Wilson's doctrines. If much of the "empire" was retained, it was scrupulously insisted that this took the form of a voluntary federation of republics, the USSR, with plenty of room for formal autonomy of peoples, even within each of the republics. And when all hope was abandoned for the mythical German revolution, Lenin turned at Baku to proclaiming a new emphasis on the "East." Marxism-Leninism in effect was moving from its origins as a theory of proletarian insurrection against the bourgeoisie to a new role as a theory of anti-imperialism. This shift of emphasis would only grow with time. In the decades that would come, it is probable that more people read Lenin on *Imperialism: The Last Stage of Capitalism* than read the *Manifesto*.

Wilsonianism and Leninism emerged thus as rival doctrines for the fealty of the peoples of the peripheral zones. Because they were rivals, each placed great emphasis in its propaganda on its differences with the other. And, of course, there were real differences. But we should not be blind to the deep similarities as well. The two ideologies not only shared the theme of the self-determination of nations;

they also believed it was immediately (if not always urgently) relevant to the political life of the peripheral zones. That is, both doctrines favored what later came to be called "decolonization." Furthermore, by and large, even when it came to the details of "who was a people" that had this hypothetical right to self-determination, the proponents of both doctrines came up with very similar lists of names. There were, to be sure, minor tactical scuffles related to passing considerations of the world *rapport de forces,* but there was no important example of fundamental empirical disagreement. Israel was on both lists, Kurdistan on neither. Neither was to accept the theoretical legitimacy of the Bantustans. Both found no theoretical reason to oppose the eventual realities of Pakistan and Bangladesh. It could not be said that fundamentally different measuring rods were being used to judge legitimacy.

To be sure, there were differences about the road to self-determination. Wilsonians favored what was termed a "constitutional" path, that is, a process of gradual orderly transfer of power arrived at by negotiations between an imperial power and respectable representatives of the people in question. Decolonization was to be, as the French would later put it, *octroyée,* that is, given. Leninism came of a "revolutionary" tradition and painted a more insurrectional path to "national liberation." Independence was not to be octroyée but *arrachée,* that is, taken. This would be incarnated in the later Maoist injunction of the need for "protracted struggle," which came to be widely repeated and, more important, to be part of the fundamental strategy of movements.

One should not exaggerate even this difference. Peaceful decolonization was not unacceptable in Leninist doctrine, merely improbable. And revolutionary nationalism was not inherently inconsistent with Wilsonian ideas, merely dangerous and thus to be avoided whenever possible. Still, the debate was real because it masked another debate: who was to lead the struggle for self-determination. And this was important, in turn, because it would presum-

ably determine the "postindependence" policies. Wilsonians saw the natural leadership of a national movement to lie in its intelligentsia and bourgeoisie—educated, respectable, and prudent. They foresaw a local movement that would persuade the more "modern" sectors of the traditional leadership to join in the political reforms and accept a sensible, parliamentary mode of organizing the newly independent state. Leninists saw the leadership to lie in a party/movement modeled on the Bolshevik Party, even if it did not accept the whole Leninist ideological canon. The leaders might be "petty bourgeois," provided they were "revolutionary" petty bourgeois. When it came to power, the party/movement was supposed to become a party/state. Here, too, one should not exaggerate the difference. Often, the respectable intelligentsia/bourgeoisie and the so-called revolutionary petty bourgeoisie were in reality the same people, or at least cousins. And the party/movement was almost as frequent a formula of "Wilsonian" movements as of "Leninist" ones. As for the postindependence policies, neither the Wilsonians nor the Leninists worried too much about them as long as the struggle for self-determination was ongoing.

Wilson, Lenin, and National Development

What then of the postdecolonization practice? Surely here the Wilsonian-Leninist antinomy would reveal its importance. In one major respect, there was no question that the two paths to independence tended to correlate with opposite postindependence policies. This was in the domain of foreign policy. In all world issues in which the United States and the USSR were locked in Cold War battle, the states outside the core zones tended to lean in one direction or the other. Some states were considered and considered themselves "pro-Western," and other states considered themselves to be part of a world progressive camp that included the USSR.

There was, of course, a long continuum of positions, and not all states were consistent over time. Nonalignment was itself a major movement. Still, when the chips were down, on unimportant matters like voting for resolutions in the General Assembly of the United Nations, many votes were easily predictable. The United States and its allies, on the one hand, and the USSR and the so-called socialist bloc on the other, spent much diplomatic energy on trying to push wavering states in one direction or the other. Wilsonian versus Leninist propaganda was incessantly purveyed, directly through government media and indirectly through scholarly discourse.

A close look at the internal realities of the various states reveals, however, that, both in the political and in the economic arenas, there was less difference than the theory or the propaganda would suggest. In terms of the actual political structures, most of the states most of the time were either one-party states (de facto or de jure) or military dictatorships. Even when states had a multiparty system in formal terms, one party tended in reality to dominate the institutions and to be impervious to change of regime other than by military coup d'état. The corollary of such structures tended to be a low level of civil rights—a powerful police structure, arbitrary arrests of opposition figures, a government-controlled press, and a long list of intellectuals in exile. There was very little difference in this regard to be found among states employing a Wilsonian rhetoric and those employing a basically Leninist rhetoric.

Nor was much more difference to be located in the economic arena. The degree to which private local enterprise was permitted has varied, but in almost all Third World states there has been a large amount of state enterprise and in virtually no state has state ownership been the only property form. The degree to which foreign investment has been permitted has no doubt varied more. In the more "pro-Western" states it has been encouraged, indeed solicited, albeit quite frequently in the form of joint ventures with a state corporation. In the more radical, or "progressive," states, foreign investment has been dealt with more cau-

tiously, although seldom totally repudiated. Rather, it has been the case that investors from OECD countries have themselves been reluctant to invest in such countries because of what they considered higher political risk.

Finally, the aid picture has not been too different. Virtually all Third World countries have actively sought to obtain aid in the form both of direct grants and of loans. To be sure, the aid-giving donors tended to correlate their assistance with the foreign policy stance of the potential recipients. A long list of countries received aid primarily from OECD countries. A smaller list received aid primarily from socialist bloc countries. A few countries self-consciously sought to emphasize the Nordic countries (plus the Netherlands and Canada) as aid sources. A large number of countries were ready to accept aid from multiple sources. In the end, most of the aid took the same form: personnel and tied grants, intended to support military structures and to fund so-called development projects.

What was most alike in all these countries was the belief in the possibility and urgent importance of "national development." National development was operationally defined everywhere as "catching up." Of course, it was assumed by everyone involved that this was a long and difficult task. But it was also assumed that it was doable, provided only that the right *state* policies were pursued. The state policies advocated, of course, covered the whole ideological gamut from facilitating the unrestricted flow of capital, commodities, and even labor across the national frontiers at one extreme to total state control of productive and exchange operations within largely closed frontiers at the other. There were, of course, a very large variety of in-between positions.

What was common however to the programs of all the noncore state members of the United Nations—from the USSR to Argentina, from India to Nigeria, from Albania to St. Lucia—was the overall state objective, increasing the wealth of the nation and "modernizing" its infrastructure. What was also common was an underlying optimism about this objective. What was further common was the sense that this objective could be best pursued by full participation in the interstate system. When any state was excluded even partially—as was the People's Republic of China for many years—it worked very hard to regain its unquestioned status of full membership.

In short, what has to be seen is that the Wilsonian-Leninist ideology of the self-determination of nations, their abstract equality, and the developmentalist paradigm incarnated in both variants of the ideology was overwhelmingly and virtually unfailingly accepted as the operational program of the political movements of the peripheral and semiperipheral zones of the world system. In this sense, the USSR itself was the first test case of the validity of the analysis and the workability of the recommendations. The postrevolutionary state was formally structured—a federation of states, most of which contained autonomous subunits—to respond precisely to the juridical formula of self-determination. When Lenin launched the slogan that "Communism equals the Soviets plus electricity," he was putting forward national (economic) development as the prime objective of state policy. And when Khrushchev, decades later, said that the Soviet Union would "bury" the United States by the year 2000, he was venting supreme optimism about "catching up."

These themes grew stronger in the interwar years—in eastern and central Europe, in Latin America, in India, and elsewhere (Love 1988; Chandra 1991). The original great boast of the USSR was that, in the 1930s, at a time of world economic depression, there was not only no unemployment in the USSR but also a program of rapid industrialization.

After 1945, the world chorus on the possibilities of national development grew stronger. The relatively rapid reconstruction of Western Europe and Japan (after massive wartime destruction of infrastructure) seemed to demonstrate that, with will and investment, it was possible to rapidly upgrade technology and

thus raise the overall standard of living. All of a sudden, the theme of economic development became pandemic among politicians, journalists, and scholars. The forgotten corners of already industrialized states (the American South, southern Italy, etc.) were targeted for "development." The Third World was to develop as well—partly through self-help, partly with the assistance of the more advanced "developed" countries. The United Nations would officially proclaim the 1970s the "development decade."

In the universities of the world, development became the new intellectual organizing theme. A liberal paradigm, "modernization theory," was elaborated in the 1950s, to be countered by a *marxisant dependista* counterparadigm elaborated in the 1960s. This was, of course, essentially the updating of the Wilsonian-Leninist antinomy. Once again, in practice, the specific recommendations for state policy may have been polar opposites, but both sets of theories involved specific recommendations for state policy. Both sets of applied practitioners, who advised the governments, were confident that, if their recommendations were implemented, national development would in fact follow and the countries in question would eventually catch up.

We know what happened in the real world. From roughly 1945 to 1970, there was considerable practical effort to expand the means and level of production around the world. It was in this period that gross national product (GNP) and GNP per capita became the principal measuring tools of economic growth, which itself had become the principal indicator of economic development.

This period was a Kondratieff A-period of exceptional amplitude. The amount of growth varied considerably around the world, but on the whole the figures were upward everywhere, not least of all in the so-called socialist countries. This same period was a period of the political triumph of a large number of movements in the Third World that had evolved the strategy of struggling for state power in order thereby to implement policies that would guarantee national development. Everything therefore seemed to be moving in the same positive direction: worldwide economic expansion, the fulfillment state by state of the Wilsonian-Leninist vision, and the almost universally upward growth rates. Developmentalism was the order of the day; there was a worldwide consensus about its legitimacy and its inevitability.

This consensus, however, suffered two shocks from which it has not recovered and, I am arguing, will not recover. The first shock was the worldwide revolution of 1968. The second shock was the worldwide economic stagnation of the period 1970–90, the economic failure of almost all the governments of the peripheral and semiperipheral zones, and the collapse of regimes in the so-called socialist states. 1968 broke the ideological crust. The 1970s and 1980s removed the rest of the ideological covering. The gaping sore of the North-South polarization has been uncovered and exposed to view. At the moment, in desperation, the world is muttering incantations about the market as remedy, as though this could solve anything. But market medicine is mercurochrome and will not prevent further deterioration. It is highly unlikely that most states now abandoning "socialist" slogans in favor of "market" slogans will see a significant improvement in the 1990s in their standard of living. After all, the vast majority of noncore states who adhered to market slogans in the 1980s did quite poorly. Reference is always made to the rare "success" stories (the current hero is South Korea), neglecting the much larger number of failures, and the fading of earlier so-called success stories, such as Brazil.

The main issue, however, is not whether specific state policies have or have not led to economic development. Rather, it is whether or not there will continue to be widespread belief in the likelihood of economic development as the result of any particular state policies.

The Paradigm Not Working

The worldwide revolution of 1968 grew out of a sense that national development had not

occurred; it was not yet the consequence of feeling that the objective itself was an illusion. There were two main themes that were common to all the uprisings (east and west, north and south), whatever the local details. The first was a protest against U.S. hegemony in the world system (and the collusion of the USSR in that hegemony). The second was a protest against the inefficacy of the so-called "Old Left" movements that had come to power in the world in multiple versions—social democracy in the West, communism in the East, national liberation movements in the South. These movements were attacked for not having truly transformed the world, as they had promised in their mobilizational days. They were attacked for being too much a part of the dominant world system, too little antisystemic (Wallerstein, 1991).

In a sense, what those who participated in the various uprisings were saying to the "Old Left" political movements is that their organizational activities had achieved the formal political objectives they had historically set themselves, most notably state power, but that they had distinctly not achieved the greater human equality that had been said to be the purpose of achieving the state power. The worldwide attraction during this period of "Maoism" was due to the fact that it expressed in the most vigorous possible way this double rejection: of U.S. hegemony (and Soviet collusion); and of inefficacious "Old Left" movements in general. However, Maoism represented the argument that the fault lay in the poor leadership of the "Old Left" movements, those who were in Maoist terminology the "capitalist roaders." Hence it was implied that, were the movements now to reject the "capitalist roaders," were they to have a "cultural revolution," then at last the objective of national development would in fact be achieved.

The significance of the worldwide revolution of 1968 was not in the political change it brought about. By 1970, the uprisings had been suppressed or had fizzled everywhere. Nor was the significance in the new ideas it launched. Maoism had a short career in the 1970s but disintegrated by mid-decade, and first of all in China. The themes of the new social movements—cultural nationalism of "minorities," feminism, ecology—have had somewhat more staying power than Maoism but have yet to find a firm ideological footing. The significance of 1968 was rather that it punctured the consensus around Wilsonianism-Leninism by questioning whether the developmentalist ideology had in fact achieved anything of lasting importance. It sowed ideological doubt and corroded the faith.

Once the faith was shaken, once the consensus viewpoint was reduced to the status of merely one viewpoint amid others in the arena (even if still the one most widely held), it was possible for day-to-day reality to have the effect of stripping that ideology bare. This is what happened in the next two decades. The world economic stagnation, the Kondratieff B-phase, has thus far been played out in two major dramas. The first was the OPEC oil price rise of the 1970s. The second was the debt crisis of the 1980s.

The OPEC oil price rise was thought at first to give renewed credence to the possibilities of national development. It seemed to be a demonstration that primary producers in the South, by concerted action, could significantly affect the terms of trade. An initial hysteria in Western public opinion abetted such an interpretation. It was not long for a more sober assessment to take hold. What had really happened? The OPEC countries, under the leadership of the Shah of Iran and the Saudis (the leading friends of the United States, be it noted) raised the price of oil dramatically, thereby drawing a significant percentage of world surplus into their hands. This represented a very significant drain on national accounts for all Third World and socialist countries that were not themselves oil producers, at a time when the world market for their own exports was weakening. The drain on the national accounts of the major industrialized countries was also important but far less significant as a percentage of

the total and more temporary since these countries could more easily take steps to restructure their energy consumption.

What happened to the world surplus funneled through the oil-producing countries? Some of it, of course, went into the "national development" programs of oil-producing states, such as Nigeria, Algeria, Iraq, Iran, Mexico, Venezuela, and the USSR. Some of it went into heavy luxury consumption in oil-producing states, which meant it was transferred to the OECD states as the purchasing of commodities, as investment, or as individual capital flight. And the remaining money was placed in U.S. and European banks. This money that was placed in the banks was then refunneled to Third World and socialist states (including even the oil-producing states) as state loans. These state loans solved the immediate problems of the balance of payments of these states, which were in particularly bad shape precisely because of the oil price rise. With the state loans, the governments were able to stave off for a time political opposition by using the money to maintain imports (even while exports were falling). This in turn sustained world demand for the manufactured goods of the OECD countries and thus minimized the effects on them of the world economic stagnation.

Even during the 1970s, a number of Third World states began nonetheless to feel the effects of a decline in the growth rate combined with an exhaustion of monetary and social reserves. By the 1980s, the effects were felt everywhere (with the exception of East Asia). The first great public expression of the debt crisis was Poland in 1980. The Gierek government had played the 1970s like everyone else, borrowing and spending. But the bill was coming due, and the Polish government sought to reduce it by increasing internal prices, thereby making the Polish working class assume the burden. The result was Gdansk and Solidarność. Solidarność could then incarnate Polish nationalism (and hence both anti-Russianism and anti-Communism). But Polish nationalism was not new. It was the debt crisis that made the difference. In 1982, Mexico announced it could not service its debt. And now at last the world acknowledged it had a "debt crisis." It is noteworthy that it was relatively strong and relatively industrialized countries outside the core—Poland and Mexico—where the collapse started, or at least where it attracted attention.

The 1980s saw a cascade of economic difficulties for peripheral and semiperipheral countries. In virtually all, two elements were the same. The first was popular discontent with the regime in power, followed by political disillusionment. Even when regimes were overthrown—whether by violence or by collapse of a rotting regime, whether they were military dictatorships or Communist parties or one-party African regimes—the pressure for political transformation was more negative than affirmative. It was less out of hope than of despair that the changes occurred. The second common element was the hard financial face of the OECD countries. Faced with their own economic difficulties, they exhibited little patience for the financial dilemmas of Third World and socialist governments. The latter were handed harsh IMF conditions to fulfill, given risible assistance, and subjected to sermonizing about the virtues of the market and privatization. Gone were the Keynesian indulgences of the 1950s and 1960s.

In the early 1980s, the Latin American countries saw a wave of dismantling of developmentalist military dictatorships and discovered "democracy." In the Arab world, developmentalist secular regimes were under sharp attack from Islamists. In black Africa, where one-partyism was once the sustaining structure of developmentalist hopes, the myth had become ashes in the mouth. And in Eastern and Central Europe, the dramatic transformations of 1989 came as a great surprise to the world, although they were clearly inscribed in the events of 1980 in Poland.

In the Soviet Union, where in some senses the developmentalist trek began, we have witnessed the disintegration of the CPSU and of the USSR itself. When developmentalism failed in Brazil or Algeria there was still the argument possible that it was because they had not followed the political path of the USSR. But when it fails in the USSR?

Elegy and Requiem

The story of 1917–89 deserves both elegy and requiem. The elegy is for the triumph of the Wilsonian-Leninist ideal of the self-determination of nations. In these seventy years, the world has been largely decolonized. The world outside Europe has been integrated into the formal political institutions of the interstate system.

This decolonization was partly octroyée, partly arrachée. In the process, an incredible political mobilization was required across the world, which has awakened consciousness everywhere. It will be very difficult ever to put the genie back in the box. Indeed, the main problem is how to contain the spreading virus of micronationalism as ever smaller entities seek to claim peoplehood and therefore the right to self-determination.

From the beginning, however, it was clear that everyone wanted self-determination primarily in order to make their way to prosperity. And from the beginning the road to prosperity was recognized as a difficult one. As I have argued, this has taken the form of the search for national development. And this search for a long time found itself relatively more comfortable with Leninist than with Wilsonian rhetoric, just as the struggle for decolonization had found itself relatively more comfortable with Wilsonian rhetoric.

Because the process was in two steps—first the decolonization (or comparable political change), then the economic development—it meant that the Wilsonian half of the package was always waiting for its Leninist fulfillment. The prospect of national development served as the legitimization of the world system's overall structure. In this sense, the fate of Wilsonian ideology was dependent on the fate of Leninist ideology. To put it more crudely and less kindly, Leninist ideology was the fig leaf of Wilsonian ideology.

Today the fig leaf has fallen, and the emperor is naked. All the shouting about the triumph of democracy in 1989 around the world will not long hide the absence of any serious prospect for the economic transformation of the periphery within the framework of the capitalist world economy. Thus it will not be the Leninists who sing the requiem for Leninism but the Wilsonians. It is they who are in a quandary and who have no plausible political alternatives. This was captured in the no-win dilemmas of Mr. Bush in the Persian Gulf crisis. But the Persian Gulf crisis is only the beginning of the story.

As the North-South confrontations take ever more dramatic (and violent) forms in the decades to come, we shall begin to be aware how much the world will miss the ideological cement of the Wilsonian-Leninist ideological antimony. It represented a glorious but historically passing panoply of ideas, hopes, and human energy. It will not be easy to replace. Yet it is only by finding a new and far more solid utopian vision that we shall be able to transcend the imminent time of troubles.

The World System after the Cold War[†]

Introduction

The certainties of the post-1945 era are now over, in particular two. (1) The United States dominated the capitalist world economy, being the most efficient producer and the most prosperous country. This is no longer true. (2) The United States and the USSR were engaged in an all-encompassing "cold war," which shaped all interstate relations. The cold war is no more. Indeed, the USSR is no more. To understand what this portends, we have three relevant pasts: the past of the U.S. hegemonic era, 1945–90; the past of liberalism as the dominant ideology of the capitalist world system, 1789–1989; the past of capitalism as a histori-

cal system, which started in 1450 and will perhaps be no more by 2050.

The Three Relevant Pasts

The story of the U.S. hegemonic era is the easiest to tell. At the end of World War II, the United States found itself in an exceptional position. Its basic economic forces had been growing steadily stronger in terms of technology, competitiveness, and quantitative share of world production for one hundred years. World War II resulted in enormous physical destruction throughout the Eurasian land mass, and thus among all the potential economic rivals of the United States, both those who had been allies and those who had been foes during the war.

The United States was thus able to establish a new world order, a Pax Americana, after the long disorder of 1914–45. The Pax Americana had four pillars. The first was the reconstruction of the major industrial powers, not only its longtime allies in Western Europe, but its recent foes, Germany and Japan. The motives were multiple. The world economy needed the reentry of these countries both as major producers and as major customers for U.S. production. The United States needed a network of associates to maintain the world order. And, ideologically, the United States needed to propagate the idea of a "free world" that was prosperous as a symbol of hope and therefore of moderation for the world's lower strata.

The second pillar was an arrangement with the only other serious military power in the world, the USSR. The Soviet Union was ostensibly an ideological rival and potentially an expanding power. In fact, it was quite easy to come to an arrangement in which the Soviet Union had its reserved zone (the "socialist bloc"). There were four conditions to the deal: there would be absolute peace in Europe; the two blocs would be territorially fixed; the two great powers would maintain internal order in their blocs; the socialist bloc would expect no help in reconstruction from the United States. There were, to be sure, many noisy quarrels, but since none of them ended in breaking the arrangement, we may assume that their purpose was largely for show.

The third pillar was U.S. internal unity built around the acceptance of U.S. "responsibility" in the world system, anti-Communism at home and abroad, and the end of racial segregation. The fourth pillar was the slow political decolonization of the Third World and modest efforts for its so-called economic development. The emphasis was on the adjectives "slow" and "modest."

If we turn to the second past, that of 1789–1989, we start with the geocultural shock of the French Revolution and its Napoleonic aftermath. The French Revolution changed France less than we believe, but it changed the world system fundamentally. The French Revolution changed mentalities by imposing the belief that political change was "normal" and legitimated by "popular sovereignty." The attempt to deal with this new reality took the form of the creation of the three ideologies: conservatism, liberalism, and socialism. The ostensible difference was in their attitude toward such normal change: the conservatives dubious and wishing to slow it down maximally, the liberals wishing to manage it rationally, and the socialists wishing to speed it up maximally. In theory, all three ideologies looked with disfavor on the state. But, in practice, all three ideologies found that they had to strengthen the state vis-à-vis society in order to achieve their objectives. In the end, all three ideologies united around the liberal program of orderly "reform" enacted and administered by "experts." The conservatives became liberal conservatives and the socialists became liberal socialists.

In the nineteenth century, in Europe, liberalism promoted two great reforms: the extension of the suffrage and the creation of the social welfare state. By 1914 both reforms were in place or in process, and widely accepted as legitimate throughout Western Europe and North America. The object of the reforms was the integration of the working classes in a way that would tame their anger but not threaten the continuing functioning of the capitalist world economy. This program was superbly successful, for two reasons. The governments could mobilize their working classes around a double nationalism: an intra-European nationalism and the nationalist superiority of the "Europeans" to the "backward" peoples of the world. And, second, the costs of the social welfare state could be borne without too much disruption because of the expanded exploitation of the periphery.

World War I marked the beginning of a long intra-"European" struggle between Germany and the United States as the successor hegemonic power to Great Britain. It would end with U.S. victory and world hegemony in 1945. World War I also marked, however, the moment when the peoples of the periphery began to try to reassert themselves against the European domination of the world system. The North-South struggle we know today took shape then. The ideological response of the North to this new political reality was Wilsonianism, or the liberal program applied on a world scale. Wilsonianism offered the world equivalent of suffrage, the self-determination of nations. And twenty-five years later Roosevelt added the world equivalent of the social welfare state, the program of the economic development of the Third World, assisted by Western "aid." Leninism, which posed itself as the radical opponent of Wilsonianism, was in fact its avatar. Anti-imperialism was self-determination clothed in more radical verbiage. The construction of socialism was economic development of the Third World clothed in more radical verbiage. One of the reasons "Yalta" was possible was that there was less difference in the programs of Wilson and Lenin than official rhetoric maintained.

In the heyday of U.S. hegemony after 1945, this world liberalism also seemed superbly successful. The decolonization of Asia and Africa was rapid and, for the most part, relatively painless. The "national liberation movements" were full of hope for the future. The United Nations proclaimed the 1970s the "Development Decade." But something essential was lacking in the attempt to repeat in the twentieth century at the world level what had been the nineteenth-century success of liberalism within Europe. There was no Third World for the Third World. One could neither mobilize the "patriotism" of the Third World against a "Third World" nor count on the income from exploiting a periphery to pay for their social welfare state. The taming of the working classes, so successful within Europe, was a chimera at the world level.

If we now turn to the third past, that between 1450 and today, we see a third "success story," that of capitalism as a historical system. The raison d'être of capitalism is the endless accumulation of capital. The historical system that has been built, slowly and steadily, has been remarkable in its accomplishments. It has sustained a constant expansion of technology permitting an incredible growth in world production and world population. The capitalist world economy was able to expand from its initial European base to incorporate the entire world and eliminate all other historical systems from the globe. It has developed a political framework of "sovereign" nation-states within an ever more codified interstate system which has developed the right proportion of state power vis-à-vis the market so as to permit the maximal accumulation of capital. It has developed a complex system of the remuneration of labor, combining wage and nonwage forms, thereby keeping world labor costs down but offering incentives for efficiency. It has institutionalized both sexism and racism, enabling the construction of a hierarchical labor force which is self-sustaining politically.

Capitalism has been a dynamic system. It has been based not on a stable equilibrium but on a pattern of cyclical swings wherein the "animal spirits" of the entrepreneurial classes, in pursuing their own interests, regularly and inevitably create minicrises of overproduction which lead to downturns or stagnations in the world economy. This is in fact very functional for the system, weeding out the weak producers and creating constraints on the ability of the working classes to pursue their incessant claims for greater reward.

There are, however, some basic contradictions in this historical system, as in all historical systems. The dynamic of the system requires constant spatial expansion; this has reached its limits. The dynamic of the system requires constant externalization of costs by individual producers; this may be coming close to reaching its limits. The dynamic of the system requires the constant, if slow, proletarianization of the working classes of the world; but proletarianization is a negative process from the point of view of the capitalists, in that it increases labor costs and creates political risks. Liberalism as an ideology was a very effective means of containing unrest and "democratization," but over time it inevitably has put enormous strains on state budgets and created a public debt pyramid which threatens the stable functioning of the system.

The Transitional Present

The late 1960s was a turning point in many ways. It marked the beginning of the downturn ending the incredible post-1945 Kondratieff A-phase expansion. The basic economic reason was obvious. The remarkable economic recovery of Western Europe and Japan plus the economic development of the Third World led to such a great increase in the production capacities of the previously most profitable industries (steel, automobiles, electronics, etc.) as to create a profit crunch. We have been living in this Kondratieff B-phase ever since. What has happened is what always happens in B-phases: acute competition among the core powers in a situation of contraction, each trying to maximize its profit margins and minimize its unemployment at the expense of the others; a shift of capital from seeking profits in production to seeking profits in financial manipulations; a squeeze on governmental balance of payments, resulting in debt crises (of the Third World, the ex-socialist bloc, and the United States). There has been a relocation of production at the world level. There has been an intensive search for new product innovations which can be the basis of future quasi monopolies. As in all B-phases, the effects of the downturn have not been felt evenly; some do better than others. In this downturn, the relative success story has been that of Japan and the East Asian "dragons," which are linked.

At the same time, in 1968, there began a world revolution which, it is now clear, was a revolution against liberalism as the dominant ideology of the world system. At the time, the social unrest, which occurred throughout the world—France and Germany, the United States and Japan, Czechoslovakia, and China, India and Mexico—seemed to have two common themes everywhere: opposition to U.S. hegemony in the world system and Soviet collusion; denunciation of the so-called Old Left (Communist and social-democratic parties, national liberation movements) for their complicity with the dominant forces. This revolt of 1968 in fact culminated with the overthrow in 1989–91 of the Communist governments in Eastern Europe and the USSR. It is today clearer than it was in 1968 that the two themes—opposition to U.S. hegemony and opposition to the Old Left—are in fact but a single theme, the opposition to reformist liberalism as a justification of the workings of the world system.

The two principal changes in the geopolitics of the world system in the 1970s and 1980s have been the decline of the relative power of the United States and the great disillusionment with developmentalism in the Third World. The first is a normal cyclical occurrence. The economic strengths of the European Community and Japan have been steadily rising since the mid-1960s, and the United States has not been able to keep pace. This has of course political and cultural implications. The world policy of the United States has for the past twenty years been centered around ways to slow down this loss of hegemony by exerting pressure on its allies. The second is not a cyclical occurrence at all. It marks the breakdown of the Wilsonian liberal enticement to the working classes of the periphery. The collapse of "sta-

tism" in both the Third World and the ex-socialist bloc is the collapse of liberal reformism, and hence the undermining of a crucial pillar in the stability of the capitalist world economy.

The collapse of the Communist bloc is thus a double setback for the world system. For the United States, it is a geopolitical catastrophe, as it eliminates the only ideological weapon the United States had to restrain the EC and Japan from pursuing their self-defined objectives. For the capitalist world economy as a historical system, it marks the onset of an acute crisis, since it lifts the Leninist justification of the status quo without replacing it with any viable substitute.

The Uncertain Future

We have now entered into the post-American era, but also the postliberal era. This promises to be a time of great world disorder, greater probably than the world disorder between 1914 and 1945, and far more significant in terms of maintaining the world system as a viable structure. What may we expect?

On the one hand, we may expect the capitalist world economy to continue to operate in the short run in the way it has been operating for five hundred years, but operating in this way will only exacerbate the crisis. Once this current Kondratieff B-phase is finally over (which will only be after one last downward swing), we shall as previously enter into a new A-phase, in which Japan, the United States, and the EC will struggle to obtain quasi-monopolistic control over the new leading industries. Japan stands a good chance of coming out on top, and it is probable that it will make a world economic alliance with the United States as junior partner to ensure this. In this new era of prosperity, the new main areas of economic expansion will be China for the Japan-U.S. grouping and Russia for the EC. The rest of the periphery will be largely excluded from any benefits, and the polarization of world wealth will grow markedly more acute, as will the polarization of population growth.

A further problem is that the collapse of Wilsonian liberalism has led worldwide to a collapse in the faith in the "state" as the central locus of social change and progress. It has also meant the collapse of long-term optimism, which has long been a key stabilizing political factor in the operation of the system. Polarized wealth without hope leads to generalized fear and the search for structures of security. These are being sought in identity politics, whose meaning is ambiguous but whose force is quite apparent.

There are three obvious sources of major instability in the world system over the next fifty years. One is the growth of what I shall call the Khomeini option. This is the assertion by states in the periphery of total otherness and rejection of the rules of the interstate system as well as the geocultural norms governing the world system. This particular option has been largely contained for the moment in Iran, but it is quite likely that other states will resort to it (and not only Islamic states), and it will be much more difficult to contain it if several states try it simultaneously.

The second source of instability is what I shall call the Saddam Hussein option. This is the attempt to challenge militarily the dominance of the North in the world system. While Saddam Hussein's attempt was stopped cold, it took an extraordinary mobilization by the United States to do it. It is not at all clear that, as the decades go by, this can be repeated, especially if there are several such attempts simultaneously. U.S. military strength will decline because the United States cannot sustain it either financially or politically. The states of the North are looking for a long-term substitute, but there is no clear one in sight. And acute economic and political competition among the core powers during the next upturn of the world economy may not render such military collaboration too likely.

The third source of instability will be an unstoppable mass movement of people from South to North, including to Japan. The growing polar-

ization of wealth and population makes this an option which no amount of border guards can successfully police. The result will be internal political instability in the North, coming doubly from right-wing anti-immigrant forces and from the immigrants themselves demanding political (and hence economic) rights; and all this in a context where all groups will have lost faith in the state as a means of solving social inequities.

This is a picture of world turmoil, but it is not necessarily a pessimistic one. Obviously, such world disorder cannot go on indefinitely. New solutions will have to be found. This will undoubtedly mean creating a new historical system to replace the one that has been so efficacious for five hundred years, but which is now crumbling because of its very success. We come therefore to the historical choices before us: what kind of new historical system to build, and how? There is no way to predict the outcome. We shall find ourselves in what scientists today are calling a bifurcation far from equilibrium, whose resolution is intrinsically unpredictable, but in which every intervention has great impact. We are thus in a situation of "free will." The world of 2050 will be the world we create. We have a considerable say about that creation. The politics of the next fifty years will be the politics of this restructuring of our world system.

Notes

*   From *American Behavioral Scientist* 35, nos. 4/5 (March/June 1992): 517–29, by permission of Sage Publications. Copyright 1992 by Sage Publications.

†   From the *Journal of Peace Research* 30, no. 1 (1993): 1–6, by permission of the author and Sage Publications. Copyright 1993 by Sage Publications.

References

Arrighi, Giovanni, Terence K. Hopkins, and Immanuel Wallerstein. 1989. *Antisystemic Movements.* London: Verso.

Chandra, Bipan. 1991. "Colonial India: British versus Indian Views of Development." *Review* 14:81–167.

Jennings, Sir W. Ivor. 1956. *The Approach to Self-Government.* Cambridge: Cambridge University Press.

Love, Joseph L. 1988. "Theorizing Underdevelopment: Latin America and Romania, 1860–1950." *Review* 11:453–96.

Wallerstein, Immanuel. 1991. "1968: Revolution in the World-System." In *Geopolitics and Geoculture: Essays on the Changing World-System,* 65–83. Cambridge: Cambridge University Press.

Wallerstein, Immanuel M. 1991. *Geopolitics and Geoculture: Essays on the Changing World-System.* Cambridge: Cambridge University Press.

———. 1992. "The Concept of National Development, 1917–1989: Elegy and Requiem," pp. 79–88, in Gary Marks and Larry Diamond, eds, *Reexamining Democracy: Essays in Honor of Seymour Martin Lipset.* Newbury Park, CA: Sage.

———. 1992. "The Collapse of Liberalism," pp. 96–110, in Ralph Miliband and Leo Panitch, eds, *Socialist Register 1992: New World Order?* London: Merlin.

The Structure of Dependence*

Theotonio Dos Santos†

What Is Dependence?

By dependence we mean a situation in which the economy of certain countries is conditioned by the development and expansion of another economy to which the former is subjected. The relation of interdependence between two or more economies, and between these and world trade, assumes the form of dependence when some countries (the dominant ones) can expand and can be self-sustaining, while other countries (the dependent ones) can do this only as a reflection of that expansion, which can have either a positive or a negative effect on their immediate development [7, p. 6].

The concept of dependence permits us to see the internal situation of these countries as part of world economy. In the Marxian tradition, the theory of imperialism has been developed as a study of the process of expansion of the imperialist centers and of their world domination. In the epoch of the revolutionary movement of the Third World, we have to develop the theory of laws of internal development in those countries that are the object of such expansion and are governed by them. This theoretical step transcends the theory of development which seeks to explain the situation of the underdeveloped countries as a product of their slowness or failure to adopt the patterns of efficiency characteristic of developed countries (or to "modernize" or "develop" themselves). Although capitalist development theory admits the existence of an "external" dependence, it is unable to perceive underdevelopment in the way our present theory perceives it, as a consequence and part of the process of the world expansion of capital-ism—a part that is necessary to and integrally linked with it.

In analyzing the process of constituting a world economy that integrates the so-called national economies in a world market of commodities, capital, and even of labor power, we see that the relations produced by this market are unequal and combined—unequal because development of parts of the system occurs at the expense of other parts. Trade relations are based on monopolistic control of the market, which leads to the transfer of surplus generated in the dependent countries to the dominant countries; financial relations are, from the viewpoint of the dominant powers, based on loans and the export of capital, which permit them to receive interest and profits; thus increasing their domestic surplus and strengthening their control over the economies of the other countries. For the dependent countries these relations represent an export of profits and interest which carries off part of the surplus generated domestically and leads to a loss of control over their productive resources. In order to permit these disadvantageous relations, the dependent countries must generate large surpluses, not in such a way as to create higher levels of technology but rather superexploited manpower. The result is to limit the development of their internal market and their technical and cultural capacity, as well as the moral and physical health of their people. We call this combined development because it is the combination of these inequalities and the transfer of resources from the most backward and dependent sectors to the most advanced and dominant ones which explains the inequality, deepens it, and transforms it into a necessary and structural element of the world economy.

Historic Forms of Dependence

Historic forms of dependence are conditioned by: (1) the basic forms of this world economy which has its own laws of development; (2) the type of economic relations dominant in the capitalist centers and the ways in which the latter expand outward; and (3) the types of economic relations existing inside the peripheral countries which are incorporated into the situation of dependence within the network of international economic relations generated by capitalist expansion. It is not within the purview of this paper to study these forms in detail but only to distinguish broad characteristics of development.

Drawing on an earlier study, we may distinguish: (1) Colonial dependence, trade export in nature, in which commercial and financial capital in alliance with the colonialist state dominated the economic relations of the Europeans and the colonies, by means of a trade monopoly complemented by a colonial monopoly of land, mines, and manpower (serf or slave) in the colonized countries. (2) Financial-industrial dependence which consolidated itself at the end of the nineteenth century, characterized by the domination of big capital in the hegemonic centers, and its expansion abroad through investment in the production of raw materials and agricultural products for consumption in the hegemonic centers. A productive structure grew up in the dependent countries devoted to the export of these products (which Levin labeled export economies [11]; other analysis in other regions [12][13]), producing what ECLA has called "foreign-oriented development" (*desarrollo hacia afuera*) [4]. (3) In the postwar period a new type of dependence has been consolidated, based on multinational corporations which began to invest in industries geared to the internal market of underdeveloped coun-

tries. This form of dependence is basically technological-industrial dependence [6].

Each of these forms of dependence corresponds to a situation which conditioned not only the international relations of these countries but also their internal structures: the orientation of production, the forms of capital accumulation, the reproduction of the economy and, simultaneously, their social and political structure.

The Export Economies

In forms (1) and (2) of dependence, production is geared to those products destined for export (gold, silver, and tropical products in the colonial epoch; raw materials and agricultural products in the epoch of industrial-financial dependence); that is, production is determined by demand from the hegemonic centers. The internal productive structure is characterized by rigid specialization and monoculture in entire regions (the Caribbean, the Brazilian Northeast, etc.). Alongside these export sectors there grew up certain complementary economic activities (cattle raising and some manufacturing, for example) which were dependent, in general, on the export sector to which they sell their products. There was a third, subsistence economy which provided manpower for the export sector under favorable conditions and toward which excess population shifted during periods unfavorable to international trade.

Under these conditions, the existing internal market was restricted by four factors: (1) Most of the national income was derived from export, which was used to purchase the inputs required by export production (slaves, for example) or luxury goods consumed by the hacienda and mine owners, and by the more prosperous employees. (2) The available manpower was subject to very arduous forms of superexploitation, which limited its consumption. (3) Part of the consumption of these workers was provided by the subsistence economy, which served as a complement to their income and as a refuge during periods of depression. (4) A fourth factor was to be found in those countries in which land and mines were in the hands of foreigners (cases of an enclave economy): a great part of the accumulated surplus was destined to be sent abroad in the form of profits, limiting not only internal consumption but also possibilities of reinvestment [1]. In the case of enclave economies the relations of the foreign companies with the hegemonic center were even more exploitative and were complemented by the fact that purchases by the enclave were made directly abroad.

The New Dependence

The new form of dependence, (3) above, is in the process of developing and is conditioned by the exigencies of the international commodity and capital markets. The possibility of generating new investments depends on the existence of financial resources in foreign currency for the purchase of machinery and processed raw materials not produced domestically. Such purchases are subject to two limitations: the limit of resources generated by the export sector (reflected in the balance of payments, which includes not only trade but also service relations); and the limitations of monopoly on patents which leads monopolistic firms to prefer to transfer their machines in the form of capital rather than as commodities for sale. It is necessary to analyze these relations of dependence if we are to understand the fundamental structural limits they place on the development of these countries.

1. Industrial development is dependent on an export sector for the foreign currency to buy the inputs utilized by the industrial sector. The first consequence of this dependence is the need to preserve the traditional export sector, which limits economically the development of the internal market by the conservation of backward relations of production and signifies, politically, the maintenance of power by traditional decadent oligarchies. In the countries

where these sectors are controlled by foreign capital, it signifies the remittance abroad of high profits, and political dependence on those interests. Only in rare instances does foreign capital not control at least the marketing of these products. In response to these limitations, dependent countries in the 1930s and 1940s developed a policy of exchange restrictions and taxes on the national and foreign export sector; today they tend toward the gradual nationalization of production and toward the imposition of certain timid limitations on foreign control of the marketing of exported products. Furthermore, they seek, still somewhat timidly, to obtain better terms for the sale of their products. In recent decades, they have created mechanisms for international price agreements, and today UNCTAD and ECLA press to obtain more favorable tariff conditions for these products on the part of the hegemonic centers. It is important to point out that the industrial development of these countries is dependent on the situation of the export sector, the continued existence of which they are obliged to accept.

2. Industrial development is, then, strongly conditioned by fluctuations in the balance of payments. This leads toward deficit due to the relations of dependence themselves. The causes of the deficit are three:

a.   Trade relations take place in a highly monopolized international market, which tends to lower the price of raw materials and to raise the prices of industrial products, particularly inputs. In the second place, there is a tendency in modern technology to replace various primary products with synthetic raw materials. Consequently the balance of trade in these countries tends to be less favorable (even though they show a general surplus). The overall Latin American balance of trade from 1946 to 1968 shows a surplus for each of those years. The same thing happens in almost every underdeveloped country. However, the losses due to deterioration of the terms of trade (on the basis of data from ECLA and the International Monetary Fund), excluding Cuba, were $26,383 million for the 1951–66 period, taking 1950 prices as a base. If Cuba and Venezuela are excluded, the total is $15,925 million.

b. For the reasons already given, foreign capital retains control over the most dynamic sectors of the economy and repatriates a high volume of profit; consequently, capital accounts are highly unfavorable to dependent countries. The data show that the amount of capital leaving the country is much greater than the amount entering; this produces an enslaving deficit in capital accounts. To this must be added the deficit in certain services which are virtually under total foreign control—such as freight transport, royalty payments, technical aid, and so forth. Consequently, an important deficit is produced in the total balance of payments; thus limiting the possibility of importation of inputs for industrialization.

c. The result is that "foreign financing" becomes necessary, in two forms: to cover the existing deficit, and to "finance" development by means of loans for the stimulation of investments and to "supply" an internal economic surplus which was decapitalized to a large extent by the remittance of part of the surplus generated domestically and sent abroad as profits.

Foreign capital and foreign "aid" thus fill up the holes that they themselves created. The real value of this aid, however, is doubtful. If overcharges resulting from the restrictive terms of the aid are subtracted from the total amount of the grants, the average net flow, according to calculations of the Inter-American Economic and Social Council, is approximately 54 percent of the gross flow [5].

If we take account of certain further facts—that a high proportion of aid is paid in local currencies, that Latin American countries make contributions to international financial institutions, and that credits are often "tied"—we find a "real component of foreign aid" of 42.2 percent on a very favorable hypothesis and of 38.3 percent on a more realistic one [5, II-33]. The gravity of the situation becomes even clearer if we consider that these credits are used in large part to finance North American investments, to

subsidize foreign imports which compete with national products, to introduce technology not adapted to the needs of underdeveloped countries, and to invest in low-priority sectors of the national economies. The hard truth is that the underdeveloped countries have to pay for all of the "aid" they receive. This situation is generating an enormous protest movement by Latin American governments seeking at least partial relief from such negative relations.

3. Finally, industrial development is strongly conditioned by the technological monopoly exercised by imperialist centers. We have seen that the underdeveloped countries depend on the importation of machinery and raw materials for the development of their industries. However, these goods are not freely available in the international market; they are patented and usually belong to the big companies. The big companies do not sell machinery and processed raw materials as simple merchandise: they demand either the payment of royalties, and so forth, for their utilization or, in most cases, they convert these goods into capital and introduce them in the form of their own investments. This is how machinery which is replaced in the hegemonic centers by more advanced technology is sent to dependent countries as capital for the installation of affiliates. Let us pause and examine these relations, in order to understand their oppressive and exploitative character.

The dependent countries do not have sufficient foreign currency, for the reasons given. Local businessmen have financing difficulties, and they must pay for the utilization of certain patented techniques. These factors oblige the national bourgeois governments to facilitate the entry of foreign capital in order to supply the restricted national market, which is strongly protected by high tariffs in order to promote industrialization. Thus, foreign capital enters with all the advantages: in many cases, it is given exemption from exchange controls for the importation of machinery; financing of sites for installation of industries is provided; government financing agencies facilitate industrialization; loans are available from foreign and domestic banks, which prefer such clients; foreign aid often subsidizes such investments and finances complementary public investments; after installation, high profits obtained in such favorable circumstances can be reinvested freely. Thus it is not surprising that the data of the U.S. Department of Commerce reveal that the percentage of capital brought in from abroad by these companies is but a part of the total amount of invested capital. These data show that in the period from 1946 to 1967 the new entries of capital into Latin America for direct investment amounted to $5,415 million, while the sum of reinvested profits was $4,424 million. On the other hand, the transfers of profits from Latin America to the United States amounted to $14,775 million. If we estimate total profits as approximately equal to transfers plus reinvestments we have the sum of $18,983 million. In spite of enormous transfers of profits to the United States, the book value of the United States's direct investment in Latin America went from $3,045 million in 1946 to $10,213 million in 1967. From these data it is clear that: (1) Of the new investments made by U.S. companies in Latin America for the period 1946–67, 55 percent corresponds to new entries of capital and 45 percent to reinvestment of profits; in recent years, the trend is more marked, with reinvestments between 1960 and 1966 representing more than 60 percent of new investments. (2) Remittances remained at about 10 percent of book value throughout the period. (3) The ratio of remitted capital to new flow is around 2.7 for the period 1946–67; that is, for each dollar that enters $2.70 leaves. In the 1960s this ratio roughly doubled, and in some years was considerably higher.

The *Survey of Current Business* data on sources and uses of funds for direct North American investment in Latin America in the period 1957–64 show that, of the total sources of direct investment in Latin America, only 11.8 percent came from the United States. The remainder is in large part, the result of the activities of North American firms in Latin America (46.4 percent net income, 27.7 per-

cent under the heading of depreciation), and from "sources located abroad" (14.1 percent). It is significant that the funds obtained abroad that are external to the companies are greater than the funds originating in the United States.

Effects on the Productive Structure

It is easy to grasp, even if only superficially, the effects that this dependent structure has on the productive system itself in these countries and the role of this structure in determining a specified type of development, characterized by its dependent nature.

The productive system in the underdeveloped countries is essentially determined by these international relations. In the first place, the need to conserve the agrarian or mining export structure generates a combination between more advanced economic centers that extract surplus value from the more backward sectors, also between internal "metropolitan" centers and internal interdependent "colonial" centers [10]. The unequal and combined character of capitalist development at the international level is reproduced internally in an acute form. In the second place the industrial and technological structure responds more closely to the interests of the multinational corporations than to internal developmental needs (conceived of not only in terms of the overall interests of the population, but also from the point of view of the interests of a national capitalist development). In the third place, the same technological and economic-financial concentration of the hegemonic economies is transferred without substantial alteration to very different economies and societies, giving rise to a highly unequal productive structure, a high concentration of incomes, underutilization of installed capacity, intensive exploitation of existing markets concentrated in large cities, and so forth.

The accumulation of capital in such circumstances assumes its own characteristics. In the first place, it is characterized by profound differences among domestic wage levels, in the context of a local cheap labor market, combined with a capital-intensive technology. The result, from the point of view of relative surplus value, is a high rate of exploitation of labor power. (On measurements of forms of exploitation, see [3].)

This exploitation is further aggravated by the high prices of industrial products enforced by protectionism, exemptions and subsidies given by the national governments, and "aid" from hegemonic centers. Furthermore, since dependent accumulation is necessarily tied into the international economy, it is profoundly conditioned by the unequal and combined character of international capitalist economic relations, by the technological and financial control of the imperialist centers, by the realities of the balance of payments, by the economic policies of the state, and so on. The role of the state in the growth of national and foreign capital merits a much fuller analysis than can be made here.

Using the analysis offered here as a point of departure, it is possible to understand the limits that this productive system imposes on the growth of the internal markets of these countries. The survival of traditional relations in the countryside is a serious limitation on the size of the market, since industrialization does not offer hopeful prospects. The productive structure created by dependent industrialization limits the growth of the internal market.

First, it subjects the labor force to highly exploitative relations which limit its purchasing power. Second, in adopting a technology of intensive capital use, it creates very few jobs in comparison with population growth, and limits the generation of new sources of income. These two limitations affect the growth of the consumer goods market. Third, the remittance abroad of profits carries away part of the economic surplus generated within the country. In all these ways limits are put on the possible creation of basic national industries which could provide a market for the capital goods this surplus would make possible if it were not remitted abroad.

From this cursory analysis we see that the alleged backwardness of these economies is not due to a lack of integration with capitalism but that, on the contrary, the most powerful obstacles to their full development come from the way in which they are joined to this international system and its laws of development.

Some Conclusions: Dependent Reproduction

In order to understand the system of dependent reproduction and the socioeconomic institutions created by it, we must see it as part of a system of world economic relations based on monopolistic control of large-scale capital, on control of certain economic and financial centers over others, on a monopoly of a complex technology that leads to unequal and combined development at a national and international level. Attempts to analyze backwardness as a failure to assimilate more advanced models of production or to modernize are nothing more than ideology disguised as science. The same is true of the attempts to analyze this international economy in terms of relations among elements in free competition, such as the theory of comparative costs which seeks to justify the inequalities of the world economic system and to conceal the relations of exploitation on which it is based [14].

In reality we can understand what is happening in the underdeveloped countries only when we see that they develop within the framework of a process of dependent production and reproduction. This system is a dependent one because it reproduces a productive system whose development is limited by those world relations which necessarily lead to the development of only certain economic sectors, to trade under unequal conditions [9], to domestic competition with international capital under unequal conditions, to the imposition of relations of superexploitation of the domestic labor force with a view to dividing the economic surplus thus generated between internal and external forces of domination. (On economic surplus and its utilization in the dependent countries, see [1].)

In reproducing such a productive system and such international relations, the development of dependent capitalism reproduces the factors that prevent it from reaching a nationally and internationally advantageous situation; and it thus reproduces backwardness, misery, and social marginalization within its borders. The development that it produces benefits very narrow sectors, encounters unyielding domestic obstacles to its continued economic growth (with respect to both internal and foreign markets), and leads to the progressive accumulation of balance-of-payments deficits, which in turn generate more dependence and more superexploitation.

The political measures proposed by the developmentalists of ECLA, UNCTAD, BID, and so forth, do not appear to permit destruction of these terrible chains imposed by dependent development. We have examined the alternative forms of development presented for Latin America and the dependent countries under such conditions elsewhere [8]. Everything now indicates that what can be expected is a long process of sharp political and military confrontations and of profound social radicalization which will lead these countries to a dilemma: governments of force which open the way to facism, or popular revolutionary governments, which open the way to socialism. Intermediate solutions have proved to be, in such a contradictory reality, empty and utopian.

Notes

*   From the *American Economic Review* 60, no. 2 (May 1970): 231–36, by permission of the author and the American Economic Association. Copyright 1970 by the American Economic Association.

†   This work expands on certain preliminary work done in a research project on the relations of dependence in Latin America, directed by the author at the Center for Socio-Economic Studies of the Faculty of Economic Science of the University of Chile. In order to abridge the discussion of various aspects, the author was obliged to cite certain of his earlier works. The author expresses his gratitude to the researcher Orlando Caputo and Roberto Pizarro for some of the data utilized and to Sergio Ramos for his critical comments on the paper.

References

[1]   Baran, Paul. *Political Economy of Growth* (Monthly Review Press, 1967).

[2]   Balogh, Thomas. *Unequal Partners* (Basil Blackwell, 1963).

[3]   Casanova, Pablo Gonzalez. *Sociología de la explotación,* Siglo XXI (México, 1969).

[4]   Cepal, *La CEPAL y el Análisis del Desarrollo Latinoamericano* (1968, Santiago, Chile).

[5]   Consejo Interamericano Economico Social (CIES) O.A.S., Interamerican Economic and Social Council, External Financing for Development in L.A. *El Financiamiento Externo para el Desarrollo de América Latina* (Pan-American Union, Washington, 1969).

[6]   Dos Santos, Theotonio. *El nuevo carácter de la dependencia,* CESO (Santiago de Chile, 1968).

[7]   — — —, *La crisis de la teoría del desarrollo y las relaciones de dependencia en América Latina,* Boletín del CESO, 3 (Santiago, Chile, 1968).

[8]   — — —, *La dependencia económica y las alternativas de cambio en América Latina,* Ponencia al IX Congreso Latinoamericano de Sociología (México, Nov., 1969).

[9]   Emmanuel, A. *L'Echange Inégal* (Maspero, Paris, 1969).

[10] Frank, Andre G. *Development and Underdevelopment in Latin America* (Monthly Review Press, 1968).

[11] Levin, I. V. *The Export Economies* (Harvard University Press, 1964).

[12] Myrdal, Gunnar. *Asian Drama* (Pantheon, 1968).

[13] Nkrumah, K. *Neocolonialismo, última etapa del imperialismo,* Siglo XXI (México, 1966).

[14] Palloix, Cristian, *Problemes de la Croissance en Economie Ouverte* (Maspero, Paris, 1969).

Population: Analysis and Advocacy

We title this section "Population" in hopes that it will imply to the reader a broad range of subtopics all rooted, at least to some extent, in demography. Today, population implies resources, environment, peoples, places. And demography is much more than census taking. It encompasses a veritable host of topics and extends its focus beyond statistics to serious efforts to explain continuity and change in the size, composition, and condition of human populations.

Perhaps the most fascinating of the topics of current interest in this broad field is the "demographic transition." Born of modernization and industrialization, the demographic transition, in one form or another, has characterized virtually every industrialized and industrializing country. Briefly, a country begins with high mortality and fertility rates. At some point in its modernization process, the country will begin to experience a decline in its mortality rate. Then, at some point, lagged in time—a lag that can be short, medium, or long—the fertility rate begins to decline. As a consequence, the country's population rises rapidly but then stabilizes at a low, or even negative, rate of growth. No two countries exhibit exactly the same pattern. There are marked variations, and possibly some exceptions. In a general sense, however, the phenomenon has become axiomatic within the context of modernization.

In our first selection Nathan Keyfitz, one of the giants in this field, offers an expansive overview of the history and development of the science of demography. From the first English population estimates at the end of the seventeenth century to the contemporary study of the demographic transition, Keyfitz describes how the world once "pushed against the ceiling of food," as described by Malthus, and now "pushes against the ceiling of space, air, water, minerals."

In our next selection Kingsley Davis, another towering figure in the field, explores the relationship between population and resources and elaborates the formal demography that relates the two, including the important concepts of "carrying capacity" and "limits to growth." In this essay Davis makes a compelling case for infusing ideas about human culture into the theory of population and resources. He seems very dubious about the usefulness of the concept of carrying capacity, an idea adapted from consideration of the grazing of cattle, for the understanding of human population growth. Davis also thoroughly explores the fascinating modern phenomenon known as the demographic transition.

Our last selection is an eye-opener from the executive director of the United Nations Children's Fund (UNICEF). In this excerpt from *The State of the World's Children 1993,* James Grant proposes that spending $25 billion per year for ten years can control the major childhood diseases, halve the rate of child malnutrition worldwide, bring clean water and sanitation to all the world's communities, make family planning services universally available, and provide nearly every child with at least a basic education. Grant then goes on to demonstrate the workability of this extraordinary plan.

Population Theory and Doctrine: A Historical Survey*

Nathan Keyfitz

The number of people in the city, the nation, or the world—what determines that number and how in turn it affects power and welfare—has been a persistent theme of social science. Philosophers, theologians, counselors to princes, and legislators have espoused population doctrines and promoted policies based on them, or else promoted policies and created doctrines to buttress them.

We can learn from all of them, ancient and modern, even where the views of a particular society are hardly appropriate for us. Most premodern thought was pronatalist. The Romans wanted men to fill the legions that would extend the boundaries of the empire. The mercantilists wanted workers on the land or in manufactures, who would produce goods to sell abroad and so add to the riches of the prince. Imperial and mercantilist thought was directed toward turning people into power or into gold. High death rates made populations seem fragile, in danger of dying out if not fostered and encouraged from above.

In the late eighteenth century the center began to shift from the emperor or prince to the people. Sincerely or not, the arguments in population debate came to revolve around the prosperity or misery of the masses. The optimum population for high average income is a smaller number than the optimum for the wealth and power of the ruler. When people ceased to be regarded as the property or instrument of the ruler, restrictions on growth could be seriously argued. The following paragraphs sketch the historical course of discussion. They are especially indebted to Vialatoux (1959), the United Nations (1953, chap. 3), and Sauvy (1956).

Antiquity

Greek thought on population developed in city-states with constitutional rule by the minority who were citizens. According to Plato (*Laws,* Book V, para. 637), a population must be sufficient to defend itself against its neighbors, and the optimum thus depends partly on the strength of these neighbors; but no city should exceed its capacity to provide materially for its citizens. Effective rule and civil order depend on the citizens knowing one another, which sets another limit to size. In his discussion he used the arbitrary figure of 5,040 landholders, a number sufficient for the various specialities the state requires. This total is divisible by fifty-nine numbers, and so would facilitate the allocation of tasks and the division of property. When more or fewer children were needed to attain the ideal, the change in fertility could be realized by appropriate honors or negative sanctions; fostering immigration or dispatching citizens to the colonies were also acceptable policies for influencing the total. Aristotle was especially concerned that the city not be too large; he advocated abortion, rejecting infanticide except as a eugenic measure (*Politics,* Book I, para. 1; Book VII, para. 4; see Barker 1959: 407–8; United Nations 1953).

In India not long after Plato—around 300 B.C.—Kautilya wrote *Arthasastra* (Book VII, chaps. 1, 11; Book VIII, chap. 3; Book XIII, chap. 4; cf. Spengler 1963), which discussed population as a source of political, economic and military strength, the necessary complement of land and mines. Though a given territory can hold too many or too few people, the latter is the greater evil. Kautilya restricted asceticism to the aged, favored the remarriage of widows, opposed taxes so high as to provoke emigration.

With their tightly administered land empire and ceaseless wars on their borders, the Romans needed men even more than did China or India. Being superior to their neighbors in the arts of warfare, they could send any excess men across their frontiers to conquer the lands that would sustain them. Women were useful for producing warriors. Roman writers condemned celibacy and advocated monogamous marriage as the type that would produce the most offspring. Vice leads not only to individual ruin but to collective depopulation (Cicero, *De republica,* Book IV, para. 5). The literary emphasis on virtue and on Rome's need for men did not prevent small families, especially in the upper and middle classes, or an increasing dependence on hired barbarians.

Christian Thought

Christian thought developed in the declining Roman Empire, but encouraging population growth to meet the secular needs of the empire formed very little part of it (Noonan 1965). To the church fathers virginity was the ideal; only for those too weak to abstain from temptation of the flesh was marriage recommended. Augustine reacted against the pessimistic heresies of Gnosticism and Manicheism, which condemned marriage and procreation as producing material human bodies in which the Light would be imprisoned. He sought a justification for marriage, and found it above all in procreation. His doctrine of the marital goods—offspring, fidelity, symbolic stability—dominated Christian thought for a thousand years, during which marriage remained the second-best state. "I am aware," Augustine wrote, "of some that

murmur, 'What if all men should abstain from sexual relations, whence will the human race subsist?' . . . I answer, so much more speedily would the City of God be fulfilled and the end of the world hastened."

The contrast to the prior Hebrew teaching is striking. The early Christian theologian did not refer to the injunction of Genesis to increase and multiply, nor did he speak of spreading Christianity by having children. The less austere Thomas Aquinas reintroduced the Aristotelian concept of nature; just as it is the nature of the eye to see, so it is the nature of the genitalia to procreate—the very word tells that. It is right and pleasurable to do what is according to nature.

In 1930, the encyclical *Casti Connubii* synthesized a variety of themes from many historical epochs. It condemned contraception on the grounds of the need to propagate the human race and to bear children for the Church of Christ, as well as on Augustine's three goods of marriage. It recalled Aristotle and Aquinas in arguing that "no reason can make congruent with nature what is intrinsically against nature." It used nineteenth-century theology to condemn the sin of Onan (Noonan 1965: 508). Following the lead of the Lambeth Conference, which in 1930 opened the door to contraception in the Anglican Church, most other Protestant groups have found little difficulty in reversing their previous stand against birth control. But Catholic doctrine up to this writing has yielded only the theologically confusing concession of the rhythm method, sanctioned by Pius XII in 1950 after much debate within the church, which seemingly shifted from the intention of contraception to the method. Insistence at the highest level that contraception is wrong has proved incomprehensible to many priests and laymen.

The Cycle of Population and Empire

Ibn Khaldûn, who lived before the eighteenth century invented the idea of progress, saw history as the rise, prospering, and fall of states and civilizations (Mahdi 1957: Part 4). When a tribe becomes numerous under an aggressive chief, it enters on a career of conquest, builds or captures a capital city, and adapts its tribal religion in order to strengthen loyalty to the chief. The tribal chief's successors make themselves absolute rulers of an expanding state, build palaces and temples, and sponsor the arts and the sciences. Rule comes to depend less on the respect for a senior kinsman and more on a tightly organized bureaucracy and army. The city expands with the expansion of the hinterland supplying its food.

Later generations of rulers, attracted to luxury, lose their martial virtues. The original population declines; foreign mercenaries are hired for the army, and foreign officials for the administration. These can be paid only by high taxes, levied on both the artisans and the surrounding peasantry. The absorption of the rulers in luxury, the decline of the native population, and the spread of intrigue in the bureaucracy and army lead to the loss of the provinces on whose food and other raw materials the state depends. Having broken the original bonds of kinship and perverted religion to the service of the state, the rulers are helpless when the artificial military and civil structure dissolves. In the last phase the provinces have fallen away, commerce is undercut by taxes and insecurity, and the birth rate declines further. If it is not conquered by a newly rising population, the state burns out like a lamp wick when the oil is exhausted.

Machiavelli, also a counselor to princes and a political realist, lived about a century after Ibn Khaldun, and like him saw population growth as initiating new cycles of history. He gave as an example the demographic expansion of the barbarians beyond the Rhine and the Danube. A community that became numerous would divide into three parts, each containing the same proportions of nobles and people, rich and poor, and draw lots to see which third would move out of its native country, generally toward the south. The migrating masses destroyed the Roman Empire. Population was indeed a matter for the ruler to be concerned about: "I think those princes capable of ruling," said Machiavelli, "who are capable, either by the numbers of their men or by the greatness of their wealth, to raise a complete army and bid battle to any enemy that shall invade them" (*History of Florence,* quoted by Malthus 1960b: 195).

In Europe of the sixteenth to eighteenth centuries, states competed ceaselessly for military, political, and economic power. Absolute rulers had an interest in maximizing their territories' populations, from which both armies and manual workers could be recruited. The monarch's wealth was seen as a function of the total value produced by his kingdom less whatever was paid in wages. Since the wage per worker would always diminish as the number of workers increased, people were an unqualified asset to their masters. A king could no more have too many subjects than a modern farmer can have too many cattle. Any limit is set by food in the one case and pasture in the other. "One should never fear there being too many subjects or too many citizens," wrote Jean Bodin, "seeing that there is no wealth nor strength but in men" (*La République,* Book V, chap. 2). The goods they produced could be exported for gold or silver, and so people were money. For Frederick the Great it was a certain axiom that "the number of the people makes the wealth of states" (Stangeland 1904: 131). For Süssmilch (1788, 1: 17 ff.), a chaplain in Frederick's army, the interests of the sovereign coincided with the divine order, and both would be furthered by more Germans (Mackenroth 1953: 301–2). With minor exceptions, other French, Italian, and Spanish mercantilists favored population growth unanimously. Botero (1956) offered advice on how larger populations might be attained: agricultural and especially industrial production should be encouraged; the export of raw materials should be forbidden and that of manufactured goods fostered. The English writers were more qualified in their populationism; Petty accepted the thesis that men create wealth but also feared the poverty and social turmoil consequent on too great numbers.

Political Arithmetick and the Physiocrats

The numerical study of population starting in the seventeenth century, rather than earlier speculations, marked the beginning of the demography. When John Graunt (1662) worked up bills of mortality, he observed many constant features of deaths and births. Estimating that the ratio of deaths to births was fourteen to thirteen in London, as against fifty-two to sixty-three in the countryside, he calculated the immigration from the countryside needed to maintain and increase London's population. The statistics were poor, but Graunt made what reasoned adjustments he could and did not hesitate to draw conclusions. The concept of a cohort that is diminished by death as it goes through successive ages was clear to him, though his estimates of its diminution were too high. (The life table implied in his calculations has an expectation of life at birth of about 17.5 years, as against the 27.5 years of Halley's [1693] table for Breslau. The European urban average of the time was probably between these two figures.) He calculated age distributions from the life table, although he did not quite understand the notion of a stable (for a steadily increasing or decreasing population) as against a stationary age distribution, apparently first stated precisely by Euler in 1760. He made some corrections for misstatement in the bills' totals by cause of death, and noted that aside from the plague, the distribution by cause did not change greatly from year to year. The records of baptisms, which he also analyzed, showed a slight but constant excess of males over females at birth, and he considered that this excess held in the population as a whole. Childbearing women "one with another, have scarce more than one childe in two years," a birth interval close to that computed by present-day scholars from data on seventeenth-century Europe.

It is not clear, however, whether the credit for initiating demography goes to Graunt or to his more imaginative younger contemporary, Sir William Petty. Even the original authorship of the *Observations on the Bills of Mortality* has been attributed to Petty. At least, "Petty may have stimulated Graunt's initial interest in this sort of enquiry; he later carried through somewhat similar, but more superficial, observations on the Dublin bills of mortality; and he edited a posthumous edition of Graunt's *Observations,* published by the Royal Society" (Lorimer 1959: 126; Glass 1963).

Petty's new science of Political Arithmetick (1691), based on empirical work by Graunt among others, raised exciting perspectives in the Royal Society of London. Toward the end of the seventeenth century, Gregory King assembled enough data to produce a realistic estimate of England's population—5.5 million. Such work as that of Graunt, Petty, Halley, and King, who made good use of the crude data at hand, when combined with later theorizing on population convinced legislators of the need for censuses and vital statistics.

By the eighteenth century the mercantilists' emphasis on numbers was tempered by the recognition of poverty. Cantillon, standing between the mercantilists and the physiocrats, saw that an overcrowded state could acquire some relief by exporting manufactured goods and importing food—a frequent mercantilist theme (Hoselitz 1960: 26–42; Spengler 1942). Cantillon's masterpiece, *Essai sur la nature du commerce en général* (1952: 1), made land or nature the source of all wealth. Population is created by the means of subsistence, which depend not only on nature and such institutions as property rights in land but also on the decisions that princes and landowners make. If those who control the land want horses for hunting and war, the human population will be smaller than if they prefer domestic retainers. That French landowners preferred Dutch cloth reduced France's population and increased Holland's. The prince's way of living sets the style for smaller landholders. Cantillon does not moralize, but by implication he tells the rulers by what personal sacrifices they could increase population. Horses were the means of transport favored in Europe; that in China bearers carry travelers on litter chairs explains why compared with Europe the human population is larger, the horse population smaller.

The Enlightenment and Malthus

Some mercantilists feared a growth of population beyond the subsistence already in sight, but most expressed confidence that any number of new subjects could produce their own subsistence. The latter view was incorporated in the very different framework of the eighteenth century's new theory of progress and human perfectibility. Among others, Condorcet, Godwin, and Daniel Malthus held that the numbers of men determine available resources, rather than vice versa. In the era that they saw dawning, such past coercive institutions as property, the family, and the punishment of criminals would disappear, their objectives to be realized through the individual consciences of perfected men. No growth of population in an adequately organized society could conflict with progress, in Godwin's view, for the new City of Man (like Augustine's City of God) would harmonize all social classes and the whole of society with its material base. "There is in human society a principle whereby population is constantly maintained at the level of the means of subsistence," for "the goods of the world are a common fund from which all men can satisfy their needs" (Godwin 1793: 466, 520; Hutchinson 1967).

These views, which he heard first from his father, stimulated Thomas Robert Malthus (1960b) to seek a more realistic analysis of how population relates to resources. By his famous "principle of population," the number of people, if unchecked, grows in geometric pro-

gression, while the resources on which they depend at best increase arithmetically. Moreover, the capacity of men to multiply, and through their multiplying to make themselves miserable, would be accentuated by the very changes in institutions designed to attain an earthly paradise. Malthus's persistence in opposing this thesis to the optimism of the *philosophes* established him as the central figure of population doctrine. For his immediate predecessors — Hume, Wallace, Adam Smith, and Quesnay — population growth was primarily a sequel to an increase in produce; demand for labor (as for shoes) produces the supply in a self-regulating system (Coontz 1957; Smith 1921, 1: 82–83). Malthus opposed to Smith's natural harmony the conflict between population and its means of subsistence.

To ascertain the power of population one had to look at a territory where good land was plentiful. America showed a doubling in less than twenty-five years. In countries settled longer the pace was much slower, and most of Malthus's writing and research concerned the nature of the checks by which the rate of growth is held down. He found that in Europe late marriages made for small families. This moral restraint, incorporated in custom and in individual responsibility, he termed a *preventive* check. Also included under preventive checks were vices such as homosexuality, adultery, birth control, and abortion, and these Malthus certainly did not recommend (Petersen 1969: 149). When preventive checks were inadequate, such *positive* checks as wars and epidemics would supplement them. The ultimate positive check was famine; that did not often come into operation, but had always to be taken into account as a potential danger.

Malthus remains one of the most controversial figures in social thought. Regarded as a reactionary by those who dreamed of an earthly paradise, he in fact helped develop the economic theories that propelled the revolutionary social changes of the nineteenth century. The traditionally pious accused him of blasphemy for urging men to take responsibility for the size of their families; had not the Creator himself enjoined all to be fruitful and multiply? Had not Luther declared that any man hesitating to start a family because he lacked property or a job showed a want of faith? One of the most vigorous attacks came from Proudhon, who held that early marriage is the surest guarantee of good morals. To defer love in the name of moral restraint would restrict marriage to superannuated spinsters and aging satyrs. Like other socialists, Proudhon argued that the imprudence of the working classes was not the cause of their misery but a consequence; with the institution of a society based on justice people would not want more children than could be provided for (Vialatoux 1959, 2: 375–98).

In the English language "Malthusian" or "neo-Malthusian" came to designate a proponent of contraception. This is despite the fact that Malthus explicitly disavowed birth control. In an appendix to the *Essay*'s fifth edition he wrote: "Indeed I should always particularly reprobate any artificial and unnatural modes of checking population, both on account of their immorality and their tendency to remove a necessary stimulus to industry. If it were possible for each married couple to limit by a wish the number of their children, there is certainly reason to fear that the indolence of the human race would be very greatly increased." In recent years a similar opposition to contraception was expressed by Gandhi: "If Indians made the necessary effort, they could grow all the food they need; but without the stimulus of population pressure and economic need they will not make the effort" (Clark 1964: 283).

Contraception goes back to the beginning of human history, with references to it in the Kahun Papyrus, the Bible, the writings of Charaka (an Indian physician of the first century B.C.), Herodotus, al-Razi (A.D. 900), and other Islamic scholars (McCleary 1953: 83; Himes 1936). Nearly all known human cultures have had sufficient knowledge of the facts of human reproduction to be able to use at least coitus interruptus, and most have had other de-

vices as well. Among moderns it appeared in the writings of Moheau, Condorcet, and especially Francis Place (1822), who was followed by Richard Carlile, Charles Bradlaugh, and Annie Besant. These did not share the puritanical view that hunger and sex were the stick and carrot without which men would be slothful, and they found in contraception the full answer to the problem Malthus had posed. "Contraception . . . is both old and new; old in the sense that the *desire* dates back half a million years and some *practice* nearly as long; . . . new in the sense that democratized knowledge is an ultramodern phenomenon . . . that we have been able, more effectively than our ancestors . . . to winnow out the reliable, the harmless" (Himes 1936: 422).

In one of his last statements on the matter, a "summary view" published in 1830, Malthus (1960a: 13) went one step toward applying his principle to nonhuman populations. The principle of population was a direct forebear of the theory of evolution. "I happened to read for amusement Malthus on *Population*," Darwin (1961: 58) noted in his autobiography, "and being well prepared to appreciate the struggle for existence which everywhere goes on from long continued observation of the habits of animals and plants, it at once struck me that under these circumstances favorable variations would tend to be preserved, and unfavorable ones to be destroyed. The result of this would be the formation of new species. Here then I had at last got a theory by which to work." Wallace, who developed a theory of evolution independently of Darwin, also acknowledged a debt to Malthus. The directions in which Malthus's thought changed from the slim book of 1798 to the elaborate empirical studies of subsequent editions is the subject of Keyfitz (1982, chapter 2).

The Biological Perspective

The tendency of species to outreproduce their means of support exerts a constant pressure toward differentiation. Each species seeks to adapt to a niche in which it will have some degree of shelter from competition. Some species become complementary to others and enter into symbiotic relations with them. "We can dimly see why the competition should be most severe between allied forms, which fill nearly the same place in the economy of nature" (Darwin 1962: 88). In Spencer (1867, 2: 406–10, 479–508) this leads to an escape from the original Malthusian predicament by way of biology: organisms become more complex in the process of adaptation, and complexity reduces the animal's drive to reproduce. Human individuation is a continuation of animal evolution: the nervous system becomes more active, with a consequent further reduction in reproductive activity. The theory has been used to explain why bacteria are more prolific than mice, why men are among the least prolific of the higher animals, why the Victorian upper classes had fewer children than the lower classes. In every case the group comprising more differentiated, more elaborately adapted individuals has a lower reproduction combined with greater adaptability. In Spencer's optimistic view, the evolutionary process that population growth initiated would persist until both fertility and mortality had reached a low-level harmony.

More immediately suggestive for our subject is the recent observation of ecologists and ethologists that fertility in many species of birds and animals depends on density. We all know that beyond a certain point mortality is density-dependent through the ultimate check of starvation. But starvation is not very often seen in nature and, even combined with predators, disease, harsh weather, and other disasters, does not seem to exercise the continuous control that would explain the relative constancy of numbers in most species of higher animals. The constancy has been explained by a territorial mechanism of reproductive control, to accord with long-term food supplies. Among some species of birds, at the beginning of the breeding season each male lays claim to an area of suitable size and keeps out other males; all of the available ground is thus parceled out as individual territories. The often

furious competition for an adequate piece of ground takes the place of direct competition for food. This territoriality is a special case: some species compete merely for membership in a hunting group, and only so many are accepted. Those without territory, or left out of the hunting group, have no opportunity to reproduce. The pecking order among birds has the same function: those low on the scale are a reserve than can fill in for casualties among the established members or be dropped, as circumstances require (Wynne-Edwards 1962).

By such territorial and similar mechanisms population is maintained comfortably below the ceiling imposed by resources. The analogy to Malthus's preventive check comes as close as is conceivable for species lacking human foresight. Man has indeed the possibility of foresight, yet he offends more than most species in overgrazing, overfishing, and generally overexploiting his habitat.

Population and the Gifts of Nature

The classical school of economics developed from Malthus the law of diminishing returns: more work applied to given land produces less than proportional returns, and indeed increments of any one factor of production eventually generate lessening amounts of income. The doctrine was given mature expression in Mill (1876, Book I, chap. 13, 2): "The niggardliness of nature, not the injustice of society, is the cause of the penalty attached to overpopulation. An unjust distribution of wealth does not even aggravate the evil, but, at most, causes it to be somewhat earlier felt. It is vain to say that all mouths which the increase of mankind calls into existence bring with them hands. The new mouths require as much food as the old ones, and the hands do not produce as much." The operation of the law may be long postponed if there is vacant land to which people may move and, subsequently, if technical improvements are developed, but over the longer run its course is seen as inexorable. The law is applied to an increase in the land under cultivation through the presumed fact that rational men would start to till the most fertile and accessible portions first, so that any new lands added to the nation's agriculture would be less and less productive. As population grows in any country closed to trade, poorer lands will necessarily be brought into use, and any excess over the return to labor on marginal land will be taken as rent by landowners in the natural operation of the market. Population growth beyond a certain point would provide landlords with an increasing proportion of the national product. The model supposes an agricultural community of fixed land and techniques with a growing population.

But quite different conditions apply in industry, where the factors of production are extensible and the division of labor advantageous. True, industry depends on the availability of raw materials, but the limits of these are more distant than the coming shortage of agricultural land. If in some sectors of the economy returns increase with added effort while they diminish in others, then there will be a certain size of population at which overall production per head will be a maximum (Cannan 1895). It is useful to consider production a function of population whenever the economy is relatively static while population grows—

the situation of many countries today. In Figure 35.1 the three curves represent, respectively, total, A; marginal, B; and average production, C. The maximum point on B is at the inflection point along A, where the slope of total production ceases to increase and begins to decrease, the maximum on C at the point of A tangent to a line drawn from the origin. The curve B can be shown to cut C at its maximum point; where the marginal product equals the average, the latter is at its peak. This is demonstrated by considering the output of the last man; if it is greater than the average, the average will be raised by the presence of this last man. The reverse is true if the last man's output is lower than the average. Only if the last man's output is equal to the average will the average be at its peak and the population optimum from a welfare viewpoint. Call this optimum population N_0.

Consider now the curve of marginal production B along with line D, representing the minimum that will keep individuals alive, assumed to be equal for all sizes of population (Figure 35.2). The area below B and above D can be called a surplus, which is at a maximum for the population where B and D cross, or N_1. A technically primitive and static state that wants to maximize its armed strength or any other entity not dependent on immediate consumption will aim at population N_1 in its coun-

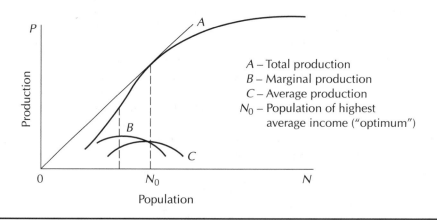

FIGURE 35.1   Production as a function of population, and location of the welfare optimum of population.

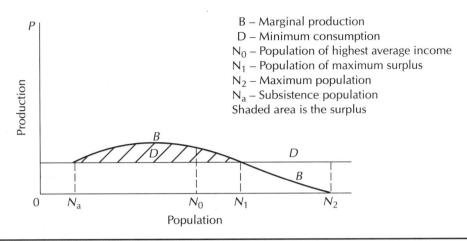

FIGURE 35.2   Optimum population and the surplus.

tryside. The surplus will be drained off and used to support an urban court, artisans, and armed forces, including the police and tax collectors who remove the surplus. The mechanism for this removal will vary and may include resident or absentee landholders taking rents. In modern times, a well-entrenched, development-minded government determined on heavy investment for industrial growth will appropriate the surplus for that purpose; it will be inclined to favor a population N_1, larger than the optimum N_0. But any diminution in the authority of government, reflected in a rise of the level D regarded as subsistence, lowers N_1 and moves it closer to N_0.

A state seeking the maximum population will aim at N_2—placed so that areas between curves B and D are equal in the intervals N_aN_1 and N_1N_2. Under mild assumptions the welfare optimum N_0 is smaller than the power optimum N_1, which in turn is smaller than the maximum population N_2 (Sauvy 1956, 1: 60). Fixed costs raise the optimum population, while lowering average income.

Nineteenth-century English economists tried to adapt these arguments, which apply to a closed economy, to one heavily based on foreign trade. Some thought that Britain could increase per capita production indefinitely; any excess population could emigrate to distant

lands, there to grow food that would be exchanged for British manufactured goods. But since that time freely available lands have been appropriated by population growth elsewhere, and agricultural countries want to develop their own industry.

In the 1920s England and some other advanced countries seemed to have passed their optimum and arrived at the point of rapidly diminishing returns (Keynes 1920; Wright 1923; Overbeek 1970: 141–63). The best coal deposits were being exhausted, cotton was attacked by the boll weevil, and for these and other commodities prices could only rise in response to increasing scarcity, with a resultant fall in the standard of living. The question of resource adequacy raised in the nineteenth century by Jevons has been intermittently asked in the twentieth century. Population control is an important part of the answer.

The optimum depends on the criterion used and will be very different if it is national power or real income per capita. Even with the best of statistics on the present and past, the optimum is not readily calculable; it can be determined only if we know what income would accord with various levels of population. This lack of empirical applicability contrasts with the sharply defined theory. Any curve relating population and production may "for large spaces have a very level course" (Myrdal 1940: 142). Even if one proved that, for instance, a given country has double its optimum population and has also the power to reduce it by emigration, a sharp reduction might be a disaster; for the disadvantages of the change—particularly since most emigrants would be young adults, whose rearing their native country had paid for up to the age when they began to produce—could more than offset any advantages of arriving at the optimum level.

The Environment

Contemporary ecologists are interested in optimum population, but they sharply reject the gradually diminishing returns and easy adaptations of classical economics. Their writings constitute a radical attack on the modern system of production and consumption (Ehrlich and Ehrlich 1970). At best, the kinds of damage not now entered in private or national accounting schemes must be deducted from our calculation of national product and income. At worst, the word *production* itself is seen as an ironic misnomer for such a process as depleting supplies of irreplaceable crude oil (that ought to be saved for lubrication), consuming it in an inefficient way of moving people from place to place, and creating unbreathable air that may well raise mortality rates. If the population of Malthus's time was pushing against a food ceiling, that of today seems to be pushing against a ceiling of space, air, water, and mineral resources (Wright 1923; Brown 1954).

The problem for us is whether such complaints really have a bearing on population. Parking space is short not because there are too many people in the country, or even too many automobiles, but because people want to live in large cities, or because they all want to go to the same place at the same time. The air is polluted either because automobiles are badly designed, or because some other solution to the transport problem should replace them. The

present system of production would quickly direct itself along lines that preserve the environment and enable it to take care of far more people if manufacturers were charged for the damage their products cause. They receive income for their goods and should pay for their bads, as Kenneth Boulding says. He proposes (1966:9) to rescue nation-income accounting by distinguishing "that part of the Gross National Product which is derived from exhaustible and that which is derived from reproducible resources, as well as that part of consumption which represents effluvia and that which represents input into the productive system again."

Socialist Writers on Population

Marx was generally well disposed toward the classical economists, of whose school he was a wayward member. But he repeatedly attacked not only Malthus's doctrines but also his motives and personality:

Malthus . . . asserts that population constantly exerts pressure on the means of subsistence. . . . If there are too many people, then in one way or another they must be eliminated. . . . Now the consequence of this theory is that since it is precisely the poor who constitute this surplus population, nothing ought to be done for them, except to make it as easy as possible for them to starve to death. . . . The giving of alms would be a crime, since it would encourage the growth of surplus population. (Meek 1953: 59)

Malthus had propagated a "vile and infamous doctrine, this repulsive blasphemy against man and nature." No general law of population could be valid for all societies; each had its own law. The irreducible opposition between population and welfare, far from being universal, was in Marx's view the special predicament of capitalism, with its impoverishment of the proletariat. The reproduction of the working class made new workers cheap and so permitted the bourgeoisie to extract surplus value from their work. But to ask the proletariat to be more responsible was futile, for the very degradation inherent in capitalism ruled out an appeal to their higher natures. The transformation of capitalist to socialist institutions would eliminate the Malthusian dilemma. As on other points, Marx started with the classical premises and reached a conclusion very different from the classical harmony.

The history of capitalist society, as he viewed it, is divided between a period of original accumulation and one of maturity and imperialism. In the period of original accumulation all the conclusions of Adam Smith and Ricardo are valid, with only a change of terms and some simplification. Marx divided capital into constant, C (for example, buildings and machinery), and variable, V (comprising consumer goods such as food bought with workers' wages). Constant capital is so called because it is merely reproduced without a quantitative change in the product; all surplus is imputed to labor. The capitalist tries to use all the labor he can employ, for thus he makes the largest profit. If it costs six hours per day to produce labor—the amount of time the average worker requires to feed, clothe, and house himself and his family at a subsistence level—and if the goods he produces sell for the equivalent of twelve hours' time, then the capitalist's surplus value is six hours multiplied by the number of workers he employs. The rapid increase of population in early capitalism was due to the demand for labor, just as Adam Smith had said.

For the second or "imperialist" period, however, Marx diverged sharply from the classical economists. The wage rate is V/P, variable capital divided by population, as before. But now as technical progress and competition force capitalists to substitute machines for men, the "reserve army" of the unemployed grows continually. Workers respond by lowering their birth rate as less labor is demanded, and Marx pictured a struggle around the ratio V/P, with the capitalists trying to shift the resources they control from V to C, and the workers seeking to counter this effort by reducing P.

Unfortunately for the system as a whole, the birth rate cannot fall fast enough to prevent capitalism from producing the surplus workers that are its grave diggers.

That labor-saving methods of production make an increasing fraction of the population redundant has been a popular fear before and since Marx. Today the identification of surplus population with unemployment is found in underdeveloped countries, while the countries with the largest stock of capital have more often encountered a labor shortage.

The world at large sees Malthus and Marx as "the two great antagonists, battling eternally" (Sauvy 1963:13). But the very vehemence of Marx's attack stemmed from the lack of a substantive rebuttal, as his *Critique of the Gotha Program* admitted: "If [Malthus's] theory of population is correct, then I can *not* abolish this [iron law of wages] even if I abolish wage-labor a hundred times, because this law is not only paramount over the system of wage-labor but also over every social system" (Marx and Engels 1959: 124). Marx and Malthus agreed that the condition of the proletariat was miserable and that its misery should be alleviated (Petersen 1964: 72–89). Malthus's solution relies on individual responsibility, Marx's on a collective condition called socialism; but both were better at posing the problem than at solving it.

Marx and Malthus agreed profoundly on the material base of social existence. At Marx's graveside Engels summed up his collaborator's contribution: "Marx discovered the law of evolution in human history: the simple fact, previously hidden under ideological growths, that human beings must first of all eat, drink, shelter, and clothe themselves, before they can turn their attention to politics, science, art, and religion" (ibid.). Malthus (1960a) made the same point with equal clarity in his own summing up, published four years before his death: "Elevated as man is above all other animals by his intellectual faculties, it is not to be supposed that the physical laws to which he is subjected should be essentially different from those which are observed to prevail in other parts of animated nature." Says Mehring (1962: 149) of the Marxist view:

This theory, the contention that the capitalist mode of production impoverishes the masses wherever it prevails, was put forward long before the *Communist Manifesto* was published, even before either Marx or Engels put pen to paper . . . first of all by bourgeois economists. The *Essay on Population* written by Malthus was an attempt to refine this "theory of increasing misery" and turn it into an eternal natural law.

That the workingman can avoid increasing misery, both collectively and individually, by restricting his family, that mothers should in effect become a trade union and declare a childbearing strike, was a theme of leftist social reform in the writings of John Stuart Mill, Bernstein, and others. But Marxists insisted that advanced capitalism could always undercut the workingman with more efficient equipment; in the race between voluntary reduction of the workforce and substitution of laborsaving devices, the latter would necessarily win. Relief must be sought in revolution rather than in contraception.

Marx bequeathed his opposition to Malthus to succeeding Marxist thinkers. Lenin in particular stressed that evolving technique would undercut the law of diminishing returns. Much of Stalin's argument has the tone of the mercantilists: the growth of population facilitates economic advance. Recent Soviet writings on population include a study of Europe's population increase during the past century (United Nations 1953, chap. 3). The increasing growth under industrial capitalism was followed by a slower rate during the "imperialist" stage; and since private property in land or other means of production in itself diminishes fertility, Western birth rates will continue to fall. Although Soviet society was supposedly immune to these pressures, its birth rate over the past two decades has followed very closely that of the United States. Hungary's birth rate fell to four-

teen per thousand, well below that of the capitalist countries of Western Europe. Evidently, fertility differs less between socialist and capitalist than between industrial and traditional societies.

Density and the Division of Labor

Durkheim (1902) marked society's change from a small undifferentiated clan or tribe to the complexity of his day, noting that interdependence increases with the greater specialization of groups and individuals. The complex society, he concluded, comes with population growth. As a tribe increases in volume and density, individuals and groups compete more and more intensely; only by specialization can they find shelter from competition. "In the same city the different professions can coexist without having to harm each other, for they pursue different objectives. The soldier seeks military glory, the priest moral authority, the statesman power, the industrialist wealth . . . ; each can thus reach his goal without preventing the others from reaching theirs" (ibid.: 249–50). For Durkheim population growth, through the "moral density" that arises from it, is responsible for the advance from a simple segmented society to a complex organic one.

Among peasant populations, one that is small and stationary is more likely to stay with slash-and-burn agriculture, which under many circumstances of low density produces more with less labor. Higher density forces a shorter fallow and ultimately annual crops, even though these mean more work. A "gradual adaptation to harder and more regular work is likely to raise the efficiency of labor in both agricultural and nonagricultural activities; the increasing density of population opens up opportunities for a more intricate division of labor" (Geertz 1971: chap 2; Boserup 1965: 75).

Population and Development

If a poor country somehow does manage to cut its birth rate, this improves its development prospects, in the theory worked out by Coale and Hoover (1958) and others. From alternative projections for India and other countries Coale (1969) concluded:

Any low-income country that succeeds in initiating an immediate reduction in fertility would in the short run enjoy a reduction in the burden of child dependency that would permit a higher level of investment and more immediately productive uses of investment

After 25 or 30 years the advantage of reduced dependency would be enhanced by a markedly slower growth of the labor force, making it possible to achieve a faster growth in capital per worker from any given investment, and making it easier to approach the goal of productive employment for all who need it. . . . In sum, a reduction in fertility would make the process of modernization more rapid and more certain.

Between two countries with different birth rates, the one with a higher rate will initially be at a disadvantage by its lack of industrial capital rather than of food. For the underdeveloped countries, the choice is whether to use resources in order to produce more capital rather than more labor, so that each unit of labor will be better equipped in the next generation. This concentration on capital accumulation has dominated professional thinking on population and development (Ohlin 1967).

And yet it is far from universally accepted. Latin Americans argue that their empty spaces can hold many millions, and that the internal migrants to those spaces can construct their own agricultural and other capital. According to Nurske (1953), a dense rural population positively helps the development of a country with a sufficiently strong and single-minded government. Everyone in the countryside may appear to be working, at least for part of the year, yet some of the rural population constitutes disguised unemployment in the pertinent sense that it could be removed, even with no substituted technical improvements, without a loss in production. Such persons could engage in the construction of buildings, roads, and urban industrial projects that do not require much capital. Since they all somehow obtained a minimal

diet before, the shift would entail merely transporting their food to the city. But it is not clear that fewer agriculturists can produce the crop merely by reorganizing the task and without major technical improvements (Schultz 1964). If there were genuine surplus of labor, moreover, it would not be easy to hold per capita consumption fixed in a half-starving countryside; and if those remaining on the land simply eat better, the expected surplus from the land disappears with the out-migrants. This was the famous "scissors" problem in the Soviet Union of the 1920s; it has never been solved, for the punitive measures used to mitigate it generated new troubles.

Global development may be prevented by too many people, not through the difficulty of accumulating capital but by the absolute shortage of raw materials. After showing what large quantities of metals and fuels are now required to keep the advanced economies in operation, and noting the rate of increase in world population, Harrison Brown (1954: 226) considers it unlikely that the agrarian underdeveloped regions of the world will be able to attain their goal of industrialization. "The picture would change considerably if Western machine civilization were to collapse, thus giving the present agrarian cultures room into which they could expand. But the collapse of Western culture would have to come well in advance of the time when high-grade ore and fuel deposits disappear." The raw materials in the earth's crust set a limit on the volume of development, on the number of people—or more exactly the number of person-years—that can exist in the developed condition, as that condition is understood today in the United States. How the volume of development will be apportioned among peoples, and over time, could well be the major question of national and international politics in the next generation.

For the advanced countries population has often been seen as an aid to growth. Writing in the 1930s, Keynes and Hansen saw an increasing population as a guarantee of markets. Housing demand, for example, varies with the rate of growth of a population. Investors know that even a product that does not quite fit consumers' tastes still finds buyers in an expanding economy. But in recent decades it has been noted that an expanding economy could be arranged more easily by an increase of purchasing power than of population.

The basic prerequisite to expanding the economy is a high level of investment, and the chief argument against rapid population growth has been that it diminishes savings and hence investment. But expenditures on children do not necessarily reduce savings, for at least in advanced countries expenditures on children may be a substitute not for savings but for more consumer goods or more leisure (Kuznets 1960: 332). Looking into the past, Hicks (1939) asked whether the whole industrial revolution of the last two centuries has been nothing but a vast secular boom, largely induced by the unparalleled rise in population (Bladen 1956: 115). Myrdal (1940:161–66) held that the cessation of population increase "will have a restrictive effect upon young people's opportunities for advancement," and Coale (1968) also opposed any immediate policy to bring about a zero population growth in the United States.

These theories relating population and the economy in a macroeconomic model say nothing about how individual parents are motivated. The route from micromodels that describe individual behavior to an explanation of aggregates was traveled at least as far back as Adam Smith. In his view, the demand for labor increases population by permitting individuals to marry earlier and to raise a larger proportion of the children born to them (Coontz 1957: chap. 4). But different mechanisms have been proposed in recent years to account for the quite different phenomena now observed.

The Economic Theory of Fertility

In a microeconomic framework the decline of the birth rate with economic development can be analyzed in relation to the utilities and costs of children to their parents (Leibenstein 1963). With increasing income the cost of a child of a given order rises, let us say in proportion to the family income. The consumption utility—that is, the pleasure of having the child in the house—is difficult to assess and can be estimated as fixed independently of income. The utility of the child as a source of security certainly declines: parents with more income can provide for their own security, or a wealthier state provides it for them; and if increased income is accompanied by weakening of family discipline, parents are less likely to be able to exercise claims on their children even if they are in need. The child is less valuable as a producer as income increases, because schooling is extended and the household ceases to be the unit of production (Figure 35.3). If these four elements (one of cost and three of utility) are exhaustive and correctly portrayed, then the individual family is likely to have fewer children as per capita income increases and as development proceeds. At any given stage, moreover, richer families would be inclined to have fewer children than poorer ones.

One can start with the opposite view, that the price per child does not go up with the parents' income. The rich could spend as little on their children as the poor, but *choose* to dress them better, send them to better schools, and so on; in effect, they purchase higher-quality children (Becker 1960). By this view the cost curve in Figure 35.3 for a given quality of child becomes horizontal. Thus, Becker comes to the opposite conclusion from Leibenstein: people have more children as they become richer, just as the well-to-do have not only better cars than the poor but more per household. In any large population the relation is hidden by the fact that the rich practice contraception more effectively; and among contracepting couples, according to data that Becker cites, income is related directly to family size, as his theory demands. Duesenberry (1960), Leibenstein (1963), and Okun (1960) reject Becker's distinction between price and cost, on the grounds that each family is constrained to house, clothe,

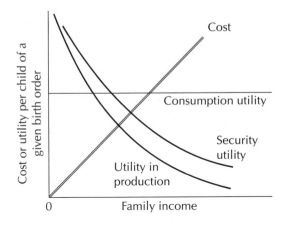

FIGURE 35.3 Cost and utility curves for a child of a given birth order (after Leibenstein 1963: 162).

and feed its children in accordance with the norms of its income group. If custom requires richer families to spend more on each of their children, one cannot conclude from their larger income that they will also want more children. If one controls for the differential knowledge of contraception, not by comparing the family sizes of birth control users but by using surveys of ideal family size, the correlation with income is negative. From such data, the poor *want* more children than the better off (Blake 1967).

These are microexplanations in that they reason from individual behavior to certain aggregate phenomena of the community or country taken as a unit. Economics (like physics) tries to explain the mass in terms of the atoms, but such explanations cannot be successfully detached from the cultural and social context.

Social Capillarity and Family Structure

The decline of the birth rate in industrial countries has followed a decline of the death rate. The populations involved have undergone a more or less uniform transition: first a slow and accelerating fall in mortality, followed at

some interval by a corresponding fall in fertility. The pace varies from country to country; the later the fall in the death rate, the more rapid it is. In one country, France, the fall of births very nearly coincided with the fall of deaths; elsewhere there has been a considerable lag. Whatever its local variation, the phenomenon has been so widespread, and commented on by so many writers, that it has acquired a name: the demographic transition (Notestein 1945; Taeuber 1960; and others).

Both the fall in deaths and the slower fall in births may be a concomitant of modernization (Notestein 1945), or the decline of fertility may be a response to the earlier decline of mortality (Davis 1963). In either case, the literature is incomplete concerning the causal mechanisms operating. In particular, there is no answer to the big question: will the fall in mortality that by now has taken place in the underdeveloped countries by itself produce a fall in fertility, or will it do so only in the presence of development? Must poor countries wait for development before their birth rates can fall? If high fertility prevents capital accumulation and so development, then they will have to wait a long time.

A French social scientist, Arsène Dumont (1890), tied declining fertility to the structure of society and to the individual's desire to rise in the world. Trained as an anthropologist, Dumont was a passionate nationalist who saw in France's depopulation a harbinger of her downfall, and devoted his life to analyzing the familial conduct of his countrymen. (He never married, and at the age of fifty-three took his own life!) "All men," he wrote, "tend to raise themselves from the lower functions of society to higher ones. . . . Guided by an unerring and inescapable instinct, each social molecule strains with all the energy at its command . . . to rise unceasingly toward a luminous ideal which charms and attracts it" (ibid.:106). This ascent is not by income alone, but in every field of manual work, of intellect, and of art (Sutter 1953). In the competition for higher places, the man with few or no children has as certain an advantage over the father of many as the liquid in a narrow tube has over that in a wide one. This is the law of social capillarity.

Social mobility gradually intensified over a century or more in Europe and America. It was functional for economic development, but signs of change are appearing:

> One does not have to be a prophet to foresee that our present passion for demographic and economic growth will some day be superseded by a concern for population quality and ecological balance. When this inevitable adaptation is effected—inevitable, that is, barring the catastrophe that will forestall all adaptation—perhaps it will seem more natural to espouse a hierarchy of values in which our assessment of men will not depend so heavily on their ability to "get ahead." (Duncan 1969:365)

The Use of Past Doctrines

This account has sketched population ideas and doctrines that appear in writings over 2,500 years. Some of the ideas are thoroughly obsolete, some keep recurring and are to be heard on the street or read in newspapers today. The advantage of knowing the antecedents of what people are now saying is that one then knows the context in which they fit and the criticism that they aroused. When we hear someone say that more people will add to national power, we remember the Romans and appreciate how the then-current techniques, especially the organization of men, enabled the Romans to conquer the lands of their neighbors. When someone says that masses of people can be set to making goods for export, we think back to the mercantilists and the treasuries of their princes. To locate the argument in its setting may not dispose of it, but it is an aid to clear thinking.

Note

* From *Population Change and Social Policy,* by Nathan N. Keyfitz (Cambridge, MA: Abt Associates, 1982), 3–26, 245–54, by permission of the author and Abt Associates, Inc. Copyright 1982 by Abt Associates, Inc.

References

Adelman, I. 1963. "An Economic Analysis of Population Growth." *American Economic Review* 53: 314–39.

Arthur, B. 1981. Personal communication.

Artle, R. 1980. "The Economics of an Aging Population: Regional and Interregional Implications." Paper presented at the International Congress of Arts and Sciences. Cambridge, Mass.

Balinski, M. L., and Young, H. P. 1982. *Fair Representation: Meeting the Ideal of One Man, One Vote.* New Haven: Yale University Press.

Barker, E. 1959. *The Political Thought of Plato and Aristotle.* New York: Dover.

Barr, N. A. 1979. "Myths My Grandpa Taught Me." *The Three Banks Review* 124: 27–55.

Becker, G. S. 1960. "An Economic Analysis of Fertility." In National Bureau of Economic Research [editor]. *Demographic and Economic Change in Developed Countries.* Princeton, N.J.: Princeton University Press.

Bell, D. 1973. *The Coming of Post-Industrial Society: A Venture in Social Forecasting.* New York: Basic Books.

Bellamy, E. 1951 (1887). *Looking Backward.* New York: Modern Library.

Berelson, B. 1969. "National Family Planning Programs: Where We Stand." In *Fertility and Family Planning: A World View.* S. J. Behrman, L. Corsa, and R. Freedman, eds. Ann Arbor, Mich.: University of Michigan Press.

Bixby, L. E. 1977. Statistical Data Requirements in Legislation. Prepared for Committee on National Statistics, Assembly of Behavioral and Social Sciences, National Research Council. Washington, D.C.: National Academy of Sciences.

Bladen, V. W. 1956. *An Introduction to Political Economy,* rev. ed. Toronto: University of Toronto Press.

Blake, J. 1967. "Income and Reproductive Motivation." *Population Studies* 21: 185–206.

Bonar, J. 1885. *Malthus and His Work.* London: Macmillan.

Boserup, E. 1965. *The Conditions of Agricultural Growth: The Economics of Agrarian Change under Population Pressure.* Chicago: Aldine.

Botero, G. 1956 (1589). *The Reason of State.* D. P. Waley, ed. New Haven: Yale University Press.

Boulding, K. E. 1955. "The Malthusian Model as a General System." *Social and Economic Studies* 4: 195–205.

———. 1964. *The Meaning of the Twentieth Century.* New York: Harper and Row, Inc.

———. 1966. "The Economics of the Coming Spaceship Earth." In *Environmental Quality in a Growing Economy.* H. Jarrett, ed. Baltimore: Johns Hopkins University Press.

Bourgeois-Pichat, J. 1978. "Le Financement des retraites par capitalisation." *Population* 6: 1115–36.

Brackett, J. W. 1968. "The Evolution of Marxist Theories of Population: Marxism Recognizes the Population Problem." *Demography* 5: 158–73.

Brown, H. 1954. *The Challenge of Man's Future.* New York: Viking.

Brown, L. R. 1968. "New Directions in World Agriculture." *Studies in Family Planning* 32. New York: The Population Council.

Cannan, E. 1895. "The Probability of a Cessation of the Growth of Population in England and Wales." *Economic Journal* 5: 505–15.

Cantillon, R. 1952 (1755). *Essai sur la nature du commerce en général.* Paris: Institut National d'Etudes Démographiques.

Chen Huan-Chang. 1911. *The Economic Principles of Confucius and His School.* 2 Vols. New York: Columbia University Press.

Chenery, H. B. et al. 1974. *Redistribution with Growth.* London: Oxford University Press.

Chesnais, J. C., and Sauvy, A. 1973. "Progrès économique et accroissement de la population: Une expérience commentée." *Population* 28: 843.

Choucri, N. 1974. *Population Dynamics and International Violence: Proportions, Insights, and Evidence.* Lexington, Mass.: Lexington Books.

Clark, C. 1940. *Conditions of Economic Progress.* London: Macmillan.

Clark, C. 1964. "Overpopulation—Is Birth Control the Answer?" In *Population, Evolution, Birth Control.* G. Hardin, ed. San Francisco: Freeman.

Clark, C. 1967. *Population Growth and Land Use.* London: Macmillan.

Clark, R. L., ed. 1980. *Retirement Policy in an Aging Society.* Durham, N.C.: Duke University Press.

Coale, A. J. 1956. "The Effects of Changes in Mortality and Fertility on Age Composition." *Milbank Memorial Fund Quarterly* 34: 79–114.

———. 1957. "How the Age Distribution of a Human Population Is Determined." *Cold Spring Harbor Symposia on Quantitative Biology* 22: 83–89.

———. 1968. "Should the United States Start a Campaign for Fewer Births?" *Population Index* 34: 467–79.

———. 1969. "Population and Economic Development." In *The Population Dilemma,* P. M. Hauser, ed. 2nd ed. Englewood Cliffs, N.J.: Prentice-Hall.

———. 1970a. Man and His Environment. *Science* 170: 132–36.

———. 1970b. "Review of Ehrlich and Ehrlich." *Population, Resources, Environment. Science* 170: 428–29.

———. 1978. "T. R. Malthus and the Population Trends in His Day and Ours." Ninth Encyclopaedia Britannica Lecture. Edinburgh, Scotland: University of Edinburgh.

———. 1979. "The Use of Modern Analytical Demography by T. R. Malthus." *Population Studies* 33: 329–32.

Coale, A. J., and Demeny, P. 1966. *Regional Model Life Tables and Stable Populations.* Princeton, N.J.: Princeton University Press.

Coale, A. J., and Hoover, E. M. 1958. *Population Growth and Economic Development in Low-Income Countries: A Case Study of India's Prospects.* Princeton, N.J.: Princeton University Press.

Cohen, J. E. 1975. "Livelihood Benefits of Small Improvements in the Life Table." *Health Services Research* (Spring): 82–96.

Coontz, S. H. 1957. *Population Theories and the Economic Interpretation.* London: Routledge and Kegan Paul.

Darwin, C. 1961 (1876). *Autobiography.* Sir F. Darwin, ed. New York: Collier.

———. 1962. (1859). *The Origin of Species.* New York: Collier.

Davis, K. 1955. "Malthus and the Theory of Population." In *The Language of Social Research.* P. F. Lazarsfeld and M. Rosenberg, eds. Glencoe, Ill.: Free Press.

———. 1963. "The Theory of Change and Response in Modern Demographic History." *Population Index* 29: 345–366.

———. 1967. "Population Policy: Will Current Programs Succeed?" *Science* 158: 730.

Doll, R., and Hill, A. B. 1952. "A Study of the Aetiology of Carcinoma of the Lung." *British Medical Journal* 2: 1271–86.

Dorn, H. F. 1950. "Pitfalls in Population Forecasts and Projections." *Journal of the American Statistical Association* 45:311–34.

Duesenberry, J. 1960. "Comment on Becker," op. cit., pp. 231–34.

Dumont, A. 1890. *Dépopulation et civilisation: Etudes démographiques.* Paris: Lecrosnier et Babé.

Duncan, O. D. 1969. "Inequality and Opportunity." *Population Index* 35: 361–66.

Dupâquier, J. 1980. "Avez-vous lu Malthus?" *Population* 35: 280–90.

Durkheim, E. 1960 (1902). *De la division du travail social*. Paris: Presses Universitaires de France.

Ehrlich, P. R., and Ehrlich, A. H. 1970. *Population, Resources, Environment*. San Francisco: Freeman.

Ekanem, I. 1972. "A Further Note on the Relation between Economic Development and Fertility." *Demography* 9: 383–98.

Enke, S. 1963. *Economics for Development*. Englewood Cliffs, N.J.: Prentice-Hall.

Euler, L. 1970 (1760). "A General Investigation into the Mortality and Multiplication of the Human Species." N. Keyfitz and B. Keyfitz, trans. *Theoretical Population Biology* 1: 307–14.

Feldstein, M. 1974. "Social Security, Induced Retirement, and Aggregate Capital Accumulation." *Journal of Political Economy* 82: 905–26.

———. 1976. "Savings Behavior: New Influences and Consequences." *Journal of the American Economic Association* 66: 77–86.

Freedman, R., and Takeshita, J. Y. 1969. *Family Planning in Taiwan: An Experiment in Social Change*. Princeton, N.J.: Princeton University Press.

Frejka, T. 1981. "World Population Projections: A Concise History." Center for Policy Studies Working Paper no. 66. New York: The Population Council.

Friedlander, S., and Silver, M. 1967. "A Quantitative Study of the Determinants of Fertility Behavior." *Demography* 45: 30–70.

Furstenberg, G. M. von, ed. 1979. *Social Security Versus Private Saving*. Cambridge, Mass.: Harper and Row, Ballinger.

Geertz, Clifford. 1971. *Agricultural Involution*. Berkeley: University of California Press.

Glass, D. V. 1963. "John Graunt and His *Natural and Political Observations*." *Proceedings of the Royal Society* 159 (Series B): 2–37.

Glick, P. C., Heer, D. M., and Beresford, J. C. 1963. "Family Formation and Family Composition: Trends and Prospects." In *Sourcebook on Marriage and the Family*. M. B. Sussman, ed. Boston: Houghton Mifflin.

Godwin, W. 1793. *An Enquiry Concerning Political Justice and Its Influence on General Virtue and Happiness*. London: G. G. J. and J. Robinson.

Gonzalez, M. E. 1978. "Statistics for Allocation of Funds." *Statistical Reporter* 78: 217–20.

Gonzalez, M. E., and Waksberg, J. 1973. "Estimation of the Error of Synthetic Estimates." Prepared for Presentation at the First Meeting of the International Association of Survey Statisticians, Vienna, Austria. Washington, D.C.: U.S. Bureau of the Census, Census Vertical File, Staff Papers.

Goode, W. J. 1963. "The Role of the Family in Industrialization." In United Nations, Conference on the Application of Science and Technology for the Benefit of the Less Developed Areas. *Social Problems of Development and Urbanization* 7: 32–38. Washington, D.C.: U.S. Government Printing Office.

Graunt, J. 1964 (1662). "Natural and Political Observations . . . Made upon the Bills of Mortality." Republished with an introduction by B. Benjamin, *Journal of the Institute of Actuaries* 90: 1–64.

Halley, E. 1693. "An Estimate of the Degree of the Mortality of Mankind." *Philosophical Transactions of the Royal Society of London* 17: 596–610.

Hawley, A. H. 1950. *Human Ecology: A Theory of Community Structure*. New York: Ronald Press.

Heer, D. M. 1966. "Economic Development and Fertility." *Demography* 3: 423–44.

Henry, L. 1968. "Essai de calcul de l'efficacité de la contraception." *Population* 24: 265–78.

Henry, L., and Gutierrez, H. 1977. "Qualité des prévisions démographiques à court terme: Etude de l'extrapolation de la population totale des départements et villes de France, 1821–1975." *Population* 32: 625–47.

Hicks, J. R. 1939. *Value and Capital*. Oxford: Oxford University Press.

Himes, N. E. 1936. *Medical History of Contraception*. Baltimore: Williams and Wilkins.

Ho, Ping-Ti. 1959. *Studies on the Population of China, 1368–1953*. Cambridge, Mass.: Harvard University Press.

Horlick, M. 1979. "The Impact of Aging Population on Social Security." In *Social Security in a Changing World*. Washington, D.C.: U.S. Department of Health, Education, and Welfare, Social Security Administration, HEW Publication (SSA) 79–11948.

———. 1980. "Private Pension Plans in West Germany and France." Research Report No. 55. Washington, D.C.: U.S. Department of Health and Human Services, Social Security Administration.

Horlick, M., and Skolnik, A. M. 1978. "Mandating Private Pensions: A Study of European Experience." Research Report No. 51. Washington, D.C.: U.S. Department of Health, Education, and Welfare, Social Security Administration.

Hoselitz, B. F. (ed.) 1960. *Theories of Economic Growth*. Glencoe, Ill.: Free Press.

Hutchinson, E. P. 1967. *The Population Debate.* Boston: Houghton Mifflin.

Jacobson, P. H. 1959. *American Marriage and Divorce.* New York: Rinehart and Co.

Jaffe, A. J. 1966. "Education and Automation." *Demography* 3: 35–46.

Janowitz, B. S. 1971. "An Empirical Study of the Effects of Socioeconomic Development on Fertility Rates." *Demography* 8: 383–98.

Keech, W. R. 1979. "Elections and U.S. Public Pension Policy: A Working Paper." Paper presented at the Second International Workshop on the Politics of Inflation, Unemployment, and Growth, University of Bonn, West Germany.

Keyfitz, N. 1971. "Migration as a Means of Population Control." *Population Studies* 25: 63–72.

———. 1977a. *Applied Mathematical Demography.* New York: Wiley.

———. 1977b. "What Difference Would It Make if Cancer Were Eradicated? An Examination of the Taeuber Paradox." *Demography* 14: 411–18.

———. 1980. "Why Social Security Is in Trouble." *The Public Interest* 58: 102–19.

Keyfritz, N. 1982. *Population Change and Social Policy.* Cambridge, Mass.: Abt Books.

Keyfitz, N., and Flieger, W. 1968. *World Population: An Analysis of Vital Data.* Chicago: University of Chicago Press.

———. 1971. *Population: Facts and Techniques of Demography.* San Francisco: W. H. Freeman.

Keynes, J. M. 1920. *The Economic Consequences of the Peace.* London: Macmillan.

———. 1936. *The General Theory of Employment, Interest and Money.* London: Macmillan.

———. 1937. "Some Consequences of a Declining Population." *Eugenics Review* 29: 13–17.

———. 1972. "Economic Possibilities for Our Grandchildren." In *Essays in Persuasion,* Vol. 9 of *The Collected Writings.* London: Macmillan.

Kuznets, S. 1960. "Population and Aggregate Output." In National Bureau of Economic Research, *Demographic and Economic Change in Developed Countries.* Princeton, N.J.: Princeton University Press.

Ladejinsky, W. 1970. "Ironies of India's Green Revolution." *Foreign Affairs* 48: 758–68.

Landry, A. 1909. "Les Idées de Quesnay sur la population." *Revue d'Histoire des Doctrines Economiques* 2: 41–87.

Lee, E. S. 1966. "A Theory of Migration." *Demography* 3: 45–57.

Lee, E. S. et al. 1957. *Population Redistribution and Economic Growth, United States:* *1870–1950.* 2 Vols. Philadelphia: American Philosophical Society.

Lee, M. P. 1921. *The Economic History of China, with Special Reference to Agriculture.* New York: Columbia University Press.

Lee, R. D. 1978. "Appraisal of the Fertility Assumptions Employed in the Social Security Projections." Unpublished manuscript.

———. 1980. "Aiming at a Moving Target: Period Fertility and Changing Reproductive Goals." *Population Studies* 34: 206–26.

Leibenstein, H. 1963. *Economic Backwardness and Economic Growth.* New York: Wiley.

———. 1974. "An Interpretation of the Economic Theory of Fertility: Promising Path or Blind Alley?" *Journal of Economic Literature* 12: 467–79.

———. 1975. "The Economic Theory of Fertility Decline." *Quarterly Journal of Economics* 89: 1–31.

Léridon, H., and Henry, L. 1968. "Influence du calendrier de la contraception." *Population* 24: 1009–54.

Leslie, P. H. 1945. "On the Use of Matrices in Certain Population Mathematics." *Biometrika* 33: 183–212.

Lipton, M. 1977. *Why Poor People Stay Poor: Urban Bias in World Development.* Cambridge, Mass.: Harvard University Press.

Lorimer, F. 1959. "The Development of Demography." In *The Study of Population.* P. M. Hauser and O. D. Duncan, eds. Chicago: University of Chicago Press.

Lotka, A. J. 1907. "Relation between Birth Rates and Death Rates." *Science,* n.s., 26: 21–22.

———. 1939. *Théorie analytique des associations biologiques. Part II. Analyse démographique avec application particulière à l'espèce humaine.* Actualités Scientifiques et Industrielles, No. 780. Paris: Hermann & Cie.

Mackenroth, G. 1953. *Bevölkerungslehre.* Berlin: Springer.

Mahdi, M. 1957. *Ibn Khaldûn's Philosophy of History.* Chicago: University of Chicago Press.

Malthus, T. R. 1959. *Population: The First Essay.* Foreword by K. Boulding. Ann Arbor, Mich.: University of Michigan Press.

———. 1960a. (1798). *On Population.* G. Himmelfarb, ed. New York: Modern Library.

———. 1960b. (1830). "A Summary View of the Principle of Population." In Malthus et al. *Three Essays on Population.* New York: Mentor.

Marx, K., and Engels, F. 1959. *Basic Writings on Politics and Philosophy.* L. S. Feuer, ed. New York: Doubleday.

McCleary, G. F. 1953. *The Malthusian Population Theory.* London: Faber and Faber.

McKeown, T. 1976. *The Modern Rise of Population.* London: Edward Arnold.

McNeill, W. H. 1963. *The Rise of the West.* Chicago: University of Chicago Press.

———. 1977. *Plagues and Peoples.* New York: Anchor Press/Doubleday.

Meek, R. L. 1953. *Marx and Engels on Malthus.* London: Lawrence and Wishart.

Mehring, F. 1962. *Karl Marx, The Story of His Life.* Ann Arbor, Mich.: University of Michigan Press.

Mill, J. S. 1876. *Principles of Political Economy.* 5th ed. New York: Appleton.

Morgan, J. N. 1977. "Myth, Reality, Equity, and the Social Security System." *Economic Outlook USA* 4: 58–60. Ann Arbor, Mich.: University of Michigan, Survey Research Center.

———. 1978. Summary Statement for the Public Assistance Subcommittee Hearings, Senate Finance Committee May 1. Ann Arbor, Mich.: University of Michigan, Institute for Social Research.

Myrdal, G. 1940. *Population, A Problem for Democracy.* Cambridge, Mass.: Harvard University Press.

Nee, V. 1980. "Post Maoist Changes in a South China Production Brigade." Unpublished manuscript, Ithaca, New York: Center for International Studies, Cornell University.

Nelson, R. R. 1956. "A Theory of the Low Level Equilibrium Trap in Underdeveloped Economies." *American Economic Review* 46: 894–908.

Noonan, J. T., Jr. 1965. *Contraception: A History of Its Treatment by the Catholic Theologians and Canonists.* Cambridge, Mass.: Belknap-Harvard University Press.

Notestein, F. 1945. "Population—The Long View." In *Food for the World.* T. W. Schultz, ed. Chicago: University of Chicago Press.

Notestein, F. et al. 1944. *The Future Population of Europe and the Soviet Union: Population Projections 1940–1970.* Geneva: League of Nations.

Nurkse, R. 1953. "Population and the Supply of Capital." In *Problems of Capital Formation.* Oxford: Basil Blackwell.

Ogburn, W. F. 1964. "Why the Family Is Changing." In *William F. Ogburn on Culture and Social Change.* O. D. Duncan, ed. Chicago: University of Chicago Press.

Ohlin, G. 1967. *Population Control and Economic Development.* Paris: Development Centre of the Organisation for Economic Cooperation and Development.

Okun, B. 1960. Comment on Becker, op. cit.: 235–40.

Overbeek, J. 1970. *Comparative Thoughts on Overpopulation between the Two Wars.* Rotterdam: Drukkerij Princo.

Pan Ku. 1950. *Food and Money in Ancient China.* N. L. Swann, trans. Princeton, N.J.: Princeton University Press.

Peacock, A. T. 1952–54. "Theory of Population and Modern Economic Analysis." *Population Studies* 6: 114–22; 7: 227–34.

Petersen, W. 1964. *The Politics of Population.* New York: Doubleday.

———. 1969. *Population,* 2nd ed. New York: Macmillan.

———. 1971. "The Malthus-Godwin Debate, Then and Now." *Demography* 8: 13–26.

———. 1979. *Malthus.* Cambridge, Mass.: Harvard University Press.

Petty, W. 1691. *Political Arithmetick.* London: Clavel.

Pitts, A. M. 1976. *Some Notes on the Collection of U.S. Multiple Cause of Death Data with Illustrative Multiple Cause Tabulations for 1969.* Durham, N.C.: Duke University Center for Demographic Studies.

Place, F. 1822. *Illustrations and Proofs of the Principle of Population.* London: Longman, Hurst, Rees, Orme, and Brown.

Pollard, J. H. 1979. "Factors Affecting Mortality and the Length of Life." Proceedings of an IUSSP conference on science in the service of life, Vienna. In *Population Science in the Service of Mankind.* Liège, Belgium: International Union for the Scientific Study of Population.

Population Council, The. 1970. "Governmental Policy Statements on Population: An Inventory." In *Reports on Population-Family Planning.* New York: The Population Council.

Potter, R. G. 1960. "Some Relationships between Short Range and Long Range Risks of Unwanted Pregnancy." *Milbank Memorial Fund Quarterly* 38: 255–63.

———. 1967. "The Multiple Decrement Life Table as an Approach to the Measurement of Use Effectiveness and Demographic Effectiveness of Contraception." In *Proceedings,* International Union for the Scientific Study of Population, Sydney (Australia) Conference.

———. 1970. "Births Averted by Contraception: An Approach through Renewal Theory." *Theoretical Population Biology* 1: 251–72.

Potter, R. G., Jain, A. K., and McCann, B. 1970. "Net Delay of Next Conception by Contraception: A Highly Simplified Case." *Population Studies* 24: 173–92.

President's Commission on Pension Policy. 1980. *An Interim Report.* Washington, D.C.: 736 Jackson Place N.W.

Preston, S. H., Keyfitz, N., and Schoen, R. 1972. *Causes of Death: Life Tables for National Populations.* New York: Seminar Press.

Quesnay, F. 1908. Hommes. *Revue d'Histoire des Doctrines Economiques* 1: 14 ff.

Ryder, N. B. 1964. "The Process of Demographic Translation." *Demography* 1: 74–82.

Ryder, N. B., and Westoff, C. F. 1967. "The Trend of Expected Parity in the United States; 1955, 1960, 1965." *Population Index* 33: 153–68.

Rogers, A. 1975. *Introduction to Multiregional Mathematical Demography.* New York: Wiley.

Sauvy, A. 1956. *Théorie générale de la population,* 2 Vols. Paris: Presses Universitaires de France.

———. 1958. *François Quesnay et la Physiocratie.* Paris: Institut National d'Etudes Démographiques.

———. 1963. *Malthus et les deux Marx.* Paris: Denoel.

———. 1968. "Population Theories." *International Encyclopedia of the Social Sciences.* 12: 349–58. New York: Macmillan and Free Press.

Schultz, T. W. 1964. *Transforming Traditional Agriculture.* New Haven: Yale University Press.

Shepard, D. S. 1976. "Prediction and Incentives in Health Care Policy." Doctoral dissertation. Cambridge, Mass.: John Fitzgerald Kennedy School of Government, Harvard University.

Shepard, D., and Zeckhauser, R. 1977. "Interventions in Mixed Populations: Concepts and Applications." Discussion Paper Series, 49D. Cambridge, Mass.: John Fitzgerald Kennedy School of Government, Harvard University.

Sheps, M. C. 1967. "Uses of Stochastic Models in the Evaluation of Population Policies." San Francisco: *Proceedings of the Fifth Berkeley Symposium on Mathematical Statistics and Probability* IV: 115–36.

Sheps, M. C. and Menken, J. A. 1973. *Mathematical Models of Conception and Birth.* Chicago: University of Chicago Press.

Sheps, M. C., and Perrin, E. B. 1963. "Changes in Birth Rate as a Function of Contraceptive Effectiveness." *American Journal of Public Health* 53: 1031–46.

———. 1966. "Further Results from a Human Fertility Model with a Variety of Pregnancy Outcomes." *Human Biology* 38: 180–93.

Shubik, M. 1981. "Society, Land, Love, or Money: A Strategic Model of How to Glue the Generations Together." Unpublished Manuscript.

Siegel, J. S. 1975. *Coverage of Population in the 1970 Census and Some Implications for Public Programs.* Washington, D.C.: U.S. Bureau of the Census, Current Population Reports. Special Studies, Series, P-23, No. 56.

Siegel, J. S. 1977. *Developmental Estimates of the Coverage of the Population of States in the 1970 Census: Demographic Analysis.* Washington, D.C.: U.S. Bureau of the Census, Current Population Reports, Special Studies, Series P-23, No. 65.

Smith, A. 1921 (1776). *The Wealth of Nations,* 2 Vols. London: G. Bell.

Spencer, H. 1867. *The Principles of Biology,* 2 Vols. New York: Appleton.

Spengler, J. J. 1942. *French Predecessors of Malthus: A Study in Eighteenth-Century Wage and Population Theory.* Durham, N.C.: Duke University Press.

———. 1963. "Arthasastra Economics." In *Administration and Economic Development in India.* R. J. D. Braibanti and J. J. Spengler, eds. Durham, N.C.: Duke University Press.

———. 1966. "Values and Fertility Analysis." *Demography* 3: 109–30.

Stangeland, C. E. 1904. *Pre-Malthusian Doctrines of Population.* New York: Columbia University Press.

Statistics Canada. 1954. Memorandum on the Projection of Population Statistics, 1954. Ottawa: Dominion Bureau of Statistics.

Stockwell, E. G. 1972. "Some Observations on the Relations between Population Growth and Economic Development during the 1960s." *Rural Sociology* 37: 628.

Stoto, M. A. 1979. "The Accuracy of Population Projections." Working paper 79–75. Laxenburg, Austria: International Institute for Applied Systems Analysis.

Stouffer, S. A. 1940. "Intervening Opportunities: A Theory Relating Mobility and Distance." *American Sociological Review* 5: 845–67.

Süssmilch, J. P. 1788. (1741). *Die göttliche Ordnung in den Veränderungen des menschlichen Geschlechts, aus der Geburt, dem Tode und der Fortpflanzung desselben Erwiesen,* 3 Vols. Berlin: Verlag der Buchhandlung der Realschule.

Sutter, J. 1953. "Un Démographe engagé: Arsène Dumont (1849–1902)." *Population* 8: 79–92.

Taeuber, C., and Taeuber, I. B. 1958. *The Changing Population of the United States.* New York: Wiley.

— — —. 1971. *People of the United States in the Twentieth Century.* Washington, D.C.: U.S. Government Printing Office.

Taeuber, I. B. 1960. "Japan's Demographic Transition Re-examined." *Population Studies* 14: 28–39.

Tietz, C., 1959. "Differential Fecundity and Effectiveness of Contraception." *Eugenics Review* 50: 231–34.

— — —. 1967. "Intra-uterine Contraception: Recommended Procedures for Data Analysis." *Studies in Family Planning* 18 (Supp.): 1–6.

Tufte, E. 1978. *Political Control of the Economy.* Princeton, N.J.: Princeton University Press.

United Nations. *Demographic Yearbook,* annual series.

United Nations. 1953. *The Determinants and Consequences of Population Trends.* Population Studies No. 17. New York: United Nations Press.

— — —. 1958. *The Future Growth of World Population.* Population Studies No. 28. New York: United Nations Press.

— — —. 1966. *World Population Prospects as Assessed in 1963.* Population Studies No. 41. New York: United Nations Press.

— — —. 1973. *World Population Prospects as Assessed in 1968.* Population Studies No. 53. New York: United Nations Press.

— — —. 1979. *World Population Trends and Policies. 1977 Monitoring Report.* Volume 1. *Population Trends.* Population Studies, No. 62. New York: U.N.

U.S. Bureau of the Census. 1965. *Projections of the Population of the Communist Countries of Eastern Europe, by Age and Sex, 1965–1985.* J. L. Scott. International Population Reports, Series P-91, no. 14. Washington, D.C.: Government Printing Office.

— — —. 1975. *Population Estimates and Projections: Projections of the Population of the United States: 1975 to 2050.* Current Population Reports, Series P-25, no. 601. Washington, D.C.: Government Printing Office.

— — —. 1980. *Statistical Abstract of the United States.* Washington, D.C.: Government Printing Office.

U.S. Department of Health, Education, and Welfare. 1964. *Smoking and Health.* Report of the Advisory Committee to the Surgeon General of the Public Health Service, Public Health Service Publication No. 1103. Washington, D.C.: Government Printing Office.

U.S. Department of Commerce. 1978. Statistical Policy Working Paper 1: Report on Statistics for Allocation of Funds. Prepared by Subcommittee on Statistics for Allocation of Funds, Federal Committee on Statistical Methodology. Washington, D.C.: Office of Federal Statistical Policy and Standards.

Vaupel, J., and Yashin, A. E. 1982. "The Deviant Dynamics of Death in Heterogeneous Populations." Working Paper 82–47. Laxenburg, Austria. International Institute for Applied Systems Analysis.

Vialatoux, J. 1959. *Le Peuplement humain,* 2 Vols. Paris: Editions Ouvrieres.

Waite, L. J. and Stolzenberg, R. M. 1976. "Intended Childbearing—Labor Force Participation of Young Women: Insights from Nonrecursive Models." *American Sociological Review* 41: 235–52.

Waugh, W. A. O'N. 1971. "Career Prospects in Stochastic Models with Time Varying Rates." *Fourth Conference on the Mathematics of Population.* Honolulu: East-West Population Institute.

Westoff, C. F. 1978. "Marriage and Fertility in the Developed Countries." *Scientific American* 239 (December): 51–57.

Whelpton, P. K. 1963. "Cohort Analysis and Fertility Projections." In *Emerging Techniques in Population Research.* New York: Milbank Memorial Fund.

White, C. L. 1965. "Geography and the World's Population." In Ng, L. K. Y., and Mudd, S. (eds.), *The Population Crisis: Implications and Plans for Action.* Bloomington, Ind.: Indiana University Press.

Widjojo Nitisastro. 1970. *Population Trends in Indonesia.* Ithaca, N.Y.: Cornell University Press.

Wright, H. 1923. *Population.* New York: Harcourt, Brace.

Wright, Q. 1965. *A Study of War.* Chicago: University of Chicago Press.

Wrigley, E. A. 1969. *Population and History.* New York: McGraw-Hill.

Wynne-Edwards, V. C. 1962. *Animal Dispersion in Relation to Social Behaviour.* Edinburgh: Oliver and Boyd.

Population and Resources: Fact and Interpretation*

Kingsley Davis

The interrelation between population and resources is a difficult subject. For this there seem to be several reasons. First, the two interacting sets of phenomena (resources and population) come from different universes of discourse. To bring them together in a common frame of reference is not like comparing apples and oranges, which at least are both fruit, but more like comparing, say, houses and trees, or horses and bacteria. The category "resources" itself includes a huge and diverse miscellany of things having little in common. Copper and fresh water, for example, have nothing in common except that both are used by man. Further confusion arises from the fact that mankind's use of resources is not just a phenomenon to be observed and understood scientifically, but a matter of major political and economic significance and therefore of controversy and popular opinion (Teitelbaum and Winter, 1985).

Further, no one specializes in the study of population and resources as an integrated discipline. One is either a demographer or a natural scientist, but not both at once. Demographers are baffled by the encyclopedic knowledge they think the natural scientists must possess, and the environmental specialist often has only a sketchy view of human demography.

Demography itself is a peculiar subject. It has developed analytic tools that can be applied to nonhuman as well as to human entities—for instance, to telephone poles, rabbits, machines, and cells. Scholars in the social sciences, however, are not used to dealing with human beings in abstraction from ideas, motives, and, in general, subjective aspects of behavior. As a result, the demographer is often regarded in social science circles as a mere provider of statistical facts, while the economist, sociologist, and social psychologist provide the interpretation. It frequently turns out, however, that the best person to interpret the facts is the scholar who produced them in the first place.

On the environmental side, the wide array of disciplines that must somehow be drawn upon is intimidating. Since no one individual could possibly master all the fields involved, the best course is to bring different specialists together. Specialization is a necessity, not a fault.

As things stand, despite the intense public interest in population and resources, the subject receives little direct attention from demographers. The reason is not that they regard it as unimportant, but rather that they take its importance for granted. For instance, during the last three decades, a field of study much favored by demographers has been fertility in Third World countries. The most expensive survey ever undertaken—the World Fertility Survey—was carried out during this period, as were countless other surveys and studies. The reason for this interest is not a preoccupation with human fertility per se, but rather an unquestioned belief that high fertility is causing too much population growth in the Third World, straining limited resources. But demographers have tended to rule themselves out of the direct study of environmental and ecological questions. They feel that mastering the voluminous literature on human demography is hard enough, without trying to cross the barrier separating social from natural sciences.

In the present article, I shall briefly examine four concepts that have been used in the field of population and resources. These are the search for scientific "laws" linking population and resources, the idea of "carrying capacity," the related notion of "limits to growth," and the concept of the "demographic transition." In considering these overlapping ideas, or principles, I shall be quite critical but not malicious because the subject is too important to be buried under needless controversy. My perspective is that of a demographer.

The Search for Laws Linking Population and Resources

In view of the difficulties of focusing on the linkages between population and resources, it is not surprising that scholars have sought a way out. One way they have pursued is to find scientific "laws," or "principles," that can order and simplify an otherwise chaotic subject. This has been accomplished in what is variously called "formal demography," "mathematical demography," or "stable population theory."[1]

In fact, however, mathematical demography has little to do with resources. It has, so to speak, kept away from messy population-resource problems by dealing almost exclusively with "inside variables" rather than with "external" ones. In the meantime, those demographers willing to tackle resource questions have kept looking for helpful generalizations of one sort or another.

One demographer who was willing to state generalizations about population was Malthus. In his *Essay* (p. 12), he says: (1) Population is necessarily limited by the means of subsistence. (2) Population invariably increases where the means of subsistence increase, unless prevented by some very powerful and obvious checks.

Unfortunately, these are two of the most confusing propositions in social science. If

they are taken literally, as empirical findings, they are patently false. Population is not in fact "necessarily limited" by a scarcity of the means of subsistence. It is limited by whatever contributes to mortality, such as wars, epidemics, overeating, alcohol consumption, smoking, and so on. On the other hand, if Malthus's statements are taken as hypothetical, they are true only by definition. A "check" to population must be defined as whatever impedes population growth. The proposition in effect, therefore, is a simple tautology: population growth is impeded by whatever impedes it.

Another example of the search for laws is provided by two articles by E. G. Ravenstein in the *Journal of the Royal Statistical Society,* 1885 and 1889, on "The Laws of Migration." One rule is that people move no farther than they have to, and as a result there are more short-range than long-range migrants. A further rule is that a migratory stream always produces a countercurrent of lesser strength. A third rule is that women predominate among short-range migrants. Finally, he maintains that migration tends to increase with the development of manufactures and commerce.

Under criticism for calling his rules "laws," Ravenstein admits they are not laws in the scientific sense. They are characterized by unexplained exceptions and are not logically connected with other propositions in a system of reasoning (Davis, 1989: 248).

Although Ravenstein searched for laws of migration in order to lay the foundations of a science of migration, and though he is often cited, there was no follow-up building upon his work.

One problem with the search for empirical regularities is that the regularity is viewed as operating mechanically, thus overlooking perhaps the most important trait of the human animal—namely, his possession of culture. We can ask why it is that the human organism requires very little material to subsist and yet, in fact, has transformed the world in its ceaseless search for material goods. It is mankind's possession of culture that has given him his accumulative technology and his language for social organization. It is this that has ultimately allowed an explosion of the Earth's human population. And it is this that now paradoxically gives mankind the ability to satisfy wants that have little to do with the simple needs of the human animal. Indeed, it is amazing how, starting only about ten thousand years ago with the spread of agriculture, this once-inconspicuous mammal, hunting and gathering for a living, was soon able to create nation-states with tens of millions of citizens and with social structures and procedures so complicated that a system of sciences (the social sciences) has evolved to try to understand them. It is equally amazing that this inconspicuous animal has been able to build huge cities and can make airplanes that fly faster and farther than any bird.

What drives the creation and maintenance of this complex civilization? Whatever it is, it is surely not the primary, or absolute needs of the species, but the secondary and tertiary needs that have been created. People have transformed goods into symbols of status, and symbols into material forms. Instead of using the powerful new engines of production to give themselves more leisure and freedom from drudgery, the citizens of today's industrialized nations admonish one another to work harder, to compete in an unremitting struggle to "get ahead," to "insure one's future," to "succeed," Yet, increasingly, new inventions and devices are made simply to overcome the noxious effects of inventions and devices already in place. We build cars, for instance, with anti-smog devices, but the manufacture of antismog equipment itself contributes to air pollution. The solution of one problem nearly always creates new problems or makes old problems worse. People become enmeshed in a complicated system of paperwork, regulatory requirements, bureaucratic rituals, escalating taxes, and countless other tasks. It seems that human beings had more leisure and were under less "pressure" when they were hunters and gatherers than is the case now in civilized societies (Lee, 1968; Howell, 1979).

But the story of man's unique reliance on culture has often been told. Why repeat it here?

The answer is clear. If I am right—if the main feature that most clearly distinguishes humans from other mammals is their ability to make and use tools, to exchange goods, and to organize groups—then certain conclusions must follow. Perhaps the most important of these, and certainly the most elementary, is the principle that any theory of population and resources that overlooks cultural phenomena is very likely to be deficient. Yet in much of the literature, this is exactly what is done. The role of cultural factors is either minimized or distorted, often by unconscious assumption.

This is not a demand that every study in demography somehow inject cultural considerations into its analysis. Far from it. I am not talking about demography in general but about the study of the relationships between population and resources. It is this particular subject that requires close study of cultural and motivational factors. It is this field that exhibits some of the most glaring illogicalities.

"Carrying Capacity"

If the search for scientific laws linking population and resources has not succeeded, perhaps another kind of approach will serve better. Let us take the concept of "carrying capacity" as an effort to build a bridge between demography and the environment. The general idea is that by analysis of soil and other elements of the environment, one can estimate how many people can be supported on a given amount of land. A recent symposium (Lee et al., 1988) provides us with an example of the reasoning. One of the chapters—by the economist T. N. Srinivasan—deals with the question of "carrying capacity" in the rural areas of currently developing countries. His analysis is thoroughgoing and thus provides a good basis for discussion.

Srinivasan defines carrying capacity as "the maximum population that can be sustained indefinitely into the future" (p. 13). The built-in, unconscious bias of such a definition is readily apparent. Why should we be concerned only with the "maximum" population? Why not consider the "minimum" population as well? In some counties of western Texas, for example, there are not enough people to man the existing infrastructure. The same individual may therefore have to occupy more than one post. Yet few would claim that this population is too small to be "sustained." An animal species may suffer extinction if its numbers fall below a certain critical level, but hardly anyone would maintain that this is true of the human species today. If the population of a region is extremely scarce in relation to resources, people adjust their institutions and behavior to the situation. Australians and Canadians, for example, do not find their sparse populations to be an obstacle to maintaining a high level of living. On the contrary, in today's world a high population density is generally associated with poverty while a low density is associated with prosperity.

As a matter of fact, considerable attention has been given to areas that have lost population. Such loss is characteristically viewed by the business community as a calamity rather than a blessing. For example, on 3 January 1990, the *New York Times* ran a long story under the headline: "With Rural Towns Vanishing, States Choose Which To Save." The article, by Isabel Wilkerson, focused on Sheridan County, North Dakota, and its county seat, McClusky, as prototypes of what is happening across the rural areas of the United States. In North Dakota alone, there are ten "deeply distressed" counties.

Complicating the problems of these counties is that their populations are steadily shrinking and aging. . . . While the population in the United States has doubled since 1930, the population in Sheridan County has dropped by two-thirds, from a peak of 7,373 people in 1930 to about 2,500 last year spread out over nearly 1,000 square miles.

The article does not blame the economic plight of the rural towns on their loss of people, but it clearly regards the exodus as making things worse. In the words of the mayor of McClusky, "Watching shops close and towns disappear is like sitting there dying and waiting for someone to set the date for your funeral."

The assumption is that the depressed rural counties would be better off if they had not lost population, but no evidence is offered. One can argue the opposite—given the slender and uncertain resources of the "distressed" counties, if the population had grown as fast as that of the nation at large, it would have been a disaster. The exodus of people from rural areas is clearly a demographic adjustment to economic change. For the people who stay, as well as for those who leave, it helps to restore the balance between people and resources. If observers find vacant houses and stores depressing, bulldozers can quickly reduce these structures to rubble and green crops can be planted for profit and beauty.

Another bias of the definition reported by Srinivasan lies in the word "sustained." The quotation says "carrying capacity" is "the maximum population that can be *sustained* indefinitely. . . ." Evidently, the word refers to commodities wholly or partially necessary for the individual to live, but from the context one gathers that the commodity really being considered is food. That is why I call the usual "carrying capacity" reasoning the "bread-alone fallacy." As we saw above, humans do not live simply to sustain themselves. Instead, they have a culture heritage, a set of beliefs, attitudes, and instilled desires, a cumulative technology, and an identity within a group structure.

What does the "carrying capacity" theorist, if we may call him that, do with the sociocultural aspects of human existence? The chances are that he will ignore them and concentrate on calculations presumably showing how many human beings could have enough to eat under the stipulated conditions. For instance, the following quotation describes the procedures and results of a major study of this type by FAO, UNFPA, and IIASA. It demonstrates the weaknesses of this kind of reasoning.

The study "combines a climate map . . . with a soil map . . . and then divides the study area into grids of 100km² each . . . the 15 most widely grown food crops were considered. . . . Three alternative levels of farm technology were postulated." Given these estimates of potential production, along with the calorie and protein requirements of the human body as recommended by FAO and WHO, the investigators computed "the maximum population which can be supported." (Srinivasan, 1988: 14–15)

The findings were as follows (ibid.:16–17) (in billions of people):

Farm Technology	Carrying Capacity	Projected in 2000 A.D.
Low	5.6	3.6
Intermediate	14.9	3.6
High	33.2	3.6

Bear in mind that these are not estimates for the whole population of the earth, which is projected to be 6.12 billion by the year 2000. They are figures only for the currently developing countries, with the largest country of all, China, omitted. For this reason, the estimates of "carrying capacity" are even more extreme than they seem at first to be. If the developing countries were to concentrate all resources on food production, the calculation implies, they could possibly feed 40 or more billion people.

Such calculations are clearly mere exercises having little or no relation to reality. They appear to assume that the goal of mankind is to maximize the number of people, and that in order to do so, every available resource must be turned into food. Yet there is no country in the world in which people are satisfied with having barely enough to eat.

Why, then, do writers on population concentrate so single-mindedly on food? I am not sure I know the answer, but I can make some pertinent observations. Not only is food necessary for existence, but it is intimately, continuously, and appetitively involved with the individual organism. It is consumed two or more times each day and is tied to a plethora of rituals and cultural associations. It is therefore of-

ten unconsciously viewed as a surrogate, or proxy, for population itself. Thus, to explain why a given region is populous, an observer may simply point out that the soil there is unusually fertile. The special role of food in an individual's life thus makes it easy, in reasoning about population and resources, to confuse a necessary cause (food) with a sufficient one.

The food bias in "carrying capacity" reasoning leads to other distortions—for instance, unwarranted and largely unconscious assumptions concerning the nature of demographic change. The biggest mistake of this sort, in my opinion, is the automatic tendency to view mortality as the chief mechanism by which human numbers are adjusted to resources. If, for example, the discussion concerns contemporary sub-Saharan Africa, the usual reasoning goes as follows: If the production of food in Central Africa continues to fall, the result will be more famines. These will drive up the death rate and thus slow the rate of population increase.

The preoccupation with food gives rise to another distortion—the assumption that self-sufficiency in food production is desirable. Actually, and for good reason, international trade in foodstuffs has been gaining. Since people must eat every day and since most foodstuffs are perishable or seasonal, international trade in food may have more advantages than it does in many other commodities. If, instead of food, we were to talk about, say, gold watches, what would be the carrying capacity? Perhaps it should be set at two gold watches per capita. Next, one could take hats—three hats per capita, and so on through the hundreds of items involved in modern human consumption. Obviously, if a country has certain advantages in nonfood trade, it can use these to buy food. A policy of self-sufficiency in food makes no sense for countries like England and Wales, Japan, Taiwan, the United States, or any other country that has access to international trade. The Earth is becoming one large trading system; and so the "carrying capacity" must refer not just to what food could be raised within national borders, but to the total of what could be gained in all ways.

Frequently, "carrying capacity" is treated as a norm, or optimum that should be sought. To say, for instance, that the world could "support" 33 billion people is to imply that below that figure they would be all right because they would have enough to eat, but above the 33 billion they would starve. Apparently, the idea is that as the increase in population reaches a high level, it automatically stops itself—mainly through diseases caused principally by malnutrition. According to this view, people are automatons, passively waiting to be killed by their own reproductive success. Overlooked is the possibility that the increase in human numbers may be stopped by the people themselves at a point far below the theoretical "carrying capacity," not because of a scarcity of food and other necessities, but because of a love for the frills and foibles of advanced civilization and a distaste for the arduous tasks of bearing and rearing children.

In short, the notion is false that each region has a carrying capacity that can be calculated and used in making projections and formulating policies. This idea is more applicable to cattle grazing in a pasture than to human beings.

"Limits to Growth"

Our next concept, commonly used but highly ambiguous, is "limits to growth." As with "carrying capacity," use of this term without specifying the frame of reference or the level of abstraction is confusing. For instance, there is often uncertainty as to whether an alleged "limit" refers to a potential (theoretical or hypothetical) constraint or to an actual one. It is also difficult to tell whether a supposed limit to population growth is a goal or a simple fact. If it is a simple fact, does it occur automatically or as a result of human volition?

Given these ambiguities, one should not be surprised to find that the idea of limits has for centuries given rise to acrimonious, confusing, and inconclusive debate. The confusion and ac-

rimony occur despite the fact that, at bottom, both sides of the debate agree. They agree that in a finite world the human population cannot continue to grow forever, but they disagree sharply about the time and circumstances of an ultimate limit.

On the one side of this great debate are the alarmists—people who believe that the limits to population growth are rapidly being approached and therefore that action should be taken now to reduce or reverse world population growth and thereby prevent a catastrophe. On the other side are the skeptics—those who think the Earth is big enough to accommodate a much larger population than it now has and that there is no need to worry.

The first group—the worriers, or environmentalists—claim that the supply of several indispensable resources is already running low and will soon be insufficient to sustain the present population, much less the population projected for the future. They also claim that the addition of approximately 85 million persons to the Earth's population each year is resulting in ever more ruthless and shortsighted handling of the resources that remain. It therefore seems only a matter of time until some essential but scarce resource gives out and stops population growth by causing widespread disease, famine, war, or some other calamity. The particular resource whose scarcity in relation to population size might become critical could be any one of a number of possibilities—topsoil, fresh water, clean air, forests, sites for safe waste disposal, or a particular species.

There is thus, according to this view, a collision course between, on the one hand, an expanding population and rising per capita consumption and, on the other, a diminishing resource base. Given this impasse, say the concerned scientists and activists, population growth cannot continue much longer. One way or another it will be halted, perhaps quite suddenly and catastrophically, perhaps gradually, as the necessary resources disappear. In the meantime, the longer population growth continues, the more painful and drastic must be the manner by which the growth is finally stopped. Already there are signs of acute stress from the swelling numbers and poverty of the world's people. About 85 percent of all children live in the Third World, where they are least likely to learn the skills necessary for work in a modern economy. Further, a high proportion of the world's people live within a few feet of sea level, a zone likely to be inundated if the polar icecaps are melted by global warming. Finally, according to this view, the driving force behind the world's population explosion has been a cheap but essential resource—energy from fossil fuels. This magical gift has been available for only the cost of extraction and transportation, but the price seems likely to rise rapidly in the future. Already fossil energy is too costly for ordinary people in less developed countries, leading them to continue to burn another resource (wood) that is becoming scarce and costly too.

On the other side are those who think the alarmists are wrong and who either do not see or refuse to discuss the possible exhaustion of any essential resource. These skeptics point out that the very growth of the world's population proves that the necessities for human existence are being met, and in abundance. The skeptics also recall the predictions of disaster made in the 1940s to 1970s—disasters that were supposed to result from population growth but that never occurred. In addition, the skeptics are quick to note the irony of talking about limits and scarcities when we live in a technological wonderland. By its very nature, they say, technology has no inherent limits that can be known in advance. So there is no reason to think that the world will run out of some essential resource and thus reach a limit to population growth, at least not soon enough to affect the present or the next generation.

This debate over limits to population growth may never be resolved, except by facts as time goes along. It is also a debate over a metaphysical concept that is only potentially, or theoretically, defined, and that therefore has little value in understanding the real world.

Most people, when they speak of a "limit to growth," have in mind a number that the actual population may approach but never quite reach. It is an upper asymptote, determined post hoc but not before.

In the early 1970s, it was widely believed that the alarmists had won the debate. At that time a book entitled *The Limits to Growth* (Meadows et al., 1972) reported the findings of a team of scholars connected with the Massachusetts Institute of Technology and working under the auspices of a loose group intriguingly called the Club of Rome. Essentially the team selected five major variables and, with the help of a computer (not as familiar a tool then as it is now), traced out how changes in one variable would affect changes in the others. The five basic variables were land, food, industrialization, nonrenewable resources, and pollution. To determine causal relationships among these and between them and other variables involved in development, they used the actual trends during the period from 1900 to 1970.

In the "standard run" the researchers assumed that the 1900–70 trends would continue as long as possible. The result was "overshoot and collapse," brought on by the scarcity of nonrenewable resources. With population and industrialization both growing, the drain on resources quickly becomes so large that within a century, rising mortality brings massive population decline. One of their most startling claims was the speed at which collapse would arrive. If 3.18 billion hectares (7.86 billion acres) is taken as the potentially arable land on Earth, and if per capita land requirements and population growth rates remain as they are today (Meadows et al., 1972: 51), there will be "a desperate land shortage before the year 2000." Quadrupling soil productivity would merely postpone the shortage by about fifty years.

In another computer run the researchers asked what would happen if, through technological advance, available resources were doubled and energy became limitless. Population decline, the model indicated, would start about ten years earlier than in the standard run, due not to depletion of resources but to pollution. Provisionally released from the resource restraint, the growth of population and industrialization would poison the environment and drive up the death rate sharply.

But suppose that new technology reduced pollution by a factor of four. What then? There would be no pollution crises before 2100 but there would be a loss of population, due this time to a shortage of food.

Now suppose both that agricultural yields were doubled and the pollution per unit of industrialization were reduced by a factor of four. The world's population would still reach a limit and decline, paradoxically because of pollution. Even though pollution per unit of industrialization was reduced by a factor of four, industrialization would be so enormous that it would overload the environment, raising the death rate.

Thus, all variants of the model, incorporating different assumptions, suggest that if population and industrialization continue to expand, population will rise temporarily above some limit and then collapse, probably in less than 130 years. The only way to avoid this outcome, the Club of Rome suggested, would be to pursue a deliberate policy of limiting growth before the population reaches a natural limit. If population growth were stabilized by 1975 and industrialization by 1985, resource depletion and pollution would be sufficiently reduced to avoid collapse before 2100.

Limits to Growth caught the world's imagination overnight. For the first time in intellectual history, science was being used to confirm a long-held instinctive fear that mindless demographic and economic increase is leading the world to disaster. Further, the book preached a sermon: the only way to avoid catastrophe was to pursue a deliberate policy of curtailing growth. If this is not done in time, the Earth will become choked with people and pollution.

Doubtless *Limits* made many new converts to the environmentalist side. Soon, however, the book was subjected to intense criticism.

For instance, a group at the University of Sussex, England, published a symposium called *Models of Doom* (Cole et al., 1973) devoted to refuting the Club of Rome study. As time went by without a letup in world population growth and without such consequences as "overshoot" and "collapse," it became fashionable to dismiss the study as being unsound in its methods, biased in its assumptions, and extreme in its conclusions. In general, its greatest weakness was not only that it dealt with the future, but that it dealt with future technology, which is notoriously unpredictable. For instance, if a fourfold improvement of land productivity is achieved, a food crisis will obviously be postponed. But why stop at quadrupling soil productivity? There is no proof that it could not be raised twenty times, or for that matter that food could not be manufactured rather than caught or grown. Although population can hardly grow forever, setting any particular time for its demise is a dubious enterprise.

It is now two decades since *The Limits to Growth* was published. This is too brief a period to test the accuracy of even the short-term theoretical predictions, much less the long-term ones that were the main focus of interest in the project. Nevertheless, one cannot ignore developments in the last two decades that tend to support the study's findings. For instance, the world's population has grown faster during these years than it did between 1900 and 1970, and (to a lesser extent) so has industrialization. According to the Club of Rome study, this continuation of business as usual would lead to massive and deadly pollution, and that is what is happening now. On a global scale the atmosphere is being contaminated by the products of combustion from automobiles, forests, and factories; acid rain is spreading from industrial regions to many other parts of the globe; the protective ozone layer of the upper atmosphere is gradually being depleted; the problem of waste disposal has not been solved, especially the problem of nuclear waste; cities are engulfed in smog; the world's climate is being altered, with potentially grave consequences; and death rates in some countries are rising. Thus the grizzly truth may turn out to be that *Limits* was more prophetic than its detractors and even some of its defenders thought possible. In fact, during the last three decades several basic developments have occurred that together amount to a revolution in environmental concerns. First, the sheer number of discoveries of environmental problems has increased precipitously; second, the long-term seriousness of the problems has been increasingly recognized as more of the consequences of growth are felt; third, many problems formerly thought to be local in character are in fact global or near-global in scope; fourth, the involvement of science in understanding the causes of environmental change has increased rapidly; and fifth, the international scope of environmental damages has led inevitably to strong demands for conservationist policies.

It seems doubtful whether the debate over limits to growth will be resolved any time soon. Not only is the disagreement about the future; it is also about a concept that is only potentially, or theoretically, defined and that therefore has little value in understanding the real world.

The literature on population is filled with hypothetical reasoning. "The ultimate check to population," wrote Malthus, "appears then to be a want of food, arising necessarily from the different ratios according to which population and food increase" (Malthus, 1888: 6). But a potential limit is not necessarily realizable in the actual world. It is an imaginary concept like the "life span" of a species or the "reproductive potential" of the human female. Its use fails to enlighten us. We do not learn much by speculating on the potential or ultimate check to population growth. We learn a great deal more by analyzing the historical trends and circumstances of actual populations. This is what the Club of Rome tried to do. If it was not wholly successful, the fault lay less in the method (some kind of global system analysis seems called for) than in the application.

Discussions of population often envision a limit created by scarcity. They overlook the possibility of a limit rooted instead in abundance, as the failure of city populations to replace themselves suggests. They also overlook another kind of "limit to growth"—namely, a limit set by political fiat. At first glance one might think it easy to set an arbitrary limit (the authorities simply decide what they want and enforce it); but in practice this has proved difficult to do.

All told, then, concepts like carrying capacity and limits to growth teach us little about population and resources. Neither concept gives us a vision of the future. Neither gives us analytic power, or foresight instead of hindsight. Although they and similar ideas have sometimes hinted at an "iron law" or "general principle" by which population and resources are related, the truth is that this branch of science (in contrast to, for example, stable population theory) has not advanced beyond description and explanation of empirical regularities. These are less rigorous than the theorems found, say, in physics and chemistry, but they are nonetheless helpful in understanding the population-resources field. To see why, we can turn to one of the most widely known and respected concepts—the "demographic transition."

The "Demographic Transition"

This particular regularity was first publicized in the 1930s by Warren Thompson, the foremost American demographer of his day. He and other experts noted that the transition was being repeated in country after country. This allowed observers to put together not only two or three, but a whole system of variables. Also, instead of winding up with an equilibrium model (in which change is a distortion), transition theory made change its central focus. Finally, transition theory could be used to suggest new questions about population and new lines of research. In any study of population and resources, then, the demographic transition cannot be ignored. It represents a powerful tool for connecting demography with "outside" factors in a process of change.

Stripped to its essentials, "demographic transition" refers to a shift from a regime of high mortality and fertility to one of low mortality and fertility. Because the decline of mortality precedes the decline in fertility, there is a period during which population grows rapidly. As time goes by, however, fertility declines faster than mortality, with the result that the country's population growth stabilizes at a low or negative level.

Table 36.1 shows the stylized pattern of change; Figure 36.1 presents an actual example of the demographic transition, that in Singapore.

On the fertility side, a noteworthy feature of the post–World War II era has been the enormous difference between the more advanced and the less advanced countries. The latter, comprising more than two-thirds of the globe, have had five to seven births per woman, while the highly advanced nations, despite their postwar baby boom, have had a drop in births so drastic as to portend reproductive failure.

Scientific interest in the transition is thus not confined to petty debates over whether a given country does or does not fit the pattern. Although no two countries behave exactly alike, none appears to have become urban-industrial without passing through, or at least entering, the demographic transition.

But the more profound question is why the transition occurs in the first place. Why, with the process of economic and social modernization, does the demographic transition always occur? Why are there no real exceptions? Further, with respect to the dynamics of the transition, why does mortality decline first? Why

does fertility eventually start down and then later stop falling? Does the drop in mortality somehow trigger mechanisms that reduce the birth rate? If so, are the mechanisms automatic or motivational? Finally, why does the demographic transition vary from one country or region to another? In particular, are there systematic and significant variations according to when, in history, the transition occurs? If these questions are answered, it may solve puzzles that have intrigued social scientists for some two hundred years.

If the demographic transition always occurs as a country becomes more highly educated, urbanized, and economically developed, the cause must be nothing less than the Industrial Revolution, broadly conceived. Indeed, the theory of the demographic transition is part of a general theory of economic change. Beginning in the eighteenth century, continuing until today, and gradually spreading around the world, the Industrial Revolution has substantially raised the standard of living of people in the industrializing nations. Using ever more sophisticated machinery to harness stored-up fossil energy, the revolution was so fundamental that it affected everything else. Its first demographic effect was to increase longevity. By raising the per capita consumption of goods and services, it probably had a greater impact on human life than the invention of agriculture. Indeed, it accomplished what human beings had been unsuccessfully trying to do for thousands of years: it dramatically extended the average length of life. It did this in two ways—first, by providing better and more reliable diets, clothing, shelter, and other elements of consumption; and second (after approximately 1850) by developing better sanitation and better medicine.

Why does mortality decline first? In some northwest European countries the first sustained drop in the birth rate did not come until approximately a century after the first sustained fall in the death rate. Why such a long gap? The answer, I believe, is that longevity was what people wanted, whereas small fami-

TABLE 36.1   Vital Rates in Transition

Phase	Death Rate	Birth Rate	Rate of Natural Increase
Early	High	High	Low
Middle	Low	High	High
Late	Low	Low	Low

FIGURE 36.1 Crude birth and death rates: Singapore, 1930–88.

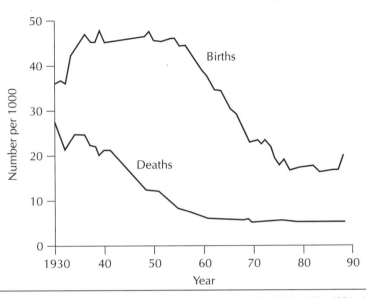

Sources: United Nations, *Demographic Yearbook* (issues for 1951, 1955, 1966, 1971, 1974, 1980, 1986, 1988); *Demographic Yearbook Historical Supplement,* 1978; *Population and Vital Statistics Report,* Series A, Vol. XL, No. 2, April 1988.

lies were not. Reproduction was governed by strong institutional controls that did not leave individuals free to do as they pleased. Furthermore, since the decline in mortality was sharpest in infancy and childhood, it had much the same effect as a rise in the birth rate. People responded by exercising their options. They migrated to towns and cities, moved to the New World, postponed marriage or never married at all, and relied on abortion and homemade contraceptive practices to reduce fertility within marriage (Davis, 1963). These adjustments took time, however, and while they were occurring Europe experienced a fairly rapid population growth.

Once the birth rate started downward, it fell faster than the death rate, with the result that eventually the population either ceased to grow or grew very slowly. As a further consequence, the proportion of the older population grew significantly. This was the demographic transition as it first occurred in northwest Europe and in overseas nations of European settle-

ment. Although the process differed in detail from one country to another, and although it was disturbed by two world wars, the Great Depression, the widespread adoption of pronatalist policies, and other political and economic interferences, the general outline of the transition in the older industrial countries matched the model remarkably well. For instance, in two countries as different as Norway and the United States the pattern of mortality change was much the same, except for the fact that the United States entered the cycle some fifty years after Norway did. As expected, then, the United States made the change more rapidly, as illustrated by levels of life expectancy shown in Table 36.2.

There were profound differences in the transition according to when in history it occurred. The classic model, which can be called "demographic transition A," was tightly linked to the rise and spread of the Industrial Revolution and was essentially completed by the end of World War II. Countries entering the transition after World War II followed a model that can be called "demographic transition B." These countries are moving through the entire trajectory much more rapidly than did the older industrial countries. As a consequence, the distortion among the phases of the transition is greater. The drop in mortality is more abrupt, and the fall in fertility, starting from a higher level, is sharper once it gets under way. As a result, the growth of population is two to three times what it was historically in transition "A."

This acceleration surprised most observers because the prevailing wisdom of the early postwar period was that economic development, not medicine or sanitation, determined the death rate. Only gradually was it recognized that public health measures could lower death rates independently of economic development. A typical case is that of Costa Rica. In 1950 that country had a life expectancy of fifty-six years. During the subsequent thirty-five years, it added eighteen years to that figure. The rate of improvement was nearly three times that of the United States starting at a comparable level. Mexico's experience was similar. Its life expectancy improved at a rate nearly twice that of the United States from the same starting level.

The precipitous fall of death rates in the less developed world since World War II is perhaps the most profound change ever to occur in human population history. It was, for instance, the main cause of the unequaled world population growth in the postwar era. In the forty years from 1950 to 1990, the Earth's inhabitants increased by 2.78 billion, or 110 percent, a far faster gain than ever before. It is often assumed that the acceleration in population growth was caused by high birth rates, but in fact the main cause was declining mortality.

The rapid fall in Third World death rates after 1945 was mainly due to the achievements of medical science in the advanced countries and to the unexpectedly low cost of applying these achievements in developing countries. The advanced countries made large investments in medical research, teaching, and appli-

TABLE 36.2 Speed of Trends from Similar Starting Levels: Life Expectancy at Birth in Norway and the United States

	Start	Year	End	Year	Change per Year
Norway	47.6	1855	76.3	1986	.22
United States	47.6	1900	75.4	1986	.32

Sources: Central Bureau of Statistics (Oslo): *Historical Statistics 1968*, p. 57; *Statistical Yearbook of Norway 1988*, p. 65; US Department of Health and Human Services, *Vital Statistics of the United States, 1986, Life Tables*, Vol. II, Section 6, p. 14.

cation. By having access to the yield of these investments, the developing countries received a free ride, so to speak. The latest techniques were transferred to them quickly at low cost, and thus their death rates were dramatically reduced in a short time.

The rapid fall in mortality had the effect not only of multiplying the population but also of making families larger than they otherwise would have been. Reproduction in the developing world continued for some time to be governed by preindustrial mores. As a result, population growth in these countries was approximately double that of the now-industrialized nations when they were in the middle of their demographic transition. Countries like Sweden and Great Britain achieved at their peak a rate of natural increase of barely fifteen per thousand population per year, whereas now, for countries like Kenya, Egypt, Mexico, Pakistan, and El Salvador the rate is between twenty-five and forty per thousand.

The "Demographic Transition" and the Future

As a model for predicting the future, the demographic transition has undeniable limitations. In a field where there are many variations from one time and place to another, the transitional model is too crude, and as a consequence it has a poor track record in clairvoyance. It did not enable the experts to predict the spectacular fall in death rates in developing countries after World War II, nor did it lead them to anticipate the baby boom in advanced nations. More recently, the transition model failed to predict the remarkable drop in fertility that has been occurring in much of Asia. For making projections the model is less satisfactory than relying on the particular history and idiosyncrasies of the country in question.

With such a record, one might wish to adopt other methods for projecting the population. One might, for instance, perform some mechanical extrapolation of recent trends. But for purposes of *understanding* what is going on, the theory of demographic transition still offers the best starting point.

According to stylized theory, the transition is finished when birth and death rates are both low and equal and zero population growth has been achieved. Most of the projections prepared by the United Nations, the U.S. Bureau of the Census, and the World Bank, for example, seem to assume that the demographic transition will conform to this stylized pattern and, accordingly, the growth of world population will by and large cease sometime around the middle of the next century (United Nations, 1982; U.S. Bureau of the Census, 1985; World Bank, 1984).

Actually, there is no compelling reason for equilibrium ever to be reached. For all we can tell, population growth may continue for a long time to come, and, as a result, the world may be teetering on the verge of the greatest calamity it has ever faced. The purpose of population projections is not simply to tell us how many people will be in the world according to present trends, but to tell us how many under various assumptions. In the literature, scant attention is given to catastrophic or other dire events. The reason for this inattention is easy to discern. In view of the many drastic, improbable, massive, and uncontrollable things that could happen to mankind, there is no way to pick the most likely. Also, anyone who pursues the question of what will actually happen gets branded as either a pessimist or an optimist and is shunned by those in the mainstream.

In speculating about the future world population, one should examine carefully those countries that appear to have recently completed the transition. A special group of nations, mostly Asian, demonstrate how rapidly a country can advance through the demographic transition despite adverse conditions. These countries, sometimes referred to as "miracle countries" due to their rapid development, include Hong Kong, Japan, Singapore, South Korea, and Taiwan. At the end of World War II these countries faced a bleak picture. Their economies had traditionally been heavily dependent on agriculture, yet their territory included little or no agricultural land. As a consequence, their population density on the land was extremely high, as tends to be the Asian pattern. To be sure, Japan had faced such conditions and moved through most of its demographic transition, but the other countries seemed to be mired in labor-intensive activity that supported high numbers of people at or near the subsistence level.

To the surprise of everyone, however, these countries recovered with incredible speed. On the demographic side, Figure 36.2 shows that in a mere thirty-five years, from 1950 to 1985, their total fertility rate dropped from around five to seven births per woman to below replacement. Figure 36.2 also shows how similar these countries are in their demographic behavior. If these countries were able to quickly reach a fertility rate below replacement, others can do it too, regardless of the starting conditions.

Naturally, there is keen interest in what the miracle countries will do next. Will they serve as a role model for the rest of the developing world—"demographic transition C," if you will—or will it prove impossible for many poor countries to travel that path? No one knows the answer, but from a demographic point of view the options are few. The prodigious growth of the Earth's population must soon stop somehow. It may stop because of a return to high mortality due to some catastro-

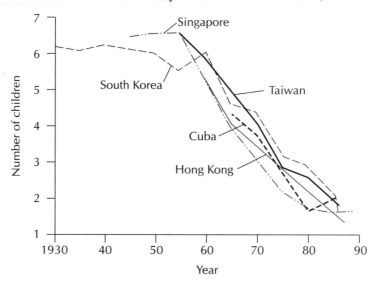

FIGURE 36.2 Total fertility rates in selected countries, 1930–87.

Sources: See note 2.

phe such as warfare, a worldwide epidemic, loss of an essential resource, or other disaster, perhaps induced by human crowding. Or, it may be stopped because of a birth rate continuously too low to replace the population, a condition possibly brought on by an increasing complexity of human society that makes childbearing more costly in time and money and less rewarding.

If virtually all less developed countries acquire below-replacement fertility, will there be a strong effort to raise the birth rate by deliberate policy? Will governments provide positive incentives for childbearing? If the answer is yes, the policy will be dubious, owing to the changed conditions that prevail. In the first place, precisely because the highly advanced nations have now reached near-zero rates of population growth, their low fertility characterizes an ever smaller portion of the world's population. In 1950 approximately one-third of the human population lived in the advanced regions. By 1985, the proportion had fallen to just under a quarter. According to the medium variant of the UN projections, the proportion

will be down to one-fifth in the year 2000 and to one-sixth in the year 2025 (United Nations, 1988). If the advanced nations want a higher birth rate merely to get a larger population, they can rely instead on immigration from the poor and crowded areas of the world. Admittedly, few advanced countries are currently willing to encourage immigration on a grand scale, but they may feel such extreme pressure from the Third World that mass migration occurs anyway. A relatively low rate of outmigration from the perspective of the Third World could be a major rate of immigration for the industrialized nations. Governments in the developed world might feel that acceptance of immigrants would be a small price to pay for temporary peace. At the moment, however, most of the advanced nations expect to continue to restrict rather than facilitate immigration.

These thoughts, I trust, demonstrate that simple or mechanical formulas do not exist for understanding the relation between population and resources. Formal demography has shown little interest in this relationship. The idea of carrying capacity is seriously biased, and conveys a grotesquely lopsided notion of human welfare. The idea of limits to growth knowable in advance is promising, but it requires more research than anyone now seems ready to undertake. As an organizing and stimulating principle, the demographic transition is virtually indispensable, for it brings "outside" and "inside" variables together in a creative fashion. Although it is too tied to historical and idiosyncratic factors to serve as a means of predicting future trends, it is nevertheless useful in comparative analysis and in comprehending the broad sweep of human demography. Such comprehension provides no comforting reassurance that a balance between population and resources can be trusted to come about through spontaneous convergence to a stabilized global population enjoying a high level of material affluence.

Notes

*   From *Resources, Environment, and Population: Present Knowledge, Future Options,* edited by Kingsley Davis and Mikhail S. Bernstam (supplement to *Population and Development Review,* vol. 16, 1990; New York: Oxford University Press, 1991), 1–21, by permission of Oxford University Press. Copyright 1991 by the Population Council, Inc.

1. The foundation of these disciplines, laid early in the twentieth century by the mathematician and biologist Alfred J. Lotka, deals with mathematical relations among the elements of population and has been enormously successful. Indeed, Lotka's work and that of his colleagues and successors is the heart of demography as we know it today. Lotka's main work is contained in his treatise, *Théorie Analytique des Associations Biologiques.* One of the best accounts of his contribution to the field is contained in David V. Glass, *Population Policies and Movements in Europe* (Oxford: Clarendon Press, 1940). Other authors who have contributed significantly to the development of population theory are Brass, Coale, Das Gupta, Keyfitz, Pollard, and Schoen.

2. Sources for Figure 36.2 are as follows: Tai Hwan Kwon et al., *The Population of Korea,* Population and Development Studies Center,

Seoul National University, 1975, p. 12; Ansley J. Coale, Lee-Jay Cho, and Noreen Goldman, *Estimation of Recent Trends in Fertility and Mortality in the Republic of Korea,* Committee on Population and Demography, Report No. 1, National Academy of Sciences, Washington, D.C., 1980, p. 2; Saw Swee-Hock, *Population Control for Zero Growth in Singapore,* Oxford University Press, 1980, p. 161; Lee-Jay Cho, Fred Arnold, and Tai Hwan Kwon, *The Determinants of Fertility in the Republic of Korea,* Committee on Population and Demography, Report No. 14, National Academy Press, Washington, D.C., 1982, p. 38; Benjamin Mok, "Recent Fertility Trends in Hong Kong," in *Fertility Transition of the East Asian Populations,* ed. Lee-Jay Cho and Kasumasa Kobayashi, University Press of Hawaii, 1979, pp. 178–97; T. H. Sun and Y. L. Soong. "On its way to zero growth: Fertility transition in Taiwan, Republic of China," in Cho and Kobayashi, 1979, p. 120; Directorate of Budget, Accounting, and Statistics, Executive Yuan, *Statistical Yearbook of the Republic of China 1986,* p. 3; United Nations, *Demographic Yearbook,* 1986, pp. 554, 558–63.

References

Brass, W. 1971. *Biological Aspects of Demography.* Symposia of the Society for the Study of Human Biology, Vol. X. New York: Barnes and Noble.

Cole, H. S. D., et al. (eds.). 1973. *Models of Doom.* New York: Universe Books.

Davis, Kingsley. 1963. "The Theory of Change and Response in Modern Demographic History." *Population Index* 29, no. 4: 345–66.

———. 1987. "The World's Most Expensive Survey." *Sociological Forum* 2, no. 4: 829–34.

———. 1989. "Social Science Approaches to International Migration," in Teitelbaum and Winter, 1989, pp. 245–61.

Glass, David V. 1940. *Population Policies and Movements in Europe.* Oxford: Clarendon Press.

Howell, Nancy. 1979. *Demography of the Dobe !Kung.* New York: Academic Press.

Keyfitz, Nathan, and Wilhelm Flieger. 1971. *Population: Facts and Methods of Demography.* San Francisco: W. H. Freeman.

Lee, Richard B. 1968. "What Hunters Do for a Living," in *Man the Hunter,* ed. Richard B. Lee and Irven DeVore. Chicago: Aldine, pp. 30–48.

Lee, Ronald D., et al. 1988. *Population, Food and Rural Development.* Oxford: Clarendon Press.

Lotka, Alfred J. 1934–39. *Théorie Analytique des Associations Biologiques: I, Principes; II, Analyse Démographique avec Application Particulière à L'Expece Humaine.* Paris: Hermann et Cie.

Malthus, Thomas Robert. 1888. *Essay on the Principle of Population,* 9th edition. London: Reeves and Turner.

Meadows, Donella H., et al. 1972. *The Limits to Growth.* New York: University Books.

Pollard, A. H., Farhat Yusaf, and G. N. Pollard. 1974. *Demographic Techniques.* Ruschcutters Bay, NSW: Pergamon Press.

Srinivasan, T. N. 1988. "Population Growth and Food—An Assessment of Issues, Models, and Projections," in Lee et al., 1988, pp. 11–39.

Teitelbaum, Michael S., and Jay M. Winter. 1985. *The Fear of Population Decline.* Orlando: Academic Press.

——— (eds.). 1989. *Population and Resources in Western Intellectual Traditions.* Cambridge: Cambridge University Press.

United Nations. 1982. *United Nations Demographic Indicators of Countries: Estimators and Projections as Assessed in 1980.* New York, pp. 3–28.

———. 1988. *World Population Prospects.* New York.

U.S. Bureau of the Census. 1985. *Population Profile of the United States 1983/4,* Current Population Reports, Special Studies, Series P 23, No. 145. Washington, D.C.: U.S. Government Printing Office, pp. 4–6.

World Bank. 1984. *World Development Report 1984.* New York: Oxford University Press.

CHAPTER THIRTY-SEVEN

The State of the World's Children 1993: The Age of Neglect and the Age of Concern*

James P. Grant

Amid all the problems of a world bleeding from continuing wars and environmental wounds, it is nonetheless becoming clear that one of the greatest of all human aspirations is now within reach. Within a decade, it should be possible to bring to an end the age-old evils of child malnutrition, preventable disease, and widespread illiteracy.

As an indication of how close that goal might be, the financial cost can be put at about $25 billion a year. (In 1990, UNICEF estimated at $20 billion a year the extra financial resources needed to meet the health, nutrition, education, and water and sanitation goals agreed at the World Summit for Children. Estimates for the additional resources required to also meet family planning goals have since become available[1] and this has increased the overall estimate to approximately $25 billion a year.) That is UNICEF's estimate of the extra resources required to put into practice today's low-cost strategies for protecting the world's children. Specifically, it is an estimate of the cost of controlling the major childhood diseases, halving the rate of child malnutrition, bringing clean water and safe sanitation to all communities, making family planning services universally available, and providing almost every child with at least a basic education.[2]

In practice, financial resources are a necessary but not sufficient prerequisite for meeting these basic needs. Sustained political commitment and a great deal of managerial competence are even more important. Yet it is necessary to reduce this challenge to the denominator of dollars in order to dislodge the idea that abol-ishing the worst aspects of poverty is a task too vast to be attempted or too expensive to be afforded.

To put the figure of $25 billion in perspective, it is considerably less than the amount the Japanese government has allocated to the building of a new highway from Tokyo to Kobe; it is two to three times as much as the cost of the tunnel soon to be opened between the United Kingdom and France; it is less than the cost of the Ataturk Dam complex now being constructed in eastern Turkey; it is a little more than Hong Kong proposes to spend on a new airport; it is about the same as the support package that the Group of Seven has agreed on in 1992 for Russia alone; and it is significantly less than Europeans will spend this year on wine or Americans on beer[3] (Figure 37.1)

Whatever the other difficulties may be, the time has therefore come to banish in shame the notion that the world cannot afford to meet the basic needs of almost every man, woman, and child for adequate food, safe water, primary health care, family planning, and a basic education.

A 10 Percent Effort

If so much could be achieved for so many at so little cost, then the public in both industrialized and developing countries might legitimately ask why it is not being done.

In part, the answer is the predictable one: meeting the needs of the poorest and the least politically influential has rarely been a priority of governments. Yet the extent of present ne-

FIGURE 37.1   Affording the cost.

It is no longer possible to say that the task of meeting basic human needs is too vast or expensive a task. With present knowledge, the task could be accomplished within a decade at a cost of an extra $25 billion per year. Some comparisons of annual and other expenditures versus the cost of meeting basic human needs are found in this chart.

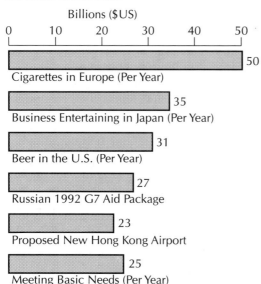

Billions ($US)

Cigarettes in Europe (Per Year) — 50

Business Entertaining in Japan (Per Year) — 35

Beer in the U.S. (Per Year) — 31

Russian 1992 G7 Aid Package — 27

Proposed New Hong Kong Airport — 23

Meeting Basic Needs (Per Year) — 25

$25 billion is UNICEF's estimate of the extra resources required to control the major childhood diseases, halve child malnutrition, reduce childhood deaths by 4 million per year, bring safe water and sanitation to all communities, provide a basic education for all children, and make family planning universally available.

Source: UNICEF, derived from various sources.

glect in the face of present opportunity is a scandal of which the public is largely unaware. On average, the governments of the developing world are today devoting little more than 10 percent of their budgets to directly meeting the basic needs of their people.[4] More is still being spent on military capacity and on debt servicing than on health and education.[5]

Perhaps more surprising still, less than 10 percent of all international aid for development is devoted to directly meeting these most obvious of human needs (Figure 37.2).[6] According to one study, for example, as little as 1.5 percent of all bilateral aid goes to primary health care, 1.3 percent to family planning, 3.2 percent to "other health care," and only 0.5 percent to primary education.[7] Because national aid programs are not broken down into common or comparable categories, such figures can only be approximate; but 10 percent is probably a generous overall estimate of the proportion of bilateral aid allocated to such purposes.[8] And as total bilateral aid from the Western industrialized nations is approximately $40 billion a year,[9] this means the amount given for nutrition, primary health care, water and sanitation, primary education, and family planning comes to about $4 billion a year. This is less than half as much as the aid-giving nations spend each year on sports shoes.[10]

It could therefore fairly be said that the problem today is not that overcoming the worst aspects of world poverty is too vast or too expensive a task; it is that it has not seriously been tried.

A Watershed

With the beginning of the 1990s has come new hope that the age of neglect may be giving way to the age of concern.

The evidence for this new hope, amid all the seismic shifts in the political and economic landscape of recent years, is a series of quieter changes which have not made the nightly news but which have affected the daily lives of millions of people.

The first of these changes is the entirely new priority that has been given to the task of immunizing the world's children. For a decade, national health services, UNICEF, the World Health Organization (WHO), and many thousands of individuals and organizations have struggled toward the goal of 80 percent immunization coverage in the developing world. In 1990, that goal

FIGURE 37.2   Percentage of bilateral ODA (OECD countries) allocated to meeting basic needs, 1990

The overseas aid given by governments is known as official development assistance (ODA). Some 80% of this aid is "bilateral"—given directly from one government to another. The other 20% is "multilateral"—given through international organizations. The table shows what percentage of bilateral aid is allocated to basic needs related to children—nutrition, water, sanitation, primary health care, primary education, and family planning.

	Net bilateral ODA (US$ millions)	Percentage Allocated to basic needs	Amount allocated to basic needs (US$ millions)	Amount available for basic needs if 20% allocated (US$ millions)
Norway	756	19.7	149	150
Switzerland	551	18.1	100	110
Finland	498	15.7	78	100
Canada	1690	10.9	184	340
Denmark	695	10.6	74	140
Netherlands	1901	9.4	179	380
United Kingdom	1483	8.8	131	300
Italy	2112	8.5	180	420
United States	8370	8.3	695	1670
Austria	299	8.1	24	60
Sweden	1384	7.1	98	280
Belgium	548	6.5*	36	110
Ireland	23	6.5*	1	5
New Zealand	82	6.5*	5	16
France	7829	4.0	313	1570
Japan	6786	2.7	183	1360
Australia	753	2.0	15	150
Germany	4479	1.9	85	900
Total	40239	6.3[†]	2530	8061

*Figure not available. Average share of 6.5% has been applied.
[†]Statistical work on the percentage of aid allocated to basic needs is still at a rudimentary stage and there are many problems of definition and international comparability still to be resolved. For this reason, the text of this report uses a figure of "approximately 10%" as the basic needs portion of aid flows, rather than the more precise figure yielded by this table.

Source: Human Development Report 1992, Table 3.14, UNDP, New York, 1992. *Development Co-operation*, OECD, Paris, 1991.

FIGURE 37.3   Deaths prevented and still occurring from vaccine-preventable diseases in all developing countries, 1991.

Immunization coverage in the developing world has been increased to approximately 80% in the last 10 years. As a result, 3 million deaths from vaccine-preventable diseases are now being prevented each year.

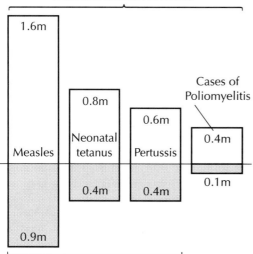

3 Million Deaths Prevented

1.7 Million Deaths
Still Occurring

3 million deaths prevented is less than the figure reported in last year's *State of the World's Children* (3.2 million). This is as a result of recent changes in the method used by the World Health Organization for calculating the number of measles deaths prevented by immunization.

Source: WHO and UNICEF, July 1992.

was reached. The result is the saving of over 3 million children's lives each year (Figure 37.3), and the protection of many millions more from disease, malnutrition, blindness, deafness, and polio. Second, the number of child deaths from diarrheal disease has been reduced by over 1 million a year through empowering one-third of the developing world's families to use the technique of oral rehydration therapy (Panel 5).

[Panels may be found in the Appendix at the end of this chapter.—*Ed.*]

The significance of these achievements goes beyond even the extraordinary numbers of lives saved and illnesses prevented. Eighty percent immunization means that approximately 100 million children are being reached by a modern medical technique on four or five separate occasions during their first year of life. As a logistical achievement, it is unprecedented; and it shows beyond any doubt that the outreach capacity now exists to put the most basic benefits of scientific progress at the disposal of the vast majority of the world's poor. Secondly, it demonstrates that, with sustained political commitment, progress can now be made toward basic social goals even by the poorest of developing countries; over the last five years, immunization coverage has been lifted dramatically in many nations with per capita incomes of less than five hundred dollars a year, including Bangladesh, the Central African Republic, Equatorial Guinea, Myanmar, Nepal, the Sudan, Uganda, Vietnam, and Zambia.[11]

Other advances in knowledge and technique are now lining up outside the door that immunization has unlocked. And the potential remains enormous. Thirty-five thousand children under five die in the developing world every day. Almost 60 percent of those deaths, and much of the world's illness and malnutrition, are caused by just three diseases—pneumonia, diarrhea, and measles—all of which can now be prevented or treated by means which are tried and tested, available and affordable (Figures 37.4 and 37.5 and Panels 1 and 5). Similarly, the vitamin A deficiency which threatens up to 10 million of the world's children with death, serious illness, and loss of eyesight could now be brought under control at a cost which is almost negligible in relation to the benefits it would bring (Panel 3).[12] Or to take another example, the iodine deficiencies that lower the mental and physical abilities of up to a billion people and are the world's single biggest cause of mental retardation could also now be eliminated at a total cost of approxi-

FIGURE 37.4 Under-five child deaths, by main cause, in developing countries, 1990.

Over 60% of the 12.9 million child deaths in the world each year are caused by pneumonia, diarrheal diseases, or vaccine-preventable diseases, or by some combination of the three.

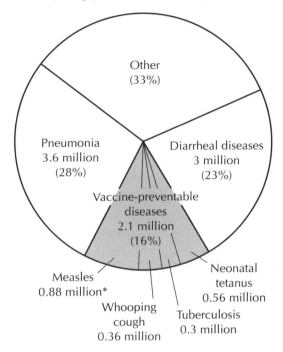

In practice, children often die from multiple causes or from the interrelated effects of frequent illness and malnutrition. For the purpose of this chart, each child death has been allocated to only one cause.

* Including measles with diarrheal disease and measles with pneumonia.

Source: WHO and UNICEF.

mately $100 million—less than the cost of two modern fighter planes.[13]

Even those aspects of poverty which have traditionally been considered the most expensive and the most logistically stubborn—the lack of adequate nutrition, safe water supply, and basic education—are also now becoming susceptible to a combination of new technolo-

gies, falling costs, and community-based strategies. The cost of providing clean water in Africa, for example, has been halved since the mid-1980s and now stands at an average figure of about twenty dollars per person per year.[14] Similarly, countries such as Bangladesh and Colombia have demonstrated that a basic, relevant education can be provided at a cost of approximately twenty dollars per child per year.[15] Equally large-scale trials in Africa and in India have shown that the incidence of child malnutrition can also now be halved at a cost of less than ten dollars per child per year.[16] "A direct attack on malnutrition is needed" says a World Bank report, "and governments willing to make that effort now have effective and affordable measures to make it happen."

New Goals

These advances in technology and strategy, and the extraordinary potential they have revealed, were the principal concern of the World Summit for Children held at the United Nations in September 1990—at about the same time as the immunization goal was being reached. The summit was attended by approximately half the world's presidents and prime ministers and resulted in a set of specific commitments which, if implemented, would indeed mark the beginning of a new era of concern.

Those commitments, designed to reflect the potential of the new knowledge and the new technologies now available, were expressed as a series of specific goals to be achieved by the end of the present century. These goals include control of the major childhood diseases; a halving of child malnutrition; a one-third reduction in under-five death rates; a halving of maternal mortality rates; safe water and sanitation for all communities; universally available family planning services; and basic education for all children.

To give these commitments a more permanent purchase on political priority, all the countries represented at the summit, and many more who have subsequently signed the Declaration

FIGURE 37.5   Percentage of under-five child deaths preventable by low-cost methods, in developing countries, 1991.

The table shows the number of child deaths each year by main cause, and the proportion of those deaths that could now be prevented by relatively simple and inexpensive means such as vaccines, antibiotics, oral rehydration therapy, and the proper management of diarrheal disease.

In practice, children often die from multiple causes or from the interrelated effects of frequent illness and malnutrition. For the purpose of this chart, each child death has been allocated to only one cause.

Cause	Annual number of child deaths (thousands)	Proportion of deaths preventable at low cost (percent)	Number of deaths preventable at low cost (thousands)
Diarrhea	3000	90	2700
Pneumonia	3560	70	2492
Measles*	880	85	748
Whooping cough	360	80	288
Neonatal tetanus	560	90	504
Tuberculosis	300	65	195
Malaria	800	70	560
Other peri- and neonatal	2470	25	618
Other	970	—	—
Total	12900	63	8105

* Includes measles with diarrheal disease and measles with pneumonia.

Source: WHO and UNICEF.

and Plan of Action, also agreed to draw up detailed national programs for reaching the agreed goals. As of September 1992, such plans have been completed in over fifty countries and are nearing completion in more than eighty others. In June of 1992, the United Nations Secretary-General reported to the General Assembly that thirty-one countries have so far indicated they will restructure budgets to increase the proportion of government spending devoted to primary education, basic health care, nutrition, water, and sanitation.[17]

The drawing up and financing of such plans is inevitably a bureaucratic process, and too much should not be expected too soon. But most nations have made a start toward keeping the promises that have been made to the world's

children. Immunization levels have been sustained (Figure 37.6 and Panel 4 in the Appendix) and in some cases, notably in China, lifted above the new goal of 90 percent (at which point very significant decreases in the incidence of disease can be expected). Polio has almost certainly been eradicated from Latin America and the Caribbean (Figure 37.7), where a year has now passed since the last confirmed case of the virus. Reported cases of the main vaccine-preventable diseases are declining (Figures 37.7 and 37.8), and WHO believes there is a reasonable chance that the 1995 goal of eliminating neonatal tetanus will be met. Countries such as Bangladesh, Bolivia, Ecuador, Malawi, Namibia, Sri Lanka, Tanzania, and possibly Brazil have already begun serious efforts to

FIGURE 37.6 Immunization coverage, children under one year, in developing countries, 1981–91.

The goal of 80% immunization by 1990 has been achieved after a determined worldwide effort. Now the question is whether that effort can be sustained. So far, the fall-off has been slight, and many nations have begun the push toward 90% coverage.

Year	BCG	DPT3	Polio3	Measles	TT2*
1981	31	27	24	18	14
1984	36	37	36	25	14
1985	40	38	38	28	17
1986	51	49	50	37	19
1987	69	60	60	53	27
1988	75	68	69	60	39
1989	85	77	79	73	44
1990	90	83	85	79	56
1991	85	78	80	77	54

Note: 1981–85 exclude data for China.
* For pregnant women.

Source: WHO and UNICEF, July 1992.

halve the rate of malnutrition. Similarly, several countries are moving determinedly toward the goal of water and sanitation for all—including Bangladesh, Burundi, China, Ghana, India, Nigeria, Paraguay, the Sudan, Togo, Vietnam, and virtually all the countries of Central America.[18] And to achieve the summit goal of empowering all families with today's knowledge about the importance of breast-feeding, hundreds of hospitals and maternity units have begun to change institutional policies and to use their enormous influence to reverse the trend toward the bottle-feeding of infants.

Not least, the promise of the summit is being kept by the rapid spread of acceptance for the Convention on the Rights of the Child, which seeks to lay down minimum standards for the survival, protection, and development of all children. The convention was adopted by the General Assembly of the United Nations to-ward the end of 1989 and came into force, with the necessary twenty ratifications, on the eve of the 1990 World Summit for Children. Usually, such conventions require many decades to achieve the stage of widespread international recognition; but in this case, the summit urged all national governments to ratify as quickly as possible and more than 120 have so far done so.

In some nations, the process of translating the convention into national law has begun. In many nations, it is becoming the accepted standard for what is and is not acceptable in the treatment of the young. In all nations, its mere existence gives citizens, journalists, and non-governmental organizations (NGOs) an agreed platform from which to remind political leaders of their promises and to campaign against the neglect and abuse of children in all its forms.

Finally, it is clear that these promises made to the world's children have now established themselves on the international political agenda. Over the last two years virtually every major summit meeting of the world's leaders—the Ibero-American, the Islamic States, the francophone countries, the nonaligned movement, the Commonwealth, the Organization of African Unity, the South Asian Association for Regional Cooperation, the League of Arab States, and finally the United Nations Conference on Environment and Development—has formally confirmed the commitment to achieving the basic social goals that were agreed at the World Summit for Children.

Promises on Paper

The importance of the convention, the summit goals, and the national programs of action that have been drawn up should neither be overestimated nor underestimated. At the moment they remain, for the most part, promises on paper. But when, in the mid-1980s, over one hundred of the world's political leaders formally accepted the goal of 80 percent immunization by 1990, that, too, was just a promise on paper. Today, it is a reality in the lives of tens of millions of families around the world.

One lesson to be learned from that achievement is that formal political commitments at the highest levels are necessary if available solutions are to be put into action *on a national scale.* But a second lesson is that such commitments will only be translated into action by the dedication of the professional services; by the mobilization of today's communications capacities; by the widespread support of politicians, press, and public; and by the reliable and sustained support of the international community. Most of the countries that succeeded in reaching the immunization goal, including many that were among the poorest and the hardest hit by problems of debt and economic adjustment,[19] succeeded primarily because large numbers of people and organizations at all levels of national life became seized with the idea that the goal could and should be achieved. Many developing countries could provide examples, but it will be sufficient to cite the case of Bangladesh: against formidable internal and external difficulties, one of Asia's poorest and most populous countries succeeded in lifting its level of immunization coverage from only 2 percent in 1985 to 62 percent in 1990. "Never in the country's history," wrote a UNICEF officer in Dhaka, "had so many groups come together for a single social programme: the President, eight social sector ministries, parliamentarians, senior civil servants, journalists, TV and radio, hundreds of non-governmental organizations, social and youth clubs, religious leaders, film and sports stars and local business leaders all worked successfully towards a common goal."[20]

The question for the years immediately ahead is whether people and organizations in all countries and at all levels are prepared to breathe similar life into new goals that have been agreed on, and into the national programs of action that have been drawn up for achieving them. Only by this degree of popular participation, by the practical and political energies of literally millions of people and thousands of organizations, will the new commitments and the promises of the 1990s be given a priority in national life. And only by such means will a new age of concern be born.

Wider Changes

All of these developments, and the hopes to which they have given rise, come at a time of extraordinary change in world affairs. And it is possible to hope that the cause of overcoming the worst aspects of poverty will also draw sustenance, for the long haul ahead, from the changed political and economic environment of the 1990s.

At the moment, that environment remains extremely difficult for most nations of the developing world. There is as yet no sign that the ending of the cold war is leading to any increase in the resources available for development. Indeed, much of the developing world is today facing its worst financial famine of the modern era, starved of resources by its own high levels of military spending, by the continuing debt crisis, by the further falls in commodity prices, by the restrictive trade policies of the industrialized nations, by the lingering recession in large parts of the world, by the costs of postwar reconstruction in the Persian Gulf, and by the channeling of new aid, credit, and investment to the nations of Eastern Europe and the former Soviet Union.

But despite all of these problems, the prospects for progress have been profoundly improved by the enormous political and economic upheavals of recent years: the advance of democracy throughout Latin America; the liberation of Eastern Europe; the collapse of the Soviet Union; the ending of the cold war; the spread of democratic political reform through most of Africa (including the erosion of apartheid); the almost worldwide retreat from the ideology of highly centralized government control over all aspects of economic life; and the growing acceptance of the necessity of joint international action in response to both humanitarian and environmental problems.

FIGURE 37.7　Percentage fall in reported cases of polio, by region, 1981–91 (1989 for Sub-Saharan Africa).

In the 1990s it is essential to monitor not just the level of immunization reached but the impact on the target diseases. The *World Summit for Children* set the goal of eradicating polio by the year 2000. The chart shows that reported cases are on the decline, with Latin America and the Caribbean leading the way.

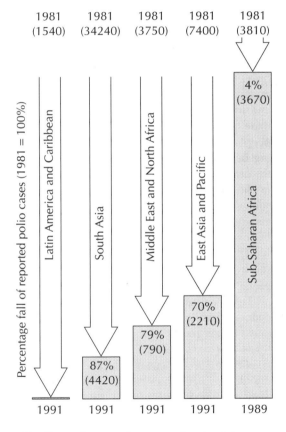

The figures in parentheses are the absolute numbers of reported cases.

WHO estimates that the actual number of polio cases in 1991 was approximately 100,000 worldwide, almost 10 times the number of reported cases. The relationship between reported cases and actual cases depends on the merits of the surveillance system.

Source: WHO.

These changes amount to one of the most sudden and fundamental transformations in history. And for all the suffering that is surfacing in the turbulent wake of these changes, from Somalia to the former Yugoslavia, it can still be said that this is a transformation which holds out new hope for world development. If the various forms of free-market economic policies now being adopted are not crushed under the weight of military spending, debt repayment, and trade protectionism, then there is real hope of achieving sustained economic growth. And if the steps now being taken toward democracy do not falter under the assault of continued poverty and social unrest, then there is also real hope that the poor will eventually begin to share more equitably in the benefits of that growth.

These developments are changing the overall environment in which the developing world must earn its living and within which its people must struggle to meet their own needs. Whether those needs are met or not depends, first of all, on whether families have jobs and incomes. Second, it depends on whether governments fulfill their responsibilities for providing the essential services and safety nets to support families so that even the most disadvantaged do not suffer from preventable malnutrition, from disease borne by unsafe water and sanitation, or from the lack of even basic health care and education. The great changes of the last five years by no means make such progress inevitable or automatic; but they do make it more possible and more likely.

This coming together of both general and specific developments means that a new threshold in the struggle to overcome the worst aspects of poverty has been reached in the early years of the 1990s. Broad-scale political and economic change is creating an environment more conducive to a renewal of progress against poverty; and advances in technology, in strategy, and in political commitment to meeting basic social goals have given that challenge both a specific focus and a new impetus.

FIGURE 37.8   Annual reported cases
of measles, by region, 1981–91.

The *World Summit for Children* set the goal of a
90% reduction in measles cases (and a 95%
reduction in deaths) by the year 2000, compared
with pre-immunization levels. The number of
reported measles cases is now declining in all
regions, with East Asia showing the steepest fall.

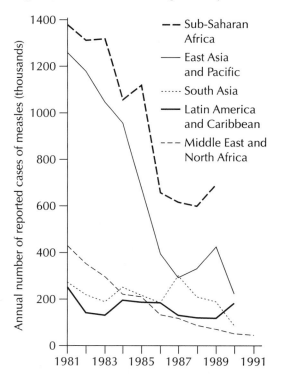

The relationship between reported cases and
actual cases depends on the merits of the
surveillance system. This system is weakest in
Africa, where the number of reported cases
should be considered as only broadly indicative.

Source: WHO.

Symptom and Cause

If there is one area of the development
process that is more widely misunderstood
than any other it is the relationship between
these two factors — between the long-term processes of overall development and the specific,
deliberate, targeted interventions such as are
represented by the basic social goals that have
been agreed. And it is the nature of this relationship which should also give a new urgency
to meeting essential human needs.

With sufficient public and political support,
it is clearly now possible to control those aspects of poverty that bring the greatest suffering to the greatest number. In particular, it is
possible to close some of the most obvious, the
most shameful, and the most damaging gaps
between today's knowledge and today's needs.

Closing these gaps will not solve the problems of economic development; it will not remove the burden of debt or restructure inequitable economic relationships; it will not
bring an end to oppression and exploitation or
eradicate the many causes of unemployment
and low incomes; nor will it meet the legitimate aspirations of hundreds of millions of
people in the developing world who are not living in absolute poverty but who do not enjoy
the amenities of life that are taken for granted
in the industrialized nations. It has therefore
sometimes been argued that such specific, targeted interventions address only the symptoms
of poverty and leave the causes undisturbed.

This is an argument which is no longer de-
serving of the politeness extended to it in the
past.

It is an unacceptable argument on two
counts. First, it is an inhuman argument. How
much longer must the poorest families wait before it is decided that the world has reached the
level of socioeconomic development at which a
few dollars per capita can be afforded to help
them prevent millions of their children from becoming malnourished, blinded, crippled, mentally retarded?

Second, it fails to recognize that frequent illness, malnutrition, poor growth and illiteracy
are some of the most fundamental *causes* as
well as some of the most severe symptoms of
poverty. It fails to take into account that the
pulse of economic development is weakened
when millions of children suffer from poor mental and physical growth; that the march toward

equality of opportunity is slowed when the children of the very poor drop out of school and into a lifetime of illiteracy; that the productivity of communities is enervated by hours spent carrying water from unsafe sources and by the time, energy, and health that are lost to the diseases it brings; that the prospects of finding a job and earning an income are crushed by preventable disabilities such as polio or nutritional blindness; that a family's capacity to save and invest in the future is the less when a child is born mentally retarded by iodine deficiency; and that the contribution of women to economic development cannot be liberated if women remain chained to long years of childbearing, long days of attendance on illness, and long hours devoted to the fetching and carrying of water and fuel.

In these and many other ways, the worst symptoms of poverty help to crush the potential of the poor, to reduce their control over circumstance, to narrow the choices available to them, and to undermine the long-term process of development.

The struggle for social justice and economic development, both within and between nations, must continue — just as the poor themselves will continue to struggle, as they have always done, to meet most of their own needs by their own efforts. But it is a tragic mistake not to recognize that those efforts can be enhanced by reductions in disease, disability, malnutrition, illiteracy, and drudgery. Today's advances in knowledge and technology could therefore augment future prospects as surely as they could diminish present suffering. And the argument that making today's advances widely available is dealing only with symptoms is an argument as destructive to the future as it is insensitive to the present.

The Vulnerable Years

These links between poverty's causes and effects lend special weight to the case for doing what could now be done to protect young children from the worst aspects of poverty.

There are many external causes of that poverty. And the process of development must address all of those causes, whether they be rooted in accidental geographical circumstances or exploitative economic relationships. But one of the most intractable of those causes is the fact that the children of the poor do not usually receive the kind of start in life which will enable them to take advantage of the opportunities that do become available. And one of the main aims of development must be to break into this insidious "inner cycle" of malnutrition and disease leading to poor mental and physical growth; leading to poor performance at school and at work; leading to reduced adult capacity for earning an income, initiating change, responding to new opportunities; leading to poor and often large families which are vulnerable to the malnutrition and disease that close the cycle and allow the current of poverty to flow from one generation to the next.

The place at which to make that break is before the child is born and during the early years of his or her life. *If* the mental and physical growth of the child can be afforded special protection at this time, *if* families and communities and government can prevent the worst aspects of poverty from affecting the child's normal growth and development, *if* special measures can be taken to give those vulnerable months and years something of the protection which is given to children fortunate enough to be born into a higher socioeconomic class, then a major contribution to the breaking of the cycle will have been made.

This is the kind of protection for the vulnerable years which millions of parents the world over make sacrifices to provide. From the point of view of those parents, it is special protection given from love and common sense. From the point of view of the effects of poverty on growth and development, it is special protection given in order to artificially and temporarily lift a child to a higher socioeconomic level, for the vulnerable early years, so that the poverty into which that child is born will not, as far as is possible, inflict long-term damage.

To illustrate the thesis still further, this is also the kind of special protection that nature itself tries to provide to those vulnerable years in the form of breastmilk. In almost all circumstances, breastmilk means that during the first six months of life a child is well nourished whether he or she is born into the meanest slum or the most opulent mansion. Nature, too, is here attempting to neutralize the fortunes of birth by providing a standard of nutrition that does not reflect, and is not affected by, the socioeconomic level of the family into which that child is born.

The capacity for extending this special protection, and for protecting the period of most rapid physical and mental growth from the most damaging aspects of poverty, has now been vastly increased by advances in knowledge and communications capacity. By such means as immunization, growth monitoring and promotion,[21] the proper management of diarrheal diseases and respiratory infections, supplementing vitamin A and iodine, targeted food subsidies, and low-cost water and sanitation services, it is now possible to broaden and strengthen this basic protection for the most vulnerable years of life. With today's knowledge and communications power, families, governments, and the international community could now build a shield of basic protection around the early years for *all children*. And in so doing, a major contribution could be made not only to meeting immediate human needs but to breaking the "inner cycle" of poverty and underdevelopment.

The present opportunity to meet the most basic and obvious needs of children in the poorest quarter of the world must therefore also be seen in the context of this profound relationship between the physical and mental needs of children and the social and economic development of their societies. "I think it is time," says Professor Muhammad Yunus, founder of Bangladesh's Grameen Bank Movement, "to come out

boldly to insist that children should be placed at the centre stage in all development thinking."[22]

Outreach Capacity

To these arguments must be added two other reasons which add weight to the idea that the time is now right for a decisive advance against the worst aspects of poverty.

One of the most important common factors uniting today's means of protecting lives and health and growth is that almost all of them are able to be put at the disposal of families by a community health worker with only a few months of training. A well-trained, well-supervised, and well-supported community health worker can, for example, help to provide family planning information and services; advise on prenatal care and safe birth practices; inform families of the advantages of breast-feeding; organize immunization and record-keeping services; diagnose acute respiratory infections and prescribe antibiotics; teach oral rehydration therapy and the proper management of diarrheal diseases; promote home hygiene and disease prevention; organize growth-monitoring sessions; promote today's knowledge about the special feeding needs of the young child; organize protection against malaria; distribute the most essential drugs and medicines; provide vitamin A, iodine, and iron supplements where necessary; and refer more difficult health problems to more qualified health professionals. In short, they can demystify today's basic health knowledge and put it at the disposal of communities. And if they are supported in that task by the full range of today's communications capacities, schools and teachers, religious leaders and local government officials, the print and electronic media, retail outlets and professional organizations, NGOs and women's groups, then the trained health worker can be the central span of the bridge between present knowledge and present need.

There are many problems involved in the deployment of large numbers of community health workers—in their recruitment and retention, in their career structure and motivation, in their regular training and supervision, and especially in the organization of the essential referral services. But such problems can be and have been overcome when the political commitment has been sustained and when the financial resources have been made available.[23]

Above all, it can no longer be claimed that putting a trained health care worker within reach of every family is not a practical and affordable proposition. Assuming a ratio of one health worker for every two hundred families, for example, it would require approximately 2 million such health workers to serve the world's poorest 2 billion people (it is not possible, in practice, to reach only the poorest 20 percent). At an average cost of approximately $1,000 per year, to cover salaries and regular in-service retraining, the total cost would be in the region of $2 billion dollars a year. Such a sum represents approximately 2 percent of the amount the developing world now spends every year on the salaries of its soldiers.[24]

For a wider range of services, the point has been elaborated by Amartya Sen, Lamont University Professor at Harvard and former Drum-

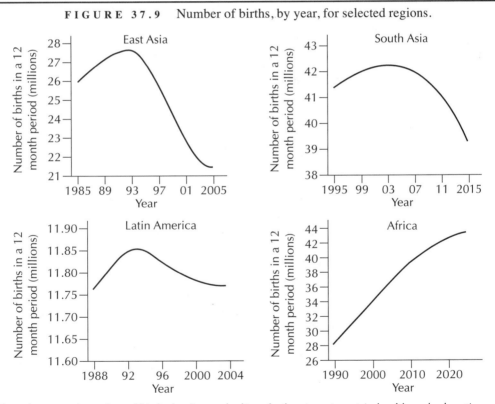

FIGURE 37.9   Number of births, by year, for selected regions.

When the annual number of births begins to decline, further investment in health and education can be used to improve the quality of services and increase the *proportion* of people reached. All regions of the developing world, except Africa, are now at or near that point. In Africa, the rate of increase begins to slow only in 2010.

Source: World Population Prospects 1992, United Nations Population Division, New York.

mond Professor of Political Economy at the University of Oxford:

> The question must also be raised . . . as to whether a poor country should have to wait many decades before it has enough resources generated by economic growth to undertake ambitious public programmes of health care and education. It is not illegitimate to wonder whether a poor country can "afford" to spend so much on health and education.
>
> In answering this question we must not only note the empirical reality that many poor countries—such as Sri Lanka, China, Costa Rica, the Indian state of Kerala, and others—have done precisely that with much success, but also understand the general fact that delivering public health care and basic educational facilities is enormously cheaper in a poor country than in a rich one. This is because both health and education are labour-intensive activities and this makes them much cheaper in poor countries because of lower wages. Thus, even though a poor country is tremendously constrained in expending money on health and education because of general poverty, the money needed to pay for these services is also significantly less when a country is still quite poor.[25]

Demographic Change

Lastly, the great demographic change taking place in our times also adds its weight to the idea that the time is now right for a determined effort to overcome the worst aspects of poverty.

Fertility rates have fallen in almost every region of the world. In Latin America, the annual number of births has now begun to decline; in Asia, births will reach a peak in the mid-1990s and begin to fall; even in South Asia, a peak will be reached within a decade (Figure 37.9). Only in Africa will the annual number of births continue to rise until well into the next century.[26] A turning point in the modern era will therefore soon be reached. For once the annual number of births is stable or declining, any further investment in such services as health and education can be used to improve the quality of the services offered and to increase the proportion of people reached. In other words, the task of providing such services will no longer be a case of "running to stand still," and the goal of meeting basic human needs will no longer be a target that is forever moving away.

Twenty Percent for Basics

As the end of the twentieth century approaches, there is therefore an accumulation of reasons for believing that ending the worst aspects of poverty is an idea whose time may finally have come.

New strategies and low-cost technologies are available. Specific goals which reflect this potential have been agreed upon. The commitment to those goals bears the signatures of more presidents and prime ministers than any other document in history. The plans for achieving them have been or are being drawn up in most nations. And there is a growing acceptance of the idea that targeting some of these worst effects of poverty, particularly as they affect children, is an essential part of long-term development strategy.

In the wider world, the ground being gained by democratic systems means that the long-starved concerns of the poor may begin to put on political weight; providing basic social services for poor families with the vote is, after all, good politics. At the same time, economic reforms may also create the kind of environment in which a new effort to meet basic human needs would have a much greater chance of success. Meanwhile, the powerful tide of demographic change is also beginning to turn.

For all of these reasons, a new potential now exists for moving toward a world in which the basic human needs of almost every man, woman, and child are met. But it is equally clear that this attempt will not gather the necessary momentum unless the political commitment is sustained and the extra resources begin to be made available.

If advantage is to be taken of the political commitments that have been made, and of the national programs of action that have been drawn up, then those extra resources must begin to become available in the next twelve months to two years.

Some nations have already begun the process of finding the necessary funds from their own resources. In most cases, this is almost certainly going to mean an increase in the proportion of government expenditures allocated to nutrition, primary health care, clean water, safe sanitation, basic education, and family planning services. UNICEF strongly supports the United Nations Development Programme's suggestion that at least 20 percent of government spending should be allocated to these direct methods of meeting priority human needs.[27] If implemented, such a restructuring of government budgets would enable the developing nations as a whole to find several times the $25 billion a year that is needed to achieve the agreed goals.

In practice, such a shift in present patterns of resource allocation will not be easy to bring about. All governments, however well intentioned, have limited room for maneuver as political pressures push them against the walls of economic constraint. Currently, the governments of the developing world as a whole are spending over one-third of their combined budgets on the repayment of debt and on the financing of the military.[28] Such distortions do not happen by accident. And the internal and external forces which have shaped such spending patterns will not disappear overnight. Nor will the pressure to devote disproportionate amounts of public resources to more advanced and more expensive health and education services for the wealthier and more influential sections of society.

But even in the face of all such pressures, it should be possible to allocate 20 percent of government spending to the task of helping the poor meet their needs for food, water, sanitation, basic health care, family planning, and the education of their children.

Restructuring Aid

There remains the question of whether the industrialized nations are prepared to assist in this effort. Following the commitment made at the World Summit for Children, every developing country which draws up a detailed program of action for reaching the agreed goals — no matter what label is attached to the process — should now be able to expect that some proportion of the cost will be met by increased or reallocated aid. That proportion will vary from less than a quarter in East Asia and Latin America, to between a quarter and a half in South Asia, and up to two-thirds in the least developed countries and sub-Saharan Africa. For the developing world as a whole, the additional external assistance required will be in the region of an additional $8 billion a year.

So far there is no significant sign that the industrialized nations will make additional resources available on this scale. Aid continues to stagnate. And there have been few serious attempts to restructure existing aid allocations. Government-to-government assistance cannot easily shuffle off the coil of foreign policy considerations, economic vested interests, and historical associations, which means that the richest 40 percent of the developing world's population receives twice as much aid per head as the poorest 40 percent,[29] and that the nations which account for two-thirds of the world's child deaths receive only one-quarter of the world's aid. More positively, it would be a mistake to imply that all the aid not used for directly meeting basic human needs is irrelevant to this cause. Roads also help to meet basic needs. Jobs even more so.

But again, it is not too much to expect that 20 percent of development aid should be allocated to directly helping people to meet their most basic needs for food, water, health care, family planning, and primary education. Such a restructuring of aid expenditures would, on its own, make available the extra $8 billion a year required. It would be an increase in the kind of aid that the majority of people in the developing world want to receive, and in the kind of aid that the majority of people in the industrialized world want to give. And it is an increase which should now be offered to any developing country that commits itself to a program of action to meet basic human needs.

The same commitment must also be expected from the multilateral organizations which currently disburse approximately $12 billion a year. In particular, the United Nations could play an increasingly central role in international efforts to achieve agreed social goals and to lay a new foundation for human development in the twenty-first century. And it is a role that could also provide a focus for the impending reform of the United Nations system and lead to the kind of changes which would make sense to, and meet with the approval of, a worldwide public.

The Fading Excuse

Above all, this is an opportunity that must not be allowed to evaporate into the perennial atmosphere of pessimism about the prospects for world development. The necessary task of drawing attention to human needs has unfortunately given rise to the popular impression that the developing world is a stage upon which no light falls and only tragedy is enacted. But the fact is that, for all the setbacks, more progress has been made in the last fifty years than in the previous two thousand. Since the end of the Second World War, average real incomes in the developing world have more than doubled; infant and child death rates have been more than halved; average life expectancy has increased by about a third; the proportion of the developing world's children starting school has risen from less than half to more than three-quarters (despite a doubling of population); and the percentage of rural families with access to safe water has risen from less than 10 percent to almost 60 percent. Yet even these extraordinary statistics cannot capture the true dimensions of the change that has occurred in only a few decades. Much of the world has also freed itself from colonialism, brought apartheid in all its forms to the edge of extinction, and largely freed itself from the iron grip of fascist and totalitarian regimes. And underlying all of these

changes is the slow and even more fundamental change from a world organized almost exclusively for the benefit of a privileged 10 or 20 percent, in almost all societies, to a world in which the needs and the rights of all people are increasingly recognized. Only a few decades ago, it did not seem a matter of great concern that the poor majority had no right to vote, no freedom of expression or religion, no right to due process of law, or that their children were not educated or immunized and received little or no benefit from advances in hygiene and health care. In many nations, it even seemed natural that the children of the poor could be sold or bonded or made to work fourteen hours a day in field or mine or factory. And almost exactly fifty years ago, when more than a million people starved in the Bengal famine, they died in a world which raised no murmur of protest.[30]

Seen from this longer perspective, the fact that two-thirds of the world's people now have the right to vote, or that 80 percent of the world's infants are immunized, or that there is such a thing as a worldwide Convention on the Rights of the Child, is a symptom of a remarkable change. And in the face of such progress, pessimism is a sign less of sagacity than of cynicism. In the decade ahead, a clear opportunity exists to make the breakthrough against what might be called the last great obscenity — the needless malnutrition, disease, and illiteracy that still cast a shadow over the lives, and the futures, of the poorest quarter of the world's children.

It is almost unthinkable that the opportunity to reach these basic social goals should be missed because the political commitment is lacking or because the developing world and the donor nations cannot, together, find an extra $25 billion a year. The technologies and strategies are available and affordable. The outreach and communications capacity are there to be mobilized. The political commitments have been made. And the broader context of political, economic, and demographic change is probably as favorable at this time as it is ever likely to be. The difficulties are enormous. But they shrink beside the difficulties that can be and have been overcome in the course of all the many great achievements of our times.

In the industrialized world, neither recession nor competing claims on resources can justify the failure to find the extra $8 billion a year which would be required to support the developing nations that decide to make meeting basic social goals into a national priority.

In the developing world, underdevelopment is a fast-fading excuse for failure to make that commitment and to begin mobilizing the necessary financial and human resources.

It is time that the challenge replaced excuse. If today's obvious and affordable steps are not taken to protect the lives and the health and the normal growth of many millions of young children, then this will have less to do with the lack of economic capacity than with the fact that the children concerned are almost exclusively the sons and daughters of the poor—of those who lack not only purchasing power but also political influence and media attention. And if the resources are not to be made available, if the overcoming of the worse aspects of poverty, malnutrition, illiteracy, and disease is not to be achieved in the years ahead, then let it now be clear that this is not because it is not a possibility but because it is not a priority.

Appendix
Panel 1
Pneumonia: 3.5 Million Deaths

Respiratory infections account for more than a quarter of all illnesses and deaths among the children of the developing world. They are also responsible for 30 to 60 percent of all visits to doctors and clinics and for about a third of all hospital admissions. The toll on both health and health services is enormous; and it is levied on almost every poor country.

In over 90 percent of cases, the problem is the common cold, for which there is no known cure. But this does not prevent up to one-third of the developing world's budgets for drugs and medicines being swallowed up in the prescribing of unnecessary antibiotics. Nor does it prevent families worldwide from spending an estimated $3 billion a year on the more than two thousand cough and cold remedies now on the market.

Meanwhile, a small minority of respiratory infections, probably only 2 or 3 percent, strike at the tissue of the child's lung. The result is pneumonia, and without an antibiotic there is a 10 to 20 percent risk that the child will die within days. But because the victims are usually children from the poorest families, without easy access to doctors and hospitals, antibiotics are often not available at all, or not available in time. The result is that approximately 3.5 million children die each year.

In 80 to 90 percent of cases, the problem is bacterial pneumonia, which can be controlled by a course of antibiotics, usually cotrimoxazole, lasting for five days and costing twenty-five cents. But if the scientific problems are relatively simple, the logistical problems are not. How can the right care and the right drugs be made available to the right children at the right time?

In recent years, a clear answer to this question has been tested and found to work. Parents can be educated to recognize the first danger signs, and community health workers can be trained to diagnose pneumonia, prescribe on-the-spot antibiotics, and recognize the small minority of emergency cases that need to be urgently transferred to the nearest hospital.

In many countries, the medical profession is still reluctant to allow health workers to prescribe drugs. But a recent study by WHO has concluded: "The answer to one question is clear: this strategy . . . has been effective. The reduced mortality rates speak for themselves. Studies of ARI (acute respiratory infections) interventions in Bangladesh, India, Indonesia, Nepal, Pakistan, the Philippines and Tanzania show reductions in pneumonia mortality ranging from 25 to 67 percent."

Over sixty developing countries now have national programs to try to put the new strategy into effect. The aim is to reduce deaths from pneumonia by at least one-third in this decade.

In addition, about 20 percent of acute respiratory infections could still be prevented by immunization. Over a third of a million children die each year from whooping cough, and hundreds of thousands succumb to the pneumonia that frequently follows an attack of measles.[31] Other known risk factors are low birth weight and malnutrition. Research in Brazil and Peru has shown that the risk increases by between three and five times if children are bottle fed. And from Indonesia has come the finding that risks are doubled by even mild vitamin A deficiency (Panel 3). Overcrowding and a smoky environment (including wood smoke and cigarette smoke) also increase the likelihood of respiratory infections.

Panel 2
Mexico: From Words to Deeds

Some fifty nations have now drawn up national programs of action (NPAs) aimed at reaching the targets agreed at the World Summit for Children. Those targets, to be reached by the year 2000, include a halving of child malnutrition, control of the major childhood diseases, a one-third reduction in under-five death rates, a halving of maternal mortality, the provision of safe water to all communities, the universal availability of family planning services, and a basic education for all children.

In Latin America, almost all countries have completed NPAs. Mexico, in particular, has made a determined start; a detailed NPA has been drawn up, and its progress is being monitored every six months under the personal chairmanship of President Carlos Salinas de Gortari. The main points:

- As the debt crisis has eased and the country has returned to economic growth, the deep cuts in social spending of the 1980s are being reversed. As a percentage of GDP, social spending has risen from 6.4 to 9 percent in the first two years of the 1990s.

- An ambitious immunization program has already reached more than 90 percent of the country's 11 million under-fives. More than 1,000 rural clinics have been built. Approximately 1,300 health centres and 140 hospitals have been refurbished. And specific programs have been launched to control two of the biggest threats to the life and health of Mexico's children—diarrheal disease and acute respiratory infections.

- To reduce malnutrition, a growth-monitoring program has begun with the aim of reaching all preschool children. Food supplements are beginning to be made available to children from families where low income and lack of food is the main cause of malnutrition (in many cases, the main cause is frequent illness).

- The baby-friendly hospital initiative has moved ahead rapidly, and thirty maternity units or hospitals have so far been awarded "baby-friendly" status. The practice of free distribution of commercial infant formulas, common in many countries of the developing world, has been suspended, and a training program is under way to explain the advantages of breast-feeding to both nursing staff and general public.

- Following the cuts made in the 1980s, the last four years have seen a 70 percent increase in the resources earmarked for education. As a result of the new National Agreement on the Modernization of Basic Education, a special effort is being made to reduce educational disparities. In the country's ten poorest states, support has been provided to 1,000 schools, including 270,000 financial "scholarships" designed to stop children from dropping out of school because their families are too poor to keep them there. With the support of the World Bank, and the cooperation of UNDP, UNESCO, and UNICEF, the government has also begun a program of non-formal initial education for 1.2 million children.

- Over 1 million copies of *Facts for Life* have been published, and 600,000 are now in use in the educational system. The *Facts for Life* booklet, jointly published by UNICEF, UNESCO, UNFPA, and WHO, sets out today's essential child health knowledge on such subjects as timing births, safe motherhood, breast-feeding, child growth, immunization, diarrhea, coughs and colds, home hygiene, malaria, AIDS, and child development.

- A program for the Protection of Street Children has begun in Mexico City and in thirty-one states.

- Government spending on clean water supplies has more than doubled to over $1 billion, and the number of people served has increased by 8 million since 1990.

Panel 3
Vitamin A: Suspicion Confirmed

The 1986 *State of the World's Children* report drew attention to a startling new proposal for protecting the lives and the health of many millions of children. New research in Indonesia had indicated that the lack of vitamin A might be responsible for a large proportion of illnesses and deaths among the under-fives. The findings of the study were summed up by the principal investigator, Dr. Alfred Sommer: "We know that five to ten million children develop mild xerophthalmia, hence vitamin A deficiency, every year. Given these figures, and the increased risk of death among children with mild, and probably even with subclinical vitamin A deficiency, it may account for as much as 20–30 per cent of all pre-school-age deaths in developing countries."

It had long been known that a quarter of a million children were going blind each year from the lack of this particular vitamin. But since the announcement of the controversial findings from Indonesia, other investigations in other parts of the world have sought to expose the deeper relationship between vitamin A and the health and survival of young children. "If the findings are confirmed," said a 1990 report by the Commission on Health Research, "the strategic implications would be astounding."

Early in 1992, thirty experts and researchers met in Bellagio, Italy, to consider all the studies undertaken so far and to pull together conclusions.

Overall, the group confirmed that even mild vitamin A deficiency substantially increases the death rate among children between the age of six months and six years. In particular, vitamin A deficiency significantly increases the severity and risk of the three main health threats facing children in the developing world—diarrheal diseases, measles, and pneumonia. It was also confirmed that these findings hold good even when the lack of vitamin A is so mild that it does not show up in the eyesight problems which until now have been the accepted indicator of vitamin A deficiency. "Therefore," says the group's report, "the definition of vitamin A deficiency for public health purposes must be revised and made more sensitive to milder degrees of deficiency."

Turning to the question of whether giving vitamin A supplements to children can reverse the risks, the Bellagio group considered the results of six separate investigations in the last decade—two each in India, Indonesia, and Nepal. The studies, involving a total of more than 100,000 children, confirm that giving children extra vitamin A can reduce child deaths by about one-third in many areas of the developing world.

There are three main ways of tackling the problem. Parents can be educated about the importance of vitamin A in their children's diet (plenty of green leafy vegetables). Or foods that everybody eats—such as sugar or salt— can have vitamin A added to them at the point of processing. Or vitamin A capsules can be given every six months to young children at risk. All of these strategies are inexpensive. Vitamin A capsules, for example, cost as little as five cents each. And with vaccines now regularly reaching over 80 percent of the world's infants, it should be possible to add vitamin A to immunization services.

There is no longer any reason to wait. Vitamin A supplements have taken their place alongside the handful of other low-cost strategies that could now significantly reduce illness and death among the children of the developing world.

Panel 4
Immunization: Sustaining Success

By September 1991, the World Health Organization and UNICEF were able to report to the UN Secretary-General that the goal of immunizing 80 percent of the world's children had been achieved. The result of this decade-long effort, involving many thousands of individuals and organizations worldwide, is that over 3 million child deaths and over 400,000 cases of paralytic polio are now being prevented each year.

The intense drive to reach the goal by the end of 1990 led many to question whether such an effort was sustainable and whether it would distract from the task of building more comprehensive systems of primary health care. Two years after the achievement of the goal, it is possible to begin answering those questions.

Some fall-off from the unprecedented levels of immunization achieved by the target date—the end of 1990—was to be expected. But the figures for the end of 1991 show that the fall has been slight—approximately 3 percent in the developing world as a whole. One hundred and one developing countries maintained or increased immunization levels in 1991, and twenty-eight countries recorded a fall in coverage.

In Asia, there has been little or no fall-off. Bangladesh has overcome enormous odds in raising immunization coverage from almost zero in 1980 to 62 percent in 1990 and has maintained coverage at 60 percent in 1991 despite every conceivable difficulty. Even Vietnam, which has had difficulties in obtaining enough vaccine, was able to maintain coverage.

In the Middle East and North Africa, almost all countries have sustained their levels of immunization coverage despite the disruption caused by the Gulf War.

In the Americas, coverage has remained stable with the important exceptions of Brazil and Venezuela, which recorded lower immunization rates in 1991 than in 1990. Nonetheless, the polio eradication campaign in the region is on the verge of victory, with not a single case of paralytic polio being recorded in the last twelve months.

It is in sub-Saharan Africa that the steepest decline has occurred. Overall, the immunization level fell by approximately 10 percent in 1991, with coverage falling below 50 percent for polio, measles, and DPT. Most of this decline is accounted for by the 1991 figures from Cameroon, the Central African Republic, Ethiopia, Ghana, Mozambique, Nigeria, and Sierra Leone, where health systems are generally weaker or have been disrupted by social and political unrest. Countries with stronger health systems such as Botswana, Burundi, Cape Verde, the Gambia, Namibia, and Rwanda have maintained high levels of coverage and are witnessing dramatic declines in the incidence of disease.

As important as the achievement of the immunization target itself is the setting up of an outreach system capable of delivering vaccines to over 100 million children on four or five separate occasions in their first year of life. In most countries, that system is now being used for other essential services. In Asia, in particular, the immunization network is being used to combat diarrheal diseases (Panel 5), acute respiratory infections (Panel 1), and vitamin A deficiency (Panel 3). India is using the system for its safe motherhood initiative, and Bangladesh has begun using immunization outreach services to strengthen family planning services.

Rather than waiting behind clinic doors to serve a minority, many health services have been inspired by the idea of using all available means to reach out into the community to establish regular, ordered contact with an entire population. In the long run, that may prove to be the most fundamental change brought about by the immunization effort of the 1980s.

Panel 5
Diarrheal Diseases: A Strategy
for the Nineties

Ten years ago, diarrheal disease was the biggest killer of the world's children, claiming almost 4 million young lives each year. Most of the victims died of dehydration. And although a cheap and simple method of preventing and treating dehydration had been available for many years, it was known to few outside the scientific community.

Today, thanks to a decade of promotion, some form of oral rehydration therapy (ORT) is known and used by approximately one family in three in the developing world. The result is the saving of approximately 1 million lives each year and the demotion of diarrheal disease to second place among the causes of child death.

This success in the last decade has reshaped the challenge for the next. ORT still needs to be promoted; a majority of the developing world's families still do not use the technique; and dehydration still causes over 1.5 million deaths a year. But it is becoming more and more clear that the campaign against diarrheal diseases must now be broadened.

The rapid reduction in dehydration deaths brought about by ORT means that an increasing proportion of the remaining deaths are caused by dysentery and persistent diarrhea, which normally require appropriate antibiotic treatment in addition to ORT. Ten years ago,

two-thirds of all diarrhea-related deaths were caused by dehydration; today that proportion has fallen to less than half. At the same time there is a growing realization that diarrheal disease is also a major cause—perhaps even the major cause—of malnutrition among the developing world's children. Study after study has shown that frequent diarrheal disease stunts the child's normal growth by reducing the appetite, inhibiting the absorption of food, burning up calories in fever, and draining away nutrients from the body.

A strategy for the 1990s must therefore give new priority to clean water and safe sanitation and to educating parents about preventing diarrheal diseases and minimizing the impact on their children's health and growth. Today's knowledge makes prevention possible on a large scale and at a low cost. The principal means are: breast-feeding; immunizing against measles; using a latrine; keeping food and water clean; and washing hands before touching food. The main ways of preventing diarrhea from causing malnutrition are continued feeding throughout the illness (especially breast-feeding) and giving the child an extra meal a day for at least a week after the illness is over. In addition to knowing about the importance of food and fluids, all parents should know that trained help is needed if there is blood in the child's stool or if the diarrhea persists or is more serious than usual.

Reducing child deaths by one-third and child malnutrition by half were two of the most important targets agreed on by the world's leaders at the 1990 World Summit for Children. Neither target can be achieved without a widening of the battle against diarrheal diseases and a reduction in the toll they take on both the lives and the normal growth of many millions of the world's children.

Notes

*   From *The State of the World's Children 1993*, by James P. Grant for UNICEF (New York: Oxford Press for UNICEF, 1993), 1–23, by per-

mission of the author and UNICEF. Copyright 1993 by UNICEF.

1. World Bank. *World Development Report 1992.* Washington, D.C.: World Bank, 1992, p. 26.

2. United Nations Children's Fund. *Children and Development in the 1990s: A UNICEF Sourcebook.* New York: UNICEF, 1990.

3. All figures from *The Economist,* 1992.

4. Derived from United Nations Development Programme, *Human Development Report 1991.* New York: UNDP, 1991, p. 41, Table 3.1.

5. United Nations Children's Fund. *Patterns of Government Expenditure in Developing Countries During the 1980s—The Impact on Social Services,* Paper No. 18, UNICEF, International Child Development Centre, Florence, Innocenti Economic Policy Series, 1991.

6. United Nations Development Programme. *Human Development Report 1992.* New York: UNDP, 1992, p. 43, Table 3.15.

7. Kanda, Chiyo, "Trends in Bilateral Official Resource Flows to Social Sectors 1985–1988." New York: UNICEF, 1990.

8. UNDP. *Human Development Report 1992,* p. 43, Table 3.14. United Nations, "Implementation of General Assembly Resolution 45/217 on the World Summit for Children." Report of the Secretary-General to the 47th Session of the General Assembly, 17 June 1992, A/47/264, United Nations, New York.

9. Development Center for the Organisation for Economic Co-operation and Development. *Development Co-operation 1991.* Paris: OECD, 1991, Table 14.

10. "The Maecenas Touch," p. 9 of "A Survey of the Sports Business." *The Economist,* July 25, 1992.

11. Mehrotra, Santosh, "Immunization Coverage in an Economically Unfavourable Environment," UNICEF Planning Office, UNICEF, New York, 1992.

12. "Ending Hidden Hunger," A Policy Conference on Micronutrient Malnutrition, Montreal, Canada, October 10–12, 1991, Sponsored by the Canadian Agency for International Development, the Food and Agriculture Organization of the United Nations, the United Nations Children's Fund, the United Nations Development Programme, the United States Agency for International Development, the World Bank, and the World Health Organization.

13. Haxton, David P., "Defeating Iodine Deficiency with a Grain of Salt," *First Call for Children,* No. 2. New York: UNICEF, April–June 1992, pp. 8–9.

14. Donaldson, Lloyd A., "Rural Water and Health: The Challenge to Water and Sanitation Sector Professionals," *WATERfront,* No. 1. New York: UNICEF, February 1992, p. 3.

15. The figures for the number of schools and pupils in the BRAC scheme are estimates for December 1992 provided in August 1992 by the Senior Programme Coordinator, UNICEF Dhaka. The figure of $18 per child is taken from *Together for Education,* Dhaka, Bangladesh, BRAC, February 1992. See also Lowell, Catherine H., *Breaking the Cycle of Poverty—The BRAC Strategy,* Kumarian Press, 1992.

16. Yambi, O. and Mlolwa, R., *Improving Nutrition in Tanzania in the 1980s: The Iringa Experience,* Innocenti Occasional Papers No. 25, International Child Development Centre. Florence: UNICEF, March 1992. Shekar, M., *The Tamil Nadu Integrated Nutrition Project: A Review,* Cornell Food and Nutritional Policy Program Report, November 1991.

17. United Nations, "Implementation of General Assembly Resolution 45/217 on the World Summit for Children."

18. These examples provided by the Nutrition Cluster and the Water and Environmental Sanitation Section of UNICEF, New York.

19. Mehrotra, 1992.

20. McKee, Neill, "Social Mobilization: Lessons from Bangladesh," *First Call for Children,* No. 2. New York: UNICEF, April–June 1992, pp. 8–9.

21. For a full discussion of growth monitoring and promotion, see "Going for Growth," *The State of the World's Children 1987.* New York: UNICEF, 1986, pp. 64–80.

22. ul Huq, Mujibul (ed.), *Near Miracle in Bangladesh.* Dhaka: University Press Ltd., 1991, Foreword.

23. Gill, Walt, "CHWs: Are National Programmes in Crisis?" *Health Policy and Planning,* Vol. 3, No. 1, 1988, pp. 1–21.

24. "Let Them Eat Guns," *The Economist,* November 2, 1991, p. 99.

25. Sen, Amartya, "Public Action to Remedy Hunger," Fourth Annual Arturo Tanco Memor-

ial Lecture, Queen Elizabeth II Conference Centre, London, 2 August 1990.

26. United Nations Population Division. *World Population Prospects 1992.* New York: United Nations, 1992. Hill, Kenneth, "Babies of the Future: Setting the Scene." Baltimore: School of Hygiene and Public Health, Johns Hopkins University, in press.

27. UNDP. *Human Development Report 1992,* p. 89.

28. United Nations Children's Fund. *Patterns of Government Expenditure in Developing Coun-tries During the 1980s.* New York: UNICEF, World Bank, *World Debt Tables 1991–92.* Washington, D.C.: World Bank, 1992.

29. UNDP. *Human Development Report 1992,* p. 44.

30. Sen, Amartya, *Poverty and Famines: An Essay on Entitlement and Deprivation.* Oxford: Oxford University Press, 1981.

31. Measles vaccination, which is normally given at the age of nine months, could not prevent the 50 percent of pneumonia deaths which occur before that age.

Attitudes and Values

Comparative studies of attitudes and values have grown substantially since the 1950s and 1960s, when technology began to make large-scale survey studies practical. Along with the needed survey "infrastructure," the necessary know-how soon followed as dozens of survey organizations sprang up not only in academia but also as profit-making enterprises. Suddenly everyone wanted to know what everyone else's attitudes and values were, some just to sell more soap; others to advance the fortunes of their political, economic, and social policies; and some just to advance knowledge about human affairs.

Today, in the 1990s, the funding may not always be sufficient to finance large-scale cross-national studies, but the computers and statistical methods are in place. Perhaps inevitably, these relatively new capabilities have lent themselves to the study of an extraordinarily diverse number of attitudes and values in many combinations of nations and subpopulations. To name just one of these subjects, several researchers have turned their attention to exploring "national character," that is, the way people in given nations think or, in popular parlance, "what makes them tick."

In our first selection, Alex Inkeles describes a major cross-national study assessing individuals' attitudes, values, and behaviors regarding the roles typical of a modern industrial society. By administering a complex questionnaire to six thousand young men in six countries of differing development levels, the study explored the question: Is there a modern man, and if so, what causes him to be such? The answer was yes, one can distinguish a set of attitudes and values that form a clear-cut syndrome of individual modernity that has much the same character in all the countries studied. One of the principal sources making men modern is shown to be education. Despite great cultural variation the study found "striking stability in education, factory experience and urbanism vis-à-vis their impact on individual modernization."

Our next selection, by Masamichi Sasaki and Tatsuzo Suzuki, used a new Bayesian cohort analysis to test the secularization thesis by studying data on religious commitment in the United States, Holland, and Japan. Despite notably different attitudes toward religion and God held in Japan as against the United States and Holland, the authors develop theoretical and methodological approaches that make possible meaningful cross-national retrospective comparison of these very subjective attitudes. They found that the secularization thesis, while supported in some instances, is not a universal global phenomenon.

Our final selection is by Ronald Inglehart. In this paper Inglehart revisits his extraordinarily widely cited original work on "postmaterialism" and asks what has occurred during the economically insecure decade of the 1970s. Drawing on data gleaned from about one hundred national surveys conducted during the 1970s, all of which asked questions about postmaterialism, he finds relative stability in the older groups but there is some evidence for backsliding, with fewer postmaterialists emerging in the youngest age-groups.

Making Men Modern: On the Causes and Consequences of Individual Change in Six Developing Countries*

Alex Inkeles†

Since 1962 a group of my colleagues and I at Harvard University have been working to understand the impact on the individual of his participation in the process of modernization. In the pursuit of this goal we devised a complex and comprehensive questionnaire touching on a wide variety of life situations and intended to measure a substantial segment of the range of attitudes, values, and behaviors we conceive as particularly relevant to understanding the individual's participation in the roles typical for a modern industrial society.[1] This questionnaire we then administered to some six thousand young men in six developing countries: Argentina, Chile, India, Israel, Nigeria, and East Pakistan. All three of the continents containing the overwhelming majority of developing nations are represented. The sampled countries cover the range from the newest nations which have only recently won their independence to those with a long history of self-governance; from those only now emerging from tribal life to those with ancient high cultures, and from those furthest removed from, to those most intimately linked to, the European cultural and industrial social order. The men interviewed were selected to represent points on a presumed continuum of exposure to modernizing influences, the main groups being the cultivator of the land still rooted in his traditional rural community; the migrant from the countryside just arrived in the city but not yet integrated into urban industrial life; the urban but nonindustrial worker still

pursuing a more or less traditional occupation, such as barber or carpenter, but now doing so in the urban environment even though outside the context of a modern large-scale organization; and the experienced industrial worker engaged in production using inanimate power and machinery within the context of a more or less modern productive enterprise. To these we have added sets of secondary school and university students who enjoy the presumed benefits of advanced education. Within and across these sample groups we exercised numerous controls in the selection of subjects and in the analysis of our data, both to understand the influence and to prevent the uncontrolled effects of sociocultural and biosocial factors such as age, sex, education, social origins, ethnic membership, past life experience, and the like.

Our interview included almost 300 entries. Some 160 of these elicited attitudes, values, opinions, and reports on the behavior of others and oneself, touching on almost every major aspect of daily life. The questionnaire included various tests of verbal ability, literacy, political information, intelligence, and psychic adjustment. In some cases it took four hours of interviewing to complete—a demanding experience for both interviewer and interviewee.

We completed our fieldwork near the end of 1964, and since that time have been engaged in processing and then later analyzing the very substantial body of data we collected. At this time our analysis is sufficiently far advanced so that we can discern the main outlines of some of the conclusions we must draw. To present these within the rigorous limits of the time and space currently allotted for scholarly communications requires imposing a telegraphic style and forgoing the presentation of detailed evidence to support my arguments. Each of my conclusions will address itself to one of the main issues to which our research was directed. Each issue is presented in the form of a question to which I will assay an answer. The four main issues dealt with here should not be understood as being the only ones to which we addressed ourselves; neither should it be assumed that our data provide answers only to these questions.

1. *How far is there an empirically identifiable modern man, and what are his outstanding characteristics?*—Many social scientists have a conception of the modern man, but few have submitted this conception to an empirical test to ascertain whether this type really exists in nature and to determine how often he appears on the scene. Important exceptions may be found in the work of Kahl (1968), Dawson (1967), and Doob (1967). We too have our model of the modern man, a complex one including three components which we refer to as the analytic, the topical, and the behavioral models, all of which, we assumed, might well tap one general underlying common dimension of individual modernity.[2]

We believe our evidence (presented in some detail in Smith and Inkeles 1966) shows unmistakably that there is a set of personal qualities which reliably cohere as a syndrome and which identify a type of man who may validly be described as fitting a reasonable theoretical conception of the modern man. Central to this syndrome are: (1) openness to new experience, both with people and with new ways of doing things such as attempting to control births; (2) the assertion of increasing independence from the authority of traditional figures like parents and priests and a shift of allegiance to leaders of government, public affairs, trade unions, cooperatives, and the like; (3) belief in the efficacy of science and medicine, and a

general abandonment of passivity and fatalism in the face of life's difficulties; and (4) ambition for oneself and one's children to achieve high occupational and educational goals. Men who manifest these characteristics (5) like people to be on time and show an interest in carefully planning their affairs in advance. It is also part of this syndrome to (6) show strong interest and take an active part in civic and community affairs and local politics; and (7) to strive energetically to keep up with the news, and within this effort to prefer news of national and international import over items dealing with sports, religion, or purely local affairs.

This syndrome of modernity coheres empirically to meet the generally accepted standards for scale construction with reliabilities ranging from .754 to .873 in the six countries.[3] Looking at the range of items which enters into the scale, one can see that it has a compelling face validity. In addition, the empirical outcome accords well with our original theoretical model and, indeed, with those of numerous other students of the problem. Evidently the modern man is not just a construct in the mind of sociological theorists. He exists and he can be identified with fair reliability within any population which can take our test.[4]

To discover that there are indeed men in the world who fit our model of a modern man is comforting, but perhaps not startling. After all, we can probably somewhere find an example of almost any kind of man one might care to delineate. It is important to emphasize, therefore, that men manifesting the syndrome of attitudes, values, and ways of acting we have designated "modern" are not freaks. They are not even rare. On the contrary, there are very substantial numbers of them in all six of the countries we have studied.[5]

Furthermore, we consider it to be of the utmost significance that the qualities which serve empirically to define a modern man do not differ substantially from occupation to occupation, or more critically, from culture to culture. In constructing our standard scales of modernity we utilized a pool of 119 attitude items.[6] In each country these items were then ranked according to the size of the item-to-scale correlation, and the subset of items having the highest correlations was then selected as defining the modern man for the given country. Using this "coherence" method to construct the national modernity scales, we might have found a totally different set of items defining the syndrome of modernity in each of our six national samples. Indeed, if we used only the twenty items ranking highest in the item-to-scale correlations for each country, we could theoretically have come out with six totally different syndromes, one for each country, no one overlapping in the least with any other. The actual outcome of the analysis was totally different. The probability that even one item would come out in the top fifty in all six countries is approximately five in a thousand. We actually had ten items which were in the top fifty in all six countries, sixteen more in the top fifty in five countries, thirteen more which were in this set in four of the six countries. The probability that the same thirty-nine items would by chance be in the top fifty in four of the six countries is so infinitesimal as to make our results notable indeed.

This means that what defines man as modern in one country also defines him as modern in another. It argues for the actual psychic unity of mankind in a structural sense and the potential psychic unity of mankind in the factual sense. In speaking of the unity of mankind in terms of psychic structure, I mean that the nature of the human personality, its inner "rules" of organization, is evidently basically similar everywhere. That is, the association of the elements or components of personality do not—and I think in substantial degree *cannot*—vary randomly or even relatively freely. There is evidently a system of inner, or what might be called structural, constraints in the organization of the human personality which increase the probability that those individuals—whatever their culture—who have certain personality traits will also more likely have others which "go with" some particular

basic personality system. So far as the future is concerned, moreover, I believe that this structural unity provides the essential basis for greater factual psychic unity of mankind. Such a factual unity, not merely of structure but of *content,* can be attained insofar as the forces which tend to shape men in syndromes such as that defining the modern man become more widely and uniformly diffused throughout the world. This point requires that we consider the second issue to which our research addressed itself.

2. *What are the influences which make a man modern? Can any significant changes be brought about in men who are already past the formative early years and have already reached adulthood as relatively traditional men?*—Education has often been identified as perhaps the most important of the influences moving men away from traditionalism toward modernity in developing countries. Our evidence does not challenge this well-established conclusion. Both in zero-order correlations[7] and in the more complex multivariate regression analysis, the amount of formal schooling a man has had emerges as the single most powerful variable in determining his score on our measures. On the average, for every additional year a man spent in school he gains somewhere between two and three additional points on a scale of modernity scored from zero to 100.

Our modernity test is not mainly a test of what is usually learned in school, such as geography or arithmetic, but is rather a test of attitudes and values touching on basic aspects of a man's orientation to nature, to time, to fate, to politics, to women, and to God. If attending school brings about such substantial changes in these fundamental personal orientations, the school must be teaching a good deal more than is apparent in its syllabus on reading, writing, arithmetic, and even geography. The school is evidently also an important training ground for inculcating values. It teaches ways of orienting oneself toward others, and of conducting oneself, which could have important bearing on the performance of one's adult roles in the structure of modern society. These effects of the school, I believe, reside not mainly in its formal, explicit, self-conscious pedagogic activity, but rather are inherent in the school as an *organization*. The modernizing effects follow not from the school's curriculum, but rather from its informal, implicit, and often unconscious program for dealing with its young charges.[8] The properties of the rational organization as a hidden pursuader—or, as I prefer to put it, as a silent and unobserved teacher—become most apparent when we consider the role of occupational experience in shaping the modern man.

We selected work in factories as the special focus of our attention in seeking to assess the effects of occupational experience in reshaping individuals according to the model of the modern man. Just as we view the school as communicating lessons beyond reading and arithmetic, so we thought of the factory as training men in more than the minimal lessons of technology and the skills necessary to industrial production. We conceived of the factory as an organization serving as a general school in attitudes, values, and ways of behaving which are more adaptive for life in a modern society. We reasoned that work in a factory should increase a man's sense of efficacy, make him less fearful of innovation, and impress on him the value of education as a general qualification for competence and advancement. Furthermore, we assumed that in subtle ways work in a factory might even deepen a man's mastery of arithmetic and broaden his knowledge of geography without the benefit of the formal lessons usually presented in the classroom. Indeed, the slogan for our project became, "The factory can be a school—a school for modernization."

Although our most sanguine hopes for the educational effects of the factory were not wholly fulfilled, the nature of a man's occupational experience does emerge as one of the strongest of the many types of variables we tested and is a quite respectable competitor to education in explaining a person's modernity. The correlation between time spent in factories and individual modernization scores is generally about .20.[9] With the effects of education controlled, the factory workers generally score eight to ten points higher on the modernization scale than do the cultivators.[10] There is little reason to interpret this difference as due to selection effects since separate controls show that new workers are not self- or preselected from the village on grounds of already being "modern" in personality or attitude. Nevertheless, we can apply a really stringent test by making our comparisons exclusively within the industrial labor force, pitting men with few years of industrial experience against those with many, for example, five or more. When this is done, factory experience continues to show a substantial impact on individual modernization, the gain generally being about one point per year on the overall measure of modernization (OM).

It is notable that even when we restrict ourselves to tests of verbal fluency and to tests of geographical and political information, the more experienced workers show comparable advantages over the less experienced. To choose but one of many available examples, in Chile among men of rural origin and low education (one to five years)—and therefore suffering a double disadvantage in background—the proportion who could correctly locate Moscow as being the Soviet Russian capital rose from a mere 8 percent among the newly recruited industrial workers to 39 percent among those with middle experience and to 52 percent among the men who had eight years or more in the factory. Even among those with the double advantage of higher education (six to seven years) and urban origins, the proportion correctly identifying Moscow decidedly rose along with increasing industrial experience, the percentages being 68, 81, and 92 for the three levels of industrial experience, respectively. Summary evidence from all six countries is presented in Table 38.1. It should be clear from these data that the factory is serving as a school even in those subjects generally considered the exclusive preserve of the classroom.[11]

To cite these modernizing effects of the factory is not to minimize the greater absolute impact of schooling. Using a gross occupational categorization which pits cultivators against industrial workers, we find that the classroom still leads the workshop as a school of modernization in the ratio of 3:2. Using the stricter test which utilizes factory workers only, grouped by length of industrial experience, it turns out that every additional year in school produces three times as much increment in one's modernization score as does a year in the factory, that is, the ratio goes to 3:1. The school seems clearly to be the more efficient training ground for individual modernization. Nevertheless, we should keep in mind that the school has the pupil full-time, and it produces no incidental by-products other than its pupils. By contrast, the main business of the factory is to manufacture goods, and the changes it brings about in men—not insubstantial, as we have seen—are produced at virtually zero marginal cost. These personality changes in men are therefore a kind of windfall profit to a society undergoing the modernization process. Indeed, on this basis we may quite legitimately reverse the thrust of the argument, no longer asking why the school does so much better than the factory, but rather demanding to know why the school, with its full-time control over the pupil's formal learning, does not perform a lot *better* than it does relative to the factory.

Our experience with the factory enables us to answer the secondary question posed for this section. Since men generally enter the factory as more or less matured adults, the effects observed to follow upon work in it clearly are late socialization effects. Our results indicate that substantial changes can be made in a man's personality or character, at least in the sense of attitudes, values, and basic orientations, long after what are usually considered the most important formative years. The experience of factory work is, of course, not the only form which this late socialization takes. It may come in the form of travel or migration, by exposure to the media of mass communication, or

through later life in the city for men who grew up in the countryside.[12] We therefore combined our explanatory variables into two main sets, one representing *early* socialization experiences—as in formal schooling—and the other reflecting *late* socialization experiences—as in one's adult occupation. We may observe (from Table 38.2) that the late socialization experiences stake out a very respectable place for themselves in the competition to account for the observed variance in individual modernization scores.[13] In five countries the set of late socialization variables explained as much or more of the variance in modernization scores as did the combined early socialization variables, each set explaining between one-fourth and one-third of the variance.

In India the early socialization variables were decidedly more powerful—accounting for 52 percent as against 31 percent of the variance explained by the late socialization variables. But in absolute terms, the late experiences are still doing very well.[14] All in all, we take this to be impressive evidence for the possibility of bringing about substantial and extensive changes in the postadolescent personality as a result of socialization in adult roles.

3. *Are there any behavioral consequences arising from the attitudinal modernization of the individual? Do modern men act differently from the traditional man?*—Many people who hear of our research into individual modernization respond to it by acknowledging that we may have discovered what modern man *says,* but they are more interested in knowing what he *does.* This view overlooks the fact that taking a stand on a value question is also an action, and one which is often a very significant one for the respondent.[15] Our critics' comment also tends implicitly to underestimate the importance of a climate of expressed opinion as an influence on the action of others. And it probably assumes too arbitrarily that men use speech mainly to mislead rather than to express their true intentions. Nevertheless, the question is a legitimate one, and we addressed ourselves to it in our research. Although this part of our

TABLE 38.1 Percentage of Low-Educated Industrial Workers Giving Correct Answers on Information Tests (by Country and Months of Factory Experience)

Question	Argentina		Chile		India		Israel		Nigeria		East Pakistan	
	3	90	2	96	2	72	3	84	3	48	1	48
Identify electrical apparatus†	37	63*	33	62***	44	76***	80	88	91	91	50	70**
Identify movie camera	60	69*	6	8	29	51**	84	88	68	70	9	37***
Cite three or more city problems	5	18	15	32***	0	1	24	25	30	22	52	52*
Identify international leader‡	26	67**	47	85***	1	31***	80	81	11	17	2	26**
Identify local leader	33	51	27	81***	15	52***	67	92	70	78	52	79*
Identify Moscow	36	60*	17	67***	1	16***	86	86	11	17	2	2
Name three or more newspapers§	12	21	81	92	6	28**	75	61	81	91	20	44**
Approximate N cases	40	70	90	130	75	130	25	100	60	25	65	120

Note: Data for high education groups on these seven questions in each country provide an additional 42 tests of which 33 were in accord with the conclusion that men with more factory experience score higher on information tests, 7 were inconclusive, and 2 contradictory.

*t-test score significant at the .05 level.
**Significance at the .01 level.
***Significance at the .001 level or better.

†In Pakistan, India, and Nigeria a picture of a radio was shown; in Argentina, Chile, and Israel, a picture of a tape recorder was used instead.
‡Respondents were asked to identify Lyndon Johnson in Chile, Argentina, and Israel; John F. Kennedy in Pakistan and India; Charles de Gaulle in Nigeria.
§In Argentina, "name books" was substituted for "name newspapers."

TABLE 38.2   Variance in Scores of Individual Modernization (OM-3) Accounted for by Early and Late Socialization Influences in Six Developing Countries (%)

Variable	Argentina	Chile	India	Israel	Nigeria	Pakistan
Early socialization	28.8	26.0	52.4	22.1	23.0	22.2
Late socialization	31.6	34.4	31.4	22.4	28.2	28.3

analysis is least advanced, we can offer some tentative conclusions on the basis of preliminary analysis.

We have the definite impression that the men we delineate as modern not only *talk* differently, they *act* differently. To explore this relationship we constructed a scale of modernization based exclusively on attitudinal questions, rigorously excluding those dealing with action rather than belief or feeling.[16] This measure of attitudinal modernity we then related to the behavioral measures in our survey. In all six countries we found action intimately related to attitude. At any given educational level, the man who was rated as modern on the attitudinal measure was also more likely to have joined voluntary organizations, to receive news from newspapers every day, to have talked to or written to an official about some public issue, and to have discussed politics with his wife. In many cases the proportion who claimed to have taken those actions was twice and even three times greater among those at the top as compared with those at the bottom of the scale of attitudinal modernity. Table 38.3 presents the relevant evidence. We should note, furthermore, that the items included in Table 38.3 are illustrative of a larger group of about thirty individual questions and a dozen scales selected on theoretical grounds as appropriate tests of the relation between expressed attitudes and reported behavior. The items used for illustration were not arbitrarily selected as the only ones supporting our assumptions.[17]

The particular behaviors we cited above are all "self-reported." The question inevitably arises as to whether then we are not merely testing attitudinal consistency—or merely consistency in response—rather than any strict correspondence between modernity of *attitude* and modernity of *behavior.* The answer is partly given by considering the relation of attitudinal modernity to our several tests of information. These questions did not deal with "mere" attitudes, but obliged the respondent to prove objectively whether he really knew something. Quite consistently the men who were more modern on the attitude measures validated their status as modern men by more often correctly identifying a movie camera, naming the office held by Nehru, and locating the city of Moscow. Men with the same education but with unequal modernity scores performed very differently on these tests, with those more modern in attitude scoring high on the tests of information two or more times as often as those classified as traditional in attitude. The details are summarized in the lower part of Table 38.3, which presents summary scale results.

We conducted a further and more exact check on the extent to which self-reported behavior is fact rather than fantasy by comparing what men claimed to do with objective tests of their actual performance. For example, we asked everyone whether or not he could read. Individuals certainly might have been tempted to exaggerate their qualifications. But later in the interview we administered a simple literacy test, asking our respondents to read a few lines from local newspaper stories we had graded for difficulty. In most settings less than 1 percent of the men who had claimed they could read failed the literacy test. They proved objectively to have been accurately and honestly reporting their reading ability. Similarly, men who claimed

T A B L E   3 8 . 3   Percentage of High-Educated Workers Engaging in Various Forms of Modern Behavior (by Country and Modernity† Score)

Form of Behavior	Argentina Low	Argentina High	Chile Low	Chile High	India Low	India High	Israel Low	Israel High	Nigeria Low	Nigeria High	East Pakistan Low	East Pakistan High
Joined two or more organizations	26	48	50	61	32	31	2	6	86	97	0	6
Voted often	54	54	44	57	60	65	76	86				
Talked politics with wife	40	57*	29	61***	74	80	46	72**	50	65	65	83*
Contacted official about public issue	2	9	4	17**	20	26	17	27	11	21	5	15
Read newspapers daily	40	77***	31	53**	32	61**	36	81	63	84***	35	42
High on geographic information scale	44	78***	23	60***	20	51***	29	75***	7	48***	9	53*
High on political information scale	22	56***	18	37***	22	65***	36	72***	20	48***	7	39**
High on consumer information scale	10	21**	7	39***	67	94*	29	53**	84	89	23	52***
High on opposites test	50	76	36	63***	59	86***	31	57***	59	71	47	78***
Approximate *N* cases‡	50	150	60	160	55	115	40	110	60	120	45	125

Note: In each country the total sample was divided at the median into a "high" and "low" educated group. The average number of years of education for the high group was: Argentina: 7.6; Chile: 6.6; India: 10.2; Israel: 8.6; Nigeria: 8.6; and Pakistan: 4.8.

t-test based on the extremes of the continuum on each form of behavior significant at the .05 level.

**Significance at the .01 level.

***Significance at the .001 level or better. All other *t*-tests of the relation were below the .01 level.

†The range of Overall Modernity Scores was split into "low"—bottom 25%, "middle"—middle 50%, and "high"—top 25% for each country's *entire* sample. Modernity scores are highly correlated with education. Since in this table only the high educated are represented, more men fall into the category of those with high as against low modernity scores.

‡*Ns* are approximate due to the disqualification of part of the sample on certain questions, e.g. those legally under age could not be expected to "vote often."

T A B L E 3 8 . 4 Percentage of Low-Educated Workers Whose Performance on a Test of Behavior Accords with Their Oral Claim (by Claim and Country)

Objective Behavior and Claim	Argentina	Chile	India	Israel	Nigeria	East Pakistan
Naming three newspapers among those who claim to read papers:						
Rarely/never	NA	73†***	13***	68	59***	38
		(356)	(582)	(28)	(71)	
Daily		98***	60***	90	85***	45
		(85)	(63)	(119)	(152)	
Correctly identifying international leader among those claiming mainly interested in:						
Other news	43**	59	8	79	7	4
	(299)	(414)	(668)	(216)	(276)	(459)
World news	73**	76	12	84	8	10
	(30)	(29)	(26)	(68)	(73)	(10)
Correctly identifying international leader who claim on total information media exposure they are:						
Low	14***	45***	1***	73	4*	0**
	(51)	(196)	(71)	(45)	(78)	(85)
High	79***	79***	18***	84	17*	10**
	29	76	(11)	(38)	(18)	(40)
Correctly identifying Washington who claim on total information media exposure they are:						
Low	14***	43***	3	64*	3***	2
	(51)	(196)	(71)	(44)	(78)	(85)
High	72***	70***	7	90*	28***	3
	(29)	(76)	(28)	(38)	(18)	(40)
Who can read at least a little among those who claim they can read	NA	NA	99	99	99	74
			(408)	(266)	(346)	(80)

Notes: NA = not available. *N* is in parentheses. Percentages are a proportion of the cells' base *N* who manifested a given behavior. These cell *N*s (in parentheses) represent all those of low education who made the indicated behavioral claim, e.g., claimed to read a newspaper daily. The average number of years of education by country was Argentina: 4.5; Chile: 3.7; India: 1.0; Israel: 5.1; Nigeria: 6.2; and Pakistan: .2.

*.05 level of significance reached in *t*-tests of the difference in the proportion manifesting a given behavior in the case of those falling at the extremes of the continuum on each "claim."

**.01 level of significance.

***.001 level of significance.

†Includes "a few times a week" in "rarely or never" category.

to use the mass media regularly were—as they should have been—better able to correctly identify individuals and places figuring prominently in world news. In Nigeria, for example, among experienced workers of low education, the proportion who could correctly identify de Gaulle as the president of the French Republic was 57 percent among those who claimed to pay only modest attention to the mass media, 83 percent among those who asserted they listened or read more often, and 93 percent among those who claimed to read a newspaper or listen to the radio almost every day. Many additional examples which test the internal consistency of attitude and behavior are summarized in Table 38.4.[18] Clearly, the men who claim to have the attributes we score as modern give a better account of themselves on objective tests of performance. We may conclude not only that modern is as modern does, but also that modern *does* as modern *speaks*.

4. *Is the consequence of the individual modernization inevitably personal disorganization and psychic strain; or can men go through this process of rapid sociocultural change without deleterious consequences?*— Few ideas have been more popular among the social philosophers of the nineteenth and twentieth centuries than the belief that industrialization is a kind of plague which disrupts social organization, destroys cultural cohesion, and uniformly produces personal demoralization and even disintegration. Much the same idea has been expressed by many anthropologists who fear—and often have witnessed—the destruction of indigenous cultures under the massive impact of their contact with the colossus represented by the European-based colonial empires. But neither the establishment of European industry in the nineteenth century, nor the culture crisis of small preliterate peoples overwhelmed by the tidal wave of colonial expansion may be adequate models for understanding the personal effects of industrialization and urbanization in developing nations.

To test the impact on personal adjustment resulting from contact with modernizing influ-

ences in our six developing countries, we administered the Psychosomatic Symptoms Test as part of our regular questionnaire. This test is widely acknowledged to be the best available instrument for cross-cultural assessment of psychic stress.[19] Using groups carefully matched on all other variables, we successively tested the effect of education, migration from the countryside to the city, factory employment, urban residence, and contact with the mass media as these modernizing experiences might affect scores on the Psychosomatic Symptoms Test. No one of these presumably deleterious influences consistently produced statistically significant evidence of psychic stress as judged by the test. Those who moved to the city as against those who continued in the village, those with many years as compared to those with few years of experience in the factory, those with much contact with the mass media as against those with little exposure to radio, newspaper, and movies, show about the same number of psychosomatic symptoms.

In each of six countries, we tested fourteen different matched groups, comparing those who migrated with those who did not; men with more years in the factory with those with fewer, and so forth. Because some of these matches did not apply in certain countries, we were left with seventy-four more or less independent tests of the proposition that being more exposed to the experiences identified with the process of modernization produces more psychosomatic symptoms. Disregarding the size of the difference and considering only the sign of the correlation between exposure to modernization and psychosomatic symptoms as (+) or (−), it turns out that in thirty-four instances the results are in accord with the theory that modernization is psychologically upsetting, but in forty other matches the results are opposed to the theory. Very few of the differences in either direction, furthermore, were statistically significant. Indeed, the frequency of such statistically significant correlations was about what you would expect by chance. Of these significant differences, furthermore, only two supported the hypothesis while two contradicted it. This again suggests that only chance is at work here. We must conclude, therefore, that the theory which identifies contact with modernizing institutions and geographical and social mobility as certainly deleterious to psychic adjustment is not supported by the evidence. Indeed, it is cast in serious doubt. Whatever is producing the symptoms—and the test does everywhere yield a wide range of scores—it is something other than differential contact with the sources of modernization which is responsible.

Life does exact its toll. Those who have been long in the city and in industry but who have failed to rise in skill and earnings are somewhat more distressed. But this outcome can hardly be charged to the deleterious effects of contact with the modern world. Perhaps if we had studied the unemployed who came to the city with high hopes but failed to find work, we might have found them to have more psychosomatic symptoms. If we were faced with this finding, however, it would still be questionable whether the observed condition should be attributed to the effects of modernization. The fault would seem to lie equally in the inability of traditional agriculture to provide men with economic sustenance sufficient to hold them on the land.

We conclude, then, that modernizing institutions, per se, do not lead to greater psychic stress. We leave open the question whether the process of societal modernization in general increases social disorganization and then increases psychic tension for those experiencing such disorganization. But we are quite ready to affirm that extensive contact with the institutions introduced by modernization—such as the school, the city, the factory, and the mass media—is not in itself conducive to greater psychic stress.

Men change their societies. But the new social structures they have devised may in turn shape the men who live within the new social order. The idea that social structures influence the personal qualities of those who participate in them is, of course, as old as social science and may be found in the writings of the earliest social philosophers. Its most dramatic expression, relevant to us, was in the work of Marx, who enunciated the principle that men's consciousness is merely a reflection of their relation to the system of ownership of the means of production. The rigidity of Marx's determinism, and the counterdetermination of many people to preserve an image of man's spiritual independence and of the personal autonomy and integrity of the individual, generated profound resistance to these ideas. The idea that ownership or nonownership of the means of production determines consciousness is today not very compelling. To focus on ownership, however, is to concentrate on the impact of macrostructural forces in shaping men's attitudes and values at the expense of studying the significance of microstructural factors. Yet it may be that these microstructural features, such as are embedded in the locale and the nature of work, are prime sources of influences on men's attitudes and behavior.

In reviewing the results of our research on modernization, one must be struck by the exceptional stability with which variables such as education, factory experience, and urbanism maintain the absolute and relative strength of their impact on individual modernization despite the great variation in the culture of the men undergoing the experience and in the levels of development characterizing the countries in which they live.[20] This is not to deny the ability of the macrostructural elements of the social order to exert a determining influence on men's life condition and their response to it. But such macrostructural forces can account for only one part of the variance in individual social behavior, a part whose relative weight we have not yet measured with the required precision. When we attain that precision we may find some confirmation of popular theories, but we are also certain to discover some of them to be contradicted by the data—just as we have in our study of microstructural factors. The resolution of the competition between these two theoretical perspectives cannot be attained by rhetoric. It requires systematic measurement and the confrontation of facts however far they are marshaled in the service of ideas. The facts *we* have gathered leave *us* in no doubt that microstructural forces have great power to shape attitudes, values, and behavior in regular ways at standard or constant rates within a wide variety of macrostructural settings.

Notes

* From the *American Journal of Sociology* 75, no. 2 (September 1969): 208–25, by permission of the University of Chicago Press. Copyright 1969 by the University of Chicago Press.

† This paper was presented at the Dallas meeting of the American Association for the Advancement of Science in the section on "Comparative Sociology and Contemporary Social Issues," December 29, 1968. My chief collaborators from the early days of the project were Howard Schuman and Edward Ryan, who served, respectively, as field directors for Pakistan and Nigeria, and David H. Smith, who was my assistant in Chile and later was assistant director of the project in Cambridge. The fieldwork and later analysis were greatly facilitated by the work of our local collaborators in all six of the countries. We owe particular debt to Juan César and Carlotta Garcia, Perla Gibaja, and Amar Singh who were field directors for Chile, Argentina, and India, respectively, and to Olatude Oloko who was assistant field director in Nigeria. In its different aspects, stages, and settings, the research has been supported by the Rockefeller Foundation, the Ford Foundation, the National Science Foundation, and the National Institute of Mental Health. The Cultural Affairs Division of the Department of State provided local currencies to support our fieldwork in India, Israel, and Pakistan, and the Office of Scientific Research of the U.S. Air Force supported technical exploration in problems of translation and computer analysis undertaken in Cambridge. All these organizations gave their support through the Center for International Affairs of Harvard University, which is the sponsor and institutional home of our pro-

ject on the social and cultural aspects of economic development.

1. Some sixty-eight of the questions are listed, in abbreviated form, in Table 1 of Smith and Inkeles 1966. A complete copy of the questionnaire may be obtained by ordering Document 9133 from the Chief, Auxiliary Publication Project, Photoduplication Service, Library of Congress, Washington, D.C.

2. This model has been sketched in a preliminary way in Inkeles 1966.

3. Reference is to the reliabilities of the long form of the scale (OM-2) containing 159 items. Reliabilities for some of the various short forms were sometimes lower but were generally in the same range. See Smith and Inkeles 1966, p. 367.

4. On the basis of our experience with the longer versions of the questionnaire, we have been able to devise several short forms which permit rapid identification of the more modern and more traditional men in any population. Details on the construction and content of these short forms are given in Smith and Inkeles 1966. One of these short forms (OM-12) which has proved a highly reliable instrument is currently being used in more than twenty pure- and applied-research programs in over a dozen developing countries.

5. Of course, when you use a scale score to designate a "type" of man, the number of men who fit your typology depends entirely on your decision as to a cutting point on both the items and on the scales as a whole. For example, in one form of our modernity scale (IM-6) a representative subset of thirty-three items is scored so that only by affirming the most decidedly modern position at the end of the theoretical continuum of alternative answers does a man get a point toward his modernity score. On this strict test, getting as many as half the answers "right" would qualify 37 percent of our Nigerian sample as "modern." If we set a higher standard, and reserve the term modern for men who get two-thirds or more of the answers "right," then only 6 percent qualify. Raising the standard still higher to require that a man get three-fourths or more of the answers "correct" reduces the pool of modern men to 2 percent of the sample. The comparable proportions qualifying as modern by this standard in our Pakistani sample are much lower, being 14 percent, 2

percent, and 0 percent, respectively. Changing the scoring standard for the individual questions would, obviously, also affect the proportions classified as modern.

6. These included *all* questions which in our opinion measured attitudes and could be unambiguously scored as having a "modern" and a "traditional" answer. Queries which did not meet these criteria were excluded from consideration. This meant mainly background questions, information-testing items, behavioral measures, adjustment measures, and the like. For details see Smith and Inkeles 1966.

7. The correlation (Pearsonian) between education and the overall measure of modernization ranges from .34 in Pakistan to .65 in India. The size of these coefficients is substantially affected by the educational "spread" in each sample. That spread is largest in India, with the cases rather evenly distributed from zero to thirteen years of education.

8. In much of the current discussion of the effectiveness and ineffectiveness of our schools, this aspect of the school's impact has been generally neglected. For an important exception see Dreeben 1968.

9. However, in India it was only .08. We believe this to be not a condition peculiar to India, but to our industrial sample there. Everywhere else we sampled from fifty to more than one hundred factories, including all types and sizes of industry, but in India our sample was limited to eleven factories, mostly large, and two of these were not truly industrial; they processed minerals.

10. Keep in mind that the test has a theoretical range from zero to 100, and an observed range in our samples almost as great. With samples of our size, differences so large are significant at well above the .01 level. This test of significance and many of the other statistics presented in this report require that one meet certain conditions, such as random sampling, which our data do not meet. Nevertheless, we present such statistics in order to provide a rough guide or standard of judgment, in the belief that to do so is preferable to leaving the reader without any criterion by which to evaluate one figure as against another. The reader must be cautioned, however, not to interpret any single statistic too literally. Conclusions should be drawn not from single figures but from the whole array of evidence across the six countries.

11. It will be noted that the pattern manifested in the other five countries is not shown in Israel. There the new workers are as well informed as the experienced. We attribute this not so much to the qualities of Israeli industry as to the nature of Israeli society. In that small, mobile, and urbanized environment, information tends to be rapidly and more or less evenly diffused throughout the nation and to all classes.

12. The distinctive effectiveness of each of these potentially modernizing experiences, and others, is assessed in the general report of our project in Inkeles and Smith 1974.

13. In this regression analysis we utilized as the dependent variable a long form of the modernity scale OM-3, not as described in Smith and Inkeles 1966. Using seven principal predictor variables selected on theoretical and empirical grounds, we obtained multiple correlation coefficients of from about .57 to .76 in our six countries. We could thus account for between 32.5 percent and 59.0 percent of variance in the modernity scale scores. We then grouped the predictor variables in two sets. The set of early socialization variables included ethnicity, father's education, and own formal education. Late socialization variables included occupational type, consumer goods possessed (as a measure of standard of living), a measure of mass media exposure, and age. Each set was then used alone to ascertain what portion of the variance it could explain, as indicated in Table 38.2. A discussion of the rationale for selecting these particular variables and grouping them so, as well as details of the linear multiple regression analysis, are presented in Inkeles and Smith 1974.

14. An alternative approach to estimating the relative contribution of the two sets of variables is to consider the decrement in the total variance explained when either set is withdrawn from the total pool of predictors. When this was done, the late socialization variables again emerged as more powerful everywhere except in India. The following set of figures presents, first, the decrement in the total variance explained resulting from withdrawal of the early socialization variables, and second, the decrement resulting from withdrawal of the late socialization vari-

ables from the total predictor pool: Argentina .127/.155; Chile .100/.184; India .276/.066; Israel .101/.104; Nigeria .068/.120; East Pakistan .070/.131. The fact that these decrements are so much smaller than the proportion of variance explained by each set alone indicates that to some extent the sets overlap, and when one set is dropped the other "takes over" for it in explaining some part of the variance.

15. For example, it is an act of substantial civic courage for a young man in a traditional village to tell our interviewer he would be more inclined to follow the local coop leader than the village elders, or that he considers himself more a Nigerian than an Ife, or whatever is the local tribal basis of solidarity.

16. In the project identification system this scale is designated OM-1. It includes only seventy-nine items selected from the larger pool by a panel of expert judges on the grounds that (a) they dealt only with attitudes, not information, political orientation, or action, and (b) they clearly were appropriate to test the original theoretical conception of modernity as more or less "officially" defined by the project staff.

17. This assertion is supported by consideration of the relevant gamma statistics on the relationship of attitudinal modernity (OM scores) and

	Country		
Tests	Argentina	Chile	India
Based on items			
Average gamma	201	232	342
Number of tests	60	62	58
Based on scales			
Average gamma	305	296	449
Number of tests	24	24	24
	Israel	Nigeria	Pakistan
Based on items			
Average gamma	244	205	303
Number of tests	52	46	29
Based on scales			
Average gamma	313	276	339
Number of tests	28	24	10

information tests. For this purpose low- and high-education groups were tested separately (except in Pakistan), hence the number of gamma statistics obtained is twice the number of items used. The average gamma statistics shown below are based on three-part tables which included middle as well as low and high OM. Separate results are given for items and for scales, since the scales show the combined effects of groups of items and hence are not truly "independent" additional tests of the hypothesis under scrutiny.

18. For lack of space, Table 38.4 shows the percentage whose behavior validated their oral "claim" only in the case of those falling at the extremes of the continuum on each "claim," and the t-tests are based on these same extremes. To leave no doubt that this outcome was not a fortuitous result of considering only the extremes, we note the gamma statistics for the full cross-tabulations including all steps in both the oral claim and the behavioral test. The five tests of the relation between claim and behavior applied in six countries yield a potential thirty tests, but some were inapplicable in certain instances. The procedure was repeated separately for the "low" and "high" educated, divided at the median in each country. For the low educated, where twenty-seven of the tests were applicable, the association of claim and behavior was in the expected direction in all cases, and the gammas ranged from .011 to .877, with a mean of .351 and a median of .334. For the high educated, the hypothesis could be tested in twenty-three full cross-tabulations. All but two of the associations were in the expected direction, the gammas ranging from $-.123$ to .690, and over this range the mean gamma was .309 and the median .276.

19. Variants of the test were used with the Yoruba as reported by Leighton et al. 1963, and the Zulu as reported by Scotch and Geiger 1963–64. Details on the form of the test as we used it and the results of our investigation were presented by Alex Inkeles and David Smith to the Eighth Congress of the International Anthropological Association at Tokyo-Kyoto in September 1968 under the title "The Fate of Personal Adjustment in the Process of Modernization," and will appear in the *International Journal of Comparative Sociology,* 1970.

20. This idea is more fully elaborated in Inkeles 1960.

References

Dawson, J. L. M. 1967. "Traditional versus Western Attitudes in Africa: The Construction, Validation and Application of a Measuring Device." *British Journal of Social and Clinical Psychology* 6(2):81–96.

Doob, L. W. 1967. "Scales for Assaying Psychological Modernization in Africa." *Public Opinion Quarterly* 31:414–21.

Dreeben, R. 1968. *On What Is Learned in School.* Reading, Mass.: Addison-Wesley.

Inkeles, A. 1960. "Industrial Man: The Relation of Status, Experience and Value." *American Journal of Sociology* 66:1–31.

———. 1966. "The Modernization of Man." In *Modernization,* edited by M. Weiner. New York: Basic Books.

Inkeles, A., and David H. Smith. Forthcoming. "The Fate of Personal Adjustment in the Process of Modernization." *International Journal of Comparative Sociology.*

———. 1974. *Becoming Modern.* Cambridge: Harvard University Press.

Kahl, J. A. 1968. *The Measurement of Modernism, a Study of Values in Brazil and Mexico.* Austin and London: University of Texas Press.

Leighton, Alexander H., T. A. Lambo, C. G. Hughes, D. C. Leighton, J. M. Murphy, and D. B. Macklon. 1963. *Psychiatric Disorder among the Yoruba.* Ithaca, N.Y.: Cornell University Press.

Scotch, Norman A., and H. J. Geiger. 1963–64. "An Index of Symptom and Disease in Zulu Culture." *Human Organization* 22(4):304–11.

Smith, David H., and Alex Inkeles. 1966. "The OM Scale: A Comparative Socio-Psychological Measure of Individual Modernity." *Sociometry* 29:353–77.

Changes in Religious Commitment in the United States, Holland, and Japan*

Masamichi Sasaki and Tatsuzo Suzuki[†]

Changes in religious commitment over age, historical period, and generation are a controversial and recurrent issue in the sociology of religion and gerontology. Abundant but contradictory research exists, for instance, on religious commitment and age in the United States. Bahr (1970) classified this research into four different models: traditional, stability, family cycle, and disengagement. According to Bahr, the traditional model identifies a sharp decline in church attendance between the ages of eighteen and thirty, a decline that bottoms out between ages thirty and thirty-five. Beyond age thirty-five, however, a steady increase in church attendance is observed until old age. The stability model, however, identifies stable church attendance throughout an individual's lifetime; that is, aging and church attendance are not related. In the family-cycle model, church attendance is tied to the family life cycle. Finally, in the disengagement model, decreasing church attendance is seen as beginning in middle age. Bahr was careful to point out, in constructing these models of the existing research, that societal changes have never been superimposed on the models to test their validity.

In testing the validity of the relationship between age and church attendance, Wingrove and Alston (1974) attempted to place twenty different studies into Bahr's four models. In so doing, they were forced to conclude that most of the studies had used inappropriate methodologies (either cross-sectional or retrospective).

For religious commitment over time, adherents of the "secularization thesis" state that traditional religion has been experiencing declining involvement and commitment (e.g., Durkheim 1893; Sorokin 1956; O'Dea 1966; Wilson 1966, 1976a; Berger 1967, 1969; Luckmann 1967; Stark and Glock 1968). The identified root causes of the decline include urbanization (Yinger 1963; Weigert and Thomas 1974; Martin 1978), industrialization (Hertel and Nelsen 1974; Martin 1978), decline of community as well as changes in social control from moral or religious to technical and bureaucratic (Wilson 1976b), modernity (Berger 1977; Bibby 1979), social and geographical mobility—including the rise of the sensualist and materialist cultures (Acquaviva 1979), and rationalization (Berger 1967; Wilson 1976a, 1976b). Wuthnow (1976), however, pointed to an age-strata phenomenon (e.g., the counterculture of the late 1960s) as being responsible for the "discontinuous" process of the secularization of religious patterns.

While the preceding remarks have been principally relevant to the U.S. experience, many proponents of the secularization thesis also see secularization as prevalent in Europe. These include White (1956), Wilson (1966), Luckmann (1967), Berger (1969), Schneider (1970), and Mol (1972). Certainly not all observers are inclined to agree with the secularization thesis. Greeley, for example, concludes that "the available statistical data simply do not indicate a declining religiousness in the United States" (1972, p. 7). Others who can be included here are Davis (1949), Herberg (1955), Parsons (1967), Martin (1967), and Bell (1977).

The conflict that thus emerges is no doubt partially due to the lack of appropriate longitudinal data on religious commitment and to the lack of legitimate methodologies that are able to separate age, period, and cohort effects, a separation that is imperative for testing the secularization thesis. The common means to measure secularization has been to compare data at time t (some point in the past) and $t + 1, t + 2, t + 3$, and so on (for more recent times) on a given measure of religious commitment. If an overall decline persists over these time periods, then secularization exists. However, because three variables (age, historical period, and cohort) are logically confounded with one another, it is difficult to determine that the decline is attributable to one (or more) of these three variables. The secularization thesis can be fully supported if there exist both negative, overall, progressive period and cohort effects on religious commitment, and it can be partially supported if there exists either negative, overall, progressive period or cohort effects. In general, however, cohort effects have greater impact on secularization than do period effects because period effects are temporal phenomena while cohort effects are persistent, remaining influential throughout one's life. (In this respect, Ryder [1965] states that new cohort effects provide an opportunity for social change.)

In addition to the lack of appropriate data and adequate methodologies, the secularization thesis has been tested only on Western forms of religion. The need for international comparative studies has ben expressed, in particular by Turner: "The third limitation of the contemporary sociology of religion is its narrow empirical focus on western forms of religion. In practice, the sociology of religion is very largely the sociology of Christianity" (1983, p. 5).

Looking to the East, we can identify a number of studies of religion in countries whose religious traditions differ from those in the West (e.g., Japan; see Morioka 1975; Yanagawa and Abe 1978). However, comparative sociological analyses of religion between East and West are few and far between, especially empirical studies. There is no question but that this is owing, at least in part, to the obvious difficulty of comparing ideas of religious commitment between East and West[1] as well as the difficulty of comparing religions in varying cultural contexts. Yanagawa and Abe (1978), for instance, argue that Japanese religion cannot be explained in terms of the church-centered concept of religion in the West.

In the international comparative studies that do exist, two different methods have been common. The first involves collecting data simultaneously—using the measures relevant to the country in question—and then translating the resulting questionnaire as precisely as possible. Comparing the results in this way stresses a common questionnaire that transcends the language barrier; nonetheless, because of societal differences (particularly with regard to religion and politics) that are embedded in all social structures and social and cultural institutions, there is often little benefit in comparing the contents of such questionnaires, however accurate their translation. For example, in the United States, it is legitimate to ask about religious practices (such as whether one attends church regularly), but this question is frequently irrelevant in non-Christian countries such as Japan, where, contrary to the West, religious practices are more or less obligatory. (The majority of Japanese Buddhist temples and Shinto shrines emphasize funeral rites and memorial services.)

It is, however, inappropriate to ask in the United States whether a respondent has religious beliefs. Consistently, in the United States, 95 to 98 percent of those responding to public polls believe in God (Glock and Stark 1965; Herberg 1967; Demerath 1968). Indeed, according to a Gallup poll, if a person has no religious beliefs, he or she will be subject to a negative image. Herberg (1967, p. 474) states that over 95 percent of Americans regard belief in God as essential to being a good American. If, for longitudinal analysis, the percentage of those responding to some question (say, on religiosity) is quite high (say, over 95 percent with consistently low variance), then the use of that question is inappropriate as an indicator of religiosity. Conversely, in Japan, studies (e.g., Suzuki 1970) have shown that only about one-third of respondents say they have religious faith. Thus, there would be little or no meaning to such a comparison between the United States and Japan. Indeed, one of the most important tasks of international comparative research is to ascertain whether the same dimension of a given concept, such as religious commitment, can commonly be used as a relevant social indicator.

The second method compares the structure of responses among subgroups in the relevant societies. This method is believed to increase comparability vis-à-vis the first method. Nonetheless, this method suffers from the same drawback as the first in that it requires simultaneous conduct of the surveys and thus enormous time and expense.

The implication is that yet a third method is desirable for international comparative studies. This third method would recognize that, while the content of questions may differ somewhat (accounting for social-structural, cultural, and historical differences), their use in an appropriately sequenced manner is a more meaningful way of comparing changes in the structure of responses over time in the countries being compared. Cohort analysis suggests itself as being very useful to this third method of comparison, provided that it is used properly (i.e., the analysis is capable of legitimately separating age, period, and cohort effects).

The purpose of the present study therefore is to adopt this third method in conjunction with a newly developed Bayesian method, which provides a powerful analytic tool for cohort analysis by overcoming the serious shortcomings in previous cohort analysis, in order to test the validity of findings regarding religious commitment as it relates to age, historical period, and generation in modern industrialized societies: the United States and Europe (which have predominantly Western forms of

religion) and Japan (which has an Eastern form of religion). To elaborate on the purposes of the present study, we note that it was designed to test the validity of Bahr's four models of the relationship between church attendance and age for the United States (by taking into account generational and sociohistorical changes) as well as the validity of the secularization thesis for three societies in question, all of which exhibit the various causes suggested for secularization (modernity, urbanization, industrialization, etc.).

There are several reasons supporting the selection of Holland as an exemplar of the European experience. First, "Holland has never witnessed the general religious indifference found in many neighboring countries (Scandinavia, France, and England); church and religion belong to the most important molding forces which have given the whole pattern of Dutch social life a characteristic stamp. Nowhere in the surrounding European countries is vertical pluralism (organizational segmentation along denominational boundaries) or high rate of formal non-membership in the church (a paradoxical indicator of religious involvement) more striking. For the sociology of religion the Netherlands is thus particularly interesting" (Laeyendecker 1972, p. 325). Second, Peterson (1967) points out that, because religion is an important social institution in the Netherlands, sociologists have tended to concentrate much research effort in that country. Finally, to summarize the validity of this selection, Larkin states that ". . . in contradistinction to developments in most other comparable industrial societies, religious institutions and ideologies occupy a central place in the social structure of the Netherlands" (1974, p. 401).

We use Greeley's definition of secularization in the present study: "a decline in religious enthusiasm, belief, and activity—a decline brought on by the higher level of religious sophistication of ordinary people" (1979, p. 175).

With regard to the definition of religious commitment, Glock and Stark (1965; Stark and Glock 1968) claim that, for all world religions, there are five "universal" dimensions (belief, practice, knowledge, experience, and consequences). Our study adopts this multidimensional approach.[2] In any international, cross-cultural comparison (in this case, East-West), it is likely that common global dimensions will not exist, and thus it is often inevitable that different dimensions be compared. For religious commitment, it has been shown above that the most salient questions involve somewhat differing dimensions in the countries being compared. Thus, even though it may be theoretically ideal to test the validity of the secularization thesis using identical dimensions, the present context suggests the empirical impossibility of such a task. Wilson's argument is correct in this respect: "It is sociological bias—and an unwarranted bias—to suppose that comparative analysis should always lead to unified theory and universally valid formulations. Such a conclusion can be produced only by ignoring the importance of empirical evidence and the historical diversity of societies and their cultures, and only by subsuming factually diverse contents under highly abstract summary propositions which obscure by their abstraction as much as they illuminate about social reality" (1982, p. 147).

In sum, the most relevant means to test the secularization thesis is to use the most salient dimension of religious commitment in each society over time. These salient dimensions must be determined by looking at what questions have been used repeatedly within each society to measure religious commitment over time. On the basis of their repeated or recurrent use, we can assume that these questions are then salient indicators of religious commitment for a given society.[3]

Data and Method

Because most existing data were not gathered for the purpose of cohort analysis, it is inevitable that these data carry certain restrictions and limitations, such as the use of different or slightly modified questions over time, missing data because of surveys not having been conducted during certain periods, and, for data on religious commitment over time, the overall scarcity of such data. Greeley comments on these issues: "In popular writings there is some difficulty in distinguishing between long-range and short-range terms, with one group of authors arguing apparently that secularization, or at least dramatic secularization is a relatively recent event. . . . Other writers, however, would see a much longer trend and in this respect, I think, would be closer to men like Berger" (1979, p. 21). It is empirically impossible to test the secularization thesis over the long run because there simply are no data. The present study used the data described in the following paragraphs.

For the United States, the survey data of the archives of the Institute for Social Research at the University of Michigan were used. This survey was conducted every two years from 1952 to 1982, except for 1954, for a total of fifteen periods. The data contain religious practice only as a dimension of religious commitment, which was measured by the following questions: "Do you go to church regularly?" (1952–68) and "Do you go to church every week?" (1970–82). Glock and Stark elaborate on the reasoning behind the use of these questions: "The saliency of belief is more appropriately studied in terms of the kinds of religiosity individuals express on other dimensions. . . . Reliance is usually placed on church membership and frequency of church attendance as indicators of religiosity within the ritualistic dimension, and there exists a plethora of studies describing the social correlates of these indicators" (Glock and Stark 1965, pp. 25, 28).

For Holland, data derived from the national surveys carried out by the Central Bureau of Statistics of the Netherlands from 1899 to 1969 were used (the same as those used by Cobben [1976]). The survey was terminated in 1969. Religious practice as the only available indicator of religious commitment was used here as well, with the question asking respondents whether they had any religious affiliation (questions about church attendance were not asked). Here, too, the vast majority of the Dutch people believe in God (Martin 1978, p. 201), thus minimizing the usefulness of any data that might result from that question. The social and cultural circumstances are relevant here as well (see Peterson 1967; Laeyendecker 1972). Finally, Bagley stated: "In Dutch society religious affiliation seems to be an important determinant of the degree and manner of interpersonal relationships" (1973, p. 8).

For the Japanese data, the National Character Surveys conducted by the Institute of Statistical Mathematics, Tokyo, at five-year intervals between 1953 and 1983 were used. As discussed above, temple and shrine attendance are not relevant issues in the Japanese setting, and thus religious belief is used as the relevant dimension of religious commitment. The relevant question in the survey was, Do you have any religious faith?

Used frequently in demography, cohort analysis implies a group of methods designed to separate cohort, age, and historical period effects (see Hobcraft, Menken, and Preston 1982). In our study, the meaning of "cohort" is restricted to a collection of people born in the same period, which is more or less synonymous with "generation" (Glenn 1977).

Many cohort analysts (Mason et al. 1973; Glenn 1977; Fienberg and Mason 1978; and Mason and Fienberg 1985) have, however, pointed out an identification problem. The three variables—age, historical period, and cohort—as usually measured, are logically confounded with one another. Their joint use to predict a dependent variable is therefore problematic. One suggestion has been that cohort analysis can be meaningful only if one of the three independent variables is ignored. However, as Mason et al. have suggested, "If age, cohort and period have distinct causal interpretations, then an analysis which omits one of these variables is subject to spurious findings" (1973, p. 243). Other possible assumptions are based on the fact that each variable can be linearly related to the dependent vari-

able and that, at the same time, age, historical period, and cohort are linearly related to one another. Also, any two consecutive ages, historical periods, or cohorts can have identical effect parameters. Nonetheless, these assumptions and their attendant restrictions do not represent a general solution to the age-historical period-cohort problem. The use of such assumptions is, of course, situationally dependent; at one time they may be valid, while at others they will not be.

In this new approach, a logit cohort model for qualitative data under the binomial sampling model and a normal-type cohort model for quantitative data under the normal sampling model are adopted. This approach is so flexible that both the logit cohort model and the normal-type model can be applied not only to standard cohort tables (see Glenn 1977) but also to general cohort tables.

The Bayesian procedure in Nakamura's new method can provide a satisfactory explanation for the data almost automatically, without the identification specification that has occurred in previous cohort analysis and resulted in misleading findings. In fact, Mason et al.'s (1973) constrained multiple-classification analysis (MCA) and Feinberg and Mason's (1978) logit cohort model are special cases of Nakamura's Bayesian cohort model.[4]

Findings and Discussion

All data are displayed in Tables 39.1 through 39.6, with the results of the Bayesian cohort analyses shown in Figures 39.1 through 39.3. For the U.S. case, first of all, we can examine church attendance trends from 1952 to 1982 (without age classification) in Table 39.1. There, we see that church attendance remained stable over the thirty-year period. However, when we classify the data by age distribution (Table 39.2) and use the newly developed Bayesian cohort analysis (results shown in Figure 39.1), we see a clear trend that exhibits no historical period effects but does exhibit weak age effects and moderate cohort effects.[5]

TABLE 39.1 U.S. Consecutive Data on Church/Synagogue Attendance

Year	Percent
1952	38.4
1956	42.5
1958	43.0
1960	44.1
1962	44.6
1964	44.0
1966	39.8
1968	38.3
1970	39.5
1972	39.2
1974	40.1
1976	40.0
1978	39.2
1980	40.5
1982	40.0

Note: From 1952 to 1968, the question was, Do you go to church/synagogue regularly? Since 1970, the question has been, Do you go to church/synagogue every week? The percentages from 1952 to 1968 represent regular attendance, while the percentages since 1970 reflect a combination of attendance "every week" and "almost every week." *Source:* P. E. Converse, J. D. Dotson, W. J. Hoag, and W. H. McGee III. (1980), *American Social Attitudes Data Sourcebook, 1947–78.* For 1980 data, *American National Election Study, 1982.* Both: Principal Investigators, Warren Miller and the National Election Studies; Center for Political Studies, The University of Michigan, Inter-University Consortium for Political and Social Research, 1982 and 1983, respectively.

These findings do not support claims about historical period effects on religious commitment in the United States (e.g., for the postwar religious revival, see Glock and Stark [1965]; the fourth great awakening from 1960 on, see McLoughlin [1978]; and fluctuations in religious commitment usually attributed to socioeconomic and political conditions). Nor do these findings support claims about the influence of factors identified by secularization thesis proponents (e.g., modernization, urbanization, industrialization, and social and geo-

graphic mobility).[6] Indeed, these factors have no direct effect on secularization in the three-decade period under scrutiny in the United States (1952–82).

The finding of weak age effects on church attendance means that the percentage of those who attend church regularly beyond age forty-five increases steadily into old age, which partially supports Bahr's traditional model. This finding can also be explained by Glock, Ringer, and Babbie's "comfort" hypothesis, which states that "parishioners whose life situations most deprive them of satisfaction and fulfillment in the secular society turn to the church for comfort and substitute rewards" (1967, pp. 107–8).

Strong cohort effects are seen in the U.S. case, based on the high value of the range of parameter variation (.719). The general tendency here is that the percentage of those born before 1897 who go to church regularly has increased, the percentage born between 1897 and 1927 who go to church regularly has fluctuated, but the percentage of those born after 1927 who go to church regularly has decreased. The steady negatively increasing cohort effects after 1927 indicate that church attendance in the United States has been dropping over the past few generations. Thus, in terms of religious practice (i.e., church attendance), the cohort factor does play a critical role in secularization, although for a comparatively short span of recent generations. If we at least partially adopt Ryder's (1965, p. 843) factors, which differentiate successive cohorts, then these findings imply that generational difference factors (peer-group socialization, idiosyncratic experiences, especially early on in life, and so forth, as well as religious socialization through family and personal religious experiences) have negative effects on religious behavior in later life among those cohorts born after 1927. The secularization thesis, therefore, is partially supported over recent generations in the United States.

From Table 39.3, where the Dutch data are displayed in their original opposite configura-

TABLE 39.2   U.S. Consecutive Data on
Church/Synagogue Attendance: Period × Age (%)

Year	18–24	25–34	35–44	45–54	55–64	65–74	75–84
1952	37.3	34.4	40.5	37.9	42.5	38.5	35.7
1954	NA	NA	NA	NA	NA	NA	NA
1956	32.4	46.9	44.4	40.4	41.9	39.4	44.4
1958	32.6	41.5	46.0	42.5	49.2	41.8	30.5
1960	56.9	41.1	48.4	46.0	42.0	42.6	25.7
1962	40.0	39.4	49.3	41.8	43.4	55.5	43.3
1964	19.3	44.2	47.3	41.7	45.6	55.8	48.9
1966	33.9	33.9	38.6	41.4	45.1	47.1	35.5
1968	31.8	34.6	43.1	35.4	42.4	38.4	43.6
1970	30.2	37.1	36.9	39.7	44.8	46.9	46.3
1972	28.4	35.6	41.9	38.6	47.2	43.4	45.8
1974	27.5	32.9	41.6	42.2	48.7	47.2	50.4
1976	31.7	31.7	40.0	40.0	50.9	46.1	48.0
1978	25.8	35.5	39.7	43.5	43.4	47.8	50.9
1980	23.4	34.2	45.0	46.1	43.2	50.6	47.3
1982	36.7	32.1	33.1	40.0	49.5	56.2	42.2

Note: From 1952 to 1968, the question was, Do you go to church/synagogue regularly? Since 1970, the question has been, Do you go to church/synagogue every week? The percentages from 1952 to 1968 represent regular attendance, while the percentages since 1970 reflect a combination of attendance "every week" and "almost every week." NA = not available.
Source: P. E. Converse, J. D. Dotson, W. J. Hoag, and W. H. McGee III. (1980), *American Social Attitudes Data Sourcebook, 1947–78.* For 1980 data, *American National Election Study, 1982.* Both: Principal Investigators, Warren Miller and the National Election Studies; Center for Political Studies, The University of Michigan, Inter-University Consortium for Political and Social Research, 1982 and 1983, respectively.

tion (i.e., religious nonaffiliation) and are not partitioned by age, we see a significant increase in religious nonaffiliation, which is a paradoxical indicator of religious commitment over the seventy-year period in Holland. However, from Table 39.4 (partitioned by age) and Figure 39.2 (results of the cohort analysis based on Table 39.4), we see strong period effects exhibited by the high value of the range of parameter variation (1.848). However, weak age effects, which bottom out between ages thirty and thirty-nine, can be identified, despite the general trend seen in Table 39.4, which shows that, as the Dutch age, there is a greater tendency for them to have religious affiliation. The Dutch cohort effects are more distinct than

are those in the United States. So far as period effects are concerned, this would indicate that, at the time the 1899 survey was conducted, socioeconomic and political conditions were already having substantial negative effects on religious affiliation for the Dutch, and this phenomenon continued from that time through 1929. However, the period effects did weaken after 1929 and stayed weak until 1969, when the survey was terminated.

Martin discusses a factor that he feels affects this phenomenon of declining affiliation: "A factor affecting non-affiliation which should be emphasized even though it is part of more general processes is the diminution in social functions experienced by churches, since

Hyper-Parameters and ABIC

	Hyper-Parameter	Square of M.S.D.	Range of P.V.
Period =	.2500	.044	.235
Age =	1.0000	.105	.274
Cohort =	.5000	.062	.719

ABIC = 221.5656

(SIGMA = 0.016996)

Grand Mean

−.4338
(39.32)

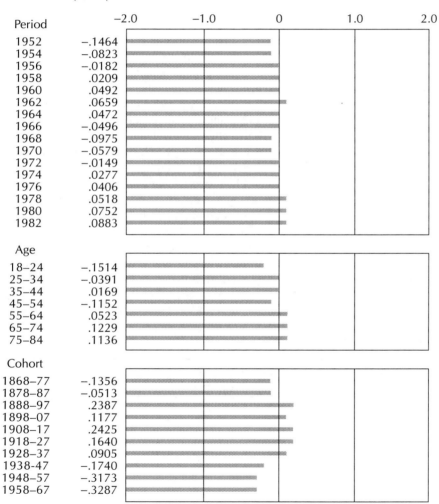

Period	
1952	−.1464
1954	−.0823
1956	−.0182
1958	.0209
1960	.0492
1962	.0659
1964	.0472
1966	−.0496
1968	−.0975
1970	−.0579
1972	−.0149
1974	.0277
1976	.0406
1978	.0518
1980	.0752
1982	.0883

Age	
18–24	−.1514
25–34	−.0391
35–44	.0169
45–54	−.1152
55–64	.0523
65–74	.1229
75–84	.1136

Cohort	
1868–77	−.1356
1878–87	−.0513
1888–97	.2387
1898–07	.1177
1908–17	.2425
1918–27	.1640
1928–37	.0905
1938-47	−.1740
1948–57	−.3173
1958–67	−.3287

FIGURE 39.1 Bayesian cohort analysis for U.S. data, based on Table 39.2. (Square root of mean square difference = $\sqrt{[\sum_i(\mu_i^p - \mu_{i+1}^p)^2/(I-1)]}$ for period effect. Range of parameter variation = $\max_i\mu_i^p - \min_i\mu_i^p$ for period effect. If the values of the SQR of M.S.D. and/or the range of P.V. become larger, then the effects become stronger. Generally speaking, if the SQR of M.S.D. is larger than .1, then we can assume that the effect exists. Also, if the range of P.V. is larger than .3, then we can assume that the effect exists. Sigma is a geometric mean or the sampling distribution of the binomial distribution of each cell.)

TABLE 39.3   Consecutive Data on Religious Nonaffiliation for Holland

Year	Estimated Percentage
1899	1.8
1909	4.5
1919	7.1
1929	13.4
1939	15.8
1949	17.7
1959	18.8
1969	23.0

Note: Data for ages less than 19 and greater than 80 are not included in this analysis.
Source: Cobben 1976. Table 3 and Table 4, p. 28 and p. 29, respectively.

this attenuates the motives for gathering together in a church context. . . . At any rate nonaffiliation is higher than it is in neighboring west European countries where it rarely rises above 5 per cent. This suggests that the 'pillars' not only define and hold people within the churches but ensure that whoever is outside those pillars is highly secularized" (1978, p. 199).[7] Larkin also talks about this phenomenon: "In so far as 'secularization' will occur in

the Netherlands, this is in the Catholic case most likely to be the outcome of a change in the balance of power and prestige between Catholic and other groups in Dutch society" (1974, p. 416).

The finding that there are weak age effects on religious affiliation in Holland means that the percentage of those who have religious affiliation beyond age thirty increases steadily into old age, a trend similar to that seen for church attendance in the United States.

For cohort effects on religious nonaffiliation, the general tendency is for increased percentages among those born before 1890, no change among those born between 1900 and 1939, and increased percentages among those born after 1940. Therefore, the explanation given above for the U.S. case (generational difference factors) applies here as well.

The overall increases in both historical period and cohort effects on the absence of religious commitment (i.e., religious nonaffiliation) for the seven decades support the secularization thesis for Dutch society, indicating that the Dutch have gradually been giving up religious affiliation over both historical periods and generations from the time the survey was begun in 1899 until its termination in 1969. In this regard, the progress of Luckmann's (1967)

TABLE 39.4   Consecutive Data on Religious Nonaffiliation for Holland: Period × Age (Estimated %)

Year	20–29	30–39	40–49	50–59	60–69	70–79
1899	2.4	2.2	1.7	1.2	.9	.6
1909	5.8	5.6	4.2	3.2	2.4	1.6
1919	8.4	8.9	7.1	5.3	3.9	2.7
1929	15.0	16.2	14.1	11.0	8.1	5.8
1939	16.9	18.3	17.0	14.6	11.2	8.0
1949	18.0	19.5	19.0	17.5	14.3	10.4
1959	18.3	20.2	19.8	19.2	17.8	14.2
1969	24.7	23.0	23.3	23.1	21.4	19.2

Note: Data for ages less than 19 and greater than 80 are not included in this analysis.
Source: Cobben 1976. Table 3 and Table 4, p. 28 and p. 29, respectively.

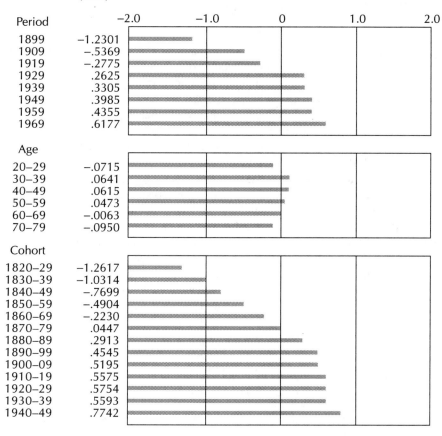

Hyper-Parameters and ABIC

	Hyper-Parameter	Square of M.S.D.	Range of P.V.
Period =	2048.0000	.355	1.848
Age =	256.0000	.077	.159
Cohort =	2048.0000	.201	2.036

ABIC = 1590.3608

(SIGMA = 0.000020)

Grand Mean

−2.4372
(8.04)

Period

		−2.0	−1.0	0	1.0	2.0
1899	−1.2301					
1909	−.5369					
1919	−.2775					
1929	.2625					
1939	.3305					
1949	.3985					
1959	.4355					
1969	.6177					

Age

20–29	−.0715
30–39	.0641
40–49	.0615
50–59	.0473
60–69	−.0063
70–79	−.0950

Cohort

1820–29	−1.2617
1830–39	−1.0314
1840–49	−.7699
1850–59	−.4904
1860–69	−.2230
1870–79	.0447
1880–89	.2913
1890–99	.4545
1900–09	.5195
1910–19	.5575
1920–29	.5754
1930–39	.5593
1940–49	.7742

FIGURE 39.2 Bayesian cohort analysis for Dutch data, based on Table 39.4. See legend for Figure 39.1.

TABLE 39.5 Consecutive Data for
Japanese Religious Faith

Year	Percentage
1958	33.5
1963	29.4
1968	28.8
1973	22.8
1978	31.8
1983	30.2

Note: Data for ages above 70 were not included in the analysis.
Source: Japanese National Character Survey, the Institute of Statistical Mathematics, Tokyo, 1984.

"invisible religion" can be located in Holland during the period.

From Table 39.5, which has no age partitioning, we can see that religious belief among the Japanese between 1958 and 1983 (except 1973) is relatively stable, with no tendency toward religiosity or secularization.

From Table 39.6, with age distribution, and Figure 39.3, which presents the results of the cohort analysis based on Table 39.6, moderate period effects can be identified; however, there is no overall trend toward religiosity or secularization. From 1958 to 1973, historical period had negative effects on religious belief. This

trend, though, reversed itself in the period 1978–83. Therefore, this finding does not support the secularization thesis over historical period.

Strong age effects (the value of the range of parameter variation is high, 2.187) indicate that the aging process tends to influence the Japanese people to become progressively more religious, with the younger Japanese being potential religious believers.[8]

The cohort effects are slight, indicating a relative stability in religious belief over generations (those generational groups born after 1888 but before 1927 and those born after 1957), with a propensity toward neither greater religiosity nor greater secularization. Most religious nonbelief cohort groups are those born between 1938 and 1942. This finding implies that, unlike the United States and Holland for religious practice, generational difference factors (acquired early in life) have not had a significant effect on Japanese religious belief. Therefore, the secularization thesis is not supported for Japan over generations. Also, the findings for Japan (that there is no tendency toward religiosity or secularization over historical period or generations) do not support the assertions of those who have stated that the Japanese are becoming externally religious but internally secular (see Ikado 1969). This assertion no doubt resulted from seeing only partial

TABLE 39.6 Consecutive Data for Japanese Religious Faith: Period × Age (%)

Year	20–24	25–29	30–34	35–39	40–44	45–49	50–54	55–59	60–64	65–69
1958	10.6	18.9	27.3	33.3	36.5	46.1	54.2	47.6	67.4	64.9
1963	7.5	18.6	17.4	23.2	36.2	44.8	44.0	42.1	49.7	60.2
1968	9.8	14.8	19.8	22.8	30.8	32.9	46.2	49.5	55.7	57.0
1973	8.1	11.1	15.4	17.4	23.0	31.3	32.4	37.2	47.2	47.1
1978	17.1	19.8	21.4	24.9	27.7	43.9	39.4	49.6	52.0	57.9
1983	12.6	17.5	18.0	24.8	30.2	32.2	35.7	44.3	53.0	59.5

Note: Data for ages above 70 were not included in the analysis.
Source: Japanese National Character Survey, the Institute of Statistical Mathematics, Tokyo, 1984.

Hyper-Parameters and ABIC

	Hyper-Parameter	Square of M.S.D.	Range of P.V.
Period =	2.0000	.250	.520
Age =	4.0000	.270	2.187
Cohort =	.2500	.045	.312

ABIC = 100.5189

(SIGMA = 0.027310)

Grand Mean

−.7495
(32.09)

Period		−2.0	−1.0	0	1.0	2.0
1958	.2131					
1963	.0005					
1968	−.0200					
1973	−.3069					
1978	.1103					
1983	.0031					

Age						
20–24	−1.2568					
25–29	−.7521					
30–34	−.5479					
35–39	−.3138					
40–44	.0042					
45–49	.2821					
50–54	.3661					
55–59	.5041					
60–64	.7874					
65–69	.9286					

Cohort						
1888–92	.1476					
1893–97	.1434					
1898–02	.0997					
1903–07	.1082					
1908–12	.1260					
1913–17	.1051					
1918–22	.0268					
1923–27	−.0483					
1928–32	−.1192					
1933–37	−.1593					
1938–42	−.1642					
1943–47	−.1340					
1948–52	−.0896					
1953–57	−.0269					
1958–62	−.0153					

FIGURE 39.3 Bayesian cohort analysis for Japanese data, based on Table 39.6. See legend for Figure 39.1.

aspects of religious commitment (i.e., religious belief only) among the Japanese.

Summary and Conclusions

Although the controversial issues of religious commitment over age and the well-known secularization thesis have been discussed in the literatures of the sociology of religion and gerontology, most previous empirical studies were unable to test them properly because of methodological shortcomings, particularly in cohort analysis. While cohort analysis is appropriate, lack of relevant longitudinal data, lack of specification of the dimensions of religious commitment, and lack of cross-cultural studies have all worked against these research efforts. In addition, in the literature on the secularization thesis, age, historical period, and cohort effects have never been treated distinctively.

Based on the need for a multidimensional approach in specifying the differing dimensions of religious commitment (because of the absence of a common global dimension), the present study, to resolve the controversial issues of religious commitment over age and the secularization thesis, used a newly developed Bayesian cohort analysis to analyze data from three industrialized nations: the United States, Holland, and Japan (where religious traditions differ significantly from those in the West). Two different dimensions of religious commitment, each regarded as one of the most suitable indicators for religious commitment in the respective countries, were employed: church attendance (religious practice) for the United States, religious affiliation (practice) for Holland, and religious belief for Japan.

So far as the relationship between age and religious commitment is concerned, the findings for the United States, where people beyond age forty-five consistently exhibit greater church attendance, partially support Bahr's traditional model, although the age effects are weak. Similarly, this is true of religious affiliation among Dutch over age thirty. Japan, however, shows the strongest age effects on religious belief among the three countries examined, with the aging process tending to influence people in Japan to become progressively more religious.

For the secularization thesis, it was found that it is fully supported over generations and periods for Holland in the seven-decade study, is partially supported for recent generations in the United States, but is not supported for historical period or generation in Japan. These findings imply that generational difference factors, such as religious socialization as well as peer-group socialization and idiosyncratic experiences that people have during their sensitive childhood years and youth, have had significant effects on secularization for people in the United States and Holland in later life. (In Holland, the cohort effects are more distinct, and the decline in religious commitment seems to have begun much earlier, a fact that points to the need for longer-term data for the U.S. experience.) Such is not the case for Japan.

Holland also exhibits distinct historical period effects on secularization. This is not true, however, for the United States or Japan, indicating that domestic sociohistorical events are often sufficient to affect religious commitment significantly. Thus, the strong historical period and cohort effects for Holland imply that the secularization thesis is most relevant to Dutch society.

In conclusion, although data are needed to test the validity of the secularization thesis over a longer period (as some proponents of the thesis, such as Berger, might claim), the available short-term data used here do not validate the general claim of the secularization thesis—which is rooted in the assumption that scientific, rational, technological man cannot really accept the mythological and the sacred—that secularization is simply part of a worldwide trend toward industrialization, modernity, rationalization, and urbanization. Secularization cannot be viewed as a global phenomenon of modern societies. Our findings suggest that the major causes of secularization are generational difference factors, such as religious socialization, peer-group socialization, and idiosyncratic experiences that people have during early childhood and youth. In addition, domestic sociohistorical events themselves can sometimes be sufficient causal explanation for the process of secularization, depending on their degree of significance to the total social structure at the time the events occur (or at some time afterward), on their significance for religious institutions and change, and finally, on the functional importance of people's religious commitment in a society during a certain period.

Notes

* From the *American Journal of Sociology* 92, no. 5 (March 1987): 1055–61, 1063–76, by permission of the University of Chicago Press. Copyright 1987 by the University of Chicago Press.

† This article is a revision of a paper presented at the 27th world congress of the International Institute of Sociology, held at the University of Washington, 1984. We wish to thank Howard Taylor, Robert Wuthnow, Gisela Trommsdorff, and the anonymous reviewers for *AJS* for extremely helpful suggestions and comments on an earlier draft of this paper. We are also grateful to Jean Stoetzel for informing us of the existence of the Dutch data and to D. J. van de Kaa and Frans van Poppel for providing these data (which were used for N. P. Cobben's master's thesis). Finally, we wish to thank Takashi Nakamura for making his program available for the present study and Saeko Tanaka for her computational assistance. Authors' names are in alphabetical order.

1. For religious commitment, Glock and Stark (1965) point out that the real challenge probably lies in its cross-cultural study.

2. Glock and Stark (1965) state, however, that the indicators of religiosity most often used fall into the religious-practice and religious-belief categories.

3. From the point of view of the researcher in the field doing longitudinal studies, extreme caution must be taken to avoid disrupting the relationship between the interviewer and interviewee, in particular by avoiding such things as repeated asking of irrelevant or difficult questions or ones that simply do not fit the prevailing social and cultural circumstances and conditions.

4. The computer program is given as app. C in Nakamura's (1986) article.

5. The small fluctuations in the period and age effects in the United States seem to be attributable to an insufficient number of sampling areas (i.e., 112), as well as to the fixing of the sampling areas for a long period. The design effect of the multistage-area probability sampling used by the Institute for Social Research at the University of Michigan is generally about one and one-half times greater than that of a simple random sampling.

6. According to Luckmann (1967, p. 38), it is more consistent with general sociological theory to view industrialization and urbanization as specific sociohistorical processes.

7. He also states (Martin 1978, p. 198): "Nonaffiliation is least in the southern Catholic provinces (2 percent) and greatest in the northern and urbanized regions, where it rises to just under or just over a third."

8. The findings from the Japanese National Character survey show that age effects are more dominant than period and cohort effects for questions other than those related to religious belief (Hayashi and Suzuki 1984).

References

Acquaviva, S. S. 1979. *The Decline of the Sacred in Industrial Society.* Oxford: Blackwell.

Akaike, H. 1980. "Likelihood and the Bayes Procedure." Pp. 143–66 in *Bayesian Statistics,* edited by J. H. Bernardo, M. H. DeGroot, D. V. Lindley, and A. F. M. Smith. Valencia: University Press.

———. 1985. "Prediction and Entropy." Pp. 1–24 in *A Celebration of Statistics,* edited by A. C. Atkinson and S. F. Fienberg. New York: Springer.

Bagley, C. 1973. *The Dutch Plural Society: A Comparative Study in Race Relations.* London: Oxford University Press.

Bahr, H. M. 1970. "Aging and Religious Disaffiliation." *Social Forces* 49:60–71.

Bell, D. 1977. "The Return of the Sacred: The Argument on the Future of Religion." *British Journal of Sociology* 28:419–49.

Berger, P. L. 1967. *The Sacred Canopy.* Garden City, N.Y.: Doubleday.

———. 1969. *A Rumor of Angels.* Garden City, N.Y.: Doubleday.

———. 1977. *Facing Up to Modernity.* New York: Basic.

Bibby, R. W. 1979. "Religion and Modernity: The Canadian Case." *Journal for the Scientific Study of Religion* 18:1–17.

Cobben, N. P. 1976. *Generatie-Kohort,* vol. 3, *En Kohortanalyse von Onkerkelijkheid.* Master's thesis. Tilburg, Catholic University of Tilburg.

Converse, P. E., J. D. Dotson, W. J. Hoag, and W. H. McGee III. 1980. *American Social Attitudes Data Sourcebook, 1947–78.*

Davis, K. 1949. *Human Society.* New York: Macmillan.

Demerath, N. J., III. 1968. "Trends and Anti-Trends in Religious Change." Pp. 349–445 in *Indicators of Social Change: Concepts and Measurements,* edited by E. B. Sheldon and W. E. Moore. New York: Sage.

Durkheim, Émile. (1893) 1964. *The Division of Labor in Society.* New York: Free Press.

Fienberg, S. E., and W. M. Mason. 1978. "Identification and Estimation of Age-Period-Cohort Models in the Analysis of Discrete Archival Data." Pp. 1–67 in *Sociological Methodology, 1979,* edited by K. F. Schuessler. San Francisco: Jossey-Bass.

Glenn, N. D. 1977. *Cohort Analysis.* Beverly Hills, Calif.: Sage.

Glock, C. Y., and R. Stark. 1965. *Religion and Society in Tension.* Chicago: Rand McNally.

Glock, C. Y., B. B. Ringer, and E. R. Babbie. 1967. *To Comfort and to Challenge.* Berkeley: University of California Press.

Greeley, A. M. 1972. *Unsecular Man.* New York: Schocken.

———. 1979. *Crisis in the Church.* Chicago: Thomas More.

Hayashi, C., and T. Suzuki. 1984. "Changes in Belief Systems, Quality of Life Issues and Social Conditions over 25 Years in Post-War Japan." *Annals of the Institute of Statistical Mathematics* 36:135–61.

Herberg, W. 1955. *Protestant, Catholic, and Jew.* Garden City, N.Y.: Doubleday.

———. 1967. "Religion in a Secularized Society: The New Shape of Religion in America." Pp. 470–81 in *The Sociology of Religion: An Anthology,* edited by R. D. Knudten. New York: Appleton-Century-Crofts.

Hertel, B. R., and H. M. Nelsen. 1974. "Are We Entering a Post-Christian Era? Religious Belief and Attitude in America, 1957–1968." *Journal for the Scientific Study of Religion* 13:409–19.

Hobcraft, J., J. Menken, and S. Preston. 1982. "Age, Period and Cohort Effects in Demography: A Review." *Population Index* 48:4–43.

Ikado, F. 1969. "Constitution of Religion in the United States [Amerika Shūkyo no Taishitsu]." Pp. 307–36 in *Lecture: American Culture, I [Koza: Amerika no Bunka I].* Tokyo: Nanundo.

Laeyendecker, L. 1972. "The Netherlands." Pp. 325–63 in *Western Religion,* edited by H. Mol. The Hague: Mouton.

Larkin, G. 1974. "Isolation, Integration and Secularization: A Case Study of the Netherlands." *Sociological Review* 22:401–18.

Luckmann, T. 1967. *The Invisible Religion.* New York: Macmillan.

Martin, D. 1967. *A Sociology of English Religion.* London: SCM.

———. 1978. *A General Theory of Secularization.* Oxford: Blackwell.

Mason, K. O., W. M. Mason, H. H. Winsborough, and W. K. Poole. 1973. "Some Methodological Issues in the Cohort Analysis of Archival Data." *American Sociological Review* 38:242–58.

Mason, W. M., and S. E. Fienberg, eds. 1985. *Cohort Analysis in Social Research.* New York: Springer.

McLoughlin, W. G. 1978. *Revivals, Awakenings, and Reform.* Chicago: University of Chicago Press.

Mol, H., ed. 1972. *Western Religion.* The Hague: Mouton.

Morioka, K. 1975. *Religion in Changing Japanese Society.* Tokyo: University of Tokyo Press.

Nakamura, T. 1982. "A Bayesian Cohort Model for Standard Cohort Table Analysis." *Proceedings of the Institute of Statistical Mathematics* 29:77–97 (in Japanese).

———. 1986. "Bayesian Cohort Models for General Cohort Table Analyses." *Annals of the Institute of Statistical Mathematics* 38 (part B): 353–70.

O'Dea, T. F. 1966. *The Sociology of Religion.* Englewood Cliffs, N.J.: Prentice-Hall.

Parsons, T. 1967. "Christianity and Modern Industrial Society." Pp. 33–70 in *Sociological Theory, Values, and Sociocultural Change: Essays in Honor of Pitirim A. Sorokin,* edited by E. A. Tiryakian. New York: Harper and Row.

Peterson, W. 1967. "Religious Statistics in the United States." Pp. 57–68 in *The Sociology of*

Religion, edited by R. D. Knudten. New York: Appleton-Century-Crofts.

Ryder, N. B. 1965. "The Cohort as a Concept in the Study of Social Change." *American Sociological Review* 30:843–61.

Schneider, L. 1970. *Sociological Approach to Religion.* New York: Wiley.

Sorokin, P. 1956. *Fads and Foibles in Modern Sociology and Related Sciences.* Chicago: Regnery.

Stark, R., and C. Y. Glock. 1968. *American Piety: The Nature of Religious Commitment.* Berkeley: University of California Press.

Suzuki, T. 1970. "A Study of the Japanese National Character, Part IV—Fourth Nation-Wide Survey." *Annals of the Institute of Statistical Mathematics,* Suppl. 6, Pp. 1–80.

Turner, B. S. 1983. *Religion and Social Theory: A Materialist Perspective.* London; Heinemann.

Weigert, A. J., and D. L. Thomas. 1974. "Secularization and Religiosity: A Cross-National Study of Catholic Adolescents in Five Societies." *Sociological Analysis* 35:1–23.

White, W. H., Jr. 1956. *The Organization Man.* New York: Simon and Schuster.

Wilson, B. R. 1966. *Religion in Secular Society.* London: Watts.

———. 1976a. *Contemporary Transformations of Religion.* New York: Oxford University Press.

———. 1976b. "Aspects of Secularization in the West." *Japanese Journal of Religious Studies* 3:259–76.

———. 1982. *Religion in Sociological Perspective.* Oxford: Oxford University Press.

Wingrove, C. R., and J. P. Alston. 1974. "Cohort Analysis of Church Attendance, 1939–69." *Social Forces* 53:324–31.

Wuthnow, R. 1976. "Recent Patterns of Secularization: A Problem of Generations?" *American Sociological Review* 41:850–67.

Yanagawa, K., and Y. Abe. 1978. "Some Observations on the Sociology of Religion in Japan." *Japanese Journal of Religious Studies* 5:5–27.

Yinger, J. M. 1963. "Religion and Social Change: Problems of Integration and Pluralism among the Privileged." *Review of Religious Research* 4:129–48.

CHAPTER FORTY

Postmaterialism in an Environment of Insecurity*

Ronald Inglehart†

A decade ago it was hypothesized that the basic value priority of Western publics had been shifting from a materialist emphasis toward a postmaterialist one—from giving top priority to physical sustenance and safety, toward heavier emphasis on belonging, self-expression, and the quality of life. This shift was traced to the unprecedented levels of economic and physical security that prevailed during the postwar era (Inglehart, 1971). Since this first exploration, the materialist/postmaterialist value change hypothesis has been subjected to further analysis by dozens of investigators using fieldwork carried out in the United States, Canada, Australia, Japan, and fifteen West European nations.[1] Measurements at multiple time points are now available for a number of these countries; in all, well over one hundred representative national surveys have measured the prevalence of materialist/postmaterialist value priorities among the publics of advanced industrial societies. A disproportionate share of this research has taken place in Germany and Japan—two countries that have experienced rapid economic growth in recent decades, and relatively rapid value change. Less evidence has been gathered in the relatively stagnant United States, despite the dominant position this country has held until recently in empirical social research.

Our data now span a decade. Implications for political change that were suggested by the original cross-sectional analysis can be tested in diachronic perspective. We can begin to distinguish between: (1) intergenerational value change, based on cohort effects; (2) life cycle change based on cohort effects; (2) life cycle or aging effects; and (3) period effects; in particular, we can ask: have the economic uncertainty and the deterioration of East-West détente in recent years produced a sharp decline in postmaterialism? As we will see, the answer is no. Overall there was remarkably little change in the ratio of materialists to postmaterialists among Western publics. But, like Sherlock Holmes's dog that did not bark in the night, this lack of dramatic change has crucial implications. Much of the literature on postmaterialism deals with whether it is a deep-rooted phenomenon having a long-term impact on political behavior, or simply a transient epiphenomenon. We will reexamine this issue in the light of recent evidence. If a society's basic values change mainly through intergenerational population replacement, we would expect them to change at a glacial pace. But though short-term changes may be small, close examination of their societal location can provide valuable insight into their long-term implications. Contrary to what some observers have assumed (Kesselman, 1979), postmaterialism has not dwindled away in the face of diminished economic and physical security. In most countries its numbers grew, and in some ways its political influence seems greater now than a decade ago; but its character and tactics have changed significantly.

One of the most important changes derives from the simple fact that today, postmaterialists are older than they were when they first emerged as a major political factor in the 1960s. Initially manifested mainly through student protest movements, their key impact is now made through the activities of young elites. For the students have grown older, and postmaterialism has penetrated deeply into the ranks of young professionals, civil servants, managers, and politicians. It seems to be a major factor in the rise of a "new class" in Western society—a stratum of highly educated and well-paid young technocrats who take an adversary stance toward their society (Ladd, 1978; Gouldner, 1979; Lipset, 1979; Steinfels, 1979). The current debate between those giving top priority to reindustrialization and rearmament, versus those who emphasize environmentalism and the quality of life, will not be easy to resolve: it reflects persisting value cleavages.

Reexamining the Theory of Value Change

Before turning to time series evidence, let us reexamine our theoretical framework in the light of recent findings. It is based on two key hypotheses:

1. *A scarcity hypothesis.* An individual's priorities reflect the socioeconomic environment: one places the greatest subjective value on those things that are in relatively short supply.
2. *A socialization hypothesis.* The relationship between socioeconomic environment and value priorities is not one of immediate adjustment: a substantial time lag is involved, for, to a large extent, one's basic values reflect the conditions that prevailed during one's preadult years.

The *scarcity hypothesis* is similar to the principle of diminishing marginal utility, in economic theory. A complementary concept— Abraham Maslow's (1954) theory of a need hierarchy underlying human motivation—helped shape the survey items we used to measure value priorities. In its simplest form, the idea of a need hierarchy would probably command almost universal assent. The fact that unmet physiological needs take priority over social, intellectual, or aesthetic needs has been demonstrated all too often in human history: starving people will go to almost any lengths to obtain food. The rank ordering of human needs be-

comes less clear as we move beyond those needs directly related to survival. But it *does* seem clear that there is a basic distinction between the "material" needs for physiological sustenance and safety, and nonphysiological needs such as those for esteem, self-expression, and aesthetic satisfaction.

The recent economic history of advanced industrial societies has significant implications in the light of the scarcity hypothesis. For these societies are a remarkable exception to the prevailing historical pattern: the bulk of their population does *not* live under conditions of hunger and economic insecurity. This fact seems to have led to a gradual shift in which needs for belonging, esteem and intellectual and aesthetic satisfaction became more prominent. As a rule, we would expect prolonged periods of high prosperity to encourage the spread of postmaterialist values; economic decline would have the opposite effect.

But it is not quite that simple: there is no one-to-one relationship between economic level and the prevalence of postmaterialist values, for these values reflect one's *subjective* sense of security, not one's economic level per se. While rich individuals and nationalities, no doubt, tend to feel more secure than poor ones, these feelings are also influenced by the cultural setting and social welfare institutions in which one is raised. Thus, the scarcity hypothesis alone does not generate adequate predictions about the process of value change. It must be interpreted in connection with the *socialization hypothesis.*

One of the most pervasive concepts in social science is the notion of a basic human personality structure that tends to crystallize by the time an individual reaches adulthood, with relatively little change thereafter. This concept permeates the literature from Plato through Freud and extends to the findings of contemporary survey research. Early socialization seems to carry greater weight than later socialization.

This, of course, doesn't imply that no change whatever occurs during adult years. In some individual cases, dramatic behavioral shifts are known to occur, and the process of human development never comes to a complete stop (Levinson, 1979; Brim and Kagan, 1980). Nevertheless, human development seems to be far more rapid during preadult years than afterward, and the great bulk of the evidence points to the conclusion that the statistical likelihood of basic personality change declines sharply after one reaches adulthood. Longitudinal research following given individuals over periods as long as thirty-five years, shows strong correlations (as high as .70) between people's scores on standardized personality scales from young adulthood to middle age, or even old age (Block, 1981; Costa and McCrae, 1980).

Taken together, these two hypotheses generate a coherent set of predictions concerning value change. First, while the scarcity hypothesis implies that prosperity is conducive to the spread of postmaterialist values, the socialization hypothesis implies that neither an individual's values nor those of a society as a whole are likely to change overnight. Instead, fundamental value changes takes place gradually, almost invisibly; in large part, it occurs as a younger generation replaces an older one in the adult population of a society.

Consequently, after a period of sharply rising economic and physical security, one would expect to find substantial differences between the value priorities of older and younger groups: they would have been shaped by different experiences in their formative years. But there would be a sizable time lag between economic changes and their political effects. Ten or fifteen years after an era of prosperity began, the age cohorts that had spent their formative years in prosperity would begin to enter the electorate. Ten more years might pass before these groups began to occupy positions of power and influence in their society; perhaps another decade would pass before they reached the level of top decision makers.

The socialization hypothesis complements the scarcity hypothesis, resolving objections derived from an oversimplified view of how scarcity affects behavior. It helps account for apparently deviant behavior: on one hand, the miser who experienced poverty in early years and relentlessly continues piling up wealth long after attaining material security, and on the other hand, the saintly ascetic who remains true to the higher-order goals instilled by his culture, even in the face of severe deprivation. In both instances, an explanation for the seemingly deviant behavior of such individuals lies in their early socialization.

The socialization hypothesis also explains why certain experimental tests of the need hierarchy have found no positive correlation between satisfaction of a given need at one time, and increased emphasis on the next higher need at a later time (Alderfer, 1972; Kmieciak, 1976). For these experiments are based on the implicit assumption that one would find almost *immediate* changes in an individual's priorities. But if, as hypothesized, an individual's basic priorities are largely fixed by the time he or she reaches adulthood, one would not expect to find much short-term change of the kind that was tested for.

This does not mean that an adult's value priorities are totally immutable—merely that they are relatively difficult to change. Normally, the rewards and deprivations employed in experimental psychology are modest, and the treatment is continued for a fairly brief time. Only in unusual experiments has the treatment been extreme enough to produce evidence of changed priorities among adults. In one such experiment, for example, a conscientious objector was kept on a semistarvation diet for a prolonged period under medical supervision. After several weeks, he lost interest in his social ideals and began to talk about, think about, and even dream about food (Davies, 1963). Similar patterns of behavior have been observed among inmates of concentration camps (Elkins, 1959; Bettelheim, 1979).

Marsh (1975) finds that postmaterialists do not express higher satisfaction with their incomes than do materialists. This is illogical, he argues: presumably, the former are postmaterialists *because* their material needs are satisfied—so why don't they express relatively high levels of subjective satisfaction with their material circumstances? Once again the confusion is based on the implicit assumption that value change reflects an *immediate* response to one's environment. In the short run, one normally *does* experience a subjective sense of satisfaction when one satisfies material needs. But if these needs have been satisfied throughout one's formative years, one takes them for granted and develops higher expectations. In the long run, the fact that one has enough oxygen, water, food, and clothing does *not* produce a subjective sense of satisfaction—which is precisely why the postmaterialists seek satisfaction in *other* realms.

Because their incomes are higher than those of the materialists, and yet they are still dissatisfied, Marsh concludes that postmaterialists are actually *more* acquisitive than materialists. Their emphasis on nonmaterial societal goals reflects mere lip service to fashionable causes, he argues, not their true personal values. Subsequent findings by Marsh himself refute this interpretation. To test his hypothesis, he developed an index of "Personal Post-Materialism"; he finds a correlation of +.22 between it and my index of societal postmaterialism (Marsh, 1977, p. 180). While his discussion emphasizes the fact that this correlation is "only" .22, the crucial point is that the correlation is *positive*—and not negative, as he argued earlier. When one is dealing with survey data, a product-moment correlation of +.22 is fairly strong, particularly when it is found between two sets of items that were designed with the expectation that they would show a *negative* correlation.

Time Series Evidence from the Postwar Era

Our hypotheses imply that the unprecedented prosperity prevailing from the late 1940s until the early 1970s, led to substantial growth in the proportion of postmaterialists among the publics of advanced industrial societies. We would need a time machine in order to go back and test this proposition, using the battery specifically developed to measure materialist/postmaterialist values. Though this is impossible, some available data *do* seem to tap the relevant dimension.

Data on the priorities of the German public, for example, cover more than twenty years, from 1949 to 1970. In these surveys, representative national samples were asked, "Which of the four Freedoms do you personally consider most important—Freedom of Speech, Freedom of Worship, Freedom from Fear, or Freedom from Want?" In 1949, postwar reconstruction had just begun, and "Freedom from Want" was the leading choice by a wide margin. But in the following years, Germany rose from poverty to prosperity with almost incredible speed. In 1954, "Freedom from Want" was still narrowly ahead of any other choice, but by 1958 "Freedom of Speech" was chosen by more people than all other choices combined (EMNID, 1963, 1970).

These changes in the German population's value priorities seem to reflect the concurrent changes in their economic environment. And there is clear evidence of an age-related lag between economic change and value change. In 1962, 59 percent of the Germans from 16 to 25 years old chose "Freedom of Speech"; the figure declines steadily as we move to older groups; among Germans aged 65 and older, only 35 percent chose "Freedom of Speech." The fact that the young are much likelier to give "Freedom of Speech" priority over "Freedom from Want" fits theoretical expectations neatly. The original data have been lost, and it is not possible to perform an age cohort analysis in order to determine how much of this age difference is due to generational change. But the magnitude of the overall shift is so great that each age-group must have *deemphasized* "Freedom from Want" as it aged during this period: the age differences *cannot* be attributed to life cycle effects. Further persuasive evidence of an intergenerational shift toward postmaterialist priorities among the German public is found in the massive and definitive analysis of German survey data from 1953 through 1976 by Baker, Dalton, and Hildebrandt (1981).

The most dramatic example of economic change in modern history is Japan–a nation that rose from harsh poverty to astonishing prosperity in a single generation. Indicators of the Japanese public's values are available in the Japanese national character studies carried out at five-year intervals, from 1953 through 1978. Analysis of these surveys indicates that Japanese culture changed along *several* different dimensions during this period, with the perceived sacredness of the emperor declining and emphasis on individuation and political participation rising (Ike, 1973; Hayashi, 1974; Nisihira, 1974; Richardson, 1974; Research Committee on Japanese National Character, 1979; Flanagan, 1979; Inglehart, 1982). One of the changes, it seems clear, was a shift from materialist to postmaterialist priorities. Among the available survey questions, the most unambiguous indicator of materialist versus postmaterialist priorities is the following: "In bringing up children of primary school age, some think that one should teach them that money is the most important thing. Do you agree or disagree?" In 1953, a strong majority (65 percent) of the Japanese public agreed that financial security was the most important thing. This figure declined steadily in subsequent surveys: by 1978 only 45 percent of the public still took this view. As was true of Germany, the trend is in the predicted direction—but in this case, the original data have been preserved and we can carry out a cohort analysis. Table 40.1 shows the results.

In any given year, the young are a good deal less likely to emphasize the importance of money than are the old. Does this simply reflect an inherent idealism of youth that will disappear as they grow older? Apparently not— for when we follow given age cohorts as they age during this twenty-five year period, we find no indication whatever of increasing materialism. Quite the contrary, we find a tendency for a given cohort as it grows older to place

less emphasis on money: the five cohorts for which we have data throughout the twenty-five-year period show an average shift of six points *away* from giving top priority to money. Almost certainly this was a period effect, with the sharply rising prosperity of the postwar era producing a diminishing emphasis on money within each age cohort, quite independently of generational change or aging effects. As closer examination of Table 40.1 indicates, this period effect operated rather strongly from 1953 to 1973 and then reversed direction, so that from 1973 to 1978 each age cohort came to place slightly *more* emphasis on the importance of money. This pattern reflects changes in the economic environment rather faithfully: the extraordinary rise in prosperity that took place in Japan from 1953 to 1973 was mirrored in a gradual deemphasis on money within each age cohort; and the economic uncertainty that followed the oil shock of 1973 was accompanied by a partial reversal of this trend.

But these period effects are dwarfed by the intergenerational differences. While period effects seem to account for a mean net shift of 6 percentage points away from emphasizing the importance of financial security, we find a difference of 44 points between the youngest and oldest groups in 1978. Since these data show no evidence whatever that aging leads to increasing emphasis on money, there is a strong prima facie case for attributing this forty-four-point difference entirely to intergenerational change. It is conceivable that a life cycle tendency toward increasing materialism with increasing age *also* exists, but is totally concealed by stronger period effects working in the opposite direction: the complexities of distinguishing between aging effects, cohort effects, and period effects are such that we can not totally exclude this possibility (Glenn, 1976; Knoke and Hout, 1976). But belief in such an aging effect must depend on faith alone; it is totally unsupported by empirical evidence.

Indications of intergenerational change, conversely, seem incontrovertible. In 1953, even

TABLE 40.1 Cohort Analysis: Percentage of Japanese Public Agreeing That Financial Security Is Most Important

Age Group	1953	1958	1963	1968	1973	1978	Change within Given Cohort*
20–24	60	—	43	34	22	18	
25–29	66		55	49	36	26	
30–34	63		58	58	42	37	
35–39	62		56	59	43	43	
40–44	65		63	59	46	49	
45–49	66		62	62	46	56	−4
50–54	72	—	68	65	49	51	−15
55–59	72	—	72	67	60	56	−7
60–64	77	—	76	66	59	62	0
65–69	78	—	72	73	59	62	−3
Spread between youngest and oldest:	+18	—	+29	+39	+37	+44	

*Mean = −6.

Source: Japanese National Character Surveys carried out by the Institute of Statistical Mathematics, Tokyo.

the *youngest* group showed overwhelmingly materialistic priorities—because at that time, *all* adult age cohorts had spent their formative years during World War II or earlier. These cohorts show only modest changes as they age during the ensuing quarter century. It is only from 1963 on—when the postwar cohorts begin to enter the adult population—that we find a clear rejection of financial security as a value having top priority among the younger cohorts. The shift of the Japanese public from a heavy majority giving money top priority, to a minority doing so, seems to reflect intergenerational population replacement above all, with only a minor component due to period effects. By 1978, there was a tremendous difference between the priorities of younger and older Japanese. As the leading example of economic growth in the postwar era, Japan constitutes a crucial case for testing our hypotheses. The time series data are unambiguous: from 1953 to 1978 there was an intergenerational shift away from materialism among the Japanese public.

Materialist and Postmaterialist Values from 1970 to 1979

Our data from Western countries cover a shorter period than those from Japan, but they were specifically designed to measure materialist/postmaterialist value priorities. It is difficult to measure values directly. But their presence can be inferred from a consistent pattern of emphasis on given types of goals. Accordingly, we asked representative samples of citizens from Western nations what they personally considered the most important goals among the following:

1. Maintain order in the nation.
2. Give people more say in the decisions of the government.
3. Fight rising prices.
4. Protect freedom of speech.
5. Maintain a high rate of economic growth.
6. Make sure that this country has strong defense forces.
7. Give people more say in how things are decided at work and in their community.
8. Try to make our cities and countryside more beautiful.

9. Maintain a stable economy.
10. Fight against crime.
11. Move toward a friendlier, less impersonal society.
12. Move toward a society where ideas count more than money.

Our earliest survey (in 1970) used only the first four items, in six countries. The full twelve-item battery was first used in 1973 in the nine-nation European Community and the United States (Inglehart, 1977). Both batteries were administered in numerous subsequent surveys. Items A, C, E, F, I, and J were designed to tap emphasis on materialist goals; theoretically, these values should be given high priority by those who experienced economic or physical insecurity during their formative years. The remaining items were designed to tap postmaterialist goals; they should be emphasized by those raised under relatively secure conditions. If so, certain respondents would favor materialist items consistently, while others would consistently emphasize the postmaterialist ones.

Survey results support these theoretical expectations. Those who give top priority to one materialist goal tend to give high priority to other materialist goals as well. Conversely, the postmaterialist items tend to be chosen together. Hence, we can classify our respondents as pure materialists (those whose top priorities are given to materialist goals exclusively); pure postmaterialists (those whose top priorities are given to postmaterialist items exclusively); or mixed types based on any combination of the two kinds of items. Though for simplicity of presentation we will usually compare the two polar types, we are dealing with a continuum having numerous intermediate categories.

The predicted relationships with social background are also confirmed empirically. Within any given age-group, those raised in relatively prosperous families are most likely to emphasize postmaterialist items, and the predicted skew by age-group is manifest. Figure 40.1 depicts this pattern in the pooled

FIGURE 40.1   Value type by age-group, among the publics of Britain, France, West Germany, Italy, Belgium, and the Netherlands in 1970.

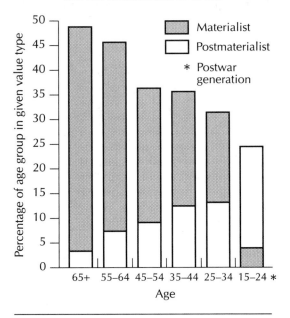

Source: European Community survey carried out in Feb.–Mar. 1970, sponsored by Commission of the European Communities; principal investigators were Jacques-René Rabier and Ronald Inglehart.

sample of six West European publics interviewed in our initial survey. Significant cross-national differences exist, but the basic pattern is similar from nation to nation: Among the oldest group, materialists outnumber postmaterialists enormously; as we move toward younger groups, the proportion of materialists declines and that of postmaterialists increases.

A major watershed divides the postwar generation (in 1970, those 15 to 24 years old) from all other age-groups. While materialists are still more than twice as numerous as postmaterialists among those 25 to 34 years old, when we move across the World War II watershed, the balance shifts dramatically, with postmaterialists becoming more numerous than materialists.

The materialist and postmaterialist types have strikingly different opinions on a wide variety of issues, ranging from women's rights, to attitudes toward poverty, ideas of what is important in a job, and positions on foreign policy. Within each age-group, about half the sample falls into the mixed value types. On virtually every issue, their position is between the materialists and postmaterialists: they seem to be a cross-pressured group that could swing either way.

By 1970, postmaterialists had attained numerical parity with materialists *only* among the postwar generation. Furthermore, they were concentrated among the more affluent strata of this age-group: among university students, they heavily outnumbered the materialists. In this light, perceptions of a generation gap in the late 1960s and early 1970s are understandable. Even among the postwar generation, materialists were about as numerous as postmaterialists. But in this age-group's most articulate and most visible segment—the students—there was an overwhelming preponderance of postmaterialists. The students lived in a distinct milieu: they had highly developed communications networks with other students but were largely isolated from their nonstudent peers. The priorities prevailing in this milieu were fundamentally different from those shaping the society as a whole.

The existence of such a milieu can play an important part in the evolution and propagation of a given set of values. Indeed, Habermas (1979) argues that the rise of postmaterialism is not due to the different formative experiences of different generation units, but to exposure to the specific worldviews inculcated by distinct communications networks (cf. Jaeggi, 1979). This explanation seems to complement, rather than substitute for, the one proposed here. It helps account for the spread of values in a given milieu, but provides no explanation why given generation units were disposed to accept given values in the first place, while others rejected them. Nevertheless, it seems clear that in virtually all Western nations, the student milieu of the late 1960s *did* constitute a distinct communications network, propagating a distinctive viewpoint. Given these circumstances, it is not surprising that the student elite saw themselves as part of a counterculture that was engaged in an irreconcilable clash with the culture of an older generation: From their viewpoint, the dictum, "Don't trust anyone over thirty" seemed plausible. Our hypotheses imply that as time went by, the postmaterialists became older and more evenly distributed across the population. But in 1970, conditions were optimal to sustain belief in a monolithic generation gap, with youth all on one side and older people all on the other.

Clearly, there are large empirical differences between the priorities of younger and older groups in Western Europe (and, as subsequent research revealed, the entire Western world). But one can advance various interpretations concerning the *implications* of this finding. Though our own hypotheses point to intergenerational change based on cohort effects, we must acknowledge that any given pattern of age differences could, theoretically, result from (1) aging effects, (2) cohort effects, (3) period effects, or some combination of all three.

1. Aging Effects versus Cohort Effects. Perhaps the most obvious alternative interpretation is one based on aging effects. It would argue that for biological or other reasons, the young are inherently less materialistic than the old. As they age, however, they inevitably become just as materialistic as their elders; after fifty years, the youngest group will show the same overwhelming preponderance of materialists that the oldest group now displays. The aging interpretation, then, holds that the pattern found in 1970 is a permanent characteristic of the human life cycle and will not change over time. The cohort interpretation, on the other hand, implies that the postmaterialists will gradually permeate the older strata, neutralizing the relationship between values and age.

The most dramatic change from one age-group to the next, in Figure 40.1, is the sudden shift in the balance between materialist and postmaterialist types that occurs as we move from the second-youngest to the youngest group. Our hypotheses imply the existence of a significant watershed between the postwar generation and the older groups that had experienced the world wars, the Great Depression and their associated threats to economic and physical security. The gap between the two youngest groups in 1970 fits the historical change theory neatly. But this gap could *also* be interpreted as a permanent feature of the human life cycle. For in 1970, the dividing line between the postwar generation and all older groups happened to coincide with the boundary between those twenty-five years of age or older, and those who were twenty-four or younger. Since we know that people tend to get married, have their first child, and begin a permanent career at about this age, it might be argued that what we have identified as a historical watershed between the postwar generation and the older ones merely reflects the stage in the life cycle when people get married and settle down. Time series data are needed to determine which interpretation is correct.

2.   **Period Effects.** Both the German data and the Japanese data reviewed earlier show period effects: the economic environment of the period up to 1973 apparently induced *all* age-groups to become less materialistic as time went by, quite apart from any processes of aging or generational change. These surveys were executed during a period of dramatic improvement in living standards, particularly in Germany and Japan. But even in the United States (where economic growth was much slower) the real income of the American public approximately doubled from 1947 to 1973.

From 1973 on, however, economic conditions changed drastically. Energy prices quadrupled almost overnight; the industrialized world entered the most severe recession since the 1930s. Economic growth stagnated and Western nations experienced extraordinarily high levels of inflation *and* unemployment. By

1980, the real income of the typical American family was actually *lower* than in 1970.

Western publics were, of course, acutely aware of changed economic circumstances, and responded to them. The most amply documented case is that of the American public, whose economic outlook is surveyed each month. In mid-1972, the University of Michigan Survey Research Center's Index of Consumer Sentiment stood at 95, only slightly below its all-time high. By the spring of 1975, the SRC Index had plummeted to 58—the lowest level recorded since these surveys were initiated in the 1950s. With the subsequent economic recovery, consumer confidence revived—only to collapse again in the wake of the second OPEC price shock in late 1979; in April 1980 consumer confidence had reached a new all-time low, with the SRC Index at 53. Similar patterns of declining confidence in the economic outlook were recorded among West European publics (Commission of the European Communities, 1979).

The sense of physical security has also declined. The Soviet arms buildup, their invasion of Afghanistan, and the Western response to these events led to an erosion of East-West détente. This, too, had a pronounced impact on the outlook of Western publics. In the fall of 1977, the publics of the European Community nations were asked to assess the chances of a world war breaking out within the next ten years. Only 26 percent of the nine publics (weighted according to population) rated the likelihood at 50 percent or greater. This was roughly comparable to the results obtained when a similar question was asked in July 1971. In April 1980, however, fully 49 percent of the nine publics rated the danger at 50 percent or greater: such pessimism had almost doubled since 1977 (Euro-Barometer 13, 1980, p. 16).

Clearly (as the scarcity hypothesis implies), the period effects of recent years should inhibit the development of a postmaterialist outlook. And the socialization hypothesis implies that current conditions would have their greatest impact on the youngest and theoretically most malleable respondents—those aged 15 to 24, who are still in their formative years.

Which of these three processes was most important during the 1970s? Given the severity of the economic decline and the almost total disappearance of student protest and other dramatic manifestations of a counterculture, one might assume that postmaterialism has been swept away completely by a new, harsher environment. Or—as the socialization hypothesis suggests—are these priorities sufficiently deep-rooted among the adult population to weather the effects of the current socioeconomic environment?

Table 40.2 provides part of the answer. It shows the distribution of the two polar value types from early 1970 to late 1979, in the six countries for which we have data covering this entire time span, and in the United States from 1972 to 1980. Of necessity, we use the original four-item index here. By contrast with the cataclysmic changes that took place in consumer confidence indices and in perceptions of the danger of war, the changes here are remarkably small: for the most part, the shifts from year to year fall within the range of normal sampling error. Moreover, only modest and nonlinear cumulative changes took place from 1970 to 1980, and they vary cross-nationally. In four of the seven countries—Great Britain, Germany, France, and the Netherlands—there were fewer materialists and more postmaterialists at the end of the decade than at its start. In two countries (Belgium and the United States) there was virtually no change. Only in the seventh country—Italy—do we find a shift toward the materialist pole.

The fact that Italy is the deviant case is not surprising. During the 1970s Italy not only experienced exceptionally severe economic difficulties, but also severe political disorder. Probably for this reason, there was a substantial net shift toward materialism among the Italian public. But in the other six countries, the pro-

TABLE 40.2 Changes in Prevalence of Materialist and Postmaterialist Value Types, 1970–80

	1970	1973	1976	1979
Britain:				
Materialist	36	32	36	27
Postmaterialist	8	8	8	11
Germany:				
Materialist	43	42	41	37
Postmaterialist	10	8	11	11
France:				
Materialist	38	35	41	36
Postmaterialist	11	12	12	15
Italy:				
Materialist	35	40	41	47
Postmaterialist	13	9	11	10
Belgium:				
Materialist	32	25	30	33
Postmaterialist	14	14	14	14
Netherlands:				
Materialist	30	31	32	28
Postmaterialist	17	13	14	19

	1972	1976	1980
United States:			
Materialist	35	31	35
Postmaterialist	10	10	10

Note: Percentage falling into the two polar types.
Source: European Community surveys carried out in February–March 1970; September 1973; November 1976; and November 1979; and postelection wave of the U.S. National Election surveys carried out in each respective year by the Center for Political Studies, Institute for Social Research, University of Michigan.

cess of population replacement outweighed the effects of economic and physical insecurity. The net result for the seven countries as a whole is that postmaterialists were slightly *more* numerous at the end of the 1970s than they were at the start.

The impression of remarkable stability that the aggregate national data convey conceals an extremely interesting underlying pattern. For, as hypothesized, the distribution of values across age groups has changed over time. Table 40.3 shows this relationship, from early 1970 through late 1979. Figure 40.2 depicts these data in graphic form. As these data reveal, the overall stability shown in Table 40.2 is the result of two opposing processes that largely cancel each other.

On one hand, the youngest group shows a substantial *decline* in the ratio of postmaterialists to materialists. In 1970, postmaterialists were four percentage points more numerous than materialists among this group: in other words, the group showed a percentage difference index (PDI) of +4. This fell to a PDI of −1 in 1973 and fell further to a PDI of −5 in 1976. Although the trend then reversed itself, with a partial recovery to an index of −3 in 1979, this youngest group showed a net shift of seven points in the materialist direction during the 1970s.

But this shift was more than offset by shifts in the *opposite* direction among the older groups.

The socialization hypothesis implies that period effects would have their greatest impact on the youngest group. Empirically, it turns out that the youngest group was the *only* group on which period effects had a significant negative net impact: the older ones moved in the postmaterialist direction. The American data show a similar pattern: younger respondents became more materialist but the older ones became *less* so. In Europe, this countervailing tendency was especially strong among the second-youngest group, which showed a steady rise in the proportion of postmaterialists even during the depths of the 1970s recession; despite economic uncertainty and the erosion of détente, by 1979 this group had registered a net shift of eight points toward the postmaterialist pole.

This seemingly counterintuitive development reflects changes in the composition of the 25- to 34-year-old group, due to population replacement. In 1970 this group contained no one born after 1945; but by late 1979 its members were recruited entirely from the postwar generation. The World War II watershed now fell between the *two* youngest groups and all of the older ones.

TABLE 40.3   Changes in Prevalence of Materialist (M) and Postmaterialist (PM) Values, 1970–79 by Age-group (Percent)*

Ages	1970		1973		1976		1979	
	M	**PM**	**M**	**PM**	**M**	**PM**	**M**	**PM**
15–24	20	24	21	20	25	20	24	21
25–34	31	13	28	13	29	16	27	17
35–44	35	12	35	9	35	11	33	13
45–54	36	9	39	7	39	8	41	10
55–64	45	7	43	6	47	6	41	8
65 and over	48	3	45	4	52	5	49	5
All ages	35	12	34	10	37	12	35	13
Percentage difference index	−23		−24		−25		−22	

*Combined results from six European nations.
Source: Surveys sponsored by the Commission of the European Communities, carried out in February–March, 1970; September 1973; November 1976; and November 1979.

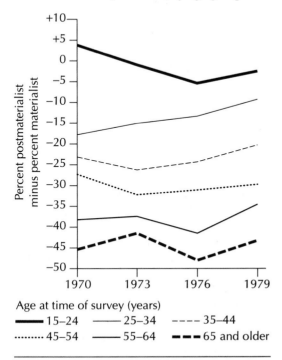

FIGURE 40.2 Change in value priorities in six nations, 1970–79, by age group.

Age at time of survey (years)
▬▬ 15–24   ——— 25–34   ─ ─ ─ 35–44
········· 45–54   ——— 55–64   ■ ■ ■ 65 and older

Source: European Community surveys carried out in February–March 1970; September 1973; November 1976; and November 1979 in Britain, Germany, France, Italy, Belgium, and the Netherlands: since data from only these nations are available for 1970, only these data are used for the subsequent time points. Surveys were sponsored by the Commission of the European Communities; principal investigators were Jacques-René Rabier and Ronald Inglehart.

Let us examine Figure 40.2 more closely. In 1970, by far the widest gap between adjacent age-groups was that between the youngest and second-youngest groups. This gap was a prominent feature of the value distributions in each of the six nations surveyed in that year. At that point, it was unclear whether this gap should be interpreted as a World War II watershed, or as the reflection of a major life-cycle transition that takes place in one's midtwenties.

That uncertainty has now vanished. During the 1970s, the still-malleable 15- to 24-year-

old group became progressively more materialist until the recession bottomed out, and then staged only a partial recovery. But the 25- to 34-year-old group became steadily more postmaterialist throughout the 1970s. By the end of 1979 the largest gap no longer was located between these two youngest groups, but between the 25- to 34-year-old group, and those aged 35 to 44. This accords perfectly with the fact that members of the postwar generation had now reached 34 years of age.

It is virtually impossible to interpret this pattern in terms of aging effects—unless one believes that the human life cycle changed radically between 1970 and 1979: the crucial life stage transition that took place at age 25 in 1970, had somehow shifted to age 35 in 1979. Furthermore, there is no indication that aging has an inherent tendency to produce a Materialistic outlook. Despite the economic uncertainty of this period, only the 15- to 24-year-old age group became significantly more materialist; among older groups, the downward pressure of period effects was more than offset by the upward pressure of the population replacement process. Furthermore, not even the youngest category showed a *continuous* downward trend: plummeting steeply until 1976, it began to reverse itself with recovery from the recession. It seems far more plausible to attribute this nonlinear pattern to period effects than to the aging process (which presumably is continuous).

The economic and physical uncertainty of the 1970s produced a significant period effect. The net movement toward postmaterialism that would be expected from population replacement slowed to a crawl. By the decade's end, the 15- to 24-year-old group was significantly less postmaterialist than their counterparts a decade earlier had been. This is congruent with impressionistic observations that the student population no longer seems as nonconformist as it once was. For while young people have become more materialistic, those in their thirties and forties have become less so: the notion of a generation gap, already an oversimplification in 1970, was even farther from reality in 1979 due to this convergence.

Postmaterialism and Political Change

The evidence indicates that postmaterialism is a deep-rooted phenomenon. Despite the recession of recent years, it not only persisted but increased its penetration of older groups. What are the political implications? The remainder of this article will focus on that question.

One would expect that, despite their favored socioeconomic status, postmaterialists would be relatively supportive of social change, and would have a relatively high potential for unconventional and disruptive political action. The reasons can be summarized as follows: (1) Materialists tend to be preoccupied with satisfying immediate physiological needs; postmaterialists feel relatively secure about them and have a greater amount of psychic energy to invest in more remote concerns such as politics. (2) As a recently emerging minority whose highest priorities have traditionally been given relatively little emphasis in industrial society, postmaterialists tend to be relatively dissatisfied with the established order and relatively supportive of social change. (3) The disruption and property damage that sometimes result from unconventional political action seem less negative to postmaterialists, since they threaten things they value less than materialists do. In short, postmaterialists have a larger amount of psychic energy available for politics, they are less supportive of the established social order, and, subjectively, they have less to lose from unconventional political action than materialists. Consequently, the rise of postmaterialism has made available a new, predominantly middle-class base of support for the left.

Is it empirically true that postmaterialists tend to be relatively change-oriented and ready to engage in unconventional political protest? One measure of support for social change is

now a standard feature of the European Community surveys carried out twice each year. Representative national samples of the publics of the European Community countries are asked:

On this card are three basic kinds of attitudes toward the society we live in. Please choose the one which best describes your opinion. (1) The entire way our society is organized must be radically changed by revolutionary action. (2) Our society must be gradually improved by reforms. (3) Our present society must be valiantly defended against all subversive forces.

These alternatives might be described as revolutionary, reformist, and conservative.

The reformists constitute a clear majority—63 percent of those responding—in the European Community as a whole, and this holds true for all value types. But there is a pronounced difference between materialists' and postmaterialists' attitudes toward social change. Table 40.4 shows the relationship between value type and attitudes toward social change among the publics of the European Community as a whole. Among materialists, only 4 percent endorse the revolutionary option; nearly ten times as many (38 percent) support the conservative option. Among postmaterialists, by contrast, the revolutionary option draws *more* support than the conservative one. For both, the reformist option is the leading choice—but postmaterialists are only about one-third as likely to hold conservative views as are materialists, and about four times as apt to favor radical social change.

Despite their relatively privileged social status, postmaterialists are markedly more favorable to social change than are other value types. But how far are they ready to go on behalf of their values?

A central feature of an eight-nation survey carried out during 1974–76 was a scale designed to measure an individual's potential for participation in political protest activities (for details of field work, see Barnes, Kaase et al., 1979). This scale is based on whether the re-

TABLE 40.4 Support for Social Change versus Resistance to Social Change, by Value Type, 1976–79 (Percent)

Respondent's Value Type	Support for Revolutionary Change	Support for Gradual Reform	Support for Defense of Present Society	N
Materialist	4	57	38	18,292
Mixed	8	62	30	26,694
Postmaterialist	17	69	14	6,098

Note: Results are weighted according to size of each nation's population.
Source: Pooled data from Euro-barometre surveys, 1976 through 1979, from all nine European Community nations.

spondent has done, or would do and approves of, a series of acts ranging from circulating petitions to occupying buildings and disrupting traffic. Tested and applied in eight countries, the scale has remarkably good technical characteristics and seems to measure, in a straightforward way, just how far an individual is willing to go in order to carry out his or her beliefs.

Do postmaterialists show a relatively high propensity for unconventional political activities as measured by the Protest Potential Scale? On one hand, Marsh (1975) has argued that postmaterialist responses tap nothing more than a form of radical chic among a basically conservative elite. If so, the answer would be no. On the other hand, if our typology reflects basic value differences, the answer should be yes. The Protest Potential Scale was developed, in part, to test whether postmaterialist values go no deeper than lip service to fashionable goals, or whether they have behavioral implications. The answer is unequivocal.

Table 40.5 shows the relationship between protest potential and value type in each of the eight nations surveyed in 1974–76. A score of 3 is the cutting point for this table: Those scoring below this level are (at most) ready to circulate petitions or to march in peaceful demonstrations; a good many of them have done nothing at all and are not willing to do anything. Those scoring higher are willing to do all of the above *and* engage in boycotts; many are ready to go still farther — to take part in rent strikes, illegal occupation of buildings, or to block traffic.

As Table 40.5 makes clear, people's value priorities have a strong relationship to their level of protest potential. In Great Britain (where the relationship is weakest), only 21 percent of the materialists are ready to engage

TABLE 40.5 Protest Potential, by Value Type in Eight Western Nations, 1974–76 (Percent)

Respondent's Value Type	The Netherlands	Great Britain	United States	Germany	Austria	Italy	Switzerland	Finland
Materialist	27	21	38	23	17	20	17	20
Mixed	42	31	48	36	21	38	27	34
Postmaterialist	74	55	72	74	48	69	61	58

Note: Figures represent percent scoring 3 or higher on Protest Potential Scale. Values index is based on items A–L cited above.
Source: Eight-nation survey, carried out 1974–76; for details of fieldwork and a report of findings from five of these eight nations, see Samuel H. Barnes, Max Kaase et al., *Political Action* (Beverly Hills, Calif.: Sage, 1979).

in boycotts or go beyond them in protest against some form of perceived political injustice; among the postmaterialists, 55 percent have done so, or are willing to do so. The linkage between values and the potential for protest is particularly strong in Italy, where only 20 percent of the materialists rank high on protest potential—as compared with 69 percent of the postmaterialists. In all eight countries postmaterialists are far readier to engage in political protest than materialists.

In multivariate analyses, when we control for the effects of age, education, income, and one's level of ideological sophistication, a strong relationship persists between postmaterialist values and a predisposition for unconventional protest. A relatively high potential to use unconventional and disruptive techniques in order to intervene in the political process seems to be directly linked with the postmaterialist outlook; it is not merely a spurious correlate, resulting from the fact that postmaterialists tend to be young and well educated.

This might seem paradoxical. On one hand, we have seen that the economic uncertainty of the 1970s did not cause postmaterialism to disappear—on the contrary, its support seems to have grown in most Western countries. On the other hand, the dramatic political protest movements of the late sixties and early seventies have disappeared in the United States (though not in Western Europe): why did this happen, if a relatively high protest potential characterizes the postmaterialists?

The main answer is that people don't protest in a social vacuum. The postmaterialists did not protest for the sake of protesting— they responded to specific issues, above all the war in Indochina. The fact that there no longer is a war in Indochina (or, at least, no *American* war) makes a big difference. Almost nothing can compare with war, in terms of violence, drama, and human tragedy, and nothing on the current scene can command sustained mass attention in the way the Vietnam War did. In the absence of any political cause fully comparable

to the war, it is only natural that much of the attention and energies of postmaterialists have been diverted into other channels.

For some, this means seeking self-actualization through development of the inner self, rather than through social action. The human potential movement is an example. For those who remain politically active, this turning inward seems like desertion of the cause; the current crop of youth has been characterized as the Me Generation, practicing a culture of narcissism. There is some truth and even more misapprehension in this view. As we have seen, at the close of the 1970s the 15- to 24-year-old group *was* more materialistic than their counterparts at the start of the decade had been— but the difference was modest. If the potential for political protest generally remained only a potential, it may have been because none of the current political causes were as compelling as those of the earlier decade.

Post-Materialist Penetration of Elite Groups

But another major factor has also affected how postmaterialism manifests itself politically. It springs from the simple fact that the average postmaterialist is substantially older than he or she was in 1970. Postmaterialists are no longer concentrated in a student ghetto. They have moved into positions of influence and authority throughout society. Despite their minority status in society as a whole, they outnumber the materialists in certain key sectors.

Table 40.6 shows how the two pure value types are distributed by age and occupation among the publics of the European Community countries. This table pools the data from six surveys carried out in all nine countries in the late 1970s, in order to provide reliable data for certain small but important elite groups. A national sample survey normally contains only a handful of professionals, for example; but here we have large enough numbers that we not only can compare this occupational category

TABLE 40.6　Materialist (M) versus Postmaterialist (PM) Values by Respondent's Occupation and Age Group in Nine European Community Nations, 1976–79 (Percent)

	Age Less than 35			Ages 35–49			Age 50 and Over		
	M	PM	*N*	M	PM	*N*	M	PM	*N*
Top management + top civil servants	20	30	565	22	22	702	28	16	374
Students	20	25	3,800	—	—	—	—	—	—
Professionals	25	21	280	21	19	218	29	12	162
Nonmanual employees	26	18	4,591	34	13	2,918	38	9	1,569
Unemployed persons	24	16	875	38	9	279	48	6	321
Self-employed business persons	35	13	1,329	41	10	1,109	43	7	855
Manual workers	32	11	4,673	40	8	3,264	44	5	2,255
Housewives	38	9	3,469	46	6	3,763	50	5	4,755
Farmers	42	10	347	44	5	528	48	4	778
Retired persons	—	—	—	—	—	—	51	5	7,018

Note: N = base number for percentages.
Source: Based on combined data from the nine-nation European Community surveys carried out from 1976 through 1979.

with others, but can break it down by age group.

The pure postmaterialist type comprises only about 8 percent of the manual workers, and 7 percent of the farmers; in these occupational groups, pure materialists outnumber postmaterialists by ratios of at least five to one. On the other hand—despite the recent decline in postmaterialism among the student-age population—postmaterialists continue to outweigh materialists in the student milieu. This is significant but not particularly surprising. What *is* surprising is the fact that among those less than 35 years old with jobs that lead to top management and top civil service posts, postmaterialists outnumber materialists decisively: their numerical preponderance here is even *greater* than it is among students. This is all the more astonishing since these young technocrats are older, on the average, than the students. This phenomenon reflects the fact that the young managers and officials are a highly select stratum, recruited according to considerably more demanding criteria than those for admission to a university: there are many more students than young technocrats. In social background, the

latter correspond to the students at the most prestigious schools, rather than to the student population as a whole. In general, the more selective our criteria become, the higher the proportion of postmaterialists—and the young technocrats represent the elite of the recent university graduates. Already occupying influential staff positions, many of them should reach the top decision-making level within the next decade.

Apart from the students, the young technocrats are the only category in which postmaterialists hold a clear preponderance over materialists. But postmaterialism has also made impressive inroads in certain other elite categories. In the free professions, postmaterialists are almost as numerous as materialists—not only in the under-35 age group but in the 35- to 49-year-old category as well. And there is an even balance between materialists and postmaterialists among those aged 35 to 49 in top management and top civil service posts.

Among those 50 and older, the materialists hold a clear preponderance in *every* occupational category. Among self-employed people in business and trades in this age-group, materialists are six times as numerous as postmaterialists. And even among the self-employed under 35, materialists predominate by a ratio of nearly three to one: young technocrats may be postmaterialistic, but young self-employed business people definitely are *not.*

By the end of the 1970s, postmaterialism had become a powerful influence among technocrats and professionals in their thirties and forties. This does not mean that it will automatically become the dominant influence in Western societies. Postmaterialists remain a numerical minority, better equipped to attain their goals through bureaucratic institutions or the courts than through the electoral process. They may encounter the backlash of resurgent materialism, as recent political events in the United States suggest. Nevertheless, by the late 1970s postmaterialism had not only made deep inroads among young technocrats; but it had *also,* to a surprising degree, penetrated the West European political class.

Table 40.6 may actually *understate* the degree to which younger Western elites had become postmaterialist. For these data are based on representative national samples; even when we break them down into relatively fine categories as in Table 40.6, even the top management and civil service group is fairly heterogeneous, ranging from relatively modest levels to the truly elite stratum. Theoretically, the latter should be more postmaterialistic. For an indication of the values prevailing among West European political elites, let us turn to some data from interviews with the candidates running for seats in the European Parliament in 1979. This sample includes candidates from all significant political parties in all nine countries, drawn in proportion to the number of seats each party holds in the European Parliament (for details of fieldwork, see Inglehart et al., 1980). In background, these candidates are roughly similar to members of the respective national parliaments (in which many of them hold seats). Though somewhat younger than the average member of the national parlia-

ments, they seem to provide a reasonably good sampling of the West European political elite.

The candidates for the European Parliament were asked to rank their priorities among the twelve-item set of societal goals described above. Those who gave top priority to one materialist item tended to give high priority to the other materialist items as well; the same was true of postmaterialist items. Table 40.7 shows how the twelve items fell into two clearly defined clusters on the first dimension of a factor analysis. The structure of the candidates' choices shown here is virtually identical to that found among the publics of these same nine countries (compare the results in Inglehart, 1977, p. 46). Empirically, all six of the items designed to tap materialist priorities show negative polarity, while all six items designed to tap postmaterialist priorities show positive polarity.

T A B L E   4 0 . 7   Value Priorities of Candidates to the European Parliament, 1979*

Materialist/Postmaterialist (24%) Goals	Factor Loadings
Postmaterialist	
More say on job	.660
Less impersonal society	.478
More say in government	.472
Society where ideas count	.408
More beautiful cities	.315
Freedom of expression	.254
Materialist	
Control of inflation	−.436
Fight against crime	−.442
Stable economy	−.450
Economic growth	−.566
Maintain order	−.588
Adequate defense forces	−.660

*First factor in principal components factor analysis.
Source: Interviews with 742 candidates for seats in the European Parliament, carried out March–May, 1979, as part of the European Election Study organized by Karlheinz Reif. Principal investigators were Ian Gordon, Ronald Inglehart, Carsten Lehman Sorensen, and Jacques-René Rabier.

The materialist/postmaterialist dimension proves to be remarkably robust—not only cross-culturally but also across time, and from the mass to the elite level. We used responses to these items to construct a value priorities index, coding those candidates who chose materialist items for both their first and second priorities as pure "materialists"; coding those who chose two postmaterialist items as "postmaterialist"; and those who chose other combinations as "mixed." Table 40.8 shows the distribution of value types among our sample of the European Parliament, weighted in proportion to how many seats each party and nationality obtained in 1979.

In the Parliament as a whole, materialists narrowly outnumber the postmaterialists. But while postmaterialists (as defined here) constitute little more than one-eighth of the general public of these countries, they make up nearly one-third of the European Parliament. And when we break our sample down by age-group, we find a pronounced skew. Among those 55 years of age and over, materialists are almost twice as numerous as postmaterialists. But among those under 55, the postmaterialists outnumber the materialists.

Clearly, postmaterialism is no longer a student phenomenon. When the postwar generation first became politically relevant in the 1960s, the universities may have been the only major institutions in which they were the dominant influence. Their youth, their minority status in society as a whole, and their relative lack of representation at decision-making levels dictated a protest strategy. Postmaterialists had little access to key decision-making posts; but they were highly motivated and articulate. They could not control decision making, but they *could* disrupt it—and they made use of unconventional political protest techniques.

Postmaterialism and the Rise of the New Class

The relative youth and powerlessness of the postmaterialists may have dictated a strategy of student protest in the 1960s. But postmaterialism has moved out of the student ghetto. By 1980, a postmaterialist outlook had become more common than a materialist one among young technocrats, professionals, and politicians of Western countries. As experts, congressional staffers, and members of ministerial cabinets, postmaterialists had direct access to the command posts of the sociopolitical system. Protest was no longer their most effective tool. The impact of postmaterialism was no longer symbolized by the student with a protest placard, but by the public interest lawyer, or the young technocrat with an environmental impact statement.

In recent years, a growing number of Western intellectuals have focused their attention on the rise of "the New Class." In contrast with the establishment-oriented New Class of Eastern Europe described by Djilas (1966), the New Class in the West is an elite characterized by it adversary stance toward the existing social order (Podhoretz, 1979; Bruce-Briggs, 1979); by its "culture of critical discourse" (Gouldner,

TABLE 40.8 Value Type by Age Group, among Candidates for European Parliament, 1979 (Percent)

| | Ages | | |
	25–54	55–86	Total
Materialist	31	43	35
Mixed	34	34	34
Postmaterialist	36	23	32
N	439	221	660

Note: Percentages are weighted in proportion to actual number of seats each party and nationality had in the European Parliament as of June 1979. Accordingly, candidates from parties that won no seats are excluded from this table. Unweighted Ns appear at foot of each column. One column does not add up to 100 because of rounding.
Source: Interviews with sample of candidates running for seats in European Parliament, interviewed in March–May, 1979. This sample includes 62 percent of those actually elected in June 1979.

1979, pp. 28–29); and by a "new liberalism" (Ladd, 1978, pp. 48–49). Broder (1980) describes the emergence of a new generation of political elites that have many of these characteristics as a "changing of the guard."

There is no clear consensus on the criteria that define the New Class. Ehrenreich and Ehrenreich (1977) describe it as those in the census categories of "professional and technical," plus "managers and administrators"—precisely the categories we have found to be most heavily postmaterialist. But Ladd (1978) extends its limits to include anyone with a college education. There is even less consensus concerning *why* this well-paid and increasingly powerful stratum of society is critical of the existing economic and political order and participates in leftist political movements. There is a tendency to view an adversary culture as something *inherent* in higher education or in certain occupations, but the reasons are not altogether clear. Highly educated groups have existed for a long time, but in the past they generally were politically conservative. High levels of education and information are the *resource* that enables the New Class to play an important role—but they do not explain why today, an increasing share of the most highly educated and informed strata take an adversary stance toward their society.

I suggest that the rise of postmaterialism and its subsequent penetration of technocratic and professional elites has been a major factor behind the emergence of the New Class. For this group is distinctive not only in its occupational and educational characteristics, but also in its values. And the ideology attributed to the New Class reflects postmaterialist values rather closely (Ladd, 1976, 1978). If this is true, it explains why a New Class having these specific characteristics has emerged at this particular point in history.

For the distinctive values of the New Class reflect a historical change that cannot be attributed simply to a changing educational and occupational structure. Rising levels of education and a shift of manpower into the "knowledge

industries" have played a major role in the rise of this new elite, as Bell (1973, 1976), Lipset and Dobson (1972), Lipset (1979), and others have argued. But—as Table 40.6 makes clear—an "adversary culture" is not an *inherent* concomitant of the education or adult role of professionals and technocrats. *Older* professionals and technocrats are preponderantly materialist; it is only among the younger segments of these groups that postmaterialist priorities outweigh materialist ones.

Because both the political environment and the social location of postmaterialists have changed significantly, their tactics have also changed. Though the war in Indochina no longer plays an important role in Western politics, some of the most important movements on the current scene reflect the clash of materialist and postmaterialist worldviews—among them, the women's movement, the consumer advocacy movement, the environmental movement, and the antinuclear movement. These movements involve questions of whether one gives top priority to economic growth, or to the individual's right to self-realization and the quality of life.

Environmentalism and Economic Growth

Until quite recently, it was taken as self-evident that economic growth was inherently good; though there were sharp disagreements on how its benefits should be allocated, the pro-growth consensus embraced both labor and management, capitalist and communist. Only recently has this assumption been called into question, with the environmental movement holding that economic growth does not always justify the impact it makes on the environment; and with some segments of the movement arguing that economic growth is now becoming either undesirable or even impossible, because of the scarcity of natural resources. When environmentalism raises questions of environmental quality versus economic growth it pits postmaterialist priorities squarely against materialist ones. Thus in 1977, among the materialists in the European Community publics, 36 percent expressed a "very high" opinion of the environmental movement—while 53 percent of the postmaterialists did so. And while 3 percent of the former claimed to be members of some environmentalist group, 7 percent of the postmaterialists did so.

It is significant that the environmental movement has *not* collapsed, in the post-1973 setting of severe strains on Western economies due to skyrocketing energy costs that exacerbate inflation and drain away immense sums of capital that might otherwise be invested to produce fuller employment. Despite this economic crisis, and a subsequent backlash against environmentalism, environmental protection standards were not abandoned—on the contrary, they became more stringent after 1973, when the energy crisis became manifest. Currently, cross-pressured groups seem to be wavering, but postmaterialist support for environmentalism remains firm and the movement continues to win some victories. Stricter limitations were enforced on the mining and burning of coal, and on automotive emissions in the late 1970s. Although the amount of hydroelectric power produced in the United States could be doubled fairly readily, environmentalist opposition has made construction of major new hydroelectric projects next to impossible. In 1980, a proposed Energy Mobilization Board—designed to facilitate the development of energy resources in the face of environmentalist opposition—died in Congress; and millions of acres of land were added to wilderness areas that are largely closed to exploration for natural resources.

But the most dramatic and emotionally charged confrontation between materialist and postmaterialist priorities was the struggle over nuclear power. One can conceive of a world in which postmaterialists favored the development of nuclear power on the grounds that it disturbs the natural environment less than coal mines, petroleum wells, or hydroelectric dams, and that it produces less pollution and has a better safety record than conventional energy sources. This is conceivable—but the reality is quite different.

Nuclear power has come to symbolize everything the postmaterialists oppose. It carries connotations of the bombing of Hiroshima, reinforced by fears that nuclear power plants might facilitate the spread of nuclear weapons. Based on complex technology, nuclear power was developed by large corporations and the federal government, in the name of economic growth. Postmaterialists were disproportionately active in the antiwar movement, tend to be suspicious of big business, and big government—and give low priority to economic growth. They form the core of the opposition to nuclear power. And, despite the current energy crisis, opposition to nuclear power plants has not died away—on the contrary, it has brought the development of nuclear power almost to a halt in the United States, West Germany, and several other countries. In 1968, nuclear power produced less than 1 percent of the electricity used in the United States; by 1978 it was providing nearly 13 percent of all electricity consumed. After the Three Mile Island accident this development halted: in 1979 nuclear sources produced only 11 percent of the nation's electricity. Facing protracted and unpredictable delays, no new nuclear power plants are currently being ordered and many of those already ordered have been canceled. In South Korea, where environmental and antinuclear groups have virtually no impact, a nuclear power plant can be built in four years. In the United States, construction time now averages about twelve years. It seems possible that the American power plant industry, which led the world until recently, may shut down completely.

Other nations have chosen to pursue the nuclear option vigorously, and a number of them (including Belgium, Sweden, Switzerland, France, and Great Britain) are already far ahead of the United States in the percentage of electricity they produce from nuclear sources. By 1985 nuclear power plants will supply

TABLE 40.9 Support for Development of Nuclear Power among Nine
West European Publics, by Value Type, 1979 (Percent)

	Great Britain	France	Germany	Belgium	Italy	Luxem-bourg	Ireland	Nether-lands	Denmark
Materialist	79	77	69	56	57	53	52	59	41
Mixed	75	64	58	57	47	59	45	36	40
Postmaterialist	52	44	46	46	45	36	35	27	20

Note: Question: "Could you tell me whether you agree or disagree with . . . the following proposal? . . . Nuclear energy should be developed to meet future energy needs." Figures show percentage who said they "agree" or "agree strongly."
Source: European Community survey (Barometer 11) carried out in April–May 1979. Values index is based on top two priorities selected from items E–H, cited in text.

about 40 percent of Sweden's electricity and 55 percent of France's electricity. The Soviet Union will quintuple its production of nuclear power between 1980 and 1985. The contrasting American record reflects technological problems to some extent, but above all it is a question of political and ideological factors.

Like the environmental movement, the struggle over nuclear power reflects a clash of worldviews. For materialists, the use of nuclear energy is viewed as desirable insofar as it seems linked with economic growth and full employment. For them, highly developed science and industry symbolize progress and prosperity. Among postmaterialists, nuclear power tends to be rejected not only because of its potential dangers but because it is linked with big business, big science, and big government— bureaucratic organizations that are evaluated

negatively because they are inherently impersonal and hierarchical, minimizing individual self-expression and human contact. The ideologues of the antinuclear movement argue for a return to a simpler, more human society in which energy is used sparingly, and what is needed comes directly from nature— symbolized by solar power (Nelkin and Pollak, 1981).

Tables 40.9 and 40.10 show the relationship between value type and support for developing nuclear energy, among European Community publics and among candidates for the European Parliament. In every country, materialists are far more favorable to developing nuclear energy than are the postmaterialists. At the mass level, a majority of the materialists support the development of nuclear power and a majority of the postmaterialists oppose it in

TABLE 40.10 Support for Developing Nuclear Power among Candidates
to European Parliament, by Value Type, 1979 (Percent)

	France	Germany	Great Britain	Italy	Belguim	Ireland	Luxem-bourg	Denmark	Nether-lands
Materialist	95	98	77	55	100	54	71	86	64
Mixed	85	65	54	54	40	29	25	14	35
Postmaterialist	49	40	24	44	24	0	0	9	5

Note: Figures show percentage who said they "agree" or "agree stongly." The question about nuclear energy included an "in-between" option (not proposed to the mass publics) that was selected by 6 to 26 percent of given national samples: only in the Netherlands, Denmark, and Luxembourg were pluralities opposed to developing nuclear energy.
Source: European Elections Study survey of 742 candidates for the European Parliament, interviewed in spring 1979; respondents' value type is based on top two priorities selected from items A–L cited above.

eight out of nine nations. The differences are even more pronounced at the elite level; a majority of materialists support nuclear power and a majority of postmaterialists oppose it among candidates from *every* one of the nine countries. And the percentage spread between materialists and postmaterialists is at least forty-six points in every country but Italy, where nuclear power has not become a major political issue.

This emerging axis of polarization cuts squarely across traditional left-right lines. On the antinuclear side one finds intellectuals, some socialists—and much of the upper middle class. On the pronuclear side, one finds big business—and the AFL-CIO; Gaullists—and the French Communist party. It is not a traditional class struggle, but a polarization based on materialist versus postmaterialist values.

One of the most striking features of the nuclear power controversy is the extent to which well-informed members of the public and even competent experts, when exposed to the same body of information, draw totally different conclusions. We believe this reflects a process of cognitive screening in which given facts are retained and weighted in accord with the individual's basic values. Though support or opposition to nuclear power is usually justified in terms of objective costs, benefits, and risks, an underlying factor is a clash of worldviews.

Materialists take it for granted that economic growth is crucial, and weigh the costs and risks of nuclear energy against the costs and risks of alternative energy sources. Postmaterialists take economic security for granted and weigh the costs and risks of nuclear power against various no-cost alternatives—among which, reduced material consumption seems not only acceptable but, to some, actually desirable: insofar as it might lead to a more decentralized, less impersonal society that allows freer play for individual self-expression, it has a very positive image (see Schumacher, 1973; Lovins, 1977; Sale, 1980). Thus the debate over nuclear power is based on contrasting visions of the good society, with pronuclear and antinuclear advocates talking past each other

because their arguments are implicitly based on different value priorities. To a considerable degree, each side is insensitive to the basic premises of the other.

Conclusion

A decade's time series data indicate that postmaterialism is a deep-rooted phenomenon with important political consequences. Persisting in an atmosphere of insecurity, postmaterialism has come to manifest itself in new ways under new circumstances; what was a student subculture in the 1960s has evolved into the ideology of the New Class. And conflict between those seeking materialist and postmaterialist goals has become the basis of a major dimension of political cleavage, supplementing though not supplanting the familiar polarization between labor and management.

There are ironies on both sides. For generations, predominantly materialistic elites took it for granted that nature had infinite resources to withstand consumption and environmental pollution, for the sake of industrial development. But growth did *not* inaugurate the "politics of consensus in an age of affluence." Instead, after a certain lag, it led to the emergence of new sources of discontent while a blind emphasis on growth that depended on cheap oil undermined its own future.

More recently, some postmaterialist elites adopted a mirror image of this view, taking it for granted that industry had infinite resources to support taxation, and regulation—sometimes in a needlessly punitive spirit. The irony here was that in the long run, postmaterialism is contingent on material security; the insecurity of recent years arrested its growth and gave impetus to a renewed emphasis on reindustrialization and rearmament.

The rise of postmaterialism was accompanied by a wave of legislation designed to advance the cause of human equality, raise social welfare standards, and protect the consumer and the environment. There were pervasive changes in national priorities. Prior to 1965, over half of the American federal budget was spent on defense and only about one-quarter on health, education, and welfare. By the end of the 1970s, these proportions had been almost exactly reversed. That reallocation of resources is now under attack.

It would be gratifying to be able to identify one side as totally right and the other as utterly wrong. Unfortunately it is not that simple. Both materialist and postmaterialist goals are essential elements of a good society, and neither emphasis is automatically appropriate, regardless of circumstances. A healthy economy and defense forces adequate to deter attack are essential to the realization of *both* materialist and postmaterialist goals. But they are not the only legitimate political concerns. Beyond a certain point, a military buildup tends to generate countermeasures. The Soviet Union is militarily stronger than ever before, but faces suspicion and opposition from China, Afghanistan, Poland, the West, and much of the Third World. And beyond a certain point, material production produces growing social costs and a diminishing payoff. When there are two cars in every garage, a third adds relatively little; a fourth and a fifth would be positively burdensome. From this perspective, a shift to postmaterialist priorities, with more time, thought, and resources going into improving the social and natural environment, is simply a rational response to changing conditions.

A statesman's task is to seek a reasonable balance between a variety of social goals. That task is complicated in any case, but all the more so if the goals themselves can change.

Notes

*   From the *American Political Science Review* 75, no. 4 (December 1981): 880–900, by permission of the author and the American Political Science Association. Copyright 1981 by the American Political Science Association.

†   The author thanks the following for stimulating comments and suggestions: Samuel Barnes, Russell Dalton, Kenan Jarboe, Max Kaase, Hans D. Klingemann, Shinsaku Kohei, Rex Leghorn, Warren Miller, Ichiro Miyake, Sigeki Nisihira, Tadao Okamura, Jacques-René Rabier, Tatsuzo Suzuki, and Joji Watanuki. The European public opinion surveys were sponsored by the Commission of the European Communities; the American data are from the National Election surveys carried out by the Center for Political Studies, Institute for Social Research, University of Michigan. Interviews with candidates to the European Parliament were sponsored by the European Parliament, the Commission of the European Communities and the Volkswagen Foundation. The data used in this article are available from the ICPSR survey data archive, the Belgian Archive for the Social Sciences and the Zentralarchiv für empirische Sozialforschung. This research was supported by grant SOC 79-14619 from the National Science Foundation.

1.   For representative examples, see Ike, 1973; Kerr and Handley, 1974; Marsh, 1975, 1977; Kmieciak, 1976; Lafferty, 1976; Hildebrandt and Dalton, 1977; Zetterberg, 1977; Watanuki, 1979; Inglehart, 1977; Jennings, Allerbeck and Rosenmayr, 1979; Lehner, 1979; Kaase and Klingemann, 1979: Heunks, 1979; Pesonen and Sankiaho, 1979; Kemp, 1979; Flanagan, 1979, 1980; Nardi, 1980.

References

Alderfer, Clayton P. 1972. *Existence, Relatedness and Growth: Human Needs in Organizational Settings.* New York: Free Press.

Baker, Kendall L., Russell Dalton, and Kai Hildebrandt. 1981. *Germany Transformed.* Cambridge, Mass.: Harvard University Press.

Barnes, Samuel, Max Kaase et al. 1979. *Political Action.* Beverly Hills, Calif.: Sage.

Bell, Daniel. 1973. *The Coming of Post-Industrial Society.* New York: Basic Books.

– – –. 1976. *The Cultural Contradictions of Capitalism.* New York: Basic Books.

Bettelheim, Bruno. 1979. *Surviving.* New York: Knopf.

Block, Jack. 1981. "Some Enduring and Consequential Structures of Personality." In A. I. Rabin et al. (eds.), *Further Explorations in Personality.* New York: Wiley-Interscience.

Brim, Orville G., Jr., and Jerome Kagan, eds. 1980. *Constancy and Change in Human Develop-*

ment. Cambridge, Mass.: Harvard University Press.

Broder, David S. 1980. *Changing of the Guard.* New York: Simon and Schuster.

Bruce-Briggs, B., ed. 1979. *The New Class?* New Brunswick, N.J.: Transaction Books.

Commission of the European Communities. 1979. *Survey of Consumer Confidence in the European Community Countries.* Brussels: European Community.

— — —. 1980. *Public Opinion in the European Community: Euro-Barometre 13.* Brussels: European Community.

Costa, Paul T., Jr., and Robert R. McCrae. 1980. "Still Stable after All These Years: Personality as a Key to Some Issues in Adulthood and Old Age." In Paul B. Bates and Orville G. Brim, Jr. (eds.), *Life-Span Development and Behavior,* Vol. 3. New York: Academic Press.

Dalton, Russell J. 1977. "Was There a Revolution? A Note on Generational versus Life-Cycle Explanations of Value Differences." *Comparative Political Studies* 9, no. 4: 459–75.

Davies, James C. 1963. *Human Nature and Politics.* New York: Wiley.

Djilas, Milovan. 1966. *The New Class.* London: Unwin.

Ehrenreich, Barbara, and John Ehrenreich. 1977. "The Professional-Managerial Class." *Radical American* 2: 7–31.

Elkins, Stanley. 1959. *Slavery: A Problem in American Institutional and Intellectual Life.* Chicago: University of Chicago Press.

EMNID. 1963. *Pressedienst,* cited in *Encounter* 22: 53.

Flanagan, Scott C. 1979. "Value Change and Partisan Change in Japan: The Silent Revolution Revisited." *Comparative Politics* 11: 253–78.

— — —. 1980. "Value Cleavages, Economic Cleavages and the Japanese Voter." *American Journal of Political Science* 24, no. 2: 178–206.

Glenn, Norval D. 1976. "Cohort Analysis' Futile Quest: Statistical Attempts to Separate Age, Period and Cohort Effects." *American Sociological Review* 41: 900–904.

Gouldner, Alvin W. 1979. *The Future of the Intellectuals and the Rise of the New Class.* New York: Seabury.

Habermas, Jurgen. 1979. "Einleitung." In Jurgen Habermas (ed.), *Stichworte zur "Geistigen Situation der Zeit."* Frankfurt: Suhrkamp.

Harrington, Michael. 1979. "The New Class and the Left." In B. Bruce-Briggs (ed.), *The New Class?* New Brunswick, N.J.: Transaction Books.

Hayashi, Chikio. 1974. "Time, Age and Ways of Thinking—From the Kokuminsei Surveys." *Journal of Asian and African Studies* 10, nos. 1–2: 75–85.

Heunks, Felix J. 1979. *Nederlanders en hun Samenleving.* Amsterdam: Holland University Press.

Hildebrandt, Kai, and Russell Dalton. 1977. "Die neue Politik: Politischer Wandel oder Schönwetter Politik?" *Politische Vierteljahresschrift* 18: 230–56.

Ike, Nobutaka. 1973. "Economic Growth and Intergenerational Change in Japan." *American Political Science Review* 67: 1194–203.

Inglehart, Ronald. 1971. "The Silent Revolution in Europe: Intergenerational Change in Post-Industrial Societies." *American Political Science Review* 65: 991–1017.

— — — 1977. *The Silent Revolution: Changing Values and Political Styles among Western Publics.* Princeton: Princeton University Press.

— — —. 1982. "Changing Values in Japan and the West." *Comparative Political Studies* 14: 445–79.

— — —, Jacques-René Rabier, Ian Gordon, and Carsten J. Sorenson. 1980. "Broader Powers for the European Parliament? The Attitudes of Candidates." *European Journal of Political Research* 8: 113–32.

Jaeggi, Urs. 1979. "Drinnen and draussen." In Jurgen Habermas (ed.), *Stichworte zur "Geistigen Situation der Zeit."* Frankfurt: Suhrkamp, pp. 443–73.

Jennings, M. Kent, Klaus R. Allerbeck, and Leopold Rosenmayr. 1979. "Generations and Families: General Orientations." In Samuel H. Barnes, Max Kaase et al. (eds.), *Political Action.* Beverly Hills, Calif.: Sage.

Kaase, Max, and Hans D. Klingemann. 1979. "Sozialstruktur, Wertorientierung und Parteiensysteme." In Joachim Matthes (ed.), *Sozialer Wandel in Westeuropa.* Frankfurt: Campus Verlag.

Kemp, David A. 1979. "The Australian Electorate." In Howard R. Penniman (ed.), *The Australian National Elections of 1977.* Washington, D.C.: American Enterprise Institute.

Kerr, Henry, and David Handley. 1974. "Conflits des Générations et Politique Etrangère en Suisse." *Annuaire Suisse de Science Politique,* pp. 127–55.

Kesselman, Mark. 1979. Review of "The Silent Revolution." *American Political Science Review* 73: 284–86.

Kmieciak, Peter. 1976. *Wertstrukturen und Wertwandel in der Bundesrepublik Deutschland.* Gottingen: Schwartz.

Knoke, David, and M. Hout. 1976. "Reply to Glenn." *American Sociological Review* 41: 906–8.

Ladd, Everett C., Jr. 1976. "Liberalism Upside Down: The Inversion of the New Deal Order." *Political Science Quarterly* 91: 577–600.

———. 1978. "The New Lines Are Drawn: Class and Ideology in America." *Public Opinion* 1: 48–53.

Lafferty, William M. 1976. "Basic Needs and Political Values: Some Perspectives from Norway on Europe's 'Silent Revolution.'" *Acta Sociologica* 19: 117–36.

Lehner, Franz. 1979. "Die 'Stille Revolution': zur Theorie und Realität des Wertwandels in hochindustrialisierten Gesellschaften." In Helmut Klages and Peter Kmieciak (eds.), *Wertwandel und gesellschaftlicher Wandel.* Frankfurt: Campus Verlag, pp. 317–27.

Levinson, Daniel J., et al. 1979. *The Seasons of a Man's Life.* New York: Knopf.

Lipset, Seymour Martin. 1979. "The New Class and the Professoriate." In B. Bruce-Briggs (ed.), *The New Class?* New Brunswick, N.J.: Transaction Books, pp. 67–88.

———, and Richard B. Dobson. 1972. "The Intellectual as Critic and Rebel." *Daedelus* 101: 137–98.

Lovins, Amory. 1977. *Soft Energy Paths: Toward a Durable Peace.* New York: Harper.

Marsh, Alan. 1975. "The Silent Revolution, Value Priorities and the Quality of Life in Britain." *American Political Science Review* 69: 1–30.

———. 1977. *Protest and Political Consciousness.* Beverly Hills, Calif.: Sage Publications.

Maslow, Abraham H. 1954. *Motivation and Personality.* New York: Harper.

Meadows, Donella H., et al. 1972. *The Limits to Growth.* New York: Universe.

Nardi, Rafaella. 1980. "Sono le condizioni economiche a influenzare I valori? Un controllo dell'ipotesi di Inglehart." *Rivista Italiana di Scienza Politica* 10: 293–315.

Nelkin, Dorothy, and Michael Pollak. 1981. *The Atom Besieged: Extraparliamentary Dissent in France and Germany.* Cambridge: MIT Press.

Nisihira, Sigeki. 1974. "Changed and Unchanged Characteristics of the Japanese." *Japan Echo* 1: 22–32.

Pesonen, Pertti, and Risto Sankiaho. 1979. *Kansalaiset je kansanvalta: Soumalaisten kasityksia poliittisesta toiminnasta.* Helsinki: Werner Soderstrom Osakeyhtio.

Podhoretz, Norman. 1979. "The Adversary Culture and the New Class." In B. Bruce-Briggs (ed.), *The New Class.* New Brunswick, N.J.: Transaction Books, pp. 19–32.

Research Committee on the Study of the Japanese National Character. 1979. *A Study of the Japanese National Character: The Sixth Nation-Wide Survey.* Tokyo: Institute of Statistical Mathematics.

Richardson, Bradley M. 1974. *The Political Culture of Japan.* Berkeley, Calif.: University of California Press.

Sale, Kirkpatrick. 1980. *Human Scale.* New York: Coward McCann Geoghegan.

Schumacher, E. F. 1973. *Small Is Beautiful.* New York: Harper.

Steinfels, Peter. 1979. *The Neo-Conservatives.* New York: Simon and Schuster.

Watanuki, Joji. 1979. "Japanese Politics: Changes, Continuities, and Unknowns." In Joji Watanuki, *Japanese Politics.* Tokyo: Tokyo University Press.

Zetterberg, Hans. 1977. *Arbete, Livsstil och Motivation.* Stockholm: Svenska Arbetsgivareforeningen.